MW00527960

DUTCH CHICAGO

THE HISTORICAL SERIES OF THE REFORMED CHURCH IN AMERICA, NO. 42

DUTCH CHICAGO

A History of the Hollanders in the Windy City

ROBERT P. SWIERENGA

A. C. VAN RAALTE INSTITUTE
HOPE COLLEGE

WILLIAM B. EERDMANS PUBLISHING COMPANY
GRAND RAPIDS, MICHIGAN / CAMBRIDGE, U.K.

Wm. B. Eerdmans Publishing Co.
255 Jefferson Ave. S.E., Grand Rapids, Michigan 49503 /
P.O. Box 163, Cambridge CB3 9PU U.K.
www.eerdmans.com

Printed in the United States of America

07 06 05 04 03 7 6 5 4 3 2

Library of Congress Cataloging-in-Publication Data

Swierenga, Robert P.
Dutch Chicago: a history of the Hollanders in the Windy City / Robert P. Swierenga.
p. cm. — (Historical Series of the Reformed Church in America; no. 42)
Includes bibliographical references and index.
ISBN 0-8028-1311-9 (pbk.: alk. paper)
1. Dutch Americans — Illinois — Chicago — History. 2. Dutch Americans — Illinois — Chicago — Social conditions. 3. Chicago (Ill.) — History. 4. Chicago (Ill.) — Social conditions. 5. Chicago (Ill.) — Ethnic relations. I. Title. II. Series.

F548.9.D9 S9 2002
977.3′110043931 — dc21

2002035234

The Historical Series of the Reformed Church in America

The series was inaugurated in 1968 by the General Synod of the Reformed Church in America acting through the Commission on History to communicate the church's heritage and collective memory and to reflect on our identity and mission, encouraging historical scholarship which informs both church and academy.

For

great-grandfather Jan Hendriks Swierenga (1847-1899)

grandfather Bouwko (Robert) Swierenga (1887-1949)

father John R. Swierenga (1911-1999)

uncles Ralph Swierenga (1919-1987)

Henry R. Swierenga (1924-1998)

Paul Tuitman (1908-   )

John Davids (1914-1951)

and all the Groninger teamsters on Chicago's West Side

Contents

Preface

My paternal great-grandfather, Jan Swierenga (1847-99), a canal bargeman in the Netherlands, died thirty-six years before my birth, but his decision in 1893 to emigrate to Chicago from the province of Groningen had a direct bearing on his descendants. Instead of hauling grain in Groningen, Jan's sons and grandsons became teamsters and produce wholesalers in Chicago, except for a son and daughter who farmed.

Jan Swierenga's ancestors were humble peasant folk of Reformed persuasion who devoted themselves to family and faith. For at least nine generations since the late 1600s, the family, despite frequent moves, lived clustered within an eight-mile radius of Stedum, which is located about twelve miles north of the city of Groningen, the provincial capital. They sometimes married cousins and even in-laws, which suggests that the clan shared a social life. Until the nineteenth century, the family belonged to the national Reformed *(Hervormde)* Church. But after a spiritual revival and secession in the 1830s, some joined and served as officers in the more orthodox Christian Seceded Church *(Christelijk Afgescheiden Kerk),* later renamed the Christian Reformed Church *(Christelijk Gereformeerde Kerk).* Jan and his family joined the Christian Reformed Church in 1876.

Over the centuries the Swierengas worked as farm laborers, farm operators, and, in the last three generations in the nineteenth century, as canal bargemen and grain brokers. These last hauled wheat and other grains to market in the city of Groningen and set prices for the various grades at the national board of trade in the city.

The wheat-producing region of Groningen and Friesland suffered a severe depression in the 1880s, due to falling prices in world markets caused by the glut of new production on the rich American and Canadian prairies. The agricultural crisis forced Dutch farmers to mechanize and consolidate land holdings in order to compete with North American growers. Farm laborers and small farmers were cast off by the tens of thousands, and emigration to America offered the best long-term prospects.

Jan owned a canal barge and tow horse and transported grain from a windmill known as *Olle Widde* ("Old White"), which stood among fertile grain fields beside his rented red brick home on the outskirts of a small village in the north of the country. Across the road was the canal, the Damsterdiep, which ran directly to the national grain market in the city of Groningen.

The precipitating event in Jan's decision to emigrate to Chicago was a financial blow caused by a canal shipping accident. While hauling a full load of wheat to the Groningen grain market, Jan had to pass through a *sluis* ("lock") on the canal. He followed the usual procedure of tying his barge to the side of the sluis but failed to allow enough slack line. When the water level in the lock dropped suddenly and unexpectedly, the rope became taut and caused the boat to tip, and the entire load, about twenty tons, was soaked and ruined. This disaster drained Jan financially. He decided to start over in Chicago, where his older brother had settled on the West Side eleven years earlier, having followed a paternal uncle who immigrated shortly after the Civil War. It was a typical "chain migration," in which members of an extended family follow and assist one another over time.

Jan and his wife and eight children arrived amidst the great Columbian Exposition. Like most immigrants, they had left a pinched existence for the promise of a better future in an expansive new land. Chicago was a burgeoning metropolis, dubbed the "lightning city" because of the unbelievable pace of growth that came with its strategic location as the gateway to the West. Jan again took up transport work, buying a horse and wagon to haul limestone and commodities of all kinds. But 1893 was not a good year to arrive in the United States. One of the periodic business panics struck that year and set off a depression second only to the Great Depression of the 1930s. The Swierenga family suffered greatly, living in a damp basement and lacking adequate food. Before the economic crisis had run its course, Jan's wife Katrijn had died in 1897 of "consumption," or tuberculosis; and Jan succumbed two years later to the same wasting disease; this was the plague of poverty. The parents left seven orphans, three boys and four girls, since the oldest daughter had married.

Jan and Katrijn emigrated and sacrificed their lives for the sake of their children, all of whom married Dutch Reformed spouses and prospered. The oldest son farmed in South Dakota, and the other two sons together operated a wholesale produce house at Chicago's Randolph Street market. The food business provided a solid middle-class living for their families and launched several of the children on the road to even greater success in the trucking business in Chicago. They lived out the promise of America, and in their memory I dedicate this book.

Figures

Tables

Acknowledgments

"Many hands make light work," says the old adage, and I experienced its truth in writing this book. Most helpful was the assistance in transcribing, translating, and reviewing Dutch-language church records, periodicals, and newspapers. Hendrik Harms transcribed thousands of pages of consistory minute books, thus making often obtuse, handwritten text eminently clear. Henry Lammers read these copies, and many more in the original form, and summarized or translated relevant items. His knowledge of Reformed Church history and polity gave him a sharp eye to hone in on important trends and turning points, and to see the deeper meaning of seemingly routine consistorial work. Lammers also reviewed microfilmed files of the important Dutch-language Chicago newspaper, *Onze Toekomst.* Huug van den Dool and Simone Kennedy translated several items from other newspapers and sections of books published in the Netherlands. Dirk Hoogeveen translated the remarkable Chicago letters of Bernardus De Bey. I also benefited from the translation by William Buursma and Nella Kennedy, under the auspices of the A. C. Van Raalte Institute, of the minutes of the Classis of Wisconsin of the Reformed Church in America for the years 1856-90. This classis included the immigrant congregations of greater Chicago until 1918. Ginger Evenhouse Bilthuis shared genealogical information from her voluminous records of West Side families.

Martin Stulp, a friend and fellow member of my Timothy Christian School Class of 1949, recorded on videotape more than twenty hours of reminiscences of native westsiders, including Jake Bakker, Dirk Brouwer, Effie Dwarshuis, Ben Essenburg, Ben and Martha Heslinga, Mike and Lena Keizer, Tom Oldenburger, Ralphina Roeters, John R. Swierenga, and Hank and Marie Tameling. Essenburg drove Stulp around the Ashland

Avenue district of the Old West Side for two hours. With Stulp's camera running, they traversed every street, and Essenburg recounted from his incredible memory which Dutch families lived in which houses in the 1930s and 1940s, where the boys played baseball, life on the schoolyard and in the churches, and favorite soda fountains and watering holes. Since most of the buildings are gone and the streets stand empty and largely deserted, Essenburg's memories are a time warp that recreates a time when life was lived on the front porches, and the streets were alive with activity.

I interviewed a number of other westsiders on audio- and videotape, including Dick Blaauw, Henry Martin Stob, Clarence and Anna Boerema, and Robert Vander Velde. Above all, I mined the vivid memories of my late father, John R. Swierenga, a Chicago cartageman and churchman who knew everyone and could recall the most minute details of people, places, and events. I only wish he had lived to see the end product of this research.

Many men who know the Chicago scavenger industry firsthand shared with me their knowledge, family and business records, and photographs. I am particularly indebted to Calvin Iwema for making available for the first time the minute books of the Chicago & Suburban Ash and Scavenger Association for the years 1935-43. William Buiten, Sam Hamstra, Jr., Peter H. Huizenga, the brothers Edward and John Evenhouse, and William Zeilstra read all or parts of chapter 12 and offered advice and information.

Ross and Peggy Ettema, with the valued assistance of Randy Bosma, freely provided genealogical information on Roseland families from their treasure trove of data extracted from church, school, and social records. William Prince and Jackie Vander Weide Swierenga Vogelzang shared books and photos of early Roseland.

Jane Wezeman Smith and her brother Fred Wezeman kindly made available the voluminous files of their father, Frederick H. Wezeman, principal of Chicago Christian High School and Chicago Christian Junior College. The files included rare photographs and documents and a nearly complete run of Wezeman's newspaper, the *Chicago Messenger*, 1934-36. William Buiten shared his firsthand knowledge of the Timothy Christian School imbroglio with the Lawndale Christian Reformed Church. Arnold Hoving provided valuable information on Timothy Christian Schools in the 1970s and 1980s. Peter H. Huizenga, Timothy alumnus extraordinaire, provided a publication subvention that made this effort feasible. His can-do attitude nudged me to "get it done." A number of "FOPs" (Friends of Peter) generously provided funds to ensure that the book reaches the hands of the children and grandchildren of the "greatest generations," whose story is told here. These benefactors are Ken and Gwen Hoving, Dick and Pixie Molenhouse, Martin and Janet Ozinga, Jr., Martin and Ruth Ozinga III, Rob and Sally Petroelje, Steve and Joan Tameling, Terry and Linda Van Der Aa, Jack and Carolynn Van Namen, and Wayne and Barbara Vriesman.

I owe much to the cooperation and expertise of the directors of the premier archives for the study of the Midwestern Dutch in America, Geoffrey Reynolds and his predecessor Larry Wagenaar of the Joint Archives of Holland, and Richard Harms and his predecessor Herbert Brinks of the Calvin College Archives. They let me photocopy materials with abandon and suggested sources to use. This work rests heavily on these guides and their rich storehouses of records. Reynolds and Harms also enhanced the quality of the many photographs from their collections that complement the text by scanning them electronically. Reynolds gave countless hours to this tedious task, as did my student assistant, Christina Van Regenmorter. Timothy Ellens designed the jacket cover in his imaginative style, and my nephew Richard Boomker applied his computer graphics training at Trinity Christian College to draw maps and figures.

My colleague, Elton J. Bruins, former director of the A. C. Van Raalte Institute and a constant source of encouragement and support, read the entire manuscript. So did Ben and Martin Essenburg, Timothy Douma, and William Zeilstra, all of whom have special gifts of insight and reflection on the meaning of growing up on the Old West Side and Cicero. Donald Bruggink, professor emeritus at Western Theological Seminary and the general editor of the Historical Series of the Reformed Church in America, under whose auspices this book is being published, put his sharp pencil to the text, as did his copy editor, Laurie Baron. Klaas Wolterstorff shepherded the book through the production process at the Wm. B. Eerdmans Publishing Company, as did editor Jennifer Hoffman and others on the staff. Gordon De Young also read the final text with his trained editorial eye and saved me from a number of errors and muddled passages, for which I am deeply appreciative. Others who read and commented on various chapters are William D. Buursma, John Dryfhout, Henry J. Hoeks, Fred W. Huizinga, Arnold Hoving, Hans Krabbendam, Willliam Prince, Richard Schuurman, Jackie Vander Weide Swierenga Vogelzang, and Homer J. Wigboldy. My daughter Suzanna Swierenga Breems red-penciled grammatical and other problems in various drafts. Needless to add, I am solely responsible for the mistakes that careful readers will doubtless find in this book. There would be many more, were it not for the eyes of so many.

Finally, I am grateful to the A. C. Van Raalte Institute of Hope College for providing me with a congenial place to work in a research center devoted to the study of the Dutch in America. The institute has generously supported my research and given encouragement at every turn. What more can a scholar ask for than the unfettered opportunity to follow one's head and heart? And telling this story of my own community and family has given me more satisfaction than any previous writing project.

Introduction

In 1980 an estimated 250,000 Chicagoans out of 5,000,000 in the greater metropolitan area (5 percent) claimed Dutch birth or ancestry, and the Windy City was second only to Grand Rapids, Michigan (with 20 percent), as a Dutch center. Yet the Chicago Dutch have remained an invisible people to historians and journalists for 150 years, and no wonder. At the high point of ethnic identity in 1930, the Dutch ranked only tenth among foreign-born residents, far below Germans (32 percent), Irish (11.5 percent), Swedes, and Poles (9 percent each). In 1893, after fifty years and a dozen Dutch Reformed churches, the Reverend Peter Moerdyke of Trinity Reformed Church in Chicago could lament in his weekly column in the *Christian Intelligencer,* the denominational weekly, that the Dutch "unhappily remain unknown in this metropolis."[1]

The Chicago Dutch were a polyglot population from all social strata, regions, and religions of the Netherlands. Three-quarters were Calvinists; the remainder included Catholics, Lutherans, Unitarians, Socialists, Jews, and the nominally churched. By all expectations, the Dutch should have Americanized rapidly, intermarried, and disappeared as an ethnic group. Indeed, this happened to Protestants who preferred American denominations such as the Presbyterians, and to Dutch Jews and Catholics who joined German congregations. A Holland Presbyterian and

1. Peter Moerdyke, "Chicago Letter," *Christian Intelligencer,* 17 May 1893, p. 11; Cornelius Bratt, "Our Churches in Grand Rapids," ibid., 9 July 1890, p. 11; Robert P. Swierenga, comp., "Dutch in Chicago and Cook County 1900 Federal Census" (1992); William Harms, "Dutch settlers share heritage with the suburbs," *Chicago Tribune* (Daily Suburban edition), 26 April 1983, p. 5; Chicago Department of Development and Planning, *The People of Chicago: Who We Are and Who We Have Been* (Chicago, 1976), 12-45.

a Holland Unitarian church also served the westsiders briefly, but both collapsed. Only one Catholic parish of some two hundred families, St. Willibrord in Roseland-Kensington, which was formed in the 1890s, preserved a Dutch Catholic identity in the twentieth century.

The Dutch Reformed were concentrated in four enclaves until the 1920s: the Old West Side, Englewood on the near South Side, and Roseland and South Holland on the far South Side. From these "nests" eventually came many other Dutch settlements in greater Chicago. Of the four core areas, the Old West Side was "in almost every respect the most interesting of them all," according to Amry Vandenbosch in his book, *The Dutch Communities of Chicago.*

The West Side was the quintessential working-class district. It was always the most congested and ethnically mixed, with the highest proportion of immigrants, the least attractive housing, and the slowest and least developed public transportation. The development of the west division lagged that of the rest of the city. Such neighborhoods are always in flux and pass through a natural cycle of growth, maturity, deterioration, and out-migration. The West Side Dutch community fits this classic pattern; it began near the city center and then relocated five times toward the suburbs, due to the encroachment of noisome factories and ethnic groups it considered uncouth and threatening. The westsiders relocated almost every generation, and in each cycle of "Dutch flight," they bought or built new churches, homes, schools, stores, and shops. By contrast, Englewood was stable for seventy-five years, and the Roseland and South Holland colonies remained intact for more than one hundred years.

The Reformed Dutch survived against all odds in the metropolis of Chicago primarily because of their religious institutions. They experienced the full force of Americanization on their families and institutions, but they coped and even flourished by ghettoizing themselves as a cognitive minority (to use sociologist Peter Berger's phrase). This strategy worked for four generations and more, but since the 1950s many young adults have left the ethnic community behind for other climes or succumbed to the city's allure. Today, all of the Reformed congregations in greater Chicago count only twenty-three thousand members, or 10 percent of the city's quarter million Dutch.

A major focus of this book is the emergence of the Groninger Hoek on the West Side in the years after the Civil War, but the Englewood and Roseland communities also share the story. Out of cultural diversity came unity, out of spiritual indifference came Calvinist orthodoxy and intense loyalty to the Reformed churches, and out of poverty came middle-class respectability. General prosperity took two or three generations. Less than one in seven Dutch families in Chicago owned their own homes in 1900. Economic competency for most did not come until after the First World War, but it was the Second World War and its aftermath that brought real prosperity and even great wealth for some. Today the Dutch live comfortably in the far suburbs and worship in imposing churches. They enjoy the fruits of the sacrifices of their immigrant forebears, who gave up everything for freedom and opportunity in America.

This is the story I have recounted here in all its splendid detail. Those with roots in the Dutch sub-cultures of Chicago, especially the Reformed communities, will find their history rescued from near oblivion. Without history there can be no memory, and without memory there is no self-understanding. Above the entrance to the National Archives is inscribed the words, "Past is Prologue." Knowing the past enables one to understand the present and chart the future. For parents and grandparents this book offers a feast of recognition and nostalgia; it will jog their memories and kindle reminiscences about the "old days" among themselves and especially with their children and grandchildren. These conversations, hopefully, will create in the next generation a collective memory of families, churches, schools, and communities that has vanished. Such memories may help them avoid past failings and face the future with greater confidence.

In short, this is a memory book for "insiders," although others are invited to look in. It tells the story, warts and all. Ethnicity and religion are a powerful adhesive, but they can also divide and exclude. I have described those divisions and setbacks, and also noted the triumphs and accomplishments. But I have not attempted to balance the strengths and weaknesses or to analyze the complicated interaction between faith and folk. Neither have I compared the Chicago Dutch to their compatriots elsewhere in the United States, or placed them in the midst of other ethnic groups in the city. Is there a Chicago Dutch character that sets them apart from Hollanders in Grand Rapids, Michigan? How do they differ from Chicago's other northern European immigrant groups, such as Germans and Swedes? Such analytic questions are worthy of study, and readers are invited to use this detailed narrative account to build larger generalizations and conclusions.

CHAPTER I

Dutch Chicago Takes Shape

Chicago and the state of Illinois in general never appealed to the Dutch immigrants as did Michigan, Iowa, and Wisconsin. Land for farming was expensive, and the population was increasing rapidly with the influx of peoples from every country in Europe. Most important, however, was the absence of trusted preachers to direct and promote the immigration. In other states, the colonists had eloquent clerics to write pamphlets and let-

Chicago Fire of 1871, looking east along Randolph Street from Market Street (now Wacker Drive). Gutted building is the county courthouse and city hall.

(Courtesy of Chicago Historical Society)

ters to newspapers in the Netherlands to recruit settlers. The Chicago settlements had to rely on their own *spekbrieven* ("bacon letters"), which were not without impact.

Dutch settlers drifted into the Windy City in ones and twos as early as 1839, only two years after the city's founding. Leonard Falch (Valk), a soapmaker and chandler (candle maker) on La Salle Street in 1839, and his Dutch-born wife were the first Dutch family living in Chicago, and their eldest son Charles, born in 1840, was the first recorded Dutch birth in the city. In 1850 Falch reported real estate worth $10,000, which made him the wealthiest Hollander in all of Illinois. He was still a soapmaker in the 1860s, living near the north city limits at Hubbard Street.[1]

In the 1840s three distinct Dutch neighborhoods emerged in Cook County – the "city Dutch" on the near West Side, and the "country Dutch" in Roseland (first called High Prairie) fourteen miles south and South Holland (first called Low Prairie) twenty miles south. The country Dutch were truck gardeners, while the city Dutch became teamsters and trash collectors. All three "cocoons," to use church historian Martin Marty's guiding metaphor, were centered around their Reformed churches, which marked the Dutch as a people of faith who took their Calvinist heritage seriously.[2]

By 1900 Chicago's Hollanders had collected in four areas – three thousand on the Near West Side, three thousand in Englewood, seven

1. *Fergus' Directory of the City of Chicago for 1839* (Chicago: Fergus Printing Co., 1876), 14. The 1850 federal population census of Chicago and Cook County lists Falch and his wife as Dutch-born. The 1850 census is the first to record the nationality or state of birth of all inhabitants. See Robert P. Swierenga, comp., *Dutch Households in U.S. Population Censuses, 1850, 1860, 1870: An Alphabetical Listing by Family Heads,* 3 vols. (Wilmington, Del.: Scholarly Resources, 1987), 1:326 (also in CD-ROM format in Swierenga, *Family Tree Maker's Family Archives, Immigration Records: Dutch in America, 1800s,* CD #269 (Broderbund, 2000). In the Chicago city directories, 1839-1861, Falch is variously listed as a soap and candle maker or chandler, and a grocer. He lived for many years on the northwest corner of Little Fort Road and Hubbard Street, and his shop was on La Salle Street.

2. Amry Vandenbosch, *The Dutch Communities of Chicago* (Chicago: Knickerbocker Society of Chicago, 1927). This hundred-page book, Vandenbosch's master's thesis, is the only study of the Chicago Dutch. It provides a brief sketch of the West Side community (pp. 16-28, 45-46, 54-56, 96-97). The two standard histories of the Dutch in America devote only a few pages to the West Side settlement. See Jacob Van Hinte, *Netherlanders in America: A Study of Emigration and Settlement in the Nineteenth and Twentieth Centuries in the United States of America,* Robert P. Swierenga, gen. ed., Adriaan de Wit, trans. (Grand Rapids: Baker, 1985), 153-56, 792-94; and Henry S. Lucas, *Netherlanders in America: Dutch Immigration to the United States and Canada, 1789-1950* (Ann Arbor: Univ. of Michigan Press, 1955, reprinted Grand Rapids: Eerdmans, 1989), 227-32, 322-28.

thousand in Roseland, and one thousand in South Holland. The rest were scattered across the city center and North Side. The West Side covered a broad band between Van Buren (400 south) to 18th streets westward to the city limits and into Cicero and Berwyn. Four Dutch Reformed churches served the area. Englewood, which ran from 55th to 75th streets, and Roseland, which extended from 99th to 115th streets, were both annexed in 1889. These densely packed Dutch centers eventually each had four Reformed and four Christian Reformed congregations. South Holland remains a separate village that only in recent decades became part of the greater metropolitan area.[3]

Upward Mobility

The census manuscripts provide a factual picture of the economic life of the Dutch in Chicago. Unlike many immigrant groups, they began one or two rungs up on the job ladder. In 1850, ten breadwinners were skilled craftsmen (carpenters, cabinetmakers, blacksmith, etc.), and eight were wooden shingle makers, a semi-skilled job that offered ready work in the thriving lumber industry. Several farmed and six were laborers and hands. Eight young women, ages 12 to 22, were boarding out as maids, which was a common way to augment the family's income until marriage. Only three families reported owning real estate. Wages at the time ranged from 75 cents a day for unskilled labor to $2 a day for skilled craftsmen.

Within five years, by 1852, several adult sons of the pioneers had moved into entry-level trades at the city newspaper, the *Democratic Press.* Hiram Vanden Belt was a printer and Henry Van Zwol an apprentice printer at the plant. In 1858 Vanden Belt had risen to foreman of the pressroom.

Vanden Belt personified the rising status of the Dutch, evident by 1860. Three-fourths of all households had reportable wealth ($50 or more in real estate and personal property), and the average surpassed $500 per household. Even most laborers owned property; one had $2,000. Three were teamsters, the first of their fraternity to take the reins. Craftsmen comprised nearly one-half of the Dutch work force, led by carpenters and painters, and one in five held "white collar" jobs as shopkeepers, dealers and brokers, clerks, police and firemen, a physician, and a ship captain.

3. Richard A. Cook, *South Holland, Illinois: A History, 1848-1966* (South Holland: South Holland Trust and Savings Bank, 1966).

One of these pencil pushers was the thirty-year-old surveyor, Henry Hospers, a son of Jan Hospers of the Pella, Iowa, Dutch colony. Henry Hospers became a prime mover in the Orange City Dutch colony in northwestern Iowa a decade later. Other notables in Chicago were Albert Malefyt and Theodore G. Kimman, both master carriage builders, who owned and operated a carriage factory at West Madison and Green Streets.

The Dutch profited from the economic buildup of the Civil War, along with the rising economy of the city generally. The total value of the real and personal property of the Chicago Dutch in 1870 surpassed $500,000, and the average property value per household doubled in ten years from $530 in 1860 to $1,013 in 1870. The Reverend Bernardus De Beij (Bey) of First Reformed Church slightly exaggerated when he reported that "many own a house or will soon own one," but he was correct that most "earn a good living."[4] Hundreds of new immigrants arrived from the Netherlands as soon as the war ended in the spring of 1865. By 1870 Chicago's Dutch population had jumped fivefold over 1860 (from 400 to 2,095).

Most of the newcomers were farm laborers from northern Groningen who joined the ranks of the city's unskilled workers. Of the 655 Dutch males in the labor force in 1870, one-third were day laborers, the same proportion as in 1860. Laborers in 1870 earned $1.50 to $2 a day or $36 to $48 a month. Few could find work for the entire year, however, so average annual earnings for laborers ranged only from $170 to $200. One company, the Illinois Central Railroad, employed as laborers the heads of twenty-two families in Hyde Park, which was about one-third of all the Dutch households in the township. This was the most concentrated Dutch job site in the Chicago area. Almost all the Hyde Park families emigrated from the province of Zuid Holland.[5]

The occupational data reveal a Dutch characteristic — the desire to be "one's own boss." Half of the Dutch work force in 1870 was self-

4. Bernardus De Bey letter, *Provinciale Groninger Courant,* 13 Feb. 1869. De Bey's invaluable letters were published in ibid., 1869-1871. Dirk Hoogeveen translated these letters. Very few Chicago Dutch are known to have served in the Civil War. One who did was John C. Goemans, who immigrated to Chicago from Rotterdam in 1853 (obituary, *Onze Toekomst,* 2 Apr. 1909).

5. Hyde Park Township, 1870, in Swierenga, *Dutch Households in U.S. Population Censuses;* letters of De Bey, *Provinciale Groninger Courant,* 10 Dec. 1869; 8 June 1870; Letter of K. Boersma, Englewood, to E. Mussenga, Kloosterburen, Groningen, 19 Dec. [1880], Archives, Calvin College, trans. Henry Lammers.

employed; only 5 percent worked in factories, foundries, mills, and the like. Skilled craftsmen and building contractors were dominant, comprising 40 percent of the work force. Another 25 percent were clerks, dealers, and retailers of all kinds. Carpenters earned $15 a week and store clerks $8.[6] Fifteen Dutch were farming, market gardening, and dairying on the outskirts; that number increased rapidly in the next decades. The Dutch were clearly upgrading themselves.

Several excelled in business. Sieds De Vries, an 1861 immigrant, opened a lumberyard in Englewood that was carried on by his sons. Henry Bosch, a member of the Reverend Bernardus De Bey's church in Middelstum, Groningen, emigrated to Chicago in 1862 and opened a wallpaper and paint store in Hyde Park. It was so successful that he expanded to leading cities across the country. Another Dutch entrepreneur in Hyde Park was Marinus Vander Kloot, a blacksmith who immigrated in 1868 from the Amsterdam region and started the Vander Kloot Iron Foundry. By the 1920s the list of prominent Holland-American firms in real estate, wholesale produce, and teaming had grown considerably.[7]

Very few Dutch women were in the workforce. According to a Dutch adage, "a woman's place is in the home." In 1870 when census marshals for the first time were required to report the occupation of females, not one Dutch wife was employed, except for two widows – a washerwoman and a boarding house operator. But 82 unmarried young women were working full-time. Three-fourths were boarding out as servants, 15 were seamstresses and dressmakers, one was a professional singer, one was peddling perfume ("Avon calling"?), one was a store clerk, another a hairdresser, and one worked in a factory stripping tobacco. All left the workplace when they married.

The pay for servant girls ranged from $1.50 to $2 per week, including room and board. And in Chicago, as recent immigrants Abel G. and Hinderkje Bouws reported to family in the homeland, girls "don't have to work as hard here as they do over there and they get better food and drink. Generally speaking it is much better here for the working class than where you are."[8]

6. William J. Elzing, Chicago, to Jelle Elzing, Irnsum, Friesland, 11 Sept. 1870, Archives, Calvin College, trans. Henry Lammers.

7. Vandenbosch, *Dutch Communities of Chicago,* 77; Robert P. Swierenga, comp., "Dutch in Chicago and Cook County 1900 Federal Census."

8. Letter of Abel G. and Hinderkje Bouws, Chicago, to "Brothers, sisters, nephews, and nieces," 6 Mar. 1890, Archives, Calvin College, trans. Henry Lammers.

Chicago, the "Lightning City"

Dutch settlement in Chicago began near the city center and spread out into the new neighborhoods and suburbs of Cook County; it eventually reached the adjacent counties of Will and Du Page in Illinois and Lake County in Indiana.

The infant city that received these newcomers was still very primitive, but it was on the verge of a massive growth spurt. Hendrik Van Eyck, an immigrant from Zwolle who visited Chicago in 1848, recorded in his diary that Chicago already had twenty-five thousand inhabitants, and its commerce and industries were developing in an "extraordinary fashion." Van Eyck noticed a "bustle here like that in the largest commercial cities of the Old World. Here I found many Hollanders whom I had known some time ago. They were all doing well. There is much trade here in wood for building purposes, etc."[9]

Van Eyck's upbeat evaluation is echoed by the English visitor, John Lewis Payton, who toured Chicago the same year. "A kind of restless activity prevailed," said Payton, "which I had seen no where else in the west except in Cincinnati." But Payton also noted the dismal living conditions:

> The city is situated on both sides of the Chicago River, a sluggish, slimy stream, too lazy to clean itself, and on both sides of its north and south branches, upon a level piece of ground, half dry and half wet, resembling a salt marsh, and containing a population of 20,000. There was no pavement, no macadamized streets, no drainage, and the three thousand houses in which the people lived were almost entirely small timber buildings, painted white, and this white much defaced by mud. . . . To render the streets and sidewalks passable, they were covered with deal boards from house to house, the boards resting upon cross sills of heavy timber. This kind of track is called "the plank road." Under these planks the water was standing on the surface over three-fourths of the city, and as the sewers from the houses were emptied under them, a frightful odor was emitted in summer, causing fevers and other diseases, foreign to the climate.[10]

9. Hendrik Van Eyck Diary, entry of 16 Aug. 1848, Holland Museum Collection, Joint Archives of Holland, Hope College.

10. Payton's description is quoted in Harold M. Mayer and Richard C. Wade, *Chicago: Growth of a Metropolis* (Chicago: Univ. of Chicago Press, 1969), 28-172, quote 32. This section relies heavily on this excellent work.

No wonder Chicagoans suffered from severe cholera outbreaks in the summers of 1849 and 1850.

Not only was the city unhealthy, its highways were impassable and there was not a single mile of railroad track in 1850. This was about to change, however. Chicago's central location made it the market of the Midwest and the jumping-off point for immigrants from Europe and the East Coast. By 1854 Chicago was the hub of the nation's transportation systems by water and rail. It was also a center of meatpacking, grain elevators, and farm implement factories such as the McCormick Reaper works. In 1856 ten trunk rail lines ran into Chicago, with 58 passenger and 38 freight trains arriving daily.[11]

Chicago harbor rivaled the railroads in traffic. It received three hundred ships daily by the 1860s, carrying lumber from northern Wisconsin and Michigan, iron ore from Lake Superior, and manufactured goods from the East. Timber vessels choked the harbor, and lumberyards extended for miles along the south branch of the Chicago River from Halsted to Western avenues. In 1867, 50 million pine boards were sold, and total wood sales reached 1.5 billion feet. Chicago's seventeen grain elevators in 1870 bulged with 60 million bushels of grain. As early as 1856, some of the wheat went directly to England by ship via the Mississippi River. Already in 1865 the Union Stockyards on the southwest side sprawled over 355 acres (one-half of a square mile), and quickly it became the slaughter capital of the world, taking in two hundred rail cars of live animals per day. On the north branch of the river in the 1860s stood the McCormick Reaper and Mower Works and the steel works of the North Chicago Rolling Mills.[12]

Between 1850 and 1870, Chicago's population grew tenfold to 300,000; more than half the increase was foreign-born. State Street, the east-west division line, extended up to eight miles long, traversed by horse-drawn streetcars in all directions. In one generation, Chicago passed from Indian territory to large metropolis. To capture the speed of the transformation, a foreign visitor in 1870 called it "the lightning city." Everywhere the city was expanding, particularly the West Side, which seemed to be "heaved up out of the mud by a benevolent earthquake."[13]

Chicago's four fashionable neighborhoods in the 1860s to 1880s were south along Indiana, Prairie, Calumet, and South Park Avenues around

11. Ibid., 30-35, quote 35.

12. Ibid., 44-53.

13. British visitor Sara Jane Lippincott, quoted in Mayer and Wade, *Chicago,* 35.

22nd Street; west along Washington Boulevard around Union Park; Ashland Boulevard between Monroe and Harrison Streets; and along north La Salle and Dearborn Streets.

The newly built home of Adriaan Vander Kloot on West Congress Street east of Laflin Avenue in the Ashland-Harrison district exemplified the opulence. "The house truly excels among the beautiful houses of which there is no lack on W. Congress Str.," reported the Chicago Dutch-language newspaper, *De Nederlander,* in 1885:

> The front features multi-colored glass that tastefully contrasts with the Anderson pressed brick. There are three stories. The hall, library, and reception room have been finished with hard polished wood. The rest of the house is finished with the finest light wood, partly naturally polished, partly painted in three different colors. Beautiful furniture has been ordered. Both inside and out, this will be one of the most beautiful houses occupied here by a Dutchman – and certainly the most expensive.[14]

While the wealthy lived along the avenues and boulevards, the crowded and dirty "workers' districts" consisted of huddled, pine cottages in poor neighborhoods: west of Wells Street (200 west) on the North Side, west of Ashland (1600 west) from Kinzie (440 north) to Harrison (600 south) on the West Side, and west of State Street on the South Side. The West Side population quadrupled between 1863 and 1873, thanks in part to new Dutch arrivals after the Civil War. In the workers' districts there were often two houses per lot – one facing the street and one on the alley. In contrast, the avenues had spacious lots.[15]

The Chicago fire of 1871 put a temporary halt to this development, but it also gave the city a chance to remake itself. The fire devastated the city center and north coast from Halsted Street (800 west) to Lake Michigan, because the winds were from the southwest (see figure 1.1). It claimed 250 lives, consumed 17,000 homes, left one-third of the population homeless, and created property losses of nearly $200 million.[16]

The Dutch westsiders were spared. Only two Reformed families and perhaps twenty other families were burned out, according to Bernardus

14. *De Nederlander,* 16 Sept. 1885, reprinted in *De Grondwet* (Holland, Mich.), 22 Sept. 1885, trans. Huug van den Dool.

15. Mayer and Wade, *Chicago,* 63-64.

16. Irving Cutler, *Chicago: Metropolis of the Mid-Continent,* 3rd ed. (Dubuque, Iowa: Geographic Society of Chicago, 1982), 30.

Figure 1.1 Reformed Churches on the Old West Side

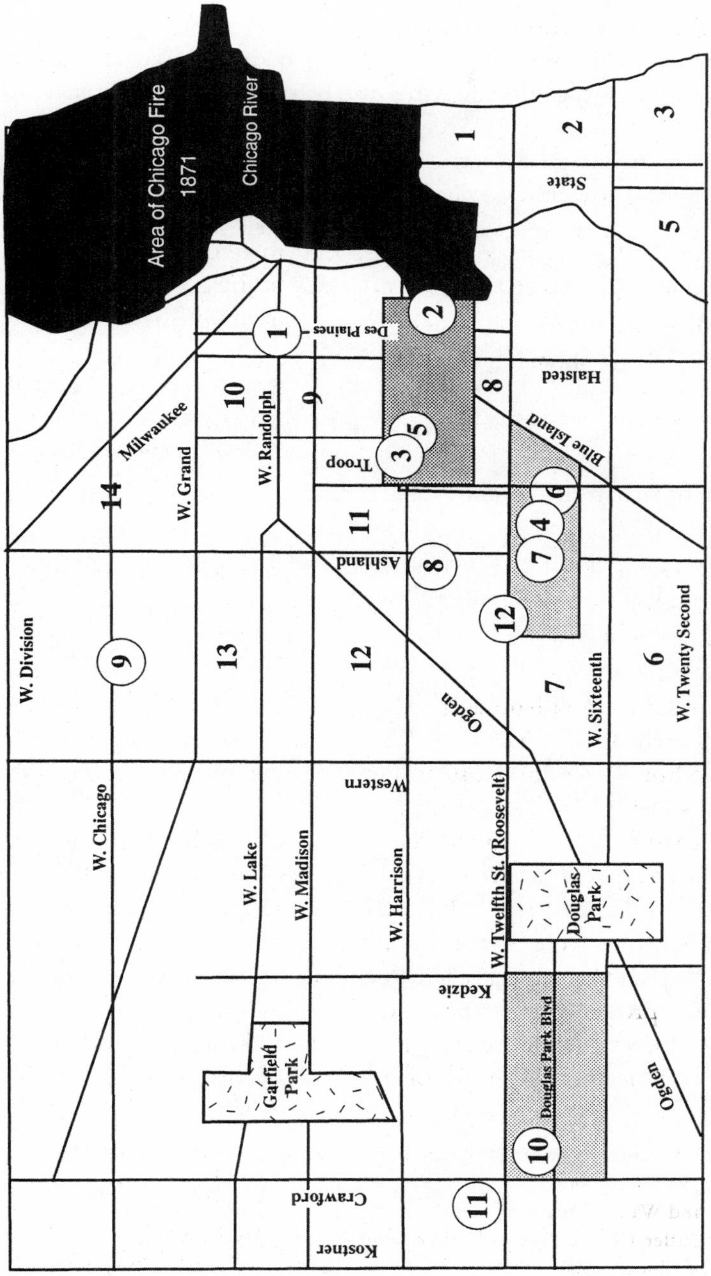

1. First Reformed, 1853–56
2. First Reformed, 1856–69
3. First Reformed, 1869–94
4. First Reformed, 1894–1944
5. First Christian Reformed, 1867–83
6. First Christian Reformed, 1883–1923
7. First Christian Reformed, 1923–45
8. Trinity Reformed, 1891–1919
9. Northwestern Reformed, 1892–1926
10. Douglas Park Christian Reformed, 1899–1927
11. Third Christian Reformed, 1912–24
12. Fourth Christian Reformed, 1923–46

De Bey, pastor of the First Reformed Church at the time. Rebuilding the city, said De Bey in a letter to the homeland, created all the more job opportunities for unskilled laborers who knew how to work.[17]

After the fire, Chicago became a modern metropolis, with modest "skyscrapers," railroad stations, and cable cars running in all directions into new subdivisions. K. Boersma, a recent immigrant to Englewood, could hardly believe the speed of the electric cable cars. "Here they run cars that if you ever saw them you would certainly be amazed," he wrote to friends in Groningen, "because there are no horses in front. There is no locomotive up ahead or anything; they go so fast that horses cannot keep up to them." Another newly arrived Groninger, Geeske Bandringa, wrote home in 1884: "Oh Jantje, you will never believe how big a city this is. It is said that there is hardly an end to it. And how big the houses are; I have seen houses with at least 100 panes of glass in them. If you were here you would be amazed. It is said that here in Chicago live eleven thousand Dutchmen."[18]

These Dutch, like most new immigrant groups, knew at first hand the underside of urban life. The Reverend Peter Moerdyke of Trinity Reformed Church complained in 1899 of the "corruption, the gross materialism, the abominable filth of streets and alleys, the vile politics, the shallow religion, . . . [and the] vulgar and glaring inequities . . . in this bragging city." In 1900, city officials finally recognized the dire need of the West Side and improved many miles of streets with brick and asphalt.[19]

The city's population, mostly foreign-born, doubled from one-half to one million between 1880 and 1890 and its land area covered 160 square miles.[20] The Dutch kept pace, rising from 3,100 to 21,500 (table 1.3). They were concentrated on the South Side; by 1900 nearly one-half resided in the Englewood and Roseland districts. Ward 31, which encompassed Englewood, had 2,228 of Dutch birth or parentage, and Ward 34, which included Roseland, had triple that number at 7,208 (figures 1.6 and 1.7).

17. Herbert J. Brinks, "Netherlanders in the Chicago Area," *Origins* 1, No. 1 (1983): 3; Brinks, "Bernardus De Beij (1815-1894)," ibid., 9-13.

18. Letter of Geeske Bandringa to Jantje Borgman, Pieterburen, Groningen, [1884], published in unnamed Netherlands newspaper; Letter of K. Boersma, Englewood, to E. Mussenga, Kloosterburen, Groningen, 19 Dec. [1880s], both in the Archives, Calvin College.

19. Moerdyke, "Chicago Letter," *Christian Intelligencer* (hereafter *CI*), 18 Oct. 1899, p. 9; 21 Nov. 1900, p. 752.

20. Mayer and Wade, *Chicago,* 144 (quote), 171-172; *Chicago Daily News Almanac,* 1900, 99; Melvin G. Holli and Peter d'A. Jones, eds., *Ethnic Chicago: A Multicultural Portrait,* 4th ed. (Grand Rapids: Eerdmans, 1995), 5.

Table 1.1 Number of Dutch-born and Dutch Parentage, by Ward, Chicago, 1850-1900

Ward	1850	1860	1870	1870*	1880	1900
1	3	20	61	0%	16	91
2	2	24	37	0%	95	49
3	6	15	88	0%	39	99
4	1	2	21	0%	47	195
5	29	61	19	0%	87	264
6	36	84	89	15%	351	190
7	7	13	304	46%	242	105
8	14	27	194	50%	201	204
9	3	5	403	10%	40	1,330
10		148	68	0%	33	778
11			28	0%	52	215
12			211	80%	97	566
13			48	94%	105	573
14			57	78%	185	435
15			266	59%	35	267
16			56	0%	52	97
17			47	0%	45	17
18			23	0%	31	38
19			42	5%		81
20			33	18%		38
21						82
22						33
23						39
24						69
25						82
26						172
27						280
28						398
29						131
30						1,182
31						2,228
32						332
33						173
34						7,208
35						221
Total	101	399	2,095	34%	3,120	21,537

*Column indicates percent Groninger, i.e., Groningen-born and their U.S.-born children, identified by linkage to Netherlands emigration records and by family names.

Source: Compiled from U.S. Population Censuses of Chicago, 1850-1900.

The exact Dutch proportion of the population in these neighborhoods is difficult to ascertain, but the number present in 1920 can be estimated, based on a published study of federal census tracts, which breaks down the data to areas of one square mile or less. Chicago in 1920 comprised some 500 census tracts. Three cover the main Dutch communities: Tract 256 in the Old West Side (Taylor to 16th Street from Laflin to Wood), Tract 430 in Englewood (Halsted to Loomis from 71st to 79th streets), and Tract 483 in Roseland (State to Halsted streets from 103rd to 111th streets). From this data, I calculated the Dutch proportion of the population in 1920 as 60 percent in the heart of Roseland, 20 percent in the core of Englewood, and 17 percent in the Groninger Hoek on the Old West Side. The Roseland Dutch shared their neighborhood primarily with Swedish Protestants; Englewood had many Irish Catholics and Protestant Germans and Swedes. The entire West Side was dominated by Russian and Polish Jews, who outnumbered the Dutch by at least twenty to one.[21]

Antecedents of the Groninger Hoek

Dutch settlement took shape in the 1840s and 1850s in the region immediately west of the Chicago River around Randolph and Clinton streets; the area later became known as Haymarket Square. In 1850 two-thirds lived west of the Chicago River, half north of Randolph Street and half south of it (see figure 1.1). These were the vanguard of a mass emigration from the Netherlands that began in 1846 due to a religious schism and a potato famine.[22]

The first five Dutch families arrived in 1847, when Chicago was barely ten years old. Within three years, the federal census enumerator listed one hundred Dutch-born in the city. Compared to the homogeneous southside colonies, the city Dutch hailed from many parts of the Netherlands and were culturally diverse. They scattered widely and lacked

21. Ernest W. Burgess and Charles Newcomb, eds., *Census Data of the City of Chicago, 1920* (Chicago: Univ. of Chicago Press, 1931). I calculated the percentage of Dutch-born and Dutch parentage by multiplying the number of Dutch-born by a factor of five on the West Side and Englewood and by a factor of 3.5 in Roseland. The lower factor for Roseland takes account of the later immigration and hence fewer U.S.-born children. The number of Reformed Church members in the three neighborhoods in 1920 was also used to estimate the total Dutch stock population. For Roseland the total was 5,100, Englewood 2,800, and for the Old West Side 2,200 (see appendix 5 for exact totals).

22. Vandenbosch, *Dutch Communities of Chicago,* 93.

cohesion for many years. Unlike South Holland and Roseland, the Groninger Hoek did not begin with the group migration of a *dominie* (the Dutch term for a clergyman that literally means "Lord"), such as the Reverend Willem Wust of South Holland. It even lacked a dominant lay leader like Jakob de Jong in Roseland.

From unpromising beginnings, the westside Dutch Calvinists evolved into a socially homogeneous, religiously orthodox, and economically prosperous community that has continued for more than 150 years. While they shared their neighborhoods and rubbed elbows on the job with "outsiders," culturally and religiously they lived their lives from the cradle to the grave within the cocoon of their families, churches, Christian schools, social organizations, shops, and offices. Distinctive traits were a "love of home, love of the Bible, and patience and persistence."

The earliest Dutch settlers hailed not from Groningen but from the provinces of Zeeland, Friesland, Zuid Holland, Noord Holland, Gelderland, and Utrecht. The first families in 1847 were the households of Herman Van Zwol, R. G. Kroes, Lucas Vanden Belt (Bilt), Henry Pelgrom, and Ale Steginga. All lived along the north branch of the Chicago River.[23]

Van Zwol was a key person because he took the lead in gathering the few families for worship services in his home. He arrived in Chicago due to a transportation mistake, having intended to settle in Albertus C. Van Raalte's Holland, Michigan, colony, founded in 1847. Instead, Van Zwol landed in Chicago and decided to stay, after readily finding work in his carpenter's craft. The family rented a home on North Clark Street, near the blacksmith Kroes and his family. Vanden Belt and Steginga, both bargemen in the Netherlands, were making shingles, along with their unmarried sons. Pelgrom, who had been a merchant, was also a shingle maker. Vanden Belt lived in a houseboat moored on the river at Canal Street. Steginga and Pelgrom resided west of the river north of Randolph Street near the lumberyards and wood products factories that lined the banks.

Other 1847 arrivals who worshiped at Van Zwol's home, according to

23. Pelgrom and his wife and seven children were from Baambrugge, Utrecht; Van Zwol with his wife and two children were from Deventer; Vanden Belt with his wife and four children were from Hasselt, both in Overijssel; Kroes and his wife were from Harlingen, and Steginga and his wife and two children from Workum, both in Friesland. Information on place of origin and religion are in Robert P. Swierenga, comp., *Dutch Emigrants to the United States, South Africa, South America, and Southeast Asia, 1835-1880: An Alphabetical Listing by Household Heads and Independent Persons* (Wilmington, Del.: Scholarly Resources, 1983); and Swierenga, *Dutch Households in U.S. Population Censuses.* Both lists are in Swierenga, "Dutch in America, 1800s," CD #269.

a 1904 semicentennial history of the First Reformed Church written by George Birkhoff, Sr., are the families of Ede Sipke Meter, Sr., a merchant from Friesland; Hendrik Albertse, a saddler from the city of Utrecht; Barend Snitseler, a farmer, and wife from Gelderland; Hendrik Sterenberg, an unmarried laborer from Groningen; Nicholas (Klaas) Van Heest, a laborer from Zuid Holland; J. Labots; and one Wieland. The families Albertse, Snitseler, and Sterenberg were members of the Christian Seceded Church. Sterenberg was the first known Groninger in Chicago.[24]

The immigrants of 1848 and 1849 were the Frisians Maas Vander Kooi, a dairyman who painted houses in Chicago and served as the first treasurer of First Reformed Church, and Gosse Vierstra, a ship carpenter's hired hand who advanced to become a ship carpenter. From Zeeland came the house painter Willem Goosen, the tailor Isaac Van't Hof, and the workman Jannis Schaap. Zuid Holland sent out Adam Ooms, a village policeman who had to accept a common laborer's job in Chicago. All these emigrated with wives and children. Other 1849 arrivals were the families of Rudolf Keun (Kuin), a carpenter from Groningen; Simon Nederveld from Zuid Holland; Roelof Pieters, an unmarried farmer from Drenthe, who later succeeded Van Raalte as pastor of Holland's First Reformed Church; Nicholas (Klaas) Voute (Foute), a painter from Noord Holland; and Thomas Vander Zee.[25]

Additional pre-1850 immigrants, whose places of origin remain unknown, were J. De Glopper, a cabinetmaker; Marion De Jong, a farmer; Henry Muller, a laborer; Isaac Schelling, a mechanic; William Carson, Chicago's first Dutch grocer; and five unmarried hired hands – Philip Van Nieuwland, Henry Handkolk, Isaac Schryter; and the brothers Harry and John Roelofs. Finally, there was a Prins whose wife and two oldest children died of cholera in Chicago, leaving the widower with three young children.

Families arriving in 1850-52 were Ernest Klokke, a Lutheran from the city of Utrecht, who was a broker but found work as a clerk in Chicago; Jan Slotboom, a weaver from Gelderland, who became a railroad ticket agent; and Daniel Gordon, a bricklayer's hired hand from Zuid Holland, who was a stonemason.[26]

24. G. B. Sr. [George Birkhoff, Sr.], "Historische Schetsen," *De Hope* (Holland, Michigan), 25 May 1904, p. 4, trans. Huug van den Dool. None of the 1847 arrivals named by Birkhoff are found in early city directories or the 1850 federal census.

25. Birkhoff, "Historische Schetsen"; First Reformed Church Minutes, 1853-1867; Swierenga, *Dutch Emigrants to the United States.*

26. Listed in Swierenga, *Dutch Emigrants to the United States;* and Swierenga, *Dutch Households in U.S. Population Censuses.*

The organization of a Reformed church in 1853 made Chicago a more attractive destination for many Dutch immigrants. A church was a prerequisite for a viable settlement. In the next years the Dutch population of Chicago saw its greatest increase, including four Groninger families who arrived in 1853. These were the farm laborers Nicholas (or Harm) Ronda, with his wife and daughter, and his younger brother Henry and his wife. A dozen other newcomers in 1853 were D. Van Berschot from Zuid Holland; Berend Boterman, a baker, and B. Vander Kolk, a farmer, both from Overijssel; J. Blankenzee; Hermannus Fabries, a plumber, and wife from Zuid Holland; Willem Goossen, an unmarried painter from Zeeland; Daniel Schipperus (Schippers); the family of Cornelis Vander Wolff, a cook from Noord Holland; John Brink; and B. Van Wijnkoop.[27]

The next year, 1854, seven more Groninger families arrived, plus an equal number from other provinces. The Groningers were the blacksmiths Cornelius Bos and Peter Kooi, shoemaker John Evenhuis (Evenhouse), carpenter Bernardus Postema, laborer Eisse Broekema, and two Sellinga families. Bos, Kooi, Evenhouse, and Ronda are household names on the West Side. Other newcomers in 1854 were John Van Ballegooyen from Gelderland; John Tris, a carpenter's hired hand from Zeeland; Casper Pelgrim, a retired military officer and a Lutheran from Zuid Holland; and Peter Bunning, Marinus Hoogbruin, Henry Nyenhuis, and William Jansen, whose origins are not yet known. Thus, 1854 was the premier year for the Chicago Dutch prior to the Civil War.[28]

By 1860 the West Side contained over half (53 percent) of all the city's Hollanders (see figure 1.4). Most lived in the area bounded by Harrison Street (800 south) on the north, 12th Street (renamed Roosevelt Road in 1919) on the south, the south branch of the Chicago River on the east, and Loomis Street (1400 west) on the west. Another one-fifth lived on the northwest side and the remaining quarter were scattered east of the river and north and south of the city center.

The 1870 Chicago census, which counted 2,095 Dutch-born and their native-born children, reveals a much greater concentration on the West Side, where most of the Reformed Dutch resided (see figure 1.5). Over 60 percent of Chicago's Hollanders lived west of the river and south of Lake Street; only 20 percent were north of Lake Street. Two small nuclei were in the same regions as in 1860: between Harrison and 12th Streets to Loomis (Ward 9), with 403 Dutch (20 percent), and a vast, newly opened region

27. Birkhoff, "Historische Schetsen"; Swierenga, *Dutch Emigrants to the United States.*
28. Swierenga, *Dutch Emigrants to the United States.*

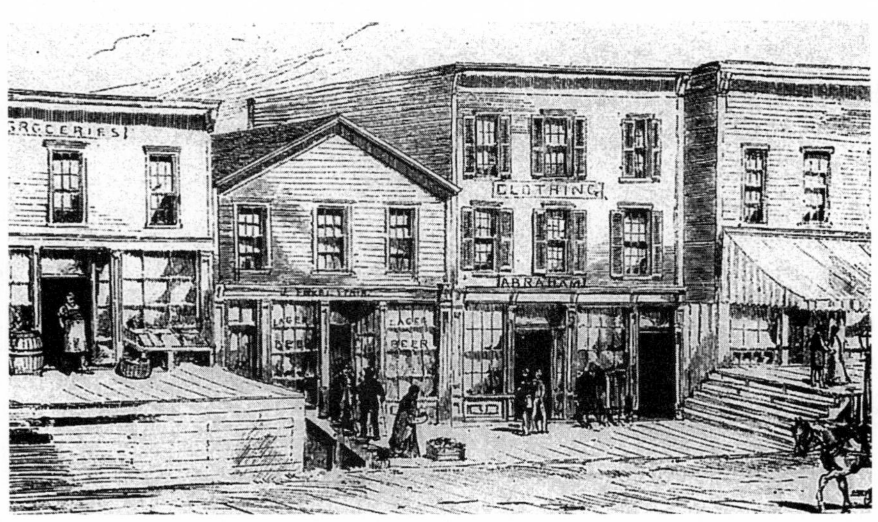

Jewish-owned stores, Clark Street, 1857
(Courtesy of Chicago Historical Society)

south of 16th Street to the Illinois-Michigan Canal and west to Crawford Avenue (Ward 7) with 304 Dutch (15 percent). The area in between, from 12th to 16th Streets (Ward 8), which by the 1880s was the geographic center of the Reformed settlement, had only 194 Dutch (9 percent). West of Loomis between 12th and Lake Street (Wards 12 and 13) had another 259 (12 percent).

Apart from the West Side wards, which were heavily Reformed, Dutch Jews lived in the city center and immediately west of the river (Wards 10 and 11). In the central business district, they owned second-hand clothing stores and pawnshops on Wells and Clark streets, several cigar shops on Washington Street, and tailor shops on Randolph Street. Henry S. Haas, a retail clothing merchant located at 718 S. Wabash Avenue, owned $37,000 worth of property in 1870 and was by far the wealthiest Hollander in Chicago. About 4 percent of the Dutch in Chicago were Jews, which was twice the percentage of Jews in the Netherlands. Their story is told in chapter 15.

Dutch Catholics were underrepresented in Chicago and widely dispersed (see table 1.2). They composed about 10 percent of Dutch, whereas in the Netherlands, Catholics numbered over 36 percent of the population. Father Arnold Damen, the founder of Holy Family Parish and St. Ignatius High School (later College) on West 12th Street at May Street, was the most famous Dutch Jesuit in America. Damen Avenue and Damen Bridge were named in honor of his pioneering work in church and school

Table 1.2 Dutch Catholics in Chicago, by Ward, 1870

Ward	Households	Individuals
3	16	47
4	2	11
6	15	80
7	13	45
8	10	38
9	17	61
10	4	23
14	2	6
15	11	42
16	16	56
17	7	31
18	5	8
19	4	14
20	2	8
Total	124	470

Source: These figures are estimates compiled from the Chicago 1870 federal population census manuscripts. Wards not listed (e.g., 1, 2, 5, 11, 12, 13) had no Dutch.

in Chicago.[29] The nearby St. Francis of Assisi Church on West 12th Street at Newberry Avenue also had two Dutch priests, Ferdinand Kalvelage and Bernard Baak, and a few Dutch Catholics lived in that locale. The largest Dutch Catholic parish in Chicago, St. Willibrord, took shape in the 1890s in Roseland's Kensington district. This two-hundred-family parish remained predominantly Dutch until the 1960s.[30]

Beginnings of the Groninger Hoek

The Reformed immigrants formed a unique subset of Chicago's Dutch population, centered in their churches and schools. In the 1856 they built their first sanctuary, a modest 20- by 45-foot structure, costing $540 for

29. Joseph P. Conroy, S.J., *Arnold Damen, S.J.: A Chapter in the Making of Chicago* (New York: Benzinger Brothers, 1930); Thomas M. Mulkerins, S.J., *Holy Family Parish, Chicago: Priests and People* (Chicago: Universal Press, 1923), 109-41.

30. Harry C. Koenig, S.T.D., ed. *A History of the Parishes of the Archdiocese of Chicago,* 2 vols. (Chicago: Archdiocese of Chicago, 1980), 1: 45, 2: 987-90; Lucas, *Netherlanders in America,* 457; Van Hinte, *Netherlanders in America,* 857.

the lot and building. It stood on the southwest fringe of the city, on Foster Street (later Law Avenue) (625 west) between Harrison and Polk streets (600 to 800 south) (figure 1.6, site 2). Here some thirty Reformed Dutch families staked their claim![31]

These families hailed from many parts of the Netherlands and were culturally diverse. Soon, however, one region came to dominate, that of Groningen, a northern province. By 1859 the Foster Street neighborhood was being described as the "Groninger Hoek" (literally corner, or neighborhood). The first Groninger family, that of Hendrik Sterenberg, had arrived in 1847, and many more followed in the next decades.[32]

Harrison Street — the Groninger Hoek Takes Shape

In the late 1850s a new Dutch community formed west of the key intersection of Harrison, Halsted, and Blue Island Avenue, which is now the campus of the University of Illinois at Chicago. Newcomers included Gerrit Vastenhouw, a carpenter from Amersfoort (Utrecht); John Oosters; Henry Otte, a farmer from Zaandam (Noord Holland); Jacob Martin, a baker from Willemstad, Noord Brabant; Jacob Vander Wall, a laborer from Goedereede (Zuid Holland); and the previously mentioned Schipperus, Foute, and Van Berschot. Others whose place of origin is not yet known included Henry Van Ouwen, Andrew De Boer, and Arie Van Deursen.

The core group that had launched the First Reformed Church in 1853 managed to run it for seven years without a resident pastor. They nurtured the historic Reformed faith in the city under very adverse circumstances. One of the challenges was a schism in 1867, the fallout of events in western Michigan a decade earlier. Some fifteen families seceded to form the True Holland (later Christian) Reformed Church of Chicago.[33] Such

31. First Reformed Church of Chicago, *A Century for Christ, 1853-1953* (Chicago, 1953), 4-5; First Reformed Church of Chicago, Minutes, 7, 20 May 1856.

32. Van Hinte, *Netherlanders in America,* 156.

33. While grammatically it would once have been unacceptable to use the word *of* when *in* was appropriate (for instance, the True Holland Reformed Church *of* Chicago), common American usage has tended to blur the distinction. Theologically, a church is *in* a place, it is not the creature *of* a civil entity, whether local or national. However, a literal translation of the Dutch *van* would be *of,* so it was only natural that the Dutch, when translating their church names into English, would use *of.* Out of respect to history, we will follow this usage throughout this volume, unless a congregation specifically uses the preposition *in* to describe its location.

First Reformed Church of Chicago
(Chicago Sunday Tribune, 30 October 1898)

fractious behavior could be expected because the province of Groningen had been a hotbed for rebellion against the state church in the 1830s, and Groningers led the most conservative wing of the Christian Seceded Church (chapter 2). These ardent traditionalists in Chicago built a small frame edifice three blocks west of First Reformed Church, on Gurley Street (one block south of Harrison Street) between Miller and Sholto streets (1000 west) (figure 1.6, site 5).[34]

The next year, the First Reformed Church followed its members to the same neighborhood and built a new church on the southwest corner of Harrison at May Street, a block from the True Church. From this time on, the Reformed Dutch in Chicago had rival churches facing one another or within sight and sound of each other's bells. In doctrine, worship, and life, non-members would be hard pressed to see any differences

34. First Reformed Church of Chicago, *A Century for Christ,* 3-5; First Christian Reformed Church of Chicago, *Seventy-Fifth Anniversary, 1867-1942* (Chicago, 1942), 11; De Bey letter in *Provinciale Groninger Courant,* 10 Dec. 1869.

between them. Both were Dutch-speaking, conservative, and traditional. But for the insiders, the minor differences were serious indeed.

The two congregations on the West Side flourished during the flowering period in the 1870s and 1880s with the steady arrival of hundreds of Groninger families. The True Church, which attracted the most conservative immigrants with its Dutch ways, suffered at first from short pastorates and long interims in between. First Reformed Church, on the other hand, captured its share of the immigration because of the capable leadership and energy of the Reverend Bernardus De Bey. He emigrated in 1868 directly from the Christian Seceded Church at Middelstum, Groningen. The previous year, two dozen Middelstum families had departed in the midst of an agricultural slump in the northern Netherlands, with more than half coming to Chicago. The next year they called their esteemed pastor to follow. De Bey accepted and another seventeen families accompanied him. Several dozen more families followed in the next five years. Altogether, nearly 20 percent of the Middelstum congregation emigrated, and the number of Groninger families on the West Side by 1869 exceeded one hundred.[35]

De Bey was a strong person mentally and physically. For two decades he made his parsonage on Harrison Street the headquarters for the resettlement of Dutch immigrants. As his wealth grew from judicious real estate investments, he helped immigrants with small loans to start businesses. Some of these men became leaders in the city.[36]

De Bey also worked to promote more Dutch immigration. For twenty years he wrote a series of letters for the *Provinciale Groninger Courant,* the major newspaper of the province, in which he urged those with "an iron will and a pair of good hands" to come where laborers were urgently needed, especially after the Chicago Fire of 1871.[37]

On the other hand, De Bey warned those who work with their heads – clerks, bookkeepers, small merchants, teachers, and gentlemen – to stay at home. "Our new Hollanders are cutters of wood and drawers of water. They perform the roughest and heaviest labors."[38] Only farm hands,

35. Hans Krabbendam, "Serving the Dutch Community: A Comparison of the Patterns of Americanization in the Lives of Two Immigrant Pastors" (M.A. Thesis, Kent State University, 1989), 48-93; Brinks, "Bernardus De Beij," 9-13; Van Hinte, *Netherlanders in America,* 373.

36. Vandenbosch, *Dutch Communities of Chicago,* 17.

37. De Bey's famed Chicago Fire letter of 8 June 1871, in English translation, is in *Origins* 1, no. 1 (1983): 10-13.

38. De Bey letter in *Provinciale Groninger Courant,* 13 Feb. 1869.

day laborers, craftsmen, and maids need apply. Anyone who "expects a bed of roses will be disappointed." Nearly 90 percent of all emigrant households from Middelstum in the years 1864-1873 fit this description.[39]

De Bey's letter of June, 1870, caught the flavor:

> Those who belong in America are those who understand from the beginning that they are just like a tree planted in rich soil; first they have to live through a life struggle and also have the desire to do so. The ones who can and want to work and do not hesitate to take on anything, be it unusual or strange, or of little attraction, will succeed very well here. Later they have the opportunity and capability to improve themselves after they have learned the language, customs, and have obtained some financial reserves. Many, even hundreds, who were impoverished when they arrived here, would not like to change their situation with the well-to-do farmers in the Netherlands. This does not happen, however, in two or three years.[40]

De Bey thus became the most influential link between the Old and the New World, and his "America letters" left little doubt that Groninger farm laborers would greatly benefit by coming to Chicago. Needless to say, the Groninger Hoek and the Reformed churches grew by leaps and bounds with such effective appeals from a trusted native who had himself worked as a farm laborer before entering the ministry later in life.

To help his followers get out of the crowded city and back to the soil they loved, De Bey in the 1870s talked of buying a large tract of land twenty miles west of Chicago (in what is now Forest Park) for a Groninger farming colony. But his people demurred, not wanting to leave steady jobs and the promise of advancement in the city.[41] Nevertheless, some Groningers on their own did take up truck farming on the outskirts (chapter 11). In the 1890s they moved into Bellwood and Maywood and in the 1920s into La Grange, Western Springs, and Des Plaines. But cartage, not farming, would bring the Groningers economic prosperity. Hauling garbage, general freight, ice, and coal and peddling produce and milk became employment mainstays (chapter 12).

39. Letter of J. Molenaar Akkerman, Roseland, to "Brother-in-law and sister and godparents," 3 Mar. 1878, in the Archives, Calvin College, trans. Henry Lammers. The social classes of Middelstum emigrants are analyzed in Krabbendam, "Serving the Dutch Community," 58.

40. De Bey letter in *Provinciale Groninger Courant,* 8 June 1870.

41. Vandenbosch, *Dutch Communities of Chicago,* 22-23, 101.

Homes on 14th Place under the Paulina station of the Douglas Park "El," 1941

Ashland Avenue: The Heart of the Groninger Hoek

After the fire the Reformed Dutch moved to the renowned Ashland Avenue area, also known as the Old West Side, a one-square-mile area that from the 1880s to the 1930s was the heart of the Groninger Hoek. This mixed blue-collar neighborhood, interspersed with Jews and Catholics, was the tightest Dutch Reformed community ever on the West Side. It ran from Racine Avenue (1200 west) to Damen Avenue (2000 west) and from Harrison Street (600 south) south to the railroad tracks at 15th Street.

The retail corridors of 12th Street, 14th Street, and Ashland Avenue held the shops, stores, banks, and professional offices to serve the Dutch, Bohemians, Jews, and various other European groups with whom they shared the neighborhood. Jews and Greeks owned most of the shops and businesses. In Amry Vandenbosch's mixed metaphor, the Groninger Hoek in the 1920s was a "handful of Hollanders in a sea of Jews." Little Italy stretched north of 12th Street, and Poles and Bohemians dominated the area south of 16th Street.[42]

If one street stood out as a veritable Dutch row, it was 14th Place in the two-block stretch from Ashland Avenue to Wood Street; Hollanders

42. Ibid., 79.

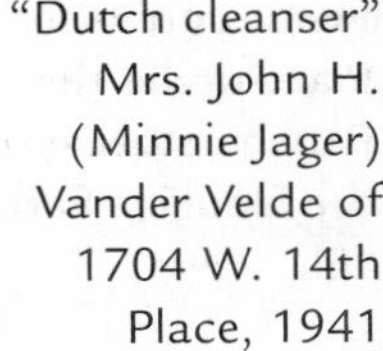

"Dutch cleanser" Mrs. John H. (Minnie Jager) Vander Velde of 1704 W. 14th Place, 1941

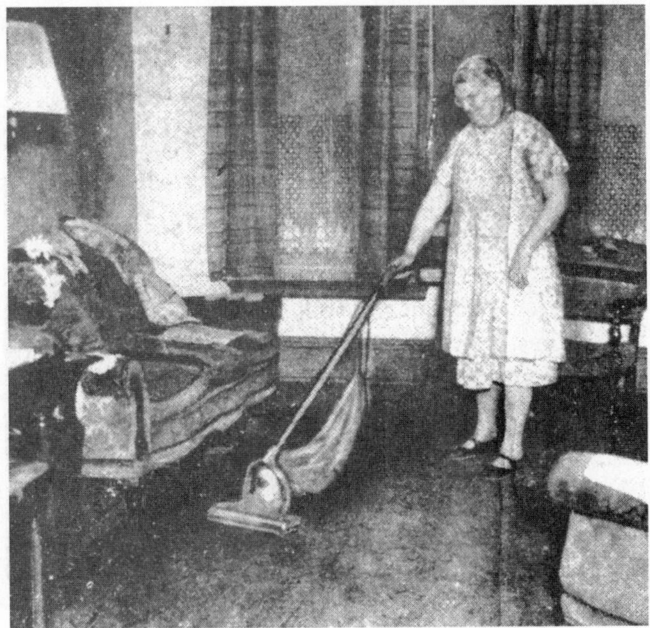

occupied virtually every house. No wonder that the locals called it "Wooden Shoe Boulevard." Houses stood cheek by jowl on twenty-five-foot lots, some with less than a foot between them. Everyone knew everyone and shared in the joys and tragedies of life from the front porches and stoops. They were poor but "didn't know any better," as resident Mike Keizer recalled. Even today, seventy years later, old timers can drive down the streets and recall which family lived in which house, even though most are now only empty lots.

Dutch homes were mostly one- and two-story "flats" set close together, many standing six to eight feet below the present street level, with "bridge stairs" leading to the front doors. The streets had been raised to get them out "of the mud." Access to the second floor was by stairs that ran up from the sidewalk. Trees and lawns were scarce and fondly cherished. Some homes had white fences to protect the prized flower gardens, and Dutch lace curtains adorned the front windows.

To call the homes and lots clean would be an understatement. The Dutch prized cleanliness next to godliness; everything inside and out was kept spick-and-span. This despite the Dutch penchant for smoking pipes, cigars, and cigarettes, and chewing tobacco. If homes were scrubbed and polished, personal hygiene was another matter. Dr. A. S. Riedel, a medical doctor who wrote a regular column on health in Chicago's Dutch language newspaper, *Onze Toekomst* [Our Future], urged readers in 1927 to change their underwear several times a week. "Americans are in this respect generally ahead of the Dutch," lamented the good doctor.[43]

Bess De Boer Figel described life in the Groninger Hoek in her reminiscences, *Once Upon a Time.*

> We lived at 1714 W. 13th Street, Chicago, Illinois, in a two story house. Mrs. Knoiheusen [Knooihuizen] and her son lived upstairs in the front apartment and we kept the two bedrooms in the back. There was no heat in these bedrooms, so we had "krooks" filled with hot water, to keep our feet warm. Sleeping three to a bed also helped. There was a pot under the bed if we had to use it. Since I was still young, I didn't always find the pot and would wet the bed. This also kept us warm.
>
> On the first floor, there was a living room and a large dining room where we had our meals, and a kitchen where Ma did her laundry and cooked our meals on a coal stove. The flatiron that she used to iron was also heated on the stove. There was always a barrel of apples in the kitchen because you know the saying, "An apple a day keeps the doctor away." The washing machine had a wringer on it to prepare the clothes to dry. Andrew and Louie [her brothers] had the job of wringing out the clothes. They also had the job of emptying the ashes. All of this had to be done before school in the morning.
>
> We used kerosene lamps until Mr. Dekker came to install electricity. This meant that Ma didn't have to heat water on the stove for our weekly baths. We had a cat in the house to keep out the mice. John had pet rabbits, but they multiplied so fast that they were put in a tub of water and drowned.
>
> I played with Annie Hoekstra and Margaret Decker who lived on our block. Clark School was only a half block away so we would go there to play in the playground. Then we would go across the street to the candy store to buy a glass of soda water or a pickle for a penny. Sometimes, we would play Jacks or Jump Rope, or we would make costumes from crepe paper to have a show. Everyone was invited; but nobody came except our mothers. On Saturday, we were allowed to go to 12th Street to Katrina's Fancy Goods Store and she would teach us to crochet or stitch. Everyday during recess or lunch time, we would sit on the neighbor's steps and stitch until the school bell rang. . . .
>
> Now we must talk about the most important room in our house,

43. "Health Education," *Onze Toekomst,* 20 July 1927, trans. Henry Lammers.

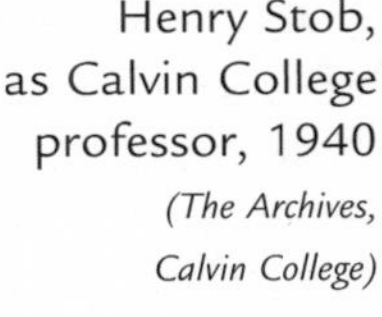

Henry Stob, as Calvin College professor, 1940 *(The Archives, Calvin College)*

the dining room. This is where Ma cooked the dinner for twelve people. The menu was primarily pot roast, potatoes, beans, and carrots. This was all prepared on a coal stove. Before we prayed, we had to get rid of the gum in our mouths. What better place to get rid of it than to stick it under the table. Then Pa would pray the "Lord's Prayer" in Holland [Dutch], and the younger children would say "Heere Seigen Deize Spys, Amen."[44]

Four churches and a Christian day school anchored the tight-knit neighborhood. Hollanders who lived there in the 1920s and 1930s hold poignant memories of this "golden age" of Chicago's Dutch Calvinists. "If you didn't live on the Old West Side, you never lived," Jack Essenburg remarked at his fiftieth wedding anniversary years later.[45]

Henry Stob, a product of the Groninger Hoek in the 1920s, recalled that the Dutch were an "industrious and thrifty" lot, but "few of them were rich." They "spoke Dutch at home, worked hard, and harbored intense loyalties" to their churches and Christian schools. Benjamin Essenburg, pastor of the First Christian Reformed Church, echoed these thoughts; the Dutch are "not wealthy, but they are hard working, earnest, faithful, and friendly." Even the boys and girls kept busy delivering newspapers, In Cicero in the 1940s, they earned about $6 per month (10 cents per customer, plus bonuses of $1 for not being absent and $2 for not more

44. Bess De Boer Figel, *Once Upon a Time . . .* (Chicago, nd).

45. Ben Essenburg, 2 Nov. 1998; Mike Keizer, 12 May 1998, video interviews by Martin Stulp.

than three customer complaints). If they had to collect for the papers, earnings went up to $10 a month.[46]

For professional services the Dutch preferred fellow church members, but as consumers they willingly patronized non-Dutch merchants if the price was right or they had no other option. Most Dutch took their savings to Dutch-owned banks, bought homes through Dutch realtors, drew up their wills with Dutch attorneys, went to Dutch doctors and dentists with their hurts, and patronized fellow merchants and craftsmen. Employers preferred to hire relatives and fellow church members. As Stob recalled, "Some heads of families in the community worked in shops and factories, others held office jobs, and a number ran their own businesses." Many were teamsters and haulers of cinders and garbage (see chapter 12).[47] Novelist Peter De Vries captured the Dutch character of the 1920s best in his renowned autobiographical novel, *The Blood of the Lamb.* De Vries recites this street rhyme: "Oh, the Irish and the Dutch, Don't amount to very much."[48] But they were on the way up.

The Chicago public transit network of streetcars and elevated trains provided mobility at a time when few families owned cars and many streets were unpaved and full of potholes. The Dutch rode the "cars" and the "el" for work, school, church, visiting, shopping, and recreation. The Ashland Avenue Dutch had a convenient stop on the Douglas Park Elevated Line right at their doorstep at 14th Place and Paulina Street. The trains took them "downtown" in ten minutes. Even more useful were the streetcar lines that ran on 14th Street from Western Avenue to Canal Street (near the Maxwell Street market), and the 12th Street line that ran from the Chicago Natural History Museum (Field Museum) at the lake front to the city limits and later to Austin Boulevard at the Oak Park border. Public transport was the norm until family cars became common in the 1920s.

46. Henry Stob, "Recollections," *Origins* 1, No. 1 (1983): 3 (quote); 9, No. 2 (1991): 14; 10, no. 2 (1992): 18. Stob's fuller account is *Summoning Up Remembrance* (Grand Rapids: Eerdmans, 1996); chaps. 1-3; William H. Fort, "Dutch Corner of Valley Brightens West Side," *Chicago Daily News,* 1 Mar. 1941; Ralphina Roeters nee Klooster and son John Roeters, video interview, 1 Dec. 1997, by Martin Stulp; interview with Martin Essenburg by the author, 16 May 2001. For Roseland, see Richard R. Tiemersma, "Growing Up in Roseland in the 20's & 30's," *Origins* 5, No. 1 (1987): 2-19. Stob was professor of philosophy in Calvin College, and after 1951 professor of philosophical and moral theology in Calvin Theological Seminary. Both are institutions of the Christian Reformed Church.

47. John Vander Velde, "Our History," Ebenezer Christian Reformed Church, *Centennial Booklet, 1867-1967* (Berwyn, 1967), 6-7; Stob, "Recollections," *Origins* 9 No. 2 (1991): 15-16.

48. Peter De Vries, *The Blood of the Lamb* (New York: Little Brown, 1961), 23.

Peter De Vries, as Calvin College student, ca. 1931 *(The Archives, Calvin College)*

Below: Traffic congestion, Chicago, 1910 *(Courtesy of Chicago Historical Society)*

As in all Dutch Reformed settlements, life centered around the church. In 1883, the First Christian Reformed Church, successor of the True Holland Reformed Church, was the first planted in the Ashland Avenue district. The congregation purchased a spacious building from the Presbyterians on 14th Street east of Ashland Avenue (figure 1.6, site 6). The

Old Fourteenth Street (First) Christian Reformed Church of Chicago, purchased 1883, parsonage on right *(The Archives, Calvin College)*

edifice affectionately became known as the "Old Fourteenth Street Church," and it served the congregation for forty years, until 1923.[49]

This congregation relocated because its old sanctuary on Gurley Street could not accommodate the immigrant rush of the 1880s, when groups of seventy-five to one hundred arrived. In the summer of 1893, at the end of the big wave, the church received seventy-five families! The newcomers appreciated its genuine Dutch *gezelligheid* and traditional ways.[50]

First Reformed Church, the mother church, relocated in 1892 from Harrison Street some fifteen blocks southwest to the heart of the Ashland Avenue Dutch neighborhood. The congregation chose a site on Hastings Street (13th Place) just east of Ashland Avenue (figure 1.6, site 4).[51] This was only two blocks west of the 14th Street (First) Christian Reformed Church.

49. First Christian Reformed of Chicago, *Seventy-Fifth Anniversary Booklet,* 11.
50. Moerdyke, "Chicago Letter," *CI,* 25 May 1892, p. 11; 31 Mar. 1893, p. 10.
51. Ibid., 8 Apr. 1891, p. 11; 6 Jan. 1892, p. 10.

First (Hastings Street) Reformed Church of Chicago, erected 1894

In the 1890s two new congregations sprang up in the Ashland Avenue district. In 1891 young families desiring English-language worship left First Reformed Church and organized Trinity Reformed Church on the north fringe of the area (figure 1.6, site 8). In 1893 other members of First Reformed Church living on the far North Side transferred to the Northwestern Reformed Church on Superior Avenue (figure 1.6, site 9), which congregation of 240 parishioners had that year left its Presbyterian affiliation.[52]

In 1892, of eight thousand Hollanders on the West Side, one-fourth (2,200) belonged to the four Reformed congregations – First Reformed, Fourteenth Street (First) Christian Reformed, Northwestern Reformed, and Trinity Reformed (American). The rest were a "multitude dispersed, irreligious, and adopted by other denominations," according to Moerdyke. These latter included Dutch Jews, Catholics, and Unitarians.[53] Worship

52. Ibid., 11 Nov. 1891, p. 11; 3 Mar. 1893, p. 10.

53. Ibid., 11 Nov. 1891, p. 11.

services in all the Reformed churches except Trinity were in Dutch until the 1910s, but First Reformed in 1890 had begun English-language Sunday school and catechism classes and young people's societies.

First Reformed Church was the "established, large, and powerful institution among the Hollanders," but the forces of Americanization were at work. Young second-generation families who wanted English-language worship services for their children were siphoned off to Trinity Church. By contrast, the Fourteenth Street Christian Reformed Church, the "purely and thoroughly Dutch Church, . . . fattened" on fresh arrivals from the Netherlands. The congregation's day school, Ebenezer Christian School, established in 1893, was an added inducement.

The Unitarian body attracted a smattering of free thinkers; it was "insignificant and so strangely officered and led as to be at present of no account," said Moerdyke in 1891. Three years later he announced its demise with sarcastic glee. "Without a tear or so much as a sigh, we chronicle the 'poor, dying rats,' of that Holland Unitarian organization of our city, and, as far as we can learn, its death. Defunct, at last, yes, so early, to all appearances. Died – of starvation, being without the Bread of Life."[54]

By 1920 First Reformed Church (commonly called Hastings Street Church) had six hundred members, and First (Fourteenth Street) Christian Reformed Church had twelve hundred members. In 1923 the latter body bought from the Lutherans a beautiful edifice a stone's throw from First Reformed Church on the very visible corner of Ashland Avenue and Hastings Street. Thus, it became known as the Ashland Avenue Christian Reformed Church. The former facility served a black congregation until it succumbed to a wrecking ball to make way for public housing in 1941.[55]

Douglas Park – Lawndale

Beginning in the 1880s, the more affluent Dutch on the Old West Side moved into Douglas Park and Lawndale on the "Far West Side," attracted by the new homes on larger lots. Always they were also escaping from the press of newer ethnic groups, especially the Jews driven out of Russia by the czarist pogroms. These eastern Europeans were considered a decided cut below the more assimilated German Jews who had long dominated

54. Ibid., 11 Nov. 1891, p. 11; 24 Jan. 1894, p. 10.

55. First Reformed Church of Chicago, *Century for Christ*, 5; First Christian Reformed of Chicago, *Seventy-Fifth Anniversary Booklet*, 11; Vander Velde, "Our History," 5.

the West Side but likewise fled to newer neighborhoods to the north and south.

Moerdyke caught the fluid nature of city life and its negative impact on religious life:

> The situation here is one of rapid and significant changes for all the Reformed churches. Neighborhoods undergo some vital transformations, our people scatter to find homes where property is cheaper or rents lower, or privileges greater for the same outlay. Consequently, a large proportion of the parishioners live at considerable distances, involving expense, much time and difficulty and sacrifice in attending those churches on the West Side. That all the congregations suffer losses in strength and attendance from these causes is inevitable. Though the elderly people are ordinarily loyal to the Reformed Church and flock to their own banner, if possible, there are other tendencies, and every year will give a new aspect to this problem. "The times change and we change with them."
>
> Happy are the Dutch settlements, such as Roseland, of our city, and numerous towns, small cities, and rural districts of the West where our pastors experience no difficulty whatever in getting large congregations, inasmuch as their people are all around them in compact settlements. Long may such easier conditions bless all parties concerned! When worshipers travel from two to eight miles in our city to fellowship with their own beloved people, it may mean far more in many ways than the devotion of hosts who take a few steps, or in a ten or fifteen minute comfortable and cheap walk reach their seats in the sanctuary.
>
> And, besides, do not overlook the formidable and expensive task of pastoral visiting over such a wide territory to find the distantly separated homes of parishioners. Half-days count for no more than an hour in the rounds of an ordinary minister.[56]

Douglas Park, named after the famed Senator Stephen Douglas, and Lawndale, immediately adjacent to the west, were then upscale neighborhoods developed on the high prairie lands in the 1870s. Home prices, including lots, ranged from $3,000 to $8,000, and included all city utilities.[57] This area of tree-lined streets, boulevards, and parks between Kedzie

56. Moerdyke, "Chicago Letter," *CI,* 17 Dec. 1902, p. 840.

57. Chicago Times, *Our Suburbs: A Resume of the Origin, Progress, Present Status of Chicago's Environs* (Chicago, 1873), 39-40.

and Cicero Avenues was the fourth Calvinist enclave. Between 1891 and 1923, three congregations and a Christian day school were established in the area – the Douglas Park Christian Reformed (1899), and the English-speaking Third (1912) and Fourth (1923) Christian Reformed churches. Timothy, the second Christian school on the West Side, opened in 1911.

The South Side – Englewood, Summit, Evergreen Park, and Oak Lawn

Soon after the Civil War, Groningers from the Old West Side and fresh immigrants from the province of Groningen began settling as market gardeners on the open prairies of Englewood. As the city encroached, some farmers turned to urban work while others in the late 1880s moved five or six miles west to Summit. A major employment center for Englewood men was in nearby "Packingtown," the vast Union Stock Yards and especially its numerous meat packing plants, such as Swift and Company, and Libby, McNeill and Libby, which employed thousands of unskilled immigrants.[58]

Englewood's main hub was the intersection of 63rd (6300 south) and Halsted Streets (800 west). Around the hub, lots were platted for inexpensive, $1,500 bungalows on tree-lined streets. In 1880 the township had 2,850 inhabitants, but it was still very rural and surrounded by truck farms. In 1882 Englewood had an official cow puncher to herd 110 cows belonging to the inhabitants to pastures to the southwest and the fresh spring at 63rd and Ashland Avenue. Julius Petersen's wooden shoe factory turned out *klompen,* "which were largely used at the time by farmers and laborers."[59]

During the 1880s the farm fields gave way to homes, schools, and churches. The area was an easy commute to downtown Chicago on the Rock Island Railroad or horse-drawn streetcars. The State Street line was completed in 1882, the Wentworth Street line in 1883, and the Halsted Street line in 1884. By then eight railroads and interurban lines connected Englewood with the city center, several stopping at the junction hub at 63rd Street and Wentworth Avenue.

58. Ebenezer Christian Reformed Church, *Centennial Booklet, 1867-1967,* 11; Mayer and Wade, *Chicago,* 160, 163, 213, 230.

59. This and the next paragraph rely on Gerald E. Sullivan, *The Story of Englewood, 1835-1923* (Chicago: Englewood Business Men's Association, 1923), 16-37, quote 28.

The First Reformed and First Christian Reformed churches in Englewood were founded the same year, 1887, to serve the Dutch Reformed population, which numbered about one hundred families and was growing rapidly. By 1900 First Reformed had more than a thousand souls, and First Christian Reformed numbered eight hundred souls. Both churches spun off daughter congregations, Second Reformed in 1902 and Second Christian Reformed in 1903. In 1915, when the Dutch population of Englewood was at its apogee, the two Reformed congregations numbered 1,160 souls, and the two Christian Reformed congregations counted 1,575 souls. Most were Groningers.[60]

The Dutch in Englewood were concentrated in two areas. The larger area was a 108-block region bounded by 66th and 75th streets and Halsted (800 west) and Loomis (1400 west) streets. An eighteen-block subdistrict within this area, ranging between 71st and 73rd streets and Green (832 west) and May (1132 west) streets, counted some 170 Dutch families. A smaller fifteen-block Dutch area was found a mile north, bounded by 60th and 63rd streets and Peoria (900 west) and May streets.[61]

Englewood was the first colony of the Groninger Hoek, and it quickly became a major Dutch Reformed enclave and intellectual center. Englewood boasted the only Christian high school from 1918 to 1945, and for several years in the 1930s the first college as well, Chicago Christian College. Dutch youth commuted daily from throughout the city and suburbs to attend these institutions, which attracted prominent leaders and serious scholars to their faculties.

From Englewood the Dutch moved west and southwest in the late 1880s into Summit and surrounding areas (figure 1.7). These were small farming and market gardening centers on leased lands that supplied Chicago tables with fresh fruits and vegetables. Summit was linked to the "big" city ten miles distant by the Joliet interurban line, but the Dutch farmers used the muddy trunk road, Archer Avenue, which ran diagonally southeast from Joliet. Along this lonely stretch, farmers carted their crops by horse and wagon to the Chicago produce markets. Those in Evergreen Park and Oak Lawn later did the same but had farther to travel.

These Groninger truck farming settlements that ringed Chicago were inherently ephemeral. Few of the immigrants had money to buy the

60. Christian Reformed Church, *Jaarboekje,* 1889, 33; 1900, 37; 1915, 19; *Acts and Proceedings of the General Synod of the Protestant Dutch Reformed Church in America,* 1887, 428; 1900, 886; 1915, 584.

61. Vandenbosch, *Dutch Communities of Chicago,* 4.

Figure 1.2 Map of Chicago and Environs, 1967

high-priced lands near the city, which were largely in the hands of real estate developers. Most could only rent the lands until the city encroached and they were subdivided for housing. Some developers required tenants not only to build their own homes but to be prepared to remove them when the leases ran out; such homes could hardly be substantial. Few Groninger truck farmers thus benefited from rising land values in the city and suburbs.[62]

Despite the uncertain future, the Dutch truck farmers founded churches and Christian day schools in their locales that provided religious sustenance. Most continue today, but several have disbanded in recent

62. The land tenure system is explained in "Chicago Letter," *Banner*, 21 Mar. 1912.

years. The survivors adapted as the farms gave way to housing subdivisions and an urban work force. In the 1950s the Hollanders in Englewood and environs fled a black influx by moving to southern Cook County and northern Indiana. They were joined by Roseland Hollanders, who were the next to be uprooted in the 1970s.

The Far South Side – Roseland

In 1849 a small band of forty-five devout Dutch Seceders from the province of Noord Holland founded the "Holland Settlement" on the ridge west of Lake Calumet that became known as the Dutch Settlement Road. The area was first called High Prairie, then Hope, and, after 1875, Roseland. Unlike the Groningers, these pioneers had money. The group immediately bought 160 acres of land from private owners for $5 per acre between State Street and Indiana Avenue and divided it into smaller plots for dairying and market gardening. The three Madderom families who arrived in 1853 introduced the cultivation of vegetables, notably onions, for the Chicago market.[63]

In 1855 the Dutch purchased, also for $5 per acre, all 640 acres of the Lake Calumet Township "school lands" (Section Sixteen). This square mile, from State to Halsted Streets between 103rd and 111th Streets, became the center of Roseland. Later the farmers settled the prairies to the south up to 117th Street and west of Halsted Street to the railroad tracks at Vincennes Road.

Cornelius Kuyper opened the first general store at 103rd Street, and in 1854 he took on Goris Vander Syde as partner. Eventually, Vander Syde bought out his partner and moved the store to the center of town on Michigan Avenue at 110th Street; it was called the Calumet Store. An early landmark was Jan (John) De Young's huge windmill on 103rd and State that drew water from a seventy-two-foot depth. "The whole neighborhood came down to our farm to get water," recalled son John, Jr. The windmill

63. Ross Ettema, ed., *Down an Indian Trail in 1849: The Story of Roseland* (Palos Heights, Ill.: Trinity Christian College, 1987). This work reprints the centennial account by Marie K. Rowlands, published under the same title in serial form in the *Calumet Index*. The first of fifty-seven installments began 20 June 1949. Rowlands was the daughter of the town photographer, Henry Koopman, Jr., and granddaughter of its first minister, Henry Koopman of the First Reformed Church. A historical novel of Roseland by an American inhabitant is Arthur G. Lindell, *School Section Sixteen* (New York: Vantage Press, 1983).

of Al Vanden Berg at 111th and State streets stood ready to grind grain for many years.

For a century, until the white flight of the 1970s, Roseland was the major Dutch colony in the Chicago area. In the early decades Roseland served as a stopping point for farmers from the sister colony of South Holland, six miles to the south, who were en route to the produce houses at South Water Market. The favorite watering hole for man and beast was the Eleven Mile House at 93rd and State streets. The Roseland Dutch supplied garden vegetables for the same Chicago wholesale market. The community grew slowly to eight hundred inhabitants by 1882, most of whom were still engaged in general farming and stock raising. But the population exploded in the 1880s due to a large influx of Frisians who were pushed out of the northern Netherlands by a severe agricultural depression. Over fifteen hundred dwelling units were constructed during the 1880s and 1890s, and the village population grew accordingly: thirty-five hundred in 1890, seven thousand in 1900, and ten thousand in 1920.

After 1900 some 240 Dutch Catholic families from the provinces of Noord Brabant and Zeeland opened truck farms on the south fringe of Roseland and in Kensington, which stretched south of 113th Street and east of State Street. This group of 1,100 souls in the 1920s worshiped at St. Willibrord Church on Edbrooke Avenue (134 east) at 114th Street, which the archdiocese founded in 1900 for the Dutch Catholics in the Calumet district (see chapter 15). The Catholic and Calvinist Hollanders, while both Dutch-speaking, lived insulated lives and had no contact with one another.

In Roseland itself, the encroaching city of Chicago and industrial development in the Lake Calumet district, especially the Pullman Palace Car Company, transformed the "idyllic village," as an early resident described Roseland, into a hustling, bustling retail hub that supplied workers for commerce and industry. Developers bought out the Roseland farmers for up to $500 per acre for industrial plants and residential subdivisions. "Houses went up like mushrooms in all directions, and the boom kept up for several years," recalled Harry Eenigenburg in 1935. The pioneers of 1849 "became rich overnight" in the 1880s; "it was the best period for making money that I have ever lived through."[64]

This financial windfall ensured that the Noord Holland families – the Madderoms, Kuypers, De Jongs (De Youngs), Dalenbergs, Eenigen-

64. Harry Eenigenberg, *The Calumet Region and its Early Settlers* (Chicago, 1935), 26.

burgs, and Vander Sydes – would be dominant in Roseland business and social life. The Frisians, who came en masse in the 1880s, had an entirely different experience. They left the homeland in poverty and could ill afford to buy farmland in Roseland priced above $100 per acre. Their only option was to seek work in the new factories and heavy industries and live in Pullman company housing or rent homes on small lots in Roseland. The road to home ownership was a long one for the Frisians, but they made it.

Some Dutch continued to farm on the outskirts of Roseland into the 1920s, but most sought employment in town or in the large factories "down the hill" from Michigan Avenue – the Pullman Works with ten thousand workers in the 1920s, the Illinois Central Railroad shops at Burnside with five thousand, the Plano Works of International Harvester with two thousand, the Sherwin Williams paint plant employing one thousand, and a dozen other large factories.[65]

Here the Dutch rubbed shoulders with other nationalities and felt the power of organized labor. At the time of the great Pullman strike of 1894, Hollanders comprised 12 percent of the workforce. They generally rejected unions, opposed strikes, and crossed picket lines whenever possible; they were Pullman's kind of employees. Industrial work made the Roseland Dutch particularly vulnerable to economic downturns. No Chicago-area Hollanders suffered more in the Great Depression than they did, especially when all three banks, including the Wiersema State Bank, Roseland's oldest, failed and wiped out the savings of families, businesses, and even churches. This disaster was the great leveler between the first-wave Noord Hollanders and the second-wave Frisians, because it placed at risk the capital gains from real estate that the Noord Hollanders had won in the 1880s.[66]

Along with the Frisians came many other immigrants from Europe, Poles and Italians, Swedes and Germans, who established their churches and social clubs. "Instead of the peaceful village," another Dutch pioneer noted, "we have, since 1900, become the polyglot part of a great town." Thus, the Roseland Dutch had to make way for other groups, although

65. Jacob Brouwer's reminiscences in "Garden Farming in Roseland," *Origins* 14, no. 1 (1996): 25-31; Vandenbosch, *Dutch Communities of Chicago,* 14-15; Cornelius Teninga, *The Roseland District of Chicago: Some Facts* (Chicago: Teninga Bros., 1924), 6.

66. Stanley Buder, *Pullman: An Experiment in Industrial Order and Community Planning, 1880-1930* (New York: Oxford Univ. Press, 1967), 90 (Table 2), 175, 194; Almont Lindsey, *The Pullman Strike* (Chicago: Univ. Chicago Press, 1942); J. R. Brink, "Roseland and the South District," *Banner,* 20 May 1932; 24 Mar. 1933.

they continued to dominate the community. In the 1920s ten thousand Hollanders lived in the greater Roseland region.[67]

Life in Roseland for the Dutch Reformed revolved around their eight churches, two Christian schools, societies, stores and shops, and for the youth, playing in the streets and alleys. Richard Tiemersma, retired English professor of Calvin College and a native Roselander, delightfully recounted growing up in the "good old days" of the 1920s and 1930s, when work and play, schooling and dating, took place in keeping with the strict Dutch Calvinistic "manners and mores" of the community.[68]

Cicero – Berwyn – Oak Park

During World War I, the fifth Dutch hub on the West Side took shape in the nexus of Cicero, Berwyn, and Oak Park, the suburbs immediately to the west of the city and several miles from Douglas Park and Lawndale (figure 1.2). A large migration of blacks from the South to Chicago's Old West Side set off massive white flight after incidents of purse snatchings, muggings, and even rapes of Dutch residents. Their children were also harassed on the walk to and from school. "We didn't feel safe anymore among the coloreds," was the common refrain. The Dutch had lived in harmony among the old northern blacks, but the newcomers from Dixie were more aggressive and threatening to whites. Moreover, property values began to plummet, and this too aroused racial animosity. The climax came in the mid-1940s, when realtors went door to door to induce panic selling.

By 1935 one Reformed and three Christian Reformed churches and Timothy Christian School dotted Cicero's Warren Park district. The remnant at Chicago's First Reformed and First Christian Reformed churches sold their buildings to black congregations in 1944 and 1945 and built new edifices in Berwyn. Fourth Christian Reformed Church of Chicago likewise sold its building in 1945, and most members affiliated with the Oak Park Christian Reformed Church. Ebenezer School was closed in 1946.

The remaining families moved west quickly after that, leaving behind only a handful of elderly folk. The 12th Street car line conveniently

67. Ann Durkin Keating, *Building Chicago: Suburban Developers and The Creation of a Divided Metropolis* (Columbus: Ohio State Univ. Press, 1988), 21; Eenigenburg, *Calumet Region,* 26; *Onze Toekomst,* 30 Aug. 1922.

68. Tiemersma, "Growing Up in Roseland in the 20's & 30's," 2-19.

linked the Hollanders of the Ashland Avenue district with those of Douglas Park-Lawndale district and later also with those in Cicero and points west, as the tracks were extended to serve the expanding city.

Elmhurst – Lombard

In the 1960s the westsiders pulled up stakes for a fifth time in the face of incursions by Italians, Poles, and a few blacks. The Dutch bought homes more than ten miles further west in Elmhurst and environs, where in the 1970s three of the Cicero area churches relocated, as did Timothy Christian School – its third location.

Factors in the migration from Cicero in the 1960s were somewhat different from those pushing the Dutch out of the Old West Side in the 1940s. Cicero was still "lily white" when the Dutch began moving to Elmhurst, unlike the interracial situation in the Ashland Avenue district. Upward mobility, rather than fearful flight, largely explains this later move. The Cicero case also differs from that in Englewood and Roseland in the 1960s and 1970s; these communities experienced sudden and profound social changes, as did the Old West Side earlier.

"Westward Ho!"

Mobility was the defining characteristic of the West Side Groningers; "Westward Ho!" seemed to be their motto. Over the course of 150 years each generation uprooted itself, moving from the city center to the upscale and then nonintegrated suburbs.

In each of these mass upheavals, both push and pull factors were at work, although the relative forces changed. As much as the Dutch felt pushed out by unwelcome neighbors, they were also pulled out by a desire for upward mobility. The first two relocations, from Foster to Harrison Street and then to Ashland Avenue, primarily stemmed from a desire for better housing and safer neighborhoods. Pull factors were stronger than push factors in these instances. In the Ashland Avenue neighborhood, however, the Dutch first encountered blacks in substantial numbers, and hence push factors predominated in the move to Cicero and Berwyn. The same forces caused the flight from Englewood and Roseland. But the migration to Elmhurst and Lombard was prompted more by upward mobility than white flight.

For the westsiders, the path of least resistance flowed along the commercial and streetcar artery of 12th Street (Roosevelt Road), because major trunk railroad lines and industrial districts hedged them in to the south and north. Later, when the automobile was king of the road, the Eisenhower (formerly Congress) Expressway channeled the Dutch into the far western suburbs.

In each cycle of "Dutch flight," they bought or built new churches, homes, schools, stores, and shops. The shopkeepers, merchants, morticians, lawyers, doctors, and dentists stayed close to their customers and clients. First, the Dutch left the city; then, the Cook County suburbs; and finally, the county itself. This migratory habit was very different from life in small towns and rural communities, where the residents experienced stability over many generations. The Dutch in Englewood stayed put for seventy-five years, and the Roseland and South Holland colonies remained intact for more than one hundred years. Thus, the habit of constant migration gave the city Dutch a unique character.

Becoming Americans

The cohesion of Chicago's Dutch Reformed immigrant community and their clear sense of identity came from their churches and theological convictions, especially the concept of covenant. They believed that God had covenanted with them as with Abraham, the father of all believers. God had written his law in their hearts; he would be their God, and they would be his people. The meaning and purpose of this covenantal relationship was explained weekly in sermons that were heavy on doctrine and piety. Their "Christian world and life view" was lived out during the week in countless church and Christian school activities. They organized men's and women's societies and feeder groups for young people, choirs and bands, mission clubs, Sunday school fests and church picnics, men's softball and bowling, and many similar activities.

But America assimilates all its children, although some resist longer than others, depending on religious and cultural factors. The two Reformed denominations ranged along the continuum from separation to assimilation. Christian Reformed folk chose separation and held the forces of assimilation at bay through their churches and Christian day schools. They maintained an ethnocultural identity five and six generations after immigration, thus defying many assumptions of scholars, notably that grandchildren of immigrants are no longer "hyphenates" but fully American. Reformed Church members, on the other hand, chose quasi-acculturation by favoring the public schools. Their outward-looking emphasis put them on a faster track to Americanization, and they were largely assimilated by the third and fourth generations (chapter 7).

The Christian Reformed churches blunted cultural forces by channeling the social life of their children into an exclusively ethnoreligious track, keyed to private Christian schools. Outside of school, the Young Calvinist League served Christian Reformed high schoolers, as did the Calvinist Cadet Corp for boys and Calvinette Club for girls. By contrast, Reformed Church youth attended public schools, joined Boy Scout and Girl Scout troops at church, and on Sunday evenings high schoolers participated in Christian Endeavor. These affiliations speak volumes. The Christian Reformed Church stressed Dutch Calvinist roots, while the Reformed Church "endeavored" to be simply Christian, whether in scouting or in church life.

The differing approaches to schooling and social life resulted in Reformed youth more often marrying outside the ethnoreligious circle than did Christian Reformed youth. Both churches, however, sternly warned against intermarriage with Catholics, which was the greatest perceived threat. Author Peter De Vries tells of seriously dating an Italian girl while attending Chicago Christian High School, but finally he broke the relationship. Why? "Religious reasons," he quipped with tongue in cheek, "our faith doesn't allow us to intermarry."[69] By "faith" he meant Dutch Reformed, and by "intermarry" he meant Protestant-Catholic. De Vries was correct. Both Reformed and Catholic clerics counseled strongly against such marriages, largely because of the issue of which church would baptize the children.

Church membership records, while incomplete, are instructive. The First Reformed Church of Chicago between 1860 and 1900 lost 9 percent (67 of 730) of its confessing members – a third to the Christian Reformed Church; a third to other denominations; and a third were "erased" or "dropped" after several years of nonattendance. A handful were excommunicated. Fully one-third of two hundred baptized members were also dropped from the rolls; they had been sprinkled as infants but as adults never became confessing members or participated in the life of the church. The First Christian Reformed of Chicago, by contrast, lost only 3 percent (22 of 691) of its confessing members between 1890 and 1920 and one-fifth of its baptized adult members, the latter mainly by erasure. The

69. De Vries, *Blood of the Lamb,* 30.

Robert Swierenga family in parlor: Dutch *gezelligheid* (warm coziness), 1346 S. Crawford Avenue, ca. 1914
l-r: Grace Dykhuis Swierenga, daughter Henrietta (age 1), son John (age 3), Robert Swierenga

Reformed thus experienced a loss rate three times as high as the Christian Reformed, and this was in the early period before the full impact of Americanization hit after the First World War.[70]

Christian schooling had a great impact on this divergence. One hundred years ago, at their inception, both denominations on the West Side were equal in strength. But today Reformed Church membership in the western suburbs is less than one-fourth that of the Christian Reformed Church.

For the successful professional and business elite, social clubs such as the Holland Society and the General Dutch League provided an opportunity to boast of one's heritage.[71] Such outward and often shallow displays of ethnic pride, however, ultimately testified more to the extent of

70. The records of the First Reformed Church of Chicago are in the Joint Archives of Holland, and those of the First Christian Reformed Church of Chicago are in the Archives, Calvin College.

71. See the Chicago Dutch-language weekly newspaper *Onze Toekomst,* 1894-1953 (incomplete files), and its successors, the *Illinois Observer* (monthly) 1954-59 and *Church Observer* (monthly) 1960-64.

assimilation than they did of "Dutchness." Political life conveyed the same message. The Chicago Dutch were passive Republican voters who supported the party ticket and seldom ran for office themselves. And the few Reformed Dutch candidates could not count on the support of their fellow ethnics unless they ran as party-backed Republicans (chapter 14). The editors of *Onze Toekomst* tried repeatedly to generate bloc voting for "our" Holland candidates, but they found a spirit of cooperation "non-existent among our people."[72]

In the workaday world, the Dutch accommodated quickly; they had to earn a living. They easily became part of the fabric of American society. To the non-Dutch they appeared, at least by the 1940s, to be indistinguishable in dress and speech, in the work place, the voting booth, and the rows of neat brick bungalows. But secondary associations and even language are not the prime markers of ethnicity. One must look to primary associations – the worshiping community, separate schools, home life, marriage, and recreation. Here the Dutch confessionalists carry on in America's second city, although the ethnic glue has loosened since the 1950s.

72. *Onze Toekomst,* 7 Sept. 1906; 26 Feb. (quote), 3 July 1909; 18 Mar., 1 Apr. 1910.

Figure 1.3 Dutch in Chicago, 1850

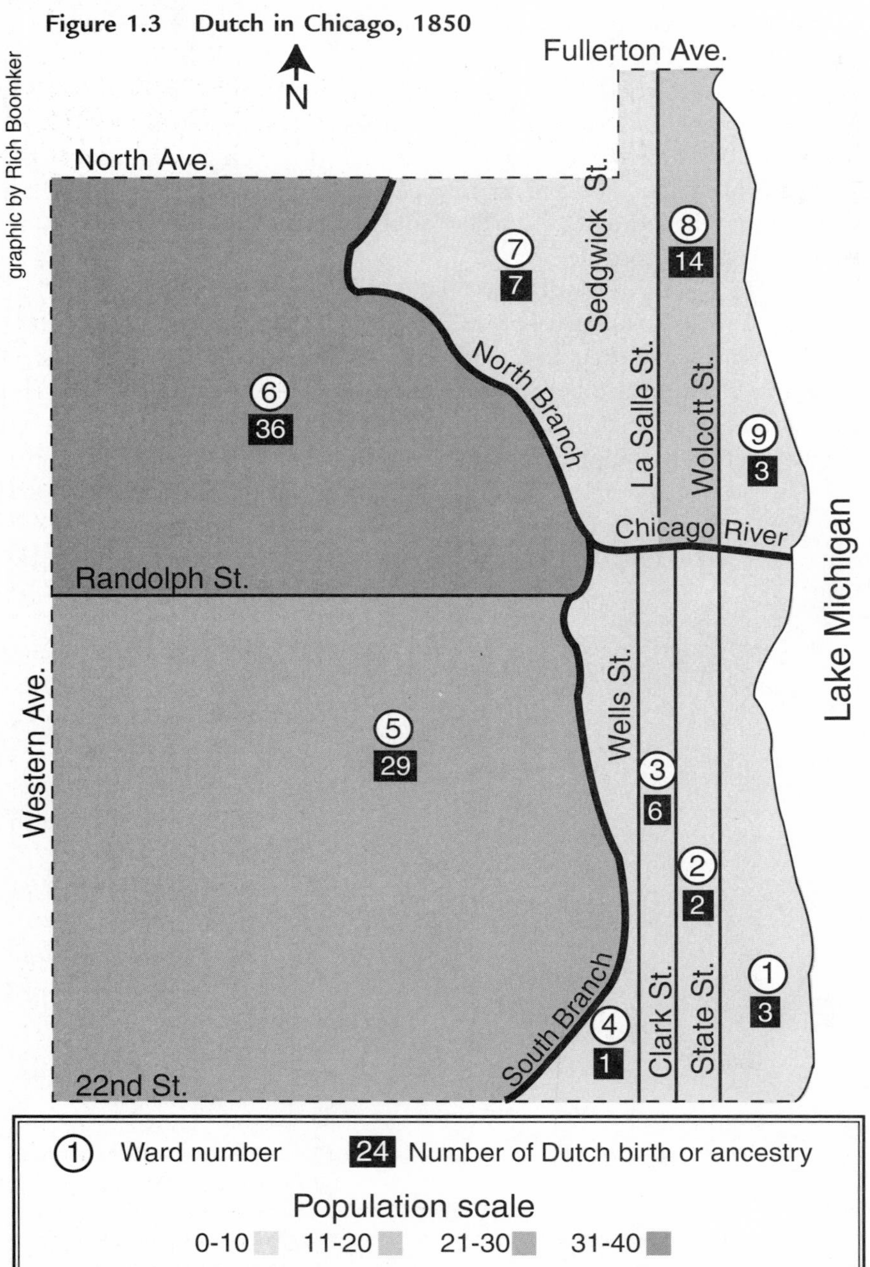

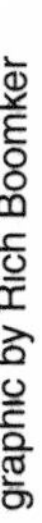
graphic by Rich Boomker

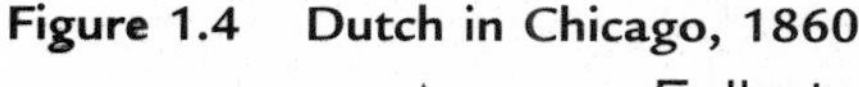
Figure 1.4 Dutch in Chicago, 1860
N
Fullerton Ave.
North Ave.
Western Ave.
Randolph St.
Harrison St.
North Branch
South Branch
Chicago River
La Salle St.
Wolcott St.
Wells St.
Clark St.
State St.
Lake Michigan
31st St.
7
13
8
27
6
84
9
5
5
61
3
15
10
148
2
24
1
20
4
2

1 Ward number
24 Number of Dutch birth or ancestry
Population scale
0-10
11-20
21-80
81-120
121-160

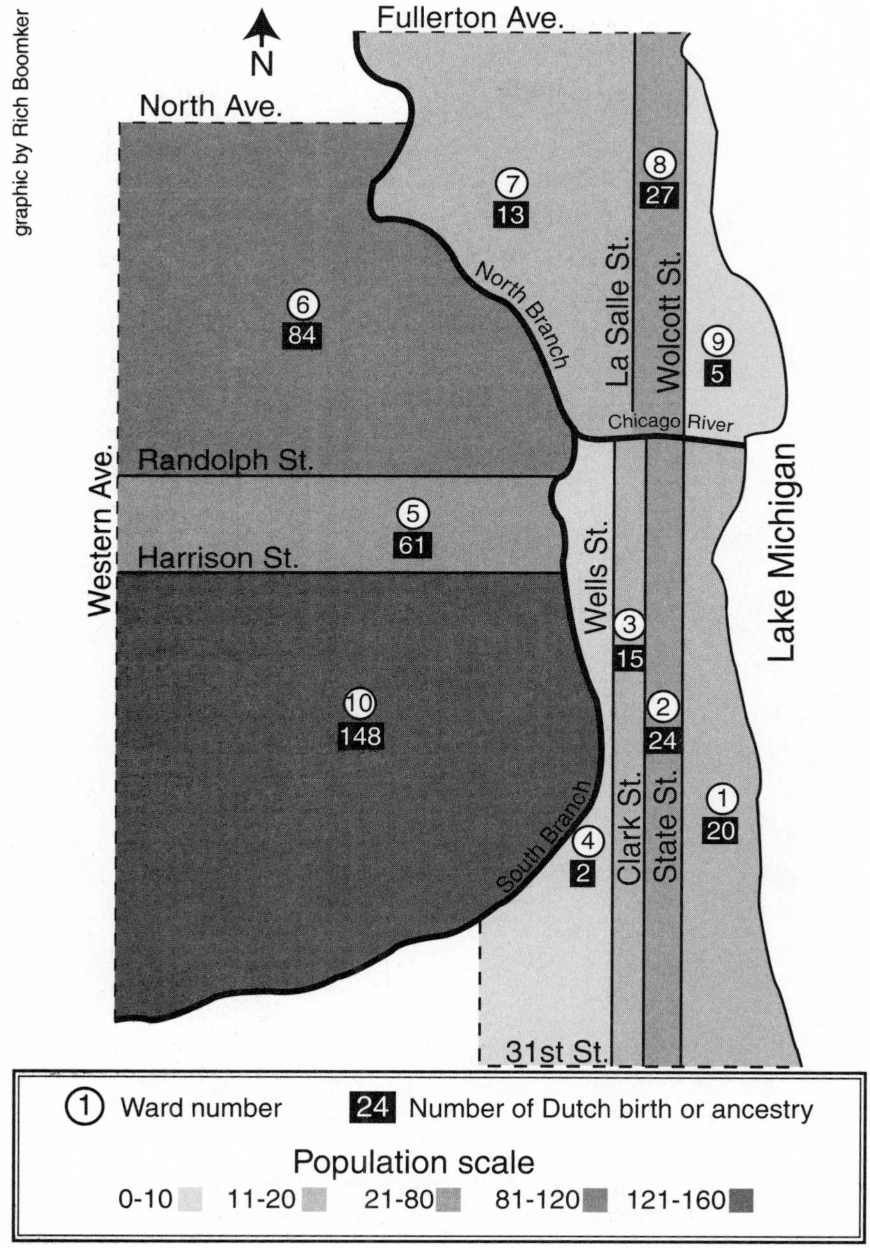

Figure 1.5 Dutch in Chicago, 1870

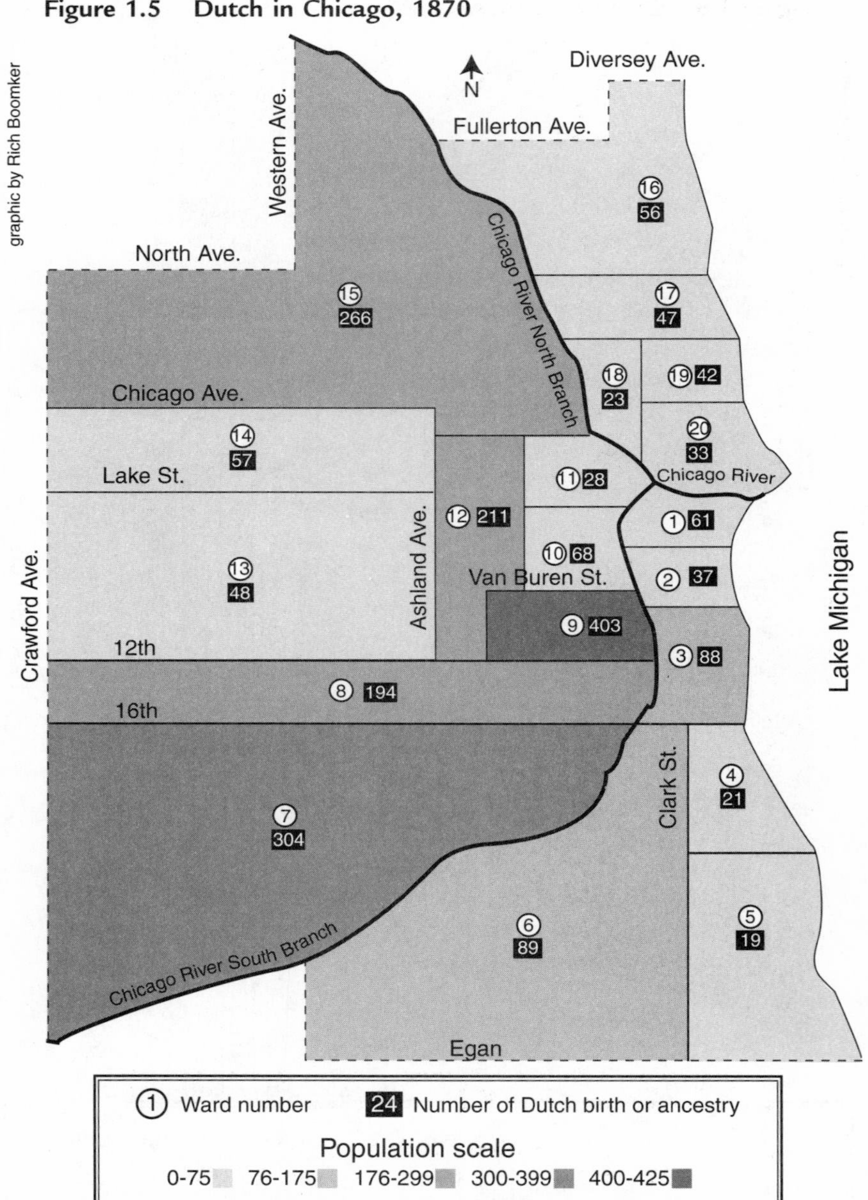

Figure 1.6 Dutch in Chicago, 1880

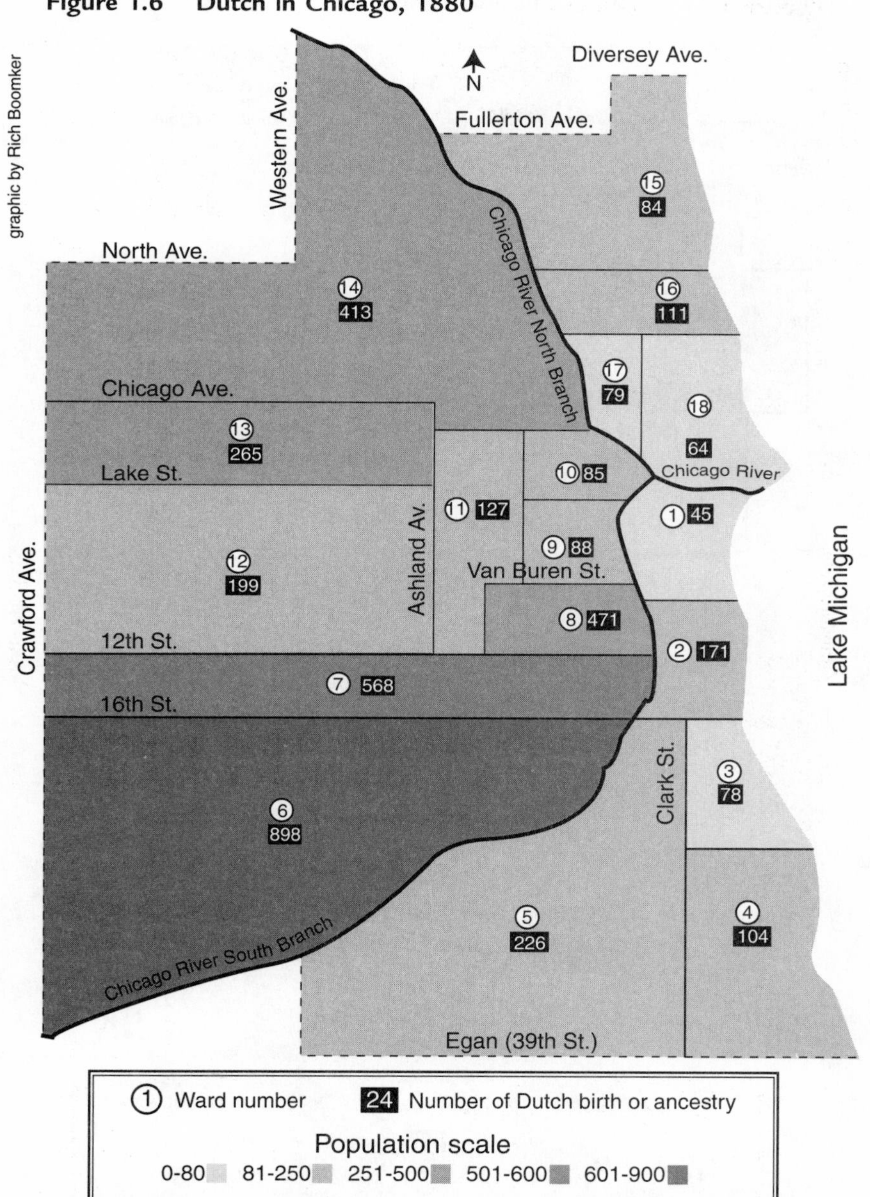

Figure 1.7 Dutch in Chicago, 1900

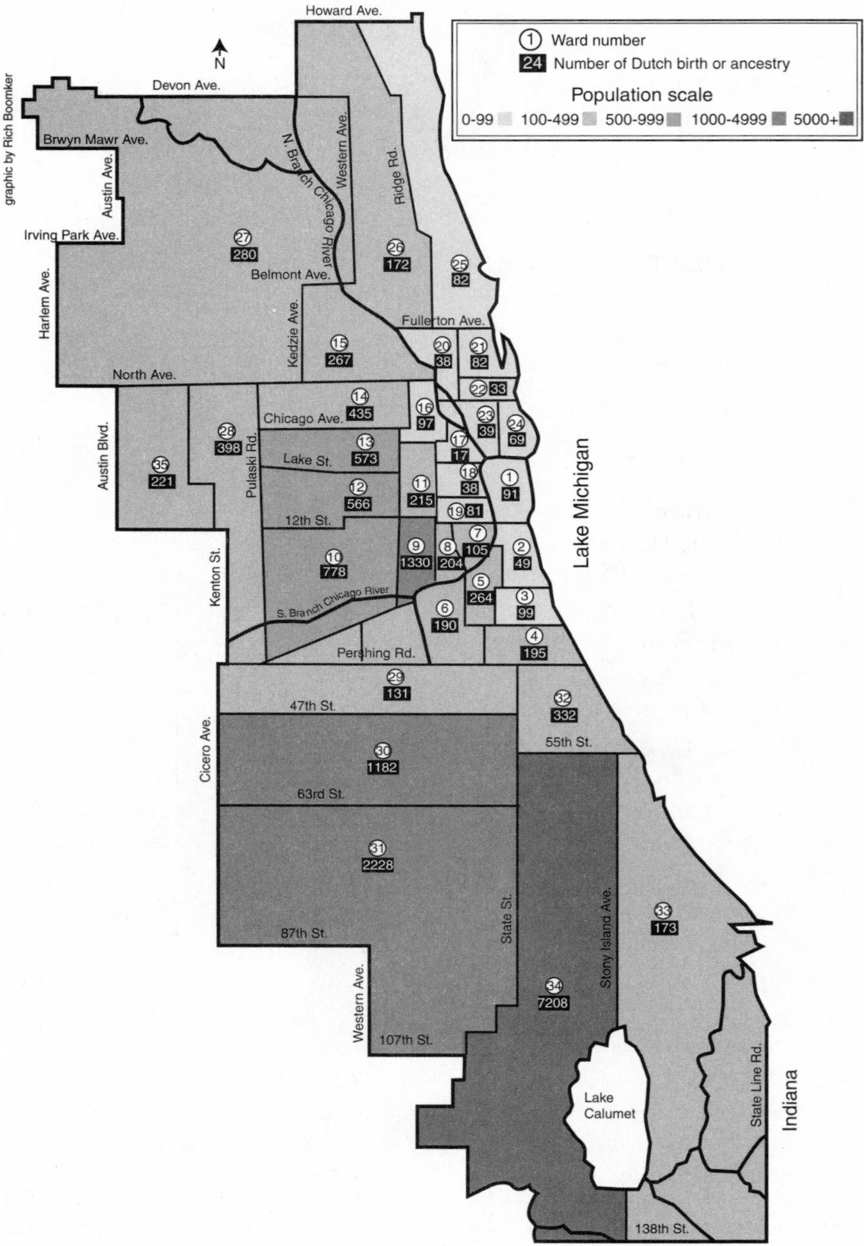

CHAPTER 2

"Like Mother, Like Daughter": Dutch Calvinism in America

For a generation or more, the immigrant churches in Chicago and throughout the United States were mirror images of the churches in the homeland. Every "changing wind" of doctrine in the mother churches echoed in its daughter churches in America. Conflicting interpretations of the historic church order of the Synod of Dort (1618-1619) also troubled the churches in America. For this reason, Reformed history in America is intimately connected to old-world religious history. Attempts to reform the national Reformed (Hervormde) Church form a critical backdrop to the struggles in America.

Two major reform movements took place in the Netherlands. The first, the Secession of 1834 (known as the *Afscheiding*), was a precursor to the schism in western Michigan in 1857. The second, the *Doleantie* or neo-Calvinist revival of 1886, headed by theologian and political leader Abraham Kuyper, reverberated in America after 1900.[1]

The Secession of 1834 tapped two strains in Netherlandic religious life, one pietist and the other doctrinal. Pietism, a strain of simple-hearted

1. Masterful analyses of the cultural roots of these movements are James D. Bratt, *Dutch Calvinism in Modern America: A History of a Conservative Subculture* (Grand Rapids: Eerdmans, 1984); Henry Zwaanstra, *Reformed Thought and Experience in the New World: A Study of the Christian Reformed Church and Its American Environment, 1890-1918* (Kampen: J. H. Kok, 1973); Gerrit J. ten Zythoff, *Sources of Secession: The Netherlands Hervormde Kerk on the Eve of the Dutch Immigration to the Midwest* (Grand Rapids: Eerdmans, 1987); and Hendrik Bouma, *Secession, Doleantie, and Union: 1834-1892* [translation of *De vereniging van 1892* (1917) by Theodore Plantinga] (Neerlandia, Alberta, and Pella, Iowa: Inheritance Publications, 1995).

Abraham Kuyper
(1837-1920)

faith, arose in medieval times and flourished in the seventeenth-century "conventicles" or house churches, where pious people gathered under local teachers for private devotionals and teachings. The lay preachers called the faithful to Godly living, to abstain from "the things of the flesh and the world." Standard puritanical admonitions against worldliness included abstaining from "strong drink"; playing at cards and throwing dice; going to dances, theaters, and fairs; and desecrating the Sabbath with everyday activities other than works of necessity.

The doctrinal strain was a product of the Calvinist reformation and harked back in the Netherlands to the Synod of Dort. This wing of the Seceders stressed theology, "head knowledge," and assent to true doctrine, as the essence of biblical faith. The lead question in the old formulary for "Profession of Faith" asked: "Do you heartily believe the doctrine contained in the Old and the New Testaments . . . ?" This simple doctrinal tradition, which blended easily with an experiential piety, resonated in Chicago among leaders of the Reformed churches.

The Seceders of 1834 drew on both the pietist (heart) and doctrinal (head) traditions as an antidote to the theological liberalism, religious formalism, and ecclesiastical power struggles to which much of the national

Reformed Church succumbed after 1815. Their house churches became centers of resistance in the 1820s and 1830s, when religious change swept across the land. In the economic crisis of the 1840s, the Seceded congregations sent a disproportionate share of their members to America. As we will see, the Dutch churches of Chicago, especially in the twentieth century, were nothing if not daughters of the Secession of 1834. Piety and orthodoxy have always characterized the Dutch Reformed of Chicago.

The neo-Calvinist, Kuyperian movement had its roots in the Anti-Revolutionary Party of Guilliaume Groen van Prinsterer (1801-76). This party arose in the 1840s as a response to the secularism that pervaded the Netherlands after French armies in 1795 introduced the ideals of the Revolution of 1789 and its humanistic, Enlightenment ideology. The goal of the Anti-Revolutionary Party was to battle the spirit of secularism in public life and institutions, including the government itself, by building a network of separate institutions, especially Christian schools, with the goal of reforming society along Christian, rather than socialist, lines.

In the 1890s, Kuyper modified the anti-revolutionary program to make a place for all religious worldviews, not only the Reformed. After winning the prime ministership in 1901, Kuyper reordered "every sphere of life" according to the three main religious communities – Reformed, Catholic, and liberal-socialist. His system, known as *verzuiling* (literally "columnization" or "pillarization"), placed the three faith communities on an equal basis at law and allowed for tax-supported separate schools and universities, newspapers, trade unions, media outlets, health and welfare agencies, and sports associations. Thus, Dutch society was segmented into religiously based blocs, each valuable in its own right and together indispensable in supporting the national structure.[2] The Kuyperian vision, as we will see, found very few advocates among the Dutch Reformed in Chicago.

In sum, immigrants brought both the Seceder and Kuyperian traditions to America, where advocates of each mind-set jostled for position in the churches. Often the devotees lived harmoniously, but just as often they differed sharply over the question "How, then, shall we live?"

2. James E. McGoldrick, *God's Renaissance Man: The Life and Works of Abraham Kuyper* (Auburn, Mass.: Evangelical Press, 2000); and Frank Vanden Berg, *Abraham Kuyper* (St. Catherines, Ont.: Paideia Press, 1978); D. H. Kromminga, "The Dutch Reformation in 1886," *Banner*, 10 July 1936; Johan Goudsblom, *Dutch Society* (New York: Random House, 1967), 32-33, 50-51, 102-04, 118-27.

Religious Seceders and Overseas Emigration

The Seceder impact on the American settlements was so pronounced because Seceders dominated the first wave of emigration in the 1840s. Many of the early Dutch settlers in Chicago, and in the Midwest colonies generally, were Seceders who brought a piety and independent spirit that was characteristic of their movement.

It is difficult to imagine what life would have been like among the Dutch Calvinists in America if there had been no Secession in 1834 in the Netherlands. Without the religious upheaval, fewer families would have left the homeland. The Dutch never caught "America fever" like the Irish or Germans. They value *gezelligheid* (cozy conviviality) and believe in the adage: *"Oost, west, t'huis best"* ["East, west, home is best"]. Had there been no religious turmoil, the overall Dutch emigration might have been reduced up to 25 percent – seventy-five thousand people.

Religious estrangement was a dislocating force in numerous villages and hamlets. The people experienced "cognitive dissonance," to use a modern term, which prepared hearts and minds for the unthinkable – leaving the fatherland permanently for overseas colonies. The Seceders were thus the most prominent of all Dutch emigrants. In 1849 they numbered only 1.3 percent of the Netherlands population but contributed 65 percent of all emigrants in the peak years of emigration, 1846-1849. In these years eighty of every thousand Seceders in the Netherlands emigrated to America. Fully 60 percent of the thirteen thousand Seceders who emigrated before 1880 left in the decade 1847-1857.

This Seceder dominance in the first wave of the great nineteenth-century Dutch emigration had a multiplier effect, like a rolling snowball, which prompted other families and friends to follow. Members of the Reformed Church and Catholics were also inclined to emigrate because of the example of the Seceders, who first made migration a normal response to troubles at home.

But it took an economic crisis, which struck hardest in the very same regions and among the same social groups as the religious unrest, to actually instigate the emigration. In the 1840s plant diseases hit the potato and rye crops, which were staples of the diet for the working poor. This, coupled with rising taxes and license fees and widespread unemployment and underemployment, sparked a localized "America fever" in Seceder regions, where many already felt dispossessed as outcasts for rejecting the standing order of church and state.

The straitened economic circumstances and a general spirit of malaise seemed to offer no hope for the future. The religious declension and fear that the nation was losing its very soul and would soon feel the wrath of a just God added to the sense of despair. This worst-case scenario of Seceder preachers became real in the bloody and violent revolutions of 1848 in neighboring Germany and France, which spilled over into the Netherlands and caused a constitutional crisis. It was high time to escape the fury to come.

Seceder clerics like Albertus C. Van Raalte and Hendrik P. Scholte organized and led the emigration in order to establish colonies where the believers could band together and not be scattered and lost to the faith. Seceder networks funded and directed the movement, and their letters back and forth kept the whole process on track and created a migration chain of kith and kin. The result was that between 1847 and 1860, eight Calvinist colonies were planted in America, including South Holland and Roseland near Chicago.[3] By 1900 there were one hundred such enclaves in the nation; all acted as magnets. It is estimated that between 1846 and 1900 three-quarters of all Dutch emigrants settled in Reformed enclaves. They include urban centers in Chicago, Grand Rapids, Paterson (N.J.), Rochester (N.Y.), Milwaukee, Cincinnati, and elsewhere.[4]

The intense and focused migration of Dutch Calvinists gave them a strong presence in America that was far out of proportion to their numbers. In 1920 there were over five hundred immigrant congregations of the Reformed and Christian Reformed churches, many still worshiping in the Dutch language. These bodies experienced a much slower and less intense Americanization process than did the nonenclaved immigrants, who tended to be nominally Reformed, Roman Catholics, and Jews. The ethnic cohesion in the Reformed colonies and their continuing ties to the mother churches preserved the Dutch identity for many generations.

Ironically, by colonizing in America, the Seceders, "who had been marginalized in their native villages, became dominant in their transplanted settlements," where they "assumed a cultural authority that was much like that of the Reformed Church they had spurned in 1834." They preserved old values and practices and became "more Dutch than the Dutch."[5]

As table 2.1 shows, Seceder emigrants outnumbered Reformed Church emigrants in 1845, 1846, and 1847, but overall, members of the Reformed

3. The other colonies were Holland, Mich.; Sheboygan and Alto, Wis.; Pella, Iowa; Pultneyville (later East Williamson) and Clymer, N.Y.

4. Herbert Brinks, ed., *Dutch American Voices: Letters from the United States, 1850-1930* (Ithaca: Cornell Univ. Press, 1995), 2-3; Lucas, *Netherlanders in America,* chap. 5.

5. Thus argues Brinks, *Dutch American Voices,* 15, 11.

Table 2.1 Emigration by Year, Reformed Church and Seceded Church Members, 1835-1857

	Reformed Church		Seceded Church		Total
Year	N	%	N	%	N
1835-44	152	61	99	39	251
1845	210	49	216	51	426
1846	349	27	957	73	1,306
1847	835	21	3223	79	4,058
1848	837	52	779	48	1,616
1849	1,006	59	691	41	1,697
1850	333	81	77	19	410
1851	565	83	118	17	683
1852	764	93	60	7	824
1853	801	84	152	16	953
1854	2,457	86	402	14	2,859
1855	1,376	80	342	20	1,718
1856	1,300	81	311	19	1,611
1857	1,191	89	142	11	1,333
Totals	12,176	62	7,569	38	19,745

Source: Robert P. Swierenga, *Faith and Family: Dutch Immigration and Settlement in the United States, 1820-1920* (New York: Holmes & Meier, 2000), 178 (Table 8.2), which also notes the specific groups included in each category.

Church made up 58 percent of all Dutch emigrants in the period 1835-1880, compared to the 20 percent who were Seceders.[6] Some devout Reformed Church members also emigrated under Seceder auspices or joined Seceder colonies. Others joined the Seceders in America because they alone offered a "touch of home," social cohesiveness, and church benevolence in times of need. But most Reformed Church emigrants scattered far and wide, and often chose large cities, where they quickly assimilated; some 10 percent even settled in the Dutch East Indies and other parts of the world. So the Reformed Church immigrants are important – they outnumbered Seceders two to one – but Seceders deserve the top billing when we think about the founding of the Dutch Calvinist churches in America.

6. Robert P. Swierenga, *Faith and Family: Dutch Immigration and Settlement in the United States, 1820-1920* (New York: Holmes & Meier, 2000), 177-78, Tables 8.1, 8.2.

Secession of 1834

Given the concern in the conventicles for a warm and vibrant orthodoxy, it is not surprising that these pietists became alarmed when the secular spirit of the French Enlightenment gained the upper hand in the Netherlands in the early nineteenth century. Signs that the National Church leaders "had fallen asleep" were everywhere. Few protested when the French revolutionary army came into the Netherlands in 1795 and purged traditional Calvinism from public life.[7]

The crowning blow came after the restoration of the House of Orange, when King Willem I in 1815 convened another national synod, the first since 1618, and hand-picked delegates who reflected the modern temper, thereby bypassing local congregations and provincial assemblies. With little debate, this synod made a number of momentous changes that threatened completely to undo the Reformed Church, particularly its creedal basis and representative governance. Thus, given the close bond between church and state, any future reform movement in the church, as in 1834, was quickly perceived as a threat to the social order.[8]

When a few intellectuals within the Reformed Church, centered in Amsterdam and Leiden, raised their voices in protest against theological heterodoxy, they were met with vicious counterattacks by church leaders. The protesters were influenced by the religious revival, known as the *Réveil,* that began in Geneva, Switzerland, around 1810. The *Réveil* made resistance to rationalism intellectually respectable and sparked a spirit of renewal and piety in Dutch Reformed circles.[9]

In the next years pious folk in the pews joined in passive resistance to the new regime by abandoning the Reformed Church or joining the few "faithful" congregations nested within it. Devout elders organized informal worship services in homes and barns, where they read sermons of the revered founders of Reformed theology, the "old writers" of the seventeenth century, as they fondly called them. Here the people heard the pure *Staten Bijbel* read and expounded, and memorized the Heidelberg Catechism and the Dutch version of the Psalms, which alone were sung in the services.[10]

7. Ten Zythoff, *Sources of Secession,* 1-42, 103-04.

8. Ibid., 25-42; Albertus Pieters, "Historical Introduction," in *Classis Holland Minutes, 1848-1858* (Grand Rapids: Eerdmans, 1950), 10-12.

9. J. Vree, "De Nederlandse Hervormde Kerk in de jaren voor de Afscheiding," in *De Afscheiding van 1834 en haar geschiedenis,* 30-61, eds. W. Bakker, O. J. de Jong, W. van't Spijker, L. J. Wolthuis (Kampen: J. H. Kok, 1984), 47-52.

10. Ten Zythoff, *Sources of Secession,* 45-48; Lucas, *Netherlanders in America,* 45-46.

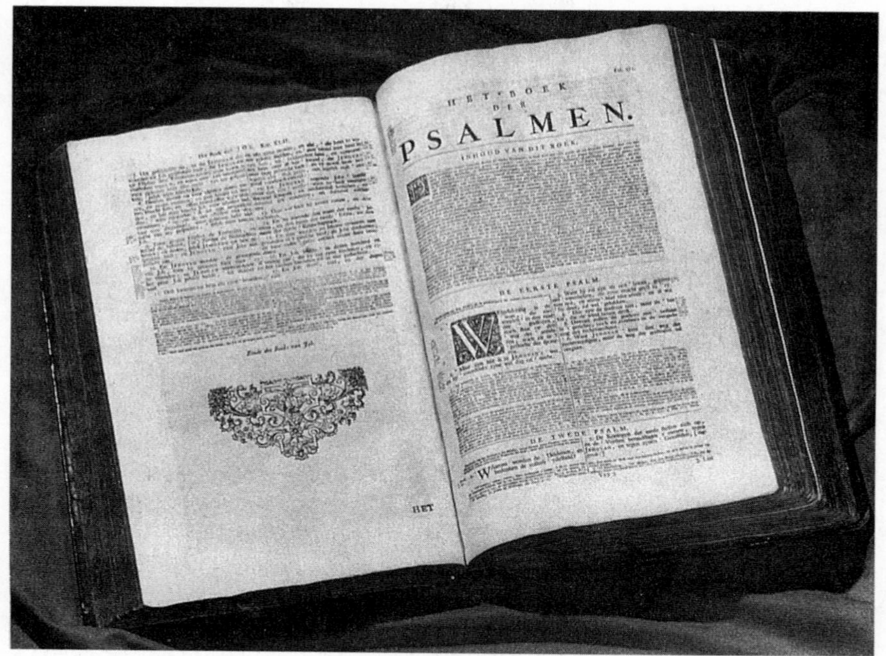

Staten Bijbel (Official Dutch Pulpit Bible) used in First (Gurley St.) Christian Reformed Church from 1867

Some parishioners actually won over their pastors, as happened at Ulrum with Hendrik De Cock, a graduate in theology of the University of Groningen, where religious humanism was the norm. De Cock's revitalized preaching touched a nerve, and believers who were dissatisfied with their own pastors flocked to Ulrum by the hundreds to hear his sermons and have him baptize their children. Reformed Church leaders declared De Cock to be "the most dangerous man in society" and suspended him. He and most of his congregation of 137 members then seceded and declared that they had "returned" to the "true church" of "the Fathers." In the next year De Cock planted sixteen seceded churches throughout the provinces of Groningen and Drenthe.[11]

De Cock found allies among members of the "Scholte Club," a small coterie of former theological students at the University of Leiden led by Hendrik Scholte, which included Anthony Brummelkamp, Simon Van

11. Ten Zythoff, *Sources of Secession,* 104-10; P. N. Holtrop, "De Afscheiding – breekpunt en kristallisatiepunt," in *De Afscheiding van 1834 en haar geschiedenis,* 62-99.

Velzen, and Albertus Van Raalte. Scholte pastored the Reformed Church congregation at Doeveren in Noord Brabant and was suspended from his pulpit two weeks after De Cock's secession; nearly three hundred members of his congregation withdrew with him. Van Velzen preached in Friesland and Amsterdam, and Van Raalte planted congregations in Overijssel.

Soon the Seceders counted 128 congregations, mostly in rural reaches of the land. But they had only six pastors, which shows the bottom-up character of the revival. Its foot soldiers came from the lower ranks of society, the disinherited, those of low culture and little formal education. Most were rural laborers and village craftsmen, whom Abraham Kuyper later affectionately called *de kleine luyden* (literally, "the little people").[12]

Persecution

The government moved swiftly to suppress the Seceder threat. King Willem I issued a royal decree in 1836 denouncing the Seceders as schismatics, fomenters of unrest, and secret agitators. He demanded that they obey the law and submit to the "established and recognized church."[13] This order they could not in good conscience obey and all were deposed or forced to resign.

The king's officials resorted to a Napoleonic law that forbade unauthorized political gatherings of twenty or more persons and applied the law to Seceder worship services. This banned all but the very smallest gatherings. The authorities levied exorbitant fines on pastors and consistory members, cumulatively totaling hundreds of thousands of guilders; they even briefly jailed some pastors, including De Cock and Van Raalte. The fine for conducting an "illegal" service was *f*100 ($40), plus *f*50 ($20) for each consistory member and *f*100 for the owners of a house or barn used for worship. Van Raalte spent twelve days in jail in 1837; his fines totaled *f*40,000.[14]

12. Peter Y. De Jong and Nelson D. Kloosterman, eds. *The Reformation of 1834: Essays in Commemoration of the Act of Secession and Return* (Orange City, Iowa: Pluim Publishing Co., 1984), 28; ten Zythoff, *Sources of Secession,* 125-27; Bratt, *Dutch Calvinism,* 6-7.

13. J. Weitkamp, "De vervolgingen," 246, 255-57, 264, in *'Van scheurmakers, onruststokers en geheime opruijers . . .': De Afscheiding in Overijssel,* ed. Freek Pereboom, H. Hille, and H. Reenders (Kampen: Uitgave Ijsselakademie, 1984). An English translation of this chapter by Elizabeth Dekker is available at the Van Raalte Institute.

14. Lucas, *Netherlanders in America,* 42-53, 119-20; Henry Beets, *Life and Times of Jannes Van de Luyster, Founder of Zeeland, Michigan* (Zeeland, Mich.: Zeeland Record Company, 1949),

Seceder pastors carried on, preaching to as many as a thousand spiritually thirsty people at a time. The government went so far as to mobilize police and soldiers to prevent unauthorized worship services, which they termed "riots." Seceder leaders were forced to quarter the soldiers in their homes and their wives had to feed them. No wonder that in America the Seceders cherished freedom of religion as such a precious right!

Persecution, which strengthened the movement, peaked in the years 1836-1840 but continued until King Willem II promulgated a new constitution in 1848 that guaranteed complete religious freedom. By 1849, forty thousand people belonged to the Christian Seceded Church, and the Reformed Church had lost 5 percent of its members. Many more sympathizers stayed because they could not face the official repression, family splits, and public ridicule hurled at the dissenters. Seceders continued to suffer social ostracism, economic boycotts, and job blacklists long after the official suppression stopped.

Religious reformation is difficult to channel in constructive paths. At least this was the case in the 1834 Secession, which consisted of a series of locally oriented reformations rather than a centrally organized movement. Strong personalities in the center and extremists and bigots at the fringes also plagued the Seceders, as they do in many popular movements.[15] The fissures came to a head in the early 1840s, and immigrants carried the disputes to America.

The differences gradually crystallized around the major issue of the role of the church in society. Was it to establish the religion of the realm (*Corpus Christianum* – "Body of the Christened") or to be a fellowship of true believers (*Corpus Christi* – "Body of Christ")? The Reformed Church clearly was a "realm-religion," but most Seceders were wary of the heavy hand of the state and desired a true covenanted church.[16]

The Seceders coalesced into three major factions. At the "center" was an urban and liberal "southern party" led by Brummelkamp and Van Raalte, based in Overijssel and Gelderland. On the "right" stood the rural and very orthodox "northern party" or "Cocksians" led by De Cock and

12. Ten Zythoff, *Sources of Secession,* 49, quotes in English translation the relevant articles 291, 292, and 294 of the Napoleonic Code.

15. Herbert J. Brinks, "Religious Continuities in Europe and the New World," 209-23, in *The Dutch in America: Immigration, Settlement, and Cultural Change,* ed. Robert P. Swierenga (New Brunswick: Rutgers Univ. Press, 1985).

16. Leonard Verduin, "CRC: Hewn from the Rock," *Banner,* 8 Oct. 1984, 9. Verduin further elaborated the distinction in his booklet, *Honor Your Mother: Christian Reformed Church Roots in the Secession of 1834* (Grand Rapids: CRC Publications, 1988).

Van Velzen, based in Groningen, Friesland, and Drenthe, with allied groups in Zeeland. Scholte, whose base was in Utrecht and Noord Brabant, held the extreme "left," espousing a separatist, premillennial, nonconfessional Christianity — "no creed but the Bible." He ventured into nontraditional paths that led to "ecclesiastical anarchy" — to use Van Raalte's words, where few others would follow.[17]

The northern party defended the doctrine, liturgy, and polity of Dort as biblically grounded; it was made up of strongly traditional Calvinists who stressed the need for Christian schools and catechetical instruction of the youth to combat the "godless influence" in the public schools. The southern party was more broad-minded, inclusivistic, and even-tempered; they stressed experiential piety and evangelism to the point that some charged them with Arminian leanings.

These factions in the Seceder churches presage the future divisions in America, which were merely a continuation of old battles, with a new issue thrown in, that of Americanization. Among the Seceders who emigrated in the crucial 1840s, the southern element was stronger. After the American Civil War, however, the northern contingent became predominant, and this spurred the growth of the Christian Reformed Church. The more open mind-set of the Van Raalte camp was evident at the First Reformed Church of Chicago, while the Cocksians were firmly rooted at Chicago's First Christian Reformed Church.

Thus, the Secession of 1834 was a reformation in the Dutch Reformed Church that started small but had a far-reaching impact at home and abroad. Despite regional struggles and personal rivalries, the leaders renewed the Dutch church and planted a branch in America. The Dutch Reformed churches in the Midwest are truly daughters of the Secession of 1834. We cannot understand them without knowing their mother, the Christian Seceded Church and its successor, the Christian Reformed Church (Christelijke Gereformeerde Kerk). By 1869, this mother had grown to 100,000 members and more than 325 churches.[18]

17. Henry Beets, *De Chr. Geref. Kerk in N.A.: Zestig Jaren van Strijd en Zegen* (Grand Rapids: Grand Rapids Printing Co., 1918), 34-36, 45-48; John Kromminga, *The Christian Reformed Church: A Study in Orthodoxy* (Grand Rapids: Baker, 1949), 30-31; Earl William Kennedy, "Eden in the Heartland," *Church Herald* 54 (March 1997): 8-10, 15.

18. J. van Gelderen, "'Scheuring' en Vereniging," in De *Afscheiding van 1834 en haar geschiedenis,* 100-46; J. A. de Kok, *Nederland op de breuklijn Rome-Reformatie* (Assen: Van Gorcum, 1964), 292.

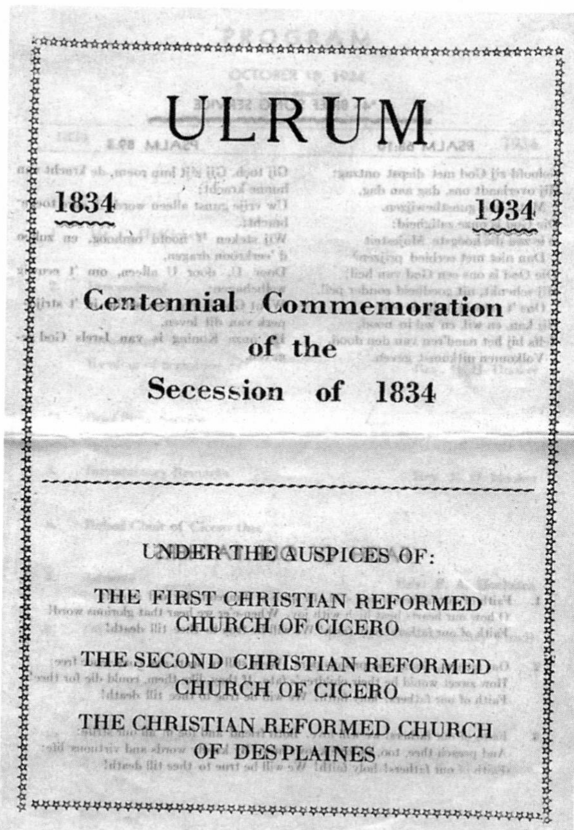
ULRUM

1834 1934

Centennial Commemoration of the Secession of 1834

UNDER THE AUSPICES OF:

THE FIRST CHRISTIAN REFORMED CHURCH OF CICERO

THE SECOND CHRISTIAN REFORMED CHURCH OF CICERO

THE CHRISTIAN REFORMED CHURCH OF DES PLAINES

Ulrum Centennial Commemoration program, 1934

Reformed Church in America, 1628-1850

If developments in the Netherlands Reformed churches since the 1830s shaped the immigrants, so did the nature of the Reformed Church in America, with which the nine congregations of the Classis of Holland formally affiliated in 1850. The Reformed Church began in the New Netherland Colony in 1628 as a branch of the Classis of Amsterdam, under the auspices of the Dutch West India Company, which had established a trading center at the mouth of the Hudson River.[19] For a hundred years

19. Gerald F. De Jong, *The Dutch Reformed Church in the American Colonies* (Grand Rapids: Eerdmans, 1978); John Beardslee III, "The Reformed Church and the American Revolution," in *Piety and Patriotism: Bicentennial Studies on the Reformed Church, 1776-1976,* ed. John W. Van Hoeven (Grand Rapids: Eerdmans, 1978), 17-33.

and more the body remained very Dutch in its religious culture and thoroughly committed to the Dort church order. This was possible because the Articles of Surrender offered by the English government in its military takeover in 1664 guaranteed freedom of religion to the Dutch. As Firth Haring Fabend, an expert on the Reformed Church, has stated:

> The colonial church continued to be overseen by the Amsterdam Classis. Reformed clergymen continued to be educated and ordained in the Netherlands and supplied to New York and New Jersey congregations by the Amsterdam Classis. Church services continued to be conducted in the Dutch language. And worship, doctrine, polity, and church order continued to be governed by the canons, creeds, confessions, and catechisms established at the Synod of Dort in 1618-1619.[20]

Moreover, the English civil and church authorities took over the public welfare tasks that had earlier been the obligation of the church. This allowed the Dutch to distance themselves further from the new English regime and culture. As a result, Dutch ethnic identity persisted, says Fabend, "despite the establishment of English law, the English language, and English manners and customs; in fact, it prospered – actively nurtured by Reformed clergymen and laity determined to honor their religious roots and to keep faith with the churchmen of Dort."[21]

In the eighteenth century, however, the inevitable process of Americanization, made evident in the Great Awakening, divided the Dutch Reformed Church into factions – progressives versus traditionalists. The progressives advocated an independent American church while the traditionalists demanded one with continuing ties to the Netherlands. The Americanizers gained the upper hand during the Revolutionary War because they supported the patriot cause, whereas the conservatives or Tories condemned revolution as a non-Christian solution. In fact, one-third to one-half of the Dutch Reformed in the New York–New Jersey area were Tories, but only four ministers out of forty-one dared to come out openly against the War.[22]

20. Firth Haring Fabend, "The Synod of Dort and the Persistence of Dutchness in Nineteenth-Century New York and New Jersey," *New York History* 77 (July 1996): 273-300, quote on 276; Firth Haring Fabend, *Zion on the Hudson: Dutch New York and New Jersey in the Age of Revivals* (Albany: Univ. of New York Press, 2000), 13-14.

21. Ibid., 278.

22. Ibid., 278-79, 285, quote on 279; A. C. Leiby, *The Revolutionary War in the Hackensack Valley* (1966), cited in Beardslee, "American Revolution," 18, 21-23, 165.

In 1792 the Dutch Reformed Church in America, in keeping with the new democratic era, exercised its right to declare independence from the Classis of Amsterdam and adopt its own constitution. The preface included a most significant clause, which gave church members the freedom to worship God "according to the dictates of their own consciences." This phrase mimicked the religious freedom clause of the American Bill of Rights adopted the previous year. In effect, it was an abandonment of the creedal basis of the church and a "sharp departure" from the Dort church order. It allowed clergymen to remain in good standing even when they reinterpreted cardinal Reformed doctrines such as election and limited atonement in favor of the rising spirit of Arminianism that came to full fruition in the Second Great Awakening. Weekly sermons from the Heidelberg Catechism also fell away in many churches.[23]

The result was that in 1822, under the leadership of theology professor Solomon Froeligh, a number of New Jersey churches seceded from the Reformed Protestant Dutch Church – the name adopted in 1819 to distinguish it from the German Reformed and other Reformed bodies – and formed the True Reformed Dutch Church. This offshoot, organized as Classis Hackensack, many years later, in 1890, merged with the Christian Reformed Church.[24]

Meanwhile, the Dutch Reformed Church cooperated with Presbyterian and Congregational churches in frontier home missions efforts, adopted Sunday schools like the English, and looked favorably on the new revival techniques of Charles G. Finney, which included altar calls and other emotional styles of worship. A "quickening of the Lord's people" in 1843 brought three thousand souls into the Reformed churches, which was double the number added in any previous year in the history of the denomination.[25]

By the 1840s, when the new immigrants arrived, they found that the Reformed Church had adapted itself to American revivalism and interdenominational societies. To a certain extent it had become "methodized." By 1848, for example, nearly every Reformed Church had a Sunday school, and ten thousand children were enrolled. More remarkably, two-thirds of the schools were not affiliated with the Reformed Church but with the American Sunday School Union, an ecumenical body the Re-

23. Fabend, "Persistence of Dutchness," 284-91, quote on 285.

24. Dick L. Van Halsema, "Hopkins, Hackensack, and Haan," *Reformed Journal* 7 (Jan. 1957): 7-9.

25. James W. Van Hoeven, "The American Frontier," in *Piety and Patriotism,* 44.

formed Church had joined in 1828. Further evidence of Americanization is that, in 1848, of 276 active ministers, barely one-half were born in the denomination. The others were mainly English and Scottish Presbyterian in background.[26]

In 1840 Reformed Church leaders considered dropping the word Dutch from the denominational name, arguing that it gave the church a detrimental "foreign image" and was un-American. The Reformed Dutch Church, in their view, could not hope to keep pace with the rapidly growing Presbyterian Church, which was similar in organization and beliefs, unless it cast off its "foreign badge." In 1867 the offending word was excised in the name of progress, although it still resonated emotionally with many in the pews. These developments provided the backdrop for the arrival of the "young Dutch" in the mid-nineteenth century and the founding of immigrant Reformed churches throughout the Midwest.[27]

Union of 1850 and Secession of 1857

The American denomination that the Classis of Holland joined in 1850 was quite unlike the Christian Seceded Church in the Netherlands. Dissatisfaction with this decision was, therefore, quite predictable, and for several generations, until the 1920s at least, the Dutch Reformed community was racked with conflict over the pace of Americanization. The pressure to adapt to the host culture and yet maintain a sense of Dutchness created tensions that had to be faced. The force of Americanization could not be stayed but it could be delayed. The Reformed Church continued on its well-worn path of acculturation, accepting and even welcoming the opportunity to be a player in the broader Protestant world. The Christian Reformed Church, on the other hand, sought to remain as true as possible to its Netherlandic heritage and to wall itself off from American Christianity and culture, or at least to slow the inevitable process of conforming to it.

Another secession rent the Dutch immigrant church in North America and led to competing congregations in almost every colony and urban neighborhood — the Reformed Church in America and the Chris-

26. Fabend, "Persistence of Dutchness," 291-93.

27. Gerald F. De Jong, "The Controversy over Dropping the Word Dutch from the Name of the Reformed Church," *Reformed Review* 34 (Spring 1981): 158-70. It is worth noting that the Classis of Holland, under the leadership of Van Raalte, voted 21 to 9 in favor of dropping the word Dutch, but the more traditional Classis of Wisconsin, which included the Chicago churches, voted 15 to 8 against the name change (167).

tian Reformed Church in North America. The schism of 1857 had a distinctly 1834 flavor because some issues were similar and some of the same players were involved, notably Van Raalte. But 1857 was not an exact parallel of 1834 because the immigrants were living in a foreign land and they had affiliated with an American denomination.[28]

The Reformed Church in America, founded in 1628 in New Amsterdam and centered in New York and New Jersey, had in 1850 welcomed the nine churches of the Classis of Holland (Michigan) with their one thousand members into a thoroughly Americanized fellowship. Van Raalte and his fellow clerics had formed the classis in 1848 as an independent church organization.

The Union of 1850 led some Seceders to replay the debates of the 1830s and to secede again in 1857 to form the True (Christian) Reformed Church. All future Reformed immigrants consequently had to choose which denomination to join. The immigrants from the outset were of two minds, one separatist and oriented to the mother church, and the other ecumenical and desirous of reaching out to fellow Reformed believers in the new homeland. The central issue was that of Americanization. Would the immigrants remain faithful disciples of the 1834 Secession and keep their ties to the mother Seceded Church, or would they cut themselves loose and quickly integrate into American Reformed Christianity? Van Raalte pushed them in the direction of assimilation by the Union of 1850, but one in ten refused to go along.

The Union of 1850 seemed to be a natural outgrowth of ties that developed when the old Dutch gave assistance to the young Dutch who arrived at New York harbor. Leaders in the Reformed Church met the newcomers at customs; provided temporary lodging; gave food, clothing, and money to the destitute; and even loaned several thousand dollars to purchase land in the West. Needless to say, these acts of kindness engendered much goodwill among the first contingents of Seceders during their "time of troubles."[29]

While the aid from the East was much appreciated, many in the Michigan colony were very uneasy about union with the Reformed Church, which under the impact of the Second Great Awakening had seen many congregations move away from a strict Calvinist theology toward

28. Kromminga, *Christian Reformed Church,* 23-39; Albert Hyma, *Albertus C. Van Raalte and his Dutch Settlements in the United States* (Grand Rapids: Eerdmans, 1947), 193-238: Lucas, *Netherlanders in America,* 506-15.

29. William O. Van Eyck, *Landmarks of the Reformed Fathers, Or What Dr. Van Raalte's People Believed* (Grand Rapids: Reformed Press, 1922), ch. 25.

more evangelical themes.[30] The Seceder tradition of separatism and suspicion of autocratic synods also made them wary.

Gysbert Haan, elder in the Grand Rapids church, reflected the suspicious spirit. After worshiping for a time in Reformed churches in Albany and Rochester, he had in 1850 settled in western Michigan, where he brought reports of purported "irregularities" in the eastern churches. Haan charged that many ministers and elders held membership in "secret societies" (Masonic lodges) and that churches practiced "open" (i.e., unregulated) Communion, used choirs in worship services to the detriment of congregational singing, sang hymns rather than the psalms, and neglected catechism preaching. In 1855 Haan attacked Van Raalte himself for promoting free-will doctrines. More than those of any other individual, Haan's complaints "fed the fires of discontent."[31]

Underlying all of Haan's grievances was the suspicion that the Reformed Church in America, like the Reformed Church in the Netherlands to which it had been attached until the American Revolution, was similarly tainted with heterodoxy. The leaders of the Classis of Holland adamantly refuted this charge as groundless. Van Raalte tried to dissuade Haan but failed, and Haan in 1856 withdrew from his congregation before the classis could discipline him.[32]

But Haan had posed the critical question: Why not abandon the tie to the Reformed Church in the East and remain linked to the Seceded Church in the Netherlands? Van Raalte's answer, after sitting in on a classical assembly at New Brunswick, was that the theology of the Reformed Church was compatible with that of the Seceders and its American ways were not something to be feared but emulated. Haan and his allies disgreed on both points.

The subsequent arrival of colonists fresh from the Netherlands brought reinforcements for Haan's position. A key dissenter was Dominie[33] Koene Vanden Bosch, who emigrated in 1856 in response to a call from the Noordeloos, Michigan, congregation. Even before leaving

30. Fabend, *Zion on the Hudson,* 215-16.

31. So says John Kromminga, *Christian Reformed Church,* 32. See also R. John Hager, "Gysbert Haan: A Study in Alienation," *Reformed Journal* 13 (Nov. 1963): 7-10, 13; 13 (Dec. 1963): 12-15; 14 (Jan. 1964): 15-18.

32. *Classis Holland Minutes,* 203-07, 225-26; Kromminga, *Christian Reformed Church,* 33, 37.

33. "Dominie" (Dutch, *dominee,* derived from the Latin "master" or "lord") is the common title for Reformed clerics in the Netherlands (D. H. Kromminga, "Dominee," *Banner,* 24 July 1936). It has since fallen into disuse in the United States.

the Netherlands, Vanden Bosch had heard from dissatisfied brothers in Michigan about the supposed apostasy of the Reformed Church.[34]

The end result was a schism in 1857 and the creation of the True Dutch Reformed (later Christian Reformed) Church. A majority in five West Michigan congregations seceded, totaling 750 persons, or 10 percent of the Classis of Holland.[35] Vanden Bosch's withdrawal letter typified their sentiments. He declared that the Reformed Church was not a "true church of Jesus Christ" because of the "abominable and church-destroying heresy and sins which are rampant" in it. The formula of subscription "was not binding," "many Freemasons were in the church," the church sang hymns in worship, etc. To belong to a church infected with such "extreme wickedness" was unconscionable, Vanden Bosch declared, and "consequently, I renounce all fellowship with you and declare myself no longer to belong to you."[36] This open condemnation of the Reformed Church was broadcast widely.

The Reverend Hendrik Klyn's more irenic letter of withdrawal urged the end to a spirit of bitterness. We were "together ministers of the secession" of 1834, he reminded his colleagues, who had separated in the conviction that "the Church, the Bride of Christ, is a garden enclosed, a well shut up, and a fountain sealed." The words "enclosed," "shut up," "sealed," capture the essence of the Seceder fortress mentality that gave rise to the later "motto" of the Christian Reformed Church: "In isolation is our strength." Thea Van Halsema acknowledged this ethnocentric worldview in her centennial history, *I Will Build My Church* (1956): "In our hearts we were still a church walled-in."[37]

These acts of secession "grieved" Van Raalte deeply, and he responded on the floor of Classis to the "serious (and) unsubstantiated accusations . . . which are the fruit of a lust for schism already for a long time manifested by a few leaders." Joining the Reformed Church in 1850 in no way abandoned the 1834 Secession, he insisted, because the Reformed Church, contrary to the Netherlands Reformed Church directorate of 1816, upheld the traditional principles of Dort.

34. Noordeloos Christian Reformed Church, *Centennial, 1957,* 11, in the Archives, Calvin College. An excellent treatment of Vanden Bosch is Brinks, "Religious Continuities," 209-23.

35. Robert P. Swierenga and Elton J. Bruins, *Family Quarrels in the Dutch Reformed Churches in the Nineteenth Century* (Grand Rapids: Eerdmans, 1999), 89-90.

36. *Classis Holland Minutes,* 240.

37. Ibid., 240-41, 245. Klyn was quoting from the Song of Solomon 4:12; Thea B. Van Halsema, "*. . . I Will Build My Church*" (Grand Rapids: International Publications, 1956), 188.

The True Church was a weak reed for many years. Vanden Bosch was the only ordained minister among the five charter congregations, and several were plagued with instability and conflict.[38] Yet, the struggling seceders survived the rocky first decade and eventually flourished. In the nearly thirty years from 1873 to 1900, the Christian Reformed Church grew eight-hundred fold, compared to a one-hundred-fold increase in the immigrant congregations of the Reformed Church in America. The younger denomination grew from twelve thousand souls in 1880 to forty-seven thousand by 1900; it appealed to immigrants who wished to preserve their Dutchness and their strict Reformed orthodoxy.

In the 1880s the old issue of Freemasonry in the Reformed Church fed rapid growth in the junior denomination. All of the Midwestern immigrant congregations of the Reformed Church, including Van Raalte's pioneer church in Michigan, condemned Freemasonry as incompatible with church membership. But Reformed Church synods, some of whose officers in the East were Freemasons, persistently for twenty years refused to make this pronouncement, despite repeated overtures by the Midwestern church assemblies imploring it to do so. The controversy reflected transatlantic differences in Freemasonry. In America the lodge lived comfortably with Christianity and marked one's patriotism; but in Europe it was viewed as antithetical to Christianity and a nest for freethinkers.

The upshot was that in 1882 several thousand members, representing 10 percent of total membership of the Particular Synod of Chicago, withdrew in frustration and joined the junior denomination. This 1882 secession was a greater defection by far than in 1857, and it had wider ramifications.[39]

The failure to bar Freemasons cost the Reformed Church in America its close relationship with the mother church in the Netherlands, the Christelijke Gereformeerde Kerk Nederland (CGKN), which had always barred Freemasons. After 1882, it would send membership papers with its approbation only if immigrants affiliated with Christian Reformed congregations. Thus, the immigrant members in the Reformed Church, who themselves stemmed from the mother church, had to suffer the outright repudiation of that heritage by their American denomination. And the ju-

38. Ibid., 91-97.

39. This and the next paragraph rely on Elton J. Bruins, "The Masonic Controversy in Holland, Michigan, 1879-1882," 53-72, in Peter De Klerk and Richard R. De Ridder, eds., *Perspectives on the Christian Reformed Church: Studies in Its History, Theology, and Ecumenicity* (Grand Rapids: Baker, 1983). In 1894 the Reformed Church in America established formal ties with the Hervormde Kerk Nederland. See *Acts and Proceedings of the General Synod of the Protestant Dutch Reformed Church in America,* 1894, 115, 136.

nior denomination thereafter captured the bulk of the big immigrant wave of the 1880s, totaling more than eighty-five thousand souls, many of whom came from the strongly Calvinistic northern provinces.

Choosing a Church Home

The decision to affiliate with one or the other Dutch Reformed denomination in America was the most critical choice an immigrant family had to make. The effect lasted for generations. It determined not only the church fellowship but also the circle of friends, pool of potential marriage partners, and educational choices. Although churches of the sister denominations often faced one another on the same street or were only blocks apart, members had little social contact. Christian Reformed children attended Christian schools while Reformed children enrolled in the public schools (see chapter 7). Differing life paths flowed from these educational choices.

Mentalities of Chicago's Dutch-American Community

The Chicago Groningers were products of the Secession of 1834 more than of the Doleantie of 1886. This was largely a by-product of the fact that most had emigrated earlier. Moreover, they had been nourished in the Seceder conventicles and believed in restoring doctrinal orthodoxy and the historic confessions. Those who emigrated after 1886 included Kuyperian triumphalists, who worked to create Christian day schools and other social institutions.

The 1834 Seceders, in James Bratt's words, were "vigilant for orthodoxy among themselves and content to let the rest of the world go by." Their religion had a "warm" character that stressed the "importance of the heart" more than the intellectual work of building God's kingdom on earth. Fearing worldliness and believing the "antithesis" or sharp division between the church and "the world," they formed themselves into culture islands, a "handful of Hollanders in a sea of Jews, with whom the Dutch do not mix."[40] Their Calvinism was largely limited to preserving purity in

40. Bratt, *Dutch Calvinism,* 3-54, note 4; ten Zythoff, *Sources of Secession,* 99-127; Bratt's schema was foreshadowed in Zwaanstra, *Reformed Thought,* ch. 3, and in Nicholas Wolterstorff, "The AACS in the CRC," *Reformed Journal* 24 (Dec. 1974): 9-16.

Table 2.2 Mentalities of Chicago's Dutch Reformed Churches

	SECEDERS/ PIETISTS	NEO-CALVINISTS/ KUYPERIANS
	Reformed Church "West"	**Positive Calvinists**
OUTGOING OPTIMISTIC	*Christian Intelligencer* Bernardus De Bey Peter Moerdyke Marinus E. Broekstra	*American Daily Standard* J. Clover Monsma Ralph Dekker (layman) Dick T. Prins (layman) Richard Fennema (layman)
	Confessionalists	**Antithetical Calvinists**
DEFENSIVE ISOLATION	*De Wachter* Harm Douwstra Frank Welandt J. H. Mokma John O. Vos Benjamin Essenburg Herman Bel	*Onze Toekomst* John Van Lonkhuyzen William Heyns Evert Breen Cornelius De Leeuw Sjoerd S. Vander Heide Jacob Manni Klaas Schoolland

Schema adapted from Bratt, *Dutch Calvinism in Modern America,* 47.

the home, church, and school; it did not extend to transforming "every sphere of life." They contended with the culture more than they challenged it.

As these predominantly Seceder pietists sorted themselves out theologically in Chicago under the influence of their parsonage-trained dominies, they divided again into revivalist and confessionalist camps, to use Bratt's schema of four "mentalities" (Table 2.2). First Reformed Church was pulled between an optimistic, revivalist faction and the defensive, confessionalist immigrant majority. The dominant leader, Bernardus De Bey, who pastored the body for twenty-three years (1868-1891), clearly identified with the Americanizing wing. Despite his strong Seceder background, De Bey viewed immigration as a chance to jettison Dutch theologizing for American ecumenism. As Herbert Brinks explained, De Bey deliberately emulated local preaching styles and adopted the "spiritual rhythms of American evangelism — conversion, backsliding, and renewal," despite the fact that his first-generation immigrant members were less than enthusiastic.[41]

De Bey continued to preach in the Dutch language and managed to hold the factions in his congregation together. Immediately after he retired, however, the most acculturated members followed Peter Moerdyke into the English-language Trinity Reformed Church, where "seasons of refreshing" were also *de rigueur*. Some revivals, marked by fervent prayer and personal testimonies, mainly by the young people, ran nightly for three weeks or more. As Moerdyke explained: "The older people of our Western Holland Churches do not, as a rule, contribute to the life and power of this [prayer] meeting, but our young people are fast being Americanized in their training for usefulness at this service."[42] De Bey's successors, especially Marinus Broekstra, continued to push these practices of American evangelicalism at the First Reformed Church of Chicago.

Moerdyke, the optimistic pietist, also saw no way for Kuyper's Calvinist political ideals to succeed in Chicago. "Had he understood our people's prevalent, conscientious and prudent abhorrence of corrupt politics," he might change his mind, Moerdyke suggested. "The European situation is not ours." Political reform could only come when all evangelical Christians joined hands to push one or the other major party to enact needed laws and programs.[43]

By contrast, Christian Reformed clerics condemned American evangelical techniques and remained committed to Dutch confessional orthodoxy. In 1897, clerical writers in *Onze Toekomst*, according to Moerdyke, "attacked the prayer-meeting as an anti-Calvinistic feature of Church life . . . [and warned] against the 'Arminian' or 'Methodist' institution – our 'sweet hour of prayer.'"[44]

During the Progressive era, neo-Calvinists made their move. They had been energized by a visit to Chicago of Kuyper himself in 1898, following his famed Stone Lectures at Princeton University. The Dutch leader received a hero's welcome from those of his persuasion among the city's twenty thousand Hollanders. He lectured in Dutch in a packed Englewood church and urged his followers to be both loyal Americans and good Netherlanders. Accept a rapid and wholesale Americanization,

41. Herbert J. Brinks, "The Americanization of Bernardus De Beij (1815-1894)," *Origins* 6, No. 1 (1988): 28.

42. Moerdyke, "Chicago Letter," *Christian Intelligencer* (hereafter *CI*), 30 Jan. 1895, p. 10; 16 June 1897, p. 9.

43. Ibid., 16 Nov. 1898, p. 14; 23 Nov. 1898, p. 4.

44. Ibid., 6 Oct. 1897, p. 8.

he advised, but also hold to the mother tongue, history, and culture. You are now Americans, he declared, and you must be such in language, sympathy, and ambitions, if you wish to have any influence in public affairs. "A mere Hollander is a ten cent man; the Americanized Hollander is a dollar man." The latter can bring his light out from under the Dutch bushels and let it shine all around, transforming the secular institutions into Christian beacons. Kuyper's visit was a shining moment.[45]

Four successive Kuyperians served as pastors of the First Christian Reformed Church of Chicago and its daughter, the Douglas Park Christian Reformed Church, after 1900: William Heyns (1900-02), Evert Breen (1903-09), Sjoerd S. Vander Heide (1909-18), and Dr. John Van Lonkhuyzen (1918-28) at First Church; and Cornelius De Leeuw (1905-10) and Jacob Manni (1910-16) at Douglas Park. Heyns became professor of Old Testament at Calvin Theological Seminary, and John Van Lonkhuyzen, a graduate of the Free University of Amsterdam and disciple of Kuyper, used his pulpit and his pen as editor of *Onze Toekomst,* Chicago's only Dutch-language newspaper (3,500 circulation in 1922), to promote Kuyper's vision in the Windy City. For example, Van Lonkhuyzen strongly pushed Christian secondary education at the newly established Chicago Christian High School (1916). Support for separate Christian schools marked Van Lonkhuyzen and his associates as defensive Kuyperians.

Some leaders on the West Side held a variant of Kuyper's world view. The motto of Calvin College professor Klaas Schoolland resonated among them: "In our *isolation* and in our independent action be our strength and our purpose for the future." They would construct a holy Dutch community within as a bulwark against the "world."[46]

While the boundaries between Seceders and Kuyperians sometimes blurred, one mindset had little influence, that of the cosmopolitan, positivist Calvinists. These were led by the Christian Reformed clerics B. K. Kuiper and Henry Beets in Grand Rapids, and in Chicago by the Reverend J. Clover Monsma of Englewood and several laymen, including Ralph Dekker, an electrician and member of the Second Englewood church; Dick Prins, an accountant and member of the Second Cicero church; and Richard Fennema of Roseland. Dekker advocated a Christian labor movement, Fennema a Christian political party, and Prins called for groups to

45. Ibid., 16 Nov. 1898, p. 14.

46. Bratt, *Dutch Calvinism,* 51; "Dr. John Van Lonkhuyzen," obituary, *Banner,* 8 Jan. 1943, 38; "Rev. S. S. Vander Heide," obituary, ibid., 27 Sept. 1929; Lucas, *Netherlanders in America,* 851, 920, 936, 917. I am indebted to Herbert J. Brinks and the late Marinus Goote for providing information on the religious orientation of the Chicago Christian Reformed pastors.

study the writings of Kuyper, "the interpreter of Calvinism par excellence," a practice he hoped would lead to the founding of a university in America like the Free University of Amsterdam. "We are an army without a general," Prins lamented, and a "Calvin-Kuyper University" would produce such leaders.[47]

Chicago's Groningers seemed to have no vision to build Christian labor and political movements or a Christian university. Few attended Chicago Christian High School or the Kuyperian stronghold of Calvin College, and few read the triumphalist periodicals. J. Clover Monsma's *American Daily Standard,* modeled after Kuyper's newspaper, went bankrupt within months in 1921 (chapter 14). Van Lonkhuyzen's editorials had little impact on the Groningers because their dominant spirit was Seceder pietism. This was also the perspective of his own successor at the First Christian Reformed Church, the very popular Benjamin Essenburg, who renewed the pietist mentality with great vigor during his sixteen-year pastorate (1929-45).

P. H. Holtman, the first editor of *Onze Toekomst,* had sounded the Seceder themes already in 1894 before Kuyper's visit. Holtman exposed the dangers of Americanization and the loss of the Dutch language, especially in religious life, and denounced public schools as "un-Christian." He charged that churches that jettison the Dutch language risked "casting off Calvinism, our confessions, and the form and spirit of Reformed worship," and thus succumbing to theological modernism. Such churches, he continued, "discard everything that is sound and conservative," deliberately cast their youth "adrift" by denigrating Reformed doctrines, and "fling away" their honor as Hollanders and even despise their heritage.[48]

Churches committing the egregious errors that Holtman had in mind were in the Reformed Church in America. Of 191 churches in the Particular Synod of Chicago in 1905, which included all of the congregations in the Midwest and West, 29 (15 percent) were entirely English-speaking and many more had introduced an evening English service for the youth. Trinity Reformed's Peter Moerdyke reported further that the "number of ministers that cannot preach in English is small and diminishing, and those who use the English with greater ease than the Dutch are rapidly on the increase."[49]

47. D. T. Prins, "Kuyperianism and Calvin-Kuyper Clubs," *Banner,* 9, 23 Dec. 1937; Richard Fennema, "A Christian Political Party," ibid., 22 Sept. 1933.

48. Quoted by Moerdyke, "Chicago Letter," *CI,* 28 Mar. 1894, p. 11.

49. Ibid., 28 June 1905, p. 411.

From Moerdyke's perspective, which stood diametrically opposed to that of Holtman, "one of the most urgent, sacred duties of leaders is to lead youth out of bondage into the fullest and freest possession of the land that God has given them." English is in reality the native tongue of the youth. "Their associations, school, books, papers, surroundings are so irresistibly English as to replace the Dutch." Therefore, he concluded, "trying to keep our youth partially foreign to our country and her religious movements will handicap them in many ways and relations, and must of necessity discount their future standing and influence. We believe in a safe, Christian, rapid Americanization of all our young people."[50]

Thus, rapid Americanization was "safe" and "Christian" for Reformed churches, but for Christian Reformed churches it was "un-Christian" and involved "risk." The juxtaposition of differing perspectives could not be starker than the statements of Moerdyke and Holtman.

While the Reformed Church progressed on the path of Americanization by mimicking the Yankee Presbyterians and Congregationalists, the Christian Reformed Church continued to value its vaunted conservative traditions. As Moerdyke described the body in 1907:

> They are thoroughly Dutch, retain foreign ways, have a true Dutch ministry, get nearly all of the immigrants from the old country, instruct the youth of their congregations and govern the parish very strictly, maintain parochial "Christian Schools" in very many charges, and so bind their boys and girls to their own Church by teaching Dutch as well as English, and the tenets of their creeds and confessions. . . .
>
> Their own men and leaders share offices, honors and distinctions equally, and their whole constituency without sectional division or cleavage originate and shape and execute the policy and plans of their Church. Their aggressiveness, with this independent, unanimous and homogeneous make-up is remarkably successful as their rapidly growing institutions at Grand Rapids prove. Their periodical literature is bright, ably edited, widely read, in both languages. In this respect they surpass us. And yet they are a decidedly foreign Church, with their field inevitably limited to Hollanders and their descendants, which, however, is about as true of our Church in the West.[51]

50. Ibid., 11 Aug., p. 9; 15 Dec. 1897, p. 10.

51. Moerdyke, "Indiana Letter," *CI,* 18 Sept. 1907, p. 606, citing Henry Beets's editorial in the *Banner,* 3 Oct. 1907, pp. 484-86.

Despite this "foreign" character, the Christian Reformed Church went through the process of Americanization in tandem with the Reformed Church, only lagging by a generation or two. The immigrant church experienced transition and change by gradually adopting ways that it had once eschewed. Examples are Sunday schools; the use of organs, choirs, and hymns in worship; and most importantly, English-language services. However reluctantly, the Christian Reformed Church followed the path blazed by its older sister, the Reformed Church.

This behavioral pattern was recognized already a century ago. "It is noteworthy," said Moerdyke in 1906:

> that, whilst our dear brethren are so staunch and loyal in their conservatism, their churches are nevertheless progressing in many ways of initiation and transitional adoption of new ideas and methods. It is inevitable. Not a few of our plans and methods and developments against which their people protested years ago are no longer foreign to them, but now followed. It is often remarked that they are simply a generation behind us in Americanization. We honestly hope this process will continue only along the line of careful, prayerful, orthodox acclimatization.[52]

During the Christian Reformed Church semi-centennial in 1907, the denomination held special festivities and celebrations around the country and counted their blessings. The junior denomination numbered 167 churches grouped into 10 regional assemblies (called classes), with 130 ministers and 52 "vacant" pulpits (i.e., churches without a regular pastor), and its membership totaled 66,122 souls. It boasted a college and seminary with a faculty of 10 and 153 students, of which 144 were preparing for the ministry. The denomination published three periodicals, *De Wachter, The Banner of Truth,* and *De Heidenwereld,* and it had begun intensive missionary work among the Navajo Indians in New Mexico. These accomplishments served to vindicate its Seceder birth and nurture its strong sense of in-group loyalty.[53]

At the same time, the junior denomination saw the "spirit of our land" make "deplorable inroads among us." As the immigrant generation gave way to their children, interest in Dutch Reformed doctrine and life slipped noticeably. As Henry Beets lamented in 1907: "Love for the sanctuary displayed in frequent and diligent attendance upon the means of

52. Moerdyke, "Chicago Letter," *CI,* 11 July 1906, p. 448.

53. Statistics summarized in ibid., 10 Apr. 1907, p. 233.

grace, is as a rule not on the increase but rather the opposite in circles which use the American language as the tongue of religious exercises." Americanization had its downside.[54]

Conclusion

The West Side Groningers, like Dutch Calvinists elsewhere in the United States, were shaped and molded by the "brothers' quarrels" in the homeland. They carried the religious controversies with them and kept the issues alive. Doctrinal discourse was the coin of the realm in their circles, and the incessant debates over fine points of doctrine served as a means of self-definition and a way to set them apart from American society.

Religious mentalities divided the Dutch Calvinists into rival churches, often within earshot of one another. Members of the Reformed Church were optimistic about the promise of American life and eager to assimilate with it, while most Christian Reformed members looked inward and tried to hold American cultural influences at bay. They were defensive isolationists with a strong pietist bent. The Secession of 1834 resonated far more with them than did the Doleantie of 1886. Few in either denomination entered the mainstream in order to transform it along the Calvinistic lines that Abraham Kuyper modeled in the Netherlands. But some did step forward to build separate Reformed institutions for education, works of mercy, even recreation.

An economic gulf also divided the two Dutch denominations in Chicago. At least in the value of churches and parsonages, the properties of the Reformed churches far surpassed those of the Christian Reformed churches. According to the national religious census of 1906, Reformed church properties in Chicago valued at $156,000 were worth three times as much as the $51,000 value of Christian Reformed properties. The latter's buildings also carried much higher mortgage indebtedness. This was at a time when the six Christian Reformed congregations in greater Chicago outnumbered the eight Reformed congregations 5,000 members to 4,500 members. These data indicate a higher wealth and income status for Reformed church members. It paid to Americanize, but it was at the expense of membership.[55]

54. Beets, *Banner,* 3 Oct. 1907, p. 485. Moerdyke in a remarkable editorial concurred with "Brother Beets" ("Indiana Letter," *CI,* 23 Oct. 1907, p. 686).

55. "Editorials," *Banner,* 3 Oct. 1918, 708. RCA parsonages were also worth 25 percent

In church life and teachings, many subtle differences marked the rival Dutch Reformed denominations in Chicago, but both bore the three "marks of the true church" — the faithful preaching of the Word, the regular administration of the sacraments, and the diligent exercise of discipline by the elders. In facing the pressures of Americanization, however, the Christian Reformed Church deliberately held back.

In the end, the Christian Reformed Church adopted the same practices as the Reformed Church. In recognition of this melding together, the two denominations in 1976 for the first time since 1857 entered into an official relationship called "ecclesiastical fellowship." This historic decision enabled the churches that shared a common heritage to work together in evangelism, church education, and worship.[56] But the matter of Christian day schools remains a differentiating marker.

---

more. Membership data were compiled from the respective denominational annual reports of 1918. At the time of the 1916 national religious census, these disparities were much reduced.

56. "CRC-RCA," *Banner,* 27 Aug. 1976; Tymen E. Hofman, "RCA and CRC — 119 Years Later," ibid., 29 Oct. 1976.

CHAPTER 3

Guided by God Is Guided Well: The Founding Years

The lives of Chicago Dutch Calvinists revolved around their churches. The church stood at the center of the community and defined the religious culture that differentiated the Dutch from other groups. While mannerisms, dress, lace curtains, and a miniature windmill on the front lawn might betray their Dutchness, it was in the religious realm that it came to fullest expression. The church was the one institution brought from the motherland that they could preserve. The Dutch language almost immediately gave way to English in the streets and workplaces, as did American style dress and demeanor. But within the ethnic community and its many societies, services, and extended families, one could live from the cradle to the grave among fellow believers and enjoy a measure of security not available to those outside the pale.

The Dutch Calvinists in Chicago held their cherished doctrinal beliefs and practices close to their hearts and would make any sacrifice to preserve the faith of the fathers. Against tremendous odds, because of their lowly immigrant status and extreme poverty, they hoarded pennies and dimes to pay pastors' salaries, build churches and parsonages, care for the widows and orphans, and run church societies and programs. Their faith sustained them in adversity; they drew inspiration and fortitude from the Scriptures and especially the Dutch Genevan Psalter that they treasured in their hearts.

No matter the disappointments and disagreements, singing the psalms each Sunday sustained them. Every consistory meeting was opened and closed by singing a familiar but moving verse from the Psalter. Following the opening psalm one of the elders prayed for God's blessing on the meeting, and following the closing psalm another elder offered a prayer of thanks *(dankzegging)*. The first consistory meeting in the First Reformed Church of Chicago opened with Psalm 25:2 and closed with Psalm 86:6. Psalm 25 expressed the deepest yearnings of the heart:

> Teach me to walk in your way.
> I will walk in your truth.
> Make my heart submissive and prepare it,
> in order to fear your name.
> Lord my God I will praise you,
> and lift my heart on high.
> I will honor your name and majesty
> unto eternity.

Religion was not only doctrines and liturgies but social relationships, wedding and funeral ceremonies, Christian day schools, Sunday schools and youth clubs, sporting activities, and even picnics and vacations. The Dutch counted on their religious heritage to preserve their ethnic identity. A Dutch Reformed presence remains today in Chicago, as Amry Vandenbosch wrote in 1927, due "in large part . . . to their attachment to the church, as well as to their strong race [i.e., nationality] consciousness."[1] The same held true, of course, for the other European immigrants among whom the Dutch lived cheek by jowl – Poles, Bohemians, Italians, Germans, and Jews.

Because of the centrality of the Reformed faith, the intellectual battle between *colonizers,* who wished to preserve their Dutchness, and *immigrants,* who were willing and even eager to give it up for American ways, took place inside the sacred precincts. Clerics, teachers, and editors of church periodicals were the opinion makers. They found that a desire to preserve old ways came naturally, but a willingness to accept new ways took much persuasion. The immigrants carried in their cultural baggage a deeply rooted attachment to the church and community. Their social background played a large a part in this.

As farm laborers, the West Side Groningers shared a strong sense of localism and family loyalty that was almost tribal in character. Their desire was to transplant trusted institutions and the familiar culture, and above all to preserve the beloved language. The memories of one's native village, church, and dialect took on special significance in America. For

1. Vandenbosch, *Dutch Communities of Chicago,* 2.

these reasons, conservative religious values and the traditional ethnic clannishness were mutually reinforcing.

The founding of Dutch institutions and societies reflected core beliefs and values and was a response to the pressures of Americanization. This chapter provides an overview of these key developments and describes the planting of the Reformed churches in Chicago. The fundamental fault line was the division between the historic Reformed Church in America, dating from 1628 in the New Amsterdam colony, and its offshoot of 1857, the Christian Reformed Church in North America. Church edifices of these rival denominations faced one another in almost every Dutch Protestant immigrant settlement.

The Reformed Churches of Low and High Prairie

Between 1846 and 1852, several hundred Dutch immigrant families and single adults settled in Chicago or opened farms twenty miles south of the city in South Holland (first called Low Prairie) and fifteen miles south in Roseland (first called High Prairie). Roselanders originated in the province of Noord Holland, and South Hollanders, as the name signifies, hailed from the province of Zuid Holland.

South Holland and Roseland had clerical leadership from Willem Wust, a renegade Seceder pastor, who had been deposed and his congregation "disfellowshiped" for acting in arbitrary ways. The banning prompted Wust and his band of followers from Giessendam, Zuid Holland, to emigrate and join the nascent South Holland settlement.[2] Wust organized the congregation there in 1848 and the Roseland body late the next year. The pioneer "Dutch Church" in Roseland, however, only had Wust's services for the sacraments and to supervise the consistory. Elder Jakob De Jong conducted Sunday worship and read the sermons from an approved book of sermons that all Dutch Reformed churches had on hand for just such purposes.

In 1850 Wust suddenly returned to the Netherlands, leaving both congregations to fall back on lay leaders. De Jong continued in the Roseland church, and South Holland appointed elder Jakob Duim as lay

2. Gerrit Bieze, "W. C. Wust: Founding Father of the Netherlands Reformed Church in America," *Origins* 3, No. 1 (1985): 30-37; Arie Blok, "W. C. Wust: an extraordinary ministerial career!" *Historical Highlights* (Newsletter of the Historical Society of the Reformed Church in America) 4 (summer 1983): 5-20.

preacher. But when Duim baptized an infant and made up his own sermons for a time, some objected to the irregularity. The Reverend H. G. Klyn of the Milwaukee church mediated, and Duim and the church agreed that he must only read sermons and not perform the sacraments.[3] Both congregations thus carried on for years as *lees kerken* (literally, "reader churches," where elders read printed sermons).

The two congregations decided in 1853 to seek wider ecclesiastical fellowship and regular pulpit supply. In a decision that must have been much debated, they asked to be placed under the spiritual care of the Classis of Holland of the Reformed Church in America, which Albertus C. Van Raalte of Holland and his associate Cornelius Vander Meulen of the Zeeland congregation had organized in 1848. Since the South Holland group, according to classis minutes, was "at the moment too weak to be able to elect a consistory," they did not affiliate officially with the Reformed denomination until 1855.[4]

Five years passed after Wust departed before the Roseland and South Holland churches, known simply as the "Prairies," obtained an ordained pastor. They succeeded only because they agreed to share a pastor on a biweekly basis and thus could pay a living wage. In 1855 Marten A. Ypma of Milwaukee accepted their call. He was a Frisian who in 1847 had brought many in his Seceder congregation at Hallum, Friesland, to establish the Vriesland, Michigan colony.

Founding of the First Reformed Church of Chicago

The religious situation among Dutch Reformed immigrants in the central city was far more tenuous than in the Prairies. Van Raalte visited Chicago in 1852 and reported "the ravages wrought by error, worldliness, and quarrels to be great. Some had joined the so-called Spiritualists, one young man had gone over to the Romanists, others dispersed themselves among all kinds of denominations, many lived in indifference and sought the world, while others who confessed the name of the Lord lived in isolation.

3. First Reformed Church of South Holland, *Centennial, 1848-1948* (South Holland, 1948), 23-26; First Reformed Church in Roseland, *Ninetieth Anniversary Historical Booklet and Directory, 1849-1939* (Chicago, 1939), 5-10; Thorn Creek Reformed Church (formerly First Reformed Church of Roseland), South Holland, Illinois, *125th Anniversary, 1849-1974* (South Holland, 1974), 5-7.

4. *Classis Holland Minutes, 1848-1858* (Grand Rapids: Eerdmans, 1950), 110-11; First Reformed Church of South Holland, *Centennial,* 25.

One of the chief causes of all these woes," Van Raalte continued, "was to be sought in the lack of the ministry of the word and pastoral care."[5]

Most of the first Dutch settlers in Chicago had been members, at least nominally, of the national Reformed (Hervormde) Church, but Seceders, Catholics, and Jews were also represented. Several Reformed and Seceder families brought "attestations" (membership papers) from their home churches.

In 1847, within months of coming to Chicago, several Seceder families who took their faith seriously began meeting for worship as a *lees kerk.* They had to act on their own because the nearest Reformed church was at Low Prairie (South Holland) twenty miles away; High Prairie (Roseland) had not yet come into being. Herman Van Zwol collected a dozen families to meet on Sunday mornings at his home on North Clark Street, including Ale Steginga, Lucas Vanden Belt, Albert J. Kroes, Nicholas (Klaas) Van Heest, J. Labots, Ede Sipke Meter, Sr., Hendrik Albertse, Berend Snitseler, Wieland, Hendrik Sterenberg, and others. The Reverend Cornelius Vander Meulen of Zeeland, Michigan, encouraged the group by preaching whenever he was in Chicago. From time to time other preachers came to "lift their hearts and minds."[6]

In 1849 several new arrivals augmented the fledgling church, including the families of Simon Nederveld, Gosse Vierstra, and Timas Van Zee. Let Birkhoff tell the story:

> This increase in numbers made for a well filled home of H. Van Zwol. Rev. Van Raalte (later Dr.), the father of all Hollanders, especially in Michigan, driven by his warm heart and religiosity, came to preach every once in a while and would pay his own expenses. In the same year, one Jan Koppejans organized so-called religious services on Sundays in the home of Lucas Vanden Belt. Unfortunately, the mentioned "oefenaar" [lay preacher] could not satisfy the needs of his audience.[7]

Albert Kroes next opened his home for the place of worship, but it was so cramped that people had to stand. This led to a problem of fatigue,

5. *Classis Holland Minutes,* 111. Spiritualism was a "new age" religion that gained popularity in the 1840s and 1850s as a form of public entertainment. It involved communicating with the spirit world in séances, rapping and banging on tables, consulting mediums, and other "body reforms." See Ronald Walters, *American Reformers, 1815-1860* (New York: Hill and Wang, 1978), 163-71.

6. G. B. Sr. (George Birkhoff, Sr.), "Historische Schetsen," *De Hope* (Holland, Mich.), 25 May 1904, p. 4, trans. Huug van den Dool.

7. Ibid.

because the written sermons were too long to be read in one session. The solution was simple — find a book with shorter sermons! Services still exceeded by far the now customary one-hour format.[8]

The Chicagoans in 1852 took the next step in organizing their congregation. Seven men, including Kroes, Vanden Belt, Van Zwol, Philip Van Nieuwland, a Mr. Leister, Roelof Pieters, and Jan Rypkes Vander Kooi, formed a steering committee and asked Dominie Van Raalte to come and formally organize their nucleus as part of the Reformed Protestant Dutch denomination. Van Raalte reluctantly agreed to come, "to free his soul from a burden," as he put it. "The need of the Hollanders there impelled him to labor there."[9] All three Chicago area churches were small and isolated from the stronger congregations in West Michigan.

In February 1853, Van Raalte traveled to Chicago to constitute the steering committee, and together they convened a congregational meeting to vote on organization and elect a consistory. The first elders were Kroes, Van Zwol, and Vanden Belt, and the first deacons were Pieters and Vander Kooi, who was named treasurer. Morning worship would be at Brother Henry Pelgrim's home and the afternoon service at Brother Kroes's home, plus a Wednesday evening Bible study. The men agreed that the oldest elder, Van Zwol, would chair the consistory meetings. Van Raalte's coming was much appreciated but costly. Article 1 of the minutes of the first consistory meeting, held February 15, 1853, reports a discussion about how to pay his traveling expenses. The decision was predictable — take a collection at both services the next Sunday! Securing a larger meeting place was also high on the agenda. But the group was very poor, and the collections for Van Raalte were woefully insufficient. In the end, he largely paid his own way.[10]

Elders Van Zwol and Vanden Belt brought the formal application of the Chicago congregation to the classis at its April 1853 meeting in Zeeland, which granted approval with thanksgiving.[11] Van Raalte was the midwife of the First Reformed Church of Chicago, as he was for many other congregations in the Midwest.

Thus, after five years as an independent body, Chicago joined the

8. First Reformed Church of Chicago, *A Century for Christ*, 3.

9. *Classis Holland Minutes*, 110-11.

10. Birkhoff, "Historische Schetsen"; First Reformed Church of Chicago, Minutes, 1853-1945, Western Seminary Collection, Joint Archives of Holland. Volume two (1867-1881) is missing. Henry Lammers translated key parts of the Dutch-language minutes and summarized other items.

11. First Reformed Church of Chicago, *Century for Christ*, 3.

historic and Americanized Reformed Church in America, of which its members knew next to nothing except what the trusted Van Raalte told them. Classis, however, was made up of kindred spirits, and that body was the primary focus of ecclesiastical fellowship, not the church in the East. Nonetheless, after the union in 1853 the Chicago body was often tugged in two directions; they treasured the familiar Dutch ways but had to be open to their American friends.

First Chicago practiced benevolence from the outset, as did all churches in the Reformed tradition, by regularly collecting offerings for the poor in its congregation. Within six months of organizing, the body also decided to take a collection every three months for Van Raalte's hoped-for preparatory school "for the training of ministers." An acute need for their own minister – a need that was shared by all the western immigrant churches – demanded this sacrifice for the broader mission of the denomination.[12] The school, called the Holland Academy, was founded in 1857 and became Hope College and Western Theological Seminary. Van Raalte had no way of knowing that deacon Roelof Pieters would go on to study for the ministry at his new school and then follow him into the pulpit at the seminal First Reformed Church in Holland, Michigan, in 1869.

Elder Kroes represented the small Chicago congregation as sole delegate to the classis in September of 1853. This was the last classis meeting in Michigan attended by any Chicago delegates, however; the distance was too great. In April 1855 Chicago and the Prairie churches transferred to the Classis of Wisconsin, which four Wisconsin churches had organized a year earlier. It met conveniently in Milwaukee. Elder Van Zwol was Chicago's delegate to this and many subsequent classis meetings for the next three years.[13]

That the Reformed immigrants started holding worship services shortly after their arrival, without the benefit of clerical leadership, weakens the contention of the noted historian Henry Lucas that the westside Dutch "manifested little interest in religion and church life" and that they were "different from the majority of Dutch immigrants" elsewhere.[14]

12. First Reformed Church of Chicago, Minutes, 8 Aug. 1853.

13. *Classis Holland Minutes,* 146, 169-70; Classis of Wisconsin, Minutes, 25 April 1855, Art. 3, typescript, English translation by William D. Buursma and Nella Kennedy, Van Raalte Institute, Hope College, Holland, Mich. In 1856 the Classes of Illinois, Michigan, Holland, and Wisconsin were organized as the Particular Synod of Chicago at a meeting in Chicago's Third Presbyterian Church. *Acts and Proceedings of the General Synod of the Protestant Dutch Reformed Church in America,* 1856, 91; 1857, 133-34.

14. Lucas, *Netherlanders in America,* 323.

Also, Chicago Hollanders affiliated with the Reformed Church *before* the Prairies did, despite Van Raalte's generally dismal picture of Reformed vitality in the city. Chicago very likely had neither more nor fewer religiously indifferent newcomers of Reformed origin than did other urban centers. Cities attracted more young people and "rolling stones" than did homogeneous rural colonies, and the loose urban environment made it difficult to exert social control.

Within months of organizing, in May 1853, three families joined – Rudolph Kuin (Keun) of Veendam (Groningen), B. Vander Kolk, and Berend Boterman. In October four more families affiliated – including Nicholas (Klaas) Foute (Voute), B. Blankenzee, Willem Goossen, and B. Van Wijnkoop – and five men were added by public profession of faith, including Daniel Schipperus, Cornelis Vander Wolff, D. Van Berschot, Hermannus Fabries, and John Brink.[15]

This rapid growth compelled the congregation to seek its own place of worship and pastor. "After many struggles, exploiting in the extreme whatever little force and talent they had," they rented an empty store on Randolph and Des Plaines streets, located immediately west of the Chi-

15. Families and single members of the First Reformed Church of Chicago, 1847-1866, included, among others, Hendrik Albertse, Begerdekerk, Adrianus Beyzy, B. Blankenzee, P. Boeleman, Ralph Borgman (Boogmans), Cornelis Bos, P. Bosloper, Berend Boterman, Bouman, B. Braschler (Brasselaar), John Brink, Jan Brouwer, H. J. Bruggeman, H. Buis, Wim Dammers, Sijbert De Jong, C. P. De Neve, A. De Roo, Elizabeth and Jantje De Roo, N. De Wit and wife, Jelle De Vries, John Drent (Drenth), John Evenhuis, Hermannus Fabries, Conrad D. Foute, Nicholas Foute, R. Foute, Richard Gerritsen, Willem Goossen, Daniel Gordon, A. Hendrikse and wife, C. Hes, Cornelius Hillegonds, Marinus Hoogbruin, Huizenga, Rudolph Kamphuis, Kerk . . . , Johannes Keersemaker and wife, John Kooi, Rudolph Kuin (Keun), Klein, Koning, Jan Koppejan, Albert J. Kroes, B. Kroes, J. Labots, Liester (Luister), G. Lyse (Tyde), Jan J. Lormier, Jacobus Martha, G. Meinardi, Ede Sipke Meter, Sr., Helene Mulder, Derk Natelborg, Simon Nederveld, Nanne None, Adam Ooms, Oosterhoudt, John Oosters, Henry Otte, Henry Pelgrim, Roelof Pieters, Nicholas Ronda, Peter Ritzema, Isaac Schelling, Daniel Schippers (Schipperus), A. Seilmeyer, C. Smit, Berend Snitseler, Steffens (Leffers), Ale Stegenga (Steginga), E. Stegenga, F. Stegenga, J. Stegenga, Hendrik Sterenberg, Swart, Johanna Christiana TerHaar, Sophia Trenthop, A. J. Tris, D. Van Berschot, Hiram Vanden Belt, Lucas Vanden Belt, Jan Vanden Belt, Gerrit Vanden Burg, Vander Hout, B. Vander Kolk, John Rypkes Vander Kooi, Maas P. Vander Kooi, K. Vander Plas, H. Vander Sloot, Cornelis Vander Wolff, Arie Van Deursen and wife, Nicholas (Klaas) Van Heest, Barend Van Mynen, Philip Van Nieuwland, Abraham J. Van Persyn, Van Winden, A. B. Van Wijnkoop, Timas Van Zee (Vander Zee), Herman Van Zwol (Zwoll), Gerrit Vastenhouw, Klaas Vechter (Vegter), Verdoot and wife Sophia Van Winden, Gosse Vierstra, Josephine Vis, and Wieland. See First Reformed Church of Chicago, Minutes, Book 1, 1853-1866; Birkhoff, "Historische Schetsen."

Downtown Chicago, looking west between Randolph and Washington streets, 1858. First Reformed Church worship site (upper left) on Randolph Street just beyond Chicago River

(Courtesy of Chicago Historical Society)

cago River on the near West Side (Figure 1.6, site 1). Later the group moved less than a block east to "a large room" in the Seeley Building at the corner of Randolph and Clinton Streets. Times of worship for the simple services were 9:30 AM and 2:30 PM.[16] The location indicates that the center of

16. *Chicago City Directory*, 1856-1857, Appendix; First Reformed Church of Chicago, *Century for Christ*, 3.

the small Dutch Reformed community in the early years was immediately west of the Chicago River along Randolph Street.

Finding a pastor was more difficult, although the members "more and more . . . felt a need for a shepherd and teacher." Like the Roseland and South Holland churches, Chicago could not afford a full salary. So its consistory proposed that the three congregations share a pastor. He would live in Chicago and preach on a rotating schedule – two weeks in Chicago, one in Low Prairie, two more in Chicago, one in High Prairie, etc. The tripartite proposal was untenable from the start. The centennial history of First Church says simply: "Difficulties arose in regard to the regulations of the preaching services and the combination was dissolved." No doubt, the Prairies felt that the proposed sharing was hardly equitable. So Chicago struck out on its own.

The consistory considered the tiny pool of a half dozen ordained ministers in the Classis of Holland and formed the customary "trio"; it included Van Raalte, Cornelius Vander Meulen, and Seine Bolks of Grand Haven. After due deliberation, the members convened and voted to call Bolks. He received eight votes to Vander Meulen's seven and Van Raalte's one. Doubtless, the congregation realistically did not expect Van Raalte to accept a position in Chicago.

The call letter specified the salary in cash and kind, preaching expectations, and other conditions. To raise the monies, the consistory set a goal of $300 in pledges and assigned deacons Pieters and Vander Kooi to canvass the congregation. The American Second Reformed Church of Chicago, founded in 1854 by the Reverend John M. Ferris (1854-1862) to serve the Old Dutch from the East, offered to cover any shortfall. With this guarantee the letter went out to Bolks. The pledge method, in lieu of free-will offerings, seemed so satisfactory that the consistory decided to use it on a regular basis. Thus did the congregation move toward a fixed system of budgeting.[17]

Bolks had prepared for the ministry under Van Raalte and followed him to America in 1847 with a large part of his Christian Seceded Church at Hellendoorn in Overijssel, to found the colony of Overisel, Michigan. There, says historian Henry Lucas, Bolks was the "soul of the enterprise. Not only was he minister, teacher, and physician, but he served also as surveyor, architect, and agent for the settlement." Bolks was clearly a multitalented man, as well as a pious Christian and gifted preacher. But his tenure at Overisel ended in disgrace after only four years, when in 1851

17. First Reformed Church of Chicago, Minutes, 11 Sept., 6 Nov. 1853; 13 April 1854.

Bolks admitted to the sin of adultery. Upon his full confession and the urging of the Grand Haven church that had called him, classis readmitted him to the ministry after a suspension of six months. He served Grand Haven until 1855.[18]

Bolks declined First Chicago's call in early 1854 "to everyone's disappointment." The body wondered "what to do now? Everyone's assurance was the Triune God and, in complete surrender, many a prayer rose to the Lord from the pained bosom of the congregation. Their faith was steady. Financially, the congregation was poor; all were youthful emigrants." The next year the congregation decided to call Bolks a second time, but again he declined. Three years later, in 1858, the persistent congregation queried Bolks yet again about a call but he discouraged it. Then, in 1861, the congregation called him a third time. He was then pastor of the Milwaukee church, and finally he accepted. But he remained for less than two years. Despite the high regard that the Chicago Dutch had for Bolks, he did not seem to reciprocate the feelings.

Foster Street: Inception of the Groninger Hoek

New families continued to come in a slow steady pace. Five members joined the congregation in July, 1855, including Pieter Ritzema and John Drenth of Ulrum (Groningen); Klaas Vechter (Vegter), a farmhand from 't Zandt (Groningen); B. Braschler; and John Oosters, a carpenter.[19] By the next year First Church had grown to about thirty families and desperately needed its own sanctuary and pastor.

In February the consistory bought a lot for $375. It was located one mile to the south, on Foster Street (later Law Avenue) (625 west) between Harrison and Polk streets (600 to 800 south) (Figure 1.6, site 2). This was near the south branch of the Chicago River, a major commercial waterway. To pay for the lot and the construction of a small frame building, the brothers decided to canvass the membership in hopes of raising $250.

The consistory then struggled to select one of its number as a solicitor to canvass the congregation for the building drive. The discussion

18. Lucas, *Netherlanders in America,* 144-47; *Classis Holland Minutes,* 70-78, 87-88. The Grand Haven congregation, where Bolks's adultery actually took place, voted 27 to 15 to call him. The classis vote to readmit was 28 to 5. Classis was concerned about the sizable opposition of one-third of the Grand Haven congregation but acquiesced to avoid a possible schism.

19. Birkhoff, "Historische Schetsen."

went on for some hours and everyone made excuses. Marinus Hoogbruin, Daniel Schipperus, and Hiram Vanden Belt were too busy, and Van Zwol felt his English was not good enough. B. Blankenzee and Nicholas Foute said nothing. The counselor, the Reverend Ferris, suggested casting a secret ballot, but Hoogbruin said they should choose the most competent person and pay for his services, to which D. Van Berschot agreed. The idealistic Lucas Vanden Belt stated that the congregation should not pay for what ought to be done out of love. Rejecting the high road, the consistory, "after further discussion," by motion decided by majority vote to pay $1.50 per day for canvassing, which terms Hoogbruin and Blankenzee were delighted to accept.[20]

Hoogbruin made periodic reports and encouraged the brothers to proceed in faith and "above all to give due honor to God." The consistory turned first to its classis, but without success. The minutes of April 30, 1856 state:

> The brothers of Chicago inform the gathering of their current desperate situation as far as their physical facilities are concerned. Appropriate places for worship are almost unobtainable. The congregation requests Classis to consider whether something can be done to assist them. A lengthy discussion follows. Classis has empathy for the pressing circumstances of the Chicago situation, but, since all of the congregations in the Classis are new and are overwhelmed by the pressure of their own needs, the requested assistance cannot be given. The brothers from Chicago are encouraged to remember how good and blessed it is for the congregation to provide for its own needs in a spirit of sacrifice for the Kingdom. They are also advised to contact a church in the East for assistance.[21]

So the classis gave Chicago little more than empty platitudes about sharing the pain and the joy of sacrificial giving.

The consistory did follow up on the suggestion to appeal to the Reformed Church in the East. Through Ferris, they sent an urgent request for a denominational loan to John Gerritsen, corresponding secretary of the Board of Domestic Missions for the Midwest region. Classis minutes report that the brothers also sent Hoogbruin and Lucas Vanden Belt to ask Ferris's congregation for a special collection. But when the body discussed contacting the Presbyterian church for financial help, Lucas

20. First Reformed Church of Chicago, Minutes, 4 Feb. 1856.

21. Classis of Wisconsin, Minutes, 30 April 1856, Art. 8.

Vanden Belt expressed strong misgivings. After much discussion, the consistory decided that, given the great need and the common mission of spreading the gospel, they had the freedom to do so based on the word of God. So they assigned two church members to translate the request letter into good English. At the next consistory meeting, however, Van Berschot reopened the issue and it quickly became clear that the majority, including their collection agent, Hoogbruin, opposed contacting the Presbyterians.[22]

During this time of stress, the consistory often closed their meeting by singing Psalm 90:9:

> May Thy grace enrich us with Thy comfort,
> And reveal Thy work to Thy servants;
> May Thy bounty never leave Thy children,
> May Thy love and power keep us from faltering.
> Strengthen our hand and bless our industry,
> Crown our work now and forever![23]

The building campaign ran through the spring of 1856 with a measure of success. The willingness and generosity of the people "gladdened" the leaders. This spirit was put to the test when other denominational needs intruded at the same time. In March the Reverend Marten Ypma, pastor of the Prairie churches, came as examiner to the Chicago consistory by classical appointment, and he brought an urgent letter of appeal from Van Raalte requesting a special collection for founding the Holland Academy. After singing Psalm 119:105, "Thy word is a lamp unto my feet, and a light before my path," the consistory, despite their own building campaign, called a special Thursday evening prayer service to have a collection for the Michigan school.[24]

By May 1856 the brothers realized that their building plans were too ambitious, so Van Berschot, who was in charge of construction, recommended scaling back the sanctuary to twenty feet by thirty feet (half the original design), buying used lumber, and asking members to donate their time. Adopting these measures would cut the cost to only $165. Failing to come up with a more feasible plan, the brothers accepted this minimal concept, but when construction actually began in the fall of 1856, they

22. First Reformed Church of Chicago, Minutes, 8 April, 22 April, 6 May 1856.

23. Ibid., 18, 26 Feb., 25 Mar. 1856. Henry Lammers made the free translation of Psalm 90:9.

24. Ibid., 21 Mar., 25 Mar., 20 May 1856.

had sufficient monies to put up a frame building, twenty feet by forty-five feet, with the pulpit raised in good Reformed practice. Thus, in the end, the building was two-thirds of the original plan. The Dutch Reformed in the city had finally staked their claim![25]

The church was little to boast about. The walls were of "raw planks without plaster," recalled Birkhoff. Yet there "they worshiped the Triune God, and Christian love tied them together. No carpet, no fine seats, no well-sounding organ could be found there. In this most minimal tabernacle, the congregation met with hearts that glowed with brotherly love and piety." Birkhoff added that a "lack of harmony and a desire for secession were not yet present" to mar this idyllic picture.[26]

Even this scaled-back version caused financial problems for the poor Hollanders, and deacon Hiram Vanden Belt loaned $200 to stretch out the debt payments. By the spring of 1857, the elder delegates to the classis reported that the mortgage was in default and a sheriff's sale on the property was pending unless they received help. Classis was "deeply moved with the situation, but, because every congregation in the classis is totally preoccupied with its own needs, it regretfully concludes that nothing can be done to provide the necessary assistance."[27] Given this same old refrain, the church in the fall of 1857 considered selling the property to get out from under the crushing debt, but they managed to stave off the day of reckoning. Action was needed for another reason; the building had become too small.[28]

While struggling to build the sanctuary, the congregation also pursued a pastor, but that took many years longer to accomplish. They raised $324 for a salary and called a Seceder minister, the Reverend G. B. Mos, from the Netherlands, a Groninger by birth and follower of De Cock.[29] He declined after waiting a year to reply! And the congregation had the fortitude to call him again but with no better result. Meanwhile, the body wrote Bolks again and learned of his lack of interest.

During the decade without an ordained teacher and leader, consistory members carried all of the responsibilities in this *lees kerk*. The consistory by 1855 had grown to four elders and four deacons, who met jointly at least once a month according to the Dort Church Order. Elders who

25. First Reformed Church of Chicago, *Century for Christ*, 4-5; Minutes, 7, 20 May 1856.

26. Birkhoff, "Historische Schetsen."

27. Classis of Wisconsin, Minutes, 23 April 1857, Art. 19.

28. First Reformed Church of Chicago, Minutes, 29 July, 9 Sept. 1856.

29. *Honderd veertig jaar gemeenten en predikanten van de Gereformeerde Kerken in Nederland* (1974), 238; J. Wesseling, *De Afscheiding van 1834 in Groningerland*, 3 vols. (Groningen: Vuurbank, 1972-78), 3:152.

carried the load during the years of "vacancy" were Lucas Vanden Belt (president), D. Van Berschot (clerk), Herman Van Zwol, and Marinus Hoogbruin. They faithfully led worship (including a Wednesday evening service), comforted the sick, visited every family *four* times per year, heard professions of faith, examined prospective members "in a simple but dignified way," and admonished the delinquent "with the purpose of promoting peace." The goal of the family visits in 1855 was to "admonish each one to walk a faithful Christian life and to urge faithful attendance at the Sabbath services." The elders also supervised the Thursday evening catechism classes by visiting in person from time to time. Deacons controlled financial matters and set up a poor fund to take care of needy families.

At first the elders took turns leading worship and reading the sermons, but in 1855 they asked Van Zwol to be the leader *(preeklezer)* at every service. Within six months of his appointment, however, Van Berschot criticized him in a consistory meeting for choosing too lengthy sermons of the "old writers." He urged Van Zwol to delete parts, or better yet to substitute a book with shorter sermons. After much persuasion by the brothers, Van Zwol reluctantly agreed, but the traditionalist "found it quite hard to put aside his dearly beloved book." The consistory also authorized Van Berschot to inquire at the American sister church, Second Reformed, whether any of its elders could preach. It is not known if anyone came over to help the immigrants.[30]

Marriages of members posed a unique problem because the church had no one licensed by the state to perform weddings. This forced members of the congregation, such as Wim Dammers in 1856, to request permission of the elders to be married in the Dutch way, with official ceremonies before a civil magistrate and then a service in the church. The consistory accepted this reasonable solution, which was nonetheless irregular in America.[31]

Because of the close working relationship among the elders, when disagreements erupted between them in 1856 and again in 1857, and harsh words were spoken, the situation was so serious that the consistory took pains to resolve it. "God's Word must stand in the middle and this should not happen in our midst," the parties were admonished. This conviction prompted them to be reconciled in both instances.[32]

30. First Reformed Church of Chicago, Minutes, 3 Oct., 3, 13 Dec. 1855; 4 Feb., 20 May, 2, 16 June, 15 July, 23 Dec. 1856; 14 Apr. 1858; Lucas, *Netherlanders in America,* 45-46.

31. First Reformed Church of Chicago, Minutes, 7 July 1856.

32. Ibid., 12 Aug. 1856; 10 Nov. 1857.

In late 1856 the situation improved, when the church was able to hire temporarily as minister the Reverend Willem Van Leeuwen, who had served four Seceder congregations in the Netherlands before he emigrated to America without a call in 1856.[33] Van Leeuwen was needed to preach the Word and also, as the consistory minutes ominously report, to "mediate disputes . . . help avoid problems." The congregation held a special subscription to pay Van Leeuwen, amounting to $37.25 per month.

The Chicago flock viewed Van Leeuwen's coming as providential because he brought leadership and a trained mind, but it later turned out, after he went to the Holland, Wisconsin, church, that his credentials had not been in good order. He also had a somewhat contentious nature. The dominie stressed the importance of mission work and the need to honor the Lord's Day. "Some confessing members," he reminded the elders, "have been found to associate with the wrong crowd in the city," and the overseers must "explore ways to bring this problem to the congregation in order to obtain compliance to keep the Sabbath and to ask God for forgiveness for having broken this law."[34]

Van Leeuwen also raised the controversial church order issue of membership transfers from the Hervormde Kerk, the national church. At his urging, the consistory decided not to accept such attestations (membership papers) but to require applicants "to submit to an examination to find out if their faith is based on the infallible Word of God as revealed in the Bible and also to ascertain if these people subscribe to the teaching of the 1834 Secession in the Netherlands before accepting such souls to become members of our congregation."[35]

The second part of this line of inquiry speaks volumes about the Seceder character of the Chicago congregation. It was a more rigid policy than that of Van Raalte or any congregation in Michigan. Not accepting the membership papers of those in good standing in the national church was a hard stance, but adding the additional qualification to be of one mind with the secessionist principles in doctrine and polity was radical indeed. Nothing less than Dortian orthodoxy was acceptable.

Van Leeuwen forced yet another point of church order on the fledgling congregation. He "felt strongly" that at the installation service of an

33. *Gereformeerde Kerken in Nederland,* 233. Van Leeuwen's last charge was at Zaandam, Classis of Amsterdam. Classis of Wisconsin, Minutes, 9-10 Sept. 1857, Articles 7-11, report extensively on the Van Leeuwen case, which turned on his refusal to admit that he had left Zaandam without a proper dismissal.

34. First Reformed Church of Chicago, Minutes, 9, 16 Sept., 28 Oct. 1856.

35. Ibid., 11 Nov. 1856.

elder, the minister should "also use the laying on of hands." This ran counter to normal practice under the Dort church order, which reserved "laying on" only for ministers and professors of theology, but "after some discussion" led by one strong dissenter, the consistory agreed. The next year, after Van Leeuwen's departure to Wisconsin, the consistory asked classical advice on this matter and also the procedure for replacing office bearers whose terms have expired. Classis said that these decisions were best left in the hands of local churches. With this freedom the elders decided to end the laying on ceremony. They also sought advice on another issue that had troubled the Seceders since 1834 – that of covenantal baptism. Specifically, may nonconfessing parents present their infants for baptism? Classis said no; only confessing members who accept the covenant or believing godparents may do so.[36]

Van Leeuwen stayed in Chicago about six months, until the spring of 1857. At his departure the consistory worked diligently to raise the necessary funds and fill the pulpit again. In August that year, the body unsuccessfully called the Reverend Pieter J. Oggel, who had emigrated a year earlier to pastor the Grand Haven church. Because this call letter was sent without first obtaining the approval of the classis, the higher assembly issued "a gentle but earnest reprimand, because, once again, they [the Chicago consistory] have placed the horse after the wagon and followed improper procedure."[37]

Thereafter, the consistory decided to wait until spring and then call a new seminary graduate from the Netherlands. Monthly pulpit supply had to suffice in the interim for the morning service, but for evening worship the elders employed John Ferris of the Second Reformed Church, who could preach in Dutch.[38] Ferris's training at New Brunswick Semi-

36. Ibid., 7 Jan., 10 Aug. 1857; Classis of Wisconsin, Minutes, 9-10 Sept. 1857, Art. 20, Art. 22 (trans. William Buursma). The remarkable decision on who may present an infant for baptism reads as follows: "The answer of Classis is only those who are members of the congregation and those who accept the covenant of grace for themselves and their offspring. If this belief is not present, there should be no baptism unless they are godparents." Allowing godparents to take the vows in place of parents harks back to the historic practice in the Netherlands national church, which the Christian Seceded Church continued. In that state church tradition, elders or other confessing members could "stand in" for parents who were baptized, but not confessing, members. See Swierenga and Bruins, *Family Quarrels* (Grand Rapids: Eerdmans, 1999), 28-29.

37. Classis of Wisconsin, Minutes, 9-10 Sept. 1857, Art. 20. Van Leeuwen was later ordained after a complete confession of guilt (ibid., Art. 10; 14 Apr. 1858, Art. 9), but in 1859 he was deposed for adultery (18 May 1859, Art. 5).

38. First Reformed Church of Chicago, *Century for Christ,* 4-5; Minutes, 9 Sept., 16

nary and Rutgers College gave him an American style that must have appealed to the young people. His work also tied the congregation more closely to the denomination and speeded the pace of acculturation. Ferris gave generously of his time to the immigrant congregation during the seven years he ministered at Second Church. Since the Particular Synod of Chicago, which was organized in 1856, met frequently at Second Church, the immigrant congregation in Chicago had many opportunities to learn at close hand about the work and history of their denomination.[39]

The elders at First Reformed Church faithfully carried out family visitation. In June 1857 the theme of the visits was the "observance and maintenance of the truth and the importance of immortal souls." For some this topic was "met with comfort," but for others it "fell short of expectations."[40]

Uncouth behavior in church concerned the consistory in these years as well. The minutes in 1857 report:

> The children as well as grownups do not behave themselves in church. The young men are in the habit of laughing at each other, while others when coming into church do not listen but turn their backs while coming in late when the preacher has already started with prayer, instead of standing to wait till the prayer has been concluded, they walk in as if walking on the street, move chairs noisily while prayer is going on, thus disturbing everyone present.

Catechumens were similarly unruly and the teaching elders struggled to keep order.[41]

There is no record of charter families or early membership books, but the semi-centennial history of 1903 and consistory minutes in the

---

Sept. 1856; 27 Nov. 1857. Second Reformed Church was in financial trouble in 1859, and the Particular Synod of Chicago urgently asked all the churches to take up a collection "to release these brethren from their embarrassments" (*Acts and Proceedings of the General Synod of the Protestant Dutch Reformed Church in America,* 1859, 429). First Reformed responded generously (Minutes, 24 May 1859), even though one would have expected the need to flow in the other direction, toward the new immigrants. Despite continued denominational assistance and loans of $20,000, Second Reformed succumbed in 1880. Its failure did not have the negative impact that Reformed Church leaders in the East feared, because the First Reformed Church of Chicago was thriving.

39. Reformed Church in America, *125 Years of the Synod of Chicago, Reformed Church in America, 1856-1981* (1981), 52-53.

40. First Reformed Church of Chicago, Minutes, 25 June 1857.

41. Ibid., 3 Nov. 1857; 23 Feb. 1858.

years 1853-59 list some eighty families who joined the congregation or pledged monies in various subscription campaigns for building the church or calling a minister (see note 15).

Pledging monies was easier than actually collecting them, however, particularly after the national financial panic of 1857 brought hard times. The economic situation reached the point that in early 1859 the Classis of Wisconsin called on all churches to hold a day of prayer the first Wednesday of March, which the Chicago consistory made a day of fasting as well as prayer. The benevolent fund in Chicago was stretched to the limit, and the deacons had to watch every penny. Nevertheless, when they learned of the desperate need for food by a large family who had sporadically attended services, they scheduled a special offering the next Sunday to "extend Christian charity." Then the husband died, leaving a widow with five small children, and the church felt compelled to continue providing assistance.[42]

The Chicago congregation took no official notice of the schism in the Classis of Holland in the spring of 1857 that led to the founding of the True Holland Reformed Church (De Ware Hollandsche Gereformeerde Kerk). They were well aware of the schism, however, and it was much discussed at classis meetings, which took great pains to reaffirm the doctrinal soundness of the denomination. The Classis of Wisconsin even dispatched the Reverend Marten Ypma of the South Holland church to travel all the way to Paterson, New Jersey, to seek to dissuade a number of families from seceding.[43]

Chicago's elder at the April 1858 meeting of the Classis of Wisconsin also reported that the delegates had discussed at length the matter of Freemasonry, and "the greater majority was against membership." This pleased the Chicago congregation, which consistently barred lodge members. But the classis muted its voice, because it voted to allow congregations, by way of exception, to accept Freemasons into church membership provided they are "able to give proof that [lodge] membership is not in conflict with the true Christian faith and the Reformed confessions of our church." The nature of such proof was not spelled out. Classis also discussed millennial teachings that had been stirred up by the Millerites, a religious sect in the 1840s that had set a fixed date for the bodily return of Christ.[44]

Eleven years after its founding and seven years after joining the Re-

42. Ibid., 11 May, 8 June 1858; 2 Feb. 1859.

43. Classis of Wisconsin, Minutes, 8 Sept. 1858, Art. 30; 9 Feb. 1859, Art. 36.

44. Ibid., 14 April 1858, Art. 17, 18.

Rev. Cornelius Vander Meulen (1800-1876) *(Western Seminary Collection, Joint Archives of Holland)*

formed denomination, First Chicago in May 1859 welcomed its first regular pastor, the Reverend Cornelius Vander Meulen, founder of the Zeeland, Michigan, church and faithful associate of Van Raalte. Vander Meulen's son Jacob recalled that his father was "lured [by] the prospect of building a congregation in that great city." The church building on Foster Street was "small and unsightly," Jacob Vander Meulen noted, yet it was a "central point for the Dutch churchgoers of that time." The frontage for both church and manse was only fifty feet (twenty-five feet each), with a depth of fifty-three feet. The challenge was to increase the membership from the twenty-four families that greeted the new dominie.

"My father was surprised that so few came to hear him," Jacob recalled,

> for there indeed were many Netherlanders in that great city who, generally referred to as "Hollanders of the Groninger Section," were quite indifferent in the matter of religion. It was said that these people would have nothing to do with it.
>
> Father decided to call on these people and invite them to his ser-

> vices. Their answer was evasive: the church was too far distant, etc. He therefore suggested that he preach in their neighborhood in one of their homes. He went to this place every week, one week conducting evening service, the following giving catechetical instruction to the grownup folk. Soon there were conversions, and many joined the congregation.[45]

Vander Meulen's negative characterization has long stigmatized the Groninger Hoek, and it is a difficult point to disprove. It seems, however, that the Michigan clerics, Van Raalte and Vander Meulen, underestimated the Chicago Dutch.

Vander Meulen was a strong leader, plain spoken, warm, and humble in spirit, and the church thrived. Indeed, its size doubled in three years to forty-eight families by 1860. The Holy Spirit was doing His "quiet work," said the dominie. "There also exists an eagerness to come to the worship services and the teachings; if the devil and our own corrupted nature do not spoil this, we may have something beautiful – something that may grow." Vander Meulen's salary was $600 a year (the denominational board of missions paid one-half), and the overjoyed members contributed additional monies to buy a new pulpit and pews. The pastor temporarily left his family in Michigan and boarded with an elder to spare the expense of renting a parsonage, "because of the scarcity of money." The congregation was so poor that total contributions for the church budget were only $12 per month. But the body did rent a manse for their pastor and family. In 1860 the yearly giving totaled $425, plus $71.58 for benevolence.[46]

On the Monday evening before the installation of its first dominie, the consistory in "heartfelt gratitude" met in special session to pledge support for "our new servant of God." They solemnly vowed "to accord him our high esteem and lend him our loving assistance so that he may be able to carry out his ministry among us with gladness and not with sighing or heaviness of heart."[47] It was a honeymoon time for the Chicago congregation.

45. "Jacob Van der Meulen's Life of His Father," *De Grondwet,* 5 Sept. 1911, published in Henry S. Lucas, ed., *Dutch Immigrant Memoirs and Related Writings,* 2 vols. (Assen, 1955, rev. ed. Grand Rapids: Eerdmans, 1997), 2: 369-70.

46. First Reformed Church of Chicago, Minutes, 31 March, 1859; Classis of Wisconsin, Minutes, 9 Feb. 1859, Art. 34, 39; letter of Rev. Cornelius Vander Meulen, 7 Feb. 1860, published in *De Hollander,* 20 Feb. 1860 (trans. Simone Kennedy); Birkhoff, "Historische Schetsen."

47. First Reformed Church of Chicago, Minutes, 2 May 1859.

Vander Meulen soon challenged the people to expect growth and make plans to build a new or enlarged church. The consistory, which had grown to sixteen, acknowledged the need, but financial concerns forced them to postpone the project for a year. The new pastor, with advice from Ferris, also helped the church start a Sunday school, that quintessential American institution, "to protect the children from strange teachings." They likely had in mind the Arminian theology of Methodism that was taking the country by storm. Reformed church leaders in the East had in 1859 urged every immigrant congregation in the West to take this step. While the Sunday school curriculum would be informed by Reformed theology, it could if not guarded slip into the same moralistic teachings that characterized Yankee-style schools.[48]

Vander Meulen himself taught Sunday school and catechism, thus relieving elders Hoogbruin and Gerrit Vastenhouw, a carpenter from Amersfoort, who had served for many years. The Sunday school began with thirty-eight pupils and grew to more than one hundred in the next decade. Although the church adopted the American system of Sunday Bible education for the youth, it did not observe the American Thanksgiving Day until many years later.[49]

Late in 1859 the consistory caught Vander Meulen's enthusiasm and, in an emotional meeting, the members individually pledged some $360 plus labor and materials for a building project.[50] Every meeting for months was devoted to the topic. The body agreed on the need for a larger edifice, but should it be on the old site or a new one farther west? The controversy came to a head at a congregational meeting in January 1860, where a bare majority of five members favored relocating, as Rev. Vander Meulen urged. The consistory then appointed a committee with the power to sell the old church and lot to raise funds. But after checking lot prices on prominent streets, the majority concluded that they could not "really afford a new church at this time." Said Vander Meulen ruefully, quoting a Dutch proverb, "the herring has not yet been caught." In the end, the congregation widened the old building by ten feet, to thirty by forty-six feet, and remodeled it extensively. At the dedication of this "greatest jewel of the congregation," the body had the "rare privilege" of hearing the father and his two sons preach, "all in one day, all from one

48. Ibid., 3 Nov. 1857; 7 Mar., 11 Mar., 13 May, 24 May, 16 Aug., 1 Nov. 1859; Classis of Wisconsin, Minutes, 9 Feb. 1959, Art. 8.

49. First Reformed Church of Chicago, *Century for Christ,* 5; *Acts and Proceedings of the General Synod of the Protestant Dutch Reformed Church in America,* 1860, 544.

50. First Reformed Church of Chicago, Minutes, 14 Nov. 1859.

pulpit" – the father in the morning, the eldest son in the afternoon, and the youngest son in the evening. The sons were both students at New Brunswick Theological Seminary, Jacob (born in 1834) and John (born in 1838).[51]

The remodeling killed the dream of a new church for ten years, during which time the country went through the throes of the Civil War. Vander Meulen showed his disappointment by leaving for the Grand Rapids Holland church, which needed him because it was racked by schism. His tenure in Chicago was barely two years.

Vander Meulen's son Jacob later gave voice to his father's thinking. "There was need of another church building at a point more central to the Dutch population. Finally, a new church was erected on the site of the old. Father thought that this was unfortunate from the standpoint of evangelizing among the Dutch population, throttling the growth of the congregation. This is one of the reasons why he accepted a call from the Second Reformed congregation in Grand Rapids."[52] Seine Bolks took Vander Meulen's place at First Chicago, to the great satisfaction of the congregation, but he stayed only until 1863.

After the Confederate states seceded in 1861, President Lincoln called for a national day of fasting and prayer on January 4, 1861, "to explore ways that the threatening disaster of the War may by the grace of God cease." First Reformed wholeheartedly agreed with this "fitting request by the leader of the United States," and the congregation continued to endorse the war effort. In the summer of 1863, during the darkest time in the war, the congregation devoted a Wednesday evening service to prayers for national repentance and God's deliverance of both church and nation. Then on August 6, after the glorious triumphs at Gettysburg and Vicksburg, the consistory unanimously approved President Lincoln's call for a national day of thanksgiving "to commemorate the victory over the enemy of this republic."

Several special offerings were taken for sick and wounded Union sol-

51. Quotes by Rev. C. Vander Meulen, "Dedication of the church building in Chicago," *De Hollander,* 11 July 1860 (trans. Simone Kennedy); and by Jacob Vander Meulen, cited in letter of C. M. Budde-Stomp (Burlington, Iowa) to J. Wormser-Van der Ven (Amsterdam, Netherlands), undated (likely late 1860 or early 1861), in J. Stellingwerff, *Amsterdamse emigranten: onbekende brieven uit de prairie van Iowa, 1846-1873* (Amsterdam: Buijten & Schiperheijn, 1975), 307, trans. Walter Lagerwey; Russell Gasero, ed., *Historical Directory of the Reformed Church in America, 1628-2000* (Grand Rapids: Eerdmans, 2001), 412.

52. "Jacob Van der Meulen's Life of His Father," in Lucas, *Dutch Immigrant Memoirs,* 2: 369-70.

diers, with the final one in March 1865, just weeks before the war's end. One collection to purchase religious books for Union soldiers was made on a national day of prayer and fasting on April 30, 1863. The consistory also made special arrangements to hear the confession of faith of a soldier from the congregation, Johannes Keersemaker, who was home on leave, and to baptize his two children. It is clear that Chicago's Dutch Calvinists, even though citizens of America for less than a decade, wholeheartedly supported the war effort.[53]

Discipline cases seemed to multiply during the tenures of Vander Meulen and Bolks. The consistory closed the Lord's Supper to a member charged with drunkenness, and several others were admonished for selling milk with horse and buggy on Sunday. A husband was condemned for abusing his wife and children, even after having been jailed for domestic violence. A couple was made to answer for infidelity. Another wished to marry in church, but the consistory refused because the bride-to-be a few years earlier had given birth to an illegitimate child that was found dead in her home under suspicious circumstances, and she had yet to confess her sins. The issue of baptizing an adopted child required a "lengthy discussion," but the consistory, despite reservations by some members, gave permission "in the same way as Abraham would have done in his time."[54]

The old problem of unruly behavior in church recurred in 1861 and compelled Vander Meulen to preach a catechism sermon on Lord's Day 47 of the Catechism, which teaches reverence during worship services. The weak spiritual condition of the congregation may also explain why Vander Meulen and Bolks departed after very short pastorates; indeed, Bolks only stayed for seventeen months!

Within months of Bolk's departure, the classis assigned the elderly H. G. Klyn as stated supply, and a year later the congregation called him in a nearly unanimous vote to become the regular pastor. The denominational Board of Domestic Missions subsidized Klyn's salary. He remained for six years until retiring in 1868 and was the first long-term minister of the congregation. Klyn had a beautiful voice, "worthy of a servant of the Word," and "his work was a real blessing." The body thrived under his leadership, although the workload was heavy. In 1867 Klyn told classis that "in his old age he finds the labor in the congregation burdensome."

No wonder! The church was rent by schism at the same time that it

53. First Reformed Church of Chicago, Minutes, 11 Aug., 29 Dec. 1863; 12, 26 Jan. 1864; 21 Mar. 1865.

54. Ibid., 22 June, 18 Aug. 1862.

Rev. Hendrik G. Klyn (1793-1883) *(Western Seminary Collection, Joint Archives of Holland)*

was making critical property decisions. Klyn had to preside over the secession of fifteen families led by elders Vastenhouw and Van Deursen (see below). Despite the turmoil, the congregation nearly doubled between 1866 and 1868, growing from 64 to 105 families. This gave it the confidence to proceed with plans to buy a parsonage and build a new church. The church bought a house for $850 at 331 (new numbering 1114) West Adams Street and a lot on the southwest corner of Harrison and May streets for $3,300. The sanctuary to seat 400 was completed in the first year of Klyn's successor, the Reverend Bernardus De Bey, in 1869. Meanwhile, the consistory asked the city fathers to improve the street in front of the church, which was little more than a footpath, and they complied.[55]

Klyn was mission minded, and once a month at the Sunday evening service he read accounts of mission work around the world. This prompted the church to join a new mission project with all of the Mid-

55. Ibid., 19 May, 2 June 1863; 19 April 1864. By October 1866 the church and school were too small, and the consistory decided to sell them, plus the parsonage and empty lot, and to relocate to the west (ibid., 15 Oct. 1866). See also Classis of Wisconsin, Minutes, 26 Sept. 1866; 26 Sept. 1867; and Classis of Wisconsin membership reports for June 1866, 1867, and 1868.

western congregations. The consistory raised the necessary support by canvassing every household. Klyn also involved the congregation directly in the selection of consistory members by obtaining permission from the classis to hold a "free election" by the congregation, instead of the customary nomination by the consistory.[56]

Dominie Klyn faithfully called on the church families, but because many lived at a distance on the northwest side the consistory rented a horse and buggy for him. The same year the church rejoiced to send the first son of the congregation, Peter Schipperus, to study for the ministry at Holland Academy. The body provided financial aid for his studies.

That same year the consistory modified the standard practice of renting entire pews to one of renting individual seats. They also insisted on faithful attendance at consistory meetings and levied a fine of 25 cents for being "unlawfully absent." When members lagged in paying their pew rentals and pledges, the deacons decided to "approach them in a friendly manner next Sunday." The consistory also agreed, at the general urging of the synod "in these expensive times," to raise the pastor's salary by $100 and to stop charging rent on the parsonage. To meet this obligation the consistory canvassed the congregation once again. Another internal matter for the consistory was a report by Dominie Klyn that he was the target of women's gossip; the offending women were admonished to refrain. This matter "will be kept in check from now on," the brothers promised.[57]

The congregation remained committed to Reformed orthodoxy. Klyn continued the policy instituted under Van Leeuwen that required new immigrants with papers from the Dutch national church to be examined by the elders before being accepted as members. A member was excommunicated for drunkenness after ignoring repeated visits by the elders. Elder Cornelis Hillegonds, who taught catechism, was challenged for unilaterally scratching out the section regarding infant baptism from the compendium. He was teaching from the book of Dutch cleric Jakobus Borstius, which had served Reformed youth for more than two hundred years. When Hillegonds refused to recant after many meetings, the church censured him. The elders then rejected his letter of resignation, in good Dortian practice, and declared that only death or excommunication can separate a confessing member from the church. In the end, after the

56. Classis of Wisconsin, Minutes, 25 Sept. 1867.

57. First Reformed Church of Chicago, Minutes, 8 Mar., 14 June, 13, 25 July, 6 Sept. 1864, Classis of Wisconsin, Minutes, 26 Sept. 1866.

brother was rebaptized in the Baptist church, the elders acquiesced and released him.[58]

To strengthen the indoctrination of the youth, Klyn proposed in late 1865 to establish a congregational school, which the body accepted. Member Hiram Vanden Belt sold a house with an adjacent empty lot near the church for the school building. At this time, the Reformed Church had embarked on a denominational campaign, funded by elder Samuel Schiffelin of New York City, to establish parochial schools. The Classis of Wisconsin readily endorsed the project and provided grants of $100 in 1865 and again in 1866 to help launch the school. Upon the recommendation of Philip Phelps, Jr., principal of the Holland Academy, and with the concurrence of Van Raalte himself, the consistory called "brother" Huizenga as schoolmaster and he accepted. Huizenga addressed the parents and teachers at the dedication of "onze school," and classes began in September 1866. Chicago had its first Dutch Reformed day school, with instruction in the Dutch language, but enrollment was restricted because the location was too far to walk for children in the northwest part of the city.[59]

That year the consistory also created a committee to sound out the Dutch throughout the city about establishing a cemetery exclusively for Hollanders. This idea bore fruit later with the designation of the Dutch section at the Forest Home Cemetery in suburban Forest Park.[60]

Another expression in the Chicago congregation of Seceder pietism, blended with American evangelicalism, was an emphasis on spiritual renewal. The Wednesday evening Bible exposition by the pastor was made biweekly to allow for a weekly Monday evening prayer service to bring revival, especially among the upcoming generation, and to pray for repentance by the erring elder who denied infant baptism.[61]

A refusal to use civil courts to settle disputes between fellow believers was also normative among Seceders, so when a business dispute erupted in 1866 among three elders in which two threatened legal action, the consistory intervened to prevent the "worldly" civil court getting involved. A soap

58. First Reformed Church of Chicago, Minutes, 29 Nov., 13, 27 Dec. 1864; 10 Jan., 7 Feb., 14 Nov. 1865; 8 Mar., 10 April, 26 June 1866. Borstius of Dordrecht (1612-1680) was a Dutch clergyman whose catechetical book, based on the Heidelberg Catechism, for more than two hundred years gave Dutch youth their first introduction to the Reformed faith.

59. Ibid., 23 Jan., 24 June 1865; 7 Feb., 21 Mar., 16 May, 30 May, 24 July 1866; Classis of Wisconsin, Minutes, 26 Apr. 1865; 25 Apr. 1866.

60. First Reformed Church of Chicago, Minutes, 16 May, 30 May, 24 July 1866.

61. Ibid., 27 Mar. 1866.

factory owned by G. Vanden Burg, Sr., and A. De Roo, on which Abraham Van Persyn had lent $1,000, was failing, and the partners agreed to sell it. Vanden Burg wanted to sell the business to his son, without first paying off Van Persyn's note, so Van Persyn threatened legal eviction. This prompted Vanden Burg and his son, without De Roo's knowledge, one night to carry off all the equipment and goods of the factory. But De Roo discovered the secret maneuver, and the next morning he began legal action to protect his share of the business. This got the consistory involved. They confronted Vanden Burg "with his wrong action," and he admitted his guilt and agreed to negotiate with De Roo a mutually acceptable agreement to make the sale to his son. The consistory then sent a committee, including Klyn, to confront Vanden Burg's son, also a church member, in order to obtain his confession of sin and consent to the agreement.

Despite the apparent reconciliation, the parties continued to disagree sharply, and the consistory had to assemble two more times to mediate terms of a settlement. Vanden Burg was admonished at one point for his "contemptible attitude" and for turning the conflict into a "vicious affair." Van Persyn finally agreed to buy the entire enterprise for $1,300, and the two partners had to share the losses equally. Thus did the elders broker a business deal between their members to uphold the good name of the church.[62]

Harrison Street: The Groninger Hoek Takes Shape

By 1866, a year after the Civil War ended, First Reformed had outgrown its church and school because of the rush of Groninger immigrants, and the congregation got serious about selling and relocating. For more than a decade, its members had been moving west along Harrison Street beyond Halsted Street (800 west). Harrison and Halsted was a key intersection because it stood at the terminus of Blue Island Avenue, a major diagonal traffic artery serving the entire southwestern part of the city, including the docks and lumber warehouses along the south channel of the Chicago River. The booming Harrison-Halsted-Blue Island nexus was immediately west of the destructive path of the 1871 Chicago fire and totally escaped harm. But one hundred years later it was leveled to make way for the new campus of the University of Illinois at Chicago.

The consistory of First Reformed in late 1866 set a price of $4,000-

62. Ibid., 15 Oct., 30 Oct., 5 Nov., 9 Nov., 13 Nov. 1866.

5,000 on its Foster Street property and formed a committee to sell it and select a new location. Since cash on hand of $1,865 was too little to launch a building campaign, the leaders decided unanimously to ask each member to pledge $20, to be paid over time, for a building fund.[63] This raised $6,000 within three years to fund the construction of a new frame church and parsonage at 404 (new numbering 1117) West Harrison Street (figure 1.1, site 3). In the spring of 1868, when Bernardus De Bey (1868-91) arrived from the Netherlands to take on the pastorate, the work on the church was far enough along for the service of installation to be held on the ground floor, where the congregation worshiped for the next eighteen months, until the main floor was completed in August of 1869. This imposing structure announced that the Dutch in Chicago had arrived! Klyn participated in De Bey's installation, along with Adrian Zwemer of the First South Holland church and Peter Lepeltak of the First Roseland church. It was a proud moment for the Chicago congregation and the beginning of a renowned, twenty-three-year pastorate, the longest in its history.[64]

The Schism of 1867 in Chicago

While still in the Foster and Harrison neighborhood, the Chicago Dutch Reformed community experienced its first church schism. In its theological and cultural aspects, the division bore a resemblance to the Secession of 1834 in the Netherlands that many had experienced firsthand. Personalities and church issues again were intertwined. In the summer of 1867, fifteen mostly Groninger families (seventy-five souls) from the mother church, First Reformed, led by elder Gerrit Vastenhouw and his associate Arie Van Deursen, seceded to form the True Holland (later Christian) Reformed Church of Chicago. These ardent traditionalists, mostly Netherlands Seceders, were "not satisfied with conditions" in the Dutch Reformed church and "did not feel at home there." They decided to follow the lead of like-minded brethren in western Michigan who had seceded ten years earlier (1857) and established the new denomination.[65]

Vastenhouw had twice represented the First Reformed Church of Chicago at the Classis of Wisconsin in 1857 and 1858, just as the secession

63. Ibid., 13 Nov., 26 Nov. 1866.

64. Birkhoff, "Historische Schetsen."

65. *Seventy-fifth Anniversary of the First Christian Reformed Church of Chicago, 1867-1942* (Cicero, 1942), 7; untitled typescript history, First Christian Reformed Church of Chicago, Jan. 1913.

of 1857 in Michigan broke out. In 1857 he heard letters read from Van Raalte and from Peter J. Oggel, pastor of the Grand Haven church, reporting on the momentous events in Michigan. He also heard Seine Bolks, president of the classis and delegate to the recent Reformed Church General Synod, go out of his way to testify to the doctrinal soundness of the denomination. Classis itself reaffirmed the confessional integrity of the denomination and declared that "no brethren or congregation will be given reason for concern." Classis even decided to copy into the minutes the formula of subscription and then have all the ministers sign it, which they gladly did. But Vastenhouw also remembered the double-minded decision of the classis in 1858 concerning Freemasonry.[66]

De Bey, who arrived a year after the secession in his Chicago congregation, gave an entirely different explanation of Vastenhouw's defection and of the birth of the True church in a polemic book he co-authored with Adrian Zwemer in 1871, entitled *Stemmen uit de Hollandsch-Gereformeerde Kerk in de Ver. Staten van Amerika (Voices of the Dutch Reformed Church in the United States of America)*. In this account, which contains the only detailed, firsthand report of the Chicago secession, De Bey asserted that the cause was primarily sour grapes by Vastenhouw, disputes over pew rentals, and other petty grievances. Until shortly before January 1867, said De Bey, the consistory minutes reveal not a single trace of Vastenhouw "registering a protest against the Church's doctrine or government."[67]

The controversy, according to De Bey, began the previous year when the congregation divided into two groups over the issue of whether their seventy-four-year-old minister should retire and on what financial terms. The dispute entered the consistory room during the nomination and election of officers, when Vastenhouw tried in an unethical way to influence the outcome in favor of his man, J. De Jong, over Andrew Van Zwol, whom he opposed. Interestingly, Vastenhouw and Van Zwol were co-workers in

66. "After lengthy discussions," the classis ruled that consistories must bar lodge members from church membership, except for "those who have been able to give proof that membership is not in conflict with the true Christian faith and the Reformed confessions of our church" (Classis of Wisconsin, Minutes, 14 Apr. 1858, Art. 18). The Milwaukee and Bethlehem congregations had members secede (ibid., 30 Apr. 1856, Art. 5; 14 Apr. 1858, Art. 14, 15).

67. (Groningen, 1871), section IX, "In the Chicago Congregation," 198-200, English translation typescript, Archives, Calvin College; Hans Krabbendam, "Serving the Dutch Community: A Comparison of the Patterns of Americanization in the Lives of Two Immigrant Pastors," (M.A. thesis, Kent State University, 1989), 72-73.

the same store, and issues on the job might have soured their friendship. In any case, according to De Bey, Vastenhouw "spread false, malicious slanderous reports about the minister, the consistory, and certain church members." When these actions became public, the consistory had no choice but to begin taking steps to suspend him from office. "This was too dreadful a humiliation for a man who so long has enjoyed the honor and respect of the majority of his acquaintances," De Bey opined.

Vastenhouw announced at the March 26, 1867, consistory meeting that he was resigning "because of the confusion presently rife in the congregation." De Bey's account continues:

> [When Klyn and two fellow elders] admonished him and pled with him to recant his decision lest he lay the groundwork for a secession in Chicago, Vastenhouw solemnly promised never to set a secession in motion. . . . With that assurance he left the parsonage. But when Sunday rolled around Vastenhouw conducted services in his own home on the very first Sunday after his solemn promise. On the following Sundays an increasing number of people who were somewhat disgruntled began to meet with him. One was dissatisfied because pews were rented in the church; another because De Jong had not been elected; a third because he felt he had no status with the Zuid Hollanders; a fourth because he was tied to Vastenhouw's leash; a fifth because. . . . But why add more? All withdrew because they wanted to, not because they had good grounds for it. This continued for several weeks. After a while the group felt it was large enough to be organized into a congregation.

Out of this pettiness came the new church. So declared De Bey.

The validity of De Bey's explanation, which he claimed found support in the consistory minutes, can never be confirmed because the record book covering this crucial period is lost. But De Bey came to Chicago only one year after the secession, and he could talk to members who had lived through the troubles. He also provides a wealth of details that seem plausible. That the seceders raised no complaints, doctrinal or otherwise, at classis or synod, or against Klyn personally, is also confirmed in the classis minutes. Surprisingly, Klyn made no official report to classis about the split in his congregation and the loss of fifteen member families. The minutes are silent as the grave.[68]

On the other hand, De Bey, when still in Middelstum, had condemned

68. Classis of Wisconsin, Minutes, 1867-68.

the 1857 secession in Michigan, and he did not mellow upon his arrival in Chicago. His and Zwemer's *Voices* was the first full-fledged polemic against the True church and contained a biting attack on its legitimacy.

Vastenhouw and Van Deursen offered their interpretation of 1867 in a statement published in the denominational periodical, *De Wachter,* in 1868. It breathed an irenic spirit that seemed to belie De Bey's account. Many years later, Henry Beets, editor of the English-language church weekly, the *Banner,* noted the "Christian spirit" that pervaded this statement. For Beets the issue was simple: "The fact appears that several people who had come from the Christian Reformed Church in the Netherlands *did not feel at home* in the Dutch Reformed Church of Chicago."[69] They acted largely out of a desire to remain connected to their Netherlandic roots rather than take the fast track toward Americanization in the Reformed Church in America. This cultural explanation ignores any personal shortcomings or theological concerns of the seceders and simply attributes their actions to a desire for churchly *gezelligheid,* a feeling of warmth and coziness in familiar religious ways.

Doubtless, there is some truth on both sides. Vastenhouw, as a "watchman on the walls of Zion," believed that the Reformed Church was deserting its doctrinal heritage, but his pettiness in church polity stirred up needless strife in the fellowship. Klyn's age and pending retirement also gave the dissidents a freer hand to act, given the weakness at the top.

Early Years of the First Christian Reformed Church of Chicago

The seceders met for mutual edification in Elder Vastenhouw's home, where he read sermons and prayers of the Old Fathers. Within weeks, and without consulting the classis of the Christian Reformed Church, they urgently requested the Reverend William H. Frieling of the Vriesland, Michigan, church to come and organize a church. He agreed to do so and arrived July 28, 1867, to greet the heads of the fifteen families assembled. This after Klyn had informed him, "These people had seceded entirely without grounds and were even subject to church discipline." Frieling, as a disciple of De Cock and the northern wing of the Christian Seceded Church, disregarded the views of Klyn, an ally of Van Raalte and the southern wing. Indeed, Frieling, according to De Bey, "told the people

69. Emphasis mine; *De Wachter,* 4 Dec. 1868; *Banner,* 22 April 1909.

that the Reformed Church was even more corrupt than the Hervormde Kerk of the Netherlands. His speaking and influence therefore added many new members to the secession ranks."[70]

Frieling had served three Seceded churches in Groningen before taking a call to Michigan a year earlier and was known and trusted by the Chicago Groningers. Vastenhouw and Sijbert De Jong were chosen as the first elders, and Jacob Bos and Klaas Reitsma as the first deacons.[71] The thankful brethren sang the words of Psalm 118:25, as set to music by Louis Bourgeois in the Dutch Psalter. Dewey Westra's 1931 translation renders the verse this way:

> Save, O Jehovah, we implore Thee.
> Save now Thy people, e'en today;
> Prosperity send Thou in mercy,
> And favor us upon our way.

At the next Christian Reformed classis meeting, Frieling admitted that he acted too hastily in organizing the Chicago church but "the need demanded it." The assembly excused him. "Under certain conditions Ministers may proceed as they see fit," the body concluded.[72] Thus did the Christian Reformed Church become rooted in Chicago. Within seventy-five years, the seventy-five souls increased to twelve thousand, and the one congregation multiplied to twenty. The prayer sung by the first consistory had been answered beyond their fondest hopes.[73]

Gurley Street

But the church did not let any grass grow under its feet either. Less than two weeks after its organization in September, 1867, the body decided to build a small forty- by fifty-foot frame church on Gurley Street (one block

70. De Bey and Zwemer, *Stemmen,* 199-200.

71. J. G. Vanden Bosch, "Willem Hendrik Frieling," *Reformed Journal* 6 (Dec. 1958): 19-22. Jacob Bos (1841-1910) immigrated to Chicago from Meeden, Groningen, in 1872, with his wife Andrea and three children. He arrived "just after the big fire, when hands enough could not be found to rebuild the city" (obituary, *Onze Toekomst,* 9 Dec. 1910). The obituary of Andrea Bos differs in some details (ibid., 27 Feb. 1920).

72. "Christian Reformed Church, Classical and Synodical Minutes, 2-3 Oct. 1867," Art. 40. An English-language typescript of the minutes for the years 1857-80 is in the Archives, Calvin College.

73. "First Christian Reformed Church, Chicago, Ill.," *Banner,* 22 April 1909.

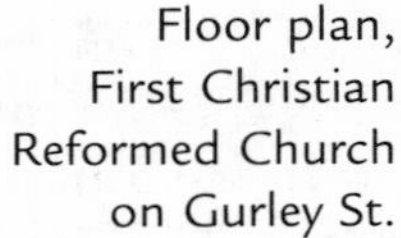

Floor plan, First Christian Reformed Church on Gurley St.

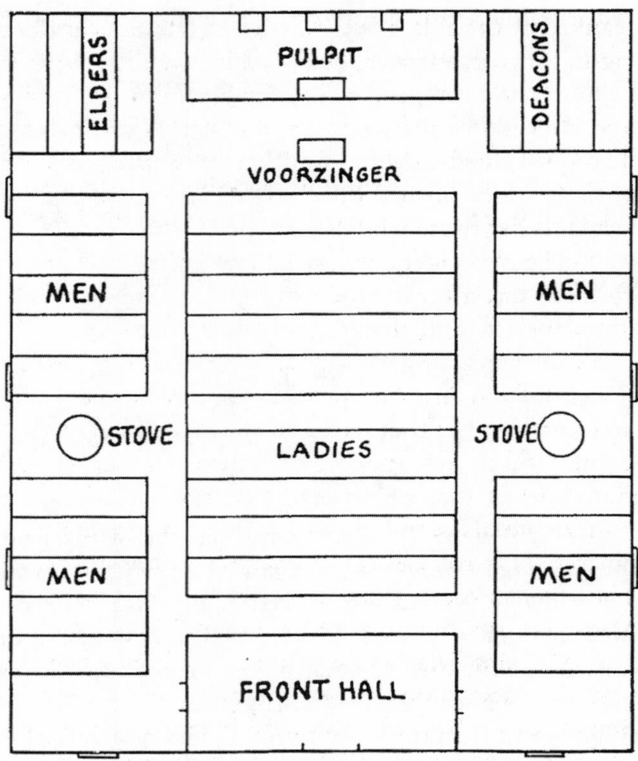

south of Harrison Street) between Miller and Sholto (1000 west) (figure 1.6, site 5). Construction began immediately, and before the end of the year they dedicated the new facility.

The Gurley Street site stood between the First and Second Reformed churches, and today also lies under the University of Illinois campus. It was three blocks west of the Foster Street building and only one block east of the First Reformed Church's Harrison Street building, which opened two years later. So the rival congregations shared the same small neighborhood, and their churches were within sight of each another.[74]

The rectangular sanctuary on Gurley Street was typical of Reformed churches in the Netherlands. The elevated pulpit stood front and center,

74. First Reformed Church of Chicago, *Century for Christ,* 305; First Christian Reformed Church of Chicago, *Seventy-Fifth Anniversary,* 7; De Bey letter, *Provinciale Groninger Courant,* 10 Dec. 1869, trans. Dirk Hoogeveen. No photograph of the Gurley Street edifice is known to exist. The word *voorzinger* in the floor plan should properly be *voorzanger.*

flanked by the elders' benches on the left and the deacons' benches on the right. Singing was a cappella, led by the *voorzanger,* who stood below the pulpit facing the people. The congregation sat in pews, with the women and children in the warmer center section and the men along the sides. Two pot-bellied stoves midway on each side provided minimal heat. The entrance door opened into a "front hall," where Psalters and Bibles were available for those who did not bring their own.[75]

The new elders organized not one but three catechism classes. The children met after the morning service, adults assembled after the afternoon service, and the young people gathered on Thursday evening. To carry the increasing workload, two more elders and deacons were elected, Klaas Rol and Arie Van Deursen, and K. Rikkers and John Swierenga. In an unusual move that reflected the precarious situation of the new immigrants, the church appointed member Dr. Metjes as their "official physician." Gerrit Vastenhouw often represented the congregation at the denominational assemblies in Michigan, including the first time Chicago answered the roll call at the Holland, Michigan, meeting in January, 1868. The classis assigned the Reverend Koene Vanden Bosch of Noordeloos, Michigan, as Chicago's "pulpit supply" in the spring.[76]

Without delay and undaunted by a huge debt, on New Year's Day of 1868 the eager group called the prominent Netherlands Seceder pastor, Bernardus De Bey, who during a twenty-two-year tenure at Middelstum, Groningen, had built a thriving congregation. But Vastenhouw and his cohorts did not realize that De Bey strongly disapproved of their secession. His letter of decline shocked them; he declared them to be "zealots without love, and makers of sects."[77] Not only did the Middelstum dominie chastise the Chicago seceder church in his strident letter, but he punctuated his NO by accepting a call a few months later from the mother church, First Reformed, and he induced many congregants to follow him to that church. The True church now had to deal with this strong leader in the community, who worked to stymie the nascent congregation.

75. Floor plan in Ebenezer Christian Reformed Church, *Dedication Booklet* (Berwyn, 1949), 26.

76. Klaas Rol, Arie Van Deursen, and Derk Natelborg were Chicago delegates to subsequent Christian Reformed denominational assemblies. Rol (1825-1910) was born in Middelstum, Groningen, married, migrated to Chicago in 1867, and lived at 503 W. 16th St. for thirty-seven years. He was also a board member of the Ebenezer Christian School (obit., *Onze Toekomst,* 11 Feb. 1910).

77. Van Hinte, *Netherlanders in America,* 373, citing G. K. Hemkes, *Het Rechtsbestaan der Holl. Ger. Kerk in Amerika* (1893), 67.

First Christian Reformed Church of Chicago next called its counselor, the Reverend Frieling, but he was not ready to leave his Michigan congregation. The third call happily succeeded and brought the church its first pastor, Jan Schepers (1868-71). Barely thirty years of age, Schepers had just completed his theological studies under the Reverend Douwe Vander Werp at Graafschap, Michigan. Schepers, the first Christian Reformed minister to receive his entire training in the U.S.A., was rooted, like Frieling and Vander Werp, in the De Cock wing of the Secession of 1834. Schepers was born in the province of Drenthe and came to Drenthe, Michigan, as a teenager with his parents in 1848, where he married and farmed until his wife died. This freed him in 1864 to answer a call to the ministry that had tugged at him.

Schepers brought a conservative, separatist mentality to the ministry. His father, Harm, an elder in the Drenthe church, had disapproved of the Union of 1850. In 1853, together with pastor Roelof Smit, Harm had led that congregation to secede from the Classis of Holland and join the Associate Reformed or "Scottish" Church, a conservative, psalm-singing body that in 1858 entered into a merger that began the United Presbyterian Church. In Chicago, Schepers thus stood in sharp contrast to the more latitudinarian and outward-looking De Bey, who was many years his senior, and who had built an enviable reputation serving the large congregation in Middelstum. Schepers's Chicago congregation numbered only fifteen families when he began his ministry.[78]

The pioneer Reformed and Christian Reformed churches in Chicago were so alike and yet so different. Groningers dominated in both, but one was outward looking and ready to interact with the American scene, while the other looked inward and guarded its Dutch theological and cultural treasure.

The First Christian Reformed Church provided pastor Schepers, who came in October 1868, with a new two-story parsonage built in five weeks for under $1,000; it stood on the back of the church lot. The congregation also fulfilled the law of love, as the deacons canvassed the congregation for contributions to help a needy family buy a house. And after the devastating fire that destroyed most of Holland, Michigan, in 1871, the consistory again canvassed the congregation to help the poor victims.

78. *Classis Holland Minutes,* 43, 123, 125. Biographical sketches of Jan Schepers, including an obituary in the Christian Reformed Church *Jaarboekje,* 1903, are in the Archives, Calvin College. See also J. G. Vanden Bosch, "John Schepers," *Reformed Journal* 6 (July-Aug. 1956): 14-16.

This was in the face of the tremendous fire losses in Chicago itself, which struck at the same time but only wiped out the few Dutch dwellings and businesses on the North Side (see Fig. 1.6). Caring for their poor was a mark of Reformed diaconates, and the Chicago church met the standard. This despite the fact that the building committee had to install louvers on all the church windows to deter "naughty boys in the neighborhood [who] repeatedly threw stones through the windows."[79]

The Christian Reformed congregation grew slowly but steadily under Schepers, and people were sad to see him go to another Groninger congregation at Lafayette, Indiana, after less than three years. He was a soft-spoken, kindly, and wise man who preached from the heart a simple gospel of grace and saw to the faithful exercise of church discipline. His legacy in Chicago was a parochial school he established at the church in 1870, taught in the Dutch language by a Mr. Albers, who was paid $7.50 per week. Children in the congregation attended for free, but children of nonmembers were charged 15 cents per week. The latter likely included children from the Reformed church, since its school had closed.[80]

Remarkably, the First Christian Reformed Church obtained another pastor in only four months. This was the talented Frederikus Hulst, a Groninger, who had studied in the parsonage of the Reverend Walter H. Kok at Hoogeveen and served five Seceder churches in Groningen before emigrating to pastor the Holland (Michigan) congregation in 1868. Another Cocksian, Hulst fit in well in the Groninger Hoek in Chicago. The council raised his annual salary to $700 in 1873, and that year the congregation started an American Sunday school, sixteen years after the First Reformed Church of Chicago had done so.

Hulst's ministry, unfortunately, was scarred by a sex scandal in the congregation, which eventually divided the consistory, undermined his ministry, and may well have undermined his health as well. Barely two years into his ministry in Chicago, during Christmas week in 1874, Hulst developed a throat infection and died within two days, on December 22.

The scandal broke in October 1871, when a housewife reported seeing two married church members carrying on an illicit affair. The matter, as customary in Reformed fellowships, came before the church consistory. Elder Vastenhouw confirmed that he had had similar suspicions and had

79. *Seventy-Fifth Anniversary,* 8. Deacons at this time were John Vastenhouw, C. Van Deursen, C. Bos, Derk Natelborg, G. Veltman, J. Bos, J. Mendelts, Hendrik Bulthuis, and J. Haan.

80. First Christian Reformed Church of Chicago, Minutes, 27 June 1870.

warned the man involved more than once. The elders called the offending parties for questioning at a special meeting; and in a mark of the seriousness of the problem they invited the deacons, who ordinarily had no part in "discipline matters." At the interview, in which first the man and then the woman were questioned before the face of God, both adamantly denied everything, except that the woman admitted kissing in a closet. The council rejected their claims of innocence, took the first step of discipline by closing the Lord's Table to them, and requested them to appear for further examination at the next consistory meeting, but to no avail.

For more than a year the consistory dealt with the scandal numerous times, but witnesses gave contradictory testimony and no one brought absolute proof of adultery. So the consistory decided to put the case to rest and warned all members to stop spreading the poisonous rumors that caused so much grief. The elders also determined to be more prudent in the future, and they chastised the husband of the woman who had first reported the tryst for bringing a "false testimony." Presumably, peace would now return to the troubled flock.

However, the accused man did not let the matter rest. He canceled his membership by baptism and demanded that the consistory and pastor apologize publicly for mistreating him. After a personal visit from a committee consisting of the Reverend Hulst and elders Vastenhouw and J. Haan, the man "calmed down and has withdrawn his resignation," so the minutes report, provided that the consistory apologize and admit guilt.[81] But the body would not do this; rather, it accepted his resignation and announced it to the congregation. A classical committee that was appointed to assist the consistory concurred in the action.

Now the case took a more dangerous turn by dividing the consistory into factions. At a meeting attended by the accused ex-member, who could yet be reconciled with a formal apology, two elders and a deacon asked the brethren to state, "In so far as I am guilty, I confess." All agreed, some reluctantly, but Hulst would have none of it. The accused, he said, also harbored guilt and refused to admit it and to "grasp a brother's hand and no longer to speak about the part." Hulst stood on the Apostle Paul's principle (1 Tim. 5:19): "Do not entertain an accusation against an elder unless it is brought by two or three witnesses."[82]

After two years, the issue continued to fester and the pastor had become the target, even drawing a formal grievance from the accused man's

81. Ibid., 9, 26 Dec. 1872 (quote, 26 Dec., Art. 4).

82. Ibid., 11 Aug. 1873, Art. 6.

wife about "unchurchly treatment," which the consistory dismissed.[83] Another member accused the pastor of having wrongly alluded to the affair in a sermon early on. The majority of the consistory, led by the deacons, continued to pressure Hulst to apologize, and he just as adamantly refused. Not "into eternity" would he admit guilt. Hulst finally felt he could not enter the pulpit in good conscience, and he refused to preach. The classical committee offered its counsel again, but with little affect.

In the final stage, the dispute intruded into the process of nominations for office bearers and nearly split the congregation. In an attempt to lower the voices, the consistory deleted from the list of nominees the most vocal leaders of the two factions, elder Arie Van Deursen, a church founder, and deacon G. Meinardi. But the voting procedure in the consistory was highly irregular, and both men protested vehemently; the deacon even accused the pastor of "blatantly influencing" the voting. Just as the matter seemed to be spinning out of control, and the congregation had voted on the controversial slate of nominees, Hulst took sick and died at age forty-six.

This stunning event so shocked the congregation that it closed ranks in mourning for its "powerful, faithful, and diligent preacher and defender with mouth and pen of the Gereformeerde Kerk and standards here on earth."[84] Former pastor William Frieling of the Ridott, Illinois, congregation, conducted the funeral, held Saturday, December 24, 1873, and led the worship services the following day. The congregation took a collection to pay the funeral expenses, and the council granted the widow and children free use of the parsonage with free coal until such time as a new pastor arrived. This turned out to be nearly a year. They also granted a stipend of $25 per month. The deacons scheduled two offerings per year to raise the funds. The final shoe dropped when several members, led by Arie Van Deursen, who had raised a protest against the classis, returned to the Reformed Church.[85]

Hulst was succeeded by the highly esteemed Willem (William) Greve, who like Schepers was tied to the Cocksian wing of the Afscheiding and had trained in the parsonage of Douwe Vander Werp in Graafschap, Michigan. Greve, who was born in Graafschap Bentheim in Germany,

83. Ibid., 17 May 1875. A year later the wife again wrote to the consistory, and the pastor and an elder visited her and "she was satisfied." Coincidentally, her husband, the subject of the original investigation, had just left her (22 May, 19 June 1876).

84. Ibid., 23 Dec. 1873, Art. 2.

85. "Christian Reformed Church, General Assembly Minutes," 3 June 1874, Art. 25, 38; 2-4 June 1875, Art. 24.

came from his first charge in Cincinnati and served from 1874 to 1878. These were years of rapid growth in the congregation, despite a severe national economic depression. Construction of the school building was completed at this time and the deacons decided to look after the poor and if necessary to cover burial expenses.

In February 1877, Greve led the congregation to take a major step toward meeting the demands of the youth by starting a Sunday school following the afternoon worship service. Support was overwhelming. More than seventy students turned out for the first session. Old and young returned home with grateful hearts, the minutes report. Greve further endeared himself to the congregation by donating $100 in a debt-reduction drive for the Gurley Street church building in 1877. The next year the council had gas lights installed in the church and made other improvements. When Greve received a call from Passaic, New Jersey, the council unanimously urged him to stay but to no avail.[86]

In marked contrast to the stocky and vibrant "German pastor" came the aged and frail Koene Vanden Bosch, at a salary of $700 per year plus free housing. The two men were friends; Vanden Bosch had organized the Cincinnati church and appointed Greve as its pastor. Vanden Bosch was a revered elder statesman in the denomination. He had been the prime mover in the 1857 secession in the Classis of Holland and the sole cleric in the Christian Reformed denomination for its first seven years. The General Synod honored him as president in 1873 and vice president in 1878. His sermons were strong and practical, like the man himself.[87]

Vanden Bosch dealt firmly with a protest in 1879 concerning the nature of profession of faith. A member, Jan Meeter, believed that a personal testimony of his conversion was sufficient, but Vanden Bosch demanded a Reformed creedal confession as well. In fact, Vanden Bosch throughout his ministry had always insisted on a literal mastery of the Compendium. That the dispute ended peacefully indicated that the dominie had mellowed with age, but that it ended without a final resolution spoke to his legendary touchiness and unwillingness to compromise. Vanden Bosch also had the consistory take firm control of the Sunday school after complaints about disorderly teachers' meetings. Not all the teachers were happy with

86. First Christian Reformed, Minutes, 5 Feb., 24 Dec. 1877; 29 Apr., 28 May, 15 July 1878; Obituaries, "Rev. William Greve," *Banner,* 6 Apr. 1906; "Rev. Willem Greve 1836-1906," Christian Reformed Church in America, *Jaarboekje,* 1907, 119-23; J. G. Vanden Bosch, "Willem Greve," *Reformed Journal* 10 (Jan. 1960): 19-21.

87. First Christian Reformed Church of Chicago, Minutes, 29 Aug. 1878; J. G. Vanden Bosch, "Koene Vanden Bosch," *Reformed Journal* 4 (Sept. 1954): 13-15.

Rev. Koene Vanden Bosch (1818-91) *(The Archives, Calvin College)*

this ruling. In 1879 the classis sent Vanden Bosch to De Motte, Indiana, to organize a congregation there among recent Dutch farm settlers, some of whom came from Chicago. Jan (John) Meeter left Chicago to farm on the Ridge Road in Lansing, Illinois/Munster, Indiana, and became one of the leading men in church and school in the Illiana area.[88]

Vanden Bosch, the aged icon of the 1834 Secession who had answered the call to the ministry under the very preaching of Hendrik De Cock himself, served the Chicago congregation well for three years. Then a bronchial infection, contracted while doing family visiting, sapped his strength and forced him to request emeritation at age sixty-three. After a year his nephew, Tamme M. Vanden Bosch, who was born in the province of Drenthe and fought in the American Civil War, accepted the call to Chicago as his first charge. He revived the Sunday school that had languished and orchestrated the church's move to the Ashland Avenue district. Growth forced the congregation to leave its small Gurley Street church.[89]

88. First Christian Reformed Church of Chicago, Minutes, 31 Mar., Art. 4-6; 5 May, Art. 5; 19 May, Art. 4; 11 June, Art. 29; 22 Sept. 1879, Art. 4. Clarence Boomsma, "Meet Mr. Meeter," *Origins,* 16, No. 1 (1988): 43-45.

89. J. G. Vanden Bosch, "Tamme M. Vanden Bosch," *Reformed Journal* 10 (Nov. 1960): 17-19; First Christian Reformed Church of Chicago, Minutes, 3, 22 Jan. 1883. Male teachers were Boswinkel, Jakob Bos, Sabelis, Jan Meeter, and Velthuizen; females were Vanden

During the younger Vanden Bosch's year in Chicago, October 1882–October 1883, the denomination took some of the sting out of its name by dropping the word "True." De Ware (True) Hollandsche Gereformeerde Kerk became De Hollandsche Christelijke Gereformeerde Kerk (later Christian Reformed Church in North America).[90] This name change coincided with a relocation program that was not without controversy.

In the decades after the great fire of 1871, Dutch families had gradually spread out across the expanding city. One cluster formed on the northwest side along Erie Street and the other expanded from the Harrison-Halsted hub in a southwesterly direction along Blue Island Avenue as far as 18th Street. The church had to go with the population flow and relocate. But where? Everyone wanted the church in his neighborhood, and a bitter struggle ensued, especially by the northsiders.

What settled the issue was the availability in 1883 of a splendid church building being vacated by the Presbyterians on the south side of West 14th Street in the 1400 block (new numbering) between Throop and Loomis streets (figure 1.1, site 6). This site two blocks east of Ashland Avenue lay one mile southwest of the Gurley-Harrison Street enclave. It stood close to the Blue Island corridor but was still accessible to those on the northwest side. Dutch families had gradually moved into the district in search of better housing in the 1870s. The numerous Dutch immigrants flooding into Chicago in the 1880s also found homes there.

The North Side contingent filed a formal protest with Classis Illinois against the dealings of the building committee and demanded a share of the proceeds of the Gurley Street building to start its own congregation. But the classis, after "lengthy debate," exonerated the consistory and building committee but did appoint a committee to help negotiate a monetary settlement.[91] The congregation the same year bought the vacant lots on each side of the new church for $2,300 and issued $2,800 in five- and six-year promissory notes at 7 percent interest to fund a new parsonage.[92]

Vanden Bosch was a restless man and remained only one year to the day at First Church. He left for the newly organized, and presumably more peaceful, congregation at New Holland, South Dakota. These were trying

Bosch's wife, and Mrs. Generaal, A. Bruining, J. Walters, and J. Broersema. *Seventy-Fifth Anniversary,* 10-11.

90. Jan Meeter, a lawyer and notary who had crossed swords with Tamme's uncle Koene Vanden Bosch years earlier, saw to the legal aspects of filing for the name change.

91. First Christian Reformed Church of Chicago, Minutes, 15 Oct. 1883.

92. Ibid., 19 Feb., 19 Mar. 1883.

times for the True church in Chicago, but it persevered. The church's conservative image and the negative fallout in the Reformed Church from the Freemasonry controversy (see below) enabled the congregation to grow rapidly by sweeping in the bulk of the heavy immigration after 1880. First Christian Reformed Church of Chicago grew to 425 members by 1875, 1,000 by 1886, and 1,200 in 1895. It also gave birth to five daughter churches: First Englewood (1887), Douglas Park (1899), Archer Avenue in Summit (1911), Third Chicago (1912), and Fourth Chicago (1923).

The De Bey Era (1868-91)

Bernardus De Bey came to Chicago with a reputation for effective leadership in church and society. In his previous charge at Middelstum, Groningen, he had built a new sanctuary for his growing flock, organized various church societies such as a choir and young men's society, started a Christian elementary school in town, and took an active part in local and national politics. Critics accused him of acting "pope-like," but the Groninger congregation grew by leaps and bounds under his "pious and practical" direction until it included almost one-third of the town inhabitants (625+ souls). At the farewell service, the church was so full that ladders were placed against the outside walls so people could look in through the windows and hear their beloved dominie.

De Bey was fifty-two years of age when he emigrated and ready for a change after preaching in Middelstum for twenty-two years. In a retirement speech many years later, he summed up his reasons for accepting the post in Chicago:

> In your unanimous call, according to my conviction a call from God, I left my fatherland and a congregation dear to me. Chicago was the place of my desire, a place where I thought I could work fruitfully. A people was there that had known me in the Netherlands and of which I was convinced that they would receive me with open arms. And I have not been disappointed in this.[93]

93. Krabbendam, "Serving the Dutch Community," 48-59, long quote 57; Herbert J. Brinks, "The Americanization of Bernardus De Beij (1815-1894)," 6, No. 1 (1988): 26-27; "The Story of My Life by Siewert Bus, 1854-1938," p. 3, Archives, Calvin College. The travel route from Groningen to Chicago at the time was via the Frisian port of Harlingen, across the English channel to Hull, then by train to Liverpool, where the steamer took them to New York, and then by train to Chicago. The entire trip took one month (Siewert Bus, p. 4).

Rev. Bernardus De Bey (1818-94) *(Courtesy of First Reformed Church of Chicago in Berwyn)*

The First Reformed Church of Chicago could seat five hundred, but it was soon overcrowded, thanks to De Bey, and he laid plans to build a new sanctuary with twice the seating capacity.[94] In the year of the great revival, 1877, the congregation had the joy of receiving 120 members by confession of faith, and three years later it paid off the $6,000 remaining on its building debt, despite the economic hard times in the 1870s. One member set off the campaign to burn the mortgage by pledging to pay 10 percent, if the congregation would cover the remainder. The successful "challenge grant" freed the congregation from "this pressing burden" and opened new opportunities for ministry.[95]

First Reformed Church reached a thousand souls by 1879 and twelve hundred at its high point in 1884 before birthing daughter congregations

94. De Bey letter in *Provinciale Groningen Courant,* 10 Dec. 1869, 13 Feb. 1869; First Reformed Church of Chicago, *Century for Christ,* 5.

95. Classis of Wisconsin, Minutes, 17 Apr. 1878, Art. 34.

in Englewood (1886), the English-speaking Trinity (1891) in Chicago, Bethel in Summit (1899), West Side in Cicero (1911), and Calvary in Berwyn (late 1930s).

Church life at First Reformed under De Bey took on more and more aspects of American style. He was much taken with popular preaching methods and attended a nearby Presbyterian church every Sunday night to practice the language and pick up tips on sermonizing. De Bey particularly admired Yankee ministers for focusing on the central idea of the text and applying it in practical ways to everyday life without much biblical exegesis, analysis, or synthesis. He also marveled at the full-orbed ministry of American Protestants. In a personal letter to his cousin in Groningen, A. P. Lanting, De Bey reported:

> In our churches here we have something going on virtually every evening of the week – prayer meetings, preaching, catechism, youth societies, choral groups. . . . I could no longer feel at home with some of the pious customs and exclusively Sunday Christianity which characterized my life in Groningen. Here Christianity is more a way of life, an active love, a devotion to God – preaching his Word and laboring for the kingdom.[96]

During his pastorate, De Bey dispensed with several practices of standard Reformed polity. He canceled the yearly schedule of formal "family visits," believing that such "superficial chats" were a "waste of time." He substituted informal Bible studies on Saturday evenings at the vestry. In 1888 the consistory gave up its customary prerogative of nominating elders and deacons in favor of the more democratic congregational selection by vote. But other changes he wanted were blocked, notably the purchase of a church organ and the singing of half notes in the Psalter along with the customary whole notes. After many years he won the organ battle but only after donating $600 toward the purchase.[97]

Clearly, the dominie from Middelstum had become the American preacher. He was enamored with the practice of taking the faith into the public square, unlike the "Sunday Christianity" of the Netherlands. His six children lived out these convictions; three entered the profession of medicine and became community activists. Only three remained in the

96. Letter of B. De Bey to A. P. Lanting, 9 Mar. 1871, quoted in Brinks, "Americanization of Bernardus De Beij," 27-28.

97. Krabbendam, "Serving the Dutch Community," 76, 80; Vandenbosch, *Dutch Communities of Chicago,* 23.

Reformed Church, including a daughter who married a Reformed Church minister after first experiencing a painful divorce. One son died before age thirty, and another was an alcoholic who lived outside the church for several years. The four children who married chose Dutch-born spouses, but most of the grandchildren left the Reformed church; two joined the liberal Fountain Street Church in Grand Rapids, and one became Congregational.[98]

By 1874 De Bey was even more explicit in accepting the tenets of American evangelism. Reformed orthodoxy was needed, he averred, but not a dogmatic kind that lacked a warm heart. Revival fires burned regularly in Chicago under the father of urban revivalism, Dwight L. Moody, pastor of the nondenominational Illinois Street Church. De Bey adopted these spiritual rhythms of American evangelism – conversion, backsliding, and renewal.[99] When Moody's understudy, George F. Pentecost, held revival meetings in the neighborhood in 1878-79, De Bey signed on as a counselor and encouraged those members of his congregation who understood English to attend. The spiritual condition of his congregation was languishing, he wrote Lanting, and Pentecost brought the hope of revival.

> He is a blessed awakening whom my people (as many as understand English, and most do) attend regularly. I also attend as often as possible. He holds meetings four times each day: from 12 noon to 1 p.m., an hour of prayer; from 3 to 4 p.m., Bible study; from 4 to 5, dialogue and testimonies; and from 7:30 to 9:00 p.m., preaching. Hundreds remain until 10 p.m. to receive added counsel from Pentecost and other pastors, and I am also among the counselors. Here in this land our divine worship is a lively activity. Conversion and renewal are the fruits of Rev. Pentecost's work.[100]

Thereafter, De Bey's biannual reports to the regional church body, the Classis of Wisconsin, concerning the spiritual condition of his congregation, were couched in the idiom of revivalism. An 1881 report was typical:

98. Krabbendam, "Serving the Dutch Community," 81-83.

99. George M. Marsden, *Fundamentalism and American Culture: The Shaping of Twentieth Century Evangelicalism, 1870-1925* (New York: Oxford Univ. Press, 1980), 32-39.

100. Letter of B. De Bey to A. P. Lanting, 2 Feb. 1879, quoted in Brinks, "Americanization of Bernardus De Beij," 28; Krabbendam, "Serving the Dutch Community," 74.

> Chicago reports a good attendance upon the means of grace and points to evidences of their good effect in general. There is a spirit of mutual appreciation, peace, love, and labor of love. Of the many conversions resulting from a general revival a few years since, some have persevered, others give but feeble tokens of full consecration, others seem quite worldly minded. At present it seems children of the covenant do not understand what God has sealed to them upon their foreheads [i.e., in the sacrament of baptism]. Conversions and returns to God are scarce. Planting and watering is however continued in obedience and faith that God will give the increase.[101]

For De Bey, First Church was clearly in a "dry season" in terms of conversions.

Another of the "fruits" of revivals was ecumenism, which De Bey adopted wholeheartedly:

> We have here a number of churches or denominations, and in very many of these the gospel is preached, and they contain a good Christian element. The best denominations are included in the general category of evangelical churches – the Presbyterians, the Dutch Reformed, Baptists, Methodists, Congregationalists, Reformed Episcopalians, Lutherans, and others. Besides working in their own circles, these churches work together for the general promotion of Christianity. Thus, there are combined gatherings, prayer meetings, and other occasions in which there are no references to particular denominations. Together, then, they preach, speak, and pray to influence the unbelieving world and lead sinners to Jesus.
>
> I have a high regard for that work because, after all, faith in Jesus, turning to God, and renewal of the Holy Spirit are really what counts where Christianity and eternity are concerned. Fighting for one's own church and the remote, unimportant, and speculative doctrines has no significance for true Christianity and eternity. . . . A practical Christianity – faith, living, and doing – is earnestly recommended everywhere. Further, it is actually taken to heart in many excellent ways. . . .
>
> Now, you must not read between the lines that certain doctrines are denied in these evangelical churches and, even less, that I, if it were so, would approve. Still, it goes without saying that each church has individual practices – in baptism, customs, congregational management

101. Classis of Wisconsin, Minutes, 21 Apr. 1881, Art. 21 (quote); cf. 17 Apr. 1878, Art. 34; 17 Apr. 1883, Art. 27.

— but these matters have nothing to do with Jesus Christ. I tell you, cousin, I feel genuinely at home in this Christian life.

After quoting this very telling letter at length, historian Herbert Brinks concluded: "Though not explicitly embracing the nondenominational dictum 'No creed but the Bible,' De Bey's perspective clearly encompassed the essence of that peculiarly Anglo-American anticredal expression." Even the Lutherans fell within the pale of his ecumenism. Immigration had happily offered him the opportunity to throw off the old Dutch Reformed ways and associate with conservative American churches. Brinks put it succinctly: "Fine theological distinctions, denominational boundaries, and traditional piety were, from his perspective, no longer crucial." De Bey did not even subscribe to the religious periodical of his mother church. "I do not get the *Bazuin* or the *Wekstem,* he wrote. "All I receive from the Dutch press is the *Provinciale Groninger Courant.*"[102]

De Bey's views about American Christianity were in step with those of his denomination, which had earlier embraced the revivalism of the Second Great Awakening. He had come a long way from his religious roots in the Afscheiding of 1834. No wonder that he criticized "our separated brothers" in the Christian Reformed Church for "proceeding along the old paths." They were, in his words, "beneath criticism." Ignore the self-righteous "True Brothers" and they would quickly disappear. "They can say and write what they want," he declared, "and no one pays any attention to them. That is the best and quickest way to kill them off."[103]

During the 1880s, the fruits of De Bey's ministry at First Reformed Church were less evident than in the 1870s, although in 1886 he reported another revival in the church, especially among the young people. The Sunday school thrived and enrollment surpassed three hundred, which was more than double the numbers when De Bey began his labors.[104] But in the 1880s, more members transferred to other denominations or were excommunicated than joined by confession or transfer. Many of the outtransfers joined the Christian Reformed denomination, along with most of the newly arriving immigrants. These "little brothers," after all, were holding on tenaciously to the Dutch Reformed heritage of 1834, while the

102. Letters of B. De Bey to A. P. Lanting, 3 Jan. 1878, 13 Sept. 1870, quoted in Brinks, "Americanization of Bernardus De Beij," 28-30.

103. Letter of B. De Bey to A. P. Lanting, 26 May 1873, quoted in ibid.

104. Enrollment figures, along with membership data, were reported annually in the *Acts and Proceedings of the General Synod of the Protestant Dutch Reformed Church in America.*

Reformed Church in America was content to fit into the American scene.[105]

Another concern at First Reformed was more mundane. The Harrison Street neighborhood had become industrialized and seedy and was in rapid decline. The congregation sought police protection to control rowdies in front of the church during Sunday morning worship but was turned down. To increase security, members surrounded the property with a six-foot fence and screened the windows with wire mesh. The handwriting was on the wall; soon it would be time to relocate. In the meantime, the aging De Bey continued to lead a grateful congregation, who in 1882 surprised its beloved pastor with a cash gift of $100.

In the years 1880-84, the explosive issue of Freemasonry came to a head in the Reformed Church in America (see chapter 2). Some 10 percent of all the members of the Particular Synod of Chicago, made up of the two Midwestern immigrant classes of Wisconsin and Michigan, went over to the Christian Reformed Church because of this issue. De Bey was in the middle of the controversy, which was on the agenda of almost every session of the Classis of Wisconsin for four years.[106]

The problem in the Particular Synod of Chicago was that while it condemned the "God-dishonoring sin of Freemasonry" in the strongest terms and would not admit a Freemason to membership in any congregation; nevertheless, the denominational synod centered in New York insisted that Freemasonry was entirely permissible in congregations elsewhere. This "local option" policy did not satisfy the Midwestern congregations, who saw it as forcing them to be "unequally yoked" to those who had joined an "anti-Republican," "anti-Christian," and "anti-Reformed" organization. Many congregations were torn and saw members secede over "this evil in the church." Moreover, the mother church in the Netherlands held the same views and henceforth would commend its departing members only if they joined the Christian Reformed congregations.[107]

Before the issue wreaked havoc in the Midwestern churches, De Bey was a moderate who accepted the denomination's longstanding policy of letting local consistories decide the question individually. He believed

105. Krabbendam, "Serving the Dutch Community," 76, 68; First Reformed Church of Chicago, *Century for Christ,* 5.

106. Elton J. Bruins, "The Masonic Controversy in Holland, Michigan, 1879-1882," 53-72, in Peter De Klerk and Richard R. De Ridder, eds., *Perspectives on the Christian Reformed Church: Studies in Its History, Theology, and Ecumenicity* (Grand Rapids: Baker, 1983).

107. Classis of Wisconsin, Minutes, 18 Feb., Art. 59; 21 Apr., Art. 42; 22 Sept. 1880, Art. 19; 20 Apr. 1881. Art. 8, 13, 14; 17 Apr. 1883, Art. 34.

that Freemasonry in the United States was not irreligious like its European counterpart, but a quintessential American social club that had proven to be compatible with Christianity. Lodge members should not be disciplined by the consistory but rather educated as to the dangers of lodge membership.

But in the 1880s, De Bey came to see that his denomination was losing members by the thousands to the Christian Reformed Church because of its acquiescence in Freemasonry. This pained him deeply. So, on practical more than principial grounds, he concluded that it was unwise for the Reformed Church to accept Freemasons, since this was having a most negative impact on the Reformed Church. After some eight months of vacillation, De Bey's consistory condemned secret oath-bound societies and warned members that to be polluted *(besmet)* by Masonry is incompatible with being a Christian.

People in the mother Dutch church did not understand, said De Bey, that the split between the two daughter denominations in the United States on issues of Americanization was irrevocable. The Reformed Church would soon abolish the Dutch language and join the American Protestant mainstream, while the Christian Reformed Church would keep the language and stay isolated. Netherlanders, De Bey charged, are too idealistic:

> They think that the Hollanders [in America] are still Hollanders like them, without sympathy for unification with the American Christian church. But we want to remind them that Secession does not inspire us; that we love the association with the civilized American Christian people and do not consider to break away; that it is unthinkable that the present day Seceders [i.e., the Christian Reformed Church in North America] will ever unite.

In De Bey's mind, American Christianity was civilized, whereas traditional Reformed churches in the Old Country presumably were not.[108]

De Bey's willingness to adopt American ways is revealed in several minor but symbolic actions. In 1887 his consistory decided to dispense with collecting offerings with the traditional Dutch *zakjes,* a small sack at the end of a long pole, and instead used baskets. The congregation also became involved in the 1893 Chicago World's Fair, the Columbian Exhibition, by agreeing to participate in the Columbian Sunday Association, a

108. Quoted in Krabbendam, "Serving the Dutch Community," 79-80.

Yankee "blue nose" effort to maintain strict Sunday observance on the Midway. Congress had mandated that all attractions and rides be closed on Sunday, but many in the general public strenuously objected to this and tried to override the ruling. The mainline Protestant churches of Chicago vowed to protect the Christian Sabbath.

The most divisive issues that De Bey faced late in his ministry were the "language question" and hymn singing, which for all his Americanizing ways he had forestalled for years. The old Dutch Psalms from the Genevan Psalter tugged at the heartstrings. De Bey humored the congregation by selecting only a few dozen favorite psalms from the opus of 150, notably those that had singable tunes and were committed to memory. Two Reformed congregations in Chicago, but not First Church, had adopted the controversial Evangelical Hymnbook of the Reformed Church in the Netherlands (Hervormde Kerk Nederland), which the youth favored because of the contemporary tunes and quicker tempo. These and other "gospel hymns," however, were used at First Church only in the evening English services for several decades.[109]

The language issue came to a head in 1885 "to save our young people," as it was said. Already in 1883, De Bey had chaired a classical committee to push for English-language worship, on the grounds that the young people prefer it and were voting with their feet in droves because no such church existed in Chicago. "They disappear gradually in all kinds of English churches and are thus lost to our denomination," lamented the committee in its report.[110]

On this matter, however, De Bey's eagerness to enter the American Protestant mainstream was sorely tested. He stubbornly held to Dutch language worship at First Church, despite signing his committee's report. When his own consistory decided to hire an English-speaking "evangelist" to preach "on occasion" in the evening service, De Bey stymied the plan by refusing to share the evening pulpit. Two years passed before seminarians Charles J. Sonnema and Albertus Pieters (a son of the congregation) were engaged on a regular basis.

When attendance at the English worship did not grow as expected, Rense H. Joldersma, the Chicago-based superintendent of Domestic Missions for the Reformed Church, seized the opportunity and obtained the consistory's approval in 1890 to start an English-speaking "mission" sta-

109. Moerdyke, "Chicago Letter," *Christian Intelligencer* (hereafter *CI*), 10 May 1893, p. 10; 3 Jan. 3 1900, p. 8.

110. Classis of Wisconsin, Minutes, 17 Apr. 1883, Art. 28.

tion. De Bey again resisted splitting off a new congregation; "Father must live too," he insisted.

That year, at the age of seventy-six, De Bey chose to retire after twenty-three years at the helm. Very likely the Trinity secession had a part in the decision. And he did not need the salary; he retired with an "independent livelihood," it was noted.[111] In September 1891, First Reformed gave its renowned Dominie De Bey an emotional farewell. The clerk recorded De Bey's farewell speech to the consistory, chaired on behalf of classis by the Reverend Jacob P. De Jonge, of the First Reformed in Englewood:

> When I recall in my mind the long period of 23 years and some months of service in the midst of this congregation, I feel the urge to express my gratitude to God and my recognition of consistent good health and desire to lead, and strength provided by Him during all those years. With love I have brought God's word every Sunday and Wednesday evening. I wish to express my gratitude for the esteem, love, and cooperation I have received from you brothers of the consistory and also not in the least by those who were before His throne during all those years in the past in spite of my shortcomings.
>
> I look back with satisfaction on a congregation that changed places of worship twice and has given me a large place in her heart as well as providing a place of love and honor to my family, giving appreciation and esteem. Nothing is permanent on this earth, including the congregation who called me in 1868 in the Netherlands, after which we moved here along with several other families. The present situation in the congregation allows me to retire from this place of work and to lay down my shepherd's staff. My task is to be carried on and continued by a capable young minister, I hereby kindly request to be relieved of my duties as pastor, asking for an honorable discharge from this congregation to start the first week in November 1891, with the prayer that the brotherly love may remain.
>
> Done in Consistory September 3, 1891.

De Bey preached his farewell sermon November 1, 1891, on the text of Acts 20:32, quoting the words of the Apostle Paul: "I commend you to

111. Moerdyke, "Chicago Letter," *CI*, 11 Nov. 1891, p. 11; 20 Aug. 1891, p. 10. Moerdyke predicted correctly that the language issue was the "irrepressible conflict [which] will ere long be the burning question of the majority of our Western churches" (ibid., 20 Jan. 1892, p. 11).

God." The Classis of Wisconsin emeritated De Bey with many words of praise for this "man of influence in the Fatherland" who "remained faithful to his convictions on this side of the Atlantic." The classical resolution went on to describe the impact of De Bey's sermons: "The character of his preaching, always intensely evangelical, did not fail to permanently impress hearts and form character and lives."[112]

Two discordant notes surrounded De Bey's retirement. One was the demand of his youngest daughter Cornelia (Tryntje), known as "Katy," for payment for services rendered as the regular church organist. The other was the consistory's offer to reimburse De Bey $100 for leaving the parsonage carpets, curtains, and stove, which amount the dominie judged insufficient. Then his successor Bloemendal deemed the items "out of fashion," so De Bey was left to take them away for nothing.

Cornelia was attending Illinois Normal School to become a teacher. She later studied medicine and became a leading Progressive reformer and feminist in Chicago, even holding a seat on the Chicago Board of Education.[113] The headstrong Cornelia, who became the most famous of De Bey's six children, demanded respect even as a teenager. The dominie himself first brought her sensitive payment request to the consistory in 1888, which was the same year that De Bey proudly boasted of the new $2,000 organ. The brethren followed standard practice in such tender matters and appointed a committee, which recommended reimbursement in the form of a yearly present or gift at the annual Christmas program. The consistory agreed, but congregants, who had never paid for any services in the church except those of the dominie, gave stintingly in a special offering for the purpose.

Finally, after three years had passed and a new minister was in place, Cornelia submitted a bill to the consistory. The brethren judged it "too high" and called Cornelia to appear in person in hopes of reaching a "mutually harmonious" (no pun intended) settlement. At the face-to-face meeting, both parties agreed to the sum of $325, provided Cornelia played until the end of the year. This money covered more than three years of service, perhaps 175 Sundays and 525 worship services, or nearly $2 per week. Cornelia was vindicated, but her successors, Jelle Engelsman and Effie Nienhuis, were satisfied with a yearly "present" rather than a weekly fee,

112. Ibid., 30 Sept. 1891, p. 11; 18 Nov. 1891, p. 11.

113. Mary Pieroni Schiltz and Suzanne Sinke, "De Bey, Cornelia Bernarda," 214-16, in *Women Building Chicago: A Biographical Dictionary, 1790-1990,* Rima Lunin Schultz and Adele Hast, eds. (Bloomington: Indiana Univ. Press, 2001); *Onze Toekomst,* 10 Sept. 1909; Krabbendam, "Serving the Dutch Community, 84-88.

and the amount was half that paid to Miss De Bey, $25 each or only $1 per week. The brothers Vander Weg were given a present of $5 each for pumping the organ bellows, and they better not fall asleep while on duty![114]

Following his retirement, De Bey moved with his wife to a home on Perry Avenue in Englewood, across the street from his son William and family. Here within three years, De Bey passed away full of honor on a cold winter day in February 1894. He died peacefully at age seventy-eight, conscious to the last, after a touching farewell to his loved ones by his side. By his count, he had preached four thousand sermons in his Chicago congregation – the last the previous October, taught two thousand catechism classes, and led seventeen hundred prayer meetings. The obituary in *De Hope* called him a "spiritual father," and the Chicago newspaper, *The Daily Inter Ocean,* a paper for the city's immigrant community, in an overstatement called De Bey the "Founder of the Dutch Reformed Church" in Chicago and "beloved by all the Hollanders of America."[115]

De Bey's noon funeral coincided with the worst winter storm Chicago had experienced in many years and, fittingly, the service was the first to take place in the newly completed Hasting Street sanctuary. Since the pews had not yet been installed, chairs were brought in from Trinity Church for the large gathering. The Reverend Ralph Bloemendal led the service with the participation of his dear friends and colleagues Peter Moerdyke of Trinity, Balster Van Ess of First Roseland, and E. C. Oggel of Pullman Presbyterian.[116]

Certainly, the role of Dominie De Bey and his parsonage as a receiving center and focal point of Dutch life in Chicago would be sorely missed. He had drawn many hundreds of Groningers from across the sea and introduced them to the American social and economic world without apology, and he ardently promoted the more ecumenical Reformed Church in America rather than the principles of the Seceders of 1834 and 1857.

In De Bey's last years, it had became clear that First Church's loca-

114. First Reformed Church, Minutes, 1, 15, 29 Oct. 1891; 25 Mar. 1895.

115. Quoted in Krabbendam, "Serving the Dutch Community," 90-91, which relies on De Bey's own calculations in his *Eene laaste getuigenis. Afscheidswoord uitgesproken in de Eerste Gereformeerde Kerk te Chicago. Op Zondag den 1. November 1891* [A last testimony. Farewell address given in the First Reformed Church of Chicago. On Sunday November 1, 1891] (Chicago, 1891), 16; Moerdyke, "Chicago Letter," *CI,* 19 Apr., p. 11; 29 Nov. 1893, p. 11; 14 Feb. 1894, p. 14. Mrs. De Bey died within five years. In her eulogies, the "beloved *juffrouw*" [the term for a dominie's wife] was called a "mother in Israel" (ibid., 25 Jan. 1899, pp. 8-9).

116. Moerdyke, "Chicago Letter," *CI,* 21 Feb. 1894, pp. 10-11.

tion was "not sufficiently central," and the congregation decided to sell the Harrison Street church and parsonage that had given thirty years of faithful service. Early in 1891, the consistory began a subscription campaign to fund the move; members pledged generously – one opened the list with a $1,000 donation. But they decided to wait with the final decision until securing a new pastor, which happened quickly when the youthful but eloquent Bloemendal (1891-94) accepted their call in August 1891.

Almost simultaneously, realtor Van Vlissingen brought an offer from a developer for the church properties of $25,000, one-third in cash, which the congregation accepted by unanimous vote. Unfortunately, the buyer in December forced the congregation to accept $5,000 less. A church, after all, is a difficult building to sell at top dollar. Things got

Marble baptismal font, gift of the De Bey children in memory of the ministry of Bernardus and Anje Schuringa De Bey, 1899. Now in First Reformed Church of Chicago in Berwyn

(Photo by Hans Krabbendam)

worse. More than a year later, in late 1892, the hard-nosed buyer pushed the price down to only $15,500. When the bottom fell out of the American economy the next year, the congregation counted its blessings after all.

Subsequently, the frame church on the corner of Harrison and May streets suffered an ignominious fate. Moerdyke's depiction is classic:

> The wood building has had quite a history in these years of new ownership, having been a deaconess home, a mission, partly a religious book and tract "shop," a lodging house of charity, an old rookery, with windows for the hoodlums' targets, an eyesore and offense to the neighborhood, and finally a condemned building. For the past fortnight a gang of wreckers has reduced it to its original timbers and beams and boards, etc., and I know of one, and there may be many others, who for years met God and His beloved people there, to whom the old place was still sacred, who at the first attack of the destroyers reverently visited the scene of those blessed years and piously reviewed the history of his own conversion and development there as a disciple.[117]

Bloemendal carried the relocation plan forward energetically, and in early 1892 the congregation chose a site in the heart of the Ashland Avenue Dutch neighborhood, one mile south and west of the old site. Here the committee found several adjoining lots at 1533 West Hastings Street (13th Place) just east of Ashland Avenue (figure 1.1, site 4) for a price of $10,600.[118] The lots were only two blocks west of the First Christian Reformed Church. Thus, seven years after the First Christian Reformed congregation had purchased the Fourteenth Street church, First Reformed, with its nearly eleven hundred members, erected a new church to seat a thousand in the same locality.

Building in the Ashland Avenue district was dictated by the concentration of member families within walking distance, but the entire West Side was already showing signs of decline. By 1900 the neighborhood around First Reformed began to deteriorate rapidly. Already in 1895, the building had been burglarized and the clocks stolen. This prompted the

117. Ibid., 28 Oct. 1903, p. 689.

118. Ibid., 8 Apr. 1891, p. 11; 6 Jan. 1892, p. 10. The eleven-member site committee included S. J. Baar, E. Ter Maat, P. De Jong, W. Dykema, Rolf Engelsman, G. Eimers, H. Smith, Nick Knol, P. Ritzema, Peter Kelder, and Cor Brouwer. An obituary of Bloemendal is in *Minutes of the General Synod of the Reformed Church in America,* 1930, 603-04.

building committee to fence in the property and demand that the city police step up patrols, especially to quell disturbances out front during worship services.[119]

Well-to-do families soon began moving to the suburbs and selling their homes to newer ethnic groups – eastern European Jews and Roman Catholics. First Reformed Church had bought some time, but hardly more then two generations, before it would once again have to follow its members ever westward.

As Moerdyke observed despairingly:

> Our West Side neighborhood has been undergoing such radical changes in character of its population as to affect the churches very materially. . . . Several congregations of this vicinity are, therefore, vexed with the problems of existence, of support, of growth, of new methods. But Hebrews and Roman Catholics come to fill up this community, and methods seem futile.[120]

119. Moerdyke, "Chicago Letter," *CI,* 11 Sept. 1895, p. 9.
120. Ibid., 18 Jan. 1899, p. 9.

CHAPTER 4

Pulpit and Pew in the Heyday of the Groninger Hoek

The Ashland Avenue Dutch district remained the center of the Groninger Hoek for sixty years, and the churches were always the focal point of daily life. As the mother congregations reached maturity and the younger generation clamored for English-language worship, daughter churches were established. Sometimes this went smoothly, but often it did not.

First Christian Reformed Church, 1886-1910

Once the First Christian Reformed Church got past its shaky founding period and was well established, the body reached maturity under a run of able pastors. In 1886, after the bitter debate over relocation and a pulpit vacancy of two and a half years, the Reverend Willem Greve (1836-1906) happily returned for a second pastorate and restored the lost harmony. Greve came from a similar second pastorate in Cincinnati.

That Greve should be called to serve two congregations twice is a testimony to his gifts for ministry. In physical appearance he was clean shaven and stocky, as befitted his German blood (he was from Graafschap, Bentheim). Greve preached fluently in a clear strong voice, and his sermons were eminently practical and dealt with salvation as experienced. His theological training had been limited, and he stood in the pulpit in the years before expository preaching came into vogue.[1]

1. J. G. Vanden Bosch, "Willem Greve," *Reformed Journal* 10 (Jan. 1960): 19-21.

Growth continued at the First Christian Reformed Church of Chicago, despite the transfer of numerous families to the First Christian Reformed Church of Englewood in 1887. Seating was at a premium, and in 1893 the balcony was reconfigured to increase the capacity. The congregation weathered the depression of 1893-97, the so-called "Cleveland hard times," under the Groninger, Harm (Henry) Douwstra (1890-92), and the Frisian, Jan (John) Riemersma (1893-99).

Douwstra and Riemersma led the 14th Street congregation in taking very controversial steps without stumbling. Under Douwstra in 1891 a pipe organ was installed, and under Riemersma the Sunday school started English-language classes, and the congregation established a Christian school. On the organ issue, only thirty years earlier the Scottish Presbyterian church had gone through the throes of an "organ controversy," which pitted those wanting to make worship services more attractive to

Rev. John Riemersma (1857-1930)

the youth against those desiring to preserve "purity" of worship. Chicago's problem, remarkably, was more with its organ as an instrument than with the principle itself. The strong psalm-singing of the Hollanders so overpowered the organ that it had to be replaced with a more powerful model. The organ, the salesman averred lamely, was designed "to accompany the singing of four hundred people, not their shouting!"[2]

Within a month of Riemersma's arrival in January 1893, the consistory allowed the elementary-age Sunday school classes to switch from Dutch to English, because the children were no longer sufficiently proficient in the mother tongue. Riemersma also helped found the congregation's first Christian school in 1893. Morning classes were taught in Dutch, and afternoon subjects in English. Ebenezer Christian School opened on the cusp of the worst economic downturn of the nineteenth century, but the faithful congregants and teachers made heroic sacrifices to carry on. The deacons scheduled frequent collections for the "*suppletie* fund," a fund to help indigent parents pay tuition. To save money, the school moved into the church basement in 1895.

In 1901 a parent-controlled Christian school association took over the institution from the consistory. But the organization remained independent in name only; society members and church members were one and the same, and the clergy led both. The school thrived for the next forty years in a two-story brick building constructed in 1906 at 1626 West 15th Street. The history of Ebenezer Christian School is related in chapter 7.[3]

The decisions of 1893 clearly showed the press of Americanizing influences, but First Christian Reformed Church remained a "Holland congregation." The organ and language issues did not jeopardize the faith; therefore, accommodations could be made with the host culture. But establishing a Christian school was a proactive step to train covenantal youth for life as Reformed Christians in a hostile, secular society (chapter 7). This was a move rooted in the antithetical thinking of the Kuyperian revival in Dutch Calvinism (chapter 2), and it had major ramifications for the future direction of the Dutch community in Chicago. A separate school system would hold the threatening forces at bay and safeguard the children from a too-rapid adoption of alien American values. This shelter-

2. John S. Moir, "How Presbyterians dealt with introducing the organ," *Christian Courier*, 2 Jan. 1998, 12-13. The article only dealt with the Canadian Presbyterians, but the story was much the same south of the border. A Mr. De Koe became the first organist at the First Christian Reformed Church of Chicago (*Seventy-Fifth Anniversary, 1867-1942* [Chicago, 1942], 11-12).

3. "Historical Sketch of the Ebenezer Christian School," in Ebenezer Christian School, *Fiftieth Anniversary, 1893-1943* (Chicago, 1943).

ing aspect appealed to those in the pietist tradition, and the religion classes satisfied the doctrinalists.

In the 1890s, the Christian Reformed churches, including First Chicago, also debated whether to continue the Netherlandic custom of gathering for public worship again on the "second Christmas," "second Pentecost" or "Whitsunday," and "Second Easter," that is, the following day. But work schedules in an industrial age meant that, increasingly, the men could not attend on a Monday. Reformed churches had already dropped this custom, and the Christian Reformed would eventually follow suit, but not yet. There was no debate about the American custom of meeting for worship on Thanksgiving Day. All Reformed churches did so. They also held their annual congregational meetings on the afternoon of the holiday, because the men were free to attend. Only male confessing members could vote for office-bearers and adopt the new budget.[4]

In other ways, Riemersma reached out across the "big divide" to First Reformed Church. In 1894 his congregation took the unusual step of cosponsoring with First Reformed the Persian missionary Isaac Adams to work in his native land (present-day Iran). The program lasted for only one year, however, until Adams came home on furlough under charges of fraud, and First Reformed dropped its support. First Christian Reformed then took Adams under its wing, further educated him, and sent him back to the field. To this the Reverend Peter Moerdyke of Trinity Reformed Church and regular columnist for the *Christian Intelligencer* commented wryly: "Our own people and churches should now have the grace to exercise inter-denominational comity, and permit our sister Church to monopolize him and make him their own missionary, especially since in this line their hands are empty and ours are full." Thus did Moerdyke rebuke the Christian Reformed churches for their minimal foreign missions programs and at the same time dismiss Adams as a rotten egg.[5]

The Adams affair did not hinder continued cooperation between the two First churches. In 1895, when the Christian Reformed church's facilities were being repaired and remodeled, Riemersma encouraged his members to worship with the Reformed congregation. This unusual gesture so moved their new pastor, Rense H. Joldersma, that he opened his pulpit to Riemersma, "which was fraternally accepted." To this Joldersma's colleague Peter Moerdyke declared: "If mutual and reciprocal pulpit ex-

4. Peter Moerdyke, "Chicago Letter," *Christian Intelligencer* (hereafter *CI*), 1 Jan. 1896, p. 10; 30 Nov. 1904, p. 770.

5. Ibid., 11 Dec., p. 10; 25 Dec. 1895, p. 10.

changes could become the general practice out here, the cause of Christ would be materially promoted."[6] The two denominations cooperated in Chicago more than many other places, but pulpit exchanges never became the norm.

Riemersma's very effective leadership came to a calamitous conclusion after four years, due to alcoholism and adultery. His abuse of alcohol first came to public attention in December 1897, although he had confessed his guilt in the consistory room a number of times. After the morning worship service on December 12, when the Lord's Supper was celebrated, Riemersma drank so much of the Communion wine that he was visibly inebriated during the afternoon service. Most elders wanted to take immediate action, but the body was persuaded by Riemersma's supporters to give him another chance before invoking broader ecclesiastical procedures. Riemersma promised not to abuse alcohol again and agreed with the consistory's stipulation that, since his sin was public, he must confess it before the entire congregation. The pastor did so Sunday, the twenty-fourth of December, one day before Christmas.[7]

This decision did not quell the matter but rather, according to the consistory minutes, caused "great confusion and unrest in the congregation and also caused great consternation outside the church." This prompted the consistory, after further discussion among themselves and with Riemersma, to ask the consistory of the First Christian Reformed Church in Englewood to meet in a "double consistory." Here Riemersma dissembled and made excuses, and the body unanimously decided to ask the regional assembly (classis) to depose him. Meanwhile, the elders suspended him immediately and cut off his salary as of December 30, 1897.[8]

Moerdyke commented on the sad news in his weekly "Chicago Letter" in the *Christian Intelligencer:*

> An impressive object lesson on intemperance was recently given to the Hollanders of this region. After years of tippling, a prominent minister of the Chicago Holland Christian Reformed Church became enslaved to his drinking habits, was intoxicated on the Lord's Day, and is suspended. It is a painful and public scandal, by which the name of Christ and His Church will be blasphemed. Such a warning may, however, do good just where it is sorely needed.[9]

6. Ibid., 10 Apr. 1895, p. 10.
7. First Christian Reformed Church of Chicago, Minutes, 14 Dec. 1897.
8. Ibid., 27, 30 Dec. 1897.
9. *CI,* 5 Jan. 1898, p. 9.

Classis Illinois met in Roseland in January 1898, and decided to give Riemersma one more opportunity to repent and change his behavior. At a morning service conducted by the Reverend Lubbert Van Dellen of the First Englewood Christian Reformed Church, Riemersma was asked a specific set of questions composed by the classical committee, modeled after the form for the public confession of faith. He solemnly promised "with all my heart" to change and was allowed to lead the afternoon service.[10]

But the classical decision did not sit well at First Christian Reformed of Chicago. "The unhappy affair continues to disturb the congregation," Moerdyke reported, because a substantial minority "has lost faith in his usefulness among them." Riemersma proved them right. Four months after his reinstatement, he again preached "under the influence." This time, the classical councilor advised the consistory to ask for its pastor's resignation, which Riemersma submitted by letter. But no sooner did the consistory accept the resignation than Riemersma recanted and claimed the process was illegal. He even circulated a petition of support throughout the congregation. The matter landed in the lap of the classis again.[11]

While Classis Illinois equivocated, the final shoe dropped. In August 1899, a member of the congregation came to the consistory to accuse Riemersma of committing adultery with his wife during the past four months. Within a month, the classis met and deposed Riemersma for a minimum of six months because of his "lies, deceit, and dishonorable behavior — adultery and abuse of alcohol." Riemersma's actions had rocked the church for over a year and prompted a number of families living farther west to transfer their papers in 1899 to the newly formed Douglas Park church. Through it all, the consistory had acted with patience, forbearance, and grace.[12]

First Christian Reformed of Chicago set about to fill its pulpit, but for more than a year it received one *bedankje* ("letter of decline") after another. The reputation of the church had suffered, and prospective pastors were wary of the troubled congregation. The able William Heyns (1900-02)

10. First Christian Reformed Church of Chicago, Minutes, 21 Jan. 1898.

11. Moerdyke, "Chicago Letter," *CI,* 2 Feb. 1898, p. 9; First Christian Reformed Church of Chicago, Minutes, 24, 28 Apr. 1898.

12. First Christian Reformed Church of Chicago, Minutes, 2 June, 31 July, 31 Aug., 24 Sept. 1898. Riemersma moved to Sioux Center, Iowa, in July and soon began preaching in the First Christian Reformed Church there, whose pulpit was open. In 1902 this congregation called him, after he obtained a halfway reinstatement from Classis Illinois — to the pulpit but not to the denomination (ibid., 22 Apr., 11 May 1902; Moerdyke, "Chicago Letter," *CI,* 19 July 1899, p. 9).

finally agreed to come, and he brought much wisdom and a renewed sense of calm. But his tenure was cut short after eighteen months by an appointment as professor of practical theology at Calvin Theological Seminary, the denominational school.

The sturdy Evert Breen (1903-09) followed Heyns and brought an evangelistic spirit that boosted the Sunday school enrollment to 250 under superintendents Lambert Hofstra and then Henry Jacobsma. Hofstra also directed the "Singing Society" of fifty members.[13] From Breen's previous pastorate in northwestern Iowa, he had organized so many congregations in the region that he had earned the title, "Bishop of the West." In Chicago he found the Dutch living "like an island in a sea of Jews," whose friendship he cultivated as children of Abraham. Breen gained their respect and preached at the nondenominational Chicago Hebrew Mission, which was founded in 1887 to reach the sixty thousand Jews in Chicago's West Side ghetto.[14]

In the larger religious sphere, Breen was honored in 1904 to be elected president of the denominational synod. He edited the church periodical, *De Calvinist,* and was associate editor of *De Heidenwereld,* the precursor of the *Missionary Monthly.* Like many Christian Reformed clerics, he also promoted the National Christian Association, an anti-Masonic organization whose monthly organ was the *Christian Cynosure.* In 1906, the Chicago congregation eased its pastor's life by installing a telephone in the parsonage. But his parishioners could not protect him from being "touched" by a thief and having his "pocket lightened."[15]

13. Christian Reformed Church, *Jaarboekje,* 1900, 73; 1903, 64; 1907, 79.

14. The Christian Reformed Home Mission Board, through the agency of the Reverend John Fles, head of the Jewish Mission Board, contributed $500-2,500 annually to the mission. Breen preached regularly at the evening worship services and served on the board during his years in Chicago, along with Fles, Reformed Church cleric Cornelius Kuyper, and Simon Dekker of the Second Christian Reformed Church in Roseland and a well-to-do landlord. Both Fles and Kuyper were pastors of churches in Michigan. Dekker was also a member of the executive committee. Young men from Breen's congregation volunteered in the teaching ministry at the mission. In its first four years, the mission rented four different "reading rooms," on or near Halsted and 12th Streets. In 1892 the mission purchased a two-story brick building at 22 (new numbering 1425) W. Solon Place for its ministry. See Mrs. T. C. Rounds, "The Chicago Hebrew Mission," *Banner,* 1 Aug. 1907; 5 Feb. 1914; 25 Nov. 1915.

15. Henry Beets, "Rev. E. Breen Celebrates Twenty-five Years in the Ministry," *Banner,* 3 Sept. 1914; obituaries, Christian Reformed Church, *Yearbook,* 1922, 167-70; and *De Wachter,* 2 Feb. 1921; First Christian Reformed Church of Chicago, Minutes, 29 Nov. 1906; Moerdyke, "Chicago Letter," *CI,* 12 Sept. 1906, p. 592.

Trinity American Reformed Church

Trinity American Reformed Church grew out of a mission station founded by the Classis of Wisconsin for "the preservation of our own youth" in Chicago who were drifting into English-speaking churches. In 1885, the classis welcomed a request from several members of First Reformed and other evangelical churches, together with a "substantial number" of unchurched Dutch immigrants in the area, to found an English-speaking Reformed church. But First Chicago's leaders forestalled the classis for several years, much to the chagrin of the petitioners and the regional assembly.[16]

Finally, in March 1891, the "little band" won classical approval, but not the blessing of First Church, to organize as the Trinity Reformed Church. The classis wished to stem the loss of many "choice young friends and families" who felt "compelled to find homes in other denominations," mainly Presbyterian and Episcopalian. The Trinity congregation also provided a home for members of the defunct American (Second) Reformed Church, which stood in the same locale and had failed in 1876.[17]

The parting was not amicable. "Agitations of the last decade to organize a church such as ours were squelched by that, alas! too well-known opposition to change of language," reported the first pastor, Peter Moerdyke, who was installed in July, 1891. Yet, "in spite of opposition most bitter, in the face of threats, prophesies of evil, boycotting of mercantile leaders and such intimidating influences, our little bark is launched." The decision to "go English" took courage. Such families, said Moerdyke, are "discouraged, dissuaded, or, if they persist, branded by clannish people as 'ashamed of being Dutch,' etc. It really requires a brave heart to be a come outer," Moerdyke continued, and to "run the gauntlet" of petty criticism.[18]

One sore spot was that the progressives had first planned to open their mission near 16th Street, almost within sight of the planned reloca-

16. Classis of Wisconsin, Minutes, Art. 17, 14 Apr. 1885; 20 Apr. 1886, Art. 49; English translation by Nella Kennedy, A. C. Van Raalte Institute, Hope College.

17. Moerdyke, "Chicago Letter," *CI,* 18 Aug. 1894, p. 10. The eighteen charter members, all from either the First or Second Reformed church in Chicago, were Anthony Biemolt, Dr. David Birkhoff, William Broekema, Mr. and Mrs. Sievert Bus, Elizabeth Dimnent, Mr. and Mrs. John Doornbos, Charles W. Griggs, Nicholas Kelder, Mr. and Mrs. John Nanninga, Bessie Smith, Mr. and Mrs. Henry Smith, Sr., Minnie Stompe, Peter Ter Maat, and John Tilbuscher. Biemolt and Griggs were chosen as elders and Bus and Birkhoff as deacons (Trinity Reformed Church, *Twenty-Fifth Anniversary,* [Chicago, 1916], 13).

18. Moerdyke, "Chicago Letter," *CI,* 4 Dec. 1895, p. 14.

Trinity Reformed Church, erected 1892 *(Herrick Public Library, Holland, Michigan)*

tion site of the mother church around 14th Street and Ashland Avenue. Ultimately, Trinity built an edifice north of 12th Street, at 440 (new numbering 913) South Marshfield Avenue (one block west of Ashland) between Taylor and Polk Streets (figure 1.1, site 8). This was just a half mile west of the old Harrison Street church, but more than a mile from the new Ashland Avenue district; 12th Street, which served as a demarcation line, lay in between.

Trinity broke ground in November 1891 on a $16,000 brick building, 93 by 70 feet in size and designed to seat five hundred, with a Sunday school room in the rear. The beautiful Portland brown stone facade featured a copper cornice. The cornerstone ceremony took place in an impressive service on New Year's Day 1892, and the joyous "feast of dedication" followed in July.[19]

Meanwhile, Bernardus De Bey, who with his entire consistory had declared that they would "never agree" to the new church plant, tried to smooth troubled waters by inviting Trinity members to a union Thanksgiving Day service at the mother church in 1891. In the evening,

19. Ibid., 6 Jan. 1892, p. 9; Rev. S. Streng, "Classis of Illinois," ibid., 13 Jan. 1892, p. 11.

he hosted Moerdyke and his flock at the manse for "a feast of reason and a flow of soul. . . . It was an inspiring family reunion," Moerdyke noted happily.[20]

The *taal questie* ("language question") at the First Reformed Church was played out in every Reformed immigrant congregation between 1890 and 1930, to the consternation of the leaders. All had to deal with demands for bilingual worship services. While parents and grandparents clung to the mother tongue, the young people lost interest in it and threatened to vote with their feet if the church did not introduce an English service. A temporary solution was to spin off English-only daughter congregations like Trinity, but in the long run the mother churches also had to change. Ideally, an intergenerational agreement allowed the first generation immigrants to retain Dutch in the main morning service, while allowing the second generation to have an English service in the evening. Eventually, after the first generation died off, the order would be reversed. This agreement required both sides to "make haste slowly"; parents had to yield and children had to be patient. But many would do neither, and that caused innumerable problems.[21]

Moerdyke, Trinity's energetic pastor for its first sixteen years (1891-1907), gave the body much visibility by writing a regular column, entitled "Chicago Letter," in the denominational weekly, the *Christian Intelligencer.* A former professor of theology at Hope College, his ready acceptance of the American religious scene, coupled with a fearless mind and long tenure as stated clerk of the Particular Synod of Chicago, made him a force to be reckoned with in Chicago and in the denomination. Indeed, in his first eighteen months, the church grew from 22 to 100 members, and the Sunday night Christian Endeavor (C.E.) youth ministry reached 75. By 1894, 175 to 200 worshipers gathered twice a Sunday, and the flourishing Sunday school surpassed 200 students. In three and a half years, the membership had increased fivefold, and attendance rose sixfold.[22]

Yet, Trinity Church struggled to survive and required denomina-

20. Classis of Wisconsin, Minutes, 21 Aug. 1885, Art. 9; Moerdyke, "Chicago Letter," *CI,* 11 Nov., p. 11; 9 Dec. 1891, p. 11; 31 Aug. 1892, p. 11.

21. Rev. C. H. Post, "Holland or American – Which?" *CI,* 23 Apr. 1902, p. 268.

22. Moerdyke, "Chicago Letter, *CI,* 21 Mar., p. 11; 10 Oct., p. 11; 12 Dec. 1894, p. 11; 2 Sept. 1896, p. 9. To obtain copy for his informative weekly missives, which ran for sixteen years from 1891 to 1907, Moerdyke read half a dozen Dutch language newspapers, including Chicago's *Onze Toekomst, De Hope, De Grondwet,* and the *Leader* of Holland, Michigan, and *De Volksvriend* of Orange City; all denominational periodicals; classical and synodical reports and minutes; plus his extensive personal correspondence.

Rev. Peter Moerdyke (1845-1923) *(Herrick Public Library, Holland, Michigan)*

tional subsidies for years. Not a single member of Trinity Church "is rich or has money," said pastor Peter Moerdyke, and "very few . . . have any home or property of their own." They are the "hardworking poor" and "dependent on wages mostly." Yet, these young, blue-collar families met their church budget obligations faithfully.[23]

One of Trinity's leading elders was "Father" Arend De Roo, "a loyal and sterling officer" of "exemplary piety" who held office for more than forty years. Others were Anthony Biemolt, Sievert Bus, and clerk Harry Bierma. Nurse Effa Hofma, a daughter of the congregation and graduate

23. Ibid., 13 Mar. 1901, p. 169. Consistory members in 1916 included elders William Baar, Anthony Biemolt, E. Nienhuis, Henry Smith, and J. T. Cox, and deacons J. Engelsman, H. Mulder, John Nanninga, and C. H. Smith. The choral director was Henry Doornbos; organists were Anna Nanninga and Mary Smith (Trinity Reformed Church, *Twenty-Fifth Anniversary*).

of the Moody Bible Institute, went to the American Indian field in Arizona with her husband, the Reverend Andrew Vander Wagen, under the auspices of the Christian Reformed Home Mission Board. "She is well known for her ability and unusual consecration," noted pastor Moerdyke. Another son of the congregation to win future renown was Edward D. Dimnent, who became professor of Greek (1898-1946) and president (1918-31) of the denomination's liberal arts college, Hope College, in Holland, Michigan. The famed Hope chapel was named in his honor. Edward's father Daniel was for many years a stalwart leader in Chicago's First Reformed Church and, after 1892, in Trinity Church. Biemolt endowed a chair at Western Theological Seminary.[24]

The young Trinity congregation experienced a scare in early December of 1895, when the furnace overheated and a fire broke out in the church basement. But the fire department contained the blaze within an hour, and the damages of about $1,000 were limited mostly to smoke and water. The sanctuary was cleaned up and repainted within two weeks, just in time to proceed with the Christmas program and avoid disappointing the children. "Burned with fire but not consumed," declared Moerdyke thankfully in his weekly column. The total church indebtedness had been reduced to only $4,000 by this time.[25]

One high point in Moerdyke's tenure came at the outset with the Chicago Columbian Exposition in 1892-93. As the only English-language Dutch Reformed church on the West Side, Moerdyke used his weekly "Chicago Letter" columns in the denominational periodical to invite Eastern Reformed Church members to "worship with us" at our "thriving, progressive, active" Trinity Church. Moerdyke also took an active part in the "Reformed Headquarters" of the World's Fair, a free comfort station for Reformed visitors in the Siegel, Cooper & Co. Department Store on State Street.[26]

Moerdyke was an unabashed believer in America, and he particularly adored the Hollanders' own Theodore Roosevelt, who prided himself on his Dutch Reformed heritage. Roosevelt worshiped at the English-speaking Trinity Church a number of times, beginning in 1900 when, as

24. Moerdyke, "Chicago Letter," *CI,* 12 Dec. 1894, p. 11; 5 Feb., p. 9; 2 Sept., p. 9; 10 Oct. 1896, p. 9; 22 June 1898, p. 12; 10 Oct. 1900, p. 653; 13 Nov. 1901, p. 733; 15 Jan., p. 41; 17 Mar., p. 185; 28 May 1902, p. 349. De Roo died in 1905 at ninety years of age. He served as elder first at the Keokuk, Iowa, church until 1862, then at First Reformed of Chicago, and finally from 1891 at Trinity Church (obituary in ibid., 20 Sept. 1905, p. 604).

25. Ibid. 11 Dec., p. 10; 18 Dec., p. 10; 25 Dec. 1895, p. 10; 18 Mar. 1896, p. 10.

26. Ibid., 11 Jan., p. 14; 31 Mar., p. 11; 21 June 1893, p. 11.

governor of New York, he came unannounced and created more than a passing sensation. "His loyalty to his own Church delighted our people," said Moerdyke, who named Roosevelt an "honorary parishioner."[27]

On September 7, 1901, Roosevelt returned to Trinity Church as vice president of the United States, and this time Moerdyke asked him to deliver a sermon. The vice president obliged, giving a homily from the New Testament book of James on being doers of the Word and not hearers only. The day was fraught with emotion, because President William McKinley lay fatally injured in Washington at the hand of an anarchist assassin the day before. (McKinley died on the 14th.) No wonder Trinity Reformed became known as "Roosevelt's church."[28]

Moerdyke's report of the president's visit glows with pride:

> VICE-PRESIDENT Theodore Roosevelt was again most cordially welcomed as our occasional "parishioner" on last Sunday morning. The congregation of Trinity Church were anew confirmed in their admiration of our distinguished fellow-worshipper because of his loyalty to his own church, his manly declaration in the midst of public political life and friends that he is a Christian, and his charming humility in meeting with us and not seeking the sanctuaries of the wealthy or aristocratic.
>
> He had not forgotten his promise to preach a lay sermon at his next visit, and, upon our reminder, gave us a forty-minute address on being doers of the Word and not hearers only. It was marked by his characteristic strenuous and sound sense and plain, direct speech, and was received by a full house with decided satisfaction. After the service all gathered about him to honor and thank him, and to make his acquaintance. His attendance with us is never announced by him in the published program for the Lord's Day, since he wishes his movements during hours of worship to be "strictly private." At this sadly critical juncture, while the nation entreats the All-Ruler to spare our noble Chief Magistrate, there is relief, in the midst of a threatened blow, by reason of a possible successor so eminently qualified and deservedly popular.[29]

Moerdyke's pride in his lineage exceeded that of Roosevelt; Moerdyke was a Netherlander by birth. When the new Queen Wilhelmina was mar-

27. Ibid., 11 July, p. 445; 19 Sept., p. 605; 17 Oct. 1900, p. 669-70.
28. Trinity Reformed Church, *Twenty-Fifth Anniversary,* 13.
29. Moerdyke, "Chicago Letter," *CI,* 11 Sept. 1901, p. 589.

ried in 1901 to German Duke Heinrich, who became Prince Hendrik of the Netherlands, Moerdyke had the Ladies' Aid Society arrange a banquet at Trinity Church to celebrate the royal wedding with toasts and speeches by "able and ardent admirers of the Dutch." Three hundred guests came to hear *Onze Toekomst* editor Henry Uden Marsman, Chicago attorney Herman Vander Ploeg, and several clergymen. Elder George Birkhoff, Sr., of the Northwestern congregation paid a fine tribute on behalf of the queen. The event "was the most delightful gathering of Dutch American citizens we ever attended in this city," enthused Moerdyke.[30]

The future of Trinity Church looked less bright. Jews were flooding into the neighborhood and wanted to buy the sanctuary for a synagogue. By 1904, up to 90 percent of the neighbors were Jewish, Moerdyke noted. The familiar process of relocation was facing the congregation, because, said Moerdyke with some disgust, "this land of Canaan has become the conquest of the children of Israel. No fewer than five synagogues now occupy the ground where not one was found when we in 1891 built in what seemed the ideal spot for our work." In 1905, Trinity negotiated the sale of its building to a Hungarian Jewish congregation from the "ghetto." But the Jewish group, after signing a contract, broke it without notice and proceeded to build its synagogue on a nearby lot. So Trinity had no choice but to stay put; they even redecorated the sanctuary for $600.[31]

When the founding pastor left for the South Bend church in the spring of 1907, after sixteen years of excellent leadership in the congregation and as clerk of the regional synod, Trinity members felt some fear and trepidation. George Niemeyer of the nearby Northwestern church noted:

> Trinity Church of Chicago is perplexed but not discouraged. A congregational meeting for the free exchange of opinion was called. At this meeting unanimity prevailed; the members are unanimous in the conviction to carry on the work, and at an early date to call a new Pastor. Love and loyalty for this church is very strong, and they entertain the hope and expectation some time to see this church prosper and become strong.[32]

Reading between the lines, one senses foreboding about the future prospects of the church. Nevertheless, within months, the congregation

30. Ibid., 9 Jan., p. 26; 23 Jan., p. 57; 30 Jan., p. 73; 13 Feb. 1901, p. 101.

31. Ibid., 9 Mar. 1904, p. 153; 17 May, p. 315; 13 Sept. 1905, p. 586; 19 Oct. 1904, p. 670.

32. Ibid., 17 Apr., p. 249; 22 May 1907, p. 331.

managed to complete a two-year goal of being debt-free. At a special social hour, elder Biemolt held up his hands and shouted: "'Here are all the notes, all paid' . . . and the people applauded." They also moved promptly to call another pastor, but met with several letters of decline.[33]

Moerdyke's successors, John Van Peursem (1908-12) and Jacob Heemstra (1914-18), paled by comparison to him, although Heemstra had done graduate work at Princeton and the University of Chicago and later became a professor at Central College in Pella, Iowa. Despite its promising beginning, Trinity's light flamed only for twenty-eight brief years. English-language services and an ecumenical outreach were not sufficient in themselves to grow a church. The Chicago Dutch Reformed community was not ready for a high-brow, intellectual, "American-style" church such as Trinity aspired to be. Within a dozen years of Moerdyke's departure, in 1919, the congregation disbanded.[34]

Northwestern Reformed Church

Two years after Trinity began, in 1893, the remaining contingent of seventeen northside families at First Reformed, who still wanted Dutch services but were inconvenienced by its removal further south, transferred to the Northwestern Reformed Church on West Superior Street (750 north) between Robey Street and Hoyne Avenue (figure 1.1, site 9).

This influx pushed to capacity the 250-seat frame church, which had begun in 1870 as a Holland Presbyterian Church. A McCormick Seminary student, Emanuel Van Norden, had rounded up its sixteen members after several years of mission work under the Presbytery of Chicago. The Presbyterian Home Missionary Society paid $800 of the pastor's annual $1,000 salary, and a new church edifice was constructed on the corner of Noble and Erie Streets. Jacob Post succeeded Van Norden in 1873, and he induced the body to switch the evening service to the English language, which step attracted some non-Dutch worshipers. But it also split the

33. George Niemeyer, "Illinois Letter," ibid., 12 June 1907, p. 382.

34. Russell L. Gasero, ed., *Historical Directory* (Grand Rapids: Eerdmans, 2001), 512; Moerdyke, "Chicago Letter," *CI,* 29 Apr., p. 10; 3 June, pp. 10-11; 8 July, p. 11; 12 Aug. 1891, p. 11. Information on Moerdyke, Van Peursem, and Heemstra is in their obituaries in the *Minutes of the RCA,* 1924, 675-76; 1966, 308; 1959, 215-16. Moerdyke's home, a news center for Reformed church life in Chicago, stood at 689 (new numbering 1610) W. Harrison Street, until 1894, when he moved to 446 (new numbering 919) S. Marshfield Avenue, directly next door to the church.

congregation into Dutch and English factions, who worshiped separately and simply shared the same sanctuary. The Dutch continued to run the church and controlled all offices.[35]

When Post left in 1878, the struggling congregation sent a letter to the Wisconsin Classis of the Reformed Church in America, then meeting in Chicago, with a request to affiliate with it. The classis demurred, believing the body "does not seem to be viable at this time." The classis urged the congregation to review its plans and in 1881 appointed a committee to work with the congregation. But progress was slow. Meanwhile, various McCormick seminarians who could preach in Dutch filled the pulpit, notably the Reformed Church student Rense Joldersma in 1882-83.[36]

In December, 1884, the Reverend John Vanden Hook answered the call of the 235-member congregation. He managed to bridge the cultural division, and he led the congregation in 1892 into the Reformed Church. "Royally do we welcome . . . [the congregation's] return to the mother church," exclaimed Moerdyke. It was a "mistake" that they became Presbyterian in the first place.[37]

Theodore Zandstra was a leading elder in the early years, as was George Birkhoff, Sr. In 1886, P. Fisher was the Sunday school superintendent for nearly a hundred students.[38] After Vanden Hook left for Montana in 1896 for health reasons, the congregation had a succession of relatively short pastorates for fifteen years. For another decade, the classis assigned "stated supply" and finally "pulpit supply" to the dwindling body until it disbanded in 1926. The pastors, all Dutch-born but American-trained, were Seth Vander Werf (1896-99), Henry K. Boer (1900-02), Bernard De Jonge (1902-04), the genial George Niemeyer (1905-08), James

35. Alfred T. Andreas, *History of Chicago from the Earliest Period to the Present Time,* 3 vols. (Chicago: A. T. Andreas, 1884-1886), 3: 801. The congregation was part of the Presbyterian Church – United States of America, later United Presbyterian Church.

36. Classis of Wisconsin, Minutes, 16 Apr. 1879, Art. 8; 20 Apr., Art. 11; 21 Sept. 1881, Art. 8; 19 Apr. 1882, Art. 20.

37. Moerdyke, "Chicago Letter," *CI,* 27 Apr. 1892, p. 10; 1 Mar. 1893, p. 10.

38. On Zandstra, whose son and grandson became Reformed Church clergymen, see *Missionary Monthly* 59 (May 1945): 144. Zandstra in 1946 was the oldest living member of the Emmanuel Reformed Church in Roseland. Consistory members reelected in 1886 were a Mr. Swieringa as elder, a Mr. Mulder as deacon and treasurer, and E. Bierma as church warden. Because of the growth of the congregation, George Birkhoff was appointed as a fourth elder (report by member M. Van Kloot in *De Grondwet* [Holland, Michigan], 19 Jan. 1896). In 1910, elders of the sixty-family church were J. Zeilstra and L. Verschuur, and deacons were B. Fennema and J. Woltman. Nick Fisher was also a member (*Onze Toekomst,* 28 Oct., 23 Dec. 1910).

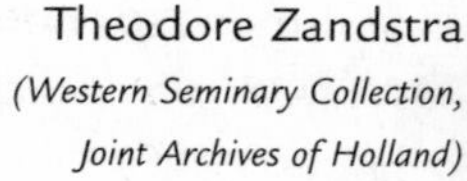

Theodore Zandstra
(Western Seminary Collection, Joint Archives of Holland)

Vander Heide (1911-14), and stated supply pastors W. Teeuwissen (1916-17) and John Huiser (1918).[39]

Vander Werf brought a brief flurry of enthusiasm and renewed growth; he heard thirteen confessions of faith in his first months and welcomed thirty new members. The next year another ten members joined. The growth forced the body to enlarge the seating capacity, and at the same time they replaced the "worn out little organ" at a cost of $300 and converted the oil lamps in the chandeliers to natural gas.

For another decade, under pastors Boer, De Jonge, and Niemeyer, the congregation carried on. Boer brought the body to organizational ma-

39. Obituaries of Boer, De Jonge, Niemeyer, and Van Der Heide are in *Minutes of the RCA,* 1914, 249-50; 1920, 274-75; 1952, 168-69; 1965, 283.

turity in 1902, when it was able to "get off the bottle" of denominational support and become self-supporting. When De Jonge came, the church was "prospering and full of hope," and under Niemeyer the body extensively repaired its facilities. But the pastorates were short, and the upward momentum could not be maintained. "This church is not strong," Moerdyke noted when reporting on Niemeyer's installation in 1906, but it is "loyal, pays the minister very promptly, keeps its property ever in finest condition, respects the pastor and his family, seeks peace, fills a place and performs a mission."[40]

Niemeyer conducted the first English-language service in 1907. The young people had donated a new Communion table, and upon its first use for the sacrament, the pastor spoke in English "for the benefit of a large element of young people, who are able to understand the services in this tongue only."[41]

Chicago's North Side became increasingly Jewish and Scandinavian; it never attracted many Dutch. So Northwestern Reformed, and its English-speaking sister congregations of Trinity, Norwood Park (organized in 1871), and Irving Park (organized in 1874), failed to grow. Norwood Park and Irving Park were Old Dutch congregations that became Presbyterian in 1916 and 1913, respectively, and Trinity disbanded in 1919. This ferment led a committee of the Classis of Chicago in 1925 to try again to organize a Reformed church on the North Side for unchurched Hollanders. But Classis concluded in 1930 after two years of fruitless work there by home missionary Rev. Herman Vander Ploeg that "no Macedonian call can be discerned even faintly," and limited funds could better be spent in other promising areas. In 1938 yet another Dutch Presbyterian Church was founded at Armitage and Hamlin Avenues.[42] A Holland Presbyterian church that P. Court Van Woerden, an Englewood physician and lay cleric, founded in 1913 on the South Side was also short-lived.

40. Moerdyke, "Chicago Letter," *CI,* 3 March 1893, p. 10; 27 May 1896, p. 9; 6 Jan., p. 8; 17 Feb. 1897, p. 8; 13 Apr. 1898, p. 9; 29 Mar. 1899, p. 14; 4 June 1902, p. 368; 27 Jan. 1904, p. 57; 15 Feb. 1905, p. 106; *De Grondwet,* 18 Jan. 1886; *Onze Toekomst,* 27 Apr. 1892; *De Hope,* 25 May 1904, p. 5.

41. Niemeyer, "Illinois Letter," *CI,* 12 June 1907, p. 382.

42. Classis of Chicago Minutes, April 1925, April 1930. Trinity, Northwestern, Norwood Park, and Irving Park churches were part of the American Classis of Illinois, as was Second Chicago (called American Reformed after 1870), which disbanded in 1880, and the short-lived (1872-78) Leyden Center congregation in Jefferson Township (near the present day University of Chicago). Gasero, *Historical Directory of the Reformed Church in America,* 305; Moerdyke, "Chicago Letter," *CI,* 23 Apr., p. 11; 4 June 1890, p. 9. Dutch Presbyterian churches are noted in the *Banner,* 26 June 1913, and in *Onze Toekomst,* 21 Mar. 1938. The Norwood Park Church had only one Dutch family in 1904, that of Herman Kelder, who

Hastings Street (First) Reformed Church, 1890s-1920s

The final service in the Harrison Street edifice, which had been the church home for nearly twenty-five years, took place on the evening of March 19, 1893. The highlight was the return of the Reverend De Bey, the revered former pastor, to present an historical overview of the church. The very next day, workers began transforming the building into a Mennonite hospital. For the next year, First Reformed worshiped in rented quarters ($40 per month) at Curran's Hall on Blue Island Avenue and 14th Street. Midweek meetings were held at another rented building on Henry Street for $13 per month.[43]

In a noteworthy change, the congregation voted during the transition to end the traditional practice of renting pews to meet the church budget. Henceforth, all pews would be "free" and contributions would be monitored by numbered envelopes. To take this step showed First Reformed's strength, since the free seat system was not popular among the immigrant congregations. That year, 1893, First Reformed Church took a special collection to pay for distributing Bibles at the World's Fair. The consistory also convened a meeting of all three Reformed churches in Chicago to deal with the overwhelming needs of poor Hollanders, due to the severe national depression. In a special collection, First Reformed raised more than $1,100 for relief.

Yet another ambitious decision was the launching of a monthly church newspaper, *De Boodschapper* (The Messenger), in August of 1893. It was "born out of need," said the first issue, to keep the hundreds of members informed about church life. It carried news articles, personals, obituaries, upcoming church programs and activities, and even several pages of block advertisements to pay for the venture. John Engelsman was the advertising director, Albert Klei the collector, and J. Esnorf the editor. The paper was distributed free to members of the congregation, but they and other readers were asked to contribute 50 cents per year.[44]

Although the nation was in the throes of a major depression, the Hastings Street congregation proceeded in faith with the construction of its new church. The cornerstone was laid on August 31, 1893, and the modern brick edifice, with seating for 650, was dedicated six months later, on

---

originally belonged to First Reformed Church of Chicago and then became a charter member of Trinity Reformed before joining Norwood Park in 1901 (Moerdyke, "Chicago Letter," *CI,* 20 Jan. 1904, p. 41).

43. Moerdyke, "Chicago Letter," *CI,* 29 Mar. 1893, p. 10.

44. The sole issue known to be extant is in the author's possession.

February 18, 1894. Ralph Bloemendal led both joyous services of music and praise. A Mrs. Vander Ploeg was hired to play the organ for the "feast of dedication," since her skills exceeded those of the regular organist. In the evening service, all of the Dutch Reformed ministers in Chicago participated, including John Riemersma of the Christian Reformed Church and the family of the late Bernardus De Bey, who had regrettably died only a week earlier. In 1896, the church built an elegant manse for $6,000 on the adjoining lot to the west. The relocation was complete.[45]

When Bloemendal took the helm of First Chicago, this "mother of many churches" stood at a crossroads, declared the editor of the *Christian Intelligencer.* "If centralization and Americanization from within, by gradual introduction, be the policy of the mother church, it may result only in disintegration." Bloemendal's challenge was to cling to the Dutch heritage and yet help the congregation adapt to its location in the heart of urban America. He and the consistory, led by veteran elder Abraham J. Van Persyn, met the challenge admirably. Under Bloemendal's pastorate (1891-95), said the *Intelligencer,* "this old church is renewing her youth. Prayer meetings, Sabbath-school, and catechetical classes have all the vigor of new life." Indeed, forty-six adults joined the church by confession in early 1892. In 1893, the congregation held its collective breath when Bloemendal took seriously ill and was laid up for three months.[46]

The First Reformed Church, whose membership peaked at eleven hundred souls in 1896, continued to thrive under Bloemendal's successors – the home missionary Rense Joldersma (1895-99), the renowned Henry Harmeling (1900-06), the Reformed church leader Nicholas Boer (1907-09), the persuasive preacher Henry P. Schuurman (1910-13), the evangelically minded Henry Schipper (1913-18), and the Dutch-born Marinus E. Broekstra (1918-29), who had earlier served the First Englewood Reformed Church (1905-08). But these able pastors could not prevent a gradual slippage in membership over the thirty years; from eleven hundred in 1896 to six hundred in 1929. The mother church, of course, had also given birth to several daughter churches.[47]

45. The "elegent Baptismal font," gifted by De Bey's children, graced the sanctuary from 1899. Moerdyke, "Chicago Letter," *CI,* 27 Sept. 1899, p. 8.

46. Ibid. 23 Sept. 1891, p. 11; 10 Mar. 1892, p. 11; 26 July 1893, p. 10; 19 Dec. 1894, p. 11; 1 July 1896, p. 9; 12 Feb. 1902, p. 105. Van Persyn died in 1902 at seventy-two years of age. He immigrated in 1856 and came to Chicago from New York City in the early 1880s.

47. The parsonage in these years was variously at 683 (new numbering 1702) S. Ashland Ave. (1894-95), 631 (new numbering 1530) S. Ashland Ave. (1896), and 195 (new numbering 1537) West Hastings St. (1897ff.).

Joldersma graduated from the Presbyterian McCormick Theological Seminary in Evanston, a town north of Chicago; Harmeling studied at New Brunswick Theological Seminary in New Jersey, the flagship of the Reformed denomination; and Broekstra attended the Theological School at Kampen in the Netherlands. The latter two, however, graduated from Western Theological Seminary in Holland, which served the western wing of the Reformed Church. Joldersma and Broekstra had taken their preseminary training on the same campus at the denomination's Hope College.

Joldersma took charge of a congregation in transition. It was committed to the process of Americanization and yet needed to welcome fresh immigrants or lose them to the rival Christian Reformed congregation down the street. To lead such a congregation "peacefully and healthily," said his colleague Moerdyke, "requires sagacity, tact, and force."[48]

Joldersma was equal to the task. Early in his tenure, he and the consistory had to deal with charges by various members that the denominational youth program, Christian Endeavor ("C.E." in popular parlance), was un-Reformed, i.e., Arminian. (Jacob Arminius [1560-1690] was a professor of theology at the University of Leiden, whose moderate predestinarian teachings were condemned at the National Synod of Dort, 1618-19.) The Christian Endeavor Society was a nondenominational American youth ministry founded in 1881 by a Congregational pastor. It became a big success, with 500,000 members in 7,000 local societies by the late 1880s. The Synod of the Reformed Church in America endorsed the program in 1888 and strongly recommended it to all pastors and churches. Each local chapter reflected the distinctiveness of its church and denomination. Nevertheless, the national C.E. program, with its focus on prayer meetings and missionary outreach, bore the unmistakable marks of American evangelicalism, rather than the traditional Reformed emphases on God's sovereignty and covenantal faithfulness.[49]

48. Moerdyke, "Chicago Letter," *CI*, 27 Feb. 1895, p. 11.

49. *Acts and Proceedings of the General Synod of the Protestant Dutch Reformed Church in America*, 1888, 569; 1890, 153. The 1890 proceedings state that C.E. is "markedly increasing throughout the denomination." Again in 1894, the Home Missions Board reported being "highly gratified with the effective work of the Christian Endeavor Missionary League of our Church during the past year; and that this excellent method of arousing and maintaining Missionary zeal be proposed for adoption to all our Young People's Societies." The Christian Endeavor Missionary League, founded in 1893, was the RCA arm of the C.E. movement. The General Synod declined to make the program mandatory but continued to push it. By 1900 almost every RCA congregation had a society (ibid, 1895, 191; 1896, 445;

The issue of C.E. festered for months at First Reformed. For a time the consistory considered disaffiliating, but finally the body reaffirmed its support of the program after one of its most prominent members, attorney George Birkhoff, Jr., Netherlands Consul General in Chicago, wrote a strong letter demanding continuing affiliation.

Joldersma pushed English-language preaching and, in 1898, he gained consistorial approval on a trial basis to deliver the Sunday evening sermon in English. This proved less than successful, however, and after a year the service was changed to an hour of prayer. The church also began a local mission outreach in Riverside, a truck-farming area west of the city. It asked Nick Knol to teach catechism at his home to children in this neighborhood and explored starting a Bible school there.[50]

First Reformed at this time also allowed a representative of the American Tract Society to speak in an evening worship service and take up a collection for the work. Another sign of acculturation was the decision to schedule a season of prayer with three evening sessions the first week and each Wednesday evening thereafter.[51]

The Sunday school also strongly supported mission outreach. The children were encouraged to put their pennies in jars, and once a year in the spring, a "jug-breaking" (*kruikjes breken*) service of celebration was held on a midweek evening. At the 1902 jar-breaking fest, the pennies totaled $1,000, making it a banner year. Customarily, about half that amount was tallied. Two-thirds of the monies went to support foreign missions and one-third funded Chicago projects, such as the Hebrew Mission, Tract Society, Bible Society, and the Cook County Sunday School Association.[52]

Joldersma left Chicago in August 1899, and Henry Harmeling soon took his place. Harmeling enjoyed the city and served four of its Reformed congregations: First Chicago, 1900-06; First South Holland,

---

1900, 824). For C.E.'s history and purpose, see Timothy P. Webber, "Christian Endeavor Society," 256-57, in *Dictionary of Christianity in America,* ed. Daniel G. Reid (Downers Grove: InterVarsity, 1990).

50. First Reformed Church of Chicago, Minutes, 5 Apr. 1898; Moerdyke, "Chicago Letter," *CI,* 27 Apr. 1898, p. 5.

51. First Reformed Church of Chicago, Minutes, 26 Mar., 24 Apr., 24 July 1900, 11 Dec. 1906; Timothy P. Weber, "Christian Endeavor Society," in *Dictionary of Christianity in America,* 256-57.

52. Moerdyke, "Chicago Letter," *CI,* 19 Apr. 1899, p. 9; 28 Jan. 1903, p. 56; John W. Brooks, "Chicago, Ill.," ibid., 3 Apr. 1907, p. 218; "Uit Chicago, Ill.," *De Hope,* 20 Apr. 1904, p. 5.

1906-09; First Roseland, 1921-29; and Archer Avenue, 1928-38. Twice he was elected president of the denomination's Particular Synod of Chicago, and he retired in the city and died there in 1946. Harmeling's pastorate at the First Reformed Church was marked by a great affliction, the death of his wife and newborn child in 1901. It also coincided with the South African Boers' "righteous" war for independence (1899-1902), when politically active members, again led by Birkhoff, assembled often in the church basement for rallies and fundraisers. The Dutch strongly condemned the British resort to force and prayed for victory by the Boers, their "beloved brethren and kindred in blood and faith" who fought for the "Lord's cause."[53] But the Dutch crusade and related relief effort for the Afrikaaners was very low key, compared to that of the Swedes, who at the same time mounted a very public campaign to save their compatriots famishing in the fatherland. "The Scandinavians here are, as a whole, a very valuable element and prosperous, and begin to assert and put themselves forward more and more from year to year," Moerdyke reported. "Their present relief effort is greatly encouraged by the press and people of the city. How different and quiet and churchly was the late relief effort of the Hollanders in behalf of the Dutch in South Africa. In that movement there was little, if any *display* of benevolence."[54]

In church business, Harmeling and the consistory managed to reduce the property debt of $10,000 by 30 percent, after canvassing the congregation around Thanksgiving Day and selling several building lots no longer needed. Economic good times had returned after the harsh depression of the 1890s, and the members were now able to put church finances on a surer footing. The congregation also repaired and redecorated its sanctuary for $800, "which was cheerfully contributed by the people."[55]

Harmeling resigned late in 1906 to pastor the First South Holland congregation, although "his people were very loath to let him go." First Chicago then called the Reverend Nicholas Boer of Grand Rapids at a salary of $1,200 per year, with four weeks vacation. He must preach three times – morning and afternoon services in Dutch and the evening service in English. Boer declined the call, which shocked the congregation because he was the first minister to do so in its fifty-year history. This record was most exceptional indeed. Three months later, the congregation re-

53. Moerdyke, "Chicago Letter," *CI*, 9 May 1900, p. 302; 13 Sept., p. 12; 20 Sept. 1899, p. 9; 18 Apr. 1900, p. 268; 31 July 1901, p. 492.

54. Ibid., 25 Feb. 1903, p. 127.

55. Ibid., 13 Nov. 1901, p. 733; 1 Jan. 1902, p. 10; 9 Dec. 1903, p. 806.

Rev. Henry Harmeling (1864-1946)

solved to ask him again, and this time Boer accepted. The grateful members welcomed him enthusiastically; they spruced up the parsonage and even installed a telephone! But his short tenure of only thirty months was a big disappointment and hardly warranted the expense.[56]

Boer's legacy was one of quiet support for the local Christian day school, Ebenezer, even though most youth in the congregation attended Clark Public School on Ashland Avenue at Hastings Street. First Reformed began scheduling collections for Ebenezer, allowed graduation exercises to be held in the auditorium on occasion, and opened the church for "propaganda" meetings by Christian school advocates in the Reformed Church, such as Western Theological Seminary professor Nicholas Steffens, a neo-Kuyperian.[57]

56. Ibid., 7 Nov., p. 721, 26 Dec. 1906, p. 849; George Niemeyer, "Illinois Letter," ibid., 22 May 1907, p. 331; First Reformed Church of Chicago, Minutes, 14, 26 May 1907.

57. First Reformed Church of Chicago, Minutes, 30 Nov. 1915; James D. Bratt, *Dutch Calvinism in Modern America: A History of a Conservative Subculture* (Grand Rapids: Eerdmans,

Henry Schuurman of Iowa followed Boer in 1910, after also declining the first call and accepting the second three months later. First Chicago would simply not take no for an answer! The church raised Schuurman's salary 16 percent to $1,400, plus free coal for the parsonage, reimbursement for his life insurance premium of $20, and the promise to pay for pulpit supply if the workload became too heavy. Besides preaching three times on Sunday, the pastor had to teach catechism, lead societies and the midweek prayer service, and assist the elders in annual family visitations. Once in office, Schuurman realized that the congregation was too large for him to make annual rounds, so the membership was divided into six districts, and the elders had to carry more of the load.

It was also on Schuurman's watch that church members living on the far west side successfully pushed for the organization of a new congregation in Cicero, which cost the congregation more than thirty of its families. That the birthing of West Side Reformed Church (discussed below) occurred with minimal friction is a testimony to the spiritual health of the body.

But this development only speeded up the decline of the mother church, which was fighting urban blight. In fact, the consistory in 1912 sent a delegation to the First Christian Reformed Church to discuss the problem of the many saloons in the neighborhood, whose inebriated patrons caused disturbances during Sunday evening worship services. The two bodies sent a joint petition to the city council demanding that the police keep the peace on Sundays. They even considered deputizing some of their members as private security guards. Schuurman departed in 1913 for the South Holland congregation, just as the consistory had to deal with four members who admitted belonging to the Masonic Lodge and saw no sin in this.[58] After discussing the issue at length and reaffirming the church's stand against secret societies, teams of elders met with each of the lodge members. In every case, the recalcitrants chose the lodge over the church and resigned or were excommunicated.

Recruiting members from among the two thousand Holland-American families living in the five West Side wards that surrounded the First Reformed Church was a challenge shared by the other two Reformed

1984), 46, 60. In 1916, First Reformed scheduled four collections per year for Ebenezer Christian School. How many children of the congregation attended is not yet known, but the Mulder and Evenhouse families sent their children. Interview by the author with former members Dick Blaauw and Robert Vander Velde (since deceased), Hudsonville, Michigan, 10 Mar. 1998.

58. First Reformed Church of Chicago, Minutes, 12 Aug., 26 Sept. 1912; 1 Mar. 1913.

and three Christian Reformed churches in the area. Together, the six congregations numbered seven hundred families, and nine hundred families attended other congregations, including Roman Catholic and Jewish. This left four hundred Dutch-American families with no religious affiliation. Clearly, the mission field was teeming on the West Side, especially for the two English-speaking churches.[59]

Under Schuurman's successor, Henry Schipper (1913-18), the Hasting Street Church made the transition from Dutch to English as the primary language. Schipper, who grew up in Grand Rapids and served three South Dakota churches before coming to Chicago, guided the congregation "into further paths of Americanization" during the patriotic First World War. In early 1915, the church switched the primary morning service and all catechism classes to English. In 1918, it also introduced English in the afternoon service every other week, which in effect reduced Dutch services to two times a month. This momentous change, according to a classical report, in what must have been the understatement of the year, "slightly ruffled the calm" of the congregation.[60]

Schipper supported the war effort from the pulpit, which led one member to protest by walking out during the service because, as the consistory minutes note, he "did not want to hear any preaching about the War." The elders rebuked him for humiliating Pastor Schipper, but he insisted that the pastor's remarks were inappropriate. In an unrelated procedural matter, the consistory decided regarding infant baptism that when only one parent is a confessing member, that parent will present the child. Ordinarily, however, the father presented the infant within a few weeks of birth, while the mother was still recuperating at home, in the Dutch practice known as *vroeg doop* ("early baptism"). The consistory graciously honored David Groeneveld at the conclusion of thirty-five years of leadership, seventeen as deacon and eighteen as elder; and the body gave full approbation to the church choral society, "Concordia."[61]

59. The figure of two thousand families in 1913 was calculated by an anonymous member of the Twelfth Street Christian Reformed Church, based on the Chicago school census of 1912, which counted 5,774 pupils of Dutch birth or ancestry. Estimating three pupils per family (a low estimate) gives the number of families as 1,925. How the estimate of nine hundred families who were affiliated with "other denominations" was calculated is not known, but it appears to be reasonable. See "Twelfth Street Christian Reformed Church, Chicago," *Banner,* 27 Mar. 1913, p. 205.

60. Gasero, *Historical Directory,* 342, 350; Reformed Church in America, *Minutes of the Particular Synod of Chicago,* 1-2 May 1918, 7.

61. First Reformed Church of Chicago, Minutes, 15 Sept., 17 Nov. 1914; 16 Mar. 1915; 2

To modernize its facilities, the congregation borrowed several thousand dollars to put toilets in the twenty-year-old church and parsonage, as well as to wire the parsonage for electricity and to install a gas water heater so the pastor's family could draw warm bath water. This was a big step up for the Schipper family, after the years of privations in South Dakota. To protect the improved properties, the consistory increased its fire insurance policy to $25,000. First Reformed was clearly progressing as it celebrated its sixtieth anniversary!

Marinus Broekstra, formerly of First Englewood Reformed Church (1905-08), welcomed the soldier "boys" home from the war and led First Reformed in the "roaring twenties" (1918-29). In contrast to Schipper, he preached in fluent Dutch and loved to sing the Dutch psalms in worship, but his ministry did little to hold back the process of acculturation. In 1919, the appreciative congregation took the very American step of buying a car for his use. Did Dominie Broekstra drive a Model T? The car created an unanticipated problem – the alley behind the parsonage had to be improved to accommodate the vehicle.

In other concessions to modern ways, the congregation substituted plates for the offering "sacks" at the end of long poles, allowed women members to vote in congregational meetings, and deacons to come to the front of the church for a pastoral prayer before the collection. The churches also appointed a "reception committee" for morning worship services to "look out for strangers . . . [and] to shake hands," and switched to English for the New Year's Eve service in 1921. And in keeping with the more relaxed atmosphere of the postwar era, the elders decided "for the time being" to suspend the exercise of discipline, but within months they began visiting delinquents to give them a six-week grace period to return to worship or risk termination of their memberships.[62]

Immigrants continued to arrive from the Netherlands in the 1890-1920 decades, sometimes in groups of seventy-five to a hundred, and First Christian Reformed gathered most of them in by offering more Dutch *gezelligheid* than could First Reformed. "The pastor of the Seceders is commendably prompt and zealous to welcome these strangers," admitted Moerdyke, "and he is gathering nearly all that kind of material into

---

Feb., 31 July 1, 3 Oct., 19 Dec. 1917; 20 Nov. 1918; First Reformed Church of Chicago, *Century for Christ,* 5, 7; *Minutes of the RCA,* 1913, 893-94; 1934, 735; 1936, 441; 1940, 565; 1947, 188-89.

62. First Reformed Church of Chicago, Minutes, 16 Sept. 1919; 23 Oct. 1921, 25 Nov. 1930. In a concession to the old timers, the New Year's Eve service of 1923 was again in Dutch (Minutes, 8 Sept. 1922).

his church, where they find a really Holland congregation, and feel at home."[63]

Many immigrants also drifted away from their religious heritage. The most important home mission project of the Chicago pastors and consistories was one they could do only with great difficulty – to seek out the many compatriots who lived in religious indifference or attended American churches with English preaching. This, at least, was the opinion expressed in 1913 by a Christian Reformed leader in the denominational weekly, the *Banner.* He rightly observed that pastors and elders who had to nurture the spiritual life of five hundred to one thousand members, which was common in Chicago-area churches, were so overburdened by the routine of running church programs, making regular family visits, and dealing with numerous discipline cases, that they could not adequately tend to stragglers.[64]

By the 1920s, First Reformed considered relocating farther west. The edge of the black ghetto had reached Ashland Avenue from the east by this time. In 1923 the matter came up directly, because the newly organized Fourth Christian Reformed Church (see below) needed facilities. First Reformed offered to sell its Hastings Street building for $50,000, provided the congregation could use it for another three to five years. Peter Woldman, Fred Mulder, and John Medendorp represented First Reformed to negotiate with their counterparts of Fourth Church, James De Boer and George Ottenhoff.

The Fourth Christian Reformed Church consistory tentatively accepted the offer, but the deal fell through because the buyer set two conditions – first, to use the church jointly and share expenses in the interim, and second, to gain possession of the parsonage within six weeks of the sale. First Reformed did not wish to share their church building or give immediate possession of the parsonage, since the Broekstra family still occupied it. The church did talk of relocating just inside the border of Cicero in the target area of 49th Avenue between 16th and 22nd Streets, but this idea became moot when Fourth Church withdrew its offer and built a church and parsonage elsewhere. First Reformed remained in the Hastings Street facility for another twenty-two years, until 1945.

63. Moerdyke, "Chicago Letter," *CI,* 25 May 1892, p. 11.

64. "Chicago Letter," *Banner,* 26 June 1913.

Douglas Park Christian Reformed Church, 1899-1927

The more affluent families in the Ashland Avenue district continued the pattern of moving into newer neighborhoods with more open spaces and larger lots. Some went south of the vast Chicago Union Stockyards to Englewood (1880s) and southwest to Summit (1890s), but most went into the adjacent Douglas Park–Lawndale district, then called the "Far West Side," which became the third Calvinist enclave.[65]

This district of tree-lined streets, boulevards, and the city-owned Douglas Park ran west from Western (2400 west) to Cicero (4800 west) Avenues and ranged between 12th and 16th streets. Douglas Park anchored the east part and Lawndale the west part, with Kedzie Avenue the demarcation line. The area boasted Timothy Christian School (1911) and three Christian Reformed churches – Douglas Park (1899), Third (1912), and Fourth (1923).

Douglas Park was very much a Dutch church; its official name said as much: "Douglas Park Hollandsch Christelijke Gereformeerde Gemeente," which the *scriba* ("clerk") conveniently wrote as "D.P.H.C.G.G." The rationale for forming the congregation was the concern that the young people might "drift away from the church," because the Old Fourteenth Street Church was too far away for the youth to participate in midweek catechism and society life. The same thinking drew to Douglas Park Church some families from First Reformed who lived nearby. For the first fifteen years after its founding in 1899, Douglas Park was bound by a territorial agreement laid down by the mother church, First Christian Reformed, that it would only recruit families living west of Western Avenue (2400 west).[66]

The first consistory included elders Hendrik Bulthuis, Roelf Dykhuis, and Roelf Tinge, and deacons Freerk Brands, George Slager, and Martin Hoekstra. Bulthuis was elected chair and also named Sunday school superintendent, which placed a big load on his shoulders until the installation of the first pastor, the Reverend Frank Welandt (1899-1905). Before emigrating, Welandt had joined the Christian Seceded Church in Groningen and studied at the Theological Seminary at Kampen. His starting salary in Chicago was $500, plus the use of the parsonage, free fuel, and stable rental for his horse. This stoutly orthodox congregation

65. William Dryfhout, "Chicago's 'Far West Siders' in the 1920s," *Origins* 9, No. 2 (1991): 18-22.

66. "Douglas Park Christian Reformed Church, Chicago, Illinois," *Banner,* 29 Apr. 1909; "Report of Classis Illinois," ibid., 6 Feb. 1913. *Warren Park Christian Reformed Church, Golden Anniversary, 1899-1949* (Cicero, 1949), 4-9, 32.

First Consistory, Douglas Park Christian Reformed Church, 1899
l-r, seated: Freerk (Fred) Brands, deacon; Rev. Frank Welandt; Hendrik (Henry) Bulthuis, elder; standing: George Slager, deacon; Roelf (Ralph) Dykhuis, elder; Roelf (Ralph) Tinge, elder; Martin Hoekstra, deacon

met a real need and quickly grew to five hundred members during Welandt's six years.[67]

After worshiping eighteen months in a store at 1732 (now 3410) West 12th Street, near Homan Avenue, the Douglas Park church in September 1900 dedicated a new brick edifice on a triple lot at 1329 South Harding Avenue (3932 west) (figure 1.1, site 10). To cover the costs beyond funds on hand, the consistory borrowed $3,500 from the Holland Building and Loan Association of Chicago at 7 percent interest. A number of Reformed and Christian Reformed clerics spoke at the joyous Sunday evening service of dedication. The most touching moment in the otherwise solemn occasion came when Welandt paid tribute to "a mother in Israel" who was closely related to some fifty fellow members of the congregation and who was present that day in good health and a thankful heart on her seventy-eighth birthday! It was a nice touch and also showed the clannish nature of Dutch immigrant church life.[68]

The congregation next constructed a parsonage next door to the church. The two buildings and lots together cost $13,000. Taking on this

67. "1883 – Rev. F. Welandt – 1923," *Banner,* 1 Nov. 1923; J. J. Weersing, "Rev. F. Welandt," obituaries, ibid., 13 Jan., 3 Feb. 1938.

68. Unfortunately, Moerdyke did not name the woman. Moerdyke, "Chicago Letter," *CI,* 3 Oct. 1900, p. 636; Douglas Park Christian Reformed Church, Minutes, 24 Sept. 1900.

debt required a step of faith, because the consistory minutes report that at the end of 1899, cash on hand totaled only $51.26. At one point, Roelf Dykhuis had loaned the church $18.92 to meet its obligations. He also took care of the church sign and made sure that the horse stables were well secured. Member Jan Vander Mei was hired as a "silent" policeman to safeguard the properties and the worshipers. The consistory delegated elder Bulthuis and pastor Welandt to attend the spring session of Classis Illinois in 1902, with the express request that Bulthuis ask classis to judge whether he violated the Christian Sabbath by slaughtering pigs on Sunday, March 2. The elders claimed this was true, but when Bulthuis demurred, they did not want to pass judgment on their leading elder, so the decision was handed to the classis, which body concurred. Bulthuis would not repeat the deed.

Since pipe organs had become the norm in the Dutch Reformed churches, Douglas Park in 1901 installed the "king of instruments" to lead the psalm-singing. Lambert Dykhuis, elder Roelf's son, was paid a stipend of $10 per year to be the regular organist. For a time he shared the console with pastor Welandt's two daughters. The singing society of fifty members, "Harmonia Christiana," directed by G. Dekker, was forbidden to participate in worship, under a 1904 synod ruling. It might be detrimental to congregational singing and a form of self-glorification for the musicians.

Douglas Park Christian Reformed Church, erected 1899, with parsonage, person unknown

The congregation enjoyed the concerts nonetheless, such as the performance of the sacred choral cantata, *Bethlehem,* on Christmas Day of 1911. The congregation's "Excelsior Brass Band" performed every Thanksgiving evening and gave concerts in area churches throughout the year; all collections went to support the local Timothy Christian School.[69]

The recollections of Mrs. Harmina Doot (nee Bos), a progressive daughter of the congregation whose father spearheaded the founding of the Third Christian Reformed Church (see below), recalls the staid style of worship services:

> The Dutch speaking Douglas Park Church had two rows of benches on either side of the minister, where the consistory members sat facing the congregation. When the minister got up to say his long prayer, the consistory members in their dark suits stood with him. There was no choir in those days because such singing was seen as self-glorification. There were three services on Sunday, each ninety minutes long.
>
> Many of the westsiders were laborers, teamsters, and worked very hard during the week. Clothing material was heavy, pews were crowded, sermons were long, buildings poorly ventilated; not surprisingly, some heads nodded, sonorous breathing was heard. To combat this, with the absence of speech amplifying devices, "dominies" often tended to orate at higher decibel levels. Pounding the pulpit was used to emphasize a point and to arouse the audience's attention level above that of semi-slumbering agreement.[70]

The demeanor of the consistory had the same impact on Mrs. Martha (Cornelius) Kickert as it did on Doot. "One memory I have of the Douglas Park church," Kickert recalled, "was of the two rows of the consistory members who stood to the right and left of the minister when he preached his long prayer. They were very awesome in their dark suits and somber faces. Religion in those days, I believe, was a fearsome thing."[71]

The all-time favorite psalm from the Dutch Psalter was Psalm 68, verse 10:

69. Warren Park Christian Reformed Church, *Golden Anniversary,* 6, 10; Moerdyke, "Chicago Letter," *CI,* 19 Sept. 1900, p. 605; Christian Reformed Church, *Jaarboekje,* 1906, 29; "Douglas Park, Chicago," *Banner,* 12 Jan. 1911.

70. Harmina Doot memoirs, quoted in Lombard Christian Reformed Church, *Celebrating Seventy-Five Years, October 9, 1987* (Lombard, Ill., 1987), 3. Doot was a daughter of elder Jacob Bos.

71. Mrs. Cornelius Kickert, "Last Meeting at Coffee Hour at Cicero I Church – 1976," typescript manuscript, p. 2, Archives, Calvin College.

Geloofd zij God met diepst ontzag!
Hij overlaadt ons, dag aan dag,
Met zijne gunstbewijzen: Die God is onze zaligheid!
Wie zou die hoogste Majesteit
Dan niet met eerbied prijzen?

An English translation of this psalm by the Reverend Benjamin Essenburg reads as follows:

Let God be praised with reverence deep;
He daily comes our lives to steep
In bounties freely given.
God cares for us; our God is He;
Who would not fear His majesty?[72]

Spiritual oversight of the congregation fell primarily to the elders, who took their office very seriously. Clerks reported in tedious detail the discussions and decisions of the consistory, and the handwritten minute books are replete with reports about "slackers." Some unfaithful members gave as their excuse the fact that the church lacked ventilation. Elders trudged through the mud to the house of another delinquent member only to be met at the door with a string of invective.[73]

In 1913, members elected to this august body were elders Henry Bulthuis, Fred Brands, and Roelf Dykhuis, and deacons Klaas Veldman, John Van Slooten, and Edward Swierenga. Elections of officers and adoption of the budget always took place in the afternoon of Thanksgiving Day, when all the men were free to attend. Dykhuis did not finish his term; death took him unexpectedly in 1914, leaving a widow and twelve children![74]

That Welandt was much loved at Douglas Park was demonstrated after his wife, the mother of his four children, died in 1903 and he remarried the next year at age fifty-four. The joyous congregation greeted the returning newlyweds with a special social at the church, which was newly decorated for the occasion. The young people's society composed a cheery welcome song, and the surprised couple was given several costly gifts. An

72. Only the first lines are quoted here. The entire verse 10 is in the Ebenezer Christian Reformed Church, *Centennial Booklet,* 23.

73. Warren Park Christian Reformed Church, *Golden Anniversary,* 10.

74. Four Dykhuis children were married when their father died. "Douglas Park, Chicago, Notes," *Banner,* 4 Jan., 4 Dec. 1913, 25 June 1914. Dykhuis was a paternal great-grandfather of the author.

Favorite Dutch Psalm Verse (Ps. 68:10) translated by Rev. Benjamin Essenburg

A DUTCH PSALM VERSE

Probably the all-time favorite of the Dutch psalmsinging congregations was Ps. 68, verse 10. We print it here in the original:

The English translation of this verse, listed as stanza five of number 124 in our Psalter Hymnal, was made in 1931 by the Rev. B. Essenburg, who was our pastor at the time:

Let God be praised with reverence deep;
He daily comes our lives to steep
In bounties freely given.
God cares for us, our God is He;
Who would not fear his majesty?
In earth as well as heaven?
Our God upholds us in the strife;
To us He grants eternal life,
And saves from desolation.
He hears the needy when they cry,
He saves their souls when death draws nigh,
This God is our salvation.

elder happily noted how good it was for the people to see a wife in the manse again, "a privilege we did without for so long." It was a moving moment and gave evidence of the affection toward Welandt and the spirit of love and unity in the congregation.[75]

75. "From Douglas Park, Chicago," *De Grondwet,* 2 Aug. 1904, trans. Huug van den Dool; "1883 – Rev. F. Welandt – 1923."

Just before Welandt departed in 1905 for a new charge in Sheboygan, Wisconsin, Douglas Park dedicated a new $1,500 organ in a special service of praise. The mother church had not yet taken this expensive and somewhat controversial step, which shows the progressive spirit of the daughter congregation. Similarly, Douglas Park invited as speakers the ministers from First and Trinity Reformed churches, Henry Harmeling and Peter Moerdyke. This reaching out "across the divide," which the congregation had also done five years earlier at its building dedication, reflected the ecumenical spirit among the Reformed folk in Chicago.[76]

The language issue also surfaced for the first time just before Welandt's departure. Elders Nick Knol, George Slager, and Omke Groot and their wives came to the consistory and asked for permission to send their children to an English Sunday school in a nearby church. They likely had in mind Trinity American Reformed Church. This request by several leading elders demanded a clear and unambiguous response by the consistory. It decided at the next month's meeting, upon the recommendation of the committee of pastor Welandt and elder Roelf Dykhuis, that it was "not good to send their children to a Sunday school outside our church." When some parents did so anyway, the consistory asked Classis Illinois for advice. It affirmed that the decision was correct, so the consistory held firm.

Nick Knol also crossed swords with the consistory over his unilateral decision as leader of the Young Men's Society to allow the use of English-language Bibles. The consistory charged that Knol had "humiliated" them by acting without first obtaining permission. When he received the reprimand, Knol threw the letter in the street. Since he and his young charges would not yield, the consistory removed Knol and censured him and barred the young men from meeting on church premises. The young men demanded that Knol be reinstated as their leader, and several allies of Knol in the congregation threatened to bring their complaint to the classis. After more ugly confrontations, with elder Roelf Dykhuis caught in the middle and estranged from the rest of the consistory, the two sides softened and then made peace. Knol was reinstated as the leader. In the end, the young men forced the consistory to back down. The conflict roiled the congregation for nearly three years, 1904-06, and was a harbinger of future conflicts involving the Young Men's Societies (see chapter 8).[77]

76. Moerdyke, "Chicago Letter," *CI,* 22 Mar., p. 185; 29 Mar. 1905, p. 202.

77. Douglas Park Christian Reformed Church, Minutes, 27 Feb. Art. 12; 27 Mar., Art. 2-3; 23 Apr. 1905, Art. 4, 7.

The continuing language struggles at Douglas Park show that the second generation was Americanizing rapidly and pressuring their parents for English-language teaching. It was an issue that could not be avoided, only postponed until the pressure became intolerable.

Candidate Cornelius De Leeuw followed Welandt in the years 1905 to 1910, and then Jacob Manni (1910-16) and the revered John O. Vos (1917-26). De Leeuw, a shy but wise counselor, came from Princeton Theological Seminary, where he earned a Bachelor of Divinity Degree after finishing studies at Calvin Seminary.[78] De Leeuw's salary *(tractement)* was $800, or $67 per month. Since a day laborer was then happy to earn $2 per day or $50 per month, the dominie's salary reflected his honored position. Members pledged their tithes for the church budget, and every three months the elders and deacons, and later only the deacons, made the rounds to collect what was treated as a debt. Ex-members who moved out of state or returned to the Netherlands and left an unpaid tithe could expect a letter to follow.

Jacob Manni graduated with Evert Breen (1863-1921) from Calvin Seminary in 1889 in a class of two, the smallest ever. Just before entering the seminary, Manni's home congregation in Grand Rapids had gone through the turmoil of seceding from the Reformed Church over the issue of Freemasonry, which deepened his devotion to the Christian Reformed Church. He was a fearless man with common sense, business smarts, and the gift of administration, who aligned himself with the progressive wing of the denomination by pushing mission outreach and the change to English. Douglas Park was his sixth charge, and he accepted it after turning down fourteen calls while serving the East Saugatuck, Michigan, congregation. Clearly, he was at the height of his considerable powers in 1910, both in the pulpit and in leadership roles in the denomination.

Manni was delegated to *every* denominational synod during his forty-six years of active ministry, except for a time of serious illness around 1900. The synod in 1914 chose him as president for the third time. For years, he also served on the board of Calvin College and Seminary, for a considerable time as president. He wrote editorials for the denominational weekly, *De Wachter,* and the church periodicals *De Calvinist* and *Gereformeerde Amerikaan,* and contributed a regular "Chicago Letter" to keep *Banner* readers abreast of local church news. Both in Muskegon and Chicago, Manni used his considerable leadership skills to promote the or-

78. See De Leeuw obituaries, *Banner,* 17 Aug. 1963, and Christian Reformed Church, *Yearbook,* 1964.

ganization of English-speaking daughter congregations. In Breen and Manni the Groninger Hoek boasted two of the most powerful churchmen in the denomination.[79]

Manni helped resolve the pressure for English at Douglas Park and at the Fourteenth Street Church by leading an effort to start the first "American" congregation among the Christian Reformed. During a two-year period from 1910 to 1912, in a series of cautious steps coordinated by committees of the two mother congregations, the Third Christian Reformed Church of Chicago was launched (see below). Although thirty families transferred from Douglas Park, its membership held steady at 675 souls, "nearly without exception all of Groninger descent," and the tithes and offerings easily met Manni's salary of $2,212 and other budgeted needs. Growth came thereafter mainly from a high birth rate. Between 1899 and 1942, the records list 898 baptisms, mostly of infants, for an average rate of one baby a year for every five families.

By 1915, the shortage of seating became so acute that the Douglas Park consistory proposed to replace its sanctuary with a larger one. The congregation, however, judged it better to sell and relocate further west. The consistory then appointed a committee to try to sell the building, but without success, and the issue was shelved for another decade.[80]

In the 1920s so many families joined the "Cicero movement" that by 1927 the congregation had decided to relocate there as well. Membership still totaled 690 souls at that point, but internal growth was slowing. In 1948, the baptism rate was only one baby for every eleven families, which was only about one-third of the 1899 annual rate of one baby for every four families.[81]

John Vos, a Groninger who entered the ministry at fifty years of age without seminary training because of "exceptional gifts," led Douglas Park in the seminal decade 1917-26, in tandem with Van Lonkhuyzen at First Chicago. Vos spent twenty-two years as a Christian school teacher and principal in the Groninger settlement of Muskegon before entering

79. Henry Beets, "Rev. J. Manni's Silver Jubilee, 1899 – Nov. 3 – 1914," *Banner,* 29 Oct. 1914; obituaries by H. J. Kuiper and Edward Masselink in ibid., 25 Jan. 1935; Christian Reformed Church, *Yearbook,* 1936, 169. Manni's wife was seriously ill during his tenure at Douglas Park, but she recovered and the couple celebrated their thirty-fifth wedding anniversary ("Douglas Park Notes," *Banner,* 20 Mar., 17 July 1913).

80. "Douglas Park Notes," *Banner,* 16 Dec. 1915; 9 Mar. 1916.

81. C. De Leeuw, "Douglas Park Christian Reformed Church, Chicago, Illinois," ibid., 9 Apr. 1909; Warren Park Christian Reformed Church, *Golden Anniversary,* 30, 32, 34; *Onze Toekomst,* 10 Jan. 1913.

Rev. John O. Vos (1862-1937)
(The Archives, Calvin College)

the ministry. He then served in the Illinois Groninger churches of Fulton and Summit (Archer Avenue) before coming to the city. Eventually he retired in Cicero where the Douglas Park congregation had relocated, and he could chat with the old timers in the native "Gronings" dialect. In a gesture of esteem, the Douglas Park church elected him honorary elder. When the congregation celebrated its twenty-fifth anniversary in 1924, Vos composed a festive song for the occasion, but was too ill to participate along with the former pastors who had returned for the service of thanksgiving. A hallmark of his ministry was ardent support of the congregation's fledgling Christian school, Timothy, then only five years old.[82]

82. "Quarter Centennial, Douglas Park, Chicago," *Banner,* 4 May 1924; Vos obituary, ibid., 6 Jan. 1938; *Onze Toekomst,* 30 Apr. 1924.

Fourteenth Street (First) Christian Reformed Church and *De Taal Questie* ("the Language Question"), 1910-30

The mother church on Fourteenth Street continued in its traditional ways during the era of the First World War and the 1920s, led by the philosophic Sjoerd Vander Heide (1909-18) and the brilliant Dr. John Van Lonkhuyzen (1918-28). Vander Heide was much loved for his practical messages that urged believers to combine work and prayer, which idea he gladly borrowed from his hero Abraham Kuyper. "In Unity is Strength," Vander Heide declared, quoting Kuyper and also the motto of the Reformed Church in America. "We could do much more, as Christians of Dutch stock in the second city of the Union, if we were to co-operate more in matters educational and philanthropic [with the Reformed churches]."[83]

Vander Heide's ready wit and leadership gifts helped him deal with the language controversy that erupted just before Evert Breen left for a Grand Rapids church. Trinity Reformed Church had offered English-speaking services since 1891, but the church was not located in the heart of the Dutch neighborhood, and it was affiliated with the "American" denomination. Thus, many Christian Reformed parents of younger children for years had been pressing for English-language worship services and catechism classes. Ebenezer School had accommodated them but not their churches. Dutch was taught at Ebenezer only for one hour on Friday afternoon. But many adult church members had difficulty understanding the English language, especially the mothers who lived in a closed ethnic world. They spoke only Dutch at home, when visiting family and friends, and buying from the Dutch grocer, butcher, and milkman. In 1911, when the elders of the Fourteenth Street church repeatedly chastised a mother for her sporadic attendance at divine services, her defense was that she understood little of it. And so it was.[84]

Since the pressure was on both the Fourteenth Street and Douglas Park churches, the consistories in 1909 decided to start combined English services once a month on Sunday evenings in each church, on an alternating basis. Thirty-five families participated, and it soon became apparent that an exclusively English-language church was needed. It took three years and much acrimony and tension before the idea of a "Yankee

83. First Christian Reformed Church of Chicago, *Seventy-Fifth Anniversary,* 13; "Chicago News," *Banner,* 11 Dec. 1913.

84. Obituary of Vander Heide, *Banner,* 27 Sept. 1929; Tena Huizenga, "The Life Story of Harm (Harry) Huizenga, 1869-1936," typescript, p. 12; First Christian Reformed Church of Chicago, Minutes, 31 July 1911.

Dutch" church bore fruit. By 1912, forty families plus twenty single adults (about two hundred souls) had signed petitions, and the Fourteenth Street consistory agreed that the church-plant was viable – it had sufficient strength and capable leaders.[85]

In 1912 the sponsoring churches agreed to read the following announcement in their morning services on April 28, 1912: "On Sunday morning, May 5, 1912, your consistories, in co-operation with a committee of Classis Illinois, will begin a Mission Station for the purpose of having the Gospel preached in the English language, and if enough interest is shown, to organize a Church." Classis Illinois endorsed the project and obtained funding from the denominational Home Mission Board.[86] The upshot was the founding of the Third Christian Reformed Church of Chicago (see below).

By this time, the neighborhood around the Fourteenth Street Church was getting thick with Russian Jewish immigrants, who made an offer to buy the property, including the church and parsonage. The congregation considered the offer and saw a possibility to buy a modern and beautiful church building on Ashland Avenue, but the German Lutheran congregation decided to stay put. The deal was consummated finally in 1921, nine years later.[87]

Vander Heide's pastorate spanned the years of World War I, but the consistory minutes make scant mention of the tumultuous times, other than to schedule several special collections at the behest of the Dutch consulate in Chicago for the suffering Reformed Church congregation in Brussels, Belgium, which country was under German conquest. A request from the Federal Council of Churches to promote the Liberty Loan crusade from the pulpit on a Sunday in April, 1918, was declined, but the consistory did refer the matter to the church societies, who subscribed a modest amount of $6.30.[88]

The consistory had to deal with thorny discipline problems brought on by the complexities of modern life. For example, confessing member Sam Postema was a milk wholesaler who delivered seven days a week to retailers. The consistory ordered him to keep the Sabbath day holy, but city authorities told him he would lose his license if he did so. Postema asked for advice, but the consistory was stumped. Another member attended an

85. Ibid., 11 Jan., 8 Feb., 16 Nov., 7 Dec. 1909; 12 Feb., 11 Mar., 12 Apr. 1912.

86. Lombard Christian Reformed Church, *Celebrating Seventy-Five Years,* 2.

87. "Chicago Letter," *Banner,* 23 Jan., 20 Mar. 1913.

88. Douglas Park Christian Reformed Church, Minutes, 1 Apr. 1918.

50th Anniversary Consistory, First Christian Reformed Church of Chicago, 1917.
l-r seated: Frederick Goosens, Derk Doornbos, John Stouwie, Klaas Wierenga
row 2: John Blauw, James De Boer, Harold Toren, Rev. Sjoerd Vander Heide (center, behind lectern), E. Vander Meulen, Martin Halbersma, Jacob Dykstra
row 3: Albert Hoekstra, George Speelman, Harold Van Der Molen, William Vander Kamp, John Hoekstra, John H. Vander Velde

English church "where she did not belong," while a young man went to socialist meetings and neglected divine worship and catechism classes. The elders admonished both but with little effect.[89]

That the work of the elders in all the Reformed congregations was admirable is evident from reading the consistory minutes.[90] The elders were faithful in their oversight and willing to go after the wayward. Every meeting included at least one "discipline case" and often three or four. In dealing with human failings, they showed great patience and persistence. For example, in 1915 the elders at the First Christian Reformed Church had to deal with a marriage breakdown in the congregation. The breakdown was caused by the husband's alcohol problem and the physical abuse of his wife to the point of knocking her unconscious once with his fists, for which she had to be hospitalized. The family's dirty laundry, of course, became public knowledge and pained the entire church fellowship.

89. First Christian Reformed Church of Chicago, Minutes, 12, 26 Jan., 9 Feb. 1914; 17 Mar., 14 May, 23 Nov. 1915.

90. The discipline account in this and the following paragraphs is recorded in ibid. May 1915–May 1918.

For the next three (!) years the elders diligently worked with the family to resolve a seeming intractable situation. For one full year, they visited this dysfunctional home virtually every other week, in hopes of restoring the marriage and the family. Thereafter, they made regular contacts but were often spurned by one or the other spouse. The minutes of every consistory meeting from May of 1915 to May of 1918 tell the ongoing saga.

At first, the elders urged the wife and teenaged children to be patient, while they took the initial step of barring the husband and father from the table of Holy Communion, a practice known as "silent censure." The wife was subsequently barred as well, because of her bitter and angry spirit. When after a year she moved out of the home and refused to work for reconciliation, as did her husband, the consistory proceeded with the "first step" of formal excommunication of the pair. They announced to the congregation on three Sundays, but without naming the parties, the "nature of the offense and obstinacy of the sinner" and urged the body to pray for and admonish the sinners, lest they be cut off from the church, and by implication, from the body of the Christ.

With the formal process of excommunication underway, the wife accused the consistory of "unfair treatment" and refused to repent, even while the husband softened and expressed a willingness to be reconciled with his wife and the church. He even attended church again and claimed to have stopped drinking. But just as the wife appeared willing, the husband resumed heavy drinking. The church put him under the "second step" of excommunication.

Meanwhile, the wife said that she intended to file for divorce, at which the elders warned that this would also bring her under the second step of discipline. This consisted of publicly naming the offenders before the congregation, an action that required the prior approval of the higher assembly, Classis Illinois. The consistory then had the right, after a reasonable time, to take the third and final step of reading in public worship the denominational "form for excommunication," which completed the expulsion. But the consistory of the First Christian Reformed Church continued to deal patiently with the pair.

In the later stages of the affair, after the wife filed for divorce, the focus of church discipline shifted entirely to her. The elders strongly condemned her action and urged her with repeated visits not "to walk in her sinful way" but to seek to reconcile with her husband. From the moment the wife used the "D word," the elders treated the wife as the more guilty party. His drunken fits and pattern of spouse abuse seemingly paled in comparison to the act of divorce, although the elders continued to work on his alcohol addiction.

The wife finally played her trump card and charged her husband with adultery. If she could prove the charge, it would give her both biblical grounds and a church sanction for divorce. But she could not do so, and the consistory proceeded to excommunicate her after her divorce became final. The court acted solely on the grounds of her husband's "persistent drunkenness," not adultery.[91]

Attitudes in the Reformed churches and in society at large were clearly much different seventy-five years ago. In 1934, when a female member of the First Reformed Church divorced her husband for cruelty and then remarried, the elders excommunicated her for entering into a "sinful relationship," namely her second marriage. In another example of conscientiousness, two men who applied for membership in 1935 were denied because they were members of the Moose Lodge, to which "no true Christian could belong." The congregation historically and under synodical rules of local autonomy, had always held this view of Freemasonry.[92]

Third Christian Reformed Church of Chicago

The Third Christian Reformed Church, as noted earlier, began in 1912 as the English-language "12th Street Mission" of the Fourteenth Street (First) and Douglas Park congregations. It was the first American congregation of that denomination in Chicago. The name, Twelfth Street Church, was dictated by the church's rented store front at 2231 West Twelfth Street (near Ogden Avenue), which lay midway between the two mother churches. Worship services began with sixteen families, who sat on folding chairs and sang with a piano. Seminarians Abram Dekker and Henry Meeter ministered during the summer months, while committees canvassed every family of the two mother congregations to recruit prospective members. The church steering committee included James De Boer and Garret Bossenga of Fourteenth Street and H. Brands and Jacob Bos of Douglas Park.[93]

91. Ibid., 13 May, 10 June, 1 July, 26 Aug., 11 Nov. 1918. The elders continued to be plagued by this woman until she died in 1920, after remarrying another church member in 1919. The husband was then free to remarry as well (26 May, 27 Oct. 1919; 25 Jan., 1, 16 Mar., 12 Apr. 1920).

92. First Reformed Church of Chicago, Minutes, 6 Dec. 1934, 30 Apr. 1935.

93. Dekker and Meeter alternated between the Twelfth Street and Evergreen Park

The need for the church was obvious. For several years, the young people had been scattering to English-speaking churches of different denominations. The only way to stem the loss was for the Dutch immigrants to found a similar congregation. The venture was a big success. In September 1912, Classis Illinois granted permission and forty-three families, 202 souls in all, gathered on October 3 to organize and to witness their membership letters being handed over. About half came from Fourteenth Street and half from Douglas Park. After a lengthy worship service, the male members then elected the first consistory of six men: elders Jacob Bos, Garret Bossenga, and George Slager, all prime movers, and deacons Herman Bos, Douwe J. Rietdyk, and John Tuls. Thus began a Dutch church with a distinctly American flair.[94]

Although the leaders of both mother churches gave the daughter congregation their wholehearted blessing, not everyone was happy with it. Mrs. Martha Kickert recalled hearing, as a seven-year-old, how angry her uncle Ralph Euwema was when he learned that her parents had joined the English-speaking church. But the reason was obvious. "None of the children could understand the minister's Dutch – evidently our parents thought it was time we understood what the church was for."[95]

Within two months the nascent group outgrew the storefront and leased space at the Mayflower Church on Sacramento Boulevard at Fillmore Street, beginning on Thanksgiving Day, 1912. Visiting ministers

---

congregations. Meeter was studying at the University of Chicago prior to returning to Princeton University in the fall. Dekker took a call to the Cincinnati, Ohio, church ("Chicago Letter," *Banner,* 1 Aug., 26 Sept. 1912); First Christian Reformed Church of Cicero, *Commemoration of the Twenty-Fifth Anniversary, October 3, 1912–October 3, 1937* (Cicero, 1937), 6; Third Christian Reformed Church of Chicago, *Directory,* 1926.

94. "Chicago Twelfth Street, New Church Organized," *Banner,* 17 Oct. 1912. Charter members, by transfer, from the First Christian Reformed Church of Chicago were: John Balk and wife, Dirk D. Lenters and family, Klaas De Vries and family, Harm Bos and family, Henry Bos and family, Jantje Bos, D. H. Lenters and wife, Arie Bremer and family, Gerrit Vanden Burg and family, John Tuls and wife, Arnold Lenters and family, Gerrit Boeringa and family, Willem Zylstra and family, Auke De Boer and wife, Albert Koelikamp and family, Bonne Iwema and family, Peter Bulthuis and wife, Melle Balk, Jr., Melle Balk, Hanna Tillie Balk, Grietje Balk, Hendrikje Balk, Effie Doornbos, Clara Doornbos, Pieter Doornbos, Bertha Venhuizen, Jurrien B. Huiner, Jacob Vander Molen, Annette Gerda Lenters, Alexander Lenters, Otto Lenters, Maria Francis Lenters, Riena Lenters, Van Dyk and child, Jan Optholt, and Siebrand Batjes. First Christian Reformed Church of Chicago, Minutes, 30 Sept. 1912.

95. "Twelfth Street Christian Reformed Church," *Banner,* 28 Nov. 1912; Mrs. Cornelius Kickert, "Last Meeting at Coffee Hour at Cicero I Church – 1976."

filled the pulpit for more than a year, until the Reverend John H. Mokma (1913-19) of the Munster, Indiana, church accepted the call; he was the fifth pastor solicited. By classical appointment Mokma had coincidentally preached the sermon and installed the consistory at the first worship service after formal organization in October 1912. In the interim, Elder Bos normally hosted the visiting pastors, known in denominational jargon as "pulpit supply." They arrived on Saturday evening and, due to a ban on Sunday travel, would remain till Monday.[96]

For the parishioners, the entire week revolved around Sunday services. Harmina Doot, a daughter of Elder Bos, recalled:

> I remember Sunday as a day completely immersed in the Word. Not only because we attended three worship services, but in between, after services, during dinner, the conversation was always biblical, theological. I think then, at the very beginning, is where this church began the tradition of fine preaching. I did not know it at the time of course, but my father was paid a small sum to have these visiting pastors stay with us. He saved all that money, and, finally, used it to start the church library.[97]

Under Mokma, the congregation in 1914 built a basement church, with the intention to add the superstructure later. But that time never came. The congregation also erected a parsonage. Both buildings stood on five lots in the 4100 block of Grenshaw Street (between Keeler and Karlov) (figure 1.1, site 11). The building committee consisted of George Slager, Henry J. Bos, Gerrit Vanden Burg, Henry Bos, and Jacob Doornbos. Grenshaw ran parallel to 12th Street and one half-block north, and was only a few blocks from the Douglas Park Church, which bade godspeed to those who wished to join the new body, now named Third Chicago. Families walked to church, even those few who had moved to Cicero, a distance of several miles, because they believed paying streetcar fares desecrated the Christian Sabbath.

From the beginning, Third Chicago boasted an *avant garde* "choral society" for those who wished to "develop the gift and art of song in the glory of God." John Tuls was the first director, followed by Gerrit Vanden Berg and John M. Bolt. The choir of thirty-five voices performed sacred cantatas, but it did not perform in the worship services. The denomina-

96. First Christian Reformed Church of Cicero, *Commemoration,* 6-7.

97. Harmina Doot memoir, quoted in Lombard Christian Reformed Church, *Celebrating Seventy-Five Years.*

Worship service at Third Christian Reformed Church of Chicago, the "basement church." Rev. Herman Moes preaching. Bonne Iwema family in back row

(Courtesy of Calvin Iwema)

tional synod had long discouraged this, although local consistories had the final say. Third Chicago would not break this tradition.[98]

Candidate Herman Moes, a Chicago boy who had pursued graduate studies at Princeton University for a year after completing the ministerial course at Calvin Seminary, followed Mokma as pastor from 1920 to 1924. Moes was a deeply pious man of firm but quiet convictions who solved intricate calculus problems and studied astronomy for relaxation. His successor, Jacob J. Weersing, whose father shared in the secessions of 1834 and 1857, then began a stint of eight years (1924-33). Weersing's forte was dynamic doctrinal preaching and promoting Christian education.

Growth at Third Chicago was phenomenal during the 1920s because of the mass migration of families from the declining Ashland Avenue

98. "12th Street Singing Society," *Banner,* 12 June 1913; Christian Reformed Church, *Jaarboekje,* 1920, 137-38; Third Christian Reformed Church of Chicago, *Directory,* 1927; "Synodical Report Regarding Choir Singing," *Banner,* 24 Jan. 1930.

neighborhood into the Lawndale district and further west into Cicero. By 1925, the congregation counted 465 members and a third worship service was added to lessen the press.[99]

Third Chicago during Weersing's tenure outgrew its facilities and decided to relocate. Already in 1924, some members of the consistory had the foresight to "go west" by buying a large lot at 1220 South 60th Court in Cicero. The next year, Third Chicago sold the Grenshaw facilities to a Jewish congregation and began construction of a large and impressive church and parsonage in Cicero. Weersing spearheaded the fund drive for the new building with organ, which raised $3,800 in an intense two-day campaign.[100] Third Chicago subsequently became the First Christian Reformed Church of Cicero. It is presently the Lombard Christian Reformed Church.

Dr. John Van Lonkhuyzen: The Abraham Kuyper of Chicago

Dr. John Van Lonkhuyzen directed the Fourteenth Street (First) Christian Reformed Church during the upbeat postwar decade (1918-28), when the forces of Americanization were in full swing. But he was thoroughly Netherlandic by birth and education, a product of Abraham Kuyper's Doleantie movement (see chapter 2) and the Free University of Amsterdam, and thus he often seemed out of step. Though small in stature, Van Lonkhuyzen was an intellectual giant, fluent in six languages — Dutch, English, Greek, Hebrew, German, and Spanish. The latter he mastered while organizing Reformed congregations in Argentina. Van Lonkhuyzen was the most educated and traveled pastor ever to serve the congregation and also its last Dutch dominie. He was a throwback to fifty years before, when all the Christian Reformed pastors were foreign born.

Van Lonkhuyzen left a pastorate in the Netherlands in 1911 to serve the Alpine Avenue congregation in Grand Rapids, Michigan, and he returned to his homeland in 1928, after resigning his Chicago position in extreme grief upon the death of his wife and the mother of his six children. He had met and married his beloved Katie ("Kaatje") Dykstra at the Alpine Avenue church. His thick accent and Dutch mannerisms made him stand out during his seventeen years in America.

99. Obituary of Moes by C. M. Schoolland in *Banner,* 27 Apr. 1981; obituary of Weersing by Frank De Jong in ibid., 26 Mar. 1976.

100. *Onze Toekomst,* 1 Dec. 1926.

But nothing exposed him more than an article he published in the denominational weekly, *De Wachter,* in 1915, which was quickly picked up by the *Grand Rapids News.* Following the German U-boat sinking of the British passenger liner, *Lusitania,* at the cost of 1,198 lives, 124 of them Americans, Van Lonkhuyzen strongly protested against president Woodrow Wilson's condemnation of the German government, in a piece entitled "Playing with Fire." Wilson, in the dominie's judgment, was tilting American foreign policy in favor of England in the World War at the expense of Germany. "What were these people [the passengers] doing on a ship loaded with ammunition in the war zone showing a hostile flag?" he declared. "They might as well sit on an ammunition wagon and enter a firing zone. It was recklessness in the extreme. . . . On the English side, obviously, it showed the same meanness that led them to place women and children of the Boers in front of canons during the Boer War." Van Lonkhuyzen's antipathy to the British, because of what they did to his beloved Boers fifteen years earlier, clearly colored his judgment about Ger-

Rev. Dr. John Van Lonkhuyzen (1873-1942)

many. Many Hollanders agreed and signed a petition that the dominie circulated to instruct the American Wilson.[101]

The *News* editors found the learned Dutch dominie's opinions to be uninformed and dangerously inflammatory and said so in a pointed editorial response. Van Lonkhuyzen not only failed to understand the "spirit of American patriotism in all its depth and fullness," but he had no right as a foreigner to speak up. At this crude attack on his honor and character, Van Lonkhuyzen filed a libel suit against the *News* for $20,000. Following the trial testimony, however, as the case was set to go to the jury, the judge declared, on motion of the newspaper's attorney, that the cleric had "no cause for action" and dismissed the suit. The newspaper, said the judge in his written opinion, was well within the bounds of its free speech rights to criticize the views of a public man. Van Lonkhuyzen appealed the decision, but to no avail.[102] This sour experience in American political discourse in Grand Rapids the dominie doubtless carried to Chicago.

Van Lonkhuyzen left a positive mark in Chicago, nonetheless, where he served as pastor, churchman, and journalist. Van Lonkhuyzen guided the First Christian Reformed Church in the purchase of a new church and parsonage and led the churches of Chicago into new mission endeavors. For nine years (1919-28), he edited Chicago's Dutch-language newspaper, *Onze Toekomst,* which circulated widely in the city and throughout the midwestern region. In pulpit and press, Van Lonkhuyzen taught a Kuyperian world view, and he provided leadership for the entire Reformed community in Chicago during the 1920s.

With more than twelve hundred souls in 1920, the First Christian Reformed Church of Chicago had outgrown its "Old Fourteenth Street Church," as the edifice was affectionately called in the following poem.

The Street of the House of God (Ezra 10:9)

Within this vast metropolis
There is a calm retreat;
As unpretentious edifice.
'Tis known as **Fourteenth Street**.
Though by the busy world ignored,
It is a sacred place;

101. This and the next paragraph relies on "Speelen met vuur," *De Wachter,* 16 June 1915; *Grand Rapids News,* 2, 29 July, 2, 3, 4 Nov. 1915. I am grateful to Huug van den Dool for translating this article.

102. Report in *Banner,* 11 Nov. 1915.

Many who know and fear the Lord
Seek here His gracious face.

Immanuel's messengers proclaim
The truths to Zion dear.
Dwell on the glories of that name
Which Zion loves to hear.
Within their walls the Gospel Song
Oft animates the Saints,
Confirming, building up the strong
Encouraging the faint.

Sweet spot, and fragrant even now
With memories of the just!
Still do they speak, though long ago
Committed to the dust.
And, though those valiant ones are gone,
A noble few remain,
Who, with their Lord's bright armor on,
Boldly His cause maintain.

With glowing hearts they oft record
The victories of their king;
And tidings of their glorious Lord
Fresh from His hand they bring.
Many who rest in heaven above
Drank from the river here –
The river of eternal love
Pure, crystal, deep, and clear.

Long may this hallowed place be known,
And for the truth renowned;
Long may the trumpet here be blown,
And thousands bless the sound!

Part II

When in the busy scenes of life,
The noise, the tumult, and the heat,
How comforting, amid the strife,
Has been the thought of "Fourteenth Street!"
There I have listened with delight,

And felt a heavenly peace within,
A brief cessation in the fight,
A moment's rest from worldly din.

How many burdened souls have stepped
Within this precious room for prayer,
And tears of self-abhorrence wept
And found the King of Israel there!

What is it makes the place so dear?
'Tis not the many friends I see
But Jesus meets His people here,
And here, I trust, has met with me.

And in the sleepless hours of night
When favored at the mercy seat,
One's heart cries out: "O King of light,
Shine on thy fold at **Fourteenth Street**!"

Banner, 25 March 1915 (anonymous)

In 1921 the congregation sold its building to the Chicago Jewish Mission of the Christian Reformed Church for $16,000. It then took advantage of an opportunity to buy from the German Evangelical Lutherans a stately brick edifice on the northeast corner of Ashland Avenue at Hastings Street (1319 South Ashland Avenue) (figure 1.1, site 7).[103]

This location was barely two and one-half blocks west and only a stone's throw from the First Reformed Church. The Zion Lutheran congregation wished to go further west, "where Israel's hosts do not push us aside." The Dutch took advantage of the German antipathy toward Jews. The congregation paid only $75,000 for the sanctuary with stained glass windows, an ornate nave, an $8,000 pipe organ, all furnishings, and an adjacent brick parsonage. It was a steal; the property was worth at least $200,000! No wonder the members voted "almost unanimously" to accept the deal.[104]

103. The mission ended up selling the building for $25,000 after remodeling it for its own use. The sales agreement is appended to the First Christian Reformed Church of Chicago, Minutes, 25 Apr. 1921; "Proceedings of Classis Illinois," ibid., 24 May, 4 Oct. 1923. The Old Fourteenth Street Church fell to the wrecking ball in 1943 to make way for a Chicago public housing complex.

104. *Onze Toekomst,* 16 Dec. 1921; First Reformed, *Century for Christ,* 5; First Christian Reformed Church of Chicago, *Seventy-Fifth Anniversary,* 11; "Eerste Christelijke Gerefor-

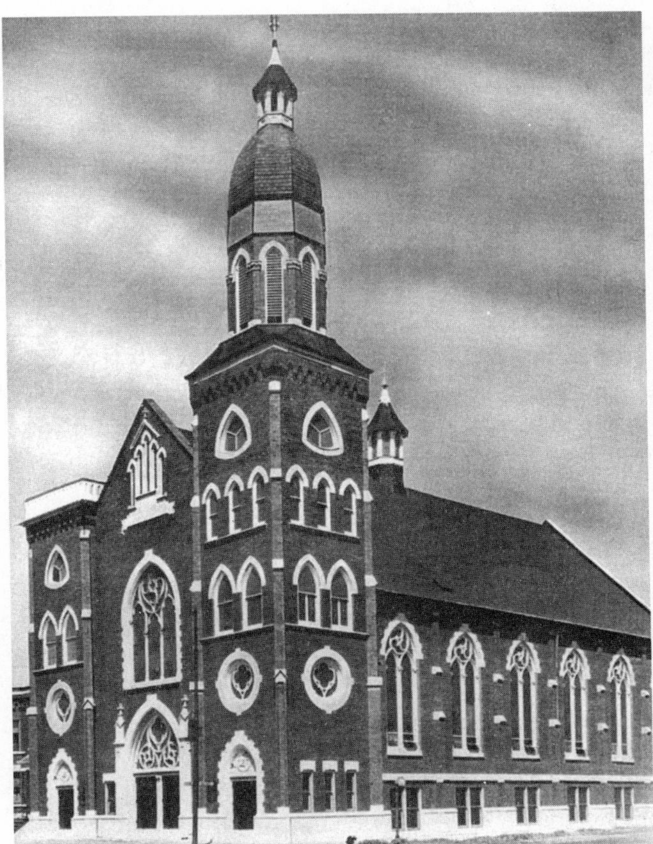

First (Ashland Avenue) Christian Reformed Church of Chicago, 1942

To help pay for the new edifice, the congregation sold $50 shares to members at 6 percent interest.[105] It is notable that this and the Old Fourteenth Street edifice, both of which the congregation had purchased from other denominations, were far more lavish and ornate than the spare wooden structures that this and other Dutch Calvinist congregations in the city themselves built. Since the new building stood on Ashland Ave-

---

meerde Gemeente te Chicago," *De Wachter,* 7 Oct. 1923; John Vander Velde, "Our History," Ebenezer Christian Reformed Church, *Centennial Booklet* (1967), 5. As a condition of the sale, the German congregation reserved the right to use the edifice for eighteen months after the sale, until June 1923.

105. The church paid $15,000 at signing, $20,000 after six months, $15,000 after twelve months, and the remaining $25,000 within twenty-four months, all without interest (First Christian Reformed Church of Chicago, Minutes, 12, 27 Dec. 1921).

nue, it was commonly referred to by that street name, just as with the former building.

The Fourteenth Street facility became the site of a Christian Reformed outreach ministry to the Jews in 1919, begun under the auspices of Classis Illinois and spearheaded by Van Lonkhuyzen. This Chicago Jewish Mission, renamed the Nathanael Institute in 1932 to blunt bitter opposition from local rabbis against Jewish evangelism, was independent of the nondenominational Chicago Hebrew Mission that Reformed Hollanders had long supported. The first superintendents were the Reverends John Beld (1919-20) and John Rottenberg (1920-24). The West Side at this time counted 150,000 (60 percent) of Chicago's 250,000 Jews.[106]

Jewish evangelism, despite bitter resistance by local rabbis, went so well that Van Lonkhuyzen's congregation experienced a most unusual Sunday school program on Christmas Eve of 1922 with eighty Jewish children. As Van Lonkhuyzen reported in *Onze Toekomst:*

> The church building was filled with Jewish children and mothers and as many of the congregation as could find room. Old pillars of the church who had a great deal of experience in the doings of the church said that they could not remember having spent a more beautiful evening in the church. . . . Imagine, right in front of the pulpit half way up in the auditorium, where usually sit the well-known, round, fair-haired and blue-eyed Groninger men and women I saw before me the dark-faced, small and grown-up Semites! . . .
>
> They behaved so reverently, even better than our own children. They recited Christmas recitations and sang Christmas songs. What a surprise in the eyes of the congregation when one girl rose, came forward and recited in a load, clear voice the whole plan of salvation, using in alphabetical form New Testament passages!
>
> What an inspiration to hear all the children sing: "Silent Night, Holy Night," in tender and earnest voices, and to hear a little boy recite: "What can I do for the Savior?" With gratitude, praise, and thanksgiving the congregation went home, believing that God had begun a mighty work among the Jews of the Chicago Jewish Mission district.[107]

106. "Chicago Jewish Mission," *Onze Toekomst,* 20 Feb. 1920; "Classis Illinois," ibid., 3 Oct. 1930; Albert Huisjen, "Our Chicago Jewish Mission," ibid., 3 Mar., 22 Dec. 1938.

107. Issue of January 13, 1922, quoted in *Souvenir of the Nathaniel Institute, 1919-1929* (Chicago, 1929), 20.

Helping Hand Gospel Mission on Chicago's "Skid Row,"
ready for first open air meeting 1915
l-r: J. Slager (board member), John Vande Water (mission superintendent),
Rev. Peter J. Hoekenga (Chicago city missionary),
Gerrit Bossenga (board member);
seated, John Dekker (board member)
(The Archives, Calvin College)

On Labor Day in 1923, however, the mission learned how difficult the work could be. While preparing to transport seventy-five children and their mothers on a picnic outing to Highland, Indiana, violence broke out. "We started out in two trucks in the midst of a shower of eggs and stones, so bitter were the Jews against us, particularly a woman living next door to the mission." So reported the director, John Rottenberg and his assistant, the Jewish Christian pastor, Elias Newman.[108]

Albert Huisjen, director for four years (1920-24) of the Helping

108. "From and For the Chicago Jewish Mission," *Banner,* 30 Nov. 1923.

Nathanael Institute, erected 1927

Hand Gospel Mission on West Madison Street's "Skid Row,"[109] was appointed evangelist at the Chicago Jewish Mission (later Nathanael Institute) in 1924. He replaced Newman, who took a call to Damascus, Syria. The next year William Yonker, a medical doctor also trained in theology, was named director, and he opened a full-time medical clinic at the mission to treat indigent Jews. The Great Depression cut funding from the

109. R. B. Doornbos, "Chicago Helping Hand Mission Silver Jubilee," ibid., 15 Mar. 1940; Gilbert Haan, "Fifty Years on Skid Row," ibid., 14 Feb. 1964; William P. Brink, "Chicago North News," ibid., 18 May 1945. The Helping Hand Mission at 848-50 W. Madison Street was begun in 1915 to offer religious services, overnight lodging, and meals for homeless and destitute men and day programs for women and families. The official name until 1929 was the City Mission of the Christian Reformed Church of Chicago. It was closed in 1984 when its building was torn down for an urban renewal project. For many years in the 1930s and 1940s, there was also a South Side Branch of the Helping Hand Mission in Englewood. In 1945 it was replaced by the South Side Community Church at 83rd Street and Calumet Avenue.

Superintendents of the Madison Street facility were Peter Hoekenga (1914-16), John Vande Water (1915-32), Albert Huisjen (1920-24), George Steenstra (1930-34), Jelke Nauta (1934-35), the Rev. George Weeber (1935-38), Nick Youngsma (1938-47), Henry Jager (1947-49), Jelke Nauta (1949-52), and Clarence Laning (1952-82). Other volunteer staff included Louis Alexander, Chris Baker, Jennie Deckinga, Miss A. Hamstra, Ed Ottenhoff, Harry Overset, Johanna Pilon, Grace Plum, Samuel Post, Mr. Romein, the Rev. Aletinus Rus, Minnie Spiers, Nellie Terborg, and Ida and Johanna Vander Weide.

Above left,
Edith Vander Meulen;
above right, Albert Huijsen;
left, William Yonker, M.D.

supporting churches, and Yonker was forced to go into part-time private practice, although veteran nurse Bena Kok continued to staff the clinic full time. Edith Vander Meulen from 1925 directed the teaching staff for

Nathanael Institute Board, 1944
l-r, seated: Rev. Renze O. De Groot, Rev. John Van Beek,
Rev. Benjamin Essenburg; standing: George Ottenhoff,
Dr. William Masselink, Lambert Bere

more than thirty-five years, with a brief hiatus in the early 1940s due to ill health.[110]

The Jewish Mission Board in 1932 appointed Huisjen superintendent. He had studied rabbinic and Talmudic theology and literature, mastered the Hebrew language, and spoke such fluent Yiddish that Jews mistook him as one of their own. He was the leading expert on Old Testament Judaism in the denomination and refocused the institute's ministry on evangelism and social activities. In 1945, Classis Chicago North ordained him

110. Other long-time missionary nurses were Tina Delis and Marie De Bruin. This and the next paragraphs rely on B. Essenburg, "Chicago, Englewood, and Cicero Churches," *Banner,* 21 Apr. 1933; "Chicago Jewish Mission," ibid., 21 Aug. 1942; "Nathanael Institute of Chicago Has New Workers," ibid., 29 Oct. 1943; John C. De Korne, "Silver Jubilee of Mr. Albert Huisjen," *Missionary Monthly* 54 (Jan. 1949): 15; J.G.V.D., "William J. Yonker, M.D.," ibid., 56 (Dec. 1951): 325; "Grateful Patients Say Farewell to Dr. W. Yonker," ibid., 57 (Jan. 1952): 9, 18; "New Doctor at Nathanael, Reception for Dr. E. Van Reken," ibid., 57 (April 1952): 74; Gerben Zylstra, "Ministering to the Jewish People in Chicagoland," *Banner,* 25 Mar. 1960. See also Classis Illinois reports and the annual reports in the Christian Reformed Church *Acts of Synod* (e.g., 1934, 73-74), which contain budget recommendations. The Rev. Peter A. Hoekstra of the Second Cicero Christian Reformed Church chaired the synodical committee on Hebrew Missions during the 1930s.

Rev. Jack Zandstra (1904-84)

Rev. John Rozendal (1899-1982)
(Courtesy of Dorothy Rozendal Meyer)

upon his request. Huisjen served for twenty-four years (1924-47), the last fifteen as superintendent, along with Dr. Yonker, who provided medical care for twenty-six years (1925-51). George Ottenhoff was the long-time treasurer of the board.

Huisjen's best efforts were undermined for a time by the rise of Adolf Hitler in Germany in 1933, which aroused a hostile spirit among the Jews toward Christians in general. The local Jews reproached Huisjen and his volunteer staff "time and again as friends of Hitler." In one Bible class of a dozen boys, three flew into a rage at hearing the name of Jesus, and everyone "left the room in violent passion." The missionaries were perplexed but did not despair. After the war, passions subsided. In 1947, the Reverend Jack Zandstra took Huisjen's place. He was a son of the Highland, Indiana, Christian Reformed Church and had served in the Orthodox Presbyterian Church. The Reverend John Rozendal, formerly of the Paterson, New Jersey, Hebrew Mission, succeeded Zandstra in 1951, and Dr. Everett Van Reken, a former medical missionary in China, took up Yonker's stethoscope and blood pressure cuff in 1952.

Despite the total commitment by these dedicated missionaries, and

Ben-Zion Tabachnick, first convert, Nathanael Institute

the many hundreds of Jews who participated in mission activities and weekly worship services, adult converts were few over the years and could be counted on the fingers of both hands, even after fifty years. Ben-Zion Tabachnick was the first to be baptized. The solemn occasion for the sixty-year-old man took place in 1923 at the Third Christian Reformed Church of Chicago. Tabachnick assisted in the mission's reading room for years and later transferred to the First Cicero congregation. Another convert was Samuel Basner, who in 1935 was baptized and also joined the First Cicero Church. William Kooistra gave voice to the frustrations of the ministry when he noted in 1949 that Jewish evangelism was a "very important but in so many ways disappointing work."[111]

Meanwhile, in the pages of *Onze Toekomst* Van Lonkhuyzen addressed the key issues of the day – Christian schools, the language change from Dutch to English, and the rising premillennial movement. The denomination stood solidly in support of Christian schools, but friction arose over the issues of English usage and millennial teachings. The conservatives "wished to maintain the Dutch language in the worship services, fearful that a change to the English language would break down the

111. *Souvenir of the Nathanael Institute,* 22; W. H. Rutgers, "Nathanael Institute: Chicago Jewish Mission," *Banner,* 21 June 1935; E. Kooistra, "Albert Huisjen's Twenty-Fifth Anniversary at Nathanael Institute," ibid., Feb. 1949.

barriers to the inroads of modernism, while the younger generation growing up in an American climate of English usage would be lost to the church."[112] One stalwart elder of the congregation expressed the sentiments of many, declaring (in Dutch): "When English is preached, the Devil is in the pulpit."[113]

After being stymied for two years, the English faction, feeling the urgency to worship in "the language of the land," pushed ahead without the approval of the consistory. The group was led by one of those very consistory members, elder James De Boer. He was described later as the group's "guide, philosopher, and friend whose counsel was eagerly sought and faithfully followed." The group circulated a petition to organize a church, obtained more than one hundred signatures, and presented it to the regional assembly, Classis Illinois. With this affront to its authority, the First Church consistory suspended De Boer and another elder who backed him, and placed all the signatories under censure.[114]

The classis, to the surprise of the consistory, sided with the seceders and allowed them to organize, over the strong objections of the Ashland Avenue Church delegates, namely Van Lonkhuyzen and his elder, who considered the new church to be "unnecessary, unorderly, and unlawful." The classis also ordered the reinstatement of the two suspended elders. The consistory had to acquiesce, but not before filing a protest for allowing the faction to circumvent church order provisions and thereby undermine its authority. The main concern may well have been more financial than cultural. The leaders argued that the full complement of twelve hundred members was needed to pay for the new edifice, and that the petitioners should wait at least seven years before leaving.[115]

After getting approval from the classis, the petitioners quickly organized the Fourth Christian Reformed Church of Chicago. It was a dramatic moment at the Sunday service in February, 1923, when Van Lonkhuyzen read the names of the 45 families with 135 souls who were transferring. Chicago "is sufficiently large," said a member of the new body, "to permit the healthy development of this church, the growth of which should mean added resistance against the encroachments of the

112. Ebenezer Christian Reformed Church, *Centennial Booklet, 1867-1967,* 6.

113. The elder was John (Jense) Blaauw. This anecdote, which was vividly recalled for years at First Christian Reformed Church, was told by the Rev. Eugene Bradford in an interview with the author in Holland, Michigan, on 16 Mar. 1998.

114. The quote is in Andrew De Boer, "Brief History of Fourth Christian Reformed Church of Chicago" (1990), manuscript in possession of the author.

115. "Press Report of the Meeting of Classis Illinois," *Banner,* 1 Feb. 1923.

forces of evil."[116] The turmoil and bitter recriminations of the church's birth took some years to fade away on the Old West Side.

Over the next years, Van Lonkhuyzen gradually introduced English, but only by doubling the number of services from two to four – Dutch at 9:00 AM and 3:00 PM, and English at 1:30 PM and 7:30 PM. Usually a guest pastor conducted one or two of the services, but Van Lonkhuyzen's successor, the energetic Benjamin Essenburg (1929-45), led all four. Even more amazing, a few zealous, bilingual members could boast of attending all of them.

Because the language issue pitted the older generation against the younger, the transition to English could come only in small steps. The Reformed congregations introduced English a generation ahead of the Christian Reformed congregations, but the first step in the mother churches of both denominations in Chicago was the same – to release pressure and buy time by establishing English-language daughter congregations. Eventually, the mother congregations themselves adopted English, usually first in the evening service, which was geared to young people. The Reformed churches simply replaced Dutch with English, while the Christian Reformed churches often added English services. Over time, however, as the older generation dwindled, Dutch was relegated to the afternoon service until it was no longer needed.

The First Reformed Church of Chicago, as already noted, in 1891 began the transition to English in the Sunday school, catechism classes, and young people's societies; and by 1915 the changeover was nearly complete in the worship services as well. Only the Wednesday evening prayer meeting remained in Dutch until 1925, when English and Dutch were alternated. The use of English helped First Reformed retain established families, but it turned away fresh immigrant families with children who only knew the Dutch tongue.

Among the Christian Reformed churches, the Third and Fourth Chicago congregations spoke English from their inception in 1912 and 1923, respectively. But the major congregations, First and Douglas Park, worshiped entirely in Dutch until the late 1920s, when English services were added in the afternoon and evening at First and in the evening only at Douglas Park. The Sunday schools were permitted to adopt English much earlier, however. First Christian Reformed Church did so in 1893, and Douglas Park changed around 1915. By 1921, English-speaking men's and women's societies were organized. Attendance at the Dutch service de-

116. "New Congregation in Chicago," ibid. 5 Apr. 1923.

clined steadily in the 1930s; in 1938, First Christian Reformed dropped the second (3:00 PM) Dutch worship service, and ten years later, in 1948, the 9:00 AM Dutch service was moved to the afternoon, with English in the 9:30 AM and 7:00 PM services. The last Dutch worship was on Christmas Day, 1955. Douglas Park in the early 1930s switched the main Dutch morning service to the afternoon slot, where it continued until the early 1940s.

There was no more emotional issue than pushing the mother tongue out of church life. Peter Moerdyke put the matter in colorful terms:

> This transition process must, like a child, pass through the series of teething, chicken pox, measles, whooping cough, and all sorts of fevers and rashes, and you never know what next will break out; and they are all signs of growth, if this evolution does not destroy life. . . .
>
> The sound religious constitution of our Holland Reformed Churches has, within our distinct recollections, healthily passed through ailments and excitements and agitations. Scores of collisions between European and American forms, methods, aims, and customs have ended in the adoption of the latter. So must it be; so shall it be.[117]

In 1928 Van Lonkhuyzen returned to a pastorate in his homeland with his children, now all American citizens. His oldest son remained in America, and two sons re-emigrated. After Germany occupied the Netherlands in 1940, the dominie and his family came in harm's way because he openly spoke against the Nazis. As an American citizen, the dominie also faced imprisonment in a concentration camp, should the United States enter the war. In desperation, Van Lonkhuyzen in early 1941 appealed to the Christian Reformed denomination for $1,200 to pay the fare of his family of five. The church leaders in Grand Rapids responded promptly and opened the Van Lonkhuyzen Fund to receive contributions. By June of 1942, Van Lonkhuyzen and his family were safely in Grand Rapids for the duration of the war. But within six months he died of a blood clot after a fall on the ice. Henry Beets, director of missions for the Christian Reformed church and a close friend, mourned the loss of his "loyal intellectual companion," a "man of keen judgement and a real theologian," one whose "vision and original leadership" would be sorely missed in the church.[118]

117. Moerdyke, "Chicago Letter," *CI,* 18 Aug. 1894, p. 10.

118. "Appeal for Help for Dr. Van Lonkhuyzen," *Banner,* 21, 29 March, 4 Apr. 1941; "Two Appeals in One," ibid., 25 Apr. 1941; "Van Lonkhuyzen Announcement," ibid., 27 June 1941. Some church members condemned the leadership for officially funding the cleric, on the grounds that he had left the United States in 1928 "because he did not like it" ("Voices

Fourth Christian Reformed Church of Chicago

As noted above, early in 1923 forty-five families of the First Christian Reformed Church, especially those on the northern fringe around Harrison Street, organized another English-language congregation, the Fourth Christian Reformed Church (often called Chicago IV). It was a controversial beginning, spearheaded by elder James De Boer. When he died suddenly the next year, the fledgling group was devastated. Fortunately, the congregation (after two letters of decline) had just welcomed its first pastor, Herman Bel, who preached his inaugural sermon in December 1923. It was a good partnership. "Congregation and pastor liked each other immediately, [and] a happy, cordial, blissful life resulted," said James De Boer's son, Andrew.[119]

For the first two years, Fourth Chicago leased Salem Church for Sunday services, until it built a chapel on Roosevelt Road near Cypress Street, just west of Ashland Avenue. The congregation soon outgrew the chapel and next purchased an empty building four blocks west at 2040 West Roosevelt Road (figure 1.1, site 12), which was popularly known as the "pickle factory," in reference to its prior usage.

Like those of Third Church, these Hollanders wanted to speed up the transition to the American way of life. They found the old ways at First Church "irritating," and church "policies and actions caused difficulties continually," noted Andrew De Boer. The insistence of the old timers on Dutch-language services was "intolerable," declared another son, Henry De Boer. And the attempt to banish the church choir was wrong-headed. Given such feelings of mutual antipathy, it is no wonder that the mother church regarded the request to organize as "heresy."[120]

Fourth Chicago from the outset was known as the "church of the teachers"; among its members were nine Christian school teachers. These included Professor John J. De Boer, Dr. Frederick Wezeman, and Maurice Vander Velde, of the faculty of the Chicago Christian High School, and Ebenezer Christian school teachers Albert Cleveringa, Harry Wassink, and

---

in the Church," ibid., 9 May 1941); obituary by Henry Beets, "Dr. John Van Lonkhuyzen," ibid., 8 Jan. 1943.

119. Fourth Christian Reformed Church of Chicago, *Official Directory,* 1925; "Our History," Faith (Elmhurst) Christian Reformed Church, *Dedication Program* (Elmhurst, 1977); Andrew de Boer, "Fourth Christian Reformed Church of Chicago, Early Church History, 1923-1927," [1927], based on consistory minutes, typescript in possession of author.

120. Henry De Boer, "Recollections of the James De Boer Family" [February 1971], typescript, p. 2, courtesy of John H. Evenhouse; Edward Vander Molen, *Memoirs* [ca. 1970], courtesy of Everett Van Der Molen.

First consistory, Fourth Christian Reformed Church of Chicago, 1923. Seated, l-r: Albert Hoekstra, William Beamer, Rev. Herman Bel, George Ottenhoff; standing l-r: Henry Van Der Molen, Nick Wieringa, James De Boer, George Speelman, Peter Huiner, Edward Groenboom, Albert Hoeksema

Peter Berkhout. The latter two later became professors at Calvin College. Progressive thinkers all, these academics were tapped for the educational ministries of the congregation. They found ready allies among successful businessmen in the congregation, including George Ottenhoff, Peter Huiner, the De Boer brothers (George, Henry, Andrew, Clarence, and James — all sons of James), the Wieringa brothers Nick and Ben, Bonne Iwema, George Speelman, and others. Together, the teachers and businessmen made up a dynamic duo that worked to open the Christian Reformed community to the larger world.[121]

121. Fourth Christian Reformed Church of Chicago, *Official Directory, 1925.* Nick Wieringa is an example of a business and church man. With his brother Ben, Nick operated Wieringa Bros Cartage. He was president of the Christian Press Association and member of the board of Chicago's Dutch newspaper, *Onze Toekomst;* he served on the Timothy Christian School Society board, where many of his ten children attended; and he was an elder and leader in the church. He was born in Bedum, Groningen, immigrated to Chicago at age twenty-one, and died in 1929 at age fifty-three, after twenty-six years in the cartage business. His funeral was held in the large sanctuary of the First Christian Reformed Church of Chicago. "Christian education, city dispatching, and the Fourth Christian Reformed Church have lost much in him," said an obituary writer in *De Grondwet* (21 May 1929, p. 8).

Rev. Herman Bel (1886-1971)
(The Archives, Calvin College)

Herman Bel was the first pastor from 1923 to 1928, followed by the studious James Putt (1929-40), and finally Dr. Renze De Groot (1941-46). Bel was an educator at heart who later joined the faculty of the Chicago Christian High School as teacher of Bible. Putt during his tenure did postgraduate work at McCormick Seminary and Pikes Peak Theological Seminary, earning the doctorate in 1940 from the latter institution for a thesis on "The Future of the Jews." De Groot also earned a doctoral degree. Fourth Chicago installed a pipe organ in 1939 and boasted a choral society whose fifty-five members were directed by the well-known musician, Frans Kramer of Englewood, and accompanied by Catherine Wieringa.[122]

Given its constituency, Fourth Church, along with the Second Englewood Church (see below) and to some extent the Third Chicago Church, developed a reputation for cultural and theological "liberalism," within the givens of a conservative classis and denomination, of course. The church's leaders seemed to relish challenging the status quo of clerical dominance that had typified the Reformed churches. Indeed, the edu-

122. Benjamin Essenburg, "Chicago, Cicero and Englewood Churches," *Banner,* 17 Oct. 1930; Essenburg, "West Side News," ibid., 26 Oct. 1939, 1 Nov. 1940; "Chicago Four Choral Society to Render Annual Concert," *Chicago Messenger,* 22 May 1936.

Rev. James Putt (1898-1965)
(The Archives, Calvin College)

Rev. Renze O. De Groot (1908-91)
(The Archives, Calvin College)

cators at Fourth Church were in the vanguard of a lay revolution then sweeping the churches. For the first time, the laity could match wits with an educated clergy.

Professor De Boer led the charge in Chicago, attacking the local Christian Reformed ministerial organization, *Inter Nos* ("Between Us"), as a secret cabal. De Boer and his allies also took over the programs of the city-wide League of Reformed Young Men's Societies and used them as forums to introduce "radical" ideas, such as President Franklin Roosevelt's big government programs, naval disarmament, a new league of nations, and the like (see chapter 8). Condemning rugged individualism, calling "profit" a dirty word, and urging the collectivization of basic industries did not sit well with the staunch Republicans in the Chicago Christian Reformed churches.[123]

123. See, for example, "De Boer At Voters' League Calls N.R.A. But A Start," *Chicago Messenger,* 1 June 1934; "On Second Thoughts," ibid., 15 Nov. 1935; "Choral Society at Chicago IV," ibid., 20 Sept. 1935.

In the mid-1930s, De Boer's cousin and soul mate, Frederick Wezeman, whom Fourth Chicago named as its associate pastor, came under withering fire for his theological teachings at Chicago Christian High School. As chapter 7 describes in detail, both Classis Illinois and the Synod of the Christian Reformed Church condemned his teachings and put the congregation on notice for not correcting him.

The years under the wise and genial Bel were rich and the congregation flourished, only to wither during the depression years under Putt, as members moved "toward the setting sun" – to Cicero, Berwyn, and points west – to escape the "negro influx" pressing from the east. Residential segregation was a given among the Dutch, as it was among most European immigrant groups in the city. "We believe the negro would rather not live with the white and vice versa. Both races are most happy when far apart," noted Edward Groenboom, clerk of the council in 1935.[124]

That year Putt and the consistory, who saw the membership rolls drop from ninety to sixty-eight families, decided to establish a branch church in Cicero, with the idea of eventually moving the mother church as well. In 1939, however, the leaders of Fourth Church had second thoughts about abandoning the old neighborhood and decided to stay. They spun off the western branch as an independent congregation. This only delayed the inevitable. Fourth Chicago continued to decline and the new church plant to grow.

The last hurrah was the pastorate of Renze De Groot, who came in 1941 after Putt went to the Fulton, Illinois, congregation. The first pastor, Herman Bel, officially introduced De Groot at the service of installation by recalling that "the happiest days in my ministry were passed in Fourth Chicago." When Wezeman rose to conclude the "long to be remembered service," the sense of euphoria and joy was overwhelming. "Our congregation now again is enabled to go forward," declared the consistory.[125]

Alas, it was not to be. De Groot was the last pastor at Fourth Church. When in 1945 he accepted a call to an Iowa church, the congregation sold its Roosevelt Road building and relocated to Oak Park. That story is told below.

124. "4th Christian Ref. Church Branches Out," ibid., 23 Aug. 1935; E. Groenboom, "News About Fourth Christian Reformed Church of Chicago," *Banner,* 23 Aug. 1935.

125. Ibid., 20 Sept. 1935; "Fourth Christian Reformed Church of Chicago," ibid., 14 Apr. 1938; "Berwyn Christian Reformed Church," ibid., 26 Apr. 1940; "Fourth Chicago Rejoices," ibid., 25 July 1941 (quotes).

Benjamin Essenburg and First (Ashland Avenue) Christian Reformed Church (1929-45)

The long pastorate of the Reverend Benjamin Essenburg at the First (Ashland Avenue) Church marked both the high point and the end point for the Groninger Hoek on Ashland Avenue. Essenburg and his congregation shared first the glory years and then the "empty nest syndrome," as one after another of the Dutch families fled the deteriorating Old West Side, leaving only a remnant behind. Essenburg's ministry began in the Great Depression and ended with the allied victory over Germany. The Depression years were both the worst of times and the best of times. Families faced hardships beyond imagining, but the community came together like never before to help those made destitute. The challenge of survival forced the Hollanders to practice what they proclaimed weekly in the Apostles' Creed: the "communion of the saints."

The much-heralded Essenburg began his work at the new church edifice on Ashland Avenue in early 1929 at a salary of $3,500. His style and facility in both English and Dutch, including the Gronings dialect, made him a good fit for the bilingual congregation. Further, he understood the working world because he had been a farmer for some years before entering the ministry.[126]

Essenburg was the most effective pastor ever at First Church. Unlike his predecessor, Van Lonkhuyzen, who was brainy but stiffly formal, as Dutch dominies are wont to be, Essenburg mixed with the people in a warm folksy way that endeared him to all. He nurtured with a firm but effective hand up to one hundred children at a time in eight (!) catechism classes, including one in Dutch, with a total enrollment of 417 in 1930. A former pupil, Tom Oldenburger, recalled that Essenburg actually made catechism "fun," even though he was a strict disciplinarian who "ruled with a ruler." He guided the teenagers in their church societies and cheered the elderly with frequent visits. Essenburg was truly a shepherd of his flock.[127]

Getting to the same level as his parishioners actually took some doing. The problem, complained the new dominie, was that the pulpit in

126. Essenburg had a sixth-grade education, a wife and child, and a farm near Holland, Michigan, when he applied to Classis Holland for student aid to attend Calvin College and Seminary to prepare for the ministry. Classis approved and supported him for ten years (three to complete high school, four in college, and three in seminary).

127. The Rev. B. Essenburg, "The Chicago, Cicero and Englewood Churches," *Banner,* 21 Feb., 17 Oct. 1930; video interviews, Tom Oldenburger, 19 Nov. 1998; Ben Essenburg, Jr., 17 July 1998, both by Martin Stulp.

this "Lutheran" church was hung high up on the front wall under a large sounding board. How could he preach behind this confining "girdle" of a pulpit that was only accessible by climbing a ladder? He needed to walk around and "connect" with his hearers.

The solution to the problem was memorable indeed, as every old timer will attest. Only two days after the Essenburg family moved into the parsonage, and eight days before his scheduled service of installation, a boiler explosion in the dead of winter damaged the pulpit and the front of the sanctuary and caused extensive smoke damage throughout the newly redecorated church. "The lofty pulpit, so dear to some and so detestable to others, could no longer be used," according to the historical account. Wags quipped that the new preacher must have set the fire. But Essenburg used the opportunity to redesign the front to provide a large platform with an open pulpit, behind which he could range at will.

During the services, the pastor's wife and eight children always sat in a reserved pew near the front of the sanctuary, as was the practice in every Reformed and Christian Reformed congregation. When the family pa-

Rev. Benjamin Essenburg (1889-1976)
(The Archives, Calvin College)

Rev. Essenburg teaching catechism class,
First Christian Reformed Church of Chicago, 1941

raded to their pew, all eyes were on their dress and demeanor. No wonder the children wore the label of PK, preacher's kids; they could never escape the public gaze. Essenburg's musically talented children all added in their own ways to the worship experience by playing the organ, piano, and marimba, and by singing. Five daughters were church organists. They also performed special midweek concerts of singing and instruments directed by their enthusiastic father.

Essenburg was a very popular preacher, a "pulpit pounder," who drew large audiences with his dynamic, popular messages. Significantly, attendance at the evening service more than doubled. He sometimes modeled his sermons after those of the renowned British evangelist, Charles Spurgeon, much to the chagrin of the some "amateur theologians" in his congregation who thought Spurgeon's Reformed Baptist theology too Arminian.[128]

128. Ben Essenburg, video interview, 11 Nov. 1998, and reminiscences, video, Ebenezer Christian Reformed Church Rally, Berwyn, 17 July 1998, both by Martin Stulp. Two members of the congregation, Martin LaMaire and Edward Stouwie, wrote letters to the *Banner* in 1944 attacking Arminianism in general and specifically the preaching of American evangelist Gypsy Smith, but neither mentioned their pastor by name or implied any criticism of him (21 Apr., 26 May, 7 July 1944).

Church auditorium, front and rear views, 1942
First Christian Reformed Church of Chicago

To prepare himself mentally and spiritually for entering the pulpit, Essenburg arose early on Sunday mornings. Before mounting the platform, he would bow in a brief silent prayer, as was the custom in all the churches. The parishioners likewise prayed silently after taking their seats in the pews. Quiet and decorum were the order of the day in the church worship. This is one reason the congregation spent $3,500 to line the interior walls with acoustical material, which was designed to eliminate an annoying echo in the sanctuary that had long bothered preachers and listeners.

Blessed with "leather lungs" and the stamina of a work horse, Essenburg's voice carried clearly throughout the large sanctuary, even when the windows and doors were open on hot summer Sundays and the Ashland Avenue street cars clanged by every few minutes. Sermons of one hour or more were normal. Only the need to leave time for the next worship service – there were four in all until 1938 – forced him to stop.[129]

Elders ruled the church in those days, and they participated in worship by leading the psalm singing and reading the Law and the Scripture text of the day. The designated elder stood on the "little" platform, which was separate from the "big" pulpit platform. Elders sat in benches on the right front side and stood during the congregational "long" prayer, often fighting to stay awake. Deacons sat on the left front side and gathered the weekly offerings with collection baskets or plates, one set to meet the church budget and another for the poor. During the Depression, the needs were so great that the deacons dispersed the benevolent offering to needy families immediately after the service. Caring for the community of faith was the norm in Dutch Reformed circles.

The thorny issue of working on Sunday also came up again. On a long Labor Day weekend, a faithful church member pulled his truck out on Sunday to deliver ice to families with little children, so their milk and other perishables in the icebox would not spoil in the summer heat. Elder Clarence Leenhouts, the leading local undertaker, noticed the truck on the street and at the Monday evening consistory meeting raised his concerns about Sabbath desecration. At this, fellow elder John Blaauw brought him up short. In a thick Dutch accent, Blaauw said: "Clarence, last Sunday I saw you get up and leave in the middle of the church service. Now tell me, is it better to bring ice to a living being or to fool around

129. First Christian Reformed Church of Chicago, *Seventy-fifth Anniversary,* 14. The second Holland service was discontinued in April 1938. B. Essenburg, "Chicago, Englewood, and Cicero Churches," *Banner,* 25 Aug. 1938.

with a dead body?" The stunned Leenhouts had nothing more to say, but Essenburg, who chaired the meeting, could hardly suppress an audible "Amen, brother."[130]

To accommodate the overflowing afternoon English service, the balcony was expanded in a U-shape to seat twelve hundred, and the lighting system was upgraded. Liberated teens preferred the balcony, where they could eye one another and prepare for the traditional courting walk after the evening service along Ashland Avenue in front of the stately mansions north of 12th Street to Harrison Street. Unattached women walked in pairs or trios for the half mile, while the men viewed them from cars or on foot in what was crudely called the "fish market." Some serious relationships began in this infamous way. Roseland's Wentworth Avenue served the same purpose for its young people.[131]

Essenburg was an activist pastor with a heart for community outreach and Christian political action. He had his congregation organize the Community Mission in 1931, which included a Sunday school and evening gospel meetings for the white underclass in the neighborhood. In 1941, the congregation purchased Bethel Hall on West 13th Street from the Chicago Hebrew Mission to carry on the work. Fifteen volunteers from the congregation staffed the ministry under Superintendent Clarence Leenhouts. Some sixty neighborhood youngsters attended the mission Sunday school, and more than fifty came out for the gospel meetings. Although the "church kids" and "mission kids" played in the streets together, the church elders kept them separate in religious activities.[132]

On a wider scale, Essenburg served on the boards of the Chicago Jewish Mission and the Helping Hand Mission, and he was treasurer of the denominational radio program beamed from Chicago, the *Back to God Hour*. He also headed the National Christian Association, a society founded in 1868 by Jonathan Blanchard, president of Wheaton College, to "point to Jesus Christ as the only Redeemer and to warn against the paganism of secret societies" (Freemasonry). The association's headquarters was next door to the Helping Hand Mission, and the city's Reformed and Christian Reformed churches promoted it and backed it financially.

130. Recollection of Ben Essenburg, shared with the author, 1 Oct. 2001.

131. Interview by the author with Dick Blaauw and Robert Vander Velde, 10 Mar. 1998; video interviews, Henry and Marie Tameling, 2 Feb. 1998; Effie (Mrs. Len) Dwarshuis nee Klaassens, 8 Aug. 1998, both by Martin Stulp.

132. B. Essenburg, "Chicago, Englewood, and Cicero Churches," *Banner*, 4 May 1934; C. Leenhouts, "About a Chicago Mission," ibid., 1 Dec. 1938; B. Essenburg, "West Chicago News," ibid., 7 Mar. 1941.

Essenburg was president of the association board in 1932 and for forty years served on the editorial board of its official organ, the *Christian Cynosure.* Gerard Van Pernis, pastor of the First Reformed Church in Fulton, Illinois, was editor-in-chief.[133]

Essenburg led First Chicago in 1932 in its sixty-fifth anniversary and in 1942 in its seventy-fifth birthday amid the trying times of war. The 1932 celebration included an all-day program before a capacity crowd, before whom Essenburg recited the proud past. Since 1867, the congregation counted 13 ministers, 58 elders, and 80 deacons; and the number of families increased from 15 to 200 in the mother church, plus 902 in daughter and granddaughter churches. "We have not yet grown old and weary in the service," Essenburg noted, "but, like the eagle, may renew our strength. With new courage and zeal, we go forward, determined to do more than ever for his service out of love and faithfulness."[134]

This Essenburg did with single-minded determination. At his farewell service in 1945, he reported that in his sixteen years at First Chicago he had preached 2,981 sermons – missing only one Sunday because of illness, baptized 471, heard confessions of faith of 354, married 208 couples, conducted 163 funerals, and gave 224 public addresses. He did not mention the numerous reports on Chicago church news that he wrote every few months for the denominational weekly, *The Banner.*[135]

This "iron man" pastor had touched the lives of an entire generation of Christian Reformed families in the Ashland Avenue district, and to this day old timers fondly recall the Essenburg era. He caused church life to flourish in his eleven-hundred-member congregation. The weekly schedule included three men's and three ladies' societies, an equal number of young men's and young ladies' societies, a choral society led by Dr. John Minnema and capable of performing Handel's *Messiah* annually, a church band, and a Sunday school staff of 22 teachers and 275 students.

133. George Marsden, *Fundamentalism and American Culture: The Shaping of Twentieth Century Evangelicalism, 1870-1925* (New York and Oxford: Oxford Univ. Press, 1980), 29, 31; B. Essenburg, "Chicago, Englewood, and Cicero Churches," *Banner,* 17 June 1932; 25 Oct. 1935; "National Christian Association at Work Abroad," ibid., 24 Nov. 1938. The association was organized in Pittsburgh but incorporated under Illinois law in 1874.

134. B. Essenburg, "Sixty-fifth Anniversary of First Chicago," *Banner,* 7 Oct. 1932; Consistory, "First Church of Chicago Celebrates Anniversary," ibid., 16 Oct. 1942.

135. Benjamin Essenburg, "Farewell Message from the Pastor," *First Christian Reformed Church Bulletin,* 8 Apr. 1945. Essenburg missed a Sunday in June, 1932, because of tonsillitis. "This was a strange experience," he noted (B. Essenburg, "Chicago, Englewood, and Cicero Churches," *Banner,* 17 June 1932).

World War II banner, 1942. First Christian Reformed Church of Chicago. Blue stars for each serviceman, gold stars for those "killed in action"

The congregation also single-handedly supported Ebenezer Christian School.[136]

In his last years in Chicago, Essenburg also led the congregation through the trying times of the Second World War, when it sent 135 men into the armed forces. A banner was hung on the wall behind the pulpit, and a blue star was stitched on it for each man who went to war. Before the war ended in 1945, four gold stars replaced blue ones to signify those who gave their all. These were Jacob Buikema, Gerrit Peters, Koert Stulp, and Henry Vander Kamp.[137]

Essenburg's colleague, Edward Masselink of Cicero's First Christian Reformed Church, in an obituary in the *Banner* spoke for many:

136. First Christian Reformed Church of Chicago, *Seventy-fifth Anniversary,* 15; William P. Brink, "Chicago North News," *Banner,* 23 Mar. 1945; obituary by Edward J. Masselink, ibid., 3 Dec. 1976. Essenburg officially retired in 1961 after forty years of ministry and returned to Chicago, living in Berwyn. But he continued to preach and write for another twelve years. He died at age eighty-six.

137. Martin LaMaire, "Our History," in Ebenezer Christian Reformed Church, *125th Anniversary, 1867-1992* (Berwyn, Ill., 1992).

> We shall remember Rev. Benjamin Essenburg as one of the most colorful and dynamic preachers of his generation. He had a sharp and scintillating mind, which he dedicated to his work in the ministry. He was keen in analyzing and understanding people, and always had an eye for the incongruities of life. Altogether he was an individual whose person and work will not soon be forgotten.
>
> His consuming passion was to be a minister of the Word of God. His life long, he never lost his sense of amazement that God should have called him to this work. The pulpit to him was more than a lectern. It was a place from which to proclaim the greatest message the world has ever heard.[138]

Hastings Street (First) Reformed Church, 1930s-1940s

Contemporaries of Essenburg at "Old First," as the flagship congregation was familiarly known, were Marinus Broekstra in 1929 and then Jacob Brouwer (1930-32) and Bart Van Zyl (1933-43). These men had to endure the harsh economic times of the Great Depression and to watch the membership decline rapidly with transfers to more westerly churches. Already in 1925, Broekstra declared that his family could no longer live in safety in the neighborhood, and he requested housing elsewhere. The church responded by raising his salary from $2,500 to $3,400 and telling him to buy or rent his own home. During Sunday worship, men of the church had to patrol the street to protect parishioners' automobiles.

That same year, 1925, the Hastings Street consistory discussed buying property in Berwyn on either Ridgeland or Home Avenues between Roosevelt Road and 22nd Street for a future church site. The action was prompted by an offer from a congregation of "coloreds" to buy the church and parsonage for $70,000 on land contract. The consistory put the offer to a congregational vote and set a two-thirds majority to pass. It failed, and the congregation remained in the Ashland Avenue district.

During the Depression, in 1932, Jacob Brouwer raised the language issue again but with little success. At the time, the morning service was in Dutch and the afternoon in English. "The future welfare of the church would be firmer if we had all English services," he noted. The context was the financial struggle to pay the salaries of the church staff. Brouwer was paid $4,000 with no housing or automobile allowance, but when he left in

138. Edward J. Masselink, "Rev. Benjamin Essenburg, 1890-1976," *Banner,* 3 Dec. 1976.

1932 after only two years, the congregation cut the salary on the next letter of call by 25 percent, to $3,000. That man declined, so the congregation raised the stipend on the next call to $3,500, with no better result. The next two call letters went out with the $3,000 stipend, and both were refused. This forced the consistory to raise the salary to $3,500 on the fifth call, to Bart Van Zyl, and he accepted. The choir also was told to get by without a paid director "for the time being owing to financial conditions." Under Van Zyl in 1937, the congregation voted two to one in a secret ballot to eliminate the Dutch service. Van Zyl was the last minister to serve in the Hastings Street location. Then the church relocated to Berwyn.[139]

Conclusion

By the late 1930s, the heyday of the Groninger Hoek on the Old West Side was passing. Although the older generations hung on until after the Second World War, the incessant movement of the Dutch into nicer neighborhoods drained off the up-and-coming families. Between 1920 and 1940, total membership in the Reformed churches on the Old West Side and Douglas Park declined from twenty-eight hundred to two thousand, while the Cicero-Berwyn churches increased from five hundred to twenty-five hundred, and the Englewood churches grew from twenty-eight hundred to thirty-seven hundred. Another mass migration of the Chicago Groningers was in full swing.

139. First Reformed Church of Chicago, Minutes, 25 Jan., 28 June (quote), 8 Sept., 7 Nov. 1932; 21 Feb., 17, 25 July 1933; 14 Jan. 1937; *Minutes of the RCA,* 1949, 206; 1971, 259.

CHAPTER 5

White Flight: Reformed Churches Seek the Suburbs

The constant population shift to the suburbs in large cities nationwide forced many Protestant congregations to face the question: "Should the church follow its members?" As the old neighborhoods spiraled down socially and economically and became increasingly dysfunctional, church members fled to the suburbs and did not wish to commute for worship. Soon the city churches, faced with shrinking memberships, could hardly meet their budgets. Every generation of Dutch Reformed congregations in Chicago found themselves in this situation. Their answer was simple: relocate. Sell the old churches and parsonages and build or buy new ones where the members had relocated.[1]

In Chicago, the option of keeping an old church for mission outreach, in obedience to the scriptural mandate to preach the gospel to every creature, was given short shrift. The two mission stations, the Helping Hand Mission and Nathanael Institute, served this purpose adequately, and funding these programs took priority. The Helping Hand Mission began ministering to black children as early as 1942, and in 1956 the former Nathanael Institute on Crawford Avenue was converted from a Jewish mission into a church for black families, becoming the Lawndale Chris-

1. Peter Y. De Jong, "Should the Church Follow its Members?" *Torch and Trumpet* 10 (April 1961): 19; Derk Bergsma, "A Tale of Two Churches: An Analysis and Critique of the Process of Decision Leading to Relocation from City to Suburb," unpublished seminar paper, University of Chicago, n.d.

tian Reformed Church. This congregation in the 1970s founded a Christian day school and developed a full-orbed ministry.[2]

The Christian Reformed churches of Chicago came closest to the ideal of inner-city mission outreach by creating the Roseland Christian Ministries Center in 1975, based in the former *Back to God Hour* building. The center, under the Reverend Tony Van Zanten, first focused on outreach to children. It expanded in the 1980s to include an overnight shelter and food service for men and the restoration of old houses for transitional housing for families. To nurture the center's social programs, the Roseland Christian Reformed Church was established in 1987 in the former Immanuel Reformed Church facility. Rounding out the ministry was the Roseland Christian School, which enrolled the black children who moved in as the white children moved out.[3]

Cicero-Berwyn-Oak Park

During World War I, the fourth Dutch hub on the West Side took shape in the nexus of Cicero, Berwyn, and Oak Park, the suburbs immediately west of the city and two to three miles from the "Island" on the Old West Side. Upwardly mobile Dutch began moving beyond the city limits before the war, but the Great Migration during the war from the South to northern cities, including Chicago, set off massive white flight. In the previous thirty years, Chicago's black population had increased slowly and was quite integrated, except for a narrow "black belt" on the South Side where four out of five lived. But the Great Migration during the war doubled the black population, and whites as well as middle-class blacks fled before the newcomers, whose very different socioeconomic status and consequent behavior were perceived as overly aggressive.[4]

The West Side, which in 1910 counted only 3,400 blacks (7.5 percent), came under pressure for the first time. Blacks soon dominated the area east of Ashland Street, which put the Hollanders west of the line on the very fringe of the encroaching ghetto. This situation, added to the rising incomes of the Dutch during the war and subsequent "prosperity decade"

2. B. Essenburg, "North Chicago News," *Banner,* 23 Oct. 1942.

3. Martin LaMaire, "Roseland Christian Ministries Thrives on Serving Needy," *Banner,* 12 Mar. 2001.

4. James R. Grossman, "African-American Migration to Chicago," 303-40, in Melvin G. Holli and Peter d'A. Jones, eds., *Ethnic Chicago: A Multicultural Portrait,* 4th ed. (Grand Rapids: Eerdmans, 1995).

of the 1920s, accelerated the so-called "Cicero movement," as did the new "automobility." Hollanders in all of the West Side churches joined the exodus, and by 1935 one Reformed and three Christian Reformed churches, as well as Timothy Christian School, were opened in the Warren Park district (figure 5.1).

That the suburban churches would grow "strong and rich" at the expense of the core city churches was not surprising, noted Peter Moerdyke with a tinge of chagrin. They receive the "best families from the city proper" while the "once commanding popular, great church[es] are hard pressed to maintain themselves. They must in order to live at all adjust themselves to the needs of an almost wholly new constituency of a far different character."[5]

The first Dutch Reformed congregation in Cicero was the **West Side Reformed Church of Chicago**, established with thirty-three families in December 1911 as a "mission church" of the First Reformed Church of Chicago. As with similar mission stations of Chicago's Dutch churches, it was not designed for community outreach as much as to serve Dutch families who had moved or were contemplating settling in the area. This is evident in the demand of the classis, at the behest of the mother church, that a geographical "dividing line" at 55th Avenue must be drawn. Members would be directed to one church or the other depending on their place of residence. West Side Reformed Church began with thirty-two communicant members, all but one transferred from First Chicago. The Nicholas Knol, Sr., family, including adult sons Albert, George, and John and his wife, transferred from the Trinity Reformed Church. Knol, Sr., provided sterling leadership until his untimely death in 1917 at age fifty-three. Elder Theodore Zandstra was the first clerk.[6]

At first the body worshiped in a vacant store at 5737 West 12th Street and then in a home and later a garage on Austin Boulevard (6000 west) at 13th Street. Within three months of organizing, the resolute members bought for $1,300 a large lot a few hundred feet to the south, at 1321 Austin Boulevard (figure 5.1, site 6). On this prestigious boulevard, the main thoroughfare of Cicero, the congregation constructed a church edifice.

5. Moerdyke, "Chicago Letter," *CI,* 21 Mar. 1900, p. 185.

6. First Reformed Church of Chicago, Minutes, 27 June, 25 July, 29 Aug. 1911; *Onze Toekomst,* 3 Jan. 1913; West Side Reformed Church, *Program and Historical Sketch of the Twenty-Fifth Anniversary, 1911-1936* (Cicero, 1936), 5; West Side Reformed Church, *Fiftieth Anniversary Program and Historical Sketch, 1911-1961* (Cicero, 1961), 7-17. The exploratory meeting, held in Jacob Nienhuis's home in Cicero on 2 August 1911, proved promising. Nienhuis was the main church organist.

Figure 5.1 Churches and Schools in Cicero, Berwyn, and Oak Park

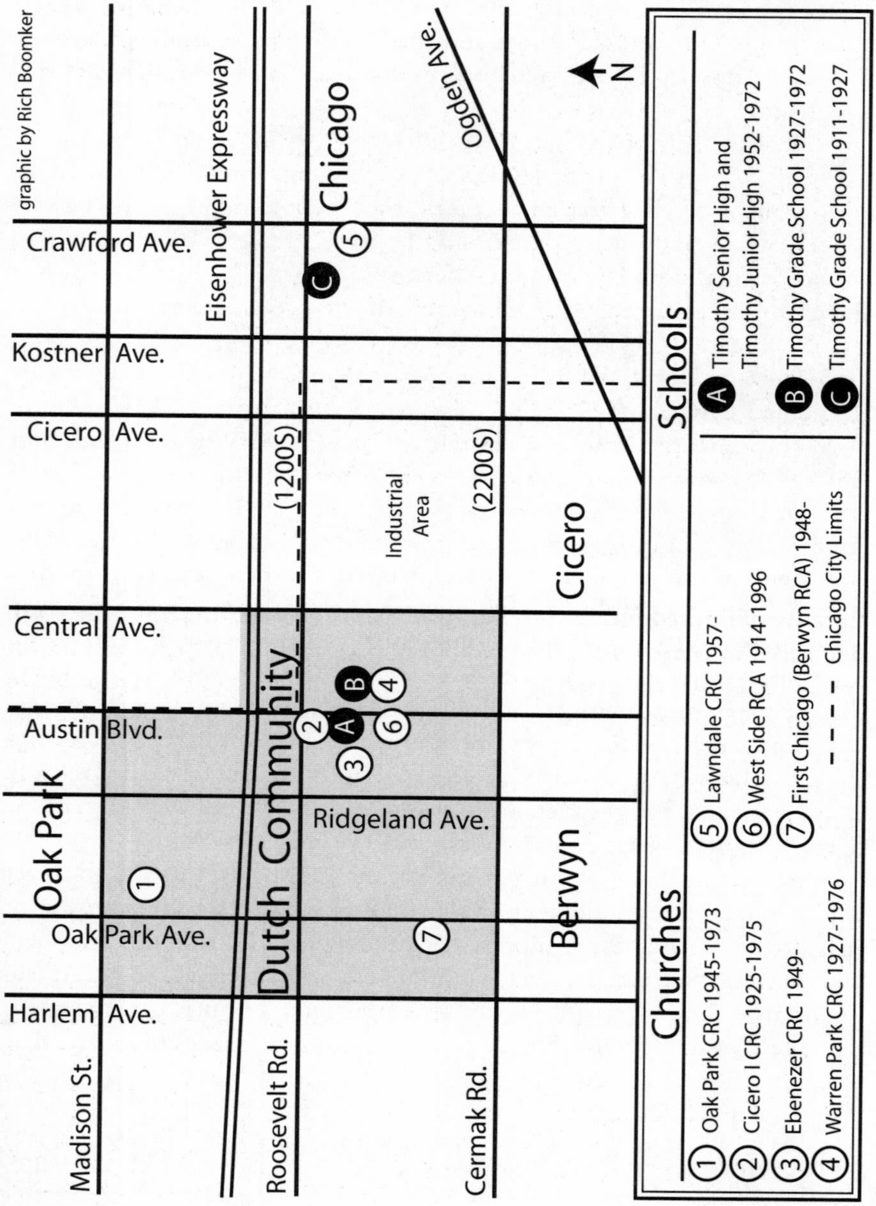

graphic by Rich Boomker

Madison St.
Eisenhower Expressway
Roosevelt Rd.
(1200S)
Industrial Area
(2200S)
Cermak Rd.
Ogden Ave.
N
Harlem Ave.
Oak Park Ave.
Ridgeland Ave.
Austin Blvd.
Central Ave.
Cicero Ave.
Kostner Ave.
Crawford Ave.
Oak Park
Dutch Community
Berwyn
Cicero
Chicago

Churches

1 Oak Park CRC 1945-1973
2 Cicero I CRC 1925-1975
3 Ebenezer CRC 1949-
4 Warren Park CRC 1927-1976
5 Lawndale CRC 1957-
6 West Side RCA 1914-1996
7 First Chicago (Berwyn RCA) 1948-
- - - - Chicago City Limits

Schools

A Timothy Senior High and Timothy Junior High 1952-1972
B Timothy Grade School 1927-1972
C Timothy Grade School 1911-1927

West Side Reformed Church, Cicero, erected 1924 *(Courtesy of John Dryfhout)*

Because of limited funds, they initially built only the basement, which was dedicated in March, 1914. The denomination loaned $2,500 of the $5,950 cost. This served the growing flock for ten years, until 1924 when, aided by a $15,000 loan from the denomination, the 430 members added the impressive super-structure, in the English Tudor style, costing $65,000. Already in 1916 they had built the adjoining parsonage for $5,000. After two more land purchases, the frontage totaled two hundred feet, which provided abundant space for car parking.

In the summer of 1912, a seminary intern, Henry Pasma, helped the infant congregation until the arrival of the first pastor, the popular Frisian, Peter Braak (1912-16), who preached "a plain gospel" and oversaw the construction of the first building phase, the "basement church." Henry Pietenpol (1916-20) first enjoyed the new parsonage; West Side was his fifth charge and the pinnacle of his career. He ably led the congregation through the turbulent war years, after which they had to wait two years for another "under-shepherd," having experienced eight declines to calls. Pietenpol helped the congregation resolve the problem of lodge membership that had troubled it from the beginning; in 1918 the consistory decided no longer to accept any such members. In 1922 Henry Vander Naald, a Princeton Seminary graduate, took up the work and carried on for twenty-two years, until 1944. He was an anchor during the church's

Rev. Henry Vander Naald (1878-1969)

flourishing period and saw the completion of its edifice, but he "outstayed his welcome" and the church suffered in the 1940s.[7]

Unlike most Reformed Church leaders, Vander Naald was a strong supporter of Christian schooling, and a number of families in his congregation sent their children to the nearby Timothy Christian School. The church in 1925 also began the Stickney Sunday School on 41st Street near Oak Park Avenue, which evolved into the Faith Community Church of Stickney.

Under Vander Naald's successor, Benjamin Hoffman (1945-52), the flourishing congregation in 1946 burned the mortgage and then undertook many improvements to the building, including a costly Möller pipe organ in 1950. Hoffman, too, backed Timothy School. In 1950 the congregation numbered almost 650 souls. From the mid-fifties, the migration to

7. West Side Reformed Church, *Historical Highlights,* 11-12; Classis of Chicago Minutes, 13 April 1943.

the far west suburbs put West Side Reformed Church into a long, slow decline, and in 1995 the congregation disbanded after a ministry of eighty-five years. The remnant joined the First Reformed Church of Chicago in Berwyn.[8]

The Third Christian Reformed Church was the second body to relocate to Cicero. Late in 1924 the congregation held a momentous meeting, and the majority voted to follow the lead of many members and buy property in Cicero. A site committee selected a vacant lot near the interchange of Roosevelt Road (formerly 12th Street) and Austin Boulevard. This intersection straddled the borders of three cities – Chicago, Cicero, and Oak Park – and was the major business hub of the entire region. Austin Boulevard was also the western terminus of the Roosevelt Road streetcar line from the city center.

One year later, in 1925, the congregation sold its Grenshaw Street property and appointed a building committee to plan a new place of worship. Third Chicago lived up to its reputation for bold and innovative thinking. When the building committee first presented the plans to the congregation, they were "at once gigantic, at first blush staggering, and yet such that evidences courage and the forward look." The consistory and its committee worked with "untiring zeal" to sell the project and succeeded in putting the fears of the ninety-family congregation "to shame." An early commemorative history testifies that "a unified aim and purpose gripped the congregation as well, as they saw ambitions and visions realized."[9]

The result was a magnificent Gothic church with cathedral glass windows in the 1200 block of 60th Court, which was completed and dedicated just before Thanksgiving Day 1925 at a cost of $140,000 (figure 5.1, site 2). Thus, the first English church on the West Side successfully negotiated the twin shoals of deciding to relocate and then managing an ambitious building campaign, both of which issues had a history of ripping

8. Pastors after Hoffman were Russell Horton (1953-57), Joseph Holbrook (1957-64), William Brouwer (1965-73), Henry Elgersma (1974-82), Roger Johnson (1983-91), and Ronald Amos (1992-1994). See Gasero, *Historical Directory*, 513; obituaries in *Minutes of the General Synod of the Reformed Church in America*, 1925, 1016; 1948, 225-26; 1969, 303. Church records are now in the archives of the Reformed Church in America, New Brunswick, N.J.

9. First Christian Reformed Church of Cicero, *Commemoration of the Twenty-Fifth Anniversary*, 11; *Golden Anniversary, 1912-1962;* Neal Folgers, "From 12th Street to Lombard: The History of Lombard CRC," Senior History Seminar Paper, 1987, Archives, Calvin College. The building committee included Gerrit Bossenga, L. Buurma, George De Vries, C. Loerop, Thomas J. Stob, George Tinge, Gerrit Vandenburg, Peter Visser, and Theodore S. Youngsma.

First Christian Reformed Church of Cicero,
erected 1925; parsonage on left
(The Archives, Calvin College)

congregations apart. The Reverend Jacob Weersing deserves much of the credit for preserving harmony and unity of purpose. It helped that the congregation was familiar with the process; this was its fourth move. In Cicero, the Third Church of Chicago became the **First Christian Reformed Church of Cicero**, with the emphasis on the word "first." A new parsonage in matching brick was erected next to the church edifice.[10]

During Weersing's tenure, the congregation doubled from 445 to 885 souls. He accomplished another feat, getting the consistory to allow the church singing society to evolve into the church choir. Many Reformed folk considered church choirs frivolous and detrimental to vibrant congregational singing. Cornelius Kickert, a young music teacher and skilled organist in the congregation who had recently graduated from Calvin College, convinced the leaders to open the morning service to the choir, but the first time the fifty-voice choir sang, at least one elderly parishioner walked out in protest. This was the infamous year 1929. Weersing managed to quell the protest, and over time the people learned to appreciate Kickert's tradition of fine organ and choral music. The 1926

10. The architecture and design of the church building is described in detail in the First Christian Reformed Church of Cicero, *Dedication Program, 'Deo Gratias,'* 22 Nov. 1926, Archives, Calvin College.

Rev. Jacob J. Weersing (1879-1976)
(The Archives, Calvin College)

synod had given its blessing to choirs singing in worship services, subject to approval by the local consistory.[11]

When Weersing chose to move on in 1933, First Cicero aimed high, calling successfully a college professor and president, the Reverend Dr. William Rutgers (1933-43), who had taught at Grundy College in Iowa, an institution of the German-speaking wing of the Christian Reformed Church. Rutgers was one of only a handful of clerics in the denomination with an earned doctorate. With the full vigor of youth, he put his poetic gifts, way with words, and ready humor to good use in his ministry. The church grew, and the young people responded most enthusiastically to his warm and powerful preaching. Because of his love for high quality music, Rutgers supported Kickert's organ and choral work at the church. The

11. Lombard Christian Reformed Church, *Celebrating Seventy-Five Years, October 9, 1987* (Lombard, Ill., 1987), 4; Kickert, "Last Meeting at Coffee Hour at Cicero I Church," 5; "Report Regarding Choir Singing," *Banner,* 24 Jan. 1930.

Rev. William Rutgers (1898-1980)
(The Archives, Calvin College)

singing mortician George Mulder added his talents to the church musical scene.

Rutgers gave the church added exposure throughout the Chicago area every Sunday afternoon by broadcasting on radio station WHFC-AM his trademark Heidelberg Catechism sermons. He called the program *The Reformed Hour.* First Cicero had grown to over eleven hundred members when the congregation, after ten vibrant years, reluctantly bade Rutgers farewell in 1943. He left to become a professor at Calvin Theological Seminary.[12]

Interestingly, during Rutgers's tenure, the young men's societies of his congregation sponsored a "Psalm-Hymn program" for the societies of all four Christian Reformed congregations on the West Side. The evening featured a song service of Holland psalms and hymns, with piano and organ accompaniment, followed by a debate between two speakers from Calvin College on the issue of singing hymns in worship. That the use of

12. Lombard Christian Reformed Church, *Celebrating Seventy-Five Years,* 4; obituary of Rutgers by John T. Holwerda, *Banner,* 29 Sept. 1980; B. Essenburg, "West Chicago News," ibid., 26 Oct. 1939; "News from First Cicero," ibid., 25 Feb. 1944.

Rev. Edward Masselink (1901-99)
(The Archives, Calvin College)

Rev. Rolf Veenstra (1913-90)
(The Archives, Calvin College)

hymns, against which the founders of the denomination in 1857 had railed, should still remain open for debate eighty years later was due to the fact that the denomination in 1934 had authorized a new worship hymnal that for the first time included hymns.[13]

Another minister with a doctorate, Edward Masselink, next took the helm at First Cicero. Unlike the systematic theologian Rutgers, Masselink was a biblical theologian who interpreted the sacred text historically and applied it to everyday life in sermons that ran to fifty minutes. He continued the church's community outreach efforts during a ministry of six years (1944-50), as did his successor, Rolf Veenstra (1952-57). Veenstra's rhetorical style contrasted sharply with his predecessor; he spoke concisely and to the point in pithy, twenty-minute sermons that appealed to all. The young people especially delighted in services that often ended within the hour. Tragedy struck the congregation when Veenstra's wife, Helen Sweetman, died unexpectedly during a minor operation. In 1957, Veenstra resigned to minister in the Nigerian mission field of the denomination.

First Cicero reached its zenith in membership in the early 1950s at three hundred families, or twelve hundred souls. This far surpassed the

13. *Chicago Messenger,* 28 Feb. 1936.

capacity of even this large auditorium strung with folding chairs in the aisles. Worshipers had to come a half-hour early to avoid the basement overflow room supplied by the public address system. By the late 1950s, however, the call "Westward Ho!" again became strong, and many families began moving into the far suburbs of Bellwood, Western Springs, Elmhurst, and Wheaton, where Christian Reformed congregations had already been established.[14]

The outmigration speeded up in the 1960s, during the pastorates of Henry Erffmeyer (1957-63), Jacob Boonstra (1963-68), and John Ebbers (1969-78). Erffmeyer laid out his agenda in a letter to the congregation: "We must develop more reformed distinctiveness; cultivate more covenant consciousness and we must muster more mission-mindedness." In his sermons, Erffmeyer stood in the tradition of the "hell, fire, and brimstone" preachers. The congregation suffered another blow in the middle of his pastorate, with the death from cancer of its music leader, Cornelius Kickert, but his daughter Virginia Folgers carried on ably as church organist. "Neal," as he was known, had played the organ and led the choir at both morning and evening services for more than thirty years.[15]

Jacob Boonstra, a man in his mid-thirties, appealed to the young people, but this did not stay the outmigration. During the five years of his pastorate, the membership declined from one thousand to six hundred because of transfers to the Western Springs and Elmhurst Christian Reformed churches. Boonstra's successor, John Ebbers, brought good leadership and preaching skills, but families continued to go west and the membership dropped to a hundred families (425 souls). By 1974, the congregation and its societies were hardly viable, and the financial burden was so great that the congregation had to face giving up its beautiful and beloved sanctuary. The choices were to merge with long-time rival Warren Park (formerly Second Cicero), move west, or stay put and change the focus of ministry to a community outreach among non-Dutch. After much heated discussion over many months, the congregation voted down the

14. Wheaton Christian Reformed Church was organized in 1950 and for many years was the most westerly congregation on the West Side. Wheaton, forty miles west of the Chicago city center, was a distant commute on the Northwestern Railroad. Second Cicero was the mother church of the Des Plaines (1929) and Western Springs Christian Reformed churches (1938), both of which served Dutch truck farmers in these areas southwest and northwest of the city. Gradually all three localities came into the expanding suburban orbit of greater Chicago.

15. Folgers, "From 12th Street to Lombard." Folgers is a grandson and namesake of Cornelius (Neal) Kickert.

Second (Warren Park) Christian Reformed Church of Cicero, erected 1927

merger and chose to relocate at a cost of $600,000. They bought property in Lombard and broke ground for a new church in 1975. The turmoil hastened the membership loss, but Ebbers managed to keep the remnant together and regroup them after the move.[16]

The **Second Christian Reformed Church of Cicero** was the third Dutch congregation in town. It stemmed from the decision of the Douglas Park Church to follow its members to the suburbs, just as Third Chicago had done two years earlier. In 1927, Douglas Park constructed an imposing red brick church on the southwest corner of 14th Street and 58th Court (figure 5.1, site 4). The structure, with magnificent stained glass windows, was impressive, but it could not match the imposing presence of the First Cicero building. The project required a step of faith, because the congregation had no pastor at the time and its Harding Avenue building had been sold to a Jewish congregation before the new church was ready. So the congregation worshiped temporarily in a vacant factory on 55th Court and then in the auditorium of the just-completed Timothy Christian School, which had also relocated that same year from Tripp Av-

16. First Christian Reformed Church of Cicero, *Golden Anniversary, 1912-1962,* 8-10; Folgers, "From 12th Street to Lombard."

enue to 14th Street and 59th Court, one block west of the new church (figure 5.1, sites B and C).

During this time of transition, the Reverend Peter A. ("P.A.") Hoekstra accepted the congregation's call and came from Grand Rapids to pastor the church, known colloquially as "Cicero II" until taking the name of the area, Warren Park, in 1947. Hoekstra grew up in Roseland, Illinois, where his parents had settled after emigrating from Friesland when he was a young child. He holds the distinction of being the first Calvin Seminary student to begin ministerial studies after earning a Bachelor of Arts degree (from the prestigious University of Chicago in 1907).

Hoekstra, who had the rare ability to preach well in both Dutch and English, faced the controversial task of convincing a reluctant and strongly vocal minority that it was time to adopt English in the primary morning and evening worship services, maintaining Dutch in the afternoon service. This was the only way to prevent the next generation from becoming "oncers," i.e., those who attend only one service.[17] Hoekstra succeeded in making the switch in 1938, but at the cost for a time of his emotional health, which was restored by a prolonged leave of absence in California. The language battles in the Christian Reformed congregation in the 1920s and 1930s followed similar controversies in Reformed congregations a generation or two earlier. This is another marker of the slower pace of Americanization in the Christian Reformed Church.

Two years after the congregation took on its huge building debt, in October 1929 the stock market plunged and the Great Depression began. With Dutch fiscal conservatism, the congregation met its financial obligations during the dreary thirties and grew steadily, reaching 780 members by 1940 when Hoekstra left for the Hanford, California, church. In his thirteen years in Cicero, Hoekstra preached meaty, exegetical sermons that produced "real spiritual growth." Cornelius Schoolland, his patriotic successor, left for the military chaplaincy in 1943, after serving only nineteen months. He joined more than fifty men from the congregation then in the armed forces.[18]

Schoolland was followed by the studious and evangelical Marvin Vander Werp (1944-48), the energetic Enno Haan (1949-56), the intellectual Derk Bergsma (1958-62), the orthodox Fred Van Houten (1962-70), and fi-

17. B. Essenburg, "Chicago, Englewood, and Cicero Churches," *Banner,* 24 Feb. 1938; P. A. Hoekstra, obituary, Christian Reformed Church *Yearbook,* 1966. The rationale for two English services, so as not to produce "oncers," is given by editor H. J. Kuiper, "Church Attendance in Bi-Lingual Congregations," *Banner,* 2 June 1938.

18. "Second Cicero Bids Farewell to Its Pastor," ibid., 23 Apr. 1943.

Rev. Peter A. Hoekstra
(1886-1965)

Rev. Enno L. Haan
(1910-82)

nally the innovative Alvin Mulder (1970-77). Vander Werp preached twice monthly at the Sunday afternoon Dutch language service for the "slowly dwindling, though still active and loyal, Holland-preferring element."[19] Geraldine Ronda was the organist for twenty years (1929-49), along with Elco Ostendorp, and they were followed by Andrew Hoekstra and Angeline Ter Maat Swierenga (Mrs. Ralph).

The major growth in Cicero II came immediately after World War II, when sixty families transferred from churches closing on the Old West Side. By 1949 membership had jumped to nine hundred souls, which was close to capacity for the facilities, including the spacious balcony. This is where the "liberated" teenagers sat in the evening service, while their families were in the pews below. The teens were sometimes unruly and disturbed the peace and quiet, especially during sermons that they found boring. More than once, pastors had to stop speaking and stare at, or ver-

19. "Second Church of Cicero," ibid., 30 June 1944.

Sanctuary, Second (Warren Park) Christian Reformed Church of Cicero, 1949

bally admonish, the miscreants. The consistory took action in 1934 and assigned two young men, John R. Swierenga and Edward Wezeman, to sit in the balcony and police the teens.[20]

Mother Churches Move

By the mid 1940s, the mother churches on the Old West Side of Chicago – First Reformed, First Christian Reformed, and Fourth Christian Reformed – could no longer ignore the constant "population shift" to the suburbs. The minutes of almost every consistory meeting in these churches reported families transferring to Cicero, Berwyn, and, to a lesser extent, Englewood. First Reformed particularly suffered from a spiritual

20. Enno L. Haan, "A Golden Anniversary and Great Welcome," ibid., 19 Aug. 1949; T. D. Pals, "Growth of the Congregation," containing a line graph, in Warren Park Christian Reformed Church, *Golden Anniversary, 1899-1949,* 34; Second Christian Reformed Church, *Bulletin,* 11 Mar. 1934.

malaise, especially in its English-language services, where attendance dropped off sharply among the second and third generation. It was "a trend of the times," lamented the pastor.[21]

The churches finally had no choice but to sell their buildings to black congregations and relocate, which happened quickly in the space of two years, 1945-46. Ebenezer Christian School also closed in 1946, and its remaining pupils transferred to Timothy School in Cicero. Only a handful of elderly folk were left behind.

First Reformed Church of Chicago first positioned itself for the inevitable relocation to Cicero or Berwyn in 1934 by starting catechism classes there in the basement of elder N. Diephouse's home. The next step was to start a mission church out west, but the high cost of rental space forced them to go slowly. The relocation committee zeroed in on Berwyn, because the West Side church served Cicero well. In 1937 the congregation was able to rent the Berwyn Gospel Tabernacle for $5 for a Sunday evening service and the Christian Endeavor youth meeting that followed. The first three services went well, so Peter Rozendal was hired to conduct the services, while Bart Van Zyl preached at Hastings Street. The group temporarily adopted the name Calvary Reformed Church.[22]

Calvary Church was led by pastors Raymond Beckering (1940-42) and Henry Kik (1943-49) and worshiped at first in rented quarters. In 1944, after Van Zyl left and Kik became the sole pastor of both Hastings Street and Calvary, the mother church merged with its daughter. The next year, 1945, the Hastings Street church sold its building to the black Shiloh Baptist Church and bought lots in Berwyn at the corner of Oak Park Avenue and 19th Street (figure 5.1, site 7). The reunified congregation retained the name **First Reformed Church of Chicago**, although it was located in Berwyn.

For three years the flock worshiped in various rented places – Timothy Christian School, West Side Reformed, a store on Cermak Road, and a United Presbyterian church in Oak Park. In December 1948, the congregation finally dedicated its new sanctuary, and the unsettled years came mercifully to an end. Kik served until 1949 and was followed by Arnold Dykhuizen (1950-60), Douglas Van Gessel (1961-68), Albert Van Dyke (1970-79), and Harold Rust (1979-98).

When the First Christian Reformed Church of Chicago moved to

21. Classis of Chicago, Minutes, April 1943.

22. First Reformed Church of Chicago, Minutes, 25 Sept. 1934; 27 Oct. 1936; 14, 26 Jan., 27 Aug., 28 Sept., 14 Oct., 14, 30 Nov. 1937; 5 Jan., 22 Feb. 1938.

First Reformed Church of Chicago in Berwyn, erected 1948

(Western Seminary Collection, Joint Archives of Holland)

Berwyn in 1946, it chose the name **Ebenezer Christian Reformed Church**. The decision to relocate six miles west to the tri-cities area was prompted by "white flight" from the inner city, "due to the great influx of colored folks into the vicinity."[23] The congregation also had lost its much-beloved pastor of sixteen years, Benjamin Essenburg, whose tenure was the longest in the history of the congregation. Shortly after Essenburg left for the Jenison, Michigan, church, the shrunken flock in Chicago held a historic congregational meeting in the summer of 1945. The congregation voted to sell the Ashland Avenue church and parsonage and build a new church in Berwyn on a choice lot at 1300 South Harvey Avenue (figure 5.1, site 3). It took four years to finance and construct the new church, an imposing flagstone structure, with four columns and a soaring cupola with bell tower. Andrew Folkema (1945-52) pastored the flock during the prolonged time of resettlement.

More than a year passed before the final worship service on Ashland Avenue was held on the last Sunday afternoon of 1946. The *Centennial Booklet* of 1967 speaks of the poignant moment: "The auditorium was

23. William P. Brink, "Chicago North News," *Banner*, 27 Apr. 1945.

Ebenezer Christian Reformed Church, Berwyn, erected 1949
(The Archives, Calvin College)

crowded with members, past and present. There was a feeling of sadness as the keys were turned over to the incoming group."

The church had left an indelible mark. Over the decades, several dozen members went into full-time Christian service, fifteen as ministers of the gospel. The latter included home missionary John R. Brink and foreign missions director Henry Evenhouse; church leaders Herman Hoeksema and Harry and Ralph Danhof; evangelist John Rozendal; Calvin Seminary professors Henry and Ralph Stob, John Zwaanstra; three Veldmans – Herman and brother Richard, Sr., and his son Richard, Jr.; and Ben Essenburg, founding pastor of a charismatic congregation. Martin Essenburg, Ben's nephew, served as an educational missionary in Japan and then administered the Holland, Michigan, Christian School system and Covenant College in Georgia. Chaplain Herman Keizer became a full colonel in the United States Army. Among the nine lay evangelists were missionary nurses Tena Huizenga in Nigeria and Marie De Bruin and Edith Vander Meulen at the Chicago Jewish Mission, and street evangelist Clarence Laning of the Chicago Helping Hand Mission.[24]

24. Others included the Revs. B. Danhof, William Dryfhout, Peter Huisman, Oliver Breen, and Richard Karsten and evangelists H. Hoekstra, Peter Vander Kamp, Peter Laning,

Tena Huizenga (1907-78), late 1930s

Tena Huizenga was a graduate of the Chicago Mission Training School (predecessor of the Reformed Bible College) and the Garfield Park Community Hospital nursing program. She worked in the slums of Chicago until instructors at the Moody Bible Institute kindled a desire to "labor in darkest Africa." She left in 1937 under the auspices of the Sudan United Mission for Lupwe, Nigeria, where she ministered to "both body and soul" for seventeen years, until 1954. Tena Huizenga was the West Side's very own African missionary and no one was held in higher esteem. The Second Cicero church proudly claimed her as a member and generously supported her ministry.[25]

During the next years the congregation worshiped in seven different places. The remnant in the old neighborhood met for Holland language

Elise Dykstra, Cora Renkema, and Jacoba Tibma. For a complete listing, see *Illinois Observer,* Mar. 1956; First Christian Reformed Church of Chicago, *Seventy-fifth Anniversary,* 15, 24, 40; Martin LaMaire, "U.S. Army Chaplain (Col.) Herman Keizer, Jr.," *Banner,* 13 Aug. 2001. Other congregations on the Old West Side, of course, recounted similar lists of "heroes of the faith."

25. Shawn Brix, *In the Master's Service: The Life of Tena Huizenga* (Grand Rapids: Calvin Theological Seminary, 1994); Gerald L. Zandstra, *Daughters Who Dared: Answering God's Call to Nigeria* (Grand Rapids: Calvin Theological Seminary, 1992), 85-88, 99, 103.

services at Beacon House, a Presbyterian social center at 15th Street and Ashland Avenue, while afternoon English worship was held at the nearby Salem Evangelical Church, located at the corner of Washburne Avenue (13th Place) and Wolcott Street (1900 west). The Berwyn contingent had meanwhile begun worshiping at the Good News Center at 15th Street and Ridgeland Avenue and then at the Olympic Hall at 61st Court and Cermak Road (formerly 22nd Street). In mid-1947 the consistory moved the afternoon English service to Cicero by making use of the First Cicero Church sanctuary. The evening service at Olympic Hall continued until early 1948, when it was transferred to the Trinity Evangelical Church at Austin Boulevard and Fillmore Street. Consistory meetings and societies met at the Berwyn Bible Church on Roosevelt Road at Lombard Avenue. Finally, in late 1948, the basement of the new church was finished, and the congregation worshiped there for six months until the superstructure was completed. After so much turmoil, the congregation dedicated its new church building with great rejoicing in April of 1949. It was one of the more imposing edifices in the denomination.[26]

During this time, transition minister Andrew Folkema focused on pastoral work and sound doctrinal preaching and left much of the practical matters of church governance to the consistory. This practice encouraged solid lay leadership in the congregation. In 1949 Ebenezer and the Warren Park church in Cicero decided to alternate their Holland afternoon services, a sign of the coming end. Folkema's successor was the youngest pastor ever to serve the congregation, the "twenty something" Louis Dykstra (1953-57). Under the energetic Dykstra, eighty-five persons made profession of faith, which testified to the healthy spiritual condition of the congregation. The mission-minded Herman Hoekstra (1957-62) maintained the evangelical emphasis; his sermons, delivered in a "stentorian voice," stressed the need for repentance. Eugene Bradford (1963-69), the first minister of non-Dutch descent, took the flock in a different direction. His strong Calvinistic teachings challenged the members to take their beliefs into public life and the workplace. During his time, the congregation of nearly eight hundred souls replaced its electronic organ with a Casavant pipe organ to enhance congregational singing.

In the tumultuous decade of the 1970s, Esler Shuart (1970-80) provided steady and wise leadership for Ebenezer, but the westward movement gained momentum again and the membership dropped precipitously. Fred Gunnink (1982-85), Duane Timmermans (1986-92), and

26. "Dedication of Ebenezer Church, Berwyn, Illinois," *Banner,* 13 May 1949.

Lugene Schemper (1992-2000) maintained the congregation of just over two hundred souls. Ebenezer and First Reformed, which is slightly smaller, are the only Dutch Reformed churches remaining in the tri-city area, since West Side Reformed in Cicero closed in 1996. Their commitment to the community remains strong, although the relentless Dutch-American population movement west will eventually require the Berwyn churches to relocate or refocus their ministry on non-Dutch neighbors.[27]

Fourth Chicago Christian Reformed moved west in two steps; an initial one in 1935 and then again in 1945. In June 1935 some sixty members gathered at the church to consider a plan of the consistory to stave off the dissolution of the congregation by forming a branch in Cicero. The consistory had been grappling for some time with the "Cicero movement." Fourth Chicago declined by 100 members in just five years, dropping from 450 to 350 souls between 1930 and 1935. The consistory thus proposed that pastor James Putt conduct services every other week in Cicero at the Timothy Christian School, and that an associate pastor be hired to preach on the alternate weeks. The Timothy board offered the school auditorium rent-free. Elder George Ottenhoff made an impassioned speech in favor of the proposal, and it was adopted unanimously after he and the pastor had allayed fears that the decision would destroy the "ties of Christian fellowship and the bonds of tradition."[28]

Assurances notwithstanding, the fears proved well founded, because the consistory did not follow the prescribed denominational procedure in the calling process. It selected and installed a member of the congregation who held credentials in an Iowa classis without first obtaining the approval of Classis Illinois, to which the church was accountable. This person was the Reverend Frederick Wezeman, the principal and Bible teacher at the Chicago Christian High School. Classis Illinois declared Wezeman's appointment illegal, against the advice of a six-person synodical committee from Grand Rapids that unanimously endorsed Wezeman. Fourth Chicago appealed this decision to the national synod of 1936, but the case did not go smoothly because Wezeman was under a cloud of suspicion for theological "modernism" (see chapter 7). While the wheels of church governance ground slowly, Fourth Chicago scheduled Wezeman, an ordained elder, to preach at the mother church, and it sent pastor Putt to the Cicero

27. Ebenezer Christian Reformed Church, *Centennial Booklet, 1867-1967* (Berwyn, Ill., 1967), 9-10.

28. "Fourth Church to Hold Services in Cicero," *Chicago Messenger,* 28 June 1935; "Fourth Christian Reformed Church of Chicago," *Banner,* 14 Apr. 1938.

branch. In the end, the classis approved Wezeman's appointment as associate pastor of Fourth Chicago.[29]

Under the preaching of Putt and Wezeman, the Cicero branch grew rapidly, and soon the dual congregation was back to full strength. Eventually the Cicero branch shifted worship services to Berwyn, which was further west than the three already established Reformed congregations in Cicero. After four years, in June 1939, seventeen families organized the Berwyn Christian Reformed Church with the blessing of the mother church. The young congregation attracted a number of Reformed Church families in the area, and it worshiped in the Bohemian Baptist Chapel on Ridgeland Avenue (6400 west) at 15th Street. The first consistory members were principal John Van Bruggen of Timothy Christian School, George De Boer, and Andrew Hoekstra, elders, and John Wieringa and George De Vries, deacons.

The congregation soon called the beloved Herman Bel, the first pastor of Fourth Church, and he accepted. "Dominie" Bel had recently returned to the Chicago area to teach Bible at the Chicago Christian High School, after serving a pastorate at the prestigious La Grave Avenue Christian Reformed Church of Grand Rapids. Morning worship in this upscale Berwyn congregation was set at the late hour of 10:30, and the gifted Henry Baar directed the church choir.[30]

The mother church generously donated money to buy a parsonage for Bel, who served the Berwyn church for its first five years, until 1944, when the dual task became too great. In 1942 the congregation had welcomed nine families from the nearby Calvary Reformed Church. Bel preached his farewell sermon just as the body, which had grown to two hundred members, welcomed his successor, the Reverend Elbert Kooistra (1944-52). Bel remained with the church as an associate pastor, under the colorful and forceful Kooistra.[31]

Kooistra arrived at a major transition point in the life of the congregation. It had just purchased a beautiful church on the tree-lined Jackson Boulevard at Wesley Avenue (6700 west) in the heart of the upscale suburb of Oak Park (figure 5.1, site 1). Constructed in 1927 by a Lutheran congregation in the Gothic style with stained glass windows and "two pulpits" (actually a pulpit and lectern), it was the most imposing stone church ever

29. "Chicago IV Activities," ibid., 29 Nov. 1935, p. 5.

30. "Fourth Christian Reformed Church," ibid., 26 Apr. 1940; B. Essenburg, "West Chicago News," ibid., 15 June 1939.

31. B. Essenburg, "North Chicago News," ibid., 23 Oct. 1942; "Oak Park, Illinois (formerly Berwyn) Christian Reformed Church," ibid., 9 Feb. 1945.

owned by any Chicago-area Dutch congregation. And the Berwyn church bought it for only one-tenth of its value. The poor Dutch immigrants had arrived!

With a spacious sanctuary came a new name, **Oak Park Christian Reformed Church**, and new members. Almost the entire membership of Fourth Chicago amalgamated with its daughter congregation in 1945, and the original body disbanded and sold its facilities. The tireless and affable Kooistra now served the reconstituted congregation in Oak Park.

Oak Park Christian Reformed Church held its own under the Reverend Richard Frens (1953-58), a calm and scholarly man, and the youthful Earl Marlink (1959-66), but by the late 1960s three members left for every four who joined. Some departing members transferred to newer congregations farther west, but a disturbing number joined other denominations or simply resigned. This, together with more frequent non-Dutch marriages, signified that the cohesive ethnic community was fraying at the edges. Under John Morren (1966-70) and Oliver Breen (1970-73), the membership losses continued, dropping from 500 to 325 members.

Since Warren Park Christian Reformed Church in Cicero was experi-

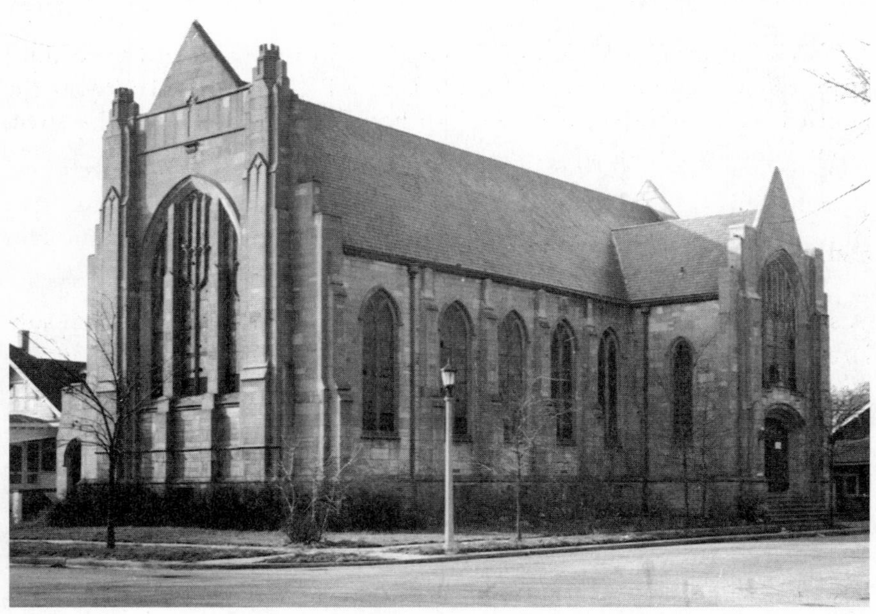

Oak Park Christian Reformed Church, 1945-73

(The Archives, Calvin College)

encing the same pattern of losses, the two congregations decided to merge and eventually to relocate west. In 1973 Oak Park, by a 95 percent margin, and Warren Park, by a 75 percent margin, approved the merger and took the name West Suburban Christian Reformed Church. But in an unusual way, the consolidated congregation continued to worship separately for three years under their pastors Breen and Mulder.

The Oak Park contingent immediately sold its majestic grey stone edifice, which had provided lavishly for twenty-eight years, to the Chicago Austin Church of the Nazarene and began services in the all-purpose room of the new Timothy Christian Grade School on South Prospect Street in Elmhurst. Breen gave the group wise leadership and counsel until he retired in 1975. The spare surroundings of the school "gym" were a bitter contrast to the "hallowed" and "stately edifice" in Oak Park. Lamented Henry De Boer:

> How can we forget the morning sun that made the great window glow with color and brilliance. . . . How can we forget the treasured organ that poured out its melodious strains. . . . How can we forget the grandeur and the elegance of the builder's art in the Gothic style and the majestic reaches of supporting beams and trusses overhead.[32]

The Warren Park contingent continued to worship in Cicero until 1976, when it sold its facilities to the Cicero Bible Church. That year the unified West Suburban congregation bought property across the street from Timothy school and began a building program.

Bellwood

A small number of Dutch Reformed folk settled in the far western suburbs of Maywood and Bellwood in the early 1940s. By the 1960s, the trickle had become a flood as westsiders pulled up stakes yet again in the face of incursions by southern Italians and Greeks and moved across the Cook County line into the Du Page County villages of Elmhurst, Lombard, Downers Grove, Villa Park, and Wheaton. In the decade 1967-76 four of the six churches in the Cicero-Berwyn-Oak Park region relocated in Du Page County, as did the Timothy Christian elementary and high schools. This was the second relocation for Timothy grade school and the fourth

32. Henry De Boer, "Recollections of the James De Boer Family" [February 1971], typescript, p. 1. Courtesy of John H. Evenhouse.

uprooting for the Dutch community. There was a similar white flight out of Englewood and Roseland, beginning in the late 1950s, into southwestern Cook County and Lake County in northern Indiana. This was more racially motivated than the West Side exodus, because inner-city blacks were flooding into those communities. By contrast, the migration of westside blacks was contained at the Cicero border for many years.

A Christian Reformed church came about in Bellwood in a most unusual way; it was started by a female pastor of Dutch ancestry who had no official connection with a Reformed church. Katherine Tessman, nee Lubben (1879-1950), was converted as an adult in the Epiphany Baptist Church of Chicago and, after studying at the Moody Bible Institute, she went to Bellwood with her second husband, Albert, in the early 1920s to begin missionary work. The couple bought a home at 3510 Monroe Street, built a high steeple in the front, and launched a Sunday school at her "Bellwood Gospel Tabernacle." Katherine's dysfunctional early life gave her a compelling "testimony."[33]

In 1924 Epiphany Baptist ordained Tessman as its first missionary in Bellwood. She renamed her church the "Light of the World Rescue Mission" and began weekly worship services and evangelism outreach activities. The work flourished, and the Sunday school soon surpassed one hundred students and strained the capacity of the home/church. Twenty years later, after her husband died in 1944 and Katherine was nearing retirement age, she looked to link up with a denomination willing to carry on the ministry.

In the previous year, the home missions committee of the Classis of

33. Great-nephew Ralph Lubben has told the largely unknown story of Katherine Tessman in "Aunt Kate 1879-1950," reprinted from the newsletter of the Lombard Christian Reformed Church, *Echoes: Newsletter of the Elmhurst Christian Reformed Church* (Feb. 1998): 8-9. See also Barbara Brouwer, "Promises, Promises: Women and the Reformation," seminar paper, Northern Baptist Theological Seminary, 1998. Katherine Lubben Tessman was born in the Netherlands in 1879, the oldest daughter of David and Tryntje Lubben, and immigrated in 1891 with her mother (her siblings and father had come earlier). The family settled on the Old West Side and then moved to a truck farm in the Maywood-Bellwood region to escape the vice police. In 1900 they lived at 1131 Davidson St. (at Franklin St.) in Naperville (Robert P. Swierenga, comp., "Dutch in Cook County Federal Population Census of 1900" [1992]). Kate married Louis Wierenga in 1902 and moved back into the city, but the alcoholic husband abused her and finally in 1912 "wagered" her in a game of cards to Albert Tessman, who won. She lived with Tessman two years before marrying him, and in early 1913 her ten-year-old son died of diphtheria and a baby boy was born dead. These tragedies began to draw the couple to the Epiphany Baptist Church on Lawndale Ave. at Iowa St., where their lives were turned around.

Rev. Katherine Lubben Tessman
(Courtesy of Fred Lubben)

Chicago North of the Christian Reformed Church decided to begin church planting in the western suburban area, where some Dutch Reformed families had settled. The classis sent the Reverend Henry Baker to spend a week canvassing the Bellwood area and contacting the scattered families. He recommended planting a church. Tessman, who may have learned of Baker's activities, decided to contact the home mission committee. The two found that they needed each other, and the classis decided to take over Tessman's church, under the auspices of the First Christian Reformed Church of Cicero. The classis assigned pastors to fill the Bellwood pulpit, and the Reverend Tessman graciously gave up her preaching ministry in deference to the Christian Reformed policy of a male-only clergy.

That Tessman turned to the Christian Reformed Church was not remarkable, since her brother George and nephews Henry and William Lubben and their families were affiliated with that denomination in Cicero, and women from First Cicero, many Lubben relatives, had long volunteered as Sunday school teachers in Bellwood.[34]

34. First Christian Reformed Church of Cicero, *Directory,* 1932. Sunday school volunteers from the First Cicero church included Katherine Tessman's nieces Henrietta Lubben

The next year, in 1945, home missionary Henry Petersen began part-time pastoral work at what was called the Bellwood Chapel, under the auspices of the classis, which bought the chapel building and paid his salary. In 1948 Renze De Groot, the former pastor of Fourth Chicago, left an Iowa congregation to take up full-time work in Bellwood and Wheaton (where Christian Reformed residents had also requested a church). He was called and supervised by First Cicero, but the classis and denomination paid his salary. De Groot earned a doctorate in theology at Northern Baptist Seminary of Chicago during these years on the subject of the Dutch Anabaptists, including their effective leader, Menno Simons.[35]

De Groot had a heart for evangelism. Within a year the **First Christian Reformed Church of Bellwood** (1949) was organized. In May 1949 some fifty adults, mostly members of Cicero congregations, signed a petition asking for this step, and the classis approved in September. Among the charter members, which included twenty-six adults and twenty-four children, were Walter Loerop, Ysbrand Meyer, and Tessman's niece Marjorie Lubben and her husband Richard Feyen. Tessman was by then dying of cancer and did not join the new church.[36]

The impressive organization service brought together "dignitaries" (i.e., ministers) from the First Cicero, Warren Park, Berwyn, and Oak Park churches, and the classical home missions committee. After the Reverend Enno L. Haan of Warren Park "delivered a stemwinder of a sermon on 1 Corinthians 3:9," the august classical committee, according to the first minutes book, "sat in the front of the chapel to carefully examine and vote on the credentials of those requesting organization." All were in order, and the members then elected as the first consistory elders Jacob Medendorp and Hubert Van Holten and deacons Jacob Smith and Dudley West. West's selection signified that Bellwood was not entirely of Dutch ancestry.[37]

Merriam, Carol Lubben Basner, Jean Lubben Lambers, plus three others – Helen Doornbos Potts, Henrietta Nauta Danner, and Stella Smith Van Tholen Lubben ("Prologue"). Carol Lubben's husband, Samuel Basner, was one of the few Jews converted at the Nathanael Institute.

35. "Installation of Chicago Home Missionary [Henry Petersen]," *Banner,* 2 Mar. 1945; "Bellwood History," in Elmhurst Christian Reformed Church, *Dedication, April 3, 1964* (Elmhurst, Ill., 1964); "An Historical Review of Elmhurst CRC," in Elmhurst Christian Reformed Church, *A Service of Dedication on the completion of new educational facilities, December 20, 1981* (Elmhurst, Ill., 1981).

36. Ralph Lubben, letter to author of 17 March 2001; Lubben, "Catherina Lubben"; "History," in Elmhurst Christian Reformed Church, *Dedication, April 3, 1964;* Elmhurst Christian Reformed Church, "Thirty-Five Years of God's Blessing, September 16, 1964."

37. Ibid.

First Christian Reformed Church of Bellwood, erected 1949
(The Archives, Calvin College)

That same year, the fledgling body sold its first edifice and built for $20,000 a larger white frame chapel on the corner of the same property, 3501 Monroe Street at Linden Street. This was an ambitious venture for the small group, who approved a weekly budget of $5 per family for the building fund and $2 for general operations. Of this, only $1.25 was available for local expenses because 75 cents went to denominational ministries under the "quota system."[38]

When De Groot left in 1953, the Frisian-born seminary candidate Bernard Byma came to serve Bellwood as its first full-time pastor (1953-60). This gladdened hearts after seven "declines." During his seven-year tenure, the relentless westward population thrust continued, and the congregation in 1958 purchased prime property several miles directly west, on the corner of Kent and Van Buren streets in Elmhurst. This was only four blocks from the Timothy Christian School property, which was a major consideration. Elmhurst was in Du Page County, so this move had symbolic importance. The Dutch had deserted the city of Chicago by 1945, but a generation later they were leaving its sprawling suburban base in Cook County itself.

38. Ibid. Quotas were voluntary annual "assessments" per family that local congregations pledged to remit for denominational ministries.

Elmhurst and Lombard

Byma's successor, Jay De Vries (1961-66), oversaw the relocation to Elmhurst when in 1964 the rapidly growing congregation dedicated its new $350,000 brick edifice surrounded by extensive classrooms in the American style. This required a "monumental step of faith" on the part of the sixty or so families, recalled one member. Since the Bellwood facility had been sold, the congregation worshiped for three months at the Reserve Savings and Loan building in Elmhurst. Upon dedicating the new church in 1963, the congregation followed the custom of naming it after the town, **Elmhurst Christian Reformed Church**. In 1965 a two-manual Möller pipe organ was installed and dedicated. That year burglars cracked the church safe and stole receipts from the previous Sunday's collections. The deacons, in order to claim the loss for which the church was insured, reconstructed the amount by contacting all the members to ask what each had given. Wags quipped that this turned out to be "the largest offering in the history of the church."

In keeping with the legacy of its female founder, women have always taken a major role in the life and ministry of the Bellwood-Elmhurst congregation. The Bellwood Ladies Club raised money for missions in the 1950s with an active program of socials, bake and rummage sales, a spice demonstration, and even a Stanley cleaning products demonstration. Several times the all-male consistory denied the club permission to use the church facilities for these mundane events. Later, at the Elmhurst church, women volunteers led the most effective mission outreach program, "Little Lambs," a weekday preschool program that ministered to 450 neighborhood children.[39]

Following in De Vries's footsteps, the Elmhurst church flourished under pastors Garrett Stoutmeyer (1967-72), Wayne Leys (1974-83), and Bert De Jong (1983-), reaching in the 1990s a membership of nearly one thousand members scattered throughout more than two dozen communities. They transferred in primarily from the First Cicero and Warren Park Christian Reformed churches. The congregation proved its strength when a fire gutted the sanctuary on June 14, 1990; they recovered and rebuilt without missing a step.[40]

The **Fellowship Reformed Church of Lombard** was second, after the Bellwood Church, to organize a congregation "out west," and it was

39. Ibid; Brouwer, "Promises, Promises."
40. "An Historical Review of Elmhurst CRC."

the first to locate in Du Page County, some eight miles beyond Bellwood and just southwest of Elmhurst. Fellowship was a daughter of West Side Reformed Church of Cicero and First Reformed Church in Berwyn, and hence a granddaughter of the First Reformed Church of Chicago. In 1957, twenty-five families formed the congregation, which the next year broke ground for a 250-seat, colonial style edifice at 1420 South Meyers Road. This site is directly west, as the crow flies, from its former Hastings Street Church in Chicago. Duane Tellinghuisen, who had been ordained in the Baileyville (Illinois) congregation, was the founding pastor and remained until 1965. During construction the body met at the Lombard Civic Club. Presently served by Christopher Piersma, the church in 1995 numbered 176 souls. Its sister congregation in the far west is **Covenant (now Community) Church of Downers Grove**, which began in 1965 and grew to 243 souls by 1996 under pastor Daniel Plasman.[41]

The third congregation in the far west was the **West Suburban Christian Reformed Church**, the result of a merger between the Warren Park and Oak Park churches. Members of the Oak Park congregation began worshiping at Timothy Christian School in Elmhurst in 1973, and in 1976 the Warren Park contingent joined them. The amalgamated body bought property across from the school and began construction of a modern octagonal edifice, which was dedicated in 1977 and renamed **Faith Christian Reformed Church of Elmhurst**. The site at 1070 South Prospect Street is just north of Roosevelt Road, which has long served as a kind of "Dutch alley." In 1978 the hard-working Kermit Rietema replaced Alvin Mulder as pastor, and church membership continued to grow, reaching more than nine hundred in the 1990s under the much loved Lee Koning. By 1996 Faith had become the largest congregation in Classis Northern Illinois.[42]

The fourth Dutch congregation to move "out west," in 1975, was the **Lombard Christian Reformed Church**, a continuation of the First

41. For Fellowship Reformed Church of Lombard, see *West Side News,* 1, 8 Sept. 1958; *Historical Directory of the Reformed Church in America,* 388, 525, 576-77. Current statistics for both congregations are in the *Minutes of the General Synod of the Reformed Church in America,* 1996. Pastors of Downers Grove Community Church were Edward Grant (1965-66), Stanley Vugteveen (1966-74), Evert Fikse (1974-88), Daniel Plasman (1989-). Pastors of Lombard Fellowship Reformed were Duane Tellinghuisen (1957-65), Ellsworth Ten Clay (1965-70), James Baar (1971-76), Paul De Vries (1977-83), Donald Den Hartog (1983-96), and Christopher Piersma (1996-).

42. "Our History," in Faith Christian Reformed Church of Elmhurst, *Dedication Program* (Elmhurst, Ill., 1977).

Cicero church. It bought property at the corner of 22nd Street and Meyers Road in Lombard, sold its Cicero facilities, and built a modern sanctuary. When the edifice was dedicated in 1976, the congregation followed the naming custom and identified with its new community. Two years later the irenic Ebbers, who had managed the move, left, and, after a two-year vacancy, Donald Negen took the helm for eight years (1980-88). Happily, the membership climbed back up to six hundred by 1988, and again reached capacity at more than seven hundred souls under Negen's successors, Vernon Vander Zee (1989-2000) and Nathaniel Elgersma (1998-).

Englewood

Beginning in the 1880s, some Groningers from the Old West Side moved south instead of west, settling in Englewood and later Summit, Evergreen Park, Oak Lawn, and beyond. So appealing was Englewood that by 1920 more than three thousand Dutch Reformed folk resided there. Four churches were founded within seventeen years – First Reformed (Dutch) in 1886, First Christian Reformed (Dutch) in 1887, Second (Hope) Reformed (English) in 1902, and Second Christian Reformed (English) in 1903 (figure 5.2).

At first the Englewood Hollanders commuted six miles for church services, either to the First Reformed Church of Chicago (Harrison and May streets) or the First Reformed Church of Roseland (107th Street and Michigan Avenue). The need for a local church was obvious, however, and in 1885 several families petitioned for one. Bernardus De Bey of First Chicago supported their effort and came out to preach in a barn on what is now Garfield Boulevard and Emerald Avenue. De Bey also arranged for one of his elders, Arie Van Deursen, to conduct weekly services and read a sermon. Van Deursen gathered some fifty people for worship in a rented house at 59th and Halsted streets.[43]

The Classis of Wisconsin somewhat reluctantly assigned ministers to supply the pulpit of the new "church plant," but few were eager to do so, believing that the group in Englewood was too small. De Bey and Van Deursen persisted, and one year after De Bey preached in the barn, in Au-

43. This and the next paragraphs rely on First Reformed Church of Englewood, *50th Anniversary Booklet* (Chicago, 1936); "Seventieth Anniversary Celebrated at First Englewood Reformed," *Illinois Observer* Oct. 1956; and First Reformed Church of Englewood, *Dedication Booklet* (Chicago, 1958), 13-20.

Figure 5.2 Churches and Schools in Englewood

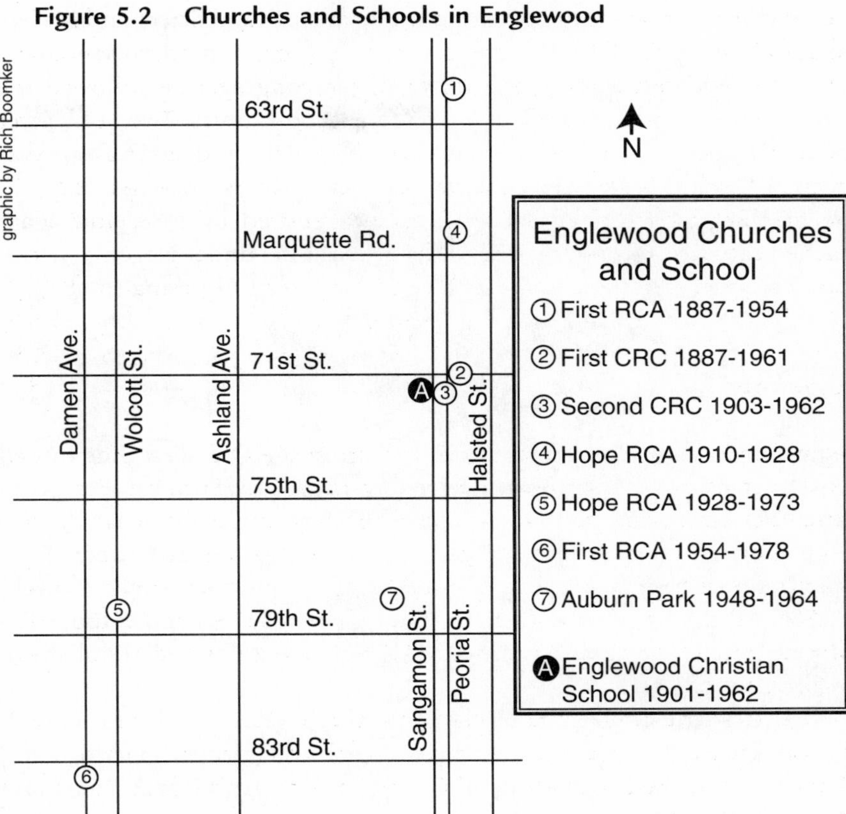

gust 1886, the **First Reformed Church of Englewood** was organized with thirty-three communicant members. The male members then elected to the first consistory Arie Van Deursen and Henry Werkman as elders and Albert Werkman and B. Toppe as deacons. Van Deursen taught the catechism classes, and the others staffed the Sunday school. The Dorcas Society for women and Young Men's and Young Women's societies were soon functioning.

The fledgling body was ambitious. Almost immediately it bought six lots on the northeast corner of Peoria and 62nd streets and began construction of a small wooden church forty feet wide by fifty feet long and an adjacent horse barn (figure 5.2, site 1). The worshipers were content to sit on chairs for three years until they could afford pews. The church cost $2,175 and the barn $380, with the first money raised by a subscription campaign. Within months the congregation bought an organ and began a

First Reformed Church of Englewood first edifice, erected 1887 *(Western Seminary Collection, Joint Archives of Holland)*

choral society. Now it was ready to call a minister, Jacob P. De Jonge (1887-93), who accepted with a salary of $900 and eight tons of coal. The arrival of a minister required the church to build a parsonage, which cost more than the church at $2,467. The final touches were to install a church clock and put in walks and a fence around the property. First Englewood had started well, thanks to the rapid influx of new members.

That growth forced the congregation to enlarge the sanctuary within five years by adding thirty-five feet to the rear; this increased the seating capacity to five hundred, which was soon filled. De Bey and his wife, Anje, were two of the newcomers, having moved to Englewood in retirement to be near their son William and wife. Bernardus died there in 1894 and Anje in 1899.

In 1893 Lawrence Dykstra (1893-99) replaced De Jonge, and early in his tenure he induced the congregation to begin English services on Sunday evenings. Allowing the process of Americanization to proceed freely kept the young people in the fold. The congregation dedicated a new organ in 1897 with an "elaborate and edifying program."[44] Dykstra had to deal with a major trauma in the congregation, the drowning of fourteen-year-old Emma Van Bergen during the 1894 church picnic. She fell overboard from the lake steamer *Cyclone,* when the group was returning from Lincoln Park (on the North Side) to Jackson Park.

44. Moerdyke, "Chicago Letter," *CI,* 31 Jan., p. 10; 16 June 1894, p. 12; 23 June, 1897, p. 12; 18 Jan. 1899, p. 7.

During the tenure of the Reverend Dr. Henry Hospers (1899-1905), First Church spun off a daughter congregation to answer the demands for an English-language congregation, the American or Second Reformed Church of Englewood. Hospers was popular with the older members, who were disappointed when in 1905 he accepted a position as professor of Hebrew at Western Theological Seminary in Holland, Michigan. Steady growth continued at First Church under his successors, all of whom had even shorter pastorates – Marinus Broekstra (1905-08), Siebe Nettinga (1908-12), Anthony Van Duine (1912-15), and John Lumkes (1916-21).

Broekstra's analytic sermons appealed to those steeped in the Reformed faith, and he used his musical talents to sing solos in the evening services, but the singing society of fifty members, led by G. Dykstra, was not permitted to join in. The young people's Christian Endeavor society flourished, and Broekstra was uncharacteristically supportive of Christian schools. Nettinga guided the congregation on a major building project, in 1911, to replace the small wood edifice with a modern brick sanctuary that cost $28,000. It stood on the same site and served well until 1957, when the building was sold to a black congregation. Nettinga later joined Hospers on the faculty of Western Theological Seminary. Having preachers of such high talents gave First Englewood a reputation for intellectual vigor and style.

The next pastor, Van Duine, had a more practical bent, and his successor Lumkes had to deal with the difficult transition days of the First World War. Lumkes prayed diligently for the forty servicemen from the congregation, all of whom returned, but the national flu epidemic of 1919

First Reformed Church of Englewood second edifice, erected 1911 *(Western Seminary Collection, Joint Archives of Holland)*

took its toll, and he had a number of funerals. The flu struck him down for many months as well. The war also pressured the Hollanders to give up their mother tongue, and in 1921 the congregation added an English service immediately following the Dutch one. Lumkes preached eloquently in Dutch but struggled to master English, which prompted him to take a call elsewhere.

After a "vacancy" of two years, the congregation obtained a bilingual pastor, Jacob Althuis, who was strongly evangelistic in emphasis. Althuis moved the English service to the afternoon and kept the Dutch service in the prime morning slot. When he left in 1935, after the longest pastorate at First Englewood, the English service was again moved to the morning, following the Dutch service. The congregation numbered 850 souls by then.

The interwar years were a time of stability before Englewood went into a rapid decline. Gradus Vander Linden (1935-44) led the congregation through the end of the Depression and the Second World War era, when two gold stars had to be sewn on the flag in front of the church, indicating members who had died in military service. Then followed Theodore Schaap (1946-49), who stressed neighborhood evangelism, and Elton Eenigenburg (1949-50), a Chicago "boy" from South Holland whom Western Seminary tapped for a professorate in theology. First Englewood's pulpit seemed to be a prime recruiting place for Western Seminary professors; Eenigenburg was the third to go.

In the late 1950s, the close-knit Dutch American community in Englewood, which was concentrated within a few blocks, broke up after an influx of blacks changed the surrounding community. In 1930 blacks comprised only 3 percent of Englewood's population, but by 1970 the number totaled 48 percent and rising. Fourteen thousand whites left the area in the 1950s, feeling threatened and unsure of their safety as they walked to church and school and visited the homes of relatives. They fled to the suburbs. The rest fled in the next two decades, and by 1980 Englewood was 90 percent black.[45]

First Reformed Church of Englewood reacted quickly, even a bit prematurely, and in 1954 relocated several miles to the southwest. The Reverend Dr. Jerome De Jong (1952-58) led the move to 84th Street and Damen Avenue, where First Church erected a new sanctuary and parsonage for $450,000 (figure 5.2, site 6). R. Jamieson Hallenbeck (1958-59), a son of the congregation, followed De Jong briefly as interim pastor, and then came

45. Dominic A. Pacyga, "Chicago's Ethnic Neighborhoods: The Myth of Stability and the Reality of Change," *Ethnic Chicago,* 615.

First Reformed Church of Englewood
Damen Avenue edifice, erected 1958
(Western Seminary Collection, Joint Archives of Holland)

John Den Ouden (1959-62), Harold Korver (1962-67), Donald Den Hartog (1968-83), and Howard Hoekstra (1984-). Under Den Hartog the congregation relocated yet again in 1978, this time many miles distant to Orland Park.[46]

Meanwhile, the **Second Englewood (later Hope) Reformed Church** followed a similar path of rapid growth and then relocation to the southwest. This American congregation was always a little brother to First Englewood. It began in 1902 with about one hundred members, meeting at first only in the evening in the mother church, which gave the birthing its blessing and support. The first consistory members were elders Fred Kruyf, J. L. Temple, and James Hoven, and deacons Professor William Zoethout, William Goedhart, and John Hospers. All transferred from First Church except Hospers (from Orange City, Iowa) and Goedhart (by confession of faith).

Soon the infant church was able to rent a Seventh Day Adventist church one-half block down Peoria Street for the Sunday morning service. But its seating limit of 150 was insufficient for the evening service, and the locale was not ideal for expanding the Sunday school program of 100 pu-

46. *Illinois Observer,* 18 Feb. 1954; First Reformed Church of Englewood, *75th Anniversary* (Chicago, 1961), 3-10; Gasero, *Historical Directory of the Reformed Church in America,* 365.

Hope (Second) Reformed Church of Englewood
Peoria St. edifice, erected 1910
(Western Seminary Collection, Joint Archives of Holland)

pils under superintendent Zoethout and then E. Takken. The facilities also limited the full bevy of active societies – Christian Endeavor for the teens, the Young Men's Society, Women's Missionary Society, and the Singing Society.[47]

The first congregational meeting authorized the purchase of lots for an edifice at 66th and Peoria Streets, but before starting construction on a $7,500 building, in 1904 a Swedish Covenant church building became available only one-half block west at 66th and Sangamon Streets, for a nominal price of $2,300, less than one third that for the proposed structure. The building needed minor repairs, and the Ladies' Aid Society took care of interior redecorating "with genuine Dutch determination." By January, 1905, it was ready for regular services.

By this time John Vander Meulen arrived as the first minister

47. This and the next paragraphs rely on Hope Reformed Church, *71 Years of Service* (Chicago, 1973); *History of the Second Reformed Church of Englewood, 1902-1914,* and *Church Directory* 1914 (Chicago, 1914); "Historische Schetsen, De 2nd Ger. Gemeente te Englewood, Chicago, Ill.," *De Hope,* 11 Feb. 1904; W. D. Goedhart, "De 'Tweede Englewood,' Ill.," ibid., 8 Jan. 1907; Moerdyke, "Chicago Letter," *CI,* 22 Oct. 1902, p. 689; Jesse W. Brooks, "Tenth Reformed Church of Chicago," ibid., 10 Dec. 1902, p. 822; J. H. Hospers, "Englewood, Ill., The Second Church," ibid., 24 Jan. 1906, p. 56.

Hope (Second) Reformed Church of Englewood, ca. 1952, Lincoln St. edifice, erected 1928 *(Western Seminary Collection, Joint Archives of Holland)*

(1903-05). He moved into a new $700 parsonage built on the Peoria Street property. The board of domestic missions subsidized the minister's salary. The congregation continued to grow, and the next pastor, Western Seminary candidate Benjamin Brinkman (1906-10), gave leadership in the decision to construct a new four-hundred-seat sanctuary on the Peoria Street site, which was dedicated in 1910 (figure 5.2, site 4). Nearly one hundred new members joined during Brinkman's tenure. After Abraham Klerk's two-year pastorate, the popular Lawrence Dykstra returned to Englewood for six years (1913-19). He dedicated new hymnbooks that added hymns to the venerable psalter and set the common Communion cup aside in favor of more hygienic individual cups.

Richard Vanden Berg (1919-26) succeeded Dykstra in the church of five hundred members. After Vanden Berg left and before Isaac Van Westenburg arrived (1927-40), the congregation decided to sell its church and relocate further south to a new and growing neighborhood. The congregation bought five lots on the corner of 78th and Lincoln (later Wolcott) streets and built a massive brick church embodying the latest in church architecture for $140,000 (figure 5.2, site 5). The church, with a Hinners pipe organ and pews to seat six hundred, was dedicated early in 1928. The makeover was completed by changing the name to Hope Reformed Church. Here the congregation worshiped until 1973.[48]

A most remarkable pastor was Raymond Beckering, who served the

48. "Chicago, Ill., en Omstreken," *De Grondwet,* 5 Mar. 1929, p. 8.

congregation twice, from 1942 to 1945 and again from 1949 to 1954. While he was ministering to a Los Angeles congregation in the interim, Hope Church had no regular pastor for two years and then Raymond Schaap served for two years (1947-49). This was a time of testing, but it made Beckering's return all the sweeter. He and his successor, Gordon Girod (1954-58), had well-earned reputations as beloved pastors and staunch conservatives in a denomination drifting toward more progressive practices and theologies.

The final three pastors at Hope Church represented that more progressive wing, including John Muller (1958-62), Robert Nykamp (1963-64), and Vernon Hoffman (1964-73). Nykamp left early for post-graduate study leading to a post at Western Theological Seminary. In these decades of social turmoil, the congregation increasingly welcomed non-Dutch neighbors as members, joined in community social ministries with the help of two full-time workers, one a woman, and began an urban studies program. Meanwhile, the members kept moving to outlying southwestern suburbs, and by 1972 it was apparent that the end was near. By a two-thirds vote of both the Hope and Palos Heights congregations, Hope Church merged out of existence after seventy-one years. The edifice was sold to a black Baptist congregation, and the final service was on November 25, 1973.

The **First (Holland) Christian Reformed Church of Englewood** was founded in 1887, one year after its Reformed counterpart, with thirty-three charter families and singles. Both of the Englewood congregations were daughters of their respective First Chicago churches.

The junior denomination was quick to capitalize on the migration of Groningers from Chicago for at least three reasons. It was an opportunity "for the extension of His kingdom in this populous neighborhood," it was compassionate to the elderly "who found it difficult or almost impossible to meet with the mother church in Chicago," and it safeguarded the "spiritual life of our young people who may now expect to find fulfillment of their needs in their own circle and vicinity." That the young people were inspired is evident, in part, from the sons the congregation later sent out into the pulpit and professorate. These included the cousins Henry and George Stob, John Weidenaar, John Steenwyk, and Homer Wigboldy, among others.[49]

49. This and the following paragraphs are based on Lambert Bere, "History of the First Christian Reformed Church of Englewood," and H. Bieze and Martin Stob, "Continuation of Church History of Englewood I," 34-47, in First Christian Reformed Church of

The push came from two elders who had moved to Englewood, Johannes Bottema and Pieter Van Dyk, together with Lubbert Wieringa, who resided in the area for some time and who had long sought a church. The first meeting of interested persons took place in the home of Johannes Kooi, and the group decided to petition the Fourteenth Street Church to ask the classis for permission to proceed. Classis agreed, and the organizational meeting was held in Wieringa's home, with pastors Greve of First Chicago, Henry Vander Werp of First Roseland, and elder C. L. Clousing of Roseland to offer counsel. Consistory members elected were elders Wieringa and Bottema, and deacons Van Dyk and Lambert Bere. Bottema moved away three months after taking office, leaving the infant church in the lurch.

The congregation immediately set about to build a church and in the meantime accepted Henry Natelborg's offer to meet for worship in the unpartitioned second story of his home. Within three months, on New Year's Eve of 1888, the new church on 71st Street between Green and Peoria streets was framed in sufficiently for the first worship service (figure 5.2, site 2). The dimensions were a minimal forty by fifty feet, but it proved adequate for eight years. The people huddled around the wood stove to keep warm. The newly founded Young Men's Society met there as well.

Securing a minister was more difficult and took nearly two years and many "declines" before the Groninger Johannes Vander Werp accepted in May, 1889. He got the weak infant church on its feet but left within three years (1889-92). Another two-year "vacancy" ensued until Lubbert Van Dellen arrived from the province of Groningen in May, 1894. He remained thirteen years (1894-1907) and provided a time of stability and great blessing.

Van Dellen's tenure was marked by three highlights. First, to stem severe overcrowding the congregation in 1896 erected a new sanctuary "with a good pipe organ." On one Sunday in 1895, twenty-three new members were admitted on profession of faith. Second, in 1900 the church gave birth to the Englewood Christian School, with considerable support from the First Reformed Church of Englewood. Finally, in 1903 it founded a daughter church for those demanding English services, the Second Chris-

---

Englewood, *Dedication Souvenir* (Chicago, 1931); "Seventieth Anniversary, The First Christian Reformed Church of Englewood, Illinois," *Illinois Observer,* Oct. 1957, p. 1; and Calvin Christian Reformed Church of Oak Lawn, *A Century of Blessings, Calvin Church, 100 Years, 1887-1987* (Oak Lawn, 1987), 8-54, quote 9.

Call letter of the First Christian Reformed Church of Englewood to the Rev. L. Van Dellen

North America
Englewood, Ill. October 23, 1893

To the Reverend L. Van Dellen
At Nieuwe Pekela
Groningen, Netherlands

Worthy Brother — Greetings!

The consistory of the Holl. Chr. congregation at Englewood, Ill. has an important matter to communicate with you. This congregation has been vacant for considerable time and the need is great for a preacher of the Word. The Consistory nominated the following brothers:

Rev. F. Welandt, Niekerk, Michigan
Rev. L. Van Dellen, Nieuwe Pekela, Netherlands
Rev. C. Kuipers, Katendrecht, Netherlands

After consultation and prayer under the leadership of the Counselor, the following was chosen by the male membership:

Rev. L. Van Dellen at Nieuwe Pekela

So herewith comes our plea to you: "Come over and help us." We hope heartily that before long we will receive your reply that you are prepared to preach to us the Word according to the forms of Unity, the Dordt Church Order, with certain stipulations of our Church.

tian Reformed Church of Englewood. Van Dellen's family ties to Englewood grew strong, and after he retired in 1914 he returned to live out his life there.

Gerrit Haan began his work in 1908 as the third pastor and stayed through the First World War (1908-18). No son of the congregation was killed, although some were wounded. Large audiences appreciated Haan's forceful Reformed preaching three times per Sunday, and catechumens noted his gift of teaching. New families continued to come from the city

Since the congregation has been vacant for a considerable time, we have great need for a leader of our own. With the Lord's blessing the congregation has many opportunities for extension.

From our side, remembering that a laborer is worthy of his hire, we promise to pay you the sum of $700.00 namely, seven hundred dollars, free housing, and $250.00 for transportation for you, yours, and your belongings, plus free fuel.

May the Lord impress this call upon your heart and give you the guidance of His Holy Spirit as you consider it.

We hope to answer any questions faithfully and truthfully that you may have in connection with this call.

May God's richest blessing rest upon us all and may God before long grant us the privilege to greet you as our pastor.

With prayer for your welfare and brotherly greetings:

Elders	*Deacons*
J. Bottema	P. Van Dyk
B. Visscher	H. Werkman
E. Bol	M. Buwalda
L. Bere	

J. Riemersma, Counselor
Chicago, Illinois, 523 W. 14th Street

Address is: P. Van Dyk
6007 Sangamon Street
Englewood, Illinois
North America[50]

and dozens arrived fresh from the Netherlands right up to the war in 1914. The latter fit in easily; they "truly live with us and love the congregation," recalled Bere.[51] Haan published a book on Jesus as the Messiah, and in 1915 he guided the birth of a second daughter congregation in Evergreen

50. Ibid, 13-14, translated from original in Archives, Calvin College, by William Dryfhout and Anna Van Dellen Dryfhout.

51. Bere, "History," *Souvenir,* 36.

First Christian Reformed Church of Englewood second edifice, erected 1896
(The Archives, Calvin College)

Park, which drew off twenty-two families. Nevertheless, First Englewood, barely twenty-five years old, counted 1,250 members in 1915 and was the largest Christian Reformed congregation in greater Chicago and, indeed, the largest nationwide, west of Michigan.[52]

After Haan left, the congregation suffered through six unsuccessful calls, during which time the national flu and smallpox epidemics of 1918-19 took twenty members, including elder W. Van Dellen, a son of Lubbert Van Dellen, the former pastor. Finally, the Reverend Peter Van Vliet (1919-23) accepted the congregation's call; he spoke Dutch and English fluently and was exactly the right man for the time. He was energetic and had a good sense of humor and a gift for teaching.

The decade of the 1920s at First Englewood under Van Vliet and Isaac Westra (1923-29) was as good as the booming national economy but not in spiritual maturity. The number of members by 1929 had increased to thirteen hundred, which pushed the church beyond capacity. It did not

52. "Chicago Letter," *Banner,* 22 May 1913.

meet ventilation, sanitation, and fire prevention codes. But the congregation for ten years turned down every attempt to launch a building program. It was difficult even to raise a building fund, since only half the families were bearing the load. The deacons knew this pattern of giving, because in 1920 they had confronted the perennial budget shortfalls by implementing a system of numbered envelopes, by which they could monitor the giving of each family.

It is quite likely that the fight over the language question was a hidden factor in the tithing problem of the 1920s. The world war had stirred patriotic feelings as never before, and the large immigrant generation at First Englewood was unable to hold back the forces of Americanization. When Van Vliet came in 1919, he immediately "finessed" the situation by starting a Sunday evening meeting in which he "lectured" in English on various biblical topics (rather than preach a "sermon"). This won over the young people and disarmed the Dutch defenders, because both the morning and afternoon services continued in the mother tongue as before. (A second service in the early afternoon, following a lunch at church, was common in the days before automobiles, when traveling was on foot, streetcar, or horse and buggy.) The consistory also Anglicized the Sunday

First Christian Reformed Church of Englewood 1920s, congregation leaving church services
(The Archives, Calvin College)

school and catechism classes, because the young people were no longer learning Dutch in the Christian school.[53]

In 1920 Van Vliet began calling the evening meetings "gospel services," thereby again giving the old guard no toehold, even though the services bore most of the hallmarks of "regular" worship services. That same year he induced the congregation to change its name from Holland Christian Reformed to First Christian Reformed Church. Three years later, in mid-1923, he left after pushing the reluctant flock as far as he could. He preached his farewell sermon only one week after the congregation had rejected a recommendation to begin English worship, even though many young people could no longer comprehend the nuances of Dutch sermons.

The next three calls were declined; few ministers wanted to enter the fray. Isaac Westra accepted the challenge to the "large and busy church," and in 1924 the congregation again refused twice to allow English in either of the two main "divine" services. By 1925 the situation was so "intolerable" that a bare majority agreed to allow two English services to be added to the schedule without subtracting either of the Dutch services. Westra would lead one Dutch and one English service, and other preachers would be hired on an ad hoc basis to cover the other two. On the first Sunday with the new arrangement, Professor Samuel Volbeda of Calvin Theological Seminary was the guest preacher for the other services.

After several years of the wearying "four service system," late in 1929 a new pastor, the thirty-three-year-old Christian Huissen, was installed (1929-41). He was a master preacher with a booming voice and dramatic style that held the parishioners spellbound and attracted many visitors. During the first round of family visitation in 1929, Huissen learned from many families of their dissatisfaction with the dual Dutch and English services, but the sanctuary could not hold everyone if one of the Dutch services was dropped. Moreover, for more than a decade the members had proven unwilling to fund a new church.

Huissen wisely gained the support of a group of thirty businessmen in the congregation, assembled by the consistory. They declared that a building program was not only feasible but necessary, if the church wanted to provide space for the families who now wished to remain, given the commitment to English worship.

The consistory in 1930 finally felt ready to bring the issue to a vote. The male members decided, first, by 136 to 66, to adopt three worship ser-

53. Bieze and Stob, "Continuation," in *Dedication Souvenir,* 42-43.

Rev. Christian Huissen
(1896-1966)
(The Archives, Calvin College)

Organist Frans Kramer
(The Archives, Calvin College)

First Christian Reformed Church of Englewood third edifice, erected 1931
(The Archives, Calvin College)

vices, with two in English, and, second, to begin a building project, once one-third of the needed $100,000 was raised. By fall, the finance committee had $31,000 in hand, and the work commenced. A wrecking crew of workmen was turned loose against the old church, and the new one was soon underway. Finally, after a decade of indecision, Huissen had managed to end the impasse. It was just in the nick of time because, although the stock market had plunged the previous September and October, it was not yet apparent that a major depression had begun.[54]

First Englewood celebrated laying the cornerstone in September, 1930, and many hands went to work, donating time and materials for the "unforgettable day."[55] The Laus Deo Band furnished the music at the ceremony. The next spring, in dedication services that ran for three successive evenings, the overjoyed congregation inaugurated its impressive brick edifice that seated one thousand. It was the largest and most attractive of all the Chicago area Christian Reformed churches, and its chimes called the community to worship. Frans Kramer was the master of the three-manual Möller pipe organ for many years, assisted by Margaret Vande Werken. Through the 1930s they were each paid $10 a year for their services.

Huissen brought "clarity, conviction, and vigor" to the church, member John Weidenaar recalled. Huissen's wise leadership also helped the congregation carry the mortgage burden through the trying times of the Depression. The church clerk, John Vande Werken, wrote in 1937: "Our pastor proved to be a captain who knew his compass, and piloted us through the turbulent sea of this building program, amidst the stress of the times." Huissen preached his farewell sermon before an overflow audience just before the outbreak of the Second World War. Most were "loath to see him leave."[56]

His successor was William Kok (1942-53), who left an administrative position at Calvin College to answer the call. Kok, then fifty years old and at the height of his powers, had a reputation for oratory. William Rutgers, an apt pulpiteer himself, noted years later in a eulogy that Kok was "skilled in drawing his fingers across the heart strings of God's people, making those hearts vibrate with jubilant song and with conviction." But Kok could shift in an instant from joyful emoting to stern re-

54. J. Sluis, "New Church at First Englewood," *Banner,* 17 Apr. 1931; "Twenty-Five Years Ago, A Report from 1st Englewood Christian Reformed Church," *Illinois Observer,* Apr. 1956.

55. Benjamin Essenburg, "Chicago, Cicero and Englewood," *Banner,* 17 Oct. 1930.

56. J. Vande Werken, "Jubilee at First Church of Englewood, Chicago," ibid., 18 Nov. 1937; George J. Bieze, "First Englewood News," ibid., 10 July 1942; *Century of Blessings,* 25.

bukes if young people were inattentive. On more than one occasion, Kok stopped in the midst of his sermon and delegated two elders to go to the balcony and maintain a proper decorum. During World War II, 160 of the "balcony guys" went off to war and seven did not return; others came back wounded or maimed. This was a tough way to grow up quickly.[57]

When the surviving boys all returned from service and married, First Englewood in 1946 reached its apogee of 1,560 members and was the largest Christian Reformed church in Chicago. That year 400 members withdrew to form a third daughter church, Auburn Park Christian Reformed Church, which built a sanctuary four blocks south.

For the next decade, First Englewood flourished under Kok's successor, Arnold Brink (1953-58), who also had been an administrator at Calvin College and Seminary. This church seemed to have a direct pipeline to the denominational school. Brink enjoyed the "Delft touch" of the church and community and recalled being enfolded there by many acts of kindness as "the best years of our life." But it was a last hurrah; the community was changing. All the Dutch-language books in the church library were disposed of in 1954, and three years later, just before Christmas in 1957, the weekly Dutch service, which had been conducted by the Reverend Oliver Breen of the Second Englewood church, met for the last time. No more would the faithful remnant gather and sing the long-meter psalms in the mother tongue.

Soon no Psalter-singing at all was heard; the members were fleeing to the suburbs, as realtors employed "block busting" sales tactics to hasten white flight when the first blacks bought homes in Englewood. In 1961, only three years after Brink's departure, under the leadership of Simon Vroon (1959-68), the beautiful church was sold for $200,000, after thirty years of blessed use, to the New Friendship Baptist Church, a black congregation. "It was a difficult time of testing and soul-searching for the congregation," recalled Vroon, as the members scattered in all directions. With the dedication of a new $450,000 edifice one year later in Oak Lawn, First Englewood began the process of reconstituting itself as the Calvin Christian Reformed Church (figure 5.3 site 7).[58]

The First Christian Reformed Church of Englewood, always the im-

57. Ibid., 18, 30. The seven who made the ultimate sacrifice were John De Witt, Leroy Dykstra, Herbert Hanko, Harry Hoogeveen, Richard Reinders, Fred Schaaf, and Gerrit Vander Schoot.

58. Ibid., 36-37; *Illinois Observer,* 15 Feb. 1954, p. 8.

Figure 5.3 Churches and Schools in Evergreen Park and Oak Lawn

graphic by Rich Boomker

Evergreen Park and Oak Lawn Churches and Schools

① First Evergreen Park CRC 1915-1931
② First Evergreen Park CRC 1931-
③ Park Lane CRC 1955-
Ⓐ Evergreen Park Christian School 1924-1986
④ First Oak Lawn CRC 1915-
⑤ Kedvale Avenue CRC 1962-
⑥ Green Oak RCA 1955-
⑦ Calvin CRC 1962-
⑧ West Evergreen CRC 1964-1974
Ⓑ Oak Lawn Christian School 1956-

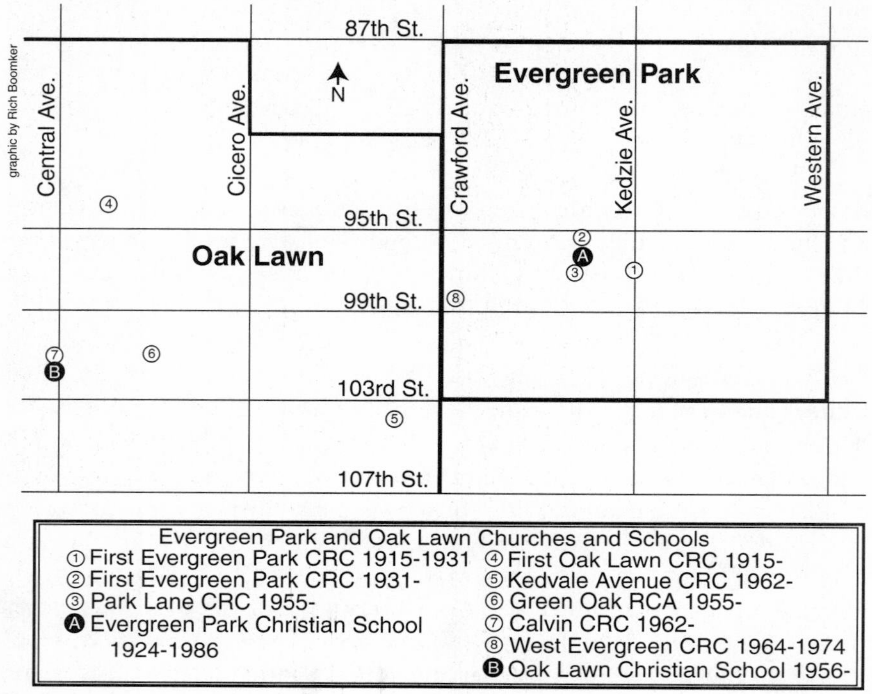

migrant church, existed in the shadow of its daughter, the **Second Christian Reformed Church of Englewood**, which was founded in 1903 to provide religious services in the English language. This "American church" was the first of that denomination in the Chicago area, and the third nationwide, to use English exclusively in all church services and activities. The parting of some sixty members was not welcomed, but First Church finally gave permission, in order to prevent those wanting English from going over to an English-speaking Reformed church that had been organized a year earlier in the same vicinity.[59]

The gifted John Natelborg was the spiritual father of the group, as Lubbert Wieringa had been at the First Englewood church. Natelborg, with the help of James Rook, visited the members of First Church and finally convinced a dozen families to work together for an English church. Classis Illinois gave its approval, and Natelborg and George Meyer were

59. So at least argues Moerdyke, "Chicago Letter," *CI,* 11 Nov. 1903, p. 721. Cf. Theodore Koelikamp, "Second Englewood's Twentieth Anniversary," *Banner,* 18 Aug. 1923.

Rev. William Kok (1892-1977)
(The Archives, Calvin College)

John Natelborg (d. 1913)

elected elders, and James Rook and John Bunning deacons. The small group worshiped in a nearby Methodist Episcopal church for a year while building its own sanctuary one block south of First Englewood at 72nd and Peoria Streets (figure 5.2, site 3). The bare-bones facility that seated 350 cost $3,557, plus $1,500 for the lots. This was a tidy sum at a time when mechanics earned $1.75 per day and church tithes in 1906 totaled only $1,533. Natelborg's untimely death from asthma in 1913 was a severe blow to the congregation.[60]

The Reverend Klaas Poppen (1904-08) arrived soon after as the first pastor. He was one of the best-educated ministers in the entire denomination, completing two four-year degree programs, at Hope College and the University of Michigan. For years he taught school in Michigan and then became principal of the Roseland Christian School in Chicago. He left teaching to earn a divinity degree at Princeton Seminary and enter the Christian ministry. During his twenty-five years of ministry, includ-

60. "From the Early History of the Englewood II Church," *Illinois Observer,* June 1955; "From Second Englewood, Chicago," *Banner,* 17 Apr. 1913; Ralph H. Dekker, "Historical Sketch," in Second Christian Reformed Church of Englewood, *Fiftieth Anniversary, 1903-1953* (Chicago, 1953).

Second Christian Reformed Church of Englewood
first edifice, erected 1904, with Rev. John R. Brink
(The Archives, Calvin College)

ing four at Second Englewood, Poppen witnessed 250 confessions of faith.[61]

The first of that number were young people in the Second Englewood congregation. These committed youth raised funds for pews, a reed organ, and even paid for paving the street out front! The most effective fund-raisers were choral performances of sacred cantatas by the Young People's Society, under Gerrit Kleinhuizen's direction. When Poppen departed for a South Dakota church, Professor E. L. Van Dellen led the worship services for more than two years. He was one of the elders and studying for a doctorate in education at the University of Chicago. So the first two pastors were also professional educators.

Second Englewood adopted American ways readily and was a more progressive church than its mother. For example, it adopted the new order of worship, one part of which included the recitation in unison of

61. "Rev. Klaas Poppen, 1864-1936: In Memoriam," *Banner,* 24 July 1936.

the Lord's Prayer in the morning service and the Apostles' Creed in the evening service. The evening worship was also preceded by a time of singing favorite hymns, none of which was included in the approved psalter. In 1914 the consistory successfully overtured Classis Illinois to urge the national synod of the denomination to buy or begin an English-language official weekly organ. Such a step was necessary, the overture asserted, "to place our American speaking churches on an equal footing with the others."[62]

The close proximity, as well as the cultural differences between the 71st and 72nd Street churches, as the two were commonly known, inevitably created some friction. Harold Hiskes, a member of 71st Street, recalled of 72nd Street: "They were always looked upon as the 'uppity' people, unjustly of course, and there seemed to develop a rivalry between the two churches."[63]

Second Englewood had the edge in its preachers. They were gifted, well educated, and widely respected. The run included John R. Brink (1911-13), Henry J. ("H.J.") Kuiper (1913-19), Edward J. Tuuk (1918-28), Edward ("E.J.") Tanis (1928-42), and William Masselink (1942-52). Brink was a "home missionary" and his task was finished once he had firmly planted the new church. Kuiper, under whom the church grew "by leaps and bounds" and became debt-free, later became the highly influential editor of the denominational weekly, the *Banner,* from 1944 to 1956. Kuiper took a leading part in the founding of the Chicago Helping Hand Mission. Masselink had an earned doctorate and left Englewood to become a professor at the Reformed Bible College in Grand Rapids. His emotional sermons earned him the name "Weeping Willie."

Tuuk had previously served the flagship congregation, Ninth Street (Pillar) Church of Holland, Michigan, which the immigrant leader Albertus Van Raalte himself had founded in 1847. Second Englewood doubled in size during Tuuk's tenure, and the growth necessitated a new church edifice. Members wept to see the beloved old church razed in 1926 to make way for a modern brick building costing $81,000 that was the envy of all. A man subject to insomnia and depression, his "thorn in the flesh," Tuuk was highly esteemed and much loved by his congregation. He worked tirelessly for Christian higher education and took a leading part in the founding of Chicago Christian High School.

62. Rev. B. Essenburg, "Chicago, Cicero, and Englewood Churches," ibid., 18 Apr. 1930; "Brief Report of the Meeting of Classis Illinois," ibid., 5 Feb. 1914.

63. Harold Hiskes, *In Memoriam* (privately published, 1996), 22.

Rev. Henry (H.J.) Kuiper
(1885-1962)
(The Archives, Calvin College)

Rev. Edward J. Tuuk
(1878-1933)
(The Archives, Calvin College)

Second Christian Reformed Church of Englewood second edifice, erected 1926
(The Archives, Calvin College)

Tuuk was also active in many denominational causes until a mental breakdown forced him to retire from the ministry. But this was not before he had to face a protest at Classis Illinois from three of his congregants, who charged him with "mutiny" against the denomination for "activities" on behalf of the deposed Calvin Seminary Professor Ralph Janssen (see chapter 7). When Tuuk's health failed in 1928, in part due to the protests, the consistory granted him a year's leave of absence with full pay! He retired before the year was out.[64]

Tanis became pastor upon earning a master's degree in sociology at the University of Chicago; he served thirteen years, the longest tenure in the history of the church, and the congregation experienced healthy growth. His ministry was so greatly appreciated that after seven years, in 1936, when he reached the twenty-fifth anniversary of his ordination, the grateful congregation organized a special celebration and gave him a new Nash automobile.[65] This generous gesture is quite common in Chicago-area churches, but atypical elsewhere. Interestingly, a synodical ruling forbade mentioning such special tokens of appreciation in church periodicals, presumably so as not to arouse jealousy elsewhere.[66]

For twenty years, beginning in the early 1930s, Tanis wrote a weekly commentary on world events for the denominational organ, the *Banner*, under the title, "The World Today." Tuuk and Tanis truly provided punch in the Second Englewood congregation. A third person in a key role was Theodore Koelikamp, the indispensable superintendent of the Sunday school for forty-three years (1894-1937).[67]

Masselink led during the Second World War, when ninety of the church's young people served in the armed forces, and one, Andrew Borgman, gave his all. The congregation attained its maximum size of 1,100 members in the immediate postwar years and reached parity with the mother church in 1949. Under Oliver Breen (1952-70), the 72nd Street

64. "Proceedings of Classis Illinois," *Banner*, 24 May 1923; E. J. Tanis, "An Appreciation of the Rev. E. J. Tuuk," ibid., 9 June 1933; E. J. Tanis, "The World Today," ibid., 27 Dec. 1940.

65. "Celebration at Englewood II," *Chicago Messenger*, 28 Feb. 1936, p. 2; "Twenty-Fifth Ordination Anniversary," *Banner*, 13 Mar. 1936. Third Roseland had also surprised its pastor, Gerrit Hoeksema, with a car in 1936, upon his completing ten years of service. First Reformed of Chicago had done the same for Broekstra already in 1919.

66. J. R. Brink, "Roseland and South," *Banner*, 18 Sept. 1936.

67. G. J. Heyboer, "In Memory of a Departed Teacher [T. Koelikamp]," ibid., 12 Feb. 1937. Tanis left Chicago for the position of teacher of Bible and church history at the Grand Rapids Christian High School.

Rev. Edward (E.J.) Tanis
(1887-1958)
(The Archives, Calvin College)

Dr. William Masselink
(1897-1973)
(The Archives, Calvin College)

church, like its mother at 71st Street, fled Englewood for Oak Lawn in 1962, becoming the Kedvale Avenue Christian Reformed Church. The Englewood properties were sold for $200,000 to the Faith Temple Church of God in Christ, a black congregation, and in 1963 it dedicated a new $400,000 church on Kedvale Avenue just south of 104th Street (figure 5.3, site 5). Six pastorates later, the three-hundred-member Kedvale congregation faithfully carries on. In 1971 the body welcomed thirty families from Third Roseland, and three years later several families joined when the West Evergreen church disbanded. In 1986 pastor Franklin Steen was killed in an automobile accident on the Dan Ryan Expressway after serving the congregation for five years.[68]

The **Auburn Park Christian Reformed Church** (Third Englewood) had a short life of twenty-eight years (1945-73). It flourished only

68. Kedvale Avenue Christian Reformed Church, *75th Anniversary, Diamond Memories, 1903-1978* (Oak Lawn, 1978). Kedvale Avenue's pastors were Oliver Breen (1952-70), John Bylsma (1971-75), Alexander De Jong (1976-80), Franklin Steen (1981-86), James Vander Slik (1987-90), H. Lamsma (1991-92), and Duane Van Loo (1993-).

Auburn Park Christian Reformed Church, erected 1948 *(The Archives, Calvin College)*

in the postwar decade, growing to five hundred members. After worshiping for three years in the Chicago Christian High School auditorium, the congregation in 1948 dedicated a new $100,000 Gothic sanctuary in the Auburn Park area on the corner of 78th and Aberdeen Streets (figure 5.2, site 7). The first pastor, Henry Baker (1946-53), was a well-known denominational "church planter" then in the waning years of his active ministry. Baker was acquainted with Chicago, because he had served the Second Roseland congregation in the 1920s. The church reached its five-hundred-seat capacity during Baker's time. Walter Ackerman followed (1954-59) and brought his considerable energy to the work, but he could not stem the steady loss of members leaving the area, nor could his successor, Robert Tjapkes (1960-66). In 1964 Tjapkes led the congregation in its transition into the West Evergreen Christian Reformed Church (see below).[69]

In three short years, 1961-64, all three Christian Reformed congregations in Englewood, two thousand members strong, had fled southwest to the suburbs of Evergreen Park and Oak Lawn. First Reformed, with its five hundred members, had set the pattern in 1954, and the equally large Hope Reformed Church was the last to relocate in 1972. The dense Dutch Reformed neighborhood of Englewood, so fondly remembered by its more than three thousand residents, disappeared with hardly a trace, leav-

69. Auburn Park Christian Reformed Church, *Dedication Souvenir* (Chicago, 1947).

ing behind only its impressive churches and school buildings. But it was reincarnated in the Evergreen Park–Oak Lawn nexus, which became a new Dutch hub on the southwest side. The six Christian Reformed churches alone had thirty-six hundred members in 1965, plus three hundred members in the sole Reformed Church (Green Oak). Preservation was the main objective of the Englewood congregations, and by relocating they achieved the goal of perpetuating their churches, socioreligious values, and lifestyles.[70]

Summit-Archer Avenue

In the late 1880s and early 1890s, some twenty Groninger market gardeners from the Old West Side and Englewood settled on the open prairies of Summit to the west of Cicero Avenue – Chicago's western boundary line – and south of 55th Street (now Midway Airport). This group was the nucleus of the Summit Reformed Church (1898) and the Archer Avenue Christian Reformed Church (1911) (figure 5.4).

At first, the farm folks traveled to church by horse and wagon, going to their respective Reformed or Christian Reformed churches on Ashland Avenue or in Englewood. But this was a real hardship for many, especially in winter. So in 1892 the mixed Reformed and Christian Reformed group, including Geert (George) Bos, George Brouwer, William Beukema, and others, organized a union congregation. They gathered in homes and chose the three men to take turns leading reading services, punctuated with an occasional visiting preacher. On New Year's Eve, 1892, in a meeting at Beukema's home, the group decided to build a one-room meeting house for worship and catechetical instruction of the youth. They made the twenty- by thirty-foot structure themselves of rough lumber for $80. It stood on the Rosenboom farm at 57th Street and Meade Avenue. For the sacraments of Holy Communion and baptism, the families traveled to their respective home churches in Chicago.

In 1896 the Summit flock upgraded its facility into a small frame church and moved it to John Schoon's farm at 55th Street and Moody Avenue. Several years later, in January 1899, the eighteen-family church obtained a regular minister as "stated supply" to preach and teach catechism in the mother tongue. He was John De Haan, a Presbyterian minister of Dutch parentage who was studying at Chicago's Moody Bible Institute.

70. Bergsma, "Tale of Two Churches," 11-12.

Figure 5.4 Churches in Summit District

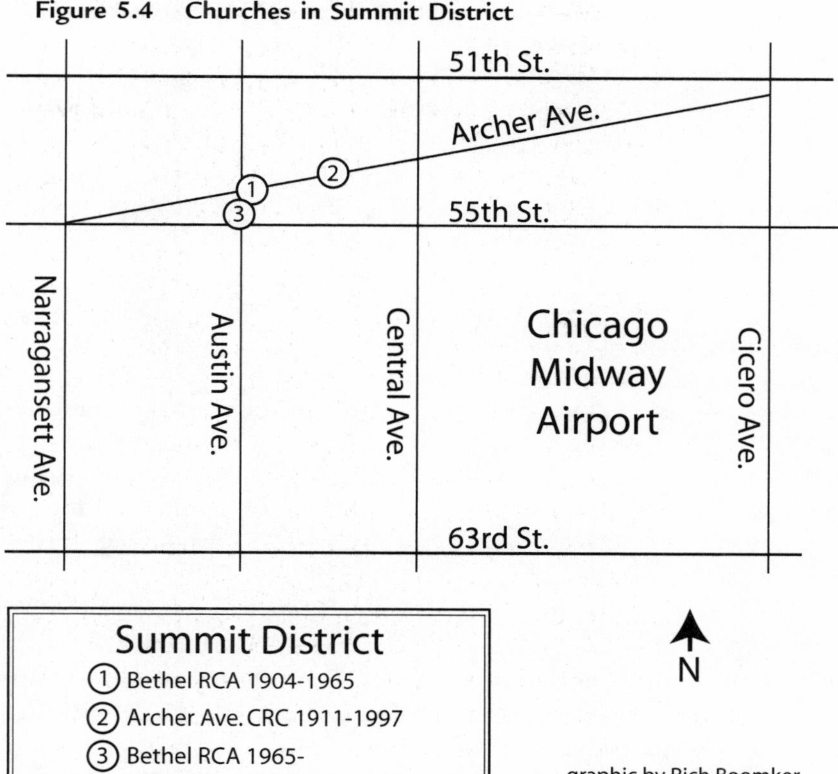

De Haan drew praise for his mastery of the native language in preaching, and the congregation gladly saw the end of the reading services.[71]

De Haan won the people's hearts and within the year was called as the first pastor (1899-1903) of the **Archer Avenue (later Bethel) Reformed Church of Summit**, which had affiliated shortly before with the Reformed denomination. The Classis of Illinois ordained him. Without any outside funds, the group built its church and paid De Haan's salary. Moerdyke, of Trinity Reformed Church, could not praise the unique union church enough: "They exhibit true Dutch pluck, and their remarkable cooperation is a model to multitudes of small settlements where sectarian division hinders religious progress." Before the year 1899 was out, De

71. Moerdyke, "Chicago Letter," *CI,* 26 Apr. 1899, p. 4; 5 Feb. 1902, p. 89; "Summit Illinois, Chr. Ref. Church," *Banner,* 26 Aug. 1915; "Church Celebrates Twenty-Fifth Anniversary," ibid., 12 Feb. 1937.

Bethel Reformed Church of Summit, after 1949 enlargement
(Western Seminary Collection, Joint Archives of Holland)

Haan instituted an English evening service to follow the morning and afternoon Dutch services. "Their enterprise is wonderful," enthused Moerdyke, who participated in De Haan's installation.[72]

Moerdyke's fulsome praise was given with a blind eye. Things at the Summit union church of forty-five families were not well. The congregation was divided down the middle by denominational loyalties that had lain dormant at first. Half of the families, those of Christian Reformed background, objected to the decision to affiliate with the Reformed Church. Once the "trouble crept in, . . . the little church was rolled away after a lawsuit over the question of who was to have the building, was settled." The half who lost the lawsuit and the building then withdrew.[73]

72. Peter Moerdyke, "Chicago Letter," *CI,* 7 Dec. 1898, p. 5; 11 Jan., p. 12, 25 Jan., p. 9, 26 July, p. 8, 11 Oct. 1899, p. 8. From 1899 to 1923 the name was the Dutch Reformed Church of Summit, from 1923 to 1948 it was the Archer Avenue Reformed Church, and from 1948 to the present the Bethel Reformed Church. Bethel Reformed Church of Chicago, *75th Anniversary, 1899-1974* (Chicago, 1974). It is surprising that until 1917 the Summit church was attached to the Classis of Illinois (American), and not the Classis of Wisconsin (Holland), which included all the other Dutch-speaking congregations except Northwestern Reformed Church.

73. "Summit Illinois, Chr. Ref. Church," *Banner,* 26 Aug. 1915; "Church Celebrates Twenty-Fifth Anniversary," ibid., 12 Feb. 1937.

Meanwhile, the original congregation carried on under De Haan. In 1901, real estate magnate Moses Wentworth, the landlord of most of the Dutch farmers in and around Summit, encouraged the congregation by donating a lot in the village for a parsonage. "This is a cheering gift," enthused Moerdyke. But the De Haan family could not adjust to country life and its one-room school. After three years, they moved back into the city, where De Haan served the Irving Park Reformed Church. Yet, he continued to conduct Sunday worship services in Summit for another year, before taking a call to Grand Rapids.[74]

The Reformed congregation moved forward energetically. It bought a half-acre lot on Archer Avenue at Austin for $500 in 1904 and moved its little church to the site (figure 5.4, site 1). With a $600 loan from the denomination, it made an addition to the church and built a parsonage, with members doing the work themselves. After a full year under effective lay leadership, the church called Maurice Ossewaarde of Clymer, New York, to its pulpit (1905-08). During the vacancy, said Moerdyke, the congregation "has suffered no lapses, no decline, and no scattering. Consistory and people, young and old, have conducted themselves most commendably. . . . They believe in thorough and unremitting devotion in the work of the Lord." In 1910 the congregation built on the site a new and larger church with stained glass windows.[75]

Seventeen pastors followed Ossewaarde in the Bethel pulpit, many staying but a few years, as is common in country churches. For some the charge was their last before retirement. Henry Harmeling (1929-38), who led the Archer Avenue church for a decade during the Depression, is a notable example. A son of Oostburg, Wisconsin, Harmeling and his family had put down deep roots in Chicago, having previously served three area churches — First Chicago (1900-08), First South Holland (1906-09), and First Roseland (1921-29). Summit was a short move from Roseland, and he worked there until he retired.

The congregation continued to grow slowly to around 175 souls, and the sanctuary of "the Friendly Church on Archer and Austin" was remodeled and expanded several times to accommodate them. In 1954 the church erected a fellowship hall to support educational and club activities. In 1965, after eight years of planning, Bethel built a new church on a

74. Moerdyke, "Chicago Letter," *CI,* 5 Dec. 1901, p. 799; 17 Dec. 1902, pp. 840-41; 4 Nov. 1903, p. 705.

75. Ibid., 1 Mar., p. 137, 8 Mar., p. 153, 29 Mar., p. 202, 13 Dec. 1905, p. 810; *Onze Toekomst,* 4 Nov. 1910.

site a mile south on 55th Street and dedicated a Möller organ the next year (figure 5.4, site 3). After the move, Bethel moved increasingly away from its Dutch immigrant roots to become a community church. The last Dutch language service was in 1946.

The **Summit (later Archer Avenue) Christian Reformed Church** had its origin in schism in 1899, as noted above, when the twenty-three families who had lost the lawsuit and the building separated themselves and resumed reading services, led by elders Beukema and Bos. They built a twenty- by thirty-foot church, an exact replica of the first, on leased land near 55th Street and McVicker Avenue (6050 West) and organized the usual activities – a Sunday school, Young People's Society, and even a choir. The Reverend Evert Breen, of the First Chicago church, a former "home missionary," took the group under his wing, and it became known as the Summit Mission Station.

When Breen left for Michigan in 1909, Gerrit Haan, of the First Englewood church, came out weekly to teach catechism, as Breen had done. Around 1910 several more families settled in Summit and joined the

Archer Avenue Christian Reformed Church of Summit
second edifice, erected 1915, parsonage on right
(The Archives, Calvin College)

mission; the meeting hall was enlarged by twenty feet to accommodate them. The influx gave the group the resources to organize as an independent congregation in 1911 with about twenty-six families. The first consistory was Beukema, Bos, and Martin De Maa, elders, and John Sterenberg and William Slager, deacons. The congregation then decided to buy an acre of land on Archer Avenue at McVicker Avenue and move its building to the site (figure 5.4, site 2). The church added a wing and built a parsonage next door, using volunteer labor over the winter months for all but the manse.[76]

The next step was to obtain a minister. After four unsuccessful attempts, the Reverend John Vos came in 1912 from the Groninger settlement in Fulton, Illinois. He was greeted with joy, because for some of the congregation his arrival marked the end of twenty years of reading services. The congregation subsequently grew to forty-two families (about two hundred souls) and then fell back to thirty-five families after losing seven, never to reach the peak again. In a pattern all too familiar, real estate developers had purchased the surrounding land for suburban subdivisions, and the Dutch tenant farmers had to change occupations or move farther out. Despite the uncertainty, the congregation in 1915 built a suitable church with steeple and bell tower that served its needs for five generations.

After Summit was annexed to Chicago, the name was changed to the Archer Avenue Christian Reformed Church, and gradually the English language took over in worship, education, and social life. In 1919 pastor J. Clover Monsma embroiled the congregation in his dream of launching a Kuyperian daily newspaper in Chicago. The body, with the concurrence of Classis Illinois, granted him an indefinite leave of absence, but when the enterprise failed in 1921 (see chapter 14), the consistory revoked the leave. Monsma thereupon resigned from the ministry, which action went directly against the church order. The next year, he sought to withdraw his hasty resignation letter, but the consistory would not hear of it, having received many sharp letters from their former cleric. Classis Illinois likewise erred in not disciplining the brother, as church order required. It simply washed its hands of this "loose cannon."[77]

76. Archer Avenue Christian Reformed Church, *Twenty-fifth Anniversary, 1911-1936* (Chicago, 1936); John O. Vos, "Enkele grepen uit de geschiedenis der Chr. Geref. Gem. te Summit, Ill.," Christian Reformed Church, *Jaarboekje,* 1916, 165-69.

77. "Report on State of Religion," Classis of Chicago, Reformed Church in America, 16 Dec. 1921; "Reports of Special Committees," April 1922; "Synodical Minutes," Fall Session, 1922. Monsma joined First Reformed Church of Chicago and sought ecclesiastical standing in the denomination, but the Classis of Chicago turned his application aside until he first justified his resignation before the synod of the Christian Reformed Church.

Under the Reverend Theodore Verhulst (1938-43), the members of Summit Church organized a school society, bought a bus, and in 1940 began sending their youngsters to Englewood Christian School. "The members are few, but the few are faithful," declared Benjamin Essenburg. The Dutch morning service also gave way to English and the common cup for Communion was ended. After 1945, new homes sprang up in the region around Midway Airport, and the congregation faced a mission challenge. The little Dutch country church evolved into a suburban American church. It expanded its facilities, reached out to its neighborhood, and brought in one-third of the members from the community. However, in the 1980s the centrifugal pressures of suburbanization pushed core families to more distant towns, and the church disbanded in 1997.[78]

In the early decades, both the Reformed and Christian Reformed churches in Summit struggled for existence, because in truth the community really had room for but one congregation. Both churches required annual subsidies from their respective regional assemblies to pay their pastors' salaries. Once past the depression decade, however, they grew and flourished for half a century and more, until the community fundamentally changed.

Evergreen Park and Oak Lawn

As in Summit a decade earlier, after 1900 truck farmers from Englewood and Roseland moved west into Evergreen Park and Oak Lawn, the next suburb to the west along 95th Street stretching from Western to Harlem Avenues. They met for worship in a little chapel at 95th Street and Crawford Avenue and filled it to capacity by 1912. In 1913 the mission chapel was organized as the Christian Reformed Church of Oak Lawn. The location seemed ideal, because Crawford Avenue was the borderline between the two suburbs. But the facility was inadequate, and the congregation split over the decision of where to build the new church. The families

78. B. Essenburg, "West Side News," *Banner,* 26 Oct. 1939; Essenburg, "North Chicago News," ibid., 26 Nov. 1943; William P. Brink, "Chicago North News," ibid., 10 Aug. 1945; Brink, "Classis Chicago North," ibid., 9 Nov. 1945. One of the teenage converts at Archer Avenue was Vincent Licatesi, an Italian Catholic, who after completing his education at Chicago Christian High School and Calvin College and Seminary, became a Christian Reformed minister. In 1970 Licatesi withdrew and formed an independent congregation in Wyoming, Michigan. In the 1990s this movement evolved into a new denomination, the United Reformed Church of North America.

in each area wanted it in their own locale, and this tore the fledgling church apart, despite the efforts of Classis Illinois to mediate. In 1914 a dozen families in Evergreen Park returned to their mother church, the First Englewood congregation, while the remnant of Oak Lawn families continued to worship at the Crawford Avenue site. This became the nucleus of the First Christian Reformed Church of Oak Lawn, organized in 1915 (see below).[79]

At the same time, sixteen farm families, mostly from Roseland, together bought a 160-acre tract in the heart of Evergreen Park. It was one mile to the east on 95th Street, running from Kedzie to California Avenues. They partitioned the tract into individual ten-acre plots, built homes, and began working the land. In 1915 the classis authorized this group, plus the families that had returned to First Englewood, together numbering twenty families, to form the **First Christian Reformed Church of Evergreen Park**.

Evergreen Park's organizational meeting took place in the barn of Henry Triezenberg, a farmer and local schoolteacher. Here the eighty-six charter members also worshiped for a few months, while their church at 97th Street and Kedzie Avenue was under construction (figure 5.3, site 1). Henry Wezeman built the little frame church for $2,100![80]

As lead elder, Triezenberg taught the Sunday school and was the *voorlezer* who read the sermons until the first pastor, Zachary Sherda, came in 1916. Sherda remained for fifteen years (1916-30) and gave the country church stability. By 1925 the body outgrew its sanctuary, even the balcony expansion that added sixty seats, but for two decades the members would not take on debt to build a larger facility. Young children were left at home to make seating for adults, and families were encouraged to worship elsewhere. These were conservative farm folks who were risk averse. However, they did sacrifice to establish a Christian day school in 1925 and build a four-room school near 97th Street and Homan Avenue that by 1931 served 156 students. The spiritual nurture of the youth was worth any sacrifice.

Sherda made another significant contribution. He introduced English worship services in 1927 without bitterness, first in the evening and

79. "Chicago Letter," ibid., 7 Nov. 1912; "Classis Illinois," ibid., 28 May 1914; Evergreen Park Christian Reformed Church, *Fiftieth Anniversary, 1915-1965* (Evergreen Park, 1965), 4.

80. This and the next paragraph relies heavily on ibid., 6-11; Evergreen Park Christian Reformed Church, *Diamond Jubilee, 1915-1990* (Evergreen Park, 1990), 5-18; "Evergreen Park, Ill." *Banner,* 25 Feb. 1915. The first consistory was Eme Meyer and Edward Torringa, elders, and Frank Ozinga and Herman Wieringa, deacons.

H. G. Triezenberg barn *(The Archives, Calvin College)*

soon in the morning as well. The two Dutch services were sandwiched in between, at 10:30 AM and 2:00 PM. In the 1930s, one Dutch worship sufficed, and in the 1940s even that was unnecessary, as the pioneer generation had died off.

The second pastor, Benjamin Spalink (1930-37), was able to accomplish the building program that had frustrated Sherda. Within days of his installation, he had formed a building committee of ten men, and within two months the congregation voted to proceed on their $40,000 recommendation. Within a week of the meeting, the members had pledged $15,000 for a down payment. In September 1931, the congregation dedicated its new church on Homan Avenue (3400 west) just south of 95th Street, replete with a two-manual Wicks pipe organ (figure 5.3, site 2).[81] The church grew to nearly six hundred members under Spalink, whose ministry of six years was "very effective and much appreciated."

The Reverend Jacob Smith led the congregation through the years of World War II (1938-44), when seventy-five of its sons served in the armed forces, three of whom died for their country. Smith maintained an active correspondence with each serviceman. The decade after the war brought continued growth, and when an enlarged balcony proved inadequate, the congregation in 1953 spun off more than three hundred members into a daughter church (Park Lane).

This happened during the pastorate of Albert Jabaay (1944-52). He was a powerful preacher who could stir the emotions, until a heart attack com-

81. "Dedication of Church at Evergreen Park, Ill.," *Banner,* 18 Sept. 1931; J. R. Brink, "Roseland and the South District," ibid.

First Christian Reformed Church of Evergreen Park: above, the building erected in 1915; below, the building erected in 1931
(Both photographs from the Archives, Calvin College)

pelled him to request early retirement. The church seemed to stumble thereafter, sending out twelve calls without an acceptance over a two-year period. Marinus Goote (1954-62) picked up their spirits, and the membership surpassed one thousand, which continued under Harvey Baas (1963-69) and Neal Punt (1969-94), who was the longest serving minister. Punt made a mark as a speculative theologian by challenging the denomination's longheld doctrine of limited atonement in favor of a more universalistic view. Over time the mother church gave pride of place to its daughter; membership dwindled to 235 in 2000, compared to 385 at Park Lane.

The **Park Lane Christian Reformed Church of Evergreen Park** began in 1953 as a full-fledged congregation of nearly four hundred members. It was also favored with a parting gift from the mother church of $37,500 cash and the deed to a large plot on Maple Street (ca. 97th Street) near Homan Avenue (figure 5.3, site 3). Renze De Groot, classical "home missionary," smoothly guided the group at its inception, along with Albert Jabaay. Dr. Benjamin Fieldhouse and Arthur Stavinga headed the steering committee, which gave way to the first consistory: elders John Brondsema, Otto Doornbos, Dr. Benjamin Fieldhouse, Harry Klunder (vice president), Leonard Stob, George Triezenberg (clerk), and John Wigboldy and deacons Henry Boss, Harold Hiskes (treasurer), George Hoekstra, Dr. John Meekma, John Teune, and Abram Vander Weit.[82] The two medical doctors lent prestige to the consistory.

Before the year was out, candidate Theodore Verseput (1953-57) was ordained and installed as the first pastor. With the dedication of the new church facility in 1955, the congregation chose the name Park Lane, to differentiate it from the mother church. The eight subsequent pastors held Park Lane on a steady course of active ministry as a blue-collar church in a working-class community.[83]

The **First Oak Lawn Christian Reformed Church** began in 1915 with less than one hundred souls, all truck farmers, and slowly doubled and then tripled from internal growth until it surpassed six hundred in the 1950s. By this time the farms had given way to new housing subdivisions, and the church had become suburbanized. When it organized in 1915, the congregation relocated to the heart of the village of Oak Lawn on 48th Avenue just

82. This and the next paragraphs rely on Park Lane Christian Reformed Church of Evergreen Park, *25 Years 1953-1978* (Evergreen Park, 1978); and *Dedication Book, March, 1955* (Evergreen Park, 1955).

83. Park Lane's pastors were William Verwolf (1957-66), Angus MacLeod (1966-74), Winston Boelkins (1974-79), Daniel Brink (1978-86) and co-pastor Ronald W. De Young (1981-86), Gary Hutt (1987-96), J. Vander Ploeg (1992-99), and Calvin Aardsma (1999-).

north of 95th Street (figure 5.3, site 4). By 1932 the sanctuary was filled to capacity. This was the year that the morning service switched from Dutch to English. The Reverend Nicholas Fokkens (1915-18) was the first in a line of twelve pastors to serve the congregation, with John Van Beek leaving the biggest imprint during a twenty-three-year tenure (1923-45). His first wife spent many years in bed as an invalid, showing "an enviable Christian patience in her trials." Since the 1970s the rolls have shrunk by half, to three hundred members, as families moved to more distant suburbs.[84]

First Oak Lawn is noted for its conservatism, and the pastors have reflected that perspective, making it the most traditional of Oak Lawn's three Christian Reformed churches. Christian education has always been a high priority for the members, and already in 1931 some fifty children were bussed to the Evergreen Park Christian School. They received their catechetical instruction at the church from the pastor, as was standard practice.

The **West Evergreen Christian Reformed Church**, formerly the Auburn Park Church of Englewood, was only a shadow of its former self in Evergreen Park. In 1964 the congregation purchased a building at 98th Street and Crawford Avenue, just south of 95th Street (figure 5.3, site 8). Its pastorates were of short duration – C. Oliver Buus (1967-69), Roger Timmerman (1970-73), and Lubbert Van Dellen (1973-74) – and membership slipped by one-third, from three hundred to two hundred, forcing the body to relocate again in 1973, this time to the far southwestern area of Palos Heights–Worth. But within months the church disbanded; too many members had remained in Evergreen Park to make the new body viable. The members joined sister churches in the two localities.[85]

The **Green Oak Reformed Church** of Oak Lawn was organized in 1955 to serve those fleeing from the two Englewood Reformed congregations. It began with only fifty-eight members and grew rapidly to three hundred members in the first decade, reaching nearly four hundred members in the early 1990s (figure 5.3, site 6).[86]

Some Englewood families bypassed Oak Lawn for the communities of Worth and Palos Heights several miles to the southwest. The **Palos**

84. J. R. Brink, "Roseland and South District," *Banner*, 24 Mar. 1931; Brink, "Roseland and the South," ibid., 18 Nov. 1932; Brink, "Roseland and South," ibid., 27 Mar. 1936; "Evergreen Park and Oak Lawn, Illinois," ibid., 26 Apr. 1940.

85. "West Evergreen Park CRC Begins New Era," ibid., 4 Nov. 1974.

86. Green Oak Reformed Church pastors were Wendell Pyle (1956-60), Donald Jansma (1961-68), Richard Welscott (1969-74), Lloyd Arnoldink (1975-86), Thomas Dekker (1987-98), and Robert Vander Putten (1999-).

First Christian Reformed Church of Oak Lawn, purchased 1915
(The Archives, Calvin College)

Heights Christian Reformed Church was established in 1955, and five years later came the **Palos Heights Reformed Church**. The former began with 150 members and the later with 91 members. Both thrived because the village became a magnet with the establishment of Trinity Christian College in 1959 and the relocation of Chicago Christian High School in 1961. By 2000 the Christian Reformed congregation had grown to 565 members, and the Reformed congregation was bursting at the seams with 500 members and contemplating a building program.[87]

Marvin Hoff served the Palos Heights Reformed Church twice, from 1966 to 1969 and again from 1981 to 1985. In the interim he held key administrative posts in the national church offices at 475 Riverside Drive in New York City, and after 1985 he left Chicago to assume the presidency of Western Theological Seminary. Bruce Laverman (1969-80) succeeded Hoff and dedicated two major additions to the worship center in 1972 and 1977, which increased the seating to 650. Donald Jansma (1986-89) pastored the Palos Heights congregation in the late 1980s, after having served the nearby Green Oak congregation of Oak Lawn in the 1960s. He and Hoff obviously enjoyed living in the area.[88]

87. Pastors who served the Palos Heights Christian Reformed Church are Peter Huisman (1957-62), Kenneth Havert (1963-69), John Vander Lugt (1970-81), James Lunt (1981-88), Calvin Hoogendoorn (1988-95), and Sam Hamstra, Jr. (1996-). Palos Heights Reformed Church pastors include Vernon Vander Werff (1960-65), Marvin Hoff (1966-69), Bruce Laverman (1969-80), Marvin Hoff (1981-85), Donald Jansma (1986-89), Robert Honig (1988-90), Peter Semeyn (1990-96), and Timothy Van Heest (1996-).

88. Palos Heights Reformed Church, *Building for Eternity: Dedication — Autumn 1972* (Palos Heights, Ill., 1972); "Illinois Church Dedicates Facilities," *Church Herald*, 14 Oct. 1977.

Western Springs Christian Reformed Church, purchased 1938 *(The Archives, Calvin College)*

La Grange and Western Springs

The movement of some fifty Dutch farm families into La Grange, Western Springs, Hinsdale, and Downers Grove in the 1920s and early 1930s spurred the founding of a mission church in La Grange in 1935. The families no longer had to drive the nine miles to the Cicero churches. The new church plant prompted more families to come, in keeping with the maxim of home missionary John R. Brink: "A church draws our people as the bee is drawn to honey." Conrad Ottenhoff and George Tameling provided the local leadership. Three years later, in 1938, the **Western Springs Christian Reformed Church** was established, and the body purchased a snug little church building at a bargain price. The first pastor, Clifford Vander Ark, left the congregation in 1942, after three years of ministry, to take an Army chaplaincy. The most notable pastor was Arthur De Kruyter (1951-65), editor of the Chicago-area news monthly, the *Illinois Observer,* and leading instigator of Trinity Christian College. He later left the denomination to found the famed Christ Church of Oak Brook, an independent body, to serve the suburban elites.[89]

89. John R. Brink, "Home Mission News and Views," *Chicago Messenger,* 29 Nov. 1935; Brink, "Western Springs Flourishing Mission," ibid., 19 June 1936; Brink, "Western Springs, Ill.," *Banner,* 12 June 1936; Brink, "Roseland and South," ibid., 7 Apr. 1938; George Ottenhoff, "Western Springs, Illinois," ibid., 16 Feb. 1940; "Western Springs, Ill.," ibid., 10 Sept. 1943.

Rev. Arthur De Kruyter (1921-)
(Courtesy of Arthur De Kruyter)

Des Plaines

The truck farmers of Des Plaines, also Groningers from the Old West Side, in 1927 prevailed on Classis Illinois of the Christian Reformed Church to send missionary Brink to plant a congregation. Brink began worship services, and in three years the **Des Plaines Christian Reformed Church** was organized with seventy-five members. Within six months, Calvin Seminary candidate Rens Hooker came as the first pastor (1930-37), and the congregation had a new parsonage built for his family. The congregation worshiped in the Carpenters Union hall in the city for more than a year, but this proved uncongenial. Consequently, in 1932, despite hard times and bank failures, the members amassed sufficient funds to build a basement church next to the parsonage. This served as their sanctuary during the Depression years until they could afford to complete the edifice. The most illustrious pastor was John Kromminga (1946-49), who shortly after was elected president of Calvin Seminary. Gerben Zylstra followed Kromminga and served for thirteen years until retiring; his was the longest pastorate. The congregation grew slowly to a high point of 277 members in 1973 under the Reverend Lloyd Wolters (1969-79), and then it declined slowly, especially after the small Des Plaines Christian School closed. In 1993 the remnant of 63 members had little choice but to disband.[90]

90. "Des Plaines, Illinois," *Banner,* 12 Dec. 1930, 25 Dec. 1931. Pastors at the Des Plaines

Des Plaines Christian Reformed Church, 1952 *(Herrick Public Library)*

Americanization

The Reformed Church in America as a denomination was more Americanized than the Christian Reformed Church, and it pushed its Midwestern immigrant congregations to reach out to the host culture. Indeed, already in 1884 its synod adopted an English language requirement. Any Holland congregation that received aid from the Board of Domestic Missions must as a condition of that aid conduct in the English language "such a portion of the Sunday services, as may be satisfactory to the Board."

Reformed congregations regularly scheduled inspirational services to encourage a "season of blessing," in which popular preachers were invited to exhort in the style of American evangelists. The nondenominational Moody Bible Institute of Chicago often furnished speakers, such as its president, the ex-actor Dr. Will Houghton, who gave his riveting personal testimony at the Bethany Reformed Church in Roseland in 1935. Conversely, Frances (Mrs. Richard) Huizenga of West Side Reformed Church in

church included Rens Hooker (1930-37), William Steenland (1937-38), Hessel Kooistra (1938-43), Albert Selles (1944-46), John Kromminga (1946-49), Gerben Zylstra (1949-62), John Draisma (1962-68), Lloyd Wolters (1969-79), Karl Wiersum (1980-83), and Robert Vander Roest (1984-93).

Rev. John H. Kromminga (1918-94)
(The Archives, Calvin College)

Cicero appeared as a regular soloist in a weekly shut-in program of the Moody radio station WMBI.[91] For many years, Joanna Hettinga sang in the ladies' trio, the King's Karollers, on the weekly Sunday evening radio program, "Songs in the Night," produced by Moody Church.

The Christian Reformed denomination, by contrast, remained an immigrant church linked to the Netherlands for a generation longer. Before the Second World War this was a plus in attracting Dutch immigrants as members, but those who arrived in the 1950s were different; they were less committed to the church and quicker to criticize and question it. This spirit of skepticism had the effect of weakening church traditions and hastening change in the Reformed community.

American-born sons of the church after World War II joined in the appeal to reach out to the American mainstream. In Chicago, the Reverend Arthur De Kruyter sounded the call in 1959:

> It is with some dismay that one searches the newspapers to find a trace of our Calvinistic and Reformed activities in Chicago. Although there are approximately 10,000 families in this area, there still seems to be an inferiority complex among us. . . . What would people think if they began to hear from the Reformed community which has been

91. *Acts and Proceedings of the General Synod of the Protestant Dutch Reformed Church in America,* 1884, 552; *Chicago Messenger,* 31 May, 27 Dec. 1935.

here for 100 years but has said and contributed so little to the cure of our metropolitan ills?

De Kruyter lamented the fact that non-Dutch people seldom attended Reformed churches in the mistaken belief that "one had to be Dutch to attend the services" and that "we still speak Dutch in some part of the service." And they were "confused about our separate school system and thought that we were anti-American in our approach."[92] De Kruyter acted on his belief in cultural openness in the next decade by leaving his Christian Reformed pastorate to open the nondenominational Christ Church in Oak Brook, which ministers to the affluent business and professional residents of the far western suburbs.

One event that added to De Kruyter's chagrin was the huge celebration in 1957 at Chicago's International Amphitheater of the centennial of the Christian Reformed Church in North America. This was the biggest event this group had ever held in Chicago. Twelve thousand of the faithful jammed the building and hundreds had to be turned away. The crowd created an immense traffic jam. A gas station attendant remarked: "Some church is having a centennial rally and has got things tied up worse than Elvis Presley!" "Never before has there been such a united effort toward a common goal — namely, the glory of God," declared De Kruyter. But neither the Chicago *Tribune* nor the Chicago *Daily News* carried a story on the rally, despite repeated contacts by the committee. "Sometimes our people wonder why we should bother with the press," declared De Kruyter. "Generally speaking, we don't need them any more than we needed them to fill the house on April 5. But because our public relations with the press have been so poor in the past, we now reap the harvest."[93] The rally helped break down the strong pride and localism among the Christian Reformed of the West Side, Englewood, and South Side (Roseland, South Holland, and Lansing), and it gave new evidence of area-wide thinking. In 1949 and 1952, South Holland–Lansing and Cicero, respectively, had founded their own Christian high schools, thus weakening the unity engendered by Chicago Christian High School. The 1957 church centenary helped prepare the way in Chicago for the founding in 1959 of a regional Reformed college, Trinity Christian College (chapter 7).[94]

92. *Illinois Observer,* Feb. 1959.

93. Arthur De Kruyter, "Discrimination by the Chicago Press," Ibid., Apr. 1957.

94. De Kruyter, "Area Interests," ibid., July-Aug., 1958.

Moody Bible Institute and Dutch Chicago

American evangelicalism also made inroads in the Reformed community, especially through the programs of the Chicago Training Institute (later Moody Bible Institute), founded in 1889. Dwight L. Moody attracted attention when he conducted a very successful crusade during the 1893 World's Fair. "Mr. Moody is aggressive and aims to introduce the Gospel and multiply such services as shall be the rivals of places of evening amusement," Moerdyke noted approvingly. "Crowds flock to hear him morning and afternoon." In Moody's 1897 revival campaign, seven thousand people attended every meeting of the four-day crusade at Moody Auditorium, and thousands more had to be turned away. "It was the old orthodox, doctrinal, evangelical preaching, now too rarely heard," Moerdyke enthused, seemingly with no concern for Moody's Baptist-leaning theology. Indeed, any criticism he labeled as "polemic sectarianism."[95]

Moody's spiritual impact on the city and its churches was noticeable. "Our own Reformed Churches have occasion to rejoice in more than the usual ingathering of souls," Moerdyke reported. "Let us hope," he added, that it will have a "sustaining influence, and may stimulate to increased fervor and zeal of all Christian forces."[96]

When Moody died in 1899, Moerdyke wrote a warm tribute.

> This city mourns the termination of Mr. Moody's labors. . . . The Christian element and forces of his beloved Chicago will miss him long. A phenomenal and unique career has ended, and millions live to bless God for the spiritual power He exerted through the evangelist. He built monuments here that will send forth blessed influences for generations.[97]

The monuments were the institute, with its academic programs to train lay missionaries, and Moody Church. These institutions over the years hosted a wide variety of speakers who drew large audiences. Famed Bible expositors, preachers, and evangelists included Dr. Arthur T. Pierson, Presbyterian mission theorist; G. Campbell Morgan, British expository preacher; R. A. Torrey, evangelist and superintendent of Moody Bible Institute; and the Reformed Church's own Wm. Walton Clark.

95. Moerdyke, "Chicago Letter," *CI,* 11 Oct., p. 9; 8 Mar. 1899, p. 8.

96. Ibid., 21 June 1893, p. 11; 12 Apr. 1899, p. 10; 24 Mar., p. 9; 7 Apr. 1897, p. 9; 7 Oct. 1896, p. 9.

97. Ibid., 27 Dec. 1899, p. 5.

Given this sterling ministry, Moerdyke concluded, the Christians in Chicago will "appreciate more and more that this Institute is a marvelous spiritual and evangelistic power. . . . The practical influence, the spiritual power of this school, is remarkable and an invaluable boon to Chicago and vicinity."[98]

Reformed pastors praised Moody Bible Institute (MBI) without reservation. Moerdyke spoke for them all in 1892:

> At the Bible Institute we always love to witness the student's manifest zeal for Christ and the Holy Scriptures, and a devotion to Bible study and work for Christ, which ought to characterize all theological seminaries, in both faculties and students. I am positive that these students will not, in later years, dwell in story upon their pranks, capers and worse during years of preparation for their life's mission.[99]

Another Moody parachurch organization, the Light Bearers Association, similarly recruited the Dutch Reformed in Chicago. William Baar, who chaired the organization in 1954, sought volunteers for ministries at the Cook County Jail, the Tuberculosis Sanitarium, the Dunning State Mental Hospital, and the like.[100]

In the 1890s already, Reformed pastors in the Chicago area employed Moody students as assistants to preach in English and assist in local evangelism efforts. Bethany Reformed Church of Roseland and its sister church in Gano both reported a "quickening and refreshing" from these students' work. Several were supported by the denominational board of domestic missions to study for the ministry in its own churches. John De Haan was one such student; he later served as pastor of the Reformed Church of Summit.[101]

A number of Reformed members, and not a few Christian Reformed, studied at Moody Bible Institute to prepare for mission work. The former received far more approbation from their home churches than did the latter. At least one Chicago-area Reformed pastor, John W. Poot of Gano, sent his son to the institute for missionary training. When nurse Effa Hofma, of Trinity Reformed Church, studied at the Moody Bible Institute in 1895 in order to qualify for foreign missionary work, her pastor, Peter

98. Ibid., 20 Nov. 1895, p. 14; 12 Nov. 1902, p. 737; 24 Nov. 1897, p. 11; 9 Jan. 1907, p. 26; 17 Mar. 1897, p. 8; 21 Jan. 1903, p. 41; 2 Feb. 1904, p. 122.

99. Ibid., 31 May 1893, p. 11.

100. *Illinois Observer,* 15 Aug. 1954.

101. Moerdyke, "Chicago Letter," *CI,* 9 Dec. 1896, p. 11; 22 Dec. 1897, p. 9.

Moerdyke, said: "We rejoice in the consecrated purpose of this estimable Christian lady." After completing her studies, Hofma in 1896 married the Reverend Andrew Vander Wagen, a recent graduate of Calvin Seminary in Grand Rapids, and the couple was commissioned to labor among the Indians in Arizona.[102]

Local Christian Reformed churches were far less willing to make such commendations. During World War I, for example, two young women from the First Christian Reformed Church of Chicago enrolled in Bible classes at the school. Jacoba Tysma earned a diploma in Sunday school teaching, and Gertrude Visser simply sought more "spiritual food" than her church offered. The elders admonished both women about the danger at Moody of being drawn away from Reformed doctrines by "foolish and dangerous" ideas. Winifred Hoekstra of the Second Cicero Christian Reformed Church evoked an equally negative reaction when, in the 1930s, she enrolled at Moody to become a missionary nurse. So opposed were the elders to the Baptist theology taught at Moody that they refused to reappoint her as Sunday school teacher. They feared she would contaminate her pupils, despite the fact that her father, Peter A. Hoekstra, was the church's pastor.[103]

But the stance of the Christian Reformed churches was inconsistent. While the Second Cicero consistory condemned Moody's theology, the Second Englewood church invited a "group of splendid Christian people" from the institute to give a program of "song and testimony" at the church on a Wednesday evening. The *Chicago Messenger* reported that "an enthusiastic crowd of young people joyously responded" to the gospel choruses and the "sincere and interesting testimonies."[104]

To offer a Reformed alternative to the Moody Bible Institute, the board of the Helping Hand Mission in 1937 founded the Reformed Bible Institute (RBI). Mark Fakkema of Roseland, director of the National Union of Christian Schools, was the point man and an instructor, along with George Weeber, mission superintendent. By the second year, enrollment in the two evening classes topped 150 and proved the desire for such training. When Weeber left Chicago the next year, his place was taken by West Side native Henry Evenhouse, a Bible teacher at Chicago Christian High School. Classes were free and the instructors taught without pay. The goal

102. Ibid., 18 Dec. 1895, p. 10; 14 Oct. 1896, p. 9; 9 Feb. 1898, p. 9.

103. First Christian Reformed Church of Chicago, Minutes, 30 July 1917; Winifred R. Dykstra nee Hoekstra, "History of Winifred R. Dykstra," typescript, Aug. 1989.

104. *Chicago Messenger,* 29 Nov. 1935.

of the institute was a full-fledged curriculum to train lay evangelists to staff the growing church mission programs in Chicago. But RBI could not compete with MBI academically or win over the hearts and minds of the Christian Reformed constituency. Classis Illinois overtured the denominational synod in 1938 to take over the institute, and when that was rejected, the board of RBI decided in 1940 to move it to Michigan.[105]

In 1941 the Chicago RBI resumed a few evening classes on the Old West Side, Cicero, and Roseland, but serious evangelism training in Chicago was left to the Moody Bible Institute, whose influence mounted, much to the chagrin of the ardent Calvinists. Essenburg, for one, was greatly disappointed in the decision. "To locate the day school in Grand Rapids is like Jacob's taking Esau's birthright and blessing," he charged. "Moreover, our chief competitor is in Chicago – and why? Chicago affords unlimited opportunity for practical work which should constitute a vital part of the training."[106]

The Christian Reformed churches in Chicago first took city mission outreach seriously in the 1910s, when they banded together to hire a full-time evangelist, the Rev. Peter Hoekenga. He engaged in street preaching and tract distribution, jail and hospital ministries, and held chapel services in various slum districts. He even labored evenings in Chicago's "red light" district. The churches provided Hoekenga with a Model T Ford automobile in 1914 to traverse the city more easily. He was probably the first Christian Reformed pastor in Chicago to benefit from the new automobility. A coalition of five West Side consistories also launched the Helping Hand and Hebrew missions in these years. A new era of evangelism was clearly gaining ground. Rather than merely planting new churches among scattered Hollanders, home mission work now truly met the dictum: "Preach the gospel!"[107]

105. The organizing committee consisted of laymen Nick Youngsma, Albert Reitsma, and George J. Stob. Church leaders were Weeber, Fakkema, and Edward Tuuk. "The Reformed Bible Institute," *Banner*, 3 June 1937; "Students Praise the Reformed Bible Institute of Chicago," ibid., 20 Jan. 1938; "A Friendly Debate on the Question, 'Is the M.B.I. Reformed?'" ibid., 19 May 1938; "Classis Illinois," ibid., 2 June 1938; "The Rev. George Weeber Leaves the Institute," ibid., 3 Nov. 1938; "Reformed Bible Institute," ibid., 27 Apr. 1939; "Reformed Bible Institute to Open in Grand Rapids," ibid., 10 Aug. 1939.

106. B. Essenburg, "West Chicago News," ibid., 24 Aug. 1939; 7 Mar. 1941.

107. "Chicago Letter," ibid., 12 Feb. 1914; "Chicago Items," ibid., 30 Apr. 1914; "Douglas Park News," ibid., 3 Sept. 1914; "Chicago News," ibid., 10 Sept. 1914; "Classis Illinois," ibid., 1 Oct. 1914. Hoekenga periodically reported on his activities in a newsletter, "The Gospel Trumpet" (1914-??), which local mission supporters mailed to every family in the denomination.

Rev. Peter Hoekenga, street preaching
near Helping Hand Gospel Mission, 1915
(The Archives, Calvin College)

The work had mixed results, however, and the missionaries could never count on the wholehearted support of the broader church constituency. Yet the base was laid, and the Reformed congregations continued various programs of city evangelism. By 1949 the Christian Reformed churches of Chicago supported twelve missions in the city and organized an annual Chicago Mission Workers' Conference. The Reformed churches had a half dozen missions as well.[108]

In the 1950s the churches began evangelism to "colored" people. This plan first surfaced in 1954, when the Lawndale Gospel Chapel at 1432 Pulaski Road, which had ministered to unchurched whites for more than a decade, faced the prospect of closing because whites had fled before the rising black influx. This forced the Christian Reformed churches either to close the mission station or to use it for a ministry to the newcomers. Since the building was available and the need for evangelism to blacks seemed obvious, the home missions committee of Classis Chicago North decided to take this bold step. The West Side Reformed had finally addressed the "Negro question," but realistically, asked Arthur De Kruyter, editor of the *Illinois Observer,* would they willingly accept converts into

108. "Chicagoland Mission Workers' Dinner," *Banner,* 9 Dec. 1949.

their churches and Christian day schools? The answer was yes, but with serious reservations (see chapter 7).[109]

In 1956 the denominational board of evangelism based in Grand Rapids, Michigan, raised the stakes by making available the just-vacated Nathanael Institute, which was a commodious, two-story structure with a gymnasium. After renovations, the Lawndale Chapel moved late in 1957. The classical committee helped the fledgling body launch an after-school Bible school and junior high boys' and girls' clubs. The chapel grew slowly, and in 1963 it matured into a full-fledged congregation, the Lawndale Christian Reformed Church, under pastor Peter Huiner, a son of the First Cicero church.[110]

In 1950 Classis Chicago North began a program to evangelize Chinese students attending the University of Chicago, which soon evolved into a mission congregation in the city's famed Chinatown on West 22nd Street. In 1956 the Chinese chapel moved nearer to the university, and in 1974 the Hyde Park Christian Reformed Church was organized to serve mainly Asian students and professors. The worship services are bilingual; an interpreter on the pulpit translates the English into Chinese.[111]

In 1958 the First Christian Reformed Church of Cicero started an outreach program to American Indians in Chicago. Two laymen from the congregation, Art Jongsma and Aldrich Evenhouse, began meeting at the Isham Memorial YMCA on north Ashland Avenue. It was an area where thousands of Indians lived in poverty and alcoholism, having left the reservations at the urging of federal officials. The ministry was extremely difficult, but within four years the men regularly gathered fifty for Sunday worship and an equal number of children for Sunday school.

This success induced the Christian Reformed denomination to take over the Chicago Indian Mission, with Jongsma as superintendent, aided by his wife. The ministry was a fitting urban counterpart to the denomination's long-standing mission program at Rehoboth and Zuni, New Mexico, among the Navajo and Zuni tribes. With the help of native converts, the Chicago Indian Mission offered teachings and songs in the Na-

109. *Illinois Observer,* 15 Dec. 1954, July, Oct. 1955, Dec. 1956. The Lawndale Chapel previously was located at 1304 S. Karlov Avenue, and Peter Reitsma was the superintendent (William P. Brink, "Chicago North News," *Banner,* 16 Nov. 1945).

110. *Illinois Observer,* Dec. 1956, Dec. 1957; Scott Hoezee and Christopher H. Meehan, *Flourishing in the Land: A Hundred-Year History of Christian Reformed Missions in North America* (Grand Rapids: Eerdmans, 1996), 137.

111. *Illinois Observer,* May 1956; Paul Han, "Hyde Park, Chicago: Church with a Mission," *Banner,* 17 Sept. 1976.

vajo tongue and classes in silver-smithing and other native crafts. The staff assisted Indians in finding work, distributed nonperishable foods, and met physical and emotional needs. Evangelist Howard Bielema succeeded Jongsma as superintendent in 1964 and, with his wife, Doris, carried on for seventeen years (1964-82) at three different locations. The Reverend Russell Van Antwerpen served the final five years until 1987, when the chapel on Wilson Avenue was closed. This significant cross-cultural outreach affected the lives of hundreds of native Americans and increased the Dutch Reformed awareness of their needs and promise.[112]

Conclusion

"Westward Ho!" seemed to be the motto of the Groningers until they had entirely deserted Chicago and even Cook County for the upscale and nonintegrated suburbs in Du Page County. For decades the path of least resistance flowed westward along the commercial and streetcar artery of 12th Street (Roosevelt Road after 1919), because major trunk railroad lines and industrial districts hedged them in to the south and north. After 1960, the Eisenhower (formerly Congress) Expressway, which paralleled Roosevelt Road, channeled the Dutch into the far western suburbs. Whether within the city or beyond its borders, the Dutch Calvinists clustered around their churches and schools in order to preserve an ethnoreligious solidarity.

But the passing of the generations has taken a toll on the Dutch Reformed churches of the Chicago area. They no longer stress the importance of the Reformed heritage and historic Calvinist creeds. The weekly preaching from the Heidelberg Catechism, which had long been mandated by the church order, has become more sporadic. And the hour-long catechetical instruction of all teenagers by the minister has given way to briefer Sunday school classes. In some congregations the pastor and elders neglect the time-honored tradition of family visiting, and they are reluctant to discipline delinquent members.

Worship styles have also changed. Organists, choir masters, praise bands, and soloists increasingly select contemporary Christian music,

112. "Indian Mission in Chicagoland," *Church Observer,* Sept. 1962; John Zeilstra's notes, based on classical Home Mission Committee minutes and reports, in letter of William Zeilstra to the author, 21 March 2001. The source materials are now in the Archives, Calvin College.

which is broadly evangelical and charismatic in origin. For congregational singing, the denominationally sanctioned hymnal, which used to reign supreme, is now supplemented by generic Protestant songbooks. The Dutch Reformed in Chicago thus are becoming part of the American evangelical mainstream.

In a curious twist on the themes of flight and Americanization, however, the Christian Reformed churches of the Chicago area in 1987 decided to reestablish a presence in the central city by forming Loop Christian Ministries (LCM). Financing came from the sale of the Helping Hand Mission property on Madison Street, which had fallen to urban renewal and changing protocols for the treatment of alcoholic addiction. LCM's pastor, Timothy Douma, is a son of the former Oak Park congregation. The small but dynamic Loop congregation plans to purchase property near Canal and Harrison streets, which by sheer serendipity lies near the original Groninger Hoek and the site of the First Christian Reformed Church in the 1860s. If the congregation had held on to its property that cost $540 in 1867, LCM would not have to raise more than $5 million to buy land in the current market![113]

Coming full circle, Loop Christian Ministries founded a Christian day school (Daystar) that draws students from a variety of Christian backgrounds and ethnic groups, and the congregation has witnessed more conversions in its short history than did the Nathanael Institute in fifty years. Adult converts are baptized by immersion in Lake Michigan in the summer. In an interesting reversal of the process of Americanization, several joined because they had married Dutch Reformed mates. A Kuyper Club draws business, academic, and church leaders together for a monthly discussion of the Reformed "world and life view." The club is reminiscent of the Calvin Fellowship Club, which was organized in 1935 "to provide an hour of fellowship and instruction for young men of Reformed persuasion, working in and about the loop."[114] Thus, the Dutch Reformed have returned to the city center after fleeing it fifty years earlier, but the former congregants might not recognize the current embodiment as one of their own.

Despite their stellar efforts at mission work in the city since 1900, the Dutch Reformed of Chicago gave little thought to maintaining their churches in the changing neighborhoods left behind. With the exception

113. For the information in this and the next paragraph I am indebted to the Rev. Timothy Douma's e-mail letter of 25 June 2001.

114. J. R. Brink, "Roseland and the South," *Banner,* 20 Dec. 1935.

of the Nathanael Institute and Roseland Christian Ministries, they sold their beloved edifices to black or Jewish congregations and moved on. As a practical matter, they needed the money to rebuild in the suburbs. And segregated worship was the norm for them as for Protestant churches generally. Mission stations served the lost (preferably whites); churches served the saved. Not until the 1960s and 1970s did such thinking begin to change. Today the suburban Dutch Reformed churches maintain numerous inner-city ministries and programs, of which the Lawndale Church, Roseland Christian Ministries, and Loop Ministries are fitting examples. Americanization, for all its negative aspects, nudged the Dutch to open their church doors to non-Dutch neighbors and thereby to mirror more closely the true church.

CHAPTER 6

Churches of Roseland: The Frisian Settlement

Persons with Dutch blood comprised about 85 percent of Roseland's population in 1920, which made it the premier Dutch district of greater Chicago. Some ten thousand Dutch lived in Roseland, including Kensington and Calumet, at its high point at the end of the last big wave of Dutch immigration. Thereafter, Dutch dominance in Roseland gradually gave way to an increasingly diverse populace. Nevertheless, the Dutch set the tone of community life until they migrated out in the 1970s.[1]

Roseland lay outside Chicago proper until 1889, and its character and development are quite different from the West Side and Englewood. Roseland began as an isolated farming settlement and evolved into a bedroom community, first of the Calumet industrial district and then of greater Chicago. Until the 1880s Roseland was a tightly knit colony, in contrast to the city Dutch who lived widely dispersed.[2]

1. *Onze Toekomst*, 30 Aug. 1922. The 1920 census counted 1,475 foreign-born Dutch, or 43 percent of all foreign-born, in tract 483, the heart of Roseland (State to Halsted Streets and 103rd to 111th Streets). See Ernest W. Burgess and Charles Newcomb, eds., *Census Data of the City of Chicago, 1920* (Chicago: Univ. of Chicago Press, 1931), 572. I multiplied the number of foreign-born Dutch in tract 483 by five (1,475 × 5 = 7,375) to obtain an estimate of the number of Dutch ancestry. This is based on the ratio of foreign-born to foreign-parentage Dutch in Cook County, Illinois. The total population of tract 483 was 8,759.

2. For histories of Roseland, see Ross Ettema, *Down an Indian Trail in 1849: The Story of Roseland* (reprint of Marie K. Rowlands's serial account in the *Calumet Index* in 1949 [Palos Heights, Ill.: Trinity Christian College, 1987]), 210; Simon Dekker, "History of Roseland and Vicinity," typescript, 1938; Harry Eenigenburg, *The Calumet Region and Its Early Settlers* (published by the author, 1935). A complete genealogical history is Ross Ettema and Peggy

Roseland crossroads, Michigan Ave. & 111th St., 1908
(The Archives, Calvin College)

Roseland's heritage was also unique in that its people hailed not primarily from Groningen but from the neighboring province of Friesland. Frisians came to Chicago in the 1880s to escape an agricultural depression at home, after hearing news about the opening of the Pullman Car works.[3] As a result, Roseland has many Frisian family names, which tend to end in "ma" and "stra" or have "de" prefixes. A register of the Netherlandic provincial backgrounds of families and single adults listed in the 1900 manuscript federal census shows that Frisians were the largest group at more than 40 percent; Noord Hollanders were second with 15 percent, Groningers third with 12 percent, and Zuid Hollanders fourth with 10 percent.[4]

Goodwin Ettema, comp., *The Dutch Connection in South Cook County Since 1847* (Chicago: privately printed, 1984). I am indebted to the Ettemas for providing genealogical information on Roseland families.

3. Dekker, "History of Roseland," 93.

4. Derived from Swierenga, "Dutch in Chicago and Cook County, 1900 Federal Manuscript Census," and Swierenga, *Dutch Emigrants to the United States.* Each family name in the census was cross-checked with the Netherlands emigration records, which give the province of origin. These lists also can be consulted in *Family Tree Maker's Family Archives,* "Immigration Records: Dutch in America, 1800s," CD #269, 2000.

Before the rise of the modern Netherlands, the region along the coast of the North Sea was inhabited by bands of bold, sea-faring Frisians noted for their tall people and fearsome paganism. Groningers and Frisians thus share a common ancestry, but since the Middle Ages they have diverged. Living in separate provinces with differing farming systems and languages gave them a markedly divergent history and culture. Frisians proudly kept their unique language; Groningers speak a low Dutch dialect called "Gronings." Frisians are "inclined to the intellectual life"; Groningers are known as "naive and realistic."[5]

Frisians are known for dairying; Groningers for raising wheat and other grains, although Frisian farmers along the North Sea coast also cultivate grains. Dairying was a stable industry worked by family labor. Grain prices fluctuated, farms tended to be large, and its cultivation required many hired hands. "Groot boeren," or landed magnates, owned much of the rich sea clay soils of Groningen and exploited the labor of the landless proletariat, who languished on the edge of survival. In short, Frisians enjoyed a higher social standing and reputation than did the lowly Groningers.

This Frisian heritage and the isolation of the Roseland colony explain why the Dutch in Roseland were the first in the Chicago area to establish churches, Christian schools, and cultural clubs. Groningers put less emphasis on church, school, and club, and more on making a living. They were a scattered minority in a polyglot city population and had to scratch for survival. Roselanders in large numbers also joined the industrial workforce of Calumet, whereas Groningers preferred going into business for themselves as teamsters or building contractors.

Roseland was also distinctive, compared to Chicago and Englewood, in that membership in the four Reformed congregations far outnumbered that in the four Christian Reformed congregations. Reformed Church membership rose from 53 to 62 percent of the whole between 1900 and 1945, the dominant congregation being Bethany Reformed with more than twenty-four hundred members. The Christian Reformed percentage declined from 47 to 38 percent, and the largest congregation, First Roseland, counted thirteen hundred members in 1945, barely half that of Bethany Reformed (Appendix 5). On the West Side and Englewood, the opposite trend prevailed; the Christian Reformed proportion increased over time.

5. Vandenbosch, *Dutch Communities of Chicago,* 20-21, citing Henry Beets, *De Geref. Kerk in N. A.: Zestig Jaren van Strijd en Zegen* (Grand Rapids: Grand Rapids Printing, 1918), 79-100.

This preponderance of Reformed Church members gave Roseland a special educational mix and cultural ambiance. Reformed youth attended public schools primarily, which placed them in the cultural mainstream and involved them in such social activities as school dances, movies, circuses, and theatrical plays, all activities shunned by Christian school pupils in keeping with Christian Reformed policy until the 1950s (chapter 2).

Until the 1950s more public high school students enrolled in college than did those from Chicago Christian High School, many of whose male students dropped out at age sixteen to go to work. As adults, public school graduates participated in city clubs and social activates, such as the Roseland Women's Club, the Roseland Men's Club, the Roseland Music House, and the Roseland Band. By contrast, Christian Reformed adults, products of the Christian schools, generally filled their leisure time with activities sponsored by the schools and churches (see chapter 8). The heavy Reformed Church presence in Roseland thus tended to make Dutch cultural life more diverse, cosmopolitan, and sophisticated than in the heavily Christian Reformed locales of Englewood and the West Side.

Beginnings

The Roseland colony began in July 1849, following the arrival of eleven families and two young men (forty-five persons) from the province of Noord Holland above Alkmaar, by way of Rotterdam and New York. The group had a schoolmaster to lead them but no cleric. Seventeen family members, more than one-quarter, died at sea from cholera. Klaas Pool, an acquaintance who had emigrated in 1847 and was living in Low Prairie (South Holland), met the group as expected on the Chicago docks. He arranged temporary shelter and directed them to explore land in the Lake Calumet area.[6]

From the Chicago city limits at Twelfth Street, along the Vincennes Road and then the Indian Trail to the high ridge at 111th Street, the scouting party of four men encountered only three residences, the last of which was that of Hamilton Lopp (Lob) at what is now Michigan Avenue and 111th Street. After a week of careful investigation, the scouts selected a choice 160 acres, which they bought for $5 per acre from three private owners. The tract ran east from State Street to Indiana Avenue and from

6. The group included Johannes Ambuul, Jan Bras, Klaas and Pieter Dalenberg, Jacob and Pieter De Jong, Gerrit and Hark Eenigenburg, Jan Jonker, and Pieter Oudendijk.

103rd to 111th streets; it was bisected by the Indian Trail (now Michigan Avenue, the business street of Roseland). Seven families subdivided the quarter section and hauled lumber from Chicago by oxcart to build their shanties, which they set atop the ridge; they farmed the fertile but often waterlogged lowlands below the hill to the east.[7]

The Dutch developed dairying and sold milk, butter, and cheese on the Chicago market. Soon they added vegetables to the trade. In the off season, they took railroad construction jobs in the locale. New settlers arrived steadily. In 1855, when the state put up for sale the school land, Section Sixteen, running west from State to Halsted Streets between 103rd and 111th Streets, the Dutch bought the entire section (640 acres) for $5 per acre. This square mile became the heart of Roseland.

First Reformed Church of Roseland — 1849

The settlers at first went to South Holland to worship under the Reverend Willem Wust. But traveling six miles by oxcart was too difficult, and within two months, in September 1849, the newcomers formed their own church. It was first called simply the Holland Church at "Junction Station" (named after a key railroad junction nearby) or "High Prairie," the preferred name. Wust effected the organization and the election of Jacob (Jakob) De Jong as elder to lead worship and read sermons and his brother Peter (Pieter), a *schoolmeester,* as deacon and clerk.

Charter families included Cornelius Kuyper, Peter and Klaas Dalenberg, Jan Ton, Peter and Jacob De Jong, John Bras, Hark and Gerrit Eenigenburg, and Abraham De Koker. The group, led in worship by Jacob De Jong, met in Klaas Dalenberg's barn until 1850, when Peter De Jong donated land for a church on Michigan Avenue at 107th Street, and the members erected a small edifice with their own hands, aided by the experienced carpenter De Koker.[8]

In 1852 the Reverend Albertus Van Raalte of Holland, Michigan, stopped on his way to Chicago to round up the "scattered Hollanders." He promised that the Classis of Holland would assign pastors to travel to the "Prairies" and minister to them on occasion. The next year the High Prairie congregation asked to join the classis, as did the city congregation.

7. Ettema, *Down an Indian Trail,* 23-24.

8. Robert Vander Ploeg, "Historical Sketch," in First Reformed Church of Roseland, *Ninetieth Anniversary, Historical Booklet and Directory, 1849-1939* (Chicago, 1939), 5.

Both were gladly received in April 1853, and in 1855 they joined the newly created Classis of Wisconsin, which was more convenient.[9]

The High Prairie Church (later named *De Eerste Hollandse Gereformeerde Kerk,* or the "First Dutch Reformed Church") carried on without a regular pastor for five years, until 1855. During that time the four-man consistory held the small body together. The teacher Peter De Jong taught catechism and conducted reading services, and together with fellow deacon Gerrit Eenigenburg, he dispensed alms. The elders, Jacob De Jong and Peter Prins, made the yearly rounds of *huis bezoek* ("family visitation") and administered discipline, both spiritual and secular. Even minor disputes among members came before the consistory to be resolved — the "fair" fee for one man to borrow another's horse, the value of a shipment of hay, the damages of cows trampling a cornfield, and a family angered by a raid on its melon patch by children of another family. One of the complainants in a monetary case was the widow Antje Paarlberg of South Holland, made famous in Edna Ferber's historical novel, *So Big.*[10]

With no minister, however, the High Prairie congregation could not celebrate the Lord's Supper, baptize infants, or enter into holy matrimony. They rejoiced when the Reverend Hendrik Klyn of Milwaukee came once in 1851 to provide the sacraments; Van Raalte did the same in 1852 and 1853. By 1855 the group so desired regular preaching that it agreed to share a pastor with the Low Prairie congregation. The Reverend Marten Ypma was called, and he implemented the unique arrangement of preaching on alternate Sundays in Low and High Prairie.

The High Prairie congregation in the next years grew to nearly one hundred members. It benefited particularly from twenty-three conversions, the fruit of a revival in 1857 that spread across the country from weekly prayer meetings at the Fulton Street Reformed Church in New York City. Van Raalte promoted the great spiritual awakening in the Midwestern churches. High Prairie thus quickly got into the rhythm of American evangelicalism. In 1857 the church had also observed the first Thanksgiving by gathering for worship to acknowledge the "Almighty's favor and blessings," especially for the new church building. Ypma's effective ministry ended in 1861 when he accepted a call to Alto, Wisconsin; Seine Bolks, then serving the First Chicago congregation, replaced him in 1862.

9. *Classis Holland Minutes, 1848-1858* (Grand Rapids: Eerdmans, 1950), 65, 106, 110-11, 171-72; Van Hinte, *Netherlanders in America,* 155.

10. Arie Van Proyen, "Yesterday," in Thorn Creek Reformed Church, *125th Anniversary, 1849-1974* (South Holland, Ill., 1974), 5-6.

Rev. Henry R. Koopman (1824-84)

During the interim, High Prairie broke its compact with Low Prairie in hopes of obtaining its own pastor. Failing in this, however, the congregation resumed sharing Bolks until 1865, when it became independent, built a parsonage, and called a pastor. He was Peter Lepeltak (1865-69), a New Brunswick Theological Seminary candidate. Under Lepeltak, the growing flock built a larger church in 1867, the third on the site, at a cost of $2,600. Nearly one-third of the funds was contributed by the denomination. As the sole Dutch church in High Prairie for three decades, the congregation gathered in all the pioneer immigrants. The membership doubled in the 1860s to more than four hundred.

Hendrik (Henry) Koopman (1870-77) succeeded Lepeltak. He was a product of the northern wing of the 1834 secession and entered the ministry with a strong dose of pietism and no formal theological training. For sermon material he borrowed heavily from the "old writers," a small group of seventeenth-century pietist preachers much revered by the Seceders. Koopman served three Christian Seceded congregations in the province of Zuid Holland before accepting a call to the troubled South Holland (Low Prairie) Church in 1865. There he greatly satisfied the pietistic faction who had left in 1862 but returned when he came. When Koopman resigned three years later, in 1868, the South Holland congregation again split.[11]

For two years Koopman had no charge. So the Roseland church

11. Herbert J. Brinks, "The Calumet Region," *Origins* 2 No. 1 (1984): 12-13.

asked him to fill its vacant pulpit one Sunday in 1870. After the service, by a one-vote majority, the congregation called him to be pastor. Koopman introduced a number of practices common in American Protestantism and coming into vogue in Dutch Reformed churches as well; he started a Sunday school and had the congregation purchase a pump organ to enhance congregational psalm singing at the expense of the *voorzanger.* One might think that such practices would alienate the pietists, but the dominie more than satisfied them by often closing his sermons in the old style, with calls for repentance and renewal. He was their kind of preacher. He also stood firm against secret societies; no Freemason was permitted to join the congregation.

The narrow majority in favor of calling Koopman showed that First Reformed Church was not of one mind regarding his theological orientation, cast of mind, and reputation. This made his pastorate very stressful, even though the congregation grew to six hundred souls under his care. In 1876 several dozen members circulated a complaint against him, which they submitted to the Classis of Wisconsin. The complaint charged that Koopman did not "serve our church with his heart, but contrarily, that he would do well to join the 'Afgescheidenen' [namely, the True Holland (later Christian) Reformed Church] to whom he is closer in feeling and would feel more comfortable there." He invited to his home those of that persuasion, "to the irritation of the congregation." Further, he "associated extensively" with them in South Holland and "instead of visiting his colleague there" (the Reverend Ale Buursma of the First Reformed Church), Koopman cultivated a "cordial relationship" with the True Church minister, Ede L. Meinders, "a man known as one of the strongest and most fanatical forces of the 'Afscheiding.'"[12]

Two of the thirty-seven complainants attended in person the fall 1877 classis meeting in Milwaukee, as did Koopman and two elder delegates from the First Roseland Church, Willem Prins (Prince) and Harmon Tien. After a lengthy discussion as a committee of the whole, the classis upheld the petitioners, even though the petition did not come before them in accord with proper church procedures. The classis took no note of this breech and by vote asked Koopman to resign, "since there is neither a solution for the congregation nor for the pastor." Classis then urged Koopman "lovingly to agree to this, and to give his heartfelt cooperation for the unity of the congregation." The resolution passed with only

12. Classis of Wisconsin, Minutes, 16 Apr. 1879, Art. 25, trans. Nella Kennedy, A. C. Van Raalte Institute, Hope College.

two dissenting votes, that of Prins and Tien; Koopman and one elder delegate from Wisconsin abstained.[13]

Koopman complied, but in an "unusual way." After a month's vacation with his family in Pella, Iowa, he announced upon his return to the pulpit, at the end of the second (afternoon) service, that the congregation "had heard him the last time as their pastor." The Koopmans then returned to the Pella area, where he entertained two calls from Presbyterian congregations in northwest Iowa. His mistake was to leave without asking the classis formally to dissolve his relationship with the First Roseland Church, as required by the denominational constitution. Koopman also departed without "being commended to a specific place."

Perhaps Koopman felt it best to leave Roseland abruptly because his supporters in the congregation pressed him to lead a secession into the True Church; this he declined to do. The group, numbering about one-quarter of the body (thirty-three families) and led by elders Prins and Tien, then seceded on their own and formed the True Holland (later First Christian) Reformed Church of Roseland.[14]

Subsequently, Koopman asked the classis to transfer his attestation (statement of membership) to the Presbyterian Church, but the brethren refused on the grounds that he had "left the congregation of High Prairie in a disorderly way, and has behaved as a schismatic at the end." The classis blamed him for the split in the congregation and demanded that he appear in person to "justify himself." When Koopman did so in 1879, the classis asked Bernardus De Bey, of First Chicago, to present the case against him.

De Bey had experienced secession in his own congregation in 1867 and was in no mood to coddle the troublemakers. Koopman, De Bey declared, had acted *"willfully and high-handedly, unecclesiastically and unconstitutionally, disorderly and ungodly."* Further, "there is proof that he is guilty of *schism*" (italics in original). No Christian, "least of all a minister," ought to behave in such a way. De Bey then asserted that it was "more than likely, yes, even quite clear, that the life, the association, the action and doctrine and way of preaching – actually all of Rev. H. R. Koopman's ideas – were prepared and fed to found the secession there."[15]

13. Ibid., 19 Sept. 1877, Art. 32-33.

14. Ibid., 16 Apr. 1879, Art. 24-25.

15. Ibid., 17 Apr. 1878, Art. 6, 23; 16 Apr. 1879, Art. 24-32, 39; Ettema, *Down an Indian Trail,* 85; Harry Koedyker, "First Reformed Church History, 1849-1949," in First Reformed Church of Roseland, *A Century for Christ: Centennial, 1849-1949* (Chicago, 1949), 16; Van Proyen, "Yesterday," 8; Simon Dekker, "History of Roseland," 36.

In his defense, Koopman allowed that he left First Roseland without following proper procedure and for this he asked forgiveness, but the charge of schism was baseless and rested only on "rumors." Classis then polled the delegates; they convicted him on the lesser procedural error but decided that the more serious charge of schism "cannot be proven completely." Under church law, therefore, "it must be dropped." Thus, De Bey and the classis extracted their pound of flesh, and a contrite Koopman got his attestation. The affair, mercifully, was over.[16]

Following the schism, the 165 confessing members remaining at First Roseland went through a most trying time, sending out seven unsuccessful calls over a two-year period; three were so-called "second calls" to the same man. Cornelius Kriekard (1879-84) finally accepted a second call. The South Holland congregation had used the same technique to secure a pastor. The classis was not pleased with either congregation. It declared: "When a pastor has considered the first call seriously and declines such conscientiously, it is reprehensible to extend a second (if not a third) call to such a pastor." Despite the rebuke, the classis approved both calls.[17]

Kriekard restored a spirit of harmony, but his preaching and personality left something to be desired, and he left at the first opportunity. It was just the opposite with the next pastor, Balster Van Ess (1884-1900), who "knew how to get along with the people." Van Ess worked effectively for sixteen years and led in building a large new church (the fourth and last) in 1888. This magnificent structure still stands in its beauty. The much-loved Van Ess was stricken in the pulpit in 1900 while reading the baptismal form and died within a week. The Reverend Jacob Vander Meulen, who was visiting that day, came up and finished the service after he and the elders restored an uneasy calm.[18]

A macabre problem came to a head during Van Ess's tenure. Since 1849, the only cemetery in town lay in the churchyard of First Church, on the northwest corner of 107th and Michigan. In 1874 Goris Vander Syde (Zyde) and his brother-in-law, Jan Ton, had first platted the town, and side streets needed to be opened up. Unfortunately, 107th Street would run

16. Ibid., 18 Sept. 1878, Art. 28-31, 39. Koopman's son and namesake, Henry R. Koopman, returned to Roseland in 1884 and became its first photographer. His classic photos are featured in Ettema's *Down an Indian Trail.*

17. Ibid., 23 July 1879, Art. 4.

18. Dekker, "History of Roseland," 37; Vander Ploeg, "Historical Sketch," 7-11. This Jacob Vander Meulen was either the son or grandson of the Reverend Cornelius Vander Meulen, founder of the Zeeland, Michigan, congregation and former pastor of the First Reformed Church of Chicago (1859-61).

First Reformed Church of Roseland, erected 1888.
Old edifice on right, erected 1867
(Western Seminary Collection, Joint Archives of Holland)

right through the cemetery, where every family in town had loved ones buried. The solution was to move graves to the new Mount Greenwood Cemetery, which in 1880 was opened out in the country on 111th Street west of California Avenue. But the cemetery could only accept bodies with certification, which was lacking in many cases because the church gave no deeds to individual plots. Although janitor Johannes Ambuul had tried to keep careful records, some early graves were unmarked, and descendants had moved away.

In 1928 the church sold the land for commercial development and a huge steam shovel moved in. When it turned up human bones, the locals protested vehemently, and the Chicago health department forced the excavating company to dig by hand. Remains found were then placed in a mass grave at Mount Greenwood donated by the cemetery. But it is certain that bodies of some pioneer Hollanders lay under 107th Street to this day.[19]

First Roseland under Van Ess surpassed fifteen hundred members in 1897, despite the steady transfer of members after 1890 to the English-

19. Ettema, *Down an Indian Trail,* 119-121.

Sanctuary, First Roseland Reformed Church, 1930

speaking Bethany Reformed Church (1890) and another daughter congregation, Gano Reformed (1891). Later daughters were Mount Greenwood Reformed in 1913 and Emmanuel Reformed in 1914. First Roseland reached its apogee of seventeen hundred members in 1922. Until Bethany surpassed First Church in the 1930s, it was the flagship congregation of Roseland.

Notable pastors were Dr. William Moerdyke (1900-05), who had also served the South Holland Church; Dr. Henry Hospers (1905-09), a namesake son of the Pella pioneer and founder of Hospers, Iowa, who came from the First Englewood Church; Martin Flipse (1909-13); and Henry Harmeling, an Oostburg, Wisconsin, native who held four pastorates in Chicago: First Chicago (1900-06), First South Holland (1905-09), First Roseland (1921-29), and Archer Avenue (1929-38). Moerdyke was the first to preach three times a Sunday, the third service being necessary to accommodate an evening English service first introduced in 1899. He was mission minded and commissioned to the Arabian field John Van Ess, a son of the church and the first of its foreign missionaries.[20]

20. Gasero, *Historical Directory,* passim; Vander Ploeg, "Historical Sketch," 8-19.

Hospers packed the sanctuary to overflowing in 1908 when he opened the pulpit to the famed Netherlands Reformed theologian, Herman Bavinck (1859-1920). An eyewitness recalled, "The people were seated in the aisles, windows, on the edge of the pulpit platform, and standing wherever there was available space." Bavinck also preached to a capacity audience in the Second Christian Reformed Church. Hospers's wife led in founding the Christian Endeavor Society for the young people in 1907. Hospers was the first to be paid by check from a church checking account. Previously, the deacons had brought to the parsonage a bag of paper bills and coins as the monies were collected by visits to the homes of members.

Martin Flipse endeared himself to the large congregation by diligently visiting every family once a year, going about with a horse and buggy furnished by the church. Harmeling was an able denominational leader; twice he was elected president of the Particular Synod of Chicago and once vice-president of the General Synod of 1914. He retired and died in Chicago in 1946.[21]

The *taal questie* ("language question") erupted during the First World War, under the pastorate of John Heemstra (1914-19), as it did in Dutch immigrant churches throughout the Midwest. In a poll in 1917, the congregation opposed by 62 percent a plan to introduce a second English service. But the next year, the consistory switched the afternoon service from Dutch to English anyway, thus providing two English services. War fervor and hyperpatriotism had forced the change. One serviceman from the congregation, Samuel Kooistra, made the supreme sacrifice. His somber memorial service stood in marked contrast to the joyful service of praise that marked the Armistice Day celebration.

In 1922 the main morning service became English, in keeping with a new poll that endorsed the change by 70 percent. The church choir began in 1934 and the children's choir in 1937. During World War II, 147 men went to war and five died in action. The Reverend John Klaaren (1930-44) led the congregation successfully through the difficult depression and war years in one of its longest pastorates. His impressive pulpit demeanor was enhanced by an elegant coat of full tails and striped trousers; he was the last so attired. The Dutch *namiddag dienst* ("afternoon service") for the old folks continued into the 1950s.[22]

21. Vander Ploeg, "Historical Sketch," 14-15.

22. Ibid., 16-17; Koedyker, "First Reformed Church History, 1849-1949," 28; quote in Edith Klaaren Kleinjans, "Going Home: A Pilgrimage Stopover," typescript, ca. 1997, Joint Archives of Holland.

As part of its mission program, First Roseland in 1944 began sending a monthly delegation to the West Side Rescue Mission, which was located on Monroe and Green Streets near the Helping Hand Mission of the Christian Reformed churches. Classis Chicago that year had endorsed this city ministry, which was founded in 1927. The congregation also supported the World (formerly American) Home Bible League that one of its elders, William A. Chapman, had founded in 1937. Members of the congregation served on the boards of both institutions.[23]

The two founders of First Roseland, Jacob and Peter De Jong, made a most remarkable contribution to the Reformed community in America and abroad. According to Peter's son-in-law, Simon Dekker, as recounted in Dekker's history of Roseland written in 1938, three of Jacob's grandsons and two great-grandsons graduated from Hope College and Western Seminary and became ministers in the Reformed Church, one serving as a missionary in Arabia. Similarly, Peter's son Jacob Peter and four grandsons became ministers, three in the Reformed Church and two in the Christian Reformed Church. Peter's granddaughter, Martha Hinkamp, married a Reformed Church pastor and professor at Hope College. Grandaughter Flossie was the wife and helpmeet in the manse of John Te Paske, a Reformed Church pastor. Peter's great-granddaughter, Swantine De Jong, married the Reverend Idris Jones, and they served together as missionaries in Arabia. Simon Dekker concluded: "Here we can see if parents are sincere in their religion the Lord will bless in the following generations according to his promise."[24]

At its centennial in 1949, First Reformed basked in its place as the "mother church" of all the Reformed churches in Roseland. Its twelve hundred members lived within a radius of two miles from the church in a stable Dutch neighborhood. The postwar years were good ones under the Reverends Henry Vermeer (1945-51) and Gary De Witt (1952-58), but the winds of change were evident in the departure of younger families to the Lansing–South Holland area. As Edith Klaaren Kleinjans, a daughter of the manse, recalled: "As blacks moved in from the north, whites moved out to the south and west." The eloquent preaching of Dr. William Brownson (1959-64) delayed the inevitable decline, which culminated under Warren Hietbrink (1965-87) in the decision to relocate to South Holland. Elder Chester Evers, Sr., led the decision-making process. The congregation sold the Roseland church and parsonage to the Lily-

23. Vander Ploeg, "Historical Sketch," 53-54.

24. Dekker, "History of Roseland," 281-90 (quote 288).

dale Progressive Methodist Episcopal Church for $224,000. In 1971 it dedicated the new $750,000 Thorn Creek Reformed Church at 1875 E. 170th Street, which continues to prosper today.[25]

First Christian Reformed Church of Roseland – 1877

Schism came to Roseland twenty years after the one in west Michigan that gave birth to the True Holland Reformed (Christian Reformed) Church, twelve years after the schism in the First Reformed Church of South Holland, and ten years after the schism in the First Reformed Church of Chicago. The upheaval was inevitable; only the delay needs to be explained. Simon Dekker, whose family immigrated in 1865 and joined the secession of 1877, explained in his memoirs that post-Civil War immigrants like his family brought "different opinions."[26]

After several years of agitation, in December 1877, a quarter of the families seceded from the First Reformed Church. Koopman's ouster was the immediate reason, but the causes were of long standing and stemmed from a deep suspicion of the theological orthodoxy of the Reformed Church in the East and its toleration of Freemasons. The division "caused friction and hatred between neighbors and friends. Yea even with relatives," recalled Dekker. The Classis of Wisconsin also took note of the "painful circumstances" at First Roseland "on account of which a considerable number have seceded." This was in marked contrast to the "peace and harmony" that generally prevails in the churches, the classis reported.[27]

The dissenting families, numbering sixty-one communicants, met December 28, 1877, at the home of Leendert Van Driel at Kensington (11550 S.) and Michigan Avenues for the purpose of organizing a "True Holland Reformed Church" in Roseland. The only other True Church ministers in the Chicago area, William Greve of the Chicago congregation and Ede Meinders of the South Holland church, came at the request of Classis Illinois to organize the congregation and supervise the election of officers. Willem Prins and Harmon Tien were chosen elders and Arie Dekker and Gerrit Den Besten deacons. Adriaan Van Kley submitted a report on the event to the denomination's weekly, *De Wachter*.[28]

25. Kleinjans, "Going Home"; Warren Hietbrink, "Today and Forever," in Thorn Creek Reformed Church, *125th Anniversary*, 9-10.

26. Dekker, "History of Roseland," 37.

27. Ibid.; Classis of Wisconsin, Minutes, 19 Sept. 1877, Art. 34.

28. "Christian Reformed Churches in Roseland," *Banner*, 13 June 1912. One of the

First Christian Reformed Church of Roseland, 111th St., erected 1878, remodeled and enlarged 1881

The group met for worship in a little schoolhouse behind Van Driel's home, while they built a small (thirty-two by forty-eight feet) church on a one-acre lot on the northeast corner of "hundred 'leventh" (111th) and State. Member Jan Kleinhuizen directed the construction, which cost less than $2,000 (including the land), and the congregation joyfully dedicated the frame church in May 1878 (figure 6.1, site 2). Because the steeple omitted due to lack of funds, opponents derisively called it a "barn." The consistory led the church at first, together with the deacons. One unpopular decision was to prohibit the men, who conveniently sat along the outside walls, from spitting tobacco juice on the floor during worship services. Women and children occupied the center benches.[29]

Elders Prins and Tien represented the congregation at the general assembly of the True Holland denomination held in Chicago in June 1878, where the first-time Roseland delegates received a warm welcome. They

---

charter families was that of Jacobus and Anna Clausing, who professed their faith under Koopman's instruction one year earlier. The Clausings are the author's maternal great-grandparents.

29. John Clausing, "Seventy-fifth Anniversary" [of the First Christian Reformed Church of Roseland], pp. 3-4, typescript in author's possession.

Figure 6.1 Churches and Schools in Roseland

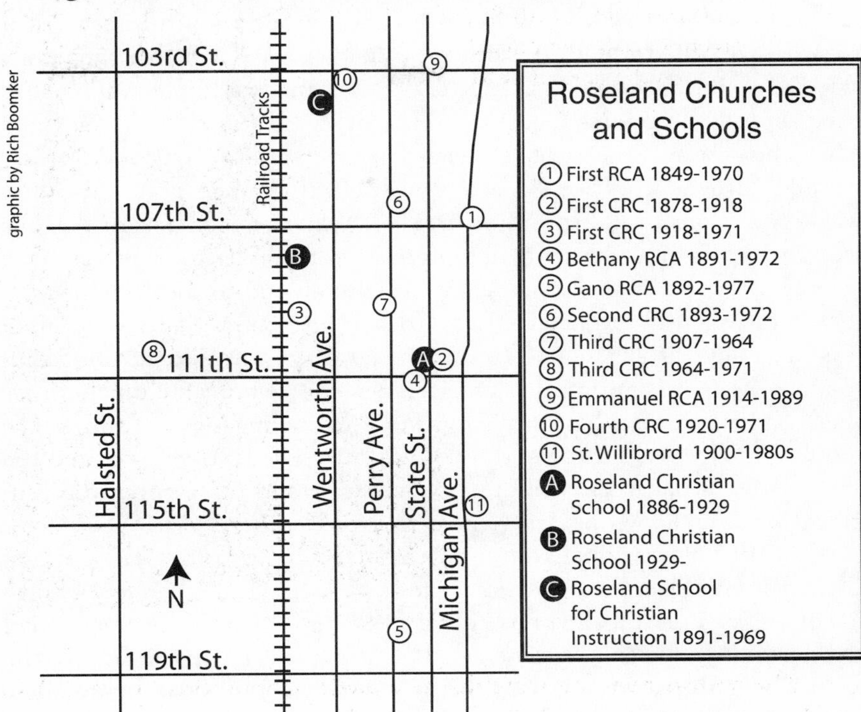

made their presence known immediately by asking the assembly to draft a petition "concerning the abuse of the Sabbath Day in general, and by the railroads in particular, and sent to the proper authorities." The assembly assigned several men the task of formulating a petition, which the body approved right away and forwarded to the churches and to Chicago area railroad and government officials. Presumably, the petition asked that all unnecessary work on the railroads stop on Sunday. This action would relieve the pressure on the many Reformed men who held construction and maintenance jobs on the several railroad trunk lines running through the Lake Calumet district.[30]

In the congregation, the elders read the services for nearly a year before a pastor, Geert Broene of the flagship Noordeloos, Michigan, congre-

30. "Minutes of the Highest Assembly of the Christian Reformed Church, 1857-1880," 6 June 1877, Art. 38, English-language translation by Richard Harms in Calvin College Archives.

gation, accepted the call to be their first pastor. To accommodate the pastor's family, the consistory rented a vacant house on 109th Street, but it was torched, due to "enmity from the outside," the day before the family arrived. A church member, C. Santefort, then made a home available for the pastor while a parsonage was built quickly next to the church.[31]

The nestor of the True brothers, the Reverend Koene Vanden Bosch, installed Broene in office. Broene was an effective pastor; "to know him was to love him," recalled Simon Dekker, a charter member. In 1881 the church had to be enlarged by adding twenty-four feet to the front. The steeple with a bell was also added, which put an end to the derisive comments and allowed the True believers to call the community to worship in (dis)harmony with First Reformed. The addition was needed to accommodate many Frisian immigrants seeking work, who came on the news that George Pullman had broken ground for his massive car shops. For more than five years, Broene (1879-84) faithfully led worship, visited the sick, started a parochial school (see chapter 7), and represented the congregation, usually with elder Tien, at the yearly general assemblies.

At the 1880 national synod, Broene presented a protest on behalf of Classis Illinois, over his signature as clerk, objecting to a statement of professor Gerrit Boer of Calvin Theological Seminary, in which Boer called the Reformed Church a "sister church." This was a "slap in the face" to the founders of the denomination, the Seceders of 1857, said the protesters. Acknowledging the Reformed Church in this way "is both dangerous and detrimental to our Church." Boer responded that he meant no disrespect and that both denominations "have the same confessions, although the Reformed Church does not always put it into practice, and in the association with other Church organizations often goes too far." The synod gently turned the Illinois protest aside.[32]

In 1883 the True Holland Reformed Church of Roseland unanimously decided to change its name to the Holland Christian Reformed Church of Roseland, in keeping with the new denominational name adopted in 1880. When Broene left in 1884, the church counted six hundred souls. More than two years passed before the parsonage was occupied again. During that time the church experienced a continuing fall-out

31. Dekker, "History of Roseland," 42-43; Lynwood Christian Reformed Church, *Centennial, 1877-1977* (Lynwood, Ill., 1977), 5; *Banner,* 13 June 1912. The unidentified arsonists are implied to be anti-seceders, presumably members of the First Reformed Church of Roseland.

32. "Minutes of the Highest Assembly of the Christian Reformed Church, 1857-1880," 9 June 1880, Art. 25, referencing Art. 34 of the assembly of 11 June 1879.

from the controversy over the classical protest, and some members left for the new Gano Reformed Church when the staunchly Christian Reformed cleric, Henry Vander Werp, was called.[33]

First Roseland grew rapidly under the able Vander Werp (1886-92), surpassing fourteen hundred souls in 1892. The congregation was a nest of interlocking, multigenerational families, which carried the risk that church loyalty was little more than family loyalty. Both church and school were enlarged in 1889, and more chairs had to be squeezed in within a year to cope with the "wonderful increase." A $600 pump organ was also installed in 1889, despite the threat of some protesting families to leave. Vander Werp ardently promoted Christian education and preached strongly Reformed sermons that pleased the faithful, but his pastoral work was not as effective as that of Broene.[34]

After Vander Werp's departure in 1892, the congregation received several letters of decline to its calls. Finally a minister wrote bluntly, "You will have to organize another congregation, otherwise you will not get another minister." The consistory acted on this wise advice and set the wheels in motion to form the Second Church in 1893. Meanwhile, the Reverend Jan Robbert, then serving a church in the Netherlands, accepted the call to be the church's third pastor (1892-1901). The mother church by this point had secured its premier place.

Robbert and his two successors, Bernard Einink (1902-09) and John Walkotten (1910-14), presided over a stable, mature congregation. Einink was remembered as "a man of keen mind, a challenging preacher, and a stern disciplinarian." He was the first pastor fluent in English and helped guide the founding of the English-speaking congregation, Third Roseland, which was a joint venture with First Roseland. Einink also led in forming the Society for Christian Instruction that took over ownership and control of the congregation's parochial school. Walkotten was the first minister to own a car.[35]

33. Ibid., 9 June 1880, Art. 47-48; Dekker, "History of Roseland," 44; Clausing, "Seventy-fifth Anniversary," p. 3; Lynwood Christian Reformed Church, *Centennial, 1877-1977,* 6; "Christian Reformed Churches in Roseland."

34. "Christian Reformed Churches of Roseland"; Dekker, "History of Roseland," 45. The comment about inbreeding at First Roseland was by the Reverend John Van Beek of the First Christian Reformed Church of Oak Lawn ("News from First Roseland," *Banner,* 5 Oct. 1939).

35. Lynwood Christian Reformed Church, *Centennial, 1877-1977,* 10.

Rev. Frank Doezema (1871-1967)

The Frank Doezema Era (1914-44)

In 1914 the noteworthy "Doezema era" began at First Church with the arrival of the Reverend Frank Doezema from a Grand Rapids church. This workhorse of a minister led the congregation for thirty years to new heights, as did his contemporary, Benjamin Essenburg, at the First Chicago Church. Doezema's forte was solid biblical preaching and diligent pastoral calling on the sick and aged. He defused critics who opposed the necessary decision in 1917 to relocate and build a new church and parsonage at 109th Place and Princeton Avenue, which was more centrally located (figure 6.1, site 3). The beloved old edifice was inadequate for the growing congregation, and 111th Street had become a busy commercial thoroughfare. Doezema's effective preaching increased the membership above twelve hundred in the 1920s. He also provided leadership in Christian Reformed circles in the Chicago area for decades.

Doezema's second challenge came in the 1920s, when the young people demanded English services, catechism, and Sunday school classes. The solution, as in other congregations, was to schedule two English and two Dutch services each Sunday. Doezema noted a "remarkable attendance" at all four services, three of which he normally led. The men and women's societies also had to be segregated by language. This took a tremendous

First Christian Reformed Church of Roseland, 109th Pl., erected 1918

toll on the pastor, but it met the needs of most members. Doezema encouraged the founding of young men's and young women's societies and a church choir, bringing the total to ten societies. In 1930 the individual Communion cup was introduced, except in the very traditional afternoon Dutch service. To direct the inevitable process of Americanization without serious church divisions was a major accomplishment.

That the congregation also paid off its entire indebtedness, supported several missionaries, and donated $10,000 to the Roseland Christian School shows a spiritually healthy body. All the children of the congregation, "practically without exception," were enrolled in the school. Cornelis L. Clousing served for many years as the clerk of the church and of Classis Illinois.[36]

Doezema and his wife, Celia Top, had a third challenge, to meet the public expectations that went with living in the fishbowl of the parsonage with six daughters, all of whom married and worshiped with their husbands and thirteen children in the church. The reserved pew for the preacher's family in the midst of the crowded sanctuary was a special perk; as the family grew to twenty-five children and grandchildren by 1936,

36. J. R. Brink, "Roseland and South," *Banner,* 16 Nov. 1934; J. Van Zyl, "First Roseland," ibid., 30 Nov. 1934.

a second pew was required. With the privilege came the social obligation to dress and act properly at all times so as not to set gossiping tongues to wagging. At times this was an impossible standard to meet.[37]

In 1940 the church building was extensively remodeled and enlarged to remedy a severe overcrowding problem that concerned the fire marshal. The improvements included a rebuilt organ, which Nick Prince played for many years. The morning Dutch service was also eliminated that year. In 1944, after thirty good years, Doezema officially retired, but he continued as "pastor emeritus" to call on the sick and elderly and lead the afternoon Dutch service; it was discontinued in 1955, when he was eighty-five years old. He also filled area pulpits for many years as a guest preacher. Doezema died in the Rest Haven Nursing Home in Chicago in 1967 at age ninety-four. He had given First Roseland the best years of his life and also the best of his declining years. "His loving and faithful ministry was much appreciated and will long be remembered by all," declared the *Centennial* history booklet.[38]

Doezema's ministry had spanned two generations; those he baptized as infants and guided to make profession of their faith he also married. Then he baptized their infants. Indeed, his three-decade pastorate at First Roseland was characterized as "serene, beautiful, indeed something idyllic." A key to this harmony might well be Doezema's remarkable congregational prayers. During the Second World War, the fact that every one of the more than one hundred servicemen came home was attributed to his ardent pleading with God for their safety. In cold statistics, at the twenty-five-year mark Doezema counted 3,833 sermons, 518 confessions, and 265 funerals. No tally is reported for the final five years. His farewell Sunday was described as a "red letter day," coming on top of a ringing retirement program the previous Wednesday evening that included a reenactment of key events in his life, capped by the choir's rendition of Handel's "Hallelujah Chorus."[39]

After feeding three daughter churches between 1893 and 1919, First Roseland reached an apex of 1,348 souls in 1945, the year the Reverend Marinus Arnoys (1945-54) replaced Doezema. The trend was down thereafter, to 1,200 in 1947, 1,100 in 1956, 1,000 in 1962, and 500 in 1970, the last

37. J. R. Brink, "Roseland and the South," ibid., 5 Aug. 1936. One of those grandchildren is the author's wife, Joan Boomker Swierenga.

38. Lynwood Christian Reformed Church, *Centennial, 1877-1977*, 12; "More Happy Days at First Roseland, *Banner*, 12 Apr. 1940.

39. "Happy Days in First Roseland," ibid., 21 Dec. 1939; "Rev. F. Doezema Retires," ibid., 1 Dec. 1944.

year before the church moved out of Roseland. The decline was so gradual as to go largely unnoticed amid the semblance of stability, until the 1960s, under the Reverend Thomas Van Eerden (1955-64). Society life flourished, the church budget was fat, and the body assumed the full support of three missionaries to Nigeria, as well as the work of Dick Aardsma at the Pullman Gospel Mission and the Roseland Community Gospel Mission. Most of these missionaries were sons and daughters of the congregation.[40]

The Reverend Rein Leestma (1964-90), who had the second longest pastorate after Doezema, was the last minister of First Roseland (Lynwood). He had the unenviable task of leading the dying congregation through some very difficult years, as it first left Roseland for points south and later left the Christian Reformed denomination. A break-in and robbery of $1,700 from the church safe in 1965 presaged difficulties to come, as the South Side ghetto breached the 103rd Street boundary into Roseland proper. First Roseland, like all the Reformed churches in the community, began ministries to the newcomers in Bible classes, food pantries, and other programs, but the efforts were blunted by the unspoken message of white flight. Church members began moving in increasing numbers to South Holland, Lansing, and other southern suburbs. The First Roseland congregation in 1969 decided to relocate and began holding worship services in the Illiana Christian High School in Lansing for some thirty-five members living in the vicinity. During the transition, Leestma led two worship services each Sunday, one in Roseland and one in Lansing. The next year he moved into a new parsonage in Lansing that could also accommodate church society meetings. The last worship service at First Roseland was held on the last Sunday of 1971; it was a time for deep emotions to spill out.

By then the body had purchased seven acres on Glenwood-Dyer Road in Lynwood for a new church, and in mid-1972 the congregation adopted a new name — the Lynwood Christian Reformed Church. The Church of God in Christ bought the old church and parsonage in November 1972, and the same month Lynwood Church broke ground for its new

40. The Roseland Community Gospel Mission at 10425 S. Michigan Avenue was founded in July 1927 by the four Christian Reformed churches of Roseland, under superintendents Harry De Boer and his assistant Gertrude Bos, followed by Dick Aardsma and in 1945 by Alias Dykstra. Bible teachers were Mrs. Harry Dekker and a Miss Swierenga, among others. "Quadruple consistory meetings" of the four churches set mission policy and gave direction ("Roseland Community Gospel Mission," *Banner*, 8 Jan. 1937; L. Trap, "Roseland and South," ibid., 17 Jan., 16 May, 12 Dec. 1930; J. R. Brink, "Roseland and South," ibid., 23 Sept. 1937; William Van Rees, "News from Chicago South," ibid., 13 July 1945).

edifice, which was dedicated in late 1973. In the next four years, the congregation doubled in size, from 65 to 120 families. The reconstituted body included members who continued from First Roseland and also many new members. Sixteen members over seventy years of age held baptismal certificates from First Roseland, and two church officers had familial links going back one hundred years. University educator Dr. Richard Prince, the vice-president of the consistory in the centennial year 1977, was the great-grandson of William Prins, an elder in the first consistory, and William Ooms, the church clerk, was a great-grandson of Arie Dekker, a deacon in the first consistory.[41]

This heritage was put to the test in the next decade, when Leetsma led the Lynwood church out of the Christian Reformed denomination in 1990 because of its perceived neo-orthodoxy. Subsequently, Lynwood affiliated with the newly formed United Reformed denomination.

Bethany Reformed Church — 1890

Bethany Reformed Church began in 1890 as a daughter of the First Reformed Church, in response to demands of younger families for an all-English congregation. Until Third Christian Reformed Church was founded in 1907, Bethany was the sole English-speaking church for the Dutch Reformed. From the outset Bethany was a cosmopolitan church; her mostly Dutch membership always included a non-Dutch minority, including Presbyterians from Pullman. This made Bethany unique among all the Reformed congregations in Chicago; it was truly a community church. Emmanuel Reformed Church, Bethany's daughter church on Roseland's North End in 1914, had a similar character.[42]

Bethany's founders faced determined opposition from the immigrant element at First Church but persisted for the sake of the children and young people who no longer spoke Dutch. The Reverend Van Ess and the First Church consistory gave their approval, however, as did the Classis of Wisconsin, and a group of about twenty persons began meeting

41. Lynwood Christian Reformed Church, *Centennial, 1877-1977,* 16-17.

42. This section relies on Dekker, "History of Roseland," 39-40; Elton Eenigenburg, "Fifty Years of Pilgrimage," in Bethany Reformed Church of Roseland, *Fiftieth Anniversary Historical Booklet, 1890-1940* (Chicago, 1940); *Seventy-Fifth Anniversary Historical Booklet, 1890-1965* (Chicago, 1965); Bethany Reformed Church of Lynwood, *One Hundredth Anniversary Historical Booklet* (Lynwood, Ill., 1990). I am indebted to Mary Hager for reading this section and adding some details from her personal experiences.

Bethany Reformed Church, Roseland first edifice, erected 1891, enlarged 1899

for worship upstairs of Vander Syde's Hall on the northwest corner of 111th Street and Michigan Avenue. They gathered in the morning and evening, not the morning and afternoon, as was the Dutch custom. This allowed the curious and the interested to experience an English service. To contain the crowds, Bethany obtained permission from the nearby First Christian Reformed Church to rent its auditorium on Sunday evenings, which provided a home for the congregation for a year or more. This was a magnanimous gesture of reconciliation by the seceder congregation, and it also raised added income.

At the organizational meeting in November 1890, twenty-seven adults became charter members of the Second Reformed Church (the name Bethany was adopted two months later), and they elected the first consistory: elders Frederick Wiersema, Gerrit Otto, and Abraham Madderom; and deacons David Patterson and John Nichols. Nichols was a partner in Frederick Wiersema's bank. Shortly, the group elected a board of trustees to supervise the business side of church life. This body bought property on the north side of 111th near Perry Avenue and supervised the construction of a $4,500 white frame church, forty by fifty-six feet, and later a parsonage next door. The main seating for 350 persons was expandable. It was dedicated one year to the day after the organizational meeting. In 1924 the Roseland Community Hospital was erected directly across 111th Street (figure 6.1, site 4).

In 1891 the Reverend Gerrit Hekhuis (1891-1906) began a long and fruitful ministry as Bethany's first pastor. His gifts were relational and his heart was in missions. His brother Lambertus had died as a missionary in

India in 1888. A hallmark of the church from the start was its Sunday school; in the first year it grew to 175 students and 14 teachers under superintendent John Nichols. Christian Endeavor societies for the young men and women began in 1893 and also a "singing school." The pulpit platform was extended in 1895 to make room for the choir. Bethany was clearly a progressive congregation, but the traditional catechism classes were a vital part of the educational program.

John Steunenberg (1907-12) brought outstanding organizational skills and tightened Bethany's ministry team into a "strong, consolidated unit." Under John Lamar (1912-23), the congregation went through the First World War and laid plans to replace the original edifice with one that could seat more than one thousand people and house the numerous Sunday school classes. The site was on the corner of 111th Place and Perry Avenue. The much-loved Lamar "died in the harness," so to speak, in 1923. His successor, John R. Mulder (1924-28), professor of Bible at Central College, came and carried through the building project in 1925-26. A teacher at heart, he accepted an appointment as professor of pastoral theology at Western Theological Seminary in 1928. He later became its president.

The massive new Gothic edifice with its twin towers dominated the

Bethany Reformed Church, Roseland second edifice, erected 1926 *(Courtesy of Mary Hager)*

Rev. Harry Hager (1899-1983) in the pulpit, 1941
(Western Seminary Collection, Joint Archives of Holland)

South End and fittingly announced that Bethany would be the flagship church of Roseland and the first megachurch in the denomination. Bethany's membership surpassed twenty-four hundred in the 1940s and early 1950s, before the Dutch began departing Roseland.

The glory years began in 1929, when the Reverend Harry Hager arrived for what turned into a lifetime ministry of forty-four years (1929-75). He was a rising star who had a gifted mind, great preaching skills, and strong leadership abilities. He left a professorship at Hope College after three years to accept Bethany's call and immediately began doctoral studies in the Divinity School of the University of Chicago, graduating in 1933. His themes were biblical orthodoxy, national revival, and local evangelism. "America must go back to God," he cried over and over in his sermons.[43] Hager was to his generation what D. James Kennedy, pastor of Ft. Lauderdale's Coral Ridge Presbyterian Church, is to this generation.

A year after Hager's installation, the Great Depression set in and hit the industrialized Calumet district especially hard. Soon the deacons were overwhelmed with relief needs of $800 to $900 a month. Hager appealed to farmers in Reformed and Christian Reformed churches in the Midwest to send produce. The church history recounts the operation: "Thousands of bushels of produce were brought from four different states to the

43. *Chicago Daily News,* 18 Apr. 1942. The "Sunday Section" of this issue featured Hager and Bethany Church in pictures and text.

Bethany Reformed Church worship service, 1941
Rev. Harry Hager preaching
(Western Seminary Collection, Joint Archives of Holland)

church kitchen which the ladies converted into a cannery that turned out 22,000 quarts of edibles. These rations, augmented by weekly stores of bread, baker's extras, and gifts from local merchants, supplied a continuous "bread line" throughout the winter of 1931-1932."[44] This work of mercy galvanized the congregation – the deacons, deaconesses, and C.E. societies and authenticated the ministry of the Word in the community. In the years 1930 to 1933, Bethany received into membership 403 persons on confession of faith.

Two preaching ministries augmented the food program, the summer tent revivals and a radio outreach. Hager raised the summer South End tent meetings to a new level by scheduling the top Bible expositors in America to speak – G. Campbell Morgan, James A. Gray, Wm. B. Riley, J. Gresham Machen, Billy McCarrell, Samuel Zwemer, Will Houghton, Wilbur Smith, Harry Ironside, Oswald Smith, and the list goes on.[45]

The church's weekly radio program, begun in 1933, further raised its visibility. The Bethany Bible Broadcast with Dr. Hager was a regular feature on the FM station WHIP. In six hours of programming weekly, it car-

44. Bethany Reformed Church, *Seventy-Fifth Anniversary Historical Booklet*, 12.

45. Bethany Reformed Church, *Fiftieth Anniversary Historical Booklet*, 12-13, provides a listing.

ried Bethany Church worship services, expository sermons, and Hager's homilies. The radio made Bethany the Gospel Lighthouse for Chicago's South Side. In 1944 Chicago's high powered AM station WCFL began broadcasting Hager's Sunday evening services across America at 8 p.m.

With its multifaceted ministries, the church grew so fast that the leaders could hardly keep up. In 1938 the membership hit twenty-two hundred, the Sunday school enrolled eleven hundred, and the many societies and church choirs taxed the facilities. That year the congregation also purchased an impressive manse adjacent to the church that incorporated the pastor's study, his business staff offices, and a reception room in the south wing. In six years, by 1944, the membership topped twenty-four hundred.[46]

The secret of Bethany's success was its many capable lay leaders who "shouldered the burdens" of the consistory, the board of trustees, the Sunday school, the choirs, and the societies. Over the years, these included George Dalenberg, John J. Boomker, Harry Eenigenburg, Albert Van Kuiken, Herman Teninga, J. Casper Bovenkerk, Henry Dekker, Albert Van Kempema, Henry Riemersma, Albert Bass, J. Howard Otto, and Nicholas Persenaire, among others. Bovenkerk ("Bovee") also directed the church choirs for many decades and won the love and admiration of all.[47]

The white exodus from Roseland in the 1960s suddenly thrust Bethany Church from the mountaintop to the valley. Church attendance dropped drastically, and all the programs suffered. Hager and the trustees decided to buy property fifteen miles away in Lynwood for a future church and to hold morning and evening worship services in the auditorium of the Illiana Christian High School, as well as in Roseland. The dual services continued until the Roseland property was sold in 1972 for $250,000 to the Christ Temple Cathedral, a Church of Christ (Holiness) congregation. This provided the needed money to build a new $420,000 church in Lynwood, which was dedicated in 1974. But by then the congregation in Roseland was moribund, and its role as a neighborhood church was over; everyone commuted by car. Some also believed that it was high time for the aged Hager to step aside; at seventy-five years of age, he was well past the normal age of retirement. Attendance at the morning ser-

46. The manse stood on the east side of the church at 50 W. 111th Street. It was purchased from the Larson family and had served as dentist offices, according to Mary Hager. See also *Calumet Index,* 17 Mar. 1938.

47. Bethany Reformed Church, *Seventy-Fifth Anniversary Historical Booklet,* 13. John J. Boomker is the paternal grandfather of Joan Boomker Swierenga.

J. C. Bovenkerk (1878-1935)
(Western Seminary Collection, Joint Archives of Holland)

vices in 1974 and 1975 averaged one hundred and the evening services only twenty-five. This was in stark contrast to the thousands that turned out in the 1950s. Hager announced his retirement in 1975 amid the gloom of the devastating impact of Chicago's changing demographics on his splendid ministry in Roseland.

Since the Hager era, three ministers have carried on: Robert Otto (1976-86), Brook Stephens (1987-95), and Eric Cook (1999-2001). Early in Stephens's tenure, a fortuitous contact with the Christ Temple Cathedral by Bethany members Don and Carol Westerhoff resulted in a joint worship service in the beloved edifice in Roseland. In August 1987, fifteen years after the sale of the church, more than one hundred Bethany members traveled to Roseland for a "healing service." They were warmly received and thrilled to see that the edifice was obviously loved and beautifully maintained.[48]

After Stephens left in 1995, Bethany had no pastoral leader for three years; when Cook came in 1999, he found only 129 active members on the rolls. Since Cook's departure, the Lynwood congregation has merged with the Living Springs Reformed Church of Homewood.

48. "A Healing Service," *Church Herald*, 16 Oct. 1987.

Who can fathom the impact of Bethany Reformed Church in its heyday? Statistics tell only part of the story. In seventy-five years in Roseland (1890-1965), Bethany church had 2,275 infant and 287 adult baptisms, 3,068 confessions of faith, 499 funerals, 1,160 transferred in and 1,146 transferred out, the Sunday school and annual vacation Bible schools tutored thousands of children in the faith, and 70 members committed themselves to full-time Christian service. This is a record unmatched in the Reformed community of greater Chicago.

The First Reformed Church of Gano — 1891

Gano was a subdivision directly south of Roseland, running from 115th to 119th Streets between State Street and Wentworth Avenue; it was annexed to Chicago in 1890. In the 1880s some members of the First Reformed Church settled there, working on the railroad at Kensington station or raising garden vegetables. They found it difficult to travel up to two miles for worship, and at their request in 1891, the Classis of Wisconsin gave permission to organize the First Reformed Church of Gano. The Reverend Balster Van Ess provided leadership for the group and chaired the organizational meeting. The thirty-one charter members, mostly Frisian immigrants, plus those from other provinces, elected to the first consistory elders Harm Bouwman and Tjebbe Turkstra, and deacons Eppe Toren and Art Korte. The body met for worship in elder Bouwman's Hall at 11528 S. Wentworth Avenue and then briefly in the Methodist Church.[49]

Within months of organizing, the Gano church obtained a pastor, John W. Warnshuis (1891-95), whose salary the classis subsidized, since the congregation was very poor. A Netherlander by birth, Warnshuis could preach in Dutch but was thoroughly American, having been educated at Rutgers College and New Brunswick Seminary. A month after his coming with a wife and ten children, the congregation, now having grown to ninety families, broke ground for a church, parsonage, and horse barn on four lots at 117th and Perry Avenue (figure 6.1, site 5). Including the lots and furnishings, the total cost was only $13,200. Then tragedy befell the nascent congregation. Barely six months after the dedication, the church was struck by lightning and burned to the ground.

49. This section relies on Phoebe Van Kovering, "History of the First Reformed Church of Gano," in First Reformed Church of Gano, *75th Anniversary, 1891-1966* (Chicago, 1966); Dekker, "History of Roseland," 38-39.

The firemen saved the parsonage and some church furnishings. The body immediately set to work to rebuild, and in six weeks worshipers were meeting in the basement, as they had done at first. Four months later they dedicated the new edifice; this was the second church dedication within twelve months.

Warnshuis left in 1895, and the next pastor, J. W. Poot (1896-98), was another American-trained but Netherlands-born preacher. This "powerful preacher," ordained in the Congregational church, stayed barely two years. His successors were all Western Seminary graduates. Under Peter Bouma (1989-1903) the church bought its first pipe organ from the mother church of First Roseland, which had upgraded its instrument. Seminarian Richard Douwstra (1904-10) was Gano's first American-born pastor. In terms of numbers, the congregation was at its high point above six hundred souls from 1906 to 1913. Thereafter, it experienced a long and steady decline, reaching a low of two hundred in the early 1970s.

During the pastorate of John Sietsema (1911-1919), Gano was still stuck in the mud. The village had no paved roads until the 1920s, yet the church drew families from the towns to the south – Dolton, Riverdale, and Blue Island – who came by horse-drawn buggies and in winter by sleigh. Sietsema traveled to these outlying districts each week to teach catechism in homes. During the First World War, twenty-nine sons of the congregation served in the military and two died in France – William Kooy and Adrian (Ed) Bogerd. Sietsema changed the main morning ser-

First Reformed Church of Gano *(Western Seminary Collection, Joint Archives of Holland)*

vice to English at this time, with Dutch moved to the afternoon service and English again in the evening for the young people.

The longest pastorate was that of John Kuite (1921-41), who came fresh out of Western Seminary and stayed two decades. In Roseland he found a wife in the De Young family and saw the modernization of both the church and parsonage. The city paved the street in front in 1929, and Gano entered the modern age. In keeping with the new image, the consistory in 1931 granted women the vote in church governance. In 1934 the common Communion cup went out in favor of small individual cups, and the Sunday evening song service became a popular feature of worship. In 1939 both the Christian and American flags were placed on display in front of the sanctuary.

Jacob Brouwer (1942-48) carried the congregation through its fiftieth anniversary celebration and the ensuing Second World War, when forty-five young men entered the armed forces and two never returned, Willis Hillegonds and James Korte. Brouwer knew the city well, having previously served the First Reformed Church of Chicago. One of his first acts was to start the Wednesday evening prayer service that is a hallmark of Reformed churches. He also led the mortgage-burning ceremony in 1943. In 1948 Brouwer retired from the ministry.

The next three ministers brought a true American evangelical spirit to Gano. Jacob Hellinga (1949-52) completed his undergraduate studies at Moody Bible Institute, and William Nelson (1958-66) graduated from Bob Jones University. Hellinga instituted a Friday evening program that incorporated the Wednesday prayer meeting for adults, Bible classes for children, and Junior and Senior Christian Endeavor. Robert Hector (1953-57), a Central College graduate, began a summer vacation Bible school that drew in one hundred children for two weeks each year. Nelson stressed tithing for missionaries and implemented a "visit-in-person" program to talk about spiritual matters with member families in their homes. The evangelical emphasis bore fruit; two of the three sons of the congregation who entered the ministry did so in the Baptist church. One, William Hillegonds, was for a time a Hope College chaplain.

The last pastor of the Gano Reformed Church was Lester Ter Louw (1967-72), another Central College graduate. The congregation was barely viable, so Ter Louw served two congregations – Gano and the nearby Trinity (First Italian) Reformed Church of Kensington. The latter was a mission project begun in 1914 by First Reformed among northern Italian Protestant immigrants; the small chapel was at 116th and State Street. In 1972 the Classis of Chicago merged the two congregations into the United

Reformed Church of Gano, which Ter Louw continued to serve, using the Gano facility for worship. In 1974 the Richton Park Reformed Church was also amalgamated into the United Reformed Church, but even this combination of three congregations only staved off the inevitable for three more years. In 1977, the United Reformed Church disbanded.

Second Christian Reformed Church – 1893

Space problems at First Roseland led to the formation of Second Roseland. In 1893 nearly fifteen hundred worshipers tried to squeeze into a sanctuary designed for barely half that number. The consistory posed the tough question: one congregation with two buildings for worship services, or two congregations. The vast majority chose the second option, and the consistory asked Classis Illinois to organize another congregation. At a congregational meeting on July 20, 1893, seventy families, five hundred souls, signed the charter of Second Roseland. Most lived north of 109th Street, which was designated as a dividing line between the first and second congregations. Officers elected at the same meeting included elders Peter G. De Boer, Abraham Moll, Simon Dekker, and John Zylstra and deacons R. Barlo, Henry Jacobsma, Age Vellinga, and Menno Zwart. Second Roseland soon gained the reputation of being more avant garde than the staid First Church.[50]

Despite the onset of a major depression that year, the body bought five lots on the southeast corner of 106th Place and Perry Avenue for $1,850 and hired carpenter-contractors Dick Greeuw and Nicholas Veldkamp to build a frame church for $5,000 (figure 6.1, site 6). It was furnished sparsely with a used $800 organ. A subscription campaign in the old and new congregations raised $3,000 in pledges, but many went unfulfilled because of the hard times. After two unsuccessful calls, the new flock obtained a pastor, Hendrik Van Hoogen (1894-96), from the Gereformeerde Kerk in the Netherlands. He conducted Dutch services in the morning and afternoon; the English evening service was jointly held at First Roseland.

The great Pullman strike of 1894 (see chapter 12) affected all the Re-

50. This section relies on Mark Bardolph, "Historical Sketch," in Second Christian Reformed Church of Roseland, *Fifty-fifth Anniversary Historical Booklet and Rededication Program, 1893-1949* (Chicago, 1949); Jean De Boer, "We Remember . . . ," in Second Christian Reformed Church of Roseland, *Seventy-fifth Anniversary, 1893-1968* (Chicago, 1968); and Dekker, "History of Roseland," 46-48.

Second Christian Reformed Church of Roseland, erected 1894
(The Archives, Calvin College)

formed churches in Roseland, but none more than the infant Second Church. The strike began the very day (May 11, 1894) of Van Hoogen's installation and lasted three months.[51] Many members worked at Pullman, and with the plants closed by pickets they could not support their families and the church. Every Christian at Pullman faced two moral issues — support the strike or not and, more fundamentally, be a member of the American Railway Union or not. The violence at the plant made it impossible to cross the picket lines, as the Dutch Reformed had done in the 1888 strike. This solved the first moral question.

The second issue was more difficult. Many Reformed workers in those days believed that membership in any American labor union, let alone the socialistic ARU of Eugene Debs, was incompatible with church membership. But they also felt compelled to join in order to work and support their families. Van Hoogen and the elders "labored tactfully, patiently, and prayerfully" with their Pullman members, noted Jean De Boer, and "by the grace of God our congregation was spared a severe spiritual decline." But Van Hoogen left for the less stressful Dutch colony of Holland, Michigan, late in 1895, after serving only eighteen months in Roseland.

51. Almont Lindsay, *The Pullman Strike* (Chicago: Univ. of Chicago Press, 1942), 122-23, 233-34.

A second Netherlandic minister, Klaas Kuiper, answered the call and proved to be a rock in the church and community for fifteen years (1896-1911). Kuiper came from Grand Haven's First Christian Reformed Church with his wife and eight children (six boys and two girls). He was at the height of his considerable powers and led a growing church and championed the cause of Christian education at the nearby 104th Street school. With no Christian high school in Chicago as yet, the Kuiper teens attended Morgan Park High School, and several continued college-level studies at the University of Chicago.

Kuiper's oldest son, Barend Klaas (B.K.), left the senior class at the university in 1900 to teach at the preparatory school of the Grand Rapids Theological Seminary (now Calvin College) and later at the Calvin Theological Seminary, where he was an outspoken Americanizer. The "Worldly Amusements Synod" of 1928 unceremoniously dismissed Professor Kuiper for attending the cinema and theater seemingly without moral compunction; he was made an object lesson. Two other sons, Reinke Barend (R.B.) and Herman, also became Christian Reformed ministers, R.B. as professor at Westminster Seminary and Calvin College and Seminary, and Herman in the parsonage. Son Hendrik (Henry) was a Christian educator and principal of Ebenezer Christian School in Chicago (1907-23). Henry too

Rev. Klaas Kuiper (1841-1921) family
seated l-r: wife Dena (Lubberdina), daughter Dena (Gerritdena), Klaas
standing l-r: sons Herman, John (Jan), Henry (Hendrik), Anton, R.B., B.K.
(The Archives, Calvin College)

was an Americanizer; he resigned at Ebenezer because of strong opposition to his policy of English-only instruction.[52]

The *taal questie* also embroiled father Klaas Kuiper at the Second Roseland church, where he had to deal with strident demands for English services in order to prevent young people who could not understand Dutch from drifting away. Kuiper was sympathetic, but he could not preach in English, and he had to defuse strong opposition from elderly members to guest pastors who could. The solution, which he worked out with his colleague Bernard Einink of the First Roseland church, was to organize an all-English church, Third Roseland, in 1907; its members were drawn equally from the two mother congregations. Despite the loss, First Roseland held steady above thirteen hundred members, and Second Roseland remained above one thousand. A highlight for Kuiper was to welcome his friend, Professor Herman Bavinck of the Free University of Amsterdam, to his pulpit in 1908. It was the largest attendance during his fifteen years. Kuiper in 1911, at seventy years of age (!), took a call to a Michigan congregation that he served for another eight years. He did not believe in retirement and died still preaching two years later at age 80.[53]

William Borgman (1911-19) followed Kuiper in the pulpit during a more troubled decade. Twenty-four sons of the church fought in the First World War and all returned, but the 1918 influenza pandemic, the so-called Spanish flu, claimed many lives; Borgman preached nineteen funerals that year. In just eight weeks in September and October, more than eighty-five hundred deaths were recorded in Chicago from influenza and pneumonia, double the normal death rate from all causes. Remarkably, most were in the prime of life, between twenty and forty years old. The influenza spread such panic that all public gatherings were closed, except for churches, schools, and patriotic parades.[54]

In the 1920s, the Second Christian Reformed Church under Henry Baker's ministry (1919-26) was "singularly blessed." He managed the tricky language transition with minimal conflict in the usual manner, by scheduling two Dutch and two English services each Sunday. This arrangement continued from 1922 to 1926, when the morning Dutch service was dropped. The church edifice was upgraded for $27,000, and a new Barton

52. Herbert J. Brinks, "A View from the Parsonage: Klaas Kuiper and His Family," *Origins* 4, No. 1 (1986): 3-10; Bratt, *Dutch Calvinism in Modern America,* 118.

53. L. Trap, "Roseland and South," *Banner,* 16 May 1930.

54. Peter Gomer, "Scientists believe deadly flu outbreak could strike again," *Holland Sentinel,* 9 Sept. 2001, reprinted from *Chicago Tribune.*

pipe organ with electric bellows was installed at a cost of $5,000. Richard L. Hoekstra was a master of the organ for many decades.

Such church expenditures were a faint memory in Leonard Trap's ministry (1926-36) during the stock market crash of 1929 and the Great Depression. The church historian reported that "many of our members were unemployed for as long as four years, and this caused untold hardship and distress." Some lost their homes to the banks and mortgage companies and the "poor funds were strained to the limit." The adversity knit pastor and parishioners together, and Trap was much loved and highly esteemed. A high point in Trap's tenure was the visit in 1930 by the famed Gereformeerde Kerk theologian, Valentijn Hepp, professor in the Free University of Amsterdam and a close associate of Abraham Kuyper. Hepp delivered a "masterful sermon" in the afternoon Dutch service, and the normally sparse audience overflowed the sanctuary and filled the pulpit platform.[55]

The Reverend William Haverkamp (1936-43), who at twenty-eight years of age in 1936 was the youngest pastor ever to serve Second Roseland, brought renewed energy and vision. Despite the lingering hard times, the congregation upgraded the sanctuary at a cost of $12,000. With the bombing of Pearl Harbor in 1941, the congregation bid farewell to seventy-six servicemen. It required a major effort by pastor Haverkamp and secretary Nell Bolhuis to keep in touch regularly with all these men. Haverkamp's leaving in 1943 for a church in New Jersey left a huge hole in the hearts of the members and the far-flung servicemen, all of whom returned home safely. It required nine calls over a year's time to obtain the Reverend William Van Rees (1944-51). In retrospect, this rapid-fire sending of calls must have set a record and involved the consistory and congregation in endless meetings.

With the end of the war also came the end of the afternoon Dutch service at Second Roseland. In 1949 the sanctuary was given a major upgrade both inside and out, costing $60,000. The increased seating could now accommodate the eight hundred members, without many being forced to sit in the basement under loudspeakers. The rededication was combined with a big celebration of the fifty-fifth anniversary, the fiftieth having been postponed in 1943 because of the war and Haverkamp's leaving. Bernard Van Someren (1952-58) served a stable congregation during the peaceful Dwight Eisenhower years. The next pastor, John Bylsma

55. L. Trap, "Roseland and South," *Banner,* 16 May 1930; J. R. Brink, "Roseland and the South District," ibid., 20 May 1932; Brink, "Roseland and South," ibid., 18 Sept. 1936.

Second Christian Reformed Church of Roseland, remodeled 1949
(The Archives, Calvin College)

(1960-65), seemed to favor Chicago, but his pastorates were short. He served, in order, Second Roseland (1960-65), Third Roseland (1965-71), and Kedvale Avenue Church in Oak Lawn (1971-75). Charles Terpstra was the last pastor of Second Roseland (1965-70); he saw the rapid decline as members moved south and southwest.

In 1972, the remaining 250 members held a program of celebration to mark the closing after nearly eighty years. They recalled that eleven sons of the congregation, including the author's maternal grandfather, Peter A. Hoekstra, had entered the Christian ministry, and four others were full-time missionaries.[56]

A substantial number of Second Roseland members affiliated with

56. The list included Henry Dekker, Herman Guikema, Peter A. Hoekstra, R. B. Kuiper, Herman Kuiper, three Yffs — Peter, Thomas, and George — Adam Persenaire, John Olthof, and David Zylstra. The missionaries were W. Mierop and Dr. Louis Bos on the Indian field in New Mexico, and E. Dykstra and Gertrude Bos in neighborhood evangelism in Roseland, Pullman, and Cottage Grove Heights.

the Orland Park Christian Reformed Church, which had begun in 1969. They amalgamated with Fourth Roseland members whose church also closed in 1970. Thus, Orland Park was a reconstitution of the Second and Fourth Roseland congregations, which in 1972 counted five hundred members.

The Third Christian Reformed Church of Roseland — 1907

As the American congregation, Third Roseland earned a reputation as progressive and prosperous. The congregation published a paper, the *Spectator,* and was first in the denomination to start a teacher training class for Sunday school teachers. It also boasted that per-family tithes in the early years exceeded $75, "an amount which few churches can approach."[57]

The congregation began in 1907 at a meeting in the First Roseland church, with Klaas Kuiper, of Second Roseland, presiding. The twenty-three persons present elected John Kleinhuizen as chair and R. T. Schuurman as secretary; Kleinhuizen then named to the organizing committee Harry De Boer, Abram Dekker, Simon Schoon, Thomas Thomasma, and Menno Zwart. The businessmen Arie Dekker and Bernard Vellinga, Sr., lent their support as well. Classis Illinois gave the group its blessing and within one month, in August 1907, the congregation was officially organized with 31 families, totaling 153 souls.

The first consistory included elders R. T. Schuurman and Charles Kleinhuizen and deacons Abram Dekker and Harry De Boer. The elders read sermons when visiting ministers were unavailable until the Reverend William Stuart (1908-15) arrived as the first pastor. The congregation met temporarily in a small German Lutheran church building at 114th and State Streets during the construction of the lower level, the "basement," of the new church at 10942 S. Perry Ave (figure 6.1, site 7). In this "commodious, though lowly building," the congregation worshiped for four years while completing the auditorium just in time to host the national synod of the Christian Reformed Church in 1912. Second Roseland contributed $500, but First Roseland gave not a penny toward the building program. It was a simple frame edifice. Bernard Vellinga directed the first church "singing society," and Richard Wesselius later took up the baton.

57. This and the next paragraphs rely on "Third Church Review: Do You Know," *Spectator* [issue unknown] (1917): 10; "Third Church of Roseland," *Banner,* 13 June 1912.

After ten years, in 1917, Third Roseland numbered nearly five hundred souls and claimed five of the twenty-five largest families in all of Chicago, according to school figures. These were the families J. Maatman with twelve children, Barney De Vries with eleven, and James Modder, Richard Kingma, and Frank Beezhold with ten each. With so many large families, it is not surprising that 87 percent of the members were interrelated as brothers, sisters, parents, uncles, aunts, and cousins. Third Roseland must have been the most inbred Dutch Reformed congregation in the Chicago area.

After Stuart accepted a call in 1915 to the La Grave Avenue congregation of Grand Rapids, William Trap served only two years. He then joined the chaplain's corps when America entered the First World War in 1917. His forte was not in the pulpit, and he was relieved to leave parish ministry. George Hylkema (1918-25) was installed in time to welcome the servicemen home, except for Cornelius Dekker, who died in France. Hylkema focused his efforts on church education and wrote a catechism book, together with Edward Tuuk of Second Englewood, that was widely adopted in the denomination.

The renowned Gerrit Hoeksema (1926-58) was a fixture at Third Roseland for an amazing thirty-two years, until he retired in 1958. Soundness of doctrine and church loyalty were the trademarks of his service. Hoeksema was highly respected and provided leadership in Classis Illinois for two decades, along with his contemporary Frank Doezema at First Roseland. Hoeksema, as a member of the board of Chicago Christian

Third Christian Reformed Church of Roseland, erected 1912
(The Archives, Calvin College)

Rev. Gerrit Hoeksema (1886-1969)
(The Archives, Calvin College)

High School in the 1930s, led the fight against the perceived modernist views of Dr. Frederick H. Wezeman, principal and Bible teacher at the high school (see chapter 7). The Christian Reformed denomination also tapped Hoeksema's talents, electing him twice as president of the national synod and also president of the board of trustees of Calvin College and Seminary.

Hoeksema led Third Roseland through the Great Depression and the Second World War; he only had one military funeral, the pilot Donald Smitter. In 1936 the congregation organized a church orchestra that gained renown for fine musicianship. That same year the congregation commemorated Hoeksema's tenth anniversary by giving him the keys to a new car. As noted earlier, a synodical ruling forbade reporters for the denominational periodical, the *Banner*, from "mentioning of presents of this kind," presumably to avoid one-upmanship among congregations and covetous feelings among ministers.[58]

Hoeksema guided the congregation in 1939 in a major expansion and renovation of its original 1912 edifice. The project, under the direction of Govert De Boer, resulted in an auditorium that met the needs of the stable six-hundred-member congregation for the next twenty-five years. When Hoeksema became pastor emeritus in 1958, he continued to preach and call on the sick and infirm for eleven years until his death in 1969. In this he emulated Doezema.

The Reverend John Pott, a former Bible teacher at Chicago Christian

58. J. R. Brink, "Roseland and South," *Banner*, 18 Sept. 1936.

High School, replaced Hoeksema in 1959. Under his watch the congregation, unwisely it turned out, in 1964 bought land and built a new sanctuary on Lowe Ave. at 110th Street (figure 6.1, site 8). The congregation worshiped there barely seven years under John Bylsma (1965-71) before disbanding in 1971 when Bylsma took a call to the Kedvale Avenue Christian Reformed Church of Oak Lawn. Many of the remaining families transferred with him to Oak Lawn. Money from the sale of the Roseland church and parsonage was donated for the "establishment of a new church in the southwest suburbs." In 1979 the newly organized Tinley Park Christian Reformed Church was the beneficiary of those funds, which were used to buy a ten-acre site for the church's future sanctuary.

Emmanuel Reformed Church — 1914

Emmanuel Reformed Church, a daughter of the Bethany Reformed Church, was formed to serve the needs of its members and the unchurched living in Roseland's North End. It evolved slowly out of a branch of the Bethany Sunday school that was established in 1896 in an old house on Michigan Avenue at 100th Place. The school moved often but always in the vicinity of 100th Street. This meant that the teachers from Bethany had to walk two miles rain or shine. By 1907 they were discouraged and wanted to quit, but Louis Van Vlymen of Bethany Church, one of the long-time Sunday school teachers, urged them to hold on. After renting Lem's Hall at 99th Place and Michigan, the work flourished again.[59]

In 1911, families whose children attended the Sunday school and others in the North End petitioned the Classis of Illinois (American) to appoint a missionary to begin worship services. The classis hired H. S. Vander Velde from Moody Bible Institute to lead morning and evening worship and oversee the Sunday school program. The next year the mission bought a lot and erected a basement building at 100th Place at Michigan Avenue to give the ministry a visible presence. Sunday school enrollment jumped to one hundred, and the worship services were soon full to overflowing. The successful summer tent meetings in 1914 on Michigan Avenue clinched the case for founding a church.

59. This section relies on Emmanuel Reformed Church, *The Story of Emmanuel: 1914-1939* (Chicago, 1939); *Dedication Memories: 1946* (Chicago, 1946); and *Golden Anniversary, 1914-1964* (Chicago, 1964).

Chapel, Emmanuel Reformed Church of Roseland, erected 1921 *(Western Seminary Collection, Joint Archives of Holland)*

In 1914 the classis organized the Emmanuel Reformed Church with forty-eight charter members, eighteen of whom joined upon a confession of faith. These were mostly non-Dutch converts. The first consistory included elders Richard De Young, George Adams, and Jake De Vries; and deacons Martin Housman, John Wheeler, and Gerrit Terpstra. The two non-Dutch officers reflected the multi-ethnic composition of the congregation. The body grew, and in 1915 it called Western Seminary graduate John Bennink (1915-17) as an ordained pastor. Over time, Emmanuel had more members from the province of Groningen than any other Roseland congregation, because Englewood Groningers migrated southward to the northern fringe of Roseland, a distance of two to three miles.

Under Leonard Potgeter (changed to Potter) (1918-27), the young congregation of 200 members outgrew its basement church and moved into a refurbished building at 102nd Place and State Street known as the "Chapel" (figure 6.1, site 9). In five years this was too small, so in 1926 the 370 members built a new $60,000 church on the site to seat 700, with a beautiful organ. They thought big, but in six short years, by 1932, it again reached capacity. The popular Reverend Potter laid the cornerstone personally in a joyous ceremony, but he did not live to see the edifice completed. He died suddenly four months before the dedication in 1927, which was led by John Bokma, chair of the board of trustees.

Harry Hoffs (1927-41) filled the pulpit during the dark Depression years, when it was often difficult to meet the payments on the bonds and mortgages to finance the new church and new parsonage on Lafayette Avenue built for his family. But no payments were missed, and the flock grew to 450 members by 1939. The youthful Spencer De Jong (1941-46), an Iowan like Hoffs, served the 1100-member church during the Second World War years, when more than 120 men went into the military. The Sunday school enrollment topped 700. Emmanuel had become the fourth largest Dutch Reformed congregation in Roseland, behind Bethany, First Reformed, and First Christian Reformed.

Tragedy struck during the night of March 9-10, 1944, when the entire

Top, Emmanuel Reformed Church of Roseland,
erected 1927, after fire of March 10, 1944;
bottom, the church's second edifice, erected 1946

(Both photographs from the Western Seminary Collection, Joint Archives of Holland)

edifice was destroyed in two fires within eight hours of one another. Firemen blamed the first blaze on oily rags left in the pews by painters who were redecorating the sanctuary. The second blaze was a flare-up. The estimated loss was $50,000, 80 percent of which was covered by insurance.[60]

De Jong rallied the disheartened members, and they set about to rebuild an even larger church, but first they had to persuade a reluctant War Production Board in Washington that using scarce materials for a church was a necessity. This took four months and a great deal of pressure. De Jong wielded the trowel to cement the final joint on the cornerstone in April 1945, and the sanctuary was dedicated in 1946. Its total cost, including a Kilgen pipe organ with harp and chimes, was $178,000. De Jong left soon after to serve the Youth for Christ organization.

The forty-five years from 1946 until Emmanuel disbanded in 1990 were characterized by stability and faithful ministry. Eight ministers served during those decades, and the church historians record nothing remarkable. The membership suffered a slow, steady decline – nine hundred in 1950, six hundred in 1960, four hundred in 1970, and less than two hundred after 1972. From 1972 to 1989 Emmanuel was essentially a black congregation, and two of the final three ministers were black. That it hung on so long after the Dutch members left Roseland testifies to its history and tradition as a mission-minded church.[61]

Fourth Christian Reformed Church of Roseland – 1919

In 1919, 23 families and single adults, totaling 114 souls, all members of the Second Roseland church, obtained permission from Classis Illinois to organize the Fourth Christian Reformed Church of Roseland as an "American-speaking" congregation. This would meet the needs of those living in the northwest end of Roseland who found it inconvenient to walk up to ten half blocks to the Third Roseland church at 109th and Perry. The Dutch congregations, First and Second Roseland, had recognized 107th Street as the division line, so why not use the same line for the American Third and Fourth Roseland churches? Convenience was the secondary rationale stated by the petitioners; their primary reason for an American

60. "Fire Strikes Church Twice in One Night," *Chicago Daily News,* 10 Mar. 1944.

61. Emmanuel Reformed Church pastors were Raymond Van Heukelom (1947-53), John Van Harn (1954-60), Chester Meengs (1961-67), Harri Zegerius (1968-70), Stephen Tamminga (1972), Ben Cox (1972-73), Sidney Mauldin (1974-81), and Benjamin Johnson (1981-86).

Fourth Christian Reformed Church of Roseland
"view-out" edifice, erected 1920
(The Archives, Calvin College)

congregation was evangelism — "to invite our neighbors to come with us and do as we, that our light may not be put under a bushel, but on a candlestick." The all-Dutch names in the church directories suggest that this altruistic goal was unrealized.[62]

The charter members, 90 percent Frisians, elected to the first consistory as elders Harry Dekker, John Postema, and John Spoolstra, and as deacons Louis Haan, John T. Hoekstra, and Richard Leistra. The elders catechized the youth and arranged for pulpit supply for more than a year, until Gerard Holwerda (1920-24), a candidate fresh from Calvin Seminary, came as the first minister. In Roseland he found a wife before leaving for a church in southern California. Albert Bratt (1925-28) followed. He graciously agreed to begin an evening service for which the young people were clamoring, in addition to the morning and afternoon services. The latter, which was favored by the many young parents with small children, was eventually discontinued.

Fourth Roseland worshiped in basements (actually "view-out" basements) for a decade, the first year in the 104th Street Christian School and

62. This section relies on Fourth Christian Reformed Church of Roseland, *In Commemoration of the Twenty-Fifth Anniversary, 1919-1944* (Chicago, 1944); *In Commemoration of the Fiftieth Anniversary, 1919-1969* (Chicago, 1969); "God's Hand in Fourth Roseland in the Year 1963," typescript, Calvin College Archives.

Fourth Christian Reformed Church of Roseland
with superstructure, erected 1930
(The Archives, Calvin College)

then in their own basement church that seated 350 on second-hand pews (figure 6.1, site 10). This brick facility, which was dedicated late in 1920, was damp and hard to heat evenly; it also lacked rooms for the eleven societies to meet. After a decade, in the midst of the Great Depression, the congregation took the step of faith to add the impressive brick auditorium at a cost of $45,000, including the organ. This increased the total cost to $62,000, almost all mortgaged, but the overflowing joy in the service of dedication showed a readiness to sacrifice. The hard times made it difficult to pay down the high indebtedness, but through faithful tithing, by 1944 the balance was only $35,000.[63]

Dr. Herman Kuiper (1928-44) came in 1928 upon completing doctoral studies at the Free University of Amsterdam. He was the youngest son of the Reverend Klaas Kuiper of the Second Roseland church and grew up in the parsonage. Gossipers declared indignantly, "The people of the Fourth church have a lot of nerve to call Herman Kuiper, Th.D. Such a small congregation, and not even a proper church building." Kuiper

63. The consistory reported a detailed account of the dedication in "Fourth Roseland Church Occupies New Home," *Banner,* 16 Jan. 1931. A mason named Van Leeuwen was tragically killed by lightning while putting the finishing touches on the chimney of the church.

Rev. Herman Kuiper (1889-1963)
(The Archives, Calvin College)

proved the critics wrong. He led the congregation for nearly sixteen years, through the Depression and Second World War. Along with his soulmate Hoeksema, he challenged the Bible teachings of Dr. Frederick Wezeman, principal of Chicago Christian High School.

One of Kuiper's memorable funerals was that of elder A. Zwitser, who was struck and killed in his car at one of the many train crossings in Roseland. Zwitser was president of the 104th Street School for Christian Instruction and anticipated attending the national Synod of 1930 as a delegate of Classis Illinois.[64] Kuiper also conducted an emotional military funeral when John Boersma's blue star, one of forty-four, had to be changed to a gold star. Harold Dekker, another blue star, served in the Navy chaplaincy corps; following the war, he joined the faculty at Calvin College briefly and in 1956 was named professor of missions and dean at Calvin Seminary.

Kuiper was a thoroughgoing Kuyperian who lent his considerable intellect to deepening the Calvinist worldview in Chicago and in the denomination. In 1953 he was appointed professor at Calvin Seminary to restore respect following a purge of almost the entire faculty. At Kuiper's death in 1963, the Fourth Roseland consistory noted that his impact was "one of the most formative factors in the development of our congregation."

He had dominated the pulpit of Fourth Roseland as Doezema did at First Roseland and Hoeksema at Third Roseland. Fourth Roseland was the smallest in numbers, but eventually it reached parity with Third

64. L. Trap, "Roseland and South," *Banner,* 28 Mar. 1930.

Roseland in the late 1950s at 550 members. The early years saw slow growth because Fourth Roseland began just as the U.S. Government in 1921 enacted the first quota laws that severely restricted immigration; the Dutch quota was only 3,100 per year.

The next four pastors, all with brief tenures, built on the base Kuiper laid. These included Richard Haan (1945-49), John A. De Kruyter (1950-54), Wilbert Van Dyk (1955-59), and G. De Young (1964-68). The debt was paid off in 1948 under Haan. De Kruyter took a call in 1954 to Holland, Michigan, and Van Dyk finished his career on the faculty of Calvin Seminary (1986-95).

In the late 1950s the suburban exodus from Roseland began in earnest, but Fourth Roseland gained a temporary reprieve with the influx of members fleeing from Englewood. Yet, by 1967 the congregation had dwindled to only ninety-nine families (430 souls), and the consistory appointed a committee to find a suburban site where it could direct the departing members. In 1968 the committee chose acreage in Orland Park at 75th Avenue (Catalina Drive) and 151st Street that lay next to the future site of a Chicago Southwest Christian School. The price was right – the Catalina Construction Company later donated the $7,500 site to the church. In 1969, with only forty-five families left, Fourth Roseland was no longer viable, so the congregation moved the worship services to the auditorium of Chicago Christian High School in Palos Heights for nearly two years until the new church was ready in Orland Park in late 1971. In a sense, Orland Park was Roseland revived, as Elmhurst was for the Cicero Dutch.[65]

At its end, Fourth Roseland boasted of the sons and daughters it sent into full-time church work. The list included the Reverends Louis Bouma, Harold Dekker, and Donald Postema, who for thirty-five years (1963-98) headed the Ann Arbor Chapel near the University of Michigan campus. Two Fourth Roseland missionaries were Susan Spoolstra in Nigeria and Ida Fennema (later Vander Meulen) on the Indian field in New Mexico.

Other Roseland Churches

After 1900 Roseland's population became increasingly mixed, especially with Germans and Swedes. By the 1940s, in addition to the eight Dutch

65. *Precious Heritage, Promising Future: Classis Chicago South Celebrates the 125th Anniversary of the Christian Reformed Church, 1857-1982* (Chicago, 1982), 13.

Reformed and Christian Reformed congregations, a wide variety of churches existed – three German and Swedish Lutheran, one Presbyterian, an Episcopal and Swedish Methodist, two Baptist, and four Roman Catholic, including the Dutch parish of St. Willibrord in Kensington. Several of the Dutch preached or worshiped in the Baptist churches, including Samuel Post, a son of the First Christian Reformed Church of Roseland, and the Reverend Douwe Lansma of Grand Rapids, who preached in the Dutch language twice a month at the Swedish Baptist church. This satisfied the small number of Dutch Baptists in Roseland. Lansma also ministered to the few Dutch Baptists in South Holland.

As Dutch families settled on the prairies south and west of Roseland, Reformed congregations were established at Dolton in 1904 and Mount Greenwood in 1913. The Dolton Reformed Church disbanded in 1915.

The First Reformed Church of Mount Greenwood – 1913

Mount Greenwood was a "city of cemeteries" on the prairies that lay four miles west of Roseland along 111th Street just beyond the Chicago city limits, between California (2800 West) and Crawford Avenues (4000 West). It abutted Evergreen Park on the north and Oak Lawn on the west. Mount Greenwood Cemetery, which opened in 1880, became the sole place of interment for the Roseland Dutch, after the 107th Street Cemetery adjacent to the First Reformed Church had to be excavated for the street in the 1870s.[66]

After 1900, truck farmers from Gano took up the open lands west of Mount Greenwood and Mount Olive cemeteries. Most belonged to the Gano Reformed Church, although a few attended the First Roseland and First Englewood churches. In early 1913, the families of Gilbert Boersma, Ben Scheen, Fred Teggelaar, and Jacob Aggen, Sr., among others, decided to form a church to lessen the long commute by horse and buggy. The group made ambitious plans; they bought a site on 111th Street at Drake Avenue (3550 West) and requested permission from the Classis of Wisconsin to organize a "mission station." Classis gave its approval and appointed student John Kregel of Western Theological Seminary to serve the church as his summer assignment.

66. This section relies on First Reformed Church of Mount Greenwood, *50th Anniversary Booklet, 1913-1963* (Chicago, 1963).

The church rented the Mount Greenwood school house for services, and Kregel preached on his first Sunday to fifty-seven in the morning Holland service and seventy in the evening English service. Attendance doubled over the summer and the thirty charter families asked the classis if they could graduate from mission status to become a full-fledged church. Classis concurred and organized the First Reformed Church of Mount Greenwood on July 30, 1913, under elders Ben Scheen, Fred Teggelaar, Peter Langeland, and Reinder Aggen and deacons Gilbert Boersma, Simon Piersma, and Steffen Aggen, Jr.

Within weeks the congregation voted to build a church and parsonage, and they called Kregel as their regular pastor, pending the completion of his senior year of studies. He came and saw attendance in thirty months (1914-16) jump from thirty to eighty families. Mount Greenwood was ready to grow into a congregation of nine hundred members in the 1940s, and it become the mother in 1946 of the Alsip Reformed Church, which stemmed from its mission Sunday school started in 1917.

Fourteen ministers since Kregel served Mount Greenwood Reformed Church, which today has some 350 members, and its history is

First Reformed Church,
Mount Greenwood
second edifice, 1920
(Western Seminary Collection, Joint Archives of Holland)

First Reformed Church, Mount Greenwood third edifice, 1955
(Western Seminary Collection, Joint Archives of Holland)

similar to sister Reformed congregations. It had no dominant pastor like Hager; Frederic Zandstra's sixteen-year pastorate (1919-35) was the longest, and it ended with his unexpected death at age fifty-three. His predecessor, John Dykstra (1917-18), became ill in the influenza epidemic of 1918 and had to resign to recover his health. The congregation provided Dykstra with a Model T Ford, having sold the horse and buggy supplied to Kregel. Everett De Witt (1935-47) carried the congregation through the Depression and Second World War. He was the last to conduct the weekly Holland service; it was discontinued when he left.

Under Lambert Olgers (1948-56), the congregation in 1953 realized its goal of building a beautiful new church costing $220,000, excluding the land; it was the equal of any in greater Chicago and seated 660. The edifice provided space for Mount Greenwood to accept families leaving Roseland in the 1950s and 1960s. By the same token, some thirty families in the late 1950s transferred from Mount Greenwood to new Reformed churches in the surrounding suburbs. It was a replay of the game of "church musical chairs" that is so typical in Chicago. In recent years the exodus of Dutch-American members accelerated, but the struggling congregation is committed to remain as a community church in this strongly Roman Catholic locale.[67]

67. "Newly Constructed Sanctuary, First Reformed Church, Mount Greenwood, Chicago, Illinois," *Church Herald,* 8 Oct. 1954. Mount Greenwood pastors since 1956 are Henry Poppen (1956-60), Harris Verkaik (1961-67), Robert Bast (1967-71), Franklin Spoolstra (1973-77), Jacob Dykstra (1977-84), associate Victor Folkert (1979-83), Philip Grawburg

The Reformed Church also established outreach ministries in two suburbs directly south of Roseland, Riverdale in 1947 and Dolton in 1958. The Ivanhoe Reformed Church of Riverdale received an early boost when in 1950 the energetic Robert Schuller, fresh out of Western Seminary, came to try out his ideas for neighborhood evangelism. After five years, Schuller moved to southern California and began his drive-in church in Garden Grove, which evolved into the famed Crystal Cathedral. The Community Church of Dolton flourished for several decades until the 1980s, when the town became interracial and most white families moved further south. In 2000, after forty-two years, the church disbanded, despite pastor Arlan Menninga's best efforts (1992-2000). It was another casualty of Chicago's changing demographics.

Conclusion

The "idyllic village" of Roseland was a Dutch ethnic enclave unlike any in greater Chicago except for its sister colony of South Holland. The Dutch Reformed dominated the churches, schools, businesses, workforce, politics, and cultural life there as nowhere else in Chicago. Economically, however, the Roseland Frisians were not the masters of their fate as were the Groninger teamsters; the Frisians were industrial wage laborers who drew paychecks instead of profits. Yet by frugal living and squirreling away their savings, they too attained financial security. Home ownership was higher in Roseland than in any other Dutch locale. Up to 75 percent of households owned their homes, according to the 1920 federal census report, compared to less than 50 percent in Englewood and under 25 percent on the West Side.[68]

The Netherlandic cultural heritage of the Roseland Dutch also was unique. "Hollanders" (as those from the western provinces of Noord and Zuid Holland were known) dominated the first immigrant wave of the 1840s and 1850s; Frisians made up the second wave in the 1880s. Roseland was thus a blend of Hollanders and Frisians, with the latter in the majority. Hollanders had the money, Frisians the numbers. The independent-thinking Frisians fixed the cultural tone and way of life in Roseland, but

---

(1985-89), Daniel Van Houten (1990-94), Kevin Schut (1996-99), and Harold Willemstyn (2001-). Members in recent years have moved to Lockport, Mokena, and other communities far to the southwest of Chicago.

68. Burgess and Newcomb, *Census Data of the City of Chicago, 1920,* Appendix Map 4.

the quiet values of the Hollanders also remained strong. Frisians were a "group within a group"; they spoke their own language in the home, revered their own history and flag, and clung together.

Hollanders were religious pietists, products of the Secession of 1834. Frisians were religious activists, products of the Kuyperian "Doleantie" of the 1880s (see chapter 2). Frisians wanted to build the kingdom of God on earth, Hollanders wanted to save the lost in a fallen world. It was Frisians who pushed for separate Christian schools in Roseland at the expense of public schools. In general, the Reformed congregations reflected the pietist mentality of the 1834 seceders, while the Christian Reformed congregations reflected the mentality of the Kuyperian triumphalists. The two Christian schools were a product of that thinking.

The Frisian influx of the 1880s understandably caused friction as they elbowed their way into the colony at the expense of Hollanders. But over time, all the Netherlanders lost their provincial loyalties, dialects, and customs and blended into a people that Americans called simply Dutch or Hollanders. The Dutch sense of ethnic identity that was shared in the twentieth century was thus forged on American soil in response to the pressures of Americanization. In Roseland, this process was speeded up because, unlike on the West Side and in Englewood, public-school-minded Reformed families outnumbered Christian-school-minded families in the Christian Reformed churches. Schooling, as the next chapter explains, was the key factor for hastening or retarding assimilation into American society.

CHAPTER 7

Feeders of the Church: Christian Schools

"The growth of our church is to a great extent due to two causes, to the Christian school for its *intensive* [growth] and to the home mission work for its extensive growth." Thus wrote the Reverend J. R. Brink in the *Banner.* Christian school advocates used a number of metaphors to make this point; they spoke of Christian schools as the "feeder of the church," the "nursery of and for the church," and a crucial link in a "chain." Parent-run Christian schools were equal partners with the church. The church nurtured "children of the covenant" – a cardinal Calvinist doctrine – in the community of faith, while the school prepared them for a life in society. One immigrant complained of the financial drain of the Christian schools; *"De school vreet de kerk op"* ("The school will devour the church"), he declared. The fit rejoinder was: *"Hoe meer de school vreet, hoe meer de kerk groeit"* ("The more the school eats, the better the church will grow"). This exactly captures the spirit of Christian school advocates.[1]

Attendance and Literacy Rates

The Dutch were products of an excellent school system in the Netherlands. This story will be noted below, after providing some general statistics on school attendance and literacy rates among the Chicago Dutch,

1. J. R. Brink, "Roseland and South," *Banner,* 22 Mar. 1935; 27 Mar. 1937; 13 Oct. 1938; John L. Schaver, "Early History of Our Christian School Movement," ibid., 17 Nov. 1944.

which exceeded that of many immigrant populations. The 1870 federal census of Chicago registered only fourteen Dutch-born adults who could not read and write in any language; ten were women and four men. In the 1880 and 1900 censuses, 97 percent of Chicagoans of Dutch origin fourteen years and older reported that they could read and write. Women were only one point lower than men. Literacy in 1900 was 99 percent on the Old West Side (Wards 9 and 10) and Roseland (Ward 34). The more recent immigrants in Englewood (Ward 31) had a slightly lower reading rate of 92 percent.[2]

In their ability to speak English, the Dutch immigrants in Chicago and in Cook County were well on the road to acculturation. An amazing 95 percent of males age fourteen and above reported in the 1900 census that they could speak English. The women's rate was nine points lower, at 86 percent. Women did not need English in their world of the home, the church, and the local market. This language facility is the more remarkable, considering the fact that in 1900 the Dutch immigrants had lived in the United States an average of only sixteen years. In the Groninger Hoek, Englewood, and Roseland, the average was even less — fourteen years.[3]

School attendance among the Dutch in Cook County followed a normal pattern for the turn of the twentieth century. Some 57 percent of boys and 56 percent of girls reported attending school in the 1899-1900 academic year. As Figure 7.1 shows, children entered the first grade between ages five and seven and quit at age fourteen or fifteen. By age seven, 75 percent had enrolled, and 85 percent of eleven- through thirteen-year-olds attended.[4]

Among teens, quitting school to go to work was common. One-quarter of thirteen-year-olds dropped out, as did one-half of fourteen-year-olds and three-quarters of fifteen-year-olds. Only one in six sixteen-year-old males and one in seven sixteen-year-old females attended high

2. Compiled from Swierenga, "Dutch in Chicago and Cook County Federal Censuses, 1850-1870"; Swierenga, "Dutch in Chicago and Cook County 1880 Federal Census"; and Swierenga, "Dutch in Chicago and Cook County 1900 Federal Census." These lists are included in Swierenga, *Family Tree Maker's Family Archives;* report of United States Bureau of Education in *Daily News Almanac and Political Register for 1891* (Chicago: Chicago Daily News, 1891), 67. In the 1840s and 1850s, only 75 percent of Dutch immigrants had attended school in the homeland (Johan Goudsblom, *Dutch Society* [New York: Random House, 1967], 95).

3. Compiled from Swierenga, "Dutch in Chicago and Cook County 1900 Federal Census."

4. Three of 25 five-year-olds attended school, 14 of 27 six-year-olds, and almost all seven-year-olds.

Figure 7.1 School Attendance, by Age and Sex, Dutch in Chicago, 1900

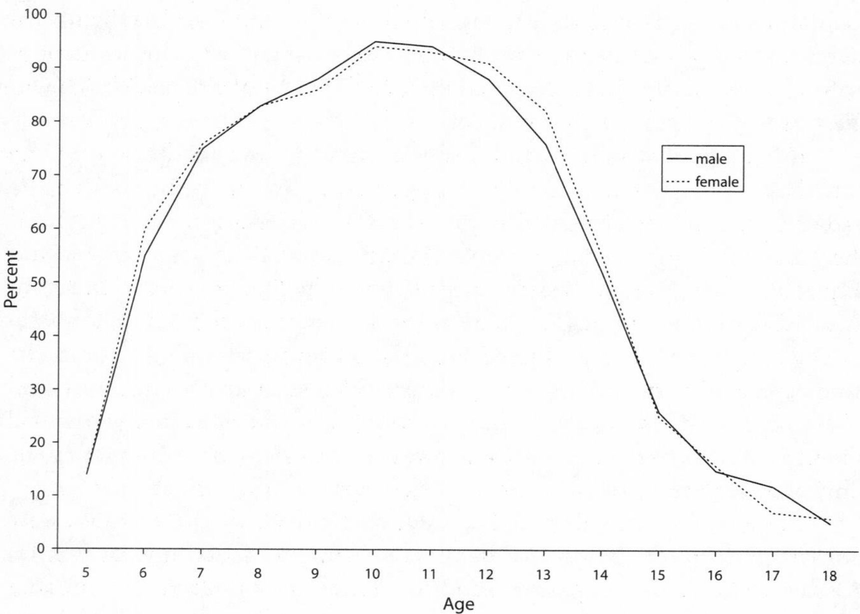

school in the 1899-1900 school year. A mere 7 percent of seventeen-year-old males went to school, compared to 11 percent of females. Among eighteen-year-olds, essentially the high school graduates, only 6 percent of men and 5 percent of women attended school. These were mostly the very wealthy and those planning to enter the professions of teaching and preaching.

Dutch young men not in school worked as apprentices, clerks, and laborers. Many fifteen-year-olds delivered telegrams for Western Union and attended the Washburne Continuation Trade School on Fridays, as the school law required until they reached age sixteen. Young women helped out at home or hired out as domestics on the affluent North Side. Some worked as live-in maids and housekeepers as far away as Evanston. There was a high demand for their services, and their parents approved, believing that idle hands were the devil's workshop.[5]

5. Dick Brouwer video interview, 25 Mar. 1998, by Martin Stulp.

Netherlandic Christian School Tradition

Dutch Calvinists and Catholics both carried to America a tradition of parochial (i.e., church owned) schools, which had sprung up after the liberal Netherlandic constitution of 1848 granted freedom of religion, education, press, and assembly. But it required long and fierce political battles to win the right to opt out of the public system.[6]

In America, Dutch Catholic youth found a congenial home in the parochial schools that virtually every parish maintained. But Calvinists had to fend for themselves. In homogeneous Dutch colonies throughout the Midwest, public schools were quite acceptable because teachers and pupils alike could and did share the faith openly. The nonsectarian "common" schools were in essence Dutch Reformed schools.

By the time the Dutch colonies opened up to outsiders later in the nineteenth century, the Christian basis had dissolved into a bland civil Christianity. But many parents were willing to tolerate this on practical grounds, and others did not see the insidious threat of secularism. The Christian ambiance of the schools lulled them into complacency.[7]

In big cities like Chicago, however, where the Dutch Reformed were a small minority in a vast and hostile environment, the impetus was far greater to establish separate schools. Teaching children the mother tongue and church history was almost as important as the four "R"s — Reading, (w)Riting, (a)Rithmetic, and Religion. Church services were conducted and catechism was taught in Dutch, and the children needed to know the language and heritage.

Also, in urban places the Protestant veneer gave way quickly under the waves of Catholic and Jewish immigration, and the schools reflected the ethnoreligious polyglot of urban culture. To counter this influence, the First Reformed Church of Chicago opened a parochial summer school as early as 1866, and the First Christian Reformed Church of Chicago did the same in 1871. Both schools were short-lived. The early immigrants did not have a sound theological rationale for the schools, and they were unwilling (or unable) to make the necessary financial sacrifices.

6. Harro W. Van Brummelen, *Telling the Next Generation: Educational Developments in North American Calvinist Christian Schools* (Lanham, Md.: Univ. Press of America, 1986), ch. 2.

7. Reformed Church in America, Committee on Educational Philosophy, "The Relationship of Public and Parochial School Education," mimeo (1957), part III, Parochial Education in the United States, 9, 13 [written primarily by the Rev. Howard Hageman]; "Brave Words on the Christian School Problem," *Missionary Monthly* 54 (Sept. 1949): 229-30, citing *Church Herald* article by Eugene Oosterhaven of 1 July 1949.

It took the next wave of Dutch immigrants, beginning in the 1880s, to build the Christian school system in America. These immigrants were the product of just such a system in the Netherlands, built by the political leader Guillaume Groen van Prinsterer and his disciple, Dr. Abraham Kuyper. Groen Van Prinsterer insisted that education was a fundamental right and responsibility of parents (especially fathers), and not a prerogative of the state or the church. His schools were "free" in the classical sense – free of the tyranny of the state and free of the tyranny of the church. They were run by parent-controlled societies.

Christian elementary schools won the legal right to confer diplomas in 1889, and in Kuyper's education acts of 1905 so did the nonpublic institutions like the Free University of Amsterdam, Kuyper's project and the capstone of the Calvinist educational system. The education acts were the ultimate triumph of Kuyper's vision; they provided tax dollars per pupil for private and parochial schools equal to those for public schools and brought nonpublic teachers into the state pension fund on an equal footing. Thus, Calvinist schools from primary to university gained full public subsidies and legal status.[8] "Free schools for a free people" was Kuyper's winning slogan.

As a theologian, Kuyper also worked out the rationale for a Christian curriculum. It must teach how God rules in history; how he structured a good creation and the laws of science; and how his beauty is shown in art, music, and literature. The curriculum must be broad, because Jesus is Lord of all and his kingdom knows no bounds. So Kuyper concluded that *everything* must be studied and brought under the Lord's sovereign control. He called this the "world and life view." The Dutch Reformed immigrants of the 1880s and 1890s brought these Kuyperian beliefs to America.

The Christian School Question

Despite the success of the Christian school movement in the Netherlands, the immigrants did not agree on the need for such a system in America. Indeed, the Christian school question became the major cause of division between the two Dutch Reformed immigrant churches, and the consequences were far reaching. The Christian Reformed Church made Christian schools an essential part of religious training, whereas the Reformed

8. Hageman, "Brave Words," 220-22.

Church committed itself to public education, although it condoned Christian schooling for parents who desired it.

The General Synod of the Reformed Church in America went on record in 1892 and again in the 1950s in favor of public schools. In 1892 the denomination first staked out its position in response to a national movement by Catholic leaders to obtain public funds for parochial schools. Said the synod:

> Whereas, The Common School is vitally essential to the fusing of the heterogeneous elements of our population into one nation, to the end, that popular suffrage may continue to be a sure buttress of our government, Resolved, . . . that . . . we request our fellow citizens to bear in mind the warnings of the farsighted, early statesmen of this land, and especially the words of General [Ulysses S.] Grant, uttered in 1876: "Encourage free schools and resolve that not one dollar appropriated to them shall be applied to the support of any sectarian school; resolve that any child in the land may get a Common School education, unmixed with atheistic, pagan, or sectarian teachings. Keep the church and State forever separate."[9]

This resolution was a reflection of the denomination's two centuries of assimilation. No Yankee Protestant could have stated it better. For the Reformed Church in America, Christian schools were un-American. Public schools were the key to building a democratic society, and Christian students there would be "salt and light."

Cornelia De Bey, the youngest daughter of the Reverend Bernardus De Bey of Chicago's First Reformed Church, exemplified this process perfectly. Baptized in a strict Christian Seceded church in Groningen, in Chicago she was educated in public schools. As an adult she became a militant member of the Chicago Teachers' Federation and won an elected seat on the Chicago Board of Education from 1905 to 1908. Christian day schools were anathema to this liberal icon of Chicago.[10]

9. *Acts and Proceedings of the General Synod of the Protestant Dutch Reformed Church*, 1892, 661-62. The synod's resolution also proclaimed that, should the Roman Catholic Church obtain any public funds, so should "every religious or anti-religious body in the land . . . have its parochial schools supported out of the public treasury."

10. Mary Pieroni Schultz and Suzanne Sinke, "DeBey, Cornelia Bernarda," 214-16, in *Women Building Chicago, 1790-1990*, Rima Lunin Schultz and Adele Hast, eds. (Bloomington: Indiana Univ. Press, 2001); Hans Krabbendam, "Serving the Dutch Community: A Comparison of the Patterns of Americanization in the Lives of Two Immigrant Pastors" (master's thesis, Kent State University, 1989), 84-86.

Given the Reformed denomination's rejection, in principle, of Christian day schools, the major debate took place primarily within the Christian Reformed churches. In 1873 the synod first "obliged" consistories to establish "Free Christian Reformed schools," but only one consistory — Grand Rapids — took action. Most members found the public schools satisfactory, as a synodical committee on Christian education acknowledged in 1898. This inspired the 1898 synod to stake out its position in hopes of "awakening an interest, and admonishing the people of the need." The synod declared: "A positive Christian education with Reformed principles is a duty for Reformed Christians." It then warned "all ministers and elders to work for the cause of Christian education in every place where such is at all possible."

The synod gave four reasons in support of its stand:

> 1. God's Word demands that our children be trained in the fear and admonition of the Lord. 2. The promises of the parents at the time of baptism. 3. There may be no separation between our civic, social, or religious life, education and training. 4. The honor of our King demands it, since all power is given him in heaven and earth, also in the realm of education and all other knowledge.

Hence, the synod concluded that "a specific Reformed education is necessary for our children."[11]

This pronouncement set off a debate that continued for two decades. The Dutch language press carried heated exchanges of opinions, and speakers and lecturers argued the case for Christian schools in numerous public assemblies. Most were ministers, who were the most respected voices in the community. The main push thus came from the pulpit rather than the pew. By 1920 the issue was settled. The Christian Reformed denomination, by an overwhelming majority, had committed itself to Christian day schools. Wholehearted support for Christian schools was a requisite for office bearers, and the few parents who objected had to answer to the consistory.

The church order and subsequent synodical rulings spelled out the official Christian Reformed position. Article 21 of the 1914 Church Order says: "The Consistories shall see to it that there are good Christian schools where the parents may have their children instructed according to the demands of the covenant." Article 41 requires that the following ques-

11. Schaver, "Early History of our Christian School Movement"; Christian Reformed Church, *Acts of Synod,* 1898, 24-25, English translation in the Archives, Calvin College.

tion be asked of each consistory delegation at each classis meeting: "Does the consistory support the cause of Christian schools?"[12] Thus, consistories must "see to it" that parents establish Christian schools.

In the throes of the Great Depression in 1932, when the Christian schools were struggling to hold on, the "Principals' Club" in Michigan appealed to the synod to help the schools survive. Synod responded positively by urging "*all* our leaders and people to lend this cause their wholehearted moral and financial support." Two years later, the synod made such support a qualifying factor for church office holders. "Although such as heartily support Christian instruction do not thereby automatically qualify for nomination as office bearers," declared the 1934 synod, "this element should be given very weighty consideration, and [the synod] advises consistories to do so." The 1936 synod was yet more direct:

> It is the duty of the consistory to use every proper means to the end that a Christian School may be established where it does not exist, and to give wholehearted and unreserved moral backing to existing Christian Schools and a measure of financial help in case of need. . . . If, in the judgement of Classis, a Consistory does not support the cause of Christian Schools, Classis should continue earnestly to admonish such a consistory publicly in its classical meeting and privately through the church visitors until it truly repents.[13]

Christian Reformed leaders acknowledged the need for salting secular society, but they saw even more clearly the threat of secularization. The rise of Darwinian evolution as the new orthodoxy in the public schools frightened them, as did the liberal social values known as modernism, taught by John Dewey to his student teachers in the education department of the University of Chicago. Parents wanted to guard their children as much as possible from these heresies. By 1905, Christian school advocates from across the Midwest met in Chicago and decided to develop their own textbooks to counter evolutionary teachings.

Peter Moerdyke, pastor of Trinity Reformed Church on Chicago's West Side from 1892 to 1907, reported the thinking of the group:

12. J. L. Schaver, *Christian Reformed Church Order, A Manual of the Church Order Adopted by the Synod of 1914* . . . (Grand Rapids: Eerdmans, 1941), 5, 8; editorial, "The Official Stand of our Church on Christian Education," *Banner,* 28 Mar. 1930.

13. Christian Reformed Church, *Acts of Synod,* 1932, pp. 26, 42 (italics in original); 1934, pp. 167-68; 1936, pp. 35-37.

> Their serious and vital objection to most textbooks now in vogue is that they all proceed from the evolutionary standpoint or hold its doctrine in solution. This they regard as full of gravest danger to the religious spiritual welfare of children and young people and hence to the church.[14]

If doctrinal beliefs dictated the founding of Christian schools, traditional cultural considerations also motivated many parents. They wanted their children, especially at the high school level, to socialize with "their own kind." The likelihood of marrying within the Dutch community was greatly enhanced by the Christian school experience.

No sacrifice was too much for *onze* ("our") school. Congregations collected offerings regularly for it, established diaconal funds to help parents meet tuition costs, musical groups staged fundraising concerts, and women's "school circles" held bake sales for school projects. Even the children lent a hand by bringing old newspapers and rags to school on "rag day," set during the proverbial Dutch housecleaning time in the spring.

In truth, not all Christian Reformed families were sanguine about the future of the Christian schools. As a Dutch import, some thought them too "foreign-outlandish" and vulnerable to the forces of Americanization. "Discard the Dutch language and you bury the Christian school," it was said. Since the schools were at first parochial, others assumed that "our schools must die out with our Holland churches." But the critics failed to reckon with the speed at which the schools left behind the Dutch language and customs for American ways, and became "free schools" under parental control and subject to state educational laws.[15]

Reformed Church leaders, however, never wavered in their rejection of Christian schools in favor of public schools, even when the evidence seemed to run counter. Moerdyke admired the consistency of the "logic of the sticklers for the mother tongue"; they inculcated their youth in the traditions so as not to lose them to the church. But at what cost! He "pitied the poor young victims of a foreign spirit that defrauds them of the superior educational advantages of our public schools, and cripples them for life."[16]

In 1894 Moerdyke castigated the editor of the new Dutch-language

14. Peter Moerdyke, "Chicago Letter," *CI,* 21 June 1905, p. 395.

15. Mark Fakkema, "The Growth of the Christian Schools," *Onze Toekomst,* 30 July 1920.

16. Moerdyke, "Chicago Letter," *CI,* 28 Feb. 1894, p. 10.

Chicago weekly, *Onze Toekomst (Our Future),* which was primarily a Christian Reformed organ, for denouncing the public schools as "un-Christian" and condemning the Reformed Church for backing them. In his regular column, "Chicago Letter," in his denomination's weekly, the *Christian Intelligencer,* Moerdyke mocked: "What an enlightener and educator this paper [*Onze Toekomst*] will be in guiding young men toward 'our future.'"[17]

Only a few months later, however, Moerdyke lampooned the Chicago public school system for banning religious and moral instruction while at the same time introducing military training for young men. "High authorities agitate and predict this as a new and universal feature in the schools," said Moerdyke sarcastically. "Then let us have uniforms for all pupils, military titles for teachers of various grades [ranks], and raise up 'mercenary troops' to play the Hessian part in any and every war agoing, or that ambitious young America can excite or encourage, providing we can't employ these skilled fighters at home."[18]

Five years later Moerdyke endorsed a stinging exposé of Chicago's public schools, which were severely underfunded and in steep decline:

> For more than a year past the educational questions connected with our city public schools have agitated the Board, the vast corps of teachers, and the perplexed host of taxpayers. Chicago is confessedly too poor to take care of its schools. One plan after another, sane, insane, commendable or disgraceful, has been suggested to cut down expenses to match available funds. The shortening of the year, abolition of fads, of ancient or modern language studies, of the high schools, of the manual training schools, of music, the deferring of the building of schools absolutely needed, the cutting of salaries, and everything imaginable have advertised all concerned in the administration of schools most unfavorably. This state of things is universally deplored, and the source of the evil clearly designated.[19]

Later the same year 1900, Moerdyke reported with disappointment that the Chicago Board of Education had refused a petition from church leaders to introduce a daily reading from an approved compilation of Bible passages. "This renewed effort to secure moral instruction from this sacred source for the children was, after careful consideration, disap-

17. Ibid., 28 Mar. 1894, p. 8.
18. Ibid., 6 Feb. 1895, p. 9.
19. Ibid., 28 Feb. 1900, p. 137.

proved by a vote of 6 to 13. Sectarian feeling and controversies were apprehended."[20]

In 1903 Moerdyke added to his lament: "The public schools of this city are on the whole sadly destitute of moral instruction, and not a few teachers often betray their infidelity or enmity by disparaging comments or insinuations regarding the Christian religion, especially the Holy Bible."[21]

The die was cast yet again in 1907, when the president of the Chicago Board of Education declared the Bible an "unsuitable" and even "dangerous" book for children "whose intellect is not completely developed." Three years later, in 1911, the Illinois Supreme Court banished the Bible and religious instruction from the public schools.[22]

The push for "value neutrality" unsettled Reformed Church leaders. H. H. Van Meter, superintendent of evangelistic work for the Christian Endeavor Union, the youth ministry in the churches, petitioned the Illinois Supreme Court to reconsider its decision. In 1937 the leaders of the First Reformed Church of Chicago were so concerned about the low moral state of the city's public schools that they sent a petition signed by 128 members to Springfield requesting that the state school superintendent permit "the reading of the Bible in the public schools."[23]

Despite this realistic appraisal of the deficiencies of the public schools in Chicago, neither Moerdyke nor any other Reformed leader reevaluated his official position on Christian schools. The consistory of the First Reformed Church of Chicago was very frank when the Ebenezer Christian school board requested that the congregation provide active ongoing support. "We are willing to comply with the request," the consistory minutes record in a classic understatement, but "it is not probable to get full support for the cause of Christian education because the attitude of our membership is not entirely in accord with the principles thereof." The deacons simply sent small contributions of $100-150 from time to time.[24] Similarly, when board members of Chicago Christian High School appealed to the First Reformed Church early in the depression crisis to budget six dollars per family annually for the school, the consistory refused,

20. Ibid., 24 Oct. 1900, p. 685.

21. Ibid., 4 Mar. 1903, p. 137.

22. *Onze Toekomst,* 25 Oct. 1907.

23. Ibid., 29 July 1910; First Reformed Church of Chicago, Minutes, 23 Mar. 1937.

24. First Reformed Church of Chicago, Minutes, 25 May 1937 (quote), 28 Jan., 25 Feb 1936, 23 Feb. 1937, 22 Feb. 1938.

although it did provide special envelopes to its members so "those who were willing to help could do so."[25]

A number of Reformed Church families were Christian school supporters in the early twentieth century, and they enrolled their children and participated in the school societies. But the Reformed churches continued to emphasize the importance of education in the church and home – in catechetical teaching, Sunday schools, and Christian Endeavor activities.[26]

In 1932 the influential Reformed Church cleric, Dr. Albertus Pieters, defended his denomination's lack of enthusiasm for Christian education in emotionally charged terms. We came out of public schools "unscathed [and] not such bad products," he declared. "The primary school was good enough for us, so it is good enough for our children." "Give us proof of the fruits of the Christian school," he demanded, but the advocates "cannot give it."[27]

In the 1950s, the Reformed Church again officially endorsed public education. The General Synod named a blue-ribbon Committee on Educational Philosophy to study the pros and cons of Christian day schools and especially their theological bases. Its report weighed in strongly on the con side. It defended public schools as integral to the democratic process, saw Christian pupils as salt and light, and insisted that parental baptism vows rested on faith and did not require any "works" such as Christian day schools. The "restricted absolutism" that dictates Christian schools produces only a "sectarianism which threatens the common life of the citizens of the community and the common life of Christians in the body of our Lord Jesus Christ." The synod in 1957 adopted this report and distributed it to every minister as "an event of major significance in our church life." At that time the Christian schools of Chicago counted one Reformed Church student for every four Christian Reformed students.[28]

25. Ibid., 28 Mar. 1930, 27 Oct., 21 Dec. 1931.

26. Moerdyke, "Chicago Letter," *CI,* 9 Mar. 1904, p. 154.

27. T.E., "Cooperation," *Banner,* 18 Nov. 1932. Pieters made his remarks in the Reformed Church periodical, the *Leader.*

28. "Relationship of Public and Parochial School Education," part IV, Theological Presuppositions of Education, 6, 16-17, 20; Mildred W. Schuppert, ed., *A Digest and Index of the Minutes of the General Synod of the Reformed Church in America, 1906-1957* (Grand Rapids: Eerdmans, 1957): 86-87. Statistics on enrollment by church affiliation, 1953-1954, are in the *Illinois Observer,* 15 May 1954.

Christian Schools in Chicago

In Chicago, as in other Dutch Reformed settlements, Christian schools passed through at least three stages. They began as parochial "Dutch schools" to teach the language and culture of the homeland. Later they became Christian schools, arms of the church, to help it and parents pass on the faith. Finally, they evolved into parent-controlled free schools to train Christian citizens to take their place in the American nation. Thus, the schools developed from Dutch to American, and from parochial to free. This was a normal progression in the process of acculturation.[29] But always the schools remained tied to the churches and homes. And just as these were patriarchal, so were the schools. Principals were always males and the teaching staff mostly young females; all were expected to live upright lives and affiliate with supporting churches.

After the Civil War, the need for instruction in the Dutch language, culture, and history was so great that consistories decided to set up their own schools to run during the summer months. As already noted, the first such school in the Groninger Hoek was founded in 1866 under the auspices of the First Reformed Church consistory. Five years later, in 1871, the First Christian Reformed Church established a school taught by a Mr. Albert. Neither survived more than a few years. First Chicago tried again in 1883 but with no better results. In 1901 the new Douglas Park Christian Reformed Church opened a Holland summer school, taught by Emanuel Welandt, the pastor's son, for five dollars per week.[30]

Until the 1890s, the West Side Hollanders lacked the leadership, commitment, and financial resources to build Christian day schools, and their children attended neighborhood public schools. But the increasing cultural diversity in the public schools and the secularization of the curriculum frightened orthodox parents. Moerdyke, a public school advocate, admitted this when he observed:

> Hosts and dense colonies of strange people by their poor, perverted, superstitious religions, or low morals and corrupting usages, are a menace to us all in direct and indirect ways. . . . The moral effect of miscellaneous association of a dozen or score of nationalities in the

29. Fakkema, "Christian Schools."

30. First Reformed Church of Chicago, Minutes, 7 Feb., 21 Mar., 16, 30 May, 24 July 1866; First Christian Reformed Church of Chicago, *Seventy-fifth Anniversary, 1867-1942* (Chicago 1942), 8; Douglas Park Christian Reformed Church, Minutes, 24 June 1901; Van Brummelen, *Telling the Next Generation,* 55.

public schools is easily perceptible and rather alarming to the observing citizen.[31]

The centennial history of Roseland Christian School spells out clearly the dread of diversity. The Hollanders had been satisfied with the public schools for forty years. Teachers opened and closed each day with prayer, read from the Bible, directed singing of Christian hymns, and recognized God as creator and sustainer of the universe. But in 1883 the Pullman shops had opened down the hill from Michigan Avenue in nearby Calumet, and suddenly the influx of thousands of new workers ended Roseland's exclusive Dutch Reformed character. Even though the public school principal in 1890 had mastered the Dutch language and joined the First Reformed Church, after marrying a woman from the congregation, the Hollanders were filled with anxiety and turned to Christian education.[32]

The Darwinian controversy and teaching of evolution in public schools energized Christian school advocates as nothing before. Other negative issues in public education were complaints of low standards by unionized teachers and mismanagement by the Chicago Board of Education. "If you approve the actions of our School Board," declared *Onze Toekomst* editor Luurt (Louis) Holstein in 1906, "you must be a jack ass, a nitwit, or a lunatic."[33] Cornelia De Bey was a leading light on the board at the time.

Because of these concerns, and a clearer understanding of the covenantal obligation of Christian education, Christian Reformed churches established regular day schools. Roseland Christian School began in 1883 under the auspices of the First Roseland church, the First Chicago church opened Ebenezer Christian School in 1893, the First Englewood church established Englewood Christian School in 1900, and the Douglas Park church founded Timothy Christian School in 1911. All these parochial schools "graduated" to an independent status run by parental societies.[34]

By 1926 the Christian school system had grown to seven schools — all accredited by the Chicago Board of Education — with two thousand

31. Moerdyke, "Chicago Letter," *CI,* 7 Nov. 1906, p. 721.

32. Roseland Christian School, *Centennial, 1884-1984* (Chicago, 1984), 14-15; Vandenbosch, *Dutch Communities of Chicago,* 43.

33. *Onze Toekomst,* 23 Nov. 1906.

34. Roseland Christian School, *Centennial;* Ebenezer Christian School, *Fiftieth Anniversary, 1893-1943* (Chicago, 1943); Englewood Christian School, *Fiftieth Anniversary, 1900-1950* (Chicago, 1950), 14-17; Timothy Christian School, *50th Anniversary, 1911-1961* (Cicero, 1961).

pupils, including a four-year secondary school, Chicago Christian High School, established in 1918, which was spearheaded by the westside leaders James De Boer and George Ottenhoff, and Henry Kuiper of Roseland. The teachers, administrators, and boards coordinated the curricula and dealt with common problems in the Chicago Christian Teachers' Association (founded in 1906) and the Board of Christian Schools, respectively. By 1953 enrollment had grown to 2,800, including 650 students in three high schools.[35] In 1959 supporters in Chicago capped the system with Trinity Christian College, a junior college in Palos Heights that quickly evolved into a four-year liberal arts college.

Roseland Christian Schools (1883-)

The First Reformed Church of Roseland began a day school for its youth almost immediately after establishing the church in 1849 on Michigan Avenue at 107th Street. *Meester* Peter De Jong, the first deacon and a teacher by profession, taught the school that met in the church. Although the language of instruction was Dutch and the Bible was at the center of the curriculum, the school was funded by property taxes and functioned for a decade as the village's only public school. In 1859 a true public school was opened at 103rd and Michigan Avenue under Professor Albert Kroon, followed by a second school in 1876 at 104th and Wallace streets under George Brennan. The famed James Van Vlissingen School, called "V.V." by locals, at 108th and Wentworth Avenue, was founded in 1892. All the graduates continued their studies either at Calumet High School or Fenger High School; these included Christian school graduates prior to the founding of Chicago Christian High School (CCHS) in Englewood in 1918. A minority of Reformed church youth also attended CCHS, but most remained in the public system.[36]

Members of the Christian Reformed churches were not satisfied with the nonsectarian public schools, even though they had the trappings of Christianity – prayer, Bible-reading, and hymns. The more orthodox parents wanted a school that was Reformed in doctrine and Dutch in language, so as to nurture both the church and the heritage. Thus, in Decem-

35. *Onze Toekomst,* 10 Mar. 1926; Henry Kuiper, "Our Christian Schools in September 1919: A Short Regime," ibid., 26 Sept. 1919; 7 Dec. 1906; *Illinois Observer,* 15 May 1954. In 1957 seven elementary schools were Roseland, Englewood, South Holland, Timothy, Evergreen Park, Oak Lawn, and Western Springs.

36. Ettema, *Down an Indian Trail,* 16, 25, 36.

ber 1882, the First Christian Reformed Church, led by the Reverend Geert Broene, decided to establish *De Hollandsche Christelijke School* ("The Dutch Christian School"). It opened the next month, in January 1883. From that time on, the Dutch in Roseland were divided by schools as well as churches.[37]

The first board of the Christian school consisted of the Reverend Broene, president; Cornelius L. Clousing, vice president; and members G. J. Vaarwerk, Jan Kleinhuizen, and Simon Dekker. Dekker was the only member not serving in the consistory, but soon that body decided to appoint only such men, presumably to share the work and avoid conflicts of interest.[38]

To accommodate the first class of sixty pupils, First Church built an addition on the rear of its sanctuary at 111th and State Streets, which doubled as the consistory room. Tuition was 60 cents a month for one child, $1 for two, and $1.25 for three or more. The board considered itself fortunate to hire for $40 a month a Mr. Aukes, an immigrant from the province of Friesland who was fluent in Dutch. But he proved to be a poor disciplinarian, and the board dismissed him after only seven months. His many Frisian compatriots at First Church complained bitterly, but they were not allowed to vote on the issue because, as former members of the Hervormde (State) Church, they had not joined the congregation.[39]

The board then hired another Frisian immigrant, Henry Jacobsma, who had just arrived to join his parents in Roseland. Jacobsma, who came with proper academic credentials, found only thirty pupils, a one-third decline, since the protesters had pulled their children out. But he soon gained the trust of the congregation and more students came. Within two years the space was too small, and the consistory built a new two-room school behind the church. Soon this again proved inadequate, and the building was moved to 110th Place, remodeled, and enlarged to six rooms.

37. The founding date is given as 1884 in Roseland Christian School, *Centennial, 1884-1984* (Chicago, 1984), but charter school board member Simon Dekker in his 1950 memoirs, "History of the Christian School at Roseland" (typescript, 2-3, Archives, Calvin College), makes the case for the 1883 date, which is consistent with other records, e.g., the copy of a consistory minute of 15 Dec. 1882, quoted in Lynwood Christian Reformed Church, *Centennial, 1877-1977,* 6; and a report by church clerk Peter Schoon, "Holl. Chr. Onderwijs," in *De Wachter,* 18 Jan. 1883.

38. Simon Dekker, "History of the Christian School at Roseland," 2-3.

39. Ibid., 2. This Mr. Aukes is very likely the bookstore owner Gerben Jelles Aukes of Dokkum, Friesland, who immigrated with his wife and child in 1879 at thirty-one years of age. His intended destination was Hampton, New York. Swierenga, *Dutch Emigrants to the United States,* 5.

Right, Henry Jacobsma, teacher-principal, 1884-93, Roseland Christian School; 1894-1921, Ebenezer Christian School; below, Roseland Christian School, 111th St., 1886-1929

Jacobsma ably led the school as teacher-principal for ten years, from 1883 to 1893, when he was unceremoniously dismissed after leaving First Church for the new Second Christian Reformed Church of Roseland. The First Christian Reformed Church of Chicago immediately hired him to direct its new school on the West Side.[40]

40. Dekker, "Christian School at Roseland," 2; Roseland Christian School, *Centennial,* 10-11.

In 1891, eight years after First Church opened its school, recent immigrants living in the northern part of Roseland opened *De Christelijke Nationale School van West Pullman* ("The Christian National School of West Pullman") on 104th Street near Wentworth Avenue. The school evolved out of a short-lived effort, led by elder Jan (John) Ton of the First Reformed Church, to instruct the youth in the Dutch language. A Mr. Venema, an "exhorter" or lay preacher in the Netherlands and in Michigan, was hired and classes began in the original church building on 107th Street, then standing vacant. But Venema lacked the gift of teaching and the building had to come down.

This prompted Ton and his supporters to approach Reformed families in the area to organize a society, buy land, and open a real school to perpetuate the faith and the mother tongue. Most were leaders in the First Reformed Church, whose pastor, Balster Van Ess, backed the effort wholeheartedly. "In education there is no neutrality," he declared. Van Ess, Ton, and the others were Kuyperians, who believed in Christian schools owned and operated under parental, not consistorial, control. Elder Dirk De Jong was the first board president (1891-98), elder Peter Grouwstra vice president, Peter Spoolstra secretary, Leendert Ton treasurer, and elder John Ton and Jacob Westerhof members. The organizational meeting took place in Westerhof's home.

Following a service of dedication in First Reformed Church, the 104th Street School opened with twenty-five students under E. Wildeman, a Chicago public school principal certified in the Netherlands, but he lacked a Reformed vision and was released after one year. The school did not flourish until the Second Christian Reformed Church was organized nearby in 1893 and got behind it. That year the board hired as teacher-principal Albert Raap, a talented young man trained in the Netherlands who later became a professor at Hope College. Raap ran the school for a decade (1893-1903) and enjoyed the enthusiastic support of pastors at First Reformed, Van Ess, and Second Christian Reformed, Hendrik Van Hoogen. An influx to Roseland of new immigrant families committed to Christian education further strengthened the school and pushed the one-room classroom designed for a maximum of 85 students to overflowing with 120. The addition of two rooms in 1899 and three more in 1901 solved the space problem for awhile.[41]

41. Roseland School for Christian Instruction, *Fiftieth Anniversary, 1891-1941: Historical Reflections* (Chicago, 1941), 4-8; Dekker, "Christian School at Roseland," 14-17. Netherlands emigration records indicate that the Wildeman family was Evangelical Lutheran.

The early history of the 104th Street School is caught up in interchurch rivalries, between Reformed and Christian Reformed and among Christian Reformed, especially the First and Second congregations. At first many families in Second Church sent their children to the "Christian Reformed school" on 111th Street. Because of the extreme hard times caused by the depression of 1893, however, Second Roseland fell behind in its contributions to the school, and the board showed little forbearance. It "laid the law down to us," recalled Simon Dekker, a charter member of Second Church: "If you want to send your children to our school you will have to pay 60c for each child." The leaders of Second Church felt aggrieved but agreed, provided they could again be represented on the board. All had resigned upon their transfer of membership to Second Church, thinking it best since the mother church owned the school.

The firing of principal Jacobsma of the 111th Street School in 1893 by the consistory of the First Christian Reformed Church, solely because he had affiliated with the daughter church, was the last straw. "Now the break was complete," said Dekker, "as practically all the children [in Second Church], with a few exceptions, were sent to the 104th St. School." Dekker succeeded De Jong as board president and served for many years, carrying his bitterness toward First Roseland to his grave. Richard Tiemersma, in his memoirs penned in the 1980s, likewise recalled that there was "little love lost" between the adult constituents of the two schools. North-south regional loyalties that were nurtured in their supporting churches sadly carried over to the schools. Dekker's taking the helm from De Jong also signaled the growing dominance of the Christian Reformed constituency.[42]

Early on, both school boards felt pressure from parents to switch instruction from Dutch to English. The church school yielded first through the efforts of pastor Henry Vander Werp (1886-92). In 1887, English was introduced in the "higher room" (grades four, five, and six); the parent-controlled school followed suit in 1889. All classes in both schools switched to English in 1906-07, but it was 1915 before teacher Katie Boersma of the 104th Street School was ordered to tell Bible stories in English. No wonder the community called it the "Holland School." Boersma taught at 104th Street from its inception, more than fifty-five consecutive years.

42. Dekker, "Christian School at Roseland," 3-4; Richard R. Tiemersma, "Growing Up in Roseland in the 20's & 30's," *Origins* 5, No. 1 (1987): 11.

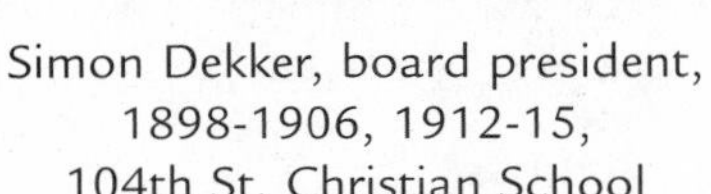

Simon Dekker, board president,
1898-1906, 1912-15,
104th St. Christian School

Katie Boersma,
teacher for 55 consecutive years,
1893-1948

The governance issue was as sticky as the language question. Should the First Church consistory yield control of its parochial school to an independent society, based on the Kuyperian principle of a "free" school? Such an action might entice the 104th Street School Society to amalgamate with it. From 1897 to 1906, many consistory meetings and congregational meetings considered the matter. Finally, in 1907, after more than ten years of discussion, the First Church consistory gave the 111th Street School its independence. The pastor, the Reverend Bernard Einink, encouraged the changeover. James Nieuwdorp was principal of the school until 1911, when Jan (John) Bovenkerk, a member of First Reformed and later Bethany Reformed Church, succeeded him (1911-15). Bovenkerk had previously administered the 104th Street School (1907-11). Both schools won accreditation and added the seventh and eighth grades, with the first graduation ceremonies in 1910.[43]

In 1911 the boards made another of several attempts to amalgamate the schools, but the union fell apart and the spirit of competition returned, although both stressed a covenantal consciousness and Kuyper-

43. Roseland Christian School, *Centennial,* 20-22; Roseland Christian School, *Golden Anniversary Program* (Chicago, 1934), "History of our School," 11.

ian worldview. The year 1927 saw another merger fail. By then the larger 104th Street School, which in 1899 was renamed the Roseland School for Christian Instruction, had over four hundred students, compared to less than three hundred at the 111th Street School, officially the Roseland Christian School. Both societies embarked on massive building campaigns. The 104th Street School dedicated a new building with eight classrooms in 1915, and the 111th Street School opened its nine-room facility at 108th and Princeton Streets in 1929, under principal John Van Bruggen. First Church contributed a generous gift of $10,000 at a critical juncture to get construction underway.

Right, John Bovenkerk, teacher-principal, 1907-11, 104th St. Christian School; 1911-15, 111th Street Christian School; below, Roseland School for Christian Instruction (104th St.), erected 1915

Roseland Christian School, 108th St., erected 1929

Both buildings were equally impressive brick, two-story structures with full "look-out" basements. They bespeak the economic power and sacrificial giving of the Christian Reformed constituency. The combined enrollment soon peaked at 920. In part this was due to an expanded curriculum; in 1934 the 108th Street school was the first in the Chicago area to introduce a kindergarten, which proved to be an excellent recruitment tool. In 1936 it started a junior high that included ninth graders.[44]

In the 1930s the fortunes of the rival schools were reversed. The 104th Street school saw enrollment fall by more than 50 percent, to less than two hundred in 1941, while the 108th Street school grew to the point of severe overcrowding. It had the better location in the heart of the Dutch neighborhood and was backed by the largest congregation, the First Roseland Christian Reformed church. Roseland Christian had a first-rate principal in John Van Bruggen (1925-37), a school alumnus, and strong board leadership from businessman J. C. Bovenkerk, brother of the former school principal. The veteran principal, A. S. De Jong (1926-38), of the 104th Street school, resigned to take a like position in Michigan, and Chris Vos replaced him.

The solution to the disparate enrollments was to merge the 104th Street school with the 108th Street school. They needed each other, but

44. Roseland Christian School, *Centennial,* 24-27; *Golden Anniversary Program,* 11; *Onze Toekomst,* 11 May 1927; J. R. Brink, "Roseland and South," *Banner,* 27 Mar., 7 Aug. 1936.

the latter was a reluctant partner. Finally in 1947, after four years of discussions and negotiations, the merger was approved and the "unique competitive spirit" died. William Brouwer, then the principal of Roseland Christian, became the "supervising principal" of the unified school and led it for fifteen years until he died suddenly in 1963. At the time the school had 693 students. During the heyday in the 1940s and 1950s, 98 percent of the Christian Reformed families sent their children to the Roseland Christian schools, and the percentage from Reformed homes was on the rise.[45]

The departure of the Oak Lawn students in 1957 eased the space crunch a bit, but the ultimate decline set in with white flight in the mid-1960s. In 1969 the 104th Street building was sold to the Chicago Board of Education, and the 108th Street facility enrolled only 196 students. At that point, the Roseland Christian School board and society made a most remarkable and visionary decision; it would continue to operate the school for all Christian families "regardless of race." Within eight years enrollment had risen to 350, and a new addition was needed. Roseland Christian continues to operate today as a largely black school, but with continuing support from the dispersed Roselanders.[46]

Ebenezer Christian School (1893-1946)

Ebenezer began as a parochial school and was operated for the first ten years by the consistory of the Fourteenth Street (First) Christian Reformed Church of Chicago. Pastor John Riemersma led the effort, following calls by parents for Christian elementary education. The church established what was called simply "The Christian School" under an appointed board.[47]

In the first two years, classes met in a store at 685 (1444 new numbering) S. Ashland Avenue, which was three blocks west of the church. Then to save money the school moved to the church basement, which was remodeled for the purpose. This walk-out space with many windows sufficed for eleven years until the congregation could afford a building. The first teachers were Mr. P. R. Holtman and Henry Jacobsma; the latter had

45. Roseland Christian School, *Centennial,* 28, 31-35; William Van Rees, "News from Chicago South," *Banner,* 23 Feb. 1945.

46. Roseland Christian School, *Centennial,* 36-42.

47. The first board members in 1893-95 were T. Dekker (president), E. Bosker (vice president), H. Boss, H. Bus, and Henry Swierenga.

been released by the Roseland Christian School and was a great boon to the fledgling school. More than one hundred pupils attended from the start; most left the nearby Clark Public School. Morning lessons were in Dutch and afternoon lessons in English.

The board raised support by creating a "5-cent society," but even contributing this much each week was difficult during the "Cleveland Hard Times," which began the year of the school's founding and lasted for five years. Unemployment in Chicago climbed precipitously from 3 percent in 1892 to 12 percent in 1893 and 18 percent in 1894.[48] By 1895 the situation at Ebenezer was so desperate that the board decided to close the school. Only a last-ditch effort to raise funds by canvassing the congregation saved the school, but instruction in English stopped because Holtman, the one qualified teacher, had resigned over poor pay. Jacobsma carried on as the sole instructor for all grades, teaching in the Dutch language. As a product of the Netherlandic Christian school system, with its emphasis on a classical curriculum, Jacobsma brought this tradition to the school.

The consistory owned and operated the school until 1902, when it turned over control to an independent society and an elected board. Ebenezer now became a "free" school directed by a society of parents and supporters. Elder L. L. Hofstra was the principal prior to its transition.[49]

The school society in 1903 chose the Old Testament name Ebenezer (*Ebenhaezer,* in Dutch), meaning in Hebrew "hitherto hath the Lord helped us." The name, suggested by church elder Bernard Huiner, captured the spirit of hope and sacrifice needed for the venture. The society, led by Abel Bulthuis, immediately began a $10,000 fundraising campaign for a new building. The society bought lots for $1,600 on 15th Street and within four years, on Decoration Day in 1906, it laid the cornerstone for an $8,000 building. The move came none too soon, since the school's booming enrollment of 225 exceeded the number the church basement could accommodate.

At the joyous groundbreaking ceremony of prayer and praise, several pastors spoke and the "large throng" of parents and supporters sang appropriate psalms (Psalm 105:5 and 100:4). The Reverend Evert Breen, of the First Christian Reformed Church, stood front and center as the lead-

48. Wesley G. Skogan, *Chicago Since 1840: A Time-Series Handbook* (Urbana: Univ. of Illinois Institute of Government and Public Affairs, 1976), table 2.

49. Edward Groenboom, "Historical Sketch of the Ebenezer Christian School," in Ebenezer Christian School, *Fiftieth Anniversary,* n.p.; Henry Stob, "Church and School on Chicago's West Side, 1913-1921, Part 1," *Origins* 10, No. 2 (1992): 19.

ing advocate of the school. In a fitting show of solidarity, two of the three main speakers were Reformed Church pastors, Moerdyke of Trinity Reformed and Henry Harmeling of First Reformed. All three stressed the importance of the endeavor. Moerdyke spoke on the topic, "Christian Instruction a Necessity for Good Citizenship," and Harmeling set forth the thesis, "The Positive Confession of God Is Necessary in the Teaching of Children." Cornelius De Leeuw, pastor of the Douglas Park Christian Reformed Church, gave the final address, which emphasized the essential connection between Christian instruction and knowledge.[50]

Moerdyke's supportive remarks surprised many, given the decidedly negative views on Christian schools that he had expressed in print for ten years, as noted above. No doubt he softened his opposition in view of the fact that several families from Harmeling's church and the Summit Church contributed liberally to the building drive and had enrolled their children, and some fathers served on the school board.[51]

That Reformed Church pastors stood front and center at the cornerstone ceremony of the Christian school speaks volumes about the special nature of interchurch relations in Chicago between the two branches of the Dutch Reformed faith. In Holland, Michigan, and many other Dutch colonies, relations remained tense for generations. But in a big city like Chicago, where Reformed Christians were a small minority and challenged on every side, the sister churches had a greater incentive to cooperate. They did so to some degree in Christian elementary and secondary education (at least until the 1950s), and they cooperated fully at the college level and in operating rest homes for the elderly, in press and periodicals, in youth recreation programs, and in other endeavors.

The new Ebenezer school, which the community commonly called the "15th Street Christian School," stood three stories tall on the north side of 15th Street facing an A&P (Atlantic & Pacific) warehouse, one-half block west of Ashland Avenue. The school of two hundred students had eight classrooms but only four teachers, so four unused rooms provided space for expansion. Faculty members in 1906 were two males: Henry Jacobsma and H. Van Dellen, and two single females: Jenney Van Weesep and Katie Venema. There was no kindergarten, and the school year ran ten months and longer, to mid-July.

The constituency at the time was justly proud of the wooden building with a brick facade, but in truth it was a firetrap. It had no fire escapes

50. *Onze Toekomst,* 8 June 1906, cited in *Origins* 10, No. 2 (1992): 16.

51. Moerdyke, "Chicago Letter," *CI,* 9 Mar. 1904, p. 154.

until the city later required them in all schools. Adjoining the school on two sides were small fenced-in playgrounds for recess activities, one for boys and one for girls. "Barricade boys" also closed off 15th Street with wooden horses during the morning and afternoon recesses to allow for roller skating and softball games.

The curriculum was heavy on the basics and the classics, and it included nearly two hours per week of Bible study, an hour per week each for devotional time and singing lessons, and up to two hours per *week* of Dutch language instruction. The Dutch lessons pale in comparison to the nearly two hours per *day* devoted to English language study. Schoolwork was done on slates until 1915, when pen and ink became the vogue, with an inkwell in every desk. Oh, what opportunity for mischief that pot provided!

The schedule of study was clearly designed to prepare children for life both in the church and in the "world." Bible study, singing, and devotional exercises were integral parts of the religious life. Each student kept

Ebenezer Christian School, ca. 1910

Second grade class, Ebenezer Christian School, ca. 1916
standing: Henry Jacobsma, teacher; Henry Kuiper, principal

a Bible in the desk, to follow the daily oral devotions by the teacher. Dutch was essential, because pastors conducted church services and taught mid-week doctrine classes (catechism) in the mother tongue until the 1920s. But mastery of English was even more necessary because English was the language of public life and the world of work. Graduates also needed English to continue their education at the nearby Medill Public High School (14th Pl. and Throop St.), at least until they reached the age of sixteen, when school was no longer mandatory. Interestingly, geography took precedence over history in the curriculum (520 to 490 minutes per eight-week term), although both subjects covered the Netherlands as well as the United States. Indeed, a framed photograph of Dutch Queen Wilhelmina adorned a prominent inner wall.

Ebenezer and its sister Christian schools took immigrant children and, by ages sixteen to eighteen, turned them into educated young adults with sufficient skills in the arts and sciences for life-long learning. The educational programs in the churches were the "finishing schools," notably the catechism classes and the young men's and women's societies, and their adult counterparts (see chapter 8). There the young people wrote position papers for discussion, publicly debated issues in the church and society, and developed skills in public speaking and logical thinking. It was a remarkable achievement for the schools and churches to take immigrants' children and prepare them for leadership roles in the churches, in the business world, and in American society in general.

Student life in the 1910s was recalled by Henry Stob, an alumnus of Ebenezer and chronicler of life in the Groninger Hoek in the 1910s and 1920s:

> Of some teachers I have only the dimmest of recollection. I recall, however, that all of them were men. . . . I distinctly remember Mr. [Henry] Jacobsma, that lovable grey-bearded teacher, who was with the school from its beginning and who taught our second-grade class to read, write, and tell time. . . . I remember that we learned the letter z by viewing a picture of a sausage sizzling in a pan. All of us respected and admired Mr. Jacobsma. On Friday afternoons he taught us Dutch, thus supplementing the adventitious foreign-language requirement I received at church, catechism, and home. . . .
>
> Of course, I remember our principal, Mr. Henry Kuiper, for though I was normally a well-behaved scholar, I was occasionally sent to him for correction and nurture. This kindly man remedied my defects — and that of others — by smartly applying two rulers to the outstretched palms of any offender sent to him. . . . I don't recall any of my regular teachers resorting to it [corporal punishment]. They usually required us to stay after school or to write some apologetic sentence fifty or a hundred times. It may as well be recorded here that my parents always took the school's side in cases of this kind and endorsed the teacher's discipline by supplementing it with their own.[52]

In addition to formal schooling, all Dutch Reformed youngsters, as Stob noted, attended a weekly, after-school doctrine class, taught by the pastor, based on a compendium of the Heidelberg Catechism.[53]

Ebenezer was a neighborhood school, and the pupils walked back and forth twice a day; all went home during the one-hour lunch period except those living more than a mile away. Students were not allowed to ride bicycles to school — they might play "hooky" — but they could use roller skates. Traversing their neighborhood of Poles, Jews, Swedes, Germans, and Irish usually was safe, but the Dutch stood out because they walked past Clark Public School and thus were labeled "oddballs."

52. Stob, "Church and School on Chicago's West Side, 1913-1921, Part 2," *Origins* 11 No. 1 (1993): 25-26.

53. Stob, "Church and School, Part 1," 16, 18.

Henry Evenhouse, Jr., recalls: "We grew up with kids of all national backgrounds around us. Mostly we played with them but we were oddballs, because we were the only ones that went to the Christian school." When he was eight or nine years old, Henry remembers being delayed in leaving school and having to walk home alone a distance of about a mile. "Some Polish kids attacked me. They hit me in the mouth and my tooth was loose. When I got home, bleeding and crying, my brother Gerrit right away said: 'Let's go find those kids.'" Fortunately, the culprits had scattered. Evenhouse concluded: "There was a lot of cantankerousness between the Polish kids and the Dutch kids." This was a reference to the traditional animosity between Protestants and Catholics in Chicago at the time.[54]

By 1914 Ebenezer's enrollment was up to 330, and tuition rates were $2 per month, with the maximum of $3.75 for families with four or more pupils. Members of the First Christian Reformed Church carried the full financial burden of Ebenezer school after 1910, and the two-hundred-family congregation even covered tuition payments from its diaconal *suppletie* ("supplementary") fund for any member family unable to do so. Teachers sacrificed too, earning an average of only $20 a week in 1919.

By the 1920s, according to Stob: "People attending the nearby Dutch Reformed Church tended to regard the Christian school as separatistic and un-American, and almost all of them sent their children to the Clark Public School, located on Ashland Avenue near Hastings."[55] First Chicago also had to get along without its more affluent members, who had moved farther west to the daughter Douglas Park congregation, which had to support its own school.

Eight men served Ebenezer as principals for its fifty-three-year history, and two stand out for longevity and influence — Henry Kuiper (1907-23) and Albert Blystra (1927-46). Kuiper led the glory years of growth and Blystra the sad years of decline. Enrollment reached 433 in 1927, but ten years later it was only 292. Kuiper was a son of the Reverend Klaas Kuiper, who is considered the "pioneer school champion" of the Christian Reformed Church and was then serving the Second Roseland Christian Reformed Church (1896-1911). Henry Kuiper was the brother of professor R. B. Kuiper, also a product of Roseland Christian School, who taught at

54. Barbara Lee, interview with the Rev. Henry Evenhouse, 10 Aug. 1989, quoted in Lee, "Gold in the Family Treasury: Hendrik and Martje Evenhouse — A Family Portrait," typescript (Chicago, 1989), p. 9, courtesy of Edward Evenhouse.

55. Stob, "Church and School, Part 2," 25.

Henry Kuiper

Westminster Seminary (1933-52) and Calvin College and Seminary (1930-33, 1952-56).

Henry Kuiper commuted to Ebenezer from Roseland every day, professionalized the staff, and secured state accreditation in 1910. Ebenezer graduates were thereafter assured admission into any city public high school or business college without examination. Kuiper also helped spike a serious suggestion to dun John D. Rockefeller, president of Standard Oil Company, for a donation. More significantly, Kuiper and the Ebenezer School Society led the effort to create the "Alliance of Christian School Associations in Chicago and Vicinity." The Alliance designed a unified curriculum for the member schools that was approved by the superintendent of the Chicago Board of Education.[56]

During World War I, with patriotic feelings rising, the administration in 1915 thought it best to eliminate all instruction in the mother tongue, except for special studies. By then, a sense of "Dutchness" was losing its appeal among the second-generation Hollanders who felt the full force of Americanization. That this generation was prospering is clear from the successful drive in 1918 to pay off the entire school building debt.

However, in 1921, after the hyperpatriotism had subsided, a strong minority of the Ebenezer constituency pressured the school board to reinstate Dutch lessons. This was the Dutch version of President Warren Harding's "Return to Normalcy" campaign. But the school administra-

56. B. J. Bennink, "Our Christian Primary Schools," *Banner,* 2 Feb. 1911, 73.

tion turned aside all the ethnic entreaties. Both during and after the war, Dutch leaders in church and school, it seemed, were all too ready to sacrifice their language and cower before public pressure and official dicta. German and Polish Christian school leaders had more backbone; they resisted at the risk of stiff fines and won. In 1923 the United States Supreme Court set aside all convictions of elementary schools for violating English-only laws.[57]

The language dispute was greater than an ethnic fight; it was a struggle for the soul of the school. Would it be a Reformed Christian school or simply a Christian school? The administration and school board increasingly in the 1920s admitted children from non-Reformed homes. This policy could only succeed if the school's ethnoreligious heritage was de-emphasized. In 1925, almost one-third (14 of 47) of new students were of "American parents who have no connection with any Reformed church," lamented John Van Lonkhuyzen, the Dutch-born editor of Chicago's influential Dutch newspaper, *Onze Toekomst,* and pastor of the First Christian Reformed Church.[58] Many parents lamented with him.

The language question (or faith issue, depending on one's viewpoint) embroiled the Ebenezer school society and board throughout the 1920s and damaged the institution, just as it did the churches. School leaders held the line firmly on instruction in English, despite great pressure generated by Van Lonkhuyzen. "It is almost a crime against parents who need the Holland language to raise their children [in the Dutch Reformed faith], to take it away from them," he declared in righteous indignation. Principal Kuiper resigned in 1923 because of the strife, and Lambert Flokstra took over for three years.[59]

Flokstra shared the viewpoint of the school board, headed by the influential Americanizers James De Boer, Edward Groenboom, and George Ottenhoff. De Boer made an indelible impression on school policies as board president from 1907 until his death in 1924. Ottenhoff served as board secretary from 1910 to 1919, vice president from 1920 to 1924, and president from 1925 to 1942. Groenboom's twenty-year term as secretary (1920-40) was sandwiched between that of Ottenhoff. Interestingly, the school board minutes were written in Dutch until 1938!

When Andrew Blystra took over in 1927, the language battle had largely ceased, and enrollment reached its peak of 433, with ten teachers.

57. John Van Lonkhuyzen, "An Important Decision," *Onze Toekomst,* 20 June 1923.

58. Ibid., 9 Sept. 1925.

59. Ibid.; "1893 – Ebenezer School – 1943," *Banner,* 15 Oct. 1943.

James De Boer

George Ottenhoff

Edward Groenboom

Andrew Blystra

Noteworthy was the kindly Benjamin Stegink, the seventh-grade teacher who came from Grand Rapids as a recent widower, leaving his five children behind in foster homes. His face carried a deep sadness for all to see.

Stegink's personality stood in sharp contrast to that of Blystra, who is remembered by all as a "marine drill sergeant," and whose favorite methods of discipline for naughty boys included a crack across the open palm with a fifteen-inch ruler and a swat across the seat with a map pointer. Those who flinched received another blow for good measure. To the chagrin of the bad boys, Blystra "ruled" the school for two decades.[60]

Graduation exercises were so well attended that only the largest sanctuary, that of the First Christian Reformed Church, could accommodate the ceremony. But clouds were on the horizon. The prosperous twenties had hastened the process of affluent families moving farther west into the upscale suburbs. Then came the devastating economic failure of the 1930s, which hit the declining old neighborhood especially hard. Ebenezer again took on debt to operate, and raises for teachers became a fond memory. Instead, the staff was cut by one-third as enrollments fell steadily every year by the same proportion, reaching 292 by 1937.

In 1932 the school faced the same question as in 1895 – should it close the doors? This time, with the strong encouragement of Benjamin Essenburg, pastor of the First Christian Reformed Church of Chicago; principal Andrew Blystra; and school board president George Ottenhoff of Hinsdale, supporters again refused to give up. When the motion was put to a vote to open for the fall term of 1932, "Shall we open next Tuesday?" the vote was a resounding "yes." The next September, in the depths of the depression, Ebenezer began the school year on time, while the Chicago public schools had to delay their opening for two weeks due to lack of funds![61]

The Ebenezer alumni song of 1940, "Memories," captured the spirit of the school. The opening lines declared: "In mem'ry I see Ebenezer/ Though years of my life are between./ It remains with a sweet recollection,/ And well do I love it, I ween./ It stood near a cold, busy corner,/ But oh, our young hearts made it warm."[62]

With the backing of First Church and, after 1940, of the Ebenezer Alumni Association, the school carried on dutifully until 1946. Declining enrollments then forced Ebenezer to join forces with the Timothy Christian School Society in Cicero. The schools were an arm of the churches

60. John Bakker, video interview, 18 Nov. 1997, by Martin Stulp. Blystra had previously served as principal of Roseland's 104th Street Christian School.

61. B. Essenburg, "Chicago, Englewood, and Cicero Churches," *Banner,* 21 Oct. 1932; 20 Oct. 1933.

62. Ebenezer Alumni Souvenir Program, First Christian Reformed Church, 15 May 1940.

and simply followed them ever westward, although the move left some families stranded in the old neighborhood. Elementary students had to ride the Roosevelt Road streetcars, although one of Timothy's school buses did serve families in the Lawndale area for the next decade, until 1956.[63]

Timothy Christian School – Tripp Avenue (1911-27)

Timothy began as a vision of several members of the Douglas Park Christian Reformed Church, led by C. F. Speckman, superintendent of the Sunday school. In a meeting at Speckman's home in April 1907, the group formed a Society for Christian Instruction and began promoting the cause among the church members.[64]

With the strong encouragement of the consistory and pastor Cornelius De Leeuw, the society doubled in two years from its initial twenty-five members. The first board members were president Abel Bulthuis, vice president George Slager, secretary Nicholas Knol, and treasurer Nick Noorlag. In 1908 the board, now headed by Slager, chose the name Timothy for the school, in honor of the New Testament evangelist who had been raised in a Christian home by a devout mother and grandmother and became the apostle Paul's spiritual son.

By August 1911, after four years of promotion, the society had sufficient members (more than seventy-five) and funds to begin the school. Classes began in a well-lighted, second-floor hall above retail stores one block south of the church on Twelfth Street (Roosevelt Road) near Harding Avenue. George Deur was hired as teacher of the thirty-four charter students.[65]

The next year the board purchased for $1,500 a double lot on the northeast corner of 13th Street and 42nd Court (Tripp Avenue), one-half mile directly west of the church, and made plans to build (figure 5.1, site C).[66] These men were pushers and promoters. The cornerstone was laid in

63. "History of the Timothy Christian School Society," in Timothy Christian School, *Twenty-five Years, 1911-1936* (Chicago, 1936).

64. Ibid.

65. "Chicago Jottings by the Way," *Banner,* 22 May 1913; Timothy Christian School, *50th Anniversary, 1911-1961,* np.

66. The site purchase committee was C. F. Speckman, Nicholas Youngsma, and Fred Brands. The building committee consisted of George Slager, Klaas Wezeman, Nicholas Youngsma, Henry Bulthuis, John Van Slooten, and Peter Stehouwer.

July 1912, and the two-room brick building was dedicated in early October. The $6,500 for the building came from the sale of unsecured promissory notes to supporters, plus a bank loan of $3,500 secured by the land. Timothy's two teachers, Deur and Nicholas Hendrikse, had sixty students, each covering four grades, and the supporting society had one hundred members. The first graduating class in 1914 boasted only two students, but it was a proud moment nonetheless.

In 1916 Timothy won full accreditation by the Chicago Board of Education. That year the school added a room in the basement, and the staff grew to three teachers, including Hendrikse, the new principal, who was paid an annual salary of $780. Tuition was increased from $1.50 to $2 per month, rising to a maximum of $4.50 for families with five children or more enrolled. Timothy did not cap the tuition for families with three or more children as generously as did the Ebenezer school board. Some families transferred their children to the public school, out of either necessity or lack of conviction. Enrollment in the years 1917-20 held steady around a hundred, and then it increased sharply by 50 percent in five years, reaching 153 by 1925.

Of Timothy's many principals, three had a major impact: Nicholas ("Nick") Hendrikse (1916-26), Richard ("Dick") Tolsma (1941-68), and Arnold ("Arnie") Hoving (1969-94). Hendrikse brought the infant plant on Tripp Street to maturity. Tolsma led the second incarnation of the elementary school in Cicero to its climax. Hoving raised Timothy in Elmhurst to a top-ranked institution in the state, first as principal of the

Timothy Christian School, Tripp Ave., erected 1911

Nicholas Hendrikse,
teacher and principal 1912-26,
Timothy Christian School

A. S. De Jong, principal 1912-17,
Englewood Christian School;
principal, 1926-38, 104th St.
Christian School

high school (1969-86) and then as superintendent of the four-school system (1986-94).

Hendrikse, a native of Oostburg, Wisconsin, won accreditation for Timothy, raised tuition to put the school on a sound financial footing, saw a second floor added to the building in 1918 for $5,500, and in 1920 had Timothy affiliate with the newly founded National Union of Christian Schools, based in Chicago. Hendrikse worked with other Reformed school administrators, particularly Henry Kuiper of Ebenezer Christian and A. S. De Jong of Englewood Christian, to establish the Chicago Christian High School in 1918 as the capstone of Christian education in greater Chicago. In 1920 he instituted a budget system and expanded the library to include books of Reformed writers. In 1923 thirty-five women from the churches banded together in a booster club, the Eunice Society, to raise funds for Timothy. That society continues to the present day.

Hendrikse ably taught grades seven and eight and had a well-deserved reputation as a stern disciplinarian, keeping the street-wise and often unruly teenage boys in check. Under his leadership the school grew from around 100 to 155 pupils under four teachers. Six pupils, it was reported, came from four families "outside our church circle." These "outsiders," in Christian Reformed parlance, referred to non-Reformed families. The Timothy board from the outset opened its school doors to such families. Symbolically, the board also decided in 1926 to write its minutes in English rather than in Dutch. That year a successful financial drive brought the school to the brink of being debt free. It was just in time, given the 1929 financial crash.

Englewood Christian School (1900-53)

In the 1870s-90s many Hollanders in the Groninger Hoek moved south to Englewood instead of west to Douglas Park and Lawndale. Englewood was a new working-class suburb south of the stockyards and yet within commuting distance to the city center. It was annexed to Chicago in 1889.[67]

In 1899 the consistory of the First Englewood Christian Reformed Church took the initiative, with the cooperation of the First Englewood Reformed Church, to form a school society for "Holland Christian instruction" during the summer vacation in the public schools. The Christian Reformed church conducted classes the first summer, in 1900, but in October it passed the torch to an independent school society. Lambert Bere spearheaded the effort and served as president of the board for the first twelve years. Tuition was set in 1901 on a sliding scale: one child, 50 cents per month; two children, 90 cents; three children, $1.20 per month. More than three went free. And the board gave teachers the choice of keeping whatever monies the pupils bring in, or a fixed salary of $8 per week; they doubtless chose the latter. The school had no formal name until 1920, when the board officially adopted the name "Englewood Christian School."[68]

In 1903 the society built a new four-room, two-story building on a double lot at 7146 S. Sangamon Street for a cost of $5,200 and converted from summer only to a full elementary program for "Civil and Biblical" education (Figure 5.2, site A). Classes in the new school began in January, 1904, with two teachers, including principal Albert Cleveringa (1904-07), who had taught at Ebenezer since 1902. In 1907 Cleveringa left Chicago to

67. This section relies on the summary of school board minutes in Englewood Christian School, *Fiftieth Anniversary*.

68. Ibid., 16; Southwest Christian Schools Association, *Family Album: Celebrating A Century of Christian Education [1900-2000]* (Palos Heights, 2001), 2-4, 8.

Lambert Bere

Albert Cleveringa

become the first principal of the Munster (Indiana) Christian School. Interestingly, Cleveringa's first graduate at the school and the only student in the 1910 class, was Cornelius Van Til, who became the famed professor of apologetics at Westminster Seminary in Philadelphia.[69]

Within two years, all four classrooms at Englewood Christian were in use. Instruction was given in both Dutch and English, with Dutch emphasized in the early grades and then tapering off after the students had mastered enough of the mother tongue to understand church services and catechism lessons. In 1919, under principal H. J. Bruinsma, the school cut Dutch instruction to one day per week in the first grade, and in 1928 Dutch was dropped entirely. It was no longer needed. A large portrait of Queen Wilhelmina, the mother of the old country, adorned the wall of a classroom opposite one of George Washington, the father of the adopted country. In 1909 the Chicago Board of Education accredited Englewood Christian School. To prepare for this outside evaluation, the school board in 1908 ordered the pupils to undergo a general examination. The board would decide who passed. Classes ran to mid-July until 1928, when the board set summer vacation to begin at the end of June.

69. *Golden Anniversary, 1907-1957* (Lansing, Ill., 1957), 6, 18. Cleveringa in 1916 became a science professor at Grundy College and taught there for many years.

Recess time, Englewood Christian School, ca. 1910 *(The Archives, Calvin College)*

Accreditation helped Englewood Christian compete academically with the D. S. Wentworth Public School three blocks away, but it did not remove the stigma of being the Dutch immigrant school. Kids on the way to Wentworth school derisively called it the "Dutch Prison," because a high iron fence ran along the entire front of the building. The Dutch youngsters would reply: "It's better than D. S. Wentworth, the Dog Dirt Wagon," or some equally offensive retort.[70] There was no love lost between Dutch Reformed and public school students in the various neighborhoods, and softball games between the two amounted to war.

To provide space for the thriving school, a second floor was completed in 1910. Other major building additions followed, in 1923, 1925, 1943, and 1950. Tuition increased from $2 per month in 1915 to $5.50 in 1929. Enrollment surpassed three hundred in 1918 and remained in this range through the hard times. The crushing building indebtedness of $65,000 and shortfall in tuition payments forced the board to cut teachers' salaries by 35 percent from 1931 to 1934. And even then teachers had to accept I.O.U.s from the board. After 1936 times improved enough to give a little back gradually, but it was 1942 before salaries climbed back to the 1930 level and teachers received their full contracted amount. The Englewood

70. Quotes in Harold Hiskes, *In Memoriam* (privately printed, 1996), 11; Grace Stob Ozinga's memories in *Family Album,* 7. Hiskes cleaned up the language (Dog S--t).

Klaas Hoeksema

staff still fared better than Roseland teachers, who suffered a 45 percent salary cut in 1933. Roseland was hit harder than any other community in greater Chicago by the Depression. Its three banks all failed, wiping out the savings of thousands.[71]

As early as 1910, the Englewood board went on record as favoring a Christian Normal School (high school) in Chicago. And in 1924 the board considered adding a junior high school, in keeping with the latest thinking among educators, but it was 1950 before it did so. The founding of Chicago Christian High School in 1918 largely obviated the need.

The principal who most shaped the school was Klaas Hoeksema. He led Englewood Christian for twenty-five years (1922-46), through the building expansions of the twenties, the financial crises of the 1930s, and the glory years of the 1940s, with record enrollments and more building additions. Hoeksema was a superb administrator who concentrated his time and energy on the essentials — assembling a skilled staff, raising academic standards, and maintaining excellent discipline. His exceptional ability blended with a humble spirit, and his favorite discipline was to have misbehaving students write "tables," rather than "lines." According to student Gerry De Horn, however, Hoeksema was also known to break rulers on the "butts of bad boys." Hoeksema's sidekick was the faithful janitor, Guys "Opa" Bulthuis, whose supply room was next door to the principal's office; Bulthuis was the students' friend for decades. Another

71. Roseland Christian School, *Centennial,* 24; J. R. Brink, "Roseland and the South," *Banner,* 18 Jan. 1935.

5th-6th-grade field trip, Evergreen Park Christian School, 1936, teacher Gertrude Vander Ark (standing), Richard (Dirk) Sluis in cab

favorite haunt was Bulthuis's store next door to the school, where students bought candy with pennies and nickels that went a long way.[72]

Early in Hoeksema's tenure, Englewood Christian could boast to its supporters that its students at Chicago Christian High School, together with those of Ebenezer Christian, earned the highest average grades – a score of 85 plus. This despite the fact that classroom size at Englewood ranged up to forty-five pupils. The teachers were pushed to the limit with paperwork and classroom control. The hallmark of the school, however, was not academics but the fourth-grade field trip to the Chicago Stockyards, where the smells and shock of the killing floor left indelible memories, not always for the better. Girls fainted at the blood and gore, and boys felt nauseated. Some could not eat the hot dog given out at the end of the tour. Maybe that is why the great fire at the Stockyards in 1934 was so unforgettable. Older students took their field trip to the Museum of Science and Industry to tour the coal mine by electric tram, which also had its dark and scary moments. The trip there and back might be equally exciting, especially when students rode on the open bed of a truck, as did the fifth and sixth graders of the Evergreen Park Christian School in 1936. Their teacher, Gertrude Vander Ark, joined them to ensure that no one fell off.[73]

72. *Family Album,* 7, 12.

73. Peter Bulthuis, *Footprints: An Autobiography* (privately printed, 1998), 39-40, gives a

Englewood Christian School, 1950

The school reached out beyond the traditional constituency. In 1907 Cleveringa admitted several children from German Protestant families in the area. In 1935 Dutch families in the Archer Avenue (Summit) area, mostly truck farmers, organized a Christian school society as a branch of Englewood Christian, and their children commuted by bus to Englewood. In 1936 Hoeksema created special classes in reading and arithmetic for "backward" children. This bold step led eventually in 1948 to the organization of Elim Christian School for children with special needs, which today serves the entire Chicago area at its Palos Heights facilities (chapter 9). In 1944 the Englewood school accepted "community children" from Christian homes, but at a 40 percent higher tuition rate.

With the major building expansion and addition of the ninth grade in 1950, Englewood Christian's enrollment surpassed five hundred. The operating budget exceeded $60,000, mostly in salaries for the teaching staff of fifteen, who labored under a heavy student/teacher ratio of 33/1. The fiftieth anniversary celebration that year honored the 7 principals, 83 teachers, and 126 board members who had led the school, and the several thousand alumni. The supporters sang two verses of the same Holland Psalm 25 as at

---

vivid description of one such class trip; Martha Wierenga Regnerus's memories in *Family Album* 26.

the organizational meeting in 1900 and with equal fervor. The school always enjoyed strong support from the three churches of Englewood (First and Second Christian Reformed and First Reformed), and from the Auburn Park and Archer Avenue Christian Reformed churches.[74]

The 1950 celebration was the last hurrah for Englewood Christian School. Most supporting families moved out of the community in the 1950s, fleeing before the advancing South Side black ghetto. The school was eventually sold to the city board of education. In the 1960s the same fate befell Roseland Christian School, although the board in 1967 decided to continue the school for "Christians of other persuasions," meaning black Christian parents.[75]

The most illustrious graduate of Englewood Christian School was the novelist Peter De Vries (1910-93), class of 1923. De Vries, the son of Dutch immigrants, grew up in the tight-knit Calvinist community in Englewood, attended the local Christian elementary and high school (see below), and then went to Calvin College in Grand Rapids, Michigan, the denominational school. All tried to imbue De Vries with the "faith of the fathers," but he rebelled and went off to New York to work in journalism and radio. This led to a position as associate editor of *Poetry* magazine in 1939 and finally to the *New Yorker,* where he developed his biting, ironic humor. Most of his satirical novels and magazine articles centered on the foibles of suburban life, but in his autobiographical novel, *The Blood of the Lamb* (Boston: Little, Brown, 1961), the protagonist deals with the tragic death of an only child without the ancestral faith to sustain him. In sharp contrast to Peter, his sister Ann ably taught the sixth grade at Englewood Christian school for many years.

Chicago Christian High School (1918-)

The initial impetus for establishing a Christian high school came from the educational leaders of the elementary schools, rather than from parents who saw little need for a high school diploma. A conversation by a Hollander heard on the street captured the point: "I ain't done no readin' since I was tooken out of the sevent' grade and set to work."[76]

In 1910 the Ebenezer and Englewood boards contacted the Chicago

74. Englewood Christian School, *Fiftieth Anniversary,* 34; *Family Album,* 14.

75. Roseland Christian School, *Centennial,* 37.

76. Quoted in S. C. Ribbler editorial, *Onze Toekomst,* 8 Dec. 1926.

Alliance of Christian Schools, a consortium of elementary schools, about the need for a Christian "Normal" school to train teachers, and they pledged to work with others toward that goal and established a fund to nurture it. Roseland's board concurred in 1911, but Timothy took no part: it was just underway and had to focus on its own survival. Little happened for three years, until 1914, when James De Boer, president of the Ebenezer board, and Englewood principal A. S. De Jong again asked the Alliance to take action. Fortunately, the Alliance was becoming more active, and it endorsed a plan for a full-fledged high school. The main purpose of the alliance was to design Reformed curricula and to raise standards to gain accreditation. In 1920 it also spawned the National Union of Christian Schools, now Christian Schools International.[77]

As a result of these renewed efforts, more than two hundred interested people gathered in 1915 and organized the Chicago Christian High School Association. It was the first parent-owned school of its kind in Reformed circles nationwide. And Reformed church ministers and members joined with Christian Reformed people in the effort. The Reformed church had a history of founding Christian academies and colleges in Michigan, Iowa, and Wisconsin.

Starting a city-wide high school in Chicago was problematic because, unlike the elementary schools, it had no single mother church to nurture it. A school owned by everyone was owned by no one. And the Dutch churches of Chicago had little experience in undertaking joint projects. Moreover, many blue-collar immigrant parents saw no need for "higher" education. De Boer and his friend Conrad Ottenhoff spent many a night discussing plans and going door to door asking people to join them. De Boer's daughter Bess recalls, "They got no response from the Hollanders on the Old West Side. They said their sons would have to work, and their daughters would have to stay home and help their mothers."[78]

When the early responses were weak, De Boer, a successful businessman and leading churchman, organized a building drive to canvass all the supporting communities, and by year's end $100,000 was pledged. De Boer's initiative and leadership in the early years earned him the accolade, "father of the school"; wags called him "high school Jim" (as in gym). His untimely death in 1924 meant the loss of a giant in the Christian school

77. Ibid., 22 July, 19 Aug. 1910; "Chicago Christian High School for Chicago," *Banner,* 30 Mar. 1916; Van Brummelen, *Telling the Next Generation,* 106, 118, 149-50; Peter De Boer, "To Train a Teacher," *Origins* 8, No. 2 (1990): 39.

78. Bess De Boer Figel, *Once Upon A Time*... (Chicago, n.d.), 15. I am indebted to Richard Schuurman, Figel's nephew, for lending me this colorful family history.

movement of Chicago. George Ottenhoff and Henry Kuiper were De Boer's main supporters.[79]

Chicago Christian High School (CCHS) was centrally located in Englewood in order to serve its four constituencies – Englewood, the West Side, the South Side (Roseland and South Holland-Lansing-Munster), and the Southwest Side (Summit-Evergreen Park-Oak Lawn). Classes began in 1918 with two teachers, including the principal Mark Fakkema, and thirteen students. They met in a large frame home converted by the Bethel Mission at 72nd Place and Loomis Street. School decorum was proper and very formal. Female students wore middy blouses with black bloomers and black stockings and the men wore dress shirts, ties, and jackets.

The student body doubled and tripled in size in a year and more space was needed. The building fund was not enough to put up a school, but it did allow the board as an interim measure to buy an old two-story building at 69th and May Streets, which served for the next seven years. The building was a former dance hall and lodge. The gym was in a garage next door, and Henry Swets was the gym teacher.

Students came by streetcar for a fare of 7 cents each way in the early days, recalled Johanna Gelderloos LaMaire and the twins, Cornelia and Henry Evenhouse, Jr. Each Monday the Evenhouse youngsters each received $1 from their parents for the weekly fare of 70 cents (7 cents per ride); they could keep the 30 cents that was left for spending money. The trip from the Old West Side took one hour each way and required some pupils to ride three cars and two transfers (Roosevelt Road to Western Avenue or Ashland, south to 63rd or 69th Street, and then east to Racine Avenue). Many young men chose to hitchhike to save time and money. Ben Heslinga recalls hitchhiking along Ashland Avenue to Englewood every day for three years; this required considerable walking on both ends of the trip. Henry Stob's parents and a few other westsiders actually moved to Englewood to be near the school. His were among the few parents who saw the value of a high school diploma in the 1920s. It was the equivalent of a college degree today and opened the doors to social and economic advancement and produced many prominent community leaders.[80]

Mark Fakkema led the school as principal for the first eight years

79. Groenboom, "Historical Sketch of the Ebenezer Christian School," *Onze Toekomst,* 22 Feb. 1932; 10 Mar. 1926.

80. H. J. Brinks, "Johanna (Gelderloos) LaMaire: Notes from and about the Past," *Origins* 11, No. 1 (1993): 30-31; Barb Lee, "Gold in the Family Treasury"; Ben and Martha Heslinga, video interview, 19 Feb 1998, by Martin Stulp.

Mark Fakkema

John J. De Boer
CCHS *Violet and Maize 1927*

(1918-26) and secured its academic standing. From the outset, school policy was to admit students who sought Christian education, regardless of their background. "It was felt that God was giving us an opportunity to let our light shine" was the thinking. As a result, a rising proportion of the student body over the years were from non-Reformed homes. The faculty was equally divided between graduates of Calvin and Hope colleges (Hope was a Reformed Church college), and almost all the Chicago students at these institutions were CCHS alumni.

Fakkema and the faculty, which included Henry Swets, Jacob Sietsema, Adriana Hammekool, G. Harry Mouw, and John J. De Boer, thought it necessary to supplement the academic curriculum in order to promote the development of "wholesome Christian character." They organized debate and oratory contests and sporting and musical activities. The music tradition was especially strong at CCHS. The a capella choir was formed in 1923 and James Baar raised it to a higher level when he took over in 1927. His son Robert and grandson David later continued his tradition of outstanding choral performances. Basketball was the premier interscholastic sport under Fred ("Fritz") Ploegman (1945-52) and his successor Wilbur ("Slug") Slager (1952-90). Slager's thirty-eight years set a record for longevity, and his 1965 team was the only undefeated club in the state of Illinois.

James Baar
CCHS *Violet and Maize 1927*

In 1925 a second building campaign raised $190,000 by the sale of bonds to construct a high school building at 71st and May streets. The bond were floated even though the initial building pledge fund had a $50,000 deficit. The bonds carried an above-market interest rate of 6 percent and promised a "well insured and safe investment," with "good lawful security" and, more important, "a righteous security from the entire Society for Christian High School Education."[81]

Construction began in early 1926, and the school, a "solid, practical building" that cost nearly a quarter of a million dollars, was dedicated in 1927, following a motorcade from the First Christian Reformed Church a mile away. The cornerstone on one side carried the words: "For God, Country, and Humanity," and on the other the pithy text from Proverbs 2:6, "The Lord Giveth Wisdom." These phrases captured the threefold school purpose: to bring all learning under the Lordship of Christ to bring "the joyous and whole-hearted dedication of our youth to His service," and to "promote wholesome, Christian character" and "trustworthy citizenship." So declared the CCHS principal in a radio address on Chicago's Mutual Broadcasting Station WGN in 1942. During the war, fifty school alumni served in the armed forces.[82]

Chicago banks had recruited graduates heavily for years. First Na-

81. *Onze Toekomst,* 2 Mar. 1927.

82. Ibid., Mar. 1927; "Radio Talk by Frederick H. Wezeman, principal of Chicago Christian High School," *Citizens of Tomorrow,* 30 May 1942; clipping from *Chicago Sunday Tribune,* 31 May 1942.

Student body, 1933, Chicago Christian High School
(Courtesy of Jane Wezeman Smith)

tional and its arch rival Continental Illinois, located on "bankers' row" on La Salle Street, were "virtually a Chicago Christian High School alumni chapter," recalled Richard Tiemersma of Roseland, who was an office boy in the mid-thirties at First National. Character and connections counted.[83]

With the opening of the new building, CCHS had eight teachers, two hundred students, and a new administrator, Dr. Frederick H. Wezeman (1927-51). As an administrator, he brought Chicago Christian High School to the pinnacle of success. And as a gifted pulpiteer, he preached effectively in Christian Reformed churches throughout Chicago and its environs. Students and faculty loved Wezeman for his irenic spirit, warm-hearted faith, and clear, Calvinistic worldview. One-quarter of the students came from the Old West Side and Cicero, which was proportionate to their share of the city's Dutch population. In 1931, only six years after the dedication of the new building, it was filled to capacity with three hundred students, and the student census continued to rise. "How wonderfully God has blessed our movement," Wezeman declared in amazement.[84]

Wezeman was a brilliant scholar and a man of exceptional influence in the Dutch Reformed community as educator, school administrator,

83. Tiemersma, "Growing Up in Roseland in the 20s & 30s," 10.

84. *Onze Toekomst,* 14 Sept. 1927, 11 Feb. 1931; annual enrollment statistics, 1927-1935, in Principal's Report, 12 Feb. 1937, Wezeman Papers.

Frederick H. Wezeman
CCHS *Violet and Maize 1927*

cleric, and editor. He had come to Chicago from Groningen in 1894 as a baby in the arms of his widowed mother, Aafke Dam, who decided in extreme poverty to take her remaining five children to the land of opportunity. The oldest son Klaas had emigrated a year earlier. The family joined the First Christian Reformed Church of Chicago and the youngest children, including Fred, attended Ebenezer School.[85]

Gifted with an encyclopedic mind and broad interests, Fred Wezeman studied science, then law, next theology, and finally educational administration. He first earned a Bachelor of Science degree from the Lewis Institute (Illinois Institute of Technology). Then in 1913 he graduated from John Marshall Law School with an LL.B. degree and began a budding law practice in Chicago as a member of the Illinois Bar and the Chicago Bar Association. Not content with law, he pursued a Bachelor of Divinity degree from the University of Chicago and then completed his studies at Calvin College and Seminary, earning his ministerial degree in 1921.[86] Finally, in 1926, he was awarded the degree of Juris Doctor from John Marshall Law School.

85. Robert P. Swierenga, compiler, "Groningen Emigrants, 1881-1901"; Henry Wezeman, Sr., "Glimpses of the Past: Recollections, Experiences, and Anecdotes, Nunica, Michigan, August 1949." The booklet was provided to the author by Maureen Cole, a descendant.

86. Wezeman was the first student to graduate with a bachelor of divinity degree from Calvin Theological Seminary *after* earning a B.D. from another seminary. This step was necessary because his denomination, the Christian Reformed Church, required at least one year of study at Calvin Seminary for anyone desiring ordination in the denomination.

Meanwhile, in 1921, Wezeman accepted an appointment to teach history and English at Grundy College, a two-year institution of the German wing of the Christian Reformed Church, located in Grundy Center, Iowa, since its founding in 1916.[87] After four years on the faculty, the College Church in 1925 called and ordained him as its pastor under the jurisdiction of Classis Ostfriesland, which classis held his ministerial credentials.[88]

In 1927 Wezeman returned to his hometown of Chicago as principal and teacher of Bible at CCHS, the school spearheaded by his brother-in-law, James De Boer. His ministerial credentials remained in the Grundy Center church, which later became a touchy issue. "Doc" Wezeman (as he was always known in Chicago) exuded self-confidence and a suave sophistication that belied his roots in the Groninger Hoek and First Chicago Christian Reformed Church. But these early ties doubtless drew him to this position, for which he was clearly overqualified.[89]

Wezeman's twenty-four years at CCHS were crucial in bringing the school to academic maturity. Under his able leadership, the school received the coveted accreditation from the North Central Association in 1931 and eventually took its place among Chicago's elite private high schools. First, however, it had to outlast the Depression and the loss of support by its church constituency due to a bitter theological controversy involving Wezeman's Bible courses. These forces, one external and one internal, forced the school in 1936 to default on its building bonds.

Fortunately, the bondholders who had not received interest payments since 1930 were all church members. Several filed suit, but in the end none would foreclose, and the board was able to refinance the debt by issuing new bonds at 50 cents on the dollar. J. Ettema forced the matter; he hired a lawyer to demand payment of his $1,000 bond plus $90 in back interest. Attorney John Ligtenberg, a member of the school board, suc-

87. Grundy College *Messenger*, Tenth Anniversary Edition, 1 June 1926, 11. I am indebted to Wezeman's daughter Jane Smith and son Frederick for important historical documents regarding their father, all of which have since been donated to the Archives, Calvin College, where they comprise the Frederick H. Wezeman Papers.

88. Christian Reformed Church, *Yearbook*, 1936, 50; R. L. Haan et al., "Report of the Committee on the Status of the Rev. F. H. Wezeman," Christian Reformed Church, *Agenda of Synod*, 1934, 1: 52-54.

89. Gerald F. De Jong, *From Strength to Strength: A History of Northwestern, 1882-1982* (Grand Rapids: Eerdmans, 1982), 123-24; Art Haverhals, "Caught in the Web," senior history seminar paper, Calvin College (1963), 3. James De Boer was married to Frederick Wezeman's sister Marie.

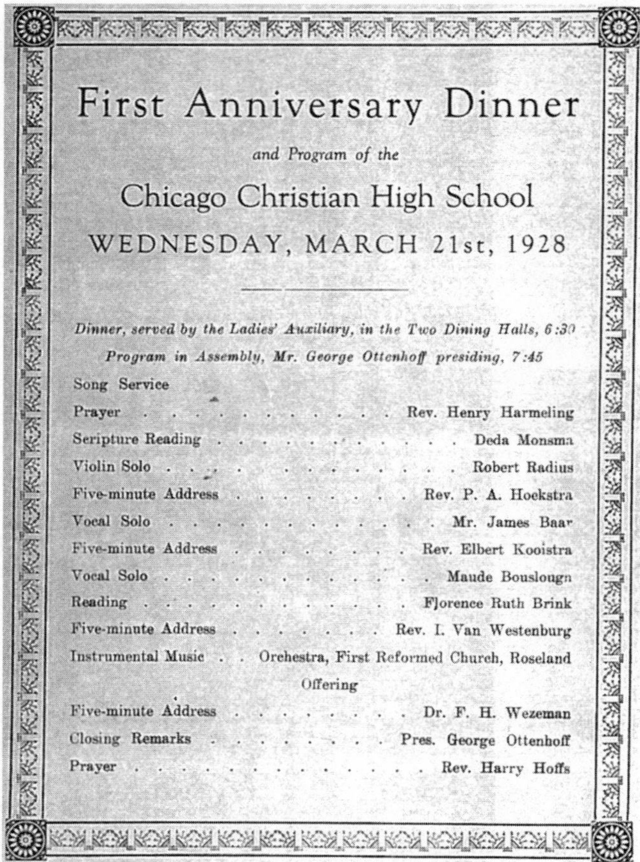

First Anniversary Dinner

and Program of the

Chicago Christian High School

WEDNESDAY, MARCH 21st, 1928

Dinner, served by the Ladies' Auxiliary, in the Two Dining Halls, 6:30

Program in Assembly, Mr. George Ottenhoff presiding, 7:45

Song Service

Prayer	Rev. Henry Harmeling
Scripture Reading	Deda Monsma
Violin Solo	Robert Radius
Five-minute Address	Rev. P. A. Hoekstra
Vocal Solo	Mr. James Baar
Five-minute Address	Rev. Elbert Kooistra
Vocal Solo	Maude Bouslougn
Reading	Florence Ruth Brink
Five-minute Address	Rev. I. Van Westenburg
Instrumental Music	Orchestra, First Reformed Church, Roseland
Offering	
Five-minute Address	Dr. F. H. Wezeman
Closing Remarks	Pres. George Ottenhoff
Prayer	Rev. Harry Hoffs

First Anniversary Dinner program, 1928 *(Chicago Christian High School)*

cessfully negotiated a settlement of Ettema's claim for half the face value. This prompted others to accept the same terms. "Fear God and do our part," urged the editor of *Onze Toekomst.*[90]

Married teachers with families, like science teacher Harry Mouw, a Hope College graduate with a master's degree from Haverford College, went unpaid for months and had to accept I.O.U.s or scrip that the board issued. He and others had to seek employment elsewhere or leave the pro-

90. "Proceedings in 77-B," Chicago Christian High School Board of Trustees, *Illuminator* [March 1936]; *Chicago Messenger,* 27 Mar. 1936; "Chicago Christian High School Saved for Now," *Onze Toekomst,* 24 Feb. 1931; "Chicago Christian High School Meeting," ibid., 22 Feb. 1932; Ken Achterhof, "A Case Study of the Bankruptcy of Chicago Christian High School in 1937," senior history seminar paper, Calvin College (1996).

G. Harry Mouw
CCHS *Violet and Maize 1927*

fession. After ten years at CCHS, Mouw in 1935 found a position in a Chicago public high school. His departure was a major loss. The next year the board could pay the teachers only 60 percent of their salaries.[91]

In 1935 the association was still in default on $148,490 in bonds and unsecured debt. To ward off expensive lawsuits, the board decided to file for bankruptcy and place the school under the protection of the federal court of Chicago, following a new law that allowed for reorganization instead of a full liquidation. When in 1936 the board presented to the bankruptcy judge its proposal to issue new bonds at 50 cents on the dollar, he called the plan "outrageous" and would accept it only if at least two-thirds of the creditors would agree. The board gave bondholders the cruel choice to accept the plan or close the school and liquidate its assets at a salvage value of $63,000 (this amounted to 42 cents on the dollar). The board succeeded only after some "friends of the high school" agreed to buy the bonds of those who objected to the plan. Doubtless, the friends included the De Boers and Ottenhoffs. In this way the board obtained the consent of a bare minimum of 67 percent of the bondholders. Thus did the school survive its greatest financial crisis ever. But it shamefully refused to repay the defaulted money in later years when the good times returned.[92]

Wezeman was a master promoter, and he did his part by valiantly trying to boost enrollment. In 1930 he helped launch a bus system to col-

91. *Chicago Messenger,* 14 June 1935; Herman Bel, "Lest We Forget," *Banner,* 11 Aug. 1936. A female teacher, Nell Bosma, who taught physiology and Bible, also left CCHS in 1936; she took a position at Wright Junior College (ibid., 28 Feb. 1936).

92. Achterhof, "Bankruptcy of Chicago Christian High School."

Archer Avenue school bus

lect students from the far reaches of the city. Parents in Roseland; Cicero, Berwyn, and Oak Park; Summit; and the far south – South Holland, Lansing, and even Munster and Highland, Indiana – organized "bus societies" to transport students to Englewood on a fleet of school buses. Bus transportation, although costly, relieved families of "many worries and the scholars from many temptations and dangers," noted the Reverend Benjamin Essenburg approvingly. No longer did they have to hitchhike, ride the streetcars, or use private cars. No school bus served students in the Ashland Avenue area, Evergreen Park, and Oak Lawn; they had to find their own way. Teachers who drove the buses needed nerves of steel and unlimited patience to put up with the endless ditties like "How Many Bottles of Beer on the Wall?"[93]

Wezeman also promoted the school in the print media. In an advertisement in the national church weekly, the *Banner*, he declared that "no parent, church, or Reformed community can afford to have any one of our youth of high school age forego the inestimable benefit of a Christian educational training." Just such a place was Chicago Christian High School, which offered "a faculty of highly qualified, consecrated men and women, a wide variety of approved courses and subjects, a strong Reformed program of moral, social and spiritual guidance, a select student constituency, [and] an ennobling system of Christian discipline."[94]

Carefully crafted statements like this touched all the right emo-

93. B. Essenburg, "News from the Chicago, Cicero and Englewood Churches," *Banner*, 11 July 1930; Essenburg, "Chicago and Vicinity," ibid. 19 Sept. 1930; "Progress of our High School," *Onze Toekomst*, 11 Feb. 1931; Brenda Prince Venhuizen's memories in *Family Album*, 57.

94. "Chicago Christian High School," *Banner*, 1 Sept. 1933.

tional chords and proved effective in slowly increasing the student body. In Fakkema's last years, only one-fourth of Dutch Reformed youth attending high school enrolled at Chicago Christian High. Wezeman raised this proportion and more than doubled the student body in his first three years. In 1931 the school was at capacity with 305 students and 14 teachers. By 1945 enrollment reached 800.

Three-quarters of the students attended one of the thirty Christian Reformed and Reformed churches in greater Chicago. The other one-quarter came from other Protestant denominations, mainly the Swedish Covenant (Evangelical Covenant Church of America, a Chicago-based Free Church denomination founded in 1885). A considerable minority of the CCHS teachers likewise did not hold membership in Reformed churches. This remarkable ecumenicity stemmed from a desire by the board and faculty from the outset to provide a quality education to all who valued a Christian perspective in academics. Economic considerations were also a factor in the openness. The school facilities needed to be utilized fully, and there were not enough Christian Reformed youth to do so.

The diversity was a constant irritant for some constituents who wished to maintain the Reformed "distinctiveness" of the school and who

Chapel service, 1933, Chicago Christian High School

(Courtesy of Jane Wezeman Smith)

feared for the spiritual well-being of the covenant youth. Nevertheless, the faculty and board upheld the policy for decades, until 1945. Then the postwar enrollment crush, with 800 students in a facility designed to hold 350, forced the board to limit student "outsiders" to those of sincere evangelical or fundamentalist convictions, as determined by personal interviews. Many hundreds of applicants were turned away. Some supporters wanted to ban all 236 non-Reformed students, but this step was rejected. The board also pushed to increase the ratio of faculty of Reformed persuasion. These moves improved the school image with its core constituency.[95]

Chicago Christian College (1931-37)

Wezeman in 1931 established the Chicago Christian Junior College as the capstone of Reformed education in Chicago. He first assembled a conference of representative Reformed and Christian Reformed leaders who were interested in higher education. This group quickly found sufficient interest and formed an advisory committee to launch the college. Classes began in 1932 and met in the high school building in both afternoon and evening sessions. Two CCHS teachers led the college, Jack P. Brouwer as registrar and English professor, and Henry A. Swets as dean and history professor. Wezeman administered both the high school and college and did it well. In 1933 the University of Illinois agreed to grant full credits for the first year of study.[96]

To increase revenue in the harsh Depression days, the college appealed to a broad spectrum of students by muting its Christian perspec-

95. Herman Bel, "Our Educational Policy," undated typescript (ca. 1945), mailed to all constituents, Wezeman Papers; William P. Brink, "Chicago North News," *Banner*, 16 May 1945; John L. Schaver, "The Churches of Chicago North," ibid., 20 May, 2 Sept. 1949. Bel made a convincing twelve-point argument for continuing to admit Christians who did not belong to Reformed or Christian Reformed churches.

96. Wezeman Papers; Don Sinnema, "The Story of Chicago Christian College (1931-1937)," in Richard Harms, ed., *The Dutch Adapting in North America* (13th Biennial Conference, Association for the Advancement of Dutch American Studies, Calvin College, 2001). Prime movers, besides Wezeman, on the advisory committee were the Revs. Edward Tuuk, chairman (he had retired in 1928 from Second Englewood CRC), Herman Moes of Third Chicago CRC, Harry Hager of Bethany (Roseland) RCA, and Jacob Brouwer of First Chicago RCA, Dr. Wm. Yonker (secretary), M. H. Chapman, Fred Kloeze, Peter Huiner, George Ottenhoff, Lambert Bere, Jacob Bosch, George De Boer, Theodore Youngsma, and J. Van Kampen. See also the Chicago Christian Junior College Minute Book, 1931-1937. Professors Enno Wolthuis and John Van Bruggen later joined the faculty of Calvin College.

Henry A. Swets
CCHS *Violet and Maize 1927*

tive in its bulletins and catalogs. The official school name was Chicago Junior College, and in 1932 Wezeman opened a downtown campus, which met in leased quarters in the Crerar Library building at 84 E. Randolph Street. This made the library's book collection of 580,000 volumes available to students. And the Chicago Public Library was located directly across the street.

The downtown campus was staffed by part-time instructors drawn from universities and colleges in greater Chicago. A 1933 listing of the faculty showed only two of twenty instructors were of Dutch Reformed background. The combined student body of 152 was even more diverse — 25 were "Dutch" (i.e., Dutch Reformed), 49 "Americans" including 11 blacks (called "Ethiopians"), and 85 represented 11 other European nationality groups. Religiously, 122 were Protestant, 27 Catholic, and 7 Jewish. The school's low tuition rates and able faculty appealed to students seeking affordable higher education. Enrollment peaked in 1933, with 152 students in the day college in Englewood and 112 in the day and evening college downtown.

It was downhill from this point. In 1934 the State of Illinois would not approve the name Chicago Junior College because there already was a school in the city with that name. More ominous was the growing pressure from the high school board, led by the Reverend Gerrit Hoeksema, to reassert a Reformed vision of the college, even if it would be small in size. Wezeman's broader policies had clearly riled church leaders. Wezeman threatened to resign but was persuaded by friends to carry on and make major changes. The board closed the downtown campus, renamed the southside campus Chicago Christian College, and openly touted its "emphatically Christian" but "nonsectarian and interdenominational" educational philosophy. The board made chapel attendance compulsory but would not require that faculty subscribe to the Reformed creeds, as Hoeksema and his colleagues demanded. One cleric who stood behind Wezeman during the troubled 1930s was the Reverend Edward Tanis of Second Englewood Christian Reformed Church, who was then president of both the high school and college boards of trustees.[97]

In the first college commencement address in 1934, board member George Ottenhoff answered the question: "Why This New Chicago College?" His four reasons were (1) to enable "covenant youth" to keep up with the trend toward higher education; (2) to serve the same needs in the wider Christian community in Chicago; (3) to advance the kingdom of God on earth; and (4) to train Christian leaders for the future well-being of the church and community. Ottenhoff, secretary of the Netherlands Building and Loan Association on the West Side and a fellow consistory member with Wezeman at the Fourth Christian Reformed Church, concluded with an even broader agenda: "We cannot be satisfied, in fact, until we have a thoroughly Christian training through the University level." Wezeman and his cohorts thought big![98]

But enrollment continued to decline, and the financial woes of the times ultimately brought the school down in 1937. In its short life, Chicago Christian College had enrolled more than five hundred students and graduated more than one hundred. To launch such an ambitious enterprise successfully in the teeth of the Depression, and with only minimal support from the people in the pews, was a testimony to Wezeman's leadership skills. Wezeman believed that he had to mute a clear Reformed vi-

97. Sinnema, "Story of Chicago Christian College."

98. "Ottenhoff Speaks to Fifty Graduates at C.C.C. Ceremony," *Chicago Messenger,* 1 June 1934; ibid., 6 Sept., 9 Aug. 1935. To help Wezeman and his cohorts finance Chicago Christian College, and as a principial matter, their consistory at the Fourth CRC of Chicago overtured the synod of 1934 to exempt the churches of Classis Illinois from Calvin College quota levies, eliminate the first two years of instruction at Calvin College, and end denominational ownership of the college with its many preprofessional programs. The immediate aim was to shift church contributions from Calvin to Chicago Christian, but the larger goal was to have the local junior college become the feeder school to Calvin and eventually to move the entire institution to Chicago (*Agenda of Synod,* 1934, part I: Reports, 173-80). Synod peremptorily rejected the Chicago IV overture and Wezeman's plans concerning Calvin College (*Acts of Synod,* 1934, 45).

sion in order to boost enrollment and recruit faculty from outside the Dutch American constituency. If he had catered to this community and accepted slower growth, the college might well have survived and eventually flourished. But his policies cost the college vital support and seemed to confirm the criticism that the college was "alien to the deepest interests of the owners of the Chicago Christian High School."[99] Twenty years passed before the Dutch Reformed of Chicago realized their hopes for a Christian college (see below).

"The Chicago Situation"

Wezeman launched the college and confronted the high school's bankruptcy while he was fighting for his reputation as a Christian Reformed cleric. That he kept so many balls in the air successfully is a testimony to his abilities and the clout of the Wezeman–De Boer family clan and his close friends, George and Ben Ottenhoff. James De Boer had helped launch the school, and, throughout the 1930s and 1940s, George Ottenhoff was the perennial president of the board and his brother Ben served as board treasurer. The three families exerted a great deal of influence on the West Side, and their backing was essential in Frederick Wezeman's battle with the Chicago Christian Reformed clerics.

The clergymen mistrusted Wezeman from the outset, fearing that he flirted with "worldliness" and "modernism." Many gave the high school only lukewarm support, and a few were openly opposed, presumably because of Wezeman, although some suspected that the critics opposed Christian higher education itself.

The first criticism surfaced in 1930, when some clerics charged that the school staff was enticing students to compromise their Christian integrity in various extracurricular activities and in student clubs that resembled fraternities and sororities. The board enlisted the help of the ministerial association of Reformed and Christian Reformed clerics, which body published a report that urged closer cooperation between the churches and the school. Wezeman undid these efforts by taking a swipe at the critics' narrow viewpoint, charging that materialism was "more destructive of the Christian life than the worldliness of play."[100] The next

99. Quoted from Paul Brouwer's final report to the college board, 4 March 1937, cited in Sinnema, "Story of Chicago Christian College."

100. *Report of the Reformed and Christian Reformed Churches of Chicago and Its Suburbs on*

year the ministers of Classis Illinois of the Christian Reformed Church met at the Y.M.C.A. in Englewood to express their concerns about the high school. They decided then and there to organize a formal Ministers' Conference that would meet monthly to keep on top of the situation.[101]

Relations with the church leaders were further roiled by Wezeman's nephew and disciple, Professor John J. De Boer, president of the League of Reformed Young Men's Societies of Chicago, who castigated the clerics as masters of priestcraft in a "Message from the President" published in the League *Yearbook* of 1933 (see chapter 8). The controversy ran until 1935, when De Boer finally stepped down, but not before the denominational synod became involved in an unsuccessful attempt to reconcile the young men's group and their ministers.

This bitter feud with the Young Men's League was a dress rehearsal for the ministers' larger battle with the board of Chicago Christian High School and its principal and Bible teacher, Dr. Wezeman. He had studied with Calvin Seminary Professor Ralph Janssen, the church's "most notable tar baby," in the colorful words of denominational historian Herbert Brinks. Janssen was dismissed in a 1922 seminary purge for bringing German higher critical methods into his lectures on biblical interpretation. "Every pastor, professor, and educator who publicly defended Janssen," said Brinks, "suffered either aspersions on their orthodoxy or severance from the denomination."[102] Wezeman was no exception.

As a "Janssen man," Wezeman was marked from the outset. The content of his Bible courses came under close scrutiny by Chicago Christian Reformed clerics, and they found it wanting. "Simon pure Modernism," they declared. As a result, Wezeman "sustained a barrage of theological examinations" in the mid-1930s that focused on lecture notes he had written and mimeographed for his students.[103] The controversy raged for three years in the local congregations and Dutch-American press of Chicago. It stirred the entire denomination in the pages of the *Banner* and twisted into knots two regional church assemblies, one in Illinois and one in Iowa, and two national synods of the Christian Reformed Church.

The first to sound the alarm about Wezeman's "modernistic-evolutionistic" teachings was A. S. De Jong, principal of the 104th Street

---

Closer Co-operation with the Chicago Christian High School (Chicago, 1930); Van Brummelen, *Telling the Next Generation,* 142.

101. B. Essenburg, "Chicago, Englewood, and Cicero Churches," *Banner,* 23 Oct. 1931.

102. H. J. Brinks, "Henry Wierenga: Sunday Isn't Sabbath," *Origins* 13 No. 2 (1993): 35-36.

103. Ibid., 36.

Frederick Wezeman's Bible class, 1933
(Courtesy of Jane Wezeman Smith)

Christian School in Roseland.[104] In 1933 he took issue with Wezeman's notes (actually the course syllabus) on the book of Amos and alerted the Reverend Gerrit Hoeksema, pastor of Third Roseland Christian Reformed Church and a school board member. Hoeksema pushed the school board to name him chair of a special committee to investigate the notes on Amos, along with fellow board members J. R. Brink, a home missionary, and principal Blystra of Ebenezer Christian School. The Hoeksema committee found "decidedly objectionable material," and that finding set off the controversy.

The board then appointed three Christian Reformed ministers not on the board to further evaluate the notes — Dr. Herman Kuiper of the Fourth Roseland church, John Van Beek of the Oak Lawn church, and Peter A. Hoekstra of the Second Cicero church. Hoekstra held an undergraduate degree from the University of Chicago and Kuiper had a theological degree from the orthodox Free University of Amsterdam, which presumably qualified them to cross swords with Dr. Wezeman. The three evalua-

104. *Banner,* 29 May 1936. De Jong subsequently wrote several long letters to the *Chicago Messenger,* criticizing the board for uncritically defending Wezeman (20 Sept., 18 Oct. 1935).

tors concurred with the Hoeksema committee that Wezeman's notes on the book of Amos were "nothing but modernism, pure and simple."

This alarming turn of events forced the board to expand the inquiry; it asked Hoeksema's committee to review Wezeman's course syllabi on all of the books of the Old and New Testaments. Kuiper replaced Brink for the task. This revised body found numerous statements "incompatible with Orthodox Christianity" and demanded that Wezeman agree to revise his notes along the lines set out by the committee. Wezeman reluctantly signed the report "to allay unrest and promote peace," but he objected to the humiliating inquiry "conducted in secrecy" as "sinister, amazing, unwarranted, unbelievable, and unethical." The whole affair was an exercise in "ecclesiastical politics" and not a "spectacular fight for 'truth,'" as portrayed by the clergy. Wezeman continued to hold his ground, but it was later claimed that he had indicted himself with his signature.[105]

Throughout the controversy, Wezeman had the unquestioned backing of most of the twenty-four board members, led by president George Ottenhoff, a realtor and vice-president of Wezeman's consistory at Fourth Chicago Christian Reformed Church; nephew George De Boer, a businessman and son of the school's founder, and also a member of Fourth church; and Roselander Fred Hanko of the Reformed Church. Fourth Chicago was the only congregation in which each family pledged to contribute $6 per year to the high school. The board in 1934 and again in 1935 by overwhelming majorities reappointed Wezeman as principal.[106] The 1935 move prompted Hoeksema and Kuiper to resign, which was a minor triumph for Wezeman, who found Hoeksema an enigma and Kuiper a man driven by an "imperialistic sense of self-importance." Their behavior provides a classic case in a textbook on abnormal psychology, Wezeman declared.[107]

The seeming defiance by Wezeman and the independent-minded school board frustrated the ministers at the very time that the board was appealing for support to deal with the school's financial difficulties. The ministers, as a group, responded to the request by adopting the following

105. Christian Reformed Church, *Acts of Synod,* 1936, 93-96; *Banner,* 13 Dec. 1935; 29 May, 19 June 1936; *Chicago Messenger,* 31 Jan. 1936; Wezeman's personal comments are appended to Haverhals's paper, "Caught in the Web," 28.

106. Herman Kuiper, *The Chicago Situation: A Word of Warning to the Churches* (Chicago: Chicago Calvin Press, 1935), 7. The vote to reappoint was 20 in favor, 3 against, and 1 abstention (32).

107. Haverhals, "Caught in the Web," 28; J. R. Brink, "Roseland and South," *Banner,* 27 Nov. 1931.

resolution in March 1935 at their monthly Ministers' Conference, referred to colloquially as *Inter Nos* ("Between Us"):

> We regret to say that we cannot support the Chicago Christian High School as enthusiastically as we might, due to a general lack of confidence in our midst in the High School, particularly in the Principal. And it is our conviction that this same lack of confidence accounts in large measure for the present lethargy among our church public.[108]

Since Wezeman was an ordained minister, his beliefs were inevitably brought for judgment before the denomination's ruling bodies, the classes and the national synod. The issue now shifted from Wezeman's willingness to revise his notes to the fundamental question of whether his beliefs were orthodox. In September of 1935, Hoeksema and his consistory petitioned Classis Illinois to investigate Wezeman's doctrinal views. Classis rejected the request on procedural grounds, and on another agenda item it disallowed the call that the Fourth Chicago congregation had extended to Wezeman to be its associate pastor.[109]

Kuiper, with the assistance of Hoeksema and Dr. William H. Rutgers of First Cicero Christian Reformed Church (another inveterate Wezeman "prosecutor"), then decided to document Wezeman's perceived failures chapter and verse. In late 1935 they published a scathing critique, *The Chicago Situation: A Word of Warning to the Churches.*[110] The booklet charged Wezeman with failing to give his students a "clear-cut statement of the fundamental doctrine of the *verbal inspiration of Scripture,*" substituting instead higher critical methods of biblical interpretation. Wezeman, they claimed, was a channel for the heresies of modernism to infiltrate the "very core and heart" of the school, its Bible courses. Two flash points were Wezeman's teachings on the place of Moses and the prophet Amos in the divine plan of revelation, which stated that "the early Hebrews" were polytheists who "finally" in Amos's day became monotheists after centuries of progressive revelation.[111]

Fifteen Christian Reformed ministers (all but three) in Classis Illi-

108. Quoted verbatim in Frederick H. Wezeman, "Grievance, Protest and Plea, To Classis Illinois of the Christian Reformed Church, in session January 18, 1937," in Wezeman Papers.

109. *Chicago Messenger,* 20 Sept. 1935.

110. Kuiper, *Chicago Situation,* 7.

111. *Chicago Situation,* 20-23; Gerrit Hoeksema, "Moses and Amos," *Banner,* 11 Dec. 1936. A complete set of Wezeman's course notes, eleven on the Bible and five on church history, are in the Archives, Calvin College.

nois affixed their names to the "Blue Book" (so-called for its blue cover), and the editors of the denominational weeklies, Henry J. Kuiper of the *Banner* and the Reverend Henry Keegstra of *De Wachter,* trumpeted the charge nationwide in scathing editorials.[112]

The school board reacted strongly, effectively keeping the critics off balance. On principial grounds, the board claimed that Classis Illinois had no right to conduct an investigation of the school, which had its own legal standing free of church control.[113] To manage the controversy and direct a counterattack, the board named a Propaganda Committee headed by Wezeman's pastor, James Putt, attorney John Ligtenberg, and businessman Peter Huizenga. Wezeman himself directed the battle in every detail, using the committee as a front.

First, the board took the unusual step of appointing a blue-ribbon committee of Michigan theologians to study Wezeman's class notes and advise the board. The board named two professors at each of the Dutch Reformed seminaries – Calvin Theological (Christian Reformed) in Grand Rapids and Western Theological (Reformed) in Holland – and asked these four to select a fifth member, who was a Christian Reformed minister and Bible teacher at Grand Rapids Christian High School. For the board to use these five Michigan hired guns, rather than ask local clerics, was taken as a further slap in the face. Moreover, since Wezeman had adroitly revised his class notes to eliminate many of the objectionable passages, the theologians fully acquitted him. So armed, the board stood by their man. The Propaganda Committee published the Michigan report and disseminated it widely.[114]

The board next scheduled a mass meeting at the high school where Wezeman "discussed" the "Chicago Situation" booklet and refuted the charges of modernism for two hours before an overflow crowd of 750. Sev-

112. Kuiper, *Chicago Situation,* 16, et passim. The Rev. Peter A. Hoekstra had endorsed Kuiper's critique of Wezeman's notes on Amos, but then had second thoughts about publishing it and so stated publicly. But shortly afterwards, Hoekstra signed his assent to Kuiper's Blue Book. See Wezeman, "Grievance, Protest, and Plea," 2. Wezeman's brother Klaas was a leading elder in Hoekstra's congregation and pressured him (phone interview with son-in-law John R. Swierenga, 8 Feb. 1999).

113. *Chicago Messenger,* 22 May 1936.

114. Ibid., 18 Oct. 1935. The Michigan committee was comprised of Professors Clarence Bouma and Henry Schultze of Calvin Seminary; Siebe C. Nettinga and Albertus Pieters of Western Seminary; and William Stuart, Christian Reformed minister and Bible teacher at Grand Rapids Christian High School, who formerly was pastor of the Third Roseland Christian Reformed Church. Chicago Christian High School Board, *The Truth About the Chicago Situation* (Chicago, 1936), 83.

eral hundred more had to be turned away. After listening to Wezeman's defense for two hours, most of the audience spontaneously rose to give him a vote of confidence. The principal clearly had wide support among laypeople, who believed that the ministers were meddling in school business. This attitude allowed the board to refuse to cooperate with an investigating committee appointed by Classis Illinois, claiming that the classis and high school had "no official connection" and that the inquiry was improper and illegal. Moreover, the majority of the ministers had never given the school "their wholehearted support, either morally or financially."

In April 1936 the board adopted as its own Wezeman's rebuttal, entitled "Grievance, Protest and Plea," and published it as *The Truth About the Chicago Situation.* This became known as the "Orange Book" (again named for its cover color). The pamphlet rejected all charges of modernism against the principal and called the Blue Book "decidedly inflammatory, opinionated, and prejudiced." Wezeman's teachings were innocent of the spirit of modernism. To prove this, the Bible course notes were offered for sale to the public at the high school bookstore.[115]

These board actions did not set well with the religious leaders, especially since Wezeman himself kept up a steady drumbeat of counterattacks on his critics. He called Herman Kuiper's Blue Book "inflammatory, sensational, and prejudicial"; "a one-sided diatribe" that "drips with self-assurance" and "arrogance." He charged Classis Illinois with meddling, and the *Banner* editor with going "on a rampage" because of his naked prejudice. This was the same editor who opened the editorial page to Wezeman's scathing response to Kuiper's booklet.

Worst of all, in Wezeman's mind, was that the clerics were a secret cabal, a grand jury, who at their Inter Nos meetings had judged him without a hearing. They were "a well-oiled political machine" that wanted to control the church and muzzle the elders. "The will and whim of Rev. Hoeksema is the decision of classis. When the Rev. Hoeksema makes a statement, Dr. Kuiper rises and echoes the sentiment." This modus operandi, Wezeman charged, ran counter to Reformed church polity, in which elders and ministers are to share authority equally over the Word and sacraments and to exercise discipline.[116]

Wezeman's mouthpiece was his newspaper, the *Chicago Messenger,* a biweekly newspaper that he launched in March of 1934 and continued un-

115. *Chicago Messenger,* 31 Jan., 13 Mar. 1936.

116. *Banner,* 7 Jan. 1936; *Chicago Messenger,* 29 Nov., 13 Dec. 1935; 28 Feb., 22 May, 22 Sept. 1936.

til the controversy ended in 1937. The paper, which was decidedly progressive in politics and religion, reported on church and school events in the Dutch Reformed community. But the primary purpose became that of putting a favorable spin on the developing church campaign against the editor's teachings and to defend his reputation. Wezeman ran articles from supporters such as nephew John J. De Boer, now professor of education at Chicago Normal College, who drummed the theme of clerical anti-intellectualism and secret conspiracies. In De Boer's opinion, the controversy was a continuation of his earlier struggle between progressive laity and narrow-minded clerics frightened of change.[117]

By 1936, hard feelings on both sides had escalated, and the Chicago area was, in Wezeman's words, "chin-deep in controversy and strife." The Third Roseland consistory asked Classis Illinois to withhold financial support for the high school, and it went so far as to advise members not to enroll their children there. First Englewood, which stood in the shadow of the school, and Fourth Roseland did the same in 1937.[118]

Classis Illinois devoted much of its four assemblies in 1936 to the Wezeman case. The classis was especially frustrated that the school board would not change its unquestioned backing of Wezeman, even after a special seven-man committee studied his Bible notes carefully and documented examples of "modernistic" and "evolutionistic" teachings chapter and verse. Wezeman's teachings, said the committee majority, began a "dangerous conflict, a conflict touching the most fundamental of all doctrines, namely, the Divine Infallible Revelation." Classis again urged the school board to "earnestly consider" its report. Until it did so, the classis "cannot give the Chicago Christian High School its full confidence."[119]

The classical committee included the only two ministers who steadfastly supported Wezeman: James Putt, his own pastor at the Fourth Chicago church; and Edward Tanis, of the Second Englewood congregation

117. *Chicago Messenger,* 27 Dec. 1935; 24 Apr., 8 May, 13 Oct. 1936. Others who voiced similar themes in published letters and articles in the *Messenger* and *Onze Toekomst* were Peter H. Huizenga, Harry Klunder, Thomas Hoekstra, John Wolthekker, B. Boerman, Benjamin Ottenhoff, George Speelman, J. Van Egmond, and J. W. Schuitema. Incomplete runs of the *Chicago Messenger* are in the Wezeman Papers and in the Dutch Heritage Center, Trinity Christian College, Palos Heights, Ill.

118. Christian Reformed Laymen's Association of Chicago, Illinois, *Shall We Have PEACE, LOVE, and UNITY or STRIFE, ENMITY, and DIVISION in our Christian Reformed Church?* (Chicago: Christian Literature Publishing Company, [1937]), 5; interview with CCHS board member John R. Swierenga, 9 Feb. 1999; "Roseland III overture," mimeo, Classis Illinois documents, Wezeman Papers.

119. "Classis Illinois," *Banner,* 31 Jan., 5, 12 June, 25 Sept. 1936; 12 Feb. 1937.

and board president of Wezeman's visionary project, the Chicago Christian Junior College.[120] Tanis had completed a master's degree in sociology at the University of Chicago. Putt shortly left Fourth Chicago for a one-year study leave at Princeton Theological Seminary. Both ministers fit Wezeman's profile of progressive thinkers.

The final pamphlet broadside came in 1937 from the newly formed Christian Reformed Laymen's Association of Chicago, a group of influential business and professional men with an anticlerical bent. The unnamed author was likely the same John De Boer who earlier had the run-in with Classis Illinois. The association apparently was formed specifically for the purpose of supporting Wezeman. It did so by publishing a "White Book" (again named after its cover), entitled *Shall We Have PEACE, LOVE, and UNITY or STRIFE, ENMITY, and DIVISION in our Christian Reformed Church?*

Reflecting on the years of controversy, the association charged that the ministers' Blue Book had been a "bomb shell which disrupted and destroyed the peace of our churches." The "violent attack" on Wezeman had caused "strife and division in our churches" instead of "peace, love and unity." Moreover, since the "vicious accusations" had severely damaged Wezeman's reputation, reconciliation between the parties was necessary in order for the churches to experience the much-needed spiritual revival. "Not the Way of Love and Peace," laconically declared the editor of the *Banner* in response. The association clearly stood in Wezeman's camp, and their White Book doubtless did little to repair the breach.[121]

The Wezeman case reached the floor of the national synod in 1936, by way of a protest by the Fourth Chicago consistory against the actions of Classis Illinois. The synod upheld the classis but chastised it for not resolving the matter of financial support for the high school at the same time. The synod also ordered Classis Ostfriesland (which still held Wezeman's ministerial credentials) to try Wezeman and named a special committee of nine men, including the esteemed Calvin Theological Seminary professors Louis Berkhof and Martin J. Wyngaarden, to "assist and advise" the classis. The rationale was that Wezeman had "given sufficient grounds of suspicion" to require "a further explanation of his sentiments."[122]

120. Other members were Hoeksema, Rutgers, Rens Hooker of the Des Plaines church, William Haverkamp of the De Motte, Indiana, church, and James Ghyssels of the Lafayette, Indiana, church (ibid., 12 June 1936).

121. *Shall We Have PEACE, LOVE, and UNITY,* 14, 3, 5, 16; H. J. Kuyper, "Not the Way of Love and Peace," *Banner,* 22 Jan. 1937.

122. *Shall We Have PEACE, LOVE, and UNITY,* 93-96, 107-10, 146-47; Christian Reformed Church, *Acts of Synod,* 1937, 107-21; *Banner,* 1 Jan. 1937.

Classis Ostfriesland took up the matter at its September 1936 sessions in Iowa. After the interrogation of Wezeman was completed and he had made his defense, the synodical committee of advice declared that it was "impossible" because of "insufficient time" to weigh the evidence and "formulate our opinion in desirable detail." It recommended adjournment until November, which the classis reluctantly agreed to do. When classis reconvened, it again found it "impossible," after hours of discussion, to reach a final decision. The essential problem was that the synodical committee believed Wezeman to be guilty of heresy and recommended his immediate suspension and deposition, but Classis Ostfriesland did not. They were satisfied with revisions Wezeman had made after the Michigan committee's investigation.

Classis Ostfriesland considered the Wezeman case for a third time at its March 1937 session, this time without the synodical committee present. After giving Wezeman another opportunity for a *mea culpa,* in which he specifically repudiated controversial sections of his course notes, the classis declared unanimously that Wezeman had "removed all grounds of suspicion," and it fully exonerated him. From the onset, Classis Ostfriesland was friendly territory for Wezeman.[123]

The synod's own investigating committee now found its spine and demanded that the synod reject Classis Ostfriesland's apparent whitewash and depose Wezeman for "false doctrine" at its 1937 assembly, barring a full confession, as Classis Illinois had demanded. The synod put the Wezeman case back on the agenda. Wezeman himself also did so by submitting a protest against the action of the 1936 synod against him. The 1937 body then tried Wezeman and unanimously concluded that portions of his course notes were "contrary to the Word of God." The synod specifically charged that the notes manifested "a false, evolutionary view of the development of revelation and of the religion of Israel, . . . [and] a purely ethical representation of the way of salvation." The body sustained these charges by substantial majorities and demanded that Wezeman recant.[124]

Wezeman realized that his future in the Christian Reformed Church and at Chicago Christian High School hung in the balance, and he wisely yielded ground. He submitted the following signed statement:

123. *Banner,* 30 Oct. 1936; 16 Apr. 1937.

124. Ibid., 20, 27 May, 3, 10, 24 June, 8, 15 July 1937; *Grand Rapids Herald,* June 26, 1937; Christian Reformed Church, *Acts of Synod,* 1937, 31-35, 51, 106, 111-12, et passim.

> You are aware of the fact that I have repeatedly stated that my Bible courses do contain a few statements that are erroneous. Synod condemns these passages. I subscribe to the judgment passed upon these passages by Synod and herewith repudiate the teaching condemned therein as being contrary to the Word of God and the Confession.

Thus, Wezeman finally admitted that some of his teachings were heretical, and Synod magnanimously, and by a vote of fifty to four, declared itself satisfied and the delegates united "spontaneously in praising God and singing the Doxology." The long ordeal was over. Several men shook Wezeman's hand warmly as a sign of reconciliation, including the president of the synod and *Banner* editor, H. J. Kuiper, who had been his leading critic outside of Chicago. Wezeman also withdrew his protest against Classis Illinois. The ecclesiastical machinery had ground slow and exceedingly fine, but it was not well-oiled. As an advanced student of the law, Wezeman well knew that his procedural rights as the defendant in a heresy trial were sometimes disregarded.[125]

The CCHS board at its next meeting unanimously resolved to "abide by the decision of the synod . . . to concur in the statement made by Dr. Wezeman in settlement of the controversy." And Fourth Chicago experienced "happy days" upon the ordination of Wezeman as its associate pastor.[126]

After three years of controversy, the protagonists had essentially called a truce. Wezeman kept his ministerial credentials, and the Chicago clerics felt vindicated, if not fully satisfied. They had fulfilled their obligation "to jealously guard our precious heritage by a careful supervision of all Bible teaching in . . . our schools for Christian instruction." However, a quarter century later, Wezeman had second thoughts about yielding his ground on the advice of faithful friends.

> Looking back I believe my procedure would have been to say to Synod: "Gentlemen, Classis Ostfriesland offers in my defense a document that is scholarly, brotherly, considerate, and constructive. The Michigan Committee too has a report that should be acceptable to you. If you refuse to accept these evidences of confidence I resign from the Christian Reformed ministry."[127]

125. Haverhals, "Caught in the Web," 31.

126. *Acts of Synod,* 1937, 115; *Banner,* 14 Oct., 2 Dec. 1937.

127. *Shall We Have PEACE, LOVE and UNITY,* 8-9; Van Brummelen, *Telling the Next Generation,* 142-43; Wezeman's comments appended to Haverhals, "Caught in the Web," 29.

At heart, the controversy reflected the traditional division in Dutch Reformed circles, described in chapter 2, between the Kuyperian triumphalists and the Seceder pietists. Wezeman and his supporters wanted to build the kingdom in Chicago, while the majority of Christian Reformed clerics wanted to guard the church and deepen the spiritual life of its members. On another level was the issue of the relationship between the institutional church and its affiliated organizations. Were Christian schools "free schools" or not? Lay leaders came to believe this strongly in Chicago and they would exert themselves.

Finally, Wezeman's theological challenge to what he deemed "an ossified type of scholarship" that was "unworthy" of the Christian Reformed Church and its seminary became for conservatives a sad marker of the encroachment of heresy within the bosom of the church. Cornelius Van Til, who grew up in the Christian Reformed Church of Highland, Indiana, and became a staunch defender of Reformed orthodoxy as professor of dogmatics at Westminster Theological Seminary in Philadelphia, in 1957 cited the "notorious Wezeman case" as a prime example of the "dual insensitivity" infecting the denomination. "First of all," said Van Til,

> Dr. Wezeman had no sense of the orthodox, let alone Reformed tradition; but nevertheless [he] had a place of honor and great influence in our circles. Secondly, the people of influence in Chicago said in effect, when they permitted him to run the whole school, "We do not care whether a man knows and loves the truth, he is a fine gentleman and a scholar, and that is enough for us." Thus for many years one of our biggest Christian High Schools, which was one of the main feeders of Calvin College, was headed by a man who forfeited every right to our confidence in his leadership.[128]

Van Til's polemical use of Wezeman as Exhibit A in his depiction of the denomination's presumed slide into heresy was simplistic and overbearing; yet he reflected the views of some in Chicago.

Wezeman carried on at Chicago Christian High School for fourteen years after the controversy ended, finally leaving in 1951 to become president of Northwestern Junior College in Orange City, Iowa. During his long tenure at CCHS, he had raised academic standards and won for the school a wide reputation, but his controversial theological views caused support for the school to erode substantially among its constituency, especially the

128. Cornelius Van Til, "The Pillars of Our Church v. Doctrinal Insensitivity," *Torch and Trumpet,* Feb. 1957, 4-7, 14-17, quote 17.

clergy he had alienated. This lack of confidence made the school's financial difficulties all the more severe, even though enrollments held firm because parents continued to believe in Christian higher education.

Wezeman's situation improved in his last decade, the 1940s, when criticism died down and enrollment surpassed 650. In 1940 the church leaders rallied behind the school, after learning that only 48 percent of the graduates of the Christian elementary schools enrolled at the high school. Every consistory sent delegates to a series of meetings to discuss the question: "How can a closer relation be brought about between the school boards, school societies, and the consistories?" Vetting the issues proved to be "very helpful in solving our problems," reported Benjamin Essenburg.[129]

The year 1942 was a high point for Christian High. It began with the "event of the century," a gala visit by Princess Juliana of the Netherlands, who was in Canada waiting out the war and the German occupation of the Netherlands. Wezeman's contacts in the Netherlandic world brought Her Royal Highness to the school, where she spoke in a chapel service and met the teachers and students socially. Everyone turned out in his or her best finery, and every nook and cranny of the building was painted and cleaned for the royal visitor!

Some weeks later Wezeman had the remarkable opportunity to explain the purposes and achievements of the school to a national radio audience on Chicago's WGN program, "Citizens of Tomorrow." In a similar vein, the school's famed A Cappella Choir under James Baar performed on the nationwide radio program, "I Hear America Singing." The next year, 1943, Wezeman led the school in celebrating its 25th anniversary with a series of observances that culminated in a festive banquet. Four years later, in 1947, the Netherlands ambassador announced that Queen Wilhelmina had knighted Wezeman into the prestigious Order of Oranje Nassau for his humanitarian relief work and for perpetuating the Dutch cultural heritage. Then, on February 10, 1949, after Wezeman completed twenty-one years at CCHS, more than five hundred alumni, board members, and friends gathered at a testimonial dinner to demonstrate their affection and esteem for "a gentleman and a scholar." The event capped a day-long celebration billed as "Doctor Wezeman Day" and "left a sweet savor never to be forgotten."[130]

129. "Classis Illinois," *Banner,* 2 Feb. 1939; J. R. Brink, "Chicago South," ibid., 2 Feb. 1939; B. Essenburg, "West Chicago News," ibid., 26 Apr. 1940.

130. "Open Jubilee at Christian High," *Chicago Sunday Tribune,* 9 May 1943, pt. 3, p. 2;

Frederick H. Wezeman Appreciation Day, 1949

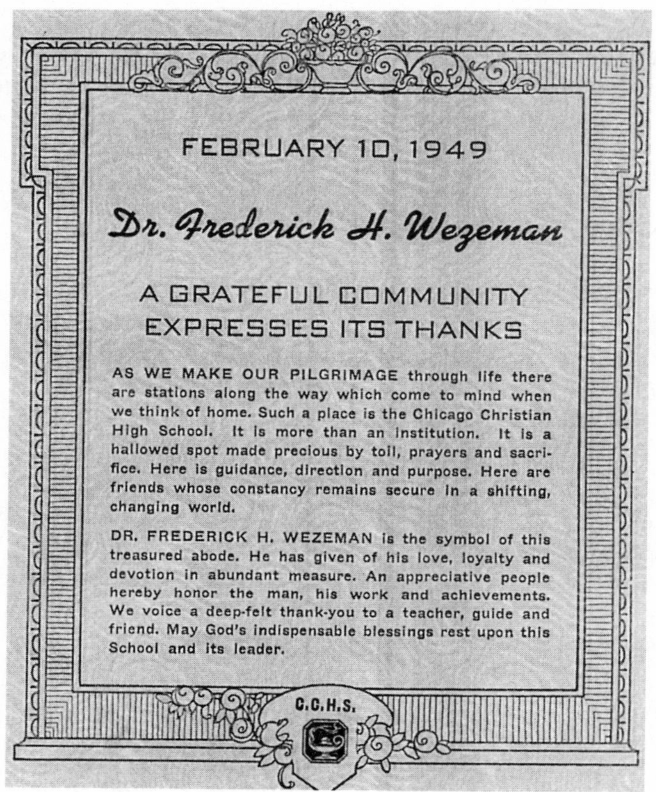

FEBRUARY 10, 1949

Dr. Frederick H. Wezeman

A GRATEFUL COMMUNITY EXPRESSES ITS THANKS

AS WE MAKE OUR PILGRIMAGE through life there are stations along the way which come to mind when we think of home. Such a place is the Chicago Christian High School. It is more than an institution. It is a hallowed spot made precious by toil, prayers and sacrifice. Here is guidance, direction and purpose. Here are friends whose constancy remains secure in a shifting, changing world.

DR. FREDERICK H. WEZEMAN is the symbol of this treasured abode. He has given of his love, loyalty and devotion in abundant measure. An appreciative people hereby honor the man, his work and achievements. We voice a deep-felt thank-you to a teacher, guide and friend. May God's indispensable blessings rest upon this School and its leader.

C.C.H.S.

In recognition of his many accomplishments and long tenure, Wezeman was also honored posthumously in 1968 at the golden (fiftieth) anniversary celebration of CCHS at the Conrad Hilton Hotel before fifteen hundred alumni and supporters. The class of 1943, the twenty-fifth anniversary class, made the presentation to his wife, Gertrude Harmeling Wezeman.[131]

Wezeman's successor was Richard Prince (1951-59), a science teacher with two degrees from the University of Chicago, a B.S. in chemistry and

"F. H. Wezeman to be Honored at Testimonial," *Southtown Economist,* 9 Feb. 1949, 6; "February 10 is Doctor Wezeman Day," *Onze Toekomst,* 2 Feb. 1949, 1; "'Dr. Wezeman Day' Celebrated by Students and Friends Today," Chicago Christian High School *Mirror,* 10 Feb. 1949; letter of Henry A. Swets, principal, Haven School, Chicago, to Dennis Tibstra, CCHS Student Council president, 9 Feb. 1949, Wezeman Papers.

131. "50th Anniversary Banquet Set by Christian High," unidentified Chicago newspaper clipping in Wezeman Papers.

Richard Prince

an M.A. in educational administration. Some years later he earned the Ph.D. in administration. Prince was a "Roseland boy" and CCHS graduate who received ready acceptance by the constituency. With a quiet and somewhat reserved demeanor, he "led from the middle" and brought no theological baggage or political agenda. The clerics could count on his loyalty to the church and school.

Prince was a strong disciplinarian who changed the atmosphere in the halls and classrooms, and he was successful in abolishing the clubs that had fostered social stratification and questionable mores. Prince also directed a much-needed building campaign in 1954 to replace the drafty wooden "portables" with an addition to the main building.

But no sooner was the upgrade finished than the Hollanders in Englewood began their flight from encroaching black newcomers. In 1961 CCHS sold its facilities to the Chicago Board of Education and relocated to Palos Heights, where many families had already resettled. The present school on State Route 83 at Oak Park Avenue was dedicated in 1963, on a campus adjacent to Trinity Christian College (founded in 1959 under a committee with Richard Prince as secretary). In its first seventy-five years, Chicago Christian graduated more than 7,000 students, myself included; and in the 1990s it enrolled nearly 450 students a year with a faculty of 27.[132]

132. *Family Album,* 56-59; "Chicago Christian High School, 1918-1993," program for 75th anniversary celebration dinner; "R. Prince Succeeds Dr. F. H. Wezeman as Principal of CCHS," Chicago Christian High School *Mirror,* 28 Sept. 1951.

Timothy Christian Schools – Cicero (1927-72)

The steady westward movement of the Reformed folk in the 1920s spelled the death knell of Timothy school in the Douglas Park–Lawndale district, just as it did later for Ebenezer School. Hendrikse led the relocation planning, and the board in 1925 bought a large corner lot (100 by 125 feet) in north Cicero for $9,400 on 14th Street at 59th Avenue (figure 5.1, site B). The site was at the geographic center of the large and growing Dutch Reformed community in the near western suburbs.[133]

Hendrikse hoped to build and move the school to Cicero immediately, but finances did not permit. At this point he resigned to go into the real estate business with his brother-in-law, Thomas J. Stob, and he entered Cicero city politics. But Hendrikse kept his hand in the school by acting as the collector for a few years (1932-34). His task was to visit the families of pupils regularly, usually monthly, to collect tuition payments. Stob succeeded him as school treasurer and served for twenty-seven years until his death.[134]

Early in 1927, after lengthy negotiations over the price, a Jewish congregation bought the Tripp Avenue school for $32,500, with a substantial down payment and the remainder on land contract. The sale required vacating the school in six months, so the Timothy building committee, headed by Theodore S. Youngsma, kicked into high gear. With the up-front money in hand, the board began construction in mid-February of the $105,000, two-story school with full basement and a gymnasium on the Cicero property. At the time Timothy was the only school, private or public, in Cicero and the only National Union–affiliated school nationwide with a gymnasium.

The cornerstone ceremony was in May, and the ten-room school opened in September of 1927 with 156 pupils in four completed rooms, amid the din of the continuing construction. It stood at 5900 West 14th Street, one block west of the relocated Douglas Park church. The school was dedicated in November and the church a month later. The Reverend Jacob Weersing, of the Third Chicago Christian Reformed Church, spoke at the afternoon school dedication service before a crowd of three hundred. The Eunice Society then fed the people a "tasty meal," after which a

133. The figure of $4,400 given in the 1961 anniversary book is likely a misprint.

134. Timothy Christian School, *50th Anniversary,* n.p. In the 1940s Hendrikse served as assistant to Henry Schultze, president of Calvin College, and addressed regional church assemblies on behalf of the college.

Timothy Christian School, 14th St. and 59th Ct., Cicero, erected 1927

standing-room-only audience of five hundred gathered in the new school assembly hall to hear an address by the Reverend P. A. Hoekstra of Second Cicero, Timothy's mother church. The collection totaled $1,700, which included a single $500 gift, and everyone was overwhelmed by the spacious and beautiful facilities.[135]

The Third Chicago congregation had also moved west by that time. Thus, the remaining six classrooms were filled within five years, by 1932, and the school benefited from efficiencies of scale with the maximum use of the building. But the gains were lost when parents fell behind on tuition payments in the 1930s.

Principal Louis Zuiderhof (1926-36), who had ably directed the move to Cicero, had to deal with the effects of the dire national economy on the school. The board accepted students of non-Reformed persuasion, and in 1932 cut salaries for the six teachers and the principal, but no one was laid off and the spirit of the staff remained strong. The board had to scramble to raise funds for salaries and mortgage payments. To increase income, new first-graders were permitted to begin in February. From then on, Timothy had both February and June graduating classes. The board auctioned off donated foodstuffs, sold Netherlands Day souvenir buttons at

135. "Dedication of the New Timothy School," *Onze Toekomst,* 23 Nov. 1927.

the Chicago World's Fair in 1933 (which brought in $135), staged an annual Rally Day dinner (which in 1936 raised $1,300!), and asked parents daily to put pennies in coin boxes for tuition.[136]

Zuiderhof's wife urged self-denial. "In the days of prosperity we have indulged. In the days of depression shall we deny ourselves? It is good for the soul." If the men gave up smoking at school board and consistory meetings, and if families stopped buying Sunday newspapers and cut back on Christmas gifts and tree decorations, they could free up hundreds of dollars for the schools. The women's auxiliary, the Eunice Society, formed clubs in 1933 and collected $180 from dues. "It doesn't seem like much today," Gertrude Iwema recalled in 1984, "but it was a start." These Friendship Clubs have meant much to the school over the years.[137]

Also in 1933, when the financial picture was darkest, the board won a four-year deferral of a $1,500 mortgage payment then due, renegotiated the interest rate from 6 to 3 percent, and extended the payment schedule. Officials of the Baker State Bank deserve credit for granting this reprieve, which saved the school from disaster.

Another factor in the money crunch was the failure of the Jewish congregation to keep current in its $11,000 note on the Tripp Avenue property. After the Timothy board began foreclosure proceedings, the Jewish congregation in 1937 offered $7,000 and all back interest as payment in full, and the board accepted the offer of 63 cents on the dollar. Times were hard for everyone.[138]

In 1938 the board had to renegotiate its bank note again and extend for five more years at 4.5 percent interest, with an annual payment of $2,000. It paid another $1,000 per year on individual notes held by society members. The school's total property indebtedness in 1937 was $50,000, and total equity was an impressive $69,000. Despite the Depression, enrollment in 1938 reached 350, and the Rally Day supper that year raised $1,200. Tuition was $66 for the 1938-39 school year.[139]

John Van Bruggen (1936-41), formerly principal of the 108th Street Christian School in Roseland, successfully led Timothy through the last five years of economic difficulties and introduced major curricular

136. B. Essenburg, "Chicago and Vicinity," *Banner,* 19 Sept. 1930.

137. Mrs. L. Zuiderhof, "Self-Denial," *Banner,* 23 Oct., 4 Dec. 1931; *Timothy Reflector,* May 1983, pp. 18-19; *Chicago Messenger,* 13, 27 Mar. 1936.

138. "Annual Report of the Secretary," Timothy Christian School, *Bulletin,* Fall Issue, 22 Sept. 1937.

139. "Annual Report of the Secretary," 22 Sept. 1937; ibid., 21 Sept. 1938; Timothy Christian School, *Twenty-five Years, 1911-1936.*

John A. Van Bruggen

Richard Tolsma

changes. He developed an integrated program for Bible study and arithmetic for all grades, and the three upper grades, six through eight, were departmentalized. This allowed teachers to specialize in several major subjects, instead of covering all subjects at one grade level. Staff morale improved, and students were better prepared for high school methods. Under the arrangement, Van Bruggen taught history and civics, Cornelius Kickert English and reading, and Neal Hulstein geography and arithmetic. Enrollment jumped from 261 in 1931 to 349 by 1937, the first full year of Van Bruggen's tenure.[140]

Principal Van Bruggen left for a position in Grand Rapids and gave way to Richard Tolsma in 1941, just as the good times were about to roll. That year the board paid $800 for the lot immediately west of the school for a playground. The city also graciously allowed the school to use a public playground across the street to the east, which was equipped with awesome giant slides, swings and seesaws, a place to play tag, and tennis courts that were perfect for softball games. The boys and girls were segregated at play inside and out, and they had to line up and reenter the school from the playground through the designated "boys" and "girls" doors.

Tolsma led Timothy for twenty-seven years (1941-1967) as an effective

140. *Timothy Bugle* 1 (Jan. 1937): 1; "Annual Report of the Secretary," 22 Sept. 1937.

administrator and leader. He enjoyed wide support in the community and brought the school to maturity and academic excellence. Just as he stepped in, the board launched a new fundraising strategy, the annual "drive," to replace the Rally Days with their suppers, plays, and sales, which had carried Timothy, Ebenezer, and the other Christian schools through the Depression. The board set a goal of $1,700 and, after weeks of hype, on the designated evening teams went out to the homes of all society members and collected $1,900! Good times had surely returned and the annual drive had proven itself. No longer would the cause of Christian education have to "go-a-begging or resort to all sorts of methods for raising funds."[141]

Tolsma and the board in 1942 also consolidated Timothy's entire indebtedness of $30,000, by issuing new first mortgage bonds at 4 percent interest, with maturities of one to fifteen years. The property was worth a minimum of $125,000 at the time. Local school supporters and Christian Reformed families nationwide bought the bonds, which freed the school from the less than tender mercies of commercial bankers.

In 1943 the board belatedly installed a telephone in the school office; how the staff had functioned without this handy device is hard to imagine. Tolsma's wife, Betty ("Bess"), taught at Timothy for twenty-five years and was highly respected. Teacher salaries during the war were a respectable $100 a month. Jane Bolt tenderly introduced kindergarten students to formal schooling for many decades, and Elsie Ten Bos taught first-graders how to read and kept order by pulling a few ears of naughty boys. She sorted the pupils by reading skills into three groups – blue birds, red birds, and black birds. Blue was best, black was bad.[142]

Tolsma was no more successful than his predecessors in gaining support from the Reformed Church. Of Timothy's 303 students in 1940-41, only 18 (6 percent) came from Reformed churches, mostly members of the nearby West Side church. The Christian school system in Chicago continued to be a bedrock Christian Reformed program.[143]

Tolsma faced three major challenges. He had to smooth the integration of Ebenezer students into the Timothy student body in the late 1940s, help develop the Timothy Christian junior and senior high schools

141. Quote of B. Essenburg, "West Chicago News," *Banner,* 2 May, 5 Sept., 1941.

142. *Timothy Reflector,* May 1983, p. 19; Martin Stulp, "Reminiscences, 1949 Timothy Class 50th Reunion, Frankfurt, IL, Sept. 1999."

143. "Annual Report of the Principal of the Timothy Christian School, September 1, 1940 to August 31, 1941," typescript, Archives, Calvin College.

in the 1950s, and deal with a gut-wrenching racial issue in admission policies in the 1960s.

Integrating 116 Ebenezer students into Timothy's student body of 350 in 1946 was Tolsma's biggest challenge. Enrollment jumped in one year by one-third, and space was at a premium. The gymnasium-auditorium and the large lunchroom in the basement were sectioned off into classrooms, and even the stage in the auditorium became a classroom. Other classes were arranged in the nearby Second Cicero church. The loss of the gym meant the end of physical education classes and indoor sports like basketball and volleyball. The loss of the lunchroom forced those who lived too far from home to eat sack lunches at their desks. And since the lunchroom had doubled as a play area during morning and afternoon recesses in inclement weather, students all too often lost their prized recess breaks. Clearly, the quality of life deteriorated at Timothy in 1946 and for the following years.

A related challenge was the social integration of Ebenezer students, who brought an inner-city mentality to the suburban school. Although all the youngsters shared the same religious beliefs and values, they showed obvious cultural differences in behavior, language, and even dress. The suburbanites thought themselves better and clearly let the city folks know it. "Oh, you're from the Old West Side," they scoffed. The Chicago kids, in turn, thought the Cicero kids were "stuck-ups." But the Cicero boys also felt intimidated. Ebenezer boys had "street smarts"; they walked with a certain swagger and knew how to defend themselves with their fists or worse, with switchblades and brass knuckles. And they carried crude nicknames. Even veteran teachers at Timothy struggled to hold the line on school discipline. One part of school life flourished, however; that was the softball team. In 1948, for the first time in the school's history, Timothy beat both St. Francis of Rome and Burnham Public School in the annual softball games.

Social differences were evident in work patterns and housing, as well. Fathers of the Old West Side students worked on garbage trucks and as factory employees; their families lived in older homes, two- and three-flats, and apartment buildings; and their children played in the streets. The cold beverage of choice was beer. Fathers of Cicero students owned the garbage and cartage trucks, operated businesses in home construction and the retail trade, and worked as skilled craftsmen or in "clean" plants like the Western Electric Hawthorne Plant in Cicero. Their families lived in spacious new bungalows with back yards and landscaped lawns, and their children played in well-maintained city parks. They preferred

Timothy Christian High School, 60th Ct., Cicero, dedicated 1952

wine to beer as a social lubricant. The inner city and the suburbs stood worlds apart, but at Timothy they came together.

The social gulf disappeared much quicker than Timothy's space problem, which could only be solved by a new building. In 1950 the board laid the cornerstone in a ceremony directed by Thomas Stob and board chair Bernard Huiner. Construction then began on a large junior and senior high school one-half mile away, at 1225 South 60th Court, directly across from the First Cicero Christian Reformed Church (figure 5.1, site A).[144] In 1952, as soon as the facility was ready, the junior high classes at the elementary school were transferred there. This relieved the overcrowding after six harrowing years. A decade later, in 1962, grades five and six were also moved to the 60th Court building. Dr. G. Roderick Youngs was principal of the Timothy Christian High School for its first decade. Like Fred Wezeman, he had a vision for developing a full-orbed Christian curriculum.

The decision to establish a junior high was easy. The need was obvi-

144. "Timothy Lays Cornerstone," *Christian Home and School Magazine,* Sept. 1960.

ous. But adding a high school was another matter, because it meant that the westsiders had to pull out of the joint, citywide Chicago Christian High School (CCHS). For a quarter century CCHS had been a unifying force in the Reformed community of greater Chicago. It brought together for four formative years the young people of all the churches, and the supporting school society and board melded members from every corner of the city. The Timothy constituency had given CCHS wholehearted support over the years, and it required tact and patience by Tolsma and the board to redirect these deep loyalties and emotional ties to the new local school. The westsiders also had to live with the fact that they had severed a special relationship with the southsiders.

There were several mitigating factors, however. CCHS was so overcrowded that wooden portables and vacant stores were used as overflow classrooms. Second, the increasing city traffic made the fourteen-mile, hour-long bus trip to Englewood time-consuming, expensive, and even dangerous. Third, the westsiders' separation was softened by the fact that Reformed families in South Holland had in 1948 made the same decision, when they founded Illiana Christian High. Finally, planning had already begun for a Christian college in Chicago, which would reunite the greater Reformed community to some degree. Those dreams came to fruition in 1959 with the founding of Trinity Christian College in Palos Heights.

The Timothy-Lawndale Controversy

Timothy elementary school and the governing board faced its greatest test from 1965 to 1972, when the 59th Street school in Cicero offered only kindergarten and grades one through four. In 1965 a group of black parents who belonged to the Christian Reformed mission church in the Lawndale neighborhood asked for admission for thirty of their young children to attend Timothy, which was the closest church-related school.[145] The Lawndale church stood just six blocks east of the border of

145. The Lawndale church was begun in a storefront at 13th Street and Karlov Avenue by Clarence Buist, a lay evangelist with the Chicagoland Board of Missions in the employ of the Warren Park Christian Reformed Church in Cicero. His ministry flourished after the mission board in 1957 gave the group the use of the nearby Nathaniel Institute building, which was vacated because the board moved its Jewish evangelism to the North Side. In 1959, Classis Chicago North approved the work among the "Negroes," which quickly grew to two hundred children in the Sunday school classes. And in 1963 the Lawndale Gospel Chapel was formally organized as the Lawndale Christian Reformed Church. In 1962 mem-

Cicero, but this crime-ridden ghetto with poor schools was beyond the pale. And Cicero citizens wanted to keep it that way. "Integration will soon mean saturation," they said.

The Lawndale parents' request came at the hands of the church's socially activist pastors, Peter Huiner (1962-65) and Duane Vander Brug (1965-69), who had urged the parents to demand their "rights."[146] Huiner, a Timothy alumnus and son of the First Cicero church, had adopted two interracial children, and he and other church families wanted Christian schooling for their children. Knowing full well the sensitivities of Ciceronians, however, in May 1964 they formally petitioned the Timothy board to open a branch elementary school at Lawndale. Despite many conversations, the proposal went nowhere. So, the next August, two weeks before Timothy's 1965 fall term opened, Huiner announced that Lawndale's parents intended to enroll their children. This set the stage for confrontation, says the board president John H. Zeilstra; it put the board "in a box." Covenant, not conflict, compelled the Lawndale parents, however, and from their perspective the board was forewarned but not forearmed.[147]

Lily-white Cicero, a town of seventy thousand European immigrants, mostly of Slavic and Italian descent, had earned a reputation as "the Selma of the North" after the first black family that tried to move into town in 1951 was driven away by a mob of four hundred neighbors. The racial protesters threw the family's possessions into the street, lit a big bonfire, and dared the city police, who had guaranteed the family protection, to intervene. The police could not or would not control the crowds, so the governor had to call out the National Guard to restore order. For this clear civil rights violation, the town of Cicero later had to pay a large sum to the family. But Cicero remained a fearful and determined white bastion, as Martin Luther King learned when, in the very summer of 1965, he challenged its citizens by marching through the town under massive National Guard protection. This was the harsh reality facing the Timothy board upon learning of the Lawndale plan.

---

bership stood at twenty-four confessing adults and thirty-five baptized children. Scott Hoezee and Christopher H. Meehan, *Flourishing in the Land: A Hundred-Year History of Christian Reformed Missions in North America* (Grand Rapids: Eerdmans, 1996), 135-37.

146. Timothy Christian School Board, *"All Things Are Lawfull; But Not All Things Are Expedient" (I Cor. 10:23); A Position Paper* (Cicero, Ill, 1969), n.p. (quote on fifth page). William Buiten, board president, authored this document, which was approved unanimously. A voluminous document file on the Timothy-Lawndale issue is in the Archives, Calvin College.

147. Letters to the author: Peter Huiner, 3 Mar. 2002; Harvey Huiner, 27 Apr. 2002; and John H. Zeilstra, 30 Nov. 2000.

The board believed it had no choice but to delay enrolling the Lawndale students. It sent a committee to explain the decision personally to the parents in a meeting at the Lawndale church on October 12. Despite the pleas of their fellow church members for Christian education, the risk of violence by angry neighbors was too great.

This assessment seemed to be confirmed in 1968 after the board polled the sentiment of 600 families living in the vicinity of the school. The response was immediate; 150 "ugly and threatening" neighbors, including many Timothy parents (!), jammed into the next board meeting at the school to demand that it not integrate the school. The chair, Albert "Swede" Kieft, could hardly maintain order, especially after he told the crowd that the board's ultimate responsibility was not to the neighborhood or the parents but to God. This prompted a neighbor to cry out: "God! Who cares about God; if the N——s come in here, my house will be worth only half." A Timothy parent responded to this outburst by breaking into applause. Another resident put it more bluntly: "My house is my God. I have $20,000 invested in that house, and my house is my God." The crowd reflected the values of the blue-collar community at large. More tragically, the responses of some of the parents showed that the board had serious internal problems as well.[148]

Of 224 replies to the board questionnaire, 93 percent opposed integrating Timothy, and many "expressed varying degrees of hostility and threats of violence." City police confirmed receiving credible threats to torch the school. Cicero's white ethnic population had already fled the "black threat" in Chicago's older neighborhoods, and they would not allow the quality of life and monetary value of their homes to fall again.[149]

"We must use sanctified common sense," the board concluded in the face of an explosive situation. Board members agreed on principle that all covenant children should be welcomed, but it was not feasible under the circumstances. Enrolling blacks in Timothy involves "dangers that all those in touch with the prevailing racial attitudes are well aware of. . . . We must take care in preserving the opportunity of Christian education and for protecting the physical well being of all our children."

148. *"All Things Are Lawful"*; interview with the Rev. Eugene Bradford, Holland, Mich., 4 Feb. 1999; letter of Donald Veurink to the author, 10 Oct. 1999; "Timothy: Crisis in Christian Education," Calvin College *Chimes,* 64, 3 October 1969, 6; Don and John Ottenhoff, "Timothy Christian Schools," *Other Side* 7, No. 2 (1971): 22-25. The historical overview by these two graduates of Timothy gently but firmly condemns the underlying racism of the West Side Dutch Reformed community.

149. "Timothy: Crisis in Christian Education," 6.

What is legitimate is not always practical or fair to others, they concluded. Even the Holy Scriptures rightly say, "All things are lawful, but not all things are expedient" (1 Corinthians 10:23), declared the board in its position paper distributed on Reformation Sunday of 1969 to the churches of the regional assembly, Classis Chicago North (Classis Illinois had by this time been reorganized). "Conditions in Cicero would not permit the safe enrollment of Lawndale children in the Cicero schools." Elsewhere in the Chicago suburbs, yes, but not in Cicero. The board also noted that the Roman Catholic hierarchy of Chicago, under liberal Archbishop John Cardinal Cody, made Cicero the sole exception to its program of integrating city and suburban Catholic schools.[150]

After the Timothy board announced its decision, based on a real fear of violence, the Cicero town council responded with a politically correct statement of its own, promising "full and complete protection. We will definitely protect students. We've got to protect everybody whether they're residents of Cicero or not; that's the law."[151] The costly federal fines levied on the city for the inadequate police protection in the 1951 racial incident dictated that officials cover their backsides, but could the police be counted on in 1968 any more than in 1951?

The Timothy board received mixed signals. In contrast to the clear public statement of some officials, others telegraphed their displeasure at the prospect of integrating Timothy. The superintendent of the park district came and demanded the key to the city playground across from the school that had long been available for Timothy students during lunch and recess breaks. And city school administrators, with whom Timothy had enjoyed good relations, suddenly turned a cold shoulder. For example, they would no longer sell surplus audiovisual equipment. The Timothy board insisted that it was not acting out of racist motives. In 1967 it admitted three Lawndale students to Timothy Christian High School, which had earlier relocated to Elmhurst. In that same year, the Des Plaines Christian School, twenty-five miles to the northwest, had welcomed nineteen Lawndale students, and Timothy provided busing free of charge. The Western Springs Christian School also invited Lawndale students to apply. In the minds of the West Side Dutch Reformed, these actions disproved charges of racism and showed their true Christian convictions.

Indeed, John H. Zeilstra, Timothy board president in 1965, declared (albeit thirty-five years after the fact) that if the board had known in May

150. *"All Things Are Lawful."* The scriptural quote is the title of the booklet.

151. *Chicago Tribune,* 11 Nov. 1969.

or June of Lawndale's intention, "We could have worked with them to enroll the children. . . . Again I would emphasize that if the Board had more time we could have prepared our people and the town as to what was happening. We did not have this opportunity but were put on the defensive where nothing positive could take place."[152] The road not taken can never be known. But, in actuality, many Timothy board members and constituents harbored a strong antipathy to living near blacks, worshiping with them, or having their children form friendships in the schools.[153]

Because the Christian schools were closely associated with the Christian Reformed churches, the standoff between Timothy and Lawndale inevitably escalated into an ecclesiastical matter. The consistory of Ebenezer Christian Reformed Church of Berwyn, a suburb directly west of Cicero, in 1968 lodged a protest against the Timothy board with the denominational synod. Most Ebenezer congregants had participated in the white flight from Chicago, and they preferred to live in segregated neighborhoods. But Ebenezer church had a pastor of strong convictions, the Reverend Eugene Bradford, who had grown up in the East. Bradford, with the biblical law of love on his side, was able with the support of forceful laymen, notably Martin LaMaire and Drewes Peters, to sway the consistory to approve his overture to synod. Many in the congregation disapproved of their pastor's crusading spirit, and the next year Bradford left the parish for a New Jersey congregation.

But Bradford had accomplished his purpose. The Christian Reformed Church synod of 1968, because of the "extreme spiritual and moral importance" of the matter, by way of exception voted to place the last-minute Berwyn overture "legally before Synod." The synod thereupon strongly rebuked the Timothy board and school society and called for ecclesiastical discipline against them. The synod declared, "Fear of persecution or of disadvantage to self or our institutions arising out of obedience to Christ does not warrant denial to anyone, for reasons of race or color, of full Christian fellowship and privileges in the Church or in related organizations, such as Christian colleges and schools." The board, therefore, was being "disobedient to Christ and [must] be dealt with according to the provisions of the Church Order regarding Admonition and Discipline."[154]

The synod seemed to be calling for the "ultimate weapon," if neces-

152. John H. Zeilstra, letter to the author, 30 Nov. 2000.

153. Ottenhoff and Ottenhoff, "Timothy Christian Schools," 23-24.

154. Christian Reformed Church, *Acts of Synod,* 1968, Art. 36; Classis Chicago North Minutes, 17 Sept. 1969, Art. 26; *Acts of Synod,* 1969, Art. 123; Classis Chicago North, Consortium of Six Consistories, "Appeal to Synod 1972," 19 Jan. 1972.

sary, of excommunication of the eighteen board members, but there was a sticking point. Dutch Reformed schools are not parochial; they are parent controlled and as such are nonecclesiastical. The consistory of each board member's local church would have to act individually to carry out the formal process of discipline.

The regional ecclesiastical body, Classis Chicago North, forestalled such action by consistently defeating motions "to declare to be sinful the present policy of the Timothy Christian Board." The first action took place September 17, 1969, when the fourteen churches of classis, by a narrow thirteen to twelve vote, rejected the synodical admonition. This drove to distraction Lawndale's pastors Duane Vander Brug and intern Karl Westerhof, George Lubben, chair of its education committee, and James La Grand Jr., who had just arrived to pastor the Garfield Chapel, another mission congregation near Lawndale that also had students applying to Timothy. Westerhof and Lubben had drafted a letter to the classis on behalf of the Lawndale Council and the black parents, demanding that the board "MAKE A WAY TO DO WHAT IS RIGHT. We believe that no Christian may choose to be disobedient whenever he judges obedience to be too risky."[155]

The school board was convinced that the white leaders of the Lawndale and Garfield churches had stirred the pot of protest. Instead of preaching the gospel of peace, they had begun an "aggressive program of social activism." The missionaries and their small band of allies in the suburban churches, mostly transfers from Michigan churches, rejected the charges in the strongest terms and accused the Timothy board and supporting churches of harboring "repression and racial hatred" and of reducing their fellow black Christians to little more than "objects of racial manipulation."[156] The rhetoric was reaching a fever pitch.

At this critical juncture, the board took some comfort in an editorial

155. Classis Chicago North Minutes, 17 Sept. 1969, Art. 26; Ottenhoff and Ottenhoff, "Timothy Christian Schools," 23; James La Grand, Jr., "An Outsider Moves In," *Calvinist Contact* 25 March 1971, 1, 12.

156. "Report of the Lawndale Subcommittee of the Home Missions Committee of Classis Chicago North," Classical Home Missions Committee Minutes, 5 Nov. 1969, Art. 5. The Lawndale Subcommittee report was drafted and signed by Eugene Bradford and Anthony Diekema. A third member, George De Boer, demurred from the strident words and resigned forthwith. See letter of George De Boer to the Home Missions Committee of Classis Chicago North, 30 Dec. 1969. In 1970 two new members joined Diekema on the Lawndale subcommittee – the Rev. George Vander Hill and elder Harry Elders of the Wheaton church.

by the influential Lester De Koster, editor of the *Banner.* De Koster, who had been visited personally by several Timothy board members, counseled the church at large that if the board is truly "*unable* to enroll these children under such circumstances, then we must at least be willing to give full consideration to this as the other side of the coin."[157]

In September 1969, William Buiten of Western Springs replaced Al Kieft as president of the Timothy board, and he was almost immediately faced with a crisis. The most dangerous day in the Timothy-Lawndale conflict came Wednesday, October 22, 1969, when four of Timothy's eleven teachers – none natives of Chicago and all new hires – expressed their moral outrage at the board's refusal to obey the synod. They resigned together the very morning that thirty-five of their supporters came from Calvin College and Seminary in Grand Rapids, Michigan, to picket the school, many wearing black arm bands. Vander Brug led the protest delegation. His last pastorate had been the Lawndale congregation, and he had recently become the denominational director of urban ministries. He felt compelled to act by duty and conscience.

The situation turned ugly that morning, as parents had to come to pick up their children after the principal closed the school. Some parents joined the school janitors and some aroused Cicero residents in heckling the quiet marchers, who had grown to more than sixty. Augmenting the Calvin College contingent were sympathetic Chicago clergy, lay leaders, and students from Trinity Christian College in Palos Heights, which was the capstone of Reformed Christian education in the Chicago area. Anthony Diekema, a Wheaton church elder and member of the classical home missions committee, alternated between the protest line and an ongoing committee meeting in the school building for which he removed his arm band; he "wore two hats" that day, so to speak. NBC newsmen covered the two-hour demonstration and taped interviews with the four teachers, which further heightened the tension. Four city police officers stood by in case of violence, but none occurred. This impromptu confrontation was a low point because it pitted Christian Reformed believers against one another. The Christian Reformed churches on the West Side had their "Selma," but it was hardly to be compared with the real Selma in Alabama.[158]

157. "Lawndale and Cicero – the other side of the coin," *Banner,* 10 Oct. 1969.

158. Hoezee and Meehan use the phase, "the CRC Selma," in their highly critical portrayal of the events at Timothy, which reflects the official denominational view of the controversy (*Flourishing in the Land,* 137-40).

The first word that picketers from Grand Rapids were departing for Cicero reached Bradford by way of a phone call at 4:30 AM from Calvin College professor Delwin Nykamp, a son of the Ebenezer church. Bradford, a member of Calvin's Board of Trustees, alerted the Timothy principal, Daniel Veurink, who had replaced Tolsma in 1967, and Veurink managed to cancel the school bus pickups so those pupils would, at least, be spared possible violence. Veurink went out to meet the street protestors in fear and trepidation. "Chaos reigned!" he recalled. Board president Buiten rescued him by directing that he close the school and send home those students who had walked to school. This defused the situation and left the protesters with no audience. By 8 AM, principal Theodore De Jong of the Timothy Christian Junior High School four blocks away had also canceled all classes for the day.[159]

The resignations of the teachers stunned the community, but the school board had been forewarned. The four – Howard Stob, Elizabeth Westerhof (both Calvin College graduates), Karen Cox, and Linda Moseson – had on October 8 written letters to the board explaining that its unscriptural policy put them in a moral "position of compromise." They demanded that the board, at its next scheduled meeting on October 16, reverse the policy and notify them in writing by October 20, 1969.

This was the background to the joint resignations of October 22, in which the four declared, "We can no longer be employed in the institution where demands of discipleship to Christ are consistently denied." In truth, Veurink was in sympathy with the four. He too resigned the next summer at the end of the contract year, after presenting a letter protesting the board's stance in January 1970 without effect.[160]

Some school supporters had the sneaking suspicion that the teachers were "plants" of denominational "do-gooders." This line of thinking –

159. Calvin College *Chimes,* 24 Oct. 1969, p. 1; "4 Teachers Quit; Cicero school shut," *Chicago Tribune,* 22 Oct. 1969, p. 7; "Cicero church school, 4 teachers resign over race policy," *Chicago Daily News,* 22 Oct. 1969; "Church School Disrupted by Race Charge," *Chicago Tribune,* 24 Oct. 1969, p. 1; "School Picketed Over Race Issue," *Berwyn Life,* 24 Oct. 1969, p. 1; public letter of Ebenezer Christian Reformed Church Consistory, Nov. 1969; interview with Eugene Bradford, 4 Oct. 1998; letter of Daniel Veurink to the author, 5 Oct. 1999.

160. Letters of Howard Stob, Elizabeth H. Westerhof, Linda A. Moseson, and Karen Cox to Timothy Christian School Board, 8 Oct. 1969, with copies to parents, clerks of consistories in Classis Chicago North, and the Commission on the Christian and Race Relations of Calvin College and Seminary. Stob, who had grown up in Grand Rapids, interestingly, was a cousin by marriage of board president Kieft, and Westerhof was the wife of Karl Westerhof, a Calvin Seminary student serving as interim pastor of the Lawndale Christian Reformed Church, the focal point of the controversy.

that Timothy was the victim of an organized plot – was encouraged by the appearance of the Michigan marchers in front of the school building. The remaining teachers were basically in agreement with the moral imperative of those who resigned, but they remained committed to the school nonetheless. Angry Cicero residents blamed Bradford for the uproar. One woman (not a school society member) called the minister and said: "Mr. Bradford, you are the one behind the effort to get black children in the school. I live across the street from the school, and when my husband comes home we're going to organize and you're going to get a bullet through your window tonight." City police stood guard that night at Bradford's parsonage, while he and his family left the city for a time. But Bradford remained adamant in chiding the school board for caving in to the threats of violence. "I cannot see how people of Christian persuasion can surrender to forces that do not permit them to operate within their teachings." Moreover, the full weight of federal law enforcement stood ready to protect the school, he averred.[161]

The Timothy board readily found four experienced "mom-teachers" who had left the classroom to raise children, and academic work continued for the benefit of the pupils. Fortunately for the administration, the annual teacher's institute fell on the Thursday and Friday following the resignations, and no classes were scheduled then or on the next Monday, which had previously been set aside for parent-teacher conferences. This gave Veurink and the board enough breathing room to get fully staffed for classes to resume on Tuesday morning. Only one school day, the infamous Wednesday, was lost.[162]

The racial dimension brought public agencies into the fracas. The state office of nonpublic school accreditation sent an investigatory team from Cook County to look into the "racist" charges, and the Internal Revenue Service ordered an audit of the school's financial records, presumably as a challenge to its tax-exempt status. Was the investigation instigated by the activists, as some supposed, or did IRS examiners merely respond to the newspaper reports about a school presumably not in compliance with civil rights laws? Neither effort came to anything. The investigating team reported that the intent of the Timothy board "is very sincere and very genuine and is certainly not one of segregation." The team

161. "Minister Received Threatening Calls," *Berwyn Life,* 26 Oct. 1969; "Church School Faces Loss of Accreditation," *Chicago Tribune,* 29 Oct. 1969.

162. "Timothy teachers resign in protest," *Calvin College Chimes,* 24 Oct. 1969, p. 1; "MCTA group discusses Timothy, asks support for four teachers," ibid., 31 Oct. 1969, p. 9.

recommended probation for accreditation and the state superintendent concurred.[163]

On the ecclesiastical front, the synod of 1970 ordered the school board and Classis Chicago North to comply with its integration orders of 1968 and 1969, on pain of being "in contempt of synod and in open disregard of the church of Jesus Christ." This is the only time in the denomination's 150-year history that the synod used the term "contempt of synod" in connection with an entire classis. The egregious behavior of Classis Chicago North and the Timothy board "is calculated to shame us all," lamented Henry Stob, a Calvin Seminary professor and synodical advisor. Stob was pained to be a native of Chicago.[164]

Classis responded positively to the synodical directive by convening a special meeting on November 10, 1970, in the Winfield church. The Lawndale church delegation, including its new pastor Richard Grevengoed, boycotted the meeting. Nevertheless, the regional assembly adopted a resolution expressing "guilt and sorrow in failing to act in accord with the declarations on race of the synods of 1968 and 1969," and it decided to send a "pastoral letter" to the Timothy board imploring it "no longer to countenance" exclusion of black children. But a crucial resolution that charged the school board with being "disobedient to Christ" by acting "out of fear" of reaction by racists, was rejected by an eighteen to eight vote, following a "long and heated debate."[165]

Unofficially, the board was angered by the synod's unprecedented use of the term "in contempt," believing such legal terminology to be wholly inappropriate. Synod, acting as the petitioner, can *charge* a classis (the respondent) with contempt, but *only a court of law* can make such a judgment, and that after petitioners have shown cause. Surely, the synod does not "wish to sit in judgment as a COURT OF LAW," declared Garrett Stoutmeyer, pastor of the Elmhurst congregation and a member of the classis.[166]

163. "Report Cicero School May Lose Its Accreditation," *Chicago Tribune,* 29 Oct. 1969; "Church School in Cicero to Get Probation on 'Bias,'" ibid., 31 Oct. 1969; "Cicero Church School Awaits State Action on 'Racist' Charge," ibid., 3 Nov. 1969.

164. Henry Stob, "Let Us Repent," *Reformed Journal* 20 (Mar. 1970): 3.

165. "Response of Classis Chicago North to Synod," 17 Nov. 1970; James Quinn, "Church School 'Rebuked' for Negro Ban," *Chicago Tribune,* 25 Nov. 1970, NW p. 10; Paul LaMaire and Donald Ottenhoff, "Latest Phase of the Racial Maze," *Calvin College Chimes,* 19 Mar. 1971. The minority votes on the crucial question included six elders and two ministers, George Vander Hill of the Wheaton church and Lloyd Wolters of the Des Plaines church. Both were Michigan-born.

166. "Response of Classis Chicago North to Synod"; LaMaire and Ottenhoff, "Latest

Nor could the board and its supporting churches shake the conviction that they faced a genuine moral dilemma, a conflict between two equally valid, equally divine requirements. Racism is sin, but fleeing out of fear is not sin; it is taking "flight for physical safety," as the patriarch Jacob did before his jilted brother Esau. For the synod to condemn the Timothy school board and its constituency is irresponsible and even wrong. "No church assembly, by demanding that families expose themselves to danger, is acting responsibly." Furthermore, "no church may demand martyrdom."[167]

When the critical vote went down to defeat, James La Grand, pastor of the Garfield Chapel and an official delegate to the classis meeting, stalked out in protest, after telling the chair that in his opinion the classis had acted in contempt of synod. For this breach of the church order (i.e, leaving without permission), plus other acts of "insubordination, bearing false witness and promoting discord and mutiny in the church," La Grand was subsequently suspended from office for three months by his sponsoring consistory, the Warren Park Christian Reformed Church of Cicero. This action further angered the Garfield congregation.[168]

Subsequently, the Timothy board wrestled with the classical admonition but felt constrained to reaffirm its policy of exclusion in the Cicero facility. To do otherwise, said the board in a letter to the classis, would pose "an unwarranted risk of bodily injury and property damage." The situation, lamented La Grand, remained a case of "left alone Lawndale and timid Timothy."[169]

The controversy continued as Classis Chicago North sought a solution acceptable to all. The primary tactic was to go on the offensive by sending overtures to Synod 1971 demanding clarity on the threat to hold the classis "in contempt" and subject to "admonition and discipline."[170] Meanwhile, a group of twelve outspoken integrationists in the classis, three clerics and nine laymen, which included the three-person Lawndale

---

Phase." A positive review of the decisions of the classis is in Garrett H. Stoutmeyer, "The Timothy-Lawndale Situation," *Outlook* (May 1971): 19-21. A negative view is Martin LaMaire, "Acts of a Minor Assembly," *Reformed Journal* (Jan. 1971), 14-18.

167. Classis Chicago North Consortium, "Appeal to Synod," 1971, pp. 6-7.

168. LaMaire and Ottenhoff, "Latest Phase"; "Black church hits voting rights loss," *Chicago Daily News*, 12-13 Dec. 1970; "Church Unit Finds School Innocent of Bias in Cicero," *Chicago Tribune*, 25 Jan. 1971; "Suspend Minister in Cicero Timothy School 'Bias' Case," ibid., 10 Feb. 1971; James Quinn, "'High Court' Plea for Rebel Minister?" ibid., 12 Feb. 1971.

169. LaGrand, "An Outsider Moves In," 12.

170. "The Response of Classis Chicago North to Synod," 17 Nov. 1970.

subcommittee of the Classical Home Missions committee, tried to blunt these moves by counterovertures to synod. Their tactic was to get the synod to declare Classis Chicago North in contempt, and then to refuse to seat its delegates. Since all but one of the members of the subcommittee were Michigan transplants living in the far western suburbs, they were conveniently dismissed as "outsiders" who simply "did not understand."[171]

The unprecedented actions of the protesters failed, although Synod 1971 chastised the classis yet again for its "failure to comply," and the classis once more sent an appeal to Synod 1972 for redress against its decisions. The classis insisted that it had always acted ethically; racial discrimination based on "hatred, is sin," but action "arising out of fear, is not sin." And in Cicero fear ruled.[172]

In the end, the westward migration of the Dutch Reformed out of the Cicero-Berwyn-Oak Park nexus into Elmhurst and Lombard in Du Page County solved the board's problem. Some fifteen hundred people of Dutch descent remained in Cicero in 1969, 2 percent of the population, but the numbers were dwindling. They had been twice as large a decade earlier.[173] Since 1962 the high school had relocated to Elmhurst, followed by grades five through eight in 1970, when the Cicero high school building was sold. In 1972 the remaining facility, the elementary school that was the focal point of the protests, was sold to the Cicero public school system, and classes were started in a new building hastily constructed on the Elmhurst property. Haste was needed because the sale was contingent on giving possession to Cicero officials in time for the new school year in September 1971, leaving barely six months to construct the new Elmhurst facility. In a Herculean effort, the board met the deadline.

171. Letter of George Vander Hill to John Kromminga, 4 Feb. 1971, and Kromminga's reply, 19 Feb. 1971; protest of Council of Wheaton Christian Reformed Church to William P. Brink, denominational stated clerk, 23 Feb. 1971; letter of James La Grand to 1972 Synod of the Christian Reformed Church (CRC), 13 June 1972; "Protest and Appeal to Synod 1971," signed by twelve individuals. The signatories are Jon R. Sharpe of Winfield CRC; Harry Elders, Leonard Sytsma, David De Mol, Russell Poel, George Vander Hill, and Anthony Diekema of Wheaton CRC, Gerald Vander Velde of Oak Park CRC, Martin LaMaire of Ebenezer CRC, Peter Vander Bent of Des Plaines CRC, James La Grand of Garfield CRC, and Henry Vellinga of Hope CRC (Oak Forest, Ill., in Classis Chicago South). Only Vander Velde was a native son. These and other valuable documents owned by George Vander Hill were graciously loaned to the author. Copies have since been donated to the Archives, Calvin College.

172. Appeal to Synod, Section II. "The Ethical Dilemma," adopted by Classis Chicago North, 19 January 1971.

173. *"All Things Are Lawful,"* 3.

The transition to Elmhurst went smoothly because Buiten, after replacing Kieft as Timothy board president, had quietly laid the groundwork for the sale of the Cicero building. But the constituency had not been ready for this step, until a precipitating event forced them to act. This was the filing in early 1971 of a lawsuit in U.S. District Court against the Timothy board by Lawndale parents, now constituted as the Chicago West Side Christian School Association. The suit charged the board with racial discrimination, demanded an immediate injunction to compel admittance of all students, and asked actual and punitive damages of $22,000 and $100,000 respectively. A national arm of the Christian Reformed Church backed the legal action. The Synodical Committee on Race Relations (SCORR), an agency centered in Grand Rapids, Michigan, paid $500 in incidental filing expenses, and the plaintiffs' Chicago lawyers, led by Christian Reformed member Case Hoogendoorn, worked pro bono.[174]

The legal action raised a firestorm of comment across the denomination because it seemed to violate the scriptural injunction against lawsuits within the church. The *Reformed Journal* editors, speaking for the liberal wing of the church, judged the litigants to be justified after having exhausted all other remedies in the previous six years. Those in the conservative wing decried the suit as sub-Christian and strongly condemned the use of church contributions to pay for brother going to law against brother.[175]

The lawsuit had a major impact locally and hastened the end game. It changed many minds among Timothy supporters and gave the board the backing it needed to conclude the sale of the Cicero building to the city school system. This action, occurring in March of 1971, rendered the suit moot, and Federal Judge Hubert L. Will, a man with impeccable civil rights credentials, dismissed the case over Hoogendoorn's heated objections. Judge Will did chastise the board, however, for its discriminatory conduct and unconstitutional policies.[176] Thus, the sorry affair ended in a bitter standoff.

With the Timothy schools safely out of Cicero, the board announced that all facilities were open to Reformed parents "without regard to race or color." In the eyes of the board, Buiten had given "Moses-

174. Memorandum, Case Hoogendoorn to Karl Westerhof, "Timothy Litigation," 12 Nov. 1971, courtesy of George Vander Hill.

175. Hoezee and Meehan, *Flourishing in the Land,* 139.

176. Ibid., 139, citing *Banner* editorial, Lester De Koster, "God Was Not Wasting His Time," 14 Jan. 1972, which quoted the ruling.

like leadership" by finding a way out of the abyss. But the embittered Lawndale and Garfield parents did not apply to Timothy, even though the relocated school was an easy thirty-minute commute on the Eisenhower Expressway. In 1970 Lawndale had already launched its own school, West Side Christian, beginning with kindergarten and grade one. They received financial help from Christian Reformed members nationwide, and two white members joined the staff in 1971, including Barbara Grevengoed, wife of the new church pastor, Richard Grevengoed. This quiet couple served the church humbly and well; they brought genuine healing.

Until the new school offered all grades, Lawndale children continued to travel by school bus to Des Plaines Christian School, despite its great distance, but many more attended the nearby Catholic school, Our Lady of Sorrows. High school students attended Timothy in Elmhurst until 1971, when they transferred to Walther High School, a theologically conservative, Missouri Synod Lutheran institution. When the Des Plaines school lost its Lawndale contingent, which had composed half the student body, it was no longer viable and had to close.[177]

The Timothy board outlasted the denomination on the Lawndale controversy because it retained the wholehearted support of the vast majority of the members of the Christian Reformed Church in the western suburbs. In one particularly tense meeting, parents gave the chair, Albert Kieft, a standing ovation after he restated the principle of expediency for refusing to admit blacks. The same thinking allowed the westsiders to dismiss the intellectual elites from Calvin College and Seminary, the denominational offices (derisively dubbed the "Pentagon"), and SCORR, all of whom came to lecture the "Cicero bigots." A biblical caption in *Chimes,* the Calvin College student newspaper that covered the story extensively, captured the attitude perfectly: "And behold, there came wise men from the east." These wise men, however, in the eyes of the locals came not with gifts but a self-righteous attitude and an unwillingness to walk in the

177. Open letter, Fall, 1971, Chicago West Side Christian School Association, signed by Luther Benton, president; author's conversation with Lloyd Wolters, then pastor of the Des Plaines Christian Reformed Church, 3 July 2001. West Side Christian School under principal Mary Post received a major financial boost in 2001 from the Bill and Melinda Gates Foundation under the sponsorship of the Grand Rapids–based Christian Schools International (CSI), the umbrella organization for all Reformed Christian schools. West Side Christian will share $4.4 million in Microsoft money with Rehoboth Christian School near Gallup, New Mexico, another Christian Reformed mission endeavor (Rick Wilson, "Christian Schools International gets $4.4 million grant," *Grand Rapids Press,* 19 Sept. 2001, D7).

shoes of others. Their children were not at risk. The Dutch proverb seemed apt: *De beste stuurman staat aan wal* ("The best pilots are on the shore").[178]

The Timothy-Lawndale confrontation is a tragic episode filled with "might have beens." If the Lawndale leaders had not been so confrontational, and if they had given the Timothy board more time to formulate a public relations campaign, might not the fearful neighbors have been persuaded to accepted the school's integration peacefully, however begrudgingly? If the denominational assemblies, the classis and synod, had exercised their discipline in a pastoral rather than a legal way, with more love and understanding than finger pointing and moralizing, might not the Timothy board and families have been persuaded to step out in faith? But history must record what actually happened, not what might have been. The Timothy board and parents might have been willing to place themselves in jeopardy for the principle of Christian fellowship they professed. But to ask them to risk the lives of their children was more than any parent would or should accept.[179]

Timothy Christian Schools— Elmhurst (1962-today)

In Elmhurst, Timothy elementary school shared a twenty-six-acre campus with the senior and junior high schools, which had relocated from Cicero in 1962 and 1970, respectively. The multimillion-dollar complex was south of the town of Elmhurst at the corner of Butterfield Road and Prospect Street. The desirable property had been owned by Cicero physician, Dr. Cornelius N. Vetten, who himself had taught at Timothy for two years under Hendrikse.

Vetten sold the prime acreage, including a brick house, for $65,000 to a syndicate of supporters who held title for some time until the school society was ready to consummate the project. In 1957, four hundred society members assembled and voted "by a large majority" to purchase the property, which the syndicate transferred at cost. At the same meeting, the society launched a $125,000 fund drive to close an operating deficit and fund the needed expansion in Elmhurst, which was projected to cost

178. "Timothy: Crisis in Christian Education," 6, 8; "Classis Chicago North," Association of Christian Reformed Laymen *News Bulletin,* July 1971, 7-8.

179. For these queries, I am indebted to William Zeilstra, Christian Reformed cleric, 1972 graduate of Timothy Christian High School, and son of board president John Zeilstra.

$600,000. The campaign, the largest in Timothy's history to that point, was led by Drive Committee chair Clarence Huizenga.[180]

The decade following the uprooting was a heady time at the high school; total enrollments rose to nine hundred by 1970. A year earlier, the board named as principal Timothy's veteran teacher Arnold Hoving. He replaced Calvin Den Besten, who had resigned to become a salesman in Michigan. Hoving was a descendant of the original West Side families, the Sterenbergs and Beukemas, and had grown up in Clearing near Midway Airport. He joined the faculty in 1958 after graduating from Calvin College and taught mathematics and science and coached boys' basketball teams. As principal, Hoving in 1970 coordinated the amalgamation into Timothy of the Western Suburbs Christian School in Western Springs (founded in 1957), and in 1976 he gained accreditation for the Timothy schools from the North Central Association. In 1978 he was named superintendent of the entire system, while continuing as high school principal.[181]

In the 1970s, Timothy Christian faced the challenge of a steep enrollment decline of more than 15 percent, largely due to the effect of oral contraception on birth rates. It took eleven years, until 1981, to get back to the 1970 student level of nine hundred, and in 1988 enrollment topped eleven hundred.

Hoving and the board accomplished this increase by broadening the school's base. First, in 1976 they began a preschool and enrolled children without requiring parents to meet the requirements of society membership. Second, they beefed up the busing program to reach high school students as far as Des Plaines. Third, with the much-coveted accreditation in hand, they targeted evangelical Protestant churches in the region and urged members to consider quality Christian education for their children at Timothy rather than public schooling. Timothy parents also helped the recruitment program by word of mouth; they recommended the school to friends and acquaintances outside the Reformed community. As a result of these ardent efforts, many people caught the vision, and the student mix at Timothy gradually became less Reformed and less ethnic, with an increasing number of minorities – blacks, Hispanics, and Asians. In 1977,

180. "Timothy Christian Schools to Expand," *Illinois Observer,* Oct. 1957. Drive committee members were Richard Evenhouse, James G. De Boer, Clarence Huizenga, Richard Schuurman, John Van Byssum, and Arnold Weersing.

181. Albert Kieft, "Mr. Arnold Hoving," *Timothy Reflector,* 30 Apr. 1969; "Chronology of Arnold Hoving's Career at Timothy Christian Schools," kindly provided the author by Arnold Hoving.

95 percent of Timothy students were of Reformed persuasion, almost all members of Christian Reformed churches. Twenty years later, in 1997, only 45 percent of Timothy students were of Reformed persuasion and nearly 10 percent were minorities.[182]

The recruitment effort restored Timothy Christian Schools to financial health, but it also fundamentally changed the ethnoreligious complexion of the school. Timothy is no longer the school of the Dutch Christian Reformed families on the West Side. The changing cultural climate caused some tensions, especially among poorer Reformed parents who felt threatened by those who could afford the high tuition costs. To remedy this problem somewhat, the board in 1978, at the urging of Peter Huizenga, created an endowment fund, the Timothy Foundation, to subsidize tuition fees. The Friendship Clubs also continued to boost the school; at their fiftieth anniversary in 1983, President Cathy Canniff tallied the total contributions of the clubs since 1933 at $640,000![183]

Hoving mastered the art of fundraising and managed a three-million-dollar budget. To meet pressing space needs, he spearheaded four capital campaigns that raised $11.5 million for additional facilities and fattened the foundation into a multimillion-dollar endowment. "Mr. Timothy" retired in 1994 with honor and acclaim after thirty-five years of service and twenty-five years in administration. Daniel Van Prooyen, the high school principal since 1986, now holds the trusted post of superintendent.[184]

In 1999 the *U.S. News and World Report* magazine recognized Timothy Christian School as one of ninety-six outstanding American high schools among more than one thousand schools in six major metropolitan areas. Timothy was the only non–Roman Catholic school to be named. "It is affirming to have a national magazine notice our mission of developing academically prepared disciples of Jesus Christ," said David Larsen, director of development at Timothy.[185]

Through its long history, Timothy Christian Schools served the Lawndale area for seventeen years, the Cicero area for forty-five years, and the Elmhurst area for more than thirty-five years. During just its first fifty years, according to the semicentennial anniversary book published in

182. Arnold Hoving reported these enrollment trends during his tenure in several phone conversations with the author, notably on 27 July 2001.

183. *Timothy Reflector,* May 1983, p. 22.

184. Ibid., April 1988. Hoving was principal of Timothy Christian High School from 1969 until 1986; he was superintendent from 1978 to 1994.

185. Report by Martin LaMaire, *Banner,* 15 Feb. 1999, p. 7.

1961, Timothy employed 160 teachers, and 340 men (yes, all men) served on the school board. Society membership over the years ran into the thousands, as do the student alumni.[186]

Trinity Christian College (1959-)

In 1952 the three Dutch Reformed high schools in greater Chicago had a total enrollment of sixteen hundred students. Until the leaders founded a Christian college in the city, the college-bound graduates went off to Calvin and Hope colleges, and few returned. In 1953 a group of clergy, businessmen, and professionals, led by the Reverend Arthur De Kruyter, pastor of the Western Springs Christian Reformed Church, formed a committee to end this "brain drain" by organizing Trinity Christian College as the apex of Reformed Christian education in Chicago. The timing was auspicious because enrollments in the Christian school system were projected to rise by 50 percent in the next five years. The initial plan was for a two-year, liberal arts feeder school.[187]

The biggest challenge for the committee was to convince the Chicago area people of the need for a *local* college. Loyalty to Calvin and Hope colleges ran deep, and many young people preferred to attend college away from home, rather than go to a commuter school. One persuasive argument was that the college would "strengthen our Reformed witness in the Chicagoland area, by consolidating the now three distinct Reformed communities."[188]

In 1959 a group of twenty society members purchased a thirty-two-acre property in Palos Heights, the Navaho Country Club, complete with an elegant stone clubhouse, for $260,000. Following a successful college fund drive in 1958 that raised $100,000, the group then sold to the college about half the acreage, including the clubhouse, which became the campus and main classroom building. The college opened for classes October

186. Listing in *50th Anniversary.* Among the board members are listed four Swierengas — the author's grandfather, father, great-uncle, and uncle. The alumni association, formed in 1939, published its first comprehensive alumni directory in 1999. See Timothy Christian High School, *Alumni Directory 1999* (White Plains, N.Y.: Bernard C. Harvis, 1999).

187. Trinity Christian College, *25 Years of Service: 1959-1984* (Chicago, 1984), *Illinois Observer,* 15 Feb., 15 Apr., 15 Nov. 1954, Dec. 1955. A survey of graduates of the three Christian high schools in Chicago in 1954 showed that four of five in college were attending Calvin College.

188. "Purposes of Trinity," *Illinois Observer,* May 1957.

1, 1959.[189] The society later sold off several acres to the Chicago Christian High School when it relocated from Englewood and an acre to the Back to God Hour radio ministry of the Christian Reformed Church when it relocated from Roseland.

Trinity's strongest support in the first decades came from the southsiders; the westsiders were lukewarm. In part, this was a reaction against a controversial, neo-Calvinistic philosophical system borrowed from the Free University of Amsterdam, which the first cadre of Trinity faculty, led by Calvin Seerveld and Robert Vander Vennen, espoused with a missionary fervor. The college constituency, in turn, reacted on the basis of historic differences that went back to the cultural roots in the Netherlands. The pioneers in Roseland and South Holland hailed from more urban and culturally developed regions (Noord- and Zuid-Holland and Friesland, respectively), whereas the westsiders and Englewood Dutch originated in the rural areas of northern Groningen.

Over time, the southsiders remained more homogeneous than did the westsiders, who rubbed shoulders with Americans at work and in the neighborhoods. The Groningers did not see the need for Reformed higher education unless the curriculum was "practical." The relative few who wanted to train for the professions, the westsiders argued, could continue to go to Michigan. But as Trinity grew and matured into a four-year, degree-granting, liberal arts college (1966), and after the board in 1972 jettisoned the narrow philosophical system that had driven the curriculum, more Timothy graduates matriculated there and attitudes slowly turned positive.

Tellingly, in 1973, the faculty approved a business major program that in 1976 ripened into B.S. degrees in Business Administration and Marketing. That year Trinity received full accreditation from the North Central Association. In 1979 the college began a nursing degree program. Clearly, the curriculum after two decades had evolved into a blend of practical and liberal courses of study, all taught, however, from a Reformed theological perspective that satisfied the constituency. In 1999 Trinity celebrated its fortieth year as a mature institution with an assured future.

Conclusion

"We love to speak of the chain consisting of three links – home, church and school; regarding it as a chain which cannot be easily broken." This

189. Ibid., May 1959.

statement by the consistory of the First Christian Reformed Church of Englewood captures the essence of the story of the Christian school system in Chicago. Christian Reformed youth were directed by church edict into congregation-supported schools at both the elementary and secondary level. Why? Because, as the axiom stated, "Our Christian schools are the feeders of our Christian churches."

These institutions were the most critical link in the chain that maintained cultural and ecclesiastical oneness in the church; they kept alive the Dutch language until the 1920s and transmitted Calvinist theological and cultural values for many generations. The schools stood in the shadow of the churches, and this naturally concentrated the families nearby, which strengthened community and church life immeasurably. The Christian high schools also provided a place to find marriage partners within the greater Chicago Reformed communities. Christian schooling thus kept the children within the cocoon of the church.

The commitment to Christian schooling in Chicago far surpassed that in Grand Rapids, the other Dutch metropolis. The seventeen Chicago-area Christian Reformed churches in 1940 averaged 89 percent attendance, compared to only 70 percent in Grand Rapids. In Chicago, it is noteworthy that the West Side surpassed the South Side; 92.8 percent of West Side families enrolled their children, compared to 86.3 percent of South Side families. The Berwyn Christian Reformed Church had a perfect record of 100 percent, and First and Fourth Chicago were close behind at 98 and 97 percent, respectively. The First and Second Cicero congregations lagged noticeably, at 88 and 81 percent, respectively. The First and Second Roseland churches stood at 96 percent, and First Englewood at 95 percent, but Third Roseland and Second Englewood fell far short at 74 percent each.[190] In most congregations, for parents to send their teens to the public high school almost guaranteed that they would be cut off from their friends at church. Such parents were often deemed to be slack Christians.

Reformed churches in Chicago, despite general denominational antipathy, cooperated in founding the Christian school system and supported it for several decades, notably at the secondary and college level. From the 1930s on, however, the commitment at the elementary level weakened, and Reformed children increasingly attended public schools. By 1940 the proportion of Reformed Church youth at Timothy Christian

190. These statistics are compiled from school attendance percentages by congregation, as reported in the National Union of Christian Schools *Yearbook* of 1940.

School had dwindled from 10 to 6 percent. This trend hastened assimilation and led to frequent outmarrying.

One hundred years ago, at the inception of the Christian schools, both denominations on the West Side were equal in strength. But today Reformed Church membership in the western suburbs is less than one-fifth that of the Christian Reformed Church. The success of the junior body in gathering in most of the new immigrants is certainly a factor. But even in the past fifty years, long after immigration ceased, the Reformed congregations continued to lose members at a rate five times greater than that of Christian Reformed congregations. From 1950 to 1999, Reformed Church membership declined by 48 percent (from 957 to 499), while Christian Reformed Church membership fell less than 10 percent (from 2,959 to 2,675). Could it be that Christian day school education made the difference in maintaining a Reformed Christian presence on the West Side? This conclusion seems warranted.

CHAPTER 8

A Covenanted Community: Church Social Life

As a covenanted community, the Dutch Calvinists of Chicago took seriously the scriptural injunction to be "in the world, but not of it" (paraphrasing John 17:15-16) and to "keep oneself unspotted by the world" (James 1:27). In the working world, they guardedly rubbed shoulders with "outsiders" out of necessity, but social life was lived among family and fellow church members. Keeping to themselves was as much cultural as religious in origin. A characteristic of European farm folk was to live in closed, corporate communities, and the Dutch immigrants carried that village mentality to Chicago.

Their clerics warned of the perils of city life and their impact on the Christian home. One lamented "the impairment, the irregularity, the resulting inefficiency of it all, on account of hurry, rush, distance, expense, weariness, outside attractions and distractions. It is next to impossible to maintain a healthy, vigorous, loyal, united, growing and fruitful church under such conditions. Many exclaim often, 'O Lord, the heathen are come into Thine inheritance.'"[1]

To facilitate fellowship among the believers and "to redeem the time," the Reformed and Christian Reformed churches organized a host of cultural, religious, musical, and sporting activities for young and old alike. As one person recalled, "Church societies were a way of life. Our three young ladies' groups were each very large. Annual socials were great occasions — mother and daughter festivities, socials for older ladies' aid

1. Moerdyke, "Chicago Letter," *CI,* 7 Nov. 1906, p. 721, quote from Psalm 79:1.

Mrs. J. C. (Elizabeth Overeem) Bovenkerk, president of first Ladies' Aid, Bethany Reformed Church, Roseland, 1913

groups, and also home-talent programs. In addition there were annual Sunday school picnics and choirs of various kinds – a full choir, a male chorus, and a ladies' chorus." Another member noted that church life "is one round of ceaseless activity."[2]

All the churches held annual summer congregational outings or Sunday school picnics, and the Christian schools put on their annual picnics as well, usually on the July 4th holiday or other summer Saturdays. Favorite venues for westsiders were in Riverside at Bergman's Grove, National Grove, and Riverside Woods, all running along Des Plaines Avenue between 26th and 29th Streets. The bands entertained from the bandstand, the children enjoyed races and games with small prizes and ice cream for all, the young men had a tug of war and played softball, as did the young women, and the older men pitched horseshoes, while the ladies talked. These picnics were a highlight of the year. On occasion, as in 1897, both Reformed denominations in Chicago held a union 4th of July picnic celebration at one of the city parks, where ministers stirred up patriotic sentiments in both the Dutch and English languages.[3]

The annual Christmas program staged by the Sunday school pupils on a Sunday evening in December was the winter counterpart to the summer picnic. Each class presented songs and recitations, the superinten-

2. Herbert J. Brinks, "Johanna (Gelderloos) LaMaire: Notes for and about the Past," *Origins,* 11 No. 1 (1993): 32; "Douglas Park, Chicago Notes," *Banner,* 5 Dec. 1912.

3. Moerdyke, "Chicago Letter," *CI,* 26 May 1897, p. 12.

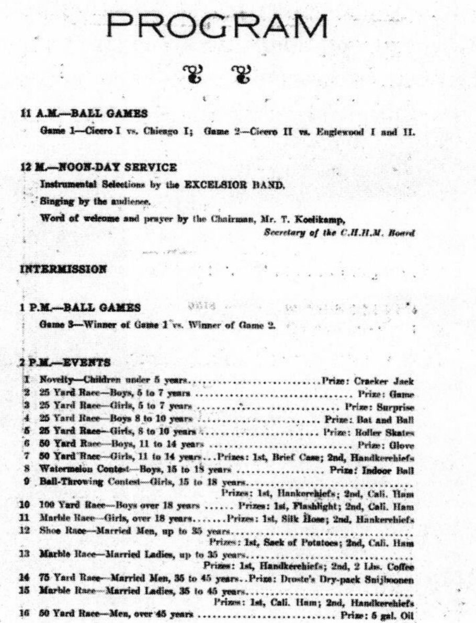

PROGRAM

11 A.M.—BALL GAMES
Game 1—Cicero I vs. Chicago I; Game 2—Cicero II vs. Englewood I and II.

12 M.—NOON-DAY SERVICE
Instrumental Selections by the EXCELSIOR BAND.
Singing by the audience.
Word of welcome and prayer by the Chairman, Mr. T. Koelikamp,
Secretary of the C.H.H.M. Board

INTERMISSION

1 P.M.—BALL GAMES
Game 3—Winner of Game 1 vs. Winner of Game 2.

2 P.M.—EVENTS
1 Novelty—Children under 5 years.......Prize: Cracker Jack
2 25 Yard Race—Boys, 5 to 7 years.......Prize: Game
3 25 Yard Race—Girls, 5 to 7 years.......Prize: Surprise
4 25 Yard Race—Boys 8 to 10 years.......Prize: Bat and Ball
5 25 Yard Race—Girls, 8 to 10 years.......Prize: Roller Skates
6 50 Yard Race—Boys, 11 to 14 years.......Prize: Glove
7 50 Yard Race—Girls, 11 to 14 years...Prizes: 1st, Brief Case; 2nd, Handkerchiefs
8 Watermelon Contest—Boys, 15 to 18 years.......Prize: Indoor Ball
9 Ball-Throwing Contest—Girls, 15 to 18 years.......Prizes: 1st, Hankerchiefs; 2nd, Cali. Ham
10 100 Yard Race—Boys over 18 years......Prizes: 1st, Flashlight; 2nd, Cali. Ham
11 Marble Race—Girls, over 18 years.......Prizes: 1st, Silk Hose; 2nd, Hankerchiefs
12 Shoe Race—Married Men, up to 35 years.......Prizes: 1st, Sack of Potatoes; 2nd, Cali. Ham
13 Marble Race—Married Ladies, up to 35 years.......Prizes: 1st, Handkerchiefs; 2nd, 2 Lbs. Coffee
14 75 Yard Race—Married Men, 35 to 45 years..Prize: Droste's Dry-pack Snijboonen
15 Marble Race—Married Ladies, 35 to 45 years.......Prizes: 1st, Cali. Ham; 2nd, Handkerchiefs
16 50 Yard Race—Men, over 45 years.......Prize: 5 gal. Oil
17 Marshmallow Race—Ladies, over 45 years.......Prizes: 1st, Double Blanket; 2nd, Handkerchiefs
18 Tug-of-War—Men, up to 35 years.......Prizes: Cigars
19 Tug-of-War—Men, 35 to 50 years.......Prizes: Cigars

EVENTS FOR ALL
BEAN CONTEST—Guess the number of Beans in jar at Refreshment Stand.....Prize: Surprise
FIND THE *DODGER*—Bring him to Mr. Henry Ottenhoff and receive a reward. Prize: Surprise

4 P.M.—AFTERNOON SERVICE
Selections by the Excelsior Band.
Singing by the audience.
Offering to be received for the POOR FUND of the Mission..
Address by Rev. P. A. Hoekstra.
Special Instrumental Selections by Miss A. Meyer and Mr. E. Vanderlaan.
Also Messrs. Korringa and Swierenga.

INTERMISSION

6:15 or 6:30 P.M.—INFORMAL SONG SING
Accompanied on the folding organ by Miss Kate Tiemersma.

7 P.M.—EVENING SERVICE
Address by one of the pastors.
Stereopticon Pictures (with Pace cartoons) by Rev. Geo. Steenstra.

THE COMMITTEE WISHES TO THANK
THE FOLLOWING DONORS

Leader Stores.......for 1st prize, event 7
Boston Store ... for 1st prizes, events 9 and 13; for 2nd prizes, events 7, 11, 15 and 17
Wm. Zylstra, *Grocer* ...... for 1st prize, event 15; for 2nd prizes, events 9, 10 and 12
Bosler Hardware & Supply Co.......for 1st prize, event 10
Van Dellen Dry Goods Store.......for 1st prize, event 11
Swierenga Brothers.......for 1st prize, event 12
C. Bulthuis, *Grocer*.......for 2nd prize, event 13
K. Wezeman, *Grocery and Market*.......for prizes, event 14 (4 jars)
Midland Oil Company.......for prize, event 16
Marshall Field & Co.......for 1st prize, event 17
J. H. Vander Velde.......for prizes, event 18
Huizenga & Son.......for prize, for Bean Contest
A Friend.......for prize, event 5
Another Friend.......for prizes, event 19
Still Another Friend.......for cash donation
Slager Auto Parts and Service.......for Programs
MISSION FESTIVAL COMMITTEE

Labor Day picnic program, Chicago Helping Hand Mission, National Grove, Riverside, 1933

dent awarded Bibles or Christian books for perfect attendance and Bible memory achievements, and afterwards everyone received a gift — an orange in the early days and later a half-pound box of chocolates. For many this was the biggest treat of the whole year, and the walls rang with the cries of the excited children.

Each Sunday school year culminated in June with the "jug-breaking" program, when the small piggy banks in which the children had saved money all year ifor the support of a particular missionary were brought to church and broken. The Christian Reformed congregations on the West Side often designated the money for one of their own, Tena Huizenga, who was a medical missionary in Nigeria for seventeen years, from 1936 to 1954. Huizenga graduated from the Chicago Mission Training School, the Garfield Park Hospital nursing program, and Moody Bible Institute.[4]

Other memorable social events on the church calendars were the Thanksgiving Day morning worship service and evening social program,

4. Brix, *Tena Huizenga;* and *The Huizenga Story: Or the Descendants of Jacob Willems and Anje Leues* (privately printed, Chicago, 1993), 23.

the annual father and son banquet and its counterpart, the mother and daughter banquet. Various church societies put on dinners and programs to raise money for missions or the local Christian schools. On average, except for the summer hiatus, church and school activities took up three evenings a week and nurtured the "fellowship of the saints."

Weddings

Weddings usually took place on a weekday evening in the sanctuary of the bride's church and were witnessed by the extended families and the entire congregation. Before the turn of the century, the ceremonies were simple affairs. The groom wore his one and only Sunday suit and the bride her best Sunday dress. The marriage of Henry [Hendrikus] Wezeman, Sr., and Clara Speelman in the 14th Street Christian Reformed Church in 1896 was typical. The couple took advantage of a spring "prayer day" service to be married and the ceremony was squeezed into the regular order of worship, complete with the long sermon.

As Wezeman recalled:

> We walked into and out of the church like the rest of the people. We had no flower girl, nor was there need of flowers but rather of the Lord's blessing and the sanction of the church upon our union. After the minister had finished reading the form [the official church formulary for marriages] and before the prayer we kneeled upon two pillows placed there so that our clothes would not be soiled, and thus we remained during the service. Before we arose I slipped a coin under the pillow as a tip for the janitor.[5]

Following the ceremony came the all-important reception, which was a major occasion for *gezelligheid,* a Dutch word for warm conviviality and fellowship. The joyous celebration was either at the bride's home, the church basement, or a nearby social hall, if the bride's family could afford it. Since the Dutch had no hall of their own, they rented such social favorites as Pilsen Hall at 1812 S. Ashland Avenue, Turner Hall on 12th Street at Western Avenue, the American Bohemian Hall on 18th Street, and the Sokol-Tabor Hall on 16th Street in Berwyn.

Wezeman described the special day:

5. Henry Wezeman, Sr., "Glimpses of the Past: Recollections, Experiences, and Anecdotes, Nunica, Michigan, August 1949," typescript courtesy of Maureen Cole.

> A carriage was waiting in front of the church to take us to the bride's mother's house, where a wedding reception was held with relatives and friends. The cab had only one horse but there was room enough for my bride and myself and our two mothers. I could have had a carriage with two horses but it would have cost four dollars. As it was, I agreed with the livery stable man at 16th St. and Blue Island Ave. to take us to the church and home again for $2.50. He did his work well! It was a cold, snowy evening and I could not have my girl walk in that weather as she had herself all fixed up so nice and the hairdresser had put her hair in many curls. People said we would get rich, for if it snowed on the bride when you married it was a sure sign. At any rate, my dear wife has been a blessing to me ever since, during more than half a century in which we have lived together.[6]

Wezeman, regrettably, did not describe the reception. Customarily, the toastmaster was an uncle or close family friend who regaled the celebrants with jokes that played on Dutch foibles or those of other ethnics, especially Jews and blacks. Potato salad and ham sandwiches were standard fare. Wine, if served at all, was offered sparingly and the music was religious or sentimental, never raucous or with a beat. A wedding dance was unheard of, except among some Reformed Church families whose teens had learned to dance in the public schools.

Following the ceremony, well-wishers would shower the happy couple with rice as they left the church for a noisy carriage ride or, later, auto parade in the neighborhood. Younger brothers and buddies decorated the wedding car and, at best, tied a string of tin cans to the back bumper. At worst, they would disable the car by stuffing a potato in the exhaust pipe, putting the car on blocks, or removing a vital part of the ignition system. Before and during the wedding ceremony, it was a cat and mouse game between the devious friends of the couple and the best man, whose duty it was to safeguard the car. Honeymoons were rare and brief at best, because grooms went to work the following Monday. Brides took up housekeeping, having quit their jobs to plan the wedding ceremony. It was now the groom's responsibility to support his bride.

6. Wezeman, "Glimpses."

Family Reunions

Beginning in the 1920s, several family clans organized annual reunions, complete with elected officers, formal programs, recreational activities, and genealogical compilations of each branch on the family tree. Such intergenerational gatherings were common in the Netherlands, where they were called *gastdagen* (literally, "guest days"). The tradition was needed even more in America, where urban immigrants scattered far and wide by the third generation. The hope was to hold the extended family together and recapture feelings of closeness experienced in the "old days." Such nostalgia was a powerful draw in the Depression decade. Most reunions were canceled during the Second World War; overtime work and military service disrupted family life, and gas rationing restricted car travel. The gatherings resumed after the war, only to be seriously diminished in the prosperous 1950s.

The Ton family of Roseland, descendants of Cornelius Ton, an 1840s immigrant from Noord Holland, was the first of many Dutch family groups to hold reunions. In 1896 the Tons first assembled at Oak Glen Woods in Lansing for what became an annual coast-to-coast celebration of their blood line. The Ton reunions were notable for their record size and formal organization; in 1920, a whopping seven hundred turned out, thanks to the energetic push of grandson C. J. Ton, a Roseland realtor and politician.[7]

The Hoekstras and Persenaires were other large Roseland families that observed annual reunion picnics for several decades beginning in the 1930s. In 1943, 350 of the 800 descendents of five sons of Lolles (Louis) Hoekstra, who had immigrated to America in the 1880s, gathered at Riverdale Park in Riverdale. Heavy rains in the afternoon drove them from the bandstand to the 108th Street Christian School in Roseland, where the picnic program continued into the evening. The American branch of the Hoekstra clan numbered 203 families that year.[8]

Among westsiders, the Stob family gathered each summer beginning in 1934. Its main progenitor was Willem Stob, who came to Chicago in 1881. He had eleven children, eighty-seven grandchildren, and hundreds of great-grandchildren. The Stob reunions continued for fifteen years and more, under the leadership of grandson Thomas J. Stob (1892-1951). In

7. Van Hinte, *Netherlanders in America,* 978-79.

8. "350 Hoekstra Descendants Join in Reunion," unidentified newspaper clipping of 1943 in possession of the author.

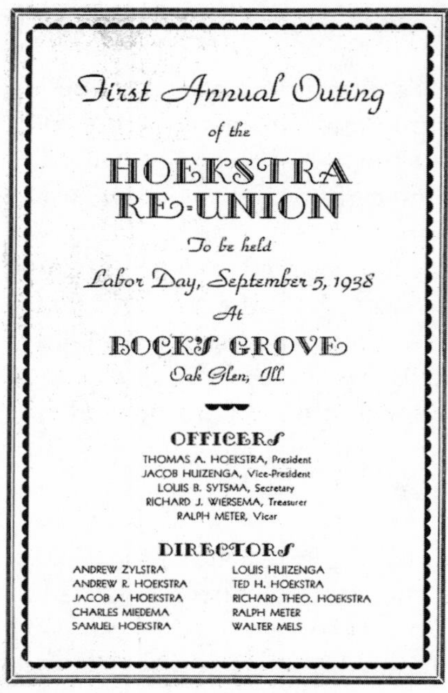

First Annual Outing
of the
HOEKSTRA
RE-UNION
To be held
Labor Day, September 5, 1938
At
BOCK'S GROVE
Oak Glen, Ill.

OFFICERS
THOMAS A. HOEKSTRA, President
JACOB HUIZENGA, Vice-President
LOUIS B. SYTSMA, Secretary
RICHARD J. WIERSEMA, Treasurer
RALPH METER, Vicar

DIRECTORS
ANDREW ZYLSTRA
ANDREW R. HOEKSTRA
JACOB A. HOEKSTRA
CHARLES MIEDEMA
SAMUEL HOEKSTRA
LOUIS HUIZENGA
TED H. HOEKSTRA
RICHARD THEO. HOEKSTRA
RALPH METER
WALTER MELS

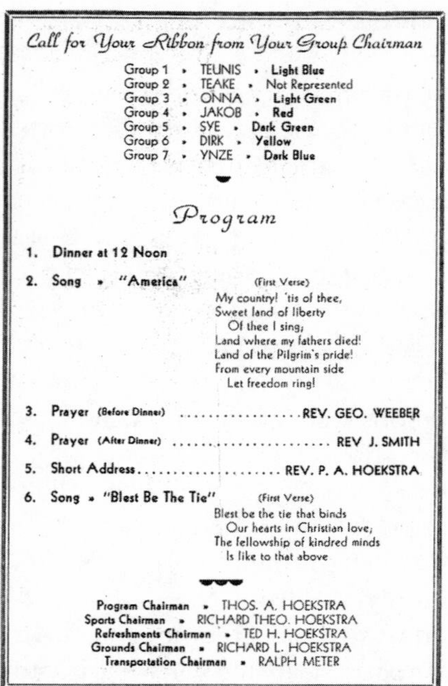

Call for Your Ribbon from Your Group Chairman

Group 1 • TEUNIS • Light Blue
Group 2 • TEAKE • Not Represented
Group 3 • ONNA • Light Green
Group 4 • JAKOB • Red
Group 5 • SYE • Dark Green
Group 6 • DIRK • Yellow
Group 7 • YNZE • Dark Blue

Program

1. Dinner at 12 Noon
2. Song • "America" (First Verse)
My country! 'tis of thee,
Sweet land of liberty
Of thee I sing;
Land where my fathers died!
Land of the Pilgrim's pride!
From every mountain side
Let freedom ring!
3. Prayer (Before Dinner) ....REV. GEO. WEEBER
4. Prayer (After Dinner) .... REV J. SMITH
5. Short Address.................... REV. P. A. HOEKSTRA
6. Song • "Blest Be The Tie" (First Verse)
Blest be the tie that binds
Our hearts in Christian love;
The fellowship of kindred minds
Is like to that above

Program Chairman • THOS. A. HOEKSTRA
Sports Chairman • RICHARD THEO. HOEKSTRA
Refreshments Chairman • TED H. HOEKSTRA
Grounds Chairman • RICHARD L. HOEKSTRA
Transportation Chairman • RALPH METER

Hoekstra Reunion program, 1933

1942 the Stob clan counted 850 members, nearly half of whom turned out for the annual love fest. That year the reunion was held indoors at the Timothy Christian School auditorium in Cicero, in order to screen 8mm movies of all the past reunions and be entertained by talented relatives. "A meeting of this kind makes for strong family ties and strengthens the bond of family relationships," noted Thomas Stob.[9]

The Stob clan was noted for intellectual acumen and leadership abilities. Thomas Stob was a leading realtor and politician in Cicero; the Berwyn-Cicero Real Estate Board elected him president and the town appointed him as its license officer. He served on the consistory of the First Christian Reformed Church of Cicero and used his financial acumen on the boards of Timothy Christian School (thirty-two years), the Chicago Helping Hand Mission (eighteen years), Chicago Nathanael Institute, the

9. "Stob Family Awaits Annual Reunion Party," newspaper clipping; "Stob Family Clan Held Interesting Meeting at Timothy Christian School May 22," *Cicero News,* 5 June 1942, with photo. Clippings kindly provided the author by Tom Stob's son Henry Martin Stob.

Chicago Tract Society, and the Reformed Bible Institute. His brother Henry Stob was a Calvin College and Seminary professor and leading intellectual in the church, as were his first cousins, Dr. George Stob and Dr. Ralph Stob, both of whom were professors at the same institutions. Ralph was president of Calvin College from 1933 to 1939. Henry Stob's book, *Summoning Up Remembrance,* is an insightful account of the family and of life in the Groninger Hoek.[10]

The Swierenga family, whose progenitor was Jan Swierenga, an 1893 immigrant with a wife and nine children, likewise met for family reunions at suburban picnic groves from the 1930s until the 1950s. The Dykhuis family, the Hoving family, and many others assembled more or less regularly in these years as well. Many of the men were small business owners and shopkeepers.

Consumerism

The Dutch Reformed held back from the cultural life of urban Chicago, but they quickly adopted the values of American consumerism. This is very evident in an 1870 "America letter" from Tijse Elzing, wife of William, to family in the Netherlands. The couple had lived in America only a few years and already they prided themselves on their new attire:

> My little girls are now dressed in American style with red stockings, white pants, and hoop skirts. . . . Last week Tjitsche and Matje got a new hat, and I made a new white hat for Tiet. Louwtje got a nice new hat with a veil and net over her hair. That is how all the girls have it here, a new dress and a pair of smooth shoes. Andries got a pair of cloth pants and smooth boots. He is a good boy and gives everything that he earns. My dear brother and sister, you should see me on Sundays with smooth boots, wearing an American hat, and a white coat. I had my hat redone; you would be quite surprised about the shape. When I go to church I wear a hoop skirt and a scarf around me. When I get back home everything comes off. You probably would say I would never be that crazy, but here no one is different.[11]

10. Thomas J. Stob, various undated newspaper obituary clippings provided the author by son Henry Martin Stob; Henry Stob, *Summoning Up Remembrance* (Grand Rapids: Eerdmans, 1995).

11. Letter, William and Tijse Elzing, Chicago, to "Dear Friends at Irnsum," Friesland, 10 Sept. 1870, Archives, Calvin College.

So Tijse and her children happily blended right into the American scene at church. Immigrants they surely were, but from outward appearances few would know it.

While young girls might glory in their church bonnets, their mothers brought down the wrath of the dominies for wearing such finery. As Moerdyke noted:

> We do vividly recall the open and frequent attacks made by Dutch ministers upon the adornment of bonnets with flowers and ribbons, in those early days of simplicity and plainness, which characterized the Hollanders in their pioneer experience here. Extravagance, luxury, fashion, vanity, were then readily suspected and repeatedly rebuked by the pulpit. . . . Incidents might be related which would amuse and amaze the generation now occupying the pews. This, too, is one of the "old things that have passed away."[12]

Young People's Societies

Beginning in the 1890s, the Reformed churches countered the emerging pop culture by promoting activities for their young people and adults that mixed social and religious teachings. The rationale was simple. As one cleric noted: "We believe our young people ought to stay among their own circle and are very glad to see our young people join our Society. In unity there is strength."[13]

First Reformed Church of Chicago inaugurated its young peoples' society, Ora et Labora, in 1893 with a big celebration that began well but fizzled badly. The church sanctuary was "full with the curious and the interested," according to a teen in attendance, and included representatives from other churches. The renowned Reverend Henry E. Dosker of Third Reformed Church of Holland, Michigan, was the featured speaker, but a teen reporter doubted whether his formal lecture on the Netherlandic writer Petrus De Genestet (1829-61) hit its target. The church's male chorus, under director R. Bol, and a recital by several church teens, were far more entertaining, as was the report of a member of the Ora et Labora.

The evening turned ugly when the church pastor, Ralph Bloemendal, formerly of North Holland, Michigan, and chair of the meet-

12. Moerdyke, "Chicago Letter," *CI,* 22 Feb. 1899, p. 12.
13. "Douglas Park, Chicago, Ill.," *Banner,* 9 Mar. 1916.

ing, curtly interrupted the young man in the middle of his oration and asked him to leave the platform because time was running out. The youth obeyed, "but only after he gave a brief but sharp disapproval of the insult." At this, "everybody expressed their indignation with body language" at the pastor's seeming lack of respect, said the eyewitness, who then added his strong opinion:

> If we are to see more of these teachers from Michigan, we suggest that they acquire some etiquette before they dare venture into Chicago. As a result of this incident, the gathered multitudes got a bad impression, the celebratory atmosphere was thoroughly spoiled, and a few more pieces that were subsequently recited, required the permission of the chair. No wonder that the audience angrily got ready to go home while the last recitals were still in progress. Nobody expected that an evening that started so lovely, with the promise of more, would end so darkly and painfully.

Amazingly, this frank report from someone who was likely not a member of First Reformed Church was published in the leading Dutch-language newspaper in America, *De Grondwet* of Holland, Michigan, right under the very nose of the esteemed Dosker.[14]

Over the next few years, the First Reformed Church followed sister congregations nationwide by adopting as its youth program the Christian Endeavor Society (known popularly as C.E.). This was an evangelical youth ministry founded in 1881 by a Congregational minister that grew into a national movement of more than seven thousand local societies in the 1880s. Christian Endeavor's motto was "For Christ and the Church," and its purpose was to integrate young people into the life of the church and prepare them for future leadership. Typically, the local chapters met in the churches each Sunday evening for instruction, inspiration, and fellowship. Topics for discussion focused on foreign missions and American evangelical crusades, such as temperance. In 1898, for example, six female members of Trinity Reformed's C.E. chapter participated in an oratorical contest for the Women's Christian Temperance Union (W.C.T.U.) medal.[15] C.E. also sponsored roller-skating, tobogganing, and other sporting activities. Many a marriage resulted from relationships begun at C.E. meetings.

14. "A Little Something from Chicago," *De Grondwet,* 7 Mar. 1893, translated by Huug van den Dool.

15. Moerdyke, "Chicago Letter," *CI,* 6 Apr. 1898, p. 14.

Soon C.E. organized city-wide rallies to bring together all the chapters for "good Dutch hospitality," music, and food. The Trinity Reformed Church sponsored the first rally in its sanctuary in 1897. The event drew delegations from seven societies and led to the formation of the C.E. Union of Chicago. The 1898 spring rally in the First Reformed Church of Englewood turned out an "inspiring audience of at least five hundred," Moerdyke reported. At the fall rally at the First Reformed Church of Chicago, young people came from all parts of the city to hear a missionary couple report on their work in India. Clearly, C.E. was a huge success. In 1899 the rallies were formalized into quarterly events under an organization headed by an executive committee, which was made up of one elected delegate from each society.[16]

The C.E. emphasis on missions led to the founding in Chicago around 1905 of the Young People's Missionary League, a regional body under clerical direction that arranged conferences featuring missionary speakers. Similar leagues were formed across the Reformed denomination in regions of concentration.[17]

The Christian Reformed counterpart to C.E. was the Young Men's and Young Women's societies, which were also formed on a congregational, city, and eventually national level. But these had no common national structure like C.E.; each local society wrote a constitution with bylaws, chose its own name, organized weekly activities, and participated in special programs. The ministers of the congregation usually led the societies and sought to integrate the participants into the life of the church locally and nationally.[18]

The Boer War in South Africa, when the Afrikaners fought for independence from British rule, provided the first big "cause" for the young people to rally around. "Chicago is alive with well nigh universal and most ardent sympathy for the cause of the two republics struggling for sacred liberty and right," declared Moerdyke. In 1900 the societies of the Fourteenth Street (First) Christian Reformed Church sponsored a city-wide

16. T. P. Weber, "Christian Endeavor Society," *Dictionary of Christianity in America,* Daniel G. Reid, ed. (Downers Grove, Ill.: InterVarsity Press, 1990): 256-57; Moerdyke, "Chicago Letter," *CI,* 13 Oct., p. 9, 10 Nov. 1897, p. 11; 9 Feb., p. 9, 12 Oct. 1898, p. 9; 1 Mar. 1899, p. 12.

17. Moerdyke, "Chicago Letter," *CI,* 19 Apr., p. 248, 24 May 1905, p. 331.

18. See, for example, the printed "Constitution and By-Laws of the Douglas Park Christian Young Men's Society, September 11th, 1924," copy in possession of author. This is a revised and translated English version of the original Dutch-language constitution of 1899.

mass meeting to uphold their cousins in South Africa who were being beaten down by the British army. Three Christian Reformed ministers spoke in the Dutch language, and Moerdyke of Trinity Reformed Church addressed the audience in English. The meeting had a "wholesome" effect on the audience, who gave a "liberal" collection for Boer relief work.[19]

Topics of most programs focused on religious, not political, issues. For example, in 1936 the West Side Division of the Young Men's Societies gathered a large audience to hear teams debate the perennial issue of whether hymns could be sung in worship services in addition to the Davidic psalms. "Even though the meeting lasted until after eleven o'clock, no one seemed to be sorry," reported the newspaper account, because it was "inspiring and entertaining." This psalm-hymn issue had been resurrected by the decision of the Christian Reformed denomination in 1934 to publish a new worship hymnal that for the first time included several hundred songs and hymns.[20]

One remarkable feature of Reformed young people's activities in Chicago was that the Reformed and Christian Reformed churches planned some joint activities, such as youth rallies and summer softball leagues. Life in the big city was threatening for the small and isolated Dutch Reformed community, and the churches felt a stronger urge to work together than did those in the homogeneous Dutch colonies like Holland, Michigan, and Pella, Iowa.

Beginning in 1905, the young men's societies in Chicago held annual rallies for all Reformed and Christian Reformed churches. The 1913 rally, for example, was hosted by the Eliezer Society of the Douglas Park Christian Reformed Church and met in the church sanctuary. According to the formal printed program of the evening, fourteen delegations attended: four from Roseland, three from Englewood, two from Summit, and five from the Old West Side. Each delegation took a turn reporting on its local activities, interspersed between musical offerings, recitations, topical reports, a break for refreshments, and a collection for the local Timothy Christian School. The adult men's society, young women's society, and even the consistory of the host church also had a part on the program. For young people from both denominations, this mixer was the highlight of the year.[21]

19. Moerdyke, "Chicago Letter," *CI,* 21 Feb. 1900, p. 121.

20. *Chicago Messenger,* 27 Mar. 1936.

21. "Programma van de 9de Openbare Vergardering van de Jongelings Vereeniging 'Eliezer' in het Kerkgebouw van de Douglas Park Gemeente, Juni 4, 1913," copy in author's

"Eliezer" Young Men's Society, Second Christian Reformed Church of Cicero, ca. 1933; row 1 on floor l-r: Tom Lanenga, William Mulder row 2 seated: Nicholas Knol (leader), Rich Lanenga, Cornelius Bos; row 3 standing: Edward Wezeman, John R. Swierenga, Jake Vander Velde, Abe Van Kampen; row 4 standing: Clarence Schoonveld, Bert Lubben, Abe Schoonveld

Some events were intradenominational only. On Labor Day, 1910, for example, the Chicagoland Young Men's Association of the Christian Reformed Church hosted the national young men's annual convention, which met that year at Palos Park, in conjunction with the National League of Christian School Societies.[22]

On the same holiday in 1910, the Young Men's Mission Association of the First Reformed Church of Chicago sponsored a city mission festival at Riverside Park. The young ladies' societies of the Reformed churches

possession. The fest of 30 April 1908, also hosted by the Douglas Park Christian Reformed Church, included eleven delegations of young men's societies with a similar program.

22. *Onze Toekomst,* 2 Sept. 1910. The National League, headquartered in Grand Rapids, was a forerunner of the National Union of Christian Schools, now Christian Schools International (CSI).

ANNUAL THANKSGIVING DAY

PROGRAM

of the

SENIOR AND JUNIOR

YOUNG MEN'S SOCIETIES

ELIEZER

SECOND CHR. REF. CHURCH OF CICERO

Thursday, November 26, 1931

1—Organ Prelude .... E. Oostendorp

2—Singing, Psalter No. 322 .... Audience

Opening .... D. T. Prins, Pres. Sr.

3—Selection .... Quartette

John R. Swierenga, John E. Swierenga
Martin J. Stob, Jacob Van der Molen

4—Debate .... Abel Van Kampen vs. Peter Huizenga

5—Singing .... Audience

6—Recitation .... Garrett Dykstra

7—Instrumental Duet .... Jerry Korringa, Herman Van der Velde

8—Essay .... Edward Ottenhoff

9—Selection .... Quartette

John R. Swierenga, John E. Swierenga
Martin J. Stob, Jacob Van der Molen

10—Recitation .... Harry Huizenga

11—Selection .... Organ

OFFERING

12—Short Address .... Rev. P. A. Hoekstra

13—Surprise Duet .... Jerry Korringa and Tom Laninga

14—Humorous Selection .... Abel Van Kampen

15—Singing .... Senior and Junior Young Men's Societies

16—Closing .... Martin J. Stob, Pres. Jr.

Annual Thanksgiving Day Program 1931, "Eliezer" Young Men's Society, Second Christian Reformed Church of Cicero

similarly met locally and regionally to promote foreign missions.[23] The Young Men's Society "Eliezer" of the Douglas Park (later Second Cicero) Christian Reformed Church organized an annual Thanksgiving Day evening program for the area youth.

23. Ibid., 16 Sept. 1925; 10 Mar. 1926; Moerdyke, "Chicago Letter," *CI,* 12 Feb. 1890; 18 Feb. 1891.

League of Reformed Young Men's Societies "Takes On" the Church

In 1930 the young men's societies formed a city-wide league, complete with elected officers, regular meetings, and a yearbook. The group took the name, "League of Reformed Young Men's Societies of Chicago and Vicinity." It immediately fell under the control of a group of educated second-generation immigrants with markedly progressive views led by the first president, John J. De Boer (1903-69), and his friends vice president Henry Wierenga and secretary August Vander Woude. De Boer had studied at Calvin and Wheaton Colleges, taught English at Chicago Christian High School (1923-31), and directed student teachers at the Chicago Teachers College (1931-44) while pursuing doctoral studies at the University of Chicago (Ph.D. 1938). He was raised in the Fourth Chicago congregation but had become a member of the Second Englewood church. Both churches had reputations for being avant garde.

Soon De Boer and the league were embroiled in a full-scale conflict with leaders in the Christian Reformed churches. The trigger was a play, entitled *The Fool,* by Channing Pollack, that the league planned to stage. The Ministerial Conference of Chicago and Vicinity, an organization of all the clerics in Classis Illinois of the Christian Reformed Church, learned from a colleague, who had been alerted by a parent, that the play contained profanity, questionable moral values, and modernist social ideas. The clerics quickly appointed a committee of two, Gerrit Hoeksema and Dr. Herman Kuiper, pastors of the Third and Fourth Roseland churches, respectively, to meet with the league officers. The meeting did not go well. "Our action," reported the committee, "instead of being received in the spirit of cooperation, met with determined opposition, and even abuse."[24]

The two pastors, nonetheless, demanded that the play be canceled or the text extensively revised. De Boer and his fellow officers took the latter course and made major alterations, but to no avail. The clerics were adamant. The play could not be redeemed; it must be canceled. In the end, two of the three officers behind the venture recanted and apologized, but not John De Boer, although he did cancel the play.

The young men took umbrage at what they perceived to be clerical interference and proclaimed that watching the play was more edifying

24. This and the following paragraphs rely on "Communication from the Ministers' Conference of Chicago and Vicinity," *Banner,* 1 Dec. 1933; "Documents in the Case of Classis Illinois vs. The League of Reformed Young Men's Societies of Chicago and Vicinity submitted to the Synodical delegates as information," 6 June 1934.

than "sitting in catechism for an hour being fed the food of Truth in the form of neat doctrinal pellets which are as unnourishing as they are unpalatable." This inflammatory statement broadened the conflict by directly attacking the revered doctrine class, the key teaching ministry in every Reformed church.

De Boer went further. He castigated the clerics in his "Message from the President," a brief, five-paragraph missive entitled, "The Mind of the Reformed Youth," which he published in the league *Yearbook* of 1933-34 and disseminated even more widely in Chicago's Dutch newspaper, *Onze Toekomst*, and in the denominational youth magazine, the *Young Calvinist*. De Boer was a master with words as well as promotion. He declared: "Arid disputations reminiscent of decadent periods of the Church have in large measure occupied the masters of priestcraft. The voice of the Nazarene . . . is lost in a welter of metaphysics and forensic exhibitionism." Reformed young men must "don the fighting vestments of faith," De Boer continued. "It will take courage to fly in the face of a withered 'orthodoxy' and the councils of the modern Sanhedrin." Reformed young men must "oppose mass murder in war" and "care more about ministering to the sick and naked and the infirm and the underprivileged than about repeating a ritual."[25]

The clerical abuse of power and the threat to "free inquiry" into the Scriptures by the "common man" set De Boer's teeth on edge. In an editorial in the *Chicago Messenger*, he declared: "I charge here that the leadership of Classis Illinois has not only been recreant to the elementary demands of Christian ethics but that they have been engaged in subversive activities which if not checked will result in the destruction of our beloved church."[26] This statement, although given to hyperbole, raised the ante. De Boer and his talented associates had thrown down the gauntlet to their spiritual overseers.

De Boer's caustic writings did not go down well. The regional church assembly, Classis Illinois, at its next meeting declared that he must recant the views expressed in his message, which seemed to be aimed at "fomenting revolt in the Church and denying that Christ is preached." This, they declared, "stirs up dissatisfaction with the spiritual guides of our youth, calls our young men to revolt against ecclesiastical authority,

25. John J. De Boer, "A Message from the President," *Yearbook No. 2 of the League of Reformed Young Men's Societies of Chicago and Vicinity* (Chicago, 1933), 3; Christian Reformed Church, *Acts of Synod*, 1934, 116-22.

26. John J. De Boer, "Concerning the Recent Meeting of Classis Illinois," *Chicago Messenger*, 22 May 1936.

and if not checked will result in 'a house divided against itself.'" Further, "taken at face value," De Boer's views "lead in the direction of Modernism"; they substitute a "social gospel" for the old gospel.[27]

Classis Illinois urged the local consistories to rein in "this type of leadership," and appointed a committee to "study the problem as to how some sort of official connection can be established between the Classis and the various leagues of church societies." But the classis made the mistake of issuing these pronouncements without first allowing De Boer to appear personally to explain his statements.

The controversy ran until 1936, a year after De Boer stepped down and the denominational synod became involved in an unsuccessful attempt to reconcile the young men's group and their ministers. On the assumption that the best defense is a good offense, De Boer and the league appealed to the synod for redress, supported by his consistory at the Fourth Christian Reformed Church. De Boer was granted the unusual opportunity to address the 1934 Synod for thirty minutes to clarify his "Message," and that body also named a high-powered "Committee on Strained Relations, etc.," all western Michigan clerics, to mediate among the classis, the league, and Fourth Church. The committee of five included the Grand Rapids clerics Herman Bel of the LaGrave Church, William Van Wyk of the Eastern Avenue Church, and William Kok of the Calvin College staff, plus Henry Keegstra of the Allendale Church and Daniel Zwier of the Maple Avenue Church in Holland.[28]

The committee met with both sides several times in 1935 and tried to get De Boer to admit that he had been inflammatory, even if inadvertently so, in attacking the clerics and promoting an overly favorable view of the modernistic social gospel. He refused, claiming that the clerics had misinterpreted his message. He had in mind churchmen in general and not specifically local church leaders. When the committee asked Classis Illinois to accept this explanation, the body refused, although it did admit

27. For this and the next paragraphs, see "Report of Committee on Strained Relations," ibid., 1936, 277-79; "Classis Illinois," *Banner,* 4 Mar. 1934.

28. *Agenda of Synod,* 1934, part I: reports, 116-23, 124, 158-62; *Acts of Synod,* 1934, 124, 158-61; "Classis Illinois," *Banner,* 25 May 1934; J. De Boer, "An Explanation of 'The Message from the President' by J. De Boer to the Synodical Committee" (Sept. 1935). The synod committee accepted De Boer's explanation and worked with the league and Classis Illinois to effect reconciliation, but neither side agreed. See "Report of the Synodical Committee Appointed to Ease the Strained Relations Existing Between Classis Illinois and the League of Reformed Young Men's Societies of Chicago and Vicinity," 1936, sixteen-page typescript, in Classis Northern Illinois file, Archives, Calvin College.

that it would have been wiser to call De Boer in before acting against him. De Boer agreed to issue a more concise statement, admitting merely that "several passages were open to misinterpretation." The classis was still not appeased. Until De Boer recanted and resigned, it would oppose the Young Men's League of Chicago.

At this, he resigned but never recanted. Indeed, his board put its finger in the eye of the clergy once more by passing two motions "while the retiring chairman was absent from the meeting." The carefully staged votes expressed a "confidence in Mr. De Boer's policies in handling the affairs of the League," and thanked him "for the work he has done as chairman of the League." Wierenga, his associate, replaced him.[29]

The league controversy with Classis Illinois in the 1930s was the opening salvo in a lay challenge of clerical control that had been the norm in Reformed churches for centuries. In the twentieth century, the clergy no longer had a monopoly on higher education. Lay persons could go "toe to toe" with them in intellectual, if not theological, issues. The laity was ready to assert its right to lead in the churches as in society in general. But with organizations such as the young men's and young women's societies, Classis Illinois and the Christian Reformed Synod in 1935 reasserted and formalized their right of supervision and control. Never again would a small group with an agenda be able to emulate De Boer and his friends. Nor did future leaders want to do so.

Young Calvinist League

The Christian Reformed youth programs were based on the Calvinism of the Netherlandic Kuyperian movement, in sharp contrast to the American evangelical Christian Endeavor movement. The Christian Reformed emphasized their heritage as Dutch Calvinists by forming the Young Calvinist League (later Young Calvinist Federation) as a national organization of young men's societies. The Federation of Reformed Young Women's Societies served the women. In Chicago, the Christian Reformed young men's societies responded to the denominational initiative by organizing the Young Calvinist League of Chicago. The Girl's Fellowship League of Chicago, also an arm of the national organization, provided a similar opportunity for young women.[30]

29. "Classis Illinois," *Banner,* 28 Sept. 1934; 20 Sept. 1935; Henry Hoekstra, "Chicago League of Reformed Young Men's Societies," ibid., 25 Oct. 1935.

30. *Illinois Observer,* 15 Nov. 1954; Sept. 1956.

Christian Reformed youth programs first went coed in 1942 with a Youth Rally Day for all young men's and women's societies. This became an annual event. Then in 1957, the centennial year of the Christian Reformed Church, the Young Calvinist Federation and the Young Women's Societies for the first time held a joint national convention in Chicago.[31] This was a harbinger of the eventual merging of two organizations. Anything but an integrated Young Calvinist Convention would be unthinkable today. Similarly, in the early 1950s a Chicagoland Christian Youth Steering Committee was formed to coordinate and schedule coed recreational activities for teens and young adults, such as hay rides, roller skating, song fests, and the like.[32]

The Christian Reformed Church provided few social activities for its youngsters below high school age until the Boy Scouts and Girl Scouts began to make serious inroads after World War II. While the Reformed Church in America encouraged scouting by forming chapters in the local churches, the Christian Reformed Synod, or governing national assembly, at its 1951 meeting created Christian alternatives to scouting, namely, the Boys Calvinist Cadet Club and the Girls Calvinette Club (now called GEMS, the acronym for "Girls Everywhere Meeting the Savior"). Within a few years every church had its Calvinist Cadet and Calvinette programs.[33]

The differing youth programs of the two Reformed denominations and the contrasting names of their organizations speak volumes. While Christian Reformed youth were indoctrinated in their Calvinist heritage, Reformed youth "endeavored" to be simply "Christian," whether in C.E. or in their church scouting troops. Thus, in time the two denominations in Chicago drifted away from their early cooperation in youth ministries. This was mainly because of differences concerning Christian day schools. Reformed youngsters increasingly attended public schools, while Christian Reformed youth went to Christian schools.

Men's and Women's Societies

Adults also had their men's and women's societies, missionary fests, and Bible conferences. The societies, all with colorful biblical names such as the women's Tryphena Society of the Hastings Street Reformed Church

31. Ibid., Sept. 1956; Sept. 1957.
32. Ibid., 15 Dec. 1954.
33. Ibid., May 15, 1954; May 1956.

and the Tryphosa Society of the First Chicago Christian Reformed Church, held weekly meetings at the churches and provided a kind of continuing adult education program, with studies of the Bible, Reformed doctrine, and theological commentary on current events. In 1935, for example, the English Men's Society "Calvin" of the First Christian Reformed Church of Chicago sponsored a lecture on "The Mark of the Beast" by William Hendriksen of Muskegon, Michigan, a New Testament theologian in the denomination. The Holland Men's Society "Nathanael," founded in 1914, met fifty-one times a year! At one time in the 1930s, sixteen men from the two societies served in the consistory.[34]

Like the young people's societies, the Reformed and Christian Reformed men's groups in 1930 formed a Chicago League of Reformed Men's Societies. For many decades, until the 1960s, the league held annual banquets and mass meetings, rotating between the two denominations and various sections of the city. This ecumenical thrust in Chicago was uncommon in other Dutch centers.

A unique mark of the Chicago area was the tradition of strong lay leadership in the church. This was evident in the founding of Chicago Christian High School and in the activism of the various church societies. A high point came in the 1950s, when the men's societies in greater Chicago formed the Christian Reformed Laymen's League (C.R.L.L.) as an arm of the evangelism ministries of the churches. The aim was to harness the latent power of the laity "to spread the gospel of our Lord and Savior Jesus Christ according to the Calvinistic and Reformed faith through the medium of secular newspapers, magazines, etc."[35]

The idea for a laymen's organization came out of the Chicago Centennial Rally at the International Amphitheater, when twelve thousand people assembled to mark the one hundredth anniversary of the Christian Reformed Church. The inspirational program so enthused the laity in Chicago that shortly afterwards a group in the Illiana area gathered to discuss a laymen's league modeled after the Lutheran Laymen's League and other such organizations, with the goal to mobilize men for mission outreach and evangelism. The Illiana effort quickly spread to Christian Reformed churches throughout greater Chicago, and in 1961 the constitu-

34. B. Essenburg, "West Chicago News," *Banner,* 23 Feb. 1939.

35. "Constitution of the Christian Reformed Laymen's League, adopted 26 May 1955"; Harold Dekker, "The Latent Power of the Laity," 1964 clipping in the *Minute Man: Bulletin of the Christian Reformed Laymen's League,* in the Archives, Calvin College. Chicago area men elected to the board of C.R.L.L. in 1964 are: Mel Dekker, William Ackerman, Ben G. Ottenhoff, Dr. Wm Venema, and John Groot.

Christian Reformed Centennial Pageant "The Light of A Century"

tion was amended to substitute the word "Chicagoland area" for "Illiana area."

In 1962 the league incorporated nationally under an Illinois charter, in conjunction with the "Minute Men for Missions," a men's group in Grand Rapids, Michigan, and moved its headquarters to Grand Rapids under the leadership of E. R. Post, a Christian school administrator. The Christian Reformed Church officially recognized C.R.L.L. in 1967, and the movement that began at the grassroots became a national arm of the denomination.[36]

League members in Chicago worked through the World Home Bible

36. E. R. Post, "The Christian Reformed Laymen's League," *Banner,* 24 Nov. 1967, pp. 20-21; letter of E. R. Post to the Synod of the Christian Reformed Church, June 1967; informational brochure, Christian Reformed Laymen's League; *Minute Man.*

League and the Back to God Hour (the international radio ministry of the Christian Reformed Church), both headquartered on the far south side. Others joined the Gideons in Bible distribution, and yet others opened wayside chapels or volunteered their skills in work projects.[37]

The men's evangelistic efforts lagged far behind those of the women, who had long been in the forefront of benevolent work and missions. The Dorcas Society of the First Reformed Church had as its main purpose to feed, clothe, and visit the sick and needy. The Golden Hour Society of the Second Cicero Christian Reformed Church for decades sewed "cancer pads" as their main work project. Such activities were typical of the women's societies. When the Ladies' Aid Society of the Second Reformed Church of Englewood, founded in 1902, celebrated its fifth anniversary in 1907, many neighboring church societies sent delegations for a gala gathering that "well nigh filled" the church.[38]

Also typical was to gather in regional missionary rallies. The Women's Missionary Society of the fifteen Chicago-area Reformed churches held its first annual conference in 1907 at the First Chicago church. Mrs. Boer, the pastor's wife, presided, and the four female speakers gave an impulse to domestic and foreign missions. Six years later, in 1913, the association added a new tradition of "Missionary Field Days" held on the nation's birthday. The Christian Reformed counterpart was the Women's Missionary Union, organized in Chicago in 1925 to meet at least yearly and promote foreign and American Indian missions (the latter among the Navajo and Zuni tribes in New Mexico).[39]

The all-day rallies often featured illustrated talks (later with slides or "home movies") by missionaries home on furlough. The Reverend Harry A. Dykstra, one of the veteran China missionaries of the Christian Reformed Church, was in great demand in the 1930s. In 1956 the speakers at a rally on the West Side were Tena Huizenga, a Nigerian missionary, and Rose Van Reken, who until 1949 had ministered in China with her husband Everett, a medical doctor.[40]

Beginning in 1956, the Women's Missionary Union also sponsored annual children's missionary rallies for children ages five through four-

37. Arthur De Kruyter, "The Birth of the Christian Reformed Laymen's League," undated clipping from the *Illinois Observer,* Archives, Calvin College.

38. Moerdyke, "Chicago Letter," *CI,* 11 Nov. 1891, p. 11; George Niemeyer, "Illinois Letter," ibid., 27 Nov. 1907, p. 791.

39. George Niemeyer, "Illinois Letter," ibid., 16 Oct., p. 670, 6 Nov. 1907, p. 717; *Onze Toekomst,* 7 Feb. 1913; 16 Sept. 1925.

40. *Onze Toekomst,* 10 Mar., 7 July 1926; Brix, *Life of Tena Huizenga.*

teen. Two rallies were held, one in a West Side church and one in a South Side church. Between twelve and thirteen hundred children turned out each year to sing evangelistic songs and catch a vision of foreign missions from a missionary speaker.[41]

In the 1930s, devout families of Reformed persuasion from greater Chicago began vacationing together at summer Bible conferences at Christian campgrounds in northern Indiana. A rally of Christian Reformed members at Billy Sunday's Winona Lake Bible Conference in 1931 attracted eighty, including seventeen clergymen. They listened with rapt attention to expositions on the Scriptures by leading luminaries such as Dr. G. Campbell Morgan, Charles R. Erdman, and Billy Sunday himself. Homer Rodeheaver entertained them with his voice and trombone and led inspirational "hymn sings."[42]

Beginning in 1937, however, the Christian Reformed Church constituency organized its own annual conference week at the Cedar Lake Bible Conference and Campground, leaving Winona Lake to the American evangelicals. The Cedar Lake program, like that at Winona Lake, combined recreation with daily morning Bible studies and evening praise services in a large tabernacle, which featured inspirational speakers and notable musical groups from within the denomination. For more than fifty years, the Cedar Lake Bible conferences provided wholesome vacations that helped unify Christian Reformed families throughout the sprawling Chicago metropolitan area.[43]

Ministerial Associations

The clerics needed fellowship as much as, if not more than, the laity. As leaders, they could never let their guard down in public without tongues wagging. And to fraternize with lay members of their congregations might engender feelings of favoritism and lead to betrayed confidences. So the clerics created ad hoc groups to meet monthly with their wives in the parsonages on a rotating schedule, with the host wife providing re-

41. *Missionary Monthly* 62 (Sept. 1957): 247; ibid., 64 (July-Aug. 1959): 18; ibid., 65 (Sept. 1960): 239-40; *Illinois Observer*, Apr. 1956; Aug. 1957; July-Aug. 1958.

42. H. J. Mulder, "Winona Lake," *Banner*, 12 June 1931; B. H. Spalink, "Winona Lake," ibid., 25 Sept. 1931.

43. J. R. Brink, "Roseland and South," *Banner*, 5 Feb. 1937; M. Van Dyke, "Christian Reformed Bible Conference Week," ibid., 2 Apr. 1937; *Illinois Observer*, April 1956. Each Bible conference was advertised and summarized in the *Banner* and later in the *Illinois Observer*.

freshments. The Reformed pastors in Chicago created their Ministerial Association in 1907 (later called the Ministerial Conference). Twelve men and their wives met at the manse of Benjamin F. Brinkman of the Second Reformed Church of Englewood. "The apparent impossible has become a fact," declared George Niemeyer. Brinkman chaired the meeting, and John Steunenberg of the Bethany Reformed Church was named secretary. "It was resolved to hold meetings once a month, and thus to spend a social as well as a profitable time, and we trust the work and interest of our Reformed Church in this great city will be better considered."[44] Christian Reformed clerics already were in the habit of socializing monthly in their group, Inter Nos, but their meetings were informal — no agenda and no secretary to take minutes.

The clerics in the parlor could speak frankly among trusted peers, while their wives conversed in the kitchen or sewing room. The opportunity was invaluable to speak frankly with one another, to share news and common concerns, and to talk "church business." At Inter Nos, the isolation that went with the job of pastor was broken down for a time; the fellowship was rejuvenating and helped prevent burnout. But some laity misunderstood the need and criticized the ministerial gatherings as secret "rump meetings," a "cabal" that gave the clergy an edge over the elder delegates in regular church assemblies. Such politicking might drive a wedge between ministers and the laity, it was claimed, and this would harm the church.[45]

Christian Friendship Clubs

The church-sponsored programs were augmented by the extracurricular activities of the Christian day schools, sponsored by the schools and their Friendship Clubs. Together, they organized musical programs, plays, interschool athletics and debate teams, high school alumni association meetings, and the like. Thus, church and school kept not only the youth busy but their parents as well. The plethora of activities eased the feeling of loss and emptiness experienced by many immigrants, who likened themselves to Israelites in exile in Babylon.

Reformed businessmen also avoided joining secular civil organizations "because of worldly activities and the ungodly atmosphere common

44. George Niemeyer, "Illinois Letter," *CI,* 6 Nov., p. 717, 27 Nov. 1907, p. 771.

45. John J. De Boer, "On Second Thought," *Chicago Messenger,* 15 Nov. 1935.

in these groups." So claimed the founders of the Chicagoland Christian Fellowship Club in 1957, which for many years held monthly businessmen's luncheons.[46]

Club luncheons were held at Kilty's Restaurant in Oak Lawn on 95th Street at Cicero Avenue. An enthusiastic group of 118 men – contractors, doctors, dentists, lawyers, clergymen, salesmen, and businessmen – gathered at the first luncheon, and within three months they had adopted a constitution of nine articles and assessed dues of five dollars annually. The threefold statement of purpose promised fellowship and networking, "mutual edification," and leadership training. The outreach goal was to be a Christian witness in business life. Membership in the first year reached 170, and a "great increase" was anticipated in the following year.

The noon luncheons began with prayer and singing, and after the meal an inspirational speaker provided the intellectual dessert. Notable guest speakers in the early years included U.S. senators Everett Dirksen and Paul S. Douglas of Illinois; State Attorney General Benjamin Adamowski; Dr. Harold Ockenga of Boston's Park Street Congregational Church; an Argonne Laboratory physicist named Dr. Winslow; Calvin College theology professor Dr. Lewis Smedes; the "flying parson" Gill Dodds, a famous track star and lay evangelist from Wheaton College; and Dr. Ted Engstrom of Chicago, among others. In 1959 the club added to its schedule an annual golf outing followed by dinner for members and their wives at the Navajo Country Club in Palos Heights, which the Reformed community had recently purchased for the site of Trinity Christian College.

Debate and Recitation Societies

Young adults at the turn of the century were encouraged to form debate and recitation societies. On the West Side, the Isaac Da Costa Recitation Society conducted public speaking contests in various Christian Reformed church auditoriums, such as an event in 1913 at the Fourteenth Street (First) Christian Reformed Church, at which the customary freewill offering went to the local Ebenezer Christian School.[47]

More than a decade earlier, the *Christelijke Reciteer Vereeniging* (Christian Recital Society) ADVENDO of Roseland had sponsored recitation pro-

46. Ibid., Nov. 1957 to Oct. 1959.

47. *Onze Toekomst,* 14 Mar. 1913. A. Hoeksema was president in 1920, Christian Reformed Church, *Jaarboekje,* 1920, 137-38.

grams, such as the one in 1898 at Madderom's Hall. Commemorating the inauguration of Queen Wilhelmina in the Netherlands, the wall behind the lectern was appropriately draped with huge Dutch and American flags, the Dutch tricolor on the left, and the stars and stripes on the right.[48]

The Dutch Dramatic Club, ADVENDO's successor, was a well-organized society of talented amateur actors on the South Side that staged plays "with much success," such as the Dutch-language play, *Jannis Tulp,* at Marquette Hall in 1907, which attracted over six hundred patrons. A member of the troop boasted of this unexpected response: "While such [a large audience] does not often occur among our Dutch people, I nevertheless deem it proper to make mention of this in *Onze Toekomst,* even though our Dutch public shows little interest in dramatic art."[49]

In 1927 another amateur drama group formed on the West Side, the Holland Dramatic Club E. & H., which kept the mother tongue alive. In 1936 the club staged a three-act comedy, *Tante Jutta* ("Aunt Jutta"), at the People's Auditorium on Chicago Avenue near Damen Avenue. John Van Zwieten, director of the group, played the lead role, along with Mrs. P. Sebel and Mr. L. Fransen. The Holland Club put on a series of plays each season on the West, North, and South Sides of Chicago, and even played before an audience of a thousand people in Muskegon, Michigan, another Groninger stronghold.[50]

Choral and Instrumental Music

The Dutch traditionally were known as a singing people, and they preferred musical activities to oratory and drama. Visitors from other denominations were astounded at the Dutch "singing congregations" that "raised the rafters" in lusty psalms of praise. Every congregation had its choral society and larger ones boasted men's and women's "singing societies."[51] The Douglas Park Christian Reformed Church choir, a twenty-five-

48. L. Holstein obituary in *Onze Toekomst,* 11 Sept. 1929, translated typescript, and photograph with descriptive notes, in L. Holstein Papers, Archives, Calvin College. The acronym ADVENDO stood for *Aangenaam Door Vriendschap En Nuttig Door Oefening* ("Pleasure through Friendship and Profit through Practice").

49. Letter to the editor, *Onze Toekomst,* 18 Jan. 1907.

50. *Chicago Messenger,* 28 Feb. 1936.

51. For listings see Christian Reformed Church *Yearbooks* of the time. In 1920 George Ottenhoff directed First Chicago's Singing Society, A. Hazenberg directed Douglas Park's Harmonia, John Fisher directed the Choral Society Harmonia Christiana of Second Cicero,

Choir, Douglas Park Christian Reformed Church, ca. 1908
George Slager, director (standing left), Rev. Cornelius De Leeuw (standing right), row 1: Albert Schoonveld, ?, ?, Robert Swierenga (assistant conductor, with baton), Molenhouse, Peter Van Dyke; ?, ?; row 2: none identified, except Grace Dykhuis (Mrs. Robert Swierenga) (2nd from right); row 3: Mabel Bulthuis (Mrs. Nick Hendrikse) (4th from left), Tillie Swierenga (Mrs. Jans Tameling) (3rd from right), John Knol (2nd from right)

voice ensemble directed by George Slager, proudly assembled with the Reverend Cornelius De Leeuw for a group photograph around 1908. The society of the First Christian Reformed Church of Roseland in the early 1920s counted seventy-four dedicated singers. It too posed for a portrait in the front of the church sanctuary. The various church choirs performed cantatas and sacred concerts but, with rare exceptions, did not assist in Sunday worship services until the 1950s, because worship was perceived as a communal activity not to be disrupted by "special performances."[52]

---

and G. Vanden Berg led the Singing Society at Third Chicago. G. Resers directed First Chicago's band Harmonia (*Jaarboekje* 1920, 137-38). In 1930 Edward Swierenga directed Second Cicero's Harmonia Christiana, R. H. Pouwsma directed the Singing Society of Fourth Chicago, M. Bolt directed the Third Chicago choir, and Gerrit Peters directed the First Chicago choir (*Yearbook,* 1930, 82-83).

52. *Contact: Monthly Newsletter of the First Christian Reformed Church of Roseland,* 12 (May 1967): 3. Cantatas performed in the 1920s included *Queen Esther, Hymn of Praise,* and *My Redeemer Liveth. Onze Toekomst,* 19 Feb. 1909; 21 May, 19 Nov. 1924; 22 Apr. 1925. The Christian Reformed Synod in 1953 gave its blessing to choirs in worship services, provided they sang from the rear or balcony of the sanctuary and were as inconspicuous as possible. See *Illinois Observer,* Mar., Apr., May, June 1955.

Choir, First Christian Reformed Church of Roseland, 1937
standing in front: Rev. Frank Doezema, John Smith,
Henry Radius, Cornelius De Vries

Regional male choruses became famous, such as the Concordia Men's Choir of the First Christian Reformed Church of Chicago led by John W. Schuitema in the 1920s, and its sister group, the Holland-American Male Chorus, which had a fine reputation and gave a splendid performance at Chicago's Orchestra Hall in 1929. Both choruses disbanded briefly in the 1930s. George Mulder, a Cicero undertaker, revived the former in 1939 as the Concordia Male Chorus, and Cornelius H. Kickert revived the latter in 1932 as the Knickerbocker Male Chorus, an award-winning ensemble. He honed the former eighty-member chorus to a serious one of fifty voices. Kickert was director of vocal music at Morton High School in Cicero and played the organ and directed the choir at the First Christian Reformed Church of Cicero. He was a gifted conductor who schooled the untrained voices of scavengers and cartagemen into a chorus famed for its blend and melodious "head tone."[53]

In 1932 the Knickerbocker Male Chorus performed its first annual Thanksgiving concert, which became an annual event at the First Christian Reformed Church of Cicero. The next year the chorus was invited to sing for the Netherlands Day program at the Chicago World's Fair. Its rep-

53. "Concordia Male Chorus at Cedar Lake Bible Conference July 4," *Banner,* 13 June 1941.

utation was assured, and Kickert directed the chorus for the next three decades (1931-1960). Besides the traditional sacred concert on Thanksgiving Day, the Knickerbockers performed on New Year's Day evening, and closed the season with a spring concert that featured sacred music, as well as patriotic and folk songs. The chorus's repertoire featured ever-popular spirituals, and the group cut two record albums that sold well among the faithful, especially the thirtieth anniversary album of 1958, *Wings of Song.* Roger Hoekstra, a medical doctor, succeeded Kickert as director in 1960, until his tragic death in a private plane crash in 1965. Robert Hoekstra and Allen Child carried on until the chorus disbanded in the early 1970s.

On the South Side, the Hamilton Park Men's Club was formed in

Concordia Male Chorus, 1923-1928 First Christian Reformed Church of Chicago l-r: row 1: George Vander Velde, Ralph Buikema, Peter Ter Maat, John Fisher (pianist), John Minnema (director), Martin Buikema, John Brondsema, John Niehoff, John Hoekstra; row 2: Nan Roon, Jack Niemeyer (?), Andrew Niehoff, Rudy Vander Velde, Paul Wigboldy, Ray Lindemulder, Aldrich Evenhouse, Peter Molter; row 3: Luke Dykstra, John H. Vander Velde, Herman Teune, Richard (?) Bos, Cornelius Van Byssum, Louis Hoekstra, Andrew (?) Voss, Charles Boersma, C. Dykstra; row 4: Sam Ter Maat, Peter Bakker, William Venema, Cornelius ("Casy") Gelderloos, John Ter Maat, Menko Hoffman, John E. Swierenga, Will De Boer, John Blauw, Dick Evenhouse, Herman Niehoff

(Courtesy of Jane Vander Velde Hoekstra, who with Angeline Ter Maat Swierenga helped identify the members)

Left, Cornelius H. Kickert
Above, Knickerbocker Male Chorus, ca. 1950
l-r row 1: Menno Zuidema, John R. Swierenga, Gerhard Otte, Jean Carlson (pianist), Cornelius Kickert (conductor), Peter Groenewold, John Hendrikse; row 2: Sam Laninga, Ben Ridder Sr., Lloyd Hoekstra, Howard Stob, Edward Vokral, John Bakker, Wilson Van Slooten; row 3: Dr. Henry Rottschaffer, Roger Hoekstra, John Auwerda, Ralph Swierenga, William Vandervelde, Frank Hovinga, Ben Slager, Henry Bulthouse; row 4: Bernard Meyer, Albie Hoekstra, Edward Bulthouse, John Meekma, Bernard Bos, Edwin Zeilstra, Lee Kickert, Lambert Bos, William Pastoor, Henry Noorlag; row 5: Martin Hoekstra, Gerald Bakker, Melvin Van Denend, Barney Auwerda, Henry R. Swierenga, Harry Boerman, Harry Huizenga, Henry Belgrave, Art Jongsma, Jeff Boerman *(Members identified with assistance of Harry Boerman)*

the 1920s, followed by the Sterling (later renamed the Netherlanders) Male Chorus, conducted for many years by Richard L. Wesselius until his death in 1958, and thereafter by Henry M. Boer. In the 1950s, George Spoolstra and later Jacob Van Eck directed the Ambassador Male Chorus of the First Roseland Christian Reformed Church, and George Zafros, choir director

Ambassador Male Chorus, Roseland, 1952
l-r, row 1: George Spoolstra (director), Wilson Van Bruggen, John Clousing (president), Harold Zeilenga, Calvin Van Lonkhuizen, Harold Boonstra, Henry Slager, Mrs. Bertha Vander Ark (pianist); row 2: Bert Krygsheld, Rudolph Norman, Gerald Hoekstra, Henry Terpstra, Jr., Henry Van Oost, John Van Schepen, Henry Terpstra, Don Tigchelaar, Jr.; row 3: Bernard Stienstra, John Krygsheld, Daniel Walstra, William De Vries, Martin Keesen, Theodore Clousing; row 4: David Vander Weide, Samuel Vander Woude, Jacob Van Eck, Jr., Bernard Clousing, Harry Vander Weide

at the Illiana Christian High School in Lansing, Illinois, led the male chorus of the Second Englewood Christian Reformed Church. Fourth Roseland Christian Reformed Church also had a male chorus. The Gloria Women's Choir of the First Roseland Christian Reformed Church and the Calvin Aeolian Choir, comprised of young women in all four Roseland Christian Reformed churches, were among the few female choruses.

From time to time, the church choruses and choirs of both Reformed and Christian Reformed churches would assemble for a mass music festival, where they performed separately and together. Throughout the 1950s, a dozen choirs from southside churches held an annual festival, as they did in the First Reformed Church of Roseland in February 1955.[54] The Christian Choral Club, organized in 1931 by James Baar, the choral director at Chicago Christian High School, similarly recruited singers from Reformed and Christian Reformed congregations city-wide to sing "the best in Christian music." This meant oratorios such as the *Messiah,* which was performed at the famed Orchestra Hall, accompanied by the Chicago Symphony Orchestra. The Christian Choral Club soon surpassed one hundred voices. Baar was one of the premier choral masters in Chicago, and he put

54. *Illinois Observer,* Feb. 1955; Feb., June 1958.

Chicago Christian High on the music map. He was succeeded by his son, Robert Baar, and then by C. Willard Clutter. In music and sports, as in church societies, the rival Dutch Calvinist churches could cooperate.

One of the most popular vocal groups in the 1930s was the Hilltop Singers, a trio composed of the Essenburg sisters, Mathilda and Marie, and Margaret Doornbos. The sisters were daughters of Benjamin Essenburg, pastor of the First Chicago Christian Reformed Church. These gifted musicians produced a call-in radio show on the Chicago station WCFL three days a week and sang by request a variety of Christian and

Gloria Women's Chorus, Roseland, 1952
l-r, row 1: Harold Boonstra (director), Mrs. Samuel (Antoinette De Jong) Vander Woude, Mrs. John Gritter, Mrs. Richard (Francis Vander Meer) Clousing, Grace Scott, Elaine Meyer, Nicholas Prince (organist); row 2: Mrs. Thomas (Corinne Hanko) Kerkstra, Mrs. Henry (Gertrude Vander Weele) Krygsheld, Pearl Clousing, Delia Van Eck, Mrs. Andrew (Hilda) Meyer, Mrs. Robert (Muriel Boomker) Vander Woude, Mrs. Henry (Jean Persenaire) Helmus, Mrs. Henry (Helen Prince) Cook, Mrs. William (Catherine Vander Weide) Prince, Mrs. Richard (Catherine Yff) Prince, Mrs. Bernard (Lena Moll) Clousing, Mrs. George (Catherine Prince) Harmsen; row 3: Anna Vree, Mrs. Melvin (Jerry) Terpstra, Marilyn Slager, Mrs. Henry (Grace Boersma) Slager, Mrs. Jacob (Grace Vander Weide) Jonkman, Jeanette Pynakker, Mrs. Marinus (Elizabeth Keegstra) Arnoys, Mrs. M. (Marion Van Oost) Meyer, Marie Clousing, Mrs. John Vander Aa, Mrs. Henry (Vera Scorza) Terpstra, Marie Vander Kodde; row 4: Joanne Norman, Lois Ericks, Pearl Vander Weide, Mrs. David (Gertrude Den Besten) Vander Weide, Elizabeth Vander Wal, Catherine Vander Weit, Mrs. M. Oostman, Frances Prince, Mrs. Richard (Sadie Meyer) Natelborg, Mrs. Frank (Bernice Doezema) Boersma, Barbara Boersma; row 5: Mrs. J. Wiersma, Ann Dykstra, Marie Aardsma, Rose Smith, Mrs. Henry (Jennie De Maar) Weidenaar, Harriet Prince, Mrs. Lawrence (Margaret De Maar) Clousing, Mrs. Dan (Bernice Jonkman) Walstra

(Members identified by William Prince and Jackie Vander Weide Swierenga Vogelzang)

Right, The Hilltop Singers — Marie ("Micky") Essenburg, Marge Doornbos, and Matilda ("Milly") Essenburg, 1930s *(Courtesy of Martin Essenburg)*

Below, Harmonie Band of First Christian Reformed Church of Chicago, ca. 1925 l-r, row 1: John Stouwie, Drew Peters, ? Wierenga, Nick De Vries, Edward Wierenga; row 2: Otto Lenters, George Van Stedum, Mike Van Erden, Edward De Vries, Peter Rispens, Gerrit Peters; row 3: M. Hoffman, Walter Ottenhoff, Neil Swierenga, Jake Van Der Molen, Gerrit Vanden Burg. *(Members identified by Fred Wiersum, son of Drew Peters, only surviving band member in 1988)*

Excelsior Band of the Douglas Park Christian Reformed Church, ca. 1912, directed by H. E. Nut; Vander Cook School of Music of Chicago Assistant Conductor Robert Swierenga, first row, second from right

popular songs. In 1936 they added a similar half-hour Saturday morning program on an ABC affiliate in Hammond, Indiana, which ran for two years. The Hilltop Singers were the talk of the town; they had made it big and put the Dutch on the map. Their father, despite a heavy workload, willingly accepted the role of driving them to the broadcast studios.[55]

Instrumental music groups were fewer in number and short lived. These included the Harmonie Band of the First Christian Reformed Church, directed by realtor George Ottenhoff, and the Excelsior Band of the Douglas Park Christian Reformed Church, directed initially by J. M. Bolt and then for a time by H. E. Nut, a faculty member of the Vander Cook School (later College) of Music of Chicago. The Golden News Youth Orchestra of the Englewood Christian Reformed churches was active in the 1930s.[56]

55. *Chicago Messenger,* 27 Oct. 1936; interview with Ben Essenburg, Jr., by author, 26 Oct. 1999, and video interview, 2 Nov. 1998, by Martin Stulp.

56. Christian Reformed Church, *Jaarboekje,* 1910, p. 103; *Onze Toekomst,* 25 Mar. 1910; 5 Aug. 1921; 15 Feb. 1922; 21 Oct. 1931; *Chicago Messenger,* 13 Mar. 1936.

Sport

The sporting craze of the progressive era also found expression among the Dutch, but never on Sunday. That was a "day of rest," and even watching a local nine or listening to the Cubs or White Sox games on the radio was forbidden. No wonder neighborhood boys taunted the Dutch Calvinists as "do nothing wooden shoes." Johnny Vander Meer, a member of a Passaic (New Jersey) Christian Reformed congregation and a star pitcher for the Cincinnati Reds in the 1940s, would go to Wrigley Field to play against the Cubs in a three o'clock game after attending the morning service at the First Christian Reformed Church of Chicago, but no young man could follow him without risking a visit by the elders. When George Zoeterman, of the Archer Avenue Christian Reformed Church, another excellent pitcher, signed in the late 1940s with the Cubs and then the White Sox, his contract specified that the coach could not schedule him on Sundays. A talented local ball player, Harold Evenhouse of the First Reformed Church of Chicago, signed with a semipro team in the Windy City League, but his consistory forced him to withdraw because of the Sunday games.[57]

Evenhouse's fellow congregant, Marvin Klein, an athlete who excelled in both softball and basketball, had his nascent career as a professional basketball player with the St. Louis Hawks nipped in the bud by his father. As Marvin's brother Peter recounted: "Marv called home to tell my Dad that he made the team and my Dad asked if that meant he would be playing on Sunday. When Marv told him, yes, he drove to St. Louis, tore up the contract and brought him home." Thus did Sunday games torpedo another all-state athlete's money career. "WOW," added brother Peter, "what a difference a generation makes."[58]

The answer to professional sports was amateur sports. In 1920 the Reformed churches of greater Chicago organized a Holland American Inter-Church Baseball (later Softball) League. Games were scheduled throughout summer evenings at local diamonds such as Altgeld Park (Harrison and Washtenaw streets) in the 1920s, and 54th and Roosevelt Road in the 1930s, 1940s, and 1950s. Speedway Wrecking Company sponsored the Hastings Street Church team, managed by Peter Klein, and furnished lettered uniforms; the Excelsior Society of the First Christian Re-

57. Dick Blaauw and Robert Vander Velde, interview by author, 10 Mar. 1998; Henry and Marie Tameling, video interview, 2 Feb. 1998; Ben Essenburg, Jr., video interview, 11 Nov. 1998, both by Martin Stulp.

58. E-mail of Pete Klein to Martin Essenburg, 23 May 2001, shared with the author.

formed Church of Chicago sponsored its church team until 1941. Then, in an unusual development, Mike Dykema, the local Dutch politico (see chapter 14), arranged for Alderman William Pacelli of the 20th Ward to sponsor the team. Thereafter, the First Christian Reformed Church team became the "Pacelli Boosters," as the uniforms proudly displayed across the back. Pacelli, an Italian Catholic, died in office in 1942 after thirteen years as an alderman.

The Pacelli Boosters competed in both the church league and the Douglas Park League, as well as playing numerous free-lance games. The team, coached by Jack Essenburg, was the premier softball team in the city in the 1930s and 1940s. With the four Evenhouse brothers, and especially Harold, in the line-up, and Ben Essenburg as the lead hitter (in 1942), they won the Holland American church league championship in 1940, 1941, and 1942. In 1941 they also captured the Douglas Park League title and won the postseason, all-city Chicago *Herald American* Tournament. The Pacelli Boosters lived for softball; they played as many as eighty-four games from April to September! It should be noted that the four Evenhouse brothers belonged to the First Reformed Church of Chicago, and yet league officials, in a remarkable spirit of ecumenicity, permitted them to play on the team of the First Christian Reformed Church. What opposing church teams thought of this "salting" is not recorded.[59]

As was customary in the city, where ball fields and empty lots were small, the softball teams used balls that were sixteen inches in circumference rather than the customary twelve inches. The balls softened quickly under the pounding of bats and did not travel as far when hit. Pitchers had to deliver the ball in "slow pitch" style, that is, thrown with an arc, and balls were caught with bare hands. In the first few innings, before the game ball was softened, the third baseman standing only forty-five feet from home plate was at great risk of having his hands painfully stung by a hard smash off the bat of a power hitter. Teams fielded ten players instead of nine, with the "short center fielder" roving behind second base. In the 1940s, the base path was lengthened to fifty feet.

The big rivalry in the early years pitted First (Ashland Avenue) Christian Reformed Church against First (Hastings Street) Reformed Church. The edifices virtually faced each other and denominational pride rode on the outcome. Later, the city-suburban rivalry between the First Chicago (later Ebenezer in Berwyn) and First Cicero Christian Reformed teams

59. I am indebted to Jack Essenburg's brother Ben and son Martin for the information in this paragraph.

aroused the most emotions; this was the Christian Reformed version of neighborhood rivalry. Huge crowds lined the base paths at the Clark Public School diamond on Paulina Street when the two teams met. Later, the First Reformed Church of Chicago in Berwyn boasted one of the best power hitters in the league, Marvin Klein, a 6′5″ giant who could send the softball over the outfield fence and hit pop-ups above the lights.

By the 1950s, the Chicago Suburban League included fifteen church teams and was organized into South and North divisions. There was also a far southside league in South Holland, Lansing, and Hammond (Indiana). Regional rivalries became the norm. Fans turned out by the hundreds and rooted for their church teams. Softball was *the* ethnocultural activity of the summer months; it was the great mixer for the Dutch Re-

Championship baseball team, First Christian Reformed Church of Chicago, 1940
l-r: row 1: Jack Essenburg (manager), Neil Benes (batboy), Ray Oldenburger;
row 2: Harold Toren, Pete ("Funny") Vander Laan, Clarence Evenhouse,
Harold Evenhouse, Raymond Evenhouse, Edward Vander Velde;
row 3: Tom Oldenburger, Meindert (Meinie) Vander Kamp, Bruce Venhuizen,
Howard Stronk, Martin Evenhouse, Herman ("Mike") Keizer, John Voss
(Courtesy of Martin Essenburg)

Bowling team, Emmanuel Reformed Church League, Roseland, 1939-40
l-r row 1: William Cook, Ben Branstra, Harry Houseman, Harry Hull, Harold Hull, Ted Raatjes, Percy De Vries, Tony De Vries; row 2: ??, John Vinke, Herman ("Hump") Bovenkerk, Neil Ruisard, Gerrit ("Lefty") Swart, Herman Vanden Berg, Roy Matzki, Harold Blom, John Post; row 3: C. Ten Hoven, Henry Vander Myde, Richard De Young, Peter Kemper, John Meyer, Andrew Raatjes, George Post, Martin Houseman, Dirk Uilenberg, John Blom; row 4: Peter Cook, Ko Lindemulder
(Courtesy of John and Harold Blom)

formed of Chicago. And the ballplayers served as role models for the young men. In the 1980s, however, sporting interests changed, and the church league dwindled until it disbanded in the 1990s.

Basketball held less appeal than baseball at first, but church teams developed after the gymnasium at Chicago Christian High School became available. In 1935 the school's athletic director, Maurice Vander Velde, organized the first annual city tournament for both junior and senior divisions. Each player had to pay a thirty-five-cent fee (twenty cents for juniors) and sell six tickets. The church pastor had to sign the roster to prevent "ringers" (i.e., non-church members). The six-day tournament drew big crowds and more than five hundred "enthusiastic fans" packed the high school gymnasium to watch the Roseland teams walk off with top honors. Besides competing in church tournaments, the young men on the West Side in the 1940s played on local teams at the Sears YMCA on West Arthington Avenue (900 south).

Despite the strong beginning, it was not until gymnasiums were built in Christian schools in each section of the city in the 1960s that every congregation sponsored a basketball team. Church league play then became a favorite winter pastime. For older men and women, there was the Holland-American Church Bowling Society, founded in 1931, which sponsored an annual "handicap" tournament of men's teams from all Reformed and Christian Reformed churches in the Chicago area. Only men of "Holland birth or descent" could participate in the meet, sponsored by Henry Kleinhuizen, an official of the society. Golf outings also came into vogue by the 1950s.[60]

For more refined recreation, including activities for young women, in 1912 some members of the society Eendracht Maakt Macht ("Unity is Strength") formed the Holland Gymnastics Society Runst en Kracht ("Skill and Strength") for gymnastics and dance. The club's first exhibition was presented in 1913 at Hamlin Hall on the North Side. This location far away from the core Dutch neighborhood on Ashland Avenue and the fact that Christian Reformed youth were forbidden to dance indicate that Runst en Kracht was drawn from secularist and Americanized families.[61]

"Worldly Amusements"

While sports gained approval, Hollywood did not. Throughout the 1920s, Dutch Calvinist church leaders warned their youth to keep away from movie houses, theaters, cabarets, and dance halls. The directive was to shun evil in all its forms, based on the principle of "spiritual separation from the world." As Harold Hiskes of Englewood recalled: "Movies for us of course were taboo. Our friends in the neighborhood could go to the Rex at 69th and Racine to see Tom Mix or others for a nickel or a dime, but not us. . . . Believe it or not, I went to the show for the first time when I was 16 years old and working." Despite the ban, "many of our boys and girls are regular patrons of the movies," lamented the editor of *Onze Toekomst* in 1922, even though the silent screen portrays sinful behavior and attracts "bad company." "Everyone is welcome – gamblers, robbers, and all other undesirables as well as honorable citizens who go to see the movies and to spend their money."[62]

60. *Onze Toekomst,* 2 July 1920; 15 July 1931; 10 May 1933; *Chicago Messenger,* 17 Jan., 14, 28 Feb., 13 Mar., 8 May 1936; *Illinois Observer,* Aug. 1955; May 1958; June-July 1959.

61. *Onze Toekomst,* 17 Jan. 1913.

62. Harold Hiskes, *In Memoriam* (privately printed, 1996), 10; *Onze Toekomst,* 8 Mar., 23 Feb. 1922; 4 May 1927.

Keeping worldliness at arm's length was a church mandate. The 1928 Synod of the Christian Reformed Church condemned "worldly amusements," that is, the "familiar trio" of theater attendance, dancing, and playing with "devil cards." Only the card game Rook was acceptable. Church pastors and elders were charged with carrying out the prohibition; they held the "keys of the kingdom" – church discipline. They diligently asked young people, in the interview prior to joining the church by a public profession of faith, this specific question: "Do you attend the movies?" A yes answer would not necessarily preclude admittance, but it would elicit a stern warning. Even so-called Christian movies only "used that blessed name to bait the devil's hook," declared the Reverend Essenburg.[63] One suspects that the waste of money on such entertainment was considered a sin equal to the fleshly temptations.

The elders, in posing the "amusements" question, were merely following the 1928 denominational directive. The rule read as follows:

> Synod instructs consistories to inquire of those who ask to be examined previous to making public profession of their faith and partaking of the Lord's Supper as to their stand and conduct in the matter of worldly amusements, and, if it appears that they are not minded to lead the life of Christian separation and consecration, not to permit their public confession. . . . Synod urges consistories to deal in the spirit of love, yet also, in the view of the strong tide of worldliness which threatens our churches, very firmly with all cases of misdemeanor and offensive conduct in the matter of amusements; and, where repeated admonitions by the consistory are left unheeded, to apply discipline as a last resort.[64]

The Reformed Church took a different tack. The Classis of Chicago warned its members against the "unwholesome and carnal influence of the theatre and the movies," but rather than to "bluntly condemn" them, the classis urged pastors and elders "frankly and intelligently" to discuss the dangers of worldliness with the youth. This decision discouraged but did not proscribe such activities.[65]

The Dutch abhorrence of the theater saved them from one particularly gruesome disaster in Chicago, the fire at the Iroquois Theater on De-

63. Christian Reformed Church, *Acts of Synod, 1928,* 86-89; *Agenda of Synod, 1928,* part I; Essenburg, "Those Christian (?) Movies," *Banner,* 9 Feb. 1939.

64. *Acts of Synod,* 1928, p. 88.

65. Classis of Chicago, Minutes, 1937.

cember 30, 1903, which killed more than six hundred people, mostly children, along with many mothers and thirty-four teachers. A standing-room crowd of two thousand was attending the afternoon matinee when fire broke out. Although the theater was new, it proved to be a firetrap. The entire city observed a day of mourning for the holocaust, and all businesses closed for the numerous funerals, which touched every neighborhood and wiped out several entire families. But the Dutch Reformed members were spared the horror. Peter Moerdyke reported: "As far as learned, not one in this harvest of death, cut down in the hours of the dying year, was from any of our Reformed churches." The cleric then added this oblique remark: "That two clergymen ended their career at this memorable show and play – for it was largely spectacular – calls out endless comment."[66] He offered none, believing that his readers would draw the proper moral lesson.

Carnivals with their gaming booths came under similar strictures by Reformed church members. Gambling, even if sponsored by the Catholic Church or the American Legion, was condemned. In 1923 the Christian Reformed churches in Roseland asked the municipal court to revoke the permit for a planned carnival by the American Legion on a nearby vacant lot at 110th Street and Indiana Avenue. When Judge Adolph J. Sabath, a Bohemian Catholic, allowed the permit to stand, the Reverend George W. Hylkema of the Third Roseland Christian Reformed Church lashed out angrily at the judge from the pulpit.[67]

There were also strictures against speculation. In the midst of the Great Depression, a Christian Reformed church member in Cicero made a "killing" of $50,000 in commodities trading at the Chicago Board of Trade. He offered to donate a tenth of the money to his financially struggling church, but the consistory refused to accept the ill-gotten gains.

Other consistorial concerns involved Sabbath desecration for work or sport, joining of labor unions, and recreational activities such as bowling and roller-skating in rinks. Such legalisms brought a degree of hair-splitting. Should the owner of an ice route sell ice to saloons? No, not if he had scruples. Should a truck driver join the Teamsters or building tradesmen affiliate with the AFL? Were unions, bound together by oaths and bred in violence, merely the blue-collar equivalent of Masonic lodges?

66. *Lest We Forget, Chicago's Awful Theater Horror* (Chicago: Memorial Publishing, 1904); Moerdyke, "Chicago Letter," *CI,* 6 Jan., pp. 9-10, 20 Jan. 1904, p. 41.

67. *Onze Toekomst,* 8 Aug. 1923; on Sabath see Westin A. Goodspeed and Daniel D. Healy, eds., *History of Cook County, Illinois . . . ,* 2 vols. (Chicago: Goodspeed Historical Association, 1909), 1: 754-55.

Many consistories said yes and at least refused to nominate union members for elders and deacons. Should men bowl? Should teens skate? The concern about bowling alleys was their "worldly atmosphere" and drinking bars, and roller-skating in skimpy costumes to popular music was lewd and akin to dancing.

The Christian Reformed Church was somewhat inconsistent, however. While enacting anti-amusement regulations, it never made an official pronouncement against smoking and drinking, as did many Yankee Protestant denominations such as the Methodists, Presbyterians, Baptists, and even some Reformed churches. These two vices caused far more harm to families and the faith than did Hollywood. Dutch young men took up the weed as a rite of passage, and it was said that "you couldn't be elected to the consistory if you didn't smoke cigars." The room was blue with the smoke.[68]

Alcohol was served at wedding and anniversary receptions, sometimes even in the church building. Many teamsters stopped off at the tavern for a beer after finishing their work. This was a custom carried from the old country. As Frisian immigrant William Elzing gossiped in 1870: "There are people from Groningen who will always be poor because they like English whiskey." Perhaps this was a bit of Frisian snobbery. Church leaders ignored these drinking habits unless it led to overt problems in church or home life. But one man who drove a beer truck for a living was not allowed to be a Sunday school teacher; he was deemed to be a bad role model. Not surprising for men who liked their beer, a number ended up on "The Street," Chicago's skid row on West Madison Street.[69]

On all these social questions, the Reformed Church in America held a more open attitude toward American society than did the Christian Reformed Church. The ideal, in Reformed Church eyes, was a "happy blending" of the rich traditional Dutch church life with "the choicest of the American traits, ideas, and ways." This, said Peter Moerdyke, of Chicago's Trinity Reformed Church, would lessen the "distractions of 'society,' amusements, clubs, etc., which play the mischief with the hearts and the time of . . . our rising generation, while yet sharpening the consciences for Christian living through a healthy, Biblical and spiritual Church life."[70]

68. Dick Blaauw and Robert Vander Velde, interview, 10 Mar. 1998.

69. Arthur De Kruyter expressed these opinions in his editorial of September 1955 in the *Illinois Observer,* entitled, "Needed: A Liquor Abatement Program." See also "On Alcohol," ibid., Feb. 1957; quote from Elzing, letter to "Dear Friends at Irnsum."

70. Moerdyke, "Chicago Letter," *CI,* 26 Dec. 1894, p. 11. In 1905 *De Volksvriend* of Orange City, Iowa, carried a debate on the use of alcohol between the Rev. Idzard Van Dellen

Thus, Reformed youth had the freedom to attend the cinema and the circus, and dance at school social events, that was forbidden to Christian Reformed youth. But, conversely, the more Americanized Reformed youth fell under the strictures of the Yankee prohibition and anti-saloon crusades.

Intermarriage

Dutch Reformed young people were well aware of the "natural aversion" their families would have for marrying an "outsider." So said a sociological study of South Holland, Illinois, in the 1930s. An "outsider" was defined in terms both national and religious as one neither Dutch nor Reformed. Social class had little bearing and language none at all. On the Old West Side, where the Dutch Reformed lived among a small nest of Italian Catholics, there were intermarriages, especially of Dutch women and Italian men. Reformed church elders spoke of this as falling into sin, even though if pushed they would admit that Catholics were fellow Christians.[71]

Leaders in the Christian Reformed churches became so concerned about "mixed marriages" that in 1939 Classis Illinois took a stand. In a three-part declaration, the pastors and elders agreed to "warn our youth against marriage to unbelievers in sermons, at home, at school, and in pamphlet form"; to "labor" with any "covenant youth keeping company with an unbeliever"; and "to encourage, support, and promote our [Christian] schools and societies, so that our youth may find adequate fellowship in them." A fourth point, which failed to find majority support, would "deny our pastors the right to solemnize mixed marriages." This most radical point was appealing in principle but "wholly untenable" in practice; "circumstances may be such that refusal would make for evil rather than for good." Moreover, consistories were not prepared to excommunicate members entering such unions.[72]

---

of the Christian Reformed Church and the Revs. Evert Stapelkamp, Jerry Winter, and James De Pree of the Reformed Church. Van Dellen argued for moderation, but the Reformed Church men demanded total abstinence. This nicely illustrates the contrasting views widely held in the sister denominations (ibid., 29 Mar., p. 202, 19 Apr. 1905, p. 248).

71. L. S. Dodson, *Social Relationships and Institutions in an Established Community, South Holland, Illinois,* Social Research Report No. XVI (Washington, D.C.: U.S. Department of Agriculture, 1939), 13, cited in Richard C. Cook, *A History of South Holland, Illinois, 1846-1966* (South Holland, Ill.: South Holland Trust and Savings Bank, 1966), 84; Ben Essenburg, video interview, 11 Nov. 1998, by Martin Stulp.

72. "Classis Illinois," *Banner,* 12 Oct. 1939.

Twenty years later, in 1955, Arthur De Kruyter, editor of the *Illinois Observer,* repeated the admonition to parents to safeguard their teens from dating non-Christians. With the breakdown of social control that policed the segregated Dutch Reformed communities of forty years ago, De Kruyter noted, young people must be warned strongly of the biblical injunction against being "unequally yoked" with unbelievers.[73]

Unbelievers were clearly "outside the pale" of the Christian church. But what about Catholic Christians? Long-standing religious and cultural taboos held sway, stemming from the bloody Eighty Years' War in the Netherlands to win freedom from Catholic Spain and the geographical and social differentiation that ensued. Reformation Day sermons reinforced the traditional failings of Catholicism, and sermons based on Lord's Day question and answer 80 of the Heidelberg Catechism condemned the "popish mass" as "idolatry." Furthermore, "Mary's priest" stands behind every Mary that a Dutch Calvinist might marry; he is a "shadow on the threshold" waiting to snatch the children and undermine the marriage. So Peter C. De Young warned in an article in the *Illinois Observer* in 1954.[74]

Some Christian Reformed members drew the definition of outsider to include spouses from the Reformed Church, a sister denomination. They labeled even these marriages somewhat tongue in cheek as "mixed," in the belief that the more open Reformed view of worldly amusements and opposition to Christian education made them second-class Calvinists. A hint of this attitude slipped into the diary of Mrs. Henry Kickert, a Christian Reformed member, when she wrote: "I married Henry Kickert from the Reformed Church but he is a good man." The "but" speaks volumes. At the deepest level, Christian Reformed parents worried that they might "lose" their children and grandchildren to the Reformed church and the public schools. In their minds, this leaving of the family church, the church of one's baptism and profession of faith, was a crossing of the line, especially if Christian education lost out.[75] Nonetheless, parents tolerated such unions as being far preferable than mating with non-Dutch Protestants, or worse with Catholics, and worst of all with unbelievers.

The Dutch Reformed held the line against marriages outside their ethnoreligious group far more successfully than did the Catholic and sec-

73. *Illinois Observer,* March 1955.

74. Ibid., 15 July 1954.

75. Quoted in Mrs. Cornelius Kickert, "Last Meeting at Coffee Hour at Cicero I Church – 1976," typescript, p. 1, Archives, Calvin College.

ular Hollanders, although even the strict Calvinists saw some slippage by the second generation. A study of the federal census of 1870 shows that of 114 first-generation Reformed couples in Chicago (which includes all whose origins were traced back to the Netherlands), *every one* had Dutch-born spouses. But among Dutch-born children and young people who married in America within the first twenty years, six out of forty-four (13.6 percent) had married non-Dutch spouses. All who "outmarried" were young men, not women. The nativity of the six wives was Prussian (2), Irish (1), Scotch (1), New Jersey (1), and Vermont (1).

The in-group marriage continued for generations, but at a slowly declining rate. In the 1950s, more than three-fourths of the marriages reported in the Dutch Reformed periodical, the *Illinois Observer*, still joined spouses of Dutch birth or ancestry, which is the remarkable fact.[76]

One result was a kinship structure so interwoven that "almost everybody was related to someone else," and a young man was "hard pressed" to find a wife who was not his cousin. This too strong statement described the tight South Holland Dutch colony, in which, according to a sociological report in 1937, "four families, including all of their relations, probably constituted one-half of the population of the village."[77]

The contrast is striking between the Reformed Dutch and other Dutch in Chicago. In the 1870 census, of 288 first-generation non-Reformed couples, 22 percent had non-Dutch spouses, and among their children the rate was far higher. Here the Americanization process was really evident. Of 122 second-generation couples, fully 75 percent had non-Dutch spouses. Of the inter-ethnic marriages, Dutch men married non-Dutch wives twice as often as Dutch women married non-Dutch husbands.

Which nationalities did the "mixed" Dutch select? Sixty percent were German-born, mainly Prussians, 14 percent were U.S.-born, 7 percent English or Scottish, 6 percent Belgian, and the remaining 15 percent were scattered among 12 European nationalities from Ireland to Italy, Sweden to France.

The areas of the city with the highest outmarriage rates were outside of the West Side Reformed hub (Wards 7, 8, 9, 12, 13). The North Side

76. Tabulated by the author from marriages reported in the *Illinois Observer*, 1954-1959. Of 347 marriages, 266 (77 percent) were between those of Dutch birth or ancestry. The figures are based only on reported marriages; it is likely that some mixed marriages went unreported.

77. Dodson, *Social Relationships*, 13, 53, cited in Cook, *South Holland*, 84.

(Wards 1-6) and South Side wards (Wards 10, 11, 16-20) both averaged 67 percent outmarriage in 1870. The Northwest Side north of Lake Street, which contained both Reformed and Catholic Dutch, only had an 8 percent rate of intermarriage.

The German-American Dr. Emil G. Hersch told the Holland Society of Chicago, in an address entitled "Dutch Homes":

> It were well if all the world had the Dutch system of regulating homes, and the Dutch plans for society were adopted. Homes consist largely of children, and the Dutch, among other industries, know how to make homes in which to properly rear children. . . . Another thing which the Dutch home illustrates is cleanliness. Let us have a little Dutch in Chicago and clean up in this city and make our influence felt.[78]

The police seldom had trouble with the Dutch Calvinists. They learned in church and school to respect the police and all those in positions of authority. Lord's Day 39 of the Heidelberg Catechism, the major doctrinal guide of the church that all youth had to memorize, read:

> Question: What is God's will for us in the fifth commandment?
> Answer: That I honor, love, and be loyal to my father and mother and *all those in authority over me* [italics added]; that I obey and submit to them, as is proper, when they criticize and punish me. . . .

The editor of *Onze Toekomst* occasionally boasted of the low Dutch crime and poverty rate. "No other race has done so much for law and order than the example of the Hollanders. . . . There are fewer Dutch criminals than those of any other race." Of the twenty thousand Dutch-Americans in Chicago in 1908, the editor observed, "not more than ten ever came in contact with the police." Of three hundred prisoners in Joliet Penitentiary in 1911, only one was Dutch. "That one Hollander is our Pieter Van Vlissingen, forger of bonds," the newspaper declared, with the intent to shame Van Vlissingen and any compatriot who similarly walked in evil ways. But one prisoner in three hundred is only 0.3 percent, whereas the Dutch comprised 1 percent of Chicago's population in 1910. Hence, the Dutch proportion of the prisoners should be three rather than one. "How is that for a record?" the editor crowed. He neglected to check

78. *Yearbook of the Holland Society of Chicago 1897-1900* (Chicago, 1901). Hersch addressed the Holland Society in March 1901.

the rolls of prisoners in the Cook County Jail, however; in 1900 there were three Hollanders incarcerated.[79]

Chicago Police Department crime reports provide the most detailed and reliable facts about crime among Chicago's major nationality groups. For the ten years from 1915 to 1924, arrests by nationality per ten thousand population (twenty-one years and over) show that Hollanders ranked second behind Canadians among twenty-one nationality groups as having the *lowest* rates. Females made up about 5 percent of the Hollanders arrested. As a proportion of total Hollanders in the city, their per capita arrest rate was only 0.1 percent. Proportionally, this was thirty times below their 3 percent level of the city populace.

Breaking down the total arrests by type of crime, 90 percent of the Hollanders were picked up for misdemeanors and only 10 percent for felonies. The per-capita felony rate among Hollanders ranked *lowest* among all twenty-one major nationality groups in Chicago. The Hollanders even beat out the Canadians on fewest felonies per capita.[80] So the hard evidence supports the boast of the Dutch newspaper editor. But there was one notorious felony, however, that took place in a Chicago suburb in 1898, when one Hollander killed another in a drunken quarrel. The criminal was "no churchman and shy of temperance," said Moerdyke, who thereby classed the man as an exception to the rule.[81]

Conclusion

Chicago Hollanders included all religious persuasions – Reformed, Christian Reformed, Presbyterian and other mainline Protestants, Catholic, Jewish, Unitarian, Socialist, and the nominally churched. But only the Calvinists, who comprised about two-thirds of the Dutch stock, created ethnoreligious communities that shared a common culture and beliefs and associated together tightly. Many of the first three generations of Calvinists, especially among the Christian Reformed, lived from the cradle to the grave within their extended families, churches, schools, and societies.

79. *Onze Toekomst,* "Knickerbocker Society of Chicago," 18 Nov. 1931; 25 Dec. 1908; 24 Mar. 1911. The Cook County prisoners in 1900 were Henry Bolt, waiter; Tony Zeebring, upholsterer; and Peter Burker, laborer (Swierenga, "Dutch in Chicago and Cook County Federal Manuscript Census of 1900").

80. Mildred Curtis, "Statistics of Arrests in Chicago in Relation to Race and Nativity, 1915 to 1924" (Ph.D. dissertation, Univ. of Chicago, 1926), numerous tables.

81. Moerdyke, "Chicago Letter," *CI,* 19 Jan. 1898, p. 9.

Dutch Catholics and Jews, by contrast, lived within religious communities that were predominantly German, so they soon lost their ethnic identity. Only Dutch Reformed, church-based societies flourished and survived beyond the first two generations.

CHAPTER 9

From Womb to Tomb: Mutual Aid Societies and Cemeteries

Mutual aid societies gave concrete expression to ethnic groupings in the United States, and they were often tied to immigrant churches that taught the obligations of love and sharing. Immigrants in the cities and the countryside alike felt the need to band together to meet physical and financial crises. Organized mutuality was dictated by economic necessity in a society with few government safety nets. Sharing resources also meshed perfectly with the religious obligation to "do good" to those of the "household of faith."[1] As a result, immigrant groups formed thousands of mutual aid societies to provide communal support and assistance during times of death, illness, accidents, and loss of family. Ethnicity, more than religion, was the glue of this mutuality, and the loss of ethnic identity sounded the death knell of the societies within a few generations.[2]

At least, that was the pattern with most ethnic groups. For the Dutch Reformed, however, religion was always the center of mutuality. They carried out their acts of benevolence within their churches; the deacons were the hands of the Lord. They collected alms through regular tithes and offerings and distributed them to the needy in the congregation for food, fuel, rent, medical bills, and unexpected expenses. Widows

1. "So then, as we have opportunity, let us do good to all men, especially to those who are of the household of faith" (Gal. 6:10).

2. Steven M. Nolt, "Formal Mutual Aid Structures among American Mennonites and Brethren: Assimilation and Reconstructed Ethnicity," *Journal of American Ethnic History* 17 (Spring 1998): 71-86.

with young children were especially dependent on the diaconate for regular assistance.

But large and expected expenses, such as those incurred at death, were beyond the normal purview of the church deacons. Members were expected to take responsibility for such costs themselves, which they did by organizing mutual aid societies as a form of life insurance for burial costs. Compared to other ethnic groups, however, the Dutch organized very few such societies. Their strong diaconal programs well met subsistence needs, except for "final expenses." Many eschewed any kind of insurance, including fire insurance, on religious grounds. There was a belief among the most orthodox Calvinists, carried from the Netherlands, that buying insurance reflected a lack of faith in God's protective care. This conviction was put to the test and found wanting in the Chicago Fire of 1871. Fire insurance, at least, came to be looked upon thereafter as a necessity.

The founding of Dutch mutual aid and benevolent societies followed a chronological pattern that reflected core beliefs and values and the pressures of Americanization. Churches always came first and then the assurance societies. Like Lutherans, Jews, and other close-knit ethnic groups with a strong sense of religious obligation, Dutch Calvinists seldom sought public charity but rather relied upon family networks, church, and Christian benevolent societies. Even widows with dependent children or disabled husbands did not avail themselves of government programs. "It is remarkable how few Dutch ask for help of the County," the editor of Chicago's Dutch language newspaper *Onze Toekomst* observed in 1921.[3]

One reason county aid was not necessary was that the Dutch took care of their own. For example, during the depression of the mid-1890s, which was only slightly less severe than that of the 1930s, the Reformed churches in Chicago formed a Joint Committee for the Relief of Needy Hollanders. Help came unexpectedly from as far away as Pella, Iowa, when the Ladies' Aid of the First Reformed Church shipped four boxes of new and "castoff" clothing. "The donation was a most agreeable surprise, and is highly appreciated," noted Peter Moerdyke, pastor of Trinity Reformed Church. "The suffering of the poor in great cities is distressing, and these generous ladies were, in this act, true daughters of Dorcas." (Many Reformed women's societies bore the name Dorcas, in honor of the New Testament Christian woman in Joppa [modern Haifa] who was renowned for her acts of charity.)[4]

3. *Onze Toekomst,* 13 May 1921.

4. Acts of the Apostles 9:36-41; Moerdyke, "Chicago Letter," *CI,* 28 Feb. 1894, p. 10.

Again in the Great Depression of the 1930s, the churches sprang into action. The First Reformed Church of Chicago appointed a "welfare committee" to "look after the welfare of families without means of support due to conditions which exist at the present time." To fund the work, the deacons designated a special offering the first Sunday of each month, for "as long as the present depression lasts." But they refused a request to establish a center in the church to distribute food and clothing to the needy. The consistory also refused an appeal by the *Chicago Daily News* "to help in its work amongst the poor people of our city," but the consistory did agree to set aside $50 for needy families "outside of our own congregation."[5]

Pride, an independent spirit, and a strong sense of familial obligation all worked to keep the Dutch a people apart. Married children took in aged parents until the founding of the first Holland Home in 1914 relieved many of that burden.

Self Help Society

The oldest and most successful Dutch benevolent society was the Zelf Hulp Burial Fund Society, founded February 20, 1879, by westsiders. It was a cooperative venture among members of both the Reformed and Christian Reformed churches. The impetus was the economic depression of the 1870s, when church benevolent funds were drained and poor Hollanders sometimes had to be buried in the potter's field. One man finally suggested that a permanent fund be started by small weekly contributions. This effort evolved into a regularly organized society, run on an actuarial basis, which was chartered by the State of Illinois February 4, 1884. Such a mutual burial fund was acceptable even to those Hollanders who, on principle, strenuously opposed buying life insurance policies.[6]

Pioneer settler Roelof Stuivenga spearheaded the organizational drive of the Zelf Hulp Society, along with Reinder (Robert) Mulder, an Englewood grocer. Stuivenga was the first executive secretary. In his old age in 1909, when he was infirm and with the "wolf at the door," society members returned the favor by building a small house for him on the rear lot of his married daughter's home on Huron Street at Western Avenue.

5. First Reformed Church of Chicago, Minutes, 28 Oct., 23 Dec. 1930; 27 Jan., 14 July, 1 Sept. 1931; 25 Feb. 1932; Western Seminary Collection, Joint Archives of Holland, Mich.

6. Vandenbosch, *Dutch Communities of Chicago,* 65; Moerdyke, "Chicago Letter," *CI,* 25 Jan. 1905, p. 58.

Jacob Wieringa (1830-1906) of Englewood, who arrived in Chicago immediately after the Civil War, was another long-time officer. Jan Toren served as the second secretary, followed by Izaak (Ike) Emmering.

The Zelf Hulp Society prospered by limiting its risk to burial expenses. It never covered illness, as many other societies did. Zelf Hulp signed up nine thousand members by 1901 and in 1913 boasted of nearly fourteen thousand members and a capital reserve of $42,000. Beginning with a payout of only $39 in its first year, the society's death benefits totaled $109,000 by 1906, and it helped one hundred or more families each year. In 1908 the annual meeting approved hiring a second clerk to handle the rising load of paperwork and ratified an increase in the death benefit from $100 to $150 for adults; the benefit for those under eighteen years was about two-thirds of that amount. "Our capital was accumulated by hard-earned money of our working people, who constitute our majority," society president R. Van Der Molen observed in 1909. Clearly, the burial society was maturing rapidly in its second quarter-century.[7]

Agents of the society collected dues weekly or monthly in pennies, nickels, and dimes by calling at the homes of members. To single out only one of the collectors who was active for many years, Ed Vander Meulen was a leader in the First and Fourth Christian Reformed congregations and served on the board of Ebenezer Christian School. He was "widely known as a man of sterling character, well read, and possessed of admirable qualities."[8]

Zelf Hulp provides proof that the individualistic Dutch were capable of cooperative ventures, but success did not come easily. As the *Onze Toekomst* editor noted in 1907, "It is worthwhile to listen to the story of those, who have laid the foundations of this mighty organization, how they had to fight apathy as well as mistrust."[9]

One source of criticism was the growing bureaucracy, administrative problems, and sharply rising costs of operations. The society suffered its first financial loss in 1909 of $2,000 on capital reserves of $40,000. The death benefit increase in 1908 apparently was too generous. And in 1910, the death rate among the members rose unexpectedly to an average of one member per month.[10]

But an issue of far greater import was the question of who could be-

7. Moerdyke, "Chicago Letter," *CI,* 13 Mar. 1901, p. 169; *Onze Toekomst,* 5, 12 Feb. 1909 (quote).

8. *Chicago Messenger,* Ed Vander Meulen obituary, 14 Feb. 1936.

9. *Onze Toekomst,* 1 Feb. 1907.

10. Ibid., 4 Feb., 1 July 1910.

long to the society. The founders had intended it for Dutch Reformed families, but over time society officials and their agents allowed Flemish (Dutch and Belgian) Catholics to become members and even persons with nary a drop of Dutch blood.

Matters first came to a head at the special meeting in June 1909 that was called to consider a proposal to amend the by-laws. Some 150 members gathered at the usual venue, Handel Hall on East Randolph Street, for what was an "emotional meeting." The by-laws committee "could not boast of a pleasant reception," reads a report of the meeting. Every one of their recommendations was rejected in favor of keeping the old by-laws, which the body ordered reprinted in both the Dutch and English languages. The slap on the board's hands could be heard all the way to the Dutch neighborhood at Harrison and May Streets.

The officers who caught the flak had been elected at the regular February 1909 meeting five months earlier, a meeting that was "well attended and nearly filled the hall." They were: Van Der Molen, re-elected president; H. Stuit, vice president; Ike Emmering, secretary; Reinder

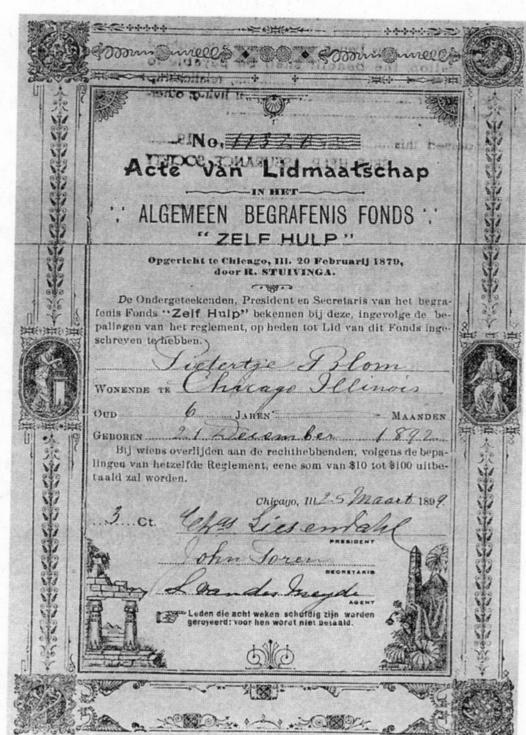

No.

Acte van Lidmaatschap

IN HET

ALGEMEEN BEGRAFENIS FONDS

"ZELF HULP"

Opgericht te Chicago, Ill. 20 Februarij 1879, door R. STUIVINGA.

De Ondergeteekenden, President en Secretaris van het begrafenis Fonds "Zelf Hulp" bekennen bij deze, ingevolge de bepalingen van het reglement, op heden tot Lid van dit Fonds ingeschreven te hebben.

Pietertje J Blom

WONENDE TE Chicago Illinois

OUD 6 JAREN MAANDEN

GEBOREN 21 December 1892

Bij wiens overlijden aan de rechthebbenden, volgens de bepalingen van hetzelfde Reglement, eene som van $10 tot $100 uitbetaald zal worden.

Chicago, Ill 25 Maart 1899

3 Ct.

PRESIDENT

John Toren

SECRETARIS

AGENT

Leden die acht weken schuldig zijn worden geroyeerd: voor hen wordt niet betaald.

Zelf Hulp (Self Help) Burial Policy, Certificate 11326, issued 25 March 1899 to Pietertje Blom, age 6, cost 3 cents, payable at death $10 to $100.

(Courtesy of John and Harold Blom)

Mulder, treasurer; and board members James De Boer, a scavenger; medical doctor Hendrik B. De Bey (son of the late Reverend Bernardus De Bey); and W. Den Herder. That February meeting had postponed acting on the report of the by-laws committee, which was obviously a hot potato.[11]

Shortly before the 1910 annual meeting, the second shoe dropped when an internal debate within the boardroom became very public. Secretary Ike Emmering wrote a strident letter (but masked his identity by signing it *Eenige Leden* ["Some Members"]) and sent it for publication to *De Grondwet* of Holland, Michigan. This newspaper regularly ran a Chicago column, and it circulated widely throughout the midwestern Dutch communities. The editor, Henry Uden Marsman, was the former editor of two Chicago Dutch papers, *De Nederlander* and *Onze Toekomst.* He ran the exposé in the conviction that Emmering spoke for many members.[12]

The society, Emmering noted, was founded by selfless men who served without pay, and it has grown "like a mustard seed entrusted to the ground into a big tree" that is the "pride of our Holland people." But the noble pioneers have been replaced by officers who "chase after little jobs," create "red tape," and do not follow the by-laws. They take stipends of $100 per year, plus fees for committee work. "If you think about it," Emmering opined, "it is a serious matter for members to pay a few pennies every week at great sacrifice while the directors are drawing stipends." They should be "ashamed to put this money in their pockets." Further, the officers operate too much on faith and routinely allow late payments, which causes a huge amount of "needless work" for the secretary.

Emmering was warming to the task and continued his indictment by warning of a "danger that is now threatening the interests of our Society that demands immediate attention." Three board members, Luurt Holstein, James De Boer, and the "family of a director," had tapped the society's reserve funds – Holstein for $2,800, De Boer for $2,000, and the third party for $2,000 – for a total of $6,800, each giving as security a mortgage on real estate.

While the insider loans were not dishonest, Emmering asserted, they were imprudent, because "should it happen that the mortgages must be foreclosed then these men would have to take themselves to court. The ridiculousness *(bespottelijke)* and danger of this situation is obvious to all."

11. Ibid., 5, 12, Feb., 18 June 1909.

12. Eenige Leden, "Een Gezonde Financiele Politiek voor Zelf Hulp," *De Grondwet,* 11 Jan. 1910, p. 6. Quotations in this and the next paragraphs were translated by Earl William Kennedy.

The secretary then drew an analogy that his readers could readily grasp; "A simple hired man may sometimes think, 'I am my own boss,' but a boss and a hired man cannot be one and the same." Emmering concluded by urging society members at the next annual meeting to vote out of office any director carrying a loan from the society. "A sound financial policy is very much to be desired."

In the next issue of *De Grondwet,* the editor identified Emmering as the spokesman for "Some Members" and promised to publish a rebuttal from the pen of director James De Boer in the following number. De Boer criticized Emmering strongly for masking his identity, but he mainly addressed the charges that he, Mulder, and Holstein had corrupted the society's good name and jeopardized its reserve funds by borrowing against mortgages. First, said De Boer, the members had been informed "of all these matters" at the 1908 society meeting. Second, the finance committee and then the full board of seven directors collectively had approved these and all such loans, which required full security backed by real estate mortgages. Third, he and the other borrowers had followed the normal practice of recusing themselves when their loans were on the table. Fourth, the note holders stood ready to pay off their loans whenever the directors so requested. And fifth, stipends had routinely been paid for committee work.

That left the question of motive. "What moved Mr. Emmering to place the board under public suspicion in this way? . . . Is this really in the interests of the Society?" Why did he not raise these concerns at the last board meeting? asked De Boer. The secretary must have hidden motives. De Boer surmised that his motive was the desire to keep his post. He was elected "with much difficulty and just barely made it," and now the board "will not support him after the things they have found out about him." In short, De Boer declared, "I think that our present secretary cannot be reelected, and I sign my own name to this."[13]

Within days of this bitter public feud between the secretary and the other officials of Zelf Hulp, the society gathered for its annual meeting at Handel Hall. *Toekomst* editor Holstein, in announcing the gathering, seemed to give Emmering some cover by recommending "a new system of bookkeeping" that would be more efficient and allow the office staff to be cut from two to one full-time person. Recall that Holstein was one of the board members carrying a loan. Nevertheless, the votes of the members confirmed De Boer's predictions. Emmering was voted out in favor of Douwe Dykstra, while Mulder was retained as treasurer. Nicholas Fisher

13. "Zelf Hulp," ibid., 18 Jan. 1910; J. De Boer, "Zelf Hulp," ibid., 1 Feb. 1910.

was elected president and H. Stuit vice president. Holstein and H. De Young were re-elected as directors, along with Henry Boss, "an old settler" and one of the charter members, and E. H. Wierenga, a "busy and reliable real estate man."[14]

This slate had been recommended in a very unusual manner. Thirty-seven leading businessmen and professionals put their names on a nominating petition and published the same in *Onze Toekomst.* The list included, among others, Ebenezer Christian School teacher Henry Jacobsma, realtors Ben and George Ottenhoff, Netherlands consul generals John Vennema and P. Court van Woerden, Ed Vander Meulen, and Alfred Oosterheerdt. These "heavy hitters" had clearly closed ranks behind the society.

De Boer was not nominated for re-election in 1910, probably by his own choice after Emmering's slashing attack. But his influence and that of the De Boer family continued for three generations. Son George was a regular on the board of directors, and son Andrew was a long-time secretary. He was succeeded in 1952 by George's son-in-law, Richard Schuurman, who ran the organization for eighteen years until it ended in a merger in 1970.

The 1911 annual meeting was pivotal. Here the members who turned out settled one of the main issues. They decided that the society would remain Dutch. They voted to amend the by-laws and limit future members to persons of Dutch or Belgian birth or descent or their spouses, from three months to fifty-nine years of age, and "in good health." Children of current non-Dutch members could also join, but not any new non-Dutch adults.[15]

In the late 1910s, the office of Zelf Hulp moved to the Oxford Building in the La Salle Street financial district (118 N. La Salle), and the annual business meetings were often held at the United Masonic Temple at 32 W. Randolph Street. Meetings again became routine, and the same cozy coterie controlled the society, along with a few new names. Continuing officers were De Bey, De Boer, Emmering, Mulder, Stuit, Vander Molen, and Wieringa. Newcomers included directors Harry Bierma, Gerrit Bossenga, Nick Fisher, and H. Kleinhuizen. Dick Driesbergen was one of the leading agents. By 1927 Zelf Hulp reported eighteen thousand members and a reserve fund of $75,000.[16]

14. Ibid., 4 Feb. 1910.

15. Ibid., 17 Feb. 1911; *De Grondwet,* 21 Jan. 1911, p. 8.

16. *Onze Toekomst,* 23 Jan., 5 Feb. 1920; "Chicago, Ill., en Omstreken," *De Grondwet,* 16 Apr. 1929, p. 8; Vandenbosch, *Dutch Communities of Chicago,* 66.

In the 1940s, the company adopted the more modern name of Self Help Life Assurance Society and moved its offices to the up-scale Monadnock Building at 53 W. Jackson Boulevard and then to the prestigious Insurance Exchange Building at 175 W. Jackson Boulevard. Bierma, Wieringa, and Kleinhuizen were still directors, along with James De Boer's son George, Lambert Bere of Clearing, D. W. Jellema, Nicholas Knol and Richard Evenhouse of Cicero, George Ottenhoff of Oak Park, J. W. Schuitema, and Peter Woldman of Berwyn. James De Boer's son Andrew served as executive secretary for many years. The company's popular slogan in the 1940s stressed its low overhead: "Security Through Net-Cost Life Insurance."[17]

In 1952 Andrew De Boer died tragically in a drowning accident, and Richard Schuurman, George De Boer's son-in-law who had joined the firm in 1948 after graduating from Calvin College, assumed the leadership role. Agents still continued to visit homes of members quarterly to collect premiums at the rate of 25 cents per month for $250 of coverage, regardless of age. "Honor Roll" agents in the period 1955-59 were: Elmer Huizinga, Bernard Laninga, Nicholas Fisher, Arnold Weidenaar, Jacob Boss, Siebert Stob, John Vander Bilt, Henry De Hoog, Lawrence Mensink, Robert L. Fluitman, Lamoire Urschel, Teade Sipling, and Bert Worries. Urshchel and Worries were non-Dutch.

Under Schuurman, the company converted to a sound actuarial basis and was rechartered as the Self Help Mutual Life Assurance Company under the general laws of the state of Illinois. Its agents could now write all forms of life insurance. In 1965 the company took the next step in its evolution by changing its name to the National Heritage Life Insurance Company and converting from a mutual charter owned by the policy holders to a public stock company. All policy holders were gifted shares of stock out of surplus funds based on the face amount of their policies. To raise capital for further growth, the company arranged with the Chicago brokerage house of McCormick & Company to float a public offering. When some twenty-six thousand shares were left unsold, Richard Evenhouse bought them to protect the company.[18]

The future in 1965 looked rosy for the eighty-six-year-old Dutch insurance company, but within five years it faced an unexpected takeover that the management could not withstand, and it was merged out of exis-

17. *Illinois Observer,* 15 Apr. 1954; Jan. 1955; Sept., Oct., Nov. 1959.

18. For the history of Self Help after 1952, I am indebted to Richard Schuurman's phone conversation of 12 November 1999.

tence in 1970. The unraveling began after Richard Evenhouse suffered several heart attacks. He decided to sell his twenty-six thousand shares because they were thinly traded and would be difficult for his wife and heirs to sell. Everett Ballard, president of the All American Life and Casualty Company, learned of Evenhouse's intent and offered to buy him out. Evenhouse agreed, believing that the company was acting in good faith, only to learn subsequently that All American was fronting for one of their star agents, Victor Saayeh, a Lebanese-American. Evenhouse felt betrayed but died before the final curtain dropped.

Saayeh quickly made a generous tender offer to all the small Dutch-American shareholders and succeeded in gaining a majority stake in National Heritage. Once in control, he abruptly fired Schuurman and took control of all the historical records – minute books from 1879, registration lists of policy holders, and certificates of burial insurance from Certificate No. 1. Saayeh merged National Heritage into a Denver-based company he controlled. He then milked both firms to support a gambling habit at Las Vegas. Eventually, the insurance adjuster for the state of Colorado had to step in and arrange for the bankrupt companies to be reinsured with the renowned Massachusetts Mutual Insurance Company, which in 1996 was merged into Conseco Life Insurance Company of Indiana. Thus did the Self Help Society meet its demise after nearly one hundred years of service. The valuable historical records, many written in Dutch, were also lost forever.

Roseland Mutual Aid Society

The origin of De Roselandsche Onderlinge Hulp Vereeniging bij Overlijden ("Roseland Mutual Aid Society in the Event of Death") was less altruistic than Self Help. Sander Van Wyngaarden, the village undertaker and furniture dealer, is generally credited with originating the idea for it, and he was its president for the first quarter century. Van Wyngaarden often had to embalm and bury indigent Hollanders at his expense. To cut his losses and ensure decent burials, as the westsiders had done, in 1884 he created the society to provide funds for final expenses. All persons in good health of Dutch birth or descent and their relatives could join, but those who failed to pay dues for thirteen weeks or more forfeited their memberships without refunds. Dues ranged from two cents a week for children below five years to twelve cents a week for adults fifty-five to sixty years. Benefits ranged from $20 for stillborns to $175 for adults. Agents collected the dues weekly or monthly and earned a commission of 25 percent. The money was invested in mortgage loans.[19]

The body thrived and reached a membership of eight thousand in the mid-1920s, with reserves of $52,000. Board members then were Fred Vos, president; Christian school principal Albert Blystra, secretary; and G. Smit, treasurer, along with six others. Madderom's Hall was the usual venue of the annual meetings, which were very popular and provided entertainment and treats – beer and cigars for the men and ice cream for the children. What the ladies received is unknown. In earlier years the meetings were held at the Knights of Pythias Hall on Michigan Avenue or the Dutch League building on 111th Street. Some Dutch Catholics in Kensington also joined the society and had full rights to vote and hold office, but none was elected.[20]

Roseland Mutual Aid had a long life of more than one hundred years, but in its 101st year, 1985, its day had passed. The society went private when Nick and Henry Wierenga, father and son insurance agents on the West Side, bought all the policies. After their deaths a few years later, the Family Protection Insurance Company bought the business and converted the policies to life insurance. Since the Roseland Mutual Aid Society never adjusted benefits for inflation, policy payouts today barely cover floral expenses.[21]

Eendracht Maakt Macht

Hollanders on the North Side organized another mutual aid society in 1894 that was pitched toward upwardly mobile Hollanders who were unchurched. The social agenda included card playing and dancing, which strict Reformed people eschewed. The members chose the name Eendracht Maakt Macht ("In Unity Is Strength"), which was the name of one of New York City's oldest (founded in 1864) and most prestigious Dutch-American organizations. The Reformed Church in America had also incorporated the phrase in its great seal. At biweekly meetings of Eendracht

19. Ross K. Ettema fortuitously saved the records in 1989 when they were "about twenty-five feet from the trash heap." He then transcribed the original documents and wrote an English-language summary in a typescript booklet in 1990. The document collection (25 vols.) with Ettema's booklet are in the Trinity Christian College Library Dutch Heritage Collection, Palos Heights, Ill.

20. Vandenbosch, *Dutch Communities of Chicago,* 66-67.

21. Ettema, typescript historical booklet.

Maakt Macht, the members took care of business and then listened to lectures that nurtured "a truly Dutch spirit."

The annual picnic was a highlight for the members and their families, which had grown to more than a hundred by 1897. That year the picnic committee, consisting of Messrs. De Graff, Arends, Straaten, and Bieze, chose the grounds of Oswald's Grove on N. Halsted Street, where they arranged music, games, and races, with prizes supplied by the famed Dutch-American retail store Siegel-Cooper & Co. on State Street. President P. Van Wanroy opened the festivities, amid unfurled Dutch and American flags, by noting the links between the fatherland and the flag, and the need for the Dutch to unite for pleasure and security. "It goes without saying," reported member Harry Meyer,

> that the picnic had a truly Dutch character. The always clean and fresh tricolor of the fatherland we left, but not forgot, mixed harmoniously with the Stars and Stripes. We heard the old cheerful folk songs, which brought back dear memories, and the young folk responded with enthusiasm to the musical invitation to the dance, every time there was an opportunity.[22]

During the South African Boer War against England in 1899-1902, the Chicago society raised money for the Boers. In 1907 it held its annual banquet at the Scbuse Hall on 12th Street, and the next year the society voted to increase dues to fifty cents per month, of which five cents went into the "aid fund." Death benefits were increased to $200 in 1908, and the next year sick benefits were raised from $5 to $6 per week. Members who moved out of Cook County lost all benefits. Early leaders of Eendracht Maakt Macht were W. Huizenga; Henry Ten Bruin, a mustard manufacturer; and John Prins, a cooper. Peter Bloemsema, a news dealer, served as president in 1909-10. Other officers were J. Meindersma, C. B. Koop, J. D. Smit, Douwe Dykstra, John Komen, Daniel Bieze, William Beerthuis, and J. Frieling. Most were businessmen. Later the society opened a Roseland branch and catered to its southside members. It was active during the First World War and into the twenties and met at the Knights of Columbus Hall on 63rd Street and Harvard Avenue in the heart of Englewood.[23]

22. "Eendracht Maakt Macht," *De Grondwet,* 24 Aug. 1897; Vandenbosch, *Dutch Communities of Chicago,* 68. Huug van den Dool translated Meyer's report, dated 19 Aug. 1897.

23. *Onze Toekomst,* 1 Mar. 1907; 29 June 1906; 19 June 1908; 15 July 1910; 30 Jan. 1920; Van Hinte, *Netherlanders in America,* 833.

Excelsior Society

In 1897 the westsiders founded a third death and disability society, which chose the English-language name "Excelsior" to symbolize their purpose – "higher yet higher with the help of all the Dutch of this city." B. Van Der Molen served as secretary in the years 1908-1911, and Hendrik B. De Bey, son of the dominie, and J. A. Riedel were the examining physicians. Excelsior grew slowly and after ten years counted only 150 members. In 1908 it took in $993, spent $728, and closed the year with a balance of only $265. But the next year the cash on hand grew to $1,494. Leaders in Excelsior were J. Vanden Berg, D. Baar, Peter Woldman, R. Huizenga, A. Heis, Dick Driesbergen, Albert Dykema, E. Heringa, R. Schuurman, R. Buikema, Ike Emmering, Nick Knol, Sr., J. Hoekstra, and D. Klei.[24]

The Excelsior Society staged annual July 4th picnics that featured the Harmonie Band of the First Christian Reformed Church, directed for many years by George O. Ottenhoff, and included foot races, boating, egg-rolling contests, and other activities. The 1908 gathering was held at Jestram's Grove in the far western suburb of Hillside. The annual business meetings usually took place at the Pilsen (Bohemian) Hall at 1812 S. Ashland Avenue, with entertainment provided by the men's choir, Concordia, directed by J. W. Schuitema, the Harmonie Band, or a similar Dutch-American musical group. The thirtieth anniversary meeting in 1927, however, featured a slide show of "moving pictures" by T. N. Huizenga, agent of the Cunard Line of steamships, presenting a trip through Europe and Holland. Excelsior covered sick benefits for 350 members in 1927, but it functioned more as a benevolent society than an insurance company like Self Help.[25]

The Excelsior Society made a significant and lasting contribution to the Chicago Dutch community when in 1911 it launched a city-wide campaign to establish a retirement home "for the benefit of our Dutch people." As Secretary B. Van Der Molen explained at the annual meeting:

> We all know that in Chicago are many aged Dutchmen who due to their old age are not capable of making their own living. . . . And very often the support of our aged by friends and relatives as a rule is short lived. And so you see, then, the poor farm is their only refuge. . . . It is especially for this reason that nearly all other Nationalities have their

24. *Onze Toekomst,* 3 July 1908; 3 July 1909.
25. Ibid., 14 Apr. 1911; 6 Apr. 1927; Christian Reformed Church, *Yearbook,* 1925, 82.

own Home for the aged. . . . And it is with the selfsame feeling, the same honor and respect for our aged, that our meeting decided to call on all our countrymen.[26]

Holland Homes

The "work of faith" succeeded, and in 1914 the Hollandsche Tehuis voor Bejaarden ("Holland Home for the Aged") opened for seventeen residents in the old parsonage of the First Reformed Church of Roseland. A member of the congregation bought the building and had it moved to a vacant lot on 107th Place. In 1925 a new fifty-room facility was constructed on an adjacent lot at 238-40 W. 107th Place. The women's societies of the various Reformed and Christian Reformed churches, organized as ladies' circles, during an eight-year period raised virtually all of the $10,500 for the new building by staging an annual Tag Day. This replaced the earlier Dutch auction, *Elk wat wils* ("Each give what he pleases"). The building was expanded several times, the last in 1958 with a $40,000 addition that increased the capacity from 90 to 150 persons and sharply reduced the waiting period of more than two years. But even this could not meet the demand for long. Subsequently, in 1970 the Holland Home was relocated in a new six-story building in South Holland.

Since the 1950s, the Chicago Hollanders also opened two additional retirement centers, three convalescent care institutions, and a school and residential facility for handicapped children and adults.[27] The homes for the elderly are the Holland Home in South Holland, Village Woods in Crete, and Saratoga Grove in Downers Grove. The convalescent homes are Rest Haven South in South Holland, Rest Haven Central in Palos Heights (1958), and Rest Haven West (Saratoga Grove) in Downers Grove (1984).

Elim School (1948), formerly the Chicago Christian School for the Handicapped, and its related Bethshan residential center in Palos Heights, provide for children with developmental and physical disabilities, mainly deaf-oral and vision-impaired. The instigator was the Rev. William Masselink and his wife Mary, leaders of the Second Christian Reformed Church of Englewood, who had a son with Down's syndrome whom the Englewood Christian School would not enroll. Cost was a factor and some

26. *Onze Toekomst,* 14 Apr. 1911.

27. Ibid., 24 Jan., 7 Feb. 1913; 27 June 1923; 24, 28 May 1924; 30 Sept. 1925; 27 Oct. 1926; *Illinois Observer,* June-July 1957; Jan., Feb., Mar., June 1958.

parents objected to "mixing" special and "normal" children. Mary had tried home-schooling Paul, but a long-term solution was needed. With the endorsement of the school board, Masselink in April 1948 began a class in the church basement with two students, under the Van Der Laan sisters, nurse Henrietta and Christine, a former bank worker. Enrollment quickly jumped to seven. That summer the sisters better prepared themselves by attending special education classes at the University of Chicago. The fall 1949 enrollment of eighteen stretched the facilities, so the Reverend William Kok of the First Christian Reformed Church seized the initiative and moved classes to his more spacious church basement. For two years the Van Der Laan sisters served as teachers, cooks, janitors, and "bus drivers" (actually, station wagons), which traveled eighty miles daily as far as Cicero to transport the pupils to and from their homes.

Kok gave forceful and effective leadership and deserves accolades as the "father of Elim." Even the name "Elim – A School for Exceptional Children" was his idea. In 1950, he and the board he had gathered conducted a national search to recruit a trained teacher-administrator. They found John Kamp, who was properly credentialed, and for the next thirty-five years, until he retired in 1985, he directed the school. In the first of many bold moves, Kok and Kamp, the dynamic duo, late in 1950 purchased an eight-acre campus in Palos Heights for $17,500. This special ministry quickly won the hearts of the Chicago-area Reformed churches. The land was paid for within one year and the farmhouse on the site provided classroom space for the twenty-seven students and four staff members until a new school was built in 1951. The next year a Work Services wing was added and Elim became a full-fledged school. The Kamps lived on the second floor of the farmhouse. Enrollment really exploded when the institution constructed dormitories and reached out nation-wide to Christian Reformed students. The denomination designated Elim as a "Recommended Cause" and gifts poured in from congregations across the country. In 1969, as the children began "aging out" of school at twenty-one years, the Elim board made the critical decision to serve adults as well as children by constructing a Work Activities Center with a dining hall. Elim is another success story in the Dutch Reformed community of Chicago.[28]

28. "The Story of Elim at Fifty" (Palos Heights, Ill., 1998); John L. Schaver, "The Churches of Chicago North," *Banner,* 20 May 1949; John Kamp's recollections shared with the author.

Hulp in Nood

The Excelsior Society worked closely with a fourth benevolent organization, Hulp in Nood ("Help in Need"), which was also a small society to provide sick and death benefits. The founding date of Hulp in Nood is not known, but it was active from at least 1913 until 1930, and probably much longer. Officers in 1913 were R. Buikema, president; D. Heslinga, vice president; R. Schreuder, vicar; Ike Emmering, treasurer; J. A. Riedel, physician; directors D. Steen, Nick Knol, Sr., and J. Hoekstra; and sergeant at arms D. Klei.[29] Since many of these men also were active in Excelsior, one can assume that Hulp in Nood was an arm of Excelsior.

In 1921 Excelsior and Hulp in Nood jointly sponsored a benefit program at the Pilsen Hall, featuring the Concordia Men's Choir and a travelogue slide show of the Netherlands. Officers of Hulp in Nood in 1925 included N. Van Zeewyk, president; Nick Rispens, vice president; A. Laning, secretary; Dick Fisher, treasurer; P. Van Wanroy, Jr., vicar; and directors J. Meidema, Albert Dykema, and J. Hoekstra. The body met every third week at 18th Street and Laflin Street.[30] Both organizations became defunct, presumably after the onset of the Great Depression in 1930.

Vriendschap en Trouw

After 1900 another Dutch benevolent society, Vriendschap en Trouw ("Friendship and Fidelity"), was organized in Englewood for the purpose of supporting "many Hollanders during their sickness." Its office was at 67th and May streets. Besides offering sickness and death benefits, the group recruited members through arranged social activities such as boat excursions, band concerts, and other entertaining programs. In early 1920, for example, the society held a big celebration at Marquette Hall on Halsted Street to honor members who served in the "Great War."[31]

29. *Onze Toekomst,* 7 Mar. 1913.

30. Ibid., 4 Mar. 1925; Vandenbosch, *Dutch Communities of Chicago,* 66.

31. *Onze Toekomst,* 23 Sept. 1910; 7 Dec. 1927; 2 Feb. 1909; 17 Dec. 1909; Vandenbosch, *Dutch Communities of Chicago,* 66.

Dutch and Belgian Catholic Societies

The westside Dutch Catholics in 1906 emulated the Calvinists and, in conjunction with the Flemish Belgians, created a benefit society for "all who speak Dutch or Flemish." The purpose was "to support members in sickness, in unemployment, and especially to lend a helping hand to new immigrants who have just recently arrived here." The first open enrollment meeting took place in 1906 at Jan Bogers Hall (located at the corner of Hastings and Loomis streets), and they chose Albert Van den Driessche as president. The official name of this Dutch Catholic group is not stated, nor is its subsequent history known.[32]

In 1907 Chicago's Dutch and Belgian priests broadened their agenda to channel new Catholic immigrants into planned church colonies and to meet the spiritual needs of their widely scattered compatriots. Their efforts and the resulting Catholic Colonization Society are discussed below.[33]

Dutch Refugees

The need to aid immigrants lessened with the sharp decline in immigration after World War I broke out in 1914, followed by the postwar American quota laws of 1921 and 1929, which reduced the Netherlands quota to 3,136 annually.[34] But forty years later, in the 1950s, a second wave of Dutch immigrants arrived in Chicago. Some fled the economic deprivation and seemingly bleak future in the Netherlands caused by the Second War, but a six-year waiting list to enter the U.S.A. diverted most to Canada and Australia.

In 1953, however, the U.S. government allowed seventeen thousand Netherlands citizens to enter this country above the quota limits, under the Refugee Relief Act of 1953. Some were victims of the massive North Sea flood of 1953 that devastated the provinces of Zeeland and Zuid Holland. But most had previously fled from the Dutch East Indies when the Netherlands Government, after strong prodding from Washington, granted independence to Indonesia under Sukarno.

In anticipation of the refugees' arrival, the Netherlands Consul in

32. *Onze Toekomst,* 21 Sept. 1906.

33. Ibid., 17 Oct. 1923; Van Hinte, *Netherlanders in America,* 730-31, 734.

34. Gerald De Jong, *The Dutch in America, 1609-1974* (Boston: Twayne, 1975), 179. In 1925, it was reported that "9,000 Hollanders were ready to sail to New York but could not be admitted because of the quota law" (*Onze Toekomst,* 8 Apr. 1925).

Chicago, working in cooperation with the Illinois Department of Public Welfare, formed in 1956 the Chicago Committee on Dutch Refugees to assist in the resettlement process. Most of the volunteers were Christian Reformed laymen who had been born in Chicago but learned to speak Dutch in their churches. Andrew Ridderhoff, a retired realtor, was appointed to coordinate the housing committee, and George De Boer, the owner of a successful rubbish removal firm, headed the reception committee.

Ridderhoff enlisted the help of large real estate firms to locate sufficient housing. As a stopgap measure, the First Reformed Church of Englewood allowed its vacant manse to be used for temporary housing. Working with Ridderhoff's committee were attorneys John Ligtenberg and Herman Ottenhoff; insurance executive Richard B. Schuurman; Tri-City banker Maurice Vander Velde; Edward Damstra, president of the Mid-America National Bank; Christian educator Nick Hendrikse; and Lambert Wieringa.

De Boer's reception committee met the immigrants at the bus stations, rail terminals, and airport and gave immediate assistance. His committee included fellow scavenger Sam Hoving, the travel agent John L. Koorman, and the Reverend Arthur De Kruyter, pastor of the Western Springs Christian Reformed Church and editor of the *Illinois Observer.* During the winter of 1956-57, a "considerable number" of Dutch refugees arrived in Chicago, and more came in the spring. Although the exact figures are not known, the numbers were great enough to overwhelm the committee, who appealed in February 1957 for more volunteers.

The ready response to the needy refugees by the Dutch-Americans prompted editor De Kruyter to boast in the *Illinois Observer:*

> Once again the Holland American community has shown it is only too eager to extend the hand of friendship to those newcomers from Holland who came here with hope and faith, much as their own grandfathers and grandmothers did two or three generations ago.[35]

Separate Even unto Death – Dutch Cemeteries

Even in death the Dutch Reformed preferred to remain separate. As the editor of *Onze Toekomst* remarked in 1925: "For some time a number of Dutch have desired a section of the cemetery for the exclusive burial of

35. *Illinois Observer,* Dec. 1956; Feb. 1957.

the remains of the departed members of Dutch families." Already in 1866, one year after the American Civil War ended, the consistory of the First Reformed Church of Chicago convened a general meeting "to explore the feelings" regarding a "cemetery exclusively for Hollanders."[36]

The response was positive, and the Hollanders made contact with an obliging cemetery company, Forest Home, in the far western suburb of Forest Park. The company responded with a clever marketing plan. It would open a large section only for the Dutch and would even donate a number of plots there to the church deacons for charity cases, provided that the church leaders would recommend the plots to its parishioners. The deal was struck, and to this day Forest Home Cemetery is the primary burial ground for the West Side Dutch. The entrance is on Des Plaines Avenue just north of Roosevelt Road.

The original Dutch section is west of the Des Plaines River in the less desirable interior of the cemetery. The charity graves were in the flood plain close to the river and were difficult to sell. When the first Dutch section filled in the 1920s and 1930s, Forest Home in the 1940s created another exclusive section nearby, complete with a small windmill. Later a third section was opened immediately to the east. Dutch-American morticians worked closely with Forest Home Cemetery for decades.

Forest Home Cemetery was located up to twenty miles west of the core Dutch neighborhoods in the city. Traveling this great distance to bury the dead was necessary for several reasons. First, space in the central city was a problem, and churchyard cemeteries gave way to rural cemeteries after the 1840s. None of the Dutch Reformed churches in the city ever had room on its lot for a cemetery. Second, the new democratic age in America demanded burial grounds that made no distinction on the basis of national origin or religion.[37] While the public espoused democratic ideals, however, clever cemetery marketers still used ethnoreligious bonds to sell plots, as Forest Home did for the Dutch.

Before the advent of the motor car in the 1920s, burials at Forest Home were all-day affairs with rituals of their own. The sad processions went by horse-drawn carriages and wagons, with a stop for a hot lunch following the committal service at a way station on Des Plaines Avenue and Roosevelt Road near the cemetery gate. For children, the coffin carriage and horses were white; for adults, they were black. The cortege

36. First Reformed Church of Chicago, Minutes, 24 July 1866, Art. 3.

37. Firth Haring Fabend, *Zion on the Hudson: Dutch New York and New Jersey in the Age of Revivals* (New Brunswick, N.J.: Rutgers Univ. Press, 2000), 208-09.

might also use special funeral coaches run on the Garfield Park Elevated Line (the "El") to Des Plaines Avenue, or use special coaches on the Roosevelt Road streetcar line to Austin Boulevard; the rest of the way was by horse. After more families owned automobiles, funerals were held in the early afternoon after the men had finished their garbage routes, and those with cars shared rides to the cemetery.

When a newborn died, which happened all too frequently, the father would go to the cemetery with the undertaker while the mother remained in the hospital for the requisite nine days. During the awful flu epidemic of 1918-19, only immediate families usually made the trip in funeral coaches.

Around 1915 motor cars could be rented from the livery, and within a decade most families used their own cars to process behind the hearse. With a police escort, the cortege was permitted to disregard traffic signals and proceed uninterrupted to the cemetery. All traffic gave way as a sign of respect for the dead. The number of autos in the procession indicated the prominence of the deceased, whose family took some satisfaction from an unusually long procession, one that might exceed one hundred vehicles.

In the 1920s the Chicago Park Cemetery Company used the same gambit as Forest Home to lure Dutch customers to its Mount Auburn Cemetery, located in southwestern Stickney (39th Street and Oak Park Avenue). In 1925 Mount Auburn set aside a "Holland section" and advertised it as a choice location "close to the main entrance and not in the rear of the cemetery." The company also donated a plot of ground within the section, sufficient for at least thirty graves, to the six westside Reformed and Christian Reformed congregations for indigent members. Clerics, elders, and the major Dutch undertaker and funeral director, Clarence Leenhouts, all recommended publicly that Hollanders purchase lots at Mount Auburn, and many did so.[38]

Englewood Hollanders also bought lots at Mount Auburn, but most preferred Fairmount Cemetery at 95th Street and Archer Avenue in Willow Springs. The Roseland Dutch used the churchyard of the First Reformed Church on Michigan Avenue until the 1880s, when the bodies were removed to open 107th Street. They were reinterred at Mount Greenwood Cemetery, which opened in 1880 just beyond the city limits on 111th Street and California Avenue, and became the primary cemetery for Roselanders. A few families, such as the Boomkers, bought burial plots at the Old Holland Cemetery in Thornton, among pioneers of the southern Calumet region.

38. *Onze Toekomst,* 3 June, 29 Apr. 1925.

The Dutch hired morticians and funeral directors who belonged to their own churches. The morticians prepared bodies for the customary three-day wake in the parlor of the family home, and they transported the casket from the home to the church. The front window might be removed to make an entry for the casket, and black crepe on the front door would mark the sad occasion for family and friends. Only in the 1950s, with rising affluence and changing customs, did wakes take place in funeral "parlors" rather than homes. But funeral services continued to be held in the home churches, although in recent years funeral homes began offering this service as well.

On the Old West Side, C. Leenhouts's Funeral Home on Ashland Avenue at 15th Street and later on Roosevelt Road at Hoyne Avenue handled most of the Dutch business from 1915 until the 1940s. Leenhouts's business evolved from a bookstore and small lending library. A member of the First Christian Reformed Church, his mortuary offered "Efficiency and Tenderness in the care of your loved ones" in a "most home-like" parlor. Louis Hasper was his embalmer in the 1930s. In Englewood, Christian Reformed families patronized George Beukema's Funeral Home on 69th Street near Sangamon and the "Dutch undertaker" J. Alberti on 63rd Street; Reformed Church families preferred Gerrit De Young's Funeral Home on Halsted near 70th Street and later Ed Damstra's Colonial Funeral Home. Likewise in Roseland, Reformed families used De Young's Roseland branch chapel on 108th and Wentworth Avenue, which seated 250, and Christian Reformed families hired the mortuaries of Wyngaarden, Gerrit (later Martin) Otto, and Milton Bos, all on the main thoroughfare of Michigan Avenue. In 1935 De Young advertised: "Your choice governs the price you wish to pay. Complete funerals as low as $100.00."[39]

In the Cicero area, Henry J. Dornbos, a plumber turned mortician, opened his funeral chapel in the early 1930s around the corner from the First Christian Reformed Church of Cicero at 6033 Roosevelt Road. His advertisements offered a "large, modern chapel for your convenience, at no additional charge." George Mulder later bought the business and operated it for many decades until he sold out to Norman Tameling. Mulder, and later Claude Klein's Funeral Chapel, catered to the Christian Reformed, while Rudolph (Rudy) Emmering's Funeral Home served Reformed members. All three were a stone's throw from one another along Roosevelt Road. Klein opened a second chapel in Evergreen Park in 1957. In the far western suburbs, Robert Van Staalduinen of Knollcrest Chapel

39. *Chicago Messenger,* 14 June 1935; *Onze Toekomst,* 16 Jan. 1920; *Pictorial Roseland, 1907.*

in Lombard now monopolizes the Dutch business, as Leenhouts did on the Old West Side long ago.

Non-observing Hollanders held their services in funeral parlors among members of their social clubs, such as that of Jan Dost in 1920, a member of Eendracht Maakt Macht. Mrs. W. Engels's funeral that same month was at a parlor on N. Lincoln Avenue among members of the Dutch Women's Society (Nederlandsch Vrouwenvereeniging) "Hollandia."[40]

That denominational rivalries would be carried over into the commercial world of funerary services is understandable, because morticians, pastors, and musicians worked closely together in coordinating funeral services in church sanctuaries, which mimicked Sunday worship services. Mortician George Mulder often sang solos in his sweet tenor voice at funeral services in the Christian Reformed churches.

A funeral service was a somber affair, with the congregation facing the casket in front of the sanctuary. The sermon warned family and friends to be ready themselves to meet their Maker, and eulogies of the deceased were frowned upon. Even the undertakers' use of cosmetics was condemned as "messing around" *(knoeien)* to make the corpse more attractive. Dr. Abraham Kuyper taught that such "tampering with the body" was unbiblical. Only God deserved glory, not humans. Cremation was also severely condemned as a "worldly or pagan" practice. At the conclusion of the funeral service, the casket would be opened, and the family and friends would file past in solemn procession for a "last look."[41]

On pleasant Sunday afternoons and especially on Memorial Day, families came from far and wide to revisit the graves of loved ones and spend hours meeting old friends. Cemeteries were social centers of a sort. By the 1950s the virtual monopoly of Forest Home, Mount Auburn, and Mount Greenwood began to break down, but they remain perennial favorites because they continue to engender a feeling of community. Westsiders were also attracted to the new Chapel Hill Gardens West in Villa Park, while Englewood Dutch used Chapel Hill Gardens South, Evergreen, and Fairmount cemeteries. Roselanders turned to Mount Hope, Thornton, Beverly, and Mount Vernon cemeteries, but most continued to retain plots in Mount Greenwood. In death as in life, it was important to be near family and friends.

40. *Onze Toekomst,* 30 Jan. 1920.

41. In 1893, a Mr. Stob appeared before the consistory of the First Chicago Christian Reformed Church to urge the body to stop the growing practice of eulogies at funerals, and the consistory concurred (Minutes of 8 May 1893); "Funerals," ibid., 1 Feb. 1928, trans. Henry Lammers.

Gerrit Scholtens's accidental shooting, 1909

(Chicago Daily News, 5 Jan. 1909)

Major Tragedies

The Dutch Reformed community experienced its share of collective tragedies over the decades, including shootings and drownings. In 1909, seventeen-year-old Gerrit Scholtens, eldest son of truck farmers Siebolt and Hendrikje (Henrietta) Scholtens, was accidently shot to death by a neighbor with a gun borrowed from his own father. The *Chicago Daily News* reported the tragedy with photos on its front page, describing the neighbor as a "hermit" who wanted the gun to "repulse blackmailers."[42]

Drownings were especially fearsome to the Dutch because few knew how to swim, even though they had lived by the sea. In 1904, four young men in Roseland drowned on Lake Calumet when both their two small boats capsized while duck hunting. Pieter Piersma and his cousins, the brothers Abraham and Teunis Slingerland, were members of the First Re-

42. *Chicago Daily News,* 5 Jan. 1909, courtesy of Albert and Virginia (Ronda) Van Der Molen; Chicago Police Department Homicide Record Index, 1870-1930, vol. 1, p. 153B; Cook County Coroner's Inquest Record Index, 1872-1911, 5 Jan. 1911, book 90, p. 81. The neighbor with the gun was not Dutch.

Eastland disaster, 1915

formed Church; the fourth victim, John Brandt, Jr., belonged to the Bethany Reformed Church. Piersma left a widow and two children and Abe Slingerland a widow and one child. The shocking tragedy pulled the entire community together in grief and forced them to draw on their faith in God.[43]

In 1912, five schoolboys on the West Side were playing tag around a tar kettle when it exploded, burning three fatally, including Ralph Hoekstra, a student at Ebenezer Christian School. The influenza epidemic of 1919 took a toll on the Dutch, as it did on the populace generally. Dirk Brouwer of the Old West Side recalled losing three siblings to the influenza. Eight years later, in 1927, his fourteen-year-old brother, John, drowned in the Douglas Park Lagoon along with his best friend, John Klein, age 15. Both were bicycle delivery boys for the Western Union Telegraph Company. It was a "tremendous shock" to the community, Brouwer noted.[44]

The *Eastland* was Chicago's *Titanic,* and the loss of life was horren-

43. "Uit Roseland, Ill.," *De Hope,* 6 Apr. 1904.

44. "Chicago, Ill.," *Banner,* 26 Sept. 1912; Dirk Brouwer, video interview, 25 Mar. 1998, by Martin Stulp; Forest Home Cemetery Record of Interments, 1 June 1927. I am indebted to Virginia (Ginger) Evenhouse Bilthuis for the cemetery record.

dous. This Lake Michigan steamer capsized in the Chicago River July 24, 1915, at the cost of 844 lives, including several Hollanders. The vessel had an unknown design flaw that made it top heavy, and when a capacity load of 1,600 passengers boarded on that Saturday morning, it listed badly and after twenty minutes capsized while still moored to the dock at La Salle Street. The Western Electric Company of Cicero's Hawthorne Plant had chartered the boat for a day excursion on the lake, and all the fatalities were company employees or their families. Most were Czech and Bohemian Catholics, but some Hollanders also worked at the plant, which made switching equipment for the Bell Telephone Company. Two of the victims were West Side Groningers – Jennie and Anna B. Evenhouse, unmarried sisters twenty-five and twenty-one years old. A brother, who was also on board, was rescued. All were children of the D. Evenhouse (Evenhuis) family, who belonged to the Christian Reformed Church.[45]

The worst tragedy by far to befall the West Side Dutch was the Labor Day drowning in 1929 of five young men, ages nineteen to twenty-four, at Long Lake, north of Chicago. The promising men from prominent families were Everett Veldman and Harry Wezeman of Cicero, Cornelius (Neal) Gelderloos and John Hoving of Chicago, and George Ottenhoff of Hinsdale. The disaster unfolded when ten couples from various Christian Reformed churches gathered at the lake for a holiday of boating and picnicking. John R. Swierenga, the author's father, planned to join them, but his steady date and future wife, Marie Hoekstra, took sick that morning. Much to Swierenga's chagrin, he had to stay home and spend the holiday with the family.

That evening Swierenga learned the awful news of the drowning of his friends, including Veldman and Wezeman, his former classmates at Timothy Christian School. Their boat had capsized after the outboard motor caught in weeds and swamped the craft in fifteen feet of water. Six men were in a boat designed for four, and none could swim. Thomas Huizenga, who was steering the boat, survived by clinging to the seat until being rescued by his older brother Peter, who was following in a second boat.

Chicago newspapers carried the awful story. The bold, black, front

45. George W. Hilton, *Eastland: Legacy of the Titanic* (Stanford: Stanford Univ. Press, 1995), 87-122, 289. The D. Evenhouse family lived at 2021 N. Avers Avenue. Their church membership in 1915 is unknown, but in 1925 they belonged to the Fourth Christian Reformed Church, which was an offshoot of First Church in 1923. Other *Eastland* victims with Dutch sounding names were Lizzie Bosch, Mary Cooper, Catherine Cooper, William Fischer, Mr. and Mrs. J. M. Hoffman, Marie Hoffman, Tillie Jansen, Otto Mares, Anna Meyer, and E. Trap ("De Ramp De Eastland," *De Grondwet,* 3 Aug. 1915, p. 8).

Labor Day drownings l-r: Everett Veldman, victim; George Ottenhoff, victim; Thomas Huizenga, rescuer; Peter Huizenga, rescuer; Cornelius Gelderloos, victim *(Chicago American, 3 Sept. 1929)*

page headline of *Onze Toekomst* cried out: "5 Hollandse Jongelingen op 'Labor Day' Verdronken" (5 Dutch Young Men Drown on Labor Day). The city newspapers showed less sympathy. The heading of the *Chicago Daily Tribune* article read: "Boys Tip Boat, Five Drown in Tragic Outing." The *Tribune* said witnesses among the three thousand people at Stanton's Resort enjoying the holiday reported that the men were "frolicking in an overloaded boat, . . . standing up and rocking their boat to amuse Miss Helen Brouwer, 1642 W. 14th Place, and Miss Jennie Dekker, 1413 S. Ashland Avenue, who were in another boat close by." Anna Klein and Hilda Sterenberg also were "forced to stand idly by during the mad thrashing of the doomed boys." The motif of recklessness was echoed in the *Chicago American,* which declared, "Chicagoans Flee Heat – Find Death." The paper ran photos of five of those involved, under a drawing of two boats alongside one another with two men standing and reaching across the sides grappling with each other, while two others did the same while seated.[46]

The editor of *Onze Toekomst* disputed the frolicking charge. "One of the girls strongly denies [it] . . . and we readily believe her. Moreover, all five boys had a good reputation and in some respects exhibited exemplary behavior," said the editor.

The *Tribune* reported there were ten men and ten women at the

46. This and the next paragraphs rely on *Chicago Daily Tribune,* 3 Sept. 1929; *Onze Toekomst,* 4 Sept. 1929; *Chicago Daily News,* 3 Sept. 1929; *Chicago American,* 3 Sept. 1929; *Chicago Herald and Examiner,* 3 Sept. 1929; and *Chicago Evening Post,* 3 Sept. 1929.

Dutch outing, but it named only the five victims and the four women. The *Onze Toekomst* account stated that "many young people came too," and identified seven men plus five women, namely Brouwer, Dekker, Anna Klein, Bertha Holtrust, and Thomas Huizenga's wife, Jennie Sterenberg. Others were Veldman's date, Anna Meyer, and possibly Peter Huizenga's date, Betty Bovenkerk. Brouwer, Dekker, and Klein had rented a cottage at Long Lake for the prior week, and this was the base for the holiday party. Tom and Jennie were the chaperones.

The disaster traumatized the West Side Dutch Reformed community like few events in the twentieth century, because it affected several congregations and their interrelated family clans. "We suddenly all feel that same shudder, all our nerves are touched with compassion, and our hearts express real sorrow and sympathy," wrote the editor of *Onze Toekomst,* as he struggled to find words of solace. The funerals were the largest and most unforgettable in the history of the churches, and friends who served as pallbearers and indeed that entire generation carried the emotional scars for the rest of their lives. Many feared water and avoided swimming and even boating for years. All became more serious about the spiritual dimension of life.

Pallbearer John R. Swierenga, age eighteen, who could not swim and might well have been in the capsized boat, took his Christian beliefs more seriously after the "shattering disaster" and close call with death. Before the year was out, he made public profession of faith in the Second Christian Reformed Church of Cicero and joined the church. Forty years later, in 1989, Swierenga testified: "I was moved to see these young men taken out of life so suddenly. It made me aware that I should be more consistent in my Christian life. God had other plans for me. This gave me motivation and incentive."[47]

Another drowning in a Lamont stone quarry in 1944 took the lives of two Evenhouse brothers — Jacob (Jake), age eighteen, and Clarence, age sixteen. Jake, an expert swimmer, drowned while trying to rescue Clarence, who could not cope with one of the whirlpools that made the quarry so dangerous. Both teens were members of the Second Cicero congregation. The same congregation experienced another tragedy in 1943 when Robert (Bobby) Mouw, a student at Timothy Christian School, was struck and killed by a high-speed Aurora & Elgin commuter train on Central Avenue while walking home from school. The Cicero community again suffered a big loss in 1952 when Andrew De Boer, the community leader and insur-

47. Robert P. Swierenga, "Robert (Bouwko) Swierenga Family History," 1997.

ance executive, drowned in a nearby lake. In 1935 three wives and mothers, all members of the Archer Avenue Reformed Church in Summit, were killed while out shopping, when their car collided with a cattle truck. In 1950 a gasoline tanker truck struck a "Green Hornet" streetcar on South State Street, killing thirty-four passengers in a huge fireball, including Carol Rudenga of Englewood and Arvis Vos of Roseland, both graduates of Chicago Christian High School.[48] Life in the big city had its tragedies.

Conclusion

As the Dutch Reformed prospered, their giving for works of benevolence grew too. Since the Calvinist reformation of the sixteenth century, supporting the work of the deacons has been a high priority in every congregation. The offerings taken up at the quarterly services of Holy Communion were always designated for the poor and needy, and additional collections were scheduled as needed.

The Dutch Reformed in Chicago also give generously for Christian education at all levels from elementary to college, and for "institutions of mercy" – the Holland Homes, Elim, various retirement and nursing homes, Christian psychiatric hospitals in Michigan and Colorado, and an alcohol treatment center in Arizona. Thus, not all benevolence monies are spent locally. In every congregation, by prior agreement with the denomination, about one-fifth of all collections are passed through to international mission programs and works of mercy.

For more predictable risks, such as burial costs, unemployment insurance, and home mortgages, the Dutch created mutual aid and benefit societies, such as the Self Help Society. By practicing mutuality, the Dutch Reformed lived from womb to tomb within the comfortable confines of their ethnoreligious community.

48. B. Essenburg, "Chicago, Englewood, and Cicero Churches," *Banner,* 3 May 1935. Gordon De Young recalls the streetcar tragedy of 25 May 1950, which took the life of the daughter of the Christian Vos family. Vos was a former principal of the 104th Street Christian School.

CHAPTER 10

The Elites: Dutch American Social Clubs

Rob Kroes noted in his sparkling book on the Dutch Calvinist colony of Amsterdam, Montana, "There is always a wide grey zone where an ethnic community tends to blur into its environment."[1] The Dutch social clubs operated in this grey zone; some were high brow, others low brow; some looked outward, others inward; some were secular, others more openly Christian. The Reformed churches and their schools and societies, by contrast, stood in the white zone, in the center of the community. The churches provided the glue of Dutch identity, built on the legacy of Dordt, De Cock, and Kuyper (see chapter 2). Church affiliation determined one's life course, beginning with the critical decision of schooling for the children, whether public or Dutch Reformed. Since the Calvinists in the Chicago area were divided into rival denominations as early as 1867, and the denominations held differing views about their place in American life, the members also lacked a unified sociocultural vision.

The founding of clubs and societies followed a sequence that reflected Dutch core beliefs and values. Churches always came first, and then mutual aid and benevolent societies. Only after the immigrants had gained a solid economic foothold and developed a sense of ethnic pride did the social climbers organize clubs. Members were recruited largely from successful new immigrants and their upwardly mobile children, along with a nucleus of Old Dutch Yorkers who had long established themselves in the Windy City. Ethnic pride was the hallmark of the clubs, whose members shared a growing interest in Dutch history and culture.

1. Rob Kroes, *The Persistence of Ethnicity: Dutch Calvinist Pioneers in Amsterdam, Montana* (Urbana and Chicago: Univ. of Illinois Press, 1992), 9.

The three most prominent clubs were the Holland Society of Chicago (1895), modeled after its aristocratic predecessor in New York City (1885); the Chicago Section (1905) of the Algemeen Nederlandsch Verbond, or "General Dutch League" (1895), a worldwide federation of Netherlanders, Flemings, and Afrikaaners that was patterned after the Alliance Francoise and the Algemein Deutscher Verbond; and the Knickerbocker Society of Chicago (1924), which also had its New York City counterpart. Lesser clubs were the William of Orange Society (1890), the Saint Nicholas Society (1906), and the Frisian Society Ut en Thús ("Away and Home") (1925). Despite the names, these clubs were more American in character than Dutch.

William of Orange Society

The first club was the William of Orange Society, named after the martyred and much revered political leader and founder of the Dutch Republic, also known as William the Silent (1533-84), a German count of Nassau by birth. The society grew out of calls in 1890 by the Reverend Bernardus De Bey, long-time pastor of the First Reformed Church of Chicago, to honor the *vader des Vaderland* on the tercentenary of the victorious Dutch Revolt against Spain, by erecting statues to Prince William in Dutch-American settlements. The Hollanders had the added stimulus of the upcoming World's Fair, the 1893 Columbian Exposition, held in Jackson Park. At a mass meeting at First Church December 9, 1890, the society was legally constituted, and the officers immediately laid plans to raise at least $15,000 to create "a worthy monument to our Washington, the idol of the Dutch, in one of the famous Chicago parks." When fair visitors from around the world admire their heroes, the founders declared, "surely the Dutch and the Knickerbockers, and all descendants of the Dutch, should see to it that this one of the foremost and grandest leaders of all ages shall then be so honored." Ten successful old settlers subscribed $1,340 to launch the project, but it came to naught.

The William of Orange Society did have the pleasure of participating at the exposition, along with a "score of genuine Dutchmen," in the raising of the Dutch flag, the beloved Tricolor, over an authentic Dutch windmill in the pavilion of Blooker & Co., the famous Amsterdam cocoa manufacturer. Speakers for the occasion were George Birkhoff, Jr., Netherlands consul general in Chicago, editor Henry Uden Marsman of Chicago's Dutch newspaper, *De Nederlander*, and the Reverend Peter Moerdyke of Trinity American Reformed Church. It was hoped that Abraham Kuyper of Amsterdam, leader of the Calvinistic political party in the Netherlands, would also take a prominent part in the World's Fair, but he was unable to do so. Abraham Kuyper did include Chicago on his big American tour of 1898, however, when he came to deliver the prestigious Stone Lectures at Princeton Theological Seminary.[2]

Another highlight of the Columbian Exhibition was "Netherlands Day," celebrated August 31, the birthday of the future "beloved little Queen Wilhelmina," in Festival Hall. The Chicago Committee planned the day's events and awakened interest among many Dutch organizations throughout the Midwest. Between six thousand and eight thousand Chicago area Hollanders turned out, plus another fifteen hundred from surrounding states.

The day's theme focused on contributions the Netherlands had made to American democracy. Speakers, all but one fluent in Dutch, included Gerrit J. Diekema of Holland, Michigan, ex-speaker of the Michigan legislature, and some twenty-two clerics, notably a priest from the large Dutch Catholic settlement of De Pere, Wisconsin, and Bernardus De Bey, the esteemed retired pastor of the First Reformed Church of Chicago, who had given leadership among the Chicago Dutch for three decades. It was his last public address.

A choir of 125 voices, directed by De Bey's son, Henry De Bey, M.D., warmed the Dutch blood of the overflow crowd with a rendition of Dutch and American national airs. And a special souvenir badge was given to all "'Vans,' 'Knickerbockers,' and lovers of the illustrious House of Orange" who turned out. The event was "a great and significant episode in the history of the Hollanders in this country," declared Moerdyke. "It is the first and only gathering of so many thousands of them in this country."[3]

Some time after the Columbian Exposition closed, the William of Orange Society disbanded without fulfilling its dream. Forty years later another club, the Knickerbocker Society, was still talking about raising a monument to William for the World's Fair of 1933.[4]

2. Moerdyke, "Chicago Letter," *CI,* 29 Mar., p. 11; 17 May 1893, p. 11; 2 Nov., p. 5; 9 Nov., p. 5; 16 Nov. 1898, p. 14.

3. Ibid., 7 June, p. 10; 23 Aug., p. 11; 6 Sept., p. 10; 13 Sept. 1893, p. 10.

4. Ibid., 3 Dec. 1890, p. 11; 25 Mar. 1891, p. 11; 31 Aug. 1892, p. 11.

Holland Society (Nederlandsche Vereeniging)

The Holland Society (Nederlandsche Vereeniging) of Chicago had broad ambitions to foster "true Americanism" and to promote Dutch ethnic pride, while enjoying "social entertainment." John Broekema, an executive of the Siegel, Cooper & Company department store and later of Marshall Field & Company, was the key organizer of the Chicago section, founded December 14, 1895.[5] Another early leader was William Van Benthuysen, the managing editor of the *Chicago Tribune.* Society members had to prove their Dutch ancestry and U.S. citizenship, the former by furnishing a "pedigree chart" to the committee on genealogy. But they did not have to prove ancestral lineage with colonial New Netherlanders, as did members of the parent New York society.

They always scheduled their annual banquets on April 16, in order to commemorate Prince William's birthday, *Oranje Dag.* In the first seven years, the Orangists assembled with their ladies "under the rafters of the old Dutch barn" at Kinsley's Hall. "Vans at a feast," trumpeted the headline of the society page of a Chicago newspaper, and the subheading proclaimed, "Speakers Laud the Dutch." The reporter described the colorful hall,

> decked out with reminders of the land of dikes and canals. A finely painted scene of the historic Hague adorned the center of the south wall; the menu cards, printed in delft blue, bore portraits of Queen Wilhelmina and Prince William, and at each plate was a Holland postal card bearing the cancellation of Amsterdam, April 16, 1533, the date of William's birth. As souvenirs the guests carried away with them little wooden shoes imported from Vianen, Holland, and church warden pipes decorated with the flag of the Netherlands.

"The society never had a happier reunion," the reporter concluded.[6]

Besides Orange Day, the Holland Society gathered in one of the

5. Broekema had arrived as a youngster with his immigrant parents in 1867. See Chicago *Record-Herald,* 9 Dec. 1908, with photo of John Broekema. The list of fifty-eight charter members is in *Yearbook of the Holland Society of Chicago, 1895-1896* (Chicago, 1897), 4, 6, 14; and a list of seventy-nine members in 1901 is in ibid. (Chicago, 1901), 208-09. See also *Onze Toekomst,* 19 Apr. 1907; 22 Apr. 1910. In 1900, D. J. Schuyler was president; George Birkhoff, vice president; Robert Van Schaack, secretary; and George E. Van Woert, treasurer (*Chicago City Directory,* 1900), John Vennema Papers, Joint Archives of Holland, Hope College, Holland, MI.

6. Unidentified Chicago newspaper clipping from 1898 in John Vennema Papers.

John Broekema, executive, Marshall, Field & Company, 1908

churches every April 1 to commemorate the Dutch defeat of the hated Spanish Duke of Alva and his army at Den Briel in Zuid Holland in 1572. The event mixed Reformed religion and Netherlandic patriotism and was designed to be "instructive entertainment." Prayers and Dutch psalm singing were interspersed with patriotic speeches, songs, and national anthems, all flanked by the Dutch and American flags. It was clear that the Chicago Dutch viewed the Netherlands and her people as "kin beyond sea."[7]

The Holland Society's social calendar included excursions and outings. In 1897 some sixty members chartered an excursion boat to Holland,

7. Moerdyke, "Chicago Letter," *CI,* 26 Mar., p. 203, 10 Apr. 1902, p. 253.

Michigan, in order to represent Chicago at the Semi-Centennial celebration of the founding of the midwestern colonies in 1847.[8] Dutch settlement in Chicago antedated that date, and the first true colony in the region, South Holland, was founded the same year as Holland.

The next year, 1898, Hollanders throughout the country celebrated the coming of age and coronation of Queen Wilhelmina, upon reaching her eighteenth birthday. "Genuine Hollanders" in Chicago organized two celebrations to express their "affectionate admiration" to the "charming young queen" and to join the universal acclaim: "Long live the Queen." Both events were well attended "by sincere people who glory in being Dutchmen," who, as Peter Moerdyke reported, enjoyed "a feast of reason and a flow of soul." The halls were decorated with a portrait of the new queen flanked by the flags of both nations, and the halls rang with the two national anthems, the "Star Spangled Banner" and "Wilhelmus van Nassouwe."[9] Speakers seized the occasion to commend the American crusade to liberate Cuba from "Castilian savagery," just as their ancestors in the Netherlands had shed their blood to end Spanish oppression. Spain, "that degenerate kingdom," will get its just deserts.[10]

In 1899 the Holland Society sponsored a float, complete with a windmill and two beautiful women in Netherlands costumes, for Chicago's huge fall festival, the "Parade of Nations," at which President William McKinley himself was the honored guest.[11]

In 1901, when the Dutch-American hero, Theodore Roosevelt, became president upon McKinley's assassination, the Hollanders had high hopes for a change in U.S. policy toward the Boers. But Roosevelt was even more pro-British than McKinley, and this tore the Hollanders apart emotionally. "For Boer and Roosevelt" proclaimed the newspaper headline of the 1901 society banquet; the "Holland Society Halts Between Two National Loves." While "heartily cheering" every mention of Roosevelt's name, the society passed resolutions deploring his South Africa policies. How could one of their own be so blind? *Oom* ("Uncle") Paul Kruger, the Boer president, and his people deserved support in their struggle for freedom. The announcement that the program committee hoped to have Kruger as a future guest of the society brought rousing applause.

8. Ibid., 26 Mar. 1902, p. 203; *Holland City News,* 21 Aug. 1897, reprinted in the *Holland Sentinel,* 21 Aug. 1997.

9. Moerdyke, "Chicago Letter," *CI,* 7 Sept., p. 9, 14 Sept. 1898, p. 8.

10. Ibid., 13 Apr. 1898, p. 9.

11. Ibid., 4 Oct., p. 9, 18 Oct. 1899, p. 9.

In the end the society had to settle for a visiting delegation of three Boer heroes, including Dutch Reformed minister, the Reverend N. Van Broekhuyzen of Pretoria, who had been imprisoned for his political activities. In 1902 the Holland Society convened a mass rally at Central Music Hall on behalf of the Boers, at which seven members gave impassioned speeches. But this was a last gasp. The cause died out with the defeat of the Boers that year.[12]

Besides the Kinsley Hall gatherings, the Holland Society gathered at places even more posh, such as the Congress Hotel, the Grand Pacific Hotel, the Union League Club, and the Chicago Athletic Club. By 1900 it was publishing classy annual yearbooks containing its speeches and resolutions. In 1902 the society carried sixty-six active members and eight honorary members, including the Dutch prime minister, Dr. Abraham Kuyper.[13]

That year, 1902, the Holland Society first set its sights on founding a Holland Home for the Aged in Chicago. Immigration had begun over fifty years before, and the need to provide for elderly parents was becoming acute. But the plan languished. "There are so many objections and obstacles as to render it more than doubtful whether the large sum required to start such a benevolent home can ever be raised among the Hollanders of Chicago," concluded Moerdyke glumly.

> The people seem too widely severed by distance of miles and minds; the churches are all poor and few out of debt; the dependent are — all honor to the system — quite generally supported by the offerings

12. Unidentified Chicago newspaper clippings, 1899-1901, in the John Vennema Papers. The *Chicago Record* was one of the papers.

13. In 1902 the society had sixty-six active members, twelve of whom lived out of the Chicago area as far away as New York City (Peter Bosch and William S. Hofstra), Boston (Henry D. Lloyd), Holland (Gerrit J. Diekema), and Grand Rapids (Anton G. Hodenpyl). Officers in 1901 were George Birkhoff, Jr., president; Dr. Daniel R. Brouwer, vice president; Benjamin T. Van Allen, secretary; and Robert Van Schaack, treasurer. Other members included William K. Ackerman, Cornelius V. Banta, Jr., Dr. David Birkhoff, Henry Bosch, John Broekema, Jule F. Brower, Edward C. Cooper, Frank H. Cooper, Holger de Roode, Volney W. Foster, Samuel Eberly Gross, Ysbrand B. Haagsma, Christian Kruizinga, H. Plasier, Daniel J. Schuyler, William L. Rooseboom, William Van Benthuysen, William F. Van Bergen, Henry R. Vandercook, Adrian Vanderkloot, Herman Vander Ploeg, J. H. Vanderpoel, Charles Van Horne, N. Van Ness Person, Peter Van Schaack, George E. Van Woert, John Vennema, and John Warnshuis. See "The Holland Society of Chicago, List of Members April 6, 1902," and "Sixth Annual Banquet of the Holland Society of Chicago, Grand Pacific Hotel, Nineteen Hundred and One, in Commemoration of the Birthday of William of Orange," John Vennema Papers.

> and diaconate of all the Dutch congregations, and the project involves an excessive expenditure in such a city as this. These are the main difficulties alleged against the enterprise, and yet probably in right hands and under distinctively churchly auspices this dream might be realized.[14]

In 1904, the Holland Society had to abandon its dream; another Dutch club, the Excelsior Society, finally brought the idea to fruition a decade later (see chapter 9).

Chicago's centennial celebration in 1903 gave the Holland Society another opportunity to call out the Dutch. As part of the six-day festivities of "Chicago Day," the society sponsored a program at the Trinity Reformed Church, followed by a banquet for the oldest Dutch settlers of Chicago. "Not a few of these date their advent back half a century," Moerdyke noted. "It would be a noteworthy story," he added, "that should faithfully describe the influence of the Hollanders in the later development of this city." The program, all in the Dutch language, was a "gratifying success," said Pastor Moerdyke. He led the audience in singing a Dutch psalm, the Trinity choir performed, society president Marsman read a congratulatory telegram from President Roosevelt, which evoked a standing ovation, and an appeal and collection was made for a Holland Home for the Aged that the society was pushing.[15]

In 1915 the Holland Society reached its apex by hosting an honored visitor, the Netherlands ambassador to the United States, His Excellency W. L. F. C. Ridder van Rappard. Fifty members gathered for an elaborate banquet at the Union League Club and dined on "Canape Hollandaise" hors d'oeuvre, "Pigeon de Philadelphia," and "Frommage de Brie" with an aperitif. Chicago mayor William Hale ("Big Bill") Thompson and Northwestern University president Dr. A. W. Harris joined the festivities. Prominent members enjoying the occasion included attorney John Vennema; John Broekema; medical doctors Robert L. Van Dellen, Frederick A. Bisdom, R. Huizenga, and Henry B. De Bey; Englewood dentist Dr. John H. Hospers; Professor Tiemen de Vries of the University of Chicago (see below) and Professor James H. Rook; attorneys Folkert Posthuma, Judge Frederick R. De Young, and Herman Vander Ploeg; Hiram Vanden Belt, grandson of Chicago pioneer Lucas Vanden Belt; and John D. and Henry R. Vandercook, who founded the Vandercook School of Music. Dr.

14. Moerdyke, "Chicago Letter," *CI,* 11 Mar. 1903, p. 153.

15. Ibid., 30 Sept. 1903, p. 625.

De Bey was likely the only member living in the lower-class West Side, and none belonged to the "Dutchy" church, the Christian Reformed Church.[16]

Although the faces of the Holland Society blue bloods preserved the "Dutch look," few were immigrants, and most members of this noble order of "Vans" gathered more for socializing. It was a passing fancy that gradually faded away.[17]

General Dutch League (Algemeen Nederlandsch Verbond)

The General Dutch League (Algemeen Nederlandsch Verbond) stood in sharp contrast to the elitist Holland Society with its largely ceremonial activities. The league was truly an effort by immigrants to foster nationalistic sentiments, preserve their language and identity, and propagate "the faith of our fathers," i.e., the Dutch Reformed worldview.[18] J. Hoddenbach van Scheltema of Roseland, an immigrant from Arnhem, inspired the idea of the league in an 1893 article in the Chicago paper *De Nederlander*, which lamented the loss of the Dutch language and called for conscious efforts to save it. With the help of Flemish Belgians, the league was launched in 1895 in Brussels and headquartered after 1897 in the famed city of Dordrecht. It grew in the Netherlands and among Dutch compatriots around the world because of rising national pride occasioned by the coronation in 1898 of Queen Wilhelmina. Interest was sparked by the revered Calvinist leader Dr. Abraham Kuyper in his lecture tour in 1898-99, and by the heralded Afrikaner resistance in the Boer War.

New York City was the eastern center of the league, with a branch in Boston. Grand Rapids led the midwestern wing, with branches in Holland and Zeeland, Michigan; Chicago, Roseland, and Fulton, Illinois; Pella,

16. Printed program, "Banquet in honor of His Excellency W. L. F. C. Ridder van Rappard, Minister Plenipotentiary of the Netherlands to the United States of America, The Holland Society of Chicago, September Fifteenth 1915, Union League Club," John Vennema Papers. Vennema served as Dutch consul in Chicago from 1914 to 1939 and was president of both the Holland Society and the Knickerbocker Society. A copy of his letter of appointment by the Netherlands ambassador in Washington, W. F. L. C. Ridder van Rappard, dated 13 Oct. 1914, and a printed program of his retirement dinner on 23 Oct. 1939 are also in the John Vennema Papers.

17. Lucas, *Netherlanders in America*, 595-96.

18. *Onze Toekomst*, 26 Jan., 6 Apr., 14 Sept. 1906; 25 Jan. 1907; 19 July 1922; Van Hinte, *Netherlanders in America*, 1002-03; Lucas, *Netherlanders in America*, 592-95; Vandenbosch, *Dutch Communities of Chicago*, 71-73.

Iowa; and Minneapolis. By 1910 the league counted nearly eleven thousand members worldwide, who were linked by the official monthly organ, *Neerlandia.*[19]

According to its by-laws, the league aimed "to foster group consciousness among Dutch people, [and] their descendants. . . . It has the spiritual, moral, and material strength of the Dutch people in view." Further, the organization planned to maintain the Dutch language, strengthen Netherlandic pride, and promote "patriotic use of the Dutch national anthem." Specific goals were to establish customs houses and Dutch chambers of commerce in American cities, to patronize Dutch bookstores and publishers, and to encourage schools to take up the study of Dutch history and culture. As an advocacy group, the league declared its determination to fight the "slanderous attacks against people of our lineage . . . [and] to step in wherever Dutch people are being threatened or oppressed.[20] This was an obvious reference to South Africa.

Van Scheltema organized the Roseland League branch in 1898 with offices at 233 W. 111th Street. In 1909 the branch under president Frank Knoll arranged a big celebration of Roseland's sixtieth anniversary. An all-day rain did not halt the elaborate parade or discourage the celebrants who lined the streets with umbrellas. Every business and organization was represented in the procession that took ninety minutes to pass. Case Kuyper was honored as parade marshal, and many old settlers rode along in automobiles, the oldest being Mrs. Jan Ton, nee Aagje Vander Sijde. All eyes followed the regal float decked in white, with six young women attending a queen seated under a canopy; the queen, who represented the Queen of the Netherlands, was Grietje Vaarwerk (later Mrs. Robert Brandsma). Attendant Jennie De Jong (later Mrs. William Vanden Berg) represented the Holland Virgin, the Dutch equivalent of the Goddess of Liberty, and Beatrice Vander Meer (later Mrs. Harry De Jong) represented Columbia, the "American Queen."[21]

In 1905 Henry Jacobsma helped found the Chicago chapter with thirty charter members. He had belonged to the Grand Rapids section until moving to Chicago. Reformed and Christian Reformed church leaders

19. The membership figure is in Luurt Holstein's 1910 address (Luurt Holstein Papers, Archives, Calvin College). See also Lucas, *Netherlanders in America,* 592-95, citing *Gedenkboek van het Algemeen Nederlandsch verbond bij gelegenheid van zijn 25 jarig bestaan, 1898-mei-1923. Geschiedenis en invloed van den Nederlandschen stam* (Amsterdam, [1923]).

20. By-laws paraphrased in Luurt Holstein's address at a 1910 rally of the Verbond (typescript in Luurt Holstein Papers).

21. Ettema, *Down an Indian Trail,* 183-84.

cooperated in the effort. The league met monthly in church basements and auditoriums and organized periodic "open meetings," picnics, and outings. "Every time the opportunity presents itself, the Dutch American again feels that he has not forgotten the land and people and especially the language which he formerly called his own," declared an enthusiast.[22] Titles of league lectures speak volumes: "The Influence of the Netherlands on America," "The Influence of the Netherlands on American Legal and School Systems," "Our Calling as Hollanders in America," etc. The speakers played on the idea that Dutch Reformed principles had guided American law and government, which views Kuyper had given impetus to in his famous Stone Lectures.[23]

The first successful league project, launched in 1907, was to push the University of Chicago to establish a chair in Dutch History, Art, and Literature. Columbia University had created such a chair in 1898 under Leonard Charles van Noppen, with generous funding from the Dutch government. Chicago was a logical site for a second professorship because, the promoters declared, the city and its celebrated university "are situated in the center of three quarters of the present Dutch immigrants of the United States of America." Not only did the university enroll several Dutch-American students, but it was destined to become the "center of Dutch civilization and influence in the United States."[24]

The campaign took five years and required a national fund-raising effort and a petition drive that mustered one thousand signatures. Endorsements were obtained from President Roosevelt, West Michigan congressman Gerrit J. Diekema of Holland, Abraham Kuyper, and Dr. Herman Bavinck, the renowned Reformed theologian of the Free University of Amsterdam, founded by Kuyper in 1880. The league also enlisted the cooperation of the Holland Society of Chicago.[25] The editor of *Onze Toekomst* waxed eloquent about the venture, saying that it refuted

22. *Onze Toekomst,* 25 Jan. 1907. The Reverend Marinus E. Broekstra of the First Reformed Church of Englewood spoke at the initial open meeting in the First Christian Reformed Church of Chicago, and its pastor, the Reverend Evert Breen, lectured at the second meeting at the First Reformed (Hastings Street) Church.

23. Lucas, *Netherlanders in America,* 593.

24. Luurt Holstein of Englewood, a salesman and agent for forty years of the Holland-America Steamship Company, was president of the league at this time. He belonged to the Christian Reformed Church. *Onze Toekomst,* 13 Dec. 1907.

25. Ibid., 13 Dec. 1907; 20 Nov. 1908; 12 Feb. 1909. Holstein's address to the Algemeen Nederlandsch Verbond rally, Chicago, 1910, is in the Luurt Holstein Papers. Alfred Oosterheerdt of Chicago led the petition campaign.

accusations often made against the Dutch, that they are too sectarian, too narrow-minded, too selfish, ever to be able to co-operate for a Dutch national purpose and much less to seek the best that the Dutch, with their glorious history, could do for the American nation. . . . Is it not beautiful for the Dutch heart, for the American of Dutch descent, yes, for every genuine American, to know that a long line of earnest men are busy with a movement to make Dutch history, art, and literature better known in the center of American national life?[26]

When University president Henry Pratt Judson and the departments of History and Art reported early in 1909 that they were favorably disposed to the idea of a Dutch Chair "as soon as finances are sufficient," the Chicago division went to work with a will. It appointed a high-powered committee that succeeded in raising $1,000 for a salary and reached an understanding with the university. If the program prospered, the chair would be made permanent.[27]

The sourest note in the campaign came when an unidentified professor at Hope College, likely Albert Raap, warned that the holder of the Dutch chair at the University of Chicago would be "like a mouse in a strange warehouse," one man among four hundred, who would be overwhelmed and compromised. The editor of *Onze Toekomst,* who had vigorously pushed the project from the outset, countered this pessimistic forecast by publishing strong letters of support from Kuyper and Bavinck.[28]

Success came in 1911 with the appointment for two years of Dr. Tiemen L. de Vries as lecturer on Dutch institutions. De Vries was a graduate in theology and law of the Free University and an early follower of Kuyper in the Anti-Revolutionary Party.[29] He was a true Calvinist, and he

26. *Onze Toekomst,* 31 March 1911.

27. The committee consisted of Chicagoans Albert Oosterheerdt, chair; Jacobsma and Birkhoff, consul general John Vennema, and Central College professor Jan Nollen, ibid., 31 July, 20 Nov. 1908; 12 Feb. 1909. League officers in 1907-09 were Birkhoff, Oosterheerdt, Jacobsma, Holstein, Henry Berends, Henry U. Marsman, John De Boer, Th. Koopmans, the Reverend Nicholas Boer, Conrad Ottenhoff, and Theo Koelikamp. Membership in 1907 totaled thirty-two.

28. Ibid., 24 Mar., 7 Apr. 1911. The editor did not identify the Hope professor, but it was likely Albert Raap, professor of Dutch from 1903 to 1924, according to Elton Bruins of Hope College in a letter to the author, 5 Nov. 1995.

29. For De Vries's career, see H. J. Langeveld, "'Een van Uwe, principieel genomen, meest trouwe leerlingen': Het tragische leven van mr. Tiemen de Vries, een vroege student van Abraham Kuyper," 77-108, in *Jaarbook voor de geschiedenis van het Nederlands Protestantisme na 1800,* vol. 1, ed. Dirk Th. Kuiper (Kampen: Kok, 1993).

fulfilled the hopes of the advocates by attracting 350 students to his lectures and several dozen students to his seminars. In March of 1912, he was invited to lecture at Calvin College and Seminary on the connection between the Netherlands and America. That same year, he published his first year's lectures with the Eerdmans-Sevensma Company of Grand Rapids, under the title *Dutch History, Art and Literature for Americans.*[30]

Despite his strong beginning, De Vries's tenure at the university was in jeopardy. The administration apparently expected that the Dutch-American community would permanently endow his chair, and, when this was not forthcoming, it refused to commit any university funds, despite strong lobbying efforts. In December 1912, in the middle of his second year, De Vries's students petitioned the administration for his reappointment. And in February 1913, the Men's Bible class of the Fourth Christian Reformed Church of Muskegon, Michigan, also sent a letter requesting that the university endow his chair. This shows that the wider Dutch Reformed community took an interest in the professorship. Nevertheless, President Judson and the university trustees placed the matter "on file" and took no further action. De Vries left in 1913 after fulfilling his contract, and the dream ended in bitter disappointment.[31] Subsequent attempts by the midwestern branches of the league to establish similar posts at the University of Illinois and the University of Michigan also failed.[32]

De Vries taught the next academic year (1913-14) at Calvin College, but that board did not renew his contract either. This was the end of De Vries's teaching career; he dabbled as an art dealer in Europe and the United States during the war years and later left Reformed orthodoxy and espoused theistic evolutionary theories. In a 1932 book, *Evidence on Christianity and Evolution,* he attempted to blend the naturalistic theories of Charles Darwin and Aldous Huxley with the biblical creation account. De

30. "Prof. De Vries in Calvin College," *Banner,* 21 Mar. 1912; Tiemen de Vries, *Dutch History, Art and Literature for Americans: Lectures Given at the University of Chicago* (Grand Rapids: Eerdmans-Sevensma Co., 1912), 15-17. De Vries claimed he was giving voice to eight million Americans "who feel Dutch blood in their veins."

31. I am indebted to Maureen Anna Harp, doctoral student in history at the University of Chicago, for searching the university archives concerning De Vries's appointment. See University of Chicago, *Annual Register, July, 1910–July, 1911* (Chicago: Univ. of Chicago Press, 1911), 54; Board of Trustees, Minutes, vol. 7 (1909-1913), pp. 242, 446; vol. 8 (1913-1914), pp. 1-2, typescript, University of Chicago Archives.

32. Vandenbosch, *Dutch Communities of Chicago,* 71-73; Lucas, *Netherlanders in America,* 596.

Vries's biographer aptly calls his life "tragic." He died at his home in Evanston, Illinois, in 1935.[33]

The league was more successful in establishing a Queen Wilhelmina Library of Dutch language books in ten American cities, including Chicago. The queen herself donated $500 in 1906 to launch the program, of which the Chicago division received $50. "Nothing else," opined the *Onze Toekomst* editor, "could serve better to teach our people Dutch grammar, knowledge, and wisdom of all descriptions, as a respectable collection of Dutch literature."[34] Queen Wilhelmina seemed to take a particular interest in the Hollanders in America. When George Birkhoff, Jr., Netherlands consul in the city, toured the Netherlands in 1907, the queen invited him to have lunch with her at the palace, and she inquired about the Hollanders of Chicago and asked him "to convey her good will to her former subjects."[35] No wonder the Chicago League proudly hung pictures of the queen in all the Dutch Christian schools, colleges, and seminaries in Chicago, Holland, and Grand Rapids.

In 1909 the society began the practice of celebrating the queen's birthday (August 31) with speeches and music by church bands. This is for "our Dutch people, a day of national rejoicing," declared *Onze Toekomst.* "It is a pity that we have been unable so far to make of this day a General Netherlands Day. It could be celebrated by all the Netherlanders irrespective of political and religious affiliations. The time for it has come now."[36] After the birth on April 30, 1909, of Princess Juliana, the first child and heir to the Dutch throne, the club also celebrated her birthday each year. The Chicago chapter could then count only thirty-eight dues-paying members at $1.50 each. Most Dutch were indifferent, believing the league to be too intellectual and "too high." The most assimilated immigrants also refused to join because they believed such nationalistic organizations to be un-American.[37]

Another opportunity to hail the Dutch heritage was the 350th anniversary of the defeat of the Spanish Duke of Alva at Den Briel on April 1, 1572. Hundreds of Chicago Hollanders turned out for a commemoration April 1, 1922, at the First Christian Reformed Church of Englewood. They heard an address by Dr. John Van Lonkhuyzen, then editor of *Onze*

33. Langeveld, "Tragische leven van mr. Tiemen de Vries," 102-03. A brief obituary appears in the *Chicago Messenger,* 26 July 1935.

34. *Onze Toekomst,* 13 Apr. 1906.

35. George Niemeyer, "Illinois Letter," *CI,* 21 Aug. 1907, p. 540.

36. *Onze Toekomst,* 23 July 1909; 26 Aug. 1910.

37. Ibid., 26 Aug., 9 Sept. 1910.

Toekomst and a Christian Reformed Church cleric. The twenty-fifth anniversary of Queen Wilhelmina's reign in September 1923 marked yet another occasion for celebration throughout the Dutch empire. Van Lonkhuyzen presided over a distinguished committee of ten, including ex-president Theodore Roosevelt, which arranged for the publication of a richly embossed album of Dutch-American historical essays that was presented to the queen at her jubilee. The Roseland division of the General Dutch League likewise celebrated the queen's birthday when the faithful assembled at Palmer Park (111th and Indiana Avenue) to listen to speeches and music amidst unfurled Dutch and American flags.[38]

The Chicago division picnic that year was held in Beverly Hills, also on the South Side. In the 1920s, the downtown branch was practically defunct, but the Roseland branch flourished for years as a social club of the nonchurched Hollanders, trying to keep the Dutch spirit alive. The members met in a new hall on 111th near Princeton Street.[39]

Besides remembering royal birthdays and Dutch national holidays, the Hollanders gathered for public lectures and concerts by visiting speakers and musicians. Artists from the fatherland were especially welcomed, such as the poet Frederick van Eeden (1860-1932) in 1909, Professor W. Martin of Leiden University in 1921, and the famed Frisian organist Abraham Alt in 1926. Alt's recital at Chicago's Orchestra Hall on Michigan Avenue filled the building with six hundred proud Hollanders who enjoyed a brilliant performance tinged with a bit of nostalgia, according to a press report. In 1913 Professor de Vries also lectured on the history of the homeland at the First Reformed (Hastings Street) Church.[40]

Saint Nicholas Society

The Saint Nicholas Society first met in 1905 as a club for "old Dutch settlers" who wished to reminisce about the "struggles of the pioneers" and to celebrate with a party the arrival of Sinterklaas (December 6). Initially, the club restricted membership to naturalized Dutch immigrants who had arrived prior to 1870. But this proved unreasonable, so in its second year the society reduced the minimum residency requirement to fifteen

38. Ibid., 5 Apr., 19 July, 30 Aug. 1922; Vandenbosch, *Dutch Communities of Chicago,* 73-74; First Reformed Church of Chicago, Minutes, 2 Mar. 1933.

39. *Onze Toekomst,* 19 July, 30 Aug. 1922; Vandenbosch, *Dutch Communities of Chicago,* 69.

40. *Onze Toekomst,* 17 Feb. 1909; 18 Mar. 1921; 13 Oct. 1926; 13 May 1913.

years. This club was for those committed to rapid Americanization, such as medical doctors Henry B. De Bey and Robert Van Dellen, professor E. L. Van Dellen, and the Illinois lawmaker Cornelius J. Ton.[41]

The annual banquet at the Bismarck Hotel December 6, 1909, drew well, especially after the very controversial dinner of 1908. The speaker, Herman Vander Ploeg, who was a prominent attorney and member of the First Reformed Church, used the occasion to lash out at closed-minded Hollanders who resisted Americanization by ghettoizing themselves and founding Christian day schools. These people, Vander Ploeg declared, came

> chiefly from small villages and country districts, where wages are low and the necessities of life dear, they arrive here with very fixed notions and prejudices, which are often the result of their birth and environment instead of a sound education and wise judgment. . . . I am afraid that the majority of them are also opposed to the study and adoption of what is best in American life and manners. They seem to have such fixed notions and habits that it is difficult for them to realize the new view of things. They wish to continue to measure and to judge things by the standard of the home they have left, and not of the home they find. So extreme is this obstinate adherence to Dutch customs and usages, that our worthy Holland people establish Dutch parochial schools in many places and would, if they could, establish exclusive small Dutch villages or settlements, even in our large metropolitan cities.[42]

The Chicago press approvingly printed a full résumé of the "old timer's" speech, but Dutch immigrants used the pages of *Onze Toekomst* to lash out angrily at Vander Ploeg's "foul imputations," "crude attacks," and "invective against everything Dutch, and everything precious to them." He not only "heaped nonsense upon nonsense" but "besmirched the character of our Dutch nation." The furor eventually blew over after an exchange of letters between Louis De Boer and Vander Ploeg in the pages of *Onze Toekomst.* In 1910 more than eighty persons attended the Sinterklaas dinner at the Bismarck Hotel.[43] But one can be certain that

41. The society was conceived by Christian Kruizinga, Herman Vander Ploeg, and John Broekema. The organizational meeting in 1906 elected Dr. David Birkhoff as president, Sietse de Vries as vice president, and J. Tillbuscher secretary. *Onze Toekomst,* 15 Nov. 1907.

42. Ibid., 25 Dec. 1908.

43. Ibid., 8 Jan., 10 Dec. 1909; 9 Dec. 1910. Other members were Edward E. Takken, John Vennema, Henry Reininga, and Harry Bierma.

few members of the large Christian Reformed community affiliated with the society. It had alienated them by demeaning the immigrant mentality.

In the 1930s, attendance at the St. Nicholas Sinterklaas banquet grew to 130 persons, and the gala affair at the University of Chicago's International House featured talks by Calvin College professor J. G. Van Andel and the Chicago businessman and humorist, Sidney T. Youngsma. Frederick Wezeman, principal of Chicago Christian High, also attended with his wife. That these Christian Reformed leaders participated suggests that some fences had been mended since the early days. But the society continued to attract only the most assimilated Dutch-Americans.[44]

Knickerbocker Society

In 1924 the Dutch-American *creme de la creme* formed a branch of the Knickerbocker Society in Chicago, with seventeen charter members, including the Netherlands consul general John Vennema, the vice consul and attorney Folkert Posthuma, and a number of prominent businessmen and professionals.[45] Like its predecessors, the Holland Society and the St. Nicholas Society, Knickerbockers had to be U.S. citizens of Dutch descent, "congenial and tolerant" and of "good moral character," a code for social ranking.[46] The Grand Rapids chapter of the Knickerbocker Society, which began twenty years earlier, also appealed to men of prominence.

Attorney Vennema, a graduate of Hope College and Chicago's Kent

44. *Chicago Messenger,* 13 Dec. 1935. Youngsma, a graduate of the University of Chicago, operated an art gallery in Oak Park during the 1930s, selling works on commission. Formerly he was a jobber for the T. S. Youngsma Paper Company, and subsequently, in 1953, he joined the development office of Calvin College, where he put his talents as a public speaker to good use until retirement.

45. *Knickerbocker Society of Chicago, 1931-1932* (Chicago, 1932), 4-7; Vandenbosch, *Dutch Communities of Chicago,* 70-71. The seventeen charter members were Dr. Frederick A. Bisdom, Luurt Holstein, Dr. Frank Hospers, Dr. John Hospers, Gabriel Heyboer, Dr. Lee Kiel, Gelmer Kuiper, Albert Oosterheerdt, Professor John Penn, Folkert Posthuma, James Rook, Professor Maurice Senstius, historian Amry Vandenbosch, John Vander Vries, James Van Pernis, John Vennema, and Theodore Yntema. A complete list of the 180 members in 1932 is in *Knickerbocker Society of Chicago, 1931-1932,* 15-19. For reports on monthly meetings, see *Onze Toekomst,* 20 Feb., 16 Apr., 30 July 1924; 15 June 1927; 20 May 1931; 26 Aug. 1936. The 1 March 1933 issue includes a history of the society. The most significant historical contribution of the society was to publish Vandenbosch's *Dutch Communities of Chicago* (1927).

46. The membership rules and constitution, adopted in April 1931, are reprinted in *Knickerbocker Society of Chicago, 1931-1932,* 12-14. Dues were $5 plus the considerable costs of each social function.

John Vennema (1871-1960), Netherlands Consul General in Chicago (1914-40)

(Courtesy of John Vennema, Jr.)

College of Law, was the most prominent Dutch-American in the city. Skilled in both Dutch and English, he was in great demand as a speaker at the Rotary Club and similar venues on the topic closest to his heart — the Kingdom of Holland and its contributions to American democracy. As the consul general of the Netherlands, he was Mr. Hollander, and he was called on repeatedly to represent his compatriots at numerous civic and cultural functions. In 1934, he addressed the Netherland's Day ceremonies at the World's Fair and was the guest speaker on the *Daily News* radio tour of station WMAQ. That special program featured Dutch songs by the Knickerbocker Male Chorus, directed by Cornelius Kickert.

Vennema resided in the fashionable north shore suburbs of Winnetka, Kennilworth, and Evanston, belonged to the Congregational church, and was a 32nd degree Mason. In 1920 Queen Wilhelmina honored him with the Officer-Cross of the Order of Oranje-Nassau, and a decade later his alma mater, Hope College, bestowed on him an honorary degree of LL.D. (Doctor of Laws). By 1939 Vennema had risen to such prominence in his church that he was elected president of the Chicago Congregational Club.[47]

The Knickerbocker Society had as its purpose the promotion of ev-

47. "John Vennema," *Who's Who in America, 1938-39,* 20: 2542. Vennema is noted in the printed dinner program of the Chicago Congregational Club, held at the Chicago Women's Club on 20 Mar. 1939. His honorary title is recognized in a letter from J. T. Cremer, Sandport, the Netherlands, 27 July 1920, John Vennema Papers.

erything Dutch. It hoped to strengthen ties with the mother country and "stimulate the study of Dutch history, art and literature, and to perpetuate the memory of honored traditions, and enlightened principles and virtues of the virile Dutch people." This heritage could be of "great influence" in the "spiritual, moral, and cultural life of our city," the society declared, and it would "further the higher principles of our fellow citizens." Besides mouthing such platitudes and touting the "virtues of the Dutch race," club members hosted businessmen and other visitors from the homeland.[48]

The years 1932, 1933, and 1934 were red-letter years in the social calendar of the Chicago Dutch-Americans, given the four hundredth anniversary of the birth of William of Orange and the year-long Chicago World's Fair. These events put the Knickerbocker Society in the limelight. In its first six years, the society had grown to 180 members under the presidency of insurance agent Gelmer Kuiper of Englewood, an official of the Pere Marquette and Chicago Grand Trunk Railroad. Dr. John H. Hospers held the secretary-treasurer post for more than ten years, and his dental office at 25 East Washington Street doubled as the club's address. James J. Van Pernis, editor of Chicago's Dutch language newspaper, *Onze Toekomst,* served as the first vice president.[49] Every part of greater Chicago was represented among the membership in proportion to the city's Dutch residential distribution; one-half lived on the South Side, one-third on the West Side, and one-tenth on the North Side.[50]

The society held monthly meetings at various hotels – La Salle, Sherman, Palmer House, and Graemere – and at the Hamilton Club, Illi-

48. "Knickerbocker Society of Chicago," *Onze Toekomst,* 21 Jan 1931; *Knickerbocker Society of Chicago, 1931-1932,* 8.

49. *Knickerbocker Society of Chicago, 1931-1932,* 5. Other presidents were Dr. Gabriel J. Heyboer (1930-32), a dentist in Englewood; Theodore S. Youngsma (1933-34); and John C. Penn of Roseland (1934-35).

50. West Side members included Jacob Baar; the Biemolts, Earl, Edgar, and Harry; Cornelius Bos; Gerrit Broekman; Siewert Bus; the River Forest building contractor L. Buurma; Abel Danhof; Peter Das of Berwyn; scavengers Andrew J. De Boer, Siert H. Huizenga, Edward Kiemel, Albert and Richard Molenhouse, Albert and Lawrence Stavenger; Harry Doornbos of Cicero; Thomas Drenthe; trucking contractor Peter Euwema of Oak Park; Jinte Grypstra; the Cicero insurance agents and partners Nicholas Hendrikse, Nick Knol, and Thomas Stob; Albert Klei of Cicero; teachers Harry Mouw and John Ten Hoor; the Mulders, Henry, John, and Thomas; Thomas Nanninga; Ezra Nienhuis; insurance agent and banker George Ottenhoff; Dr. John A. Riedel; Benjamin Ritzema; A. M. Vander Kloot of Oak Park; Hiram Vander Veen of Berwyn; Harold Weersing of Cicero; the Woldmans, Edwin, George, and Peter; and Theodore S. Youngsma.

nois Athletic Club, the City Club, and the Dental and Medical Arts Building. There the members listened to speakers such as Gerrit Diekema, former U.S. congressman from west Michigan and U.S. ambassador to the Netherlands; Illinois Supreme Court Justice Frederick R. De Young of Roseland; and the consul for the Netherlands in Chicago, A. P. van der Burch. The Netherlands ambassador to the United States, Dr. J. H. van Rooyen, also joined the chapter as an honorary member in 1931 – an announcement that was met with "loud acclaim." James Baar, choral conductor of Chicago Junior College and son of member Jacob Baar, led the singing at the banquets.[51]

A typical Knickerbocker speech touted Dutch "contributions," such as the story of second lieutenant James Strode Swearingen of Detroit, of New Amsterdam ancestry, who in 1803 led a sixty-five-man expedition to establish a military post at the future site of Fort Dearborn. Swearingen raised the Stars and Stripes, then boasting fifteen stars, on August 17, 1803. Thus, this "illustrious son of those early Dutch families which were the pioneers of civilization in America" unfurled the flag on "Chicago's birthday." "To us Americans of Dutch descent," said the speaker, this is a "glorious story with thrilling interest – a crowning event – for the development of our rich heritage, 'Chicago,' destined to become the leading city of the changing world." In such ways did the Chicago Dutch keep history "fresh."[52]

The Chicago Knickerbockers staged an annual ladies' night banquet at suitable hotel ballrooms, where members displayed Dutch heirlooms and curios. During the summer hiatus, golf tournaments brought the men together.[53] Throughout the bleak Depression years, the society sponsored Lake Michigan picnic excursion trips to St. Joseph, Michigan, with ship masts flying the Dutch flag and church bands playing Dutch music.

On April 24, 1933, the Knickerbockers, in cooperation with the Reformed churches, held a mass commemoration of the four hundredth anniversary of the birth of William the Silent, "The Apostle of Tolerance." The *Onze Toekomst* editor crowed: "In droves Dutchmen came from east, west, north and south" to the chapel of the University of Chicago to sing "Wilhelmus," "My Country, 'Tis of Thee," and Psalm 133 from the

51. *Onze Toekomst,* 12 Feb. 1931; 25 Jan. 1933; *Chicago Messenger,* 17 Jan. 1936.

52. *Knickerbocker Society of Chicago, 1931-1932,* 10-11.

53. The society was led by Gelmer Kuiper, Dr. J. H. Hospers, and James J. Van Pernis, editor of Onze *Toekomst.* See *Onze Toekomst,* 30 July 1924; 15 June 1927; Vandenbosch, *Dutch Communities of Chicago,* 70-71.

Dutch Psalter, and to listen to speeches by, among others, Dr. Henry Beets of Grand Rapids, Judge De Young of Roseland, and Rabbi Dr. Louis L. Mann of Chicago's Sinai Temple. The rabbi praised Prince William as a prophet of toleration and religious freedom, making Holland a place of refuge for Jews – in contrast to Germany. "We are highly pleased," the editor continued in the warm afterglow of the rally, "that the Dutch spirit had finally been awakened from a deep winter sleep. . . . We can hardly contain our enthusiasm and call out: 'Come Hollanders, continue on this path.'"[54]

In 1933 at the summer opening of the Chicago World's Fair, "The Century of Progress," the Knickerbocker Society went into high gear, promoting "our Dutch type of civilization" as a means to uplift the "spiritual, moral, and cultural life of our city." New president Theodore S. Youngsma early in 1933 called a meeting of all Holland American organizations and associations in Chicago to band together to organize exhibits and activities. "The project is too big for any one group," Youngsma declared, and "the cooperation of everybody is essential."[55]

Member Jacob Baar, the former postmaster of Grand Haven, Michigan, and an old Chicago settler, represented the society on the World's Fair committee and ensured the Dutch a permanent place in the "Century of Progress" exhibition. The exhibition council set aside August 31, 1933, Queen Wilhelmina's birthday, as "Holland Day" at the fair. An audience of twelve to fifteen thousand assembled that evening in the Hall of Science to welcome "Miss Netherlands," the blue-eyed Juel Yonker of Roseland, and her court of eight lovelies, all of "pure Dutch ancestry." The celebrants stood to sing lustily the Netherlands and American national anthems and then settled down to listen to speeches touting Dutch contributions to their adopted country. The talks were interspersed with singing of Dutch folk songs and favorite psalms and performances by noted musical groups.

Every Netherlandic church, school, and society was represented in this, the largest gathering ever in the United States of Holland-Americans. Mass choirs from the West Side, Englewood, and Roseland were recruited to sing sacred and patriotic music. "We surely have the numbers and the talent," declared the Netherlands Day music committee, and the five-

54. *Onze Toekomst,* 15 Feb., 2, 26 Apr. 1933; First Reformed Church of Chicago, Minutes, 2 Mar. 1933; cf. printed program, *Four Hundredth Anniversary of the Birthday of Prince William of Orange,* 24 Apr. 1933.

55. *Onze Toekomst,* 25 Jan. 1933.

hundred-voice choir proved it. The program ended with an address by J. Arthur Meeter, who represented "Uncle Sam," followed by the singing of Psalm 68, v. 10 in the Dutch Psalter.[56]

The next August 31 saw the second Netherlands Day at the Century of Progress. In an attempt to eclipse the more serious 1933 program, the 1934 committee focused on fun and frolics. It substituted "amusing plays for serious speeches, glee club novelties for somber reflections, and movie films in place of long lectures." All this would prove that "Jan Dutchman can indulge in high class wholesome amusement," noted the committee, although the repertoire of the Knickerbocker Male Chorus of the West Side and the Emmanual Church Mixed Chorus of Roseland included some sacred songs. Needless to say, mixing the sacred and the mundane drew a stinging rebuke from the editor of the Christian Reformed denominational weekly, the *Banner.* Editor Henry ("H.J.") Kuiper took a hard line on such syncretism and undoubtedly spoke for some fairgoers. "I don't believe that this is the kind of 'tolerance' which William the Silent would have approved," he insisted, much to the chagrin of T. S. Youngsma, president of the Netherlands Day Committee and a member of Kuiper's denomination.[57]

In 1942, when Princess Juliana of the Netherlands visited Chicago from her asylum in Canada during the Nazi occupation of her homeland, the Knickerbocker Society, in cooperation with the University of Chicago, honored her with a solemn program at the University Chapel. All the elites turned out for their beloved royal family. University president Robert Hutchins brought greetings, the Chicago Christian High School a cappella choir sang chorales of J. S. Bach and Johannes Brahms, and the Reverend Harry Hager, of the Bethany Reformed Church of Roseland, gave the address. It was a night to remember for the rest of one's life.

In the late 1940s, after Youngsma's era, the Knickerbocker Society degenerated into a social gathering, with a *rijst-tafel* (Chinese-Indonesian rice dinner) in the spring and *Sinterklaasfeest* in the winter, and occasional *borreluurtjes* ("cocktail hours") to fill in. In recent years it has been reincarnated by suburbanites as the Dutch Knickerbocker Society and is the only

56. Ibid., 21 Jan., 13 Feb. 1931; 25 Jan., 1 Mar., 26 June, 29 Aug. 1933; First Reformed Church of Chicago, Minutes, 2 Mar. 1933; "Rehearsals for Netherlands Day at World's Fair," *Banner,* 21 July 1933; audience photo and caption in ibid., 20 Oct. 1933; "Souvenir Program, Netherlands Day, A Century of Progress, August 31st, 1933."

57. "Dutch Festival Aug. 31 to Eclipse '33 Program," *Chicago Messenger,* 24 Aug. 1934; T. S. Youngsma, "A Letter in Regard to Netherland's Day and our Reply," with Kuiper's reply, in *Banner,* 21 Sept. 1934.

PROGRAM

FESTIVITIES AT UNIVERSITY OF CHICAGO CHAPEL

IN HONOR OF THE VISIT OF

HER ROYAL HIGHNESS PRINCESS JULIANA

OF THE NETHERLANDS

WILLIAM THE SILENT

Prince of Orange

Tuesday May the Twelfth Nineteen Hundred and Forty-two

at Seven Forty-five P. M.

Under the Auspices of

THE KNICKERBOCKER SOCIETY OF CHICAGO

In co-operation with the University of Chicago

Chapel of the University of Chicago

59th Street and Woodlawn Avenue

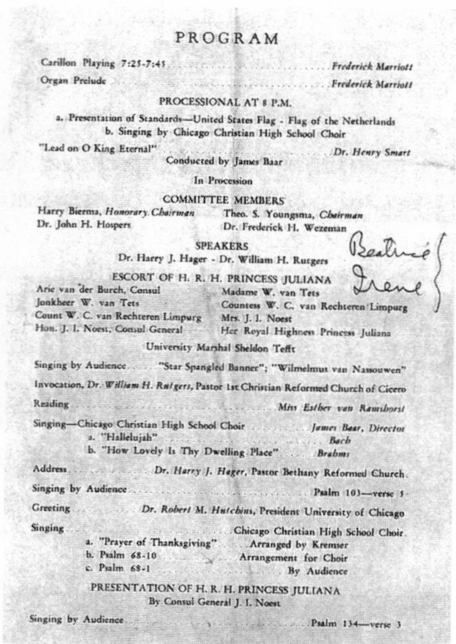

PROGRAM

Carillon Playing 7:25-7:45 .... *Frederick Marriott*

Organ Prelude .... *Frederick Marriott*

PROCESSIONAL AT 8 P.M.

a. Presentation of Standards—United States Flag - Flag of the Netherlands

b. Singing by Chicago Christian High School Choir

"Lead on O King Eternal" .... *Dr. Henry Smart*

Conducted by James Baar

In Procession

COMMITTEE MEMBERS

Harry Bierma, *Honorary Chairman* — Theo. S. Youngsma, *Chairman*

Dr. John H. Hospers — Dr. Frederick H. Wezeman

SPEAKERS

Dr. Harry J. Hager - Dr. William H. Rutgers

ESCORT OF H. R. H. PRINCESS JULIANA

Arie van der Burch, Consul — Madame W. van Tets

Jonkheer W. van Tets — Countess W. C. van Rechteren Limpurg

Count W. C. van Rechteren Limpurg — Mrs. J. I. Noest

Hon. J. I. Noest, Consul General — Her Royal Highness Princess Juliana

University Marshal Sheldon Tefft

Singing by Audience .... "Star Spangled Banner"; "Wilmelmus van Nassouwen"

Invocation, *Dr. William H. Rutgers,* Pastor 1st Christian Reformed Church of Cicero

Reading .... *Miss Esther van Ramshorst*

Singing—Chicago Christian High School Choir .... *James Baar, Director*

a. "Hallelujah" .... *Bach*

b. "How Lovely Is Thy Dwelling Place" .... *Brahms*

Address .... *Dr. Harry J. Hager,* Pastor Bethany Reformed Church

Singing by Audience .... Psalm 103—verse 5

Greeting .... *Dr. Robert M. Hutchins,* President University of Chicago

Singing .... Chicago Christian High School Choir

a. "Prayer of Thanksgiving" .... Arranged by Kremser

b. Psalm 68-10 .... Arrangement for Choir

c. Psalm 68-1 .... By Audience

PRESENTATION OF H. R. H. PRINCESS JULIANA

By Consul General J. I. Noest

Singing by Audience .... Psalm 134—verse 3

Knickerbocker Society of Chicago Program,
visit of Princess Juliana of the Netherlands, 1942

(Courtesy of Mary Wezeman Smith)

highbrow social club still active in greater Chicago. The group celebrates the national Dutch-America Heritage Day each November 16 with a dinner meeting at a distinguished venue, such as the Scandinavian Club in Arlington Heights or the Prairie Center for the Arts in Schaumburg.[58]

Dutch American Club

In the 1970s, the Dutch American Club was organized by suburban Hollanders of lesser pretensions. Jan Visser of Palos Heights, a Dutch center, was president. Members enjoyed an annual dinner and special programs with a Netherlandic flavor.[59]

58. *Onze Toekomst,* 21 Jan., Feb. 1931; *De Nieuwe Amsterdammer,* Nov. 1995; *Windmill,* 23 Oct. 2000, 13.

59. William Harms, "Dutch settlers share heritage with the suburbs," *Chicago Tribune* (Daily Suburban edition), 23 Apr. 1983.

Ut en Thús (Away and Home)

Frisians, true to form, insisted on their own *selskip* ("society"), as they did in Paterson, Rochester, Grand Rapids, Orange City, and Racine, among other places.[60] Frisians had the added incentive of a cultural crusade, the Frisian Movement, which fought for "the inalienable rights of self-preservation and self-development as a distinct people," especially the legal equality of the Frisian language. In 1925 the Frisian Society of Chicago organized and chose the name Ut en Thús ("Away and Home"), which suggested that Frisians who had left the homeland could feel at home in the club.[61] Activities included the well-known Frisian ball game of *keatsen;* singing, dancing, and singing; talks on Frisian history and heroes; and traditional foods.

The Chicago club did not continue. It lacked the Reformed Church ties that allowed the Grand Rapids–based Christian Frisian Society, Gysbert Japiks, founded in 1933, to celebrate its fiftieth anniversary (belatedly) in 1985 under the leadership of Calvin College professor Bernard Fridsma; it has since disbanded. As Fridsma lamented, "During the last twenty years we have lost many members through death, and because there has been no Frisian immigration since the sixties, we unfortunately cannot go on, at least not effectively."[62] This is the ultimate fate of all immigrant societies when the nourishment of newcomers is cut off. Even a religious and patriotic base is not sufficient to stave off Americanization.

Conclusion

The heyday of the social clubs spanned the four decades from the Columbian Exposition (1893) to the World's Fair (1933), when the immigrant community was at its high point. The clubs served the educated professionals and self-made businessmen who were largely assimilated but harbored a nostalgia, a romantic attachment, to the land of their birth.

60. "Frisian Society Commemorates 50 Years: Lack of Immigration Forces Disbandment," *DIS* [Dutch Immigrant Society] *Magazine* 16 (May 1985): 9. Utspanning toch Ynspanning of Paterson, New Jersey, was established first in 1893 and lasted seventy-five years; *Friso* of Grand Rapids, Michigan, began in 1909; Nij Fryslân of Rochester, New York, began about 1910; It Heitelân of Orange City, Iowa, was founded in 1936, as was Fier fan hûs of Springfield, South Dakota; and Us Memmetaal of Racine, Wisconsin, in 1949.

61. Ut en Thús elected Dick Driesbergen president, H. Brilsma secretary, and Piet De Painter treasurer. *Onze Toekomst,* 11 Mar. 1925.

62. "Frisian Society Commemorates 50 Years," 8-9.

Luurt Holstein, editor of *Onze Toekomst*, voiced these sentiments in an address to the General Dutch League in 1910:

> We shall always love that little patch of swampy, seaweed-covered earth across the Atlantic where we (or at least our forefathers) first saw the light of day – the place where we learned our mother-tongue in Mother's arms or on Father's knee! Are we not overwhelmed with heartfelt emotion, almost reverence, by the privilege that is ours tonight of once again seeing our beloved old red, white and blue as it is displayed beside the stars and stripes of our country?[63]

Such rhetoric provided a veneer of cultural remembrance for the elitists, but it was too intellectual and highbrow for the vast majority of immigrants, who showed little interest in Dutch national culture. Devout Calvinists were content with their humble church societies, which very well sustained the Dutch religious heritage and language. Thus, it was inevitable that the social clubs would wither and slowly disappear.[64]

In their day, however, the clubs made a valuable contribution. They passed to the second generation a sense of Dutch pride that still nourishes their descendants. They served the more secular, hyphenated Protestants of the upper crust who were largely assimilated and felt less of a need for an ethnic identity. The clubs provided a veneer of cultural remembrance that met the emotional needs of their members for a time.

63. Luurt Holstein Address, Algemeen Nederlandsch Verbond Rally, Chicago, 1910, in Luurt Holstein Papers.

64. Van Hinte, *Netherlanders in America,* 1003.

CHAPTER II

Plowing in Hope: Truck Farming and Agricultural Colonization

From the first, Chicago's Dutch immigrants mainly came from rural life in the old country. The number of farming immigrants increased even more in the 1880s under the duress of the agricultural depression in the northern Netherlands. Thousands of excess laborers came to the United States in the hope of obtaining farms of their own. Religiously devout for the most part, they believed the biblical premise, "He that ploweth ought to plow in hope" (1 Corinthians 9:10). But this was no longer possible in the fatherland.

Chicago attracted the poorest immigrants, who had no resources to move onto the land directly. They worked first in the city in order to save some money and to assess the land situation in the West. Truck farming on the city outskirts was the first step up the agricultural ladder for many.

Chicago styled itself the "Great Central Market" of the nation, with its South Water Market on 15th Street at Ashland Avenue, the livestock trading at the Union Stockyards, the grain pit at the Board of Trade on La Salle Street, and the Fulton Street Fish Market.[1] Dutch immigrants took advantage of these markets as they pursued their dream of working *het dierbaar plekje grond* ("their dear little piece of land").

Edna Ferber immortalized these Dutch truck farmers of Chicago in her Pulitzer prize–winning historical novel, *So Big*.[2] She tells of the terrific

1. Edwin Griswold Nourse, *The Chicago Produce Market* (New York: Houghton Mifflin, 1918), 8-9.

2. (New York: Crowell, 1923). The setting is High Prairie, later called Roseland.

David Leep cultivating parsnips, 112th and Halsted Streets, 1920s *(The Archives, Calvin College)*

struggle to wrest a living from the soil and how it drained the mental and physical strength of the immigrants. Any heroic portrait, however, is marred by Ferber's ridicule of the Dutch ideals, habits, and customs. She portrays their broken English as quaint, their farming methods as backward, and their stubbornness as pathetic. With their faces ground into the dirt by toil, they could only snicker at the young schoolteacher's remark, "Cabbages are beautiful." Actually, what the Dutch farmers failed to appreciate was Ferber's elevation of beauty to the sublime. In their minds, cabbages were simply one of God's good gifts, a plant to sustain life and provide income on the market.[3]

Truck farmer John Meeter exemplified that Reformed outlook. In the 1870s on a plot along Roosevelt Road he raised hay that he sold to Marshall Field for the wagon horses his draymen used to make deliveries to customers. Meeter found a kindred spirit in Field, a staunch Presbyterian, and the men frequently talked theology in Field's office when Meeter went to collect for his deliveries. As the city encroached on his farm,

3. The scathing review is by the Reverend John Van Beek, "Second Roseland," *Banner,* 16 Feb. 1940. The fact that Ferber was Roman Catholic may have added to Van Beek's antipathy.

Meeter moved to a leased farm in the Englewood area (Lake Township) and raised cabbages. He made windfall profits one year when drought wiped out his competitors' cabbages. He managed to save his crop by hiring Hungarian and Polish immigrant children living nearby to walk the long rows every day giving each plant a cup of water. Meeter sold his cabbages for the fabulous price of $40 a ton. This was the beginning of his wealth. Shortly after, in 1881, when George Pullman needed Meeter's leased farm to lay railroad tracks to his new railroad car factory in Pullman, Meeter held out and finally sold his tenant rights for a tidy sum. With this money, he built the Meeter Sauerkraut Factory on the Ridge Road in Lansing, Illinois, and became one of the wealthiest and most influential men in the Illiana area.[4]

In the early decades, hundreds of Dutch farmers like Meeter took open land on the fringes of the expanding city and raised vegetables in the rich muck soils on which Chicago sprang up. Dutch market gardeners settled in Roseland (High Prairie) and South Holland (Low Prairie) in the late 1840s, and over the next decades they spread into Englewood, Evergreen Park, Oak Lawn, Cicero, Riverside, Stickney, Summit, La Grange, Maywood, Bellwood, and Des Plaines. They generally segregated themselves by province of origin. Groningers farmed in the western and central suburbs, Noord Hollanders in Roseland and surroundings, Zuid Hollanders in South Holland, and Frisians in Evergreen Park.

Old West Side

Groninger families located on the prairies along the present-day Eisenhower Expressway. Henry Stavenger raised hay in the Lawndale area in the 1870s, John Klooster's land was on Paulina Street (1700 west), Peter and Jennie Stob and their nine children farmed at Kedzie Avenue (3200 west) just east of Garfield Park, Jacob Molenhouse's tract was west of Kedzie, and Nicholas Jannenga's farmhouse stood at 3910 West 12th Street. Jannenga had immigrated in 1867, and his large farm covered nearly a square mile stretching from Douglas Park Avenue (3000 west) to 40th (later Crawford) Avenue and from Polk (800 south) to 14th Street. His son John delivered milk, and his son Edward dealt in hay, coal, and wood,

4. Clarence Boomsma, "Meet Mr. Meeter," *Origins* 16 No. 1 (1998): 43-46, based on Boomsma's recollections of conversations with Calvin College professor Henry Meeter, John's son.

eventually with the help of John, brother-in-law Edward Bulthuis, and John Stuit. Jannenga's neighbors were the market gardeners Henry Bos (Bus, Bush), Berend Dekker, Peter Barsema, and Sieger De Vries. Barsema and De Vries mainly peddled straw.[5]

Further west in the next decades, between Cicero Avenue (4800 west) and Austin Boulevard (6000 west) along Harrison Street, were Arend Medendorp, Jacob Doornbos, and Lubbertus Stavenger at Cicero Avenue. At Laramie Avenue (5200 West) between Harrison and Van Buren were Jacob Bos, Gerrit Bakker, and William Rudenga. Rudenga employed three hands – Peter Heemstra, Joseph Vander Voort, and Peter Ter Maat. Ralph Euwema's farm was at 53rd and Lexington, and David Bakema farmed at Central (5600 West) and Harrison. Euwema's laborers were Harm Vander Woude and Nick Ketelaar, and Bakema employed his nephew Albert Cleveringa, as well as Martin Hoekstra. Bakema's farm is today part of Chicago's Columbus Park. The fresh immigrants Nicholas and Ralph De Vries and Johannes Tromp also worked the soil in this area as laborers.[6]

Cicero and Maywood farmers included Nicholas Knol, Jacob Nienhuis, Simon and John Boeringa, Nick Tillema, Henry Kooi, and their unmarried hands John Overzet, Gerrit Tiggelaar, Wicker Blaauw, Dick Van Stedum, Joseph Baker, and Joseph De Vries. Ben Dykstra farmed in Riverside.

Chicago Sanitary District

The biggest Dutch farming concentration was on Chicago Sanitary District lands on the north side of the old Illinois and Michigan Canal and the new Sanitary, Drainage, and Ship Canal, which Chicagoans simply called the Ship Canal. The latter opened in 1900, after a decade of dredging, and was called the "eighth wonder of the world." It was an engineering marvel that required moving more dirt than the Panama Canal and, even more amazing, it reversed the flow of the Chicago River to sweep Chicago's sewage inland instead of polluting its lake drinking water.[7]

5. Robert P. Swierenga, comp., "Dutch in Chicago and Cook County 1880 Federal Census" (1992), and "Dutch in Chicago and Cook County 1900 Federal Census" (1992); Evelyn Jannenga Schmidt and Paul D. Schmidt, comp., *Bulthuis-Jannenga Family Genealogy* (Holland, Mich., 1999), 597-600; Leslie Smith Powell, "The Bush/Smith/Stavenger Connection," typescript, 1978, copy from Evelyn Schmidt.

6. Swierenga, "Dutch in Chicago and Cook County 1900 Federal Census."

7. Mayer and Wade, *Chicago: Growth of a Metropolis,* 274.

The Sanitary District leased its thousands of acres to truck farmers. Dutch families filled the lands on both sides of the canals. One group settled north along 35th Street, running west of 40th Avenue to the city limits at the railroad tracks (about 4600 west). This tract, part of Ward 28 in 1900, later became a railroad yard. Sportsman's Park and Hawthorne racetracks in Cicero were built immediately to the west. Another nest of Dutch farmed south of the canals along 41st Street to the city limits at Cicero Avenue.

The Dutch families, all recent immigrants from Groningen, began working Sanitary District lands in the 1870s, and many more came later. The first families, all north of the canals, were Abel Bulthuis, George Brouwer and his unmarried brother Hendrik, Simon Van Dyke, Nicholas Auwerda, Fred Pruim, Peter Ritzema, Cornelius Smit and his married son Henry, Allan Schaap, and Adrian Vander Poel. By 1900, twenty Dutch families and as many farmhands were district tenants. These included Barney Bilthouse (Bilthuis) and sons Henry and Abel, Henry Bilthouse (Bilthuis) and son Jacob (Jake), Richard Buikema and sons John and Bernard,

David Bakema farm, 5600 W. Harrison St., Chicago, 1897;
l-r (in front): nephew Albert Cleveringa, widowed sister Grietje Cleveringa nee Bakema (Albert's mother), married niece Tryntje Auwerda (wife of Nicholas), nephew Barney Auwerda, nephew-in-law Nicholas Auwerda, widower David Bakema, laborer Martin Hoekstra on wagon, people in rear unknown (farm today part of Chicago's Columbus Park).

(Courtesy of Nicholas Auwerda)

Nicholas Auwerda farm, 3800 S. Central Ave.,
Mud Lake in Chicago Sanitary District, 1915
l-r: son Richard (Dick), wife Tryntje (Cleveringa), daughter Grace
(Mrs. Peter Winter), Nicholas Auwerda, son John ("Shorty"),
hired hand Bill Niehof, son Barney on wagon. Horses Max and Bob.
(Courtesy of Nicholas Auwerda)

Douwe Eisinga and son Peter, and Peter Poolman and son. Immigrants who joined them shortly after 1900 were Klaas Solle, Siebelt Scholtens, Peter Zylstra, Fred Rudenga, and William Eleveld. On the south side of the canals, along 41st Street, were Thomas De Boer, Peter Hillegonds, Richard Heulkamp, and Henry Venhuizen, plus farmhands Henry Dykema and Henry Vos.[8] All these families belonged to either the First Reformed or the First Christian Reformed Church of Chicago.

The Groningers gradually pushed southwest along the canals in Stickney and Summit, and to the Des Plaines River bottomlands of Lyons and Riverside. Those in Stickney, including the Siebelt Scholtens family, farmed the old bed of Mud Lake, a marsh that stretched from its head at Ogden near Austin Avenue to the river. Mount Auburn Cemetery lies in the center of that area. The Scholtens family settled later near the La

8. Swierenga, "Dutch in Chicago and Cook County 1880 Federal Census," "Dutch in Chicago and Cook County 1900 Federal Census."

Klaas Solle family in onion field in Summit, ca. 1910.
Note bundle of strings at waists to "bunch" green onions
l-r: daughter Rika, Klaas, daughter Sue,
granddaughter Jessie Jongsma, son Edward
(Courtesy of Charlotte Solle Siegers and Donna Siegers Tuls)

Grange quarry. Already in 1900, twenty-five Dutch Reformed families farmed in Riverside and Lyons.[9]

Summit

The farming colony at Summit began its rapid growth after 1900 and soon had the largest concentration in the western townships. The Dutch farmed the "school" land in section sixteen of Lyons Township, on which Chicago Municipal Airport (now Midway) grew up in the 1920s. Real estate magnate Moses Wentworth held title to this and all the other lands in and around

9. For Mud Lake, see "Des Plaines River – Part One: Description," in Nature Bulletin No. 64, May 28, 1960, Forest Preserve District of Cook County. Dutch families in Riverside and Lyons in 1900 included Rudolf Eleveld, the widow Annie Folkerts (and her hired laborers Ralph Blinkwolt, Cornelius Schmidt, and Johannes Broekema), Richard Huizenga, Fred Heyns, Peter Grima, and James Westerhof. In Lyons lived the families of Peter Abbring, Hemmo Batjes, George (Geert) Blinkwolt, Henry Boer, Hendrik Brouwer and his married son John, John Bulthuis, William Buskman, Anno Dunder, Jacob Kempes, Albert Kraai, Henry Krook, George Mulderink, Louis Rispens, Herman (Hemmo) Ruiter, Fred Schepel, William Stavenga, and Herman Warners, plus hands Martin and Abel Halbersma, Henry Modder, William Pothuis, John Spoolstra, Cent. Van Beveren, Thomas Van Dyke (Swierenga, "Dutch in Chicago and Cook County 1900 Federal Census").

Above, Siebelt Scholtens's team and wagon in front of home at Mud Lake, ca. 1908; l-r: daughter Jennie (Jantje) on wagon, Siebelt holding the horses, sons William, Peter (in arms), wife Henrietta, sons Albert, Gerrit

(Courtesy of Ginger [Mrs. Albert] Van Der Molen);

below, Henry Tholen and Jennie Scholtens, on Sears motorized bicycle, Scholtens's La Grange farm, ca. 1912

(Courtesy of Ginger [Mrs. Albert] Van Der Molen)

Herman Schutt's farm wagon on way to market,
farm on 55th Street and Central Avenue, Summit, ca. 1905
l-r: Herman Schutt, Herman's second wife (name unknown), Nick Schutt,
John Schutt (on wagon), two unknown hired hands on right
(Courtesy of Ken Van Byssum and Peter Roeters)

Summit and rented to the Hollanders. In 1900 the census marshal enumerated thirty Dutch families in Summit, including the Bulthuis, Stob, and Venhuizen families. The Herman Schutt family soon after settled at 55th Street and Central Avenue. Everyone knew Jake Bilthuis, the R.F.D. mail carrier, whose daily rounds brought correspondence, church papers, and the coveted mail order catalogs.[10] The Summit settlers organized a Reformed church in 1899 to eliminate the long commute to Ashland Avenue.

10. Moerdyke, "Chicago Letter, *CI,* 4 Dec. 1901, p. 799; Archer Avenue Christian Reformed Church, *Golden Anniversary, 1911-1961* (Chicago, 1961). Families listed in the 1900 census were Jacob Bakker, A. Bergsma, William Beukema, Frank and Joe Boekhoudt, Klaas Boerema, William Boersma, Geert Bos, Hendrik Brouwer, Nick Bulthuis, John Buis, Cor Dykman, John Iwema, Benjamin Knobbe, Richard Knol, Cornelius Koelikamp, Albert Kraai, Albert Krook, Frank Kuiper, Okko Lauwerzeel, Dick Miller, Cornelius Oosterhouse, Jelte Overset, Richard Reinders, Jacob Smit, Martin Stob, David Van Beveren, Thomas Van Voorman, Arthur Venhuizen. Farmhands included Dick Blaauw, Fred Boss, Henry Danhof, Peter Vander Kamp, Henry Schuurman, Henry Vander Weit, and Ben Workman (Swierenga, "Dutch in Chicago and Cook County 1900 Federal Census").

Far Western Suburbs

Other Groningers could be found farming west of the city to McCook, La Grange, Western Springs, Hinsdale, and Downers Grove, southwest to Willow Springs along the canals, and northwest to Des Plaines. Several Bulthuis families (Jake, Clarence, and Tony) and Ike Ridderhof worked lands along Wolf Road from 72nd to 76th Streets. In Hinsdale were the John Tameling and Henry Hoekstra families. John and Adrian Van Kooten farmed on 63rd Street in Downers Grove. To the northwest of the city was Peter Barsema in Maywood, Jacob Tazelaar on Waveland Avenue, and Richard Venema in Norwood Park. Along Mannheim Road in Bensonville and Des Plaines were found Keimpe Miedema, Peter Van Dyke, Lambert Teeuws, and Robert Folkerts, among others. After the Second World War, the expansion of O'Hare Airport and construction of the Illinois Tollway pushed them off the land.

Robert Folkerts's farm wagon loaded for market; Robert holding reins with oldest son John. In front of second wagon is Mrs. Robert (Dena, nee Hoffman) Folkerts and her daughters Etta and Frieda; others are hired hands and neighbors. Bensonville near Mannheim Rd., ca. 1920

(Courtesy of Ginger [Mrs. Albert] Van Der Molen)

Evergreen Park and Oak Lawn

Around 1915 a group of Noord Hollanders and Frisians from Roseland opened truck farms in Evergreen Park. Newcomers directly from the Netherlands and Groningers from Englewood joined them. Some leading families included those of John Adema, Neal Bloem, John Buis, William Bruinius, Abe De Vries, John Dykstra, John Hommes, Wieger Hoekstra, John Huizenga, John Iwema, Andrew Lenderink, John Leo, John Luth, Martin Ozinga, Jan Riemersma, Frank Rosier, Richard (Dirk) Sluis, Edward Solle, and Herman Triezenberg. Triezenberg earned the title of Asparagus King of Evergreen Park and Luth was known as the Cauliflower King.[11] Oak Lawn to the west also attracted Englewood truck farmers. Fertile five- and ten-acre parcels sold for $400 per acre in 1920. The locale was linked to the heart of Chicago by paved roads or a ten-cent tram fare.[12]

The truck farmers raised sweet corn, melons, cucumbers, asparagus, onion sets, pickle cucumbers, tomatoes, and potatoes. Annual cash rents at the time ranged from $5 to $20 per acre; hay fields rented for $1 to $3 per acre. "Most don't have more than 20 acres of land, on which they can make a good living," reported K. Boersma of Englewood in a letter to friends in the Netherlands. For those with know-how, even two acres were enough to make a living, Boersma added. Hands earned $1.50 to $2 per day plus board, and the demands of the job were not extreme. "Long ago in the past," said Douwe Dykstra, a farmhand, "I have seen how hard the poor had to work for the farmers and that is not necessary over here. And that is why we will not soon come back to Holland."[13]

The Groningers had farmed in the Netherlands and knew how to work the soil with their hands and their horses. In 1910, Lubbert Wieringa took first prize at the Michigan State Fair for the massive thirty-five- to fifty-pound pumpkins raised on his farm at 62nd and Whipple Streets near Marquette Park. These pumpkins were said to be "the largest ever cultivated in or near Chicago."[14]

Truck farmers brought their produce to the main Chicago wholesale

11. Mildred Semple and Virginia Wrobel, eds., *Evergreen Park: A Melting Pot of Memories* (Village of Evergreen Park, 1987), 36.

12. *Onze Toekomst,* 13 Feb. 1920.

13. Swierenga, "Dutch in Chicago and Cook County, 1880," and "Dutch in Chicago and Cook County, 1900"; letter of Douwe Dykstra, Chicago, to "Brother and Sister," 18 Dec. 1900; letter of K. Boersma, Englewood, to E. Mussenga, Kloosterburen, Groningen, 19 Dec. [1880s], both trans. Henry Lammers, Archives, Calvin College.

14. *Onze Toekomst,* 14 Oct. 1910.

South Water Market on 15th Street, 1941 *(Courtesy of Chicago Historical Society)*

Swierenga Bros Wholesale Produce House, 943 W. Randolph St., July 1942. Notice on wall (left top) an American flag, photo of Gen. Douglas McArthur, and "God Bless America" banner. l-r: cashier Joe Swierenga, customers Stanley Totura of Fox River Grove and Edward Vinicky of Elgin, and partners Mike Venterelli, Robert Swierenga, and Edward Swierenga

N. Sluis Seed Company, 851 W. Randolph St., 1910, above store of A. Huizenga & Son (third from right)
(Courtesy of Siegers Seed Company, Holland, Michigan)

market on South Water Street. Smaller centers were the West Randolph Street Market or the State Street Farm Market at 71st and State Streets. Englewood and Evergreen Park farmers found the 71st Street Market most convenient, and there many wholesalers were fellow Hollanders. One such middleman was Paul Rusthoven, who from two until five o'clock in the morning bought sweet corn, tomatoes, mustard, and other vegetables off the farmers' wagons and trucks. Rusthoven immediately resold the produce to street peddlers and retailers who served neighborhood grocery stores. Swierenga Bros. (Robert and Edward) and Omke Groot were Dutch wholesalers on Randolph Street, as was Arys Huizinga and seed dealer Nanne Sluis just down the street. In 1910 some five hundred wagonloads of produce clogged the Randolph Street Market every morning.[15]

There was a constant circulation of families between the agricultural districts beyond the city limits and the core neighborhoods within the

15. Harold Hiskes, *In Memoriam* (privately printed, 1996), 12; Robert P. Swierenga, "Robert (Bouwko) Swierenga Family History" (1997); Nouse, *Chicago Produce Market,* 23; *Onze Toekomst,* 20 Feb. 1920. N. Sluis & Sons eventually relocated to Holland, Michigan, as Siegers Seed Company. The company is now run by the fourth generation of the family.

city. Each neighborhood had its church, and families could move back and forth without leaving the ethnoreligious community. Indeed, with the coming of the motor car, farm families could commute to city churches. As late as 1932, 16 percent of the families of the Second Christian Reformed Church of Cicero were farmers who lived up to twenty-five miles away and commuted to church by car.

Truck farming around Chicago died out in the 1940s and 1950s, and most farmers were forced to retire or move out of state. Land prices rose due to urban encroachment, and the farmers faced problems marketing their produce at the Italian-controlled, wholesale commission houses. Also, by the 1950s, the big supermarket chains had built regional distribution centers in the city and had begun trucking in fresh produce from across the country on the new interstate highway system. One by one, the wholesale merchants on South Water, Randolph, and State Streets went out of business.

A few farmers held on by selling sweet corn, tomatoes, and other popular foods directly to consumers at farm stands and local farmers' markets, but this provided, at best, some extra summer income to supplement "real" jobs. Even without the massive changes in the food industry, however, the farmers could not stave off developers, who wanted to subdivide their lands for housing and industrial plants. Local farmers, who had ringed the city from the beginning and supplied its tables with fresh produce and milk, became extinct. For one hundred years they had plowed in hope, but hope ran out.

Their options were to leave farming for laboring jobs in the booming city or plant new farm colonies elsewhere. Most chose the city and found work in construction, cartage, and trash collection. But some sought land far afield.

Chicago as Colonization Depot

Chicago from the beginning was the major jumping-off point for the western agricultural frontier. Many Hollanders who had come off farms in the old country longed to get back. Tenancy was one way, but their chief goal was to live on their own land. Yet, land prices had risen to the point that few could afford to buy.

Land developers and promoters knew their situation and routinely advertised in the Dutch-language press to lure urbanites with promises of inexpensive and fertile land in the West and South. In the 1880s, for example, Close Brothers & Co. of Chicago, a firm that controlled hundreds of thousands of acres of virgin lands in northwest Iowa and southwest Minnesota, ran a large advertisement in *De Grondwet* regularly in the 1870s, seeking thousands of tenants to develop their lands. One ad in 1886 read (in translation):

> New Dutch Colony in Pipestone County, Southwest Minn., not more than 50 miles from Orange City. We have in Pipestone County alone more than 100,000 acres of outstanding lands for agriculture and cattle raising. Every sort of grain and vegetable can be grown here with the same success as in Illinois and Iowa. A fully warranteed deed of title is guaranteed. Land obtainable for cash or on easy credit.

The same issue of the paper carried an ad of A. Boysen & Co. of Chicago, offering fertile land for $7-9 per acre in the new Dutch colonies in the same areas of Minnesota that Close Bros. was pushing.[16]

Reformed and Christian Reformed Church officials likewise encouraged colonization in Minnesota, and to a lesser extent in South Dakota. The Christian Reformed church weekly, *De Wachter,* ran numerous articles and advertisements promoting Minnesota lands. In 1885, Frederikson & Co., a Chicago and Minneapolis land agency, in cooperation with the Dutch house of Prins & Zwanenburg in Amsterdam, Groningen, and Harlingen, offered thirty-four thousand acres of the "best first-rate land" at $6-8 per acre for a "Nieuwe Hollandsche Kolonie" at Olivia, Minnesota. The lands in the counties of Renville, Kandiyohi, and Chippewa lay along the Chicago, Milwaukee, & St. Paul Railroad, only twelve miles from the stations at Willmar and Kerkhoven.

In Chicago, prospective colonists were to contact J. Berghuis at 899 (new numbering 2207) W. Lake Street, who periodically took groups of prospective colonists to Minnesota for only $10 round trip. They were housed in the Hollandsche Hotel of P. Haan in Olivia, who also acted as the firm's local agent.

De Wachter editor, the Reverend Lammert J. Hulst, penned an enthusiastic boomer article that he ran in the column next to the advertisement in July 1885. It recommended the colony at Olivia in the most enthusiastic terms and announced that several Chicagoans had purchased lands after a June excursion; Jan Vander Mey bought 80 acres, Willem and George Knott 320 acres, and George Knol 120 acres. Other Hollanders in Chicago who wanted to own their own farms should take note and act promptly.

16. *De Grondwet,* 19 Jan. 1886.

By 1889 Dutch colonization in Minnesota was taken over by the Chicago-based company of Prins and Koch, headed by Theodore F. Koch and his partner, Martin Prins, both Netherlanders. Koch began in business as a partner in the firm of Prins & Zwanenburg of Groningen, exporting Holstein-Frisian cattle to the United States. At the same time, he recruited emigrants for the Holland-America Steamship Company of Rotterdam. Koch and Prins also acted as agents for several railroad companies, including the Lackawanna & Western, Nickel Plate Road, Erie, Wabash, and the Chicago and St. Paul.[17]

Koch and Prins themselves emigrated to America in 1889 and shortly thereafter jointly purchased thirty-four thousand acres in Kandiyohi County, Minnesota, from the president of the Chicago, Milwaukee, and St. Paul Railroad at $4 per acre. From their headquarters in Chicago, first at 51 S. Clark Street and later in the Unity Building at 181 W. Washington Blvd., the firm began recruiting colonists both in the Netherlands and in America for the colony of Prinsburg, Minnesota. They offered land at $6-8 per acre, one-third cash down.

These men knew that without a church it was virtually impossible to start a new Dutch Reformed community, so they contributed money to build a church. Within three years, all thirty-four thousand acres were sold, and a thriving Dutch Calvinist colony of 150 families was in place. The second to buy land in Prinsburg was the Chicago Groninger Albert Kleinhuizen, who became the leader of the colony. He served as elder in the church (which recently celebrated its hundredth anniversary) and put his sons on the land before dying at a ripe old age. Today the Kleinhuizen name is prominent in local telephone directories in the Prinsburg area. So many Chicagoans went to Prinsburg and the neighboring colony of Roseland that the latter was named after the Chicago suburb of Roseland.

After Martin Prins died in 1887, Koch incorporated as the Theodore F. Koch Land Company, with a capitalization of $400,000, and for the next twenty-five years he energetically planted Dutch colonies throughout Minnesota, Texas, Montana, and elsewhere. Koch opened an office in St. Paul and moved there himself in 1888, but his Chicago office continued to recruit Hollanders in Illinois and surrounding areas.[18]

17. Robert Schoone-Jongen, "Cheap Land and Community: Theodore F. Koch, Dutch Colonizer," *Minnesota History,* 53 (Summer 1993): 214-24.

18. Van Hinte, *Netherlanders in America,* 496; Lucas, *Netherlanders in America,* 366-70; Schoone-Jongen, "Theodore F. Koch," 214-24.

The Montana colony and Reformed church that the Reverend Andrew Wormser founded in 1894 in Wormser City also attracted some Chicago truck farmers. "Occasionally the most enthusiastic reports reach us concerning the Rev. A. Wormser's Holland colony near Bozeman, Montana," reported Peter Moerdyke. "The climate, soil, crops, and prospects of success are quite remarkable, as we repeatedly learn from eyewitnesses and reliable sources."[19]

That Wormser in 1896 recruited the Reverend John Vanden Hook of Chicago's Northwestern Reformed Church to be the minister in his colony was an added inducement. Vanden Hook's "Montana letters" were positive indeed, according to Moerdyke. "Our former beloved colleague, Rev. J. H. Vanden Hook, writes us enthusiastically about the great success of the Holland colony in Montana, in the midst of which he dwells and flourishes with his people. His ministerial and his son's farming labors yield very gratifying returns. No other Dutch settlement is so prosperous." By 1900 some Chicago farmers headed further west to a new Dutch colony in the Yakima Valley of Washington State.[20]

The most successful farm colonization by Chicago's Dutch Reformed was far closer to home, in northern Indiana, led by the Roseland real estate dealers John Cornelius Ton and his brother Richard. Early in the 1890s, the Tons bought a large parcel of swamp land near De Motte in Jasper County, Indiana, some forty miles southeast of Roseland. De Motte became a Dutch colony that continues to the present day and numbers several hundred families, most members of Reformed and Christian Reformed churches.

Encouraged by the successful Indiana venture, the Tons tried a much bolder move. They purchased muck lands a thousand miles south near New Orleans, but the Dutch did not favor the hot humid South with its hoards of mosquitoes, and the plan came to naught, with considerable financial loss to the Ton firm.[21]

Texas colonization was first promoted in Chicago in 1894 when a committee of twelve Hollanders, headed by John Broekema, an executive in the retail store of Siegel, Cooper & Company of Chicago, visited the Lone Star State. The land committee traveled free, courtesy of the Mississippi, Kansas & Texas Railroad, accompanied by its immigration agent. They bought a large tract of sixty-six thousand acres near Port Arthur in

19. Moerdyke, "Chicago Letter," *CI,* 18 Nov. 1894, p. 10.

20. Ibid., 18 Nov. 1894, p. 10; 3 Nov., p. 8; 22 Dec. 1897, p. 9; 12 Dec. 1900, p. 811.

21. Lucas, *Netherlanders in America,* 452-53.

the southern part of the state and returned to Chicago with glowing reports about the region "so highly favored by nature and civilization and commerce."[22]

The committee "made strenuous efforts to induce their countrymen to colonize in that region," going so far as to get the local newspaper, the *Port Arthur News,* to include a Dutch-language section "to boom the country and draw Hollanders as settlers." The promoters had a fair measure of success, and in 1898 there were enough colonists to organize a Christian Reformed Church at Nederland near Port Arthur. In 1900 the town counted six hundred Hollanders.

One recruit was Henry Koopman, a Chicago gardener, who was intrigued by reports of the agricultural paradise in Texas. There, he said, "most crops can be raised twice a year on the same land, even potatoes." In 1895 Koopman made the one thousand-mile train trip to Texas, but his hopes were dashed after seeing the new colony. He returned to Chicago in bitter disappointment and denounced the whole venture as misguided. As Herbert Brinks noted, the erstwhile Texan in letters to the Netherlands charged that the "promoters were worse than Judas Iscariot, for that betrayer had at least returned the blood money." Koopman canceled his subscriptions to all Dutch language newspapers and withdrew from the Reformed Church, blaming several of its ministers for having endorsed the colony.[23]

Koopman reflected on his experience to a nephew in the Netherlands:

> Two Dutch ministers sent many of their members to Texas where they had 5,000 acres belonging to a Holland organization. They put out a booklet saying it was a land flowing with milk and honey. Four Dutch ministers and a leading man in a large business signed the booklet. I went to see Dominie Dykstra [Lawrence Dykstra, pastor of the First Reformed Church of Englewood (1893-98)] and asked him many questions because he had seen the settlement and I was interested in going there. So, I took the trip, but when I got to the last stop on the railroad line, I had to stay overnight in a hotel because the settlement was still twenty-five miles away, with no railway connection.
>
> On the following day I started walking to the settlement. . . . When I saw it, I said to them, "The land is on the level with the sea [Gulf of

22. Moerdyke, "Chicago Letter," *CI,* 18 Sept. 1895, p. 8.

23. Ibid., 5 Feb. 1898, p. 9 (citing *Port Arthur News,* vol. II., no. 4); Herbert J. Brinks, "Netherlanders in the Chicago Area," *Origins* 1, No. 1 (1983): 5-6.

> Mexico], and when the sea comes up you will be flooded." They need steam plows to break up the soil; the people there were killing themselves. I lived there for two days on pancakes and coffee – they had no bread and not one piece of meat, not even beans. I went away hungry, found a hotel in Alvin where I got a good dinner, and took the train back to Chicago.[24]

On returning home, Koopman went to see Dykstra and learned to his chagrin that the dominie had never actually visited the colony, but had only gone as far as Alvin, Texas.

Koopman continued in the letter to his nephew in Drenthe:

> Then the minister had to ask me what kind of place Liverpool [Texas] was and what I thought of it. I told him that it was poor for agriculture, and that with high water from the Gulf all would be flooded and that the people would be poverty-stricken and come back to Chicago. Within one year that is what happened. They were driven off by high water and they lost everything. They had to come home begging.[25]

After dealing with lesser floods, the major tragedy actually struck in 1900, when a hurricane drove sea water far inland at Port Arthur, wiping out ten Holland families who were left with only the clothes on their backs. The destitute people appealed for help to family and friends in Chicago, and, under promoter Broekema's lead, the community raised "a handsome sum of money for immediate 'first aid.'" This disaster spelled the end of the Nederland colony and Christian Reformed Church there. Only four families remained in 1905.[26]

Six years after the flood, in 1906, the Theodore F. Koch Company opened an office in Houston and made another serious attempt to plant a colony at Winnie, Texas, some twenty miles west of Port Arthur and midway to Galveston Bay.[27] Again the firm donated land for a church and manse (fifteen acres worth $600), plus $400 cash to build the church. The advertisement read: "All industrious Hollanders who are on the lookout for a good place to settle are welcome at Winnie," where the long growing season and plentiful rain allowed one acre to outproduce three in Illinois.

24. Koopman letter in Brinks, "Netherlanders," 5-6.

25. Ibid.

26. Moerdyke, "Chicago Letter," *CI,* 9 Feb. 1898, p. 9; 10 Oct. 1900, p. 653; "Home Mission, Classis Illinois," *Banner,* 5 Jan. 1911.

27. Lucas, *Netherlanders in America,* 438-40; Van Hinte, *Netherlanders in America,* 714-15.

The Reformed Church cleric John De Spelder actively promoted the colony and preached there for a time.[28]

The ad snared a number of Dutch market farmers around Chicago to go to Winnie "to try their luck there." Quite likely these folks knew nothing of the previous disasters in Texas. The major push came in 1910. On January 4 the families of John Toren, Ben Renkema, Gerrit Hoffman, Martin Tulp, and B. Huizenga left for Texas. By April about forty families followed and all bought land. On June 7, 1910, one of the firm's Chicago agents, John Stob, who operated a feed and grain store at 1459 S. Blue Island Avenue in the heart of the Groningen neighborhood, was induced by cheap rail fares to organize a special excursion for a group of friends from the First Christian Reformed Church of Chicago. Within a month sixty families, mostly from the Chicago area but also from Michigan, Indiana, Iowa, South Dakota, and Wisconsin, had bought land and settled in Winnie, including the Chicago area families of Stob, Hoekstra, Ter Maat, Van Der Molen, Lanenga, Hoffman, Renkema, Vander Kamp, Blaauw, Teune, De Young, Dykstra, and Evenhouse, among others. On July 26 a mass meeting in Roseland at the 104th Street Christian School prompted a second exodus. On August 2 Dirk Boersema (of 1520 W. 15th Street) and Lucas Holtrop of Englewood, among others, "left with an excursion to Winnie to settle there permanently." Holtrop had already bought land there.

John Stob's son, Henry, then only an infant, described the reasons for the family's Texas venture in his book, *Summoning Up Remembrance:*

> My father and a number of his Chicago friends were taken with the idea. . . . So it happened that in 1910 my father sold his prosperous business and prepared his family for departure. He was, no doubt, excited about the prospect of living in what had been touted as an agricultural paradise. But he was also concerned to get his younger children out of a city that, in our neighborhood at least, was rife with crime and violence. The notorious Valley Gang, a number of whose members died in the electric chair, is said to have been headquartered in the district adjacent to ours.[29]

28. *Onze Toekomst,* 7 Jan., 27 May, 15, 22 July, 5 Aug. 1910; Moerdyke, "Chicago Letter," *CI,* 26 Sept. 1906, p. 624.

29. *Onze Toekomst,* 4 Jan., 7 Jan., 27 May, 15 July, 5 Aug. 1910; *De Grondwet,* 15 Feb., p. 8, 1 Mar., p. 8, 12 Apr., p. 8, 28 June 1910, p. 8; Stob, *Summoning Up Remembrance,* 6-7.

Stob home in Winnie, Texas (1910-13)

(The Archives, Calvin College)

The Stob family settled on its virgin 174-acre prairie farm, and John had a barn and home built on it. The home, Henry noted,

> was a large, two-story structure with an ample screened-in circular porch enclosing a roomy interior. It was said to be the best house in the region, and arriving visitors, including pastors occasionally sent down from Classis Pella, normally stayed under the roof. . . .
>
> Starting a farm is no small undertaking. Besides providing shelter for people and animals, one has to plow, fertilize, and sow the land, dig wells, lay ditches, and do a score of other things. One needs horses, wagons, seed, and fertilizer for the enterprise, to say nothing of muscle and will power. Because the latter qualities existed in fair supply, Father was able, with the energetic assistance of [brother] Neal, to get part of the land broken up and readied for sowing during the winter of 1910. In the spring they planted orange and fig trees; and in the ensuing years they grew sweet potatoes, corn, and cucumbers, as well as peanuts and watermelon. But the promised and hoped-for plentiful harvests did not materialize, and marketing such crops as the land yielded proved more difficult than they had anticipated.
>
> But the colonists did not immediately give up. They came together, shared their concern, and provided each other with help where needed. Father appears to have been among the leaders in the commu-

> nity. Notices appearing as early as July of 1911 disclose that he functioned as the president of the Cooperative Fruit and Tree Growers Association of Winnie, Texas. He also served as "reader" at Sunday worship services held in the little frame church that had been erected near our house on land donated by the developer.[30]

Listening to elders "read sermons" did not satisfy, so the colonists appealed to Classis Illinois to help them organize a congregation. The classis dispatched its "home missionary," the Reverend Derk Vander Ploeg, in November, 1910. He preached at the home of Ben Renkema the first Sunday, and by Thanksgiving Vander Ploeg had organized the Winnie Christian Reformed Church, numbering seventy-three souls. Renkema and John Stob were elected the first elders and Dirk Boersema and Lucas Holtrop the first deacons. Vander Ploeg started catechetical instruction and a young people's society, Ora et Labora, with K. E. Van Der Molen as president. The church had the most meager furnishings; a milk pitcher served as the wine chalice in the sacrament of the Lord's Supper, and the congregants were served in water glasses. Winnie certainly has "a good future," Vander Ploeg concluded.[31]

Other recruits agreed. A group of nineteen families from Michigan, who visited Winnie about the time that the church was organized and bought land there, declared on their return that everything the Koch firm had advertised about Winnie was proved to be "absolutely true." Crops were excellent in 1911, and the newcomers formed a Cooperative Farmers' Association. John Stob reported harvesting 125 bushels of potatoes per acre (worth $1 a bushel) on the black loam prairies, plus $150 of cabbages and 400 crates of cucumbers worth over $300. Two crops a year were normal, and orange trees were laden with ripe fruit.[32]

But Texas was not a Shangri-la after all. "Alternating periods of flooding rains and searing droughts discouraged most of the settlers," Henry Stob recalls. "In late 1913 my parents returned to Chicago." The final blow was a hurricane in September of 1915 that brought torrential rains – thirteen inches within twenty-four hours – and pushed a huge tidal wave inland. The waters devastated Winnie, and more than eighty families abandoned their farms. By May of 1916, only three families remained, and the Winnie church had to disband. The pioneers lost every-

30. Stob, *Summoning Up Remembrance,* 7-9.

31. "Home Mission, Classis Illinois," *Banner,* 5 Jan. 1911, p. 11.

32. "Good News of Winnie, Texas," ibid., 12 Jan. 1911, p. 29 (quote); *De Grondwet,* 20 Dec. 1910, p. 8; Lucas, *Netherlanders in America,* 439.

thing and the failure cost the Koch firm $100,000. Some families returned to Chicago, some went to the Port Arthur, and others were scattered widely. But a few stayed or returned and eventually succeeded.[33]

Theo. Koch & Co. had no qualms about continuing to push Texas among Chicagoans. In 1920 the company ran a full-page advertisement every week in *Onze Toekomst* touting choice lands in Riviera. Later in the decade, the company offered one free rail ticket from Chicago to Port Arthur for cash payments on forty acres of company lands at Hamshire. The ad claimed the area had good schools and churches, was ideal for dairying, and that eight Dutch Reformed families already lived there, besides some families in Winnie five miles away. Enough families fell for these offers that Classis Illinois in 1929 sent out its veteran home missionary, the Reverend John R. Brink, to organize a congregation at Hamshire. The worshipers, ranging in number from twenty-five to forty, built a small chapel with their own hands and called a minister, the Reverend Derk Mellema, who served until 1937. Mellema also preached on alternating weeks for about a dozen Hollanders at Nederland, who had remained after the hurricane in 1900, and an even smaller remnant at Port Arthur. Thus, a pitifully few dairymen carried on in Texas, but for the Chicago Dutch, the Lone Star state never delivered on its promises.[34]

An Oklahoma colonization met with no more success than the one in Texas. In 1904 sixteen families from the First Reformed Church of Roseland settled six miles from the town of Norman in Cass Township of Cleveland County. The group included the John De Valk family with eleven children, their cousins Hendrik (Henry) Knol and Henry's sister Martje Knol and her family, and Watze Buwalda and three sons. Two dozen other families joined them. All were tenant truck farmers, part of the immigrant wave of the 1880s, who hoped to get free land by homesteading. But they first had to master logging, since they found themselves in a heavily wooded region. The settlers may have learned from Reformed Church missionaries to the Apaches about the prospects in this last "land rush" state, which was also awash in oil.

The first harvest was plentiful and in 1906 more families arrived, which enabled them to found a congregation and build a little church in the village of Moore, the Sandstone Memorial Church, under the auspices

33. Stob, *Summoning Up Remembrance,* 9; Henry Stob, "Chicago's West Side," *Origins* 9, No. 2 (1991), 9-16, also recounts the Stob family saga in Winnie (1910-13).

34. *Onze Toekomst,* 21 Dec. 1927; "Hamshire, Texas," *Banner,* 25 Dec. 1931, 17 Mar. 1933, 14 Dec. 1934; 29 May, 16 Oct. 1936.

of the Classis of Oklahoma (RCA). John De Valk was the leading elder. But adverse climate conditions, drought, hail, and cyclones, discouraged them. The Reverend Siert Riepema of the Oklahoma City congregation tried to minister to their needs when he arrived in 1908, but the families gave up. The church disbanded in 1911; most families either returned to Chicago or went to South Dakota.[35]

The Chicago Dutch tried a southern colonization again in 1913, this time in Tennessee. The Chicago section of the General Dutch League organized a colonization agency, spearheaded by James De Boer and J. Berghuis, "to help Hollanders get farms, and to give those who want to go into the country the necessary information about different settlements and land offered for sale." Early in 1913 some sixty prospects attended an organizational meeting at Soustek's Hall (18th Street and Laflin Avenue), of whom twenty-two joined up. Elected as board members were James De Boer, Nick Wieringa, D. Baar, A. Laning, and Izaak Emmering. On March 4 De Boer and Berghuis headed an excursion to plant a Dutch colony in Tennessee. Apparently the plans fell through, because nothing more was heard of any Dutch colony in Tennessee.[36]

The South was unkind to Dutch farmers, who simply could not adapt to the unfamiliar climate. Perhaps this is why in 1910 twenty Dutch market gardeners in Englewood and Roseland made an inspection visit to Canada. They were not impressed, and the plan was dropped. Five or six Roseland families did follow a land agent to Lark, North Dakota, in 1906, where they planted a colony complete with a Christian Reformed Church. Dutch colonies in Wisconsin, Minnesota, and South Dakota also attracted Chicago farmers, including the Kornelius Dykstra family in Vesper, Wisconsin, near Wisconsin Rapids, and the Henry Swierenga family in Platte in eastern South Dakota. After Henry died, his widow Mary Wiersum and family returned to Chicago briefly and then settled in Prinsburg in west central Minnesota. Christian Reformed Churches were planted in Platte, Prinsburg, and Vesper in 1883, 1886, and 1888, respectively.[37]

35. Ann G. Bousema-Valkema, *Valk De Valk Valkema* (1998), 240-43, English summary, 12-17; Van Hinte, *Netherlanders in America,* 716-17; Lucas, *Netherlanders in America,* 440-41; "Uit Norman, Oklahoma," *De Grondwet,* 18 Jan. 1910, p. 6; Moerdyke, "Chicago Letter," *CI,* 20 Jan. 1904, p. 41; 7 Mar. 1906, p. 154; Gasero, *Historical Directory of the Reformed Church in America,* 325, 606; Charles E. Corwin, *A Manual of the Reformed Church in America, 1628-1922* (New York, 1922), 666.

36. *Onze Toekomst,* 3 June 1910; 7, 14, 21 Feb., 7 Mar. 1913.

37. Ibid., 3 June 1910; "Recollections of Johan Nicolay: Roseland, Illinois, and Lark,

Chicago's Dutch Catholic leaders also encouraged farm colonies in the South and West. The Association of Belgian and Dutch Priests (Belgisch-Hollandsch Priesterbond) was formed in 1907 specifically to prevent the dispersal of Flemish (Dutch-speaking) immigrants.[38] In 1909-10 Chicagoan Julius E. De Vos, with the help of Dutch priests F. F. Pieters and Vincent Tesselaar, developed the colony of Wilhelmina (named after the Dutch Queen) in Missouri on fertile swamp lands. Father Tesselaar himself emigrated and became the energetic director of Wilhelmina colony, which by 1914 boasted a church, school, and general store. The promising colony survived the war years but never grew. Dutch Catholics were more reluctant than Protestants to leave the big cities.[39]

Conclusion

The movement of Dutch Reformed farmers to the West was so extensive that during the First World War the Christian Reformed Church established an emigration commission to channel the newcomers to reputable colonies with established churches, so they would not be swindled or lost to the faith. In 1917, denominational membership statistics showed 3,800 families (29 percent) living west of the Mississippi River and 13,300 (71 percent) east of it.[40] Colonization was in full swing and remained in vogue until the dust bowl days of the Great Depression wiped out many homesteaders and drove them back east.

North Dakota," *Origins* 8, No. 1 (1995): 3; Henry Dykstra, "Two Longs and Ten Shorts" (ca. 1995); Robert P. Swierenga, "Robert (Bouwko) Swierenga Family History" (1994).

38. Lucas, *Netherlanders in America,* 453-54; Van Hinte, *Netherlanders in America,* 729-30.

39. Lucas, *Netherlanders in America,* 455; Van Hinte, *Netherlanders in America,* 734.

40. Christian Reformed Church, *Jaarboekje,* 1917, 187.

CHAPTER 12

Business Is "Picking Up": Garbage and Cartage

"How's business?" Dirk asked Siert. "Picking up," replied the proverbial Chicago scavenger. Anyone who grew up among the Dutch in Chicago heard this witticism a hundred times. Dutchmen "had garbage in their blood," it was said. But the question of why is "probably eternally lost to history," noted Peter H. Huizenga, whose grandfather went into the business in 1893, the year of the Chicago Columbian Exposition (World's Fair). "The garbage business, though it was hard work, was a very dependable business. You weren't thrown out of work. All you had to do was get out there and hustle." The adage of the men was: "Your garbage is our bread and butter." Or as a sticker on the rear of a garbage truck read: "Feed me."[1]

The Dutch knew how to hustle, and they were accustomed to hard, backbreaking work on the land. They loved to handle a team of horses, and farming was in their blood. Some went into the scavenger business directly and others as an outgrowth of market gardening on the outskirts of the city. As they hauled their produce daily to the commission houses on South Water Market and later the Haymarket Square Market on Randolph Street, they saw opportunity. People ate, and mounds of trash piled up. Someone had to clean up after the market closed each day, as well as pick up the food scraps at the downtown restaurants. All was free slop for the hogs. Collecting the trash, unsavory as it was, became the chief venue of the Dutch Calvinists.

1. Stevenson Swanson, "Lucrative lure of garbage hauling has long been a Dutch treat," *Chicago Tribune,* 29 Mar. 1993.

Their strong intent from the start was to control their own economic destinies. Like new immigrants generally, they entered the workforce at the bottom and had to work their way up. The second generation enjoyed the benefits won by the first. By the 1920s, as Henry Stob recalled, "Some heads of families in the community worked in shops and factories, others held office jobs, and a number ran their own businesses." They were an "industrious and thrifty" lot, but "few of them were rich" – at least not until the unexpected windfall in the 1970s.[2]

Early Teamstering

Teamstering, not farming, would bring the Chicago Dutch economic prosperity. Farming on rented land was a dead end. The number of truck gardeners decreased over time and all but disappeared by the 1940s, except in far distant suburbs such as Downers Grove, Des Plaines, and South Holland. In teamstering, the Dutch could indulge their love for horses by bringing a bit of the farm to the city. Hauling garbage, general freight, ice and coal, and peddling produce and milk became a mainstay of Groninger employment. By the 1930s the Dutch monopolized the waste hauling business in Chicago and its suburbs, except for homes in the city proper that were served by city crews.

We catch only a faint glimpse of this in the first generation. In 1870 the census marshals in Chicago counted only nineteen Dutch-born teamsters, drivers, and expressmen. These included John Fischer, Henry Benschop, Abel Groeneveld, Simon Heyzenberg, and Peter Maring. The latter three were West Side Groningers. Ten years later, the number had risen to thirty-two, including three "night scavengers." These pioneers of the Dutch garbage men of Chicago were John Hofman, Cornelius Mellema, and Thomas Veld. Mellema's son Melle worked with his father. The Hofman family lived near 14th and Ashland, and the Mellema and Veld families resided on the fringe of the city at Western and Grand Avenues. Others in teamstering included John Kooy, Peter Kooi, Joseph Meeter, Henry Auwinga, John and George Veld, John Vanden Belt, Jacob Vander Driest, Frederick Bultje, Roelof and George Fennema, Henry Willink, Paul Tanis, and Thomas Van Dyke.

These pioneers proved that teamstering fit the Dutch temperament, and the numbers grew rapidly between 1880 and 1900. By 1900, on the Old

2. Henry Stob, "Chicago's West Side," *Origins* 9 No. 2 (1991): 15-16.

West Side alone, the census marshal counted seventy-five teamsters, or 16 percent of all men gainfully employed. Two generations later, by the 1940s and 1950s, a thousand or more Hollanders worked "on the truck," either as owners or employees of the more than two hundred Dutch-owned scavenger and cartage companies. In the entire century 1890 to 1990, by this author's count, 450 Dutch-owned trucking companies of one kind or another operated in greater Chicago (see listings in appendices 1 and 2).

The number of scavengers increased dramatically after 1905, when the city of Chicago changed its codes to make unlawful the disposal of any waste whatever on "any street, sidewalk, alley, park, public place, drain, sewer or receiving basin." Cinders, garbage, and manure had to be kept in specially designed bins and hauled away regularly by scavengers licensed by the city, who must dispose of it only in designated places. Licenses for garbage wagons in 1913 cost $5 per year, and the city had 202 wagons under license, operated by 126 private scavengers, who principally serviced hotels and restaurants in the "Loop" district.[3]

Garbage Hauling

First we knew them as scavengers or, in humorous Yankee Dutch, *akki-pieuws,* then as garbage men or, more colloquially, "garbios," and now as solid waste haulers. These changing terms chart the evolution of the industry and the rising prestige of the work.[4] A man typically began in the business by buying a horse and wagon. For a dollar or two, he would pick up cinders and garbage from apartments, hotels, and restaurants in the Loop, and from businesses of all kinds across the city. The horse was cared for by the hauler and his family and housed in a barn behind the house, with access through the infamous alleys. Big strong horses cost up to $200 each, and tough mules about half as much, but they were notoriously stubborn.

Most of the refuse material was construction or demolition debris, industrial waste, and cinders and ashes from coal furnaces. Scavengers re-

3. City of Chicago, *Revised Municipal Code of 1905* (Chicago, 1905), Article XII, Garbage and Ashes, 507-11. The code was revised in 1910; see *Reports by the Commissioner of Public Works and Civil Service Commission, City of Chicago — 1913; Bureau of Streets Investigation* (Chicago, 1913), 40-41.

4. Timothy Jacobson, *Waste Management: An American Corporate Success Story* (Washington, D.C.: Gateway Books, 1993), dust jacket blurb. The phrase *akki-pieuws* cannot be found in a Dutch dictionary and has no direct translation in English. Lucas, *Netherlanders in America,* 324.

cycled paper, boxboard, old clothing, metal, glass, and anything else of value. Food wastes were minimal and largely became slop for the hogs. From the time of the Chicago Fire in 1871 until well into the 1900s, debris material was used as fill on Chicago's lakefront. Grant Park, Meigs Field, Soldier's Field, and much of the Midway of the Chicago World's Fair of 1933-34 was laid over rubbish and ashes hauled in by Hollanders. Less stable material and other garbage was put on scows and barges for dumping out in the lake. Ashes and cinders were spread on the dirt streets and alleys to raise the elevation and harden the mud, until the city banned this practice. Unethical drivers, to save time and money, sometimes continued to make an illegal "quick dump" in alleys. Their wagons were fitted with release levers to open the bottoms and drop the loads. The driver simply stomped on the release lever and drove off. At least one such culprit gave himself away in church, an eyewitness recalled. While dozing off during the sermon, the driver suddenly stomped his foot down for a quick dump. All his fellow scavengers in church knew exactly how to interpret the action.

During the 1910s and 1920s, drivers brought garbage to "dump stations" on Goose Island (on the North Branch of the Chicago River) and to several railway loading stations, such as the Illinois Central Railway yards at 15th Street and Loomis Boulevard. From the transfer stations, a barge or train took the garbage to distant dumps on the city's far southern and northern outskirts. Companies such as R. G. Ludy bought ashes for its parking lots in the Loop, as did the new White Sox Park at 35th Street and Shields. The city was also beginning to build incinerators at this time to reduce landfill hauling.

Later, in the 1930s and 1940s, drivers dumped garbage and rubbish in the old "borrow pits" for clay, sand, and gravel, as well as stone quarries. Clay holes at 18th Street and Damen Avenue and 35th Street and Kedzie Avenue were filled to a height of thirty feet and more, as were new holes along Cicero Avenue at 31st and 39th Streets. Dump fees were $1 for a four-wheeled truck and $1.50 for a six-wheeler, and the city's rats, the natural scavengers, thrived on the free food every night. Many loads of refuse were also dumped in the swamps around Lake Calumet and to fill in the outdated Illinois and Michigan Canal. Since this activity was entirely unpoliced, one can imagine what conglomeration of wastes went into the canal cut. It is certain, however, that the frugal Dutch salvaged useful furniture, clothing, wood, and countless other items.[5]

5. *Reports by the Commissioner of Public Works and Civil Service Commission, City of Chicago — 1913; Bureau of Streets Investigation* (Chicago, 1913), 450-53.

Hundreds of Hollanders got into the scavenger business over the years, most as sole proprietors driving their own teams and later trucks, often working with sons and other relatives. Hauling refuse was unpleasant physical labor that required a strong back and, as wags would add, a weak nose. But it brought a steady income that surpassed craft and factory wages. Peter Harsema, a teamster living on the Old West Side, boasted to his family in 't Zandt, Groningen, in 1911: "As a green one [i.e., a new immigrant], I have my own business." And little knowledge of the English language was required to get along. Harsema's success nagged at Gerrit Harm Van Dellen, his cousin with whom he boarded, because Gerrit "has to go to the factory and work for a day's wages. This may get worse next spring because we now have two wagons and hope to expand business." That summer Harsema kept four hired hands busy at $15 per week, and he often made a profit of $120 a week, "with only a horse and wagon." Harsema noted that he could never earn as much working for someone else. But he advised Melle Waalkes, a prospective emigrant from Groningen, not to come to Chicago unless he was a "strong man willing to do rough work."[6]

Peter H. Huizenga, a third-generation Dutch scavenger, spelled out the many reasons why hauling garbage was a "natural" occupation for the Dutch Calvinists.

> The rural economy of Friesland and Groningen taught these people how to work with teams of horses. . . . Their meager economy taught them to work hard and live frugally. Their Calvinistic beliefs instilled them with a dignity and respect for manual labor and a strong sense of independence, while their strange language forced them into occupations which did not require English communication, and their cultural identity provided them with a sense of community and an ability to discuss their common business interests among themselves.
>
> These people came to America to find a better economic life. They didn't want to work for the Americans, they wouldn't work on Sundays and didn't want to lose their culture and faith in the American mainstream. The garbage business was an occupation waiting for them. A lowly occupation which was disdained by most people but honored by these hard working boers, who saw their new business as the American dream. The work was steady, was not subject to the normal ups and downs of business cycles, and the growing city eliminated

6. Peter Harsema, Chicago, to Harm Harsema and wife, 't Zandt, Groningen, 12 Jan., 30 Sept. 1911, Archives, Calvin College, translated by Huug van den Dool.

Peter H. Huizenga (b. 1939)

> the strong competition to which other businesses were subject [by creating an ever growing supply of refuse]. They only needed to know enough English to collect their bills, and could live among their own people without financial worries, so long as they were strong and healthy enough to do the work.[7]

The most important attraction of the waste hauling business was that it provided a steady income through good times and bad. No wonder Huizenga could say that garbage was an occupation "waiting" for the Dutch. Handling a team and hauling heavy loads was not unlike farm work in the old country, and it far surpassed being cooped up all day in a factory or industrial plant. Above all, the Groningers could continue to work with their beloved horses and be the proud owners of teams and wagons. This was the epitome of success.

The Dutch scavengers were a true in-group. Many were related to one another, they attended the same Reformed churches, and they lived cheek by jowl around 14th Street and Ashland Avenue in the heart of the Old Neighborhood. In times of illness or death, they pitched in to help one another, just as on the farm. Conversations among the men after church, and after work on the stoops of their homes and along the side-

7. Peter H. Huizenga, "Waste Management, Its History, Growth, and Development," in *The Dutch in America, Perspective 1987* (Proceedings of the Sixth Biennial Conference, Association for the Advancement of Dutch American Studies, Trinity Christian College, 1987), 3.

walks, often turned to business concerns. They relied on informal understandings to control contracts and keep out interlopers.

Each owner had his "mark," a numbered tin emblem about 4 × 6 inches in size that was nailed to the doorpost of the customers' cinder or garbage bins. The city of Chicago required such signs, so that if any problems arose it would know the responsible party. The marker read: "These premises serviced by ______. This emblem is not to be removed under penalty of law, by ordinance number ______ of the City of Chicago." More importantly, these marks or tags served as a claim of privilege and a means of discipline. Woe be the teamster who disregarded the mark and tried to take the account away from a colleague by "low-balling" the rate. But, conversely, woe to the teamster who did not service his customers well; his mark could then be ignored with impunity by any colleague wishing to underbid. Facing an open season on one's accounts was a fearsome punishment that few wished to incur.

Pioneer Scavengers

James De Boer, Bonne Iwema, Conrad Ottenhoff, Henry Bilthuis, Herman Euwema, and Albert Folkerts led the way in the 1890s, and in the next twenty years they were joined by, among others: John Blaauw, Gerrit

City Disposal Company emblem or "mark," 1950s

(Courtesy of Edward Evenhouse)

J. De Boer office, 1444 S. Ashland Ave., ca. 1900; l-r: William Mulder, Klaas De Boer, Egbert Ronda, Nick Vander Lei, James De Boer

(Courtesy of Richard Schuurman)

Bossenga, Richard Brouwer, Joseph De Vries, Hendrik Evenhuis (Evenhouse), Henry Hoogendoorn, Sam Hoving, Peter Huiner, Harm (Harry) Huizenga, Benjamin and Frank Klein, John and Thomas Mulder, William Noorlag, George Speelman, Mark Tazelaar, Jacob Ter Maat, Ben Top, Edward Van Der Molen, John J. Vandervelde, Sr., Richard Vande Westering, John Van Kampen, and Homme (Homer) Wigboldy. In Englewood, Nicholas Deckinga and Henry P. Harms began hauling trash in the 1890s. Virtually all these families were Groningers.

James De Boer emigrated from Leens, Groningen, in 1892 and landed a job in a millworking shop on the West Side. He joined the First Christian Reformed Church, where he met and in 1897 married Maria Wezeman, daughter of a large and influential family recently emigrated from Bedum, Groningen. The family took up residence among a few other Hollanders at 1714 W. 13th Street. The next year, after James paid off his debts and sent prepaid tickets for his parents to cross the ocean, he bought a horse and wagon and launched the firm of J. De Boer Coal and Wood, Moving and Expressing. Soon he added the commodities "Hay, Grain, and Feed" to his letterhead. The first money-maker was peddling kindling wood for kitchen stoves and furnaces, which he obtained from

De Boer Bros. team and wagon, James and Andrew De Boer, 1411-1415 W. 14th Place, ca. 1905 *(Courtesy of Celia Boomker De Boer)*

the South Side Lumber Company. For $4 a full wagonload, De Boer delivered throughout the city and suburbs, making two short and one long haul six days a week.[8]

De Boer hauled coal by the basket or "carload," carrying it to basement coal bins and second- and third-floor porches. This was heavy work and required more help, so he took in a partner, Wibbe Mulder. But Mulder soon went into business for himself, and De Boer asked his younger brother Andrew, one of his employees, to become his partner under the name of De Boer Bros. At this time the brothers added garbage collection to their business, run out of a small office on 14th Place, with a hayloft and large yard out back for the horses and wagons. All the hired men were Dutch immigrants just off the boat. They came to the office every Saturday afternoon for their pay and to enjoy a free cigar with their ever-present wad of chewing tobacco.

James's three oldest sons, George, Henry, and Clarence also joined the firm after graduating from the Metropolitan Business School of Chicago. George and Clarence went out soliciting, while Henry manned the office and did the bookkeeping. Egbert Ronda, their maternal grandfather, was the janitor, but daughter Effie came in on Saturdays to wash the tobacco juice off the floor. "No wonder the boys always considered her a real saint," sister Bessie recalled.[9]

After James died of a heart attack in 1924 and was buried on his fiftieth birthday, his widow sold her half of the business to the three sons. By

8. Henry De Boer, "Recollections of the James De Boer Family," 20-page typescript, dated February 1971, courtesy of John H. Evenhouse.

9. Bess De Boer Figel, *Once Upon a Time . . .* (Chicago, n.d.).

then the family had moved to a larger home in the heart of the Groninger Hoek at 1444 S. Ashland Avenue, where they lived above the office on the second and third floors; the horses were kept out back. The building stood one block south of the church where James had been an active member and leader.

In the mid-twenties, a scourge killed all thirteen horses of De Boer Bros., and this prompted them to buy trucks and move to larger quarters at 2847 W. Harrison Street. This spacious garage even had room for the garbage trucks of Sam Hoving, a brother of Henry De Boer's wife. Sister Bessie ran the office efficiently for both firms and enjoyed bantering with the drivers.

De Boer Bros. by this time became solely a garbage company. Every month teamster's union agent Dan Tognotti, a henchman of Al Capone known as "Dago Dan," would come to collect the union dues from the drivers. "He was always friendly to us," recalled Bessie, although Dan had a reputation for ruthlessness with nonunion drivers. "He always came in a

James De Boer (1874-1924) family, ca. 1911
l-r row 1: John, Andrew, Marie nee Wezeman, Effie, Louis
row 2: Henry, James, George, Clarence.
Daughter Bessie was born in 1912.
(Courtesy of Richard Schuurman)

Harm Huizenga family, ca. 1913 l-r: seated, Tena, Harm, Pete; standing, Tammes, Aaltje nee Kremer, Siert *(Courtesy of Peter H. Huizenga)*

different car and would park it in the back of the garage. He would sit looking out the front window of the office to see if the police were following him. He would pull up his pant legs and show us the scars where the police had beaten him. . . . He always brought me a big box of candy at Christmas time. One Saturday he didn't show up. We learned that he too was murdered. So, no candy, and no Dan Tognotti." In 1939 George took sole ownership and the company grew rapidly, with the help of his sons James and John.[10] Eventually, in the 1970s, De Boer Bros. merged into the Waste Management conglomerate.

Harm Huizenga emigrated from 't Zandt, Groningen, in 1893 and settled on the Old West Side, boarding with a cousin, Harry Wierenga, and his family. Within a year he bought a horse and wagon and became a "private scavenger," hauling refuse for $1.25 per load to Lake Michigan as fill for Lake Shore Drive. This humble beginning evolved into the Huizenga companies – Huizenga & Son (Tom), Ace Scavenger (Tom), C&S Disposal (Harm and Tom with Sam as manager, later succeeded by Sam's son Clarence), and Arrow Disposal (Pete). In 1950 the Huizenga companies, together with parts of the companies of Cornelius (Neal) Groot and Jake (Jacob) Bilthuis, were merged into a reconstituted Ace Scavenger Service. This firm evolved into a cash-management company or "platform" that eventually formed the nucleus of Waste Management in 1971.

Harm ran his business out of his home and stabled the horses in the

10. Ibid., 17-18.

barn. The family lived first on 14th Place near Laflin Avenue and, after 1908, at a more prominent location on Ashland Avenue. Harm had several teams on the street until son Tom, a true entrepreneur, talked him into expanding into the western suburbs and buying a Chicago-made Old Reliable truck in 1926, which was soon paired with a $6,000 Mack truck. On both sides were emblazoned:

> Huizenga & Son
> Private Scavengers
> 1348 S. Ashland Ave.
> phone Canal 5930.

In 1928 the family could afford to move to Cicero, buying a fine brick bungalow at 1241 S. 59th Court. Tom Huizenga purchased the business from his father soon after and changed the name to Ace Scavenger, which became the flagship firm. Later, in 1943, Tom bought Citizens Service Bureau for $25,000 and added it to his empire, which also included C&S Disposal (a partnership with Dick Evenhouse, Neal Groot, George De Boer, and Charley Boersma). Brother Pete Huizenga worked in his oldest brother's companies until 1942, when Tom sold him all the Ace "stops" north of Madison Street, and Pete started Arrow Disposal. With Tom's

First truck, Harm Huizenga & Son

(Courtesy of Peter H. Huizenga)

Bonne Iwema's garbage scow *Dutton,* ca. 1912, at Goose Island transfer station, Chicago River
(Courtesy of Calvin Iwema)

untimely death in 1945, Pete again became involved in his brother's businesses, forming Metro Scavenger from some Ace accounts and selling the new company to brother Sam Huizenga and Tom's brother-in-law Jake Bilthuis as equal partners.[11]

Bonne Iwema, another scavenger, went into business in 1899 when he bought out John Karsten for $350. He was twenty-one years of age and had married Christine De Boer that year, which linked him to another "garbage family." By 1904 Iwema concentrated on cinders, but in 1907 he added excavating to his line. This was to be his main focus, although he hauled ash and garbage as well. From 1909 to 1916, Iwema bought a half interest in a "lighter," the *Dutton,* to carry dirt and cinders he picked up with his horse and wagon for dumping eight miles out in Lake Michigan. His transfer station was on Goose Island.

In 1918 Iwema bought another boat, the *Hawthorne,* and began hauling freight to Lockport on the Sanitary Ship Canal. His partner and dear friend, whom he later bought out, was Nick Niemeyer. Niemeyer and his brother Albert, who also worked on the boat, each had to obtain a

11. Tena Huizenga, "The Life of Harm (Harry) Huizenga, 1869-1936," undated typescript; Huizenga, "Waste Management"; Jacobson, *Waste Management,* 49-53; Ted Hoekstra, "Memoirs, 1927-1957"; Ted Hoekstra, Interview with Mark Volkers, 12 Aug. 1989, typed transcript, p. 5, courtesy of Peter H. Huizenga. The headquarters of the various Ace companies was in the garage at 901 W. 31st Street, and after the merger at 4750 W. Harrison Street in Chicago.

WATER-FRONT PASS.

Port of Chicago

Pass Bonne Iwema

Residence 2236 W. 13th St

Nationality Hollander Naturalized

Occupation Transportation

Employed by

Location Universal

United States Marshal.

APR 16 1918

520671

Above, Bonne Iwema's garbage boat *Hawthorne,* ca. 1918, Chicago River; below, Iwema's Water-Front Pass, 1918, required during World War I to traverse Chicago River and Lake Michigan

(Both photographs courtesy of Calvin Iwema)

"Water-Front Pass" from the United States Marshal's office because of wartime security concerns. By 1928 the firm was called Acme Lighterage Company, but in 1933 it became Bonne Iwema & Son, when Bonne took his oldest son John as a partner. By then Bonne had sold the *Hawthorne,* his pride and joy, because it could not support his growing family.[12]

Besides the boat, Iwema in the 1920s had on the streets two teams

12. Hilda Iwema Clevering to Hendrina Van Dyke, 15 Jan. 2000, for comments about the *Hawthorne,* courtesy of Hendrina Van Dyke.

and a 1923 five-ton Saurer truck (Swiss-made), all hauling ash, dirt, stone, and garbage. In 1926 he added a second truck, a used Old Reliable, purchased for $125. His federal income tax statement for 1920 reported a profit of $3,700 from his teaming business. By 1936, in the throes of the Depression, profits were down slightly to $3,400.

That year the Iwemas gained steady work at the Chicago Amphitheater at 42nd and Halsted Street with their 1926 International dump truck and 1936 McCormick-Deering front-end loader with a Trackson crawler and hydraulic high lift shovel. The work involved replacing the dirt floor surface as necessary for each successive event. The twenty-ton loader cost the princely sum of $2,114, with $500 down and eighteen monthly payments of $88.84 at 6 percent interest. Iwema was so successful that he paid off the loan within nine months.

Iwema was not the only Dutchman to find profits in moving dirt. Conrad Ottenhoff also specialized in excavating work; in the 1920s he won a $100,000 contract to dig the hole for the Tribune Building on Michigan Avenue and the Chicago River. Wigboldy Excavating, a firm started by Homme Wigboldy in 1901, survived the Depression years by working on

John Iwema driving 1936 McCormick-Deering front-end loader
Bonne Iwema & Son, ca. 1937
(Courtesy of Calvin Iwema)

Bonne Iwema & Son crew cleaning floor surface of
Chicago Amphitheater, 4200 S. Halsted St., ca. 1937
l-r by truck: John B. Iwema, Bernard Iwema, Jacob Niemeyer
(Courtesy of Calvin Iwema)

the Chicago subway project for "el" trains. Wigboldy's son John joined the firm during the First World War years, and they expanded to eight teams. In 1919 they bought their first truck for $1,000, a used Old Reliable. Another son, Albert, joined the company in the 1930s and put his mechanical skills to good use as an operating engineer. The company grew with the construction boom in Chicago after the Second World War, and by 1947 Wigboldy Excavating had a fleet of International trucks, several bulldozers, and high-lifts. The firm celebrated its one hundredth anniversary in 2001, with the fourth generation of the Wigboldy family ready to take charge.[13]

Iwema also continued to run his company until his death in 1954. In the early 1950s, he employed eight (five were family members) and had nine vehicles on the street. Dumping increasingly became a problem because of government regulations. In 1948, for example, the Chicago Commissioner of Buildings enjoined the company "AT ONCE" to "discontinue dumping or depositing garbage, refuse, or debris in the Illinois and Michigan Canal adjacent to 3501 South Kedzie Avenue . . . [and] abate nui-

13. Homer J. Wigboldy to the author, e-mail of 10 Oct. 2001; Vandenbosch, *Dutch Communities of Chicago,* 76.

Henry Evenhouse, with wife and children, moving household goods with his team and wagon, Old West Side, ca. 1915 *(Courtesy of Edward Evenhouse)*

sance odors caused by dumping noxious refuse at above location." In anticipation of such restrictions, Iwema and nine association members in 1936 had sought to buy a ninety-three-acre dump at 123rd and Kedzie Avenue for $35,000, with the cash down payment to be raised by selling shares at $500 each. The ambitious project never materialized, however.

When Iwema died in 1954, his sons and later grandsons took over the firm. But in the mid-1970s, the sons sold off the garbage routes to concentrate on the excavating side of the business. One part went to Sam Hamstra of Reliable Scavenger Service. In 1999, Iwema Excavating and Contracting celebrated its one hundredth anniversary. Remarkably, the firm has remained in the Iwema family for more than a century.[14]

Hendrik Evenhuis emigrated to Chicago in 1904 and began driving a team and dump wagon for Gerrit Bossenga, but he soon purchased his own team, operating from his home at 1637 W. 15th Street. His son Henry recalled years later "lying in bed listening to Dad's horses trotting by. He would leave for work at 2:00 a.m. He would drive his horses around through the alley, come around the next corner, and come past our house again. I would hear those horses trotting down the road as Dad was on his way downtown to pick up his load."

Picking up garbage and cinders from the cramped basements of downtown buildings was dirty and backbreaking work, and each day

14. Bonne Iwema came to Chicago from the Netherlands at age twelve in 1890 with his parents, Jan and Antje Iwema, who farmed in Summit all their lives. Sons John B. and Bernard took over the company in 1954. Interviews with son Calvin Iwema, 28 Sept., 25 Oct. 1999; letter, Sam Hamstra, Jr., to author, 13 Feb. 2001.

"Crew" of H. Evenhouse Scavenger in alley
l-r back: boarder "Uncle Fraaijema," a painter;
Hendrik and son John Evenhouse;
l-r front: Cornelia, Henry, Dick Evenhouse; three neighbor boys —
? Beerschmidt, Irv Sachman, and Evert Jensen; Aldrich Evenhouse
(Courtesy of Edward Evenhouse)

ended with the long trip to the dump at Blue Island Avenue and 18th Street. Hendrik tried to smooth the ride by straddling the streetcar tracks. Especially in the bitter winter cold and snow, he experienced a moral struggle to resist the "Devil's temptation" and join many of his fellows in one of the taverns lining the route. In less inclement weather, drivers enjoyed catching up on sleep on the way to the dump and back; their horses knew the way, even to the point of stopping for stop signs and obeying traffic lights.[15]

A turning point for Evenhuis came in 1912, when he developed an infection in his hip and could hardly walk. He was on the verge of selling his route when George Speelman, a fellow church member and scavenger, came over and said: "Don't sell your horses, and don't sell your route! Let me give you some of my work, so you can enlarge your business and hire a man to run it for you." Hendrik accepted this benevolent offer and hired

15. Barbara Geertsema Lee, "Gold in the Family Treasury: Hendrik and Martje Evenhouse — A Family Portrait" (Chicago, 1989), 19-page typescript, courtesy of grandson Edward Evenhouse; video interview, Dick Brouwer, 25 Mar. 1998, by Martin Stulp.

John Roeters to drive his wagon. In this way Evenhuis could feed his family of seven, and within a year he was miraculously healed and could take up the work again. Soon after, Hendrik bought for the family a brick two-flat at 2031 Washburne Avenue; they lived upstairs and rented the first floor to fellow Hollanders.

The recovery of his health strengthened Evenhuis's already strong Christian faith, and it also taught him the magic of expanding his business. For customer relations, Hendrik gave customers colorful ink blotters, faced with the image of a six-inch ruler above the slogan, "A GOOD RULE If your premises need a Cleaning." "Our wagons are in your immediate vicinity at all times." This entrepreneurial spirit was a far cry from the socialist thinking that Hendrik as a young farm hand had imbibed from his minister in the Reformed *(Hervormde)* Church in Groningen. However, his fiancee, Martje Blaauw, was a devout member of the Christian Seceded *(Afscheiding)* Church, and she refused to marry Hendrik unless he was willing to attend church with her and be catechized by her minister, the Reverend G. Geerds of Appingedam. Evenhuis reluctantly agreed, and soon the minister convinced him of the personal nature of salvation and the Reformed teaching of the "individual priesthood of every believer." Geerds convinced Evenhuis that Reformed Christianity was incompatible with the collectivist and materialist ethic of socialism.

"Good Rule" business card, H. Evenhuis & Son Scavengers
2031 Washburne Ave., ca. 1923

(Courtesy of Edward Evenhouse)

Nevertheless, in Chicago Evenhuis joined the Teamsters union and paid union wages to all employees, believing it his Christian duty to be a leavening influence in the rough union world and to help workers earn a fair wage by acting cooperatively. Indeed, according to son Henry, every three months when the union agent, Dan Tognotti, came to the Evenhuis house to collect the dues, his mother Martje would warn Dan about "the dangers of the work, and the need to be protective and concern himself about his way of life. Later he did get shot [to death] by one of the union men."

Evenhuis's pro-union stance reflected his earlier socialist sympathies and stood in marked contrast to his fellow Dutch Reformed owner operators, many of whom opposed secular unions on both ideological and religious grounds. Some owners had to pay a stiff price. In 1927, after Dago Dan and his union goons threatened Peter Ter Maat for refusing to sign up, he declared defiantly, "I'm bomb proof, fire proof, and shot proof." A short time later, two men pulled Ter Maat out of the cab of his truck at the dump at 31st and Cicero Avenue and backed his loaded vehicle into the abyss of the pit. It is still there. Union thugs had struck Peter Huiner some years earlier, or so the story goes; they set fire to the horse barn behind his home in the 1600 block of West 14th Street, killing his team and destroying his dump wagon.[16]

Hendrick Evenhuis received support for his unionism from, of all people, his pastor at the First Christian Reformed Church, Dr. John Van Lonkhuyzen. The Netherlands-born pastor was a disciple of the theologian, educator, and political leader Abraham Kuyper, who taught that Christians must be "in the world but not of it." Most Dutch scavengers eventually followed Evenhuis into the teamsters' union; but intimidation rather than principle impelled them. The Christian Reformed churches of Chicago, however, only begrudgingly tolerated this decision, and in 1912 their regional assembly, Classis Illinois, barred all union members from holding church offices.[17]

In 1924 Evenhuis sold his horses and purchased the first truck, a double-axle Hendrickson. On the doors of the cab he proudly painted the words, "H. Evenhouse Motor Service Phone Canal 5715." The Anglicized name Evenhouse signals that with the second generation on board, and

16. Dirk Brouwer, video interview by Martin Stulp, 26 Mar. 1998; phone conversation with the author, 7 Mar. 2002. Some recall that it was the barn and team of Ter Maat and not Huiner that was torched.

17. "Classis of Illinois," *Banner,* 18 Apr. 1912.

Specialized truck, H. Evenhouse Motor Service, ca. 1925 1924 Hendrickson 6-4-4 double-axle, 6-wheel quadri-drive w/suspension 4-wheel drive, 4-wheel brakes *(Courtesy of Edward Evenhouse)*

the switch from horses to trucks, it was time for the business image to be Americanized.

Hendrik's sons John, Richard (Dick), and then Aldrich (Al) joined the firm after they finished their schooling. When John joined his father around 1923, the name of the company briefly became H. Evenhuis & Son. Dick had business savvy and entrepreneurial skills; he took over as the manager in the early 1930s. Al had a head for figures and was the bookkeeper for a time, although George Stob held this post for many decades until Dick Evenhouse set him up with his own business, Rex Disposal, in partnership with brother John. All worked out of the business office in a bedroom off the back of the family home on Washburne Avenue. In 1932 Hendrik retired and moved with his family to a farm in Oak Lawn. He died in 1938.

Under son Dick Evenhouse, change came fast and furiously. He had an eye for expansion and soon added more trucks so he could synchronize the stops into more dense and profitable routes. In 1932 the firm had three trucks on the street, and Dick formed a new branch, Garden City Cinder Bureau. A company photo a few years later shows a line of five dump trucks, some single-axle and some double-axle, all with hard tires. In the 1930s Dick also formed C&S Disposal in order to consolidate routes in Cicero and Berwyn. This linking of Dick Evenhouse and Tom Huizenga brought together the "two big ones," the dynamic duo of hard-driving and astute entrepreneurs who led the garbage industry in Chicago.[18]

Dick Evenhouse also founded Arc Disposal, which was based in

18. Typed transcript, interview with Jay Bulthuis by Mark Volkers, 18 June 1989, p. 2, courtesy of Peter H. Huizenga.

Rosemont and serviced the northwest suburbs. Dick took in his nephew Ed De Boer as a 50/50 partner; Dick provided financial capital and Ed ran the firm. Evenhouse made similar arrangements with Ed's two brothers, Rich and Jim, who established Active Disposal in Evanston. Evenhouse continued to direct Garden City Disposal (the new name of Garden City Cinder) until his son-in-law, William Buiten, took over in the mid-1950s. About that time, Dick and his brother Al split the business, with Al forming City Disposal, which son Edward eventually took over. All these companies were merged into Waste Management in the early 1970s.

Hendrik Evenhouse's son-in-law, John Geertsema, a Dutch immigrant to Chicago in 1930, also got into the business, first as a driver for Shelte Jaarda and then for Henry Meyer. Geertsema married Cornelia Evenhouse in 1937 and, after a honeymoon in the Netherlands, his father-in-law set him up in the scavenger business just a month before he died. John bought two Ford trucks in 1938, a four-wheeler and a

Truck fleet, H. Evenhouse & Son Motor Service, ca. 1925
corner Wood St. at 14th Place
l-r: truck 1 Hendrickson – Ben Renkema, Joe Luchtenberg
truck 2 Mack – Kees Bos and John Brondsema (both waving)
truck 3 Mack – Dick Evenhouse, Hendrik Evenhouse
Joe Luchtenberg's brother (on truck), Joe Sharon (behind truck)
truck 4 Hendrickson – Peter Wiltjer, Menno Rudenga (with vest)
truck 5 Hendrickson – unidentified immigrant,
Max Helmus (on truck), Menno Rudenga's son
(Courtesy of Edward Evenhouse)

six-wheeler, and hired a driver for the second rig. He and Cornelia moved into the old family homestead at 2031 Washburne Avenue, and the business prospered. In 1946 the Geertsema family followed the rest of the West Side Dutch to Cicero, but in the early 1950s John sold his business and took up his first love of farming, buying a place owned by his uncle Dick Evenhouse in McBain, Michigan.[19]

John Van Kampen established a refuse business shortly after 1900, and his descendants have carried on for four generations until the present day. The Van Kampen family lived on Roosevelt Road near Damen Avenue and also attended the First Christian Reformed Church, as did many other pioneer scavengers. The Van Kampens were innovators; John was one of the first to switch from horses to trucks when he purchased a 1917 Nelson-LeMoon refuse truck for his route. Later, in the 1950s, his son bought the second rear-loading Leach compactor sold in Chicago. In the 1970s his grandson, John P. Van Kampen, operated two companies – South Chicago Disposal and Rapid Disposal – and John P.'s son started working in the family business.[20]

Edward Van Der Molen arrived in Chicago from Middelstum, Groningen, in 1913 and quickly found work driving a trash wagon for $3 per twelve-hour day. "There were no vacations or fringe benefits," Van Der Molen recalled, "just plain hard work." But he prospered. In 1915 he married Elizabeth Veldman (whose brother Clarence later had a garbage business), bought a modest home on Hastings Street, and went into business for himself, hauling manure and refuse with a team purchased from his brother Cornelius who had emigrated earlier. "I started with just a few customers around Milwaukee and Grand Avenues in Chicago but was happy to be my own boss and run my own business. . . . I had to work very hard and there were problems. I was the only one who knew the route. There was no one to take my place and so I could not take a day off, even for illness." The solution was to expand and hire help. Van Der Molen soon had three wagons and seven horses on the street. The animals were bedded down in his large, recently purchased barn behind an equally impressive three-flat at 1412 S. Ashland Avenue, which stood in the shadow of the Ashland Ave-

19. Barbara Lee, "Early History of the Geertsema Family," typescript, courtesy of Edward Evenhouse.

20. Eugene L. Pollock, "Chicago companies continue family's 75-year refuse business tradition," *Refuse Removal Journal,* 22 (Aug. 1979): 46, 48, 50, 82. Scavenger Edward Kiemel proudly displayed his Nelson-LeMoon garbage truck in the program of the Excelsior Band in 1930.

nue (First) Christian Reformed Church. This confirmed the Dutch saying: "Thrift and ambition will build houses like castles."[21]

In 1925 Van Der Molen moved to the upscale suburb of Cicero and got rid of the horses in favor of a truck. To cover the huge capital outlay of nearly $4,000, he kept the truck going day and night by running two shifts. In the prosperous World War Two years, he added more trucks, incorporated in 1947 as Van Der Molen Disposal Company, and began signing exclusive contracts with suburban governments for all residential trash collection. Other haulers concentrated on the more lucrative (they thought) commercial work and did not even want residential accounts. Edward Van Der Molen proved then wrong and revolutionized home refuse service in the Chicago area.

In 1948 Van Der Molen developed his own dump site, and the next year he built his own incinerator in the Proviso Yards of the Chicago and Northwestern Railway Company between Wolf and Mannheim Roads. Van Der Molen Disposal was the first family-owned waste incinerator in the nation. The steam generated by burning the refuse collected from the eighty thousand suburban homes by Van Der Molen's forty trucks powered the railway diesel shops and buildings in the yards.[22]

By 1970 Van Der Molen Bros. Disposal, under the direction of Edward's youngest son Everett, assisted by his brother George, ran more than a hundred trucks with 250 employees, serving the western suburbs of La Grange, Elmhurst, Melrose Park, and Franklin Park, among others. In the succeeding three years, Everett convinced his brothers Harold and Bernard, both with sizeable scavenger businesses of their own, to consolidate their companies under his direction and merge them into Browning Ferris Industries (BFI) of Houston, Texas, a solid waste conglomerate.[23]

John Vandervelde, Sr., began refuse collection in 1911 at age fourteen, helping his widowed mother run a firm with five wagons and thirteen horses. An innovator, Vandervelde was one of the first to hire his own geologist and buy his own landfill.[24]

21. "Memoirs of Edward Van Der Molen" (ca. 1970), courtesy of Everett Van Der Molen.

22. "Single Private Hauler Builds Own Incinerator," *Refuse Removal Journal* 1 (Dec. 1958): 6-7, 28; 2 (Jan. 1959): 32; "Railroad, Refuse Hauler Cooperate on Disposal," ibid., 2 (May 1959): 8, 29.

23. *Van Der Molen Disposal Company: Pioneers in Modern Disposal Methods for Commerce-Industry-Municipalities,* promotional brochure (ca. 1970), courtesy of Everett Van Der Molen. Edward Van Der Molen died in 1976 at age 83.

24. John J. Vandervelde, Sr., obituary, *Refuse Removal Journal* 19 (May 1976): 187.

Van Der Molen Bros. trucks
Village of La Grange city building, 1952
l-r: Everett, George, Harold, Edward Van Der Molen
(Courtesy of Everett Van Der Molen)

Sam Hoving started collecting ashes and rubbish with his team in 1914. He began with eight accounts on the North Side and expanded rapidly, specializing after 1927 in removing demolition rubble created by the building boom in Chicago. Hoving bought six Sterling dump trucks for the work and gave up the horses. Son Abe joined his father in 1939 and son Dick in 1946, and the firm became Sam Hoving & Sons. Efficiency of operations was their hallmark, and in 1958 the firm introduced the "Huge Haul" detachable containers with forty-yard capacities.[25]

John Bakker came to Chicago as a single young man just before World War I, leaving his job as a farm laborer for the garbage wagons of his uncle Jake Ter Maat in Chicago. Ter Maat sponsored him and then his brothers and parents. After the war, Bakker bought his own route and built it up into three routes when his two brothers joined him. They mainly serviced the south Loop area. His father also helped out on the truck. Bakker's first truck was a 1928 Hendrikson six-wheeler with solid tires. The truck garage was next to their home at 1623 W. 14th Place. During the Depression years, the firm survived by picking up garbage in the morning and in the afternoon hauling limestone slabs for the Lake Michigan breakwater, under the Works Progress Administration (WPA) public works program.

All these families were bound by blood and religion. They intermar-

25. "Heavy Industry Served by Big Container Idea," ibid., 4 (June 1962): 12, 14-15.

ried and worshiped in the same congregations and then passed the businesses on to their sons, in-laws, and grandsons. Hauling cinders and garbage made for a good, if toilsome, living. It brought steady work, respectable incomes, financial security in retirement, and money for widows and children. "They had worked their way solidly into America's middle class without special favor, fancy education, or exceptional intelligence. Bookkeepers, not accountants, kept their books; everything they borrowed from the bank they signed for themselves. They learned to be good citizens and neighbors. They lived in big bungalows and had few pretensions. They fit in well with Chicago."[26]

The Association

In the late 1920s, the Dutch scavengers formed an association to regulate the business and limit competition – the West Side Garbage Association. This evolved in 1933 into the Chicago Cinder and Scavenger Truck Owners Association, which in 1941 became the Chicago and West Suburban Ash and Scavenger Association. In 1959 the name was modernized to Chicago and Suburban Refuse Disposal Association. Critics aptly called it the "Dutch Mafia"; members referred to it simply as "The Association."

Sixty members strong in 1932 and more than 90 percent Dutch, the Association was in essence an informal "restraint of trade." Members agreed not to compete with each other and traded accounts to concentrate their routes for greater efficiency. This enabled them to lower their prices and still make a good profit. The arrangement helped the Dutch scavengers survive the hard times of the Depression era. In 1935 the members' gross revenue exceeded $5 million.

New Deal price controls caused the scavengers further difficulties. In 1942, President Franklin Roosevelt's new Office of Price Administration (OPA) was given the authority to approve price increases for services. Tom Huizenga fell afoul of the OPA when he raised refuse hauling rates sharply, even doubling some. A disgruntled customer filed a formal complaint with the OPA, and the bureaucrats informed Tom that he must get permission both from the customers and the OPA for any increase in rates. When Tom filed the necessary forms, the OPA disallowed the increases. He had become their "Public Enemy Number 1." The OPA subpoenaed Huizenga to appear before its board several times, and two agents

26. Jacobson, *Waste Management*, 53.

combed through his financial records for several days. They found enough cases of "illegal" (i.e., unauthorized) price increases to run up fines of more than $120,000, but Tom was able to stall the investigation for months until the war ended. The OPA office closed without the government collecting a penny![27]

Administratively, the Central Scavenger Association had a South Side division, a North Side division, and, by 1943, a Far West division and a Downtown division. The main office was at 840 N. Michigan Avenue. It also sent three representatives to sit on the board of the Rush Street Association, whose member firms serviced the restaurants and nightclubs on the famous northside strip. In 1941, twenty-two members, or 42 percent, of the Rush Street Association also belonged to the Chicago and Suburban Ash and Scavenger Association. Both groups had fifty to fifty-five members, and they honored each other's accounts and members. These associations, which fully cooperated with one another and had interlinking memberships, came to play an increasingly important role for the Dutch garbage men in the next decades.

Bonne Iwema was elected president of the Chicago Cinder and Scavenger Truck Owners Association in 1932, and he was reelected every two years by acclamation until 1944, when the body, in something of a tiff, elected Siert (Sam) Huizenga to replace him. After a brief interlude, the men smoothed things over by electing Iwema vice president.

In March 1932, in the throes of the Great Depression, Iwema gave voice to the uncertainty of the times in a speech at a North Side Association meeting, which he had penciled on the back of a membership dues list. "We feel the foundations shaking upon which we are standing," he noted, due to the farm crisis and bank failures. Scavengers were also being tested, but by organizing, he asserted, we "came out by the skin of our teeth." More cooperation and greater efficiency was needed, however.

> The tremendous rivalry in which our business has been subjected by those engaged in it should be and is being changed to more cooperation and it should be our aim to work more for a high standard of social and cooperative efficiency. The problems that confront us in our Ass[ociation] are, first I should say, removal of all distrust, suspicion. If we remove them we have a mountain of rubbish off the road. We should shake off all rules and laws which impede our going smoothly

27. Ted Hoekstra, "Memoirs, 1927-1957." Hoekstra was Tom's manager and close friend.

> [and] have no more than we must have. . . . But standpatters of individual rights are left standing alone dumbfounded by the problems confronting them. . . . We must thrash out our own problems as best we can. Many are bewildered in their intricacy, require legal guidance, political backing, organized labor approval, friendly cooperation with associations of like aims as ours is.

After making his best case for collusion in the interests of efficiency, rather than unfettered competition, Iwema laid out the road ahead.

> Our organization is to many who joined a direct appeal to their selfish instinct and for that reason does not have the sympathy of the best minds. . . . [But] we cannot stand in helpless confusion of mind and leave all the forces combine against us without raising a protest. We cannot raise our voice alone like a jackal in the woods; what good will it do. . . . We cannot adjust our old arguments and the same conclusions to the new state of things around us; we have to attack it different[ly].

Iwema's challenge was to overcome the moral objections to participating in a "muscle" organization by men who were committed Christians and leaders in their churches. He noted they were in a "competitive line of business, and meeting constantly with a perverse humanity," and yet they must try to act in a "Christian manner."[28]

Iwema also had to contend with organized labor and the moral objections of members to participating in it. But to get along in the labor-friendly era of Roosevelt's New Deal required making peace with the Teamsters union. So in 1933 the Association signed a closed-shop labor agreement with the International Brotherhood of Teamsters, Local 731. The wage scale for truck drivers was set at $8 per nine-hour day, for helpers $6.50, and for tractor operators $9.50, with payday every Saturday. Dues were $3 per month. In 1941 the union wage scale was boosted 50 cents a day for all three categories, but the Association held firm on the nine-hour day.

Iwema reported that in the prior year he had attended over eighty-six special meetings, besides twenty-four regular board meetings. Some meetings looked at the growing problem of delinquent dues; forty-eight

28. Chicago and Suburban Ash and Scavenger Association Minutes (hereafter Scavenger Association Minutes), 28 Dec. 1939, Bonne Iwema Papers, donated by son Calvin Iwema to the Archives, Calvin College.

of the sixty members in 1933 were delinquent, including Acme Cinder & Garbage for $52.50. Dues were $2.50 per truck per month, payable quarterly, but each member cast one vote, regardless of size. The largest operators — H. Evenhouse & Son, De Boer Bros., Bernard Huiner, and Shelte Jaarda — paid on three trucks. Members absent from scheduled meetings without notification were subject to fines of $1, which could eventually lead to expulsion and loss of privileges. Acme Cinder, for example, was expelled in 1935 for unpaid dues. But schedule conflicts because of Christian school board or consistory meetings were readily excused. Even free beer and sandwiches at the meetings did not ensure a full turnout. By 1941 the Association had declined to "the Noble 52" — the remnant of hardcore members who stuck it out through the Depression.

In truth, the Association operated like a church consistory, with regular meetings and detailed minutes, election of officers, disciplinary committees, brotherly admonitions, annual dinners and picnics, and the discussion of common interests. The atmosphere of the Association meetings was quite different, however. "Many of our members are humorists," the long-time secretary Edward Groenboom reported. "They like to laugh. They enjoy a good story, a snappy comeback. All of which enlivens the meeting." Of course, he added, "a glass of beer helped to promote the era of good feeling."

Iwema's presidential addresses clearly copied the style and tone of the sermons he heard each week. For example, he warned members about their sometimes unscrupulous actions against their fellows. "There are certain principles I hold as right that I want to live by. I don't want to lose my manhood in compromising to become a limp rag in time." Iwema's rhetorical skills were remarkable, given his minimal education; clearly he was an able leader.

In 1935 Iwema threatened to step down as president at the end of his term, on the grounds that it was too difficult to collect dues of members with Rush Street accounts. The body named a committee to contact the delinquents and then promptly re-elected him. He accepted, but admonished the men to "work for harmony . . . because it concerns your head and butt. . . . What would happen to our business if we had no gentlemen's agreement? We bind ourselves not to undercut. We must oppose our opponents together; we could never do this alone. Let us go on for another year."

Iwema was re-elected president and treasurer term after term for twelve years, until 1944, and he continued to urge the men to work together. "Don't fight each other," was his constant theme. "A gentlemen's agreement is a moral obligation. And we all know a moral obligation is much more binding than a legal obligation can possibly be." Iwema repeated this theme of fighting fair in a forty-one-line verse that he composed and recited at a monthly meeting:

> Our boys know all the shady tricks.
> The talk that's straight, from unctuous intermix.
> Deceit is openly laid out and bared.
> Blame then fits as near to fair and square.
> Let's keep on calling straight and pure, upright,
> Openly denounce crookedness a blight.[29]

Lost jobs and conflicts over stops were the nemesis of the industry and the topic of nearly every meeting. Conflicts between members were especially troublesome, because they divided the brotherhood. They had to be dealt with forthrightly. A typical dispute in 1931 involved Peter Ter Maat and Wolter Lindemulder. Apparently Ter Maat secured a new stop at the 305 S. Wabash Avenue building that had been vacant for several months but previously belonged to Lindemulder. Ter Maat was ordered to give it back but refused at first, claiming that another member, Dick Evenhouse, had taken work away from him at the Wrigley Building. But Evenhouse proved from his account books that Ter Maat was misinformed about the Wrigley Building. "After a lot of talking back and forth," Ter Maat was told that "for the present he is out of luck," and the decision was "final and not subject to change." Clearly, the Association was "judge, jury, and executioner."[30]

Members also routinely reported accounts lost to "outside competitors," and the board kept a list, making sure that no brother serviced them for at least the next six months. The governing regulation was "once your building, always your building – once your site, always your site." Haulers were given the first option to recover their lost accounts, and the Association backed their claim for up to two years (six months on the West Side only), provided that they were not more than six months in arrears on dues. For example, Pete Huizenga was not allowed a hearing in a

29. Latter quote is in Scavenger Association Minutes, 26 Jan. 1939.

30. Undated handwritten statement on back of 1931 license notice from the Chicago City Collector's Office; Scavenger Association Minutes, 25 Apr. 1935. Conversations with John Evenhouse, son of Aldrich and a tax accountant for many of the Association member firms, was especially helpful in tutoring me in the intricacies of the organization and its operations.

dispute with Ben Top in 1938 because of such an arrearage. Another Association rule stated that any member wishing to sell his business must give first choice to fellow members. Shelte Jaarda did this in 1941 when he sold out to Andrew Bosman.[31]

Protecting the Association members' stops from outsiders was especially crucial and led to an enormously expensive court battle (costing up to $10,000) in 1935. Denny Finn, a politically well-connected Irish American who owned a large excavating business, horned in on the scavenger business to survive the Depression because building projects had dried up. Finn's Scavenger Service Company took away many lucrative stops from Association members on Rush Street, South Shore Drive, and the Hyde Park area. Soon Finn's company had become one of the largest in the city, at the expense of the Hollanders, especially Tom Huizenga's companies, who cut prices to no avail. Finn refused to join the Association or live by its rules, and he challenged anyone to compete with him. He also flaunted the Scavengers Union Local 731 and had his drivers join a nearly defunct Teamsters Union Local 705, which he could control.

When Finn ran into stiff resistance from the Association, as could be expected, he charged it with conspiracy, but Judge Holly dismissed the case "for want of merit." However, a year later Finn won his case on appeal and the Association had to make a cash settlement. Finn's transparent blackmail had paid off. He also was behind the formation of a rival American Scavenger Association, whose name indicated that this was a move against the "Dutch Mafia." Interestingly, six years later, in 1941, Finn and two other Irish "outsiders," Emmet Flood and Frank Mahoney, asked to join the Rush Street Association, but the body split fifty-fifty and decided that "under the present attitude our association cannot take them in." Resentment over Finn's lawsuit in 1935 still rankled. In the end, Finn's company was sold to an Association Dutchman, Herman Mulder, who the *Chicago Tribune* dubbed the "King of Garbage." Mulder turned heads and made tongues wag in the Dutch community when he went out and bought five new Cadillac automobiles for himself and other family members.[32]

Ethnoreligious differences lay behind this fight, to some extent. The Dutch scavengers, and their Swedish and Norwegian Protestant associates, lived by a different set of values than the Catholic Irish. The Irish came up

31. Scavenger Association Minutes, 8 Dec. 1938; 24 Apr. 1941; 11 Nov. 1943.

32. Ibid., 10, 24 Jan., 23 May, 28 June, 22 Aug. 1935; 20 Feb., 19 Nov., 15 Oct. 1936; 27 Feb., 12 June 1941. The comments about Mulder are from a phone interview with Peter Huizenga, 9 Feb. 2000. See also Ted Hoekstra, "Memoirs, 1927-1957." Tragically, Mulder died a broken man from alcohol addiction.

through the ranks as employees and, at least in the eyes of the Dutch, wanted to make a quick buck by creating legal troubles, thus capitalizing on their political connections in city government and the courts. For the northern Europeans, hauling seemed to be in their blood, and their fabled work ethic set them on a steady course of providing a dependable service.

During the Second World War, the patriotic scavengers of Chicago hung cloth signs on their trucks reading "Save Tin Cans," compliments of the Coca Cola Company. They would do their part for the national war effort but not work on Sunday. In this, they obeyed their church leaders rather than federal officials, who urged seven-day workweeks for the duration. In a similar vein, the Association secretary, Edward Groenboom, appended the following editorial comment to the minutes of March 25, 1943. It is a paean of praise that concludes with a preacher's benediction:

> The other day, I saw one of the Noble 52, a member of our association, in action. He drove his truck, steering it like a man, like his ancestors used to drive spirited horses long ago. The look on his face was that of a contented person satisfied and happy despite priorities and gas reductions.
>
> He adores his wife, loves his children, builds for the future. He is engaged in helping to keep clean the second largest city in the Republic known as the "last best hope of earth." I could not help but trust that he will always remain encouraged with the contribution he makes to progress and civilization. May his hands never falter, never fail. May this picture fit all our members, inviting them to go their way rejoicing.[33]

The annual banquets for owners and their wives were held in the Dania Hall or Verwaerts Turner Hall on the West Side. A professional photographer took the traditional group photo of the owners as a memento of the occasion. Besides the banquet, the Association staged an annual picnic at National Grove in Riverside for all members, drivers, helpers, and their families. Helen Vander Ploeg, whose father John Groenewold drove for Charles Boersma, recalls that many families without cars rode on benches set up in the bed of the dump trucks, which were cleaned thoroughly and festooned with flags and banners for the festive proces-

33. Scavenger Association Minutes, 25 Mar. 1943; B. Essenburg, "West Chicago News," *Banner,* 27 June 1941. Unfortunately, not all Dutch-American scavengers were as patriotic; several were thought to be keeping a second set of books for unreported income to avoid federal taxes.

sion to the grove twenty miles away on Des Plaines Avenue at 29th Street. The picnic was free to all and much appreciated by the families, especially in the Depression years.[34]

The highlight of the picnic was the tug of war between laborers and "capitalists," in which the latter were "outfooted, outpulled," reported the Association's minutes. "Here rugged individualism did not avail against the united effort and united front of Union Labor. But – and this is the fine feature of it – after the contest labor and capitalist met, they shook hands, and peace and harmony prevailed while both sides pledged each other's health and happiness in foaming steins of cold beer." Beer was "to them as to their forefathers a drink for real men." These social activities ran from about 1932 to 1946.[35]

Interestingly, in 1938 member Jacob Molter recommended that the Association "cut out beer" at their meetings because "no coaxing or other foolishness must be employed to get members to meetings." The group would not hear of it; the minutes of that meeting conclude: "A glass of beer refreshed the members present. It is a drink for real men." Some members refused to attend because of the beer and the gambling after the meetings. An owner reportedly bet one of his routes on the dice, and won! The secretary reported for the first time in 1941 that "some preferred coffee." By that time problems of alcoholism were rampant among the Dutch scavengers, despite the adage to drink "in moderation."[36]

It was a former Chicago truck operator and recovering alcoholic, Barney Swierenga, who in 1963 began a shelter in Phoenix, Arizona, for suffering alcoholics. In six years the shelter had evolved into the Calvary Rehab Center. "Truckers have always been portrayed as hard workers, hard drinkers, and hard fighters," Swierenga noted. "I didn't do anything to change that image." Barney was a prototype of the self-made man, a survivor in what he called a "tough world for tough men." Some Chicago garbage haulers sought rehabilitation at Calvary Rehab.[37]

34. Interview with Helen (Mrs. John) Vander Ploeg nee Groenewold, 14 Nov. 1999, Holland, Michigan.

35. Interviews with Calvin Iwema, 28 Sept., 25 Oct. 1999; Scavenger Association Minutes, 16 July 1936; 24 Mar. 1938.

36. Ibid., 28 Apr., 28 July 1938; 23 Jan. 1941. For confirmation of drinking problems among the Dutch Reformed teamsters in Chicago, see the memoirs of Bess Figel, who "names names" (*Once Upon a Time,* 7).

37. Quotes in Dale L. Plumb, "Founder of Calvary Rehab," *Banner,* 10 Sept. 1976; Fred H. Baker, Sr., "The Church and Alcohol," ibid. Calvary Rehab Center was recently sold to a Roman Catholic health company.

From Labor-Intensive to Capital-Intensive Methods

In the 1920s, trucks slowly replaced horses and wagons in the scavenger business, although wagons were better suited to navigating the narrow alleys and sharp turns in the Loop. Peter Molter was the first member of the Association to change from a horse-drawn wagon to a motor truck. Buying the first Old Reliable or Mack chain-driven truck could be traumatic. Harm Huizenga is reported to have said to his son Tom, "When I can't do it with a wagon anymore, then I'll quit." But he let the younger generation talk him into buying an Old Reliable anyway. "It looked every inch the motorized wagon it was," Timothy Jacobson noted in his book on Waste Management, "box cab all at right angles, lantern-like headlamps, running boards, spoke wheels with hard rubber rims. The 'box' tilted back hydraulically (an innovation) but it still had to be filled by hand." Bonne Iwema thought the chain drive mechanism was too dangerous for his drivers and bought only trucks with drive shafts, such as the Swiss-made Saurer and the International.

In running the routes, drivers had to maneuver their cumbersome vehicles on busy streets and crowded alleys with care (only taxicabs and cars parked illegally in alleys were fair game) and keep the customers happy with the service. Good will, after all, was their primary asset. They also needed street smarts to deal with cops seeking a little graft. "Everyone had his hand out in those days – that's the way the world was – and every driver knew it was wise to have some money in his pocket," writes Jacobson, quoting an anonymous scavenger: "Stuff was always flying off those trucks, and they [the police] were always hauling us over, looking for a couple of bucks."[38]

Drivers also had to observe the speed limit of 10 mph for their solid-tired vehicles; in 1935 the city banned them because they destroyed the roads. Owners rewarded accident-free drivers with annual cash bonuses of $100. No wonder the custom on Saturday afternoons was to finish the work week by buying a bucket or two of beer from the corner pub and gathering for conversation and perusal of the Sunday paper while sitting on apple barrels. The Sunday paper was read on Saturday out of religious scruples.

The refuse industry changed drastically in the 1950s from a labor-intensive to a capital-intensive business. Workers were less willing to wrestle steel 55-gallon "carry-cans" filled with furnace ashes or garbage from

38. Jacobson, *Waste Management,* 70; Scavenger Association Minutes, 14 Dec. 1940.

sub-basement boiler rooms through narrow passageways and up steep staircases, hoist the cans to the truck tailgate, climb up, and finally lift them chest high and dump the contents over the top of the sidewalls into the hopper. Some trucks had ladders that allowed the men to climb up with cans on their backs, flip the ladders up to the sidewalls, and climb to the top to dump the cans. Overloaded drums of refuse or ashes could weigh 150 pounds or more, and they were proven "man-cripplers," amputating fingers and toes when dropped accidentally.

To pack more into each truckload, the men broke down boxes and crates, smashed glass bottles, and compacted the hopper load with their boots. "Walking it in," Jacobson noted, "was the name they gave to the ritual of filling the load evenly and tightly. A fellow's fitness was measured by two things: how much he could carry, and how hard he could stomp." With such traditional methods, sanitation workers had an accident rate nine times the U.S. industrial average.[39]

Beginning in the 1950s, manufacturers responded to the needs of garbage haulers by designing specialized equipment. Harold Van Der Molen conceived the concept of a one-yard steel container that would fit into hooks mounted on the rear of an enclosed collection truck that contained a packer blade. A chain attached to the packer blade hooked on the container. When the blade was activated and moved forward, it pulled the container up and unloaded the contents into the truck hopper. Since the Van Der Molen maintenance shop was unable to manufacture the containers and accessory devices in quantity and with quality, in 1954 they convinced the Leach Corporation of Oshkosh, Wisconsin, who manufactured garbage truck bodies, to also make the containers. This simple waste storage and dumping device revolutionized the waste hauling business. Residential scavengers got the next big break, when the Erlinder Company of Chicago designed an elevator lift platform, which was mounted on the rear of a truck, on which a worker could raise himself and steel drums or his "carry can" to the top of the sidewalls. Workers considered the containers and lifts gifts from heaven, but they might be a mixed blessing if bosses piled on more stops. For large quantities of industrial and construction waste, the Dempster Brothers of Knoxville, Tennessee, subsequently invented the "Dempster Dumpster," an eight- or

39. Jacobson, *Waste Management,* 70; "Overweight 55-Gallon Drum Amputates Fingers and Toes," *Refuse Removal Journal* 8 (June 1965): 24; "Accident Rate Highest for Trash Workers," ibid. (Aug. 1965): 26, 28, 56; John Vandervelde, Jr., "Disabling Injury Rate 900% Greater Than U.S. Average," ibid., 12 (Sept. 1969): 89.

Leach Company's 1-yard mobile container, developed with Harold Van Der Molen, to automate its Packmaster compacters, early 1950s

ten-yard steel container that could be hoisted aloft by hydraulic mechanical arms and skidded onto a truck bed for transport to the dump.[40]

Equipment manufacturers, such as Leach, Heil, Pak-Mor, Borg-Warner, and E-Z Pack, plied private scavengers with ever more efficient power packing systems to mount on a truck chassis. In addition to fifteen-, twenty-, and thirty-yard "roll-offs" came front-loaders, power packers, stationary compactors, bulk transfer trailers, and smaller diesel truck engines, all of which changed the nature of the business fundamentally. For residential and commercial work, Heil and Leach power packers were designed with an intake bin at the rear of the unit that was low to the ground and easily accessible for tipping large cans upside down, using the lip as a fulcrum point. The twenty-five-yard packer unit allowed the driver to pick up three times as much garbage before heading to the dump to unload and to make three loads a day instead of one.

The power equipment came none too soon, because the city of Chicago in 1970 banned the burning of garbage in coal furnaces of apartment buildings and business, and new natural gas furnaces eliminated the need for janitors to shovel coal and haulers to remove the ash residue. The carry can days had to give way to dumpsters in order to hold the garbage and improve the efficiency of operations. Landfills also had to be made environmentally sound, and incineration was needed to reduce its volume.

In 1954 the problem of shrinking landfill space seemed to be ever more acute, so forty-five member firms of the Chicago and Suburban Ash

40. "Chicago Manufacturer Has Unusual Product [Erlinder]," ibid., 1 (July 1958): 20-21; "From Steam Shovel to Industry, Public Office [Dempster]," ibid. (Sept. 1958): 16-17, 29; "Truck Makers Answer on Special Chassis Inquiry [Leach]," ibid. (Aug. 1958): 18-19; personal recollections of Peter H. Huizenga.

and Scavenger Association took a great risk to form Incinerator, Inc., capitalized at $2 million. This massive project began operations early in 1958 in the village of Stickney, seven miles southwest of downtown Chicago. Conrad Douma, a partner in Ace Scavenger, which firm was the largest investor in the venture, directed the complex operation. The state-of-the-art plant burned up to five hundred tons a day. It gave haulers peace of mind about their dumping problems by fixing the cost, cutting travel distances by 50 percent or more, and reducing the volume of waste by over 90 percent. But new air quality regulations doomed the plant after fifteen years of successful operations, despite a $1 million upgrade in 1973, and it eventually became a transfer station for solid wastes to a huge new landfill in Oak Brook, which proved to be far cheaper than incineration. The bold venture did not reach its full potential, but the Hollanders had shown their mettle by taking the risk.[41]

The Garbios

In the new era, finding capital was a greater challenge than finding help. The new power equipment and "clean" landfills were fearsomely expensive. The entire industry had to be restructured. The cost of a packer or container truck was ten times the cost of its predecessors, ranging from $75,000 to $100,000. The cans that cost $10 now became $300 steel, one-yard containers, and thousands were needed. Ace Scavenger Service in 1966 alone owned fourteen hundred containers. Dumps by law (1964) had to be covered with dirt daily to create sanitary landfills. The method ran up costs 240 percent. Instead of owners driving their own rigs, professional drivers handled the complex machines. A study in 1960 showed that Chicago-area scavengers faced increased costs of more than 450 percent in the last five years alone.[42]

While wages of refuse truck drivers went up faster than other truckers, their working hours to run the routes remained much the same — from before dawn until the afternoon trip to the dump. Pickups might take five or six hours and dumping another one to two hours. The driver's wage scale in 1965 for forty hours was $146, plus welfare and pension bene-

41. Conrad Douma, "Chicago Haulers Make History by Building First Private Incinerator," ibid., 1 (Jan. 1958): 7-8; Jacobson, *Waste Management,* 72-73.

42. "Chicago Costs Up as Much as 456 Per Cent," *Refuse Removal Journal* 3 (May 1960): 8; Harold P. Jensen, "Problems Facing Industry Today," ibid., 6 (Sept. 1964): 46; "Tailors Container Service to Construction Site," ibid., 9 (Aug. 1966): 56-57.

fits, bringing total weekly earnings to $200. The helper's cash wage was about $15 per week less. A union pension, first introduced in 1962, provided $110 per month. William T. De Boer of Roseland, one of the first eight retirees on the union pension in 1964, recalled earning just $9 a week when he began driving.[43]

A Dutch-American scavenger in the 1970s penned the following poignant recollections twenty-five years after leaving the truck:

> There has always been something about this business awfully hard to communicate. . . . My brother . . . and I would head out into Chicago's industrial district at 1 a.m. & navigate a few alleys before hitting the factories. When full, we would arrive at CID [the Waste Management landfill near Lake Calumet] about 4 a.m. in complete darkness, with the utility roads lit only by the spouts of methane gas burning off. I felt I was visiting Dante's hell! . . .
>
> The experience was intensely personal and individual. The long days. The hard work done steadily on the streets & alleys by oneself in all kinds of weather. Rubbing shoulders with men and women for whom one developed a real affection — though they may have been involved in unsavory activities — together with the easy going and genuine camaraderie experienced with the other garbios miles from home; well these things made life awfully sweet. It was hard work but good work, and the joking, pranks, and deeds of manliness I saw kept my attention.
>
> The stories are still out there: the feats of lifting heavy drums. Of steering big trucks with no power steering (. . . [the owner] was too cheap for power steering!). Of Rush Street prostitutes catching rides at 5 a.m. Of staying up all night celebrating New Year's Eve, and then with no sleep getting on the truck and meeting at Rush & Division for breakfast (with girlfriends). Of pulling the trucks over on the Gold Coast to go for a quick swim off Oak Street beach. Of getting acquainted with gay lovers and rough taverns and silver-plated 45 caliber automatic weapons in the ghetto. Of working the Puerto Ricans into the ground, but only for one day, because they worked too fast. Of getting to know the alleys of all the ghettos in the city — and the alleys of the rich neighborhoods as well. Of having your friend jumped by thugs and instead of handing over his wallet, he throws one in the

43. Ibid. 5 (Oct. 1962): 16; "Drivers Get Raise to $3.65 An Hour," ibid. 8 (Nov. 1965): 32; "Refuse Men Now Collect After Retiring," unidentified newspaper clipping, 1964, Chicago newspaper scrapbook of Henry Van Weelden, courtesy of J. C. Huizenga.

back of the truck, starts the blade (with the accompanying roar of the engine) and turns to find his partner in crime hightailing it away, so that the other can scramble out before the blade traps him. Of buying pencils from lonely policemen at 3 a.m. – for $20 per. Of traveling hundreds of miles & more a day all over the city and waving a hundred times to friends on other trucks, or friends opening a side door of a railroad car full of rotten produce in 100°+ weather – and then emptying the rail car by shoveling it [the contents] into the truck.

Of seeing bums stagger from a liquor-haze, and seeing them get beat up by angry store owners. Visiting flophouses at 6 a.m. At 4 a.m., getting chased down fire escapes by Doberman Pinchers – while carrying a 55-gallon drum – in the rain. (That was me.) Of hearing of a friend who finds dead bodies in their containers. Of getting a telephone call at home from the ghetto, after leaving info on the windshield of a car I just hit, and hearing laughter that I would do such a "proper" thing (no damage payments expected!) Of having a community leader & friend shot in his store because he bad-mouthed a drug dealer. Of playing hockey with rats. Feeling rats climb all over you. Of hearing them getting nervous in the trash piles that have to be cleaned up. Of dumping chemicals on the ground and gagging from what made it into the hopper. Of doing this 50 weeks a year, 60+ hours per week, and then being taunted by others, who tell you that you've got it made in the Dutch Mafia. If these are the stories from such a short excursion into this business as I have made, imagine all the others![44]

Picking up trash before the days of mechanical arms and packers was back-breaking work that befitted Dutch Calvinists with their strong work ethic. But the work also made widows. Heavy work required heavy food and drink. The men ate too much lard spread on sandwiches for lunch, and sausages or a roast with potatoes laden with gravy for dinner. And they enjoyed a cold beer or two after bringing the trucks to the garage.

Heart and liver problems plagued the men. The three sons of Harm Huizenga by his first wife died young of heart disease – Sam (Siert) at fifty-five, Tom at forty-four, and Pete at forty-seven. A nephew, Clarence, suffered a mild heart attack in his thirties that prompted him to leave the company. Lawrence (Lawry) Groot, a partner of Huizenga, also died in his

44. Recollections of a Dutch-American on the West Side, who drove a truck for a family member for some time in the 1970s before going to college and entering one of the professions. Letter to author, 19 January 2001. Used by permission.

forties. The Huizenga and Groot men left widows with large families to support and no knowledge of the business. The natural solution was to combine under able sons or sons-in-law, in this case Dean Buntrock, Pete and Betty Huizenga's son-in-law, who had joined the business in 1956 after college. For Tom's widow, Jennie, it was brother-in-law Sam and Jacob L. (Jake) Bilthuis who bought two Ace routes to form Metro Scavenger Service.[45]

In the next decade the individual owners (the Huizengas, Groots, Boers, De Boers, Van Tholens, Van Der Molens, Meyers, and Huiners, among others) began combining their sole proprietorships into corporations, in order better to manage the work, raise capital funds, keep accurate books, and gain legal protection. These were the "renaissance days" for the Dutch scavengers, said Peter Huizenga.

> They had finally emerged from times of horse and wagons, an immigrant society, depression, war years and backbreaking physical work. New truck bodies were being developed with loading devices eliminating the need to carry drums and cans on your back up a ladder, the Interstate expressway system was being built expanding the territory a business could operate and travel. Air transportation made distant communication and travel accessible. New kinds of dumps were being developed in old clay pits, as a business, with engineering and a new name called "landfill." The owners of garbage businesses, who had time on their hands in the 1950s, became sophisticated businessmen in the following decades, with unlimited opportunities and not enough time to seize them all.[46]

By this time, private waste hauling in Chicago had long been a "Dutch treat," except for the Danes on the North Side and Swedes on the South Side, who held on since the early days. In 1962 the 140-member Chicago and Suburban Ash and Scavenger Association represented 90 percent of all scavenger contractors in the Chicago area and controlled 98 percent of the commercial refuse business, valued at $25 million a year. Half the member firms were non-Dutch, but the Dutch had the largest operations. The national trade journal, *Refuse Removal Journal,* described the Chicago Association as "one of the most outstanding contractor's groups in the United States, . . . a model for most private organizations in the trash business."[47]

45. Jacobson, *Waste Management,* 52, 59-60, 65.

46. Huizenga, "Waste Management," 5.

47. "$500,000 Garbage Suit Filed," *Chicago Daily News,* 12 Feb. 1962; *Refuse Removal Journal* 1 (May 1958): 15. In 1963, 200 private refuse firms operated in the six-county region

An added factor in the salad days of the industry was the national trend of privatization of government services, including residential refuse collection, which saved cities millions of dollars and ended frequent labor troubles. By the 1950s the Chicago suburbs could no longer afford to have city crews pick up residential refuse, and they began opening the work to private scavengers. Some let bids and awarded exclusive multiyear contracts (known as the "contract method"), while others simply allowed homeowners to make their own arrangements. Either system provided the private scavengers with tremendous growth opportunities in the burgeoning suburbs, and the Dutch contractors scrambled to take advantage of it. Within a decade, by 1963, "privates" picked up 40 percent of the refuse in the suburbs, and the number of routes was increasing. John Vanderveld Jr.'s Barrington Trucking Company, for example, won the Palatine and Waukegan accounts in 1958.[48] The downside to municipal contracts, however, was that they inevitably tangled the haulers in local politics.

Chicago's "Garbage War"

The "pot of gold" also lured the Chicago Italian mob to try to muscle in on the waste business, as their counterparts had already done in New York and other eastern cities. The mob already controlled the lucrative business of supplying restaurants with clean linens, and it was a short step to add garbage pickups.

In 1960, syndicate leader William Daddano, alias "Willie Potatoes," formed West Suburban Scavenger Service to take over the multimillion-dollar, private refuse business in Chicago. Using threats, intimidation, and strong-arm tactics, Daddano and his operatives in the first three months took more than one hundred stops away from members of the Chicago and Suburban Refuse Haulers Association. Willie Daddano Jr.'s father-in-law, Rudolph Guy Fratto, seized sixty lucrative accounts on Rush Street, Chicago's nightclub district, and proclaimed himself the "Garbage

---

around Chicago and another 400 firms operated within the city, alongside 390 city-owned disposal trucks, ibid., 6 (June 1963): 6; "Group Leads Haulers in Union Negotiations," ibid., 9 (Aug. 1966): 18.

48. "Two Chicago Suburbs Award Private Contracts," ibid., 1 (Oct. 1958): 7, 28-29; "Private Trend Continues in Chicago," ibid., 2 (Feb. 1959): 8; "Strong Trend to Privatize Service Continues Gains," ibid., 2 (Sept. 1959): 10, 22, 28; John Vanderveld, Jr., "A Private Contractor States His Position," ibid., 4 (Apr. 1961): 14, 18; "Collection Costs Push Illinois Tax Limit Ceiling," ibid., 6 (June 1963): 6-7.

King of Rush Street." Fratto turned over the business to West Suburban, which grew tenfold the first year. Frank LaPorte, another gambling overlord, took over Association accounts in the southern suburbs.

"All they do," a scavenger owner complained, "is drop the name of a hood friend and they get the business – customers I had for years." When scavengers stopped by to ask why customers canceled, "All they tell us is, 'Please go away, we don't want to have anything to do with you.'" The mob grabbed some of the best accounts at nightclubs, restaurants, and large stores. "Within two years the Association will be out of business," Daddano boasted.[49]

The struggle had three heavy hitters – the scavenger owners Association, the Italian mob, and Jimmy Hoffa's Teamsters Local 731 (Excavating, Grading, Asphalt, Private Scavengers, and Garage Attendants). Curiously, the mob's front company, West Suburban, was nonunion, so the jobs of Hoffa's boys were at risk. But the mob and Hoffa were "in bed together," so the drivers might be sold out.

The Scavenger Association had clout too, because its members owned or controlled the dumps, and they refused to accept loads from non-Association members. Thus, the mob could not find a place to dump! This prompted at least one mob-linked firm to dump illegally on land along the Santa Fe Railroad tracks in Du Page County, for which the owners were arrested. Law enforcement officials quickly became concerned about a "war among scavengers," especially when bodies turned up, such as that of the brother-in-law of one prominent nightclub owner, who switched from his legitimate scavenger to the mob's company the same day.[50]

Organized crime fighters launched investigations and stepped up undercover work, prosecutors filed charges, and the Chicago newspapers went after the crime syndicate with a vengeance. The papers published one expose after another to smoke out the mob through publicity, naming names with addresses and mug shots. One government lawyer, Richard B. Ogilvie, former special assistant to the United States attorney general, made his political reputation fighting the Chicago crime syndicate during the garbage war and rose to the governorship of Illinois. The mobsters fought back with a $1.5 million lawsuit of their own against the Asso-

49. "Mob Cutting In, Scavengers Charge," *Chicago's American,* 10 Dec. 1960; "Hood Becomes Rush Street 'Garbage King,'" *Chicago Tribune,* 30 Jan. 1961.

50. "Garbage Turns to Gold, Gives Cops Headaches," *Chicago's American,* 10 Nov. 1960; "Fear new violence in syndicate struggles," ibid., 26 Nov. 1960. John Sexton, a very close Catholic friend of Bonne Iwema, controlled many dumps in Chicago and cooperated with the Hollanders.

ciation, forcing it to defend itself in federal courts against charges of price-fixing, collusion, and violations of antitrust laws. The local nature of the hauling rendered federal antitrust laws moot, but the mob scored some points against the Association on the issue of rigging of bids in suburban municipal contracts. After four years, the mob withdrew its suit without getting a penny.[51]

After a few years of storm and fury, the garbage war ended in a whimper. The mobsters found little gold in garbage. The expected graft and booty was minimal, due to aggressive law enforcement and the glare of newspaper publicity. They could do much better concentrating on their traditional gambling interests and loan shark rackets; the interest, or "juice," was 20 percent per month. In truth, the mobsters simply did not know how to run a legitimate and complex business like trash hauling. They set prices below cost, lacked the required refuse licenses, and their trucks were dilapidated, with the name "West Suburban" scrawled in chalk on the doors. Drivers had no work ethic, and managers could not route the trucks efficiently. They fell many months delinquent on their bank notes for trucks and equipment and generally ran the business into the ground. After only two years, in 1962, Daddano sold under duress his West Suburban Scavenger Service to Dick Evenhouse of Garden City Disposal. The Chicago mob had met their match in the Dutch garbagemen; David had slain Goliath.

Legal Troubles

The Chicago Dutch scavengers, meanwhile, had expanded into other states, including Wisconsin, Indiana, Florida, and Colorado. This interstate reach brought on legal troubles in other jurisdictions. One major blow came from the Wisconsin attorney general's office. The legal action was prompted by complaints from independent scavengers in Milwaukee, who felt threatened by the arrival of the highly efficient Chicago scavengers. Dean Buntrock, leader of Acme Disposal of Chicago, had moved into Milwaukee in 1959 after making a swap with Harold Van Der Molen, who exchanged his troubled Milwaukee routes for new routes in Chicago. Buntrock's mother-in-law, Betty Huizenga, Pete's widow, financed the venture, Buntrock's first. He formed Acme Disposal of Milwaukee and

51. Richard G. Ogilvie, "How Mob Moves in on Business," *Chicago's American*, 23 Mar. 1961; "Scavenger Bid Plot Charged," *Chicago Daily News*, 7 Feb. 1961.

hired an energetic salesman, Stan Ruminski, whom he trained to be a manager. Buntrock saw opportunity in the city's rapid industrial growth and downtown development.[52]

Troubles began in a big way in 1962, when local haulers with political connections got the state attorney general's office to launch an investigation of Acme's operation. They falsely charged that goons of the Chicago and Suburban Ash and Scavenger Association were burning their trucks and threatening their drivers, in a drive to organize the independent haulers of Milwaukee and get the same "good deal" as in Chicago. Moreover, rumor had it that the Association had put up a million dollars to provide free garbage pickups and other benefits to woo customers away from haulers who would not accept the Association.[53]

In 1962, George B. Schwahn, the assistant attorney general of Wisconsin, after a year-long, grand jury investigation, named in a temporary restraining order the Acme Disposal Company of Milwaukee, a subsidiary of Acme Disposal of Chicago, which was headquartered at 5447 West Harrison Street in the Austin district. Acme was enjoined against "monopolistic practices, threats, and violence," and "predatory price-cutting," which charges carried fines up to $10,000 against each of the directors. Schwahn also threatened further investigations leading toward criminal charges. Wisconsin led the charge because the Illinois antitrust law specifically exempted service industries such as scavengers.

The Wisconsin legal foray brought into court many of the major figures among the Chicago Dutch scavengers. The list reads like a who's who – Dean Buntrock, Harold Van Der Molen, Jacob Bilthuis, Clarence Huizenga, Conrad Douma, and John Groot. Together, these men owned or controlled at least a dozen firms in Chicago, and they were prominent in the Chicago and Suburban Ash and Scavenger Association.

The newspaper publicity unfairly tarnished the reputations of the six men; the legal case came to nothing, but this fact was never reported. The legal action did soften Acme for another Teamsters union organizing drive. Within months, after several false starts, the Teamsters in 1963 successfully organized Acme's drivers, helpers, and mechanics, making the firm the first and only unionized private waste hauler in the city for the next eight years. Since Acme had to pay higher wages and medical and retirement benefits than its competitors, it had to work smarter too. One

52. Jacobson, *Waste Management,* 80-88.

53. "Chicago-Area Men Named in Probe of Refuse Feud," *Chicago Daily News,* 17 Oct. 1962.

way was to go from two-man crews to one – the driver did it all, which new work pattern the union men grudgingly accepted. Acme also bought its own dump in Brookfield, in a former sand and gravel pit. Soon it had thirty trucks running routes in the city and suburbs. Perhaps the informal agreements among Association members also helped Acme hold its prices.

In 1971 Acme of Milwaukee again faced a firestorm of negative publicity when the city privatized its waste hauling by awarding Acme a contract to haul by rail much of the residential waste, 940 tons per day, from collection stations to distant landfills. The mayor's decision came after almost a year and a half of wrangling between the city, county, and state, amidst "recriminations, charges and counter-charges of bribery and influence-peddling, and unsavory innuendoes about 'backroom deals,' as well as outright opposition on purely political grounds." Garbage had become a hot-button issue in modern politics.[54]

The Chicago and Suburban Disposal Association handled Illinois politicians better than they did those in Wisconsin. Indeed, their attorneys for years were Mandel Anixter, Bud Delaney, and Michael Bilandic; the latter succeeded Richard J. Daley as mayor of Chicago. Bilandic's monthly retainer fee to provide political protection was money well spent.

But a major problem developed in 1968 in the suburban areas, when the Illinois State police began to harass "overweight" garbage trucks. The police ticketed the trucks for being overweight on their double rear axles, even when the overall vehicle weight was below maximum limits. The problem was trying to mesh twenty-year-old standards with the design of the modern packer trucks. The trucks had a six-thousand-pound compactor over the rear axles that crushed the refuse between metal plates and moved it forward as the truck was loaded. As a result, the first half of the load was concentrated almost entirely over the rear axles. This meant that a truck was overweight on the rear axle or axles before it was half full, even though it was well within the legal weight limits for its front axle. To comply with the law, drivers had to make so many extra trips to the dump that they worked late into the night so as not to leave residential garbage at the curb.

The haulers believed that police enforcement of such inefficient practices would put them out of business. "There is no question about it," said Everett Van Der Molen, co-owner of Van Der Molen Disposal Company. William Buiten of Garden City Disposal, the new executive director of the

54. "Milwaukee Finally Selects a Hauler for Refuse Transport," *Refuse Removal Journal* 14 (Jan. 1971): 8, 40.

Association, explained that its two hundred member firms, whose one thousand trucks serviced three million Chicago and suburban residents, were between a rock and a hard place. They could either operate within the law and go out of business, or violate the law and go bankrupt paying the $46,500 in tickets the police had written in the previous month. He predicted ominously: "All of us will be up to our necks in garbage."[55]

In desperation, seven scavenger firms filed a class action lawsuit on behalf of all private refuse collectors challenging the constitutionality of the state truck weight laws. While the legal process plodded along, Buiten and the Association pulled the political levers in Springfield and got the Illinois state legislature to raise the weight limit for garbage trucks on city and state roads from fifty-four thousand to seventy-two thousand pounds. (Interstate roads were not covered by the bill; they fell under federal jurisdiction.) Governor Ogilvie, their legal friend from the Chicago garbage wars with the mob, happily signed the bill, which had wide support from many village councils and mayors who had lobbied on behalf of the refuse haulers. Thanks to Buiten's adroit efforts, the scavengers had dodged a bullet and got the state police off their backs for good, except on the interstates. Wags noted that the officers were especially chagrined at losing a lucrative source of "payola" for their benevolent association.[56]

However, only two years later, in 1970, the Illinois attorney general, William J. Scott, pushed the 190-member Chicago and Suburban Refuse Disposal Association to the wall by charging them and forty-two member firms with illegal price-fixing and collusion. Scott had made a year-long investigation and seemed to have the goods on the Association. The scavengers saw their vulnerable position and agreed before a Du Page County district judge to pay a summary judgment of $50,000. The Elmhurst-based Association members also accepted the judge's injunction not to engage in "price-fixing, customer allocation, and collusive bidding practices." In answer to a separate suit by the A. Cherney Disposal Company of Chicago, the Association at the same time also paid an out-of-court settlement of $271,000.[57]

55. "Firms Sue to End Tickets; Predict Garbage Crisis as Result of Crackdown," undated Chicago newspaper clipping, 1968, Van Weelden scrapbook.

56. William Buiten, "Increases Granted on Illinois' Axle-Weights," *Refuse Removal Journal* 14 (Nov. 1971): 24, 62; "Unload the Trucks, Governor," undated Chicago newspaper editorial, 1969, Van Weelden scrapbook; letter, Sam Hamstra, Jr., to author, 13 Feb. 2001.

57. "Scott to Sue Garbage Collectors in 2 Suburbs for Price-Fixing," *Chicago Tribune,* 15 Sept. 1970; "Scavenger Group is Fined $50,000 Over Price-Fixing," ibid., 30 Apr. 1971; Ted Hoekstra, "Memoirs, 1927-1957."

The final blow fell when Flood Bros. Scavenger Company filed a lawsuit against the Association. Emmett Flood, Sr., had worked as a route foreman and manager for both Metro Scavenger (Pete and Clarence Huizenga) and City Disposal (Harold Van Der Molen). Although he had been treated well for two decades, he decided to go into business for himself outside of the Association. He sharply undercut the members on price and took stops at will. The members had no protection, because none of the accounts were under contract; they operated on good faith and a handshake, backed by the Association if necessary. One Association scavenger, Sam Hamstra, lost half of his business in one day when Flood signed his main account, National Food Stores, to a contract.

Flood's "betrayal" put the member firms hot on his tail; they dropped off their business cards at customers and undercut his rates. But their aggressive tactics cost them dearly. Flood complained about the concerted retaliation to the state attorney general, who forced the Association to sign a "consent decree" and pay triple damages! For many years members had to pay a special assessment to cover the fine. Flood had outfoxed the Association.

These legal setbacks sounded the death knell of the Association that the Dutch scavengers on the Old West Side had formed nearly fifty years earlier in an entirely different era. Its day had passed. With stiff fines and even jail time now a possibility at the hands of the state's legal apparatus, other methods had to be found. By 1978 the Association, still 80 percent Dutch, numbered only 116 members, down from 200 in 1971. The new solid waste conglomerates moved in and consolidated the industry, although critics charged that collusion only moved to the next level.

The significance of the Association, in some respects, was more social than economic, although business matters were in the forefront. The Association provided a place for the Dutch scavengers to meet monthly for fellowship over a beer and to exchange ideas about their customers, equipment, business trends, government regulations, and the like. In the end, the social aspect was more important than protecting stops. The reality was that the Association's regulations could not improve the bottom line of any member firm. If the firm was providing good service at reasonable rates and running efficiently, as most were, it was not possible for competitors to underbid and take away stops without hauling at a loss. Underbidding was simply not worth it in an industry where prices already were at rock bottom and owners respected one another's abilities. If, on the other hand, a member firm overcharged customers or gave poor service, no Association rules could long prevent those accounts from being picked off. Customers, after all, had the last word, and service, not rates, was the cardinal virtue.

Waste Management Incorporated (WMI) and Browning Ferris Industries (BFI)

By the 1960s, hauling waste had become so complex and capital intensive, with the high cost of power equipment, containers, landfill technology and land costs; generous labor contracts; political battles with local governments; and the rising federal environmental regulations, that a new way had to be found to manage the business and capitalize it. One- and two-truck operations were no longer viable; they had no control over spiraling dump charges set by the "big guys," they lacked the union clout that pushed labor costs higher with each new contract, and they lost the protection of the Association's "honor code" as renegades "stole" their accounts. By the 1970s, employees earned more and enjoyed better benefits than did some owners.[58]

The first step, as explained earlier, was to incorporate the family-owned companies, in order to gain liability protection, tax advantages, and continuity when principals retired or died. The second step was to consolidate to gain efficiencies of scale, and the final step was to "go public" by issuing stock and getting listed on a major exchange.

Browning Ferris Industries (BFI) of Houston, Texas, first took this step in 1969. Billing itself as "a company building an industry," it raised over $13 million through stock offerings of 750,000 shares in 1970 and 1971. The firm's shares were soon listed on the New York Stock Exchange. With these monies, BFI grew rapidly by gobbling up more than eighty local trash haulers, paying up to thirty times earnings for the larger firms. The major acquisitions in Chicago were John Vanderveld, Jr.'s National Disposal Contractors in 1971 (he was named a senior vice president at BFI), and Van Der Molen Disposal in 1972. BFI's revenues jumped from $2 million to more than $50 million within two years, and already by 1971 it was the nation's largest waste management company, operating in forty states and Canada. In Illinois alone, it controlled two hundred disposal firms, which was enough to prompt the state attorney general to file a successful lawsuit for massive price fixing.[59]

58. Letter, Sam Hamstra, Jr., to author, 13 Feb. 2001.

59. Roland B. Williams, "Browning-Ferris Industries, Inc., Candidate for Growth in

The decision of Vanderveld and the Van Der Molen brothers to sell out to BFI had a profound impact on the other Dutch scavengers and altered forever the nature of the industry. None reacted as swiftly as the Huizenga clan, who had already positioned their interrelated companies for the same evolution into a megacompany called Waste Management Inc. (WMI).

Some fifteen years earlier, Betty Huizenga's son-in-law Dean Buntrock, her nephew H. Wayne Huizenga, and her son Peter H. Huizenga, a young attorney and Hope College graduate, had linked up. Wayne grew up in Evergreen Park until his freshman year at Chicago Christian High School, when his family moved to Florida. There his father Gerrit ("Harry") eventually got him into the scavenger business in Ft. Lauderdale as manager of the routes of a Chicago Dutch pal, Herman Mulder. Soon Wayne began his own business, and, in 1962, he and his father bought the three routes of Mulder and formed Southern Disposal. Wayne's businesses grew so fast that they needed investment capital and the Chicago Huizengas, through Dean Buntrock and Peter Huizenga, supplied it.[60]

A final precursor to Waste Management was Buntrock's purchase in 1967 of 225 swampy acres near Calumet City on Chicago's far South Side for a huge sanitary landfill operation. Buntrock saw that disposal was the key to the future of the industry, and his companies, Ace and Acme Disposal, got in on the ground floor with Calumet Industrial Development (CID). His partner was Larry Beck, a Dane and, like Buntrock, a member of the conservative Lutheran Church, Missouri Synod. Beck had grown up in the trash business of his father on the South Side. Buntrock persuaded him to manage CID.

In 1968, Buntrock and Peter and Wayne Huizenga decided to reorganize their numerous businesses – Ace/Acme/the Southern companies/CID – into a holding company with combined assets of nearly $3 million. Consolidation was the trend in the industry. To go public re-

---

Solid Waste Management Services," E. F. Hutton & Company, Institutional Department Investment Report, July 1971; "Browning-Ferris notes record year," *Waste Systems Digest* (Winter-Spring, 1973): 7; "Sweet Smell of Success? In 'Solid Waste Management,' Everything's Not Coming Up Roses," *Barrons,* 23 Oct. 1972; Tom Fatjo, Jr., and Keith Miller, *With No Fear of Failure* (Waco: Word Books, 1981); James H. McCall, "Fresh Sources of Finance for the Private Hauler," *Refuse Disposal Journal* 14 (Sept. 1971): 34, 54; Will Collette, et al., *Browning Ferris Industries: A Corporate Profile* (Citizen's Clearinghouse for Hazardous Waste, Inc., July 1987). The last item is a stinging critique by a special-interest group.

60. Jacobson, *Waste Management,* 86-91, 95-117.

Dean Buntrock (right), chairman, and H. Wayne Huizenga, vice chairman of Waste Management, 1970

(Courtesy of Peter H. Huizenga)

quired a critical mass, at least $10 million in annual revenues. This was the target.

Buntrock hit on the apt name "Waste Management" and rented a suite of offices in the upscale suburb of Hinsdale. The blue-collar town of Cicero, where Ace Scavenger was located, would simply not do as a headquarters address for the company the men envisioned. Peter Huizenga, a director and corporate secretary since 1968, added the title of vice president in 1972. He handled much of the legal work in the corporate reshuffling of the twenty or more Huizenga companies. Huizenga noted that the driving factor was the urgent need for capital to seize the opportunities. "It was money that brought us to the table. We didn't have enough money to take advantage of what was right on the platter in front of us."[61]

Tom Fatjo, BFI president and founder, knew the predicament well and surprised the Huizenga clan with an offer to buy out the entire company. Fatjo's target was to become a $1 billion company, while the Huizengas thought $100 million was quite ambitious. Wayne and Peter Huizenga were tempted, after being wined and dined at BFI's lavish headquarters in Houston by top officials, including Fatjo and John Vandervelde, their fellow Chicago Groninger and friend. But Wayne Huizenga demurred, believing that Waste could be more successful by itself. He was right, although Buntrock had to be convinced to take on the awesome responsibility of top management.

61. Ibid., 96-105, quote 100.

The three Chicago entrepreneurs modeled WMI after BFI and soon surpassed it. There were twelve thousand local waste haulers in the nation, at least fifteen hundred of which were prime for acquisition and two hundred were immediate targets. With master promoter Wayne Huizinga finding hundreds of ripe targets, and backed by the financial wizardry of Don Flynn of the Big Eight accounting firm of Arthur Andersen and the underwriting prowess of the Chicago Corporation investment banking house to tap the capital markets, WMI went on an acquisitions tear. To raise the needed cash, the firm offered 320,000 shares of stock at $16 per share, bringing in $4 million. The market timing in 1971 was just right, and within months a much-larger second offering of 1.25 million shares brought in whopping $426 million in additional cash. In 1978 one million more shares were issued to willing investors, raising another $27 million.

With these funds WMI retired its equipment debt and began a rapid expansion through internal growth and acquisitions that caused the company to double, triple, and even quadruple in its early years. In the first nine months of 1972 alone, 133 firms were acquired by stock swaps and generous salaries for former owners, if they agreed to continue to run their companies under WMI oversight. Seldom was cash offered, nor was it necessary. More than three-quarters of former owners continued to run their companies; Waste needed their expertise and management skills. They had simply "joined the team."

Expansion of routes and landfills remained a linchpin of WMI for decades. As recently as 1989, the firm swallowed up nearly one hundred companies. The biggest acquisition in Chicago was Tom Tibstra's Southwest Towns Refuse Disposal Service; Tibstra was already a partner in the CID landfill. WMI went nationwide looking for companies to buy – Florida, Texas, Colorado, and elsewhere, and whenever possible they tapped the Dutch connection. In east Texas, for example, WMI acquired the large Best Waste Systems Company founded by a partnership of Chicago scavengers – Bob Drenth and his father Bernard of Clearing Disposal, Edward Evenhouse and sons Tom and Randy of City Disposal, and cousin Henry G. Evenhouse of Merchant's Disposal. The Evenhouses had earlier sold their Chicago businesses to WMI.[62]

Waste's stock, which also traded on the Big Board, rose in value even faster than its customer base, and split and split yet again. Shares traded

62. Jacobson, *Waste Management,* 52, 109-17; Andrew Webb, "Waste Management Cleans Up," *Chicago Magazine,* June 1990, 123-27, 137-43; Gail Rickey, "Bob Drenth: Garbageman doesn't waste any time," undated newspaper clipping from *Houston Chronicle,* ca. 1985.

at a multiple of up to forty times earnings. In the first two decades, Waste Management split its shares eleven times, and one share multiplied into seventy-two shares. Selling out to Waste was as profitable for former owners as for the thousands of public stockholders, including many Hollanders. Many ex-owners quickly became comfortably wealthy, although they typically continued to operate their firms as part of WMI until retirement. Van Der Molen Disposal, with more than one hundred trucks and dozens of suburban routes and an incinerator facility, reportedly was paid $15 million to become a subsidiary of Browning Ferris.

Lo and behold, the lowly scavengers and their families and friends were the first Chicago Groningers to achieve critical mass in their finances. Land developers, industrialists, and even land-rich farm owners later joined their exclusive company of wealth-holders as the city expanded and the economy thrived. In the Chicago suburban area alone in 1976, WMI and BFI together had exclusive contracts with suburban governments that controlled 75 percent of all residential trash services. The communities favored exclusive contracts to better regulate city sanitation and to cut down on the number of refuse trucks traversing the city streets.

Selling out was often the only alternative for the independents, because the directors of the conglomerates encouraged their member firms to undercut the competition. This had the unfortunate effect in Chicago of pitting fellow Dutch Calvinists against one another, just as in the days of informal regulation under the benevolent hand of the Association. One hauler would operate under the aegis of WMI or BFI, while another still ran his own business. The first followed company policy and underbid the second, thereby threatening his livelihood. Moreover, those who sold out became agents of the conglomerates to sign up others for fat commissions, and with their insiders' knowledge of routes and rates they targeted the largest accounts. Yet on Sundays, all sat in the same church pews and worshiped together. Throughout the 1970s and into the 1980s, until the independents had been shaken out, this situation caused much tension and ill will.[63] Thus, the newfound wealth came at a stiff price for the religious community.

Some independent owners refused to sell out in the "hot" 1970s, despite the blandishments of the conglomerates, and in recent years there has been a resurgence of small operators, just as in the banking business. Some are former owners now freed by the expiration of non-compete

63. Interview with Michael Van Denend, 26 May 1994; letter, Sam Hamstra, Jr., to author, 13 Feb 2001.

clauses in their sales agreements. Since the 1980s, the largest family-owned companies are all centered on the South Side. These are Wendy Yonker's Homewood Disposal, Frank Ward's Illinois Recycling, Rich Van Hattem's National Disposal, and Norm and Marv Aardema's Chicago Disposal. C. Groot & Sons in Elk Grove Village also is a large independent on the West Side. All the owners belong to Reformed and Christian Reformed churches. Thus, the pattern of religious interconnections set a century ago continues, although on a much smaller scale.[64]

Scandal also dogged the business in the 1970s, mainly as a result of the policy of exclusive city contracts. The bidders were all fellow Dutch churchgoers and members of the recently defunct Scavenger Association. The appearance of collusion among the companies, if not the actual fact, was a given. According to investigative reporter Mark Fineman of the *Chicago Daily News/Chicago Sun Times:*

> "There are certain understandings between them. Most of the people controlling both companies are of the same Dutch ancestry – many are directly related to each other," said the source who asked not to be identified to protect his job. "Ninety percent of the companies' major officeholders are members of the same church and see each other regularly on social occasions," the source added. "There probably isn't a formal, or even informal, agreement between them – they're too smart for that, and they know the law. But they're not going to compete seriously against each other. Once one of them has a contract, it stays that way." A spokesman for WMI, however, denied the charges.[65]

At issue was a refuse contract let in 1976 by the city of Berwyn. The city laid off its trucks and crews and awarded an exclusive contract to Clearing Disposal, a Waste Management subsidiary formerly owned by Bernard Drenth and his brothers, to pick up waste for $3.15 per month for single family homes. Clearing's rate beat out bids of $3.20 from Van Der Molen Disposal, a Browning Ferris hauler, and $3.55 from C. Groot Disposal of Berwyn, an independent.

Berwyn's private contract saved the city millions of dollars, but the unionized civil service workers raised the cry of collusion, and Democratic politicos chimed in. Republican city alderman John Van Tholen, Jr.,

64. Ibid.

65. Mark Fineman, "How growth profits garbage giants," a three-part series in the *Chicago Daily News/Chicago Sun-Times, Suburban Week, West Suburban Supplement,* 12-13 May 1976, 1 (quote), 19-20.

who owned his own scavenger business with ties to Waste Management, gave critics their leverage when, shortly after the contract was awarded, he took a vice presidency with the Clearing firm. "Berwyn trash pact raises stink," cried the headline of the *Daily News.* According to reporter Fineman:

> At least one inside industry source claims the WMI job [for Van Tholen] "was a reward for having made sure the Berwyn contract was given to Clearing." But Alderman Raymond Cox, the only non-Republican on the city council, rebutted the charge. "I've known John Van Tholen for years and years. He lives in my ward. . . . But that didn't enter into it at all. This contract is saving the people of Berwyn money. That's the only reason we approved it. Friendship wasn't involved."[66]

Nonetheless, Berwyn Democratic administrative officials and a private scavenger firm filed suit against the aldermen, and Circuit Court Judge Francis Delaney voided the existing contract and required re-advertising the contract. But Clearing Disposal came in again with the low bid and continued to pick up the city's garbage. Clearing's two-man crews picked up twenty-five alleys per day, compared to only eight or nine alleys by Berwyn's three-man crews. The hustling Dutch garbagemen had no use for goldbrickers. In the end, only five of twenty-six Berwyn city employees remained on the trucks.[67]

In the 1980s another collusion complaint surfaced in the village of Fox Lake, when a WMI general manager was charged with attempting to bribe the mayor to retain an exclusive city hauling contract. To keep the work, the mid-level manager had reportedly been ordered by his boss, "Do what you have to do." Little did he know that the police had wired the mayor to record the payoff. The general manager was convicted, and the company fired him, but authorities could never prove how far up the chain of command the directive had originated. And the mayor's motives were also tainted by an ongoing political scandal.

Individual scavenger operators and corporate waste executives took care to avoid any suspicions of collusive practices following the court injunction and legal actions. But in 1976 a waste industry source claimed that "the noncompetitive situation that exists today isn't much better. . . . The way things are set up now, BFI, for example, won't bid competitively

66. Ibid.

67. Jim Pokin, "Whatever happened to all those garbagemen?" *Berwyn Life,* 21 May 1976, 1, 16.

on a contract held by a WMI company because of this understanding. WMI can then raise its rates without worrying about losing the contract to another company. The residents, in turn, get ripped off." The same source claimed that BFI generally controlled suburban contracts north of the Eisenhower Expressway, and WMI dominated in suburbs to the south.[68]

Besides the exclusive residential contracts, suburban governments began licensing scavenger firms in the 1950s in order to safeguard public health and welfare. Many, but not all, preferred to deal only with the larger companies who had the best equipment, financial capital, and reputation. Independent firms were thus cut out of the most lucrative commercial hauling work, and, correspondingly, such customers were unable to seek better rates from unlicensed firms. The system was sanctioned by the Illinois Supreme Court in a landmark 1960 case that involved north suburban Deerfield. Independent haulers and small businesses complained but found it impractical to challenge the system in court. It was impractical for independents to spend tens of thousands to sue the municipalities for restraint of trade to save being overcharged by $30-40 a month. So the sweetheart licensing arrangements went on for decades, because municipalities enjoyed the efficiencies of service and government control that the exclusive contracts and licensing provided.[69]

Charges of noncompetitive practices from anonymous "industry sources" were difficult for industry leaders to refute, even when the complaints lacked credence, as many did. The Chicago area was intensely competitive. WMI, for example, in 1976 had relatively few residential contracts in relationship to the company's size and market. While it won the Berwyn contract, it had lost bids in Berkeley, Joliet, and Oak Lawn – all places south of the expressway. And the conglomerates were sometimes denied licenses in favor of local, independent haulers. In Buffalo Grove, Garden City Disposal, a WMI subsidiary, filed suit against the village for denying it a license.[70]

Besides charges of conspiracy and price-fixing, Waste Management was a favorite target of government regulators and environmentalists for malfeasance in the new era of trash awareness. Federal and state authorities cited and fined the company millions of dollars for leaking landfills

68. Fineman, "How growth profits garbage giants," 1, 9.

69. Fineman, "How licensing affects suburban scavenger rates," ibid., 19-20 May 1976, 1, 5.

70. Ibid.

and lax operations. In the 1980s alone, fines nationwide totaled $18 million, according to Greenpeace estimates. *Rolling Stone* magazine elected Waste Management to its 1989 Hall of Shame, and Greenpeace accused it of "callous disregard for the environment and for people's health." By this time, however, WMI was in the forefront of recycling and had taken serious steps to clean up its act, even to the extent of hiring in 1985 a full-time director of environmental affairs to coordinate the efforts. But in the end, landfilling is a primitive technology that is prone to seeping and leaking, despite new methods of lining the bottom with either plastic or clay and ringing the perimeter with monitoring wells. Overall, WMI's operations today are a far cry from that of earlier days.[71]

For twenty-five years, Waste Management was the largest waste disposal corporation in the world. It operated throughout the United States, Europe, and even Saudi Arabia, Argentina, and Venezuela. In 1998, however, after years of struggling to expand into other service lines (Chemical Waste, Chem-Nuclear, and Wheelabrator Technologies), the firm had a crisis of leadership in top management and a scandal that stemmed from "too aggressive accounting practices." This forced WMI to merge into USA Waste Services of Houston, Texas, the number three firm, which however retained the Waste Management name. Some $3.54 billion had been written off the books before the merger to meet government and industry standards. This came on top of a smaller write-down in 1997 of $173 million. Still, Waste's takeover value was more than $14 billion, as in $14,000 million! The next year, Browning Ferris, the number two company, which had also stumbled, was bought out by the new number three firm, Allied Waste Industries of Scottsdale, Arizona, for $7.3 billion in cash.

The final blow at Waste Management was the precipitous drop by more than 65 percent in the value of its stock in the summer of 1999, following insider selling by the new management, because of their financial malfeasance. Allied Waste stock plummeted soon thereafter. Both have since recovered some of their lost market valuations.[72]

What the frugal and hardworking Dutchmen had built up over several lifetimes, and the company that Buntrock and the Huizenga cousins had created over twenty years, was decimated in the final ten years. Wayne Huizenga had left the company in 1984 and developed Blockbuster Video and a number of other businesses and ventures, several of which became public companies. Wayne's business knowledge, drive, and energy were

71. Webb, "Waste Management Cleans Up," 124-27, 137-43.

72. *Wall Street Journal,* 17 Nov. 1997; 27 Feb., 15 May 1998; 9 Mar., 8, 30 July 1999.

sorely missed. Peter Huizenga resigned as an officer of the company in 1989 and as a director in 1997. Buntrock stayed on as chief executive officer until 1997. He had directed the company for more than twenty-five years and its predecessors for another ten years.

The "heyday" of dominance by the Chicago Dutch in the nation's waste business has passed, although some leaders in the new firms had Chicago connections. Thomas H. Van Weelden, Allied Waste's president and CEO since its founding in 1992, and his brother Jim, also a vice president, had grown up in the family business in Chicago, the firm of Van Weelden Bros. (uncle Gilbert and father Henry). Tom Van Weelden was also a former WMI employee and nephew of BFI's Everett Van Der Molen. Indeed, Chicago scavengers started businesses throughout the United States and overseas as far as Saudi Arabia and Kuwait. They knew how to handle trash and make a profit.

Cartage

While garbage held sway among the Dutch, many Groningers turned to "clean freight" to earn a livelihood. The logistics of businesses with wheels seemingly was their forte. With horse and wagon, they hauled commodities of all kinds between the rail terminals, the main post office, factories, retail stores, and commercial offices. Prior to the 1950s, many goods were delivered to one of the four depots of the Chicago Tunnel Company that ringed the Loop. From there they were transported forty-two feet underground in small electric freight cars through the web of tunnels that linked every railway terminal with every major downtown building. In 1920 the Tunnel Company carried 650,000 tons of packaged freight, besides ashes, garbage, and coal.[73]

Cartage was quite a different industry from garbage. There were no public health aspects to require city regulation; thus, it was a wide-open enterprise not given to exclusive contracts and owner associations to regulate competition. Not until the 1970s did consolidation and government regulation force the small operators out of business.

From the Civil War era, Dutch expressmen, cartmen, and drivers plied the streets of Chicago. (See listing in appendix 2.) At the turn of the century, Henry G. Haverkamp Teaming and Frederick Wesseling Teaming worked out of a shared office at 99 S. Water St., and Peter Amsterdam Ex-

73. Mayer and Wade, *Chicago,* 216-18.

John B. Swierenga, with horse and wagon, 1890s
(Courtesy of Jackie Vander Weide Swierenga Vogelzang)

pressing used his home at 537 (new numbering 1328) W. 14th St. as his base. Around 1910, the Swierenga brothers Edward and Henry hauled heavy loads, such as limestone slabs from a quarry, bound for the Lake Michigan breakwater project. At the same time, John H. Vander Velde began hauling and specialized in delivering coal and ice to private homes; he was still on the job in the 1940s, serving Hollanders in the Ashland Avenue district. George H. Camphouse Teaming likewise worked the West Side from his home at 1400 S. Crawford Avenue. Later, Andrew Post left his job on the garbage wagon to start his own coal (later oil) and ice delivery company in Cicero and Berwyn, finally selling to the City Ice Company in the late 1960s. Some drove for wages at first, like John B. Swierenga, who was a chauffeur for Mandel Brothers Department Store on State Street.[74]

In 1903 the brothers Nick and Ben Wieringa began Wieringa Bros. Cartage; this Harrison Street firm is perhaps the longest-lived Dutch-owned cartage company. In the 1950s the families split the business and formed Century and Columbia Cartage companies, and later a grandson,

74. William H. Fort, "Dutch Corner of 'Valley' Brightens West Side," *Chicago Daily News,* 1 Mar. 1941, p. 5; letter, Sam Hamstra, Jr., to author, 13 Feb. 2001.

Above, Swierenga Bros, ca. 1910, hauling limestone slabs for Lake Michigan breakwater l-r: ??, Edward Swierenga, ??, Henry Swierenga

Right, John H. Vander Velde delivering coal to John Blauw's home at 1419 S. Ashland Ave., 1941

Tom Wieringa, developed Carry Transport, a hauling company for bulk liquid food products. The enterprising Tom Wieringa developed a computerized power washing system to clean the insides of his tankers after each haul, so they could quickly and safely be put back into service carrying other products. Wieringa recently sold Carry Transport.

Leonard Gorter's Standard Cartage, established in the 1920s, specialized in hauling heavy machinery, while John B. Swierenga, owner of Swierenga Cartage Company, carried steel beams, rods, and plates. His cousin, John R. Swierenga, began hauling general freight within the Chicago area during the Great Depression. He bought for $600 a struggling firm with fifteen accounts, two decrepit trucks, and a driver with a drinking problem. John R. replaced the worst of the trucks, laid off the tippler, and hired his cousin Edward (Eddy) Swierenga for $13 per week and chose the name Excel Motor Service. The year was 1938. To save overhead costs Swierenga rented space and had his phone at Gorter's Standard Cartage office on Sherman Street in the south Loop. Gorter, a fellow church member, proved to be a good mentor and life-long friend. The office was actually a wooden shack along the southside wall of a brick building fronting at 161 West Harrison Street. (Interestingly, Loop Christian Ministries of the Christian Reformed Church was centered in this building from 1992 to 1996.)

Several of Excel Motor's original accounts, such as McCarty Letter Service, Fruit Growers Express, Burlington Refrigerator Express, and Baum Folder, proved to be valuable, but Swierenga hustled new customers. He hauled anything that he and the trucks could manage – machinery (Baum Folder and the Harris-Diebold Company, for example), bolts of woolen goods and finished garments, office water coolers (Morry Blons

John B. Swierenga, chauffeur for Mandel Brothers Store, State and Madison Sts., ca. 1910

(Courtesy of Jackie Vander Weide Swierenga Vogelzang)

International truck, Swierenga Cartage Co., ca. 1925, John B. Swierenga, proprietor *(Courtesy of Jackie Vander Weide Swierenga Vogelzang)*

Company), and paper products ranging from skids of bulk paper sheets weighing up to a ton to small packages of stationery (Monarch Printing) and advertising signs for city transit buses and trains (Chicago Advertising Company).

The firm also hauled bulk mail from insurance companies, magazine publishers, and catalog houses to the central post office on Harrison and Canal Streets. The customers placed the magazines, catalogs, and documents in large canvas mail sacks provided free by the post office. Loading and unloading dozens of these heavy sacks was a daily test of strength for drivers. Excel Motor declined to carry jewelry, tobacco, and alcohol products, because of liability concerns and the unsavory nature of the goods.

In 1940 Swierenga hired his brother-in-law, Paul Tuitman, who had recently been fired from the Jefferson Ice Company for refusing to work on Sunday. Tuitman drove for Excel for thirty years until his retirement in 1970, and for many years had primary responsibility for the Fruit Growers Express and Burlington Express accounts. These twin firms provided railroad refrigerator cars with charcoal or kerosene heaters in the winter to keep food products from freezing. The heaters had to be hauled from incoming train yards to storage areas and then trucked as needed to outgoing train yards. It was hard, dirty work in often extremely cold conditions but profitable for the company. In 1942, John hired his brother Ralph as the third driver for $35 per week. Ralph had been clerking in the Swierenga Bros. produce house of their father and uncle on Randolph Street.

In 1941 the state legislature required trucking companies to obtain an operating license or authority from the Illinois Commerce Commission (ICC). Swierenga's insurance agent and cousin, Dick Rispens, advised him to write a contract with the broadest possible authority – the right to haul general commodities within a fifty-mile radius of the city center. Fellow churchman and attorney, Ben Ottenhoff, recorded the contract with the state agency and registered the name Excel Motor Service for $1. Subsequently, when the number of trucking companies in Chicago exceeded the perceived needs of the market, the ICC sharply restricted the number and authority of new licenses issued. Excel Motor's broad license was grandfathered and became valuable.

Excel Motor Service made several small acquisitions over the years, but mostly it grew slowly by word of mouth advertising of the excellent service. In 1942 Swierenga paid $350 for a 1937 Ford truck and a few accounts and took over an office lease at the rear loading dock of the Brooks Building, 223 W. Jackson Boulevard. The location served as Excel Motor's office for the next thirty-eight years. In 1950 Swierenga paid $2,750 for a one-truck operation with four accounts, the most valuable being the Formfit Company (maker of women's undergarments).

As the volume of freight increased rapidly in the prosperous years of the Second World War, John, Ralph, and Paul Tuitman had to hustle all the more, but they would not work on Sundays except in dire emergencies. All three men were subject to military conscription, but, fortunately for the company, for various reasons they did not have to serve. Paul failed the army's physical exam and was classified 4F, Ralph was deferred due to dependents (3A), and John was deferred because he hauled vital materials such as railroad car heaters that kept food safe. The youngest Swierenga brother, Henry, after his army discharge in January of 1946 also drove for Excel Motor for seven years until taking up carpentry. In 1947 John added a fifth truck, driven in turn by Abel Korringa, Henry Van Kampen, and Paul Zaagman, all fellow Dutch Calvinists.

John R. Swierenga, proprietor Excel Motor Service, first truck, 1935 Chevrolet, with brother-in-law John Davids (left), proprietor Monroe Cartage Co., ca. 1938

In the 1950s, the company added trucks for two "steady houses" – Formfit and McCarty Letter Service (printing materials). Beginning in 1955, Ray Stuit drove the Formfit truck, whose side panels advertised in gold letters over a royal blue background, "Formfit bras and foundations." Leonard Peters, a Lutheran church member, handled the McCarty account. Peters replaced Ralph, who in 1951 took over the management of Monroe Cartage, the trucking company of brother-in-law John Davids, who died of leukemia at thirty-six years of age, leaving a widow with four children. The family decided that Ralph should operate the company, which had four trucks and three employees at the time.

At its apex in 1966, Excel Motor had nine vehicles on the street and eight employees; John continued to drive as well. Until 1951, he hired only relatives and church friends. As the business grew, the powerful Chicago Teamster's Union increased its pressure on the drivers to join up. In an early attempt to sidestep the union, John and his brother Ralph and brother-in-law Paul Tuitman in 1943 had joined the Christian Labor Association (CLA), a union based on Reformed principles that rejected the strike weapon. But Teamster officials refused to recognize the CLA and demanded that Excel drivers join the secular union. When the men refused, union goons threatened to damage their vehicles and even harm them.

Finally, in 1953 several drivers, including Tuitman and John's youngest brother, Henry, now a driver, reluctantly joined the Teamster's Local 705, as did subsequent new hires. As an owner operator, John himself was not required to be a member. But from then on, he had to hire out of the union hall and pay monthly health and welfare dues, which despite much waste and fraud provided the drivers with medical and retirement benefits. Even after the union came in, Swierenga continued to hire Dutch Calvinists whenever possible, including John Kok, Abel Schoonveld, Raymond Rozendal, Russell Erffmeyer, Bernard Weidenaar, and Abel Van Kampen.

A major crisis came in 1967 when the Teamsters went out on strike for several weeks. Tuitman and Lenny Peters took a great risk and crossed the picket lines. Within two weeks four more union drivers crossed the picket lines, but two others refused to do so until the union signed a new general contract with all independent trucking companies. The contract called for a whopping twenty-five cents per hour wage increase, plus a paid birthday holiday. The lost business and increased cost of labor forced Swierenga to lay off the last man hired, one of the holdouts. The strike left a bitter taste in the drivers' mouths, and it took some time to restore a spirit of camaraderie among them.

The strike signaled that the trucking industry had changed. In-

Ralph (Butch) and Jack Swierenga, proprietors, Monroe Transportation Co., truck fleet on new Interstate road I-53 west of Chicago, 1986

creasing government regulations and restrictive union work rules and rising wage scales forced small firms to expand or stagnate. This meant finding dependable drivers, buying or leasing more trucks, and securing bigger docking and garage facilities. Also, the operating range began to increase dramatically with the relocation of manufacturing plants and offices from the central city to the suburbs. The aggravation of the business produced ulcers, hemorrhoids, and heart attacks. John sold Excel Motor Service in 1970 to a fellow Dutchman, Bernard Mulder, one of brother Ralph's drivers, for $50,000. This included all accounts, nine trucks and equipment, the operating authority, and the nebulous but essential "good will." This sum was a pittance compared to the twenty-months' gross revenue yardstick that WMI and BFI used to buy out refuse haulers.

Ralph Swierenga, meanwhile, had to face the same labor problems and changing times at Monroe Cartage Company. Like John, he was fair and honest in his dealings, but he drove himself harder and bore the pressures of growing the company into a large business with dozens of drivers and their rigs, and a big dock facility in Addison. Sons Ralph, Jr., and Jack joined the firm and, after Ralph's death in 1987, renamed it Monroe Transportation Company and continued the rapid expansion. Today the thriving firm employs more than one hundred drivers. Ralph, Jr., died in 1999 at the young age of forty-seven; Jack Swierenga ably carries on.

The ubiquitous yellow school buses became the specialty of Terry Van Der Aa, who parlayed carrying children to school into a multimillion-dollar enterprise in the greater Chicago area since the 1960s. In 1996, Chicago's public school system privatized its bus service by signing a no-bid contract with Van Der Aa's company, Vancom of Oakbrook Terrace, and a Kansas City firm. In 2000, the joint firm transported one of every nine Chicago public school children, much to the chagrin of public sector advocates who oppose the privatization.[75] Van Der Aa also operates airport transport and specialized luxury motor coaches, and in the 1990s he even ventured overseas and purchased the entire regional bus company in the province of Groningen. He has since sold part of the school bus division to the Canadian waste conglomerate, Laidlaw, and the Groningen bus company to a Netherlands buyer. He continues to own the school bus, airport, and charter business.

The moving and storage business was a related aspect of trucking that attracted several Dutchmen. Peter Ploegman and Herman Euwema operated large businesses for many decades on the West Side. Peter Ploegman & Sons Moving and Storage was located on 22nd Street until the early 1980s as an affiliate of United Van Lines. Sons Peter and Edward Ploegman operated it the last decades. Euwema Moving and Storage of Oak Park was a worthy competitor.

Labor Union Problems

Most Hollanders were blue-collar workers, and they faced squarely the issue of unionism as Chicago industrialized, especially during the Great Depression and the Second World War when the craft and industrial unions gained great power.

Roselanders working at the Pullman Palace Car Company a half-mile down the hill near Lake Calumet first felt the power of unions in the 1880s. The magnate George Pullman, who began building his sprawling complex in 1880, hired many Dutch carpenters and laborers from Roseland, some of whom moved into the company town of Pullman. They began as unskilled laborers in the lumberyard, dry kilns, and stock rooms under bilingual foremen. As they learned the language and gained experience, they moved into better-paying skilled jobs in marquetry and finishing. Between 1885 and 1892, the number of Hollanders employed at the Pullman Works tripled, from 271 to 753, or from 3 to 12 percent of the entire workforce.

In 1886 the employees who belonged to the Knights of Labor went out on strike in sympathy with the Knights' call for a national strike on

75. Michael Martinez and Laurie Cohen, "2 probes offer divergent views of school bus service," *Chicago Tribune,* 26 July 2000.

Pullman Car Works Arcade Building with troops, 1894 strike

(The Archives, Calvin College)

May 1 for an eight-hour day. But the small Dutch contingent, not one a Knight, crossed the picket lines under police protection and helped break the strike.[76]

The 1894 strike was a different matter. The Pullman workers went out in sympathy with the American Railway Union (ARU) strike, which caused a national rail shutdown that quickly turned violent. The gates at Pullman also saw bloody and brutal confrontations between police and strikers. When Illinois governor John Altgeld hesitated to call out the state militia, President Grover Cleveland mobilized federal troops to protect the trains and the Pullman shops, which were closed for over three months. Despite the anger of seeing average wages cut by 28 percent with the onset of the depression of 1893, the Dutch opposed the strike and, amazingly, some even considered crossing the lines again as they did eight years earlier.

Fifty Pullman workers from the First Reformed Church of Roseland met at the urging of the Reverend Balster Van Ess to consider returning to work, but the meeting was broken up by union activists who flooded the

76. Stanley Buder, *Pullman: An Experiment in Industrial Order and Community Planning, 1880-1930* (New York: Oxford Univ. Press, 1967), 90, Table 2, 140-144. According to Simon Dekker, Pullman was a brother-in-law of Abraham Madderom, pioneer Roseland Hollander ("History of Roseland," 86).

room. Under heavy criticism from the strikers, Van Ess then announced publicly that he was neutral in the struggle and not opposed to unions per se. How many of the strikers were members of his congregation is unknown. Another Dutch Reformed Church immigrant pastor, the Reverend Englebert C. Oggel, who was "on loan" to the Greenstone Memorial Church (Presbyterian) of Pullman, delivered a broadside from the pulpit against the union leaders as "agitators" and admonished the workers that "half a loaf was better than none." A few weeks earlier, Oggel had praised George Pullman and his model town in a sermon based on the text, "Thou hast made him a little lower than the angels and hast crowned him with glory and honor" (Psalms 8:5). Pullman was a self-made man who "had not buried his God-given talents . . . in a napkin" but had "done his part" to create a community of "beauty and harmony, health, comfort, and contentment." With such intemperate preaching, Oggel saw attendance at the church drop sharply, and within a few weeks he left on vacation and never returned.[77]

When the strikers lost the upper hand after two months, the company began hiring replacement workers, and fully one quarter of the first eight hundred rehired were Hollanders from Roseland who had broken with the union. No wonder George Pullman liked to hire the Dutch Reformed.[78]

Independent craftsmen also experienced union troubles. Rentze Nicolay, who painted buildings in Roseland with his two sons from 1900 to 1906, was so severely harassed by union goons that he applied for a license to carry a concealed revolver. He used the gun once in 1905 to drive off two men who intended to push his ladder over when he was painting the gable of a two-story building. The incident so unnerved him that he left Chicago with his family to take up homesteading in North Dakota, through the agency of a Dakota land company in Chicago. Five or six Roseland families joined the party.[79]

For the Dutch teamsters, union problems came to a head thirty years later during the Great Depression. Beginning in 1934, the Chicago Cinder and Scavenger Truck Owners Association, whose members were almost entirely Dutch Reformed, succumbed to threats and acts of violence and agreed to closed shop contracts with Local 731 of the International

77. Ibid., 159, 174-75; Almont Lindsey, *The Pullman Strike* (Chicago: Univ. of Chicago Press, 1942), 102. Quotes from *Chicago Times,* 20 May 1894, and *Pullman Journal,* 5 May 1894.

78. Buder, *Pullman,* 175, 194.

79. "Recollections of Johan Nicolay: Roseland, Illinois and Lark, North Dakota," *Origins* 8, No. 1 (1995): 3.

Brotherhood of Teamsters (IBT). Drivers of cartage trucks and dock and warehouse workers were similarly pressured to join IBT Local 705. Hundreds of skilled craftsmen and laborers in the building construction trades had to affiliate with AFL locals in order to work. Workers in auto factories and other large industries had no choice but to join affiliates of John L. Lewis's Congress of Industrial Organizations (CIO), which made the sit-down strike its hallmark in the mid-1930s.

The Dutch Reformed had long abhorred the "socialistic" philosophies of the so-called secular or "neutral" unions. They feared that their values would be compromised by the blatant anti-Christian bias and immoral power tactics of leaders like Lewis and Jimmy Hoffa. The corrupt teamsters union was a national disgrace, Richard Tempelman declared in the *Illinois Observer* in the 1950s. Tempelman knew of the scandals from personal experience:

> The union to which I belonged was investigated by the courts. It was revealed at the hearings that no election for president was held in eleven years, and that no accounting of funds had been made in those eleven years either. When three of us Christian Reformed members went to a meeting to protest, we were told that the hall was full, there was no room to get in, and we might as well go home. This we had to do because the doors locked electronically from the inside. *And we were a full hour early.*[80]

Tempelman gave further examples of the Teamster's unions.

> Must we tell of the president of a truck-drivers local who at election time perpetuated himself in office by pointing two guns at the assembled members and declared himself elected without the benefit of a ballot? . . . Must we speak of the lewd parties which are sponsored by some unions? Must we speak of the annual masses which are being said in the Roman Catholic churches in Chicago for the prosperity of the building trade locals, masses which our church labels as "accursed idolatry"? These are said for unions to which our brothers in Christ belong by the hundreds.[81]

80. *Illinois Observer,* Nov. 1957; July-Aug. 1958. An excellent critique of the humanistic rationale governing secular unions by a leader in the Christian labor movement is Harry Antonides, "The Basis of the Secular Trade Unions: an alleged religious neutrality," *Torch and Trumpet* (Sept. 1963): 16-21.

81. Richard Tempelman, "Please Allow Me to Say," ibid., Apr. 1956, 17-19, quotes 19.

One scavenger responded very sheepishly to Tempelman's attacks on organized labor: "You correctly observe that most of us don't care what happens in our unions. . . . Our supreme interest is in enough take home pay. We live too easily on a horizontal plane. We are more interested in what we get than in how we got it. . . . These are our good people in the pews who are in the scavenger business. They [unions] are organized. You can't do business without belonging. They control things."

Tempelman retorted that even inactive members of the IBT were sinning. "The national disgrace of a corrupt teamsters Union stands as an indictment against every Christian teamster member of that Union. The Bible says: 'Come ye out from among them, and be ye separate.' It will be interesting to watch which emphasis will win, the fear of the Union (job security) or the love for Christ (trust and obey)." The outcome was not the one desired by Tempelman and the Christian Reformed Church at large.[82]

As early as 1912, Classis Illinois, the regional assembly of all Christian Reformed Churches in Chicago, made a pronouncement on the issue of secular labor unions. The church would "tolerate" membership, but individuals must resign if "a Union officially commits acts of violence or authorizes violations of God's commandments." Further, "Union members shall not be eligible for church offices." Finally, "Classis pledges its moral support to a movement aiming at a Christian Labor Organization."[83] This shot across the bow of the unions had a chilling effect in the churches, but many members felt compelled to join the Teamsters anyway.

Even pronouncements in 1943 and 1945 by the denomination's highest authority, the national synod, which condemned unions for their "unchristian practices," had a minimal impact. This was in large part because the synod condoned membership as long as a particular union gives "no constitutional warrant to sins, nor shows in its regular activities that it champions sins." What constituted sinful acts synod left to local consistories and the consciences of members themselves.[84]

By 1954 the pressing question had become very specific: "Can a Christian Reformed Church member belong to the CIO or AF of L?" The synod's study committee report recommended a "no" answer, but so many church members in Chicago, Paterson, Detroit, and other big cities belonged to these unions that the synod rejected the committee report

82. Ira Poort (pseud.), "Pewpoints," *Illinois Observer,* Oct., Nov., Dec. 1957 (quotes Nov. and Dec.).

83. "Classis of Illinois," *Banner,* 18 Apr. 1912.

84. Henry J. Kuiper, "The Labor Union Problem," ibid., 4 Mar. 1949.

and declared that such complex matters could best be decided by church leaders in the individual congregations. Membership in the church and in "so-called neutral unions" are not per se incompatible, the synod ruled, and Christian workers could be a "faithful witness" there. Preferably, the synod urged members to form Christian labor unions.

The per se clause opened the door wide for thousands of Dutch Calvinists to be "unequally yoked" with non-Christians in "worldly unions," even though the synod warned members that such membership "entails moral and spiritual danger." This warning went largely unnoticed. The church had yielded the high ground and opened its offices to union members.[85]

The Christian union that Classis Illinois and the national synod endorsed was the Christian Labor Association (CLA), which had been formed in the early 1930s by men with strong roots in the Netherlands confessional tradition. The CLA has been most successful in Ontario, Canada, among post-war Dutch immigrants, but only a few centers developed in the United States, including Grand Rapids and Chicago. The union currently represents some three thousand workers, primarily in construction and agriculture.[86]

The Chicago area CLA held rallies on a regular basis in the 1930s, usually on the South Side where the main supporters lived. Both men and women came to hear inspirational addresses by sympathetic clerics that were more philosophical than economic in focus. The meetings mimicked the traditional mass rallies of the men's and women's church societies and could hardly have appealed to blue-collar workers.

It was inevitable that CLA locals would incur the wrath of secular union bosses. It first happened in Roseland in 1937 with a CLA local at the Monarch Laundry, whose proprietor, Benjamin Vellenga (and later Cornelius "Casey" Van Beek), belonged to the Christian Reformed Church, as did many employees. Monarch, one of the largest laundries on the South Side with more than fifty trucks, was a member of the Chicago Laundry Owners Association, which had entered into a closed shop contract with the Laundry Workers International Union (LWIU). This required every inside employee at member firms such as Monarch to join

85. *Illinois Observer,* Nov. 1957; 15 Mar. 1954; Tempelman, "Please Allow Me to Say," 17.

86. "Christian Labor Organization," *Banner,* 22 May 1931. CLA members currently work for some seventy-five companies in Michigan, Minnesota, and California, according to the Zeeland, Michigan-based union. The Chicago locals have dwindled into insignificance. Interview with Mike Koppenol, CLA executive director, by Charles Honey, "No calling is too small to serve God," *Grand Rapids Press,* 2 Sept. 2000.

Monarch Laundry truck fleet, 132-40 W. 111th St., Roseland, 1920s *(The Archives, Calvin College)*

the LWIU on pain of being discharged, and to be subject to a "check-off" of dues by the employer. The LWIU refused to recognize the CLA local, and the members at Monarch refused to join the LWIU. Thus, the LWIU ordered Monarch to discharge the employees by December 31, 1937, or be subject to ruinous picketing.

When Monarch reluctantly gave notice, the CLA decided to make this a test case and filed suit in the Circuit Court of Cook County. The CLA attorneys requested an injunction restraining the LWIU from interfering with the relations between Monarch and its employees' CLA local. At stake is the "right of every man to live his own life, under the law, according to his convictions," declared CLA secretary John Gritter; it is a fight "for personal liberty." When the judge dismissed the case, the CLA attorneys appealed to the Appellate Court of Illinois early in 1938. To bear the heavy financial burden, the CLA set up a "Court Case Fund" and asked Christian Reformed members in Chicago and across the nation to send money for this righteous cause. But the Wagner Act of 1935 strengthened union closed shop agreements, and the CLA got nowhere in the courts.[87]

Richard Tempelman of Englewood was the main CLA booster in Chicago. From 1955 until his death in March 1959, he wrote a monthly column in the *Illinois Observer* under the title, "Man Under the Sun." Tempelman's columns reflect the difficulties Christian unions faced and the threat of secular unions. When the AFL and CIO merged in 1955, Tempelman described the combined union as a "juggernaut" that used "ruthless tactics of coercion and squeezed the unorganized. . . . I shudder to think of it," Tempelman declared. "So large a group without any basis

87. John Gritter, "For Personal Liberty," *Banner,* 11 Aug. 1938.

in religious ideology, which is avowedly non-Christian, which will as a matter of principle, NOT commit itself on religious issues, is indeed a fertile field for non-religious ideologies." Union president Walter Reuther, Tempelman claimed, was a third-generation socialist who had long been "associated with many red, pink, and racial movements," and he had a "hard core" of 176 Congressmen in his pocket.[88]

Two CLA locals functioned in Chicago among Christian Reformed church members, both of them organized in the late 1930s among building tradesmen and food store clerks in the Lansing–South Holland–Roseland area. The most viable was CLA Building Trades Local 12. This very fact made Local 12 the target of the Cook County Building Trades Council AFL-CIO, which fiercely opposed it by picketing work sites, organizing secondary boycotts, and filing legal challenges against its certification by the National Labor Relations Board (NLRB). The suits tied up the Christian local for many years.[89]

An AFL-CIO spokesperson declared its position in unmistakable terms: "A man has a right to choose his own union, so long as that union is the AF of L." To which Tempelman retorted: "And *that* in America, the land of the free and the home of the brave." To encourage the Calumet district locals in their fight with the AFL-CIO, the CLA held its national convention in Lansing in May of 1957. Finally, in 1958, CLA Local 12 received its NLRB certification as the exclusive bargaining agent of employees of the Calumet Contractors Association. The CLA contractors by then had formed their organization, the Christian Employers Association (CEA).[90]

The second CLA local in the Chicago area was the United Food Store Clerks Local 32. It experienced little opposition from the AFL-CIO because clerical unions were weak and small, and their contracts set no wide precedents.[91]

Despite its best efforts, the CLA had tough sledding in Chicago among the Calvinist workmen. Most were lukewarm about Christian so-

88. *Illinois Observer,* Feb. 1956; 15 Oct. 1954; July, Aug. 1958.

89. J. Gritter, "What the Christian Labor Association is Doing," *Banner,* 8 June 1939; Gritter, "Christian Building Trades Unions," ibid., 16 Aug. 1940. For two specific examples of union coercion against Chicago Dutch-owned companies, see Rein Leetsma, "Liberty Under Law?" *Torch and Trumpet* (July 1956): 11-12.

90. *Illinois Observer,* Mar., June, July 1956; Sept. 1958; Apr. 1957. CLA Local No. 12 was the first "mixed craft" construction union approved by the NLRB.

91. Ibid., Feb. 1956. CLA Local 32 officers were president John De Mik, Henry Botma, Peter Blum, and Elizabeth Rauguth.

cial action generally, and on the job they were content to affiliate with secular unions for the wage and pension benefits. Like the Apostle Paul's friend Demas, charged Tempelman, they "love this present age too much" (2 Timothy 4:10). Few Dutch union members attended meetings, ran for office, or were active in any way. They preferred, as Tempelman said, to "let George do it."[92] Rare union craftsmen were John Zeilstra, a pipe fitter, and Matt Bos, both members of the First Christian Reformed Church of Cicero. Bos for many years served as a Teamster's Union business agent, despite the risk that this sullied his reputation in the community.

Even in the construction of their churches and Christian schools, some congregations and school boards accepted "closed shop" union contractors, known as "open bid" jobs (rather than "open shop" jobs with non-union workers), in the interests of labor peace, speedier construction schedules, and perhaps more highly specialized craftsmen.[93]

The bad experience in the construction of the Hammond (Indiana) Christian Reformed Church building in 1958 showed the explosive nature of the issue. The Mission Board of the Indiana churches, Hammond's sponsoring agency, and the council of the Hammond church decided that construction would be open shop under a CLA general contractor, with the subcontractors chosen strictly by the rules of low bidding, whether workers were AFL-CIO or not. But no sooner was the site excavated and the foundation laid than the AFL-CIO threw up a ring of picketers and began secondary boycotts against the legally constituted CLA general contractor. The CLA filed a complaint with the NLRB, but AFL-CIO legal maneuvers and a tepid board response left the CLA helpless. The illegal pickets halted construction for several months, because union craftsmen, even Christian craftsmen (much to the consternation of church leaders) refused to cross the picket lines. "It is much easier to violate a moral principle than a union rule," declared Tempelman. Taking on the Cook County Building Trades Union was no picnic, but in the end the Hammond church was belatedly completed without sacrificing Christian principles.[94]

92. Ibid., Jan., Oct. 1957.

93. One South Side Christian Reformed consistory and congregation, possibly Cottage Grove of South Holland, in 1958 voted for an "open bid" shop in the construction of their new church, but a Christian school board, by contrast, declared their new building construction to be "open shop" (ibid., May, Nov., Dec. 1958). The school board might have been Timothy, Calvin, Lansing, or Oak Lawn, all of which had building programs in 1958 (ibid., Sept., Oct. 1958).

94. Ibid., Feb., Mar., Sept. 1959.

Some Dutch Reformed office workers also felt the sting of discrimination because they refused to join the Masonic Lodge. John Postema of Roseland was convinced that he and other employees at Drovers State Bank near the stockyards were denied promotions because they refused the president's repeated demands to affiliate. Only after that president died did the Reformed workers win promotions. In frustration, Postema and several associates sought out the Christian Labor Association in hopes of gaining some protection. A generation later, in the 1950s, the pattern continued; all managers from foreman up at the Acme Steel Company in Riverdale had to be Masons, and this trapped some Dutch Reformed employees.[95]

Conclusion

The Dutch made their way in Chicago with a good deal of pluck and a little bit of luck. The pluck they had to find within themselves, aided by their fabled work ethic, which for a hundred years and more put food on the table, their children through school, and their church tithes paid in full. The luck seemingly fell from the sky. As they went about making a decent living, which was all they wanted from their daily labor, the capital markets suddenly rained down cash in exchange for their garbage routes, which themselves were cash cows.

But give the haulers credit; they seized the opportunity when it came. And with the success came not only the good life but remarkable works of charity that benefited their Christian schools and colleges, their churches, and their institutions of mercy. The bottom line is that they were not in it for the bottom line.

95. Grandson Jim Postema reported on Postema in an e-mail message of 25 June 2001 on DUTCH-MIDWEST-L@rootsweb.com. The Acme example is reported by John Stegenga on the same website on 5 July 2001.

CHAPTER 13

Buying Dutch: Stores and Services

As consumers of material goods, the Dutch tended to live by the bottom line rather than the ethnic line. They did not feel inclined to "help a Hollander" in business any more than they did to vote for one in public office. They patronized the stores and businesses of fellow Hollanders if the price was right and the place was handy, but they had no qualms about trading at a Jewish-owned clothing and dry goods store or a German butcher shop. "Should we patronize our fellow Christians?" was a question much debated but never resolved.

The rise of chain stores in the 1930s brought the question to a head. Should Christians trade there to save a few cents on the dollar? Even if they knew that chain stores were ruthless in their quest for efficiency, driving small manufacturers, wholesalers, and local merchants to the wall? Even if the chains employed women whenever possible, thus undermining the home? "Chains are a detriment to our nation commercially, morally, and socially," declared Jacob Post of Roseland in a letter to the editor of the *Banner.* They are "un-American" and "I dare say in conflict with God's Word. It is power divorced from wisdom." One could even think, Post concluded, that the collectivism of the chains, their thrust toward monopoly, reflects the spirit of the Antichrist.[1] Despite such dire warnings, the Dutch Reformed did indeed buy at the chain stores.

They drew the line, however, at shopping and working on Sundays. When, in 1895, a large Chicago firm insisted on Sunday work by several scores of Hollanders under threat of dismissal, the Reformed community threatened a boycott. At this the management backed down, fearing to

1. Jacob Post, "Chain Stores and Anti-Christ," *Banner,* 13 Feb. 1931, p. 174.

lose a block of customers whom "for years they had craved and built up, and which was considerable. Presto, Sunday liberty!" crowed Peter Moerdyke in his "Chicago Letter" in the *Christian Intelligencer*.[2]

For professional services, the Dutch sought out their compatriots. It may not have mattered which store the pants or the pork chops came from, but it mattered a lot who ministered to their souls, healed their bodies and minds, birthed their children, buried their dead, drew up their wills and life insurance policies, safeguarded their meager savings and mortgages, and repaired their homes. For these very personal services, the ethnoreligious tie was all-important. Similarly, when hiring tradesmen in carpentry and masonry, milk and coal deliveries, and other services that brought men into their homes, it was necessary to deal with one's trusted friends. As employers, the Dutch Reformed also took special care to hire fellow church members, relatives preferred. The advertising section of *Onze Toekomst,* titled "Guide to Professions," filled several columns and touted the services of Dutch doctors, dentists, lawyers, bankers, insurance agents, undertakers, and tradesmen of all kinds. The foods section featured such Dutch items as rye bread, rusk, cocoa, cheeses, and cookies.[3]

The sick on the Old West Side went to the physicians and surgeons William De Bey, who died in 1891 at age forty-three, Henry B. De Bey, and J. A. Riedel on the corner of 12th Street and Ashland, or A. L. Van Dellen on the corner of 14th Place and Ashland. Dutch dentists were J. E. Hartgerink, F. J. Plankeel, and John Balk on Crawford Avenue; in Englewood, R. L. Van Dellen, S. J. Heyboer, William Lumkes, and J. Rietdyke. H. C. Barth practiced optometry and James Van Epps and Ary Arlon medicine and surgery. Arlon's ad in *Onze Toekomst* read helpfully, "Wij spreken Hollandsch." Far West Side physicians from the 1920s were Henry Rottschafer, Everett Van Reken, C. N. Vetten, Paul Wezeman, and William Yonker, who specialized in diseases of the eye, ear, nose, and throat. Peter Bardolph practiced optometry. David Birkhoff was the first immigrant Hollander in Chicago to graduate from a medical school, Rush Medical College, in the 1880s, and he practiced on the West Side after brief stints in Wisconsin and Michigan.[4]

For insurance of all kinds, the Hollanders called on Andrew De Boer in the Insurance Exchange Building on Jackson Boulevard in the Loop. Or

2. Moerdyke, "Chicago Letter," *CI,* 18 Mar. 1896, p. 10.

3. For example, see *Onze Toekomst,* 25 Mar. 1936.

4. George Birkhoff, Sr., *A Short History of the Family Birkhoff* (Holland, Mich., privately printed, ca. 1910), 33-36.

they turned on the West Side to the well-known firm of Stob, Knol, & Huizenga (Thomas J. Stob, Nick Knol, and Clarence Huizenga), who handled insurance, mortgages, and real estate, with offices on 14th Street near Ashland Avenue on the Old West Side and on Roosevelt Road in Cicero. (Ben) Wierenga & (George) Ottenhoff competed head to head and also ran multiple offices – in the old neighborhood at 1837 W. Roosevelt Road, in Englewood at 7110 S. Halsted Street, and on Roosevelt Road at Humphrey Avenue in Oak Park. Here the firm shared offices with the realty business of George Ottenhoff's brother Ben – Tri-City Savings and Loan. Competitors in Oak Park were Wezeman Realty & Mortgage Company and the Jay De Young Insurance Agency, which had moved from Wells Street downtown.

In Englewood the offices of Harry Wierenga and Andrew Ridderhoff provided real estate and insurance services in competition with Wierenga & Ottenhoff. The Van Vlissingen brothers, James and Arthur, who immigrated to Roseland after the Civil War, also opened a real estate office in Chicago in 1879 and the next year a branch in Roseland, of which Arthur took sole charge. Arthur was a major Roseland real estate promoter and developer; he platted the first addition to Roseland on four hundred acres of farmland in the heart of the village. This development confined farming to the area west of the Chicago and Eastern Illinois Railroad tracks. Arthur Van Vlissingen gained a reputation as the Dutch version of a city slicker – his contemporary, Simon Dekker, called him a "plunger," but

Hendrikse and Stob Real Estate, Cicero, ca. 1925 Thomas J. Stob (left) and Nick Hendrikse (right) *(Courtesy of Henry Martin Stob)*

Stob, Knol, & Huizenga Real Estate Office, Cicero, ca. 1937
l-r: Thomas J. Stob, John Hendrikse, Bill Bolt,
secretary Rose Morina (?), Nick Knol, and Fred Lloyda
(Courtesy of Henry Martin Stob)

Van Vlissingen won the trust of many Roselanders and carried on as the old-line realty firm in the village until he went bankrupt in the 1930s. Van Vlissingen's competitor was Teninga Brothers & Pon on Michigan Avenue, founded in 1896 by Herman and Ale Teninga and Gerrit Pon, which firm platted the Bellevue subdivision and Sheldon Heights in southwest Roseland. Other Dutch realtors in the early 1900s were Gerrit Otto and his partner N. W. Birkhoff, Bernard Vellenga, and James Van Haar. The Teningas and Pon learned the ropes by working first in the office of Arthur Van Vlissingen; Vellenga in turn was trained in the office of Teninga & Pon. All were located on the Michigan Avenue business thoroughfare, which was lined on both sides for two miles by stores, shops, and offices.[5]

5. Simon Dekker, "History of Roseland," 1938, unpublished typescript, 228-33; Ettema, *Down an Indian Trail,* 135, 203; Vandenbosch, *Dutch Communities of Chicago,* 77; *Pictorial Roseland, 1907* (West Pullman, Ill.: G. F. Robert Printing Co., 1907).

Local Shopping and Trade

Because the Dutch Reformed bought on price rather than blood or brotherhood and walked without hesitation directly past the doors of Dutch grocers or shopkeepers in order to save money, the shopkeepers' morale suffered. The grocers, whose very livelihood was threatened by chain stores, found this attitude especially discouraging. Peter Bulthuis recalls sadly how his father, who owned a grocery store in Englewood, was pained when his own minister and the principal of the Christian School shopped at a local chain store to save a few dollars. Such thoughtlessness was excused by the dictum "Business is business."[6]

Still, some businesses thrived. In Roseland the J. J. Boomker & Son Grocery and Meat Market on 111th Street (formerly 110th and 117th and Michigan) had a wide patronage; its delivery truck was a common sight on local streets. In the heart of the Dutch quarter on Wentworth Avenue at 106th Street were the competing groceries of Harry Bandstra and P. De Boer & Son. Their delivery wagons and trucks were familiar sights in town. At 103rd Place and Wentworth Avenue since 1895 stood Richard Ooms Grocery. John Vander Weit was his first customer. Ooms, who lived above the store with his family, purchased his products from two Chicago wholesale companies, each of whom had a trusted Dutch Roselander to service the account. Ooms operated the store for sixty-four years and his oldest daughter, Grace Schneider, worked behind the counter over forty years, from about 1918 until the store closed late in 1959 after her father's death. The last decades were difficult, because an A & P (Atlantic & Pacific) chain store opened two blocks east at 103rd Place and Michigan Avenue. Grace recalled that John Faber was the last customer to be served. "So we opened the store and closed the store with a John!" These neighborhood stores thrived on customer service long before the term was coined.[7]

On the Old West Side, the Dutch patronized Sid Grinker's Drug Store on Ashland Avenue at Hastings Street. "Sid the Jew" sold drugs and medicines to the elderly, and his soda fountain was a favorite teen hangout. Marvin Stob ran card games for the older guys, known as Grinker's Gang. Grinker was so respected that during the Depression many Hollanders refinanced their mortgages under the federal home loan program at his urging.

6. Peter Bulthuis, *Footprints: An Autobiography* (privately printed, 1998), 14-15.

7. Jo Ann Hofstra Stob, "A History of the Richard Ooms Grocery Store, Roseland, Chicago, Illinois," based on interviews in 1998-99 with Grace Ooms Schneider.

Above, J. J. Boomker & Son Grocery and Market, ca. 1915
J. Joseph Boomker (right), father John J. Boomker (left)
(Courtesy of Esthermae Boomker Jegen)
Below, Cornelius (Case) Ericks, driving J. J. Boomker & Son truck, 1920s *(Courtesy of William Prince)*

Grinker's store shared its key intersection with Timmy Sheehan's Tavern, where in hot weather the men went to fill their buckets with beer for twenty-five cents. In order to get a smaller "head" of foam (and thus more beer), the wily Hollanders insulated their buckets with tar. Sheehan

Above, Bandstra's Food Store, early 1920s, owner Harry Bandstra in white apron, butcher Gerrit Plantinga behind counter on right. Notice dog and cat in store

(The Archives, Calvin College)

Below, Model T delivery truck, Bandstra's Food Store, ca. 1912 Louis Bandstra (left), Harry Bandstra (right)

(Courtesy of William Prince)

married Grace Kampstra, much to the chagrin of her family and all the Reformed folks. Another favorite drinking hole with its own clientele was "Ma" Raymaker's Tavern on 15th and Loomis Streets at the fringe of the Dutch neighborhood; the Dutchmen "felt safe there," recalled Ben

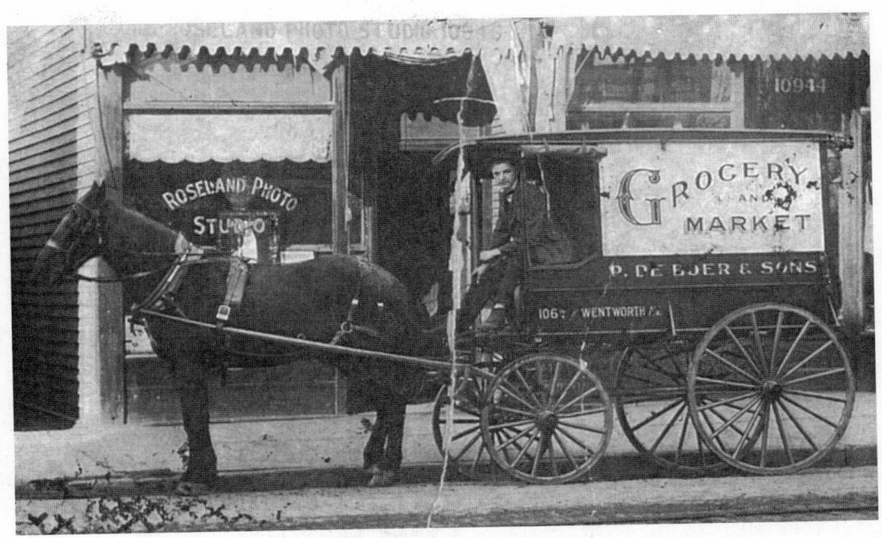

Delivery wagon, P. De Boer & Sons Grocery, ca. 1910
Louis Bandstra at the reins
(Courtesy of Arnold Bandstra)

Essenburg, because consistory members were unlikely to drop in. Teens who smoked, some as young as thirteen, bought cigarettes for a penny a piece at a store at 14th Street and Paulina Avenue.[8]

For clothing, sundries, and hardware items, the Dutch had no choice but to patronize non-Dutch stores, who sometimes hired Dutch-speaking clerks for mothers who could not speak English. The merchants liked the Dutch because they paid their bills on time. L. Klein Department Store, on 14th and Halsted Streets, and Katrina's Fancy Goods Store, on Twelfth Street (Roosevelt Road) near Ashland Avenue, were favorite haunts of the women, as was Kapper's Dry Goods and Shoe Store and the Leader Store on 18th Street, where haircuts were only twenty-five cents. Klein boasted, "Our trading stamps are best." Other popular department stores were the Albert Lurie Store on Blue Island Avenue at 18th Street, the Lion Store on Paulina and 18th Street, the Twelfth Street Store on 12th Street and

8. After her husband died, Mrs. Raymaker, nee Van Dinther, married John De Vries. Video interviews, Tom Oldenburger, 19 Nov. 1998; John Bakker, 18 Nov. 1997; Ben Essenburg, 2 Nov. 1998, all by Martin Stulp; Sarah Essenburg De Vries, "My Life on the West Side, 1929-1945," 2000, unpublished manuscript; and block advertisements in various church directories of the 1920s and 1930s.

Halsted, the Anderson Store at 16th and Paulina, the Deutch Store on 16th and Paulina, and Ginsburg's Dry Goods Store. For notions, the Dutch went to the Woolworth stores on 12th and 18th Streets. Hardware and paint were bought at B. Hirshovich's store on Ashland Avenue and Gerrit Peter's store on 14th Street. But none could beat the Maxwell Street Jewish bazaar for excited haggling over "bargains."

The Douglas Park Dutch patronized Schad Brothers and Pepper's Candy Store at 12th Street and Tripp, and Trikyl's Dry Goods Store at Crawford Avenue. During the Christmas season Trikyl's hired a Santa Claus, who provided many Dutch youngsters with their first encounter with the jolly elf.

Each Dutch neighborhood also included the usual panoply of Dutch-owned grocery and meat markets and professional services in medicine, law, realty, insurance, banking, and mortuaries. One of the first Dutch retail merchants on the West Side was Abraham Van Persyn of Hellevoetsluis, Zuid Holland, and a leader in the First Reformed Church of Chicago. By 1870 he owned a retail grocery at 72 (new numbering 735) S. Blue Island Avenue, near the major five-corner nexus with Halsted and Harrison Streets. Van Persyn's church and the First Christian Reformed Church anchored this neighborhood. Abram Pelgrim and William

Martin Otto (right) with team and wagon, delivering goods for L. Klein Department Store, 14th St. and Ashland Ave., ca. 1910

(Courtesy of Ginger [Mrs. Albert] Van Der Molen)

John Stouwie serving customers at his grocery, 1941

Campen clerked in his store and boarded with the Van Persyn family, as was the custom in the nineteenth century.

Martin Venema's grocery stood a mile to the southeast at 613 (new numbering 1324) S. Wood Street, and John Huiner and Sons' grocery and meat market was a block south of Venema's store at 703 (new numbering 1758) W. 15th Street. This was in the heart of the emerging Ashland Avenue neighborhood. Huiner featured the Dutch favorite, *gezouten snijboonen* (salted sliced green beans), "plus other foods just received by steamship from Rotterdam." In the 1920s, Huiner sold out to John Stouwie.[9]

Stouwie's store, nestled under the elevated tracks on 14th Place at Paulina Avenue, provided "quality meats and groceries." Henry Holtrust ran the meat market in the store. Stouwie, a "slim, gray-haired, and energetic" man in 1941, according to a *Chicago Daily News* reporter who visited the Dutch neighborhood, turned his business into "the nearest thing to a country store that can be found this side of Three Rivers, Michigan. Everyone knows everyone else, and the whole neighborhood trades there."[10]

Stouwie's competitor was John Olthof's grocery at 14th Place and Ashland Avenue; Albert Rispens's meat market was in the back. Jay "Butch" Broersema bought the shop and made real Dutch metwurst, and

9. Chicago City Directories, 1870-1920; Manuscript Population Censuses, Cook County, 1870-1900, *Onze Toekomst,* 16 Jan. 1920, for Huiner ad.

10. William H. Fort, "Dutch Corner of 'Valley' Brightens West Side," *Chicago Daily News,* 1 Mar. 1941, 5.

R. Dykhuis & Son Grocery 1361 (new numbering 3310)
W. Cgden Ave., ca. 1908

Hollanders came from far and wide to enjoy this traditional delicacy. Families on the western fringe of the neighborhood patronized Nicholas Rispens's grocery and meat market on 13th Street at Leavitt. Hollanders who ranked cheap prices ahead of Dutch conviviality went to Jewish competitors such as Jacobowitz's grocery store. Wezeman's grocery also provided foodstuffs, and Cornelius Van Byssum was the Dutch shoemaker. J. R. Evenhouse ran a shoe- and bootmaking shop at 1800 W. Washington Boulevard, which was north of the Dutch neighborhood.

In the Douglas Park district after 1900, Peter Dykhuis for many years operated a grocery at 666 (new numbering 1335) S. Fairfield Avenue near Ogden Avenue, which his nephew Gerrit took over in 1899.[11] In 1907 Gerrit Dykhuis's brother Roelf (Ralph) bought the grocery and meat market, running it with son John, under the name "R. Dykhuis & Son." The store was then located at 1361 (new numbering 3310) West Ogden Avenue between Homan and Spaulding Streets in a rented building. Ralph's sons Lambert and Peter clerked in the store, as did his teenaged daughters, Grace and Anna. This was a convenient arrangement, since the family of nine lived above the store. In 1909 John opened his own grocery at 2294

11. Swierenga, "Swierenga Family History."

Sluis Seed Store, Diamond T delivery truck fully loaded at rail spur on 63rd Street, ca. 1925

(Courtesy of Charlotte Solle Siegers)

(new numbering 4255) West 12th Street; his wife worked in the store, besides caring for three young children. In 1911 Ralph Dykhuis sold his store to two of his employees, Bill and Otto Rudolph, and turned to the fruit and vegetable delivery business.

The Dykhuis store, like the other Dutch grocers, bought some of their produce and dairy products from Dutch wholesale merchants such as Arys Huizenga & Sons (Richard and John), at 851 W. Randolph, and Omke Groot in the 900 block of that street. In Englewood in the 1920s, Stob & Fiet's "Great Dutch Department Store" at 68th and Halsted Streets attracted customers by offering their own trading stamps; a full book was worth $3 in gold or $3.50 in merchandize. This ploy lured the Dutch. Farmers and gardeners purchased their seeds at the Sluis Seed Store on 63rd Street and the Rock Island railroad tracks. Employees unloaded the bags of seed directly from the rail cars and delivered them by truck to their customers.[12]

12. Stob & Fiet's quarter-page ad in *Onze Toekomst,* 16 Jan. 1920; Simon J. Sluis, et al., *The Westfrisian Family Sluis* (Heiloo, 1995), English ed., 376-87. The Englewood store was established in 1908 by the brothers Joost and Pieter Sluis as a branch of the Frisian firm Gebroeders Sluis, of Laagezwaag, Friesland. Their brother, Nanne Sluis, who had immigrated to Chicago in 1906, managed the store until 1911, when he started his own wholesale seed business on Randolph Street.

J. Hofstra Bakery wagon, Roseland, 1900s, delivering Frou Frou Wafers, a Dutch pastry

(The Archives, Calvin College)

Dutch bakers featured "Holland products." The specialties of N. Hoving Bakery on Blue Island Avenue south of 16th Street were rye bread, currant bread, butter cookies, and windmill cookies. Henry ("the Baron") Labotz Bakery on Ashland Avenue at 14th Place offered similar items. In Roseland, John Hofstra's Bakery wagon advertised imported Dutch Frou Frou wafers. This three-generation firm, founded by Jan Hofstra in 1894, closed in 1990 after ninety-six years as Roseland's premier bakery.[13] For home milk deliveries, the choices on the West Side were among the Otto Woltman Dairy, John J. Vander Velde or Ralph Buikema of Union Dairy, J. D. Veldman of Wheaton Dairy, George Vander Laan of Capitol Dairy, and Huisman Milk. John H. Vandervelde, Richard Bos, and Andrew Post, among others, delivered the everyday necessities of coal, ice, and later fuel oil. All the local ice, Ben Essenburg recalled, came from Oetting's Ice Company on 15th Street, where Chicago Bears football players in the off-season could be seen handling the four hundred-pound blocks of ice; "Old Man" Oetting was a friend of Bears owner and coach, George "Papa Bear" Halas.

For building and repair work, Leonard Dwarshuis, Gerrit Peters, and Henry Roeters specialized in painting and decorating, as did Peter De

13. The Hofstra Bakery evolved from door to door peddling into a retail store, and ultimately, under his sons John H. and David and then David's son David, Jr., into a wholesale bakery. Telephone interview with Jo Ann Hofstra Stob, 6 Aug. 2002.

Young of Washburne Avenue. In Cicero, the firm of Boerman & Folgers did roofing, siding, and remodeling work. General contractors were Nick De Vries, William Stoub, and Cornelius Bierma. The latter was the largest Dutch homebuilder in Cicero and west. William Meyer of Hastings Street did cement work, besides delivering coal and ice. Kooy & Dryfhout's Wagon Repair (partners Dirk Kooy and Nicolaas [Klaas] Dryfhout) did blacksmithing and repairs in their 12th Street shop near Karlov Avenue. Later, the firm owned a car and truck repair shop at 1109 S. Crawford Avenue. In the 1940s Kooy's son John took over the farm. Blacksmiths Henry Van Der Molen and John Melvin Decker shod horses and built wagons in their shop on 14th Place. This business evolved into Decker & Van Der Molen Auto Repairs, which competed with the shop of Tazelaar & De Boer on Ashland Avenue. The gas station of Jake Gelderloos on the northwest corner of 14th Place and Ashland was a hot spot in the 1930s and 1940s.

At least one Dutch immigrant rose to the top ranks of Chicago commerce and indeed became one of the largest retail merchandisers in the United States. He was Folkert H. Kuipers (1843-1904), a Frisian Mennonite who anglicized his name to Frank H. Cooper. While working as a clothing store clerk in Leeuwarden, the Frisian capital, he decided to emigrate. He arrived in Buffalo in 1866 at age twenty-three and found the same type of employment. Later, he opened a tailoring shop in Toledo and still later in Peoria, Illinois. In 1887 Cooper joined Henry Siegel, a German drapery businessman, in opening a modest store on Chicago's State Street at Ad-

Otto Woltman (1877-1917) milk wagon

(Courtesy of Nicholas Auwerda)

Kooy & Dryfhout Auto and Truck Repairing
l-r: Klaas Dryfhout, Dirk Kooy, Dirk's son John Kooy, John's cousin John Visser and son Don, John Kooy's son Peter, 1936
(Courtesy of Evelyn [Mrs. Ralph] Kooy and son Ralph J. Kooy)

ams Street in the heart of the city retail district. The store and its entire contents were lost in a fire five years later, but the plucky entrepreneurs bought the Leiter Building three blocks south on State. The building stretched from Van Buren to Congress Streets, and the store was touted as "the largest retail establishment in the world."[14]

Siegel-Cooper was the first business of its kind in the city, and the successful partners opened a similar store in New York City in 1896. The Chicago building cost $1.5 million, and the prime lot was worth $2.5 million in 1905. Its fifteen acres of floor area, which displayed $125,000 in stock and furnishings, was contained on eight floors and a basement and was serviced by eight passenger and six freight elevators. Some twenty-five hundred employees worked in the store, and more than two hundred were fellow Hollanders, because one of Cooper's top managers, John Broekema, "always stood ready to hire a Hollander, no matter how 'green' he was." Broekema did the same when he later joined the Marshall Field store in the same capacity.[15] Siegel-Cooper "is the wonder of this wonderful city," boasted Moerdyke.

14. Swierenga, *Dutch Emigrants to the United States,* 151; Vandenbosch, *Dutch Communities of Chicago,* 76. Without the benefit of the Netherlands emigration lists, Vandenbosch incorrectly claimed Cooper as Jewish, an assumption based on the facts that large-scale retailing was dominated by Jews and his partner Siegel was Jewish.

15. Vandenbosch, *Dutch Communities of Chicago,* 76; "Frank H. Cooper," *Chicago Tribune,*

Decker & Van Der Molen blacksmiths, 1521 W. 15th Street
John Melvin Decker (center right), holding horse; others unidentified
(Courtesy of Ken Van Byssum and Peter Roeters)

> It houses everything imaginable — telegraph office, the dentist, the physician, postal clerk counter free, mammoth soda fountains, restaurant with capacity for five hundred, elegantly furnished ladies' parlor, room and care for the sick and weary, immense book department, and, in fact, the world's outfit displayed in fascinating style all around you.[16]

The Chicago store closed at Cooper's death in 1904, and, during the anti-German hysteria of the First World War, the name "Siegel-Cooper," which was carved in stone on the State Street building's ornate facade, was actually cut away! After several changes in ownership, the building became a Sears, Roebuck and Company store until the 1970s.

---

30 June 1901, p. 41; "Logic of an Aged Man: F. H. Cooper Respects Philosophy of His Father," ibid., 5 July 1901, p. 19; engraving, "De Grootste Winkel in de Wereld," *De Grondwet,* 14 Mar. 1893; Moerdyke, "Chicago Letter," *CI,* 31 Mar. 1893; Van Hinte, *Netherlanders in America,* 957; Mayer and Wade, *Chicago: Growth of a Metropolis,* 225; "Siegel, Cooper & Co.'s Mammoth Department Store," *Jewish Messenger,* 17 Apr. 1896; "Siegel, Cooper & Company," *Holland* [MI] *Daily Sentinel,* 25 Aug. 1897. In 1899 F. H. Cooper endowed a home for the aged in his hometown of Akkrum, Friesland (Moerdyke, "Chicago Letter," *CI,* 24 May 1899, p. 9). The Akkrum institution continues to the present day.

16. Moerdyke, "Chicago Letter," *CI,* 17 May 1893, p. 11.

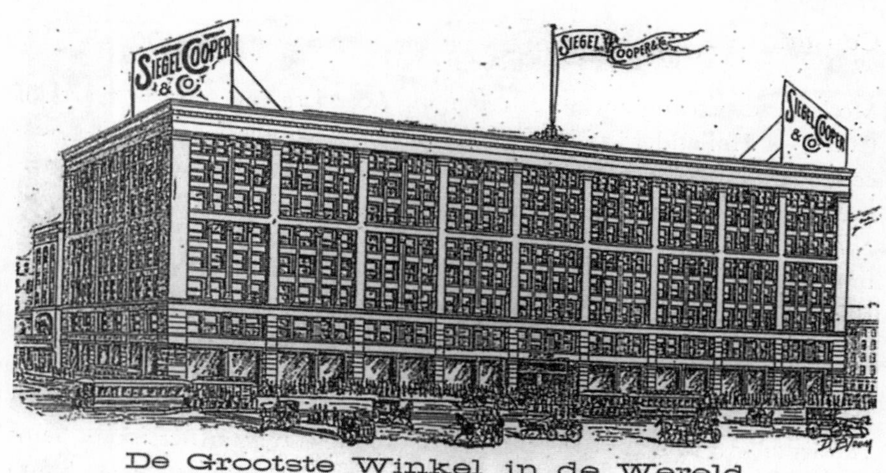

Siegel-Cooper & Co. Department Store, State Street, 1893

Roseland also had its Sears, Roebuck Store on Michigan Avenue at 114th Street, but the People's Store was the flagship department store. Owned by a Swede named Swanson, it took up most of the block on Michigan Avenue between 112th and 113th Streets and set the standard for merchandizing success. It closed in the Great Depression and, after changing hands, reopened as the Avenue Department Store. For many years, Swanson's major competitor was Boersma's Department Store on Michigan Avenue and 111th Street in the heart of Roseland, which the new Frisian immigrant, Reimer Boersma, founded in 1882.

J. C. Bovenkerk later bought the store and organized it in the modern way, with separate departments for men and women, boys and girls, and even a "self-help basement" with lower prices. Bovenkerk clearly understood the art of American merchandising; he also inherited good business instincts from his father, who was a cigar manufacturer from Weesp (province of Noord Holland) before immigrating with his family to Roseland in 1894. By the 1950s, Bovenkerk was specializing in stylish men's clothing in his Bovenkerk's Men's Wear store on 111th St., one door west of Michigan Avenue.[17]

17. Dekker, "History of Roseland," 264-65; Van Hinte, *Netherlanders in America,* 829; Swierenga, "Dutch in Chicago and Cook County 1900 Federal Census" (1992), also in Family Tree Maker's Family Archives, CD #269.

Consumerism

Modern advertising and merchandizing hoped to capture the hearts of Chicago's Hollanders as it did everyone else. The Dutch, too, were susceptible to the materialist ethic. Already in the first decades after immigration, for example, they let the deeply rooted Sint Nikolaas (Saint Nicholas) tradition wither away in favor of the American Christmas celebration. The Saint Nicholas custom involved the exchange of gifts within the family circle on December 5, three weeks before the religious celebration of the birth of Jesus of Nazareth on December 25. This preserved Christmas purely as a religious holiday. Once in America, the Dutch adopted Santa Claus as the patron saint of children, being satisfied with the argument that Santa Claus was simply the American version of Saint Nicholas. He was not. Nicholas was a Christian saint, whereas Santa Claus was a secular elf.

By the early twentieth century, Chicagoans spent twenty million dollars on Christmas buying, and some of those dollars came from Dutch pockets and purses. Christmas was bigger than ever at the department stores like Siegel-Cooper, Marshall Field, and Sears. Dutch-American parents quite readily took their children to these stores to sit on Santa's lap and tell him the toys they wanted. The parents also bought and decorated Christmas trees in their homes.

Peter Moerdyke, of Chicago's Trinity Reformed Church, aptly described the season in 1906:

> The Christmas trade, crowds, rush of shoppers, exhaustion of buyers and utter fatigue of clerks have been, are today, greater than ever in this city. The taxing of purse and time and strength and patience, the slavery and self-imposition of it all, are so extreme, as to render the popular holiday excitement a species of madness, from which this land should recover and if pure love and sincere esteem impelled all in this dreadful scramble and mania it might be justified.
>
> We shall have to return to the simpler celebration. . . . Were the St. Nicholas custom of gladdening the home circle, and possibly a few and select bosom friends, reinstated, a stupendous folly might go into the archives of history. How good sense, wise economy, a saner December, better Christian and church life in December, and healthier average business would be promoted. It is estimated that at least twenty millions will be spent here in purchasing Christmas presents. It takes a month to recover from the usual reaction, and church life

suffers just at the season when it should most flourish. This is not the true advent spirit.[18]

Dutch Financial Institutions

Home ownership was highly valued among the Dutch. As soon as they gained a measure of economic security, they bought bungalows and flats. In 1900, 28 percent of Dutch-American households citywide owned their homes. The figure was higher in Roseland at 33 percent, because property values were lower in the far suburbs. It was far lower, at 12 percent, in the vicinity around the First Reformed and First Christian Reformed churches of Chicago, but jumped to 27 percent in the upscale neighborhoods around Douglas Park Christian Reformed Church.[19]

The level of home ownership among Dutch laborers in Chicago compares favorably with that of urban workers nationally and shows that the Dutch were achieving the American dream. A 1901 survey of 25,440 urban families in thirty-two states showed that 19 percent owned their own homes. Nationally, 40 percent of all non-farm housing units were owner occupied. The Dutch disdained apartment living and avoided tenement houses at all costs. For one thing, such dwellings could not accommodate their large families. More importantly, home ownership was the dream of every young couple, and the sooner the better. Many married siblings and parents doubled up by buying two-flats or three-flats together.[20]

The key to home ownership was the Dutch building and loan associations or, more accurately, savings banks. On the West Side the most prominent was the Hollandsche Bouw en Leen Vereeniging (later the Holland Building & Loan Association of Chicago), which was formed in 1882 as a joint stock company by wealthy Hollanders. Its offices were on La Salle Street in the heart of Chicago's financial district – first at 84 South, then in 1909 at 415-84 South, and by 1914 at 10 South La Salle in the Otis Building. In 1906 the association held $150,000 in real estate mortgages and declared itself to be "very prosperous and financially

18. Ibid., 26 Dec. 1906, p. 849.

19. Compiled from Swierenga, "Dutch in Chicago and Cook County 1900 Federal Census," also in Family Tree Maker's Family Archives, CD #269.

20. Michael R. Haines and Allen C. Goodman, "Buying the American Dream: Housing Demand in the United States in the Late Nineteenth Century," Working Paper No. 5, Working Paper Series on Historical Factors in Long Run Growth, National Bureau of Economic Research, Inc., p. 1; Vandenbosch, *Dutch Communities of Chicago,* 67.

sound." Indeed, in 1927 the association boasted that it had never lost a dollar on any of its loans.[21]

In the early 1900s George Birkhoff was the president, Herman Vander Ploeg secretary, and Evert Van Herik treasurer. In the 1920s George Ottenhoff, E. H. Wierenga, Harry Bierma, J. J. Zandstra, Abel Danhof, F. Nienhuis, and Van Herik served on the board at various times. Van Herik, who lived in Englewood, was honored on his ninetieth birthday in 1936 for holding the posts of treasurer and director for more than forty years. In the mid-1930s, the bank moved from the city center to the heart of the Old West Side, into the offices of Wierenga & Ottenhoff at 1837 West Roosevelt Road. Its newspaper advertisements urged people to "start an account" and "save systematically and soundly." Hollanders hardly needed this reminder to do what came naturally.[22]

George Ottenhoff eventually became the president and led the association for decades, along with his sons Conrad, Ben, and George, Jr. In the 1920s, as more westsiders moved into the suburbs of Cicero, Berwyn, and Oak Park, the Ottenhoffs shifted the firm's main office to a choice location at 6020 West Roosevelt Road, just west of the key intersection with Austin Boulevard, where the borders of Chicago's Austin District and the towns of Cicero and Oak Park met. They renamed the firm Tri-City Savings and Loan (after the three cities), and virtually every Holland family on the West Side had a savings account or mortgage there. George Ottenhoff ran his real estate and law office from the same building.[23]

The Roseland Dutch in the late 1880s also formed a mortgage bank, the Roseland Building and Loan Association. The prime movers were the first officers: president Gerrit Otto, a realtor; and the secretary-treasurer John Nichols, a banker. Simon Dekker, who served on the board for a time, attended the monthly meetings to evaluate and approve loan applications. Investment capital came from individual shareholders who bought shares with a par value of $100, paying in at a rate of 50 cents per month for ten years. With compound interest of 6 percent, this $60 was worth par, or $100. Loans were based on a ten-year amortization schedule with monthly payments of principal and interest. The association did not

21. Vandenbosch, *Dutch Communities of Chicago,* 67-68.

22. *Chicago City Directory,* 1899; *Onze Toekomst,* 20 June 1919; 6 June 1906; 9 Jan. 1920; 9 Dec. 1936; *Chicago Messenger,* 31 Jan., 13 Oct. 1936.

23. Van Hinte, *Netherlanders in America,* 830; *Illinois Observer,* 1954ff. In the 1950s and 1960s, George Ottenhoff was president of Tri-City and Maurice Vander Velde was secretary-treasurer and office manager.

survive the "Cleveland hard times" of the 1890s because of loan defaults, and it had to be liquidated.[24]

Ale Teninga, another leading realtor, subsequently formed the Roseland Home Loan and Building Association. With Herman Teninga as secretary, the firm in 1923 had capital above $1 million. It thrived until the Great Depression, but then the value of its shares plummeted by half and the federal government bought the strongest loans to keep the association afloat. Dekker concluded from this history that such associations "are only successful in good times, but in adverse times they are absolutely no good."[25]

Banks in Roseland fared little better than mortgage companies. William Zwart's bank closed in the depression of the 1890s, paying savers thirteen cents on the dollar. In the Great Depression of the 1930s all three banks failed — the Roseland State Bank in 1931, the Wiersema State Bank in 1932, and the Roseland National Bank in 1933. The first paid 40 cents on the dollar and the second, 20 cents; only the latter paid its depositors 100 cents on the dollar.[26]

The Wiersema bank was the most prominent institution. It was founded in 1891 by Frederick Wiersema and John Nichols, and for years it operated in the Boersma block on Michigan Avenue near 111th Street. Nichols was replaced early on by Wiersema's son Asa, who won the trust of Roseland citizens. Most Hollanders put their life savings in Wiersema's hands with full confidence, and deposits exceeded $4 million. But it closed without warning January 28, 1932. The Roseland State Bank on Michigan Avenue at 114th Place was almost as old as the Wiersema Bank and also had $4 million in deposits. The sudden collapse of these two major banks was a major catastrophe for the Roseland Hollanders and made their suffering the worst in the Dutch communities of greater Chicago.

The Clearing State Bank, owned by Lambert Bere, served Hollanders along Archer Avenue in the Clearing district near the present-day Midway Airport. The Chicago City Bank and Trust Company in Englewood was the primary holder of savings for the Dutch there.[27]

24. Dekker, "History of Roseland," 234.

25. Ibid., 236; Van Hinte, *Netherlanders in America,* 829.

26. Decker, "History of Roseland," 239-45.

27. *Illinois Observer,* 1954ff.

Dutch Language Press — *De Nederlander* and *Onze Toekomst*

Newspapers bound the Hollanders together and provided advertising space for their businessmen and professionals. The first paper that old timers could recall in the 1920s appeared during the Civil War in support of Abraham Lincoln and the Union. It was edited by a Judge Entwoud (In't Woud?) and printed in the plant of the *Chicago Tribune,* Lincoln's mouthpiece.[28]

The second Chicago Dutch-language newspaper, *De Nederlander,* boasted that it was the only Dutch newspaper in the state of Illinois. It was founded in 1883 as a Republican sheet by the publisher J. Esnorf, whose offices stood at 485 (new numbering 1602) Blue Island Avenue at Throop Street. In 1889 H. M. Buhrmann, a member of the Free Dutch Congregation in Grand Rapids, Michigan, purchased the paper and moved the office a block south to 545 Blue Island. It appeared every Thursday, and the subscription price was $1.50 per year or $2 for subscribers in the Netherlands.

The paper began to flourish under the talented pen of editor Henry Uden Marsman, a university graduate and "writer of ability." His editorials and literary articles, Vandenbosch noted, "are still remembered by the older people as the acme of journalistic writing." Under Uden Marsman's watch, *De Nederlander* gained national notoriety when in 1893 it published a provocative essay by the religious immigrant, J. Hoddenbach van Scheltema of Arnhem, entitled *"Heeft de Nederlandsche taal eene toekomst?"* (Is there a future for the Dutch language?). This question so concerned the Chicago Dutch elite that it prompted them to form the Algemeen Nederlandsche Verbond (The General Dutch League) in 1898 (see chapter 10). This organization aimed to maintain contact with Netherlanders in the diaspora.[29]

Just after the close of the Chicago World's Fair, in July of 1893, *De Nederlander* suffered a devastating fire, the second in six months, which destroyed the entire printing shop, including all the type settings and the back issues. Although the equipment was fully insured, Esnorf decided to close his printery and move the production of *De Nederlander* to *De Grondwet* (The Constitution) of Holland, Michigan, America's oldest

28. No copies of this paper are extant.

29. Vandenbosch, *Dutch Communities of Chicago,* 62-63; Van Hinte, *Netherlanders in America,* 454. Another short-lived Dutch paper was *De Nederlandsche Amerikaan,* which the Chicago Holland Publishing Company began in 1891 (*CI,* 3 June 1891).

Dutch newspaper. From 1893 until 1902 *De Nederlander* was published in Michigan for the Chicago customers, but the long-distance venture did not flourish. In 1902 Esnorf closed the paper and sold the remaining list of fifteen hundred subscribers to *De Grondwet,* which began a special "Chicago Edition" that grew to eighteen hundred paid subscriptions by 1910.[30]

The rival was *Onze Toekomst* ("Our Future"). It was launched in 1894 by the Young Men's Union of the Reformed and Christian Reformed churches of Chicago, who bought and rebuilt the burned out printing plant of *De Nederlander,* under the auspices of the Rook and Bosgraaf Printing Company. The Young Men's Union sold their paper for a subscription price of 25 cents per annum. P. H. Holtman, the first editor, had a rocky start when he alienated his Reformed Church readers by criticizing the late esteemed pastor of First Church, Bernardus De Bey. Holtman charged De Bey and the Reformed churches with supporting "un-Christian" public schools. This Americanizing step, Holtman charged, would undermine Reformed orthodoxy. Faced with demands for his resignation, Holtman turned over his pen to Albert Raap and Henry Jacobsma, the principals of the two Christian schools in Roseland, who were more judicious. In 1898 A. Langeland bought the paper, reorganized it as an all-Dutch newspaper for the city, and hired Uden Marsman as editor; he ran it until the end of 1905.[31]

Uden Marsman had one tough moment. In 1899 a local Presbyterian minister threatened to sue the paper for libel over an article written by Jan Riemersma, pastor of the First Christian Reformed Church of Chicago. The nature of the charges is unknown, but one can surmise that Riemersma had questioned the moral or religious integrity of his Presbyterian colleague. The sad moment passed when Riemersma acknowledged in print that he had been guilty of "slander and defamation," and he and the paper retracted the libel. Riemersma himself was about to be defrocked at the time for preaching while drunk with communion wine, among other things.[32]

Happier responses came from Uden Marsman's efforts to enlighten *Onze Toekomst* readers about things Netherlandic. As Moerdyke noted:

30. No issue of *De Nederlander* is known to be extant. "*De Nederlander* Uitgebrand," *De Grondwet,* 8 Aug. 1893; Moerdyke, "Chicago Letter," *CI,* 30 Apr. 1902, p. 284; *Holland City News,* 18 April 1902; Henry S. Lucas, *Netherlanders in America,* 537.

31. Moerdyke, "Chicago Letter," *CI,* 31 Jan., p. 10, 18 Apr. 1894, p. 10.

32. Moerdyke reports the case in ibid., 12 Apr., p. 16, 26 Apr., p. 5, 10 May 1899, p. 9.

> To any of our bilingual ministers it may be a delight and a special line of culture to spend frequent hours with the masters of the prose and poetry of the Netherlands. As a unique feature, possible and appreciated only in a Dutch paper in America, our local weekly, *Onze Toekomst* has for months regularly contained interesting articles by Mr. L. Holstein on the grammar and rhetoric of the "Hollandsche Taal" [Dutch language]. And every week some classic Dutch poem appears in another column. This is the more gratifying to its constituency because, to tell the truth, very few of its readers possess any volumes of such literature. What few Dutch books they have are of a religious character.

Luurt Holstein, a resident of Englewood and member of the Second Christian Reformed Church, replaced Uden Marsman as editor of *Onze Toekomst* in 1906, after the latter accepted the editorship of the flagship paper, *De Grondwet.* Under Holstein's able pen, the *Toekomst* became a weekly. A board, called the Christian Press Society, provided oversight and support for the venture. Nick Wierenga was a long time member and society president. While the paper had no official connection with the Reformed and Christian Reformed churches, it essentially was their mouthpiece and featured religious and ecclesiastical news. The most popular section contained reports from all the Dutch-American communities and churches of greater Chicagoland. Holstein truly made *Onze Toekomst* Chicago's Dutch Reformed newspaper.[33]

Throughout most of its long history and until its demise in 1951, the office stood in the heart of the old neighborhood at 1315 S. Ashland Avenue. In 1917, when Holstein resigned, the paper was reorganized as a joint stock company of the Christian Literature Company. That year the Reverend Dr. John Van Lonkhuyzen, pastor of the First Christian Reformed Church of Chicago, became editor. He was a graduate of the Free University of Amsterdam and wrote interesting and pithy pieces from a strongly Reformed perspective.

In the 1920s, Van Lonkhuyzen expanded *Onze Toekomst* from four to eight pages, and the circulation grew to thirty-five hundred by 1922, with twelve hundred in Chicago. It gained subscribers in the far-flung Dutch colonies west of Chicago by introducing an extra page, entitled "Het Westen," which was written by a correspondent in Orange City, Iowa. In

33. Ibid., 13 Dec. 1905, p. 810; Vandenbosch, *Dutch Communities of Chicago,* 61-64; obituary, Nick Wieringa, *De Grondwet,* 21 May 1929, p. 8; Arthur De Kruyter, "On Being Editor of the *Observer,*" *Illinois Observer,* Oct. 1957. In 1906 there were twenty-five Dutch-language publications, weekly and monthly, religious and secular, in the United States.

this outreach, it competed with its bigger rival, *De Grondwet* of Holland, Michigan, which had a string of correspondents in Dutch centers nationwide. Van Lonkhuyzen truly made *Onze Toekomst* the most important Dutch-language newspaper in the United States.[34]

Onze Toekomst linked Dutch families and church congregations across the rapidly growing city and was a crucial vehicle to disseminate information and give the Dutch a voice. Its extensive advertisements promoted the services of Dutch professionals and businesses and pushed Dutch foods and products like rusk, roggebrood (rye bread), cocoa, cheese, and Douwe Egberts coffee.

But most readers turned first to the obituary page, especially the unique section, "Death Reports from the Old Country," which ran once a month and gave the names of those deceased in the Netherlands, listed by province with their ages and cities. Peter Moerdyke, in one of his "Chicago Letters," noted the importance of this page. "From one-half to an entire column is thus filled, and eagerly read by hundreds of people here, who in these provincially classified death-rolls find sad intelligence of the departure of old mates, chums, neighbors and friends. I am told that not a few who spent their early life in the Netherlands, whilst welcoming the whole usual page of foreign news from home, take the paper largely for that obituary column."[35]

Van Lonkhuyzen returned to his native land in 1927, and the paper continued to flourish under various editors for another twenty-five years. The first of these was Edward J. Tuuk, recently retired pastor of the Second Englewood Christian Reformed Church, who was followed by James J. Van Pernis and H. De Jong. When William Vandervelde of the Holland-American Printing and Publishing Company took over ownership in 1937, he brought in his friend, Dr. Frederick H. Wezeman, as editor. Wezeman wielded his sharp pen for two years until 1938 and brought the paper through the difficult Depression years. In the 1940s, *Onze Toekomst* gradually lost subscribers, as Dutch-language readers died and the younger generations succumbed to Americanization. By 1949 at least six of the eight pages were printed in the English language, under the rubric *Chicago Calvinist;* Wezeman's brother Henry was editor.

In 1951 the company was forced to suspend *Onze Toekomst* and replace

34. A. Oosterheert, "The Dutch Press in America," *Onze Toekomst,* 24 Oct. 1923 (reprinted from the Album for Queen Wilhelmina).

35. Moerdyke, "Chicago Letter," *CI,* 5 Mar. 1906, p. 9; *Onze Toekomst,* 30 Jan. 1920; Van Hinte, *Netherlanders in America,* 830, 915-16, 918, 921; Oosterheert, "Dutch Press."

ONZE TOEKOMST

The Holland-American Weekly — "OUR FUTURE" — $1.50 Per Year

PERPETUATE THE HONOR AND GLORY OF OUR RACE — "'t GEHEIM VAN ALLEN ZEGEN, IS IN GODS VREES GELEGEN"

Volume 56 — CHICAGO, ILL., FEBRUARY 2, 1949 — Number 5

FEBRUARY 10 IS DOCTOR WEZEMAN DAY

"FRIENDSHIP IS POWER AND RICHES ALL TO ME."

PUBLIC TRIBUTE TO NOTED EDUCATOR

NICHOLAS KNOL DIES OF HEART ATTACK; PROMINENT IN CIVIC AND CHURCH WORK

Mr. Nicholas Knol, 5040 W. 24th Place, Cicero, died of a heart attack in the office of his realty firm, Stob, Knol & Huizenga, Monday afternoon January 31, at 2:30. He was 61 years old and had been active as a business man in Cicero for 45 years. He was a member of the First Reformed Church, Berwyn, where he served as vice-president of the Men's Brotherhood. Mr. Knol was vice-president of the Self-Help Assurance Society, of which his father in the early days had been a widely known agent; a member of the Cicero Rotary, and vice-president of the All Cicero Committee. The body will rest at the Mulder Funeral Home, 6033 Roosevelt Rd., until Thursday. Funeral services will be conducted Thursday afternoon February 3, at 2 P. M. at the First Reformed Church, 19th and Oak Park Avenue, the pastor, Rev. H. Kik, officiating. Interment will be in Forest Home cemetery. Besides his wife, nee Tracy Ploegman, he leaves a daughter, Mrs. Ralph Engelsman; two grandchildren; his mother, Mrs. Herman Veldman; seven brothers, George, Albert, William, Arthur, David, Rev. Herman Knol, and Clarence; two sisters, Minnie Kieft and Angeline Hoff.

Onze Toekomst masthead

it with the English-language *Weekly Observer.* In 1954, with the subscription list down to six hundred and facing large loses, the company cut the paper to a monthly, renamed it the *Illinois Observer,* and hired a new editor, the energetic Arthur De Kruyter, pastor of the Western Springs Christian Reformed Church. The next year, 1955, with subscriptions on the rise again, De Kruyter and his friend Martin Ozinga, Jr., a successful Evergreen Park businessman, negotiated to buy the paper from the Holland-American Company. De Kruyter quickly pushed the circulation back up to its old high of thirty-five hundred, by reaching readers across the United States, Canada, and even the Netherlands.[36] But it was a last hurrah. Circulation dropped off again, and in 1960 De Kruyter changed the focus to church news under the name the *Church Observer.* The paper had become a glorified clearinghouse to publicize Chicago area church activities.

36. De Kruyter, "On Being Editor of the *Observer,*" *Chicago Calvinist,* 15 Apr. 1954.

CHAPTER 14

Help a Hollander: Ethnic Politics

"We feel it our duty to point out that the election of a Republican is more desired than that of a Democrat," declared the editor of Chicago's Dutch-language newspaper, *Onze Toekomst,* in 1910.[1] His readers readily agreed. The Dutch Protestants of Chicago were "Republican almost to a man," according to historian Amry Vandenbosch in 1927. This was a slight exaggeration, since Vandenbosch cited the calculation of Age Zylstra, a politician and member of William Hale ("Big Bill") Thompson's cabinet, who set the rate of Dutch adherence at 90 percent.[2]

Republican partisanship was even expressed in the churches on rare occasions. In 1896, just days after William McKinley had won the presidency, members of the First Reformed Church of Chicago were pleasantly shocked when parents, presenting their son for baptism, named him McKinley. Thirty years earlier, shortly after the bitter Civil War, the consistory of the same congregation had closed its pulpit to a Democrat of pronounced anti-Union sentiments.[3]

Reformed Hollanders were even urged by revered leaders from the Netherlands to reject the Democratic Party. Abraham Kuyper, head of the strictly Calvinist Anti-Revolutionary Party, when in the United States in 1898 on a big lecture tour, told his Chicago audience that the Democratic Party was an advocate of the principles of the French Revolution, and he solemnly warned them not to support that party.[4]

1. *Onze Toekomst,* 1 Apr. 1910.
2. Vandenbosch, *Dutch Communities of Chicago,* 51.
3. Peter Moerdyke, "Chicago Letter," *CI,* 11 Nov. 1896, p. 11.
4. Ibid., 24 Oct. 1900, p. 686.

The one-sided Republicanism of the Dutch Reformed in Chicago was typical of Hollanders nationwide. They had aligned themselves with the party of Lincoln ever since the Civil War. Only the Pella, Iowa, colony, where the Dutch felt the sting of nativist attacks by the Know Nothing Party in the 1850s, held to a staunch tradition of voting Democratic tickets. President Abraham Lincoln rewarded the Dutch in Roseland for their Republican allegiance by granting them a post office. The first postmaster, Goris Vander Syde, ran the station out of his general store on Michigan Avenue.[5]

Dutch Jews, along with most Jews, also voted Republican until they switched allegiance in the 1930s and joined Franklin D. Roosevelt's New Deal coalition. Dutch Catholics, by contrast, voted Democratic from the start, as did most Catholic ethnic groups. All were ardent trade unionists and many held socialist ideals. Some unchurched Dutch, called *modernen* ("modernists"), also supported the Socialist ticket.

For the Dutch Reformed, socialism was anathema. The editor of *Onze Toekomst* spoke for most in 1906:

> We are the enemy of the Socialistic principle of state or Government power. State power retards individual development and takes away from the people their individuality. Socialism for that reason is dangerous, it goes against the free development of the individual.[6]

Christian socialism had some appeal to a few liberals in the Reformed Church, but not the usual secular variety. A few thoroughly Americanized Hollanders also endorsed the Prohibition Party.[7]

National Politics – Roosevelt and the Dutch

In national politics, Chicago's Dutch Reformed held in high regard the Republican presidents Benjamin Harrison (1885-89), William McKinley

5. Robert P. Swierenga, "The Ethnic Voter and the First Lincoln Election," *Civil War History* 11 (March 1965): 27-43, reprinted in Swierenga, *Faith and Family: Dutch Immigration and Settlement in the United States, 1820-1920* (New York: Holmes & Meier, 2000), 274-89; Ettema, *Down an Indian Trail,* 57.

6. *Onze Toekomst,* 7 Sept. 1906.

7. Moerdyke, "Chicago Letter," *CI,* 18 Mar. 1910. Peter Moerdyke was one Chicago Reformed Church pastor and leader who expressed an affinity for Christian socialism, such as that of the Congregational churchman, Dr. Charles M. Sheldon, and his popular Utopian novel, *In His Steps* (1890), which coined the enduring phrase, "What would Jesus do?" (ibid., 21 Mar. 1900, p. 185; 21 Nov. 1906, p. 758).

President Theodore Roosevelt

(1893-1901), and especially the blue-blooded Dutch-American, Theodore Roosevelt (1901-09), who stimulated the Chicago Hollanders as nothing else in their memory. Roosevelt's open boasting of his Dutch ancestry made him "one of us," a revered compatriot. His frequent visits at the worship services of the First Reformed and Trinity Reformed churches in Chicago were big events, and the chair Roosevelt sat on became a relic.

The Boer War was *the* foreign policy issue at the turn of the century for Dutch-Americans in general and the Holland Society in particular. At the 1899 banquet, George Birkhoff, Jr., the Dutch vice-consul in Chicago, offered a rousing toast for the Afrikaners, who were engaged in the "same struggle for liberty and independence as were our forefathers in the 16th and 17th centuries in the struggle with Spain." Birkhoff went on to castigate the "corrupt and perfidious" American press, pro-British as it was, for reporting with such "malice and race prejudice."[8]

Reformed and Christian Reformed churches organized chapters of the newly founded Transvaal League to promote the cause. Hollanders gathered in mass protest meetings in Chicago, Grand Rapids, and across

8. *Yearbook of the Holland Society of Chicago, 1895-1896* (Chicago, 1897); ibid., *1899* (Chicago, 1901), 14, 154, 185.

the West to try to change American policies. They raised more than $13,000 for the Boer Relief Fund; Chicago Dutch contributed more than $4,000, an amount equaled only by the Grand Rapids Dutch. All their hopes were dashed in a matter of months, however, when it became clear that the cause of the Boers was lost.[9]

Harrison endeared himself to the Dutch to a greater extent after leaving the White House than during his tenure. As ex-president in 1900, Harrison strongly denounced England's "bullying of weak republics," by taking up arms to crush the Afrikaaners' independence movement for the Transvaal and Orange Free State. This earned kudos for Harrison. At his death in 1901, Peter Moerdyke wrote in his weekly column, "Chicago Letter," in the *Christian Intelligencer:*

> The Hollanders deeply lament the death of former President Harrison, whom they specially honored and loved as a true American with a heart full of boldly expressed sympathy with the Boers in their righteous contention against oppression, rapacity and imperialism. All honor to this remarkably able, wise, incorruptible statesman for his strong and genuinely American denunciation of England's "bullying of weak republics," a course she would not dare pursue against one of "the Powers."[10]

Following the American victory in the Spanish-American War in 1898, Moerdyke reveled in William McKinley's participation in Chicago's five-day celebration. "Our beloved president was our popular guest. He has greatly endeared himself to all by his wise, manly and truly American ways and words." The Trinity and Northwestern Reformed Church congregations held a joint Sunday evening service as part of the celebration. Moerdyke and Seth Vander Werf, Northwestern's pastor, gave addresses extolling America as "God's instrument," which must follow God's call to a "higher patriotism" as a "Christian Republic." The nation's future looked bright indeed at the dawn of the new century.[11]

The Dutch adored McKinley until late in his term, when some turned on him for aligning his administration with the hated British and against the freedom-loving South African Boers. In the 1900 presidential election campaign, Abraham Kuyper even urged his American followers to

9. Moerdyke, "Chicago Letter," *CI,* 1 Nov., p. 9, 8 Nov., p. 8, 13 Dec. 1899, p. 18; 3 Jan., p. 8, 7 Mar. 1900, p. 153; 29 Jan. 1902, p. 73.

10. Ibid., 27 Mar. 1901, p. 201.

11. Ibid., 26 Oct. 1898, p. 4; 23 Jan. 1901, p. 56.

"do all in their power to defeat Mr. McKinley because of his stand for imperialism and his attitude toward the Boers." Kuyper recommended the normally Republican Hollanders to vote for the Democratic candidate, William Jennings Bryan, or stay away from the polls. Following President McKinley's assassination two years later, Kuyper's government was one of the few not to send official condolences to Mrs. McKinley and the nation.[12]

Roosevelt worshiped a number of times at the Trinity Reformed Church in Chicago – twice in 1900 while governor of New York, once in the fall national election campaign after becoming the vice-presidential nominee, and several times as vice-president. Roosevelt charmed everyone at the church, including then pastor Moerdyke, who on the second visit offered "our parishioner" a "free and reserved seat." This "royal Dutchman," Moerdyke happily noted, "so unaffectedly spoke to groups about him of his Dutch ancestry, and recited snatches of Dutch nursery rhymes," that when he "bade us his friendly good-bye we all felt as if he were an old friend; and a few boys about his parting carriage could no longer restrain the cheers they had ached to give him."[13] In the minds of the Dutch, that such a "grand American" was not ashamed to worship with a small and insignificant group of recent immigrants spoke volumes about his character.[14]

Roosevelt's third visit in October 1900 was not as happy. The presidential campaign season was in full swing, and Roosevelt had joined the McKinley Republican ticket as the vice-presidential candidate. Again the congregation "most heartily welcomed him," reported Moerdyke, but this time he was expected, so the "capacity of our church was taxed by the large gathering of his admirers, who gave him an informal reception at the close of the service." So far, so good. But upon leaving the church, Roosevelt was met on the front steps by a dozen rowdy teenaged boys, who rudely shouted the name "Bryan" – the Democratic presidential candidate, William Jennings Bryan. When Roosevelt raised his hand and scolded them, saying, "Boys, be still," one or two threw sand on the colonel's trademark Rough Rider's hat as he rode off in his carriage.

The Chicago newspapers, notably the *Chicago Record,* embellished the minor incident into the "wildest, wilful, most insulting misrepresen-

12. Ibid., 17 Oct. 1900, p. 670; 25 Sept. 1901, p. 621.

13. Ibid., 11 July, p. 445, 19 Sept., p. 605, 17 Oct. 1900, p. 669.

14. Christian Reformed pastor Johannes Remein of Rochester, New York, viewed Roosevelt's humble visits in the Chicago churches as Christlike, in "Jezus en het Huisgezin," Christian Reformed Church, *Jaarboekje,* 1903, 161.

tations," cried Moerdyke. Supposedly, a mob ran after the carriage for seventy yards hurling curses and epithets, women were shrieking at the prospect of bloodshed, and the pastor was guilty of being unprepared, of calling too late for the police, etc. "Pity the poor dupe who patronizes and trusts any such unscrupulous sensationalism," declared Moerdyke angrily. "Our congregation and visitors who witnessed the whole affair are indignant, aggrieved and filled with loathing of such journalism. This campaign falsehood was almost 'created out of nothing,' as the plain facts show." Thus did Moerdyke learn at first hand the color of "yellow journalism," those "picturesque scribblers of fiction," and the rough and tumble of American politics. For weeks afterwards, he was bombarded with queries from reporters at distant newspapers seeking to follow up on the lurid story.[15]

Moerdyke was also criticized by Henry Nyenesch, editor of the staunchly Democratic *Pella's Weekblad,* who charged that Roosevelt's repeated visits to Trinity Reformed Church signaled that the candidate and the dominie had stepped over the line by bringing politics into divine worship services. The church had become a "vote-getting and political recruiting place." Not true, declared Moerdyke.

> Strange that any Western partisans should maliciously and perversely have charged both him and myself with political motives in his repeated visits last summer to our church. Men of both parties in our congregation were equally delighted with the Governor's loyal visits and never in the remotest way surmised that their pastor had the least design, inducement, expectation, or reward in simply extending heartiest welcome to our distinguished guest, who absolutely of his own free will selected his own church in Chicago. . . . He is governed by loyalty to his denomination.[16]

After the Republican victory in the November elections of 1900, Moerdyke's congregation passed a resolution of congratulations "with one heart and voice," which the members then signed and sent to Roosevelt. The resolution read as follows:

> Last Lord's Day, after the morning service, our Church adopted the following by a rising vote, and afterward requested the privilege of signing it:

15. Moerdyke, "Chicago Letter," *CI,* 17 Oct. 1900, pp. 669-70.
16. Ibid., 27 Feb. 1901, p. 137.

The Hon. Theodore Roosevelt, Governor of New York and Vice-President-elect of the United States:

DEAR SIR – The congregation of Trinity Reformed Church, Chicago, with one mind and heart extends congratulations upon your election to the Vice-Presidency of the United States, rejoicing as we do that your noble record, name and character signally influenced the expression of the people's will on November 6. And, to you, our distinguished friend, who by such loyal and cordial fellowship with us on several occasions of divine worship have greatly endeared yourself to us all, we are constrained to pledge our warmest wishes and prayers for your eminent efficiency, success and happiness in the high office of trust and responsibility to which God in His Providence exalts you.[17]

Under a Roosevelt administration, the Hollanders had high hopes for a change in U.S. policy toward the Boers. In 1902, five hundred Boer sympathizers in Holland, Michigan, signed petitions urging President Roosevelt and Queen Wilhelmina to help mediate the conflict between England and the Boer Republics. But the Dutch president was even more pro-British than McKinley, and the Hollanders were in pure anguish. Fortunately for them, the Boer cause failed and the issue gradually died with it.

Despite his failure to back the Boers, Roosevelt remained a pied piper for the Chicago Dutch. When he returned to Chicago in 1903, this time as president, Moerdyke could not contain himself:

PRESIDENT ROOSEVELT'S visit was the event of the week in this city. A royal reception was given to the Chief Magistrate, who is himself in spirit a thoroughly Western man and quite fond of Chicago as "a typical American city." As a member of the reception committee and a guest at the great dinner given to the distinguished visitor, we had the pleasure of meeting him and hearing his words. His great evening speech to an immediate audience of 6,000 and to the real audience of the civilized world was mostly read, with freedom, from manuscript or notes and without attempt at oratory.

His brave, patriotic utterances and noble American policies proved immensely popular with the hearers. There is something in our President's character, career, and ways that mightily appeals to the youth of our land and evokes a peculiar enthusiasm from all ages and classes.[18]

17. Ibid., 21 Nov. 1900, p. 752.

18. Ibid., 8 Apr. 1903, p. 220.

The final hurrah came in July 1919, when Twelfth Street was renamed Roosevelt Road in honor of Theodore Roosevelt. Many proud Hollanders stood among the fifty thousand people who attended the dedication ceremonies.[19]

For the Dutch Reformed, the Republicans represented the party of good government. In 1907, when they swept out of office the head of the Democratic machine, the Irishman Edward Dunne, Moerdyke was optimistic:

> A very unsatisfactory mayor of our city has just been defeated for re-election, and it is hoped that we shall now enjoy an immeasurably improved traction service, shall be rid of a shamelessly corrupt police service, and also of a wrangling, radical, revolutionary, political and dangerous Board of Education, that has been a disgrace to the city. A weak man, dominated and advised by dangerous elements, and one notorious leader from your city, steps down to the relief of those who long for better government and for a more creditable and safe state of things.
>
> The postmaster, [Fred] Busse, succeeds him, and the people are in no mood to be trifled with. They will insist upon the fulfilment [*sic*] of pledges and the carrying out of the reform programme. Yet how common is the disappointment of cities and states, when new officials sell out to or fall under the power of "machines," "bosses," etc., of which the Republican party also has an abundance. We hope with fear and trembling.[20]

The Chicago Dutch weekly, *Onze Toekomst,* made its first political endorsement in 1908 during the final year of Roosevelt's presidency. The president urged the Dutch to become politically active, and they backed him in turn, right through his failed third run for the presidency under the "Bull Moose" Progressive Party in 1912. P. Court Van Woerden, the minister of the Holland Presbyterian Church of Chicago, was a leader of this party in Chicago. The 1912 election was the first in which many Hollanders broke ranks with the Republican Party to mark the Progressive ticket in spite of the party's "socialistic" principles. Their admiration for Roosevelt and the obvious need for reform to limit the power of money and big business in government swayed them.[21]

19. *Onze Toekomst,* 11 July 1919.

20. *CI,* 10 Apr. 1907, p. 233.

21. Ibid., 29 Jan. 1902, p. 73; Vandenbosch, *Dutch Communities of Chicago,* 53; "Chicago

Naturalization and Participation

In order to be registered voters, the Hollanders first had to become naturalized citizens, which required five years' residence in the United States. They took this step promptly. In 1870, in the first federal census to report on naturalization, exactly one-half of all Dutch-born men were citizens. Among Reformed Hollanders, 43 percent were naturalized, reflecting the fact that many had arrived in Chicago after 1865 and were not yet eligible. This picture changed dramatically in the next thirty years. In 1900, 80 percent of Dutch-born men were citizens and another 6 percent had applied for "first papers" and would soon be citizens. These latter could vote in local elections.[22] "There is good in this Americanizing effort," Moerdyke observed, "and, unlike the English among us, of whom a heavy percentage remain shouters for the Union Jack, the Hollander generally becomes a devoted United States citizen."[23]

If eager for citizenship, the Chicago Dutch were passive as voters. "Politics? We didn't feel part of that," recalled Tom Oldenburger, an insurance agent. "We felt like foreigners."[24] Best to mind your own business and leave politics to others. This immigrant mentality was a major impediment to political life. The Dutch supported the Republican Party ticket and seldom ran for office themselves. Moreover, the few Dutch-Americans who were candidates could not count on the support of their ethnic group, unless they ran as party-backed Republicans. This was far different from the big Dutch settlement in western Michigan, where political activism was the norm and the citizens voted solidly for fellow Dutch candidates.

Only in Roseland and South Holland did the Dutch have a large enough concentration of votes to swing local races and put fellow Hollanders in office. Indeed, ever since South Holland became a village in 1894, Dutch-Americans have held the mayoral office in an unbroken string up to the present day. The Roseland pioneer, Cornelius Kuyper, held many public offices, including school director for twenty-three years.

Letter," *Banner,* 26 June 1913; Henry Zwaanstra, *Reformed Thought and Experience in a New World* (Ph.D. diss., Free University of Amsterdam, 1973), 200.

22. Twenty-one years was the age of majority. Compiled from Swierenga, "Dutch in Chicago and Cook County Federal Population Censuses, 1850-1870"; Swierenga, "Dutch in Chicago and Cook County 1900 Federal Population Census." Also in CD-ROM format in Swierenga, Family Tree Maker's Family Archives, CD #269.

23. Moerdyke, "Chicago Letter," *CI,* 22 Aug. 1900, p. 540.

24. Tom Oldenburger video interview, 19 Nov. 1998, by Martin Stulp.

In the 1900 presidential campaign, the active Republican Marching Club of Roseland turned out a group of young men to hoist the party banner in a parade down the village thoroughfare, Michigan Avenue.[25]

The Chicago Dutch never received their pro-rata share of city or county offices. The politicos, when divvying up the slates of candidates, did not have to consider the Dutch, since the Dutch did not organize like the more activist Irish and Germans. The Dutch did not vote as an ethnic group and therefore lacked clout. They paid a price for shunning the political system; fewer dollars came back to their neighborhoods to fund parks, playgrounds, street improvements, and schools.[26]

Vandenbosch identified a large part of the problem. "They are jealous of one another," he concluded. As a prospective Dutch candidate complained to Vandenbosch: "When a Hollander runs for office, the other Hollanders say, 'He is nothing but a Dutchman, let him go out and work for his living as the rest of us do. He is not too good to work,' and they go the polls and vote for some good for nothing Irish politician." The same spirit of fractiousness and independent-mindedness that caused controversies and splits in the churches crippled the Dutch politically. Nor did they have political experience in the old country to draw upon, since most as yeoman and peasants had not gained the franchise before they immigrated to America. They were political illiterates.

Vandenbosch failed to mention an equally important factor. The religious spirit of political disinterest, even distrust of government, was especially strong among the many Hollanders whose heritage lay in the pietistic Seceder tradition in the Netherlands. They tended to reject the public sphere — government offices, labor unions, schools — as Satan's kingdom and withdrew in obedience to Christ's command to "remain unspotted from the world." This isolationist mindset stemmed in part from theology, but the people's heavy persecution by Dutch authorities in the decade after the Secession of 1834 also contributed to the outsider mentality. The Seceders had been shoved to the economic and cultural margins in their home villages before deciding to depart. Then, as immigrants in Chicago, the ostracizing continued.

25. Richard A. Cook, *A History of South Holland, Illinois, 1846-1966* (South Holland: South Holland Trust and Savings Bank, 1966), lists all mayors since 1894 (78-79). Virtually all officials in the village, including the trustees, have been of Dutch ancestry. For a Kuyper obituary, see Moerdyke, "Chicago Letter," *CI,* 23 Jan. 1901, p. 57. The Marching Club is noted in the letter of Anton Kuiper, Chicago, Ill., to Barend Kuiper, Grand Rapids, Mich., 5 Oct. 1900, in B. K. Kuiper Papers, Box 2, fld 22, Archives, Calvin College, Grand Rapids, Mich.

26. Vandenbosch, *Dutch Communities of Chicago,* 58-59.

Distrust of government was also nurtured by the long tradition of corruption and intrigue that characterized Chicago politics. It made politics look, indeed, like Satan's domain! The reform-minded Peter Moerdyke expressed the frustration of many Hollanders in 1897:

> The good citizens of Chicago realize their fears, and the disappointment of . . . the administration of our present mayor. Civil service reform, after two years of purifying and reforming influence, is . . . almost completely annulled. Extreme, unscrupulous partisanship and license for the curses of gambling and the saloon . . . gratify and hold the baser element.[27]

In the city elections of 1899, Moerdyke returned to his cynical theme:

> The time has come around once again when the "sounding of brass and the tinkling of cymbals" of political aspirants and hypocrites are heard in the land, at least in our city. . . . Not a small proportion of our good citizens have so long been mocked and duped by professions and bids for their confidence and lift that they give up voting. . . . May we be forgiven the folly, the error, the innocence, the misplaced faith, that opened our mouths and lifted a finger and vote in favor of some who ought to have been excluded from office on account of their base treachery and self seeking.[28]

Imagine what Moerdyke would have said in the 1930s, when Chicago became known as the "gangster capital" of America! "This sad situation has grown to our present infamous proportions because many Christians have neglected their civic duties," declared the editor of *Onze Toekomst,* who tried repeatedly to generate a Dutch voting bloc in Chicago that would support honest Hollanders at the polls. But such endorsements of Dutch candidates often had little effect, much to the editor's chagrin. "Our Dutch voters show very little sympathy when one of our countrymen is running for nomination for a certain political job," the editor lamented in 1909, after the Dutch candidate Edward N. Jager lost in the 33rd Ward (Roseland). "If Hollanders in that ward had not supported the political machine, . . . the result would have been entirely different," the editor concluded. A few months later, the editor lamented that to promote Dutch causes "there must be cooperation, and that is usually non-existent among

27. Moerdyke, "Chicago Letter," *CI,* 9 June 1897, p. 11.
28. Ibid., 22 Mar. 1899, p. 8; cf. 24 Oct. 1906, p. 691.

our people." A political organization started on the West Side lasted "only about one season," Vandenbosch reported.[29]

Cicero, Al Capone's headquarters, was notorious for corrupt town government, but the neighborhood streets were calm and peaceful. The Dutch flocked there by the thousands and bought the solid brick bungalows with nice lawns and gardens. "Leave us alone and we'll leave you alone," was the Dutch axiom with the gangsters and politicos. Woe to those who meddled. The Reverend Edward Masselink, pastor of the First Christian Reformed Church of Cicero (1944-50), rightly saw the corruption as contrary to Christian principles. But when he spoke out at public town meetings, he received death threats, and his congregation asked him to leave political reform issues alone. Following the Cicero race riot in 1950, no Dutch Reformed church leaders spoke up. They did not regard race relations as their problem, and they believed they were too inconsequential a group to do anything anyway.[30]

Dutch Politicos

One of the earliest Dutch politicos in Chicago was John Vander Poel, Sr. (1828-1909), who arrived from Zuid Holland province in 1868 with his wife and ten children and settled on the West Side. He rose from postmaster of the Blue Island Avenue post office to chief clerk of probate court, and finally superintendent of files in the Cook County recorder's office. At his death in 1909, Vander Poel was the oldest employee in county government and "possibly the best known Dutchman in Chicago." His son John, Jr., and daughter Matilda taught at the Art Institute in 1909.[31]

Unlike Vander Poel, who never had to run for office, Republicans John Meyer and John Bos, both members of Bernardus De Bey's First Chicago Reformed Church, were the first politically active Hollanders in the city proper. Bos represented the old 11th Ward in city council for several years, and Meyer rose in the state legislature to the speaker's chair. Meyer had emigrated from De Bey's church at Middelstum in the province of Groningen and settled in Minnesota. As soon as the dominie himself immigrated to Chicago, Meyer joined him there and, in Vandenbosch's

29. *Onze Toekomst*, 7 Jan. 1931; 26 Feb., 3 July 1909; Vandenbosch, *Dutch Communities of Chicago*, 59.

30. I am indebted to Harvey Huiner for the information about Masselink; his family belonged to this congregation. Huiner to author, e-mail, 27 Feb. 2002.

31. *Onze Toekomst*, 6 Aug. 1909.

Cornelia De Bey, M.D.

words, "From that time on he became practically a member of the De Bey family." When De Bey hired an English-language tutor for his children, Meyer sat in too.[32]

With De Bey's sponsorship, Meyer became the dominant Dutch business leader on the West Side and helped found the Holland Building & Loan Association, which became the major Dutch financial institution for savings passbooks, mortgages, and business loans. Meyer entered politics in the 1880s and, from 1886 to 1890, represented the city in the state legislature. In 1894 he won another term and was immediately elected speaker of the Illinois House of Representatives, but unfortunately he died shortly after taking up the gavel at the opening session. His "ambition, pluck, and perseverance," observed Moerdyke, were a "marvel, and highly exalted him in the political world."[33]

Meyer tutored and sponsored De Bey's youngest daughter, the renowned Dr. Cornelia De Bey, in her remarkable civic and political career in Chicago. Cornelia graduated from the Cook County Normal School in 1889, a teacher training institution, and later studied science and art at the Chicago Art Institute and Northwestern University. While teaching at var-

32. Vandenbosch, *Dutch Communities of Chicago,* 54.

33. Moerdyke, "Chicago Letter," *CI,* 10 July 1895, p. 9. Moerdyke reported that Meyer in his political years "was not in any way identified with the Church, Reformed, or any other."

ious high schools and normal schools in the Chicago area, she studied medicine at Hehnemann Medical College, receiving her M.D. degree in 1895. Cornelia, who never married, served the city's poor and for a time treated immigrants at Jane Addams's famed Hull House, located on Halsted Street near Cabrini Street.[34]

Cornelia was one of Chicago's "Five Maiden Aunts," along with Addams and three other social workers. In the words of the De Bey family biographer, Hans Krabbendam, "As maiden aunts took care of the problems and worries of their nieces and nephews, so these women looked after the well-being of Chicago." A sympathetic local reform leader quipped: "If Chicago has a sore throat there's one of them running for a flannel bandage and if we work too long at night there's another of them coming around the corner with a child labor law to stop it. If they didn't look after us, who would?" The Dutch doctor, "tall, thin almost to the point of emaciation" and wearing "mannish" clothes, served as the moral conscience of the coterie.[35]

With State Representative Meyer's help, Cornelia pushed through a number of progressive reform laws, beginning in 1890 with a bill that made kindergartens part of the public school curriculum. In 1903, Cornelia was instrumental in getting the lawmakers to enact the first child labor law in Illinois. The next year she mediated in the Chicago stockyards strike and chastised the president of the yards, J. O. Armour, whom she had never met before, for causing such great suffering among the wives and children of the workers. This prompted Armour to return to the negotiating table with the labor leaders. "Within a week and single handed, she had brought an end to the strike that was causing much suffering to the laboring people."[36]

From 1905 to 1908 Cornelia held a seat on the Chicago Board of Education as an ally of Margaret A. Haley, her close friend and another of the maiden aunts, who was the militant head of the Chicago Teachers' Federation. Cornelia and her four siblings were all graduates of the city's

34. Suzanne Sinke, *Dutch Immigrant Women in the United States 1880-1920* (Urbana: Univ. of Illinois Press, 2002), 113-16; Vandenbosch, *Dutch Communities of Chicago,* 55-57.

35. Sinke, *Dutch Immigrant Women,* citing William Hard, "Chicago's Five Maiden Aunts. The Women Who Boss Chicago Very Much To Its Advantage," in *American Magazine* 62 (Sept. 1906): 482; and Robert L. Ried, ed., *Battleground: The Autobiography of Margaret A. Haley* (Urbana: Univ. of Illinois Press, 1982), 103. See also Ernest Poole, *Giants Gone: Men Who Made Chicago* (New York: McGraw-Hill Book Company, 1943), 219.

36. Vandenbosch, *Dutch Communities of Chicago,* 56; Krabbendam, "Serving the Dutch Community," 85.

public schools, and Cornelia was determined to improve the system. With her associates, Cornelia won the appointment of a reformist superintendent to head the system, and she helped convince the teachers to organize a union and affiliate with the American Federation of Labor. Cornelia De Bey also was a member of the Chicago Medical Society and the Chicago Women's Club. During the First World War, Cornelia's reputation was tarnished because she became a radical pacifist and broke federal sedition laws by criticizing the war effort. Four times federal marshals arrested her, but her reputation and political connections shielded her from severe retribution at the hands of the courts. While all of De Bey's children entered the cultural mainstream, Cornelia became more American than the Americans.[37]

A few other Dutch women took an interest in civic life. In 1927, eleven became citizens after taking advantage of free English classes offered at a local school. This prompted the editor of *Onze Toekomst* to urge four times as many of "our country women" to do the same next year.[38] But as voters, Dutch Reformed wives followed the lead of their husbands, so women's suffrage merely doubled the Republican vote in Dutch households.

The suffragist movement held no appeal whatever for the Dutch, especially the radical wing that advocated birth control. Limiting families to three children would "result in the extermination of the human race," declared Van Lonkhuyzen, "because the League of Women Suffragettes fails to realize that not even two-thirds of our children reach the age of reproduction. There is nothing more morally decadent for the younger generation than the knowledge of birth control," the editor concluded.[39]

At least one Dutch Jew in Chicago, Solomon Van Praag, was politically active before the turn of the century. He was born in Amsterdam and came to Chicago in 1860 as a youngster with his parents. In 1891-92, Van Praag served a term under the Democratic banner in the Illinois State legislature. He was a saloonkeeper on South Wabash Avenue and represented the state's 3rd District.[40]

37. Krabbendam, "Serving the Dutch Community," 85, citing *The National Cyclopaedia of American Biography* (New York: White and Company, 1930), C: 455-56.

38. "Chicago News – Free English Classes for Women," *Onze Toekomst*, 24 Aug. 1927, trans. Henry Lammers.

39. "Around Us – Against the Scriptures," ibid., 28 Dec. 1928.

40. John Clayton, comp., *The Illinois Fact Book and Historical Almanac, 1673-1968* (Carbondale and Edwardsville, IL, 1970), 249; *The Daily News Almanac and Political Register for 1891* (Chicago: Chicago Daily News, 1891), 203; Robert P. Swierenga, *The Forerunners: Dutch Jewry in the North American Diaspora* (Detroit: Wayne State Univ. Press, 1994), 285, 289, 397 n96.

Onze Toekomst came out in support of Roselander Cornelius J. Ton (1876-1915) in his Republican bid for a second term from the 13th Senatorial District in the Illinois State legislature. Ton, a grandson of the pioneer Roseland settler Jan Ton of Alkmaar, Noord Holland, was the scion of the renowned Ton family, which in 1908 gathered more than seven hundred members for its annual family reunion. The Tons gained wealth through real estate dealings in the rapidly industrializing Calumet district, where George Pullman and other entrepreneurs built their shops and factories. C. J. Ton attended Hope Preparatory School in Holland, Michigan (1890-93), and Northwestern University Law School. He ran a realty business in Roseland with his brother until 1904 and was long active in local politics. He served as Roseland road commissioner five years, school director twenty-two years, and constable seven years.[41] The Chicago Dutch newspaper declared: "All Hollanders ought to be proud of a man like Mr. Ton, and should, therefore, 'handle their tools without mittens' whenever it is necessary."[42]

Ton held a seat in the Illinois statehouse from 1906 to 1910 and focused his efforts on several Progressive reform initiatives, including stopping fraudulent employment agencies and regulating railroads. He pushed bills for full train crews and sixteen-hour service requirements. His intention was good, but such legislation served to weaken the railroad industry and led later to the major problem of union "featherbedding," that is, the policy of forcing railroad companies to carry more men on the train crews than was needed. Ton also helped reform the Chicago city charter and was one of three men to organize the "Band of Hope," which succeeded in passing the plurality primary law. In a field of many candidates, this law gave the party nomination to the person with the most votes, even if not a majority. It was touted as a means for improving the efficiency of elective politics.[43]

Ton's associates in Roseland politics were Hiram Vanden Bilt, a descendant of one of the old families who won election as village tax collector and trustee, and Jan Madderom, another of the old families. Madderom, a Civil War veteran, represented the district at the Republican

41. Vandenbosch, *Dutch Communities of Chicago,* 53, citing a biographical sketch of Ton in Alfred T. Andreas, *History of Chicago from the Earliest Period to the Present Time,* 3 vols. (Chicago: A. T. Andreas, 1884-86). Cf. Peter Moerdyke, "Indiana Letter," *CI,* 11 Sept. 1907, p. 590.

42. Van Hinte, *Netherlanders in America,* 978-79; Goodspeed and Healy, *History of Cook County,* 2: 987; *Onze Toekomst,* 3 Sept. 1907; 7 Sept. 1906; 14 Aug. 1908.

43. Vandenbosch, *Dutch Communities of Chicago,* 53-54.

state convention in Chicago in 1885. Vanden Bilt, like Ton, followed former president Theodore Roosevelt into the Progressive camp and ran for Chicago alderman on the Progressive ticket, winning two terms.[44]

In 1908 *Onze Toekomst* endorsed Garrett L. Kries for Cook County Commissioner. Kries was a second-generation Hollander, born in the Dutch colony of Holland, Michigan, who opened a successful grocery and meat market at 926 (477 old numbering) S. Western Avenue in 1892 and rose in Republican ranks to become the party leader in the 13th Ward. "He has never been ashamed of being a Hollander," and "it is the duty of every Dutchman to cast a vote . . . for our countryman," declared the editor.[45]

Kries may have been the first Hollander to serve in the Chicago city council. Peter Moerdyke reported that in the spring 1899 election, a certain Dutch Republican who had no connection "with any Holland or Reformed church, or any other, as a member," won the race as alderman in a ward "containing few Hollanders" in what was otherwise a Democratic landslide. Only Kries appears to fit this description; few Dutch lived in the 13th Ward, and Kries's name does not appear on any Reformed congregation's membership list.[46]

The next year *Onze Toekomst* backed "our countryman" H. Stuit on the Prohibition Ticket in the 11th Ward, and "our countryman" Henry Van Houten as the Republican candidate for city alderman in the heavily Democratic 30th Ward, even though the "hope of victory is nil." In 1910 the newspaper recommended "our countryman" Richard Bandringa as a candidate for precinct committeeman in Englewood's 32nd Ward. "Let us show that we are willing to help a Hollander by casting our vote for him."[47]

The Dutch sheet also endorsed the reelection in 1910 of "our countryman" Age Zylstra (1866-1948) of Roseland in the city primary for Republican alderman in the 33rd Ward. Historian Vandenbosch, who knew Zylstra personally, noted that the Roselander "controls more Dutch votes than any other politician, and he has been the only person that has really been successful in keeping a large personal following, for the Dutch are a very independent people and are not easily controlled by anybody."[48]

The editor of *Onze Toekomst* set out to change that. "It is the duty of every Dutchman in the Ward to vote for him," declared the editor. This election was more problematic, however, because Zylstra was running

44. Ibid., 53; Van Hinte, *Netherlanders in America,* 432; *De Grondwet,* 3 Nov. 1885.

45. *Onze Toekomst,* 24 July 1908.

46. Moerdyke, "Chicago Letter," *CI,* 12 Apr. 1899, p. 16.

47. Ibid., 26 Feb., 2 Apr. 1909; 18 Feb., 1 Apr. 1910.

48. Vandenbosch, *Dutch Communities of Chicago,* 57.

Herman Teninga

against a fellow Hollander, the realtor Herman Teninga, and Teninga won. The paper then quietly shifted its position and backed the victor in the general election by publishing a petition of support signed by twenty-seven community leaders and politicos on the South Side, including Ton and Jager. Teninga, a member of the Bethany Reformed Church of Roseland, later became president of the powerful Cook County Real Estate Board. He was one of the most prominent Dutch-American leaders and businessmen. At his funeral service at Bethany Reformed Church in 1924, every prominent Chicagoan attended, including the Netherlands consul general John Vennema.[49]

Two other Dutch candidates in 1910 received only passing notice, however. These were the physicians Dr. W. De Boer, candidate on the Socialist ticket for 17th Ward city alderman, and a Dr. Van Dyke, the Prohibition ticket candidate for alderman in the 11th Ward. The editor merely observed that "Dutch doctors are beginning to enter politics." Amazingly, two weeks later, the Dutch newspaper recommended a vote for the Socialist De Boer rather than the non-Dutch Democratic machine candidate. But in the 11th Ward, the editor supported the non-Dutch Republican rather than the Prohibitionist Van Dyke. These decisions were in line with the paper's policy of keeping Democrats out of office at all costs, even at the price of a little ethnic solidarity and holding one's nose at the smell of socialism.[50]

In the 1910s and 1920s, other endorsements of "our countrymen" went

49. *Onze Toekomst,* 9 Sept. 1910; 26 Nov. 1924.

50. Ibid., 18 Mar., 1 Apr. 1910.

Guy Madderom

to J. Hoekstra of Roseland as Republican candidate for township assessor in 1910; John W. Wynants as Democratic candidate for 10th Ward city alderman in 1913 (the only Democrat ever endorsed by *Onze Toekomst*); Guy Madderom, a Republican powerhouse in the 9th (former 33rd) Ward city aldermanic contests in 1919 and 1921; and South Holland Judge Frederick R. De Young, who in 1924 won a seat on the Illinois Supreme Court. Madderom sat in the city council from 1918 to 1922. De Young had been a member of the Illinois Senate for several terms, served on the state constitutional convention, and was a judge in the Circuit Court of Cook County.[51]

A number of Hollanders worked for the Cook County Sheriff's Office in law enforcement, which posts were political as well as professional. Martin Ozinga and Nick Buis of Evergreen Park were motorcycle policemen beginning in the late 1910s. Ozinga later became chief of police in Evergreen Park.[52] Sheriff William Meyering of Englewood was the chief peace officer of the superior court in the 1930s and as such was responsible for the county jail's nearly fourteen hundred inmates, which included mobster Al Capone for a time. The prohibition amendment (18th) had tripped up most of the prisoners, according to Meyering. He also had to be present at all executions.[53]

51. Ibid., 14 Feb. 1913; 28 Mar. 1919; 18 Feb. 1921; 30 July 1924; Vandenbosch, *Dutch Communities of Chicago*, 53.

52. Semple and Wrobel, *Evergreen Park*, 48.

53. "Knickerbocker Society of Chicago," *Onze Toekomst*, 18 Nov. 1931.

Age Zylstra (1866-1948)

On the West Side, George N. Knol began a career in the Cicero Fire Department in 1912, rising through the ranks from fireman to assistant chief fire marshal and, finally, to chief fire marshal. Knol was first moved to headquarters under another Hollander, chief Fred Haan, and in 1934 he took the retiring chief's place. Republicans Nick Hendrikse and Thomas J. Stob were other Hollanders active in Cicero politics in the 1930s and 1940s; both served as town clerks. Knol believed that Christians must be an influence for good in politics, as he told the 6th annual mass meeting of the Men's Societies of Chicago and vicinity in 1936. In Englewood, Mike Dykema, proprietor of a gas station near the Stockyards and a member of the Reformed Church, was the "big tie man" for the Dutch as precinct captain of the city Republican machine in the 1930s.[54]

In the 1920s Republican Age Zylstra, the former 33rd Ward alderman, was the leading Dutch politico in Chicago. He headed the McCormick-Essington-Brundage Republican political machine in the 9th Ward, which encompassed the town of Roseland, and used the post to climb the patronage ladder to positions in city and county government. For three years Zylstra served as city collector in the cabinet of Republican mayor Thompson.

Zylstra's political influence in Roseland is illustrated by an incident that pitted him against his arch rival Cornelius Ton for the 9th Ward nomination. The battle erupted in the ward convention, where Ton maneuvered among the delegates and the four candidates to secure

54. *Chicago Messenger*, 1 June 1934; 31 Jan. 1936, Frederick H. Wezeman Papers, Archives, Calvin College; Tom Oldenburger video interview, 19 Nov. 1998; Ben Essenburg, Jr., video interview, 11 Nov. 1998, both by Martin Stulp.

the nomination for himself, even though Zylstra took pledges into the meeting from fifteen of thirty-one delegates, one shy of a majority. Zylstra's Dutch followers were so outraged at their man being "cheated out of a nomination that was rightfully his" that they threatened Ton with bodily harm, and the police had to escort him home that night. In the election, Zylstra's loyalists out of spite threw their votes to the Democratic candidate, who carried the 9th Ward for the first time in many years.[55]

Reform Politics

Most politically active Hollanders worked within the Chicago Republican Party organization, but there were several efforts by clerics and lay leaders to organize political groups on specific issues, such as prohibition and Sunday blue laws. At first these efforts met opposition within the church. When the Women's Christian Temperance Union, an arm of the Republican Party, asked for the use of the First Reformed Church sanctuary for a prohibition meeting in 1887, the consistory refused. In the consistory's opinion, the organization was more political than religious. A few years later, in 1893, however, the consistory did support the Columbian Sunday Association in its quest for strict Sabbath observance at the Chicago World's Fair. The general public chafed at the congressional rule closing all rides and attractions on Sunday, and the press heaped scorn on the heads of Christian "blue noses."[56]

The Reformed churches of Chicago also prepared for the World Exposition by enlisting the Christian Endeavor youth chapters in a temperance campaign to clean up Chicago's thousands of saloons and close them on Sunday. The target was to turn away the hundreds of thousands of Christians who patronize "these rum holes," including, alas, many Hollanders, "even church members." The churches were determined to get aggressive and to educate the "community upon this vital question of morals and good government." But Moerdyke was pessimistic. "Would to God it might be! But . . . with our knowledge of the numerical and money power of 5,700 saloons, backed by gigantic breweries and a corrupt, un-

55. Vandenbosch, *Dutch Communities of Chicago*, 57-58.

56. Krabbendam, "Serving the Dutch Community," 76, citing First Reformed Church of Chicago, Minutes, 2 Nov. 1887, and 28 June 1891, Western Seminary Collection, Joint Archives of Holland, Michigan; Moerdyke, "Chicago Letter," *CI*, 31 May 1893, p. 11.

scrupulous, dangerous host of people; with Chicago's greed, and the greed of the liquor dealers, . . . what hope is there of success?"[57]

So deep was the pessimism among the civic reformers that a youth leader in Moerdyke's Trinity American Reformed Church remarked that "he sometimes felt that Christians might better leave Chicago, and abandon it to anti-Christian, degrading, destructive forces." But then, Moerdyke added, "arose the conviction that some redeeming force must endure the abuse, the toil, the strain of saving this wicked city, and he and we are called to the kingdom for such a time as this."[58]

Such a time came in 1901, when the flamboyant Carrie Nation brought her anti-liquor crusade to Chicago. Mrs. Nation's unorthodox way was to enter saloons with her infamous hatchet and lay waste to the barrels of beer. Moerdyke actually commended her direct action against private property as a "righteous opposition" to a "lawless ruinous traffic. . . . We are thankful for this new crusade," he declared, and closed by quoting from the Book of Judges: "Shimgar slew 600 Philistines with an ox goad, 'and he also delivered Israel.'"[59]

Moerdyke's reformist views mirrored those of the Social Gospel Movement that had enthralled many of his friends among Congregational and Presbyterian clerics. When Washington Gladden, the leading Social Gospel cleric in Ohio, who was also a Columbus city alderman, came to Chicago to lecture in 1903, Moerdyke was an eager listener:

> The Rev. Dr. Washington Gladden last Tuesday instructed a great concourse of our citizens at the Auditorium by treating of "The Lights and Shadows of Municipal Reform." The address was wonderfully lucid, practical, sound, and Christian. He holds and shows that the dark shadows have deepened in the cities of our land, but pointed out some gleams of light. Among these rays of hope are New York's redemption from corruption for the present; and the very materially improved membership of the Chicago Council of Aldermen, and the aroused state of the popular mind. This question is discussed as never before, which is an omen of good. The orator's own wide observation, protracted study of such problems, and aldermanic office in Columbus, O., enriched his able paper.[60]

57. Moerdyke, "Chicago Letter," *CI,* 11 Jan., p. 14; 17 May 1893, p. 11; 30 Jan. 1895, p. 10.

58. Ibid., 31 May 1893, p. 11.

59. Ibid., 20 Feb. 1901, p. 120.

60. Ibid., 18 Mar. 1903, p. 169.

By 1910 the early Dutch Reformed reluctance about bringing politics into the churches had disappeared. The issue was still prohibition of alcohol. That year many Hollanders joined the Dutch Christian Anti-Saloon League founded and spearheaded by P. Court Van Woerden, a renowned urologist and member of the First Englewood (62nd Street) Reformed Church. The initial push came from Reformed Church members, but some Christian Reformed Church members also affiliated over the next several years. The league sponsored public meetings in the various Dutch churches of Chicago, with nationally known speakers, and out of these came regional chapters – the Westside Section, Englewood Section, and Roseland Section. This activity was an outgrowth of the practice in Reformed churches of observing "Temperance Sunday" by preaching on the subject.[61]

Although the Dutch traditionally enjoyed alcoholic drinks in their homes, such as jenever (Dutch gin), beer, and wine, the Anti-Saloon League appealed to their abhorrence of the American saloon environment with its prostitution, gambling, and crime. In 1906 an *Onze Toekomst* editorial supported calls for the Chicago city council to enforce statewide Sunday closing laws for saloons. The "Chicago Letter" columns in the Reformed Church's *Christian Intelligencer* urged the same cause of the Chicago Law and Order League. The Dutch also supported $1,000 license fees for Chicago's seven thousand saloons, and state local option legislation to gave communities the right by popular referendum to close saloons permanently. Indeed, in 1909 all of the Reformed and Christian Reformed clergy in Chicago jointly took the unprecedented step of refusing to perform any marriage ceremony where "intoxicating liquor" is served. The pastors claimed that this radical step was necessary because of the "misuse" of alcohol at Dutch weddings.[62]

Prohibitionist views among Christian Reformed clerics in Chicago were at odds with sentiment elsewhere. The editor of the denomination's weekly, *De Wachter,* had already in 1907 condemned all prohibition legislation. Henry Uden Marsman, editor of *De Grondwet* of Holland, Michigan, and a Christian Reformed layman, similarly was "quite unfriendly to-

61. *Onze Toekomst,* 25 Mar., 24 June, 23 Sept. 1910; 27 Jan. 1911; 28 Feb. 1913. Court Van Woerden's photo appeared weekly in 1909-10 in an advertisement in *De Grondwet,* e.g., 5 Mar. 1910, p. 6; George Niemeyer, "Illinois Letter," *CI,* 27 Nov. 1907, p. 771.

62. *Onze Toekomst,* 12 Jan. 1906; 8 Mar. 1909; 4 June 1909; Moerdyke, "Chicago Letter," *CI,* 20 Dec. 1905, p. 828, 7 Feb. 1906, p. 90; George Niemeyer, "Illinois Letter," ibid., 27 Nov. 1907, p. 771.

wards prohibition efforts. . . . We mention this with surprise and sorrow," declared Moerdyke.[63]

One explanation for this difference of opinion is that alcohol abuse was a greater problem in large cities like Chicago, where many Hollanders worked in the streets and alleys as scavengers and teamsters and saw its harmful effects. Another explanation might be that Chicago was the home of the very influential Moody Bible Institute, a fundamentalist, nondenominational center of Yankee Puritanism, which members of both Dutch denominations and especially Reformed folks found attractive. The more the Reformed Hollanders assimilated, the more they identified with the Scottish and English Presbyterians, American Methodists, and even Baptists, all of whom pushed prohibition. When Presbyterians and other evangelical groups denounced alcohol as of the devil, the Dutch Reformed began to rethink their open views in order not to be considered "bad" Christians. They wanted respectability from their "positive reference groups," evangelical Yankee Protestants.

In 1914 the General Synod of the Reformed Church in America officially joined the crusade by appointing a standing committee and affiliating with the temperance arm of the Federal Council of Churches to work for the prohibition of the manufacture and sale of alcoholic beverages. The denomination also made contact with the temperance committee of the Presbyterian Church. Two thirds of the Reformed Church classes, or regional assemblies, formed temperance committees headed by paid agents, and they pledged to work with the Anti-Saloon League and kindred bodies. To reach the young, the church added quarterly temperance lessons in the Sunday school curriculum. And in 1915, the General Synod endorsed national prohibition and so petitioned the Congress and the President of the United States. But when the constitutional change took effect in 1919, they reluctantly substituted grape juice for wine on the Communion table. With repeal in 1932, Communion wine was restored.[64]

Most Dutch in Chicago, including Christian Reformed members, were pleased with the Prohibition Amendment to the U.S. Constitution, but Mr. and Mrs. Jacob Van Schalk, a Roseland couple, were arrested by federal agents and fined for running an illegal still in their home for whiskey, wine, and beer.[65] Curiously, the Dutch puritans objected to alcohol

63. Moerdyke, "Indiana Letter," *CI*, 18 Dec. 1907, p. 828.

64. Mildred W. Schuppert, ed. *A Digest and Index of the Minutes of the General Synod of the Reformed Church in America, 1906-1957* (Grand Rapids: Eerdmans, 1957), 211, 250-51; First Reformed Church, Minutes, 30 Aug. 1932, Joint Archives of Holland, Michigan.

65. "Chicago, Ill., en Omstreken," *De Grondwet*, 11 June 1929, p. 8.

far more than to tobacco, under the mistaken notion that smoking was less harmful to health. However, one congregation, First Reformed of Chicago, in 1937 took the unprecedented step of banning smoking in church parlors and the kitchen. Presumably, smoking continued to be the norm in the consistory room.[66]

Beer continued to be the beverage of choice of the Dutch Reformed working classes, especially among teamsters and scavengers. By the 1950s, problems of alcohol abuse reached the point that Christian Reformed leaders founded the Christian Fellowship for Alcoholics, modeled after Alcoholics Anonymous but with a stress on God as the Great Physician. The Reverend Ted Verseput, of Evergreen Park's Park Lane Christian Reformed Church, was the contact person, and the first president was Clarence Laning, the director and missionary evangelist at the churches' Helping Hand Mission on Madison Street's "skid row." Laning lamented the increasing drinking by Christian Reformed folk, especially the men who in "hot weather . . . visit taverns for a cold glass of beer." He advocated total abstinence as the only way to safeguard the "weaker brother." The Reformed monthly, *Illinois Observer*, edited by the Reverend Arthur De Kruyter of Western Springs Christian Reformed Church, also published editorials and articles by Laning and others on the evils and social "costs of beverage alcohol." An anti-drink poem published in 1955, entitled simply "Liquor," described this "road to degradation."[67]

The success of the Dutch Christian Anti-Saloon League and the rising Progressive movement throughout the United States encouraged broader efforts. In October 1910, the Reverend Siebe Nettinga, of the First Reformed Church of Englewood, invited all Dutch clerics and lay leaders in the city to meet to create an organization "to combat political and social improprieties." Out of this meeting came the Dutch-American Civic League of Chicago, formed in 1911 for the purpose of increasing "our Christian influence in the political field." Within two months, local chapters had sprung up in Englewood's Dutch wards (31, 32, and 22), but the league did not become the influential force that its founders intended.[68]

The big push came a decade later in the waning days of the Progressive reform era following World War I, with the organization of the Christian Political Society in 1920. This political action committee, led by

66. *Onze Toekomst*, 30 Aug. 1907; First Reformed Church of Chicago, Minutes, 25 May 1937.

67. *Illinois Observer*, 15 May 1954; Jan., Feb. 1955; Jan., Feb. 1956; June 1958.

68. *Onze Toekomst*, 28 Oct. 1910; 20 Jan., 3 Mar. 1911.

F. Hegeman, the Reverend Marinus Broekstra, and Henry Pothof, was modeled after the Christian Anti-Revolutionary Party of Abraham Kuyper in the Netherlands. Its inaugural meeting "filled to overflowing" the large hall above the Community State Bank at 1637 W. Roosevelt Road. Forty-five persons signed as charter members, after the mass meeting endorsed a political platform that read like a Republican sheet.

The platform called for laws against public profanity, public Sabbath breaking, prostitution and pornography, dishonesty by public officials, and "hasty unnecessary strikes before attempts at conciliation." This last was a response to the thirty-six hundred strikes that plagued the nation in the inflationary period after government economic controls were lifted in 1919. The platform also advocated laws to ban strikes by public employees in jobs "bearing on public life," tighter criminal codes, public tax support for Christian day schools, and tightening of divorce laws.[69]

The "parochiad" plank was the most controversial. It reflected the desire of the society, comprised mainly of Reformed Church members who strongly favored public education and condemned Dutch Calvinist schools as sectarian and un-American, to reach out to reluctant Christian Reformed folk, many of whom valued the Kuyperian tradition of fully tax-supported Protestant and Catholic day schools. Some of those Christian Reformed activists in later years were Dick Prins of Cicero and Martin LaMaire of Berwyn, who championed Kuyperian principles for many decades.[70]

The emergence of the Christian Political Society encouraged an idealistic Christian Reformed minister, J. Clover Monsma, to launch a national newspaper to propagate Calvinist political, social, and economic principles. The youthful Monsma, in his student days at Calvin College, had served as a "cub" reporter for a Grand Rapids newspaper. Monsma resigned his pastorate in the Archer Avenue Christian Reformed Church to devote himself to Christian journalism. He raised $120,000 of capital from pious folk, purchased a huge high-speed press to equip a plant on Ohio Street, and enlisted a string of correspondents in America and overseas.

The first issue of the *American Daily Standard* came off the press in December 1920 for five thousand initial subscribers. Monsma intentionally named the paper after Kuyper's *De Standaard,* which was a formidable mouthpiece of the Reformed community published in Amsterdam. De-

69. Ibid., 1 Oct. 1920.

70. Martin LaMaire, "Tells About the Bitter Fruits of Non-Christian High Schools," "Voices in the Church" column, *Banner,* 7 May 1943.

spite the energetic Monsma's best efforts, his Chicago paper failed to gain sufficient readers and advertising revenue to cover the $8,000 weekly operating costs. Within three months the woefully underfunded and mismanaged venture that had been touted as "God's cause" collapsed, amid recriminations by editor-in-chief Monsma and a storm of indignation from his investors, one of whom lost more than $20,000. John Van Lonkhuyzen, the editor of *Onze Toekomst* and a graduate of Kuyper's Free University, surprisingly gave no support whatsoever, perhaps fearing a competitor. Van Lonkhuyzen, pastor of the First Christian Reformed Church of Chicago, remained "as silent as a tomb," declared Monsma bitterly in a one-hundred-page polemic pamphlet he wrote in self-justification. The editor of the *Banner,* the weekly periodical of Monsma's own denomination, likewise said "absolutely nothing" about his foray into Calvinistic journalism.[71]

Within three years, Monsma launched another monthly periodical, the *New Reformation,* modeled after *Time* magazine but geared specifically for pastors. This too failed, as did a 1937 venture, the *World: An International News Weekly.* Chicago Hollanders did not see the need for a Reformed news magazine that was much too "Dutchy." Monsma moved to Grand Rapids in 1925, and, to his credit, set about to repay his backers, such as Bonne Iwema of Chicago, to whom he owed $200.[72] Whether he succeeded is doubtful. Monsma in 1922 resigned from the Christian Reformed Church and entered the Presbyterian Church pulpit, first in New York State and then in Wisconsin. Although his journalistic efforts in Chicago failed, he and his readers reflected the determination of some second- and third-wave Dutch-Americans to be a positive influence in public life.

During the Depression in 1933, Monsma's ideas bore fruit among a few Roselanders, led by the Christian school principal, A. S. De Jong, and Richard Fennema. The small group formed the South End Christian Voters' Association and contacted all the Protestant churches to stir up

71. Van Hinte, *Netherlanders in America,* 938-942; Lucas, *Netherlanders in America,* 572; Vandenbosch, *Dutch Communities of Chicago,* 61-62; Conrad Bult, "Dutch-American Newspapers: Their History and Role," 279-81, in Robert P. Swierenga, ed., *The Dutch in America: Immigration, Settlement, and Cultural Change* (New Brunswick, N.J.: Rutgers Univ. Press, 1985). Monsma's pamphlet is entitled *Why the American Daily Standard Failed and How It Is Going to Win* (Grand Rapids: Seymour and Muir, 1921).

72. Bult, "Dutch-American Newspapers," 280. Monsma's monthly budget plan for the *New Reformation,* dated 29 Aug. 1924, is in the Bonne Iwema Papers, as is the letter of J. C. Monsma (Grand Rapids) to Ben [Bonne] Iwema (Chicago), 30 Nov. 1925.

interest in forming a Calvinistic political party.[73] The idealism came to naught, but it was fun to dream.

Non-churched Hollanders from the political left also became active politically. Some twenty southsiders met in 1912 and organized the Dutch Socialist Propaganda Club. John Veltman, of 6159 S. Elizabeth Street in Englewood, served as secretary. These men may have been influenced by Daniel De Leon, the leader of the Socialist Labor Party in the 1890s. De Leon was born in Dutch Curaçao and was educated in Amsterdam. But Dutch factory workers in Chicago, Grand Rapids, Paterson, and elsewhere generally eschewed the rank materialism of socialism and its condoning of labor violence.[74] De Leon's Dutch ancestry fooled a leading Chicago newspaper editor, who in 1893 made the "reckless statement that a large proportion of the Hollanders of Chicago are Socialists." But the "very reverse is true," insisted the knowledgeable Peter Moerdyke of Trinity Reformed Church.[75]

Moerdyke was correct. There is little evidence that either the Dutch Protestant idealists or the socialists gained many adherents in Chicago. Indeed, it was more common for Dutchmen to endorse candidates of the city Republican organization than to back "outside" groups. For example, in 1927 eight Hollanders in the 26th Ward – A. Zuidema, Peter Woldman, John B. Kuyvenhoven, George Vander Laan, A. Slager, William Vennema, Dick Roelfsema, and J. Heno – publicly endorsed Bill Thompson for mayor of Chicago and Frank A. Sloan for 26th Ward Republican alderman.

Thompson was the city's last Republican mayor; he served three terms, two from 1915 to 1923 and a final hurrah from 1927 to 1931. Known as a "big builder," he pushed through the Michigan Boulevard link and dedicated numerous bridges, streets, and municipal buildings. His program appealed to middle-class voters who believed they were getting something "concrete" for their taxes. Thompson especially appealed to Germans, Dutch, and Irish voters by his tirades against the king of England.

Unfortunately, Mayor Thompson also had a dark side as a corrupt politician; he coined the infamous phrase, "vote early, vote often." During the Prohibition era of the twenties, Thompson formalized links between city government and the organized crime bosses, boasting of Chicago as a "wide open city." It was so wide open that on February 14, 1929, four of Al Capone's thugs in the South Side Gang gunned down seven rivals in

73. Richard Fennema, "A Christian Political Party," *Banner,* 22 Sept. 1933.

74. *Onze Toekomst,* 10 Jan. 1913; Lucas, *Netherlanders in America,* 573-74.

75. Moerdyke, "Chicago Letter," *CI,* 11 Dec. 1895, p. 10.

"Bugs" Moran's North Side Gang, in the St. Valentine's Day Massacre. Thompson's re-election campaign in 1931 brazenly touted his reputation for honesty, good government, and a police force that reduced crime: "Mayor Thompson is your servant – not master."[76]

Thompson's opponent and the victor in the 1931 election was the Czech Democratic Party leader, Anton J. Cermak, who was a master of one-party politics. Cermak built the modern Democratic political machine that has dominated Chicago for seventy years. He was backed by a much smaller contingent of politically liberal Hollanders, who formed the United Dutch-American Voters' League, which endorsed Cermak as a "two-fisted, untiring fighter" and friend of the foreign-born. Thus reads a political advertisement in *Onze Toekomst* signed by twenty-nine United League members, all prominent Reformed and Christian Reformed businessmen of the second generation. Officers of the United League were J. Radius, president; Dick Driesbergen, vice president; undertaker Ike Emmering, secretary; and H. Noorlag, treasurer. Other signatories included realtor Ben Ottenhoff, Martin Stob, undertaker Rudy Emmering, and teamster William Noorlag. In 1933 Cermak was shot and killed while riding in a car with President Franklin Roosevelt, who was the assassin's target, and Edward Kelly then came to power.[77]

Vandenbosch reports only one Socialist flurry among the Dutch Calvinists. That was in 1911 in Englewood, when Reverend William Stuart of the Third Christian Reformed Church addressed a Young People's Alliance rally at the First Christian Reformed Church on the topic of "Christian Socialism." A band of radical Socialists, led by L. Boersma, most of whom were recent immigrants from big cities in the Netherlands, came to the meeting, and in the middle of Stuart's speech they began singing the "International," the Communist Party anthem. A fight broke out immediately in the church sanctuary, and the radicals were forcibly ejected.

76. *Onze Toekomst,* 30 Mar. 1927; 28 Mar. 1919; 1 Apr. 1931, trans. Henry J. Lammers; Douglas Bukowski, "Big Bill Thompson: The 'Model' Politician," 74-79, in Paul M. Green and Melvin G. Holli, eds., *The Mayors: The Chicago Political Tradition* (Carbondale: Southern Illinois Univ. Press, 1987), 77; Wesley G. Skogan, *Chicago Since 1840: A Time-series Data Handbook* (Urbana: Univ. of Illinois Press, 1976), 33-40.

77. "Dutch Voters: Vote Cermak for Mayor," *Onze Toekomst,* 1 Apr. 1931. Signatories included W. Arkema, H. Bankema, G. Bor, C. Broekstra, Nicholas De Vries, Peter C. De Waard, John F. Dykstra, T. Eggenstein, Marinus Fisher, W. J. Hoekstra, Richard Laning, William Noorlag, William Rudenga, John Sluis, B. Sytsema, T. Vanden Handle, William Vander Meide, J. Venhuizen, Fred J. Vos, and A. Zuidema. For Cermak, see "Anton J. Cermak: The Man and His Career," in Green and Holli, *The Mayors,* 99-110.

Boersma then wrote a pamphlet in reply to Stuart's speech and distributed it among the Calvinists. But one can be certain that it was destined for the wastebasket. The bulk of Chicago's Dutch Reformed had their roots in the countryside, not the cities, and they left the homeland long before the rise of the socialist movement at the turn of the century.[78]

The Dutch Reformed attitude toward militant socialism was best displayed in 1927 at the height of the anti-radical crusade, when Nicolo Sacco and Bartholemeo Vanzetti, the Italian anarchists, were executed for a bank robbery and murder. Editor Van Lonkhuyzen of *Onze Toekomst* supported the government wholeheartedly: "Those that despise law and order should be banished for ever and their entry should be made impossible." The editor also commented favorably on a congressional proposal to deport aliens who created political disturbances or committed criminal acts. "Let's hope it doesn't only remain an empty threat. To now and then send back a few reds *(roden)* would certainly put the fear into the rest of them."[79] This case was clearly on the minds of the Chicago Church Federation, which sponsored a rally against "lawlessness" on a Sunday evening in May 1929; some twenty-six congregations across the city participated, including several Reformed churches.[80]

The New Deal

The victory in the 1928 presidential election of Herbert Hoover over Al Smith, the Catholic Democratic candidate, was sweet indeed. "The Lord has done great things, we are thankful to him," crowed editor Van Lonkhuyzen of *Onze Toekomst.* "We must not forget that our nation has accepted with renewed vigor the principle that national prosperity does not depend on government intervention, but for the most part it depends on personal initiative. Mr. Hoover has not warned in vain against the dangers of the principles of socialism." The editor closed with the benediction, "Praise God for the magnificent victory at the polls."[81]

Too bad that disappointment came so soon. Within months, the Hoover Administration was undermined by the stock market crash and the

78. Vandenbosch, *Dutch Communities of Chicago,* 59-60.

79. "Around Us – Sentences Executed," *Onze Toekomst,* 24 Aug. 1927; "News from Chicago, A Good Plan," ibid., 17 Aug. 1927, both trans. Henry Lammers.

80. "Chicago, Ill. en Omstreken," *De Grondwet,* 28 May 1929, p. 8.

81. "Weekly Observations – Victory Overwhelming – The Battle is Over," *Onze Toekomst,* 14 Nov. 1928.

onset of the Great Depression. The Dutch Reformed in Chicago suffered along with the rest from bank failures and massive layoffs. In September 1931, Classis Illinois joined with the Reformed and Christian Reformed classes across the country in petitioning President Hoover to "proclaim a day of humiliation and prayer." When the situation worsened, in 1933, the deacons of Classis Illinois churches formed the Chicago Deacons' Council to coordinate works of benevolence. At the suggestion of the Reverend Edward Tanis, of the Second Englewood congregation, the council set up an employment agency. Tanis likewise took the lead in an abortive effort to organize a Christian political party like that in the Netherlands. Edward Nieubuurt was elected chair and John Zwier secretary.[82]

The Depression certainly focused minds and aroused the politically lethargic Dutch Reformed community.[83] A fair number even did the unthinkable; they crossed the line to vote Democratic in 1932, having been swept up on the Franklin Roosevelt bandwagon against the discredited Hoover. But most regretted it quickly and did not make the same "mistake" again. Roosevelt quickly polarized the electorate and turned most Chicago Calvinists away from his statist policies. They hated Franklin even more than they had loved his cousin Teddy.

John R. Swierenga, owner of a trucking company, Excel Motor Service, spoke for most Dutch Calvinists when a *Chicago Tribune* reporter queried him about big government and taxes, "between passes with a cleaning rag at the windshield of his truck." Swierenga was one who in desperation had voted for FDR in 1932 but never again. Said Swierenga: "Congress has gone far enough in expanding the federal government. They should leave the aid to aged people to the individuals; it's the responsibility of families and states. We have enough government interference as it is. . . . Taxes are more than adequate if properly dispensed. Less government control would mean less taxes, and that goes for the state too. Whenever 'Uncle' does something for you and me, we pay for it. Let's face it, there's no pie in the sky." Swierenga concluded of himself, "I'm a rugged individualist."[84]

Swierenga's Hooverian view of limited government, which was typical among the Dutch Reformed, met a stiff challenge in the Depression years. Some thought it ran counter to the biblical injunction to be "thy

82. "Brief Report of Classis Illinois," *Banner,* 25 Sept. 1931; B. Essenburg, "Chicago, Englewood, and Cicero Churches," ibid., 21 Apr. 1933.

83. John Vande Water, "South Side Chicago and Vicinity Men's Meeting," ibid., 9 Dec. 1937.

84. Thomas Carvlin, "What Voters Want: Tax Cut and Economy," *Chicago Daily Tribune,* 16 Jan. 1961.

brother's keeper," although Swierenga and most church members would have considered charity to be the primary responsibility of families and the church, not the government.

Many intellectuals among the Dutch Reformed believed the Democratic Roosevelt's socialization of wealth was closer to biblical and Calvinistic tenets than was the "let-me-alone system" of the Republicans, which put a "premium . . . upon greed and selfishness and materialism." The New Deal champions of social justice included the De Boer and Stob clans. Their intellectual leaders were John De Boer, former teacher at Chicago Christian High School and professor of education at Chicago Normal College; De Boer's uncle, Frederick Wezeman, principal of the high school; and Thomas J. Stob, a Cicero realtor and politician.[85]

While James J. Van Pernis, editor of *Onze Toekomst,* took his stand on the "golden middle ground" and maintained an editorial policy of "complete neutrality," Wezeman used the pages of his biweekly newspaper, the *Chicago Messenger,* which ran from March 1934 to December 1936, to promulgate progressive politics. He enlisted as regular contributors De Boer and two like-minded Christian High faculty members, history teacher Henry Swets and language instructor Paul Brouwer.

In June of 1934, for example, Wezeman gave front-page billing to De Boer's speech praising the New Deal and condemning big business, delivered at a mass meeting of the Cook County Voters' League in the First Reformed Church of Chicago. The National Recovery Act (NRA), said De Boer, with its federal regulation of big business, was an excellent beginning to replacing rugged individualism with socialized government programs. League president Paul Wezeman, a medical doctor in Cicero and Fred's brother, chaired the meeting before a standing-room-only crowd. One suspects that the largely Reformed audience accepted De Boer's Christian socialism far more warmly than would a like audience in the First Christian Reformed Church. Fred Wezeman later had second thoughts. When the Supreme Court struck down the NRA as unconstitutional in 1935, Wezeman voiced his approval; the act was detrimental to small business and its national industrial codes were a "blunt and bold dictatorship."[86]

Wezeman condemned militarism and supported the national mili-

85. Editorial, *Chicago Messenger,* 24 Aug. 1934; Johannes Zandstra, "Is Calvinism Compatible with Democracy?" cited in John P. Vande Water, "South Side Chicago and Vicinity Men's Meeting," *Banner,* 9 Dec. 1937.

86. Editorial, *Onze Toekomst,* 26 Oct. 1932; *Chicago Messenger,* 1 June 1934; 31 May 1935.

tary disarmament programs of the League of Nations, but he was not a pacifist. He called for judges to place social justice above property rights and urged a spirit of brotherhood and cooperation among all peoples. In 1934 he recommended attending a mass meeting of the People's Political Alliance (a New Deal lobbying group) at the Chicago Christian High School, and often in his editorials he attacked "banking capitalism" and "unscrupulous, big-business racketeers." This echoed De Boer's rhetoric about World War I being the "'righteous cause' of J. P. Morgan's war," and those favoring rearmament in the 1930s as representing "the forces of greed in the temple and the royal palace."[87]

Despite his Democratic leanings, Wezeman wisely gave Republicans a voice in his newspaper alongside the Democratic broadsides of John De Boer. After all, most of his readers consistently voted Republican. He also willingly sold advertising space to Republican candidates. In the 1936 state race, the paper publicized a series of Republican rallies on the Old West Side that featured "two of their own," John H. Teune, Republican candidate for state representative, and John Vander Velde, Jr., Republican candidate for state senator. The mass meetings, held at Leenhout's Chapel on Roosevelt Road (directly across the street from the Fourth Christian Reformed Church) and at the Mission Chapel on Hastings Street at Ashland Avenue, laid the groundwork for a "rousing campaign" that promised to reach "every home and voter in the district."[88]

That same year, the national and state Republican Party appointed a Holland-American Republican Committee in Chicago, composed of professional and business leaders, to encourage "a more active interest among our own people of Holland ancestry in the political struggles of our Beloved America." Theodore S. Youngsma, president of the Youngsma Paper Company, chaired the group, and Jacob H. Hoekstra was secretary. In the fall presidential campaign, Wezeman published without comment Hoekstra's full-page diatribe against Roosevelt and the case for voting for Alfred Landon, the Republican. It was to save "our churches and our schools and our liberty" from FDR's "UnAmerican dictatorship. . . . God save our nation!"[89] Most Hollanders believed that God did so, despite Roosevelt.

The Democrats in 1936 likewise organized a Holland-American divi-

87. Ibid., 1 June 1934; 14, 28 June 1935; 17 Jan., 14 Feb. 1936.

88. Ibid., 13 Mar., 10 Apr. 1936; *Onze Toekomst,* 18 Mar. 1936.

89. *Chicago Messenger,* 10, 27 Oct. 1936. Other Republican Committee members were Dr. John H. Hospers, Albert Jellema, Dr. H. Hoekstra, Jacob Miedema, Mark Fakkema, Albert Plasman, Ben Jongsma, Nicholas Knol, Reinder Van Til, and John Woldman.

sion of the Roosevelt for President National Campaign Committee, with headquarters in downtown Chicago on North Clark Street. But the recruitment battle was uphill, especially among Christian Reformed voters. A campaign brochure, entitled "Turn Back the Pages of Memory to 'March 4, 1933!'" listed ninety-five members, mostly from the Chicago area and western Michigan. Officers were Jacob Baar, president; Gerrit Pon, vice president; Nicholas Hendrikse, secretary; and Thomas Stob, trea-

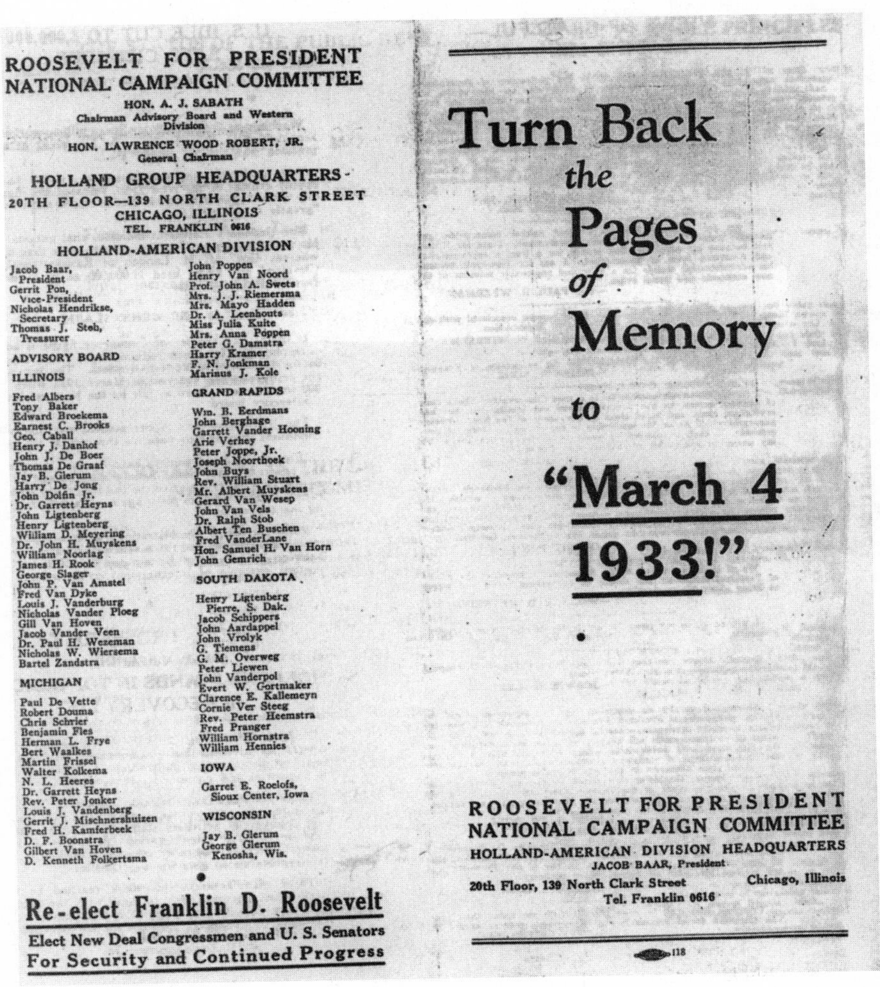

ROOSEVELT FOR PRESIDENT
NATIONAL CAMPAIGN COMMITTEE

HON. A. J. SABATH
Chairman Advisory Board and Western Division

HON. LAWRENCE WOOD ROBERT, JR.
General Chairman

HOLLAND GROUP HEADQUARTERS
20TH FLOOR—139 NORTH CLARK STREET
CHICAGO, ILLINOIS
TEL. FRANKLIN 0616

HOLLAND-AMERICAN DIVISION

Jacob Baar, President
Gerrit Pon, Vice-President
Nicholas Hendrikse, Secretary
Thomas J. Stob, Treasurer

ADVISORY BOARD

ILLINOIS

Fred Albers
Tony Baker
Edward Broekema
Earnest C. Brooks
Geo. Caball
Henry J. Danhof
John J. De Boer
Thomas De Graaf
Jay B. Glerum
Harry De Jong
John Dolfin Jr.
Dr. Garrett Heyns
John Ligtenberg
Henry Ligtenberg
William D. Meyering
Dr. John H. Muyskens
William Noorlag
James H. Rook
George Slager
John P. Van Amstel
Fred Van Dyke
Louis J. Vanderburg
Nicholas Vander Ploeg
Gill Van Hoven
Jacob Vander Veen
Dr. Paul H. Wezeman
Nicholas W. Wiersema
Bartel Zandstra

MICHIGAN

Paul De Vette
Robert Douma
Chris Schrier
Benjamin Fles
Herman L. Frye
Bert Waalkes
Martin Frissel
Walter Kolkema
N. L. Heeres
Dr. Garrett Heyns
Rev. Peter Jonker
Louis J. Vandenberg
Gerrit J. Mischnershuizen
Fred H. Kamferbeek
D. F. Boonstra
Gilbert Van Hoven
D. Kenneth Folkertsma

John Poppen
Henry Van Noord
Prof. John A. Swets
Mrs. J. J. Riemersma
Mrs. Mayo Hadden
Dr. A. Leenhouts
Miss Julia Kuite
Mrs. Anna Poppen
Peter G. Damstra
Harry Kramer
F. N. Jonkman
Marinus J. Kole

GRAND RAPIDS

Wm. B. Eerdmans
John Berghage
Garrett Vander Hooning
Arie Verhey
Peter Joppe, Jr.
Joseph Noorthoek
John Buys
Rev. William Stuart
Mr. Albert Muyskens
Gerard Van Wesep
John Van Vels
Dr. Ralph Stob
Albert Ten Buschen
Fred VanderLane
Hon. Samuel H. Van Horn
John Gemrich

SOUTH DAKOTA

Henry Ligtenberg
Pierre, S. Dak.
Jacob Schippers
John Aardappel
John Vrolyk
G. Tiemens
G. M. Overweg
Peter Liewen
John Vanderpol
Evert W. Gortmaker
Clarence E. Kallemeyn
Cornie Ver Steeg
Rev. Peter Heemstra
Fred Pranger
William Hornstra
William Hennies

IOWA

Garret E. Roelofs,
Sioux Center, Iowa

WISCONSIN

Jay B. Glerum
George Glerum
Kenosha, Wis.

Re-elect Franklin D. Roosevelt
Elect New Deal Congressmen and U. S. Senators
For Security and Continued Progress

Turn Back the Pages of Memory to "March 4 1933!"

ROOSEVELT FOR PRESIDENT
NATIONAL CAMPAIGN COMMITTEE
HOLLAND-AMERICAN DIVISION HEADQUARTERS
JACOB BAAR, President
20th Floor, 139 North Clark Street
Chicago, Illinois
Tel. Franklin 0616

Roosevelt for President Campaign Committee brochure, 1936

(The Archives, Calvin College)

surer. Hendrikse and Stob were brothers-in-law and members of the First Cicero Christian Reformed Church. They, along with John De Boer, Henry Danhof, George Slager, and Bartel Zandstra of Highland, Indiana, were among the few Roosevelt supporters who belonged to Christian Reformed churches.[90]

The social justice of the New Deal appealed to these Roosevelt Democrats. Baar cited the Federal Housing Administration program that allowed millions to refinance mortgages and thereby save their homes from foreclosure. Paul Wezeman, Fred's brother, declared: "I am for Roosevelt because I want neither communism nor fascism; neither a mob nor a bully government. . . . I am for Roosevelt because his administration stands for a sane and reasonable solution of the new economic and social order."

The Cold War changed the political parameters. Any lingering sympathy for Democratic leadership was dashed by the missteps of Roosevelt and his successor Harry Truman in dealing with the new adversaries, the Soviet Union and China. Chicago's Hollanders considered Harry Truman, the haberdasher from Kansas City, to be a "political hack" and of little account. "The present administration," said the Reverend Gerben Zylstra of the Des Plaines Christian Reformed Church, is one of "wide-spread inefficiency and corruption found in many offices and bureaus."[91] Truman picked up one lonely vote in a mock election in 1948 by the eighth grade class at Timothy Christian School in Cicero. The youngsters had clearly learned from their parents to discount Truman, while General Dwight Eisenhower's victory in 1952 brought renewed hope for the redemption of America.

A mock election among the student body at Chicago Christian High School late in the 1952 presidential campaign showed the general outlook. A male quartette sang a rousing rendition of the campaign song, "I like Ike." The song declared: "I like Ike, I'll shout it over a mike, or from the highest steeple; I like Ike, for Ike is easy to like. Why, even Harry Truman says 'I like Ike!'" Senior student and ardent Democrat Richard De Witt, son of Rev. Gary De Witt of the First Reformed Church of Roseland, then had the unenviable task of giving the Adlai Stevenson speech. He lost the straw vote resoundingly.[92]

90. This and the next paragraph rely on the Roosevelt for President Committee brochure in the author's possession; *Chicago Messenger,* 27 Oct. 1936.

91. Gerben Zylstra, "Office Seekers," *Chicago Calvinist,* Dec. 1951.

92. Martin Essenburg, a member of the quartette, along with Ronald Boss, Henry Hoeks, and the author, recalled this colorful event.

Antithetical Politics

In the relatively quiet Eisenhower era, Chicago's Calvinists tried yet again to affect city politics by forming a Christian Citizens Committee. In 1951 Ralph H. Dekker of Englewood and some thirty enthusiasts, mostly from the South Side, created the Citizens Committee to educate Calvinists on Christian political theory and practice and to encourage activism. By 1952 the group had agreed upon a constitution and appealed for members. One hundred signed up. Dekker expected that every Christian Reformed Men's Society would form a chapter, but in January 1955 he lamented the fact that only a few had done so, and their membership could be counted on two hands.

Beginning in 1954, Dekker, who was an electrician by trade, for many years faithfully wrote a monthly column in the *Illinois Observer* entitled "Christian Citizens Committee," which promoted good citizenship and informed voters. The committee always endorsed the few Dutch-American candidates, such as Frank M. Ozinga of Evergreen Park for the Illinois Senate's 6th District in 1956 (he won and served twenty-six years), and John Teune of Englewood for the State Senate's 15th District in 1958 (he lost). Occasionally, the committee also recommended Republican nominees who were not "our Hollanders," such as the 1955 mayoral candidate, Robert E. Merriam, a long-time 5th Ward alderman who ran the best campaign that Richard J. Daley ever confronted. More often, Dekker condemned the city Democratic machine for its thirst for power and influence. Politics is a dirty business, Dekker admitted, but that is no excuse for the "apparent indifference and lethargy of the average Christian in the sphere of politics."[93]

Following the 1958 mid-term elections, in which John Teune, secretary of the Christian Citizens Committee and the Republican candidate for the Illinois legislature, was swamped in a Democratic landslide, Dekker lambasted the flow of labor union money to the Democratic campaign machine and challenged the Hollanders to respond. "Our committee also stepped up our activity, despite the fact that we received few new members; or many contributors. If you do not aid us, we will be forced to cease." And that they did. Despite the valiant efforts of Dekker and his colleagues, the Christian Citizens Committee died a quiet death in the 1960s.[94]

93. *Illinois Observer,* 15 Feb. 1954; Jan., Mar., Dec. 1955; Nov. 1956; Semple and Wrobel, *Evergreen Park,* 49.

94. *Illinois Observer,* Nov. 1958. Dekker was in business with his father, G. Dekker, for many years.

Another staple of Reformed politics in Chicago was a fear of Roman Catholic power and propaganda. In the 1930s, when the Catholic hierarchy crusaded against atheistic communism, editor Wezeman of the *Chicago Messenger* read the attacks as a mere "smokescreen" by a "powerful church organization" seeking a "fascist type of political control." The real objective of Catholicism was "to protect and advance the power and privileges of organized religion."[95]

The annual Reformation Day rallies of the Christian Reformed Men's Societies in late October always sharpened the antithesis between pure Calvinism and impure Catholicism. When in 1957 the Chicago Catholic prelates "cried out in self-righteous defense" against the Protestant's TV screening of the controversial film *Martin Luther*, editor De Kruyter of the *Illinois Observer* charged that Catholic intrigue was behind the "trouble and discrimination against Protestants here in Chicago." ROMAN CATHOLIC PROPAGANDA ON THE MARCH, declared the headline. Mayor Daley (1955-76) and the powerful Catholic Church hierarchy and the media are all working together to stymie the Protestants. As a result, De Kruyter warned, "the principles of the separation of church and state are rapidly deteriorating" in Chicago.[96]

A year later, following another Reformation Day rally, De Kruyter again warned in the lead editorial of the "Catholic threat" and of the "merciless amount of propaganda favoring the Catholic political machine." This has become a "real threat to the Protestant way of life and can deal us a death blow if no check is placed upon it." The "totalitarianism" that the Roman church imposed on Spain, De Kruyter declared, is also in store here "if the U.S. becomes 51% Catholic." In 1959 the Chicago League of Reformed Men's Societies had as the featured speaker a former Catholic priest turned Protestant who revealed the "secret of Roman Catholic Power" and offered strategies "to preserve our Protestant heritage."[97]

Given the power and reach of the Irish political machine in Chicago and the large numbers and great wealth in lands and properties of the Roman Catholics there, the Protestant fears and even paranoia in the 1950s and 1960s were understandable, if not justified or clothed in Christian charity.

95. *Chicago Messenger,* 18 Dec. 1936.

96. *Illinois Observer,* Jan. 1957. In the Aug. and Sept. issues of 1955, the newspaper ran a series of articles on "The Marian Cult" written by John Mackay, moderator of the Presbyterian Church U.S.A.

97. Ibid., Nov. 1958; Apr. 1959.

Suburban Politics

The Dutch Protestants since the Second World War came into their own politically in several southwestern suburbs where they are concentrated, notably Evergreen Park and Palos Heights. Wieger Hoekstra and Edward Solle served on the Evergreen Park board of trustees, as did Louis Bruinius and John Leo in later years. Leo became so frustrated with village overspending and high taxes in the 1950s that he and a few cohorts in 1961 launched a reform movement, the Home Owners Party. The Dutch tax revolters recruited Henry "Rich" Klein to run for village president, and the Home Owners Party won 60 percent of the vote, with the help of Regular Republicans who crossed over. The reformers took over the village governing board, and Henry Klein served seven years as president (1961-68) and his son Claude four years as trustee (1969-73), along with George Triezenberg (1963-81). Leo became building commissioner, followed by Richard De Boer in 1965. Dick Sluis, another Leo ally, had been village treasurer in the 1950s.[98]

Palos Heights has had at least five Dutch city officials – aldermen Henry "Whitey" Van Heukelum 1971-81), Robert Honig (1966-69), Cal Bouma (1967-72), and John Camphouse (1987-89), and mayor Dean Koldenhoven (1997-2001). Camphouse also served in Koldenhoven's administration as city treasurer. Two controversial issues roiled the waters for Koldenhoven and the city aldermen, a casino and a mosque. When the nearby Rosemont casino opened and the city treasury grew from revenue sharing, some Palos Heights officials wanted the city to emulate Rosemont. But Mayor Koldenhoven went on record as strongly opposed to the idea. "Gambling money" is "blood money," he declared, and the city council must not "prostitute" itself to the gambling industry by accepting even a penny. At present, the city remains a casino-free zone.[99]

In 2000, Koldenhoven found himself in the middle of a bigger controversy that gained unwanted national notoriety for Palos Heights and scuttled his re-election. The Reformed Church of Palos Heights needed to expand and decided to sell its building and relocate. To the shock of everyone, the Al Salam Mosque Foundation stepped in to buy it for a mosque – the first in the city. The church leaders, not wanting to discriminate, signed the sales agreement for $2.1 million. Much to their chagrin, the act

98. Semple and Wrobel, *Evergreen Park,* 40, 52, 80, 94, 101, 168.

99. Dean Koldenhoven, "Gambling with future," letter to the editor, *Chicago Sun-Times,* 7 June 1999, p. 32.

upset many residents, both Protestants and Catholics, and some made insensitive remarks about Arabs as neighbors and Islam as a religion.[100]

The city council responded to the public pressure badly. It decided that the city needed the facility for a community youth center and threatened to take it, using the power of eminent domain. This came after the city council two years earlier had spurned the church's offer to sell the building. Worse yet, the city council, in a 5-3 vote, offered the Mosque Foundation $200,000 to walk away; the Muslims had demanded $300,000.

Mayor Koldenhoven, a graduate of Chicago Christian High School and member of the Palos Heights Christian Reformed Church, condemned the bigotry, called the payoff "an insult," and vetoed the spending bill. As a Reformed Christian, Koldenhoven believed strongly that "Christ and God are in everything, [and] in politics that can't be set aside." He took the moral high ground at great personal cost. His faith-based decision angered both the council and the mosque officials. The former gave up their designs on the building, and the latter lost their compensation for damages. The Mosque Foundation then filed a $6.2 million suit against the city of Palos Heights for discrimination and breach of contract. The Reformed Church, the innocent party, continues to worship in their too-small sanctuary, which remains on the real estate market. "When it's time to move, Christ will move us," declared Peter Semeyn, pastor of the eight-hundred-member congregation. Koldenhoven lost his re-election bid in 2001, carrying only 13 percent of the vote in a three-way race. Voting his conscience cost him dearly politically, but his courageous stand led to an unexpected international citation. In May 2002, he received a coveted John F. Kennedy Profiles in Courage Award, presented by Caroline Kennedy Schlossberg at a ceremony in the John F. Kennedy Library in Boston. Senator Edward Kennedy praised Koldenhoven for demonstrating that "the dangerous walls of religious intolerance . . . are walls that must be torn down." United Nations Secretary-General Kofi Annan was a fellow recipient.[101]

100. This and the next paragraphs rely on Shannon Bolkema, "City Conflict Blocks Church Sale, Move," *Church Herald,* Dec. 2000; Mark Skertic, "Palos Heights residents don't want mosque," *Chicago Sun-Times,* 24 May 2000; "A Lesson in Faith and Tolerance," *Chicago Tribune,* 2 July 2000; Darlene Gavron Stevens, "Mosque a religious, political tug of war," ibid., 27 July 2000. Koldenhoven was a 1954 graduate of Chicago Christian High School, one year behind the author.

101. Tom Houlihan, "Behind Koldenhoven's big plunge to defeat," *Chicago Star,* 8 Apr. 2001; Ruth Moblard De Young, "Impact of Mosque Controversy Continues," *Banner,* 7 May

In the village of Worth to the north, Walter Kerkstra was mayor for four terms (1969-77), and in the village of Crestwood to the east, Fred Hoff served two terms as mayor (1965-68). In recent years, Harry J. Klein was mayor of Burbank; Sharon Wierenga and Carl Vandenberg served as trustees in Worth and Tinley Park, respectively; Rudy Mulderink and Cheryl Bult were clerks of Palos Hills and Thornton, respectively, and D. Den Herder was a board member; and James Veld and Jack Hoekstra won seats on the village boards of South Holland and Lansing, respectively. In nearby Western Springs, Gerard Leenheer and Jeanne Vogelzang held two of six trustee seats. Richard Mouw was alderman in Hickory Hills. This list is undoubtedly incomplete, but it demonstrates that Dutch-Americans have not eschewed politics entirely.[102]

Conclusion

The Chicago Dutch were typically politically informed voters who turned out at the polls in above-average numbers, but they lacked the stomach for Chicago's political trench warfare and day-to-day organizational efforts, even in wards or suburbs where they had strength in numbers. If politics was not "of the devil," it was certainly "worldly," and power and payola tainted many of its practitioners. Exceptions that prove the rule in recent years are the south suburban mayors with Dutch roots — in the 1960s Henry Klein of Evergreen Park and Fred Hoff of Crestwood, and in the 1990s Harold Gouwens and Don De Graaf of South Holland, and Dean Koldenhoven of Palos Heights.

But even these few successful leaders could not always count on the wholehearted support of their compatriots. Helping a Hollander at the polls has never been a priority, as it has among other ethnic groups such as the Irish, Poles, Greeks, and African Americans. Politics remains for the Dutch Protestants a dirty business best carried on by "outsiders."

2001; "Palos Heights: New mayor says voters tired of council bickering," *Chicago Tribune,* 5 Apr. 2001; Theo Emery, "Courageous stand honored: Palos Heights' former mayor gets JFK award," *Chicago Sun-Times,* 7 May 2002, p. 4.

102. I am indebted for this information on elected officials to the *Directory of Cook County Elected Officials,* 4th ed., 1 June 1997; "Cook County Municipal Races, 1999," *Chicago Sun-Times,* 15 Apr. 1999; and to a letter of Dean Koldenhoven to the author, 24 Feb. 1999.

CHAPTER 15

The "Other" Hollanders: Jews and Catholics

The Dutch Reformed in Chicago lived among many other immigrant groups, two of whom shared their language and national identity.[1] Dutch Jews and Catholics made up a fifth of all Dutch overseas emigrants in the nineteenth century, and several thousand found their way to Chicago. These Hollanders did business with each other, and their children attended the same public schools and played ball together on the streets. Yet a wide gulf separated them, just as in the segmented society of the homeland.[2]

Each lived within its own cultural sphere, even while the groups shared the same streets and neighborhoods. The Reformed were clannish, the Jews and Catholics cosmopolitan; the Reformed spoke Dutch at home and in church, the Jews and Catholics were fluent in English. The Reformed were teamsters and craftsmen, the Jews shopkeepers and traders, and the Catholics business managers and factory workers. The Reformed created ethnically homogeneous churches, societies, and day schools and

1. The discussion of Chicago's Dutch Jewry is from Robert P. Swierenga, *The Forerunners: Dutch Jewry in the North American Diaspora* (Detroit: Wayne State Univ. Press, 1994), 267-89. The story of Dutch Jews in the United States suffers from a lack of primary sources. Very few immigrant letters are known, no records survive from any Netherlandic congregation, and there are no Dutch-language periodicals, newspapers, or pamphlets. Federal census records, synagogue histories, and souvenir booklets and histories are the major sources. A complete bibliography and note on sources is in ibid., 403-19.

2. A richly illustrated and detailed account is Mozes Heiman Gans, *Memorbook: History of Dutch Jewry from the Renaissance to 1940* (Baarn: Bosch & Keuning, 1971).

lived within an ethnoreligious cocoon. Dutch Jews and Catholics worshiped in multiethnic synagogues and parishes and recited universal liturgies that transcended ethnic and national boundaries. Dutch Jews and Catholics affiliated with German- and Polish-dominated synagogues and parishes, intermarried, and were assimilated by the second generation. But the Reformed kept their ethnoreligious identity for five and more generations, even to the present day.

A Dutch Reformed presence remains because of the people's religious values and clannishness. "In large part," historian Amry Vandenbosch perceptively wrote in 1927, this is "due to their attachment to the church, as well as to their strong race [i.e., national] consciousness." The Dutch Reformed were primarily a rural folk, who brought a strong sense of localism and loyalty to family and friends. They were tribal in their fierce in-group loyalties, exclusiveness, and devotion to transplanted institutions, language, and culture. But above all, they were Calvinists of the old school, dating back to the Synod of Dort (1618-19).

Fearing worldliness and believing in the "antithesis" between the church and "the world," the Reformed shaped closed communities, even as they lived cheek by jowl with Jews and Catholics. In Vandenbosch's mixed metaphor, they were a "handful of Hollanders in a sea of Jews, with whom the Dutch do not mix."[3] Henry Stob, who grew up on the West Side in the 1910s and 1920s, recalled that the elevated Baltimore and Ohio railroad tracks with their brick-walled embankments effectively separated Catholics to the south from Calvinists to the north. "These walls and tracks," Stob recalled, "minimized, if they did not eliminate, schoolboy battles between the Polish Catholics and the Dutch Calvinists. Hostilities, when they occurred, took place under the Ashland Avenue viaduct, and only the very brave ventured unaccompanied through this space." Each ethnic group had its "turf" and guarded the borders vigilantly.[4]

Jews Come to Chicago

The Jewish community first took shape in the 1840s with the arrival of a number of itinerant peddlers and petty clothiers from the East Coast. These roving merchants came to rising interior cities scratching for a start

3. Vandenbosch, *Dutch Communities of Chicago,* 2, 79.

4. Henry Stob, "Church and School on Chicago's West Side 1913-1921," *Origins* 11, No. 1 (1993): 27.

under the sponsorship of family business houses in the East. With little capital but great initiative, they brought much-needed city consumer goods to the developing frontier regions. Chicago by 1849 had emerged as a major rail and market center, and within ten years, by 1860, 1,500 Jews were found among its 109,000 inhabitants (1.4 percent). Thirty years later, in 1890, 60,000 Jews lived in Chicago's West Side ghetto; and in 1904 they made up 90 percent of the population in that locale. Indeed, the West Side by 1918 housed 150,000 (60 percent) of Chicago's 250,000 Jews. The largest part were Germans, followed by Posen (or Prussian) Poles and some eastern Europeans.[5]

Jewish businessmen were attracted by the city's bustling population, with its overwhelming demands for goods and services. They were "fairly well situated," according to an early resident. In the antebellum decades, their stores lined the streets south of the Chicago River along Lake, Randolph, Washington, Wells, La Salle, and Clark Streets. "Some had dry goods stores, others clothing stores; many were engaged in the cigar and tobacco business, and there were already a plumber and joiner, and even a carpenter here," the settler recalled. "Some – loading their goods upon a wagon, others upon their shoulders – followed the honorable vocation of peddling. . . . They made a good living for their families, and while gathering money, at the same time established a business that grew with the country." Most lived above their stores and were readily accepted in the city of immigrants that had as yet no ingrained social structure.[6]

Between 1800 and 1880, approximately sixty-five hundred Dutch Jews immigrated to the United States.[7] Most originated in the Amsterdam ghetto on the Old Side of the Amstel River, or in lesser centers in Rotterdam and The Hague. They were an overwhelmingly urban population both in the Netherlands and in the United States. Like other immigrants, Jews demonstrated the salience of national identity and preference

5. Irving Cutler, *The Jews of Chicago: From Shtetl to Suburb* (Chicago: Univ. of Chicago Press, 1996), 7-9; Hyman L. Meites, ed., *History of the Jews of Chicago* (Chicago: Jewish Historical Society, 1924), 113; Moerdyke, "Chicago Letter," *CI,* 9 Mar. 1904, p. 153; "Chicago Jewish Mission," *Onze Toekomst,* 20 Feb. 1920.

6. Leopold Mayer, "Recollections of Chicago in 1850-1851," in Morris U. Schappes, ed., *A Documentary History of the Jews in the United States, 1654-1875* (New York: Citadel Press, 1950), 310-11; Morris A. Gutstein, *A Priceless Heritage: The Epic Growth of Nineteenth-Century Chicago Jewry* (New York: Bloch, 1953), 21-24, 30; Mayer and Wade, *Chicago: Growth of a Metropolis,* 150; "Chicago," *Encyclopaedia Judaica* 5: 410-11.

7. See Swierenga, *Forerunners,* Tables 8.7, 8.8, 8.12, and 8.14 for lists of Dutch Jews in Chicago in the federal population censuses of 1860, 1870, 1880, and 1900.

for their religious and cultural institutions. They purchased cemeteries to bury their dead in consecrated ground, founded charitable and mutual aid societies to fulfill the law of love, and established Hebrew schools to train youth in the faith. In three cities Dutch Jews founded Netherlandic synagogues – Bnai Israel of New York (1847-1902+), Bnai Israel of Philadelphia (1852-79), and Beth Eil of Boston (1859-75). All were led by Dutch-born rabbis, notably Samuel Myer Isaacs of Leeuwarden and Simon E. Cohen Noot and Jacob Voorsanger of Amsterdam.[8]

In intent and desire, Dutch Jews were not much different from Calvinists and Catholics. However, because they, like Catholics, were part of an international religious community and a small minority at that, they inevitably were assimilated into American Judaism more rapidly than the majority of Reformed immigrants who planted numerous colonies and ethnic churches. Nevertheless, Dutch Jews tried to maintain their ethnicity by living in close proximity, worshiping together, and marrying fellow Hollanders. As late as 1870, three-quarters of Dutch Jewish couples in New York were both Dutch, and hundreds of families worshiped in Dutch synagogues led by Dutch rabbis.[9] But it was a losing effort, even in New York, the densest Dutch Jewish center. Between 1840 and 1870, Dutch Jewish homogeneity and orthodoxy gave way to the heterogeneity and heterodoxy that characterizes modern American Jewry.[10]

Before the Civil War, most Dutch Jews settled in East Coast cities, and they only moved inland along the trade routes after establishing themselves. New York City, Buffalo, and Pittsburgh were the main jumping-off points, with secondary staging areas being Cleveland, Toledo, Detroit, Chicago, Saint Louis, Milwaukee, Indianapolis, Cincinnati, and other interior cities.

Chicago attracted more Dutch Jews than any other interior American city. Census marshals in 1900 counted 650 Dutch Jews and they made up 3.4 percent of the total Dutch stock of 18,800. But this was only a mere fraction of the growing Jewish population, which by 1930 totaled 300,000, or 9 percent of the population. Chicago's Jews outnumbered those of any city in the world except New York and Warsaw.[11] Given Chicago's commercial and mercantile pursuits, it was inevitable that Jews found the city very attractive. Its central location and spectacular population growth made the city

8. Each Netherlandic synagogue is described in detail in ibid.

9. Ibid., 72.

10. I. Harold Sharfman, *The First Rabbi: Origins of Conflict Between Orthodox and Reform: Jewish Polemic Warfare in pre–Civil War America* (Malibu, Calif.: Pangloss Press, 1988), xxi.

11. Swierenga, *Forerunners,* Table 8.10, 279; Cutler, *From Shtetl to Suburb,* 1.

the market of the Midwest, a hub of the nation's water and rail systems, and the jumping-off point for immigrants from Europe and the East Coast.

Religious life followed economic life. On the Day of Atonement (Yom Kippur) in 1845, Chicago's Jews mustered the required ten men to constitute a *minyan* and they held their first High Holy Day service. They also fulfilled the obligation to secure a holy burial ground by forming the Jewish Burial Ground Society, which purchased an acre of land along Lake Michigan just north of the city limits. In 1847, Chicago's first Jewish congregation, Kehilath Anshe Maarab (Congregation of the Men of the West), known popularly as KAM, took charge of the cemetery.

Five years later, this mother synagogue of the Illinois region dedicated its first sanctuary in a solemn assembly led by the Frisian-born cleric Samuel Myer Isaacs of New York's Shaarey Tefila congregation. Born in Leeuwarden, Isaacs grew up in London's Dutch Jewish neighborhood and came to New York as cantor of the first German-Dutch synagogue, Bnai Jeshurun. Rabbi Isaacs was able to officiate in the English language, which impressed both Jews and non-Jews in the audience.

The *Chicago Daily Democrat* reported on Isaacs's address with considerable enthusiasm:

> No person that has made up his mind to be prejudiced against the Jews ought to hear such a sermon preached. It was very captivating and contained as much real religion as any sermon we ever heard preached. We never could have believed that one of those old Jews we heard denounced so much could have taught so much liberality towards other denominations and earnestly recommended a thorough study of the Old Testament (each one for himself) and entire freedom of opinion and discussion.

The Chicago editor, who obviously shared a tinge of Protestant anti-Semitism, concluded: "We would sooner have taken him for an independent order of free thinker than a Jew. Mr. Isaacs is an Englishman and is settled in New York City." No wonder Isaacs won acclaim as the "father of the American clergy" for his forty years of leadership in Jewish circles. No Dutch Jews were among the charter families of KAM.[12]

12. Quoted in Cutler, *From Shtetl to Suburb,* 14. Another report of Isaacs's dedication address is in the *Chicago Daily Journal,* 14 June 1851. Isaacs's career is described in Swierenga, *Forerunners,* 74-87, and in Swierenga, *Faith and Family,* 198-203; Gutstein, *Priceless Heritage,* 24-27; *The Occident* 5 (1847): 14-15; Bernhard Felsenthal and Herman Eliassof, *History of Kehillah Anshe Maarabh: Semi-Centennial Celebration, November 4, 1897* (Chicago: KAM Temple, 1897), 11-20.

Chicago's Jews experienced internecine battles, as did the Christians. Ethnic, and to a lesser extent religious, rivalries arose between the dominant group of strictly Orthodox Bavarians at KAM and the more liberal minority of Prussian Poles. In 1849, twenty Poles founded their own congregation, Kehilath B'nai Sholom (Congregation of the Children of Peace), known popularly as KBS. The Poles resented the Bavarian dominance of KAM, and they preferred the familiar Minhag Poland, or Polish worship rites, over the German Minhag Ashkenaz of KAM. Both services, however, used a combination of German, English, and Hebrew texts.[13]

By 1864 KAM boasted 125 members and its sister congregation, KBS, had 80. Two new Reform congregations, Sinai (1861) with 100 members and Zion (1864) with 60, nearly equaled in size the pioneer synagogues. These membership statistics may overstate the case, however. At least one critic, a conservative member of KAM, reported in 1859 to the *Occident and American Jewish Advocate,* a national periodical, that Judaism was not flourishing in Chicago. Indeed it was not, since 1,000 Jews lived in the city at the time and all the synagogues together had only 365 members, barely one-third. The Polish congregation in a typical Sabbath service was reportedly "mostly empty benches, since the majority of the members are attending to their business, and openly desecrate the day of rest." The critic's own KAM congregation, meanwhile, was racked by turmoil over the introduction of Reform innovations by a "small but daring minority."[14] Such problems were typical of American Judaism at this time.

To the Germans and Poseners "should be added another small group known as 'Holland Jews,'" reported Hyman L. Meites in *History of the Jews of Chicago.* The Hollanders in the 1850s and 1860s came primarily from Amsterdam, plus a few other Dutch cities. Some migrated in stages via England, as did many Dutch Jews, but most in Chicago came directly from the Netherlands. Once in Chicago, according to Meites, they "cast in their lot chiefly with the 'Polish' constituency either in its synagogue, B'nai Sholom, or in its *chevras* [benevolent organizations]. Among these 'Holland Jews' were many substantial and loyal Jewish families," Meites continued, "including the Andrews, the Van Gelders, the Van Praags, the

13. Gutstein, *Priceless Heritage,* 27-29; Bernhard Felsenthal, *The Beginnings of the Chicago Sinai Congregation* (Chicago: Chicago Sinai Congregation, 1898), 9; Morton Mayer Berman, *Our First Century, 1852-1952: Temple Isaiah Israel* (Chicago: Temple Isaiah Israel, 1952), 11.

14. The *Occident* 22 (1864): 188-91, 285; 23 (1865): 95-96; Felsenthal and Eliassof, *History of Kehillah Anshe Maarabh,* 38. The report, signed "H," is in the *Occident* 17 (1859): 65-66.

Van Baalens, and others."[15] To this list Meites might have added the families Boasberg, De Wolf, Cohen, Litt, Greenburg, and Rosenbach, among others.[16] Surprisingly, none of the Dutch held leadership positions in the KBS congregation.

These earliest Jews in Chicago, including the Hollanders, Meites explained, "not only spoke German in their daily intercourse but also transacted their various organized activities and heard their sermons preached in the language they had brought with them." There were German newspapers, theaters, and synagogue schools. "English slowly made inroads, however," says Meites, "and finally replaced the tongue that was heard practically throughout the Chicago Jewish community until the fire [1871] and for a few years thereafter."[17] If the Hollanders, perforce, spoke German in *schule* and shop, they assuredly spoke Dutch at home.

It is not known whether the Chicago Dutch ever contemplated founding a Netherlandic congregation based on the Amsterdam rite, as their brethren did in New York, Philadelphia, and Boston. They had sufficient numbers for a viable congregation, and historical precedent was in their favor. But Chicago was primarily a second-stage destination. In the eastern centers, Dutch Jews established congregations in the 1840s and 1850s. But Chicago's Dutch Jews did not arrive in strength until the 1860s, after many had first lived in the East.

A self-selection process was at work. The most assimilated ones tended to relocate in the West, while those who valued Minhag Amsterdam stayed put in the East. Adult children went west but parents remained in the East. The Dutch Jews also arrived after the Civil War, when the process of amalgamation among Ashkenazi Jews was well underway. As Meites noted, the various national groups "went their own way at first, but gradually their differences narrowed and eventually disappeared."[18] World War II helped revive the weak identities of European national groups threatened by the Nazi juggernaut. In 1940 Chicago's Dutch Jews organized the Netherlands Jewish Society to show their soli-

15. Meites, *Jews of Chicago,* 113-14; Cutler, *From Shtetl to Suburb,* 23. The complete membership list of KAM, 1847-97, in Felsenthal and Eliassof, *History of Kehillah Anshe Maarabh,* includes only three (or possibly four) Dutch Jews among its 485 members; these were Isaac Gelder, Jonas Gelder, Henry S. Haas, and possibly Lewis Cohen.

16. A listing of Dutch Jews in Chicago in 1860 and 1870 is in Swierenga, *Forerunners,* 270-74.

17. Gutstein, *Priceless Heritage,* 28. M. M. Berman, *Our First Century,* 13, also asserts that the Dutch Jews were "German-speaking."

18. Meites, *Jews of Chicago,* 114.

darity with compatriots in the homeland and their support for the war effort.[19]

Chicago's Dutch Jews joined with other Jews in religious life, particularly Germans. The process began already during immigration, when at least seven Dutch families stopped in England in the 1850s and 1860s and married and had children there. In Chicago, marriages between Jews of various nationalities increased. Two-thirds of the married Dutch-born Jews had non-Dutch spouses – one-half German, one-quarter English, and one-quarter other European or American. By 1900 nearly three-fourths (110 of 153) of married couples of Dutch Jewish birth or parentage had non-Dutch spouses. The percentage of Dutch husbands with English wives (26 percent) was nearly twice as great as for Dutch wives (15 percent), whereas the percentage of Dutch wives with eastern European husbands, especially Russians and Poles, was three times as great as that for Dutch husbands.[20]

As the Jewish pioneers prospered in the Civil War years, they moved out of the central city into newer neighborhoods. This dispersal lengthened the distance to the pioneer synagogues downtown and required the founding of new congregations. Russian-Polish Jews also came in growing numbers and desired their own congregations. As a result, by 1870 Chicago counted ten congregations, seven with synagogue buildings. Each served a particular national, neighborhood, socioeconomic, and religious group. It is estimated that two-thirds of the Jews in the city in 1870 belonged to a congregation. This was a marked rise in religious commitment since a decade earlier. Chicago had four thousand Jews at the time.[21]

The Great Fire of 1871 was a turning point in Chicago's Jewish history. The flames destroyed the homes and stores of five hundred families, the Jews Hospital on La Salle Street, and five of the seven synagogues, including the Polish-Dutch Congregation KBS. The fire spared the KAM synagogue on the West Side, but it fell to a large fire in 1874 that struck the surrounding East European Jewish quarter.[22] Jews were thus devastated by the fires, but they also benefited from the rebuilding from the ashes. Chicago thrived more than ever after the Great Fire. Large commercial buildings and industries sprang up in the city center, and residents moved to new neighborhoods in outlying districts.

19. Sidney Sorkin, *Bridges to an American City: A Guide to Chicago's Landmanshaften, 1870-1990* (New York: Peter Lang, 1993), 129.

20. Swierenga, *Forerunners,* Tables 8.3, 8.9.

21. Cutler, *From Shtetl to Suburb,* 26; Gutstein, *Priceless Heritage,* 31-32, 37, 45, 47, 71; Langer, "White-Collar Heritage," 22.

22. Gutstein, *Priceless Heritage,* 38-39, 72-74.

Kehilath Ansche Maarib (KAM) Synagogue, 33rd Street and Indiana Avenue, erected 1891

The fire disasters scattered the Dutch, as it did the other Jews. Before the fires they had lived above their stores and shops in a compact three-square-block area in the western part of the city center along Wells, Clark, and Monroe Streets. Twenty-five of the thirty-nine Dutch Jewish residences and businesses in 1870 were along Wells and adjacent streets. Eleven families lived immediately west of the south branch of the Chicago River, and four families lived along the north branch on the near North Side. All except the families west of the river were completely burned out in 1871, and the westsiders lost everything in the 1874 fire.

In the last quarter of the century, most West Side Dutch Jews moved into South Town (Wards 1-4) and Hyde Park (Ward 32). In 1900, 36 percent lived in Hyde Park and 38 percent were in South Town (Table 15.1). Only ten families (forty-seven persons) remained on the West Side (Ward 12) along fashionable Jackson Boulevard and other tree-lined avenues. A few clothiers and pawnbrokers retained their stores in the central business district and commuted to work. The two prestigious synagogues, KAM and KBS, were both situated by the 1890s in the golden ghetto on the South Side.[23]

In Chicago, as elsewhere, the Dutch Jews did not mix with the larger Dutch Gentile population. In the 1850s and 1860s, while the Jews were concentrated in the city center districts among coreligionists, Dutch Calvinists and Catholics lived in outlying wards. In the heavily Gentile wards on the West Side (7, 8, 9, 12, and 15), which in 1870 contained nearly fourteen hundred persons of Dutch origin, only two Dutch Jewish families (13 per-

23. Ibid., 78, 82.

Table 15.1: Dutch Jewish Wards in Chicago, 1870, 1900

Ward	Jewish Individuals 1870	Jewish Individuals 1900	% of Jewish Population 1870	% of Jewish Population 1900	% of Dutch Origin* 1870	% of Dutch Origin* 1900
1	37	27	22.0	4.2	61.0	29.7
2	40	5	24.0	0.8	100.0	10.2
3	11	48	7.0	7.5	13.0	48.5
4	—	161	—	25.1	—	82.6
5	—	2	—	0.3	—	0.8
7	—	10	—	1.6	—	9.5
8	9	3	5.0	0.5	5.0	1.5
9	5	—	3.0	—	1.0	—
10	27	—	16.0	—	40.0	—
11	16	13	10.0	2.0	57.0	6.0
12	—	47	—	7.3	—	8.3
13	—	5	—	0.8	—	0.9
14	—	9	—	1.4	—	0.9
15	—	6	—	0.9	—	2.2
17	—	9	—	1.4	—	52.9
18	12	3	7.0	0.5	52.0	7.9
19	6	—	4.0	—	14.0	—
20	3	9	2.0	1.4	9.0	11.1
21	—	19	—	3.0	—	23.2
22	—	10	—	1.6	—	30.3
23	—	6	—	0.9	—	15.4
24	—	5	—	0.8	—	7.2
26	—	4	—	0.6	—	2.3
30	—	6	—	0.9	—	0.5
32	—	233	—	36.3	—	70.2
34	—	2	—	0.3	—	0.0
Total	166	642	100.0	100.1	17.0	5.2

*Total Dutch residents in all wards in 1870 was 2,095, of which Dutch Jews were 8 percent; total Dutch residents in all wards in 1900 was 18,881, of which Dutch Jews were 3.4 percent.

Source: Robert P. Swierenga, "Dutch in Chicago and Cook County Federal Population Censuses," 1880, 1900; Swierenga, *Forerunners*, 279.

sons) could be found. By contrast, in the city center wards, all of the forty Dutch-origin persons in Ward 2 were Jewish, as were 61 percent in Ward 1 (Table 15.1). Only in the earliest years prior to the Civil War, when Chicago's residential areas were tightly packed in and around the city center, had Dutch Jews and Gentiles lived in proximity. But even then, a block-by-block analysis would show Jews and Gentiles clustered on different streets.

At the turn of the century, residential segregation was even more pronounced. In 1900 over 80 percent of the 642 Dutch Jews were concentrated in only five wards (1, 3, 4, 12, and 32), in two of which (4 and 32) they comprised 82.6 and 70.2 percent, respectively, of the entire Dutch population (Table 15.1). Two-thirds of the Dutch Calvinists and Catholics, on the other hand, resided on the West Side (Wards 9, 10, 12, and 13) and in the South Side suburbs of Englewood and Roseland (Wards 30, 31, and 34).

Occupationally, Chicago's Jews were mainly storekeepers and merchants, with a sprinkling of professionals and tradesmen. As soon as they learned to speak English, most went into business for themselves. Since Chicago excelled as a dry goods market, second only to New York City by the time of the Civil War, Jews became prominent in dry goods merchandizing as well as all aspects of the clothing trade – manufacturing, wholesaling, and retailing. Their shops lined the streets of the central business district until the Great Fire of 1871 caused a wider dispersal. More prosperous shopkeepers were located in the southern fringes, and later arrivals gravitated to the cheaper western edge of the city center.[24]

The Dutch Jews in Chicago dealt primarily in clothing, both new and used, but a number operated pawnshops and cigar stores. In 1860, of the seven family heads, three owned secondhand clothing outlets, one had a retail and wholesale clothing store, and one ran a dry goods store.[25] These were young men, averaging thirty years of age, who were beginning their business careers and starting with little or no capital.

Newman Levi (Levy), a storekeeper on South Clark Street, was the wealthiest Dutch Jew in 1860. He had immigrated in 1856 or 1857 and by 1860, despite a national financial crash in 1857, he reported owning real estate valued at $5,000, plus $200 worth of personal property. Levi was the only Dutch contributor in 1862 to the fund for equipping a Jewish company from Chicago in the Civil War. But his $20 was a pittance among the

24. Langer, "White-Collar Heritage," 12-13, 20. A more limited occupational study of higher-class Jews is that of Ronald Klotz, "An Economic View of Chicago Jewry, 1879-1881" (unpublished paper, Hebrew Union College, Cincinnati, 1974).

25. Swierenga, *Forerunners,* 270.

several hundred donors listed. Levi had departed the city by 1870 for destinations unknown.[26]

By then the wealthiest Dutch Jew was Henry S. Haas, whose retail and wholesale clothing store stood until the Great Fire in the 100 block of South Clark Street. His merchandise, which he valued at $2,500 in 1860, had increased tenfold by 1870 to $25,000, plus real estate (likely his store and home on South Wabash Avenue) worth $12,000. For many years in the 1860s, Haas served as the consular agent of the Dutch government in Chicago. In 1866 he contributed $50 to a fund to build a veterans hospital in Chicago. After the fire, which destroyed his business, nothing more is heard of Henry Haas. Presumably he too left the city.[27]

Not so with Solomon Andrews, Benjamin Boasberg, and the two Joseph Israel Van Baalens, who were just beginning long careers in Chicago. Andrews sold used clothing on West Monroe Street until 1870, when he upgraded to a pawnshop on South Wells Street. By 1876 he owned a jewelry store in an affluent section on South Wabash Avenue. Solomon Andrews was one of four Andrews families in the city in 1870. Perhaps they were brothers. All were pawnbrokers with stores almost side by side on South Wells Street. They likely collaborated and perhaps specialized in different merchandise, such as Solomon becoming a jeweler. One can hardly imagine that they were competitors.[28]

Benjamin Boasberg (of the Boasberg and Van Baalen clans of Buffalo) arrived in Chicago in the late 1850s and, after clerking in a clothing store for a few years, opened his own used-clothing outlet by 1869 located on South Wells Street. This was the same business his older brother Nathan Boasberg operated in Buffalo.[29] Boasberg's brother-in-law, Joseph Israel van Baalen, known as Israel, came to Chicago via Buffalo and Detroit, and by 1870 he was a prosperous clothing merchant on West Randolph

26. Cutler, *From Shtetl to Suburbs,* 20; Swierenga, *Dutch Households,* 2: 619, 717; 1: 270; *Chicago City Directory,* 1861; Meites, *Jews of Chicago,* 90.

27. Swierenga, *Dutch Households,* 1: 390; *Chicago City Directory,* 1860, 1861, 1867; Meites, *Jews of Chicago,* 103-4.

28. Leon Andrews had also moved south by 1876 to 572 South State Street. Swierenga, *Dutch Households,* 1: 13; 3: 1010-11; *Chicago City Directories,* 1861, 1867, 1869, 1876.

29. Swierenga, *Forerunners,* 232-40. Benjamin Boasberg and his wife had thirteen children, ten of whom were still living in 1900, although he was deceased. Widow Sarah Boasberg and her sons Herman, Joseph, and daughter Adaline lived in Ward 32 at 4628 S. Langley Avenue. Israel and his wife Bertha lived a block away at 23 East 48th Street. Herman was a printer, Joseph a clothing cutter, and Israel a trimmer tailor. The other children had departed the city. (See Swierenga, "Dutch in Chicago and Cook County 1900 Federal Census"; *Chicago City Directory,* 1869.)

Street with an inventory of $2,000. He had married into the prosperous Philadelphia Lit merchant family, which operated a large department store, Lit Brothers. Israel Van Baalen's son Emanuel clerked in the family store. The Great Fire wiped out the business, and Joseph became a fire insurance agent. By 1900 he lived on the fashionable South Prairie Avenue. His uncle and namesake, Joseph Israel Van Baalen, who also lived nearby, came to Chicago from Buffalo in 1865 and engaged in merchandizing until the Fire destroyed his property and pushed him into early retirement. His three middle sons in 1875 were all clerks in downtown retail stores, while his oldest son was a hatter and his youngest son a watchmaker.[30]

In 1870 the census marshal recorded the occupations and wealth of forty Dutch Jewish households. The fourteen clothiers and dry goods storekeepers still dominated, but seven men ran cigar stores and six were pawnbrokers. Five were clerks and bookkeepers, and three were peddling. The three tailors and one cigarmaker may also have run their own businesses. None of the Dutch Jews were unskilled workers. Ten years later, in 1880, the proportion of merchants and storekeepers declined (except for pawnbrokers), and salesmen, peddlers, and dealers increased threefold. The occupational distribution was similar to that of Chicago Jewry generally, but the Dutch had more merchants (both upper and lower levels), no professionals, and only half as large a proportion in the blue-collar crafts. The Dutch, therefore, were concentrated in the middle of the Jewish occupational ladder.[31]

Reported property values likewise point to men at the middle rungs of respectability. Only the Andrews clan, Henry Haas, Edward Siekel, Israel van Baalen, and Levi Van Gelder could boast of substantial wealth. Solomon Andrews in 1870 reported a total of $16,000, Andre Andrews $7,000, Aaron Andrews $2,000, and Leon Andrews $1,000. Siekel, a produce commission merchant on Kedzie Avenue at the western city limits, reported $23,000, mostly in real estate. Van Baalen was a downtown clothier worth $2,000, and Van Gelder was a lithographer worth $3,000. Sixteen family heads, 40 percent of all families, reported no property. The median wealth was $900.

Between 1870 and 1900, the many Dutch Jewish newcomers broadened the occupational distribution. The proportion of merchants declined from 68 to 55 percent, while the number of salesmen and dealers more than doubled from 10 to 20 percent. Two physicians comprised the

30. Swierenga, *Forerunners,* 156-57.

31. Ibid., Table 8.11, 270-74, 281-83.

only professionals among the Jewish Dutch in 1900. The two persons in the unskilled category were a janitor and a department store packer.[32]

These figures include only Dutch-*born* household heads. Considering also second-generation Jews, the occupational distribution widened by 1900, but it did not change substantially. Small businessmen and salesmen predominated, particularly in tobacco, clothing, and jewelry. Fewer than one in five were blue-collar workers, and only three were professionals. Specifically, of 127 persons of Jewish origin in the labor force in 1900, merchants comprised 39 percent; salesmen, agents, and dealers 31 percent; and clerks 6 percent. Together, these petty businessmen totaled 76 percent of the work force. Skilled craftsmen made up 18 percent and unskilled workers only 4 percent. In sum, in the period 1850-1900 the Dutch Jewish economic profile became more diverse. Retail clothing stores gave way first to pawnshops and then by 1900 to cigar sweatshops and retail outlets.

One reason for the relative economic success of the Chicago Dutch Jews was their residential longevity in the city. The notable clans were the Andrews, Van Gelders, Greenburgs, Litts, Rosenbachs, and Van Baalens. Single families that persisted were those of Benjamin Boasberg, Jerome Frank, George Hetzel, George Poppers, Mark Schneider, William Van Buren, Levi Van Gelder, Solomon Van Praag, and Samuel Voorsanger.

Solomon Van Praag, a saloon keeper on Wabash Avenue, is the only Dutch Jew known to be politically active, but there were doubtless others. Van Praag belonged to the Democratic Party and represented Cook County in the Illinois State legislature in 1891-92.[33]

Dutch Catholics

Six times as many Dutch Catholics as Jews immigrated to the United States. In 1920 John A. Van Heertum, a leading Dutch-Catholic prelate,

32. Ibid., Table 8.13, 285-89.

33. John Clayton, comp., *The Illinois Fact Book and Historical Almanac, 1673-1968* (Carbondale and Edwardsville, Ill.: Southern Illinois Univ. Press, 1970), 249. Philip P. Bregstone, *Chicago and Its Jews: A Cultural History* (Chicago: privately published, 1933), 314, incorrectly reports that Van Praag served in the 1887-88 legislature. Van Praag was born in the Netherlands in 1856 and came to America as a youngster in 1860. He reached Chicago in the years immediately after the Great Fire and by 1875 operated a clothing store at 597 S. State Street. By 1900 he lived with his wife and daughter at his saloon at 440 S. Wabash Avenue. See *Chicago City Directory*, 1875; Swierenga, "Dutch in Chicago and Cook County 1900 Federal Census."

counted 40,000 coreligionists "scattered throughout nearly every state of the Union." The primary concentrations were in the Fox River Valley of Wisconsin, the Bay City region of southeastern Michigan, and southwest of Minneapolis in Carver County. Dutch Catholics also could be found in the major urban centers of the Midwest – Chicago, Cleveland, Detroit, Grand Rapids, Cincinnati, and Saint Louis. The faithful were free to settle almost anywhere, because Catholic parishes were ubiquitous and the Latin liturgy was universal.[34] Dutch Catholics gravitated to German and Belgian parishes, many of whom had Dutch-speaking priests in the confessional booth, and they attended multiethnic parochial schools taught in the English language.

Religion for Dutch Catholics thus hastened assimilation and encouraged geographical dispersal, while for Protestants it slowed the process and caused them to stick together in pure Dutch churches and schools. Van Heertum notes that Dutch Catholics and their children, "of all non-English-speaking peoples, . . . have most rapidly learned and adopted the language and customs of the United States." As a result, in the 1920s there were only twenty-five Dutch Catholic congregations nationwide, compared to more than five hundred Dutch Reformed congregations. The largest urban parishes were St. Willebrord in Roseland (Kensington) on Chicago's far South Side; St. Joseph the Worker in southeast Grand Rapids, Michigan; St. John in Essexville, Michigan, near Saginaw Bay; and St. John in Little Chute and St. Joseph in De Pere, both in Wisconsin.[35]

As in the homeland, Protestant and Catholic Hollanders in Chicago had no contact, even when they shared the same neighborhood and spoke a common tongue. The pastors of both faiths had no ecumenical interchange, and they warned the faithful not to intermarry, on pain of excommunication. Even though both peoples moved along the process of Americanization, they continued to fight the old religious wars of Europe.

Irish and German Catholics were among the first settlers in Chicago, and by the 1840s some Dutch joined them. In 1844 the church assigned the first bishop to lead the growing congregations, which in 1846 totaled thirteen hundred members, one-tenth of the population of the city. That year the first two German parishes were established, St. Peter located downtown on Wells Street and St. Joseph on Chicago Avenue on the

34. John A. Van Heertum, O.P., *Regeeringsjubileum, 1898-1923: Aan haar Majesteit Wilhelmina Koningin der Nederlanden* (Chicago, 1923), 1-2.

35. Quote in Van Heertum, *Regeeringsjubileum, 1898-1923*, 1-2; Swierenga, *Faith and Family*, 160-61.

Northwest Side. Soon came other German parishes, St. Francis of Assisi on Clinton Street, St. Michael on Diversey Boulevard, and St. Boniface on Chestnut Street.

Chicago's second bishop was the Belgian-born Flemish priest, James Oliver Van de Velde (1795-1855), an eminent Jesuit who spoke fluent Dutch, along with German, French, and English. As a former president of St. Louis University and one committed to Christian education, Van de Velde established nearly a dozen parochial schools in Chicago during his tenure (1849-53). But none of the sixty-two priests serving under him was Dutch.[36]

Arnold Damen and Holy Family Church

This soon changed with the arrival in 1857 of the Dutch-born Jesuit missionary, Father Arnold Damen (1815-90). Damen was a large and impressive man with energy to match. A man of "practical and persuasive eloquence," Damen was a spiritual giant who preached "the essential truths of salvation and the peremptory duties of Christian life." His first act was to organize a spiritual retreat in all the churches, the third in five months. For three weeks, priests conducted twenty-hour daily prayer marathons, running from four in the morning until after midnight. More than twelve thousand parishioners received Communion in overflowing churches, and many Protestants converted to the faith. This deep personal piety always marked Damen's ministry. While on a preaching mission in Brooklyn, New York, in 1871, he learned by telegram of the Great Chicago Fire and immediately went to his knees and talked with God in an all-night prayer vigil. The fire, which began in the barn of one of his parishioners, the O'Learys on De Koven Street, spared the church when the winds carried the flames away to the northeast.[37]

36. Gilbert J. Garraghan, S.J., *The Catholic Church in Chicago, 1673-1871* (Chicago: Loyola Univ. Press, 1921), 119, 124-25, 137-66.

37. Garraghan, *Catholic Church,* 169-70; Garraghan, *The Jesuits of the Middle United States,* 3 vols. (New York: America Press, 1938), 2: 78. Damen was born in Leur, Noord-Brabant; studied for the Jesuit Novitiate at Florissant, Missouri (1837-40); was a professor at St. Louis University (1840-44); and a priest in St. Louis (1844-57) before coming to Chicago. A full-length biography is Joseph P. Conroy, S.J., *Arnold Damen, S.J.: A Chapter in the Making of Chicago* (New York: Benzinger Brothers, 1930); Thomas M. Mulkerins, S.J., *Holy Family Parish, Chicago: Priests and People* (Chicago: Universal Press, 1923), 109-41. The prayer vigil story is related in William Mullen, "Church that wouldn't die," *Chicago Tribune,* 6 Oct. 1995, which reports on the first mass after a nine-year restoration of the decrepit church building.

Rev. Arnold Damen, S.J., in mid-life, ca. 1855

Father Damen organized one of the largest Irish parishes on the West Side, the Church of the Holy Family, and established the Society of Jesus in Chicago, centered in St. Ignatius College (figure 15.1, site A). The imposing Gothic cathedral that Damen built at a cost of $100,000, and the college he founded in 1870, occupied a square block on 12th Street just west of Blue Island Avenue between May and Aberdeen Streets. This first Jesuit church in Chicago stood like a European cathedral on the Illinois prairie and was one of the largest churches in the country. Fortunately, it survived the Great Fire.[38]

The money for the cathedral was raised locally from thousands of small donors in the teeth of the economic panic of 1857 and ensuing depression. When Damen dedicated the cathedral with great fanfare only three years later, in 1860, he was hailed as a "Catholic Hercules." The area was then undeveloped prairie and swampland, dotted with workers' cabins and shanties. For years Damen kept several milk cows and various kinds of fowl for fresh meat behind his residence at 453 (new numbering 1144) W. 12th Street.[39]

38. George A. Lane, S.J., *Chicago Churches and Synagogues: An Architectural Pilgrimage* (Chicago: Loyola Univ. Press, 1981), 26-27.

39. Timothy Walch, "Catholic Education in Chicago: The Formative Years 1840-1890," *Chicago History* 7 (Summer 1978): 92; Garraghan, *Catholic Church,* 171-79; Mulkerins, *Holy Family Parish,* 132-34.

Figure 15.1 Holy Family Parish, 1857-1923

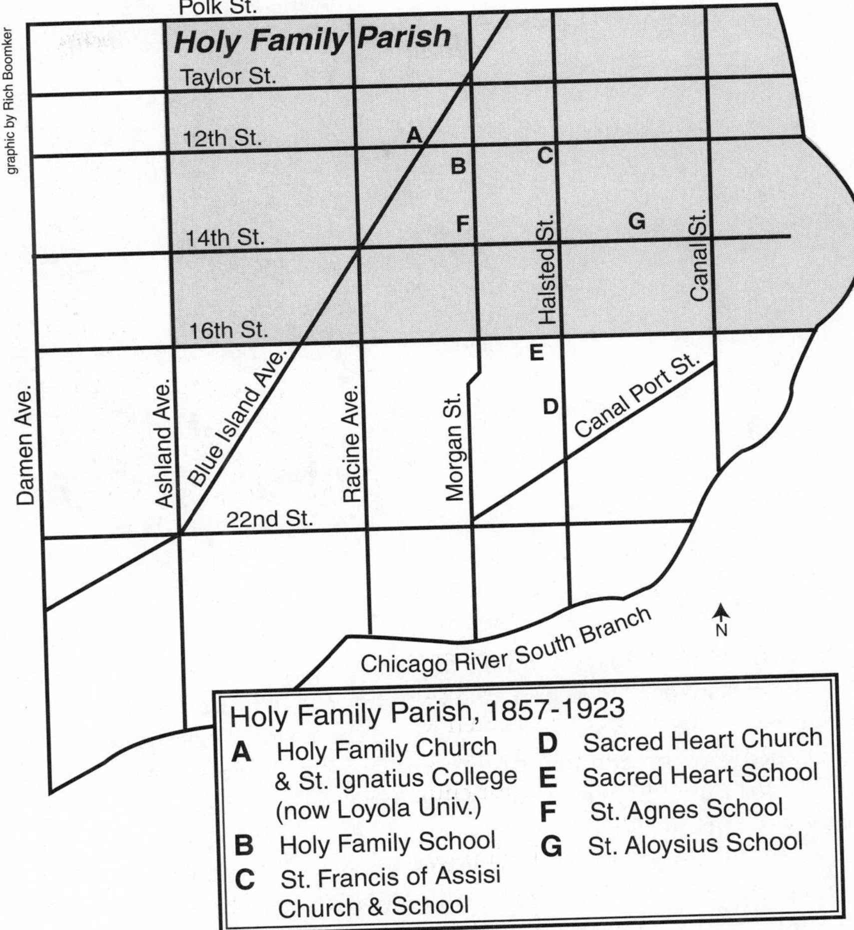

The announcement of Damen's ambitious church plans set off a real estate boom in this area southwest of the city center. Soon homes sprouted on the prairie, and lumber yards and saw mills dotted the banks of the south branch of the Chicago River, stretching west to Canal Street and from Van Buren to 22nd Streets. Railroad yards, grain elevators, and stockyards added to the mix of industry and homes on the promising West Side.[40]

40. Mulkerins, *Holy Family Parish,* 718-22.

Holy Family Church and St. Ignatius College

With Damen's driving power of leadership and eloquent preaching style, the newspaper called him "the Catholic Beecher," in flattering reference to Henry Ward Beecher, the leader of the Protestant crusade of the era. Damen was the dominant prelate on the West Side for twenty years. He founded numerous daughter congregations in Chicago, directed parish activity at Holy Family for a generation, and served as founding president of St. Ignatius College, which would become Loyola University. The college occupied a massive, five-story brick building completed in 1870 for $250,000.[41] No wonder the city fathers honored Damen by naming a major thoroughfare after him.

Damen raised most of the money to build the college on nationwide mission tours. Throughout his tenure at Holy Family, he and his associates went on numerous preaching missions throughout the country, planting new congregations, raising funds, and baptizing more than twelve thousand converts to the faith. Damen almost singlehandedly created Jesuit popular missions with their spiritual exercises.[42]

41. Garraghan, *Jesuits,* 2: 98, 102.

42. Mulkerins, *Holy Family Parish,* 124-27 (quote 124); Harry C. Koenig, S.T.D., ed.,

Rev. Peter Koopmans, S.J., in mid-life, 1860s

Even though Damen was at the head of Holy Family, it did not become a Dutch center. Among more than one thousand donors to the building campaign in 1857-60, not one was Dutch.[43] By 1890, when the mainly Irish congregation served twenty-five thousand people – the largest English-speaking parish in the United States, few Dutch attended, even though its priesthood was mainly Dutch. Damen recruited Jesuits and lay brothers from Noord Brabant and Flemish Belgium to be pastoral assistants and to staff the parish schools. Jesuits included Cornelius Smarius (1823-70) of Tilburg (Noord-Brabant), Peter C. Koopmans (1830-1902), the brothers Henry C. (1842-1918) and Martin M. (1859-1918+) Bronsgeest of The Hague, and Joseph G. Zealand (Van Zeeland) (1831-??) of Geldrop (Noord Brabant). Henry Bronsgeest immigrated with Arnold Damen in 1868 and was his traveling companion for ten years.

Koopmans was Damen's assistant for eleven years (1872-83) and succeeded him as pastor for two years (1877-79), followed by Henry Bronsgeest (1879-84), who promoted the temperance movement in the parish. Koopmans's voice was so powerful that it could be heard on Fourteenth Street, a quarter mile away. Bronsgeest, who was ordained at s' Hertogenbosch, succeeded his mentor at Sacred Heart Church in 1884.

A History of the Parishes of the Archdiocese of Chicago, 2 vols. (Chicago: Archdiocese of Chicago, 1980), 1: 369-70.

43. Mulkerins, *Holy Family Parish*, 56-80, 112.

Rev. Henry Bronsgeest, S.J., in mid-life, 1860s

Martin Bronsgeest assisted his brother first at Holy Family and later at Sacred Heart (1916-18). Zealand emigrated in 1853 and taught at a number of Catholic colleges before becoming president of St. Ignatius College in 1885 and rector of Holy Family. In 1860 Damen brought John J. Hutton (1826-86), a carpenter by trade and Jesuit lay brother, to Chicago to manage all Holy Family parish construction work, including building the cathedral.[44]

Other Hollanders who served the Holy Family church and parish schools in later years were the Breen brothers, Aloysius (1867-1960), Francis Xavier (1869-1953), and Paul M. (1873-1945); John B. Van Acken (1869-1924); Michael Van Agt (1844-96) of Eindhoven (Noord Brabant); William Vander Heyden (1842-82); John Venneman (1839-1907); and Adrian F. Van Hulst (1817-1909). Paul Breen was vice president and then treasurer of St. Ignatius College, and the superior of Loyola Academy. Francis Xavier Breen taught at St. Ignatius, as did Venneman, Van Agt, and Van Hulst. Van Acken served as assistant pastor of Holy Family and assistant chaplain at the Cook County Hospital. Van Hulst came to America in 1837, was ordained in 1847 in St. Louis, and directed the Home of the Good Shepherd there until moving to Chicago to teach at St. Ignatius for

44. Ibid., 139-42, 320-24, 381-83; Alfred T. Andreas, *History of Chicago from the Earliest Period to the Present Time,* 3 vols. (Chicago: A. T. Andreas Publisher, 1884-86), 3: 770-72; 2: 401-04.

Rev. Cornelius Smarius, S.J., in mid-life, 1860s

thirty years. At his death in 1909 at age 92, he was "supposedly the oldest Dutchman in Chicago."[45]

Van Agt spent his entire career teaching in parish schools, beginning in 1870, and ending up at St. Ignatius College. He is credited with making the Holy Family parish schools among the best in the nation. In 1876 enrollment reached four thousand, 27 percent of all parochial pupils in the city, and ten times the number of students who attended the public school in the parish. James Cardinal Gibbons aptly called Holy Family schools the "Banner Schools of America."

This ethnic firepower was enough to attract more than forty Dutch Catholic families (about 150 souls) to the vicinity of Holy Family parish by 1870. But these families had a viable alternative in the adjacent St. Francis of Assisi parish. In 1866 St. Francis relocated to 12th Street at Peoria Street, just two blocks east of Holy Family (figure 15.1, site C). The Dutch-born fathers, Ferdinand (Francis) L. Kalvelage (d. 1893) and Bernard Baak, heard confessions at St. Francis in their native tongue. The parish school stood next to the church.

Before Kalvelage's tenure, the congregation suffered from internal

45. Mulkerins, *Holy Family Parish,* 139-42, 320-44, 365-80, 412-14, 436-37, 440; Walch, "Catholic Education in Chicago," 91-92; *Onze Toekomst,* 22 Oct. 1909. The Breen brothers were born in Chicago of immigrant parents.

turmoil, when against their will the bishop sought to put Jesuits in charge. Many left and joined Emmanuel German Evangelical Lutheran Church, which was erected in 1857 on 12th Street just east of Holy Family. The bishop then appointed Father Kalvelage, a Dominican, who managed to heal the rift and stop the membership loses. It is likely that more Hollanders attended St. Francis of Assisi than Holy Family Church. Both were English-speaking, as was the case in most Catholic parishes until the 1880s.[46]

Several dozen Dutch families living in the southern part of Holy Family parish and beyond its borders as far as 33rd Street joined Sacred Heart Church (German) at 19th and Peoria Streets (1877) (figure 15.1, site D), and St. Anthony of Padua Church (German) at 28th and Canal Streets in Armour Square (1873). Damen founded Sacred Heart in 1872 and named Michael Van Agt one of the first three priests. Damen himself later led Sacred Heart (1879-84), followed in the 1880s by the Bronsgeest brothers. It was comforting for the Hollanders there to be able to confess their sins in Dutch. It is not known which Dutch priests served St. Anthony's, but by 1900 more Dutch Catholics lived in this changing neighborhood near the stockyards than anywhere else in the city.[47]

South Side Churches — St. Patrick and St. Willebrord

Dutch Catholics in the Calumet region of Hyde Park, South Chicago, Pullman, and Roseland initially affiliated with the predominantly Irish St. Patrick Church at 95th Street and Commercial Avenue in South Chicago. St. Patrick was organized in 1857 to serve everyone living south of 31st Street, which was then the southern boundary of the city. The first resident pastor of St. Patrick in 1880 was the Reverend Martin Van de Laar (1844-1906), who had attended seminary in his native Noord Brabant and

46. This is evident from an analysis of Swierenga, "Dutch in Chicago and Cook County Federal Censuses, 1850-1870." Dutch Catholic families were identified by linking the names to Netherlands emigration records or making an inference from given names, interethnic marriages, and occupations such as saloon keepers and bartenders that no Calvinist would hold.

47. Koenig, *History of the Parishes,* 2: 1674-77; Stephen J. Shaw, *The Catholic Parish as a Way-Station of Ethnicity and Americanization: Chicago's Germans and Italians, 1903-1939* (Brooklyn: Carlson Publishing, 1991), 41-42. Some thirty-five Dutch Catholic families lived in the vicinity of St. Anthony Church, based on an analysis of Swierenga, "Dutch in Chicago and Cook County 1900 Federal Census."

was ordained in 1871 to serve in his home diocese of Aalst. In 1875 Van de Laar immigrated to Chicago to seek out "strayed" Dutch Catholics and became a member of the Society of Jesus (Jesuits). But the demands of the order overwhelmed him, and he resigned to become a secular priest and was appointed to St. Columbkille Church on the northwest side of Grand Avenue at Paulina Street.[48]

Van de Laar labored at St. Patrick Church for twenty-six years as the parish economy boomed with major new industrial plants manned by thousands of European immigrants. St. Patrick flourished under his leadership. The church building was raised in 1883 to accommodate a parish school on the first floor, staffed by the Sisters of Mercy. In 1889 the sisters began St. Patrick's High School, the first Catholic coeducational high school in Chicago. Van de Laar also constructed a rectory and convent on the large property at 95th and Commercial.[49]

All of Van de Laar's efforts went up in flames in 1902 when the parish buildings were destroyed by fire under "suspicious circumstances"; a ten-year-old boy allegedly set the entire commercial district ablaze. Van de Laar, with characteristic vigor, shrugged off the $17,000 loss and immediately set about rebuilding on the same site. A new church to seat five hundred worshipers, much plainer than its Gothic predecessor, and with schoolrooms on the upper floors, was dedicated the next year. Critics derided it as the "shoe factory" because it resembled an industrial building, but the practical Dutch priest insisted that it was more important to have a large sanctuary and spacious classrooms than an ornate cathedral. The new school enrolled more than five hundred students.

Between 1882 and 1905, the parish mothered five new congregations in the area, which was gradually annexed to the city. Because so many busy trunk railroads connecting Chicago with the East ran near the church and school, to safeguard his parishioners Van de Laar did battle with the railroad companies to eliminate hazardous grade crossings by building elevated tracks.

Always a crusader, Father Van de Laar was also an outspoken critic of elaborate funeral processions with fancy horse-drawn carriages. He advocated inexpensive "streetcar funerals," and directed such for his funeral so that the poorer parishioners could participate. At his death at age

48. Koenig, "St. Patrick Church," *History of the Parishes,* 2: 760; Garraghan, *Catholic Church in Chicago,* 190-91; Annemarie Kasteel, *Francis Janssens, 1843-1897: A Dutch-American Prelate* (Lafayette, La.: Univ. of Southwest Louisiana Press, 1992), 235, n. 21; *Onze Toekomst,* 2 Mar. 1906. Kasteel incorrectly says that Van de Laar was the "first Dutch priest in the Windy City."

49. For this and the next two paragraphs, see Koenig, "St. Patrick Church," 2: 760-62.

Tower of St. Willebrord Catholic Church, Kensington

sixty-one in 1906, the *New World* reported: "The street railway company was not able to provide cars sufficient to carry the mourners. Only about 1,500 of those who followed the remains from the church were able to accompany them to the cemetery." Such was the outpouring of affection for Van de Laar by his congregation.

For decades the Catholic hierarchy in America had resisted pure nationality parishes, until the pressure from Poles and Germans (mostly Prussians) became too strong. In the 1880s and 1890s, Chicago's first archbishop, Patrick A. Feehan, a pragmatic administrator, yielded to the inevitable and, against the explicit decree of Pope Leo XIII in 1886, supervised the creation of more than fifty German and Polish parishes.[50]

Dutch immigrants from the provinces of Noord and Zuid Holland, who had settled on truck farms in the far south suburbs of Roseland and Kensington, were direct beneficiaries of this ethnic campaign. At first they attended St. Nicholas (German) Church on 113th Place at State Street, which was organized in 1890 by the Reverend Theodore Boniface. But in 1900 the Hollanders requested and received permission from Archbishop Feehan to create St. Willebrord, which was the only Dutch parish in greater Chicago. Feehan assigned to St. Willebrord the Dutch-born priest, John Lambert Broens, who was serving St. Joseph Church of De

50. Shaw, *Catholic Parish,* 12-13.

Pere, Wisconsin. Broens arranged a place of worship at St. Louis of France Church, which was no longer needed by the French Catholics. It was an eleven-year-old building in need of repair, located just east of State Street on the corner of 114th and Edbrooke Avenue.[51]

Throughout its history, St. Willebrord Church was a parish staffed by Norbertines of the Norbertine Abbey and St. Norbert College in De Pere, Wisconsin, the major Dutch Catholic colony in the United States since the 1840s. The motherhouse, the Abbey of Berne in Heeswijk, Noord Brabant, transferred its order to De Pere in 1893 and established its American seminary there in 1898 under Father Bernard J. Pennings of Gemert, Noord Brabant. Broens had trained at St. Norbert's College and served St. Willebrord "with great success" for many years until he died in 1908. He was followed by the fellow Noord Brabant priests, Matthias Vanden Elsen (1908-13) and John A. Van Heertum (1913-39).

Vanden Elsen had accepted a call to American missions in 1900 as rector of St. Norbert College; he also temporarily served the Essexville, Michigan, parish before coming to Chicago. Van Heertum was also a rector of St. Norbert College from 1903 until 1913. At St. Willebrord he supervised the construction of a new brick sanctuary and nave, complete with an imposing tower, stained glass windows, and a pipe organ. Van Heertum also founded a parish school in 1927 staffed by the Franciscan Sisters; the new two-story building stood just north of the church at 11400 S. Edbrooke Avenue. The parish of two hundred families (eleven hundred souls) clearly was prospering in the 1920s.[52]

When Van Heertum died in 1939 after serving St. Willebrord Church for twenty-six years, the editor of the Catholic periodical, *New World,* commented that although he "was widely known as a pastor and church leader, his other claim to fame is the Hollandish spirit which he maintained in people of Hollandish descent." Van Heertum's pastorate marked the apex of Chicago's Dutch parish. Under his successor, Francis Exler (1939-59), the first non-Dutch pastor, the parish grew to three hundred families, but the neighborhood gradually changed into an interracial Chicago suburb, and the core Holland families moved away. The white flight of the 1960s changed the ethnicity of the parish to black and Hispanic, and the liturgical community declined. The grammar school closed in

51. Koenig, *A History of the Parishes,* 1: 45, 2: 987-90.

52. Cornelius James Kirkfleet, *The White Canons of St. Norbert: A History of the Premonstratensian Order in the British Isles and America* (West De Pere, Wis.: St. Norbert's Abby, 1943), 221-36, 245. Broens's death is noted in *Onze Toekomst,* 26 June 1908.

1971 and the church closed in the 1980s; its members were dispersed to other Roseland churches.[53]

North Side – St. Michael Church

Dutch Catholics on the predominantly German North Side affiliated with St. Michael's Church of the Holy Redeemer (German), erected under the Redemptorist Fathers in 1853 on North Avenue at Church Street. One of the priests was Frederick Van Emstede, who heard confessions in Dutch.[54] In 1870 more than forty Dutch families lived in the vicinity of this parish, which became the largest German congregation in Chicago. Hollanders living farther west likely worshiped at St. Boniface Church (1865), at Chicago and Ashland avenues.[55] Dutch Catholics living in the fashionable Humboldt Park neighborhood on the far West Side attended the Belgian parish of St. John Berchmans, led in 1907 by its first pastor, the Belgian-born Julius De Vos.

Cicero – St. Francis of Rome

Much later, the few Dutch Catholics living in the western suburb of Cicero joined St. Francis of Rome at 15th Street and Austin Boulevard. Its senior pastor for twenty-eight years (1940-68) was George Beemsterboer, the first-born son of Dutch immigrant Louis Beemsterboer of St. Willibrord Church. A giant of a man at nearly seven feet tall, Father Beemsterboer could be seen daily walking along the boulevard with his two Great Danes on their leashes. It was a sight to behold! He taught Latin at Chicago's Quigley Preparatory Seminary for twenty-two years and built up St. Francis parish to well above a thousand families. The annual carnivals at St. Francis for its parochial school lured not a few dollars

53. Koenig, *A History of the Parishes,* 989.

54. According to the New York ship passenger manifests, Van Emstede, aged forty-five, a priest, sailed on the *Hermann of Baltimore* from Bremen to New York City, arriving 12 May 1853. No Chicago City Directory of the 1850s or 1860s lists him, but the 1860 federal census reported him as serving at St. Michael's Church in June 1860.

55. Shaw, *Catholic Parish,* 71-73, 349-50; Koenig, *A History of the Parishes,* 1: 631-68. In 1909 a Dutch-American city fireman, Simon Cooper (Kuperus), who was a member of Superior Cathedral on Superior Street, was killed fighting a grain elevator fire and buried in St. Bonifacius Cemetery. His mother was Mrs. Nycholtd-Sipma (*Onze Toekomst,* 14 May 1909).

from Dutch Reformed youth in the neighborhood, who found the Ferris wheel rides and games irresistible, despite stern warnings from their parents and church leaders to stay away.[56]

Social

Because Dutch Catholics attended parochial schools and worshiped in German, Irish, or multiethnic parishes, their rate of ethnic out-marriage was high. Already in the first decade, the 1850s, more than one-third had German or Irish spouses. In the 1860s, the rate rose above 60 percent, mostly with Germans and in a few instances with Belgians and Irish. By 1900 nearly 100 percent of Dutch Catholics in Chicago married Irish, Belgian, and German spouses. Only those who had married before emigrating had Dutch-born mates.[57]

Occupationally, Dutch Catholics held blue-collar jobs. About half filled the ranks of skilled laborers, many as carpenters, and a third worked as laborers and teamsters. Ten percent operated retail businesses, mainly as saloonkeepers and retail grocers, and another ten percent filled public posts as priests, policemen, and firemen. Thus, generally, Dutch Catholics worked in the skilled trades and as factory laborers, Dutch Jews kept shops and agencies, and Dutch Reformed operated garbage and cartage businesses. Some Reformed on the South Side favored the building trades, while those in the far suburbs worked truck farms.

Conclusion

Dutch Jewish merchants in New York, Philadelphia, and other cities penetrated the Great Lakes frontier in the antebellum decades to provide consumer goods and services to the rapidly growing region. The Van Baalen and Boasberg clans of clothiers typified the business networking that led to the establishment of branch houses from their Buffalo base in Pittsburgh, Cleveland, Detroit, and Chicago. The burgeoning cities of the interior offered these sons of the immigrants tickets to success. Already on

56. Mulkerins, *Holy Family Parish,* 328; Koenig, *A History of the Parishes,* 1: 480-81, 2: 1105-07; Swierenga, comp., *Dutch in Chicago and Cook County, 1900 Federal Census.*

57. Based on analyses of Swierenga, "Dutch in Chicago and Cook County Federal Censuses, 1850-1870"; "Dutch in Chicago and Cook County 1880 Federal Census"; and Dutch in Chicago and Cook County 1900 Federal Census."

the path to acculturation, they quickly amalgamated into the larger German Jewish community. Chicago's Hyde Park district had the largest concentration of Dutch Jews in 1900, but here too they blended into a greater Jewish neighborhood.

Dutch Catholics likewise came to Chicago for well-paying jobs in the trades. And like Dutch Jews, they had been second-class citizens in the homeland and thus held it in low esteem. Except for those in Kensington, they readily gave up their Dutchness and amalgamated into the large German Catholic communities in Chicago's western and northern sections. The "other Dutch" hardly seemed Dutch to the dominant Reformed community, who ignored them with impunity.

CHAPTER 16

The Dutch Reformed as a Covenanted Community

The cohesion of Chicago's Dutch Reformed immigrant community and the people's clear sense of identity came from their churches and their theological convictions, especially the concept of covenant. They believed that God had covenanted with them as with Abraham, the father of all believers. God had written his law in their hearts; he would be their God, and they would be his people. Their preachers explained the meaning and purpose of this covenantal relationship weekly in sermons that were heavy on doctrine and piety, and they lived out their "Christian world and life view" during the week in countless church and school activities and in the workplace.

From the beginning, the Dutch Reformed looked after one another, bore each other's burdens, and shared not only things religious but also a common social and cultural life. When parents presented their infants for the sacrament of baptism and vowed to raise them in the "fear and understanding of the Lord," the entire congregation shared those vows. They did not rest until the children became adults who also "owned the covenant" and entered the full life of the community, including its "joys and sorrows."

More than fervent piety and religious busyness, the communion of the saints meant walking together not only on Sundays but everyday. This led, naturally, to living closely, often side by side on the same block, where social life could bloom from the front porch. Formal and informal visits were the norm. Together, the Dutch Reformed went to worship, school, work, and play. Christian schools only intensified the sense of togetherness and led to lifelong friendships and marriage partners.

William Zeilstra, a Timothy School graduate, recently noted the collective impact of the triad of home, church, and school:

> When children were born, when accidents laid low, when the elderly expired, when projects were undertaken to serve the cause of religion or charity, it was a cause for the community to share the life of the heart and become more closely joined together.
>
> This is explained by the emphasis upon their lives as constituted by the covenant. They were told they were a covenant people. This meant that they were separate from all others in the world. These others, in turn, represented to them a threat of different ways, all of them false or inferior, in the demanding call to live for God's glory. This defined them as a body, and the definition stuck over several generations. It also gave them a mission. . . .
>
> Their piety consisted of cultivating this worship, these doctrines, these confessions, these sacraments in baptism (by vows) and the practice of closed Communion, and these ways reinforced this sense of separation and cohesion. Look after our own. Do all that needs to be done by ourselves. Find all, supply all, that is sensed to be important from our own resources of faith and life together.[1]

A shared worldview enabled the Reformed churches in Chicago to become national leaders in their denominations. Their "firsts" include a half dozen ministry endeavors: in 1912 city mission work at the Helping Hand Mission, in 1918 the Chicago Christian High School, in 1920 the National Union of Christian Schools, in 1921 the Missionary Training School that became the Reformed Bible College, and in 1939 the Christian Reformed denominational radio broadcast *(Back to God Hour)* on Chicago station WJJD that in 1947 moved to WGN on the national Mutual Broadcasting System.

The "M" Factor

The Dutch Reformed in Chicago shared with their compatriots nationally a common value system and worldview, but the habit of suburban migration gave them a unique character. This pattern was common to most ethnic groups in the city. As Dominic Pacyga noted in an important study of Chicago's ethnic neighborhoods, the history of every group "centers on

1. William Zeilstra, letter to author, 20 April 2001.

the reality of change, rather than on the myth of stability. . . . It was attitudes concerning race, ethnicity, and class that influenced the choices Chicagoans have historically made."[2]

No group experienced the "M-factor," mobility, more than did the westsiders. Five times and more the entire West Side Dutch community picked up, "lock, stock, and barrel," to better themselves and to escape the ever encroaching ghetto. Every generation took flight and moved farther out, reluctantly selling their homes, churches, schools, and shops. Even the Dutch in the outlying districts of Cook County, such as Roseland and South Holland, who stayed put for more than a century, eventually relocated, although they only did so once or twice. The M-factor was a distinguishing characteristic of Dutch Chicagoans, which set them apart from the Dutch in small towns and rural communities who experienced stability over many generations.

Ethnicity also played a key role in the way Chicagoans organized themselves, as Pacyga explained. "Different white ethnic groups shared the same neighborhood, but they segregated themselves socially by creating separate institutions, such as churches, schools, clubs, stores, taverns, and even street gangs."[3]

Living in America's second city and rubbing shoulders with and sharing lunch buckets with persons of other ethnic and religious groups shaped the Dutch Reformed in profound ways. But the full impact was not felt until the third generation. Language and cultural barriers segregated first-generation immigrants from the American scene, and their children were constrained by their upbringing. The tight rules of home, school, and church were legendary in Reformed circles, and the immigrant children were nurtured and educated within "ghettos" of their own making. Most willingly lived from the cradle to the grave within the cocoon of the church communities and guarded themselves against "worldliness." This behavior greatly limited their contacts with the "outside world."

But the children of immigrants also were caught between two cultures. Born and raised as "Dutch," they grew up as "Americans." Without asking for the role, they had to be "go-betweens," intermediaries between their immigrant parents and the host society. Teachers expected and en-

2. Dominic A. Pacyga, "Chicago's Ethnic Neighborhoods: The Myth of Stability and the Reality of Change," 604-17 (quote 604, in Melvin G. Holli and Peter d'A. Jones, eds., *Ethnic Chicago: A Multicultural Portrait,* 4th ed. [Grand Rapids: Eerdmans, 1995]).

3. Pacyga, "Chicago's Ethnic Neighborhoods," 617.

couraged immigrant children to teach their parents about America and its ways. Parents relied on children to translate the strange language and customs of the new homeland, while at the same time urging them to hold fast to Dutch ways and institutions. Children felt liberated by the American culture with its material benefits and looser moral constraints and shamed by their conspicuously old-fashioned parents. Taunted by their friends and criticized by their parents, the go-betweens were caught in the middle of conflicting emotions, and their roles were far more complex than that of their parents or their children.[4]

Things changed fundamentally with the rise of the third generation in the 1920s and 1930s. These grandchildren of immigrants were fluent in English, educated in American-style schools, and they moved easily into Chicago businesses, building trades, and professions. Some stepped into family businesses and raised them to the next level. Others were the first in their families to go to college. This was the cohort that broke the cultural mold.

Educator Peter Bulthuis of Englewood reflected in his perceptive autobiography *Footprints* on the significance of his going off to Calvin College in Michigan in 1942:

> I knew I was on a journey that would bring my thinking further and further from my family's traditions and practices. I had already made many choices that had brought me away from the world into which I had been born, where things were said or done because the doctrines of the church or the Dutch mores and traditions brought along from the Netherlands dictated certain behaviors and they were the established practices of the community. My parents and all of my siblings still lived within that square mile and planned to spend their entire lives there.

Bulthuis was torn by the realization of his coming of age. He continued:

> I wondered if I should quit at Christmas time and not get any further away from my family and Englewood. I loved my family and the security of living within a tight knit community. I felt that I was sitting on

4. Lyndel King and Colleen Sheehy, eds., *The Go-Betweens: The Lives of Immigrant Children* (Minneapolis: University Art Museum and Immigration History Research Center, 1986), 5; Marcus Lee Hansen, "The Problem of the Third Generation Immigrant," in Peter Kivisto and Dag Blanck, eds., *American Immigrants and Their Generations* (Chicago: Univ. of Illinois Press, 1990).

> the horns of a dilemma. Each choice had pros and cons. After considering the two choices, I decided that I wanted to embrace this new life even though it would take me further away from the rest of my family. I suddenly felt myself burst into tears and sobbed for several minutes. I wasn't sure why I was crying.[5]

Many families had a son like Peter who left hearth and home and made his own way in the world. But Peter did not drift far from his church. He became a Christian schoolteacher in a Dutch colony in Lynden, Washington, and then a church missionary in Africa. That he himself was a product of Christian schools helped bind him to the church.

The First World War had actually started the process of breaking loose culturally. More than 150 men in Chicago-area Christian Reformed congregations entered the armed forces, according to an incomplete tally in the denomination's yearbook of 1920. Reformed congregations sent out an equal if not greater number.[6] Many Dutch were not subject to the military draft in 1917-18, because they had not yet filed their naturalization papers. The Dutch also shared a cultural affinity for the Germans and still harbored anti-British feelings from the Boer War.

The World War engendered American patriotism, nonetheless, because every congregation sent sons off to battle, and members supported the war effort. The Dutch-American newspaper, *Onze Toekomst*, endorsed Victory Bonds. "How do we stand? Do the Hollanders take 1st place in subscribing to the various United States of America loans? First place among the foreign-born? These answers may be answered with a big YES," declared the editor proudly.[7]

The Second World War completed the process of cultural change. The boys went off to fight, and prosperity returned at home. An estimated 2,100 men, about 10 percent of total membership of the Reformed and Christian Reformed congregations in greater Chicago, served in the armed forces. Every church had its banner of blue stars on the front wall to designate those in service, with gold stars for those killed in action and silver for the wounded.[8]

5. Peter Bulthuis, *Footprints: An Autobiography* (privately printed, 5th ed., September 1998), 106.

6. Christian Reformed Church, *Jaarboekje*, 1920, p. 124. Eight were wounded and one from the Third Chicago congregation died, as did two from the First Reformed Church of Gano.

7. *Onze Toekomst*, 10 Feb. 1919.

8. This estimate is based on the known service figures for several congregations. The

On the home front, factories and defense plants ran at full speed seven days a week to meet war production needs. This schedule forced many workers to deal with demands for Sunday labor. The Reformed churches responded to the officially declared emergency by urging members to "abstain from Sunday labor as much as possible," unless the work was absolutely necessary. Church councils also wrote letters on church letterheads on behalf of members who so requested, asking employers for exemptions.[9] Whatever the outcome in individual situations, defense work disrupted the rhythm of the Lord's Day for many and left a permanent impact on the community.

Public support for the war effort exceeded anything seen before. Married women entered the workforce for the first time, and in many congregations women joined Red Cross clubs to sew material for the war effort. Children became involved by tending victory gardens. During the D-Day invasion of June 6, 1944, the principal of the Ebenezer Christian School, Andrew Blystra, brought a radio to school and allowed his eighth-grade class to listen to the invasion news. No one ever forgot the day. Churches held special services that evening to pray for the success of the battle.[10]

In war and peace the Dutch joined the rough and competitive commercial life of the "lightning city" and succeeded in becoming a vital part of it. The Reverend Benjamin Essenburg put it best: "If our Dutch ancestors didn't put 'Go' in Chicago, they surely did their share in making it what it is now called, 'The City of Go.'"[11] The Dutch were prudent and practical by nature and stood on their own two feet. They not only "gained a competence" and contributed in their own quiet and unique ways to the economic and social life of Chicago, but they held their heads high in pride at having "made it."

Yet the immigrant generations experienced the bane of not fitting in. They spoke a foreign tongue and their English was heavily accented. In

---

First Christian Reformed Church of Chicago, which numbered 1,152 souls in 1944, had 121 men serve, or 10.5 percent. The First Christian Reformed Church of Cicero, which numbered 1,136, had 98 men serve, or 8.6 percent (Herman Folgers, First Christian Reformed Church of Cicero *Newsette* [early 1944]). Ten percent of the 20,987 souls in the Chicago-area churches is 2,100. Some 200 alumni of Chicago Christian High School were serving in the armed forces in 1943.

9. "Classis Chicago North," *Banner,* 20 Feb. 1942; "Classis Chicago South," ibid., 13 Feb., 5 June 1942.

10. John Bakker, video interview, 19 Nov. 1997, by Martin Stulp.

11. B. Essenburg, "Sixty-fifth Anniversary of First Chicago," *Banner,* 7 Oct. 1932.

Red Cross ladies sewing volunteers, World War II, West Side Reformed Church, Cicero, l-r: Row 1: De Graaf, Grace Winter, Nellie Huizenga, Tracy Knol, Elsie Knol, Jennie Evenhouse, ?, ?; Row 2: Grace ?, ?, Jennie Klei, Theresa Ronda, ?, Florence Scholtens, Pearl Vander Lei, ?, ? Smith; Row 3; ?, Louise Niemeyer, Jenny Laning, Bess Cleveringa, Christine Hasper, Jennie Scholtens, Ann Klein, Lena Grypstra, Taulie Woldman, ?; Row 4: Tracy Bussema, Florence Knol, Catherina ?, Bertha Baar, Sophie Noorlag (?), ?, Jennie Bussema (?), Florence Engelsman

(Courtesy of Mrs. Albert [Ginger] Van Der Molen)

dress and actions, they were clearly not Yankees. Ben Essenburg, whose father was born in Holland, Michigan, recalls in the 1930s being called a "greenhorn" because of his Dutch ways. "Everyone wanted to Americanize." Yet the process could not be forced. The wise philosopher declared: "To oppose Americanization is folly; to force it is injurious. Americanization takes care of itself and runs its own course, and the prudent will simply endeavor to guide it to a happy issue."[12]

12. Ben Essenburg, video interview, 11 Nov. 1998, by Martin Stulp; quote of anonymous philosopher in H. H. Joldersma, "A Joyous Occasion," *Christian Intelligencer,* 23 Dec. 1891.

Chicago Hollanders came to blend into city life so well that they remain an invisible ethnic group. In lifestyle, language, social customs, work habits, and sports, they are indistinguishable, but not in convictions, commitments, and beliefs. The Dutch Reformed share a value system all their own. They prize hard work, business smarts, and a good laugh. They demand straight talk and are open and aboveboard in their dealings. They are suspicious of moralism, reject sanctimony, and are turned off by anyone who "puts on airs." Most drive Buicks and Chryslers, not Cadillacs and Lincolns. The highest compliment is to be called "down to earth." When one successful businessman in the late 1950s bought his first Cadillac, he lay awake for several nights agonizing over the decision, in fear that his friends at church would think he was being prideful or pretentious.

That the Dutch were acculturating is clear from the laments of church leaders in the 1920s about their young people falling prey to the "deplorable status of modern morals" and of the "ways of the world." In 1927 the Committee on Doctrine and Morals of the Classis of Chicago of the Reformed Church rang down the list of evils in these "perilous days": the use of "wine for home consumption" in the era of national prohibition, the lack of faithful "Sunday observance," the allure of commercialism and atheistic propaganda in the new-fangled radio programs, and the debasing books that had come into the homes. The next year, the committee recommended that church leaders "use extreme caution in introducing into the social life of our churches such dangerous elements as moving pictures and the drama." This was the same year that the Christian Reformed Synod issued its famous dictum against "worldly amusements," such as card playing and patronizing movie houses, theaters, cabarets, and dance halls.[13]

Although the preachers called for a life of "holy sanctification" and "complete separation" from the "spirit of worldliness," the young people saw, tasted, and touched the forbidden fruit. Only the hard times of the thirties slowed the rate of acculturation, because survival needs took precedence and placed strict curbs on discretionary spending.

Another maker of assimilation was the institutional building spree of the 1920s. Eleven of the twenty-three Christian Reformed congregations in Classis Illinois dedicated new church edifices in the "prosperity decade." Congregations in the Classis of Illinois of the Reformed Church in America had a similar pattern. Many congregations also built new manses. There were new buildings or major expansions for the Timothy,

13. Reformed Church in America, "Classis of Chicago Minutes," Sept. 1927, Sept. 1928, Sept. 1929, Sept. 1932; Christian Reformed Church, *Acts of Synod,* 1928; *Agenda of Synod,* part 1.

Englewood, and both Roseland Christian schools, the Chicago Christian High School, and the Nathanael Institute. All were impressive brick buildings designed to announce, "We have arrived!" So substantial was the construction that the school buildings are in use today by the Chicago Public School system, and various non-Dutch denominations continue to worship in the church edifices. The Dutch community was clearly prospering by the 1920s, and the desire for bricks and mortar shows that it shared in the materialist ethic of the times.

The Dutch immigrants also absorbed all the ethnic stereotypes typical of a polyglot city like Chicago, especially of Jews and blacks. Jews were shrewd, blacks inferior. Blacks were considered immoral, lazy, inept, and prone to alcoholism and petty crimes. Thieves, whatever their race or ethnicity, were said to have "gone south" with the stolen loot; Chicago's black belt was on the South Side. Such stereotyping, despite its damaging effects, did not preclude Dutch teamsters and businessmen from hiring blacks and dealing cordially with them on an individual basis, especially middle-class blacks. But their world was not "our world" and never would be; it was best to live apart. This attitude prevailed despite the fact that blacks on the Old West Side had such close relations with the Dutch that they picked up their Gronings dialect. A black laborer once remarked: "Wat is dat Gronings toch ain mooie taol; 't mos 'n wereldtoal word 'n" [That Gronings language is so nice it should become a world language].[14]

In the 1950s, ethnic pride was displayed in the annual "Dutch Day" at the Museum of Science and Industry's "Christmas Around the World" program. All the Christian schools participated, on a rotating three-year schedule. The youngsters sang the Dutch national anthem, "Wilhelmus van Nassouwe," and popular religious songs such as "Daar Rijst Langs de Wolken." By the 1970s, the Dutch import stores in Berwyn and Mount Greenwood did a thriving business in foods, china, candy, and nostalgia items. Ease of air travel made it possible to travel to the Netherlands to see old homesteads and visit distant relatives. Some boasted that they could still understand and converse in Dutch, however haltingly. But when asked if any patriotic feelings about the Netherlands still lingered in the breast, the answer was "No; I'm an American." All the ethnic symbols are thus hollow and without real content or understanding. The Dutch in Chicago today are indistinguishable from other Americans of northern European ancestry; their Dutchness is little more than a badge of identity in a multicultural society.

14. Undated tale of Gertrude Ida Marie Swierenga-Eistert, of Ten Boer, Groningen.

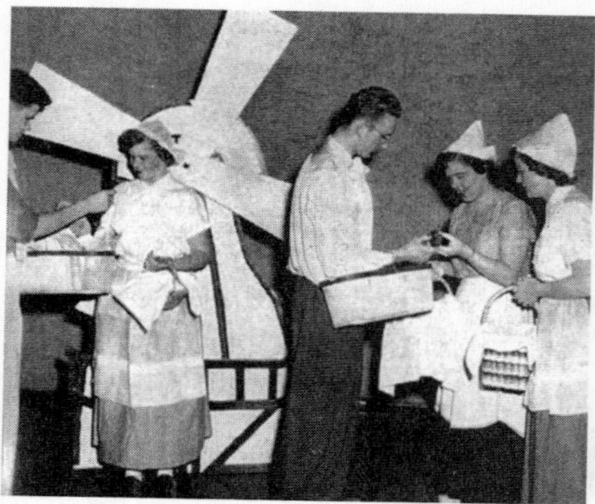

Dutch Day Pageant, "An American in Holland," written by teachers Clara Van Til and Gerda Bos, Museum of Science and Industry, December 1952, from Chicago Christian High School *Crusader 1953*
left photo l-r: Ronald Boss, Pearl Beenes Hoffman, Henry Hoeks, Melva Sievers Smith, Marlene Boomsma Biesboer
right photo l-r, row 1: Frances Zwart Terpstra (obscured), Judy Anderson Matheny, Donna Visser Venhuizen;
row 2: Gladys De Boer Voss, Glenda Racke Rickords, Gloria De Boer Hayda, Paulette Bos Camphouse;
row 3: Ronald Boss, Robert Swierenga, Curtis Youngsma, Richard Lubbers, Henry Hoeks, Martin Essenburg

An example is Jim Bere (1923-92), president of Borg-Warner Corporation and one of Chicago's best known executives. A product of Englewood's Christian Reformed community and its Christian elementary and high schools, Bere rose in the business world to a place of global prominence that far transcended his humble roots. In the early 1980s, when American industries were beginning to feel the bite of foreign competition, Bere, according to his obituary, was "one of the first Chicago CEOs to push for a national industrial policy to help essential industries survive." Bere earned both BA and MA degrees from Northwestern University in business administration and climbed the ranks at Borg Warner beginning in 1961. He became chief executive in 1972 and served as chairman of the board until his death in 1992. Fittingly, Bere joined the cosmopolitan and decidedly upscale Christ Church of Oak Brook, which was founded and led by the former Christian Reformed pastor, Arthur De Kruyter.[15]

In recent years there have been many like Bere among the Dutch of

15. Jim Bere obituary, *Chicago Tribune*, 3 Jan. 1992.

Chicago who have moved beyond the tight ethnoreligious community that nurtured them. They have found religious and cultural homes elsewhere in mainstream America and decoupled themselves from the exclusive community of their birth.

The axiom applies: "The more the community seeks its inspiration and agenda from outside its own tradition, the less will it adhere to that tradition."[16] This book has attempted for the first time to recount the rich detail of that tradition as it was lived in Chicago. Whether the Dutch Reformed heritage that was nurtured for 150 years in that city is worth preserving is a matter for this and future generations to consider. It is hoped that this story will contribute to that discussion.

16. Quoted from William Zeilstra, letter to author, 20 April 2001.

APPENDIX I

Chicago Dutch Garbage Companies

Sources

TD – Chicago telephone books – "Red Book" and Business Directory
CD – Chicago city directories
FC – Chicago federal censuses of 1900 and 1920
OT – *Onze Toekomst* advertisements
RA1933 – Chicago Cinder & Scavenger Truck Owners Association
RA1946, RA1957, RA1965, RA1978, RA1981 – Chicago & Suburban Refuse Disposal Association membership lists
RRJ – *Refuse Removal Journal,* 1958-83
Interviews or correspondence with Norman Aardema, John H. Evenhouse, Edward H. Evenhouse, Sam Hamstra, Jr., Peter Roeters, John R. Swierenga, Jack Swierenga, John Ter Maat, and William Zeilstra.

Sold to

AW	Allied Waste
BFI	Browning Ferris Industries (sold to Allied Waste)
WM	Waste Management
LL	Laidlaw
MAW	Mid-American Waste
RW	Republic Waste

Company	Owner	Sold to
A-1 American Scavenger Serv. 8717 S. Bishop Ave. TD1959	Gerrit De Vries	
A-A-A Scavenger Service 3205 W. Ogden Ave. TD1951	Herman Mulder	
Aable Scavenger Service 5813 W 102nd St., Oak Lawn RA1951	John Pierik	

A-Able Scavenger Service 1520 W. 15th St. TD1951 1315 S. Ashland Ave. TD1959 9300 Kenton, Oak Lawn TD1965	William K. Kiemel	
A-D Scavenger Service 7228 S. Sangamon St. TD1951, RA1957	Andrew De Vries	
A & W Disposal 1908 W. 60th, La Grange RA1978	Menno Workman	
A Anywhere Anytime 4384 S. Archer Ave. TD1991	??	
Aberdeen Ash Service 9206 S. Trumbull, Evergreen Park TD1951, TD1965	Claude & Nick Groendyke, & Tom Voogt	
A Best Cleaning 5106 S. Archer Ave. TD991	??	
Able Disposal West Chicago, 1970s- RA1988	Abel Meyer (son of Ysbrand) & Bruce Meyer	
Able Scavenger Service 8755 S. Peoria St. RA1933	John Lindemulder, Herman Teune, & Cornelius Wiersema	
Able West Chicago Disp. Serv. West Chicago RA1978	Abel Meyer	
A C Scavenger Service 7756 S. Paulina Ave. TD1951 7615 S. Ashland Ave. TD1965	Phillip Kiemel	
Acacia Disposal Service 2740 W. Ogden Ave. RA1978	Robert Evenhouse	
Acacia Scavenger Service 1519 S. 61st St., Cicero RA1957 2740 W. Ogden RA1978	Robert Boersema	
Ace Disposal Service 1600 Winnetka Rd., Northfield RA1957 1740 Harding, Northfield RA1978, TD1991	Louis C. Decker & son Steve	
Ace Disposal Systems Calumet City RA1978 1500 N. Hooker TD1991	Casey Dykstra	WM

Ace Scavenger Service (formerly Harm Huizenga & Son Scavenger) 1348 S. Ashland Ave. TD1927 30th & 53rd Ave. Cicero TD1965	Thos. H. Huizenga Conrad Douma, Clarence Huizenga, Dean Buntrock, Ben Essenburg, Mgrs.	WM
Acme Disposal Corp. 5447 W. Harrison TD1965	Harold Van Der Molen Emmet Flood, Mgr.	
Acme Scavenger Service (formerly Acme Cinder & Garbage) 1653 W. Hastings St. TD1926 2034 W. 13th St. TD1928 1240 S. Talman Ave. TD1930 1625 W. 14th Pl. RA1933 1705 W. 14th Pl. TD1934 1025 S. Mayfield Ave. TD1951 2740 W. Ogden Ave. TD1965 13631 S. Kostner, Crestwood RA1978, RA1988, TD1991	John De Boer Peter Bulthuis Homer A., John, Bill, & Ralph Wigboldy	AW
Acorn Disposal Service 6546 W. 28th St., Berwyn RA1965 Geneva RA1978	Thomas Huiner (son-in-law Tom H. Huizenga)	
Action Disposal Service Berwyn RA1981	Ralph Evenhouse, Jr.	
Active Disposal Service 1309 Roosevelt Rd., Broadview RA1957	Edward and Arthur Jongsma	
Active Service Refuse Disp. 9300 Kenton, Oak Lawn TD1951, TD1965 1712 Church St., Evanston RA1978 826 Foster, Evanston RA1957	Gilbert Wiersema & Bill Venema James & Richard De Boer Casey Dykstra, Dick Evenhouse Al Kieft, Mgr.	BFI
Adema, Henry 1826 W. 14th St. RA1933, TD1934	Henry Adema	
Advance Disposal Service 1528 S. Scoville, Berwyn RA1957 706 Hawthorne, Elmhurst RA1978 790 S. Euclid, Elmhurst TD1991	Dirk Brouwer (bought from Sam Hoving in 1952, sold to son James D. in 1968)	
Aero Scavenger Service 4730 W. Harrison St. RA1957	Huizenga family, Dean Buntrock, Mgr.	

Airport Scavenger Service 9906 S. Homan, Evergreen Pk. TD1951 3300 W. 99th Pl. Evergreen Pk. TD1959 became Groen Waste Services 9850 S. Spaulding Evergreen Pk. TD1957	Henry A. Groen & sons Arthur, Donald, and Roger Groen (Groen Bros Inc.)	
Ajax Scavenger Service 1423 S. Highland, Berwyn TD1959, TD1965 6241 W. Roosevelt Rd., Berwyn TD1991	Charles Ridder	
Allied Scavenger Service 16545 S. Wausau, So. Holland RA1978	Warren and Don Stienstra	
Al's Rubbish Removal 1126 Humphrey, Oak Park RA1978	Al Van Der Dyke	
Anchor Disposal 1446 S. Lombard Ave., Berwyn RA1957 1328 S. Harvey Ave., Berwyn RA1978	Sam & Russell Meyer (Ysbrand's son and grandson)	
Apex Scavenger Service 1817 S. Pulaski TD1965, RA1978	Henry De Boer, sold to nephews James G. & John G. De Boer	WM
Apollo Disposal Service Kankakee RA1978	Arend Beezhold	
Arc Disposal Service 1444 Cuyler Ave., Berwyn RA1957 5859 N. River Rd. Rosemont RA1978	Dick Evenhouse & nephew Ed De Boer, son-in-law Duane Rosendahl, Ed De Boer's sons Ed & Paul, Jack Lanenga, Mgr.	RW
Arrow Disposal Co. 4730 W. Harrison St. TD1951 1245 W. 38th, Cicero TD1965	Huizenga family Dean Buntrock, Mgr. Herman Kanis, Mgr.	WM
Arrow Disposal Service 10017 S. 53rd, Oak Lawn TA1978	James Glas & John Vander Wagen	
Associated Refuse Disposal 6035 W. Roosevelt Rd., Cicero RA1978	Ben Bosman	
Associated Scavengers Co. 1211 S. Ashland Ave. TD1934 8100 30th St., North Riverside RRJ1962	William Blauw	
Atlas Disposal Service 1512 S. Cuyler, Berwyn RA1978	Al Venema, Al Rispens, Roger Groenboom	BFI

Atlas Refuse Disposal Serv. 4300 W. Madison TD1951 1329 Highland Ave., Berwyn RA1957 16645 Crawford Ave., Markham RA1978	Thomas Tibstra, Larry Beck Albert J. De Vries Robert De Boer, Casey Dykstra	WM
B & G Scavenger Service 7258 S. Aberdeen St. RA1957 11423 S. Drake RA1978 1334 N. Central Park, Skokie RA1978	John Beukema & Wesley Greenfield Edward Cooper	
B-W Disposal Service 6207 W. 89th Pl., Oak Lawn RA1965 12500 S. Kedzie Ave., Blue Is. RA1978	Harold K. Post Thomas Mulder, Jr.	AW
Bakker, James Trucking Service 1620 S. 58th Ave., Cicero RA1957 1524 S. Ridgeland Ave., Berwyn RA1965	James Bakker son Henry Bakker sold to Peter J. Bolt, then to Cornelius J. "Charlie" Groot	WM
Bakker, John, Refuse Disposal (formerly owned by Sam Ter Maat) 1623 W. 14th Place RA1933, RA1946 7353 S. Union Ave. TD1951 3248 W. 97th St., Evergreen Pk. TD1959, TD1991	John Bakker	WM
Bakker, Peter & Sons 1316 S. Harvey, Berwyn TD1959, TD1965	Peter Bakker (brother Jacob) (ended in bankruptcy)	
Banner Refuse Disposal Joliet RRJ1962, RA1981	Melvin Brink & Ben Heslinga	
Barrington Trucking Company 419 W. Main, Barrington RRJ1959, RA1957	John Vanderveld, Jr. Peter Vanderveld, V.P.	BFI
Bee Northwest Scavenger 1516 S. 59th Ct., Cicero RA1946	John Muhlena	
Ben's Rubbish Removal 1414 S. Gunderson Ave., Berwyn RA1957	Ben Essenburg	
Bert's General Hauling 1625 W. Beech Ave. RA1957	Wilbert Tjardes	
Best Scavenger Service Cicero 1912 Lehigh, Glenview RA1978, TD1991	Arthur Vos, Sr., Art, Jr., and Don Art, Jr.'s, son Art & Don's son Kenneth	WM

Best Way Disposal Service
3056 N. Ashland Ave. TD1959
1005 W. Belmont Ave. TD1957
3550 N. Lake Shore Dr. TD1965
Alfred Venema

Bill's Disposal Service
Rt. 2, West Chicago RA1957
Bill & J. Noorlag, WM
Fred Noorlag
(sold to City Disposal)

Bilthuis, Henry, Teaming & Draying
31st & Homan Ave. CD1900
Henry Bilthuis

Blauw, John, Teaming
1522 W. 14th Pl. CD1915
John Blauw

Blauw Countryside Service
1302 S. 57th Ct., Cicero RA1957
1427 S. Maple, Berwyn RA1965
John C. Blauw

Blaauw, William
909 S. Oakley Blvd. RA1933
William Blaauw

Boer, Ben, & Son
1303 S. 61st Ct., Cicero RA1946
1446 S. 59th Ave., Cicero RA1965
Ben Boer & son Art WM

Boerema, Roger
??
Roger Boerema

Boersema, Richard, Disposal Service
10106 Devonshire Ln., Westchester RA1957
Richard Boersema

Boersma, Charles
1410 S. 59th Ct., Cicero RA1933, RA1946
Charles Boersma

Bolt Scavenger Service
1321 S. Highland Ave. RA1965
6035 W. Roosevelt Rd., Cicero RA1978
5819 W. Ogden Ave.
Peter J. Bolt
Peter J. Bolt, Jr.

Bosman, Andrew
1320 S. Lombard, Berwyn TD1951
Andrew Bosman

Bosman Bros. Scavenger Service
1160 Humphrey Ave., Oak Park RA1946
5701 Ridegwood Dr., Western Spgs. RA1965
920 Bryan, Elmhurst RA1981
Clarence & Henry Bosman
Hilda & Katherine Bosman
Matthew Bosman, Mgr.

Bossenga, G., & Teaming Company 414 S. Dearborn St. CD1915	Gerrit Bossenga	
Broadview Active Disposal Serv. 2708 S. 9th Ave., Broadview RA1978	Rich Evenhouse, Art Jongsma & son Ed, Mgr.	
Brondsema, J. 1338 S. Ashland Ave. RA1933	J. Brondsema	
Brooks Disposal Service 1335 S. 58th Ct., Cicero RA1957 Northbrook RA1978, RA1988	Don Gerrit, George Evenhouse Charles Zeilstra & son Van Henry & Kevin Tazelaar	BFI
Brouwer, Richard, Teaming & Draying 1809 Hastings St. CD1915	Richard Brouwer	
Brouwer, Dirk, Scavenger Service 1528 East Ave., Berwyn 1528 Scoville Ave., Berwyn RA1957	Dirk Brouwer sold to son James D. Brouwer, Advance Disposal	
Buffalo Grove Disposal Service Buffalo Grove RA1978	Russ Erffmeyer	
Bulthuis, Dan ??	Dan Bulthuis	
Buzy Bee Scavenger Service 4399 W. Madison St. TD1951 1239 S. East Ave., Berwyn RA1957 4754 W. Washington St. TD1959, TD1965	Clarence & Harry Huizenga (sons of Siert)	WM
C & S (Chicago & Suburban) Disp. (also Chicago Waste Disposal Co.) 5958 W. Roosevelt Rd. RA1946, TD1951 1445 S. Laramie, Cicero TD1959, TD1965	Thos. & Sam H. Huizenga Dick Evenhouse, Charlie Groot Charles "Charlie" Boersma & Allen Lenters, Geo. De Boer	WM
Capital Disposal Serv. 10001 Spaulding, Evergreen Pk. TD1965 Highland, Ind. RA1978	William Venema Ronald Venema	
Capital Refuse Disposal Serv. 10357 S. Emerald Ave. TD1965	Albert Laning	
Central Dirt Disposal 8100 S. Wolcott, Evergreen Park TD1965	??	

Central Scavenger Service 1604 S. 49th Ct., Cicero TD1951 1801 Euclid, Berwyn TD1959, TD1965 North Riverside RA1978	Henry Huizenga Clarence Evenhouse, Harold Van Dahm	 WM
Century Disposal 2740 W. Ogden RA1965	Bernard Evenhouse	WM
Chatham Dosposal 10447 Torrence Ave. RA1978	Frank Bultema	
Chicago Disposal Service Chicago, IL	Norm and Marv Aardema (sold to American Disposal)	
Chicago Disposal Systems 5447 W. Harrison St. TD1965	Harold Van Der Molen Emmet Flood, Sr., Mgr.	BFI
Chicago Garbage & Rubbish 2018 W. 21st Pl. TD1951 3900 W. 56th Pl. TD1959	Clarence Schmidt	
Circle Disposal Co. 431 S. Dearborn RA1965	Robert Molenhouse	
Citizens Disposal Systems 1146 W. Hubbard TD1959 Palos Heights RA1957	Tom & Peter Bulthuis William Venema, Mgr.	
Citizens Service Bureau Cicero	Thos. H. Huizenga	WM
City Disposal 1346 S. 60th Ct., Cicero RA1957 5859 River, Rosemont TD1959, TD1965	Aldrich Evenhouse, son Edward, & Cornelius Bussema	WM
City Refuse Service 1754 W. 14th St. TD1930	Peter Huiner	
City Waste Systems 3211 Howard St., Skokie RA1978	Marvin Van Weelden H. Van Weelden, Mgr.	WM
Clarendon Hills Disposal 270 S. Jackson, Clarendon Hills RA1957	Abe Bulthuis	
Clearing Disposal Co. 7327 S. 59th St., Summit TD1959 5245 W. 38th St., Cicero RA1978 3800 S. Laramie, Cicero TD1991	Bernard, Milton & Richard Drenth, Richard Molenhouse Richard Dykstra	WM

Clearway Scavenger Service 1404 S. 57th Ave., Cicero RA1965 1117 S. East Ave., Oak Park RA1978	George & James Van Kampen	WM
Clery Disposal 7277 S. Sawyer Ave. RA1957 608 S. Bruner, Hinsdale RA1965	Wm. Brouwer & Bernard Redeker	
Columbia Scavenger Service 1446 Lombard Ave., Berwyn TD1959 2740 W. Ogden Ave. TD1965	Bernard Meyer (son of Ysbrand Meyer)	
Consolidated Refuse Disposal Elgin RA1965	Jack Ter Maat	
Countryside Refuse Disposal 1320 S. Oak Park Ave., Berwyn RA1957 Hinsdale RA1965	Henry Roeters	
Crest Disposal Service 73rd & Rt. 83, Hinsdale TD1965	Thomas Mulder, Jr. Peter Roeters (1970s)	
Crosstown Disposal Co. 6018 W. 123rd, Palos Heights RA1978	Robert Wiersema	
Crown Disposal Co. Summit RA1957 4630 S. Vernon, Brookfield RA1978	Henry Wyma & son Robert H. Wyma	
D & H Teune Disposal Co. 10108 S. Maple, Oak Lawn RA1965	Dan & Henry Teune	
Daily Refuse Service 7639 W. 124th Pl., Palos Heights RA1957	Jacob Ter Maat	
Davids, Nick 1836 W. 13th St. RA1933	Nick Davids	
De Blecourt, Louis 1645 W. 14th St. RA1933, TD1934	Louis De Blecourt	
De Boer, James, Coal and Wood, Moving and Expressing 501 W. 15th Street FC1900 1444 S. Ashland Ave. 1915	James De Boer	

De Boer Bros. "We cover entire city" 1927 ad 1411-15 W. 14th Pl. TD1920 2847 W. Harrison St. TD1928, RA1946 1817 S. Pulaski Rd. RB1951, TD1965	James's sons George & Henry grandsons James G., George, John G.	WM
De Boer, Geo A., Disposal Service 1520 S. 61st Ct., Cicero TD1965	George A. De Boer	
De Boer, John Jr. 1626 W. 14th Place RA1933	John De Boer, Jr.	
De Boer & Stob 1315 S. 58th Ct., Cicero RA1933 1422 S. 61st Ct., Cicero RA1933	??	
Deckinga, Nicholas, Teaming 6031 S. Carpenter CD1915	Nicholas & Congo Deckinga	
Decker, A., & Son Scavenger Service 1409 S. Ashland Ave. RA1933 7157 S. Sangamon St. RA1946 7277 S. Chicago Ave. TD1965	Alfred Decker & son George John Bakker	
Decker, John 1413 S. Ashland Ave., RA1933	John Decker	
Decker, John, & Sons 1832 61st St., Cicero TD1965 1411 S. Cuyler Ave., Berwyn RA1965	John Decker & sons Herman, Melvin, & George	
Deck's Scavenger Service 939 W. 71st St. RA1957 10129 S. Green RA1965 721 S. 167th St., South Holland RA1978	Clarence Deckinga	
Dekker, Henry 6151 S. Carpenter St. TD1927	Henry Dekker	
DeGouw & Son 4938 W. Grand Ave. TD1951	? DeGouw	
Depend-On Disposal Service 5153 N. Clark RA1957, TD1965	John P. Weis Van Weelden Bros.	 LL
De Vries, Andrew 1834 W. 14th St. RA 1941 7228 S. Sangamon St. TD1951	Andrew De Vries	

De Vries, Joseph, Teaming 1519 W. 13th St. CD1915	Joseph De Vries	
De Vries & Teune 1400 S. 60th Ct., Cicero TD1951	Dan Teune & John De Vries	
De Vries, William 4431 N. Troy Ave. TD1951	William De Vries	
Diepstra, Andrew 6412 S. Kamensky TD1965	Andrew Diepstra	
Dispo-O-Waste Scavenger Serv. 1637-41 W. 14th St. TD1965	Bernard & Dodrick Huiner	WM
Disposal Service Co. 509 Pennsylvania, Glen Ellen RA198	Edward & Bernard Van Der Molen	BFI
District Disposal Service 6305 W. Ogden Ave., Berwyn RA1957	John C. Groot	
Dot Disposal Co. 2740 W. Ogden Ave. TD1965	Gerhard "Lefty" Otte, Richard & John Evenhouse Henry Evenhouse, Mgr.	WM
Downers Grove Disposal Service 1035 Curtiss St., Downers Grove RA1957	John Rot, Jr.	
DuKane Disposal West Chicago RA1978	Edward Evenhouse Glen Elders & Jake Meyer, Mgrs.	WM
Duke Scavenger Service (Refuse Disp.) 1414 S. Ashland RA1946 4300 W. Ogden Ave. TD1951 7049 S. Carpenter St. TD1959 7456 S. Halsted St. TD1965	Peter Laning, Jr.	
17804 Escanaba Ave., Lansing RA1978	Peter Lindemulder, Mgr.	AW
Dyke, John, & Son 7949 S. Lowe Ave. TD1951 7147 S. Peoria St. TD1959 10339 S. Wentworth Ave. TD1965	John Dyke	
Dykema, Mike Old West Side	Mike Dykema	
Dykinga, John 79th & South Park CD1899	John Dykinga	
Dykstra, R., Scavenger Service 9141 S. Mayfield, Oak Lawn RA1978	Richard Dykstra, Sr.	

E. & L. Scavenger Service 3504 N. Olcott Ave. RA1957	Lawrence Wiersema & Ed Plonka	
Elgin Disposal 170 E. Chicago St., Elgin RA1957	Adrian Van Weelden	LL
Elgin-Wayne Disposal Elgin RA1978	Ed Evenhouse, Jack Ter Maat Robert Molenhouse, Ed Bilthuis	WM
Elmhurst Trucking Company Villa Park RA1978	John Stob, Jr., John Scott Stob & Lawrence Stavenger	
Empire Disposal Service 9918 S. Spaulding Ave. RA1957 2740 S. Ogden Ave. TD1959 12087 Page, Calumet Pk. TD1965, TD1991	Henry Schenkel & son Jacob, Jacob & Bernard Brunius & Marvin Huisenga George Van Ryn (1970-)	
Engbers-Andersen Disposal Serv. Brookfield RA1978	Douglas Engbers & Neil Andersen sold to Groot in 1980s	
Euwema, Herman, Scavenger 1219 S. 43rd St. CD1899	Herman Euwema	
Evenhouse Bros. Disposal Service Glenview RA1957, Mt. Prospect RA1965 802 N. River Rd., Mt. Prospect RA1978 543 N. Emroy, Elmhurst RA1981	George and Don Evenhouse Donald Evenhouse Raymond Hoekstra	
Evenhouse, George 1325 S. Ashland Ave. RA1933	George Evenhouse	
Evenhouse, Henry, Teaming 1739 W. 15th St. CD1915 Evenhouse, H., Motor Service Evenhouse, Henry, & Son 2031 Wahburne Ave. CD1925 Garden City Cinder Bureau RA1933	Henry Evenhouse Henry Evenhuis (Evenhouse)	
Evergreen Scavenger Service 3145 W 87th St., Evergreen Pk TD1965	Carl Ball, Henry Stoit, & son Derk Ball	
Folkerts, Albert, Scavenger 1625 S. 41st St. CD1899	Albert Folkerts	
Folkerts, John, Teaming & Excavating 2417 W. 12th St. CD1915	John Folkerts	

Fox Valley Disposal Co. Western Springs RA1965 205 N. Lake St., Aurora RA1978	Henry and Ed Bilthouse	
Garden City Disposal formerly Garden City Cinder Bureau 2031 Washburne TD1922, TD1934 3818 N. Clark St. RA1946 2939 N. Pulaski Rd. TD1951 Rosemont CD1965, RA1978 Franklin Park TD1991	Dick & Aldrich Evenhouse, later Dick's son-in-law William Buiten and Henry Bolt, Peter Ter Maat, lastly Dick's son-in-law Cornelius Bussema, Ed Evenhouse Art Jongsma, Mgr.	WM
Geertsema, John, Scavenger 2031 Washburne Ave. RA1933	John Geertsema	
General Refuse Disposal Co. 1817 S. Pulaski Rd. TD1959 Worth BD1965, TD1991	Richard Vander Velde, Sr. Clarence & James C. De Boer Henry Ipema	WM
Glen Ellyn Disposal Inc. Glen Ellyn TD1965, RA1981	Bernard Van Der Molen Edward Van Der Molen	BFI
Glen Golf Disposal 6305 W. Ogden Ave. RA1978	John C. Groot Lee Brandsma, Mgr.	
Golf View Disposal Service 1237 S. 60th Ct., Cicero RA1957	Peter S. Venhousen	
Great Lakes Disposal 5833 S. Loomis RA1978	Robert Molenhouse Richard Dykstra, Mgr.	
Groen, August 8258 S. Morgan, TD1959	August Groen	MAW
Groen Bros. Waste Disposal Services (formerly Airport Scavenger Serv.) Blue Island TD1965, TD1991 Groen Residential Services 3100 W. Wireton Rd., Blue Island RA1988	Roger, Sr., Donald, & Arthur Groen, Marvin Hoekstra, Roger Groen, Jr., Jim Bulthuis	MAW
Groendyke, Nicholas Evergreen Pk.	Nicholas Groendyke	
Groot, C., Disposal Co. 1126 S. Mayfield TD1926, RA1933, RA1946 4730 W. Harrison St. TD1951 6305 W. Ogden Ave., Berwyn TD1959 6747 N. Elmhurst Rd. TD1991	Cornelius J. Groot sons Lawrence & John C. (from 1949-)	WM

Company	Owners	
Grove Disposal Co. 5134 S. Main, Downers Gr. RA1957, RA1978	John N. Hendrikse Ben Toebes, Mgr.	
H & H Scavenger Service 112 W. 109th St. TD1959	? Hoving	
H & R Disposal Service 11607 S. Austin, Worth TD1991	Henry E. Ipema & Rich Vandervelde	WM
Haan, Clarence 100700 S. Normal TD1951, TD1965	Clarence Haan	
Hamco Disposal 16001 S. Van Drunen, South Holland RA1981	Harold Hamstra	
Harms, Henry P., Scavenger 5012 S. Spaulding CD1899	Henry P. Harms	
Haulaway, Inc. 6305 W. Ogden Ave. RA1981	John C. Groot Lee Brandsma, Mgr.	
Healthway Disposal 928 Warren, Downers Grove RA1957 Lilse RA1978	Thomas Bulthuis Ted N. Youngsma & Robert Voss	
Henry's Disposal Service 64 W. 157th St., South Holland RA1981	Henry Toering	
Hillside Disposal Service 7501 Wolf Rd., LaGrange RA1957 4846 Butterfield Rd., Hillside RA1978, TD1991	Henry Bulthuis, Harvey & David Bulthuis, Harvey's son Rick	
Hinsdale Refuse Disposal 1422 S. 58th Ct., Cicero RA1957 19 W. Chicago, Hinsdale RA1965	Richard C. Veldman	
Hoekstra, A. RA1933	A. Hoekstra	
Hoekstra Bros. 1614 W. 15th St. RA1943, TD1965, RA1978	Lloyd, Martin, John, & George Hoekstra	
Hoekstra, Henry, Teaming 1721 W. 14th St. CD1915	Henry Hoekstra	
Hoekstra, Herman (1920s-30s) 1419 W. 14th Place	Herman Hoekstra	

Hoekstra, Samuel, Teaming 1819 Yeaton St. CD1915	Samuel Hoekstra	
Hoekstra, Thomas (with Speelman Refuse) 1250 S. Washtenaw Ave. TD1951 1629 S. Cicero Ave., Cicero TD1959	Thomas Hoekstra	
Homewood Scavenger Service 17940 Dixie Hwy., Homewood RA1957 E. Hazelcrest, Homewood TD1965, RA1988	Conrad Douma, John C. Groot Wendell E. Yonker, Mgr. Thomas J. Yonker	
Hoogendoorn, Henry, Teaming 1748 W. Hastings St. CD1915	Henry Hoogendoorn	
Hoving, Sam, & Sons (est. 1913) 833 W. Oakley Bl. TD1930 2847 W. Harrison St. RA1946, TD1951 427 N. Ashland Ave. TD1965 1220 W. Carroll Ave. RA1978, TD1991	Sam Hoving & sons Abel & Dick Abel's son Ken, son-in-law George Hoekstra, Dick's sons Dick, Jr., John, & William	BFI
Huiner, Berend, Teaming 810 W. 14th Pl. CD1900	Berend Huiner	
Huiner, Peter, & Sons Scavengers 1402 W. 14th St. CD1910 (est. 1901) 1819 W. 13th St. TD1914 1641 W. 14th St. TD1924, RA1933	Peter Huiner & sons Bernard & Dodrick	WM
Huiner, Peter, Company 1637-41 W. 14th Street RRJ1960 RA1965 Peter Huiner Co. 364 N. Harding RA1978	Bernard & Dodrick Huiner Abel Bulthuis, Mgr. Grandson William Huiner	
Huizenga, Harry, Teaming 493 W. 14th St. CD1900	Harry ("Harm") Huizenga	
Huizenga, Harm, & Son Private Scavenger 1348 S. Ashland Ave. CD1910 1546 W. 14th Place. RA1933	Harm Huizenga Thos. H. Huizenga (became Ace Scavenger Serv.)	WM
Hyde Park Scavenger Service 10638 S. Eggelston TD1951 7200 S. Chicago Ave. RB1959, TD1965 7277 S. Chicago Ave. RA1978	Henry Hoekstra, George Dekker, Peter Molter, & Milton Boomsma	

Imperial Disposal Service 10125 S. Turner, Evergreen Pk. RA1957 4754 W. Washington TD1959, TD1965 2740 W. Ogden Ave. RA1978	Harry T. Huizenga	WM
Incinerator Inc. 3815 S. Laramie, Cicero TD1959, TD1965	Pete Huizenga, William Venema, Conrad Douma, Harry Huizenga, Melvin Veenstra	WM
Industrial Disposal Co. 1146 Hubbard Ave. RA1957 6241 W. Roosevelt, Berwyn RA1978	William Venema Alfred Rispens	
Iwema, Bonne (est. 1899) Iwema Bonne & Sons 2236 W. 13th St. TD1930, TD1951 2246 W. 13th St. TD1959, TD1965	Bonne Iwema, sons John & Barney	
J & J Disposal Service Highwood RA1978	Jerry Dykstra & Jack Vos	
Jaarda, S., & H. Meyer 2246 W. 13th St. RA1933	Shelte Jaarda & H. Meyer Sold to Andrew Bosman in 1941	
Jensen Disposal Mundelein RA1978	John Obenauf & Robert Dahm	
Kampen Scavenger Service 33 Lind Ave., Hillside RA1957	Dewey & Lee Kampen	
Kampstra, Meint 1744 W. 14th Place RA1933	Meint Kampstra	
Key Disposal Evanston RA1978	Albert Kieft, Mgr.	
Kiemel Company Disposal 7756 S. Paulina Ave. RA1957 7618 S. Ashland Ave. RA1978	Philip Kiemel & John P. Van Kampen Robert Vander Laan, Mgr.	
Kiemel & Heemstra 7642 S. Loomis RA1946, TD1951	Frank Keimel & John Heemstra (father of William K. Kiemel of A-Able Scavenger Serv.)	
Kleenway Disposal Service Hinsdale RA1978	Ronald W. Tazelaar & Steve Tameling	WM
Klein, Benjamin, Teaming 1539 W. 14th Pl. CD1915	Benjamin Klein	

Klein, Frank, Teaming 234 W. 25th Pl. CD1915	Frank Klein	
Knott, J., Scavenger ?? RA1933	J. Knott	
Knott, M., Scavenger ?? RA1933	M. Knott	
Lakes Disposal Service 419 S. Main St., Barrington RA1957	P. Vanderveld & E. Obenauf	
Lake Shore Trucking 1809 S. Highland Ave., Berwyn RA1957	Martin Dykema	
Laning, Peter, & Sons 7131 S. Carpenter TD1951 4748 W. Chicago Ave. TD1959 10125 S. Green RB1959, TD1965 30 W. Washington TD1991	Peter Laning & sons Gerrit & ?	AW
Lawndale Cinder Co. 1645 W. 14th St. TD1930	Peter and Seibert Ter Maat	
Lendering, Arend Cicero 1940s-50s	Arend Lendering	
Lindemulder Bros 1345 S. 58th Ave., Cicero RA1957	Harold Lindemulder	
Lindemulder, George 1407 W. 14th Place RA1933	George Lindemulder	
Lindemulder, John, Scavenger Co. 1239 S. 59th Ct., Cicero RA1933 1319 S. 58th Ct., Cicero RA1946	John Lindemulder son Harold Lindemulder	
Lombard Refuse Disposal Co. 1S514 Chase St., Lombard RA1957, RA1978	Albert Havenga & sons Albert Jr., Harold	WM
Luchtenberg, Joe 1746 W. 14th St. RA1933	Joe Luchtenberg	
Luchtenberg, John 5208 Laramie Ave. RA1957	John Luchtenberg	
Madsen Bros. 5317 S. Ellis RA1946 10235 St. Louis RA1978	Jens Madsen Warren Kuipers	

Marengo Disposal Marengo RA1978	Henry J. De Boer	
Master Scavenger Service 12057 S. Page, Midlothian RA1965 15133 Hollyhock, Orland Pk. RA1976	Jacob Schenkel & Jacob & Bernard Brunius Martin Binnendyk	
McHenry Disposal 115 E. Third Ave., McHenry RA1957	William De Vries	
Mellema, Ben, and Sons 1716 S. School St., Lombard RA1957 3825 W. Madison, Bellwood RA1965	Ben Mellema son Jerry Mellema	
Mellema & Helmus 1845 W. Hastings St. RA1933	H. Mellema and Martin Helmus	
Merchant's Disposal Service 1337 S. Austin Blvd., Cicero RA1957 2740 W. Ogden Ave. TD1965, RA1978	Henry G. Evenhouse	WM
Mercury Waste Disposal 12450 S. Natchez, Palos Heights RA1978	Ronald Huisenga, Owen Deckinga	
Metro Disposal Service 3815 S. Laramie, Cicero RA1978	Harry Huizenga	
Metro Scavenger Service (est. 1946) 1241 S. 59th Ct., Cicero TD1959 5958 W. Roosevelt Rd. TD1951 901 W. 31st St. TD1959, RA1978 6210 S. Mayfield RA1978	Siert (Sam) Huizenga, Ted Hoekstra, & Jake (Jacob) Bilthuis Clarence & Harry Huizenga Jake's sons Jay & Lawrence Bilthuis Jay's son Mike Bilthuis	WM
Meyer Bros Scavenger Serv. (est 1955) 604 S. Campbell Ave. TD1959 7136 S. Ferdinand, Bridgeview TD1965 10324 Linder St., Oaklawn RA1978 6205 W. 101st, Chicago Ridge TD1991	John, Jacob, William, & Edward Meyer & brother-in-law George Auwema Roy Vander Klok, Mgr.	WM
Meyer, Henry 8142 S. May RA1946	Henry Meyer	
Meyer, Ysbrand, Teaming Old West Side ca. 1913 Meyer & Grypstra 1328 S. Harvey Ave., Berwyn RA1933 Meyer, Y., & Son 1328 S. Harvey Ave. Berwyn RA1933, TD1951	Ysbrand Meyer Ysbrand Meyer and Grypstra Ysbrand Meyer and son Abe	

Meyer & Meyer 559 W. Lexington Ave. TD1951 1304 S. 59th Ct., Cicero TD1959 1122 W. Harrison St. TD1959 2945 W. Lake TD1965	Ysbrand Meyer's sons Abel & Sam Meyer	
Meyer, Nick 1302 S. Highland Ave. Berwyn RA1933	Nick Meyer	
Mid-City Disposal Scavenger Service 3815 W. Madison St., Bellwood RA1946 1428 S. 58th Ct., Cicero RA1957	Ben Mellema Clarence Veldman (sold to Hillside Disp. 1980s)	
Mid City Scavenger Service 7277 S. Chicago Ave. RA1957, RA1965	Arthur Brouwer Mrs. Amadine (Peter) Molter, Mrs. Lucille Jones & Mrs. Jean Brouwer	
Mid-West Scavenger Service 3601 N. Pulaski Rd. TD1951 3733 N. Kimball Ave. TD1965 6033 W. Roosevelt, Cicero RA1978	Richard J. "Moon" & J. D. Veldman & son Richard, Jr.	
Modern Scavenger Service 1243 S. 58th Ct., Cicero RA1957 10549 S. Eggleston RA165	Dirk A. De Groot F. Robert De Groot	
Molter, Jacob, Private Scavenger 1749 W. Washburne Ave. RA1933 1538 W. 15th St. TD1925, TD1928	Jacob Molter	
Molter Disposal Co. Geneva RA1957	John Molter	
Molter, Peter, Scavenger Service (est. 1915) 2034 W. 13th St. RA1933 Rt 1 Hintz Rd., Mount Prospect RA1946 7120 S. Evans Ave. TD1951 later South Side Trash Removal 7277 S. Chicago Ave. RB1959, TD1965	Peter Molter Mrs. Amadine (Peter) Molter	
Monarch Disposal Company (est. 1949) Elk Grove Village RRJ1971, Elgin RA1981	Joe Stob & Ken Laning, Sr.	WM

Company	Owners/Managers	
Monarch Scavenger Service 7277 S. Chicago Ave. RA1957, TD1965 10447 S. Torrence, Lansing RA1978 12057 Page, Calumet Park TD1991	Ted Hoekstra George Dekker, Mgr. Henry Hoekstra & Amadine Molter, Mgrs.	
Mulder Disposal Service 3800 W. 127th, Blue Island TD1965	Herman Mulder	WM
Mulder, John L., Teaming 1408 W. 14th Pl. CD1915	John L. Mulder	
Mulder, Thomas, & Sons Excavating 1641 W. 14th St. CD1913 1655 W. Hastings St. RA1933, RA1946 3205 W. Ogden Ave. TD1951 12500 S. Kedzie, Blue Island RA1957	Thomas S. Mulder Sons Herman, Frank, & Thomas, Jr.	
National Cartage (founded 1937) (later Barrington Trucking) (later National Disposal Services) 419 W. Main, Barrington RA1957	John and Peter Vanderveld John Vanderveld, Jr. James Vanderveld	BFI
National Scavenger Service 16035 Van Drunen Rd., So. Holland RA1981 1700 W. Carroll TD1991	Richard Van Hatten, Jr. Marvin & Norm Aardema	AW
Niehoff, John 1919 W. 13th St. RA1933	John Niehoff	
Noorlag, Nick, & Son 3416 N. Southport Ave. TD1951 1801 S. Home Ave., Berwyn RA1957	Nick Noorlag	
Noorlag, Neil 1621 W. 14th Place RA1933	Neil "Happy" Noorlag	
Noorlag Refuse Disposal 104 N. Oak Park Ave., Oak Park RA1978	Wm. J. Vandervelde, Jr.	
Noorlag, William, Teaming 1623 W. 14th Pl. CD1915	William Noorlag	
Northfield Disposal Service Glenview RA1978	Rick Veldman Robert J. Venhousen	
North Shore Disposal Service 454 Central, Highland Pk. RA1965	Jack Vos, Mgr.	

Northtown Disposal 1404 S. 58th Ave., Cicero RA1981	Casey Dykstra Jerry & Randall Dykstra	
Northwest Cinder & Garbage 1935 W. 13th St. RA1946	Meint Kampstra	
Northwest Disposal Service 9212 S. 50th Ave., Oak Lawn RA1978	John H. Cooper	
Northwest Refuse Disposal 1421 S. Highland Ave., Berwyn RA1957 5245 Grand, Western Springs TD1965	Garret Teune	
Nu Way Disposal Service 9742 S. Homan, Evergreen Pk. RA1965 Mokena RA1978	Ronald Huisenga Peter, Lambert, Wm. Groendyke	
Oak Brook Disposal Service Hinsdale RA1978, RA1988	Henry & Peter Roeters sold to S. Hoving & Sons	BFI
O'Hara Field Disposal Co. 1817 S. Pulaski Rd. TD1965	George De Boer	
OK Scavenger Service 1447 S. 60th Ct., Cicero RA1957 6110 W. 26th St., Cicero TD1965	Frank Post (son-in-law Siert Huizenga)	WM
Otte & Ribbens Scavenger Service 1342 S. 57th Ave., Cicero RA1946 1437 S. 61st Ave., Cicero TD1951	Gerhard "Lefty" Otte	
Ottenhoff, C. Teaming & Excavating 1220 S. Leavitt CD1913, RA1933, TD1951, TD1965	Conrad Ottenhoff	
Page Scavenger Service 1329 S. Kolin Ave. TD1951 1237 S. 60th Ct., Cicero TD1959	Peter Venhousen	
Pioneer Disposal Berwyn RA1981	Don Mulder	
Post, C. Disposal Co. Post Scavenger Service 3031 Cicero Ave., Cicero TD1991	Ben, William, & Cornie Post Brother Harold Post	AW
Powers Scavenger 3509 S. Western RA1978	John Powers, Jr., & John Wiersema	
R & J Ash Service 1625 W. 14th Place	John Blaauw, Ralph Wiltjer	

Rapid Disposal Service (est. 1971) 1020 Buell Ct., Oak Lawn RA1978	John P. Van Kampen (wife Katherine Kiemel)	
Reliable Scavenger Service 1400 S. 61st Ct., Cicero RA1946 1325 S. Gunderson, Berwyn RA1978	John Hamstra & sons Sam, Peter, and Joseph Sam bought out Pete & Joe, Sam to son Don 1980s	WM
Rex Disposal Co. 5306 W. Lawrence Ave. TD1959 5483 N. Northwest Hwy. TD1965 419 E. Adams, Elmhurst RA1978	George Stob and John Evenhouse, later Stob's sons John G. and Albert C. Stob	
Ridder's Scavenger Service 1236 S. Maple Ave., Berwyn RA1957	Ben Ridder	
Riteway Disposal Service 5480 N. Newland Ave. RA1978	Thomas E. Cook	
River Valley Disposal Barrington RA1978	Peter Vandervelde	
Rockford Disposal Service Rockford RRJ1966	George Edema, Mgr.	LL
Roelfsema, John 1643 W. 14th Place RA1933	John Roelfsema	
Roon, Nanning 1522 W. 14th Place RA1933	Nanning (Nick) Roon Sold to Sam Hamstra 1930s	
Rot's Disposal Service Downers Grove RA1978	John, Al, & Don Rot	BFI
Rottschafer Bros 7223 S. Morgan TD1951, TD1959 124 W 104th St. TD1965	Ernest, John, & Peter Rottschaffer	
Rudenga, Martin 1412 S. 58th Ct., Cicero RA1933	Martin Rudenga	
Rudenga, Ray	Ray Rudenga died 1939	
Rusthoven, John 7245 S. Sangamon TD1951, TD1959	John Rusthoven	
S & S Disposal Service 1001 E. Park, Libertyville RA1965	James C. De Boer	

Sanitary Disposal Corp. 6200 W. 127th, Palos Hgts. RA1957, RA1978	Andrew and Paul Alkema	
Sanitation Service Gary, IN	Jay Rusthoven (son of John) Sold to Homer A. Wigboldy	
Sani-Way Disposal 267 W. Butterfield, Elmhurst RA1978	Kenneth Blauw	
Scavenger Service Corp. 1800 S. Kedzie Ave. TD1951 2740 W. Ogden Ave. TD1959	Herman Mulder	
Schaaf, Klaas, Excavating 1424 W. 73rd St., TD1924	Klaas Schaaf	
Schaaf Disposal 16557 Dobson, So. Holland TD1991	?? Schaaf	
Schoustra, Teddy, Excavating 11306 S. State TD1913 237 W. 115th Pl. CD1915	Teddy Schoustra	
Schutt & Van Der Velde 7125 S. Emerald RA1946	George Van Der Velde	
Sierveld, Henry, Excavating 1724 W. 89th St. TD1926	Henry Sierveld	
South Chicago Scavenger Service 2018 W. 21st Pl. TD1951 9607 Trumbell Ave., Evergreen Pk. TD1959	John Ter Maat Norman & Marvin Aardema	
became South Chicago Disposal Corp. 10259 S. Ave. O, South Chicago RA1965, RRJ1979	John & Helen Ter Maat	
11834 S. Ewing, South Chicago TD1991	John P. Van Kampen	AW
South Side Private Scavenger 7343 S. Cottage Grove TD1951, TD1959 7277 S. Chicago Ave. TD1965	Hank Hoekstra, George Dekker, & Peter Molter	
Southtown Private Scavenger 9310 S. May St. TD1959, TD1965	John Van Kampen, Jr.	
Southwest Disposal 7618 S. Ashland RA1978	Ronald Vander Laan	

Southwest Towns Refuse Disposal 4630 W. 95th Street, Oak Lawn RA1957 6205 W. 101st, Chicago Ridge RA1978	Thomas Tibstra Thomas Tibstra, Jr.	 WM
Speedway Scavenger Service 7143 S. Honore Ave. RA1957, TD1959 9417 Ridgeway, Evergreen Pk. TD1965	Harry Van Ryn & son George	
Speelman, George, Teaming 1217 W. 15th St. CD1915 1250 S. Washtenaw Ave. TD1930 later Speelman Trucking Service 1629 S. Cicero Ave., Cicero TD1959, TD1965 later Speelman Refuse 1629 S. Cicero Ave., Cicero TD1991	George Speelman George & Tom Hoekstra Bill Schutt	 AW
Standard Refuse Removal Service 1513 S. Highland Ave., Berwyn RA1957 1220 S. Leavitt St. TD1959, TD1965	Henry P. Ottenhoff	
Standard Service Refuse Disposal 2109 S. Winonah Ave., Berwyn RA1957 1407 Redeker Rd., Des Plaines RA1978	William, Gerald, & John Vandervelde	WM
Star Disposal Service 1321 S. 61st St., Cicero TD1951 20 W. South St., Pk. Forest TD1959, RA1978	Francis Mulder C. Huiner, Clarence Slager, & Richard Oost	
Sterling Scavenger Service 16060 Suntone, South Holland RA1978	Louis Dykstra & Harold Hamstra	
Stickney Disposal Station 3900 S. Cicero Ave., Cicero TD1951, TD1965	Ace Scavenger Service Cal Weidenaar, Mgr.	
Stob, John, Cinder and Ash Old West Side ca. 1914	John Stob	
Stob, William, Scavenger 4722 Hamlin Ave., RA1933	William Stob	
Suburban Disposal 1827 S. Clinton Ave., Berwyn RA1957 533 W. Harding Rd., Lombard RA1978	William Noorlag John Iwema, Mgr.	
Suburban Scavenger Service 16417 Evans, South Holland RA1957	Corniel Korringa & William Teune	

Superior Refuse Disposal 1405 S. Ridgeland, Berwyn RA1957, RA1978	Adrian Laning	
T & T Disposal Service 7285 Wolf Rd., La Grange RA1957	Ted & Tom Bulthuis	
T & T Scavenger Service 6052 S. Menard Ave. RA1957	Clarence J. Brouwer, Sr., & Clarence H. Brouwer, Jr.	
T.V. Scavenger Service 232 W. 108th Pl. RA1957 745 E. 75th Street RRJ1959 232 W 108th Pl. TD1965 7277 South Chicago Ave. RA1978	Thomas Ridderbos Tom Voogt	
Tameling Disposal Service 2708 S. 9th Ave., Broadview RA1978	Ben & Hank Tameling Roger Groenboom merged into Atlas Disposal	BFI
Tazelaar Disposal Service 1444 S. Marengo, Forest Pk. RA1978	Ronald W. Tazelaar bought from John Van Tholen	WM
Tazelaar, Mark, Teaming 1427 S. Tripp Ave. CD1915	Mark Taazelaar	
Teeuws, Lambert 1318 S. Austin Blvd., Cicero RA1933	Lambert Teeuws	
Teeuws, W. L. 7007 W. 19th St., Berwyn RA1957	William & Marion Teeuws	
Terborg, George, Scavenger Service Palos Heights RA1978	George Terborg	
Ter Maat, Jacob Old West Side before 1922	Jacob Ter Maat & son Sam	
Ter Maat, John P. 2018 W. 21st Pl. TD1951 9607 Trumbull TD1959, TD1965	John P. Ter Maat	
Ter Maat, Peter J. later South Chicago Disposal Corp 1647 W. 14th Pl. RA1933, TD1934 757 W. 79th St. TD1951 10259 S. Ave. O RA1978	Peter J. Ter Maat & son Peter sold to John P. Van Kampen	
Ter Maat, Peter 1540 W. 14th Place RA1933	Peter Ter Maat	

Ter Maat, Sam 1406 S. Ashland Ave. RA1933 1344 S. 60th Ct., Cicero RA1946	Sam Ter Maat sold to Meyer Bros.	WM
Terrace Disposal Service 105 May St., Elmhurst RA1978	Lawrence Stavenger, Jr.	
Teune, Dan, Disposal 1647 W. 14th Pl. TD1934 1400 S. 60th Ct., Cicero RA1933, TD1951 10108 S. Maple, Oak Lawn RA1965	Dan Teune (brother of Ed) Dan & Harry Teune	
Teune, Edward 1441 S. 61st Ct., Cicero RA1933, RA1946	Edward Teune (brother of Dan)	
Teune, Garret 5245 Grand, Western Springs TD1965	Garret Teune (son of Ed)	
Teune, Henry, & Son 1456 S. Ashland Ave. RA1933 3953 W. 49th St. TD1951, TD1959, TD1965	Henry Teune & brothers Joe, John Henry's sons Harry & Daniel	
Teune, Herman 1714 W. 13th St. RA1933, TD1934 1429 S. 59th Ave., Cicero RA1946	Herman Teune (brother of Dan)	
Teune, John 1542 W. Hastings St. RA1933, TD1934 1313 S. 58th Ct., Cicero TD1959, TD1965	John Teune	
Teune, John & Martha, Disposal Serv. 4156 N. Milwaukee Ave. RA1978	John and Martha Teune	
Teune, John H., Scavenger Serv. 7202 S. Aberdeen, Engelwood RA1957, TD1959 16550 Elm Ct., So. Holland TD1965	John H. Teune	
Teune, Peter, Scavenger Service 7318 S. Morgan, Engelwood TD1951, TD1959 16308 S. Woodlawn, So. Holland TD1965 2422 W. 100 St. RA1978	Peter Teune Clarence & Fred Schaaf	
Teune Scavenger Service 1439 S. 58th Ct., Cicero TD1959, TD1965 2740 W. Ogden Ave. RA1978	Peter Teune Harry Huizenga	

Theta Systems Rockford RRJ1977	Roy Stavenger	LL
Top, Ben, Disposal Co. 1358 S. Washtenaw Ave. CD1915 1344 S. Fairfield Ave. RA1933 1139 N. Massasoit Ave. RA1946 4850 W. Parker TD1951	Ben J. Top	
later Top, B. & Son Disposal 8412 W. Sunnyside Ave. TD1959, TD1965	Ben's son Ben J. Top, Jr.	
later Top Disposal Service 1307 S. Highland, Berwyn RA1978 Hillside RA1988	Henry & son Peter Van Tholen Peter Van Tholen, Jr. James & Steven Van Kampen	
United Disposal Service 6921 W. 157th St., Tinley Park RA1978	Dale Essenburg	
9222 S. Homan, Evergreen Park 12310 S. Austin Ave., Palos Heights	John R. Borgman & D. Craig Tuuk	
United Scavenger Service 6333 Gilbert Ave., La Grange	Louis Stalman	
Van Dahm, Simon 1917 W. 13th St. RA1933	Simon Van Dahm	
Van Der Molen Disposal Co. 4152 W. Grand Ave. RA1946, TD1951 5050 W. Lake, Melrose Pk. TD1959, RA1978	Edward Van Der Molen sons Harold, Bernard, and Everett	BFI
Van Der Molen, Harold, Scavenger 5447 W. Harrison TD1965	Harold Van Der Molen	BFI
Van Der Molen, Joseph, Scavenger 635 W. 16th St. CD1899	Joseph Van Der Molen	
Vandervelde, John J. (est. 1911) 1933 W. 13th St.	John J. Vandervelde	
Vander Velde, George (1920s) 1648 W. 14th Place	George Vander Velde & Herman Hoekstra	
Vander Velde, George (1942-51) 7134 S. Sangamon St.	George Vander Velde & Herman Schutt (sold to John Ter Maat in 1951)	
Vande Westering, Richard, Teaming 1714 W. 14th St. CD1915	Richard Vande Westering	
Van Dyke Disposal Service 824 Madison Ave., La Grange RA1957	Peter J. Van Dyke	

Van Dyken Bros. 1241 W. 74th St.	John Hornman, Mgr.	
Van Dyke's Scavenger Service 6935 W. Irving Park Ave. TD1959	?? Van Dyke	
Van Eck, Mient, Scavenger 11335 S. Michigan Ave., CD1900	Meint Van Eck	
Van's Scavenger Service 9404 S. Racine TD1951, TD1965	John Van Kampen, Jr.	
Van Kampen, G., & Sons 1404 S. 57th Ave., Cicero RA1965	George Van Kampen & sons George & James merged into Top Disposal	WM
Van Ryn Scavenger Service 4319 Butterfield Rd, Bellwood RA1978	Emil Van Ryn & sons Jerry, Charles, & Emil	
Van's Refuse Disposal 100 S. Mulberry, Oak Lawn RA1978	John & Peter Van Kampen	
Van Tholen, Henry 1307 S Ridgeland, Berwyn TD1959, TD1965	Henry Van Tholen & son Peter	
Van Tholen, John, Disposal (Acme Cinder) 1921 W 13th St. TD1930, RA1933, RA1946 1400 S. Highland, Berwyn TD1959, TD1965	John Van Tholen & sons John & Henry merged into Top Disposal	
Van Weelden Bros. 1452 N Keeler Ave. TD1951 4252 N Lincoln Ave. TD1959, TD1965	Marvin H., Gilbert, Henry & Edward Van Weelden	WM
Van Wyk Scavenger Service 7214 S. Hoyne Ave. TD1951	?? Van Wyk	
Vegter, Henry, 8507 S. Ashland Ave. TD1959	Henry Vegter	
Veldman, Clarence 1240 S. 59th Ave. RA1933	Clarence Veldman	
Veldman, Cornelius 1507 S. 57th Ct.	Cornelius Veldman	
Veldman, John D. 1185 S. Clinton Ave., Oak Park RA1946	John D. Veldman	

Venema Disposal Co. 10001 Spaulding RA1957 Geneva RRJ1962	Ronald and William Venema	
Venema, Wm. 1319 S. 58th Ct. RA1933 61st Ave., Cicero	Wm Venema	
Venhuizen, E., Scavenger ?? RA1933	E. Venhuizen	
Veteran's Scavenger Service 7277 S. Chicago Ave. RA1978	Mrs. Amadine (Peter) Molter	
Villa Park Refuse Disposal 1400 Myers Rd., Lombard RA1957	Albert Havenga Sr. sold to George Vos	
Vos Disposal Service 1 S. 478 Chase, Lombard	Jack Vos	WM
Wayne Disposal 488 Sunset, West Chicago RA1957 (see Elgin Wayne Disposal)	Edward Evenhouse, Robert Molenhouse, Jack Ter Maat, also bought John Ter Maat, Bill & son Fred Noorlag Ed Bilthouse, Mgr.	
West Chicago Disposal Co. 5050 W. Lake St., Melrose Park RA1957	Edward Van Der Molen & son, Cornelius E. Van Der Molen	
West Engelwood Private Scavenger 6412 S. Komensky Ave. RA1946, TD1951 10151 S Kolin, Oaklawn RA1978 15557 Larkspur Ln., Orland Pk. TD1991	Al Diepstra Ed Cooper & Tom Hoekstra Andy Diepstra Rich Solle	WM
Wester Disposal Service 7443 Channel Rd., Skokie RA1957	Henry P. Wester	
Western Disposal Lockport 1963-1972	Ben Heslinga, Mgr. (stockholders Ben Heslinga, Jay Bilthuis, John Bilthuis, Jack De Young, Steve Tameling, George De Vries)	WM
Westmont Disposal Westmont RA1978	Harold & Al Havenga (also Lombard Disposal)	
Westowns Trucking Company Warrensville RA1957, RRJ1962, RA1965	Robert Molenhouse Paul Van Der Molen	

West Suburban Disposal Lombard	Nick Noorlag & son Bill sold to John Iwema	
Wheaton Disposal Company Wheaton RA1957	William Vander Naald & Elmer Vos (brothers-in-law)	WM
Wheeling Disposal Wheeling RA1957, RA1978	Huizenga family, Herman Kanis Russ Erffmeyer, Ben & Ken Tameling	WM
Wiersema, Cornelius 2120 W. Hastings St. RA1933	Cornelius Wiersema	
Wigboldy Bros. Washburne Ave. 1930s-1945	Paul and Al Wigboldy	
Workman, John 7136 S. Peoria St. RA1933	John Workman	
Workman, John, & Sons 4539 Woodland, Western Springs RA1957 5616 Washington, Hinsdale RA1978	John Workman Menno & Melvin Workman	WM
Zuidema, Nick 1315 S. 59th Ct., RA1946	Nick Zuidema	

APPENDIX 2

Chicago Dutch Cartage Companies

Sources

TD – Chicago telephone directories "Red Book" and Business
CD – Chicago city directories
CCHS – Chicago Christian High School Yearbook 1928
FC – Chicago federal censuses of 1900 and 1920
CM – *The Chicago Messenger*
CP – Century of Progress programs 1933-34
KP – Knickerbocker programs
Interviews with John R. Swierenga and others

Company	**Owner**
Acme Parcel (sold to Excel Motor Serv., 1937)	Clarence Klaassens
Amsterdam, Peter, Expressing 537 W. 14th St. CD1899	Peter Amsterdam
Bandringa's Express 7153 S. Halsted St. TD1922, TD1930	
Boerema, Henry, Expressing 1405 E. 95th St. TD1930	Harry Boerema
Camphouse, George H., Teaming 1400 S. Crawford Ave. TD1922 1342 S. Keeler Ave. TD1930	George H. Camphouse
Carry Transit	Tom Wieringa & Howard Hoving
Century Cartage 1040 W. Washburn Ave. TD1952	Nick Wieringa & sons Gerrit, Ernie, & John

Clearing Cartage 5251 S. Massasoit TD1952	
Columbia Cartage 1040 W. Washburne Ave. TD1952	Peter Wieringa & sons George "Shorty" & Clarence
Davids, John, Cartage hauled for Reliable Electric 1618 Washburne Ave. (ca. 1935–ca. 1950)	John Davids
De Groot Motor Service 2130 W. Ogden Ave. TD1952	Frank De Groot & sons Clarence, Leonard, Meindert, & Frank, Jr.
De Koker Express Co. 5842 S. Robey TD1922 6256 S. Kedzie Ave. TD1930	Richard De Koker
De Vries Express & Van Co. 7751 S. Halsted St. TD1922	?? De Vries
De Vries Motor Service 716 W. Court TD1952	?? De Vries
De Vries Teaming 733 Waldo Pl. TD1930	?? De Vries
De Young Trucking 9438 S. Eggelston Ave. TD1952	?? De Young
Dornbos, Bernard J., Teaming 7214 S. Green TD1930	Bernard J. Dornbos
Dornbos, Otto, Parcel Delivery Evergreen Park	Otto Dornbos
Dykeman Bros Express & Van 6928 S. Racine Ave. TD1922, TD1930	
Eleveld Bros Motor Express 2239 W. Grand Ave. TD1930	
Engelsman, William, coal and wood, moving and expressing 5815 Roosevelt Rd., Cicero CM1935	William Engelsman
Evenhouse Motor Service 61st St., Cicero	John H. Evenhouse
Excel Motor Service (1935-59) 223 W. Jackson Blvd.	John R. Swierenga, sold to Bernard Mulder 1969, sold 1986
Folkerts, Ellerd, Trucking 1356 S. Cicero Ave., Cicero	Ellerd Folkerts

Grypstra, Jinte, Teaming 1726 W. 14th Pl. TD1930	Jinte Grypstra
Haak, Barney, Teaming 1320 S. Kolin Ave. TD1922	Barney Haak
Hartje, E. T., Motor Trucking 4817 S. Christiana Ave. TD1922	E. T. Hartje
Haverkamp, Henry G., Teaming 101 S. Water St. CD1899	Henry G. Haverkamp
Hoekstra, John, Teaming 417 W. 117th St. TD1952	John Hoekstra
Hoekstra Motor Service 536 W. 119th St. TD1952	?? Hoekstra
Hoff Bros 3501 S. Cicero Ave., Cicero	Maynard & Clarence Hoff
Huizenga, John, Cartage 2525 S. Artesian Ave. TD1952	John Huizenga
Kelder, Peter C., Cartage Service 24 N. Peoria St. TD1952	Peter C. Kelder
Korringa Cartage 1409 S. 58th Ave. KP1968	Edward Korringa
Meyer, John E., Expressing 248 W. 26th St. TD1922	John E. Meyer
Monroe Cartage Co. 620 N. Orleans St. TD1934 1130 W. Harrison St. TD1952 Addison	John Davids sold to Ralph Swierenga sons Ralph Jr. "Butch" & Jack
Meyers Express 4153 W. Rooseveld Rd. TD1930	?? Meyers
Noor, Jeremiah, Expressing 6636 S. Aberdeen St. CD1899	Jeremiah Noor
Ozinga, Martin, Trucking 400 E. 130th St. TD1952	Martin Ozinga, Jr.
Prince, Otto, Express 2754 W. Harrison St. TD1930	Otto Prince
Republic Cartage Englewood RA1957	John Roeters and son Kelly
V. J. Cartage Co. KP1958	Gary Schuil

Shoemaker, Francis S., Teaming 6009 S. Sangamon CD1899	Francis S. Shoemaker
Smith, Lawrence R., Cartage 11320 Forrest Ave. 1938	Lawrence R. Smith
Spoolstra, Peter, Expressing 355 W 109th St. CD1899	Peter Spoolstra
Standard Cartage 2056 Archer Ave. TD1922 559 W. Lexington St. TD1952 1037 W. Washburne Ave. KP1958	Leonard Gorter
Superior Cartage 1130 W. Harrison St. TD1952	
Swierenga Cartage Co. (steel) 1207 W. 37th St. TD1930, TD1934 8124 S. Hoyne Ave. TD1952	Barney Swierenga & son John B.
Tameling Bros. Motor Cartage 900 S. Menard Ave. TD1952	Nick & Herman "Bo" Tameling
Vandeberg, Lane, Expressing 156 W 111th St. CD1899	Lane Vandeberg
Vandenberg, Herman, Expressing 6944 S. Aberdeen CD1899	Herman Vandenberg
Van Der Heyden Bros 324 W. Superior Ave. TD1922, TD1930, TD1952	?? Van Der Heyden
Vander Velde, John H. 644 W. 12th St. TD1909 CCHS1928	John H. Vander Velde
Van Der Wagen Bros 4552 W. 63rd St. CCHS1928	?? Van Der Wagen
Van Eck, Kampe, Expressing 146 W 112th Pl. CD1899	Kampe Van Eck
Van Housen, F., Expressing 5335 S. Halsted TD1909	F. Van Housen
Veen Cartage 7116 S. Carpenter St. TD1952	
Verschoore's Fireproof Storage 4040 N. Kedzie Ave. TD1930	
Wesseling, Frederick, Teaming 99 S. Water St. CD1899	Frederick Wesseling

Firm	Proprietor(s)
Wierenga & Van Stedum Furniture moving and expressing 644 (1535) W. 12th St.	H. Wierenga and G. Van Stedum
Wieringa Bros. Cartage 2205 W. Harrison TD1922, TD1934 (divided into Century & Columbia Cartage Cos.)	Nick & Ben Wieringa
Wieringa Cartage 10010 Eggelston 1950s	B. L. Wieringa
Wiersum, Gerrit, Expressing 1082 (1923) N. 43rd Ave. CD1899	Gerrit Wiersum

Excavators

Firm	Proprietor(s)
Beemsterboer Excavating Roseland	Louis Beemsterboer
Bussema, John 7630 W. 25th St., Riverside KP1958	John Bussema
Elzinga & Johnson 216 W. 110th Pl. 1929	A. Elzinga and K. Johnson
Iwema, Bonne & Sons 2236 W. 13th St. TD1930	Bonne Iwema
Ottenhoff, C. Teaming & Excavating 1220 S. Leavitt CD1913	Conrad Ottenhoff
Ottenhoff C., & Sons RA1933, TD1934, TD1951, TD1965	Conrad & son Henry
Wigboldy, Homme & Sons 2109 W. 13th St. TD1919, RA1933	Homme (Homer) Wigboldy
Wigboldy, H., Sons 8344 S. Halsted St. RA1946, TD1951 8959 S. Kedzie Ave. RA1957	sons John & Albert
Wigboldy Bros. Washburne Ave. 1930s-45	Paul and Al Wigboldy

Manure Haulers

Firm	Proprietor(s)
Groen, Henry A., Trucking Manure, black soil, cinders 9319 Utica Ave., 1930s	Henry A. Groen
Huizenga, William, Hauling 116th Pl. & Crawford Ave., 1940s	William Huizenga
Klaassens Old West Side ca. 1910-15	Klaassens

Koning Old West Side ca. 1910s	Koning
Laninga, Ray Cicero, 1950-70s	Ray Laninga
Oldenburger, Sipke 1411 S. Ashland ca. 1921-30s (later D. Koning and S. Oldenburger) sold to Tameling Bros.	Sipke Oldenburger
Tameling Bros Tameling 3840 S. Laramie Ave. TD1952 7195 S. Madison, Hinsdale KP1958	Ben & sons Henry & Herman

Coal, Ice, Wood, Hay, Grain, Feed, Straw, Fuel Oil, Black dirt

Bos, Richard 1745 W. 14th St. 1930s	Richard Bos
Dykema Bros. 6926-28 S. Racine	
Dykhuis, R. Straw and hay, later fruit and vegetables Old West Side 1882-95	Ralph Dykhuis
Euwema, Herman Coal, wood, grain, and hay furniture moving 2150-52 (4043-45) W. 12th St. ca. 1900	Herman Euwema
Groeneweold, H. 1815 W. Hastings St. 1930s	H. Groenewold
Havenga, Albert coal & ice	Albert Havenga
Huizenga, Jacob Coal and coke, black dirt 10116 S. Halsted St., 1930s	Jacob Huizenga
Jannenga, Nicholaas Hay, Grain, and Feed, ca. 1900 3908-10 (2047-49 old) 12th St. became Jannenga & Fischer Coal, coke, wood, hay, and feed 1213 S. 58th Ave., Cicero ca. 1925	Nicholaas Jannenga son Edward in 1915 Edward Jannenga & Cornelius Fischer
Jousma Coal Archer & Central Aves., Summit 1900–ca. 1985	Louis Jousma & son George Dick Jousma

Kempes, Henry Hay, grain, coal, and wood 582 (2200) W. Ogden Ave., ca. 1900	Henry Kempes
Kostelyk, Cornelius Ice 231 W. 108th St., 1928	Cornelius Kostelyk
Kraai Bros Ice and coal, Roseland, 1930s	Ray Kraai
Lubbers Bros. Fuel Oil Co. Roseland, 1950s	
Mulder, W. Coal and wood 533 (1336) W. 14th St., ca. 1900	W. Mulder
Nanninga, John Dealer in hay, grain, and feed 1402-04 (641-43 old) Ashland Ave. 1903	John Nanninga
Noll, Harold Hay, grain, and coal 1510 W. 14th St. 1938	Harold Noll
Nyp, Tom 1213 S. 58th Ave., Cicero ca. 1934 became Jannenga & Fischer 1935	Tom Nyp sold to Edward Jannenga
Ozinga Bros. Coal, fuel oil (later concrete) Evergreen Park KP1958	Martin and Frank Ozinga
Post, Andrew Coal, coke, and ice 11 S. Campbell Ave. 1938	Andrew Post
Sluis Seeds 544-46 W. 63rd St., Englewood, 1920s	Jacob Sluis
Sluis, R. Evergreen Park	Richard (Dirk) Sluis
Stob, J. Hay, grain, coal, and wood 429 (1506) Blue Island Ave., ca. 1900	John Stob
Tameling Bros dirt, sand, gravel, etc. 7500 Madison, Hinsdale	Steve, Henry, and Peter Tameling then Steve Tameling
Van Der Meer, B. & Sons (coal) 403 W. 103rd St., est. 1892 CP1934	B. Van Der Meer & sons

Vander Velde, Edward 1944	Edward Vander Velde Drewes Peters, Distributor
Vander Velde, John H. 1704 W. 14th Pl. OT1920	John H. Vander Velde
Vander Velde, John H. & Son 1938	John H. & Edward Vander Velde
Vander Velde, Nick 2231 W. 13th St. 1944	Nick Vander Velde
Wichers, Thos. (Rock River Ice Co) 7043 S. Peoria St. CCHS1926 Roseland & Tinley Park	Thos. Wichers sons Will & Tom Wichers & brother-in-law Bernie Bandstra

Moving and Storage

De Vries Express & Van Co. 309 W. 106th St. TD1922 352 W. 106th Pl. TD1930	Bert De Vries
Euwema Moving 6628-32 Roosevelt Rd., Oak Park	Peter Euwema
Jamesway Express Local and long distance movers 11024 Wentworth Ave., 1928	A. J. Sieswerda and A. B. Ooms
Ploegman, P., and Sons, Movers (began 1910 as P. Ploegman coal, ice, and feed delivery) 5115 W. Cermak Rd., Cicero (since 1920s)	Peter Ploegman
Pothof, H., Moving Piano and Furniture, Coal and Wood 1714 Washburne Ave. OT1920	Henry Pothof
Van Dyke, Jno, Express & Van 1615 S. Harding Ave. TD1930	John Van Dyke
Van Dyke's Furnitue and Piano Movers 1326 S. 57th Ave. CD1936	John Van Dyke, Jr.
Van Eck, K., Moving and Storage 55 W. 109th Pl., 1930s	Kampe Van Eck

APPENDIX 3

Churches, Schools, and Missions

REFORMED CHURCHES

West Side

First Chicago — Calvary — First Chicago, Berwyn

1848-1856	met in homes and rented store fronts
1856-1869	ca. 850 S. Foster Street (between Polk and Harrison)
1869-1894	southwest corner Harrison at May Sts.
1894-1945	1535 W. Hastings St. ("Hastings Street Church")
1937-1948	Calvary, Berwyn (various rented facilities)
1948-	First Reformed of Chicago, Berwyn, 1900 S. Oak Park Ave., Berwyn

Second American Reformed ("Livingston Memorial")

1854-1858	Des Plaines St. and various places
1858-1874	northeast corner Monroe at Sangamon Sts. Disbanded 1874

Northwestern (formerly Holland Presbyterian)

1870-1885	corner Noble and Erie streets
1885-1926	1600 W. Superior St. (between Robey and Hoyne). Disbanded 1926

Trinity (American)

1892-1919	440 S. Marshfield Ave. (new numbering 913 S.) Dissolved 1919

North Side

Norwood Park

1871-1916	Ceylon and Mulberry Rd. on Wisconsin division of Chicago & Northwestern RR (became Presbyterian)

Irving Park

1874-1913	4045 N. 42nd Ave. (became Presbyterian)

Englewood

First Englewood — Calvary, Orland Park

1887-1958 NE corner 62nd and Peoria St. (new church 1911)
1958-1978 8400 S. Damen Ave.
1978- became Calvary, Orland Park, 15101 S. 80th Ave.

Hope (Second) Englewood

1902-1904 rented Seventh Day Adventist Church, 6236 Peoria St.
1904-1909 corner 66th and Sangamon St.
1910-1928 corner 66th and Peoria St.
1928-1973 corner 78th and Lincoln (later Wolcott) St.
1973- merged into Palos Heights

Roseland

First

1849-1970 10700 S. Michigan Ave.
1971- became Thorn Creek of South Holland, 1875 E. 170th St.

Bethany (Second)

1890-1891 Vandersyde's Hall, NW corner 111th and Michigan Ave. and First Christian Reformed Church at 111th and State St.
1891-1926 111th St. between State St. and Perry Ave. enlarged and basement added in 1899
1926-1972 68 W. 111th St.
1972-1973 Illiana Christian High School, South Holland, IL
1974- became Bethany Reformed (now Community) Church of Lynwood, IL

Emmanuel

1914-1915 100th Place and Michigan Ave.
1915-1989 10233 S. State St., new church edifices in 1921, 1927, 1946; dissolved 1989

First, Gano

1891-1892 in Methodist Church at 11552 Michigan Ave.
1892-1977 11623 Perry Ave.

Mt. Greenwood

1913-1914 Old school house at 111th and Homan Ave.
1914-1954 111th and Drake Ave.
1954- 3509 W. 111th St.

Summit

Bethel, Summit

1892-1896 worship in various homes, Summit
1896-1899 57th St. and Meade Ave., Summit
1899-1904 55th St. and Moody Ave., Summit
1904-1910 Archer Ave. near Austin Ave., Summit

1910-1965 6131 Archer Ave., Summit
1965- 5433 S. Austin Ave., Chicago

Cicero-Berwyn

West Side, Cicero
1911-1914 various rented facilities
1914-1996 1323 S. Austin Blvd., Cicero. Disbanded 1996

Faith Community, Stickney
1947- 4006 S. Grove (later Oak Park Ave.), Berwyn

Oak Lawn

Green Oak, Oak Lawn
1955- 10100 S. 52nd Ave., Oak Lawn

Far West and Southwest

Fellowship, Lombard
1957- 1420 S. Meyers Rd., Lombard

Tinley Park
1957- 16530 Ridgeland Ave.

Palos Heights
1960- 6600 W. 127th St., Palos Heights

Covenant (now Downers Grove Community), Downers Grove
1965- 6600 Fairview Ave., Downers Grove

Calvary, Orland Park (see also First Englewood)
1978- 15101 S. 80th Ave., Orland Park

CHRISTIAN REFORMED CHURCHES

West Side

First Chicago — Ebenezer
1867-1883 ca. 1000 W. Gurley St. (between Sholto and Miller Sts.)
1883-1921 ca. 1350 W. 14th St. ("Old Fourteenth Street Church")
1921-1946 1319 S. Ashland Ave.
1946-1949 several temporary locations in Berwyn
1949- Ebenezer, 1300 S. Harvey, Berwyn

Douglas Park — Second Cicero — West Suburban — Faith
1899-1927 1329 S. Harding St.
1927-1973 Second Cicero (Warren Park 1947-73), 1400 S. 58th Ct.
1973-1976 West Suburban, Timothy Chr. School Gymnasium, Elmhurst
1976- Faith, Elmhurst 1070 S. Prospect St., Elmhurst

Third Chicago — First Cicero — Lombard

1912-1913 2231 W. 12th St. (a rented store)
1913-1914 leased Mayflower Congregational Church, corner of Sacramento Blvd. and Fillmore St.
1914-1921 4120 W. Grenshaw St. (the "basement church")
1925-1975 First Cicero 1220 S. 60th Court, Cicero
1975- Lombard 2020 S. Meyers Road, Lombard

Fourth Chicago — Oak Park — West Suburban — Faith

1923-1946 2040 W. Roosevelt Road
1935-1939 branch church – Timothy Christian School, Cicero
1939-1945 branch church – Berwyn, 15th and Ridgeland Ave.
1945-1973 Oak Park corner of W. Jackson Blvd. and Wesley Ave.

Englewood

First Englewood — Calvin, Oak Lawn

1887-1961 842 W. 71st St. (new edifices in 1895 and 1931)
1962- 101st St. and Central Ave., Oak Lawn

Second Englewood — Kedvale Avenue, Oak Lawn

1903-1962 NW corner 72nd and Peoria St. (new edifice 1926)
1962- 10415 S. Kedvale Ave., Oak Lawn

Auburn Park

1945-1948 Chicago Christian High School auditorium
1948-1964 NE corner 76th and Aberdeen St.
1964-1974 became West Evergreen, 9800 S. Crawford Ave.

Summit

Archer Avenue

1911-1997 6059 Archer Ave., Summit (new edifice 1915)

Evergreen Park

First Evergreen Park

1915-1931 97th Street and Kedzie Ave., Evergreen Park
1931- 9547 S. Homan Ave., Evergreen Park

Park Lane, Evergreen Park

1953-1955 auditorium of Evergreen Park Christian School
1955- 3450 W. Maple Ave., Evergreen Park

West Evergreen, est. 1964, see Auburn Park

Oak Lawn

First Oak Lawn

1915-1950 9424 S. 54th Ave., Oak Lawn
1951- 9354 S. 54th Ave., Oak Lawn

Kedvale Avenue, Oak Lawn est. 1962
See Second Englewood

Calvin, Oak Lawn est. 1961
See First Englewood

Roseland

First Roseland — Lynwood

1877-1918	111th St. west of State
1918-1971	234 W. 109th Pl. (at Princeton St.)
1972-1973	Illiana Christian High School, South Holland, IL
1973-1990	became Lynwood, 1972 Glenwood-Dyer Rd., Lynwood, IL
1990-	became United Reformed

Second Roseland — Orland Park

1893-1972	10643 S. Perry Ave. (second edifice erected 1937)
1972-	amalgamated into Orland Park

Third Roseland — Kedvale, Oak Lawn

1907-1964	10942 S. Perry Ave.
1964-1971	Lowe Ave. at 110th St.
1971-	disbanded and amalgamated into Kedvale Ave., Oak Lawn

Fourth Roseland — Orland Park

1919-1920	104th Street Christian School
1920-1969	134 W. 104th St. (new edifice dedicated 1930)
1969-1971	Chicago Christian High School, Palos Heights
1971-	amalgamated into Orland Park

Cicero-Berwyn-Oak Park

First Cicero, est. 1921
See Third Chicago

Warren Park, est. 1927
See Douglas Park

Berwyn, est. 1945
see First Chicago

Oak Park, est. 1945
See Fourth Chicago

Far West

Des Plaines

1931-1993	1479 Whitcomb Ave., Des Plaines

Western Springs
1938-59 40th and Grand Ave., Western Springs
1959- 5140 Wolf Rd., Western Springs

Bellwood — Elmhurst
1949-1964 3501 Monroe St., Bellwood
1964- 905 S. Kent (corner of Van Buren St.), Elmhurst

Palos Heights
1955- 7059 W. 127th St., Palos Heights

Elmhurst est. 1964. See Bellwood

Orland Park. Formerly Second and Fourth Roseland
1971- 7500 W. Sycamore Dr., Orland Park

Tinley Park Chapel
1976-1978 Memorial School auditorium
1978-1984 Tinley Center Plaza, 177th and Oak Park Ave.

Tinley Park — Faith, Formerly Third Roseland
1979-1982 Kruse School, 7617 Hemlock Dr., Orland Park
1982-1983 Stewart Ridge Community Church, 7939 167th St.
1983- 171st St. and 84th Ave., Tinley Park

ROMAN CATHOLIC (DUTCH)

St. Willebrord
1900-1980s 11404 Edbrooke Ave., Kensington

CHRISTIAN SCHOOLS

Roseland Christian School
1884-1886 111th and State St.
1886-1929 110th Pl. and State St.
1929- 108th St. and Princeton St.

Roseland School for Christian Instruction
1891-1969 104th and Wentworth St.
(merged into Roseland Christian School, 1947)

Ebenezer
1893-1896 685 S. Ashland (new numbering 1442 S.)
1906-1946 1626 W. 15th St.

Englewood
1901-1962 7146 S. Sangamon St.

Timothy
1912-1927 13th St. and Tripp Ave.
1927-1962 14th St. and 59th Ct., Cicero
1962- Butterfield Rd. and Prospect St., Elmhurst

Chicago Christian High School
1918-1920 Bethel Mission 72nd Pl. and Loomis Blvd.
1920-1927 69th and May St.
1927-1962 7050 S. May St.
1962- 12001 S. Oak Park Ave., Palos Heights

Evergreen Park
1924-1986 Homan Ave. and 97th St., Evergreen Park

Oak Lawn
1956- Central Ave. and 101st St., Oak Lawn

Western Suburbs
1957-1970 Wolf Rd. and 55th St., Western Springs

Tinley Park
1986- 8500 W. 171st St.

MISSIONS

Chicago Helping Hand Mission (officially until 1929, City Mission of the Christian Reformed Church of Chicago)
1915-1981 848-50 W. Madison St. (building razed in 1981)
1981-1984 rented quarters on nearby street

Hebrew Christian Mission of Chicago (interdenominational)
1887-1889 264 (new numbering 713) W. 12th St.

Chicago Hebrew Mission (interdenominational)
1889-1917 425 Solon Pl.
1917-1919 1505 S. Sawyer Ave.

Chicago Hebrew Mission Reading Room
1907(?)-1917 1244 S. Halsted St.
1917-1919 1311 S. Kedzie Ave.

Chicago Jewish Mission (Christian Reformed Church) (Nathanael Institute after 1932)
1918-1921 various rented spaces

1921-1924 1324 W. 14th St.
1924-1928 1815 W. 13th St.
1928-1957 1241 S. Pulaski Rd.
1957-1966 6407 N. Leavitt St.

Chinese Gospel Church (organized as Hyde Park Christian Reformed Church in 1974)

1950-1956 Chinatown, W. 22nd St.
1956-1968 75 E. 83rd St.
1968- 5144 S. Cornell Ave.

Lawndale Gospel Chapel

1951-1956 1304 S. Karlov Ave.
1957 became Lawndale Christian Reformed Church

Lawndale Christian Reformed Church

1957- 1241 S. Pulaski Rd.

American Indian Chapel

1958-1987 Ishham YMCA (Ashland and Clyborn Aves.)
Lincoln-Belmont YMCA (Belmont Ave. just east of Damen Ave.)

APPENDIX 4

Societies and Clubs

Young people's societies:
Christian Endeavor (C.E.) (RCA)
Young Men's & Young Women's Association (CRC)
Cadets & Calvinettes (CRC)
Boy Scouts & Girl Scouts (RCA)

Adult societies:
Men's & Women's Societies
Women's Missionary Union
Christian Friendship Clubs (CRC Christian day school auxiliaries)

Summer camps:
Cedar Lake CRC Bible Conference Grounds
Billy Sunday's Winona Lake Bible Conference Grounds

Cultural societies:
Izak Da Costa Oratorical Society
AVENDO – Christian Recital Society
Dutch Drama Club
Knickerbocker Male Chorus
Netherlanders Male Chorus
Ambassador Male Chorus
Harmonie Band
Excelsior Band

Sports:
Holland-American Inter-Church Baseball (later Softball) League
Holland-American Inter-Church Basketball League
Holland-American Bowling League
Holland Gymnastics Society

Mutual Aid Societies:

Zulf Hulp (Self Help) Burial Fund Society (1879-1970)
Eendracht Maakt Macht (Unity Is Strength) Mutual Aid Society (1894-??)
Excelsior Burial Society (1897-??)
Het Huis voor Bejaarden (Holland Home) retirement and nursing home (1914-present)

1914-1925	old parsonage First Roseland RCA
1925-1970	236-248 W. 107th Pl., Roseland
1970-present	161st St. and Cottage Grove Ave., South Holland

Hulp in Nood (Help in Need) Mutual Aid Society (1913-??)
Vriendschap en Trouw (Friendship and Fidelity) Mutual Aid Society (1910-??)
Roseland Mutual Aid Society (1884-1985)
Flemish Mutual Aid Society (1906-??)

Dutch social clubs:

William of Orange Society (1890-1915)
General Dutch League (1905-??)
Saint Nicholas Society (1906-??)
Knickerbocker Society (1924-??)
Away and Home Frisian Society (1925-??)

APPENDIX 5

Church Membership, 1853-1978

Information in the following tables is derived from the *Acts and Proceedings of the General Synod of the Protestant Dutch Reformed Church in America*, 1850-1905; the Reformed Church in America's *Minutes of the General Synod of the Reformed Church in America*, 1906-2000; and the Christian Reformed Church's *Jaarboeken*, 1858-1923, and *Yearbooks*, 1924-2001. The yearbook totals are back-dated by one year; for example, the numbers reported in the year 1901 are listed for the year 1900.

An asterisk following a number indicates that it is an estimate derived by multiplying the number of families reported by five, which was reported as the average number of children in Dutch-American families in the 1900 federal census.

WEST SIDE AND FAR WEST

Year	1st Chic RCA	1st Chic CRC	Trinity RCA	N.W. RCA	D.P. CRC	3rd Chic CRC	4th Chic CRC	West Side RCA	1st Brwyn RCA	1st Cicero CRC	2nd Cicero CRC	Ebnzr Brwyn CRC	Oak Pk CRC	West Spr CRC	Lmbrd CRC	Archr Ave CRC	Dwnrs Grove RCA	Belwd CRC
1853																		
1854																		
1855	250*																	
1856																		
1857																		
1858																		
1859																		
1860	245*																	
1861	300*																	
1862	330*																	
1863	260*																	
1864	325*																	
1865	NR																	
1866	320*																	
1867	350*	NA																
1868	525*	NA																
1869	675*	NA																
1870	825*	NA																
1871	740*	NA																
1872	830*	NA																
1873	840*	430																
1874	950*	427																
1875	1050*	NA																
1876	1000*	NA																
1877	1030*	NA																

Year	1st Chic RCA	1st Chic CRC	Trinity RCA	N.W. RCA	D.P. CRC	3rd Chic CRC	4th Chic CRC	West Side RCA	1st Brwyn RCA	1st Cicero CRC	2nd Cicero CRC	Ebnzr Brwyn CRC	Oak Pk CRC	West Spr CRC	Lmbrd CRC	Archr Ave CRC	Dwnrs Grove RCA	Belwd CRC
1878	1085*	NA																
1879	1025*	NA																
1880	1000*	NA																
1881	1085	511																
1882	1003	511																
1883	1102	575																
1884	1189	600																
1885	1019	775																
1886	937	988																
1887	861*	NR																
1888	925	NR																
1889	895	NR																
1890	1112	530																
1891	1082	590																
1892	1083	590	202															
1893	1083	743	241	234														
1894	1130	1200	282	214														
1895	1068	1200	308	223														
1896	1113	1200	300	216														
1897	1114	1200	310	251														
1898	1118	1288	274	286														
1899	1159	1250	253	290														
1900	1190	882	275	289	167													
1901	1012	850	280	264	360													
1902	1027*	919	282*	267*	360													
1903	1104*	926	283*	149*	360													

Year	1st Chic RCA	1st Chic CRC	Trinity RCA	N.W. RCA	D.P. CRC	3rd Chic CRC	4th Chic CRC	West Side RCA	1st Brwyn RCA	1st Cicero CRC	2nd Cicero CRC	Ebnzr Brwyn CRC	Oak Pk CRC	West Spr CRC	Lmbrd CRC	Archr Ave CRC	Dwnrs Grove RCA	Belwd CRC
1904	774	1000	255	193	367													
1905	685	1077	235	187	500													
1907	690	1200	244	184	500													
1907	660	1200	243	191	540													
1908	655	1266	225	194	623													
1909	705	1244	232	194	660													
1910	685	1255	250	NR	675													
1911	873	1301	302	153	715													
1912	865	1263	283	133	710											54		
1913	855	1234	289	127	602	212										186		
1914	750	1134	285	118	577	288		230								200		
1915	658	1203	241	109	590	256		283								200		
1916	608	1200	249	100	625	301		302								190		
1917	581	1170	212	103	660	329		304								190		
1918	548	1173	216	86	665	322		347								219		
1919	566	1173		78	670	332		369								219		
1920	586	1200		100	680	377		416								210		
1921	599	1200		76	680	422		446								190		
1922	578	1242		76	715	426		432								189		
1923	595	1265		77	715	445		423								200		
1924	616	1150		78	715	445	315	431								216		
1925	643	1140		83	750	465	385	449								177		
1926	664	1100			740	490	418	456								181		
1927	649	1100			690	600	430	488								190		
1928	655	1100					480	515		720	690					190		
1929	658	1100					480	498		770	700					194		

Year	1st Chic RCA	1st Chic CRC	Trinity RCA	N.W. RCA	D.P. CRC	3rd Chic CRC	4th Chic CRC	West Side RCA	1st Brwyn RCA	1st Cicero CRC	2nd Cicero CRC	Ebnzr Brwyn CRC	Oak Pk CRC	West Spr CRC	Lmbrd CRC	Archr Ave CRC	Dwnrs Grove RCA	Belwd CRC
1930	627	1272					450	487		820	720					181		
1931	617	1304					450	497		841	731					166		
1932	618	1208					431	509		860	748					162		
1933	601	1176					405	533		885	756					175		
1934	541	1106					391	530		885	767					179		
1935	498	1123					350	553		1000	787					194		
1936	481	1023					375	567		1035	840					192		
1937	592	1068					397	565		1060	850					191		
1938	562	1043					405	571		1069	850					181		
1939	552	1100					420	598		1049	850			107		195		
1940	502	1153					346	585	81	1063	780		93	118		189		
1941	467	1178					310	585	120	1086	791		100	127		186		
1942	423	1121					336	601	123	1088	821		114	124		199		
1943	422	1140					335	640	64	1105	850		190	124		201		
1944	404	1152					350	659	72	1136	845		206	134		203		
1945	484	1027					312	666	NR	1142	841		217	140		206		
1946								626	476	1154	892	224	400	145		224		
1947								632	398	1128	910	750	480	130		251		
1948								627	416	1173	923	669	495	142		257		
1949								642	415	1201	901	662	366	150		252		
1950								641	416	1209	921	636	481	138		232		55
1951								635	398	1130	935	646	461	148		233		71
1952								648	406	1131	936	644	475	175		224		89
1953								639	397	1143	892	654	494	211		231		82
1954								562	353	1150	892	665	514	232		255		98
1955								572	362	1180	897	686	530	277		240		114

Year	1st Chic RCA	1st Chic CRC	Trinity RCA	N.W. RCA	D.P. CRC	3rd Chic CRC	4th Chic CRC	West Side RCA	1st Brwyn RCA	1st Cicero CRC	2nd Cicero CRC	Ebnzr Brwyn CRC	Oak Pk CRC	West Spr CRC	Lmbrd CRC	Archr Ave CRC	Dwnrs Grove RCA	Belwd CRC
1956								591	395	1095	872	721	510	317		260		136
1957								498	375	1106	871	755	497	353		262		146
1958								488	375	1074	840	748	513	387	102	272		193
1959								474	400	1087	861	743	494	394	117	266		216
1960								432	407	1061	840	763	492	452	159	240		220
1961								405	391	1063	840	775	484	495	210	231		230
1962								416	406	1017	843	776	509	549	229	223		238
1963								406	407	1002	850	781	518	626	265	212		268
1964								400	405	987	789	785	491	728	275	207		300
1965								386	404	897	789	800	481	756	340	203		398
1966								377	389	814	773	796	478	604	340	207		424
1967								379	400	752	773	792	456	789	347	200		435
1968								351	393	664	775	772	446	804	325	200	96	471
1969								355	389	606	770	730	426	793	320	207	111	539
1970								343	385	585	795	724	398	789	315	184	144	580
1971								334	364	556	816	669	405	819	326	168	149	600
1972								336	347	556	696	623	354	715	353	156	149	583
1973								328	348	497	694	590	278	792	360	166	162	582

ENGLEWOOD, EVERGREEN PARK, OAK LAWN, AND SOUTHWEST

Year	1st Eng RCA	1st Eng CRC	2nd Eng CRC	Hope RCA	Ev Pk 1st CRC	Pk Ln CRC	Summit RCA	Grn Oak Oak Ln RCA	1st Oak Ln CRC	Calvin Oak Ln CRC	Kedvale CRC	Aub Part CRC	Palos Hts RCA	Palos Hts CRC	Calvary Orl Pk RCA
1887	60*														
1888	74*														
1889	358	200													
1890	403	225													
1891	467	285													
1892	535	367													
1893	596	405													
1894	682	450													
1895	753	450													
1896	650*	648													
1897	635	700													
1898	650	760													
1899	938	760					91								
1900	1268	802					98								
1901	1045	890					90								
1902	1039*	890					94*								
1903	969*	890		186*			65*								
1904	940	970	79	140			95*								
1905	930	1020	106	179			111								
1906	841	1040	158	168			141								
1907	813	1043	158	226			161								
1908	781	1045	180	263			159								
1909	938	1037	158	265			170								
1910	1000	1037	77	300			174								
1911	1003	1215	80	308			191								

Year	1st Eng RCA	1st Eng CRC	2nd Eng CRC	Hope RCA	Ev Pk 1st CRC	Pk Ln CRC	Summit RCA	Grn Oak Oak Ln RCA	1st Oak Ln CRC	Calvin Oak Ln CRC	Kedvale CRC	Aub Part CRC	Palos Hts RCA	Palos Hts CRC	Calvary Orl Pk RCA
1912	835	1215	187	282			191								
1913	696	1248	185	304			197								
1914	750	1241	146	346			170								
1915	765	1290	146	361	130		192								
1916	685	1296	275	390	101		177		83						
1917	700	1188	281	367	138		110		113						
1918	765	1188	360	369	192		153		107						
1919	725	1208	368	294	192		171		106						
1920	730	1201	425	310	225		173		106						
1921	835	1201	458	354	325		183		110						
1922	840	1105	506	381	340		174		74						
1923	825	1120	545	400	350		170		90						
1924	804	1188	587	416	397		158		141						
1925	950	1241	640	414	415		165		174						
1926	999	1277	650	412	415		180		189						
1927	1086	1276	700	411	300		189		200						
1928	1130	1329	723	443	375		199		183						
1929	1208	1335	780	467	385		190		176						
1930	1213	1327	800	525	400		195		165						
1931	1236	1302	800	518	519		188		186						
1932	1255	1302	800	528	632		197		195						
1933	1255	1300	875	544	486		188		219						
1934	1161	1345	829	566	555		188		231						
1935	1167	1345	840	571	540		188		251						
1936	855	1300	860	565	573		189		264						
1937	867	1300	905	586	573		189		241						

Year	1st Eng RCA	1st Eng CRC	2nd Eng CRC	Hope RCA	Ev Pk 1st CRC	Pk Ln CRC	Summit RCA	Grn Oak Oak Ln RCA	1st Oak Ln CRC	Calvin Oak Ln CRC	Kedvale CRC	Aub Part CRC	Palos Hts RCA	Palos Hts CRC	Calvary Orl Pk RCA
1938	876	1300	950	608	531		196		229						
1939	864	1340	970	605	596		204		230						
1940	843	1340	1003	533	637		206		234						
1941	828	1347	1023	531	671		210		251						
1942	834	1410	1050	538	700		216		255						
1943	836	1487	1056	588	705		216		247						
1944	812	1515	1015	655	682		217		253						
1945	801	1511	1070	683	711		221		252						
1946	794	1560	1125	716	716		225		279						
1947	797	1205	1106	700	741		182		280			400			
1948	832	1205	1105	687	774		190		314			446			
1949	862	1085	656	787	787		184		303			470			
1950	801	1102	1098	618	827		223		331			515			
1951	823	1109	1097	697	886		210		343			552			
1952	824	1098	1085	713	945		267		348			562			
1953	812	1056	1066	731	1041		278		388			542			
1954	817	1033	999	735	785	445	301		450			487			
1955	807	1062	950	600	830	519	310		475			474			
1956	802	1031	879	550	892	528	312	58	490			424		150	
1957	793	1000	830	669	917	581	338	70	520			425		205	
1958	793	999	770	608	933	599	326	88	597			436		286	
1959	549	1001	708	566	955	627	313	127	647			404		319	
1960	791	939	697	608	977	674	312	164	627			368		354	
1961	781	864	678	615	980	716	316	169	654			385	91	380	
1962		760	599	615	998	729	320	209	711			363	127	416	772
1963				580	983	723	298	247	727	595	511	332	138	455	762

Year	1st Eng RCA	1st Eng CRC	2nd Eng CRC	Hope RCA	Ev Pk 1st CRC	Pk Ln CRC	Summit RCA	Grn Oak Oak Ln RCA	1st Oak Ln CRC	Calvin Oak Ln CRC	Kedvale CRC	Aub Part CRC	Palos Hts RCA	Palos Hts CRC	Calvary Orl Pk RCA
1964				562	954	699	342	247	732	578	526	293	147	493	800
1965				537	846	716	342	305	681	549	556	289	175	606	834
1966				502	853	682	346	344	648	538	564	297	199	647	826
1967				503	802	669	355	364	648	562	570	312	192	722	820
1968				493	809	667	341	332	618	559	570	287	240	781	768
1969				482	788	680	338	351	572	590	603	270	256	853	746
1970				455	9790	656	318	386	611	667	596	278	261	853	724
1971				422	742	648	351	408	569	713	561	265	276	961	675
1972				350	690	637	344	428	599	725	568	270	315	1001	644
1973				367	673	583	328	461	585	707	712	237	344	997	594
1974							338	470					571		561
1975							332	495					591		540

ROSELAND AND SOUTHWEST

Year	1st Roseland RCA	1st Roseland CRC	Bethany RCA	2nd Roseland CRC	3rd Roseland CRC	4th Roseland CRC	Emmanuel RCA	Gano RCA	Alsip-Worth RCA	Mount Greenwood RCA	Lynwd CRC	Orlnd Park CRC
1853	na											
1854	na											
1855	200*											
1856	200*											
1857	150*											
1858	150*											
1859	150*											
1860	215*											
1861	220*											
1862	250*											
1863	230*											
1864	250*											
1865	na											
1866	295*											
1867	315*											
1868	365*											
1869	445*											
1870	440*											
1871	450*											
1872	460*											
1873	485*											
1874	590*											
1875	625*											
1876	605*											
1877	620*											

Year	1st Roseland RCA	1st Roseland CRC	Bethany RCA	2nd Roseland CRC	3rd Roseland CRC	4th Roseland CRC	Emmanuel RCA	Gano RCA	Alsip-Worth RCA	Mount Greenwood RCA	Lynwd CRC	Orlnd Park CRC
1878	460*											
1879	495*											
1880	505*											
1881	555*	250										
1882	713	339										
1883	746	495										
1884	829	490										
1885	932*	600										
1886	958	965										
1887	984*	622										
1888	1100	751										
1889	1173	830										
1890	1207	984										
1891	1384	1185	65*									
1892	1404	1332	121									
1893	1367	1479	161									
1894	1433	1114	206	500								
1895	1455	1060	236	620								
1896	1514	1160	265	620								
1897	1535	1240	300	714								
1898	1513	1294	355	714								
1899	1510	1127	412	800								
1900	1220	1193	444	898				692				
1901	1315	1241	474	975				604				
1902	1307*	1160	483*	975				592*				
1903	1355*	1130	520*	975				660*				

Year	1st Roseland RCA	1st Roseland CRC	Bethany RCA	2nd Roseland CRC	3rd Roseland CRC	4th Roseland CRC	Emmanuel RCA	Gano RCA	Alsip-Worth RCA	Mount Greenwood RCA	Lynwd CRC	Orlnd Park CRC
1904	1554	1115	572	1067				429				
1905	1270	1041	589	1094				554				
1906	1270	908	561	1050				570				
1907	1225	908	567	1120				610				
1908	1370	1000	650	1168	144			650				
1909	1406	959	710	1012	185			657				
1910	1394	938	763	1034	246			660				
1911	1431	992	714	1068	282			657				
1912	1447	1063	712	1022	304			539				
1913	1436	1013	725	1066	340			542				
1914	1421	1011	760	1116	375			675		150*		
1915	1353	936	770	1114	420		79	531		283		
1916	1708	1062	815	1114	460		123	531		367		
1917	1718	1050	791	1083	450		183	482		356		
1918	1697	942	800	985	438		180	478		390		
1919	1678	942	775	935	450		190	486		391		
1920	1640	933	830	722	475	90	224	446		320		
1921	1686	822	875	835	485	149	297	457		335		
1922	1727	836	920	853	535	116	297	540		355		
1923	1632	843	881	825	510	223	332	553		381		
1924	1593	875	868	840	520	285	356	469		396		
1925	1589	954	863	876	520	290	370	485		432		
1926	1565	1070	961	905	550	314	419	514		493		
1927	1522	1042	1027	868	629	294	456	491		502		
1928	1500	1015	1066	802	655	343	497	441		511		
1929	1482	1004	1171	771	652	349	569	499		548		

Year	1st Roseland RCA	1st Roseland CRC	Bethany RCA	2nd Roseland CRC	3rd Roseland CRC	4th Roseland CRC	Emmanuel RCA	Gano RCA	Alsip-Worth RCA	Mount Greenwood RCA	Lynwd CRC	Orlnd Park CRC
1930	1425	1084	1497	750	640	370	625	413		560		
1931	1435	1084	1723	700	640	373	642	442		575		
1932	1438	1084	1697	708	640	368	657	440		574		
1933	1426	1224	1855	713	655	368	685	457		588		
1934	1395	1224	1927	713	651	383	888	451		641		
1935	1324	1244	2120	661	655	394	917	424		648		
1936	1214	1224	1937	685	655	401	950	428		567		
1937	1226	1110	2039	693	655	395	922	374		650		
1938	1219	1248	2088	707	655	393	923	368		656		
1939	1222	1232	2152	685	655	401	951	366		766		
1940	1236	1250	2303	672	675	402	991	369		789		
1942	1235	1274	2187	723	679	402	1046	350		767		
1943	1267	1301	2306	728	667	406	1095	265		780		
1944	1284	1304	2399	735	667	423	1150	288		793		
1945	1290	1331	2419	764	635	419	1119	297		887		
1946	1290	1348	2428	812	684	432	1180	405		789		
1947	1166	1242	2371	825	674	436	1185	285	64	784		
1948	1226	1210	2142	781	655	445	967	295	63	790		
1949	1279	1248	2255	780	655	492	963	290	80	802		
1950	1282	1211	2307	780	656	448	949	324	87	827		
1951	1292	1251	2320	785	638	461	964	354	104	843		
1952	1290	1263	2355	743	644	472	962	363	138	856		
1953	1232	1219	2420	690	626	502	959	356	151	867		
1954	1229	1196	2400	745	592	540	956	354	167	878		
1955	1234	1222	2366	755	586	531	879	354	179	905		
1956	1223	1148	2031	783	563	507	806	356	187	919		

Year	1st Roseland RCA	1st Roseland CRC	Bethany RCA	2nd Roseland CRC	3rd Roseland CRC	4th Roseland CRC	Emmanuel RCA	Gano RCA	Alsip-Worth RCA	Mount Greenwood RCA	Lynwd CRC	Orlnd Park CRC
1957	1180	1134	2005	788	555	547	765	328	188	859		
1958	1173	1101	2031	775	555	567	708	310	212	872		
1959	1210	1086	1845	768	549	552	699	307	262	900		
1960	1133	1055	1653	792	538	528	612	303	280	890		
1961	1188	1042	1530	786	536	503	701	291	279	796		
1962	1057	1017	1510	809	551	521	677	290	264	807		
1963	1108	1003	1499	826	532	549	645	280	270	834		
1964	1097	986	1562	850	508	509	651	267	233	854		
1965	1085	953	1537	845	533	493	642	251	243	832		
1966	1103	960	1547	812	537	496	630	264	255	838		
1967	1125	922	1562	802	571	468	449	257	220	854		
1968	1117	858	1528	733	524	430	459	255	210	849		
1969	1118	788	1229	631	465	388	435	252	188	836		
1970	951	697	1170	484	430	330	400	211	200	845		
1971		546	1075	379	350	349	349	217	152	855		
1972			1029	249			242	218	148	797		275
1973			953				181		204	778	203	351
1974			751				153		207	721	226	496
1975			529				157		203	678		
1976							133		194	668		
1977							188		194	611		
1978							205		188	619		

Bibliography

I. Archival and Public Sources

Chicago Christian Junior College Minute Books, 1931-1937, The Archives, Calvin College.

Chicago and Suburban Ash and Scavenger Association Minutes, 1934-43.

Forest Home Cemetery, Records of Interments, Newberry Library.

Holstein, Luurt, Papers, The Archives, Calvin College.

Iwema, Bonne, Papers, The Archives, Calvin College.

Kuyper, B. K., Papers, The Archives, Calvin College.

Timothy Christian School Papers, The Archives, Calvin College.

University of Chicago, Board of Trustees Minutes, 1909-14, University of Chicago Archives.

Van Eyck, Hendrik, Diary, Holland Museum Collections, Joint Archives of Holland.

Vander Hill, George, Papers, The Archives, Calvin College.

Van Weelden, Henry, Chicago Newspaper Scrapbook, 1960-75.

Venema, John, Papers, Holland Museum Collections, Joint Archives of Holland.

Wezeman, Frederick H., Papers, The Archives, Calvin College.

II. Minutes of the Churches, Classes, and Synods

Christian Reformed Church, Classical and Synodical Minutes, 1857-1880. English-language typescript in The Archives, Calvin College.

Classis Chicago North, Christian Reformed Church, The Archives, Calvin College.

Classis Northern Illinois, Christian Reformed Church, The Archives, Calvin College.

Classis of Chicago, Reformed Church in America, Western Seminary Collection, Joint Archives of Holland.

Classis of Wisconsin, Reformed Church in America, Western Seminary Collection, Joint Archives of Holland.

Douglas Park Christian Reformed Church, 1899-1927. The Archives, Calvin College.

First Christian Reformed Church of Chicago, 1867-1946. The Archives, Calvin College.

First Reformed Church of Chicago, 1853-1945. Western Seminary Collection, Joint Archives of Holland.

III. Newspapers

Berwyn Life, 1969, 1976.
Calumet Index, 1938, 1949.
Chicago's American, 1929, 1960-61.
Chicago Calvinist, 1954.
Chicago Daily Journal, 1851.
Chicago Daily News, 1909, 1929, 1940-70.
Chicago Daily News/Chicago Sun Times, 1971-80.
Chicago Evening Post, 1929.
Chicago Herald and Examiner, 1929.
Chicago Magazine, 1990.
Chicago Messenger, 1934-36.
Chicago Record-Herald, 1908 (became *Herald and Examiner*), 1929.
Chicago Star, 2001.
Chicago Sun-Times, 1976, 1999-2000.
Chicago Tribune, 1898-1901, 1929-2001.
Cicero News, 1942.
Church Observer. See *Weekly Observer.*
DIS (Dutch Immigrant Society Magazine), 1985.
Grand Rapids (Michigan) *Herald,* 1937.
Grand Rapids (Michigan) *News,* 1915.
Grand Rapids (Michigan) *Press,* 2000.
Grondwet, De (Holland, Michigan), 1860-1930.
Holland (Michigan) *Sentinel,* 1897, 1997.
Hollander, De (Holland, Michigan), 1853-76
Hope, De (Holland, Michigan), 1865-1933.
Illinois Observer. See *Weekly Observer.*
Jewish Messenger (New York), 1896.
Nieuw Amsterdammer, De, 1995.
Occident (New York), 1847-65.

Onze Toekomst. 1894-1953 (incomplete files at The Archives, Calvin Archives, and the University of Chicago Library). The Chicago Foreign Language Press Survey (1936-41), sponsored by the Chicago Public Library and funded by the Federal Work Projects Administration, hired native speakers to translate key sections of Chicago newspapers, including the Dutch-language weekly, *Onze Toekomst.* The information was initially typed on 5″ × 8″ cards and later microfilmed. The years of *Onze Toekomst* covered by the survey include 1906-13, 1919-27. Since no original issues are extant for many of those years, this is a crucial resource. For a description of the project, see *The Chicago Foreign Language Press Survey: A General Description of Its Contents.* Chicago, Ill.: Chicago Public Library Omnibus Project, Work Projects Administration, 1942.

Southtown Economist, 1949.

Wall Street Journal, 1996-99.

Weekly Observer, 1951-54, successor to *Onze Toekomst.* Became *Illinois Observer* (monthly), 1955-60, and then *Church Observer* (monthly), 1960-64.

Windmill, The, 2000.

IV. Periodicals

Association of Christian Reformed Laymen *News Bulletin.* 1971.

Banner, The, 1915-2000.

Chicago City Directories, 1856-57, 1870-1920.

Christian Home and School Magazine, 1960.

Christian Intelligencer, The. Weekly Magazine of the Reformed Church in America. 1890-1930. See Peter Moerdyke, "Chicago Letter." 1892-1907.

Church Herald, The, 1950-90.

Contact: Monthly Newsletter of the First Christian Reformed Church of Roseland, May 1967.

DIS [Dutch Immigrant Society] Magazine, 1985.

Grundy College Messenger, 1926.

Minute Man: Bulletin of the Christian Reformed Laymen's League, 1967.

Missionary Monthly, 1945-60.

Refuse Removal Journal, 1958-73. Became *Waste Systems Digest,* 1973-2000.

Timothy Reflector, 1983, 1988.

Torch and Trumpet, 1957.

Wachter, De, 1868-1930.

V. Church Anniversary Booklets, Directories, Dedications

Archer Avenue Christian Reformed Church. *Twenty-fifth Anniversary, 1911-1936.* Chicago, 1936.

———. *Seventy-Fifth Diamond Anniversary, 1911-1986.* Chicago, 1986.

Auburn Park Christian Reformed Church. *Dedication Souvenir.* Chicago, 1947.

Bethany Reformed Church of Lynwood, Illinois. *One Hundredth Anniversary Historical Booklet.* Lynwood, Ill., 1990.

———. *Seventy Fifth Anniversary Historical Booklet, 1890-1965.* Chicago, 1965.

Bethany Reformed Church of Roseland. *Fiftieth Anniversary Historical Booklet, 1890-1940.* Chicago, 1940.

Bethel Reformed Church of Chicago. *75th Anniversary, 1899-1974.* Chicago, 1974.

Calvin Christian Reformed Church. *A Century of Blessings, Calvin Church, 100 Years, 1887-1987.* Oak Lawn, 1987.

———. *75th Anniversary and Dedication, February 13, 14, 15, 1963.* Chicago, 1963.

Classis Chicago South. *Precious Heritage, Promising Future: Classis Chicago South Celebrates the 125th Anniversary of the Christian Reformed Church, 1857-1982.* Chicago, 1982.

Douglas Park Christian Reformed Church. *Ebenhaezer, 1899-1924: Vijf en Twentig-Jarig Bestaan van de Douglas Park Chr. Geref. Gemeente.* Chicago, 1924.

Ebenezer Christian Reformed Church. *Centennial Booklet, 1867-1967.* Berwyn, 1967.

———. *Dedication Booklet.* Berwyn, 1949.

———. *125th Anniversary, 1867-1992.* Berwyn, Ill., 1992.

Elmhurst Christian Reformed Church. *Thirty-Five Years of God's Blessing.* Elmhurst, Ill., 1984.

———. *Dedication, April 3, 1964.* Elmhurst, Ill., 1964.

Emmanuel Reformed Church. *The Story of Emmanuel: 1914-1939.* Chicago, 1939.

———. *Dedication Memories: 1946.* Chicago, 1946.

———. *Golden Anniversary, 1914-1964.* Chicago, 1964.

Evergreen Park Christian Reformed Church. *Fiftieth Anniversary, 1915-1965.* Evergreen Park, 1965.

———. *Dedication Souvenir, 1931.* Evergreen Park, 1931.

———. *Diamond Jubilee, 1915-1990.* Evergreen Park, 1990.

Faith Christian Reformed Church of Elmhurst. *Dedication Program.* Elmhurst, Ill., 1977.

———. *Pictorial Directory.* Elmhurst, Ill., 1981.

First Christian Reformed Church of Chicago, *Ebenhaezer 1867-1917: Herdenking van het Vijftig-jarig Bestaan van de Eerste Chr. Ger. Gem. 14th Street, Chicago.* Chicago, 1917.

———. *Fiftieth Anniversary, King's Daughters' Young Ladies' Societies.* Chicago, 1945.

———. *Seventy-fifth Anniversary, 1867-1942.* Chicago, 1942.

First Christian Reformed Church of Cicero. *Commemoration of the Twenty-Fifth Anniversary, October 3, 1912–October 3, 1937.* Cicero, 1937.

———. *Dedication Program, "Deo Gratias," 22 November 1926.* Cicero, 1926.
———. *Directory,* 1932. Cicero, 1932.
———. *Golden Anniversary, 1912-1962.* Cicero, 1962.
———. *Celebrating Seventy-Five Years, 1912-1987.* Cicero, 1987.
First Christian Reformed Church of Englewood. *Dedication Souvenir.* Chicago, 1931.
First Christian Reformed Church of Roseland. *Directory,* 1956. Chicago, 1956.
———. *Sixtieth Anniversary Directory, 1877-1937.* Chicago, 1937.
———. *Seventy-Fifth Anniversary, 1877-1952.* Chicago, 1952.
———. *Twenty-Fifth Anniversary of the Ministry of Rev. Frank Doezema as Pastor of the First Christian Reformed Church of Roseland.* Chicago, 1939.
First Christian Reformed Church of South Holland. *75th Anniversary, 1886-1961.* South Holland, 1961.
First Reformed Church of Chicago. *A Century for Christ, 1853-1953.* Chicago, 1953.
First Reformed Church of Englewood. *Dedication Booklet.* Chicago, 1958.
———. *50th Anniversary Booklet.* Chicago, 1936.
———. *75th Anniversary.* Chicago, 1961.
First Reformed Church of Gano. *75th Anniversary, 1891-1966.* Chicago, 1966.
First Reformed Church of Lansing. *Centennial, 1861-1961.* Lansing, 1961.
First Reformed Church of Mount Greenwood. *50th Anniversary Booklet, 1913-1963.* Chicago, 1963.
First Reformed Church of Roseland. *A Century for Christ: Centennial, 1849-1949.* Chicago, 1949.
———. *Ninetieth Anniversary, Historical Booklet and Directory, 1849-1939.* Chicago, 1939.
First Reformed Church of South Holland. *Centennial, 1848-1948.* South Holland, 1948.
Fourth Christian Reformed Church of Chicago. *Official Directory,* 1925. Chicago, 1925.
Fourth Christian Reformed Church of Roseland. *In Commemoration of the Fiftieth Anniversary, 1919-1969.* Chicago, 1969.
———. *In Commemoration of the Twenty-Fifth Anniversary, 1919-1944.* Chicago, 1944.
Hope Reformed Church of Englewood. *71 Years of Service.* Chicago, 1973.
Kedvale Avenue Christian Reformed Church. *75th Anniversary, Diamond Memories, 1903-1978.* Oak Lawn, 1978.
Lombard Christian Reformed Church. *Celebrating Seventy-Five Years, October 9, 1987.* Lombard, Ill., 1987.
Lynwood Christian Reformed Church. *Centennial, 1877-1977.* Lynwood, Ill., 1977.
Nathanael Institute. *Souvenir of the Nathaniel Institute, 1919-1929.* Chicago, 1929.
Palos Heights Reformed Church. *Building for Eternity: Dedication-Autumn 1972.* Palos Heights, Ill., 1972.
Park Lane Christian Reformed Church of Evergreen Park. *25 Years 1953-1978.* Evergreen Park, 1978.
———. *Dedication Book, March, 1955.* Evergreen Park, 1955.

Second Christian Reformed Church of Cicero. *Directory*, 1932. Cicero, 1932.
———. *Directory*, 1934. Cicero, 1934.
Second Christian Reformed Church of Englewood. *Forty-fifth Anniversary, 1903-1948*. Chicago, 1948.
———. *Fiftieth Anniversary, 1903-1953*. Chicago, 1953.
Second Christian Reformed Church of Roseland. *Fifty-fifth Anniversary, Historical Booklet and Rededication Program, 1893-1949*. Chicago, 1949.
———. *Seventy-fifth Anniversary, 1893-1968*. Chicago, 1968.
Second Reformed Church of Englewood. *History of the Second Reformed Church of Englewood, 1902-1914, and Church Directory, 1914*. Chicago, 1914.
———. *Fiftieth Anniversary, 1903-1053*. Chicago, 1953.
Third Christian Reformed Church of Chicago. "Brief Historical Record of Third Christian Reformed Church of Chicago," sixteen-page handwritten manuscript, no author or date, archived at the Faith Christian Reformed Church of Elmhurst.
———. *Directory*, May 1925. Chicago, 1925.
———. *Directory*, 1926. Chicago, 1926.
Thorn Creek Reformed Church, South Holland, Illinois. *125th Anniversary, 1849-1974*. South Holland, Ill., 1974.
Trinity Reformed Church. *Twenty-Fifth Anniversary*. Chicago, 1916.
Warren Park Christian Reformed Church. *Golden Anniversary, 1899-1949*. Cicero, 1949.
———. *Directory*, 1950. Cicero, 1950.
West Side Reformed Church of Chicago. *Fiftieth Anniversary Program and Historical Sketch, 1911-1961*. Cicero, 1961.
———. *Fortieth Anniversary, 1911-1951*. Cicero, 1951.
———. *Program and Historical Sketch of the Twenty-fifth Anniversary, 1911-1936*. Cicero, 1936.
———. *West Side News*. 1958.
West Suburban Christian Reformed Church of Elmhurst. *Pictorial Directory*, 1975. Elmhurst, 1975.

VI. School Histories, Anniversary Booklets, Yearbooks, Newspapers, and Publications

Calvin College *Chimes*, 1969-71.
Chicago Christian High School Board of Trustees. *The Illuminator*, 1936.
———. *The Truth About the Chicago Situation*. Chicago, 1936.
Chicago Christian High School. *50th Anniversary, 1918-1968*.
———. *75th Anniversary, 1918-1993*.
———. *Crusaders*, 1949-1953.
———. *Mirror*, 1930-51.

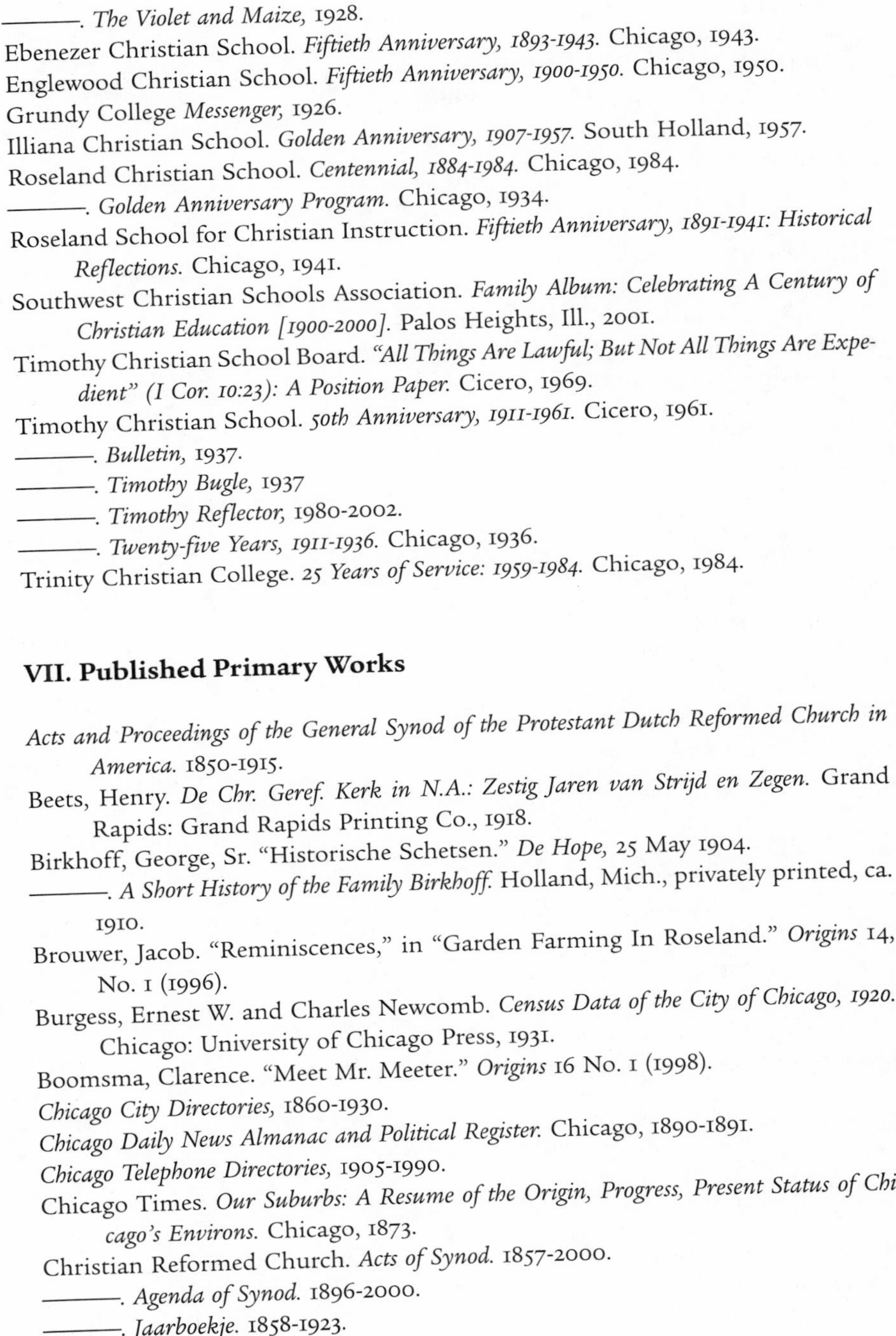

———. *The Violet and Maize,* 1928.
Ebenezer Christian School. *Fiftieth Anniversary, 1893-1943.* Chicago, 1943.
Englewood Christian School. *Fiftieth Anniversary, 1900-1950.* Chicago, 1950.
Grundy College *Messenger,* 1926.
Illiana Christian School. *Golden Anniversary, 1907-1957.* South Holland, 1957.
Roseland Christian School. *Centennial, 1884-1984.* Chicago, 1984.
———. *Golden Anniversary Program.* Chicago, 1934.
Roseland School for Christian Instruction. *Fiftieth Anniversary, 1891-1941: Historical Reflections.* Chicago, 1941.
Southwest Christian Schools Association. *Family Album: Celebrating A Century of Christian Education [1900-2000].* Palos Heights, Ill., 2001.
Timothy Christian School Board. *"All Things Are Lawful; But Not All Things Are Expedient" (I Cor. 10:23): A Position Paper.* Cicero, 1969.
Timothy Christian School. *50th Anniversary, 1911-1961.* Cicero, 1961.
———. *Bulletin,* 1937.
———. *Timothy Bugle,* 1937
———. *Timothy Reflector,* 1980-2002.
———. *Twenty-five Years, 1911-1936.* Chicago, 1936.
Trinity Christian College. *25 Years of Service: 1959-1984.* Chicago, 1984.

VII. Published Primary Works

Acts and Proceedings of the General Synod of the Protestant Dutch Reformed Church in America. 1850-1915.
Beets, Henry. *De Chr. Geref. Kerk in N.A.: Zestig Jaren van Strijd en Zegen.* Grand Rapids: Grand Rapids Printing Co., 1918.
Birkhoff, George, Sr. "Historische Schetsen." *De Hope,* 25 May 1904.
———. *A Short History of the Family Birkhoff.* Holland, Mich., privately printed, ca. 1910.
Brouwer, Jacob. "Reminiscences," in "Garden Farming In Roseland." *Origins* 14, No. 1 (1996).
Burgess, Ernest W. and Charles Newcomb. *Census Data of the City of Chicago, 1920.* Chicago: University of Chicago Press, 1931.
Boomsma, Clarence. "Meet Mr. Meeter." *Origins* 16 No. 1 (1998).
Chicago City Directories, 1860-1930.
Chicago Daily News Almanac and Political Register. Chicago, 1890-1891.
Chicago Telephone Directories, 1905-1990.
Chicago Times. *Our Suburbs: A Resume of the Origin, Progress, Present Status of Chicago's Environs.* Chicago, 1873.
Christian Reformed Church. *Acts of Synod.* 1857-2000.
———. *Agenda of Synod.* 1896-2000.
———. *Jaarboekje.* 1858-1923.

———. *Yearbook.* 1924-2001.

Christian Reformed Laymen's Association of Chicago, Illinois. *Shall We Have PEACE, LOVE, and UNITY or STRIFE, ENMITY, and DIVISION in our Christian Reformed Church.* Chicago: Christian Literature Publishing Company, [1937].

Classis Holland Minutes, 1848-1858. Grand Rapids: Eerdmans, 1950.

Clayton, John, comp. *The Illinois Fact Book and Historical Almanac, 1673-1968.* Carbondale and Edwardsville, IL: Southern Illinois University Press, 1970.

De Bey, Bernardus. *Eene laaste getuigenis. Afscheidswoord uitgesproken in de Eerste Gereformeerde Kerk te Chicago. Op Zondag den 1. November 1891* [A last testimony. Farewell address given in the First Reformed Church of Chicago. On Sunday November 1, 1891]. Chicago, 1891.

———. "Chicago letters." *Provinciale Groninger Courant.* 1869-1871.

De Bey, Bernardus, and Adriaan Zwemer. *Stemmen uit de Hollandsch-Gereformeerde Kerk in de Ver. Staten van Amerika.* Groningen, 1871. Section IX, "In the Chicago Congregation." English translation typescript at The Archives, Calvin College.

Corwin, Charles E. *A Manual of the Reformed Church in America, 1628-1922.* New York, 1922.

Directory of Cook County Elected Officials. 4th ed., 1 June 1997.

Eenigenburg, Harry. *The Calumet Region and Its Early Settlers.* Chicago: privately published, 1935.

Ettema, Ross, comp. "Roseland Mutual Aid Society." Chicago, 1990.

Ettema, Ross, and Peggy Goodwin Ettema, compilers. *The Dutch Connection in South Cook County Since 1847.* Chicago: privately printed, 1984.

Fergus' Directory of the City of Chicago for 1839. Chicago: Fergus Printing Co., 1876.

Gasero, Russell, ed. *Historical Directory of the Reformed Church in America, 1628-1992.* Grand Rapids: Eerdmans, 1992.

Gereformeerde Kerken in Nederland. *Honderd veertig jaar gemeenten en predikanten van de Gereformeerde Kerken in Nederland.* 1974.

Huizenga Story, The: Or the Descendants of Jacob Willems and Anje Leues. Privately printed. Chicago, 1993.

Knickerbocker Society of Chicago, 1931-1932. Chicago, 1932.

Kuiper, Herman. *The Chicago Situation: A Word of Warning to the Churches.* Chicago: Chicago Calvin Press, 1936.

League of Reformed Young Men's Societies of Chicago and Vicinity. *Yearbooks.* 1932-35.

Lest We Forget: Chicago's Awful Theater Horror. Chicago: Memorial Publishing Co., 1904.

Monsma, John C. *Why the American Daily Standard Failed and How It Is Going to Win.* Grand Rapids: Seymour and Muir, 1921.

Nicolay, Johan. "Recollections of Johan Nicolay: Roseland, Illinois and Lark, North Dakota." *Origins* 8 No. 1 (1995).

Pictorial Roseland, 1907. West Pullman, 1907.

Reformed Church in America. *Minutes of the General Synod of the Reformed Church in America.* 1906-2000.

———. *125 Years of the Synod of Chicago, Reformed Church in America, 1856-1981.* Chicago, 1981.

Report of the Reformed and Christian Reformed Churches of Chicago and Its Suburbs on Closer Co-operation with the Chicago Christian High School. Chicago, 1930.

Schaver, John L. *Christian Reformed Church Order, A Manual of the Church Order Adopted by the Synod of 1914. . . .* Grand Rapids: Eerdmans, 1941.

Schuppert, Mildred W., ed. *A Digest and Index of the Minutes of the General Synod of the Reformed Church in America, 1906-1957.* Grand Rapids: Eerdmans, 1957.

Stellingwerff, J. *Amsterdamse emigranten: onbekende brieven uit de prairie van Iowa, 1846-1873.* Amsterdam: Buijten & Schipperheijn, 1976.

Swierenga, Robert P., comp. *Dutch Emigrants to the United States, South Africa, South America, and Southeast Asia, 1835-1880: An Alphabetical Listing by Household Heads and Independent Persons.* Wilmington, Del.: Scholarly Resources, 1983.

———. *Dutch Households in U.S. Population Censuses, 1850, 1860, 1870: An Alphabetical Listing by Family Heads.* 3 vols. Wilmington, Del.: Scholarly Resources, 1987.

———. *Dutch Immigrants in U.S. Ship Passenger Manifests, 1820-1880: An Alphabetical Listing by Household Heads and Independent Persons.* 2 vols. Wilmington, Del.: Scholarly Resources, 1987.

———. "Dutch in Chicago and Cook County Federal Censuses, 1850-1870." 1987.

———. "Dutch in Chicago and Cook County 1880 Federal Census." 1989.

———. "Dutch in Chicago and Cook County 1900 Federal Census." 1992.

———. *Family Tree Maker's Family Archives, Immigration Records: Dutch in America, 1800s.* CD #269. Broderbund, 2000. Contains published and unpublished listings.

Teninga, Cornelius. *The Roseland District of Chicago: Some Facts.* Chicago: Teninga Bros., 1924.

Tiemersma, Richard R. "Growing Up in Roseland in the 20's & 30's." *Origins* 5, No. 1 (1987).

University of Chicago. *Annual Register, July, 1910–July, 1911.* Chicago: University of Chicago Press, 1911.

Wesseling, J. *De Afscheiding van 1834 in Groningerland.* 3 vols. Groningen: Vuurbank, 1972-78.

Yearbook of the Holland Society of Chicago, 1895-1896. Chicago, 1897.

Yearbook of the Holland Society of Chicago, 1897-1900. Chicago, 1901.

VIII. Secondary Works

Andreas, Alfred T. *History of Chicago from the Earliest Period to the Present Time.* 3 vols. Chicago: A. T. Andreas Publisher, 1884-86.

Antonides, Harry. "The Basis of Secular Trade Unions: an alleged religious neutrality." *Torch and Trumpet* (Sept. 1963).

Bakker, W., O. J. de Jong, W. van't Spijker, L. J. Wolthuis, eds. *De Afscheiding van 1834 en haar geschiedenis.* Kampen: J. H. Kok, 1984.

Beets, Henry. *Life and Times of Jannes Van de Luyster, Founder of Zeeland, Michigan.* Zeeland: Zeeland Record Company, 1949.

Berman, Morton Mayer. *Our First Century, 1852-1952: Temple Isaiah Israel.* Chicago: Temple Isaiah Israel, 1952.

Bolkema, Shannon. "City Conflict Blocks Church Sale, Move." *Church Herald,* Dec. 2000.

Bouma, Hendrik. *Secession, Doleantie, and Union: 1834-1892.* Translation of *De vereniging van 1892* (1917) by Theodore Plantinga. Neerlandia, Alberta, and Pella, Ia.: Inheritance Publications, 1995.

Bousema-Valkema, Ann G. *Valk De Valk Valkema.* 1998.

Bratt, James D. *Dutch Calvinism in Modern America: A History of a Conservative Subculture.* Grand Rapids: Eerdmans, 1984.

Bregstone, Philip P. *Chicago and Its Jews: A Cultural History.* Chicago: privately published, 1933.

Brinks, Herbert J. "The Americanization of Bernardus De Beij (1815-1894)." *Origins* 6, No. 1 (1988).

———. "Bernardus De Beij (1815-1894)." *Origins* 1, No. 1 (1983).

———. "The Calumet Region." *Origins* 2 No. 1 (1984).

———, ed. *Dutch American Voices: Letters from the United States, 1850-1930.* Ithaca, N.Y.: Cornell University Press, 1995.

———. "Henry Wierenga: Sunday Isn't Sabbath." *Origins* 13, No. 2 (1993).

———. "Johanna (Gelderloos) LaMaire: Notes from and about the Past." *Origins* 11, No. 1 (1993).

———. "Netherlanders in the Chicago Area." *Origins* 1, No. 1 (1983).

———. "A View from the Parsonage: Klaas Kuiper and His Family." *Origins* 4, No. 1 (1986).

Brix, Shawn. *In The Master's Service: The Life of Tena Huizenga.* Grand Rapids: Calvin Theological Seminary, 1964.

Buder, Stanley. *Pullman: An Experiment in Industrial Order and Community Planning, 1880-1930.* New York: Oxford University Press, 1967.

Buiten, William. "Increases Granted on Illinois' Axle-Weights." *Refuse Removal Journal* 14 (Nov. 1971).

Bulthuis, Peter. *Footprints: An Autobiography.* Privately printed, 5th ed., 1998.

Chicago Department of Development and Planning. *The People of Chicago: Who We Are and Who We Have Been.* Chicago, 1976.

Collette, Will, et al. *Browning Ferris Industries: A Corporate Profile.* Citizen's Clearinghouse for Hazardous Waste. July, 1987.

Conroy, Joseph P., S.J. *Arnold Damen, S.J.: A Chapter in the Making of Chicago.* New York: Benzinger Brothers, 1930.

Cook, Richard C. *South Holland, Illinois: A History, 1846-1966.* South Holland: South Holland Trust and Savings Bank, 1966.

Cutler, Irving. *Chicago: Metropolis of the Mid-Continent.* 3rd ed. Dubuque, Ia.: Geographic Society of Chicago, 1982.

———. *The Jews of Chicago: From Shtetl to Suburb.* Chicago: University of Chicago Press, 1996.

Davids, Clarence, Sr. *Out of Air and Onto the Ground: The Clarence Davids Story.* Enumclaw, Wash.: Winepress Publishing, 1999.

De Boer, Peter. "To Train a Teacher," *Origins* 8, No. 2 (1990).

De Jong, Gerald F. "The Controversy over Dropping the Word Dutch from the Name of the Reformed Church." *Reformed Review* 34 (Spring 1981).

———. *The Dutch in America, 1609-1974.* Boston: Twayne, 1975.

———. *The Dutch Reformed Church in the American Colonies.* Grand Rapids: Eerdmans, 1978.

———. *From Strength to Strength: A History of Northwestern College, 1882-1982.* Grand Rapids: Eerdmans, 1982.

De Jong, Peter C. "The Settlement of Roseland, Illinois." A series of fifteen articles in *Onze Toekomst,* April-July, 1949.

De Jong, Peter Y. "Should the Church Follow Its Members?" *Torch and Trumpet* 10 (April 1961).

De Jong, Peter Y., and Nelson D. Kloosterman, eds. *The Reformation of 1834: Essays in Commemoration of the Act of Secession and Return.* Orange City, Ia.: Pluim Publishing Co., 1984.

De Klerk, Peter, and Richard R. De Ridder, eds. *Perspectives on the Christian Reformed Church: Studies in Its History, Theology, and Ecumenicity.* Grand Rapids: Baker Book House, 1983.

De Kok, J. A. *Nederland op de breuklijn Rome-Reformatie.* Assen: Van Gorcum, 1964.

De Kruyter, Arthur. "On Being Editor of the Observer." *The Chicago Calvinist,* 15 Apr. 1954.

De Vries, Peter. *The Blood of the Lamb.* Boston: Little, Brown, 1961.

de Vries, Tiemen. *Dutch History, Art, and Literature for Americans: Lectures Given at the University of Chicago.* Grand Rapids: Eerdmans-Sevensma Co., 1912.

Dodson, L. S. *Social Relationships and Institutions in an Established Community: South Holland, Illinois,* Social Research Report No. XVI. Washington, D.C.: Department of Agriculture, 1939.

Douma, Conrad. "Chicago Haulers Make History by Building First Private Incinerator." *Refuse Removal Journal* 1 (Jan. 1958).

Dryfhout, William. "Chicago's 'Far West Siders' in the 1920s." *Origins* 9, No. 2 (1991).

Ettema, Ross, ed. *Down an Indian Trail in 1849: The Story of Roseland* (Palos Heights, Ill.: Trinity Christian College, 1987). A reprint of the centennial account by Marie K. Rowlands, published under the same title in serial form in the *Calumet Index.* The first of fifty-seven installments began 20 June 1949.

Fabend, Firth Haring. "The Synod of Dort and the Persistence of Dutchness in Nineteenth-Century New York and New Jersey." *New York History* 77 (July 1996): 273-300.

———. *Zion on the Hudson: Dutch New York and New Jersey in the Age of Revivals.* Albany: University of New York Press, 2000.

Fatjo, Tom, Jr., and Keith Miller. *With No Fear of Failure.* Waco: Word Books, 1981.

Felsenthal, Bernhard, and Herman Eliassof. *History of Kehillah Anshe Maarabh: Semi-Centennial Celebration, November 4, 1897.* Chicago: KAM Temple, 1897.

Ferber, Edna. *So Big.* New York: Crowell, 1923.

Figel, Bess De Boer. *Once Upon A Time. . . .* Chicago, nd.

Fort, William H. "Dutch Corner of 'Valley' Brightens West Side." *Chicago Daily News.* 1 Mar. 1941.

Gans, Mozes Heiman. *Memorbook: History of Dutch Jewry from the Renaissance to 1940.* Baarn: Bosch & Keuning, 1971.

Garraghan, Gilbert J., S.J. *The Catholic Church in Chicago, 1673-1871.* Chicago: Loyola University Press, 1921.

———. *The Jesuits of the Middle United States.* 3 vols. New York: America Press, 1938.

Goodspeed, Westin A., and Daniel D. Healy. *History of Cook County, Illinois. . . .* 2 vols. Chicago: Goodspeed Historical Association, 1909.

Goudsblom, Johan. *Dutch Society.* New York: Random House, 1967.

Green, Paul M., and Melvin G. Holli, eds. *The Mayors: The Chicago Political Tradition.* Carbondale: Southern Illinois University Press, 1987.

Gutstein, Morris A. *A Priceless Heritage: The Epic Growth of Nineteenth-Century Chicago Jewry.* New York: Bloch Publishing Co., 1953.

Hager, R. John. "Gysbert Haan: A Study in Alienation." *Reformed Journal* 13-14 (1963-64).

Hard, William. "Chicago's Five Maiden Aunts: The Women Who Boss Chicago Very Much to Its Advantage." *The American Magazine* 70 (Sept. 1906).

Harms, William. "Dutch settlers share heritage with the suburbs." *Chicago Tribune* (Daily Suburban edition). 23 Apr. 1983.

Hilton, George W. *Eastland: Legacy of the Titanic.* Stanford: Stanford University Press, 1995.

Hiskes, Harold. *In Memoriam.* Privately published. 1996.

Hoezee, Scott, and Christopher H. Meehan. *Flourishing in the Land: A Hundred-Year History of Christian Reformed Missions in North America.* Grand Rapids: Eerdmans, 1996.

Holli, Melvin G. and Peter d'A. Jones, eds. *Ethnic Chicago: A Multicultural Portrait.* 4th ed. Grand Rapids: Eerdmans, 1995.

Huizenga, Peter H. "Waste Management: Its History, Growth, and Development." In *The Dutch in America, Perspective 1987.* Proceedings of the Sixth Biennial Conference, Association for the Advancement of Dutch American Studies, Trinity Christian College, 1987.

Hyma, Albert. *Albertus C. Van Raalte and his Dutch Settlements in the United States.* Grand Rapids: Eerdmans, 1947.

Jacobson, Timothy. *Waste Management: An American Corporate Success Story.* Washington: Gateway Books, 1993.

Kasteel, Annemarie. *Francis Janssens, 1843-1897: A Dutch-American Prelate.* Lafayette: University of Southwest Louisiana, 1992.

Keating, Ann Durkin. *Building Chicago: Suburban Developers and The Creation of a Divided Metropolis.* Columbus: Ohio State University Press, 1988.

Kennedy, James Earl. "Eden in the Heartland." *Church Herald* 54 (March 1997).

Kieft, Albert. "Mr. Arnold Hoving." *Timothy Reflector,* 30 April 1969.

Kirkfleet, Cornelius James. *The White Canons of St. Norbert: A History of the Premonstratensian Order in the British Isles and America.* West De Pere, Wis.: St. Norbert's Abby, 1943.

Kivisto, Peter, and Dag Blanck, eds. *American Immigrants and Their Generations* Chicago: University of Illinois Press, 1990.

Koenig, Harry C., S.T.D., ed. *A History of the Parishes of the Archdiocese of Chicago.* 2 vols. Chicago: Archdiocese of Chicago, 1980.

Kroes, Rob. *The Persistence of Ethnicity: Dutch Calvinist Pioneers in Amsterdam, Montana.* Urbana and Chicago: University of Illinois Press, 1992.

Kromminga, John. *The Christian Reformed Church: A Study in Orthodoxy.* Grand Rapids: Baker Book House, 1949.

La Grand, James, Jr. "An Outsider Moves In." *Calvinist Contact* 25 March 1971.

LaMaire, Martin. "Acts of a Minor Assembly." *Reformed Journal* 21 (Jan. 1971).

LaMaire, Paul, and Donald Ottenhoff. "Latest Phase of the Racial Maze." *Calvin College Chimes,* 19 March 1971.

Lane, George A., S.J. *Chicago Churches and Synagogues: An Architectural Pilgrimage.* Chicago: Loyola University Press, 1981.

Langeveld, H. J., "'Een van Uwe, principieel genomen, meest trouwe leerlingen': Het tragische leven van mr. Tiemen de Vries, een vroege student van Abraham Kuyper." In Dirk Th. Kuiper, ed. *Jaarbook voor de geschiedenis van het Nederlands Protestantisme na 1800.* Kampen: Kok, 1993.

Leestma, Rein. "Liberty Under Law?" *Torch and Trumpet,* July 1956.

Lindell, Arthur G. *School Section Sixteen.* New York: Vantage Press, 1983.

Lindsey, Almont. *The Pullman Strike.* Chicago: University of Chicago Press, 1942.

Lucas, Henry S. *Dutch Immigrant Memoirs and Related Writings.* 2 vols. Assen, 1955. Rev. ed. Grand Rapids: Eerdmans, 1997.

———. *Netherlanders in America: Dutch Immigration to the United States and Canada, 1789-1950.* Ann Arbor: University of Michigan Press, 1955. Rep. Grand Rapids: Eerdmans, 1989.

Marsden, George. *Fundamentalism and American Culture: The Shaping of Twentieth Century Evangelicalism, 1870-1925.* New York and Oxford: Oxford University Press, 1980.

Mayer, Harold M., and Richard C. Wade. *Chicago: Growth of a Metropolis.* Chicago: University of Chicago Press, 1969.

Mayer, Leopold. "Recollections of Chicago in 1850-1851." In Morris U. Schappes, ed. *A Documentary History of the Jews in the United States, 1654-1875.* New York: Citadel Press, 1950.

McGoldrick, James E. *God's Renaissance Man: The Life and Works of Abraham Kuyper.* Auburn, Mass.: Evangelical Press, 2000.

Meites, Hyman L. ed. *History of the Jews of Chicago.* Chicago: Jewish Historical Society, 1924.

Mulkerins, Thomas M., S.J. *Holy Family Parish, Chicago: Priests and People.* Chicago: Universal Press, 1923.

Nolt, Steven M. "Formal Mutual Aid Structures among American Mennonites and Brethren: Assimilation and Reconstructed Ethnicity." *Journal of American Ethnic History* 17 (Spring 1998).

Nourse, Edwin Griswold. *The Chicago Produce Market.* New York: Houghton Mifflin, 1918.

Ottenhoff, Don, and John Ottenhoff. "Timothy Christian Schools." *The Other Side* 7, No. 2 (1971).

Pereboom, Freek, H. Hille, and H. Reenders, eds. *"Van scheurmakers, onruststokers en geheime opruijers . . .": De Afscheiding in Overijssel.* Kampen: Uitgave IJsselakademie, 1984.

Pollock, Eugene L. "Chicago companies continue family's 75-year refuse business tradition." *Refuse Removal Journal* 22 (Aug. 1979).

Poole, Ernest. *Giants Gone: Men Who Made Chicago.* New York: McGraw-Hill, 1933.

Post, Jacob. "Chain Stores and Anti-Christ." *Banner,* 13 Feb. 1931.

Reid, Daniel G., et al., eds. *Dictionary of Christianity in America.* Downers Grove, Ill.: InterVarsity Press, 1990.

Reid, Robert L. *Battleground: The Autobiography of Margaret A. Haley.* Urbana: Univ. of Illinois Press, 1982.

Schaver, J. L. *Christian Reformed Church Order: A Manual of the Church Order Adopted by the Synod of 1914. . . .* Grand Rapids: Eerdmans, 1941.

Schiltz, Mary Pieroni, and Suzanne Sinke. "De Bey, Cornelia Bernarda," in *Women Building Chicago, 1790-1990: A Biographical Dictionary.* Rima Lunin Schultz and Adele Hast, eds. Bloomington: Indiana University Press, 2001.

Schmidt, Evelyn Jannenga, and Paul D. Schmidt, eds. *Bulthuis-Jannenga Family Genealogy.* Holland, Mich., 1999.

Schoone-Jongen, Robert. "Cheap Land and Community: Theodore F. Koch, Dutch Colonizer." *Minnesota History* 53 (Summer 1993).

Semple, Mildred, and Virginia Wrobel, eds. *Evergreen Park: A Melting Pot of Memories.* Village of Evergreen Park, 1987.

Sharfman, I. Harold. *The First Rabbi: Origins of Conflict Between Orthodox and Reform: Jewish Polemic Warfare in Pre-Civil War America.* Malibu, Calif.: Pangloss Press, 1988.

Shaw, Stephen J. *The Catholic Parish as a Way-Station of Ethnicity and Americanization: Chicago's Germans and Italians, 1903-1939.* Brooklyn: Carlson Publishing, 1991.

Sinke, Suzanne M. *Dutch Immigrant Women in the United States, 1820-1920.* Urbana: University of Illinois Press, 2002.

Sinnema, Don. "The Story of Chicago Christian College (1931-1937)," in *The Dutch Adapting in North America,* Richard Harms, ed. Grand Rapids: Calvin College, 2000.

Skogan, Wesley G. *Chicago Since 1840: A Time-Series Handbook.* Urbana: University of Illinois Institute of Government and Public Affairs, 1976.

Sluis, Simon J., et al. *The Westfrisian Family Sluis.* Heiloo, The Netherlands, 1995.

Sorkin, Sidney. *Bridges to an American City: A Guide to Chicago's Landmanshaften, 1870-1990.* New York: Peter Lang, 1993.

Stob, Henry. "Chicago's West Side." *Origins* 9, No. 2 (1991).

———. "Church and School on Chicago's West Side 1913-1921." *Origins* 10, No. 2 (1993); 11, No. 1 (1993).

———. "Let Us Repent." *Reformed Journal* 20 (Mar. 1970).

———. "Recollections." *Origins* 1, No. 1 (1983); 9, No. 2 (1991); 10, No. 2 (1992).

———. *Summoning Up Remembrance.* Grand Rapids: Eerdmans, 1996.

Stob, Jo Ann Hofstra. "A History of the Richard Ooms Grocery Store, Roseland, Chicago, Illinois," 2002.

Stoutmeyer, Garrett H. "The Timothy-Lawndale Situation." *The Outlook* (May 1971).

Sullivan, Gerald E. *The Story of Englewood, 1835-1923.* Chicago: Englewood Business Men's Association, 1923.

Swanson, Stevenson. "Lucrative lure of garbage hauling has long been a Dutch treat." *Chicago Tribune,* 29 Mar. 1993.

Swierenga, Robert P. "Calvinists in the Second City: The Dutch Reformed of Chicago's West Side." In Gerard Dekker, Donald A. Luidens, and Rodger R. Rice, eds. *Rethinking Secularization: Reformed Reactions to Modernity.* Lanham, Md.: University Press of America, 1997.

———. *Faith and Family: Dutch Immigration and Settlement in the United States, 1820-1920.* New York: Holmes & Meier, 2000.

———. *The Forerunners: The Dutch Jewry in the North American Diaspora.* Detroit: Wayne State University Press, 1994.

Swierenga, Robert P., ed. *The Dutch in America: Immigration, Settlement, and Cultural Change.* New Brunswick, N.J.: Rutgers University Press, 1985.

Swierenga, Robert P., and Elton J. Bruins, *Family Quarrels in the Dutch Reformed Churches in the Nineteenth Century.* Grand Rapids: Eerdmans, 1999.

Tempelman, Richard. "Please Allow Me to Say." *Torch and Trumpet.* Apr. 1956.

ten Zythoff, Gerrit J. *Sources of Secession: The Netherlands Hervormde Kerk on the Eve of the Dutch Immigration to the Midwest.* Grand Rapids: Eerdmans, 1987.

"Timothy: Crisis in Christian Education." *Calvin College Chimes,* 3 October 1969.

Van Brummelen, Harro W. *Telling the Next Generation: Educational Developments in*

North American Calvinist Christian Schools. Lanham, Md.: University Press of America, 1986.

Vanden Berg, Frank. *Abraham Kuyper.* St. Catherines, Ont.: Paideia Press, 1978.

Vandenbosch, Amry. *The Dutch Communities of Chicago.* Chicago: Knickerbocker Society of Chicago, 1927.

Vanden Bosch, J. G. "John Schepers." *Reformed Journal* 6 (July-Aug. 1956).

———. "Koene Vanden Bosch." *Reformed Journal* 4 (Sept. 1954).

———. "Tamme M. Vanden Bosch." *Reformed Journal* 10 (Nov. 1960).

———. "Willem Greve." *Reformed Journal* 10 (Jan. 1960).

———. "Willem Hendrik Frieling." *Reformed Journal* 8 (Dec. 1958).

Vander Velde, John. "Our History." In Ebenezer Christian Reformed Church of Berwyn. *Centennial Booklet, 1867-1967.* Berwyn, 1967.

Vander Velde, John J. Obituary in *Refuse Removal Journal* 19 (May 1976).

Vandervelde, John, Jr. "Disabling Injury Rate 900% Greater Than U.S. Average." *Refuse Removal Journal* 12 (Sept. 1969).

Van Eyck, William O. *Landmarks of the Reformed Fathers; or, What Dr. Van Raalte's People Believed.* Grand Rapids: Reformed Press, 1922.

Van Halsema, Dick L. "Hopkins, Hackensack, and Haan." *Reformed Journal* 7 (Jan. 1957).

Van Halsema, Thea B. *". . . I Will Build My Church."* Grand Rapids: International Publications, 1956.

Van Heertum, John A., O.P. *Regeeringsjubileum, 1898-1923: Aan haar Majesteit Wilhelmina Koningin der Nederlanden.* Chicago, 1923.

Van Hinte, Jacob. *Netherlanders in America: A Study of Emigration and Settlement in the Nineteenth and Twentieth Centuries in the United States of America.* Robert P. Swierenga, general editor, Adriaan de Wit, chief translator. Grand Rapids: Baker, 1985.

Van Hoeven, John W., ed. *Piety and Patriotism: Bicentennial Studies on the Reformed Church, 1776-1976.* Grand Rapids: Eerdmans, 1978.

Van Til, Cornelius. "The Pillars of Our Church v. Doctrinal Insensitivity." *Torch and Trumpet* (Feb. 1957).

Verduin, Leonard. *Honor Your Mother: Christian Reformed Church Roots in the Secession of 1834.* Grand Rapids: CRC Publications, 1988.

Volkers, Mark. *The Huizenga Family in America, 1893-1990.* Chicago, 1990.

Walch, Timothy. "Catholic Education in Chicago: The Formative Years 1840-1890." *Chicago History* 7 (Summer 1978).

Walters, Ronald. *American Reformers, 1815-1860.* New York: Hill and Wang, 1978.

Webb, Andrew. "Waste Management Cleans Up." *Chicago Magazine,* June 1990.

Weber, T. P. "Christian Endeavor Society," in *Dictionary of Christianity in America.* Daniel G. Reid, ed. Downers Grove, Ill.: InterVarsity Press, 1990.

Wolterstorff, Nicholas. "The AACS in the CRC." *Reformed Journal* 24 (Dec. 1974).

Zandstra, Gerald L. *Daughters Who Dared: Answering God's Call to Nigeria.* Grand Rapids: Calvin Theological Seminary, 1992.

Zwaanstra, Henry. *Reformed Thought and Experience in the New World: A Study of the Christian Reformed Church and Its American Environment, 1890-1918.* Kampen: J. H. Kok, 1973.

IX. Unpublished Works

Achterhof, Ken. "A Case Study of the Bankruptcy of Chicago Christian High School in 1937." Senior History Seminar Paper, Calvin College, 1996, The Archives, Calvin College.

Bergsma, Derk. "A Tale of Two Churches: An Analysis and Critique of the Process of Decision Leading to Relocation from City to Suburb," Seminar Paper, University of Chicago, n.d.

Brouwer, Barbara. "Promises, Promises: Women and the Reformation." Seminar Paper, Northern Baptist Theological Seminary, 1998.

Clausing, John. "Seventy-Fifth Anniversary" [First Christian Reformed Church of Roseland].

Curtis, Mildred. "Statistics of Arrests in Chicago in Relation to Race and Nativity, 1915 to 1924." Ph.D. Dissertation, University of Chicago, 1926.

De Boer, Andrew. "Brief History of Fourth Christian Reformed Church of Chicago," 1990.

———. "Fourth Christian Reformed Church of Chicago, Early Church History, 1923-1927," 1927.

De Boer, Henry. "Recollections of the James De Boer Family" [February 1971]. Courtesy of John H. Evenhouse.

Dekker, Simon. "History of Roseland and Vicinity," 1938. The Archives, Calvin College.

———. "History of the Christian School at Roseland." The Archives, Calvin College.

De Vries, Sarah, "My Life on the West Side, 1929-1945." 2000. Courtesy of the author.

Dykstra, Henry. "Two Longs and Ten Shorts." Vepser, Wis., ca. 1995. Courtesy of John Dykstra.

Folgers, Neal. "From 12th Street to Lombard: The History of Lombard CRC." Senior History Seminar Paper, Calvin College, 1987. The Archives, Calvin College.

"God's Hand in Fourth Roseland in the Year 1963." The Archives, Calvin College.

Haverhals, Art. "Caught in the Web." Senior History Seminar Paper, Calvin College, 1963. The Archives, Calvin College.

Hoekstra, Ted. "Memoirs, 1927-1957." Courtesy of Peter H. Huizenga.

Hoogendoorn, Case, to Karl Westerhof. "Timothy Litigation Memorandum." 12 Nov. 1971. Courtesy of George Vander Hill.

Huizenga, Tena. "The Life Story of Harm (Harry) Huizenga, 1869-1936." Courtesy of Peter H. Huizenga.

Kickert, Mrs. Cornelius. "Last Meeting at Coffee Hour at Cicero I Church – 1976." The Archives, Calvin College.

Kleinjans, Edith Klaaren. "Going Home: A 'Pilgrimage Stopover,'" ca. 1997. Hope College Collection, Joint Archives of Holland.

Krabbendam, Hans. "Serving the Dutch Community: A Comparison of the Patterns of Americanization in the Lives of Two Immigrant Pastors." M.A. Thesis, Kent State University, 1989.

Langer, Jeffrey Ira. "White-Collar Heritage: Occupational Mobility of the Jews in Chicago, 1860-1880." M.A. Thesis, University of Illinois, 1976.

Lee, Barbara (Geertsema). "Early History of the Geertsema Family." Courtesy of Edward Evenhouse.

———. "Gold in the Family Treasury: Hendrik and Martje Evenhouse – A Family Portrait." Chicago, 1989. Courtesy of Edward Evenhouse.

Lubben, Ralph. "Aunt Kate 1879-1950." *Echoes: Newsletter of the Elmhurst Christian Reformed Church,* Feb. 1998.

———. "Catherina Lubben." Courtesy of the author.

———. "Prologue." Courtesy of the author.

Reformed Church in America. Committee on Educational Philosophy. "The Relationship of Public and Parochial School Education." Mimeo [1957].

Stulp, Martin. "Reminiscences, 1949 Timothy Class 50th Reunion, Frankfurt, Ill., Sept. 1999."

Swierenga, Robert P. "Robert (Bouwko) Swierenga Family History." 1997.

———, comp. "Groningen Emigrants, 1881-1901."

Van Der Molen, Edward. "Memoirs," ca. 1970. Courtesy of Everett Van Der Molen.

Wezeman, Henry, Sr. "Glimpses of the Past: Recollections, Experiences, and Anecdotes, Nunica, Michigan, August 1949." Courtesy of Maureen Cole.

X. Correspondence and Interviews

Bakker, Jake, video interview with Martin Stulp, 19 Nov. 1997.

Blaauw, Dick, and Robert Vander Velde, interview with author, 10 March 1998.

Boerema, Clarence, interview with author, 21 Feb. 2001.

Bradford, Eugene, interviews with author, 4 Feb., 4 Oct. 1999.

Brouwer, Dirk, video interview with Martin Stulp, 26 Mar. 1998.

Buiten, William, phone interview with author, 10 July 1999.

Bulthuis, Jay, interview with Mark Volkers, 18 June 1989, typed transcript, courtesy of Peter H. Huizenga.

Dwarshuis, Effie, nee Klaassens (Mrs. Len), video interview with Martin Stulp, 18 Aug. 1998.

Essenburg, Ben, interviews with author, 26 Oct. 1999; 8 Oct. 2001.

Essenburg, Ben, video interviews with Martin Stulp, 2 Nov. 1998; 1 Oct. 1999.
Hamstra, Sam, Jr., letter to author, 13 Feb. 2001.
Heslinga, Ben, video interview with Martin Stulp, 19 Feb. 1998.
Hoekstra, Ted, interview with Mark Volkers, 12 Aug. 1889, typed transcript, courtesy of Peter H. Huizenga.
Huiner, Harvey, e-mail letter to author, 27 Feb. 2002.
Huiner, Peter, e-mail letter to author, 1 Mar. 2002.
Huizenga, Peter H., phone interview with author, 9 Feb. 2000.
Iwema, Calvin, interviews with author, 28 Sept., 25 Oct. 1999.
Keizer, Mike and Lena, video interview with Martin Stulp, 12 May 1998.
Oldenburger, Tom, video interview with Martin Stulp, 19 Nov. 1998.
Postema, Jim, e-mail letter to author, 25 June 2001.
Roeters, Roelfina (Mrs. John), video interview with Martin Stulp, 1 Dec. 1997.
Schuurman, Richard, telephone interview with author, 12 Nov. 1999.
Stob, Henry Martin, interview with author, 21 Feb. 2001.
Stob, Jo Ann Hofstra, telephone interview with the author, 6 August 2002.
Swierenga, John R., interview with author, 9 Feb. 1999.
Swierenga, John R., video interview with Martin Stulp, ca. 1991.
Tameling, Henry and Marie, video interview with Martin Stulp, 12 Feb. 1998.
Van Denend, Michael, interview with author, 26 May 1994.
Vander Ploeg Helen, nee Groenewold (Mrs. John), interview with author, 14 Nov. 1999.
Van Dyke, Hendrina, letter to author, 15 Jan. 2000.
Wigboldy, Homer, e-mail letter to author, 10 Oct. 2001.
Zeilstra, William, letters to author, 19 Jan., 20 Apr. 2001.

Index

The Historical Series of the Reformed Church in America

Books in print, William B. Eerdmans, publisher

Dorothy F. Van Ess
Pioneers in the Arab World

James W. Van Hoeven, editor
Piety and Patriotism: Bicentennial Studies of the RCA, 1776-1976

Mildred W. Schuppert
Digest and Index: Minutes of General Synod 1958-1977

Mildred W. Schuppert
Digest and Index; Minutes of General Synod 1906-1957

Gerald F. DeJong
From Strength to Strength: Northwestern College, 1882-1982

D. Ivan Dykstra
B.D., a Biography of the Reverend B. D. Dykstra

John W. Beardslee III, editor
Vision from the Hill

Howard G. Hageman
Two Centuries Plus: The Story of New Brunswick Theological Seminary

Marvin D. Hoff
Structures for Mission

James I. Cook, editor
The Church Speaks: Papers of the Commission on Theology of the Reformed Church in America, 1959-1984

James W. Van Hoeven, editor
Word and World: Reformed Theology in America

Gerrit J. ten Zythoff
Sources of Secession: The Netherlands Hervormde Kerk on the Eve of the Dutch Immigration to the Midwest

Gordon J. Van Wylen
Vision for a Christian College

Jack D. Klunder and Russell L. Gasero, editors
Servant Gladly: Essays in Honor of John W. Beardslee III

Jeanette Boersma
Grace in the Gulf (Iraq & Oman)

Arie R. Brouwer
Ecumenical Testimony

Gerald F. De Jong
The Reformed Church in China, 1842-1951

Russell L. Gasero
The Historical Directory of the Reformed Church in America, 1628–1992

Daniel J. Meeter
Meeting Each Other in Doctrine, Liturgy and Government

Allan J. Janssen
Gathered at Albany: A History of a Classis

Elton J. Bruins
The Americanization of a Congregation

Gregg A. Mast
In Remembrance and Hope: The Ministry and Vision of Howard G. Hageman

Janny Venema, translator and editor
Deacons' Accounts, 1652-1674: Beverwijck/Albany

Morrell F. Swart
The Call of Africa

Lewis R. Scudder III
The Arabian Mission's Story

Renee S. House and John W. Coakley, editors
Patterns and Portraits: Women in the History of the Reformed Church in America

Elton J. Bruins and Robert P. Swierenga
Family Quarrels in the Dutch Reformed Church in the Nineteenth Century

Allan J. Janssen
Constitutional Theology: Notes on the Book of Church Order of the Reformed Church in America

Greg A. Mast, editor
Raising the Dead: Sermons of Howard G. Hageman

James Hart Brumm, editor
Equipping the Saints: The Synod of New York, 1800-2000

Joel R. Beeke, editor
Forerunner of the Great Awakening: Sermons by Theodorus Jacobus Frelinghuysen (1691-1747)

Russell L. Gasero
The Historical Directory of the Reformed Church in America, 1628-2000

Eugene P. Heideman
From Mission to Church: The Reformed Church in America Mission to India

Harry Boonstra
Our School: Calvin College and the Christian Reformed Church

James I. Cook, editor
The Church Speaks, Vol. 2: *Papers of the Commission on Theology of the Reformed Church in America, 1985-2000*

John W. Coakley, editor
Concord Makes Strength: Essays in Reformed Ecumenism

Robert P. Swierenga
Dutch Chicago: A History of the Hollanders in the Windy City